Footprint story

It was 1921
Ireland had just been partitioned, the British miners were striking for more pay and the federation of British industry had an idea. Exports were booming in South America – how about a handbook for businessmen trading in that far away continent? The Anglo-South American Handbook was born that year, written by W Koebel, the most prolific writer on Latin America of his day.

1924
Two editions later the book was 'privatized' and in 1924, in the hands of Royal Mail, the steamship company for South America, it became The South American Handbook, subtitled 'South America in a nutshell'. This annual publication became the 'bible' for generations of travellers to South America and remains so to this day. In the early days travel was by sea and the Handbook gave all the details needed for the long voyage from Europe. What to wear for dinner; how to arrange a cricket match with the Cable & Wireless staff on the Cape Verde Islands and a full account of the journey from Liverpool up the Amazon to Manaus: 5898 miles without changing cabin!

1939
As the continent opened up, The South American Handbook reported the new Pan Am flying boat services, and the fortnightly airship service from Rio to Europe on the Graf Zeppelin. For reasons still unclear but with extraordinary determination, the annual editions continued through the Second World War.

1970s
Many more people discovered South America and the backpacking trail started to develop. All the while the Handbook was gathering fans, including literary vagabonds such as Paul Theroux and Graham Greene (who once sent some updates addressed to "The publishers of the best travel guide in the world, Bath, England").

1990s
During the 1990s the company set about developing a new travel guide series using this legendary title as the flagship. By 1997 there were over a dozen guides in the series and the Footprint imprint was launched.

2000s
The series grew quickly and there were soon Footprint travel guides covering more than 150 countries. In 2004, Footprint launched its first thematic guide: *Surfing Europe*, packed with colour photographs, maps and charts. This was followed by further thematic guides such as *Diving the World*, *Snowboarding the World*, *Body and Soul escapes*, *Travel with Kids* and *European City Breaks*.

2009
Today we continue the traditions of the last 88 years that has served legions of travellers so well. We believe that these help to make Footprint guides different. Our policy is to use authors who are genuine experts who write for independent travellers; people possessing a spirit of adventure, looking to get off the beaten track.

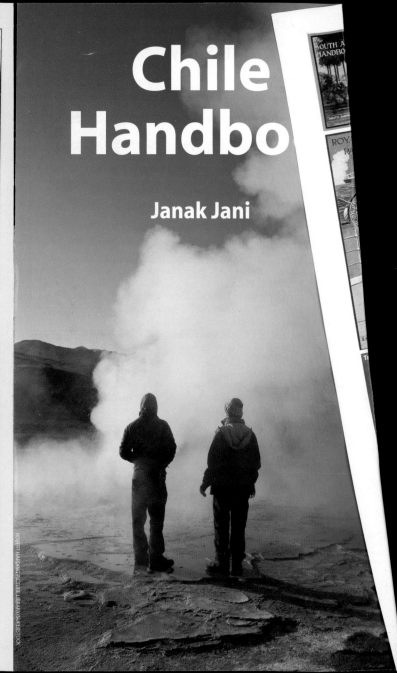

Chile
Handbo

Janak Jani

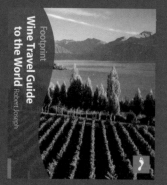
ROBERT HARDING PICTURE LIBRARY/SUPERSTOCK

Title page: The Geysers of El Tatio. At 4300 m above sea level they are the world's highest.
Above: Volcán Licancabur viewed through an arch near San Pedro de Atacama.

With an almost comical geographical shape and virtually every climate imaginable, this beautiful, memorable corner of the world is a place of extremes and contradictions. Few countries have quite such a split geographical personality. Here, you can often glimpse the snows of the high Andes from the Pacific Ocean, ski in the mountains in the morning and be drinking *pisco sours* on the beach come sundown. To the south, the country is hemmed in by thick temperate rainforest, fast-flowing rivers, icefields and glaciers, while to the north is the memorable Atacama Desert, with its endless space and pristine skies, and where some places have not seen a raindrop for centuries. The desert's geoglyphs bear testament to the ingenuity of some of prehistoric America's most complex civilizations, while an intermingling of the old world with the new has led to some of the most enduring aspects of ancient and modern Chilean culture, such as the legend of the Inca princess La Tirana, which spawned the country's biggest religious fiesta.

Map labels:

IQUIQUE, ARICA & THE FAR NORTH

ANTOFAGASTA, CALAMA & SAN PEDRO DE ATACAMA

INTO THE ATACAMA

Pacific Ocean

FROM SANTIAGO TO LA SERENA

VALPARAISO & VIÑA DEL MAR

SANTIAGO REGION

CENTRAL VALLEY

LAKE DISTRICT

CHILOE

CARRETERA AUSTRAL

FAR SOUTH

Atlantic Ocean

TIERRA DEL FUEGO

CHILEAN PACIFIC ISLANDS

Contents

Planning your trip

DAVID PRUTER/SHUTTERSTOCK

A massive cracked and creaking blue wall of ice – Grey Glacier, Torres del Paine.

Where to go

Chileans say that, when God had almost completed the act of creation, there was a little of everything left, so He threw it all down in a narrow strip of land and called it Chile. The national pride is justifiable, for this is a fantastically diverse country, but so much choice can be bewildering for the visitor. Chile is hemmed in by the Pacific Ocean, the Atacama Desert and the Andes. When combined with the country's shape, these geographical barriers rule out circular routes within the country – the choice therefore comes down to whether to go north or south.

The north is generally drier. Much of it is desert except for an occasional oasis and the verdant altiplano, and there are often large distances between places of interest. The people are slightly taciturn. Unlike the south it is pleasant to visit during the colder months of the year (May to September). Highlights include the peaceful Elqui Valley, whose green vine-laden floor contrasts with the stark metalic colours of its mineral-stained mountains where the Milky Way traces a path through a night sky filled with a billion stars. Further north is the oasis of San Pedro de Atacama, surrounded by archaeological sites and awesome natural phenomena. At the northern tip of Chile the desert rises up to meet the lush green of the altiplano, home to a dozen volcanoes and a wide variety of wildlife.

The Central Valley is the heart of the country and is where most Chileans live. Santiago has a couple of world-class museums and is a good base for many of the country's best ski resorts, while Valparaíso, the so-called Pearl of the Pacific, is a multi-coloured amphitheatre of a city with an artistic, bohemian atmosphere unlike anywhere else in Chile. Beach lovers can head

UROSR/SHUTTERSTOCK

Opposite page: Pisco vines in the lower Elqui Valley.
Above left: A typical Valparaíso *casona*, teetering on the edge of the hill.
Above right: Ice climbing on the Southern Icefield.

to the nearby resort of Viña del Mar or to any number of quiet fishing villages. A word of warning, though – the water is cold!

Stretching from Santiago to the south are Chile's prime wine valleys (see page 16). Many wineries offer tours and an increasing number are home to some of Chile's more innovative restaurants.

Southern Chile is filled with lush green forests rising up from fractured fjords, fast-flowing rivers and waterfalls, pristine lakes and smoking snow-capped volcanoes overlooked by the majestic mountain range to the east. In the Lake District adventure tourism is easy, with numerous agencies offering a dozen day-long activities in the nearby lakes, rivers, forests and mountains with all the creature comforts of Pucón or Puerto Varas awaiting you in the evening. For a taste of the real Patgonia, head south to the

Carretera Austral. The Parque Pumalín is an incredible conservation project with a diverse ecosystem and excellent trails to explore.

Towards the Argentine border, Futaleufú has the best whitewater rafting in the southern hemisphere, while further south, the azure waters of Lago General Carrera turn an even more unbelievable blue as they flow into the broad Río Baker that winds westwards, splitting Patagonia's two enormous ice fields before reaching the sea at Tortel, a streetless village where houses are connected by wooden walkways. South of the ice fields is Torres del Paine, whose glaciers and granite towers are the jewel in the crown of Chilean Patagonia.

A final word of advice: don't try to do too much; you will get more out of your travels by covering a small area properly than by rushing from one place to the next.

Itineraries

With so much to explore and with such variety in Chile, this guide makes no attempt to be prescriptive. There are, however, a number of places that stand out. These itineraries are suggested for those who want to see as much of the country as they can in the time available; but those with more time to spare could easily devote several weeks to each area of the country without running out of things to see and do.

The south

One week

Fly from Santiago to Puerto Montt, allowing two to three days to visit either the beautiful island of Chiloé or the southern Lake District. In Chiloé, visit the penguins at Puñihuil, the town of Ancud and many of the island's Jesuit churches. Visiting Chiloé in 1835, Charles Darwin found that the rolling hills reminded him of England. It has changed little since and, with its rich mythology and close-knit agricultural communities, it still evokes a bygone age. Just north of Puerto Montt is the Lake District. Use the German-founded town of Puerto Varas as a base to visit the area around Lago Llanquihue, where the Osorno volcano provides a spectacular backdrop to the lake. The impressive Petrohué waterfalls are an hour to the east. Fly to Puerto Natales and spend four days visiting the mountains and eerie blue glaciers of Torres del Paine, one of the world's greatest national parks, before flying back to Santiago.

Two weeks

After arriving in Santiago, visit the port of Valparaíso before heading south by bus and spending a few days in the Central Valley, the heart of Chile. Explore the high mountains around Vilches, or the Parque Nacional Siete Tazas. Wine buffs can sample some of Chile's best wines, while beach lovers might prefer surfing at Pichilemu. Move on to the famous

Above: Traditional palafito houses, Castro. Opposite page: Old and new, Santiago.

forests and hills around Lago Villarrica, perhaps climbing the volcano nearby, doing a day trek in the Araucaria forests of Huerquehue or Cañi, braving a day of whitewater rafting or relaxing in natural thermal springs, before flying from Puerto Montt to Puerto Natales to visit Torres del Paine (as in the one-week itinerary).

One month

Spend a further two or three days on Chiloé, visiting the Parque Nacional Chiloé, and Castro. Catch a boat to Chaitén and spend the next eight or nine days exploring the fabulous region of the Carretera Austral. See giant alerce forests in the Parque Pumalín, experience some of the world's best whitewater rafting around Futaleufú and hike around Cerro Castillo, before (if money is no object) making for Puerto Chacabuco and taking a cruise to the Laguna San Rafael glacier. Fly down to Punta Arenas and visit the nearby penguin colonies or splash out on a whale-watching trip before heading on to Torres del Paine, adding the wilds of Tierra del Fuego or the Glaciares National Park in Argentina.

The north

One week

First, fly from Santiago to La Serena to spend perhaps three days exploring the area around the city. Pick two attractions, choosing from the Elqui Valley and the public observatory, the Parque Nacional Fray Jorge, the penguins, dolphins and sea lions at Isla Damas, the cave paintings at the Valle del Encanto or the Limarí Valley. Fly on to Calama and the oasis of San Pedro de Atacama and spend three days visiting the geysers, altiplano lakes, the salt flat and the Valley of the Moon, before flying back to Santiago.

Two weeks

Head to Valparaíso before catching a bus north to La Serena, the journey providing a good introduction to the beauties of the

mountains of the semi-desert. Continue to Chañaral to see the spectacular Parque Nacional Pan de Azúcar, before moving on directly to San Pedro to continue with the one-week itinerary. Take an overnight bus to Arica, and spend two days visiting the spectacular Parque Nacional Lauca and the world's highest lake, Chungará, before flying back to the capital.

One month

A month allows you to visit some fascinating additional destinations in the north of the country. Spend two or three days exploring the hinterland around Illapel, Salamanca and Combarbalá, for example, which is spectacularly rugged country and full of minerals and ancient rock art. Heading north from Chañaral, break your journey at the attractive coast town of Taltal and then visit Chuquicamata, the largest open-cast copper mine on earth. With two extra days at San Pedro, tour the beautiful altiplano villages, before travelling to Arica. Take a four-day altiplano tour, visiting Lauca, Surire and Isluga parks and ending in Iquique where you can relax on the beach for a couple of days, jump off a cliff on a tandem paraglide over the city, or visit the nearby thermal baths at Pica.

Chile highlights

See colour maps at back of book

PERU

Arica

Parque Nacional Lauca

BOLIVIA

Iquique

La Tirana

Calama

San Pedro de Atacama

Antofagasta

Parque Nacional Llullaillaco

Taltal

Parque Nacional Pan de Azúcar

El Salvador

Chañaral

Copiapó

Vallenar

Pacific Ocean

La Serena

Parque Nacional Fray Jorge

Ovalle

ARGENTINA

Illapel

Valparaíso

Parque Nacional La Campana

SANTIAGO

Rancagua

San Fernando

Curicó

Parque Nacional Siete Tazas

Talca

Cauquenes

Parral

Concepción

Chillán

Los Angeles

Altiplano national parks

Shy vicuñas set against a backdrop of snow-capped volcanoes, page 271.

San Pedro de Atacama

A desert town surrounded by geysers, salt flats and millennia of history, page 226.

Pan de Azúcar

Where sea lions and penguins hang out on beautiful beaches and the desert blooms in spring, page 196.

Valparaíso

A UNESCO World Heritage Site waiting to be explored, page 117.

Ski resorts

The best skiing and snowboarding in South America, within easy reach of Santiago, page 106.

Wine routes

Chile's finest vintages come from the Central Valley, page 279.

Rapa Nui (Easter Island)

A remote dot in the Pacific Ocean with a fascinating cultural heritage, page 558.

Iquique

Antofagasta

Copiapó

La Serena

Valparaíso
SANTIAGO
Rancagua
Talca
Concepción

Temuco

Puerto Montt

Coyhaique

Punta Arenas

N

8 km
8 miles

Easter Island

Tahai

Ahu Tongariki

Vinapu

Pucón
Gateway to the Lake District with volcanes, fishing and whitewater rafting all nearby, page 340.

Parque Pumalín
Native temperate rainforest preserved for posterity, page 436.

Chiloé
A magical island of fishing, forests and mythical creatures, page 405.

Carretera Austral
Cycle, hike or hitch your way through spectacular scenery between Puerto Montt and Villa O'Higgins, page 429.

Torres del Paine
Quite simply one of the world's greatest national parks, page 497.

The north
One week ●▶
Two weeks ●▶
One month
extensions ●▶

The south
One week ●▶
Two weeks ●▶
One month ●▶

N

100 km
100 miles

Treks

Parque Nacional La Campana

Although not one of Chile's more fashionable national parks, La Campana is a hidden gem. Split by two *cerros* in the middle of the park, the northern side is sunbaked while the southern side lies in the shade, giving rise to two utterly contrasting ecosystems: a day-hike across the park from the northern entrance at Ocoa to Granizo in the south is like seeing Chile in microcosm. The northern half is arid semi-desert, dotted with cacti and Chilean palms, but cross the pass to the southern side and you will be surrounded by temperate forest. Spend the next day tackling the summit of Cerro La Campana, a stiff day hike with one of Chile's finest panoramic views as a reward.

Volcán Descabezado Grande

Literally translated as 'great headless volcano', this is the endpoint of a stunning trek in the heart of Chile. Accessed from Vilches, near Talca, it is a gruelling five-day return trek to the enormous ice-filled crater (an immense 1500 m in diameter). The trek is mostly walking with just a little scrambling, although outside of mid-summer to autumn, crampons and an ice axe may well be needed. The route takes you past rustic thermal springs, lagunas and an eerie field of white volcanic sand. From the summit, at over 3800 m, there are extensive views across the Andes and on into Argentina.

The Sierra Nevada, Parque Nacional Conguillio

Conguillio is the most picturesque of the Lake District's national parks. It has several well-marked trails, but the six-hour return trek to the foot of the Sierra Nevada stands out. The path climbs through dense forests of lenga and coigue, passing a series of lookouts with ever more spectacular views and down to the azure Lago Conguillio with smoking Volcán Llaima behind and the cone of Volcán Villarrica in the distance. The forest then opens to reveal an otherworldly landscape of araucaria trees with the snow-covered Sierra Nevada as a backdrop. Condors can often be seen close up. Experienced climbers can

ROBERT HARDING PICTURE LIBRARY/SUPERSTOCK

Above: The smoking crater of Volcán Villarrica.
Opposite page: Trekking the W, Torres del Paine.

continue over the Sierra Nevada and out of the park to the thermal springs at Malalcahuello to the north.

Volcán Villarrica, Parque Nacional Villarrica

Ever wanted to climb an active volcano? The Volcán Villarrica hike is probably the most popular trek in Chile and for a good reason. This snow-covered perfect cone of a mountain is a steep half-day trek with ice axe and crampons. No previous experience is required but you do need to be reasonably fit. On still days you can peer from the summit into the crater and see molten lava bubbling away, while in the distance half a dozen other volcanoes loom up from lakes and forests. The best part is still to come – forget walking back down – simply lie back and slide, toboggan style.

The W, Parque Nacional Torres del Paine

Enjoy multi-day trekking through some of the most spectacular scenery in Patagonia, among iceberg-filled lakes, valleys, waterfalls and glaciers, with the landscape all the time dominated by the imposing giant granite plugs of the Paine Massif. You'll experience four seasons in a few hours and have a warm bed and a cooked meal at the end of your arduous day's trekking. If you'd rather get away from the crowds for a real Patagonian wilderness experience pack your tent and head off around the north side of the massif on the week-long circuit trek.

Dientes de Navarino

Named after the teeth-like chain of mountains around which the trail leads, this three- to five-day fully self-contained route is only for hardy, dedicated trekkers. The southernmost trekking route on Earth winds through the Patagonian wilds where trees grow up at a 45-degree angle, sculpted by the shattering westerly winds, and where the paths often have a gradient to match. The route will take you past semi-frozen lakes and fast-flowing

rivers rivers replete with beaver dams. The views from the passes to the thick forests below and to the Beagle Channel in the north, with the outline of Tierra del Fuego in the distance, will leave you speechless with their beauty. This is trekking at the end of the world.

Wine valleys

The Central Valley offers ample scope for visits to vineyards and wine tasting, whether independently, or on a tour on one of several *rutas del vino* (wine routes). There are six main areas producing quality wines here, each with distinctive characteristics based on slight variations in soil and climate. Independent visits can be made to a number of vineyards, although a day's notice is usually required. Some give free tours, but most charge a small fee, with visitors paying for each wine they taste; some may provide lunch for an additional charge. For a full list of recommended vineyards see page 298.

Casablanca

Among the newest of Chile's wine valleys, Casablanca has a series of microclimates. To the west the coastal mist and cool sea breezes regulate temperatures to produce crisp, citric Sauvignon Blancs, while further inland, in Alto Casablanca, they are more rounded with less pronounced acidity. In this part of the valley, Pinot Noir and even corpulent Merlots are made. As a non-traditional valley, many of the wineries have extravagant, modern designs and house expensive, often innovative restaurants. Tour Operators in Valparaíso and Santiago offer tours, but independent access to most vineyards is easy, the majority being directly off the main highway linking the two cities. Recommended wineries are William Cole, Viña Mar and Casas del Bosque.

Maipo

The traditional home to Chile's top Cabernet Sauvignons and easily accessed from Santiago, the Maipo Valley is reasonably well set up for tourism. There are two main wine-producing zones, to the southeast of the capital around Pirque, where the influence of the Andes is strongly felt, and further down the valley around Isla de Maipo, much warmer and ideal for producing full-bodied Cabernet Sauvignon and Carmenère. Day tours are available from Santiago. Recommended wineries are De Martino, Aquitania and Concha y Toro.

AGE FOTOSTOCK/SUPERSTOCK

Opposite page: Viña Indomita, Casablanca, one of Chile's most modern wineries.
Above: The Alps meet the Andes – Swiss cable cars in the Colchagua Valley.

Cachapoal

This valley, to the South of Rancagua, produces a wide variety of wine, especially lively Cabernet Sauvignon, fruity Merlot and excellent Carmenère. There are also small plantations of Viognier and Cabernet Franc. There is no organized wine route as such, but independent visits can be made to several wineries. Recommended wineries are Gracia, Anakena and Altaïr.

Colchagua

Based around San Fernando and Santa Cruz, Colchagua is one of the great success stories of modern Chilean wine, with the Apalta region producing some world-beating Cabernet Sauvignons, while some of Chile's best Carmenère and Syrah is also produced in the valley. Santa Cruz is home to Chile's oldest and best-organized wine route (www.rutadelvino.cl), with several good hotels, a fascinating wine museum and the *tren del vino*, a steam train linking many of the more popular wineries. The wine route offers tours of three or six hours, from around US$40-200 per person. Independent visits can also be made. Recommended wineries are Viu Manent and Montes.

The Curicó Valley

The Curicó Valley is where the Chilean wine revolution began in 1980 with the arrival of the Spanish winemaker Miguel Torres. It now produces fruity reds in the lower valley and good-quality Sauvignon Blancs in the cooler foothills of the Andes. The valley has a wine route (www.rutadelvinocurico.cl) with circuits ranging from half-day tours to a two-day tour with meals. Recommended wineries are Miguel Torres, San Pedro and Alta Cima.

Maule

The Maule Valley, traditionally the home of the insipid País grape, has now been replanted with noble varieties, and produces decent well-balanced reds. The wine route's offices are in the Villa Cultural Huilquilemu, a well-preserved 19th-century hacienda, www.chilewineroute.cl. They offer tours and can also help arrange independent visits. Although this valley does not produce world-beating wines, the vineyards tend to be more intimate than in other valleys. A pleasant day can be had hiring a bicycle and peddaling your way at your own pace from winery to winery. Recommended wineries are Balduzzi, Gillmore and Casa Donoso.

When to go

When planning your trip you should take into account the time of year. High season is during the summer (especially January and February), when most areas are open to visitors, although the altiplano (the high plain of the Andes east of the Atacama) can experience heavy rain. It is also worth bearing in mind that many destinations are busy with Chilean and Argentine tourists at this time, especially in the far south, and bus fares and hotel prices are up to 50% higher. The north has another high season in July and August, but these are winter months in the south, meaning that many services here are closed and transport links are reduced.

Probably the ideal seasons for a visit, therefore, are spring (October to December) and autumn (March to April) when many facilities in the south are open, but less crowded, and temperatures in the northern and central regions are lower.

It is also worth arranging your travel plans to coincide with certain festivals (see page 44). In this case, it is best to book transport and accommodation well in advance. The period around the national

GARY YIM/SHUTTERSTOCK

Above: Smog-covered Santiago and its spectacular backdrop. **Opposite page**: Cerro Tronador on the border with Argentina.

Independence festivals on 18 September will be especially busy wherever you are.

Chile

Activity	J	F	M	A	M	J	J	A	S	O	N	D
Tour the altiplano			★	★	★	★	★		★	★	★	★
See the desert in bloom (weather dependent)							★	★	★	★		
Wine harvest festivals			★	★								
Ski in the high Andes or down a volcano						★	★	★	★			
Relax in thermal pools	★	★	★	★	★	★	★	★	★	★	★	★
Fish for Patagonian trout and salmon	★	★	★	★							★	★
Cycle the Carretera Austral	★	★	★									★
Trek in Torres del Paine	★	★	★	★					★	★	★	★
See southern Patagonia's penguins	★	★	★						★	★	★	★

Rainfall and climate charts

Santiago

Month	Average temperature in °C max-min		Average rainfall in mm
Jan	30	12	00
Feb	30	11	00
Mar	27	10	03
Apr	23	07	09
May	18	05	28
Jun	15	04	43
Jul	15	02	46
Aug	16	04	30
Sep	18	05	15
Oct	22	07	07
Nov	22 - 07		03
Dec	22 - 08		01

Valparaíso

Month	Average temperature in °C max-min		Average rainfall in mm
Jan	22	13	00
Feb	22	13	00
Mar	22	13	00
Apr	19	11	11
May	18	10	50
Jun	16	09	79
Jul	16	08	107
Aug	17	09	54
Sep	18	10	22
Oct	19	11	10
Nov	21	12	07
Dec	22	13	02

Iquique

Month	Average temperature in °C max-min		Average rainfall in mm
Jan	23	18	00
Feb	24	18	00
Mar	23	17	00
Apr	20	15	00
May	18	14	00
Jun	17	13	00
Jul	16	13	00
Aug	16	13	00
Sep	17	13	00
Oct	18	14	00
Nov	19	15	00
Dec	22	17	00

Arica

Month	Average temperature in °C max-min		Average rainfall in mm
Jan	24	19	00
Feb	24	19	00
Mar	24	18	00
Apr	22	16	00
May	19	14	00
Jun	18	13	00
Jul	17	13	00
Aug	17	14	00
Sep	17	14	00
Oct	19	15	00
Nov	21	16	00
Dec	22	18	00

Pucón

Month	Average temperature in °C max-min		Average rainfall in mm
Jan	24	09	17
Feb	25	09	22
Mar	22	08	43
Apr	18	06	63
May	14	06	112
Jun	12	05	157
Jul	12	05	111
Aug	13	04	91
Sep	15	04	66
Oct	17	06	66
Nov	20	07	49
Dec	22	09	35

Puerto Varas

Month	Average temperature in °C max-min		Average rainfall in mm
Jan	18	08	90
Feb	18	08	93
Mar	17	07	99
Apr	13	05	143
May	12	04	234
Jun	09	03	224
Jul	09	02	229
Aug	10	03	209
Sep	12	03	146
Oct	13	04	121
Nov	14	06	119
Dec	17	07	103

Ancud

Month	Average temperature in °C max-min		Average rainfall in mm
Jan	20	09	60
Feb	20	09	51
Mar	18	08	72
Apr	15	06	103
May	13	06	126
Jun	10	04	156
Jul	10	04	123
Aug	11	04	123
Sep	13	04	91
Oct	14	06	93
Nov	16	07	76
Dec	18	09	74

Coyhaique

Month	Average temperature in °C max-min		Average rainfall in mm
Jan	18	07	16
Feb	18	06	13
Mar	16	05	28
Apr	12	02	35
May	08	01	43
Jun	04	-02	56
Jul	04	-02	48
Aug	07	-01	43
Sep	10	00	26
Oct	12	02	23
Nov	14	04	15
Dec	16	06	21

Punta Arenas

Month	Average temperature in °C max-min		Average rainfall in mm
Jan	14	07	36
Feb	14	07	28
Mar	12	06	41
Apr	09	03	41
May	07	00	43
Jun	04	00	33
Jul	03	-01	33
Aug	05	00	33
Sep	08	02	28
Oct	10	03	23
Nov	12	04	28
Dec	13	06	31

Sport and activities

Chile might well have been designed for adventure tourism. In a country where you can often see the Andes from the coast, you are never more than a few hours' drive away from mountains. As a result, a wide range of adventure activities can be practised year-round. **CATA** (Consejo de Autoregulación de Aventura), T02-235 3646, www.catachile.cl, is an association of more reputable agencies, which regulates adventure tourism in the country. It works closely with the national park authority, **CONAF**, T02-236 1416, www.conaf.cl.

Canopy

This activity has become all the rage in Chile and can be found near most tourist destinations in the centre and south. It consists of gliding down zip lines through native forests. Runs are of different lengths and range from easy, child-friendly lines to vertigo-inducing descents from 60 m up. Check your equipment carefully.

Climbing

FEACH (The Federación de Andinismo), www.feach.cl, organizes training for local climbers, runs some expeditions and hires equipment to members. **ENAM** (Escuela Nacional de Montaña de Santiago), www.enamchile.cl, holds seminars and conferences on climbing and runs rock- and ice-climbing courses, as well as qualification courses for guides in Santiago and elsewhere. It also administers the *Carnet de La Federación de Chile*, a card which is often required to climb mountains especially where CONAF control access. To climb many mountains in border areas, permission must be obtained from the **Dirección de Fronteras y Límites**, T02-827 5900, www.difrol.cl. Apply well in advance.

There are various types of climbing available in Chile, including rock climbing, mountain climbing, ice climbing, volcano

Beware of the smoke! Protection from noxious sulphur fumes atop active Volcán Villarrica.

Southern Chile is full of opportunities to ride white water.

climbing and canyoning. There are hundreds of volcanoes to climb, ranging from the high-altitude Parinacota in the far north to the chain of much lower cones in the Lake District and along the Carretera Austral. The southern bank of the Río Petrohué in the Lake District offers many fantastic canyons for climbing. Nearby, rope ladders have been fixed in the canyon of the Río León, half an hour by boat from Petrohué on the southern shore of Lago Todos los Santos.

Horse riding

There is more of an equine culture south of Santiago than further north, but some of the best riding country is to the north and east of the capital. Horse treks are organized in Santiago, in Ritoque near Valparaíso, in the Elqui and Hurtado valleys, in the Lake District and on Chiloé, and in numerous remote areas of the south. One of the best places for hiring and riding horses is along the west coast of the island of Chiloé.

Mountain biking

Mountain biking is a popular activity, particularly on descents from the Andes and from *refugios* on volcanoes such as Antillanca and Osorno. Touring the length of the Carretera Austral by mountain bike is a great way of seeing this part of the country.

Skiing

Chile's major international ski resorts lie in the Andes near Santiago, but skiing is possible from Santiago to Punta Arenas. **Sernatur**, www.sernatur.cl, produces a leaflet on all Chilean ski resorts. Skiing elsewhere is mostly on the volcanoes to the south of Santiago. The larger resorts in the south are Termas de Chillán, Villarrica/Pucón and Antillanca.

Watersports

Watersports, such as diving and surfing, are generally practised in northern Chile, except for at Pichilemu, a resort three hours to the southwest of Santiago, which is famous for surfing. Over a dozen rivers between Santiago and Tierra del Fuego are excellent for whitewater rafting. The main ones are the Maipo, the Trancura, Fuy, Bueno, Rahue and Petrohué, the Yelcho, Futaleufú, Corcovado, Palena and Baker and the Serrano and Tyndall. The most attractive waters for sea kayaking are around the islands off eastern Chiloé or around Hornopirén in the fjords of the sheltered Gulf of Ancud.

How big is your footprint?

Travel to the furthest corners of the globe is now commonplace and the mass movement of people for leisure and business is a major source of foreign exchange and economic development in Chile. Towns such as Puerto Natales, San Pedro de Atacama and Pucón depend almost exclusively on tourism for their livelihoods, while every town south of Temuco is awash with people letting out private rooms in their homes. The benefits of international travel are self-evident for both hosts and travellers – employment, increased understanding of different cultures and business and leisure opportunities.

At the same time there is clearly a downside to the industry. Where visitor pressure is high and/or poorly regulated, adverse impacts on society and the natural environment may be apparent. This is as true in undeveloped and pristine areas (where culture and the natural environment are less 'prepared' for even small numbers of visitors) as in major resort destinations. The travel industry is growing rapidly and its impact is becoming increasingly apparent – air travel is clearly implicated in global warming and damage to the ozone layer, while resort location and construction can destroy natural habitats and restrict traditional rights and activities. Although these effects can seem remote and unrelated to an individual trip or holiday, a traveller's attitude and choices can make a big difference to his or her own impact on the region. And, collectively, travellers play a significant role in shaping a more responsible and sustainable industry.

Travel and tourism in a region can also have beneficial effects. Chile's national parks, for example, are part funded by receipts from visitors. Travellers can promote the patronage and protection of important heritage sites through their interest and contributions via entrance and performance fees. They can also support small-scale enterprises by staying in locally run hotels and hostels, eating in local restaurants and by purchasing local goods, supplies and crafts. In an attempt to promote awareness of responsible tourism, UK organizations such as **Green Globe** (T020-7930 8333, greenglobe@compuserve.com), the **Centre for Environmentally Sustainable Tourism** (CERT; T01268-795772) and **Tourism Concern** (T020-7753 3330, www.tourism concern.org.uk) now offer advice on destinations and sites that have made certain commitments to conservation and sustainable development. Generally these are larger mainstream destinations and resorts, although efforts are being made to also provide information on smaller operations.

Ecotourism has expanded astronomically in Chile over the past decade, and is probably the fastest-growing sector of the travel industry, providing access to a vast range of destinations and activities. While the eco-authenticity of some operators needs to be interpreted with care, there is clearly both a huge demand for this type of activity and also significant opportunities for travellers to support worthwhile conservation and social development initiatives. Organizations such as **Tourism Concern** (see above), **Planeta** (www.planeta.com), the **International Eco-Tourism Society** (T001-802-447 2121, www.ecotourism.org) and **Conservation International** (T001-202-429 5660, www.ecotour.org) have begun to develop and/or promote ecotourism projects and their websites are an excellent source of information. **Earthwatch** (T01865-311601, www.earthwatch.org) and **Discovery International** (T020-7229 9881, www.discoveryinitiatives.com) offer opportunities to participate directly in scientific and development projects throughout the region.

Responsible travel

▸▸ Where possible choose a destination, tour operator or hotel with a proven ethical and environmental commitment – if in doubt, ask.

▸▸ Spend money on locally produced (rather than imported) goods and services, buy directly from the producer or from a 'fair trade' shop, and use common sense when bargaining – the few dollars you save may be a week's salary to others.

▸▸ Use water and electricity carefully – visitors may receive preferential supply while the needs of local communities are overlooked.

▸▸ Learn about local etiquette and culture – consider local norms and behaviour and dress appropriately for local cultures and situations.

▸▸ Protect wildlife and other natural resources – don't buy souvenirs or goods unless they are clearly sustainably produced and are not protected under CITES legislation.

▸▸ Always ask before taking photographs or videos of people.

▸▸ Consider staying in local accommodation rather than foreign-owned hotels – the economic benefits for host communities are far greater – and there are more opportunities to learn about local culture.

▸▸ Make a voluntary contribution to Climate Care, www.co2.org, to counteract the pollution caused by tax-free fuel on your flight.

Mo'ai on Rapa Nui: there are around 600 on the island.

Chile on screen and page

Books to read

Roberto Bolaño's *By Night in Chile* (2003) is a caustic, brilliant novel. It tells the story of an ageing Chilean priest living through the last night of his life, as he recalls teaching Marxism to General Pinochet and various surreal encounters with the Chilean literary establishment – thereby exposing the complicity of so many in the 'normality' that accompanied the military government. If you read one novel about Chile, make it this one.

Pinochet in Piccadilly (2002), by Andy Beckett, is part travelogue and part reprise of almost two centuries of relations between England and Chile, seen through the prism of the Pinochet affair.

Isabel Allende's first and best novel, *The House of the Spirits* (1982), is set in an unnamed South American country and charts four generations of social and political upheavals of the Trueba family with a backdrop of magic realism, culminating in a bloody military takeover.

A series of highly evocative short stories, *Cabo de Hornos* (1941), by Fransisco Coloane, is about the harsh lives of the early 20th-century European settlers on the fjords and islands of southern Patagonia.

Films to watch

La Frontera (1991) tells the story of a Santiago teacher exiled to a desolate village for protesting against the Chilean military dictatorship. This is one of the best Chilean films ever made.

A socio-political drama, *Machuca* (2005) is centred around the friendship of two boys, one rich and one poor, during the final days of Allende's regime.

Mi Mejor Enemigo (2005) is a tragicomedy about a platoon of young Chilean conscripts and their encounter with a platoon of Argentine counterparts in the wilds of Patagonia during the Beagle Channel conflict of 1978.

The loco in *La Fiebre del Loco* (2001), is a small mollusc that's in danger of extinction but highly prized by the Japanese who pay handsomely for this delicacy. As the seasonal ban on its exploitation is lifted, all hell breaks loose.

La Batalla de Chile (1972-1979) is a hard-hitting, award-winning, three-part documentary charting the months leading up to the 1973 military coup. The film was banned in Chile until 1990.

Contents

Essentials

Getting there

Air

Long-haul flights generally allow one piece of luggage of up to 23 kg, or two pieces of 23 kg for flights from or via the USA; you are likely to be charged extra for more. If you know you are over the limit, arrive early. Weight limits for internal flights are usually 20 kg for economy class, but can be as low as 10 kg on smaller aircraft in Patagonia.

Flights from the Europe.

Flights from the UK take 18 to 20 hours, including a change of plane. It is impossible to fly directly to Santiago from London, so connections have to be made on one of the following routes: **Aerolíneas Argentinas** ① www.aerolineas.com.ar, via Madrid and/or Buenos Aires; **Air France** ① www.airfrance.com, via Paris; **British Airways** ① www.ba.com, connecting through **LanChile** in Buenos Aires; **Iberia** ① www.iberia.com, via Madrid or Barcelona; **LanChile** ① www.lan.com, via Madrid; **Lufthansa** ① www.lufthansa.com, code sharing with **Swiss International Airlines** ① www.swis.com, via Zurich; **TAM** ① www.tam.com.br, via Paris and São Paulo, or with one of the American carriers via New York, Atlanta or Miami.

Flights from North America

Flights from Miami to Santiago take nine hours and are operated by **American Airlines** ① www.aa.com, and **LanChile** direct from Miami, New York and Dallas Fort Worth. **LanChile** also has flights to Santiago from Miami and New York, as well as from Los Angeles, while **Delta** ① www.delta.com, has a service from Atlanta. Additional flights from Los Angeles, Miami and New York to Santiago are operated by **Copa** ① www.copaair.com, via Panama City. **Taca** ① www.taca.com, via San José or San Salvador. **AeroMéxico** ① www.mexicana.com, via Mexico City, have flights from several US cities.

From Canada, **Air Canada** ① www.aircanada.com, has the only direct flights, from Toronto, connecting from all other major cities. **LanChile** offers connections with sister airlines from Vancouver to Los Angeles and thence to Santiago, or from Toronto to New York and on to Santiago. Both **American** and **Delta** also have services via the US.

Flights from Australia, New Zealand and South Africa

LanChile flies from Tahiti (connections to Japan, Australia and New Zealand) to Santiago, with a stop at RapaNui/Easter Island. **Qantas** ① www.qantas.com.au, and **LanChile** have a code-sharing agreement on flights between Sydney and Santiago via Auckland. There are also several weekly flights from Auckland to Santiago via Buenos Aires with **Aerolíneas Argentinas**. From South Africa it is possible to connect to Santiago through Buenos Aires, Rio de Janeiro or São Paulo on **South African Airways** from Johannesburg.

Flights from other Latin American countries

There are about 75 flights per week to Santiago from Buenos Aires (Argentina), operated by **LanChile**, **Aerolíneas Argentinas** and **Gol**. There are also flights by **LanChile** from Bariloche, Córdoba, Mendoza and Rosario, and summer flights from Ushuaia. **LanChile** and **Pluna** run services from Montevideo (Uruguay). **TAM** connects with Asunción (Paraguay). Flights from Rio de Janeiro (Brazil) are run by **LanChile** and **Gol**. There are also

Packing for Chile

Everybody has their own list but here are a few suggestions to help you pack for your trip to Chile. Take twice as much money as you think you might need. As far as clothing is concerned, be prepared for the desert heat and mountain snow. You'll need fully waterproof clothing (essential for the south at any time of year), very warm clothes for the northern highlands and the far south, light clothing for the summer, plus a sun hat, a pair of strong shoes/boots and a pair of sandals (outside Santiago sizes over 10½/44 are very hard to find). A sarong is very useful as it can be used as a skirt, curtain, bedsheet or a towel.

Other items that you might want to take (especially budget travellers) include an inflatable travel pillow for neck support, a small first-aid kit and handbook, earplugs and airline-type eye mask to help you sleep in noisy and poorly curtained hotel rooms, a sheet sleeping bag and pillowcase, a clothes line, a nailbrush (useful for scrubbing dirt off clothes as well as off oneself), a universal plug, a Swiss Army knife, an alarm clock or watch and a torch or headlamp. Remember not to throw away spent batteries containing mercury or cadmium; take them home to be disposed of, or recycled properly. Good clothes are also available in Chile, usually at prices which are half those in Europe or North America.

It's a good idea to travel with pre-moistened wipes (such as Wet Ones) and toilet paper – cheap hotels and restaurants do not supply it. Obviously these, as well as all basic toiletries, are readily available in Chile.

services from São Paulo by **LanChile**, **TAM** and Gol. Flights from La Paz and Santa Cruz (Bolivia) are offered by LanChile. There are many flights from Lima (Peru) by **LanPeru**, **TACA** and **LanChile**. Sky has a weekly service from Arequipa. From Ecuador, **LanChile** fly non-stop from Guayaquil or Quito. **Avianca**, **AeroMéxico** and **LanChile** also fly from Bogotá (Colombia), Caracas (Venezuela) and Havana (Cuba); Mexico City is served by **AeroMéxico** and **LanChile** with that latter also having flights from Cancún.

Flights to other Chilean destinations

There are flights to Arica and Iquique from La Paz and Santa Cruz with **LanChile**. **LanChile** flies to Santiago from Stanley on the Falkland Islands (Malvinas) via Punta Arenas. **DAP** flies between Punta Arenas and Ushuaia.

Prices and discounts

The very busy seasons are 7 December to 15 January (until the end of February for flights within South America) and 10 July to 10 September. If you intend travelling during those times, book as far ahead as possible. From February to May and September to November special offers may be available. Fares vary from airline to airline and according to the time of year. Most airlines offer discounted fares of one sort or another on scheduled flights, and discounted fares are offered through specialist agencies, but always check the reservation with the airline concerned to make sure the flight still exists.

Student (or under 26) fares Do not assume that student tickets are the cheapest; though they are often very flexible, they can be more expensive than excursion or yearly fares. Some airlines are flexible on the age limit, others are strict.

Round-the-world fares Many airlines now offer code-sharing round-the-world fares. Although the cheapest ones tend to miss out South America, the Buenos Aires–Wellington and Santiago–Tahiti–Sydney flights mean that, for around US$1945 plus taxes, it is possible to include Chile on a round-the-world trip.

Open-jaw fares These are for people intending to travel a linear route, arriving at and departing from different airports. Open jaws are available as student, yearly or excursion fares. Many require a change of plane at an intermediate point, and a stopover may be permitted, or even obligatory, depending on schedules. Simply because a flight stops at a given airport does not mean you can break your journey there; the airline must have traffic rights to pick up or set down passengers between points A and B before it will be permitted. This is where dealing with a specialized agency (such as **Journey Latin America**) will really pay dividends. On multi-stop itineraries, the specialized agencies can often save clients hundreds of pounds.

Airport information

Aeropuerto Arturo Merino Benítez ⓘ *26 km northwest of Santiago at Pudahuel, help desk T02-690 1752, www.aeropuertosantiago.cl*, handles both international and domestic flights, and is the only airport in Chile with intercontinental connections. It is a modern, safe and efficient terminal, recently voted the best airport in Latin America from a sample of 70,000 international businesspeople. Domestic and international flights leave from different sections of the same terminal. Procedures at customs (*aduana*) are quick and efficient. Facilities include ATMs accepting both Visa and MasterCard, fast-food outlets, a **Sernatur** tourist information office, which offers an accommodation booking service, a *casa de cambio* (poor rates) and several car-hire offices. Left luggage is expensive at US$9 per item per day (max 60 days). Outside customs there are kiosks for minibus and taxi companies serving Santiago, as well as car-hire companies; you are likely to be approached by people offering taxi and bus services as you emerge from the customs area. ▸▸ *See Ins and outs, page 62.*

Check-in time for international flights is two hours before departure, one hour for domestic flights. Some airlines have an online check-in option, after which they require you to be at the airport just 45 minutes before departure. Remember that some airlines require you to reconfirm bookings on international flights 72 hours in advance. Airport **departure tax** is US$30 for international flights; US$11 for domestic flights, as well as occasional fuel surcharges, all of which should be included in the price of the ticket when bought by the traveller. In theory, there are **entry taxes** (officially called **reciprocity charges**) to be paid in US dollars at all international borders, for nationals of Albania (US$30), Australia (US$62), Canada (US$132), Mexico (US$23) and the USA (US$131); however, in practice, this tax is only charged at airports and is valid for the lifetime of the passport. These charges vary according to the how much is charged to Chilean citizens for tourist visas to these countries.

Discount flight agents

In the UK
Just the Ticket, Level 2, 28 Margaret St, London W1W 8RZ, T08700-275076, www.justtheticket.co.uk. All-purpose cheap ticket agency, often with excellent deals.

STA Travel, Priory House, 6 Wrights Lane, London W8 6TA, T08701-630026, www.statravel.co.uk. Good-value youth and student fares.

Trailfinders, 194 Kensington High St, London W8 7RG, T0845-0585858, www.trailfinders.com. Sometimes has

Main border crossings

To Argentina
Paso Agua Negra, see page page 170; **Paso San Francisco**, see page 191; three crossings at **San Pedro**, see page 232; **Paso Puyehue**, see page 375; and **Puerto Montt**, see page 393. There are several other main crossing points in the **Lake District**, see pages 346, and 359.

To Bolivia
Ollagüe, see page 221; **San Pedro**, see page 233; **Chungará** and **Visviri**, see page 264.

To Peru
Chacalluta, see page 263.

good deals to Latin America, especially at peak times.

Also check out websites such as www.expedia.co.uk; www.kayak.co.uk; www.opodo.com; www.skyscanner.net; www.travelsupermarket.com; and www.travelocity.co.uk.

In North America
Air Brokers International, 323 Geary St, Suite 411, San Francisco, CA 94102, T1-800 883 3273, www.airbrokers.com. Specialist on RTW and Circle Pacific tickets.
Airtech, 588 Broadway, Suite 204, New York, NY 10012, T212-219 7000, www.airtech.com.
Exito Travel, 1212 Broadway Suite 910, Oakland CA 94618, T1-800-6554053 (toll-free), www.exitotravel.com.
STA Travel, 10 Downing St, New York, NY 10014, T1-800-781-4040 (toll-free), www.statravel.com.

Travel CUTS, 234 College St, Toronto ON M5T 1P7, T1-866-246 9762 (toll-free), www.travelcuts.com.
Online agents include www.cheaptickets.com; www.etn.nl/discount.htm; www.expedia.com; www.priceline.com; and www.travelocity.com.

In Australia and New Zealand
Anywhere Travel, 345 Anzac Parade, Kingsford, Sydney, T02-96630411, www.anywheretravel.com.au.
Flight Centre, 82 Elizabeth St, Sydney, T02-133133, www.flightcentre.com.au. Also at 239 Queen St, Auckland, T09-369 1740, and in many other Antipodean cities.
STA Travel, 702 Harris St, Ultimo, Sydney T1300-733035, www.statravel.com.au. Also in other major cities and towns.
Travel.com.au, 80 Clarence St, Sydney, T130-1300481, www.travel.com.au.

Road

There are good road connections between Chile and Argentina; see above for an overview of border-crossing points. Note that any of the passes across the Andes to Argentina can be blocked by snow from April onwards (including the main Mendoza crossing, where travellers are occasionally stranded at the border posts). Travelling to or from Argentina anywhere north of Mendoza is likely to be an adventure you will not forget in a hurry.

Sea

Around 50 cruise ships, operated by the major cruise lines, visit Chile every summer. Enquiries regarding sea passages to Chile should be made through agencies in your own country. In the UK, try **Strand Voyages** ① *Charing Cross Shopping Concourse, The Strand, London WC2N 4HZ, T020-7836 6363*, or **The Cruise People** ① *88 York St, London W1H 1DP, T020-7723 2450 (reservations T0800-526313)*. In the USA contact **Freighter World Cruises** ① *180 South Lake Av, Pasadena, CA 91101, T1-818 449 3106, www.freighterworld.com*.

Getting around

Internal transport is usually straightforward. Most of Chile is linked by one road, the paved **Pan-American Highway** (or *Panamericana*), marked on maps as Ruta 5, which runs from the Peruvian border south to Puerto Montt and the island of Chiloé. However, some of the most popular destinations in Chile lie to the south of Puerto Montt, and travelling to this part of the country requires careful planning. Though much of this area can be reached by the **Carretera Austral**, a gravel road marked on maps as Ruta 7, bus services here are far less reliable than elsewhere in the country. Furthermore, the Carretera Austral is punctuated by three ferry crossings, with a further crossing at Villa O'Higgins for those on the direct overland route to the far south(summer only). Alternatives are to travel by sea and air from Puerto Montt. Ferries provide vital links in this region: notably from Chiloé to both Puerto Montt and Chaitén for the Carretera Austral; from Puerto Montt to Puerto Chacabuco (and Coyhaique); and from Puerto Montt to Puerto Natales in the far south.

Air

Travellers on a tight schedule should consider flying. Air travel can offer fantastic views stretching from the Andes to the sea, but the disadvantages, of course, are that it reduces your knowledge of the bits in between, and there are obvious environmental concerns. **LanChile** flies between Santiago and major cities under the banner **Lan Express**. There other main domestic airline is **Sky** ① *T600-600 2828, www.skyairline.cl*. Details of useful flights are given throughout the guide.

Check with the airlines for student and other discounts. Flights are generally cheaper the earlier you buy them. Note that with some fares it may be cheaper to fly long distance than take a *salón cama* bus, and also that flight times may be changed without warning; always double check the time of your flight when reconfirming. You should book several months in advance for flights to Easter Island in January and February.

LanChile sells a **South America Airpass**, which can be used on all **LAN** routes throughout South America. This is only recommended if you are planning on doing several long-distance flights; visit the website in order to assess the price implications; domestic air taxes are payable in addition for each flight. The airpass must be purchased abroad at the same time as an intercontinental ticket to South America. It is valid for six months, and must include at least three single flights; there is no maximum. Note that the airpass is more expensive if used in conjunction with an international flight with another carrier. Reservations should be made in advance; flight dates can be altered without penalty but route changes incur a charge of US$30 per change. A refund (minus 10%) can be obtained prior to travel.

Rail

In the north, only the line from Arica to Tacna (Peru) carries passengers. The main passenger service south from Santiago runs to Chillán; this journey is more tranquil than travelling by road along the *Panamericana* and it is faster than the bus. Services further south have been suspended but may re-open. There are also suburban passenger trains around Santiago and inland from both Concepción and Valparaíso, as well as the scenic line from Talca along the valley of the Río Maule to Constitución (see page 300), and a tourist steam train inland from Valdivia on Sundays in summer.

Trains in Chile are moderately priced, and snacks are available on the main Temuco line. There is a 15% discount on return tickets and a 10% discount for senior citizens aged 60 or over. For further information on all domestic lines, visit www.efe.cl.

Road

About half of the 85,000 km of roads in Chile can be used all year round, with an ever-increasing proportion well paved. Many other roads are described as *ripio*, meaning the surface is unmade gravel and/or stones; speed limits on these roads are usually lower. The region round the capital and the Central Valley has the best road connections. The main road is the Pan-American Highway (Ruta 5; see also page 30), which is dual carriageway from La Serena to Puerto Montt. This is a toll road; the toll includes towing to the next city and free ambulance in case of an accident. Good toll motorways also link Santiago with Valparaíso and Viña del Mar, and Chillán with Concepción. A coastal route running the length of Chile is also under construction.

Bus

Bus services in Chile are frequent and, on the whole, good. Buses tend to be punctual, arriving and leaving on time. Apart from at holiday times, there is little problem getting a seat on a long-distance bus and there is no need to reserve far in advance out of season. Services are categorized as *salón-cama* meaning 25 seats, *semi-cama* meaning 34 seats and *salón-ejecutivo* or *clásico* meaning 44 seats, all reclinable to a greater or lesser extent. There are also *prémium* services with seats that fully recline into flat beds. *Premium* and *salón-cama* services run between main cities and stops are infrequent; **Tur Bus** and **Pullman Bus** have nationwide coverage and are among the best companies.

With lots of competition between bus companies, lower fares are sometimes on offer, particularly just before departure, out of season. Prices are highest between December and March, and during the Independence celebrations in September. Students with ISIC cards may get discounts, except in high season; discounts are also often available for return journeys. Most bus companies will carry bicycles, but may ask for payment.

The best way of sending luggage around Chile is by *Encomienda*: your package is taken by bus from terminal to terminal and stored for up to one month at the destination (**Tur Bus** can deliver to a specified address). This means you can *Encomienda* bags when you don't need them, and pick them up when you do, which is great if you only need camping or cold-weather gear for, say, Torres del Paine.

Car

Documents Always carry your passport and driving licence. According to the Chilean **Ley de Tránsito**, a national driver's licence is acceptable, but *carabineros* may demand an international driver's licence (in the north especially). To avoid problems, obtain one before leaving home. Car drivers require the original registration document of their vehicle. Motorcyclists require the bike registration document and are also advised to carry an international *carnet de passages*. Bringing a private vehicle into Chile is a frustrating, time-consuming affair. Dozens of documents and a good deal of patience are required. The best advice is to find a good customs agent and let them do all the groundwork.

Buying a vehicle in Chile It is possible to buy a vehicle privately or through a dealer in Chile, although you will be responsible for repairs, maintenance and road taxes, and you will have to get a RUT (tax number) from any regional tax office. All Chilean cars have to undergo an annual technical revision (*revisión técnica*) to ensure road-worthiness, which can be carried out in any of the larger cities. If hiring a car, or buying through an agent with buy-back arrangements, check when its technical revision is due. Note also that all Chilean car taxes are payable in March each year; again, check who is responsible for paying tax. Failure to keep the tax up to date can lead to trouble with the police.

Insurance It is very expensive and increasingly difficult to insure against accident, damage or theft. If the car/motorbike is stolen or written off you will be required to pay very high import duty on its value. Get the legal minimum cover, not expensive, as soon as you can, because if you should be involved in an accident and are uninsured, your vehicle could be confiscated. If anyone is hurt, do not pick them up (you may become liable). Seek assistance from the nearest police station or hospital if you are able to do so.

Car hire Car hire is an increasingly popular way of travelling around Chile, although it tends to reduce your contact with Chileans. Many agencies, both local and international, operate in the country. Rates quoted should include insurance and 19% VAT, but always check first. A small car, with unlimited mileage costs about US$250 a week in high season around Santiago, a pickup much more, but shop around for a deal, as there is plenty of competition. In the Lake District prices are about 50% higher, while in Patagonia they can be double. Note that a few agencies are unwilling to rent cars to people holding driving licences from countries where cars drive on the left. Holders of (for example) UK driving licences are advised to travel with an international licence. If intending to leave the country in a hired car, you must obtain an authorization from the hire company, otherwise you will be turned back at the frontier. If you plan to leave more than once you will need to photocopy the authorization.

Information and maps Members of foreign motoring organizations may join the **Automóvil Club de Chile** ① *Av Andrés Bello 1863, Santiago, T02-431 1000, www.auto movilclub.cl, US$75 for 3 months,* and obtain discounts and roadside assistance. Road maps are available at the Santiago headquarters, or from other regional offices. Several individual maps provide greater detail than the Club's road atlas. Good maps are available from many Copec filling stations, which mark police posts; make sure you are not speeding when you pass them, as *carabineros* are strict about speed limits.
➤➤ *For details of other maps, see page 613.*

Earthquakes

It is impossible to spend much time in Chile without becoming aware of the fragility of the land beneath your feet. Earth tremors and violent quakes are a part of everyday life, and raising the matter with Chilean friends tends to lead to quick changes of the subject. The most severe earthquake in recent decades occurred in 1960, causing devastation to the Lake District around Valdivia, see box, page 364.

Quite apart from the terror of the earthquakes, tremors really are commonplace. These are most often felt at night, owing to the fact that everything is quieter. If sleeping, your first feeling may be that someone is gently shaking your bed and interfering with your dream. The vibrations of crockery and swaying flowers should alert you to the fact that this is something more. Once the tremor has passed, frightened dogs start barking, thought to be because – owing to their more sensitive hearing – they can hear the creaks and groans of the earth below.

While it is likely that visitors passing through the region will experience nothing more sinister than tremors, they should be aware that a severe earthquake is expected in Central Chile at some point in the next 10 to15 years. There is no way of telling, at the beginning of a tremor, whether it will develop into a full-scale earthquake. If you are unfortunate enough to experience an earthquake, do not panic. Rushing outside into the street leaves you vulnerable to falling masonry and objects such as flower pots. In fact, the safest place to hide really is beneath the lintel of a doorway, as in the old wives' tale.

Fuel Petrol (Bencina) costs about US$1.10 per litre, but becomes more expensive the further north and further south you go. Petrol is unleaded, 93, 95 or 97 octane. Diesel fuel (confusingly known as Petróleo) is widely available and much cheaper. Most service stations accept credit cards, except perhaps those in isolated rural areas, and the standard of facilities is generally good. When driving in the south (on the Carretera Austral particularly) and in the northern desert and altiplano, always top up your fuel tank and carry spare fuel in a steel container. Car hire companies may not have fuel cans and they are not obtainable from service stations, although some supermarkets may stock them.

Safety and security Chile is much safer than most South American countries, and you need do no more to protect your vehicle than you would at home. Remove all belongings and detach the radio panel when a car is unattended. Be sure to note down key numbers and carry spares of the most important ones (but don't keep all spare keys inside the vehicle). Wheels should be secured by locking nuts. Driving at night is not recommended; be especially careful on major roads into and out of cities in the early evening because people tend to cross the highway without warning. Watch out for cyclists without lights at night in rural areas.

Cycling

At first glance a bicycle may not appear to be the most obvious vehicle for a major journey, but given ample time and reasonable energy it is certainly one of the best. A mountain bike can be ridden, carried by almost every form of transport from an aeroplane to a canoe, and lifted across your shoulders over short distances. Cyclists can be the envy of travellers using more orthodox transport, since they can travel at their own pace, explore more remote regions and meet people who are less commonly in contact with tourists. Bring a tool-kit and as many spare parts as you can. Try not to leave a fully laden bike on its own, and always secure your bike with a lock.

Useful tips Wind, not hills, is the enemy of the cyclist. Try to make the best use of the times of day when there is little; mornings tend to be best but there is no steadfast rule. Take care to avoid dehydration. In northern Chile, where supplies of water are scarce between towns, be sure to carry an ample supply. Give your bicycle a thorough daily check for loose parts, and to see that they all run smoothly. A good chain should last 3000 km or more but be sure to keep it as clean as possible and to oil it lightly from time to time. Most towns have a bicycle shop of some description, but it is best to do your own repairs and adjustments whenever possible. Most cyclists agree that the main danger comes from other traffic. A rearview mirror has been frequently recommended to forewarn you of vehicles which are too close behind. Make yourself conspicuous by wearing bright clothing. Wearing a helmet is a legal requirement. Several good handbooks on long-distance cycle touring are available in larger bookshops. In the UK there is also the **Cyclist's Touring Club** (CTC) ① *Cotterell House, 69 Meadrow, Godalming, Surrey, GU7 3HS, T0870-8700060, www.ctc.org.uk*, for touring and technical information.

Hitchhiking
Hitchhiking in Chile is relatively easy and safe, and when a lift does come along it is often in the shape of an exhilarating open-air ride in the back of a pickup truck. However, in some regions – especially in the south – traffic is sparse, and roads in places like Tierra del Fuego rarely see more than two or three vehicles per day. Drivers will sometimes make hand-signals if they are only going a short distance beyond – this is not a rude gesture.

Taxis and *colectivos*
Taxis usually have meters and can be engaged either in the street or by phoning, though they tend to be more expensive when booked from a hotel. A minimum fare is shown on a large sticker in the windscreen, with increments (usually per 200 m or 60 seconds) below. A surcharge (typically around 50%) is applied after 2100 and on Sunday. Agree beforehand on fares for long journeys out of city centres or for special excursions; also compare prices among several drivers for this sort of trip. There is no need to give a tip unless some extra service is performed. Bear in mind that taxi drivers may not know the location of streets away from city centres.

Colectivos (collective taxis) operate on fixed routes (identified by numbers and destinations) and are a good way of getting around cities. They are usually flagged down on the street corner, although in some cities such as Puerto Montt there are signs. The fixed charges are normally advertised in the front windscreen and increase at night and weekends. It is best to use small denominations when paying, as the driver takes the money and offers change while driving along. Yellow *colectivos* also operate on some inter-urban routes, leaving from a set point when full. They compete favourably with buses for speed but not for comfort.

Sea

In the south of Chile, maritime transport is very important. Vital routes are, from north to south: Puerto Montt to Chiloé (many daily); Puerto Montt to Chaitén (several weekly) and Puerto Chacabuco (weekly); Puerto Montt to Puerto Natales (weekly); Castro or Quellón to Chaitén (several weekly in summer, fewer in winter); Quellón to Puerto Chacabuco (once weekly); Punta Arenas to Porvenir (six times weekly); Punta Arenas to Puerto Williams (twice monthly). Details of all routes and booking information are given under the relevant chapters. Note that routes and timetables change frequently.

Maps

A good map of Santiago is the *Plano de Santiago*, published annually by **Publiguías**. Maps of Santiago are also available at kiosks and bookshops in the capital. Maps of the major tourist and trekking areas are published by **Matasi**, and are sold locally at newspaper kiosks and good bookshops. However, they do contain the odd error which can be rather serious if you are stuck off the beaten path. Good trekking maps for central Chile can be ordered from www.trekkingchile.com.

Geophysical and topographical maps (US$14) are available from **Instituto Geográfico Militar** ① *Dieciocho 369, T02-698 7278, Mar-Dec Mon-Fri 0900-1800; Jan and Feb Mon-Fri 0800-1400*. The **Instituto Geográfico** has published a *Guía Caminera*, with roads and city plans (not 100% accurate). It is only available at IGM offices, although the **Biblioteca Nacional** in Santiago has an excellent collection of IGM maps, sections of which can be photocopied. **Copec** service stations sell guidebooks with good general maps (see page 613).

Stanfords ① *12-14 Long Acre, Covent Garden, London WC2E 9LP, T020-7836 1321, www.stanfords.co.uk* is the world's largest map and travel bookshop. It also has branches at 29 Corn Street, Bristol BS1, and at 39 Spring Gardens, Manchester M2.

Sleeping

Chile is still relatively behind the times with accommodation, so the swisher hotels are often part of uninspiring international chains, while the 'historic' hotels are often run down. Some characterful bed and breakfasts are cropping up, but there are hardly any places that make you think 'wow'. In most parts of Chile, however, accommodation is plentiful and finding a room to suit your budget should be easy. During the summer holiday months of January and February, rooms can be more scarce – especially in upmarket hotels in the more popular holiday venues of the south. This is also true during Easter, and at the time of the Independence Day holidays in mid-September. Even so, you should rarely have a problem in getting a roof over your head. In larger cities, the cheapest and often the nastiest hotels tend to be situated around bus terminals. If you arrive late and are just passing through, they may be OK, but better quality accommodation is often to be found near the main plaza.

Types of accommodation

The term **hotel** implies an expensive establishment in the south (but not necessarily in the north). Top-class hotels are available in Santiago and major cities, but elsewhere choice is more limited. **Hosterías** tend to be in rural areas and may have many of the facilities of a hotel, while the terms **hostal**, **residencial** and **hospedaje** usually refer to a small family-run establishment with limited facilities and services. A **motel**, especially if it is situated on the outskirts of a city, is likely to rent rooms by the hour. In the south, many families offer bed and breakfast, which may be advertised by a sign in the window. People here often meet buses to offer rooms, but the quality is variable.

Backpackers should consult www.backpackerschile.com and www.backpackers best.cl for information on suitable accommodation around the country. The former focuses on hostels charging around US$15-25 per person and are all of a good standard, while the latter features lots of hostels in a broad price range.

Camping

Camping is not always cheap at official sites. A common practice is to charge US$18 or more for up to five people, with no reductions for fewer than five; however, if a site is not full, owners will often give a pitch to a single person for around US$8. A few hostels (indicated in the text) allow camping in their garden and offer very good value per-person rates. Cheap gas stoves can be bought in camping shops in Santiago and popular trekking areas and green replaceable cylinders are available throughout the country. Campsites are very busy in January and February.

Camping wild is easy and safe in remote areas of the far south and in the *cordillera* north of Santiago. However, in much of central and central-southern Chile the land is fenced off, and it is often necessary to ask permission to camp. In Mapuche and Aymará communities it is both courteous and advisable to make for the primary school or some other focal point of a village to meet prominent members of the community first. Camping wild in the north is difficult, because of the absence of water. Note that officially it is illegal to camp on private land without permission.

Albergues (youth hostels)

Albergues spring up in summer all over the south of Chile. These are usually schools earning extra money by renting out floor space. They are very cheap (rarely more than US$7 per person) and are excellent places to meet young Chileans. Do not go to them if you want a good night's sleep, though; guitars often play on into the small hours. There is no need for an Hostelling International (HI) card to stay in *albergues*, but there is rarely much in the way of security either.

Sleeping price codes

LL	over US$200	B	US$46-65	E	US$12-20
L	US$151-200	C	US$31-45	F	US$7-11
AL	US$101-150	D	US$21-30	G	under US$7
A	US$66-100				

For a double room in high season, excluding taxes.

Hostelling International youth hostels throughout Chile cost about US$12-24 per person. The HI card (US$30) is usually readily accepted. In practice, HI hostels in Chile, while generally decent, are not necessarily better than any other hostel. Better value can more often than not be had elsewhere.

Prices
Accommodation is more expensive in Santiago than in most other parts of the country, although prices also tend to be higher in Patagonia, as well as in some northern cities such as Antofagasta. In tourist areas, prices rise in the high season (January/February, plus any local festivity), but off season you can often bargain for a lower price, though you will usually have to stay for two or more days to be successful; ask politely for a discount (descuento). Single travellers do not come off too badly in Chile compared to some other Latin American countries. In the south, hospedajes charge per person (although you may have to share your room), while in the north, single rooms are about 60-70% the price of a double.

Value Added Tax (known as **IVA**) at 19% is charged on hotel bills and should be included in any price quoted in pesos. The government waives the VAT charge for hotel bills paid in dollars or Euros but only for authorized hotels. As a result, larger hotels (but few other establishments) can offer you much lower tariffs if you pay in dollars than those advertised in pesos. However, they will often have such a poor dollar exchange rate that you can end up paying more in dollars than in pesos. Ask for prices in both currencies and see which is cheaper. Establish clearly in advance what is included in the price.

Rooms and facilities
Many hotels, but few budget places, have restaurants serving lunch and dinner. Most hospedajes offer breakfast, which usually consists of instant coffee or tea with bread and jam; but in the north, fewer hotels offer breakfast. An increasing number of cheaper establishments have kitchen facilities for guest use, but if you are relying on these you should check them out first. Most establishments will not allow you to wash and dry clothes in your room, but some offer facilities for you to do your own laundry. Many hotels have parking facilities, though in large cities this may be a few blocks from the hotel itself. Motorcycle parking is widely available.

Reception areas in hotels can be very misleading, so it is a very good idea to see the room before booking. If you are shown a dark room without a window, ask if there are rooms with windows (con ventana). In large cities the choice may be between an inside room without a window and a room with a window over a noisy street. Many middle-range establishments have rooms with private bathroom (con baño privado) and without (con baño compartido) so it is often worth asking whether there is anything cheaper than the price initially quoted. If you are not satisfied, do not be afraid of walking away and trying elsewhere.

Many hotels, restaurants and bars have inadequate water supplies. With few exceptions, used toilet paper should not be flushed down the pan, but placed in the receptacle provided. This applies even in expensive hotels. Failure to observe this custom will block the pan or drain, causing a considerable health risk. Remember to carry toilet paper with you, as cheaper establishments as well as restaurants, bars, etc, frequently do not supply it.

Eating and drinking

Chile's cuisine is varied and often delicious. The Mediterranean climate of the central regions is perfect for growing a wide variety of fruit and vegetables – avocados are especially delicious. The semi-tropical climate of northern Chile supplies mangoes, papayas, *lúcumas* and *chirimoyas* (custard apples). In the central valley, grapes, melons and watermelons abound. The lush grasslands of the south are ideal for dairy and beef farming as well as for growing grains, apples, cherries and plums, while in Patagonia, sheep roam the plains and rhubarb grows wild.

Although Chilean cuisine is mostly rooted in the Spanish tradition, it has also been influenced by the immigrant groups who have settled in the country. The pastry-making skills of the Germans have produced 'onces Alemanas', a kind of high tea with *Küchen. Pan de Pascua*, a traditional Christmas fruit loaf, also derives from Germany.

The main meals are breakfast (*desayuno*), lunch (*almuerzo*) and dinner (*cena*). Lunch is eaten any time from 1300 to 1530, and dinner between 2000 and 2230. *Las onces* (literally elevenses) is the name given to a snack usually including tea, bread, cheese, etc, eaten by many Chileans as their evening meal. Breakfast usually consists of bread, butter and jam, served with coffee (usually instant) or tea. Lunch tends to be the main meal of the day, and many restaurants serve a cheaper fixed-price meal at lunch time; when this consists of a single dish it is known as *la colación*, whereas if there is more than one course it is called *el menú*. In more expensive places, this may not be referred to on the menu. ▸▸ *For simple vocabulary related to food and drink, see page 616.*

Food

Seafood

Perhaps the most outstanding type of food is the seafood. Although there are good fish restaurants in Santiago, and fine seafood can be found at the Mercado Central, naturally the best seafood and fish is found on the coast. The excellent fish restaurants between Playa Ancha and Concón, near Valparaíso, are especially popular with Santiaguinos. Almost every port on the Chilean coast has a small market or a row of seafood restaurants where excellent seafood can be eaten very cheaply; in smaller harbours, it is often possible to eat with the fishermen. Most of these seafood restaurants receive their supplies of fish and shellfish from local fishing boats that land their catch every morning in the harbours. Watching the unloading at a port such as Talcahuano can be fascinating. If you have the courage to bargain you may be able to pick up some delicious, fresh fish from the boats or from the stalls along the harbour; whole crates of shellfish go for the equivalent of a few dollars.

Eating price codes

♈♈♈ over US$12   **♈♈** US$7-12   **♈** under US$7

For a main course or set menu for one person, excluding drinks and service charge.

In the north, great seafood can be had at Caleta Hornos, north of La Serena, and at Huasco. In the centre and south the best seafood is to be had at Concón, Valparaíso, Constitución, Talcahuano, Angelmó (Puerto Montt) and on Chiloé, where you should try the famous *curanto*, a stew of shellfish, pork, chicken and other ingredients. Beware of eating seafood that you have bought unofficially in the far south because of the poisonous *marea roja*.

The most popular fish are *merluza* (a species of hake inferior to European hake), *congrio* (kingclip or ling), *corvina* (bass), *reineta* (a type of bream), *lenguado* (a large kind of sole), *albacora* (sword fish) and *salmón*. *Merluza*, which is usually fried, is an inexpensive fish, found in ordinary restaurants. *Congrio* is very popular, and particularly delicious served as *caldillo de congrio*, a soup containing a large *congrio* steak. *Albacora* is a delicious fish, available mainly in quality restaurants. *Ceviche*, fish marinated in lemon juice, is usually made with *corvina*.

There is an almost bewildering array of shellfish. Look out for *choritos*, *cholgas* and *choros maltón* (varieties of mussel), *ostiones* (queen scallops), *ostras* (oysters) and *erizos* (sea urchins). Prawns are known as *camarones*, but these are often imported from Ecuador and can be tasteless and expensive. Chile's most characteristic products are the delicious *erizos*, *machas*, *picorocos* and *locos*, which are only found in these seas. *Machas a la parmesana* are a kind of razor clam prepared in their shells with a parmesan cheese sauce, grilled and served as a starter. *Picorocos* (giant barnacles), which are normally boiled or steamed in white wine, are grotesque to look at but have a very intense taste: it may be very disconcerting to be presented with a plate containing a rock with feathery fins but it is well worth taking up the challenge of eating it. Note, only the white fleshy part is edible. *Locos*, a kind of abalone, are the most popular Chilean mollusc, but because of overexploitation its fishing is frequently banned. The main crustaceans are *jaiba* (purple crab), *langosta* (lobster) and the *centolla*, an exquisite king crab from the waters of the south.

Packages of dried seaweed, particularly *cochayuyo* (which looks like a leathery thong), are sold along coastal roads. Both *cochayuyo* and *luche* are made into a cheap, nutritious stew with vegetables, and eaten with potatoes or rice; these dishes are rarely available in restaurants. Until recently salmon was available only in the south where the rivers and lakes are full of 'wild' salmon that has escaped from farms. It is now farmed extensively in the south and can be found on menus in many parts of the country.

Other specialities

Away from seafood, savoury Chilean dishes tend to be creative. Specialities include *humitas* (mashed sweetcorn mixed with butter and spices and baked in sweetcorn leaves), *pastel de papas* (meat pie covered with mashed potatoes), and *cazuela*, either *de ave* (chicken) or *de vacuno* (beef); it's a nutritious stew with pumpkin, potato, coriander and rice, and maybe onions and green peppers – the most common everyday dish. In central and southern Chile stews with beans (*porotos*) are common. A typical (and unhealthy) dish from Valparaíso is the *chorillana*: chips covered with sliced steak, fried onions and scrambled eggs. *Pastel de choclo* is a casserole of chicken, minced beef and onions with olives, topped with polenta, baked in an earthenware bowl. *Prieta* is a blood sausage stuffed with cabbage leaves. *Bife* or *lomo a lo pobre* (a poor man's steak) is just the opposite: it is a steak topped by two fried eggs, chips and onions. A *paila* can take many forms (the *paila* is simply a kind of serving dish), but the most common are made of eggs or seafood. In the north, *paila de huevos* (scrambled eggs with *hallulla* – a kind of bread) is common for breakfast. A *paila marina* is a delicious shellfish stew.

Chileans tend to have a very sweet tooth, and their **desserts** can be full of *manjar* (caramelized condensed milk).

Snacks

Among the many snacks sold in Chile, the most famous are *empanadas*, pastry turnovers made *de pino* (with meat, onions, egg and an olive), *queso* (cheese) or *mariscos* (shellfish). The quality of *empanadas* varies: many are full of onions rather than meat; by the coast the *empanadas de mariscos* are delicious and usually better value.

Chilean sandwiches tend to be fairly substantial: the *churrasco* is a minute steak in a bun and can be ordered with any variety of fillings. *Chacareros* contain thinly sliced steak and salad; *barros lucos* have steak and grilled cheese; and *barros jarpas* have grilled cheese and ham.

Completos are the cheapest and most popular snacks: betraying the German influence on everyday food, these are hot dogs served with plenty of extras, including mustard, sauerkraut, tomatoes, mayonnaise and *ají* (hot sauce). An *Italiano* is a *completo* with avocado and without the sauerkraut. Avocado is very popular at family *onces*, mashed up and served on bread. Bread itself is plentiful and cheap, and comes in pairs of fluffy rolls (*marraquetas*) or as a crisper slim roll (*hallullas*). Most large cities also have many ice cream stands doing a roaring trade.

Drink

Coffee and tea While Argentine cafés have excellent coffee, if you ask for coffee in many places in Chile you will get a cup of boiling water and a tin of instant coffee, even in quite high-class restaurants. There are espresso bars in major cities, elsewhere specify *café-café, espresso*. A *cortado* is an expresso with hot frothed milk served in a glass. Tea is usually served with neither milk nor lemon. If you order *café*, or *té, con leche'*, it will come with all milk; to have just a little milk ask for your tea or coffee *'con un poco de leche'*. After a meal, instead of coffee, try an *agüita* – hot water in which herbs such as mint, or aromatics such as lemon peel, have been steeped. A wide variety of refreshing herbal teas is available in sachets.

Wine The international reputation of Chilean wine continues to grow every year. The last 25 years have seen radical modernization and innovation in production techniques and processes putting Chile firmly on the world wine map. Chilean reds tend to be full bodied with lots of tannins and high alcohol content. Production centres around the great Bordeaux grapes, Cabernet Sauvignon, Merlot and Chilean wine's latest claim to fame, the lost Carmenère grape, wiped out in France over a century ago and rediscovered in Chile a decade ago. Pinot Noir is also now being successfully produced. Chilean whites are also getting better every year. Sauvignon Blancs from Casablanca and San Antonio tend to be crisp and fruity and are excellent when drunk young, while the Chardonnays have been

winning awards for years. The very best wines can sell for upwards of US$50 a bottle, while a good reserve wine might set you back around US$10. Anything over US$3 should be perfectly drinkable, and even cheaper wine sold in tetrapacks (US$2.50 a litre) can sometimes be surprisingly good. Anything cheaper than this should be avoided.
» For more on wine, see page 609.

Beer The emergence in recent years of several small independent breweries means that Chilean beer is no longer as bland as it used to be, and makes a fresh change from the previous situation whereby CCU, the country's largest brewery, had bought out the regional competition one by one and either discontinued or standardized their beers. Chile's best-selling beer is the rather insipid *Cristal*. *Escudo* is slightly more full bodied, while *Royal Guard* has a more flowery flavour. *Austral* brewed in Patagonia is good, but mediocre elsewhere. *Báltica* is good, stong and cheap. *Heineken* and *Brahma* are also good, but *Dorada* is best left for the drunks. *Kunstmann* is the best of the nationwide beers. *Malta*, a dark beer, is recommended for those wanting a British-type beer; however, there are different breweries, and the *Malta* north of Temuco is more bitter than that to the south. Of the regional beers, *Cerveza del Puerto* (Valparaíso), *Kross* (Curacaví), *Los Colonos* (Llanquihue) and *Imperial* (Punta Arenas) are all recommended. European beers are increasingly available. A refundable deposit is required for litre beer bottles (about US$0.50). Disposable bottles are sold, but these are more expensive, as are cans and smaller bottles. Draught lager is generically known as *Schop*.

Pisco and other spirits The most famous spirit is *pisco*, made with grapes, usually drunk with lemon or lime juice as *pisco sour*. *Pisco* is also often mixed with coca cola or sprite. *Pisco* is graded in strength from 30-46°; surprisingly, the stronger versions are much more pleasant and easy to drink, as they have generally had more time to mature in the barrel. Recommended brands of *pisco* are *Alto del Carmen* and *Bauzá*; avoid the ironically named *Pisco Control*, especially at 30°C. Local rum and brandy are very cheap and tend to lead to poisonous hangovers. *Manzanilla* is a local liqueur, made from *licor de oro* (like Galliano). Two delicious drinks are *vaina*, a mixture of brandy, egg and sugar and *cola de mono*, a mixture of *aguardiente*, coffee, milk and vanilla served very cold at Christmas. There are many seasonal fruit liqueurs which are delicious; *eguindado*, made from cherries, is particularly recommended. *Chicha* is any form of alcoholic drink made from fruit; *chicha cocida* is three-day-old fermented grape juice boiled to reduce its volume and then bottled with a tablespoonful of honey, while *chicha fresca* is fresh fermented grape juice. Cider (*chicha de manzana*) is popular in the south.

Other drinks Away from alcoholic drinks, Chile does not perhaps take as much advantage of its variety of fruits as it should. Unlike in Mexico, say, cheap and freshly squeezed juices are uncommon, though of course there is nothing to stop you buying a job lot of fruit from the market and preparing juices for yourself. Note that a *jugo natural* is fresh fruit liquidized with water and sugar added. If you want a 100% pure fresh juice you should ask for a *vitamina*. *Mote con huesillo*, made from wheat hominy and dried peaches, is very refreshing in summer. Families tend to drink a lot of sugary soft drinks, picking up on the usual international brands.

Eating out

Fashionable Chilean society has seen something of a gastronomic boom over the last few years. An increasing number of boutique restaurants have been opening in Santiago (and to a lesser extent in other major cities). Typically, with upper-class Chile's insecurity with its own identity they almost all shun Chilean food in favour of the flavour of the month, whether it be sushi or 'ethnic fusion'. Many of these are cliché copies of northern hemisphere new cuisine. Occasionally there are new restaurants that try to fuse uniquely Chilean ingredients with international styles and these are worth looking out for. The older established elegant restaurants rarely offer typical Chilean food either, tending to stick to Mediterranean fare.

The focal point for life in towns is the plaza, in which there will typically be a number of slightly upmarket cafés, where people tend to have a beer and snacks, but rarely go for a full meal. If you are travelling in small villages off the beaten track, it is usually possible to find someone who will cook for you; ask around. Those on a budget will want to stick to the cheaper eateries, where simple and very tasty meals can be had at a very reasonable price; a *colación* need not cost you more than US$3. The cheapest restaurants in urban areas tend to be by the transport terminals and markets or, in coastal areas, by the port. These restaurants may well have a wide choice of food for very reasonable prices, and often there is very little difference in the quality of the food between cheaper and more expensive places, the main differences being the service and the elegance (or pretensions) of the surroundings. More expensive places will, though, have a wider range of starters and desserts, which are often non-existent in cheaper eateries. Among the cheaper eating places are the *casinos de bomberos* (firemen's canteens) in most towns. Fire stations are not paid for by the state, and firemen are all voluntary. Eating at a canteen helps fund their work, and the food is usually cheap and good.

Although there are **vegetarian restaurants** in major cities, vegetarians will find that their choice of food is severely restricted, especially in smaller towns and away from tourist areas. To confuse matters, '*carne*' is understood to mean red meat, so asking if a dish has meat in it is likely to lead to disaster; or chicken, at the very least. Vegetarians should explain which foods they cannot eat rather than saying '*Soy vegetariano*' (I'm a vegetarian) or '*No como carne*' ('I don't eat meat'). To make matters worse, the bread known as *hallulas* is often made with lard (*manteca*); ask first. There are fewer problems for vegetarians if they can cook for themselves, and they may be best off looking for accommodation that has cooking facilities.

Entertainment

Bars and clubs

Nightlife in Chile varies enormously depending on where you are. Santiago and other university towns as well as major tourist resorts have a thriving nightlife. In the latter case bars may get busy at around 2000 or 2100, whereas in major cities nightlife rarely gets going before midnight. Bohemian nightlife in Santiago centres around Barrio Bellavista, below Cerro San Cristóbal, where you can listen to anything from 1980s pop to salsa, jazz or the latest fashions in both Latin and European music, and the streets are crowded with night birds until after 0500 in the morning. Valparaíso has become a centre for the Electronic music scene and in summer there are several events. Most towns and villages of any size will have a disco open at weekends and at least one bar, although invariably this will be populated by no more than two old drunks sharing a tetrapack of cheap wine. There is quite a severe alcoholism problem, especially on Chiloé and in the far south.

Cinema

With the expansion of mall culture in Chile, most of the larger cities are home to multiplex cinemas. These generally show Hollywood blockbusters and the occasional South American film. Prices are usually cheaper on weekday afternoons, and student discounts are common. Santiago has a thriving arts cinema scene and there are several repertory cinemas in the capital. Outside the capital there is an arts cinema in Viña, and in Valparaíso there are a number of film clubs with several screenings a week. Many universities throughout the country also show films. In summer there are important film festivals in Santiago, Valparaíso, Viña del Mar and Valdivia.

Dance

There are occasional performances by both Chilean and visiting groups in the capital and other culturally important cities such as Valparaíso.

Music

Concerts are common, especially in summer. Each year there are always two or three superstars (in 2009, for example, it was Madonna), who play the national stadium. The music festival in Viña also occasionally attracts rising stars. Other than that, there are several Chilean rock, pop and folk groups who are seemingly constantly on tour throughout the country. Chileans are very musical and if you go to a party in someone's house do not be surprised if someone pulls out a guitar for everyone to sing along to classic pop and folk songs.

Classical concerts are less prevalent, with Santiago naturally being the focus. In the provinces there are a few good chamber orchestras, and in summer there is a good classical festival in Frutillar as well as a series of concerts in Viña del Mar.

Theatre

Santiago is definitely the hub of Chile's theatre culture. There are dozens of small theatres showing both classic and contemporary works. Booking is best done in advance, but unless an internationally renowned group is performing, a day or two should suffice.

Festivals and events

Festivals

Festivals are held in all of Chiloé's towns, rotating from week to week, Jan and Feb (see throughout the main text for details).

20 Jan Fiesta de la Piedra Santa. Mapuche festival of the Holy Stone in the Lake District.

1st Sun in Feb Fiesta de la Candelaria. One of northern Chile's most important religious festivals, see page 194.

Mid-Feb Festival de la Canción. Viña del Mar hosts the dreaded (and often dreadful) international music festival, see page 142.

End Mar-Apr Campeonato Nacional de Rodeo. National rodeo competition in Rancagua, see page 289.

29 Jun Fiesta de San Pedro. Processions, dancing and lots of fish-eating in all coastal towns and villages in celebration of the patron saint of fishermen.

16 Jul La Tirana. This festival near Iquique, celebrating the Virgin del Carmen, is an exhilarating combination of indigenous and Catholic folklore, attended by people from all over Chile and from neighbouring Bolivia and Peru, see page 248.

13-20 Sep La Pampilla. The week-long independence celebrations in Coquimbo are the biggest in the country, see page 176.

8 Dec Fiesta de la Virgen de Lo Vásquez. The main Santiago–Valparaíso highway is closed as 80,000 faithful make the pilgrimage on foot (and sometimes even on hands and knees) to the church at Lo Vásquez.

8 Dec Día de la Virgen. Pilgrimage to Quinchao, off Chiloé, see page 417.

23-27 Dec Fiesta Grande. Vast pilgrimage to Andacollo, see page 161.

Late Dec Carnavales Culturales. 3 days of dance, music, theatre and street performance in Valparaíso leading up to the New Year celebrations.

Public holidays

1 Jan New Year's Day
2 days in Mar/Apr Easter
1 May Labour Day
21 May Navy Day
15 Aug Assumption
1st Mon in Sep Day of National Unity
18/19 Sep Independence
12 Oct Columbus Day
31 Oct and 1 Nov All Saints' Day
8 Dec Immaculate Conception
25 Dec Christmas Day

Shopping

What to buy

There is an excellent variety of handicrafts: woodwork, pottery, copperware, leather-work, indigenous woven goods including rugs and ponchos. However, many of the goods sold in main handicraft markets are from elsewhere in South America, in some cases with the country of origin labels cut off; if going on a wider South American tour, these goods are almost always cheaper in the northern Andean countries. Among the most interesting purchases will be jewellery made with the semi-precious lapis lazuli stone. There are also less well known stones unique to Chile (such as the *combarbalita*, found around Combarbalá, near Illapel), and many fine jewels and knick-knacks (such as paperweights) made with stones such as onyx. People returning home may want to buy typical Chilean foods or drinks: *pisco*, *ají chileno* or *manjar*, for instance.

Where to buy

Bargaining is rare in Chile, and often seen as impolite. You can't try the usual 'offer a half, go up to two thirds' formula, and asking for a *descuento* may be seen as implying that the goods you want to buy are defective. Instead you should ask for 'una atención', and you will often do well to knock more than 5% off the asking price. If you want to get the cheapest possible price your best bet is to go directly to the area where the object you have in mind is made, since craft specialities tend to be specific to particular places in Chile (see page 585); once there, do not go to the first craft shop you find (those nearest to the entry to the town), but look for those that are tucked away. The past decade has seen the growth of mall culture, especially in parts of Santiago, such as Las Condes.

Essentials A-Z

Accident and emergency

Air rescue T138; **Ambulance** (*ambulancia*) T132; **Fire brigade** (*bomberos*) T131; **Forest fires** (*incendios forestales*) T130; **Police** (*carabineros*) T133; **Police** – detectives – T134; **Sea rescue** T137.

Children

Chile is a good place for travelling with children as there are few health risks and children are very popular. Officials tend to be more amenable where children are concerned, and even thieves and pickpockets seem to have retained the traditional respect for families and may leave you alone because of it.

However, given Chile's geography, a lot of time can be spent travelling. On bus journeys, if the children are good at amusing themselves, or can readily sleep while travelling, the problems can be considerably reduced. Train journeys are easier, as they allow more scope for moving about, but there are few of these in Chile. On all long-distance buses you pay for each seat; there are no half-fares, so it is cheaper, if less comfortable, to seat small children on your knee for shorter trips. On urban and local buses, small children generally do not pay a fare, but are not entitled to a seat if paying customers are standing. On sightseeing tours you should always bargain for a family rate; often children can go free. Civil airlines charge a third less for children under 12.

Food can be a problem if your children are not adaptable. It is easier to take biscuits, drinks, bread, etc with you on longer trips than to rely on meal stops. You will find that people will be very friendly to children in restaurants. As far as health is concerned, remember to be very careful about sunburn in the south, due to the lack of ozone.

In hotels, try to negotiate family rates. If charges are per person, always insist that 2 children will only occupy 1 bed, therefore counting as 1 tariff. If rates are per bed, the same applies. You can often get a reduced rate at cheaper hotels.

Customs and duty free

The following may be brought into Chile duty free: 500 cigarettes or 100 cigars or 500 g of tobacco, plus 3 bottles of liquor, and all articles for personal use, including vehicles, radios, cameras, personal computers, and similar items. Chile's agricultural sector is free of many diseases, and so fruit, vegetables, meat, flowers and milk products may not be imported; these will be confiscated at all borders, where there are thorough searches. This applies even to those who have had to travel through Argentina in the far south to get from one part of Chile to another. There are also internal customs checks for all travellers going south from Región I. This is mainly to inspect for duty-free goods from Iquique but fruit, vegetables, meat, flowers and milk products may also be confiscated.

Disabled travellers

Chileans are usually very courteous, and disabled travellers will be helped and assisted where possible. The law requires that new public buildings provide disabled access and the more expensive hotels usually have dedicated facilities, transport provision is a different matter. The línea 5 subway line in Santiago has no facilitated access for the disabled and, although bus companies will certainly be helpful, and the **Transsantiago** buses are supposed to be disabled-friendly, the rest do not have any dedicated services.

Where possible, therefore, disabled travellers might be better off hiring their own transport, especially since reserved parking for the disabled is now reasonably common.

Useful organizations

Directions Unlimited,123 Green Lane, Bedford Hills, NY 10507, T1-800 533 5343. A tour operator specializing in tours for disabled US travellers.
Disability Action Group, 2 Annadale Av, Belfast BT7 3JH, T01232-491011. Information about access for British disabled travellers.
Disabled Persons' Assembly, PO Box 27-524, Wellington 6035, New Zealand, T04-801 9100, www.dpa.org.nz. Has lists of tour operators and travel agencies catering for the disabled.

Electricity

220 volts AC, 50 cycles.

Gay and lesbian travellers

In a macho culture, it is no surprise that there is quite a lot of homophobia in Chile, and gay and lesbian travellers should be aware that derogatory jokes about homosexuals (especially men) are widespread. Having said that, attitudes are beginning to loosen up, and there is a lively gay scene in most large cities. See www.puntogay.cl (Spanish only) for more information.

Health

No vaccinations are demanded by immigration officials in Chile or Argentina, but you would do well to be vaccinated against typhoid, polio, hepatitis A and tetanus. Children should, of course, also be up-to-date with any immunization programmes in their country of origin.

See your GP or travel clinic at least 6 weeks before departure for general advice on travel risks and vaccinations. Try contacting a specialist travel clinic if your own doctor is unfamiliar with health in the region. Make sure you have sufficient medical travel insurance, get a dental check, know your blood group and, if you suffer a long-term condition such as diabetes or epilepsy, obtain a Medic Alert bracelet/necklace (www.mediband.com.au).

Health risks

Temperate regions of South America, like Patagonia, present far fewer health risks than tropical areas to the north. However, travellers should take precautions against: **diarrhoea/intestinal upset**; **hanta virus** (carried by rodents and causing a flu-like illness); **hepatitis** A; **hypothermia**; **marea roja**; **rabies**; **sexually transmitted diseases**; **sunburn** (a real risk in the far south due to depleted ozone); and **ticks**.

Further information

www.btha.org British Travel Health Association.
www.cdc.gov US government site that gives excellent advice on travel health and details of disease outbreaks.
www.fco.gov.uk British Foreign and Commonwealth Office travel site has useful information on the country, people, climate and a list of UK embassies/consulates.
www.fitfortravel.scot.nhs.uk A-Z of vaccine/health advice for each country.
www.travelscreening.co.uk Travel Screening Services gives vaccine and travel health advice, email/SMS text vaccine reminders and screens returned travellers for tropical diseases.

Insurance

It is vital to take out fully comprehensive travel insurance (including medical insurance) for the duration of your stay overseas. Numerous companies offer travel insurance, including many high-street travel agents. As well as full medical insurance (including evacuation by air ambulance where necessary), it is important to check that you are covered for any special activities, as many policies exclude so-called dangerous sports (including, in some cases, trekking). Also, many cases there's a limit of cover per item, so, if you are taking something valuable and want it fully insured, you may need to pay extra.

If you do have the misfortune to be robbed (or even just to lose something), you need to make a report to the police and get a police certificate within 24 hrs in order to make a successful claim on your insurance. Be prepared for a bureaucratic nightmare. Police will either want you to make a *denuncia* (complaint), or a *constancia* (report). Beware of making a *denuncia* as you will be making a formal request to the police to follow up on the theft. As a consequence of this, if a case eventually comes to court you will be subpoenaed, and by failing to attend the trial you will be breaking the law and may well face serious problems should you visit Chile again. In most cases you should make a *constancia*. However, usually you will be presented with a stamped receipt which has no reference to the items you have reported stolen. The document you really require is called a *certificado*, and it should list all your missing goods. You may find that outside popular tourist areas the local police may not know what the *certificado* is, and you will need to explain your situation to a superior officer. Note also that every policy will have an excess amount, which you will have to pay; this varies. There is no substitute for reading the small print of a policy before signing up to it

Internet

You will have no problem locating an internet café in tourist centres, cities and towns; they are everywhere. This means that prices tend to be competitive, ranging from US$0.50-1 per hr. Other than dealing with slow connection speeds (in rural areas) and Spanish keyboards, the services are perfectly adequate, and should suit most people's needs. To access the @ symbol, you usually press the ctrl and alt keys together with 'q'.

Language

Although English is understood in many major hotels, tour agencies and airline offices (especially in Santiago), travellers are strongly advised to learn some Spanish before setting out. Chilean pronunciation – very quick and lilting, with final syllables cut off – can present difficulties to the foreigner. Chileans have a wide range of idioms that even other Latin Americans find difficult to understand. Visitors may want to buy *How to Survive in the Chilean Jungle* by John Brennan and Alvaro Taboada, a handbook for English speakers on Chilean colloquialisms and slang, available in bookshops in larger cities. In some rural areas travellers will encounter indigenous languages – Mapudungun (the Mapuche language) in the south; Aymará in the north – but most people usually also speak Spanish. For Spanish words and phrases, see page 616.

Full listings of Spanish language schools are throughout the text in the Directory sections. Many people will prefer to study somewhere other than Santiago; **Contact Chile**, Huelén 219 piso 2, Providencia, Santiago, T02-264 1719, www.contact chile.cl, offers courses throughout the country. In addition, several hostels in the provinces have Spanish schools attached.

Local customs and laws

Codes of conduct

Politeness – even a little ceremoniousness – is much appreciated in Chile. Men should always remove any headgear and say '*permiso*' when entering offices, and be

prepared to shake hands; always say
'*buenos días*' (until midday) or '*buenas
tardes*' (in the afternoon and evening) and
wait for a reply before proceeding further.
Remember that the traveller from abroad
has enjoyed greater advantages in life than
most Chilean minor officials, and should
be friendly and courteous in consequence.
Never be impatient, and do not criticize
situations in public: the officials may know
more English than you think (especially
when it comes to swearwords) and they
can certainly interpret gestures and facial
expressions. You should be aware that the
stereotype of the corrupt Latin American
official does not apply in Chile, where
most officials are scrupulously honest.

Politeness should also be extended to
street traders; saying '*No, gracias*' with a
smile is better than an arrogant dismissal.
Bargaining is not as commonplace in Chile
as in some other South American countries,
and very low offers will be seen as
contemptuous, even in markets.

Begging is rare outside Santiago.
Whether you give money to beggars is a
personal matter, but locals may provide an
indication of whether people are begging
out of genuine need. In Santiago, beggars
get onto buses and sing or sell tiny religious
calendar cards; Santiaguinos are often
generous towards them.

Dress
Urban Chileans are very fashion conscious.
You should dress reasonably smartly in the
towns and cities as scruffiness will make
things needlessly difficult. People tend to
dress smartly at bars and clubs in urban
centres – Santiago, Viña del Mar, La Serena
and Iquique being particularly swish. Away
from the cities, though, and in areas where
there are many foreign tourists, people are
less concerned about such matters.

Tipping
In restaurants 10% is a good tip, but you
should only leave about 100 pesos (US$0.15)

in bars and *fuentes de soda*. Taxi drivers are
not tipped.

Prohibitions
There are several types of police operating in
Chile: *Carabineros* (green uniforms) handle all
tasks except immigration; *Investigaciones* (in
civilian dress) are the detectives; *Policía
Internacional*, a division of the *Investigaciones*,
handle immigration and customs.

If you get into trouble with the police,
the worst thing that you can do is offer a
bribe to get yourself out of trouble. Chilean
police are very proud of their office and
will assume any attempt to bribe them is
both an insult and an admission of guilt.
Legal penalties for most offences are fairly
similar to what you might expect in a
western European or North American
country, although be advised that the
attitude towards possession of soft drugs,
such as cannabis, is very strict. If you get
into trouble, your first call should be to
your consulate, which should be able
to put you in touch with a lawyer who
speaks your language.

Media

Newspapers and magazines
Santiago daily papers are *El Mercurio*
(centre-right, a heavyweight broadsheet),
La Nación (the official state newspaper,
liberal-left and worth buying on Sun),
La Segunda (middle-market tabloid), *La
Tercera* (more serious tabloid), *La Cuarta*
(salacious and gossip-mongering) and *Las
Ultimas Noticias*. Look out for *The Clinic*, a
satirical weekly paper named after the
hospital at which General Pinochet was
arrested in 1998. Recent international
newspapers can sometimes be bought at
kiosks on the Paseo Ahumada in Santiago.

Radio
South America has more community radio
stations than practically anywhere else in

the world. Visitors to the region are recommended to bring or buy a compact portable radio, with digital tuning and a full range of short-wave bands, as well as FM, long and medium wave, as a practical means to brush up on the language, sample popular culture and absorb some regional music. International broadcasters such as the **Voice of America** (6130 or 7370 KHz), **Monitor Radio International** (operated by Christian Science Monitor in Boston, Mass (15.30 or 9.755 MHz) and the Quito-based evangelical station, **HCJB**, keep the traveller abreast of news and events, in both English and Spanish. Unfortunately the **BBC World Service** has stopped broadcasting to Chile, although it can be heard over the internet. In small regional centres, the local radio station is a very effective medium for sending a message to someone else in the area; go to the studio and make the request in person.

Television

There are 6 domestic terrestrial channels. Soap operas (*teleseries*) and soccer constitute the most popular programmes. Cable television is widely available. Channels vary from region to region, but there are usually some channels in English, French, Italian and German.

Money

→ *US$1=$548, €1=$766, £1=$883 (Aug 2009).*

Currency

The unit is the peso, its sign is $. Notes are for 1000, 2000, 5000, 10,000 and 20,000 pesos; coins come in denominations of 1, 5, 10, 50, 100 and 500 pesos. Inflation is low. Official exchange rates for many currencies are quoted in the press, and the best rates are to be had in Santiago. Travellers to rural areas should carry supplies of 1000- and 2000-peso notes; higher denominations are difficult to change. This is also good advice when

travelling on local transport or when shopping in small stores early in the day.

ATMs and exchange

The easiest way to obtain cash in Chile is by using ATMs. These are situated at the major banks and often in other locations, especially in shopping malls, bus stations, at the larger supermarkets and at many petrol stations. You can choose to be guided through the transaction in English. ATMs operate under the sign **Redbanc**; both Cirrus (MasterCard) and Plus (Visa) are accepted for daily transactions of up to US$500. The exception to this is the **Banco Estado** whose **Redbanc** machines accept MasterCard but not Visa. A full list of **Redbanc** machines in Chile is listed by town at www.redbanc.cl.

Most major currencies can be readily exchanged in tourist centres, but rates for the US dollar and, increasingly commonly, the euro, remain much better than for any other currency. US dollars and euro are widely accepted by banks, *casas de cambio* and some hotels, but rarely if ever by shops and other establishments. Foreign notes are often scrutinized carefully and rejected if torn or marked in any way. Before changing currency, check whether any commission is charged. If crossing to Argentina take some low-value US dollar bills.

Visa and MasterCard are readily accepted but American Express and Diners' Club are less useful. Credit-card use does not usually incur a commission or higher charge in Chile. In shops, identification is usually necessary to use credit cards; places accepting Visa and MasterCard usually display a **Redcompra** sticker in the window. In case of loss or theft of your card make sure that you carry the phone numbers necessary to report this; make a photocopy of the numbers and keep them in a safe place. Some travellers have reported problems with their credit cards being frozen by their bank when a charge is incurred in a foreign country. To avoid this problem, notify your bank before departure that you will be making charges in Chile (and other countries, where applicable). To avoid charges from your bank, top up your credit card account with sufficient cash before departure. If you will need to make very expensive one-off purchases, you may want to specify that your daily spending limit should not be applied to the amount by which your account is in credit, although this will prove dangerous if your card is stolen.

Exchanging traveller's cheques is possible in most large cities, although the rate will be up to 5% lower than for cash. It is generally not advisable to change cash or traveller's cheques in banks as the rate is much worse than at *casas de cambio*.

Transferring money

Before leaving your home country, find out whether any Chilean bank is correspondent to your own bank. Then, when you need funds, arrange for your bank to transfer the money to the local bank (confirming by fax). Be sure to provide the exact details of the SWIFT code of the receiving bank. Funds can be received within 48 banking hours. This is useful for transferring large amounts. Otherwise, money can be sent within minutes (and with a very large commission) through **Western Union** (in Chile operated by **Chile Express**, www.chilexpress.cl); if collecting money in a city with more than one Western Union agent, you can go to any one of them to receive the money.

Cost of living

The minimum wage in Chile is approximately US$300 per month, while the wage for relatively senior office workers may be around US$900 per month. This is low considering the general cost of living in the country. The cost of accommodation or rent is higher in Santiago than elsewhere – around US$250 per month for a basic 2-room unfurnished flat as compared with half that in the provinces. Many office workers eat out for lunch, and

you can usually find a basic meal for around US$3. City bus fares are US$0.80 in Santiago, less in the provinces. Someone living in Santiago and earning a reasonable salary (by Chilean standards) will find that they have little spare change at the end of the month; holidays and weekends away are a definite luxury.

Cost of travelling

Prices for food and other consumables tend to rise in proportion to the distance from central Chile (being highest in Punta Arenas), although accommodation is cheaper outside the capital. In Santiago itself, the eastern part of the city, encompassing Vitacura, Las Condes and to a lesser extent Providencia are much more expensive than the rest of the city.

Chile is more expensive than much of South America and southern Chile is even more expensive from 15 Dec to 28 Feb. A budget of US$300 per person per week will allow for basic lodgings, food, overland transport and an occasional tour. With a budget of US$600 a week, you will be able to stay in nice hotels, eat in smart restaurants and not stint on excursions.

Opening hours

Banks Mon-Fri 0900-1400.
Businesses Mon-Fri 0830-1230, 1400-1800.
Government offices Mon-Fri 1000-1230 (the public is admitted for a few hours only).
Shops (Santiago) Mon-Fri 1030-1930, Sat 0930-1330.

Post

The Chilean postal system is usually efficient. Airmail takes around a week from both the UK and the US. Seamail takes eight to 12 weeks from the UK. There is a daily airmail service to Europe. Letters to Europe/North America cost US$0.80. To register a letter costs US$1. Airmail rates for parcels to Europe cost US$20 for less than 1 kg; US$25 for 1-3 kg; US$150 for 10 kg. There is no overseas surface mail service from Chile. The poste restante service ('lista de correo') only holds mail for 30 days, then returns it to sender. The Lista de Correo in the Central Post Office in Santiago is good and efficiently organized, but letters are kept separately for men and women so envelopes should be marked Señor or Señora/Señorita.

Safety

While Chileans will delight in building up the prowess of Chilean thieves to nervous visitors, Chile is generally a safe country to visit. Police stations in rural areas very rarely have people in their one cell. Like all major cities, though, Santiago and Valparaíso do have crime problems. Avoid the poblaciones (shanty towns) of Santiago –– especially if you are travelling alone or have only recently arrived. The following suggestions are particularly applicable in central Santiago, in some of the hills of Valparaíso and in Coquimbo, which has a reputation for theft.

Keep valuables out of sight. Cameras should be kept in bags when not in use, and expensive watches or jewellery should not be worn. It is best to leave any valuables you don't need in the hotel safe deposit when sightseeing locally. Always keep an inventory of what you have deposited. If you lose valuables, always report to the police and note details of the report for insurance purposes.

Keep all documents and money secure. When travelling with all your gear, hide your main cash supply in different places or under your clothes; you may wish to use extra pockets sewn inside shirts and trousers, pockets closed on the outside with a zip or safety pin, moneybelts (best worn under clothes, below the waist rather than around the neck), neck or leg pouches or elasticated support bandages for keeping money and cheques above the elbow or below the knee.

Try not to appear nervous. Nervous behaviour is a clear sign to any thief that you are carrying valuables or that you are unsure where you're going. Walking confidently, but without excessive speed, is a sure way of showing that you are at home in a place – even if you are not.

Look out for tricks. Petty thieves may employ tricks to distract your attention and separate you from your possessions. One common ruse is 'the mustard trick': the victim is sprayed with mustard, ketchup or some other substance, apparently accidentally, and an accomplice offers sympathy and helps to clean your jacket, removing your wallet at the same time.

Don't fight back. If you are attacked, remember your assailants may well be armed, so it is better to hand over your valuables rather than risk injury.

Finally, bear in mind that safety awareness is not just a matter of avoiding theft or violent attack. While Chile is no worse than any other South American country as far as sexually transmitted diseases are concerned, travellers should always practise safe sex.

Telephone

→ International dialling code +56.
Centros de llamados (phone centres) are abundant and are the easiest way to make a call. They have private booths where you can talk for as long as you like and pay afterwards, the price sometimes being displayed on a small screen in your booth. They often have internet, photocopying and fax services too. From public phone boxes, local calls cost US0:20 for 3 mins and national calls cost around US$0.20 per min. A call to a mobile costs US$0.35 per min. For international calls it is cheaper to use a Centro de llamados or a pre-paid phone scratch cards, available from kioskos.

Mobile phones

International roaming is becoming more common, although buying a cheap local pay-as-you-go may be a cheaper option. Major airports and hotels often have rental desks, or can advise on local outlets.

Time

GMT -4 hs; -3 hrs in summer. Clocks change from mid-Sep or Oct to early Mar.

Tourist information

The national secretariat of tourism, Sernatur, Av Providencia 1550, Santiago, T02-236 2420, www.sernatur.cl, has offices throughout the country (addresses are given throughout this guide). Most of the larger tourist offices around the country are run by Sernatur and can provide town maps, leaflets and other useful information, otherwise contact the head office. CONAF, (Corporación Nacional Forestal) Presidente Bulnes 291, piso 1, Santiago, T/F02-697 2273, www.conaf.cl, manages national parks throughout Chile. CONAF's staff are dedicated and knowledgeable, though their offices in the parks themselves are usually much more helpful than the regional head offices. CONAF also publishes a number of leaflets and has documents and maps about the national park system that can be consulted or photocopied in its Santiago office; but these are not very useful for walking. Ancient Forest International, Box 1850, Redway, CA 95560, T/F707-323 3015, USA, www.ancient forests.org, can be contacted regarding Chilean forests. For details of other useful organizations and their publications, see page 612.

Useful websites

There are a great many sites about Chile that surfers may wish to explore, but note that you may have to weed out the sites related to chilli peppers!

Useful sites specifically covering all Chile: **www.visit-chile.org** and **www.sernatur.cl**. Other sites dealing with specific destinations in Chile include, from north to south:
www.arica.cl
www.iquique. cl
www.iquique.travel
www.sanpedroatacama.com
www.calamacultural.cl
www.municipalidaddeantofagasta.cl
www.laserena.cl
www.vinadelmarchile.cl
www.vinadelmar.cl
www.ciudaddevalparaiso.cl
www.valparaisotimes.cl (in English)
www.ciudad.cl
www.santiagotimes.cl (in English)
www.municipalidadpucon.cl
www.puconturismo.cl
www.pucononline.cl
www.sietelagos.cl
www.ptovaras.cl
www.puertovaras.org
www.puertomonttchile.cl
www.chiloe.cl
www.chileaustral.com
www.pat agoniachile.cl
www.patagonia-chile.com
www.rapanui.co.cl

Sites relating to accommodation include:
www.chile-hotels.com Reservations for many hotels in Chile (particularly upmarket ones); prices may be cheaper booking direct.
www.hostelworld.com Useful for finding cheaper accommodation.
www.backpackerschile.com and **www.backpackersbest.cl** For finding good hostels and guesthouses.

Specialist sites include:
www.ccv.cl Website of the Chilean wine-making association, for wine enthusiasts.
www.desaparecidos.org/chile Background on the Pinochet years and human-rights situation.
www.greenpeace.cl Up-to-date information on environmental issues.

www.mapuche.cl Information on Chile's Mapuche people.
www.surfchile.cl For surfers.
www.trekkingchile.com For trekking in central Chile.

Tour operators

UK and Ireland
Austral Tours, 20 Upper Tachbrook St, London SW1V 1SH, T020-7233 5384, www.latinamerica.co.uk. Specialist company with a wide range of activity holidays.
Condor Journeys and Adventures, 2 Ferry Bank, Colintraive, Argyll PA22 3AR, T01700-841318, www.condorjourneys-adventures.com. A wide range of specialist tours on offer.
Cox & Kings Travel, Gordon House, 10 Greencoat Place, London SW1P 1PH, T020-7873 5000, www.coxandkings.co.uk. Exclusive set tours all over the continent.
Exodus Travels, Grange Mills, Weir Rd, London SW12 0NE, T0870-240 5550, www.exodus.co.uk. Experience in adventure travel around the world; good trips to all parts of Chile.
Journey Latin America, 12-13 Heathfield Terrace, London W4 4JE, T020-8622 8464/ T020-8747 8315, www.journeylatin america.co.uk. Long-established company running escorted and bespoke tours throughout the region, and offering a wide range of flight options.
Last Frontiers, Fleet Marston Farm, Aylesbury, Buckinghamshire HP18 0QT, T01296-653000, www.lastfrontiers.co.uk. Tailor-made Latin American travel.
Pura Aventura, 18 Bond St, Brighton, East Sussex BN11 1RD, T0845-225 5058, www.pura-aventura.com. Small Chilean specialist with a wide range of organized and tailor-made tours.
Scott Dunn (formerly Passage to South America), Fovant Mews, 12a Noyna Rd, London SW17 7PH, T020-8682 5030, www.scottdunn.com. Wide range of tailor-made packages throughout the region.

Select Latin America, 79 Maltings Place, 169 Tower Bridge Road, London SE1 3LJ, T020-7407 1478, www.selectlatinamerica.co.uk. Specialist in tours to Latin America.
South American Experience, 47 Causton St, Pimlico, London SW1P 4AT, T020-7976 5511, www.southamericanexperience.co.uk. Books flights and accommodation, and offers tailor-made trips.
Steppes Latin America, 51 Castle St, Cirencester, Gloucester GL7 1QD, T01285-885333, www.steppestravel.co.uk. Tailor-made holidays including Patagonia escorted tours, horse-riding trips and birdwatching.
Trips Worldwide, 14 Frederick Place, Clifton, Bristol BS8 1AS, T0117-311 4400, www.tripsworldwide.co.uk. Specialists in tailor-made holidays.

North America
4 Star South America, 3003 Van Ness, NW Suite S-823, Washington, DC 20008, T1-800 747 4540 (North America)/T0870-711 5370 (UK)/T+49-700 4444 7827 (rest of Europe), www.4starsouthamerica.com. Tour operator and flight consolidator.
Discover Chile Tours, 5775 Blue Lagoon Drive Suite 190, Miami, FL 33126. T305-266 5827 (local), T1-800 826 4845 (toll-free), www.discover-chile.com. Has a range of tours, including good ski trips.
International Expeditions, 1 Environs Park, Helena, AL35080, USA, T1-800 633 4734, www.internationalexpeditions.com. Travel company specializing in nature tours.
Ladatco Tours, 2200 South Dixie Highway Suite 704, Coconut Grove, FL 33133, T1-800 327 6162, www.ladatco.com. Specialist operator based in Miami, runs explorer tours themed around mysticism, wine, etc.
Mila Tours, T1-800-367 7378, www.mila tours.com. Arranges a wide variety of tours from rafting to photography.
Mountain Travel Sobek, 6420 Fairmount Av, El Cerrito, CA 94530, T1-888-MTSOBEK (toll-free)/T1-510-527 8100, www.mtsobek.com. A specialist in Chile, offering a range of trekking tours.

Myths and Mountains, 976 Tee Court, Incline Village, NV 89451, T1-800-670 6984, www.mythsandmountains.com. Cultural, wildlife and environmental trips.

South American Explorers Club, 126 Indian Creek Rd, Ithaca, NY 14850, T1-607 277 0488, T1-800-2740568 (toll-free in USA), www.saexplorers.org. Gives good advice.

Wilderness Travel, 1102 Ninth St, Berkeley, CA 94710, T510-558 2488, T1-800-368 2794 (toll free), www.wildernesstravel.com. Organizes trips worldwide, including very good tours of Patagonia.

South America

CAT Argentina and Chile, Av Presidente Roque Sáenz Peña 615, Of 718, Buenos Aires, www.cat-travel.com. With offices in several Latin American countries, this Dutch-owned and run company offers tailor-made trips.

Australia and New Zealand

Australian Andean Adventures, Suite 201 level 6, 32 York St, Sydney, T02-9299 9973, www.andeanadventures.com.au. Specialists in trekking in South America for Australians.

South America Travel Centre, 104 Hardware St, Melbourne, T03-9642 5353, www.satc.com.au. Good, individual, tailor-made trips to Chile.

Student travellers

If you are planning to study in Chile for a long period it is essential to get a student visa in advance, which you obtain by contacting a Chilean embassy or consulate (see page 56); you will be asked for proof of affiliation to a Chilean university. Note that students are not allowed to undertake paid employment in Chile.

If you are in full-time education you are entitled to an **International Student Identity Card** (ISIC), which is distributed by student travel offices and travel agencies in 116 countries. The ISIC gives you special prices on all forms of transport, and access to a variety of other concessions and services. To find the location of your nearest ISIC office, look at www.isic.org. In Chile, student ID cards can be obtained from the ISIC offices, Hernando de Aguirre 201, of 602, Providencia, Santiago, T02-411 2000, www.isic.cl, and cost US$16 (photo and proof of status required). If you are a holder of an ISIC card and get into trouble, you can make a reverse-charge call to the helpline on T+44-20 8762 8110. If travelling with a student card, it is always worth asking for discounts for museum entry and bus tickets, although all student ID cards must carry a photograph if they are to be of any use.

Visas and immigration

Regulations change frequently, so it is imperative to check visa requirements before you travel. At the time of writing, visas are required by citizens of Cuba, Guyana, Haiti; all African and Middle Eastern countries, except Israel, Morocco and South Africa; all Asian and Pacific countries, except Fiji, Indonesia, Japan, Malaysia, Singapore, Tonga and Turkey; and all former Communist countries except those now in the EU.

A passport, valid for at least 6 months, and a tourist card, are required for entry by all other foreigners, except for citizens of other South American countries, who require national identity cards only. Those entering with just a passport and tourist card may all stay for a period of 90 days, except for citizens of Belize, Costa Rica, Malaysia and Singapore (30 days only), and citizens of Greece, Indonesia and Peru (60 days only). Tourist cards are handed out as a matter of routine at immigration offices at major land borders and Chilean airports. It is essential that you keep the tourist card safe, since you must surrender it on departure. Onward travel tickets are officially required for entry but these are rarely asked for. On arrival you may be asked where you are staying in Chile; just give the name of any hotel. Remember that it is your responsibility to ensure that your passport is stamped in and out when you cross borders. The absence of entry and exit stamps, or passports stamped with the wrong date of entry can cause serious difficulties, so seek out the proper immigration offices if the stamping process is not carried out as you cross. The vast majority of border crossings, though, are trouble-free.

90-day visa extensions (costing US$100) can be obtained from the **Ministerio del Interior (Extranjería)** in Santiago or from any local *gobernación* (government office). The procedure is often time-consuming and is officially supposed to include providing proof of funds and having an international record check (although these are usually missed out). To avoid hours of queuing and excessive punctiliousness when you are finally dealt with, you are advised to obtain extensions from smaller provincial offices rather than from Santiago; every provincial capital has a *gobernación*. If you must get the extension in Santiago, arrive at **Extranjería** early and consider bringing lunch. If you wish to stay longer than 90 days as a tourist, it is often easier to make a short trip into Argentina, or Peru if near Arica, and return with a new tourist card, rather than to apply for an extension, which also avoids the US$100 fee. However, if you do this once too often officials may become difficult. Usually, after 9 months or so of obvious 1-day trips to Argentina, you will be given a final warning to get a residency visa within the next 90 days or leave.

Finally, on a general note, Chilean officials are very document-minded, but also often exceptionally hospitable and helpful. In remote areas, you should register your documents with the *carabineros* (police), not only as a matter of courtesy, but also because the local police are usually a mine of information about local conditions, and may be able to help you find accommodation and transport. If staying for a while, it is also worth registering at your embassy or consulate. Then, if your passport is stolen, the process of replacing it is simplified and speeded up. Keeping photocopies of essential documents is recommended; always carry a photocopy of your passport on your person as, legally, some form of identification must always be carried.

Chilean embassies
For a full and updated list, see www.chileabroad.gov.cl.
Argentina, Tagle 2762, Buenos Aires 1425, T011-4808 8601, data@embajadade chile.com.ar. Also consulates up and down the country.
Australia, 10 Culgoa Circuit, O'Malley Act 2606, PO Box 69, Canberra, T02-6286 2430, chilemb@embachileaustralia.com. Also in Melbourne and Sydney.
Austria, Lugeck 1/3/10, Vienna A-1010, T43-1-5129208, echileat1@chello.at.
Belgium, 160 rue des Aduatiques, 1040 Brussels, T32-2-743 3660, www.embachile.be.
Bolivia, Av San Martín Esq 2 anillo, Edif Torres Equipetrol, piso 9, Santa Cruz, T591-3-334 1251, www.consulado-chile.scz.com. Note this is only a consulate; there are other consulates in La Paz and Cochabamba.
Brazil, Ses, Av Das Naçoes, q 803, Lote 11, CEP 70.407-900, Brasília, T55-61-2103 5151, embchile@embchile.org.br. Consulates throughout the country.
Canada, 50 O'Connor St, Suite 1413, Ottawa, Ontario K1P 6L2, T1-613-2354402, www. chile.ca. Also consulates in several other cities.
Denmark, Kastelsvej 15, III, 2100 Copenhagen, T45-3538 5834, www.chiledk.dk.
Ecuador, Juan Pablo Sanz 3617 y Amazonas, Edificio Xerox, piso 4, Quito, T593-2-249403. Also consulate in Guayaquil.
France, 2 Av de la Motte Picouet, 75007 Paris, T33-1-4418 5960, www.amb-chili.fr.
Germany, Mohrenstrasse 42, 10117 Berlin, T49-30-726 2035, www.embajada consuladoschile.de. Also consulates in Frankfurt, Hamburg and Munich.
Ireland, 44 Wellington Rd, Ballsbridge, Dublin 4, T353-1-667 5094 www.embachile-irlanda.ie.

Israel, Beit Sharbat, 8th floor, Kaufman 4 St, Tel Aviv 68012, T972-3-510 2750, consulad@inter.net.il.

Italy, Via Po 23, 00198 Roma, T39-6-884 1449, www.chileit.it Consulate in Milan.

Japan, Nihon Seimei Akabanebashi Building 8F, 3-1-14 Shiba, Minato-ku, Tokyo 105-0014, T81-3-3452 7561, www.chile.or.jp.

Mexico, Andrés Bello 10, Edificio Forum, piso18, Col Polanco, CP11560, DF, T52-55-280 9681, www.embajadadechile.com.mx. Also consulates in Guadalajara and Monterrey.

Netherlands, Mauritskade 51, 2514 HG, The Hague, T31-70-312 3640, www.e chile.nl. Also a consulate in Amsterdam.

New Zealand, 19 Bolton St, Wellington, T64-4-471 6270, www.embchile.co.nz.

Norway, Meltzers Gate 5, 0244 Oslo, T47-2244 8955, www.chile.no.

Paraguay, Capital Emilio Nudelman 351, Esquina Campos Cervera, Asunción, T595-21-662 756, echilepy@conexion.com.py.

Peru, Av Javier Prado Oeste 790, San Isidro, Lima, T51-1-611 2200, www.embajada chileperu.com.pe. Also consulate in Tacna.

South Africa, 235 Veale St, Brooklyn Gardens Building, corner of Veale St and Middel St, Block B – 1st floor, New Muckleneuk 0181, Pretoria, T27-12-460 8090, www.embchile. co.za. Also consulate in Cape Town.

Spain, Lagasca 88, 6 Planta, 28001 Madrid, T34-91-431 9160, echilees@tsai.es. Consulate in Barcelona.

Sweden, Sturegatan 8, 3rd floor, Stockholm 114 35, T46-8-679 8280, www.chileemb.se Also a consulate in Gothenburg.

Switzerland, Eigerplatz 5, 3007 Berne, T41-31-370 0058, embajada@embachile.ch.

UK, 12 Devonshire St, London W1G 7DS, T44-20-7580 6392, www.embachile.co.uk.

Uruguay, 25 de Mayo 575, Montevideo, T598-2-916 4090, echileuy@netgate.com.uy.

USA, 1732 Massachusetts Av NW, Washington DC 20036, T1202-785 1746, www.chile-usa.org. Also consulates across the country.

Volunteering

Opportunities for work are not limited to language teaching. There is considerable scope for volunteer work in Chile, both in inner cities and on environmental projects. Those with appropriate skills and experience may also find work by approaching foreign companies (especially engineering or financial service firms) with offices in Chile (usually in Santiago).

Volunteer organizations

Earthwatch, 126 Bank St, South Melbourne, Victoria 3205, Australia, T03-9682 6828, www.earthwatch.org. Organizes volunteer work on scientific and cultural projects around the world (also has associated offices in Oxford, UK).

Project Trust, Hebridean Centre, Isle of Coll, Argyll PA78 6TE, UK, T01879-230441, www.projecttrust.org.uk. Volunteer work for foreigners.

Raleigh International, 27 Parsons Green Lane, London SW6 4HZ, UK, T0207-371 8585, www.raleigh.org.uk. Volunteer projects for young travellers.

Voluntary Horizons, T56-9-8458 9680, www.voluntaryhorizons.com. Volunteer travel programmes in Chile and Argentina.

Weights and measures

The metric system is used.

Women travellers

Chile presents no special problem for women travellers. Most Chileans are courteous and helpful. The following useful tips have been supplied by women, although most apply to any single traveller.

When you set out, err on the side of caution until your instincts have adjusted to the customs of the country. Unless actively avoiding foreigners like yourself, don't go too far from the beaten track; there is a very definite 'gringo trail' that you can join. This can be helpful when looking for safe accommodation, especially if arriving after dark. Remember that a taxi at night can be as dangerous as wandering around on your own, particularly in Santiago. At borders, dress as smartly as possible. Buses are much easier than trains for a person alone; on major routes seats are reserved and bags are locked in the hold.

Women may, though, be subject to much unwanted attention. To help minimize this, do not wear suggestive clothing. Some readers advise not flirting. By wearing a wedding ring and carrying a photograph of your 'husband' and 'children' you may dissuade an aspiring suitor. If politeness fails, do not feel bad about showing offence and departing. When accepting a social invitation, make sure that someone knows the address and the time you left. Ask if you can bring a friend (even if you do not intend to do so). A good rule is always to act with confidence, as though you know where you are going, even if you do not. Someone who looks lost is more likely to attract unwanted attention. Finally, be aware that anywhere calling itself a 'nightclub' is in fact a brothel.

Working in Chile

It is not difficult to find short-term or temporary work as a foreigner in Chile. The most obvious opening is as a teacher of English as a foreign language; even those without the appropriate TEFL qualification should be able to find this kind of work, especially in Santiago, but also in other cities such as Viña del Mar, Concepción and La Serena. Teachers are expected to be clean-cut and well-dressed, and to have the correct paperwork. The pay is often poor; as low as US$4 per hr after tax for those without appropriate qualifications. Prospective English-language teachers should apply in mid-Feb/early Mar with a full CV and photo. A work visa should be obtained as soon as you have found a contract (see below); beware that, without this, you will be liable to deportation and fines if discovered. We have received reports of unscrupulous institutes employing teachers with 90-day tourist visas and then 'discovering', as this expires, that the teacher is not entitled to work, at which point unpaid wages may be withheld. The best-paid work for English language teachers is almost invariably private, 1-to-1 tuition, mainly found through word of mouth (although it may also be worth placing an advertisement in a newspaper such as *El Mercurio*).

The main obstacle to anyone seeking to work in Chile is the problem of obtaining and maintaining a working visa. All sorts of extraordinary pieces of paper may be asked for, and, at the very least, you will need proof of an employment offer before the visa is issued. Those planning to work may enter Chile on a tourist visa and then get a working visa on presentation of a contract with a minimum wage of 150,000 Chilean pesos per month after tax (approximately US$280).

Business people face no special problems when doing short-term business in the country, and may enter on a tourist visa. It is recommended to carry a good supply of business cards, as the first thing which many business people will do at a meeting is ceremoniously present you with their card. Business visas must be applied for by those who are buying a going concern, or are investing a minimum of US$5000 in Chile, and who wish to reside in the country. See also Visas and immigration, page 55.

Contents

Footprint features

Border crossing

Chile–Argentina
see page 107

At a glance

⊖ **Getting around** The efficient metro system is easier to use than the local bus network. Otherwise take taxis and provincial buses.

◉ **Time required** 2 days to acclimatize. Chile's highlights lie elsewhere.

☼ **Weather** Warm days and cool nights. Dry season Oct-Apr.

✖ **When not to go** Jan can be on the hot side, while smog can be a problem in winter (Jun-Aug).

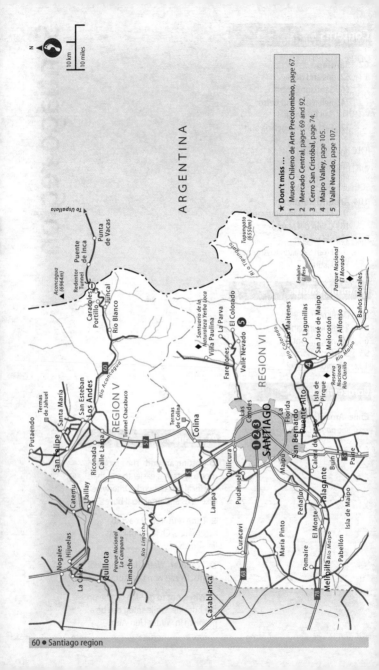

★ Don't miss ...
1 Museo Chileno de Arte Precolombino, page 67.
2 Mercado Central, pages 69 and 92.
3 Cerro San Cristóbal, page 74.
4 Maipo Valley, page 105.
5 Valle Nevado, page 107.

If you are flying into Chile, you will probably arrive in Santiago. No one can deny that the Chilean capital has an impressive setting, in a hollow surrounded by mountains, with peaks over 5000 m visible on clear days. They are most dramatic just after rainfall in winter, when the smog clears and the new snows glisten.

Santiago is a vibrant, progressive city. With its many parks, interesting museums, glittering high-rises and boutiques, it bursts with possibilities. As far as entertainment goes, there are popular scenes in everything from techno and progressive rock to Bohemian hang-outs and most of the bits in between. Certainly, those who spend an extended period of time in Santiago soon find plenty of things to do at night and at the weekends.

The region around the capital encompasses several of the country's highlights. The resorts on the coast are less than two hours away and also within easy reach are the best ski resorts in South America, which are great spots for weekend hikes in summer. Meanwhile, the area south of Santiago is perhaps the best wine-producing area in Chile. Autumn, when the grapes are being harvested, is a particularly good time to visit the vineyards.

Santiago

→ *Colour map 3, B3.*

Situated in the Central Valley and with a population of six million, Santiago has grown to become the sixth largest city in South America, as well as the political, economic and cultural capital of Chile. The city is crossed from east to west by the long-suffering Río Mapocho, into which most of the city's sewage is dumped; however, the magnificent chain of the Andes provides a more appropriate natural landmark.

It is easy to see Santiago as just another westernized Latin American city but, away from the centre and wealthier suburbs, the reality is more complicated. Street vendors are often newly arrived from rural areas, many living in appalling villas miserias on the city's outskirts (Pudahuel and La Pintana are both especially chastening barrios for those who claim that poverty does not exist in Chile). Some barrios in the south of the city have a higher concentration of Mapuche people than the Mapuche heartlands of the south.

If you are just passing through, Santiago is unlikely to be the highlight of your trip to Chile – it can take a while to get a real feeling for the city's pulse. However, if you have the time, it does warrant a visit of a few days. On top of its setting and nightlife, there are excellent museums, and you will find that the contrast with the rest of the country is stark: over a third of Chileans live in Gran Santiago, so, if you want to understand the country you are visiting, Santiago is a must. ▸▸ *For listings, see pages 80-103.*

Ins and outs

Getting there

Air International and domestic flights arrive at the Aeropuerto Comodoro Arturo Merino Benítez at Pudahuel, 26 km northwest of the city centre. Frequent bus services between the international and domestic terminals and the city centre are operated by two companies: **TurBus** ① *to/from Terminal Alameda (metro Universidad de Santiago, line 1), every 30 minutes, US$3*; and **Centropuerto** ① *to/from metro Los Héroes, T02-601 9883, every 15 minutes, first from centre 0600, last from airport 2230, US$2.50.* Return tickets are cheaper than two singles. En route to and from the airport, the buses also stop at Pajaritos metro station (where there are connections for Valparaíso and Viña del Mar). Minibus services between the airport and hotels or other addresses in the city are operated by several companies with offices in the airport. These include: **Transfer** ① *T02-777 7707*; **Delfos** ① *T02-601 0590, www.transferdelfos.cl*; and **Trans Vip** ① *T02-677 3000, www.transvip.cl.* These charge US$10 per person to/ from the city centre, US$12 to/from Las Condes. Minibuses to the airport should be booked the previous day, but taxis are cheaper if flagged down in the street. There is a taxi office inside the international terminal. Taxis to/from the centre should cost around US$20, to/from Providencia US$25; agree the fare beforehand. It is also possible to negotiate taxi fares from the airport to quite distant cities such as Melipilla and Valparaíso; rates to Valparaíso start from around US$70.

Bus and train Intercity buses arrive at one of four terminals, all located close to each other, just west of the centre and not far from the train station, along Avenida Libertador Bernardo O'Higgins. This is the main east-west avenue through the city and is within easy reach of line 1 of the metro. ▸▸ *See Transport, page 95.*

24 hours in Santiago

First, try to make sure you are here on a Saturday. Assuming you are staying in the centre, get up early and walk down to Calle San Diego for breakfast. Afterwards, walk down San Diego to the Iglesia de los Sacramentinos – Santiago's answer to Sacré Coeur – and then west through gardens until you reach the Palacio Cousiño in time for the first tour at 0930. This extraordinary building (see page 71) gives a real insight into the lives, customs and belief systems of the Chilean aristocracy and the opulence to which the upper classes became accustomed. Once the tour has finished, stroll to Toesca metro and head a few stops south to Franklin. Here you will find swarms of people all making their way to the Mercado Bío Bío. This market will show you how most of Santiago lives and it provides a striking contrast to Palacio Cousiño.

When you start feeling hungry, head back to Franklin metro and take the train north to Cal y Canto. On the opposite side of the Río Mapocho is the Vega Central, where you will find some of the best seafood restaurants in Santiago. Don't be put off by the choice – take your time and enjoy some of the best shellfish the world has to offer.

After lunch, it's time to remind yourself that Santiago has one of the most dramatic settings of any of the world's major cities. Cross back over the Río Mapocho and stroll east towards the conical hill of Cerro San Cristóbal. If it's summer, the heat may be making you feel a little tired by now – if so, you could go up the hill on the funicular railway. If you are lucky and it is a clear day, you will have an unforgettable view of the Andes. Here you can stroll through lanes that are lined with trees – a world away from the clutter of the city. There are even swimming pools to cool off in and the chance to do some wine tasting. Towards dusk, have a drink in the café near the funicular railway station and watch the sun go down over the coastal mountain range, lighting up the snows of the Andes.

After dark, go back down the hill by funicular railway (it's not advisable to walk here in the evening) in time to sample Santiago's nightlife. At the foot of Cerro San Cristóbal is Barrio Bellavista. Here you can take your pick of any one of dozens of excellent (and expensive) restaurants, before going out to one of the area's buzzing salsotecas. These don't really get going until midnight and you'll usually find that you don't leave much before five, so perhaps head back to your hotel room for some sleep after dinner and then go out dancing later on.

Getting around

The city's main avenue, Avenida Libertador Bernardo O'Higgins, is almost always referred to as the Alameda, while Plaza Baquedano, one of the city's main squares, is almost always known as Plaza Italia (in both instances, this book follows suit). Most of the more expensive accommodation is situated in the city centre or further east in the neighbourhoods of Providencia and Las Condes. Most budget accommodation is located in the city centre or further west in the vicinity of the bus terminals. Although parts of the centre can be explored on foot, you will need to master the city's transport system, which is well organized, if crowded and slow in peak periods. ▸▸ *For a metro map, see page 99.*

Moving mountains

While Santiago's smog is not too bad in spring, summer and autumn, those who arrive here during winter could be in for an unpleasant shock. It might not take more than half an hour for your throat to begin to itch and your eyes to water due to one of Santiago's biggest problems – pollution. In 2001, it was rated the eighth most polluted city in the world. When Pedro de Valdivia founded the city in 1541, between the coastal mountains and the Andes, it must have seemed like a perfect site; he could never have imagined that the city would one day engulf the whole valley, and that the mountains would become a serious problem.

The principal reason for Santiago's high levels of pollution is that it lies in a bowl, encircled by mountains, which means that the smog is trapped. This, combined with the centralization of Chilean industry in Santiago, the fact that many buses are not equipped with catalytic converters and the sheer volume of cars that choke the city's highways, conspires to create a problem that cannot easily be resolved. It is a serious issue: asthma rates are high and older people sometimes die during the winter *emergencias*, when the pollution gets particularly bad.

Over the years, all sorts of solutions have been proposed. A team of Japanese scientists once even suggested blowing up the part of the Andes nearest the city, so that the pollution could disperse more easily. Each weekday, cars that have number plates ending in one of two digits are prohibited from circulating. But, until the government finds a means of dispersing the population more widely throughout the country, the problem is likely to remain.

Tourist information

Municipal Tourist Board ① *Casa Colorada, Merced 860, metro Plaza de Armas, T02-632 7783, www.munistgo.cl/colorada, also at Cerro Santa Lucía, T02-6644216, santalucia@ munistgo.cl*. **Sernatur (Servicio Nacional de Turismo)** ① *Av Providencia 1550, metro Manuel Montt, T02-731 8336, www.sernatur.cl, open Mon-Fri 0845-1830, Sat 0900-1400, also has a basic information office at the airport, open 0900-2100 daily*. Sematur has maps, many brochures and posters. English, German and some French are spoken, and there is a good notice board. Many tourist offices in small towns, particularly in the south, are closed in winter, so stock up on information here. **CONAF (Corporación Nacional Forestal)** ① *Paseo Presidente Bulnes 285 piso 1 (metro Moneda), T02-3900125, www.conaf.cl*, publishes a number of leaflets and has documents and maps about the national park system that can be consulted or photocopied (not very useful for walking). **CODEFF (Comité Nacional Pro-Defensa de la Fauna y Flora)** ① *Luis Uribe 2620, Nuñoa, T02-274 7461, www.codeff.cl*, can also provide information on environmental questions.

Security

Like all large cities, Santiago has problems of theft. However, these tend to be exaggerated by Santiaguinos. While the central area is frequented by pickpockets and bag snatchers (who are often well dressed) - operating mostly on the metro, around the Plaza de Armas, in Barrio Brasil, near Cerro Santa Lucía and around the restaurants in Bellavista - these are easily avoided with a little common sense. The biggest risk is in unwittingly entering a dangerous *barrio* away from the centre. Parts of Pudahuel and Cerro Navia in the west, Conchalí and Renca in the north and Macul, El Bosque and La Pintana in the south have a big drug and crime problem and can be dangerous. At night, it is best to take a public bus (*micro*) rather than picking up a taxi, as you will be watched over by your fellow passengers; better still, call for a radio taxi.

Best time to visit

The Santiago area enjoys a Mediterranean climate, with long dry summers and daytime temperatures rising to over 30°C, when the heat can be uncomfortable. Rainfall is heaviest from May to August and often falls in bands lasting for two or three days at a time. In summer, rainfall is almost unknown. Snowfall is rare, although frost is not uncommon, and, as houses in Santiago rarely have central heating, you will feel the cold on winter nights. There is usually less wind in winter, making smog a more serious problem over the city (forecast levels of smog are published in the daily papers, during television weather forecasts and inside underground stations). Pollution levels vary; the west and the old city centre are much worse affected than the more expensive areas around Las Condes and the upper city to the East. Pollution is usually at its worst in July and at its lightest in September and October and after rainfall.

Orientation

The centre of the old city lies between the Río Mapocho and the city's main avenue, La Alameda. From Plaza Italia, in the east of the city's central area, the river flows to the northwest and the Alameda runs to the southwest. From Plaza Italia, Calle Merced runs west to the Plaza de Armas, the heart of the city, which is five blocks south of the Río Mapocho.

History

Santiago was founded by Pedro de Valdivia on 12 February 1541 on the site of a small indigenous settlement between the southern bank of the Río Mapocho and the Cerro Santa Lucía. During the colonial period, it was only one of several Spanish administrative and cultural centres; also important were Concepción to the south and La Serena in the north. Nevertheless, by 1647 there were 12 churches in the city but, of these, only San Francisco (1618) survived the earthquake of that year. A further earthquake destroyed most of the city in 1730.

Following Independence, the city became more important. In the 1870s, under the Intendente (regional governor) Benjamín Vicuña MacKenna, an urban plan was drafted, the Cerro Santa Lucía was converted from being a makeshift protestant cemetery into a public park and the first trams were introduced. As the city grew at the end of the 19th century, the Chilean elite, wealthy from mining and shipping, built their mansions west of the centre around Calle Dieciocho, Avenida España and República. One of these families was the Cousiños, who built the Palacio Cousiño and later donated this and what became the Parque O'Higgins to the city. Expansion east towards Providencia began in 1895. Until the 1930s, much of the city centre had colonial buildings in the style of Quito or Lima, but expansion and modernization meant that these were gradually replaced. In the latter part of the 20th century, like most Latin American capital cities, Santiago spread rapidly. Many older Santiaguinos who live in areas that are now relatively central tell how, when they first arrived in the city, their homes were right on the outskirts. In general, the more affluent moved east into new neighbourhoods in the foothills of the Andes, and poorer neighbourhoods were established to the west of the centre. This geographic division of wealth continues today.

Santiago centre

Around the Plaza de Armas

The shadiness and tranquillity of the Plaza de Armas has been disturbed by a recent remodelling of the square. Some of the taller trees were stripped away to make way for new stonework but most Santiaguinos are unhappy with the barer plaza that has resulted. On the eastern and southern sides there are arcades with shops and cheap restaurants; on the

1 Santiago orientation

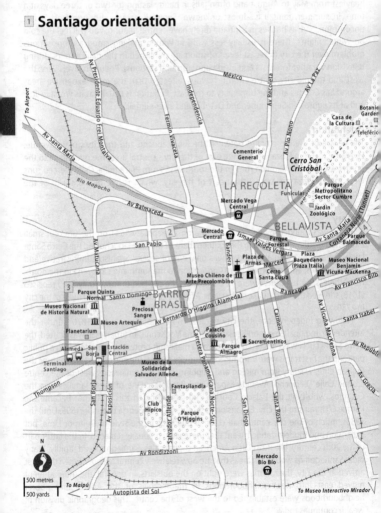

northern side is the post office and the Municipalidad; and on the western side the cathedral and the archbishop's palace. The **cathedral**, much rebuilt, contains a recumbent statue in wood of San Francisco Javier and the chandelier that lit the first meetings of Congress after Independence; it also houses an interesting museum of religious art and historical pieces. The **Museo Histórico Nacional** ⓘ *Plaza de Armas 951, T02-411 7000, www.museohistorico nacional.cl, Tue-Sun 1000-1730, US$1, free on Sun*, is located in the Palacio de la Real Audiencia and covers the period from the Conquest until 1925 and contains a model of colonial Santiago.

A block west of the cathedral is the **former Congress building**, now occupied by the Ministry of Foreign Affairs (the new Congress building is in Valparaíso). Nearby are the law courts and the **Museo Chileno de Arte Precolombino** ⓘ *Bandera 361, www.precolombino.cl, Tue-Sun 1000-1800, US$6, children and students free, booklet US$1*. Housed in the former Real Aduana, this is one of the best museums in Chile with an excellent representative exhibition of objects from the pre-Columbian cultures of Central America and the Andean region. Displays are well labelled in English. A visit is highly recommended. A further two blocks west is **Palacio de la Alhambra** ⓘ *Compañía 1340, T02-689 0875, www.snba.cl, Mon-Fri 1100-1300, 1700-1930*, a national monument sponsored by the Society of Arts. It has painting exhibitions and permanent displays.

A few metres east of the Plaza de Armas is the **Casa Colorada**. Built in 1769, it was the home of the Governor in colonial days and then of Mateo de Toro y Zambrano y Ureta, president of Chile's first national governing council. It now holds the **Museo de Santiago** ⓘ *Merced 860, T02-633 0723, Tue-Sat 1000-1800, Sun and holidays 1100-1400, US$3, students free, booklet US$0.60*, covering the history of Santiago from the Conquest to modern times with excellent displays and guided tours.

On the north side of the plaza, in the central post office, is the **Museo Postal** ⓘ *Mon-Fri 0930-1730, free*, with a collection of stamps from around the world together with old telephones, telegraph machines and post boxes. Some info in English.

From the Plaza de Armas, Paseo Ahumada runs south to the Alameda, four

Museo Rallí   Museo de la Moda

Av Vitacura

Av Presidente Kennedy

Parque Metropolitano Sector Tupahue

LAS CONDES

Av Santa María

Av Vitacura

Av Costanera

Av Apoquindo

Av Américo Vespucio

Av Andrés Bello

PROVIDENCIA

Av Tobalaba

Av Eliodoro Yáñez

Av Los Leones

Av Pedro de Valdivia

Av Antonio Varas

Senador Jaime Guzmán

To Peñalolen & Parque por la Paz

Av Irarrázaval

Av Israel

Estadio Nacional

Guillermo Mann

Rodrigo de Araya

2 Santiago centre

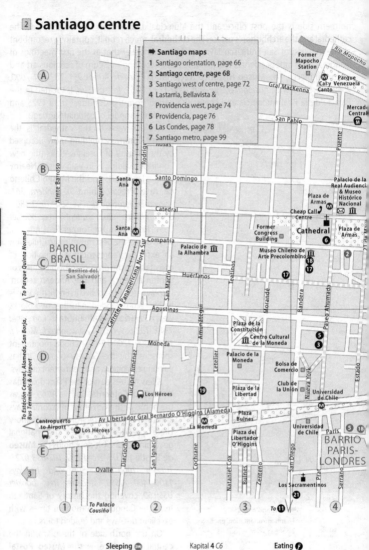

➡ **Santiago maps**
1 Santiago orientation, page 66
2 **Santiago centre, page 68**
3 Santiago west of centre, page 72
4 Lastarria, Bellavista & Providencia west, page 74
5 Providencia, page 76
6 Las Condes, page 78
7 Santiago metro, page 99

Sleeping 🏠
Andes Hostel **3** C6
El Marqués del Forestal **12** B5
Fundador **5** E4
Galerías **6** D5
Hostal Che Lagarto **1** D2
Hostal Santa Lucía **8** D5

Kapital **4** C6
Majestic **9** B2
Montecarlo **10** D6
París **7** E5
Plaza de Armas Hostel **2** C4
Residencial Londres **13** E4
Vegas **18** E4

Eating 🍴
Bar Nacional **17** C3, C4
Bombón Oriental **24** C6
Café Caribe **3** D4
Café Colonia **4** D5
Café Haltí **5** D4
Círculo de Periodistas **19** D3
Confitería Torres **14** E2

blocks away. **Ahumada** is a pedestrianized street and is the commercial heart of the centre. This is always an interesting place to come for a stroll, especially at night, when those selling pirated CDs or playing the three-card trick mix with evangelist preachers and exorcists. One block south of the Plaza de Armas, Ahumada crosses **Calle Huérfanos**, which is also pedestrianized and presents a similar spectacle, as does **Calle Estado**, one block east of Paseo Ahumada.

Four blocks north of the Plaza de Armas is the interesting **Mercado Central** ① *Av 21 de Mayo y San Pablo*. The central market is the best place to come for seafood in Santiago (see page 84), and is so prominent in the Chilean psyche that it was the setting for a recent national soap opera, *Amores del Mercado*. The building faces the **Parque Venezuela**, with the Cal y Canto metro station and, at its western end, the **former Mapocho railway station** ① *www.estacion mapocho.cl*, which is now one of the city's most important cultural centres and concert venues.

If you head east from Mapocho station, along the river, you arrive at the **Parque Forestal**. Although the park is prettily laid out, the proximity of many busy roads means that few people stroll here for long. The **Museo Nacional de Bellas Artes** ① *www.mnba.cl, Tue-Sun 1000-1900, US$1.20*, is located in the wooded grounds and is an extraordinary example of neoclassical architecture, inspired by the Petit Palais in Paris. Inside is a large display of Chilean and foreign painting and sculpture; contemporary art exhibitions are held several times a year. In the west wing of the building is the **Museo de Arte Contemporáneo** ① *www.mac.uchile.cl, US $1.20, take the Bellas Artes metro*.

The Alameda

Along the Alameda The Alameda runs through the heart of the city for over 3 km. It is 100 m wide, choked full of *micros*, taxis and cars day and night and ornamented with gardens and statuary. The most notable are the equestrian statues of generals O'Higgins and San Martín; the statue of the Chilean historian Benjamín Vicuña MacKenna who, as mayor of Santiago, beautified Cerro Santa Lucía; and the great monument in honour of the battle of Concepción in 1879 during the war of the Pacific.

At the eastern end of the Alameda is **Plaza Italia**, where there is a statue of General Baquedano and the Tomb of the Unknown Soldier. Four blocks south is the **Museo Nacional Benjamín Vicuña MacKenna** ① *Av V MacKenna 94, Mon-Sat 0930-1300, 1400-1750, US$1.20*, which records the life and works of the 19th-century Chilean historian and biographer who became one of Santiago's most important mayors. It also has occasional exhibitions.

Between the Parque Forestal, Plaza Italia and the Alameda is the **Calle Lastarria** neighbourhood (Universidad Católica metro). For those interested in antique furniture, pieces of art and old books, the area is worth a visit, especially the **Plaza Mulato Gil de Castro**. Occasional shows are put on in the plaza, and surrounding it are restaurants, a lot of cafés, bookshops, handicraft and antique shops, an art gallery and the **Museo de Artes Visuales** ① *Lastarria 307, T02-6383502, www.mavi.cl, Tue-Sun 1030-1830, US$2, free on Sun*. The museum also houses the the **Museo Arqueológico de Santiago**, with temporary exhibitions of Chilean archaeology, anthropology and pre-Columbian art.

Nearby on Calle Lastarria are the the **Cine Biógrafo** (No 131) and, at the corner with Calle Merced, the **Instituto Chileno-Francés**.

Heading west from here, the Alameda skirts Cerro Santa Lucía on the right and the Universidad Católica on the left. **Cerro Santa Lucía**, a cone of rock rising steeply to a height of 70 m, can be scaled from the Caupolicán esplanade, past the statue of the Mapuche leader, but the ascent from the northern side of the hill – where there is an equestrian statue of Diego de Almagro – is easier. There are views of the city from the top, which is reached by a series of stairs. There is a fortress, the **Batería Hidalgo** (closed to visitors) on the summit, but only its platform survives from the colonial period. The hill closes at 2100; visitors must sign a register at the entrance, giving their ID card number. It is best to descend the eastern side, to see the small **Plaza Pedro de Valdivia** with its waterfalls and **statue of Valdivia**. The area is known to be dangerous after dark. Travellers should beware of thieves here, although, with the new need to register ID cards, security in the area has been tightened up.

Beyond the hill, on the right, the Alameda goes past the **Biblioteca Nacional** ① *Av Libertador Bernardo O'Higgins 651, Santa Lucía metro, www.dibam.cl/biblioteca_nacional, Mon-Fri 0900-1900, Sat 0910-1400, free*, which contains the national archives as well as exhibitions of books, book illustrations, documents and posters. Concerts and lectures also take place here, entry to which is often free.

Beyond, on the left, between Calle San Francisco and Calle Londres, is the oldest church in Santiago: the red-walled church and monastery of **San Francisco** (1618). Inside is the small statue of the Virgin that Valdivia carried on his saddlebow when he rode from Peru to Chile. Free classical concerts are sometimes given in the church in summer; arrive early for a seat. Annexed to the church, near the cloisters, is the **Museo Colonial** ① *Londres 4, T02-639 8737, www.museosanfrancisco.cl, Tue-Sat 1000-1300, 1500-1800, Sun 1000-1400, US$1.50, take the Universidad de Chile metro, line 1, south exit*. Containing displays of religious art, one of the rooms here has 54 paintings of the life of Saint Francis. In the cloisters is a room containing Gabriela Mistral's Nobel Prize medal and there is also a collection of locks. Some of the information is in English

South of San Francisco is the attractive **Barrio París-Londres**, built in 1923-1929, now restored and pedestrianized, while two blocks north of the Alameda is the **Teatro**

Municipal ① *C Agustinas, www.municipal.cl, guided tours Tue 1300-1500 and Sun 1100-1400, US$4*. A little further west along the Alameda is the **Universidad de Chile** and the **Club de la Unión**, an exclusive social club founded in 1864. The current building dates from 1925 and houses a restaurant where wonderful meals are served at exorbitant prices. Nearby, on Calle Nueva York, is the **Bolsa de Comercio** (stock exchange). The public are allowed access to view the trading, but you will have to show your passport to get inside.

One block further west there are three plazas: **Plaza de la Libertad** to the north of the Alameda with a monument to the former President Arturo Alessandri Palma, **Plaza Bulnes** in the centre and **Plaza del Libertador O'Higgins** to the south where Chile's founding father is buried. To the north of Plaza de la Libertad, hemmed in by the skyscrapers of the Centro Cívico, is **Palacio de la Moneda** (the presidential palace) ① *guided tours of the palace 0900-1300 final Sun of every month, courtyards are open to the public (access from north side) Mon-Fri 1000-1800 unless important state business is being carried out*, containing historic relics, paintings, sculptures and the elaborate Salón Rojo used for official receptions. Although the Moneda was damaged by air attacks during the military coup of 11 September 1973, the 1805 building has been fully restored. Ceremonial changing of the guard every other day at 1000.

Just behind the Moneda is the **Plaza de la Constitución**, home to the underground **Centro Cultural de la Moneda** ① *T02-355 6500, www.ccplm.cl, Tue-Sun 1000-1930*. Like a mini version of London's Tate Modern, it houses temporary exhibitions as well as an arts cinema and an interesting gallery of Chilean handicrafts.

South of the Alameda Four blocks south of Plaza del Libertador O'Higgins is **Parque Almagro**, notable for the **Iglesia de los Sacramentinos**, a Gothic church loosely designed in imitation of the Sacré Coeur in Paris, which is best viewed from the nearby Palacio Cousiño against the backdrop of the *cordillera*. **Palacio Cousiño** ① *Dieciocho 438, www.palacio cousino.cl, admission by guided tour only (Spanish or English), Tue-Fri 0930-1330, 1430-1700 (last tour 1600), Sat, Sun and holidays 0930-1330, US$3, Toesca metro, line 2*, on the west side of the Parque Almagro and five blocks south of the Alameda, is a large mansion in French rococo style. It was built by Luis and Isadora Cousiño, part of a wealthy Chilean dynasty that made its money in the coal and silver mining industries. Furnished with tapestries, antiques and pictures imported from France, the palace startled Santiago society with its opulence and advanced technology, including its own electricity generators and the first lift in the country. Even today, the word luxurious falls short when describing the palace: one of the chandeliers is made with 13,000 pieces of crystal and the superb Italian staircase was built using 20 different types of marble. Look out also for the *indiscretos*, three-seater armchairs designed for courting couples and a chaperone. The family monogram can be seen on the curtains, mirrors and doors. Now owned by the Municipalidad, the palace is used for official receptions but is also open as a museum. A visit is highly recommended.

Parque O'Higgins lies about 10 blocks south of the Alameda, just to the west of the *Panamericana*. It has a small lake, playing fields, tennis courts, a pool (open in the summer), an open-air stage for local song and dance, a disco, the racecourse of the **Club Hípico**, and an amusement park, **Fantasilandia** ① *daily in summer, Sat and Sun only in winter, adults US$10, children US$7.50 for unlimited rides*. There are kite-flying contests on Sundays and, during the Independence celebrations around 18 September, there are many good *peñas*. There is also about 20 basic restaurants, craft shops, and three small museums: **Acuario Municipal** ① *Local 9, T02-5565680, daily 1000-2000, small charge*; **Museo de Insectos y Caracoles** ① *Local 12, daily 1000-2000, small charge*, with a collection of insects and shellfish; and **Museo del Huaso** ① *T02-556 1927, Mon-Fri 1000-1700, Sun and holidays 1000-1400, free*, with a small, interesting collection of *criollo* clothing and tools. Cars are not allowed in the park, which can be reached by metro line 2 to Parque O'Higgins station or by bus from Parque Baquedano via Avenida MacKenna and Avenida Matta.

Further west, four blocks south of the Alameda is the **Museo de la Solidaridad Salvador Allende** ① *Republica 475, T02-689 8761, www.mssa.cl, Tue-Sun 1000-1900, US$1.20, Sun free*. Located in a former military police station used as a detention centre under the military regime, it houses a collection of over 400 artworks produced by Chilean and international artists in support of the Unidad Popular government and in opposition to the Pinochet dictatorship. Artists include Alexander Calder, Joan Miró, Frank Stella, Oswaldo Guayasamín and Roberto Matta. There are also videos of interviews (in Spanish) with survivors of the 1973 coup and an information sheet in English.

③ Santiago west of centre

➡ **Santiago maps**
1 Santiago orientation, page 66
2 Santiago centre, page 68
3 **Santiago west of centre, page 72**
4 Lastarria, Bellavista & Providencia west, page 74
5 Providencia, page 76
6 Las Condes, page 78
7 Santiago metro, page 99

Sleeping
Conde de Ansúrez **2**
Happy House Hostel **1**
Hostal Americano **5**
Hostal Che Lagarto **3**
Hostal de Sammy **8**
Hostal Río Amazonas **7**
La Casa Roja **9**
Majestic **4**
Residencial Mery **11**
Residencial Sur **6**
Tur Hotel Express **12**

Barrio Brasil On the northern side of the Alameda, immediately to the west of the *Panamericana*, is the Barrio Brasil, a bohemian neighbourhood with many brightly painted houses. At the end of the 18th century, this historic part of the city was the first area to be colonized by Santiaguinos away from the centre. The area is rich in colonial architecture and is also a centre for nightlife with many underground bars, clubs and restaurants.

The heart of the *barrio* is **Plaza Brasil**, easily reached by walking straight up Calle Concha y Toro from the República metro stop (line 1). This is a narrow, winding cobbled street that passes elegant old stone homes in rococo and German Gothic styles before reaching the plaza, which is shaded by palms, lime trees and silk cottons. Just east of the plaza, on Huérfanos, is the **Basílica del Salvador**, a striking yellow- and rose-coloured church built between 1870 and 1872, with stained glass and a statue of the Virgen del Carmen. A little further along Compañía is the **Iglesia Preciosa Sangre**, a bright red church of neoclassical design, with impressive reliefs and twin towers. One block north is Calle Catedral, where there are some fine old buildings with tall double windows, wooden balconies and stone palisades.

West of centre: around Estación Central

The Alameda continues westwards across the *Panamericana* towards the impressive railway station, **Estación Central**, which is surrounded by several blocks of market stalls. Opposite Estación Central is the **Planetarium** ① *Alameda 3349, T02-718 2910, www.planetariochile.cl, US$6*, while to the north on Avenida Matucana y Diego Portales is **Parque Quinta Normal**, Quinta Normal metro, line 5. The park was founded as a botanical garden in 1830 and is a pleasant, popular spot, which gets very crowded on Sundays with families and the street entertainers who vie with one another to get their pesos.

The park contains several museums. **Museo Ferroviario** ① *www.corpdicyt.cl, Tue-Fri 1000-1800, Sat and Sun 1100-1900, US$2, free to over 60s*, contains the former presidential stagecoach and steam engines built between 1884 and 1953, including a rare Kitson-Meyer. **Museo Nacional de Historia Natural** ① *www.mnhn.cl, Tue-Sat 1000-1730, Sun and holidays 1100-1830, US$1.20, Sun free, students free*, was founded in 1830 and is one of Latin America's oldest museums. Housed in a neoclassical building, it has exhibitions on zoology, botany, mineralogy, anthropology and ethnography. **Museo Artequín** ⓘ *Av Portales 3530, T02-682 5367, www.artequin.cl, Tue-Fri 0900-1700, Sat, Sun and holidays 1100- 800, US$1.60*, is housed in the Chilean pavilion built for the 1889 Paris International Exhibition. It contains prints of famous paintings and explanations of the techniques of the great masters. Recommended.

Bellavista and Cerro San Cristóbal

Santiago's Bohemian face is most obvious in the Bellavista district, east of the centre on the north bank of the Río Mapocho at the foot of Cerro San Cristóbal. This is the main focus of nightlife in the old city; the area around Pío Nono and Antonia López de Bello buzzes,

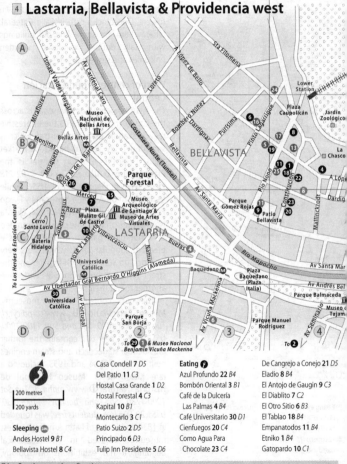

④ Lastarria, Bellavista & Providencia west

200 metres
200 yards

Sleeping 🛌
Andes Hostel **9** *B1*
Bellavista Hostel **8** *C4*
Casa Condell **7** *D5*
Del Patio **11** *C3*
Hostal Casa Grande **1** *D2*
Hostal Forestal **4** *C3*
Kapital **10** *B1*
Montecarlo **3** *C1*
Patio Suizo **2** *D5*
Principado **6** *D3*
Tulip Inn Presidente **5** *D6*

Eating 🍴
Azul Profundo **22** *B4*
Bombón Oriental **3** *B1*
Café de la Dulcería
  Las Palmas **4** *B4*
Café Universitario **30** *D1*
Cienfuegos **20** *C4*
Como Agua Para
  Chocolate **23** *C4*

De Cangrejo a Conejo **21** *D5*
Eladio **8** *B4*
El Antojo de Gaugin **9** *C3*
El Diablito **7** *C2*
El Otro Sitio **6** *B3*
El Tablao **18** *B4*
Empanatodos **11** *B4*
Etniko **1** *B4*
Gatopardo **10** *C1*

especially at weekends. In the bars is anything from live Cuban music to local imitations of Georges Brassens, while eating options range from classic Italian dishes to sushi and West African palm-nut stew. There are also theatres, art galleries and craft shops specializing in lapis lazuli, and the recently remodelled Patio Bellavista with boutiques, bars and restaurants. Also in Bellavista is **La Chascona** ① *Fernando Márquez de la Plata 0192, T02-777 8741, www.fundacionneruda.org, Tue-Sun 1000-1300, 1500-1800, guided visits only, US$4 in Spanish, US$6 in English*. This is one of the homes of the poet Pablo Neruda. The house is in three parts, built on a steep hillside and separated by gardens, and apart from numerous objets d'art it contains works by Diego Rivera, Fernand Léger and Roberto Matta as well as Neruda's Nobel Prize, Order of Lenin and Order of the French Legion of Honour. La Chascona was completed in 1955 and thereafter Neruda lived here when he was in the capital. It is in the same condition as when he lived here (it was restored after being damaged by the military) and is also now the HQ of **Fundación Pablo Neruda** ① *www.fundacionneruda.org*.

Parque Metropolitano

Bellavista lies to the northeast of the city, at the foot of the conical hill of **San Cristóbal**, which forms the **Parque Metropolitano** ① *daily 0900-2100, vehicles US$4*, the largest and most interesting of the city's parks. On a clear day it provides excellent views over the city and across to the Andes. More usually, however, the views provide a graphic demonstration of Santiago's continuing smog problem. There are two entrances: one on Pío Nono in Bellavista; the other on Pedro de Valdivia Norte, further to the east.

To ascend San Cristóbal, there is a **funicular** ① *every few minutes from Plaza Caupolicán at the northern end of C Pío Nono, 1000-2000 daily, US$3 return*; and a **teleférico** ① *from Estación Oasis, Av Pedro de Valdivia Norte via Tupahue to San Cristóbal, the funicular's upper station, summer only, Mon 1430-1830, Tue-Fri 1030-1830, Sat-Sun 1030-1900, US$4 combined funicular/teleférico ticket*. Halfway between the Bellavista entrance and the *cumbre* (summit), on the funicular, is the **Jardín Zoológico** ① *www.zoologico.cl, Tue-Sun 1000-1800, US$4*, which has a well-cared-for collection of animals. When the weather is good, the walk up the access road from Bellavista is very pleasant, providing unexpected views of distant and little-

Les Assassins **15** *C2*
Olan **2** *D4*
Opera Catedral **26** *B1*
Tercera Compañía de Bomberos **29** *D2*
Venezia **19** *B4*

Club 4-40 **24** *A4*
Jammin' Club **16** *B3*
La Bodega de Julio **13** *B4*
La Otra Puerta **17** *B4*
Tu Tu Tanga **25** *B4*

Bars & clubs ❶
Bogart **5** *B3*

visited northern parts of the city. On **Cerro Cumbre** (300 m above the city), there is a colossal statue of the Virgin, which is floodlit at night and now blighted by a giant antenna; beside it is the astronomical observatory of the Catholic University, which can be visited on application to the observatory's director.

When the teleférico is closed, the **Tupahue** sector is reached by taxi either from the Bellavista entrance (much cheaper from inside the park as taxis entering the park have to pay the entrance fee) or alternatively you could walk the kilometre from Pedro de Valdivia metro. This section of the park contains terraces, gardens and paths. One building houses the **Camino Real** ① *T02-232 1758, www.eventoscaminoreal.cl*, a good, expensive restaurant with a splendid view from the terrace, especially at night, and an *enoteca* or exhibition of Chilean wines from a range of vineyards. You can taste one of the three 'wines of the day' for US$3 per glass, and buy if you like, although prices are higher than in shops. Nearby is the **Casa de la Cultura**, with art exhibitions and free concerts at midday on Sunday. There are also two good **pools** in the park (see page 94). East of Tupahue are the **Botanical Gardens** ① *daily 0900-1800, guided tours available*, with a collection of Chilean native plants.

5 Providencia

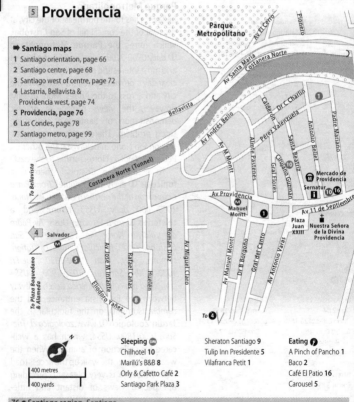

➡ **Santiago maps**
1 Santiago orientation, page 66
2 Santiago centre, page 68
3 Santiago west of centre, page 72
4 Lastarria, Bellavista & Providencia west, page 74
5 Providencia, page 76
6 Las Condes, page 78
7 Santiago metro, page 99

Sleeping 🛏
Chilhotel 10
Marilú's B&B 8
Orly & Cafetto Café 2
Santiago Park Plaza 3
Sheraton Santiago 9
Tulip Inn Presidente 5
Vilafranca Petit 1

Eating 🍴
A Pinch of Pancho 1
Baco 2
Café El Patio 16
Carousel 5

Cementerio General

From the top of Cerro San Cristóbal the Cementerio General can be seen, situated in the *barrio* of La Recoleta to the north. This cemetery contains the mausolea of most of the great figures in Chilean history and the arts, including Violeta Parra, Victor Jara and Salvador Allende. There is also an impressive monument to the victims of the 1973-1990 military government; their names, ages and dates of detention or disappearance are listed in two sections: those who disappeared and those executed for political reasons. See www.cementeriogeneral.cl for more details. The cemetery can be reached by any Recoleta bus from Calle Miraflores or by metro, Cementerios, line 2.

East to Providencia and Las Condes

East of Plaza Italia, the main east-west axis of the city becomes known as **Avenida Providencia**, as it heads out towards residential areas at the eastern and upper levels of the city. On the south bank of the Mapocho, beneath Parque Metropolitano is **Parque Balmaceda**. It is one of the more attractive parks in Santiago with well-laid-out gardens

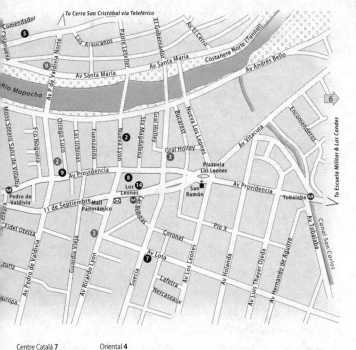

and fountains. The park houses the **Museo de los Tajamares** ⓘ *Av Providencia 222, T02-340 7329, Mon-Fri 0900-1400, 1500-2100*, an exhibition of the 17th- and 18th-century walls and subsequent canalization developed to protect the city from flooding.

Providencia

The neighbourhood of Providencia is the upmarket commercial centre of Santiago, a busy area of shops, offices and smart restaurants congregated around Pedro de Valdivia and Los Leones metro stations, line 1. The head office of **Sernatur**, the national tourist board, are located here. **Calle Suecia**, near Los Leones, is the focal point for nightlife in this part of the city, with a dozen 'pubs' offering European beers on tap, Tex-Mex food and live music.

⑥ Las Condes

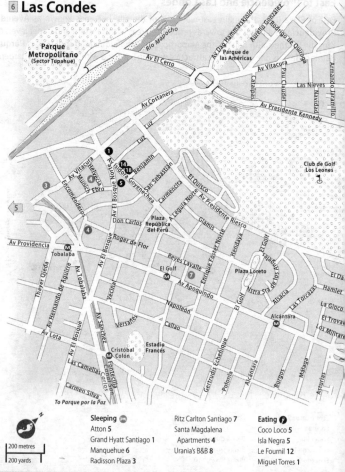

Sleeping		Ritz Carlton Santiago 7	Eating ⑦
Atton 5		Santa Magdalena	Coco Loco 5
Grand Hyatt Santiago 1		Apartments 4	Isla Negra 5
Manquehue 6		Urania's B&B 8	Le Fournil 12
Radisson Plaza 3			Miguel Torres 1

Las Condes

At Tobalaba metro, Avenida Providencia becomes **Avenida Apoquindo**, which heads on past Avenida Américo Vespucio – Santiago's ring road – and out towards the exclusive neighbourhoods of Las Condes, Vitacura, Lo Curro, Lo Barnechea and La Dehesa. Here you will find walled residential compounds, houses with servants and top-of-the-range cars, and expensive US-style shopping malls such as **Alto Las Condes** and **Parque Arauco**. Anyone who is anyone in Chilean society lives in this part of town.

Las Condes is home to two museums. **Museo de la Moda** ① *Vitacura 4562, www.museodalamoda.cl, Tue-Sun 1000-1830, US$6 including optional guided tour*, is South Americas only fashion museum. **Museo Rallí** ① *Alonso Sotomayor 4110, Vitacura, Tue-Sun 1100-1700, closed in summer, free*, has an excellent collection of works by modern artists, including Dalí, Chagall, Bacon and Miró. Recommended. There are art galleries on Avenida Nueva Costanera and Alonso de Córdova, Vitacura, in the Barrio Alto. Here, four or five private galleries showcase contemporary Chilean and Latin American art. All galleries are within a couple of blocks of each other. Try **Galería Tomas Andreu** ① *Av Nueva Costanera 3731, T02-228 9952*; **Galería de Arte Isabel Aninat** ① *Alonso de Córdova 3053, T02-263 2729*; and **AMS Marlborough** ① *Av Nueva Costanera 3723, T02-228 8696*.

South of Las Condes

Parque por la Paz ① *Av Arrieta 8401, www.villagrimaldicorp.cl*, the new peace park in the southeastern suburb of Peñalolén, stands on the site of **Villa Grimaldi**, the most notorious torture centre during the Pinochet regime. The Irish missionary, Sheila Cassidy, has documented the abuses that she underwent when imprisoned without trial in this place. The walls are daubed with human rights graffiti and the park makes for a moving and unusual introduction to the conflict that has eaten away at the heart of Chilean society for the past 30 years. To reach the park, take a metro to Tobalaba and then any bus marked Peñalolén heading south down Tobalaba. Get off at the junction of Tobalaba y José Arrieta and then walk five minutes up Arrieta towards the mountains.

➡ Santiago maps
1 Santiago orientation, page 66
2 Santiago centre, page 68
3 Santiago west of centre, page 72
4 Lastarria, Bellavista & Providencia west, page 74
5 Providencia, page 76
6 **Las Condes, page 78**
7 Santiago metro, page 99

Pinpilinpausha **14**
Puerto Mariska **18**

Bars & clubs 🍸
Flannery's Irish
Geo Pub **4**

La Florida

To the southeast of the centre, La Florida is a typical lower-middle-class residential neighbourhood that would not merit a visit were it not for the excellent **Museo Interactivo Mirador (MIM)** ① *Punta Arenas 6711, Mirador metro, line 5, T02-280 7800, www.mim.cl, Mon 0930-1330, Tue-Sun 0930-1830, US$6, concessions US$4*. This is a fun, interactive science and technology museum; perfect for a family outing. There is also an aquarium in the grounds.

Maipú

The suburb of Maipú, 10 km southwest of Santiago, is a 45-minute bus ride from the Alameda. Here, a monument marks the site of the Battle of the Maipú, 5 April 1818, which resulted in the final defeat of the Spanish royalist forces in mainland Chile. Nearby is the monolithic **National Votive Temple of Maipú** ① *daily 0830-2000, summer mass Mon-Fri 1700, Sat and Sun 1200 and 1700, winter mass Mon 1830, Tue-Sun 1200 and 1830*. This is a fine example of modern architecture and stained glass (best viewed from the inside). It is located on the site of an earlier temple, built in 1818 on the orders of Bernardo O'Higgins to commemorate the battle. The walls of the old construction stand in the forecourt, having fallen into ruin due to successive earthquakes. Pope John Paul II gave a mass here on his visit to Chile in 1987. The **Museo del Carmen** ① *Tue-Sun 1000-1800*, is part of the same building and contains carriages, furniture, clothing and other items from colonial times and later.

① Santiago listings

Hotel prices
LL over US$200 **L** US$151-200 **AL** US$101-150
A US$66-100 **B** US$46-65 **C** US$31-45
D US$21-30 **E** US$12-20 **F** US$7-11
G under US$7
Restaurant prices
♦♦♦ over US$12 ♦♦ US$7-12 ♦ under US$7
See pages 35-42 for further information.

Sleeping

Most of the more expensive accommodation is situated in the city centre or further east in the neighbourhoods of Providencia and Las Condes. The expensive hotels listed tend to be slightly characterless but with good service. Most budget accommodation is located in the city centre or further west in the vicinity of the bus terminals. There are an increasing number of hostels of varying ambiance and quality. Another good option is to stay in a family-run guesthouse. There are many basic hotels on Morandé, San Martín and San Pablo in the centre, and particularly on Gral MacKenna 1200 block, but bear in mind that this is the red-light district district and these are probably best avoided.

Accommodation in Santiago is generally about 20% more expensive than elsewhere in the country. Check if breakfast is included in the price quoted. Most 3-, 4- and 5-star hotels do not charge the 19% tax to foreigners who pay in US$ cash. However, the exchange rate given is often so punitive that it may be cheaper to pay in pesos. Several websites offer hotel booking services for Santiago and the rest of Chile, but most charge a sizeable commission.

If you are staying for weeks or months rather than days, staying with a family is an economical and interesting option. For private rentals, see the classified ads in *El Mercurio* – where flats, homes and family *pensiones* are listed by district – or in www.elRastro.cl, or try the noticeboard at the tourist office. Rates for 2-bed furnished apartments in a reasonable neighbourhood start at around US$250 per month. A month's rent and a month's deposit are normally required. Some offer daily and weekly lets. Estate agents handle apartments.

Around the Plaza de Armas *p66, map p68*

AL-A Majestic, Santo Domingo 1526, T02-695 8366, www.hotelmajestic.cl. With breakfast, pool, US-chain standard. The rooms, while spacious, retain their 1970s decor and are rather careworn. First-class Indian restaurant. English spoken.

B Kapital, Merced 433, T02-638 1624. Small, understated hotel. Rooms are clean and of decent size. Less street noise from upper floors. Some rooms have full jacuzzis. Great value although somewhat lacking in character.

B-C Andes Hostel, Monjitas 506, T02-632 9990, www.andeshostel.com. In one of Santiago's more interesting neighbourhoods. **E** per person in dorms, some rooms with bath, bar downstairs with pool table, barbeque nights on the roof terrace, kitchen facilities. Well run if slightly formulaic.

B-C Plaza de Armas Hostel, Compañía 960, Apt 607, T02-671 4562, www.plazade armashostel.com. **F** per person in dorms. Some rooms with bath, bright with fantastic views over the Plaza, high enough for noise from the street not to be an issue. Pleasant terrace, kitchen facilities, quieter rooms in an annex. A decent choice.

Along the Alameda *p69, map p68*

LL-AL Fundador, Paseo Serrano 34, T02-387 1200, www.hotelfundador.cl. Central, in a pleasant area, with helpful staff, conference rooms and banqueting halls. Pool, bar, restaurant, internet. Some rooms on the small side. Look for special internet rates. Universidad de Chile metro, line 1, south exit.

LL-AL Galerías, San Antonio 65, T02-470 7400, www.hotelgalerias.cl. Large rooms, good location, generous breakfast. Good value if booked over the internet.

A-B Conde de Ansúrez, Av República 25, T02-696 0807, www.ansurez.cl. República metro. Convenient for airport, central station and bus terminals, spacious rooms, clean, helpful, safe, luggage stored, good car hire deals and occasional special offers.

A-B Montecarlo, Victoria Subercaseaux 209, T02-639 2945, www.hotelmontecarlo.cl, at foot of Cerro Santa Lucía. Interior design is like some sort of art deco gone wrong, common areas showing their age. Small singles charged at the same rate as much bigger doubles.

A-B Vegas, Londres 49, T02-632 2514, www.hotelvegas.net. Standard 3 star. Nice location, very convenient for centre. Slightly brusque staff. Also rents out apartments.

B El Marqués del Forestal, Ismael Valdés Vergara 740, T02-639 4157, www.hotel marques.cl. Good value, apartments.

B-C Hostal Che Lagarto, Tucapel Jiménez 24, T02-699 1493, www.chelagarto.com. South American chain hostel, HI affiliated. **E** per person in dorms, some rooms with bath, comfortable common areas, kitchen facilities, internet.

B-C Hostal Santa Lucía, Santa Lucía 168, T02-664 8478, www.hostalsantalucia.cl, opposite Cerro Santa Lucía. **D** singles, **E-F** per person in dorms. With breakfast, some rooms with bath, friendly, fine views from upstairs rooms and the roof terrace, Wi-Fi, some English spoken.

B-C Residencial Mery, Pasaje República 36, off 0-100 block of República, T02-696 8883, www.residencialmery.virtuabyte.cl. Art deco building down an alley, some rooms with bath, breakfast extra, friendly owners, quiet, Wi-Fi.

C Hostal Forestal, Santiago Bueras 122, T02-638 1347, www.hostalforestal.cl. **D** singles, **F** per person in dorms. Good location, lively hostel, recently improved and expanded. With breakfast, some rooms with bath, comfy lounge with internet and big-screen TV, kitchen facilities, barbeque nights. English spoken, a decent option.

C París, París 813, T02-664 0921, carbott@ latinmail.com. **D** singles. With bath, quiet, clean, no-frills but good value, breakfast extra, luggage store. Book in advance in summer. Recommended.

C Residencial Londres, Londres 54, T02-638 2215, www.londres.cl, near San Francisco church. **E** singles, former mansion, large old-fashioned rooms and furniture, some rooms with bath, few singles, no heating so cold in winter, some English spoken, book exchange. Good value, recommended.

South of the Alameda *p71, map p72*
C Hostal de Sammy, Toesca 2335, T02-689 8772, www.hostaldesammy.com. **E** singles, **F** per person in dorms. Good-value US-run hostel with decent common areas, table tennis, good-sized pool table, and big-screen TV with hundreds of films on demand. Hearty breakfast included. Good info. Fast internet, Wi-Fi, kitchen facilities. Staff generally helpful. Recommended.

Barrio Brasil *p73, map p72*
A-B Happy House Hostel, Catedral 2207, metro Cumming or República, T02-688 4849, www.happyhousehostel.cl. **D-E** per person in dorms. In a completely refurbished mansion, this high end hostel is one of Santiago's best, with high-ceilinged spacious rooms, fully equipped kitchen, comfy lounge, internet, bar, pool room, friendly English-speaking staff. One room with en suite sauna. On the downside, some rooms facing the main street can be noisy. Expensive for a hostel, but still highly recommended.

C Hostal Americano, Compañía 1906, T02-698 1025, www.hostalamericano.cl. Nondescript brick and concrete building. Clean, comfortable rooms, some with private bathroom, friendly atmosphere, some English spoken, pleasant garden at the back. Better value if paying in US dollars. Recommended.

C Hostal Río Amazonas, Rosas 2234, T02-671 9013, www.hostalrioamazonas.cl. **D** singles. In a restored mansion with breakfast and bath, internet, good value if paying in US dollars or euro. Same owners as Hostal Plaza Italia. Recommended.

C La Casa Roja, Agustinas 2113, T02-696 4241, www.lacasaroja.cl. **F** per person in dorms. 7 years of restoration have borne fruit in this huge mansion, which now boasts a fantastic kitchen, 2 bars, swimming pool, cricket net, lots of activities and tours, and Spanish classes. Sets the standard for lively hostels in the capital. Highly recommended, but remember to pack earplugs if you want a good night's sleep.

West of centre: around Estación Central *p73, map p72*
Only think of staying near Estación Central if you are on a lightning visit or have an early or late start.
A Tur Hotel Express, Av Libertador Bernardo O'Higgins 3750, piso 3, in the TurBus terminal, T02-685 0100, www.turbus.com/turismo/TurHotel/tur-Hotel-Santiago.html. Comfortable business standard with

breakfast, cable TV, a/c, free internet. Particularly useful if you need to take an early flight as buses leave for the airport from here.
C-D Residencial Sur, Ruiz Tagle 055, T02-776 5533. **E-F** singles. Pretty grim, but a last-resort option if you arrive in the middle of the night at the bus terminal.

Bellavista and Cerro San Cristóbal
p74, map p74
AL Del Patio, Pio Nono 61, Bellavista, T02-732 7571, www.hoteldelpatio.cl. New boutique hotel in a refurbished old wooden building overlooking the lively Patio Bellavista. The location is great for bars, restaurants and nightlife, but at weekends it can be seriously noisy until late at night.
C Bellavista Hostel, Dardignac 0184, T02-732 8737, www.bellavistahostel.com. **E-F** per person in dorms. Fun, European-style hostel in the heart of this lively area. Sheets provided but make your own bed. With breakfast, kitchen facilities, free internet, satellite TV in common area, bicycles lent to guests. Good meeting place.

Providencia *p78, map p76*
LL Sheraton Santiago, Santa María 1742, T02-233 5000, www.sheraton.cl. 5-star, one of the best in town though some rooms on the small side, especially given the prices. Good restaurant, good buffet lunch, all facilities.
LL-L Santiago Park Plaza, Av Ricardo Lyon 207, T02-372 4000, www.parkplaza.cl. 5-star, another typical 'luxury hotel' geared towards business travellers. Occasional online deals.
AL Orly, Pedro de Valdivia 027, T02-231 8947, www.orlyhotel.com. Pedro de Valdivia metro. Small, comfortable, excellent location. Also more expensive suites, small café attached with reasonable food. Highly recommended.
A Chilhotel, Cirujano Guzmán 103, T02-264 0643, www.chilhotel.cl. Manuel Montt metro. Run-of-the-mill small hotel. Quiet, good value, also apartments.
A Principado, Vicuña MacKenna 30, 1 block south of Plaza Baquedano, T02-222 8142,

www.hotelesprincipado.com. Reasonable if nondescript 3-star standard. Slightly run-down.
A Tulip Inn Presidente, Eliodoro Yáñez 867, almost at Providencia, T02-235 8015, www.presidente.cl. Salvador metro. Slightly soulless, medium-sized chain hotel. Good location. Rooms vary enormously in size. The larger rooms with a desk are good value, while the smaller rooms are overpriced.
A Vilafranca Petit Hotel, Pérez Valenzuela 1650, T02-235 1413, www.vilafranca.cl. Manuel Montt metro. Homely, high end B&B. Small but impeccable rooms. Quiet neighbourhood, pleasant garden, friendly service, English spoken, Wi-Fi. Recommended.
B Marilú's Bed and Breakfast, Rafael Cañas 246 C, T02-235 5302, www.bedand breakfast.cl. Salvador metro. Comfortable, rooms with shared bathroom, very friendly owner, good beds, English and French spoken. A little overpriced.
B-C Casa Condell, Condell 114, T02-209 2343 Salvador metro, www.casacondell.cl. **D** singles. Pleasant old house, central, quiet, nice roof terrace. kitchen facilities, free local phone calls, friendly, English spoken. Recommended, but only 2 bathrooms shared between 7 rooms can be an issue in high season.
B-C Patio Suizo, Condell 847, Bustamante metro line 5, T02-474 0634, www.patiosuizo. com. Comfortable and pleasant Swiss-run B&B in a quiet area, some rooms with bath, breakfast included, Wi-Fi, English, German spoken, Spanish classes. Patio with vines and a hammock. Friendly owner with lots of tips, wine tours offered. Highly recommended.
C Hostal Casa Grande, Vicuña MacKenna 90, T02-222 7347, www.hostalcasagrande.cl. Baquedano metro. **D-E** singles. Labyrinthine *hostal* on the 2nd floor of an old high-ceilinged building. Some rooms with bath and TV, quiet, good value.

Las Condes *p79, map p78*
LL Grand Hyatt Santiago, Av Kennedy 4601, T02-950 1234, www.santiago.grand.hyatt. com. Superb, beautifully decorated, large

outdoor pool, gym, Thai restaurant. Upper floor rooms facing the Andes have great views.

LL Ritz Carlton Santiago, El Alcalde 15, T02-470 8500, www.ritzcarlton.com/en/Properties/Santiago. El Golf Metro. Newish 5-star plus hotel with all services. The most luxurious hotel in Santiago and also the most expensive.

LL-L Radisson Plaza, Av Vitacura 2610, T02-203 6000, www.radisson.cl. Metro Tobalaba. 5-star, excellent, disabled access, attentive staff, recommended.

AL Apart Hotel Santa Magdalena, office at Helvecia 244, Las Condes, T02-374 6875, www.santamagdalena.cl. Metro Tobalaba. Well-serviced apartments for 1-4 people, a/c.

AL Atton, Alonso de Córdova 5199, T02-422 7979, www.atton.cl. Comfortable, 4-star, disabled-friendly, good value. Recommended, but not convenient for the metro.

AL Manquehue, Esteban Dell'Orto 6615, T02-430 1100, www.hotelmanquehue.com. Small 4-star with pool. Rack rates overpriced but occasional very good internet deals.

B Urania's Bed and Breakfast, Boccaccio 60, T02-951 5307, www.uraniabalut.tripod.com. **C** singles. Comfortable, friendly, good beds, English and French spoken. Recommended, though not particularly convenient for public transport.

🍴 Eating

Luxury hotels have computerized information on the more expensive restaurants; particularly useful if you are not sure what to eat. There is also an excellent guide to the more exclusive restaurants at www.buenavida.cl.

For excellent cheap seafood lunches make for the **Mercado Central** (Cal y Canto metro), or the **Vega Central** market on the opposite bank of the Mapocho. Budget travellers should make the *almuerzo* their main meal. For cheap meals in the evening try the *fuentes de soda* and *schoperías* scattered around the centre.

Around the Plaza de Armas *p66, map p68*
♦♦♦-♦♦ Da Carla, MacIver 577, T02-633 3739. Intimate old-time Italian trattoria, elegant yet informal atmosphere. Good service and has maintained it quality over the years.

♦♦♦-♦♦ Majestic, see Sleeping. This hotel has one of few excellent Indian restaurants in South America, with a good range of vegetarian dishes.

♦♦ Faisan d'Or, Plaza de Armas. Good *pastel de choclo*, pleasant place to have a drink and watch the world go by. There are also many cheap eateries on the south side of the plaza.

♦ Bar Nacional, Huérfanos 1151. Good restaurants, popular, local specialities, very traditional. Another branch at Bandera 317.

♥ **El Rápido**, C Bandera, next door to Bar Nacional. Famed for its *empanadas* and *completos*, cheap, quick service, popular.

Along the Alameda *p69, map p68*

♥♥♥-♥♥ **Les Assassins**, Merced 297, Lastarria, T02-638 4280. Small family-run French bistro. Excellent food with friendly service and a decent wine list. Good-value set lunches. Recommended.

♥♥♥-♥♥ **Opera Catedral**, José Miguelde la Barra 407, Lastarria, Bellas Artes metro, line 5, T02-664 5491, www.operacatedral.cl. Very good, if expensive, French restaurant on the ground floor. Upstairs there is a minimalist pub-restaurant, usually packed at night, serving fusion food at reasonable prices.

♥♥ **El Naturista**, Moneda 846. Closes 2100. Excellent vegetarian, serving quiches, tortillas, a wide range of soups and wholemeal sandwiches. Also serves organic coffee, fruit and vegetable juice as well as beer and wine. Always full at lunchtime.

♥♥ **Gatopardo**, Lastarria 192, opposite the plaza Mulato Gil de Castro, T02-633 6420. A mixture of Bolivian and Mediterranean cuisine. Good-value lunch buffet. Recommended.

♥♥ **Lung Fung**, Agustinas 715. The oldest Chinese restaurant in Santiago. Pricey but serves decent food. There is a large cage in the centre with noisy parrots.

♥♥-♥ **El Diablito**, Merced 336, Local 2, Lastarria, Bellas Artes metro, line 5. Fashionable somewhat Bohemian bar/restaurant serving sandwiches and a wide range of beer.

♥♥-♥ **Nuria**, Agustinas y MacIver. This was a well-known Bohemian hang-out in the 1960s. Now past its heyday, it still serves a wide variety of decent food and generous sandwiches.

♥ **Círculo de Periodistas**, Amunátegui 31, piso 2. Unwelcoming entrance, good-value lunches. Recommended.

♥ **Confitería Torres**, Av Libertador Bernardo O'Higgins 1570. One of Chile's oldest bar/restaurants dating from 1879, good atmosphere, live tango music at weekends.

Cheap lunches are served in a large underground *comedor*.

Cafés

Bombón Oriental, Merced 345, Lastarria, T02-639 1069, www.bombonoriental.cl. Superb Turkish coffee, arabic snacks and sweets.

Café Caribe and **Café Haití**, Paseo Ahumada, institutions among Santiago's business community and good places to see the people who make Chile tick; also branches throughout the centre and in Providencia.

Café Colonia, MacIver 133. Splendid variety of cakes, pastries and pies, efficient if somewhat brusque service by staff who haven't changed for decades. Recommended.

Café Universitario, Alameda 395 y Subercaseaux (near Santa Lucía), Lastarria. Good, cheap *almuerzos*, lively at night, separate room for lovers of rock videos, very pleasant.

Tip-Top Galletas, for freshly baked biscuits, there are 2 branches on the Alameda just east of the Moneda, take-away only.

South of the Alameda *p71, map p72*

♥♥♥-♥♥ **Los Adobes del Argomedo**, Argomedo 411 y Lira, 10 blocks south of the Alameda, T02-222 2104, www.losadobesde argomedo.cl. Long-established traditional restaurant. Good Chilean food, floor show (Mon-Sat) includes *cueca* dancing, salsa and folk.

♥ **Las Tejas**, San Diego 234. Old-time southern Chichería. Lively, rowdy crowd, very cheap cocktails and drinks such as *pisco sour* and *pipeño*, excellent *cazuelas* and other typical dishes.

♥ **Masticón**, San Diego 152. Good service, excellent value, popular, wide range of fast food and traditional Chilean food.

Barrio Brasil *p73, map p72*

♥♥♥-♥♥ **Las Vacas Gordas**, Cienfuegos 280, T02-697 1066. Excellent *parrillada*. Very popular, so book in advance.

♥♥♥-♥♥ **Ocean Pacific's**, Cumming 221, T02-697 2413. Extremely kitsch seafood restaurant with ship and submarine-themed rooms. You can find better food elsewhere, but for over-the-top exuberance, this is hard to beat.

♼ Los Buenos Muchachos, Cumming 1031, T02-698 0112, www.losbuenosmuchachos.cl. Cavernous hall seating over 400 and serving traditional Chilean food in abundant portions. Very popular, especially at night when shows of traditional Chilean dances are held.

♼ Los Chinos Ricos, Brasil 373, T02-696 3778, www.chinosricos.cl, on the plaza. Famed Chinese. The restaurant used to be called Los Chinos Pobres, but was so popular it had to change its name. Fills up with noisy families on Sun lunchtimes.

♼ Ostras Azócar, Bulnes 37, T02-681 6109. Long-established traditional restaurant specializing in seafood and oysters.

West of centre: around Estación Central *p73, map p72*

♼ El Hoyo, San Vicente 375, T02-689 0339. Closed Sun. 100-yr-old *chichería* serving hearty Chilean fare such as *arrollado* and *prietas*, recently described by celebrity chef Anthony Bourdain as "f****** awesome".

Bellavista and Cerro San Cristóbal *p74, map p74*

Most restaurants in Bellavista close on Sun and public holidays, but this is one of the liveliest places to come out and eat at night, with many excellent and costly restaurants. There are dozens more restaurants than those listed below, with a new place seeming to open every few weeks.

♼♼♼ Azul Profundo, Constitución 111, Bellavista. Fish and seafood with a touch of invention. Good range of cocktails.

♼♼♼ Cienfuegos, Constitución 67, Bellavista. T02-248 9080. Tue-Sat evenings. Reputedly one of the best restaurants in town serving Chilean/European fusion. The food is always excellent, though portions are tiny for the hefty price tag and service can be slow, especially at weekends.

♼♼♼ Como Agua Para Chocolate, Constitución 88, Bellavista. Mexican and

Mediterranean. Slightly pretentious presentations but excellent service.

♼♼♼ El Otro Sitio, Antonia López de Bello 053, Bellavista. Upmarket Peruvian. Good service, elegant surroundings, excellent range of starters. If you are feeling brave, try the *rocoto relleno*. Recommended.

♼♼♼-♼♼ Etniko, Constitición 172, Bellavista, T02-732 0119. Sushi and Thai restaurant that also functions as a lively bar later in the night. No sign, just knock.

♼♼ Eladio, Pío Nono 251, Bellavista. Argentine cuisine, good steaks, bingo.

♼♼ El Antojo de Gaugin, Pío Nono 69 inside the Patio Bellavista. Arabic. Good *brochetas a la plancha*.

♼♼ El Tablao, Constitución 110, Bellavista, T02-737 8648. Traditional Spanish restaurant. The food is reasonable, but the main attraction is the live flamenco show on Thu-Sat nights, with Arab dance on Tue.

♼♼ Venezia, Pío Nono y Antonia López de Bello, Bellavista. Traditional Chilean home-cooked fare. Large servings, good value. One of Neruda's favourite haunts.

Cafés

There is a pleasant café at La Chascona.
Café de la Dulcería Las Palmas, Antonia López de Bello 190, Bellavista. Good pastries and lunches.
Empanatodos, Pío Nono 153, Bellavista. Serves 32 different types of *empanadas*.

Providencia *p78, map p76*

♼♼♼ Carousel, Los Conquistadores 1972, T02-232 1728. Fine French cuisine, exceptionally smart, nice garden, very expensive.

♼♼♼ Centre Catalá, Av Suecia 428 near Lota. Elegant Catalan restaurant, quiet street, pleasant decor, cheaper sal lunch.

♼♼♼ El Giratorio, 11 de Septiembre 2250, piso 16, T02-232 1827. Good French food eaten while the whole city rotates outside your window. Recommended for the view.

♼♼♼-♼♼ A Pinch of Pancho, Gral del Canto 45, T02-235 1700. Seafood and fish specialities, very good.

ŦŦŦ-ŦŦ Baco, Nueva de Lyon 113, T02-231 4444. Metro Los Leones. Sophisticated French restaurant. The food is good, but what stands out is the extensive wine list and the amount of quality wines available by the glass.

ŦŦŦ-ŦŦ De Cangrejo a Conejo, Italia 805 y Bilbao, Providencia, T 02-634 4041, www.decangrejoaconejo.cl. Metro Parque, Bustamante or Salvador. Small but varied menu, ranging as the restaurants name suggests from crab to rabbit. The food is invariably excellent. Lovely garden. Deservedly popular. No sign outside.

ŦŦŦ-ŦŦ Oriental, M Montt 584, T02-235 2389. One of the best Chinese restaurants in Santiago. Excellent service.

ŦŦ Café El Patio, Providencia 1652, next to **Phone Box Pub**. Tofu and pasta as well as fish dishes, good sandwiches, popular. Turns into a pub at night. Wide range of cocktails.

ŦŦ Eladio, 11 de Septiembre 2250, piso 5. Reasonably priced, good meat dishes. There is often karaoke on Fri and Sat nights.

ŦŦ El Huerto, Orrego Luco 054, T02-233 2690. Santiago's oldest vegetarian restaurant. Varied dishes from around the world, although slightly on the bland side. Vegan options available. Good juices. Local artwork on display.

ŦŦ-Ŧ Olan, Seminario 96A-B, Providencia. Incredibly good value tasty Peruvian food in unpretentious surroundings. Another branch opposite at No 67, slightly higher prices.

Ŧ Mercado de Providencia, Santa Beatriz, off Av Providencia. This small market has a couple of good cheap lunchtime eateries.

Ŧ Tercera Compañía de Bomberos, Vicuña Mackenna 097, Providencia, near the junction with Diagonal Paraguay. Good food, very cheap, recommended.

Cafés

Cafetto, Pedro de Valdivia 030, next to **Hotel Orly**. Upmarket café with a wide variety of sandwiches.

There are several good places for snacks and ice cream on Av Providencia, including: **Bravissimo**, No 1406; **Copelia**, No 2211;

El Toldo Azul, No 1936. Also, **Salón de Té Tavelli**, Drugstore precinct, No 2124. However the best is probably **Sebastián**, Fuenzalida 26, Los Leones Metro.

Las Condes p79, map p78
This area has many 1st-class restaurants, including grills, serving Chilean (often with music), French and Chinese cuisine. They tend to be more expensive than central restaurants. Lots of expensive eateries are located on El Bosque Norte, near the Tobalaba metro stop.

ŦŦŦ Coco Loco, El Bosque Norte 0215, T02-231 3082. Fish, seafood, good.

ŦŦŦ Isla Negra, next door to **Coco Loco**, El Bosque Norte. Seafood a speciality.

ŦŦŦ Pinpilinpausha, Isidora Goyenechea 2900, T02-232 5800. Basque specialities, good.

ŦŦŦ-ŦŦ Miguel Torres, Isidora Goyenechea 2874, T02-242 9360. Tapas bar owned by the well-known Spanish winery.

ŦŦŦ-ŦŦ Puerto Marisko, Isidora Goyenechea 2918, T02-251 9542. Renowned for seafood but also serves pasta and meat dishes. Has maintained its quality over 20 years.

ŦŦ Le Fournil, Vitacura 3841, opposite Cuerovaca, T02-228 0219. Excellent French bakery and restaurant. Particularly popular at lunchtime. Good soups. Service can be poor.

🅝 Bars and clubs

As in most of South America, a night out in Santiago begins late. Arrive in a restaurant before 2100 and you may be eating alone, while bars and clubs are often empty before midnight. Clubs and bars playing live music will generally charge an entry fee of between US$2 (for student-orientated places) and US$10 (for upmarket clubs), usually with some sort of drink included in the price.

Santiago has a good choice of restaurants, bars, discos and *salsotecas* from the reasonably priced in Bellavista (Baquedano metro) to the smarter along Av Suecia and G Holley in Providencia (Los Leones metro).

Barrio Brasil has a number of bars and restaurants dotted around Plaza Brasil and on Av Brasil and Cumming. The area is popular with Chilean students (República metro).

In **Las Condes**, El Bosque Norte is lined with chic bars and expensive restaurants for the Chilean jet-set (Tobalaba metro).

In the middle-class suburb of **Nuñoa** is Plaza Nuñoa, around which a number of good bars are dotted.

Bellavista *p74, map p74*
Clubs in Bellavista are cheaper and more downmarket than those in Providencia.
Back Stage, Patio Bellavista. Good-quality live jazz and blues.
Bogart, Antonia López de Bello 34. Rock music. 2 other similar bar son the same block.
Club 4-40, Santa Filomena 81. Named after popular singer Juan Luis Guerra's backing group from the Dominican Republic, live Cuban music, packed at weekends.
Disco Salsa, Pío Nono 223. Good atmosphere, salsa dance classes downstairs.
Heaven, Recoleta 345. Thu-Sat 2330-0500, US$15 per person.
Jammin' Club, Antonia López de Bello 49. Reggae.
La Bodega de Julio, Constitución 256. Cuban staff and Cuban cocktails, excellent live music and dancing possible, very popular, free entry before 2300, very good value.
La Casa en el Aire, Patio Bellavista. Pleasant atmosphere, live music. Recommended.
La Otra Puerta, Pío Nono 348. Lively *salsoteca* with live music. Recommended.
Tu Tu Tanga, Pío Nono 127. Busy at night, cheap beer, good value. Similar next door.

Providencia *p78, map p76*
Clubs in Providencia can be expensive; up to US$20 or more to get in.
Brannigan's Pub, Suecia 35, T02-232 7869. Good beer, live jazz, lively.
Golden Bell Inn, Hernando de Aguirre 27. Popular with expats.
Ilé Habana, Bucaré just off Suecia. Bar with salsa music, often live, and a good dance floor.

Phone Box Pub, Providencia 1670, T02-235 0303. Very popular with expats, serves numerous European beers including Pilsener Urquell, and canned British beers including Newcastle Brown Ale, Beamish Stout and Old Speckled Hen. A good place to go if you are missing home.

Las Condes *p79, map, p78*
Like Providencia, Las Condes clubs can be expensive, up to US$20 or more.
Country Village, Av Las Condes 10680. Mon-Sat from 2000, Sun from lunch onwards, live music Fri and Sat.
Flannery's Irish Geo Pub, Encomenderos 83, T02-233 6675, www.flannerys.cl. Irish pub, serving Guinness on draft, good lunches including vegetarian options, popular among gringos and Chileans alike.
Las Urracas, Vitacura 9254. US$20, free before 2300 if you eat there. Variety of cocktails.
Morena Pizza and Dance Bar, Av Las Condes 10120. Good sound system, live music at weekends, happy hour before 2200.
Tequila, Av Las Condes at Paseo San Damián. One of a few popular bar-restaurants in the area.

☻ Entertainment

Santiago *p62, maps p68, p72, p74, p76, p78 and p99*
For all entertainment, nightclubs, cinemas, restaurants, concerts, the *El Mercurio* website, www.emol.com, has listings and a good search feature. Look under the *tiempo libre* section. There are also listings in weekend newspapers, particularly *El Mercurio* and *La Tercera*, and in *Santiago What's On*.

Cinemas
A good guide to daily cinema listings across the city is provided by the newspaper *publimetro*, which is free at metro stations early on weekday mornings. Seats cost US$4-7 with reductions on Mon, Tue and Wed (elsewhere in the country the day

varies). Some cinemas offer discounts to students and over 60s (proof required).

There are many mainstream cinemas showing international films, usually in original English with Spanish subtitles. Multiplex cinemas include:

CineHoyts Estación Central, Exposición 155, www.cinehoyts.cl, in the shopping mall next to the train station. T600-500 0400.

CineHoyts Huérfanos, Huérfanos 735, T600-500 0400, www.cinehoyts.cl.

CineHoyts La Reina, Av Ossa 655, T600-500 0400, www.cinehoyts.cl. Simón Bolívar metro, line 4.

CineHoyts San Agustín, Moneda 835, T600-500 0400, www.cinehoyts.cl.

Cinemark Alto Las Condes, Av Kennedy 9001, Las Condes, T600-600 2463, www.cinemark.cl. Attached to the mall.

Showcase Parque Arauco, Av Kennedy 5413, Las Condes, T02-565 7010. Attached to the shopping malls.

'CineArte' (art-house cinemas that show quality foreign films) are also very popular and include the following:

Casa de Extensión Universidad Católica, Av B O'Higgins 390, T02-635 1994. Universidad Católica metro, south exit, line 1.

Centro Arte Alameda, Av Bernardo O'Higgins 139, Baquedano metro, line 1, T02-664 8821, www.centroartealameda.cl.

Cine Arte Normandie, Tarapacá 1181, T02-697 2979. Varied programme, altered frequently, films at 1530, 1830 and 2130 daily, students half price. Moneda metro, south exit, line 1.

El Biógrafo, Lastarria 181, T02-633 4435. Universidad Católica metro, north exit, line 1.

Tobalaba, Av Providencia 2563, T02-231 6630. Tobalaba metro, line 1.

Cultural centres

Centro Cultural Estación Mapocho, Cal y Canto metro, line 2, T02-787 0000. www.estacionmapocho.cl. Regular art exhibitions, concerts, shows.

Centro Cultural Matucana 100, T02-682 4502, www.m100.cl. Quinta Normal or Estación Central Metro. Huge new complex with spaces set aside for theatre, cinema, art galleries and live music.

Centro Cultural Palacio La Moneda, Plaza de la Ciudadanía, T02-355 6500, www.ccplm.cl. Moneda metro, north exit, line 1. Cinema and good temporary exhibitions.

Corporación Cultural de Las Condes, Av Apoquindo 6570, near beginning of Av Las Condes. T02-366 9393. Also art exhibitions, concerts, lectures, etc.

Instituto Cultural de Providencia, Av 11 de Septiembre 1995. T02-223 2700. Pedro de Valdivia metro, north exit, line 1. Art exhibitions, concerts, theatre, worth checking out the programme.

Instituto Cultural del Banco del Estado de Chile, Alameda 123. Regular art exhibitions, concerts, theatrical performances.

Performing arts

Teatro Municipal, Agustinas y San Antonio, www.municipal.cl. Stages international opera, concerts by the Orquesta Filarmónica de Santiago and performances by the Ballet de Santiago, throughout the year. On Tue at 2100 there are free operatic concerts in the Salón Claudio Arrau. Tickets range from US$10 for a very large choral group with a symphony orchestra, and US$12 for the cheapest seats at the ballet, to US$100 for the most expensive opera seats. Some cheap seats are often sold on the day of concerts.

Teatro Municipal de Nuñoa, Av Irarrázaval 1564, www.ccn.cl, T02-277 7903. Dance, art exhibitions, cinema, children's theatre.

Teatro Universidad de Chile, Plaza Baquedano, www.teatro.uchile.cl, T02-978 2203. Home of the Orquesta y Coro Sinfónica de Chile and the Ballet Nacional de Chile.

A great number of more minor theatres around the city stage plays, including **Abril**, Huérfanos 786; **Camilo Henríquez**, Amunátegui 31; **Centro Arrayán**, Las Condes 14891; **El Galpón de los Leones**, Av Los Leones 238; **El Conventillo**, Bellavista 173 and **La Comedia**, Merced 349. Events are listed in *El Mercurio* and *La Tercera*.

☸ Festivals and events

Santiago *p62, maps p68, p72, p74, p76, p78 and p99*

Mar/Apr Holy Week. Religious festivals and ceremonies throughout this time, when a priest ritually washes the feet of 12 men.
End of May Expo gourmand. A food festival, changes location every year.
16 Jul The image of the Virgen del Carmen (patron saint of the armed forces) is carried through the streets by cadets.
18 Sep Independence Day when many families get together or celebrate in *fondas* (small temporary constructions made of wood and straw where people eat traditional dishes, drink *chicha* and dance *cueca*).
19 Sep Armed Forces Day is celebrated with an enormous 4-hr-long military procession through the Parque O'Higgins.
Nov A free art fair lasting a fortnight is held in the Parque Forestal on the banks of the Río Mapocho.

○ Shopping

Santiago *p62, maps p68, p72, p74, p76, p78 and p99*

There are many shopping areas in Santiago. The shops in the centre and to the north of the Plaza de Armas are cheaper and more downmarket than the countless arcades and boutiques strung along Providencia, especially near Av Ricardo Lyon. Specialist shops tend to be grouped together, eg bikes, computer hardware and second-hand books on San Diego, new bookshops on Providencia, opticians on MacIver, lapis lazuli on Bellavista, fishing and outdoor equipment on Bulnes. Some kiosks on Paseo Ahumada/Huérfanos sell overseas newspapers and journals.

Bookshops
Book prices are very high compared with Europe, even for second-hand books.

There are many bookshops in the Pedro de Valdivia area on Av Providencia. Much

better value but with a smaller selection are the bookshops in the shopping mall at Av Providencia 1114-1120. Those looking for cheap English-language books should also try the many second-hand book kiosks on San Diego, 4 blocks south of Plaza Bulnes, next to the Iglesia de los Sacramentinos.
Apostrophes, Merced 324, www.apostrophes.cl, specializes in foreign-language publications.
Books, Providencia 1652, Local 5, in a courtyard beside the Phone Box Pub and Café El Patio. Wide selection of English-language books for sale or exchange, English spoken. On the expensive side.
Books & Bits, Av Apoquindo 6856, Las Condes, T02-210 9100. Sells books in English.
Feria Chilena del Libro, Huérfanos 623. Largest bookstore in Santiago, good for travel books and maps; also at Nueva York 3, Agustinas 859, Mall Parque Arauco and Providencia 2124.
Le Comptoir, Shopping los Cobres local F3, Av Vitacura 6780, T02-218 7368, www.comptoir.cl. French books. Good selection of literature, books ordered on request.
Librería Chile Ilustrado, Providencia 1652 local 6, next door to Books, T02-235 8145, chileil@tnet.cl. Specializes in books (nearly all in Spanish) relating to Chile, particularly flora and fauna, history and anthropology.
Librería Eduardo Albers, Vitacura 5648, Las Condes, T02-218 5371, www.texto.cl. Spanish, English and German – good selection, cheaper than most, helpful, also German and Swiss newspapers.
Librería Inglesa, Huérfanos 669, local 11, Pedro de Valdivia 47, Vitacura 5950, Providencia 2653, T02-231 9970, www.libreria inglesa.cl. Sells only books in English, good selection, stocks the *South American Handbook*.
Librería Lila, Providencia 1652, local 3. Mind/body/spirit specialists, best in Santiago in this field.
Librería Universitaria, Av Bernado O'Higgins 1050, T02-695 1529, F695 6387. Particularly for books in Spanish.

LOM Ediciones, Estación Mapocho. Mon-Fri 1000-2000, Sat 1000-1400. Sells a stock of literature, history, sociology, art and politics from its own publishing house. Also a bar and a reading room with recent Chilean newspapers and magazines.

Camping and outdoors equipment

There are a number of 'hunting' shops on Bulnes 1-2 blocks south of the Alameda, with a basic range of outdoor equipment. Also try the **Mall Sport**, Av Las Condes 13451.
Andes Gear, Helvecia 210, Las Condes, T02-245 7076, www.andesgear.cl. Good range of good-quality clothes and equipment.
Club Andino and **Federación de Andinismo** (see page 94). Expensive products, as most articles are imported.
La Cumbre, Apoquindo 5258, Las Condes, T02-220 9907, www.lacumbreonline.cl. Climbing equipment.
Lippi, Av Italia 1586, Nuñoa, T02-225 6803, www.lippi.cl. Santa Isabel Metro. Chile's premier outdoor equipment maker. Excellent-quality clothes, boots, tents, etc.
Parafernalia, Huérfanos 1973 y Brasil. Second-hand gear. Recommended.
Peregrin, del Arzobispo 0607, Bellavista, T02-735 1587. Salvador metro. Decent-quality locally made outdoor clothes.
Tatoo Adventure Gear, Los Leones 81, Providencia, T562-946 0008, outlet store at Dr Torres Boonen 686. Offers major brands of outdoor gear.

Handicrafts

Those wishing to spend a reasonable amount of money buying good-quality crafts may wish to travel to Pomaire (see page 104), where goods from all over Chile are for sale at prices cheaper than those in Santiago.

The gemstone, lapis lazuli, can be found in a few expensive shops in Bellavista but is cheaper in the arcades on the south side of the Plaza de Armas. Antique stores can be found in Plaza Mulato Gil de Castro and elsewhere on Lastarria (Merced end).

Other craft stalls can be found in an alleyway 1 block south of Av O'Higgins between A Prat and San Diego; on the 600 to 800 blocks of Santo Domingo and at Pío Nono y Av Santa María in Bellavista.
Aldea de Vitacura, Vitacura 6838, T02-735 3959. Open 1000-2000.
Centro Artesanal Santa Lucía, Santa Lucía metro, south exit. This is the best place to buy generic *artesanía* in central Santiago. Lapis lazuli can be bought here cheaply. Also has a wide variety of woollen goods, jewellery, etc.
Dauvin Artesanía Fina, Providencia 2169, local 69, www.artesaniasvdauvin.cl. Los Leones metro.
Morita Gil, Los Misioneros 1991, Pedro de Valdivia Norte, T02-232 6853.
Pueblito Artesanal Los Domínicos, Apoquindo 9805, Las Condes, www.pueblito losdominicos.com. Metro Los Domínicos. The best upmarket craft fair in Chile. A good range of modern and traditional Chilean crafts from ceramics to textiles, a pleasant central piazza, and places where the artisans can be seen working on wood, silver, glass and so on. Although more expensive than, for instance, the market in Santa Lucía, this is a good and attractive option.

Maps

Automóvil Club de Chile, Av Andrés Bello 1863, Pedro de Valdivia metro, line 1, T02-431 1000, www.automovilclub.cl. Mon-Thu 0900-1815, Fri 0900-1700. Route maps of Chile, US$6 each, free to members of affiliated motoring organizations; very helpful.
CONAF, see page 64. Maps of national parks.
Instituto Geográfico Militar, Dieciocho 369, near Toesca metro, T02-410 9463. Detailed geophysical and topographical maps of the whole of Chile, very useful for climbing. Expensive (about US$15 each), but **Biblioteca Nacional**, Av Libertador Bernardo O'Higgins 651, T02-360 5200, stocks them and will allow you to photocopy parts of each map.
Librería Australis, Av Providencia 1670, local 5. All sorts of local, regional and trekking maps.

Markets

For details of the city's craft markets, see Handicrafts, above.

Bío Bío flea market, C Bío Bío. Every Sat and Sun morning. This is the largest and cheapest flea market in the city and sells everything from spare parts for cars and motorbikes to second-hand furniture. Those trying to do up a new flat on the cheap, a car on the hoof, or who are simply interested in sharing a street with tens of thousands of others, should find their way here; just go to Franklin metro, line 2 and follow the crowds. Beware of rip-offs.

Mercado Central, Puente y 21 de Mayo by the Río Mapocho. Cal y Canto metro. Brilliant for seafood, with many places to eat cheaply, **Donde Augusto** is recommended. Otherwise an excellent range of goods, but quite expensive. See also page 69.

Vega Central, on the opposite bank of the river, is cheaper than Mercado Central, with lots of stalls selling fruit and vegetables, butchers and dozens of very cheap eateries.

Music

There are many small shops selling CDs in Paseo Las Palmas, Ricardo Lyon and Av 11 de Septiembre.

Billboard, Providencia 2314 and at La Bolsa 75 (downtown). Good source for rock, jazz and alternative music.

Feria del Disco, Paseo Ahumada. The biggest chain. Also sell tickets for rock concerts. Branches in numerous malls.

Funtrucks, Parque Arauco Mall.

Su Música, many branches in central Santiago.

Opticians

Those needing a new pair of glasses should head for MacIver 0-100 block, where there are many opticians to choose from, and prices are lower rates in Europe or North America.

Wine

There's a good selection of wines at **Jumbo**, **Líder** and **Santa Isabel** supermarkets.

El Mundo del Vino, Isidora Goyenechea 2929, www.elmundodelvino.cl. Also in Patio

Bellavista as well as the Alto Las Condes and Parque Arauco malls.

Vinopolis, Pedro de Valdivia 036, Pedro de Valdivia metro, line 1. Mon-Fri 0900-2300, Sat 1000-2300, Sun 1000-2200. Also at the airport. Exclusively Chilean wines, good selection.

Shopping malls

Generally open 7 days a week 1000-2100.

Apumanque, Apoquindo y Manquehue, Las Condes.

Centro Comercial Alto Las Condes, Av Kennedy, east of Las Condes. This is the largest and most modern mall in the city.

Mall del Centro, C Rosas 900-block, just north of the Plaza de Armas. Brings US mall culture to the centre of Santiago.

Parque Arauco, Av Kennedy 5413, Las Condes. Similar to Alto Las Condes but more variety. There is a boulevard with cafés, good restaurants and an ice trail.

Plaza Vespucio, Bellavista de La Florida metro, line 5. The next most convenient after Mall del Centro.

▲ Activities and tours

Santiago p62, maps p68, p72, p74, p76, p78 and page 99

Bowling

Bowling Center, Av Apoquindo 5012. 10-pin bowling, lots of lanes. Recommended. A 15-min walk east of Escuela Militar metro, line 1.

Cricket

There is a burgeoning cricket league based around Santiago, see www.cricketchile.cl for more information. **La Casa Roja** hostel, see page 82, has a cricket net in its grounds.

Football

There are 3 big clubs; see also box, opposite. If you decide to visit the Estadio Nacional, where international matches are played, find a space high up on the terraces

Soccer nation

Football arrived in Chile towards the end of the 19th century, courtesy of the British. The role of British workers – most of whom were employed in the construction of the railway system – is reflected in the names of several of the leading teams, notably Santiago Wanderers (who are based in Valparaíso), Everton (based in Viña) and Rangers (based in Talca). The game's popularity grew rapidly; by the 1940s most large towns boasted their own team and stadium. In 1962, Chile's importance as a soccer nation was recognized internationally when it hosted the World Cup and the national side finished third. The quarter final between Chile and Italy became known as the 'Battle of Santiago', one of the most vicious games in the sport's history (Chile won 2-1).

Although Chilean football may not enjoy the worldwide recognition given to Argentina and Brazil, Chileans follow 'the beautiful game' with as much passion as their illustrious neighbours.

The local season is split into two tournaments, the *apertura* running from March to June and the *clausura* from August to December. Most of the support (and money) goes to the big three clubs, all based in Santiago: Universidad de Chile (known as 'La U'), Colo-Colo and Universidad Católica (which tends to be favoured by the well-off). The greatest rivalry is between La U and Colo-Colo (who are also known as Los Indios, as their strip carries an image of the great Mapuche leader after whom they were named). The most fervent supporters of the former are known as *los de abajo* (the underdogs), while those of the latter are called *la garra blanca* (the white claw).

A visit to a match, especially either an international game or a clásico (local derby), is an unforgettable experience. Watching football is still very much a family affair and the supporters dance, sing and wave their team colours beneath a non-stop rain of confetti, fireworks and coloured smoke. Cheap tickets cost around US$5.

---

and you will be able to watch the sun set over the mountains behind Santiago.

Colo Colo, play at the Estadio Monumental, reached by any bus to Puente Alto or Pedrero metro, line 5; tickets from Av Marathon 5300, Macul, T02-294 7300.

Universidad Católica, play at San Carlos de Apoquindo, reached by bus from Escuela Militar metro; tickets from Andrés Bello 2782, Providencia, T02-231 2777.

Universidad de Chile, play at Estadio Nacional, Av Grecia 2001 Nuñoa, Nuble metro, line 5. Tickets from Av General Miranda 2094, Nuñoa.

Gymnasiums

Gimnasio Alicia Franke, Moneda 1481, T02-696 1681. Central location for aerobics and fitness classes (women only). There

is also another at Huérfanos 1313, T02-671 1562.

Sésamo, Los Leones 2384, Providencia, T02-204 2770. With pool and aerobics. Recommended.

Racecourses

Betting is a growing industry, with increasing numbers of **Teletrak** betting shops.

Club Hípico, Blanco Encalada 2540. Racing every Sun and every other Wed afternoon, worthwhile even if only to watch dusk fall over the Andes, entry to main stand US$5, card of up to 18 races.

Hipódromo Chile, Av Hipódromo Chile 1715, Independencia. T02-270 9237. Every Sat afternoon. *Pari-mutuel* betting.

Skiing and climbing

The 2 main climbing areas near Santiago are the Grupo Loma Larga near the Cajón del Maipo and the Grupo Plomo near the ski resort of La Parva. For ski resorts in the Santiago area, see page 106. Ski equipment hire is much cheaper in Santiago than in the resorts.

Club Alemán Andino, El Arrayán 2735, Providencia, T02-232 4338, www.dav.cl. Metro Tobalaba. Tue and Fri 1800-2000.

Club Andino de Chile, Av Libertador Bernardo O'Higgins 108, local 215, T02-274 9252, www.skilagunillas.cl. Ski club.

Federación de Andinismo de Chile, Almte Simpson 77A, T02-222 0888, www.feach.cl. Open daily. It has the addresses of all the mountaineering clubs in the country and runs a mountaineering school.

La Cumbre Ltda, Av Apoquindo 5258, T02-220 9907, www.lacumbreonline.cl. Mon-Fri 1100-2000, Sat 1100-1600. Dutch proprietors very helpful, good climbing and trekking equipment.

Mountain Service, Santa Magdalena 75, T02-234 3439, Providencia, www.mountain service.cl. English spoken, tents, stoves, clothing, equipment rental. Recommended.

Panda Deportes, Paseo Las Palmas 2217, T02-232 1840. Los Leones metro.

Skitotal, Av Apoquindo 4900, 40-42, T02-246 0156, www.skitotal.cl. Rents equipment (cheaper than at the slopes), organizes accommodation and lessons. English and German spoken. Transport provided to the ski resorts

of El Colorado, La Parva and Valle Nevado. A cheaper transport service from central Santiago is run by **La Casa Roja**, see page 82.

Swimming pools

Antilen, Cerro San Cristóbal. Open Tue-Sun 1000-1500 in summer; closed Apr-Oct, US$10. Fine panoramic view over the city.

Parque Araucano, near Parque Arauco Shopping Centre, Escuela Militar metro. Nov-Mar Tue-Sat 0900-1900. Olympic pool.

Parque O'Higgins, T02-556 9612. With 2 pools (1 for children), open summer only, US$4.

Quinta Normal, Av Portales (behind the Museo Ferroviario), T02-681 3213. Tue-Sun after 1200.

Tupahue, Cerro San Cristóbal. Large pool with cafés, US$ 10, crowded in summer.

Tennis

There are municipal courts in **Parque O'Higgins**; the national stadium, **Estadio Nacional**, Av Grecia con Av Marathon, has a tennis club that offers classes; also **Club de Tenis Universidad Católica Santa Rosa**, Andrés Bello 3782, T02-231 2777; and **Club de Tenis Stade Français**, Sánchez Fontecilla y Tobalaba, T02-233 7216.

Tour operators

Altue Expediciones, General Salvo 159, Providencia, T02-235 1519, www.altue.com. For wilderness trips including tour of Patagonia and sea-kayaking in Chiloé.

Antarctic dream, Ebro 2740 of 602, T02-481 6910, www.antarctic.cl. Operate cruises to Antarctica out of Ushuaia in Argentina.

Azimut 360, General Salvo 159, Providencia, T02-235 1519, www.azimut.cl. Salvador metro. Reasonable prices. Adventure and eco-tourism throughout Chile, including tours to the Atacama Desert. Aconcagua base-camp services and mountaineering expeditions to Parinacota and Sajama. Recommended.

Bikes and Wine, Pucara 4313A, Nuñoa, T02-209 1342, www.bikesandwine.cl. Interesting trips around the wineries of the Acongagua vally by bike.

Cascada Expediciones, Camino al Volcán 17710, T02-861 1777, www.cascada-expediciones.cl. Specialize in activity tours in remote areas.

ChileAltitudes°, T09-9022 9522, www.chilealtitudes.com. Affordable eco tours, from horse riding to skiing.

La Bicicleta Verde, Santa María 277, T02-570 9338, www.labicicletaverde.com. Sightseeing tours around the capital by bike. Also rents bicycles.

Mountain Service, Paseo Las Palmas 2209, T02-233 0913, www.mountainservice.cl, Los Leones metro. Climbing trips.

Patagonia Connection SA, Fidel Oteíza 1921, of 1006, Providencia, T02-225 6489, www.patagonia-connection.com, Pedro de Valdivia metro. For cruises to Patagonia. Also run **Puyuhuapi Lodge and Spa**, see page 445.

Reto Stockli, T02-212 4665, www.swisschile tours.com. Good independent English-speaking guide offering tours around the Santiago area.

Sportstours, Moneda 970, piso 18 T02-5495 200, www.sportstour.cl. German-run, helpful, 5-day trips to Antarctica. Another branch at San Cristóbal Tower, Av Santa María 1742.

Santiago Adventures, Guardia Vieja 255, of 403, Providencia, T02-244 2750, www.santiagoadventures.com. US-run, offering adventure day tours, wine tours, city tours, skiing and Patagonia.

Turismo Cabo de Hornos, www.turismo cabodehornos.cl. Agustinas 814, of 706, T02-664 3458. For DAP flights and Tierra del Fuego/Antarctica tours.

Travel agents

Sertur, Hernandode Aguirre 201, of 401, T02-411 2000, www.sertur.cl. For cheap student flights and youth travel, also tours, car rental, ISIC cards, medical insurance and hotels.

Passtours, Huérfanos 886, of 111, T02-639 3232, www.passtours.com. Many languages spoken, helpful.

Turismo Tajamar, Orrego Luco 023, Providencia, T02-336 8000, www.tajamar.cl. Good for flights, helpful. Recommended.

⊙ Transport

Santiago *p62, maps p68, p72, p74, p76, p78 and p99*

Air

For details of the Aeropuerto Comodoro Arturo Merino Benítez, see page 28. For domestic flights from Santiago see under relevant destinations.

Airline offices Aerolíneas Argentinas, Roger de Flor 2921 y 2907, Las Condes, Tobalaba metro, T02-210 9300, www.aero lineas.com; **Aeroméxico**, Isidora Goyenechea 2939, of 602, Las Condes, Tobalaba metro, T02-390 1000, www.aero mexico.com; **Air France**, Nueva Costanera 3420, Vitacura, T02-290 9330, www.airfrance.cl; **American**, Huérfanos 1199, Universidad de Chile metro, www.american airlines.cl, T02-679 0000; **Continental** (Chilean agents are **Copa Airlines**) Fidel Oteíza 1921, of 703, Pedro de Valdivia metro, south exit, T02-200 2100, www.continental.com; **Delta**, Isidora Goyenechea 2939, of 601, Las Condes, Tobalaba metro, T02-280 1600, www.delta.com; **Iberia**, Bandera 206, piso 8, Universidad de Chile metro, north exit, T02-870 1050, reservations T02-870 1060, www.iberia.com; **LACSA**, Dr Barros Borgoño

105, piso 2, Providencia, Manuel Montt metro, south exit, T02-235 5189, www.grupotaca.com; LanChile, Huérfanos 926, Santiago, Universidad de Chile metro, north exit, also at Av Providencia 2006, Providencia, Los Leones or Pedro de Valdivia metro and Isidora Goyenechea 2888, Las Condes, Tobalaba metro, T600-562 000, www.lan.com; Lufthansa, Av El Bosque Norte 500, piso 16, Las Condes, Tobalaba metro, T02-630 1655, airport T02-690 1112, www.lufthansa.cl; Sky Airline, Andrés de Fuenzalida 55, Providencia, Los Leones metro, north exit, T600-600 2828, www.sky airline.cl; United, Av Andrés Bello 2687, piso 16, Las Condes, Tobalaba metro, www.uni ted.com, T02-337 0000; Varig, El Bosque Norte 0177, of 903, piso 9, Las Condes, Tobalaba metro, T02-707 8020, www.varig.com.

Bicycle

For parts and repairs the only place to go is C San Diego, south of the Alameda. The 800 and 900 blocks have scores of bicycle shops with spare parts, new models and repairs all offered at prices much cheaper than you will find in Providencia or Las Condes.

Bicicletas Wilson, C San Diego 909; El Supermercado de las Bicicletas, C San Diego 921, good stock; Importadora Caupolicán, C San Diego 863, T02-697 2765, wide range, helpful, has been recommended; Luis Cabalin, Coquimbo 1114, T02-698 4193, is good for maintenance and repairs; Terrabike, C San Diego 896, does repairs.

Boat operator head offices

Check schedules with shipping lines rather than the national tourist office, Sernatur. Specific details are given throughout the text. None of the following services originate in Santiago; see throughout the text for details. Cruceros Australis, El Bosque Norte 0440, T02-442 3110, www.australis.com, for trips from Punta Arenas to Puerto Williams, Cape Horn and Ushuaia. M/N Skorpios, Augusto

Leguía Norte 118, Las Condes, El Golf metro, north exit, line 1, T02-477 1900, www.skorpios.cl, for luxury cruise out of Puerto Montt to Laguna San Rafael. Navimag, Av El Bosque Norte 0440, piso 11, Las Condes, T02-442 3120, www.navimag. com. For services from Puerto Montt to Puerto Natales and vice versa; Patagonia Connection SA, Fidel Oteíza 1921, of1006, Providencia, T02-225 6489, www.patagonia-connection.com, Pedro de Valdivia metro. For services between Puerto Montt-Coyhaique/ Puerto Chacabuco-Laguna San Rafael; Transmarchilay, Agustinas 715, of 403, T02-633 5959, www.transmarchilay.cl, for reservations www.navieraustral.cl. For services between Chiloé and the mainland and ferry routes on the Carretera Austral.

Bus

Local Transantiago, www.transantiago.cl, is the capital's new integrated public transport system. Although designed to reduce congestion and pollution, 3 years of teething troubles saw a surge in private car sales meaning that the streets are as crowded as ever, and if noise pollution has gone down, air pollution has, if anything, got worse.

The city is divided into 10 zones lettered A to J. Within each zone, buses (known as *micros*) are the same colour as that given to the zone (eg white for zone A: central Santiago). Zones are linked by trunk lines, run by white *micros* with a green stripe. The system integrates with the metro. Buses display the number and direction of the route within the system. Payment is by prepai d Tarjeta Bíp only. A card costs US$3, to which you add however much you want to pay in advance. They are most conveniently bought at Metro stations. You can travel as much as you want by bus (with 1 metro journey also allowed) in a 2-hr period for a fixed rate of US$0.70 ($0.80 at peak times).

Long distance There are frequent, good inter-urban buses to all parts of Chile. Prices are much lower outside the peak summer season. You should always book ahead in Jan and Feb, Jul, and other peak times such as Easter and on and around Independence Day (18 Sep). At other times of the year, departures are so frequent that it is usually possible to just turn up and go. Check if student rates are available, or reductions for travelling on the same day as purchasing the ticket; it is worth bargaining over prices, especially with the smaller operators shortly before departure and out of the summer season. Also take a look at the buses before buying the tickets (there are big differences in quality among bus companies); ask about the on-board services, as many companies offer drinks, sometimes complimentary, and luxury buses have meals and videos. Reclining seats are the norm and there are also *salón cama* sleeper buses.

There are 5 terminals, all located close to each other at the western end of the city centre. **TurBus** has booking offices throughout the centre, including at Universidad de Chile and Tobalaba metro stations, at Av Apoquindo 6421, T02-212 6435, and in the Parque Arauco and Alto Las Condes malls for those beginning their journeys in Las Condes.

Bear in mind that on Fri evenings in summer, when the night buses are preparing to depart, the terminals are nightmarishly chaotic and busy in the extreme.

Terminal Alameda, Av Libertador Bernardo O' Higgins 3712, T02-707 1500, Universidad de Santiago metro, has a modern extension with a shopping centre called Mall Parque Estación, several Redbanc ATMs and internet. This has the best left-luggage facilities in the city, and is a good choice as 2 of the best companies, TurBus, www.turbus.com, and Pullman Bus, www.pullman.cl, leave from here (serving all main destinations from **Arica** to **Puerto Montt**), and there are also Pullman del Sur buses to less frequented parts of the central valley, eg **Chanco** (US$10), and **Iloca** (US$8).

Terminal Santiago, O'Higgins 3878, T02-376 1755, www.terminaldebuses.

santiago.cl, just west of Terminal Alameda, Universidad de Santiago metro. Sometimes referred to as the 'Terminal Sur', this is used by services to and from the **south**, as well as buses to the central coast. It is the only terminal with services to **Punta Arenas** (48 hrs), and is also the centre for some international services (see below). There is a Redbanc ATM.

Terminal San Borja, O'Higgins y San Borja, T02-776 0645, 1 block west of Estación Central, 3 blocks east of Terminal Alameda. Estación Central metro. There are buses to destinations in the **Santiago area**, such as **Melipilla**, and many companies serving **northern Chile**. Booking offices are arranged according to destination. The entrance is, inconveniently, located through the shopping centre next to the station, and is not immediately apparent from the Alameda.

Terminal Los Héroes, Tucapel Jiménez, just north of the Alameda, T02-420 0099. Los Héroes metro. A smaller terminal with 8 companies, but useful destinations such as **Mendoza** and **Chiloé** with Cruz del Sur. Note that some long-distance bus services also call at **Las Torres de Tajamar**, which is much more convenient if you are planning to stay in Providencia.

Terminal Pajaritos, at the entrance of Pajaritos metro station, line 1. Another small terminal. All buses between Santiago and **Valparaíso** and **Viña del Mar** stop here. It is generally quicker and more convenient to take a bus from here than from the terminals in central Santiago. Shuttle buses to the airport also stop here.

Main destinations Within Chile from north to south: **Arica**, 29 hrs, US$55-90; **Iquique**, 25 hrs, US$50-80; **Calama**, 21 hrs, US$45-80; **San Pedro**, 23 hrs, US$55-85; **Antofagasta**, 19 hrs, US$40-75; **Chañaral**, 14 hrs, US$30-55; **Caldera**, 12 hrs, US$30-55; **Copiapó**, 11 hrs, US$25-55; **La Serena**, 6 hrs, US$15-20; **Valparaíso**, 1½ hrs, US$7; **Viña del Mar**, 1½ hrs, US$7; **Talca**, 3½ hrs, US$6-9; **Chillán**, 5 hrs, US$8-15; **Concepción**, 6 hrs,

US$11-23; **Temuco**, 8 hrs, US$15-46; **Villarrica**, 9 hrs, US$16-50; **Pucón**, 10 hrs, US$16-50; **Puerto Varas**, 12 hrs, US$21-50; **Puerto Montt**, 12½ hrs, US$21-50.

International Most international buses leave from Terminal Santiago (see above).

To Argentina There are frequent services through the Cristo Redentor tunnel to **Mendoza**, 6-7 hrs, US$15, many companies, eg Ahumada (recommended), Andesmar, CATA, TAC (recommended), Tas Choapa, departures around 0800, 1200 and 1600, touts approach you in Terminal Santiago. Most of these services continue on to **Buenos Aires**, 24 hrs, US$50. There are also minibuses to **Mendoza** from the Terminal Santiago, 5-6 hrs, US$20; Chi-Ar Ltda is recommended. Minibus services are less comfortable but there is generally a shorter waiting time at customs. Companies in the Terminal Santiago have connections to many other Argentine cities, including: Andesmar to **Bahía Blanca**, US$65, change in Mendoza, 24 hrs; TAC and Tas Choapa direct to **Córdoba**, US$40, 18 hrs (El Rápido not recommended); to **San Juan**, TAC, Tas Choapa, US$30. If going to destinations such as **Bariloche** or **Neuquén** in Argentine Patagonia, it is better to travel south to Temuco or Osorno and connect there.

To Uruguay To **Montevideo**, most involve a change in Mendoza, Tas Choapa and others, 27 hrs, including meals.

To Brazil To **São Paulo** and **Rio de Janeiro**, Chilebus and Pluma, Tue, Thu, Sat, 72 hrs, US$120.

To Paraguay To **Asunción**, 4 a week, 28 hrs, US$90.

To Andean destinations The biggest company is the Peruvian Ormeño in Terminal Santiago, whose buses leave on Tue and Fri at 0900 to **Lima** (Peru), where connections are made to **Guayaquil** and **Quito** (Ecuador), **Cali** and **Bogotá** (Colombia) and **Caracas** (Venezuela) – buses are good and comfortable and there are meal stops. To **Lima**, 51 hrs, US$100 (it is cheaper to take a

bus to Arica, a *colectivo* to Tacna (US$3), then bus to Lima); to **Guayaquil**, 80 hrs, US$145; to **Quito**, 88 hrs, US$165; to **Cali**, 4½ days, US$220; to **Bogotá**, US$230, 5 days; to **Caracas**, US$250, 7 days. Those heading for Bolivia are best advised to travel to one of the northern cities and then go by frequent bus from Iquique or Arica.

Car
Traffic and pollution are major problems: driving is restricted according to licence plate numbers; each day, certain plates are prohibited from circulating (numbers are given in the press). Restrictions are mostly limited to cars without catalytic converters, but when pollution levels rise to critical levels, the restrictions include all motor vehicles.
Car hire Prices of car hire vary widely so shop around. Tax of 19% is charged but check if it is included in the price. A credit card is usually asked for when renting a vehicle. Hertz, Avis, Budget and others are available at the airport.

Alameda, Av Bernado O'Higgins 4332, T02-779 0609, www.alameda rentacar.cl, San Alberto Hurtado metro, line 1, also in the airport, good value; **ANSA**, Av Eleodoro Yáñez 1198, Providencia, T02-251 0256; **Automóvil Club de Chile**, Av Vitacura 9511, Providencia, T02-431 1106, 25% discount for members of associated motoring organizations; **Avis**, San Pablo 9900, T02-331 0121, www.avischile.cl, also in Vitacura, poor service reported; **Hertz**, Costanera Andrés Bello 1469, T02-360 8600, www.autorentas.cl, has a good network in Chile and cars are in good condition; **Rosselot**, Francisco Bilbao 2032, Providencia, T02-381 3690, www.rosselot.cl, and airport, T02-690 1374, reputable Chilean firm with national coverage; **Seelmann**, Monseñor Edwards 1279, La Reina, T02-277 9259, www.seelmann.cl, mixed reports; **Trekker Ltd**, www.trekkerchile.com, has camper vans, trucks and 4WD vehicles available; **Verschae**, Manquehue Sur 660, T02-202 7266, www.verschae.cl, reasonable value, branches throughout the country.

Colectivo

Collective taxis, which operate on fixed routes between the centre and the suburbs, are a convenient form of transport. They ply the streets and carry destination signs and route numbers. Fares vary, depending on the length of the journey, but are usually between US$1.50-2.50. Higher fares at night.

Hitchhiking

Hitchhiking is generally safe, although the normal common-sense rules apply. To **Valparaíso**, take the metro to Pajaritos and walk 5 mins west. To hitch **south**, take Buses del Paine from outside the Terminal San Borja as far as possible on the highway to the toll area, about US$1.50, 75 mins.

To hitch **north** is not easy. You are better off getting a bus north to the town of La Calera, 2 hrs, and trying from there.

To **Buenos Aires** (and **Brazil**) take a bus to Los Andes (Buses Los Andes leave from Tucapel Jiménez y Moneda, behind Terminal Los Héroes), then go to Copec station on the outskirts (most trucks travel overnight).

Metro

Line 1 of the underground railway system runs west-east between San Pablo and Escuela Militar, under the Alameda, with an

⑦ Santiago metro

➡ Santiago maps
1 Santiago orientation, page 66
2 Santiago centre, page 68
3 Santiago west of centre, page 72
4 Lastarria, Bellavista & Providencia west, page 74
5 Providencia, page 76
6 Las Condes, page 78
7 Santiago metro, page 99

Line 1
Line 2
Line 4
Line 4a
Line 5
Under construction
Bus terminal
Train station

Not to scale

extension currently being built eastwards to Los Domínicos.

Line 2 runs north-south from Vespucio Norte to La Cisterna.

Line 4 runs north-south from Tobalaba to Plaza de Puente Alto with a branch to La Cisterna.

Line 5 runs southeast-northwest from Vicente Valdés to Quinta Normal with an extension being built westwards to Maipú. There are interchanges at Los Héroes, Baquedano, Santa Ana, Tobalaba, Vicente Valdés and La Cisterna.

The trains are modern, fast, quiet and very full during rush hour. At the busiest times of day it will be all but impossible to board a train with any luggage. The first train is at 0600 (Mon-Sat), 0800 (Sun and holidays), the last about 2300. Fares vary according to time of journey; there are 3 charging periods: high 0715-0900 and 1800-2000, US$0.80; mid 0630-0700, 0900-1800 and 2000-2045, US$0.70; low all other times, US$0.65. The simplest solution is to buy a **Tarjeta Bíp**, which costs US$3 (and can be topped up subsequently). For more information on the metro, see www.metrosantiago.cl.

Taxi

Taxis (black with yellow roofs) are abundant, and not expensive, with a minimum charge of US$0.35, plus US$0.15 per 200 m. Higher charges are permitted to charge more at night, but in the daytime check that the meter is set to day rates. Taxis are more expensive at bus terminals and from the ranks outside hotels – best to walk a block and flag one down. Avoid taxis with more than 1 person in them, especially at night. For journeys outside the city, arrange the charge beforehand. **Radio Taxis Andes Pacífico**, T02-912 6000, www.andespacifico.cl are recommended, but rates are above those of city taxis.

Train

All trains leave from **Estación Central**, Alameda Bernado O'Higgins 3322. There are

no passenger trains to northern Chile, Valparaíso or Viña del Mar. The line runs south to **Rancagua**, **San Fernando**, **Curicó**, **Talca**, **Linares**, **Parral** and **Chillán**. Normally the service continues west to **Concepción** or south to **Temuco** with connections to Puerto Montt, but at the time of writing these routes have been suspended indefinitely. There are 4-7 trains daily to **Chillán** (1st 0730, last 1830, 4½ hrs, US$18 *Salón*, US$32 *clase preferente*). Trains are still fairly cheap and generally very punctual, although usually more expensive than buses. Cycles can be carried, but have to be dismantled and packed. There are family and senior citizen discounts. No student discounts. There are also frequent local **Metrotren** services south to **Rancagua** and **San Fernando**. Booking offices in the Estación Central, T02-585 5000, www.efe.cl. Left-luggage office at Estación Central, open till 2300.

ⓘ Directory

Santiago *p62, maps p68, p72, p74, p76, p78 and p99*

Banks

Banks are open from 0900 to 1400, but close on Sat. Official daily exchange rates are published in *El Mercurio* and *La Nación*. There is never a problem finding a Redbanc ATM. Look for Redbanc sign. All accept VISA and MasterCard except Banco Estado (MasterCard only).

Casas de cambio

Some in the centre open Sat morning (but check first). Most *casas de cambio* charge 3% commission to change TCs into dollars. Always avoid street money changers (particularly common on Ahumada, Bandera, Moneda and Agustinas). They will show you a figure that is fractionally more than the going rate, before pulling a number of tricks, eg using the MR button on calculators to do a false calculation giving much less than you should have, or asking you to accompany them to somewhere obscure. Muggings or the passing of forged notes have also been reported.

Afex, Moneda 1148, Agustinas 1050, Pedro de Valdivia 012, Parque Arauco; **Alfa**, Agustinas 1052; **Cambios Andino**, Ocho, Agustinas 1062; **Casa de Cambio Blancas**, opposite Hotel Orly, Pedro de Valdivia; **Cambios Manquehue**, Huérfanos 1160, local 5 (Galería Alessandri); **Guiñazú**, Matías Cousiño 170, all major currencies can be bought or sold; **Exprinter**, Bombero Ossa 1053, good rates, low commission; **Inter**, Andrés de Fuenzalida 47, Los Leones metro, north exit; **Intermundi**, Moneda 896. Also several around Av Pedro de Valdivia, Providencia, eg at Gral Holley 66, good rates; **Mojakar**, Pedro de Valdivia 059.

Dentists

Antonio Yazigi, Vitacura 3082, apto 33, T02-208 7962/208 5040, English spoken, recommended; **Carlos Ulrich**, Napoleón 3565, T02-203 7390, El Golf metro. English and German spoken, recommended.

Embassies and consulates

Argentina, Miraflores 285, T02-582 2500, www.embargentina.cl; also Argentine consulate, Vicuña MacKenna 41, T02-582 2608, open 0900-1400 (visa US$25, free for US citizens), if you need a visa for Argentina, get it here or in the consulates in Puerto Montt or Punta Arenas, Australians will need a letter from their embassy to get a visa here. **Australia**, Isidora Goyenechea 3621, Torre B, piso 12-13, Las Condes, T02-550 3500, consular.santiago@dfat.gov.au; **Austria**, Barros Errázuriz 1968, piso 3, Providencia, T02-223 4774; **Belgium**, Av Providencia 2653, piso 11, dept 1103-04, T02-232 1070; **Bolivia**, Av Santa María 2796, Providencia, T02-232 8180, Los Leones metro, www.consuladogeneraldebolivia.cl; **Brazil**, MacIver 225, piso 15, T02-820 5800, www.embajadade brasil.cl; **Canada**, Nueva Tajamar 481, Torre Norte, piso 12 (Edificio World Trade Center), www.dfait-maeci.gc.ca/ latin-america/chile/, T02-362 9660; **Colombia**, Av Presidente Errázuriz 3943, T02-206 1999, www.consulbiachile.cl; **Denmark**, Jacques Cazotte 5531, Vitacura, T02-941 5100, www.ambsantiago.um.dk/la; **Ecuador**, Av Providencia 1979, piso 5, T02-231 5073, www.embajadaecuador; **Finland**, Alcántara 200, oficina 201, T02-263 4917, sanomat.snt@formin.fi; **France**, Condell 65, Providencia, T02-470 8053, www.france.cl; **Germany**, Las Hualtatas 5677, T02-463 2500, www.santiago.diplo.de; **Greece**, Jorge VI 306, Las Condes, T02-212 7900, www.greekembassy.cl; **India**, Triana 871, Providencia, T02-235 2633, www.embajada india.cl; **Israel**, San Sebastián 2812, piso 5, Las Condes, T02-750 0513, www.santiago.mfa.gov.il; **Italy**, Clemente Fabres 1050, Providencia, T02-470 8400, www.amb santiago.esteri.it; **Japan**, Av Ricardo Lyon 520, piso 1, T02-232 1807, www.cl.emb-japan.go.jp; **Mexico**, Félix de Amesti 128, T02-583 8400, www.emexico.cl; **Netherlands**, Apoquindo 3500, piso 13, Las Condes, El Golf metro, T02-756 9200, www.holanda-paisesbajos.cl; **New Zealand**, El Golf 99, of 703, Las Condes, T02-290 9800, www.nzembassy.cl; **Norway**, San Sebastián 2839, of 509, Las Condes, T02-234 2888, www.noruega,cl; **Paraguay**, Huérfanos 886, of 514, T02-639 4640, epychemb@entelchile.net; **Peru**, Bucarest 162, Providencia, T02-231 8020, www.conpersantiago.cl; **South Africa**, Av 11 de Septiembre 2353, piso 17, Torre San Ramón, T02-231 2862, www.embajada-sudafrica.cl; **Spain**, 11 de Septiembre 2353, piso 9, Providencia, T02-233 4070, cgespsantiago@correo.mae.es; **Sweden**, Av 11 de Septiembre 2353, Torre San Ramón, piso 4, Providencia, T02-940 1700, swedenabroad.com; **Switzerland**, Av Américo Vespucio Sur 100, piso 14, Las Condes, T02-263 4211, www.eda.admin.ch/santiago; **UK**, El Bosque Norte 0125, piso 6, T02-370 4100, www.britemb.cl; **Uruguay**, Av Pedro de Valdivia 711, Providencia, T02-204 7988, www.uruguay.cl; **USA**, Av Andrés Bello 2800, T02-330 3000, www.embajadaeeuu.cl.

¿Huevón, Señor?

If you spend any time in Chile, it is almost impossible not to come across *huevón*. This versatile word is used by all classes of Chilean society to describe a person. Literally meaning 'big egg', it is by turns an expression of endearment ('mate', 'buddy') and a slang expression of disgust ('idiot', 'fool'), and is used equally often in both senses. In some conversations, virtually every other word may seem to be *huevón*.

Legend has it that an expatriate living in Santiago a few years ago made the mistake of ordering a sandwich with *huevón* rather than *huevo* (egg). The waiter was so overcome that he had to finish his shift early. The hilarity with which mistakes of this sort are greeted can work to the visitor's advantage, however: tell any Chilean acquaintance that you have been to the shop to buy *huevón* and your friendship will be secured for life.

The use of *huevón* is symptomatic of the distinctiveness of Chilean Spanish, which has an unusually wide range of idioms and slang not used elsewhere in Latin America.

Anyone who is serious about getting to grips with Chilean Spanish, should get hold of a copy of *How to Survive in the Chilean Jungle*, by John Brennan and Alvaro Taboada (Ventriloc Dolmen, 2001), a handbook of Chilean colloquialisms.

Medical services

Hospitals: If you need to get to hospital, it is better to take a taxi than wait for an ambulance. **Clínica Central**, San Isidro 231-243, Santa Lucía metro, T02-463 1400, 24 hrs, German spoken; **Clínica Santa María**, Santa María 0500, Providencia, T02-461 2000. **Emergency hospital (Hospital Clínico de la Universidad Católica)**, Marcoleta 367, Universidad Católica metro, T02-354 3266 emergency, T02-633 2051 general; **Hospital de Urgencia (Posta Central)**, Portugal 125, cheapest hospital open to the public; **Hospital del Salvador**, Av Salvador 334 or J M Infante 551, Providencia, T02-274 0093 emergency, T02-340 4000 general, Mon-Thu 0800-1300 and 1330-1645, Fri 0800-1300 and 1330-1545; **Vaccinatoria Internacional**, Hospital Luis Calvo, MacKenna, Antonio Varas 360, Providencia, Manuel Montt metro, south exit, children's hospital, T02-340 1600.

Other medical services Dr Sergio Majlis Drinberg, T02-232 0853, physician available 1430-1900; **Emergency pharmacy**, Portugal 155, Universidad Católica metro, T02-631 3005. Consult www.farmaciasahumada.cl for other emergency pharmacies.

Internet

Internet cafés are ubiquitous. Prices around US$0.60 to US$1 per hr. **463@café**, Av Brasil 463, Barrio Brasil; **Anditel**, Bandera y Catedral, 1 block from the Plaza de Armas, quiet; **c@fe.com**, Av Bernado O'Higgins 0145, near Plaza Italia, good snacks; **Café Phonet**, San Sebastián 2815, Providencia, also very cheap international phone calls; **Ciberia**, Pío Nono 015, Bellavista; **Cybercafe**, Santa Lucía 0120, next to Instituto Chileno-Británico; **Cybercafe**, Cienfuegos 161, near junction with Moneda, just west of *Panamericana*, Barrio Brasil, cheap; **easy@net**, Ricardo Lyon y Providencia, Providencia; **ES Computación**, Salvador Sanfuentes 2352, Barrio Brasil, República metro, helpful staff; **Internet Virtual**, Santo Domingo 1091, also very cheap call centre; **Sonnets Ltda**, Londres 043, tea, coffee, book exchange, owner speaks Spanish, English, Dutch and German, helpful. There is also access at the **Terminal de Buses Alameda**, on the upper floor of the terminal building.

Language schools

Amerispan, PO Box 58129, 117 South 17 St, 14th floor, Philadelphia, PA19103, USA,

T1-215 715 1100, www.amerispan.com, provides information about the affiliated Amerispan school in Santiago; **Centro de Idiomas Bellavista**, C del Arzobispo 0609, Providencia, Salvador metro, T02-732 3443, www.escuelabellavista.cl; **Natalislang Language Centre**, Vicuña Mackenna 06, piso 7, of 4, Providencia, Baquedano metro, line 1, to the south, T02-222 8721, www.natalislang.com, 2-week courses are recommended as good value; **Pacífica**, Guillermo Acuña 2884, Providencia, Francisco Bilbao metro, line 4, walk 10 mins to the east along F Bilbao, T02-205 5129, pacifica@netline.cl, Anglo-Chilean agency offering cultural programmes to students, will also find accommodation with families and arrange Spanish classes either in language schools or with private teachers, minimum 1 month, US$70 commission charged.

Many private teachers: **Silvia Pöltl**, T02-235 3463, T09-353 6835 (mob), silviapol793@hotmail.com, well qualified and very experienced, recommended. **Patricia Vargas Vives**, José Manuel Infante 98, departamento 308, Salvador metro, line 1, south exit, Providencia, T02-244 2283, qualified and experienced.

Laundry

Dry cleaning At the corner of Providencia and Dr Luis Middleton there are several self-service dry cleaners (Pedro de Valdivia metro, 11 de Septiembre exit (south)). Also several just south of Universidad Católica metro including **American Washer**, Portugal 71, Torre 7, local 4, 0900-2100 including Sun, US$3, can leave washing and collect it later.

Wet-wash Lava Fácil, Huérfanos 1750, Mon-Sat 0900-2000, US$4 per load; **Lavandería Lola**, Av Ricardo Cumming y Moneda, very busy so get there before

1100, US$6 per load; **Laverap**, Av Providencia 1600 block, Manuel Montt 67; **Marva**, Carlos Antúnez 1823, Pedro de Valdivia metro, south exit, wash and dry US$10; Av Providencia 1039, full load, wet-wash, US$7, 3 hrs; **Nataly**, Bandera 572.

Post office

The main office is on the Plaza de Armas (0800-1900), poste restante is well organized (though only kept for 30 days), passport essential, list of letters and parcels received in hall of central post office (one list for men, another for women, indicate Sr or Sra/Srta on envelope).

Also sub offices in Providencia, Av 11 de Septiembre 2092, Luis Thayer Ojeda 0146, Pedro de Valdivia 1781, of 52, Providencia 1466, Moneda 1155 (downtown) and in Estación Central shopping mall. These are open Mon-Fri 0900-1800, Sat 0900-1230.

If sending a parcel, the contents must first be checked at the post office. Paper, tape, etc on sale, Mon-Fri 0800-1900, Sat 0800-1400.

Telephone

The cheapest call centres are on C Bandera, Catedral and Santo Domingo, all near the Plaza de Armas. International calls from here are half the price of the main company offices: to the US, US$0.15 per min, to Europe, US$0.25 per min, eg at Catedral 1033 and Santo Domingo 1091.

Visas and immigration

Ministerio del Interior, Departamento de Extranjería, Agustinas 1235, 1 block north of the Moneda, T02-674 4000, www.extranjeria.gob.cl. Mon-Fri 0900-1200. Visit for an extension of tourist visa or any enquiries regarding legal status. Expect long queues. Note that this can also be done at any provincial *extranjería* office.

Around Santiago

→ *Colour map 3, B3.*

This region can be divided into three: to the east are the peaks of the Andes; to the west is the coastal range; and between is the Central Valley. On the eastern edge of the Central Valley lies Santiago, its more affluent suburbs spreading east into the foothills of the Andes. Some of the highest peaks in the range lie in this region: just over the border in Argentina, Aconcagua is the highest mountain in the world outside Asia, rising to 6964 m. There is a mantle of snow on all the high mountains, while the lower slopes are covered with forests. Between the forest and the snowline there are pastures; during the summer, cattle are driven up there to graze. In this area you can ski in winter, hike in summer and soothe your limbs in thermal springs year round. The less energetic may opt for a vineyard tour, sampling en route. ▶▶ *For listings, see pages 107-112.*

Pomaire

A small town 65 km west of Santiago, Pomaire is in a charming setting surrounded by high grassy hills dotted with algarrobo bushes. The town is famous for its clayware; the main street is full of shops selling dark clay pots and kitchenware, as well as diverse *artesanía* from all over Chile including fine basketwork from the Central Valley and some lovely items made from the *combarbalita* stone from the north. There are probably few better places in Chile in which to buy general souvenirs and presents (although bargaining is not really entered into); pottery can be bought and the artists can be observed at work, before visitors retire to any one of numerous restaurants serving traditional dishes such as *humitas*, giant *empanadas* and *pastel de choclo*.

Reserva Nacional Río Clarillo

ⓘ *Reached by paved road via Av Vicuña Mackenna to Puente Alto, where it continues as Av Concha y Toro, turn right at the T-junction where the road leads to El Principal after 2 km. Open all year. US$5.*

This reserve covers 10,185 ha and is situated 45 km southeast of Santiago in the *precordillera* at between 850 m and 3000 m. It offers excellent views of the higher mountains and of the surprisingly green pastures of the foothills. The information centre is at the entrance, 2 km southeast of El Principal. There are guided trails and wildlife, including the endangered Chilean iguana, salamanders and the rare bird, torcaza. The reserve is also the only remaining home to *sclerophyllous* (hard leaved) trees in central Chile. In summer it is very hot and horse flies are a nuisance. There are no places to stay and camping is forbidden. If you are in the city for a while it is a good place to get away from the bustle for a day.

Santuario de la Naturaleza Yerba Loca

ⓘ *Park administration office, Villa Paulina, 4 km north of Route G21, 25 km northeast of Santiago, T02-321 6285, Sep-Apr, US$7.*

Reached via a *ripio* side road off the paved Route G21, 25 km northeast of Santiago towards Farellones, this park covers 39,000 ha of the valley of the Río Yerba Loca, ranging in altitude between 900 and 5500 m. It was founded in 1973. From the park administration office a four-hour walk leads north to **Casa de Piedra Carvajal**, which offers fine views. Further north are two hanging glaciers, **La Paloma** and **El Altar**. You may spot eagles and condors in the park. Native tree species include the mountain olive. Maps and information available from CONAF. There is no accommodation here.

Maipo Valley vineyards ● ➤➤ *pp110-112.*

The Maipo Valley is considered by many experts to be the best wine-producing area in Chile. Several vineyards in the area can be visited and this makes a good excuse to get away from the smog. The following is a small selection of the better tours or wineries that are easily accessible:

Aquitania ① *Av Consistoral 5100, Peñalolen, T02-791 4500, www.aquitania.cl, bus D17 or taxi from metro Quilín.* Small vineyard making high-end wines, offering interesting tours in Spanish and English, with good tastings and fine views. Call in advance. Recommended.

Cousiño-Macul ① *Av Quilín 7100, on the eastern outskirts of the city, T02-351 4175, www.cousinomacul.cl, US$10, metro Quilín.* Tours in Spanish and poor English, Monday to Friday. Call in advance if you wish to visit. Guides tend to be rather disinterested.

Concha y Toro ① *Virginia Subercaseaux 210, Pirque, near Puente Alto, 25 km south of Santiago, T02-476 5269, www.conchaytoro.cl, US$12, metro to Las Mercedes, then taxi or colectivo.* Short tours (three a day in Spanish, four daily in English). Reserve two days in advance and enquire about the specific time of tours in your language of choice. Professional but very commercial. Has been described as the McDonalds of wine tours.

De Martino ① *Manuel Rodríguez 229, Isla de Maipo, 40 km southwest of Santiago, T02-819 2062, www.demartino.cl.* Quality tours in this high-end winery with a reputation for producing excellent carmenère. Book in advance. Lunch available for large groups.

Undurraga ① *Santa Ana, 34 km southwest of Santiago, T02-372 2850, wwwundurraga.cl, US$12.* Allows entry to vistors who have made a prior reservation. Three tours daily.

Viña Santa Rita ① *Padre Hurtado 0695, Alto Jahuel, Buin, 45 km south of Santiago on the Camino a Padre Hurtado, T02-362 2520, www.santarita.cl, US$10.* Good tours in English and Spanish; reserve in advance. The vineyard has a good restaurant and a private museum. Weekend tours only available to those with restaurant reservations (lunch US$40 per head).

Cajón del Maipo ●●●● ➤➤ *pp110-112.*

This rugged and green valley southeast of Santiago provides an easy escape from the smog and bustle of Santiago. The valley is lined by precipitous mountains and the snows of the high Andes can easily be seen. There are many interesting and beautiful side tracks, such as that to Lagunillas (see page 108) or Los Maitenes, but the upper reaches of the valley around El Volcán and Baños Morales are amazingly deserted.

The road into the valley runs east from Puente Alto via Las Vizcachas, where the most important motor racing circuit in Chile is located, towards **San José de Maipo**. The mountain town of **Melocotón** is 6 km south of San José de Maipo and **San Alfonso** is 4 km further on. The walk from San Alfonso to the Cascada de las Animas waterfall is pleasant; ask at the campsite for permission to cross the bridge.

The road continues up the valley and divides 14 km southeast of San Alfonso. One branch forks northeast along a very poor road (4WD essential) via Embalse El Yeso to **Termas del Plomo**, Km 33, thermal baths with no infrastructure, but stunning scenery. The other branch continues and climbs the valley of the Río Volcán. At **El Volcán** (1400 m), 21 km from San Alfonso, there are astounding views, but little else. It is possible to cross the river and camp in the wild on the far side, surrounded by giant rock walls and with a real sense of isolation. If visiting this area or continuing further up the mountain, be prepared for military checks: passport and car registration numbers may be taken. From El Volcán the poor road runs 14 km east to Lo Valdés, a good base for mountain excursions.

Nearby are warm natural baths at **Baños Morales** ① *open from Oct, US$4*. This is a wonderful area to come and get away from it all and it is possible to spend days here exploring the paths that lead high into the mountains. (This is the old southerly horse trail linking Santiago and Mendoza, with a path still leading over into Argentina.) Some 12 km further east up the mountain is **Baños Colina** (not to be confused with Termas de Colina, see page 109) with free, hot thermal springs and horses for hire. This area is popular at weekends and holiday times, but is otherwise deserted. There are no shops so take food. Try the local goat's cheese if you can; it may be sold by the roadside or at farmhouses.

Situated north of Baños Morales, **Parque Nacional El Morado** ① *Oct-Apr, US$4, administration near the entrance*, covers an area of 3000 ha including the peaks of **El Morado** (5060 m), **El Mirador del Morado** (4320 m) and **El Morado glacier**. It is in an exceptionally secluded and beautiful place with wonderful views, well worth making the effort to reach. There is a good day hike from the park entrance to the glacier and back. Lakeside camping is possible near the glacier.

Ski resorts ⬤🔵🟡🟢 ▸▸ *pp110-112.*

There are six main ski resorts near Santiago, four of them around the mountain village of Farellones. All have modern lift systems, international ski schools, rental shops, lodges, mountain restaurants and first-aid facilities. The season runs from June to September/October, weather permitting, although some resorts have equipment for making artificial snow. Many professional skiers from the northern hemisphere come here to keep in practice during the northern summer. Altitude sickness can be a problem, especially at Valle Nevado and Portillo, so avoid over-exertion on the first day or two.

Farellones
① *32 km east of Santiago, daily lift ticket US$42 (allows access to El Colorado).*
The first ski resort built in Chile, Farellones is situated on the slopes of Cerro Colorado at 2470 m and is reached by road from the capital in an hour. From the resort there are incredible views for 30 km across 10 Andean peaks. It is a service centre for the three other

Cajón del Maipo

Border crossing: Chile–Argentina

Cristo Redentor tunnel

Traffic crosses the border through the 4-km Cristo Redentor tunnel, open Sep-May 24 hours, June-August 0700-2300, toll US$5. Note that this pass is closed after heavy snowfall, when travellers are occasionally trapped at the customs complex on either side of the border.

Just beyond Argentine customs and immigration is **Puente del Inca**, a sports resort named after the natural bridge that crosses the Río Mendoza. The bridge, apparently formed by sulphur-bearing hot springs, is 19 m high, 27 m wide and has a span of 21 m. At the resort are Hostería Puente del Inca and Residencial Vieja Estación (much cheaper), as well as camping, transport to Mendoza and information and access for climbing Aconcagua (6964 m), the highest mountain peak on earth outside Asia.

Some 17 km further east is **Punta de Vacas**, from where there is a good view of Tupungato (6550 m). The only town of any size between the border and Mendoza is **Uspallata**, from where two roads lead to Mendoza: the paved, southern branch of Route 7, via Potrerillos; and the unpaved, northern branch via Villavicencio.

resorts and provides affordable accommodation and several large restaurants. It also has a good beginners' area and is connected by lift to El Colorado. Perhaps the most popular resort for residents of Santiago, it is busy at weekends. One-day excursions, US$15, are available from **Ski Club Chile** ① *Candelaria Goyenechea 4750, Vitacura (north of Los Leones Golf Club), T02-211 7341.*

El Colorado

① *8 km from Farellones, www.elcolorado.cl, daily lift ticket US$42 (including Farellones ski lifts).*

Further up Cerro Colorado along a circuitous road, El Colorado has a large but expensive ski lodge at the base, which offers all facilities, and a mountain restaurant higher up. There are 16 lifts in total, giving access to a large intermediate ski area with some steeper slopes. La Cornisa and Cono Este are two of the few bump runs in Chile. This is a good centre for learning to ski.

La Parva

① *Daily lift ticket US$40.*

Situated nearby at 2816 m, La Parva is the upper-class Santiago weekend resort with 30 pistes and 14 lifts, running from 0900 to 1730. Accommodation is in a chalet village and there are some good bars in high season. Although the runs vary, providing good intermediate to advanced skiing, skiers face a double fall-line so it is not suitable for beginners. Connections with Valle Nevado are good. Equipment rental is from US$20-35 depending on quality. In summer, this is a good walking area, with a trail that leads to the base of Cerro El Plomo, which can be climbed.

Valle Nevado

① *16 km from Farellones, T02-206 0027, www.vallenevado.com, daily lift ticket US$40 Mon-Fri, US$52 Sat and Sun.*

Owned by **Spie Batignolles** of France, Valle Nevado was the site of the 1993 Pan-American winter games and offers the most modern ski facilities in Chile. It has been described as a deluxe hotel complex high up in the mountains. Although not to everyone's taste, it is highly regarded and efficient. There are 40 km of slopes accessed by 41 lifts. The runs are well prepared and are suitable for intermediate skiers and beginners. There's also a ski school and excellent heli-skiing.

Portillo
① 145 km north of Santiago, www.skiportillo.cl, daily lift ticket US$40, except in bad weather it is reached by any bus from Santiago, Valparaíso or Los Andes to Mendoza; you may have to hitch back.

Situated at 2855 m, Portillo lies 62 km east of Los Andes, near the customs post on the route to Argentina, and is one of Chile's best-known resorts. The 23 pistes (including one of the fastest in the world) are varied and well prepared, equipped with snow machines and connected by 12 lifts, two of which open up the off-piste areas. This is an excellent family resort, with a very highly regarded ski school, and there are some gentle slopes for beginners near the hotel. The major skiing events are in August and September. Cheap packages can be arranged at the beginning and out of season; equipment hire costs US$30.

Nearby, at an altitude of 2835 m, is the **Laguna del Inca**, 5.5 km long, 1.5 km wide and surrounded on three sides by accessible mountain slopes. This lake, frozen over in winter, has no outlet and its depth is not known. From **Tío Bob's** there are magnificent views of the lake and condors may be spotted from the terrace. There are boats for fishing; but beware, the afternoon winds often make the homeward pull three or four times as long as the outward pull. Mules can be hired for stupendous expeditions to the glacier at the head of the valley or to the Cerro Juncal.

Lagunillas
① 67 km southeast of Santiago, www.skilagunillas.cl, tow fees US$30, daily lift ticket US$25.

Lagunillas lies in the Cajón del Maipo (see page 105), 17 km east of San José de Maipo, along a beautiful *ripio* road clinging to the edge of a chasm with stunning views of the far reaches of the Andes. It is more basic than the other ski centres in the region, with less infrastructure, but the skiing is good. It is owned by the **Club Andino de Chile**, and is the only not-for-profit ski centre in the country. There are 13 pistes and four ski lifts. In winter, the *carabineros* insist that drivers have snowchains, and rent them out at US$10. Being lower than the other resorts, its season is shorter but it is also cheaper.

From Santiago to Argentina ⬤❶❷❸ ➤ *pp110-112.*

→ *Argentine phone code: +54.*

The route across the Andes via Los Andes and the Redentor tunnel is one of the major crossings into Argentina. Route 57 runs north of Santiago through the rich Aconcagua Valley, known as the Valle de Chile. The road forks at the Santuario de Santa Teresa, the west branch going to San Felipe, east to Los Andes and Mendoza. Before travelling, you should always check on weather and road conditions beyond Los Andes. It is difficult to hitchhike over the border, and Spanish is essential; try getting a ride on trucks leaving from the Aduana building in Los Andes.

Termas de Colina

Based at **Hotel Termas de Colina** at 915 m, 43 km north of Santiago (see page 111), this is an attractive, popular spa in the mountains. The temperature of the water is on the cool side (25°C) but it is supposedly good for rheumatism and nervous disorders. There is a large swimming pool, plus individual baths that can be filled with the thermal water, and a sauna. There are some pleasant short walks in the area. The springs are in a military-controlled area, so do not take photos or even show your camera when passing the military base.

San Felipe and around

The capital of Aconcagua Province, 96 km north of Santiago, San Felipe is an agricultural and mining centre with an agreeable climate. Part of the Inca Highway has recently been discovered in the city; previously, no traces had been found south of La Serena. **Curimón**, 3 km southeast of San Felipe, is the site of the Convento de Santa Rosa de Viterbo (1727), which has a small museum attached. A paved road (13 km) runs north from San Felipe to the old town of **Putaendo**; in its church there is an 18th-century baroque statue of Christ. Situated high in the *cordillera*, **Termas de Jahuel** lies 18 km by road northeast of San Felipe; see Sleeping. The mountain scenery includes a distant view of Aconcagua.

Los Andes

Some 16 km southeast of San Felipe and 77 km north of Santiago, Los Andes is situated in a wealthy agricultural, fruit-farming and wine-producing area, but is also the site of a large car-assembly plant. It is a good place for escaping from Santiago and a convenient base for skiing at nearby Portillo, see page 108. There are monuments to José de San Martín and Bernardo O'Higgins in the Plaza de Armas and a monument to the Clark brothers, who built the Transandine Railway to Mendoza (now disused, although there are tentative plans to re-establish it). There are good views from El Cerro de la Virgen, reached in an hour via a trail from the municipal picnic ground on Independencia.

The road to the border: Los Libertadores

The road to Argentina follows the Aconcagua Valley for 34 km until it reaches the village of **Río Blanco** (1370 m), where the ríos Blanco and Juncal meet to form the Río Aconcagua. There is a fish hatchery with a small botanical garden at the entrance to the Andina copper mine. East of Río Blanco the road climbs until Juncal where it zigzags steeply through 29 hairpin bends at the top of which is the ski resort of Portillo (see page 108). This is the location of the Chilean border post. If entering Chile, there may be long delays during searches for fruit, meat and vegetables, which may not be imported. Put all camera film in your hand luggage as this is not X-rayed.

Above the tunnel is the old pass, used before the tunnel was built, and above this again, at 3854 m, is the statue of **El Cristo Redentor** (Christ the Redeemer), which was erected jointly by Chile and Argentina in 1904 to commemorate King Edward VII's decision in the boundary dispute of 1902. It is completely dwarfed by the landscape. The old road over the pass is in a very poor state, especially on the Chilean side, and is liable to be blocked by snow even in summer. When weather conditions permit, the statue can be reached on foot from **Las Cuevas**, a modern settlement on the Argentine side (4½ hours up, two down). There are also 12-hour excursions to the statue from Mendoza.

For Sleeping and Eating price codes and other relevant information, see Essentials pages 35-42.

ⓢ Sleeping

Cajón del Maipo *p105, map p106*
L-AL Hostería Millahue, El Melocotón, T02-861 2020, T09-9817 6833, www.hosteria millahue.com. Accommodation in *cabañas* including full board. There is also a games room and an outdoor heated swimming pool.
A Refugio Alemán Lo Valdés, Lo Valdés, T02-220 7610, T09-9220 8525, www.refugio lovaldes.com. **E** per person in dorm. Stone-built chalet accommodation. Good restaurant. Lots of trekking and climbing information. Recommended.
A-B Cabañas Corre Caminos, Estero Morales 57402, Baños Morales, T02-269 2283, www.loscorrecaminos.com. Cabins sleeping 2-5 people. Food available, activities including horse riding and massages.
B Hostería Los Ciervos, Camino al Volcán 31411, San Alfonso, T/F02-861 1581. With breakfast, full board also available, good.
C Alojamiento Inesita, Comercio 301, San José, T02-861 1012. Good, excellent chips.
C Residencial España, Av Argentina 711, San Alfonso, T02-861 1543. Clean, comfortable, with restaurant.
C Residencial Los Chicos Malos, Baños Morales, T02-624 1887, T09-9323 6424, www.banos morales.cl. Comfortable, fresh bread, good meals. There are also *cabañas* and a campsite.
C Residencial Pensión Díaz, Manzana C, sitio 10, Lo Valdés, T02-861 1496. **F** singles. Basic, friendly.

Camping
Comunidad Cascada de las Animas, 500 m off the main road, San Alfonso, T02-861 1303. US$30 per site (up to 6 people). Also cabins with hot water, cooking equipment, etc, sauna and horse riding. There are a dozen or so other campsites throughout the valley.

Farellones *p106*
LL Farellones, Las Bandurrias 11, T02-321 1081, www.hotelfarellones.cl. Half board. Slightly careworn, heated swimming pool. Half price in summer.
LL La Cornisa, Los Cóndores 636, T02-321 1172, www.lacornisa.cl. Half board, good restaurant. Reasonably basic but comfortable, chalet style. Much cheaper in summer.
LL Posada de Farellones, T02-201 3704, www.skifarellones.com. Cosy and warm, Swiss style, satellite TV and games room. Transport service to slopes. Decent restaurant. Price includes half board.
AL Refugio Alemán, Los Cóndores 1451, T02-264 9899, www.refugioaleman.cl. **B** per person in shared rooms. Rooms with shared bathrooms, rate includes half board. English spoken. Good value.
B Refugio Universidad de Chile, Los Cóndores 879, T02-321 1595, www.dta.cl/ refugio-u.htm. Price per person in shared rooms with half board. Standard *refugio*, often fills up with university students at weekends.

El Colorado *p107*
LL Colorado Apart Hotel, Av Apoquindo 6275, of 88, Las Condes, T02-245 3401, www.skiandes.co.cl. Fully furnished apartments, half board. Also has cheaper cabins.
LL-L Edificio Monteblanco, bookings from Av Apoquindo 5555, of 905, T02-207 3700, www.ceciliawilsonpropiedades.cl. Apartments that can be rented by the day or week. Food and room service available at extra cost.

La Parva *p107*
LL-L Condominio Nueva La Parva, reservations in Santiago, El Bosque Norte 0177, piso 2, T02-339 8482 www.skilaparva.cl. Good hotel and restaurant. 3 other restaurants.

Valle Nevado *p107*
LL Apart Hotel Mirador del Inca, T02-381 3000, www.miradordelinca.cl. Fully furnished

apartments and 2 restaurants serving everything from gourmet to fast food.
LL Valle Nevado, T02-477 7000, www.valle nevado.com. 5-star resort, full board, lift ticket included. The same company runs 2 other hotels at the complex, both slightly cheaper but still **LL**. See website for details.

Portillo *p108*
LL-AL Hotel Portillo, Renato Sánchez 4270, Las Condes, T02-263 0606, www.skiportillo.com. On the shore of Laguna del Inca. Accommodation from lakeside suites with full board and fabulous views, to bunk rooms without bath. Self-service lunch, open all year, minibus to Santiago US$70 each. Cinema, nightclub, swimming pool, sauna and medical service.

Lagunillas *p108*
AL Cabañas Pura Vida, Camino a Lagunillas, T02-208 4234, Km 4 from San José on the Lagunillas road. Beautiful spot in a fantastic gorge, swimming pool, completely calm and off the beaten track. Highly recommended.
AL Club Andino de Chile, bookings at Av Bernado O'Higgins 108, local 215, Santiago, T02-638 0497, www.skilagunillas.cl. Cabins with full board.

Termas de Colina *p109*
AL Hotel Termas de Colina, T/F02-844 0990. Modern, expensive thermal baths, a beautiful swimming pool (closed Fri), US$8. Formal restaurant. Facilities open to public, crowded at weekends.

San Felipe and around *p109*
LL Termas de Jahuel, T034-582323, www.ja huel.cl, northeast of San Felipe. Luxury health resort with thermal pool, spa, and gym.

Los Andes *p109*
LL Baños El Corazón, San Esteban 2 km north of Los Andes, T034-482852, www.termasel corazon.cl. Full board, swimming pool, thermal baths, take bus San Esteban/El Cariño (US$0.50).
A Plaza, Esmeralda 367, T034-421 929. Good, expensive restaurant.

C Central, Esmeralda 278, T034-421 275. Reasonable and very friendly (excellent bakery opposite, try the *empanadas*).
C Estación, Rodríguez 389, T034-421 026. Without breakfast. Basic. Cheap restaurant.
C Residencial Italiana, Rodríguez 76, T034-423 544. Clean rooms without bath.
D Residencial Maruja, Rancagua 182. Clean.

The road to the border *p109*
A Hostería Guardia Vieja, 8 km east of Río Blanco. Expensive but untidy, campsite.
B Hostería Luna, 4 km west of Río Blanco, T034-421 026. Good value, clean, helpful, good food.

🍴 Eating

Cajón del Maipo *p105, map p106*
🍴 **El Rancho del Ché**, on the road between Puente Alto and San José, El Canelo. Excellent Argentine meat dishes.
🍴 **La Petite France**, on the road between Puente Alto and San José, nearer San José. Good French food, not cheap.
🍴 **Restaurant El Campito**, Camino al Volcán 1841, San José. Very good.
🍴 **Restaurant La Isidora**, on the plaza, San José. Smart, good, meat dishes.

Portillo *p108*
🍴🍴-🍴 **Restaurant La Posada**, opposite Hotel Portillo. Cheaper than the hotel, but open evenings and weekends only.

San Felipe and around *p109*
🍴 **La Piedra del Molino**, in the Sector Almendral, 2 km east of San Felipe on the road to Santa María. Excellent traditional food.

🚌 Transport

Pomaire *p104*
From **Santiago** take the **Melipilla** bus from Terminal San Borja, every few mins, US$2 each way, 1 hr. Alight at the side road to Pomaire, 2-3 km from town; from here there are

colectivos and micros every 10-15 mins (there are also colectivos linking Pomaire and Melipilla) – this route is easier than taking a direct bus from Santiago. En route, pastel de choclo can be obtained at Mi Ranchito.

Reserva Nacional Río Clarillo p104
Bus from **Puente Alto** to **El Principal**, 1 hr, US$3.50.

Santuario de la Naturaleza Yerba Loca p104
Colectivos with Taxis Transarrayán Ltda leave from Plaza San Enrique in Lo Barnechea. Take any bus for **Barnechea** from Alameda or Providencia in Santiago.

Maipo Valley p105
For **Undurraga**, take a Talagante bus from the Terminal San Borja to the entrance. For **Viña Santa Rita**, get a bus direct to Alto Jahuel from Terminal San Borja, T02-776 0645. For **De Martino**, get a bus direct to Isla de Maipo from Terminal San Borja.

Cajón del Maipo p105, map p106
Take line 4 metro to Floridazas Mercedes, from where there are regular bus and colectivo services as far as San Gabriel. Negotiate with the colectivo driver if you wish to go further.

Ski resorts p106
Air Alfa Helicópteros, T02-273 9999, www.alfa-helicopteros.com, 45 mins.
Bus Services from **Santiago** to Farellones, El Colorado, La Parva and Valle Nevado are run by Ski Total, Av Apoquindo 4900, Edificio Omnium, ofs 40-42, T02-246 6881, www.skitotal.cl, and leave from outside their offices, daily from 0730 in season, book in advance, US$15 return. **Skivan**, T02-219 2672, www.skivan.cl, leave for Farellones, Valle Nevado, El Colorado, Lagunillas and Portillo, daily, 0830 from The Telefónica building, Plaza Italia, Baquedano metro, book in advance.

It is easy to hitch from the junction of Av Las Condes/El Camino Farellones (YPF petrol station in the middle).

Termas de Colina p109
From Santiago take the **bus** from Av La Paz 302 (40 mins). From here a rough road leads through countryside 6 km; last return bus at 1900. **Taxi** from Colina to the hotel, US$8.

Los Andes p109
Los Héroes terminal has services to **Mendoza** (Argentina) with Tas Choapa, Fenix Pullman Norte, Cata and Ahumada. Any of these will drop passengers off at **Portillo**, US$10.

The road to the border p109
Saladillo buses hourly from Los Andes to **Río Blanco**; there are also services from Santiago, Ahumada, 1930 daily, direct, 2 hrs, US$2. For Transport into Argentina, see page 98.

❶ Directory

San Felipe has similar facilities to Los Andes, but there is little infrastructure elsewhere.

Los Andes p109
Banks ATMs on the Plaza de Armas. Cambio Inter, Plaza Hotel, good rates, changes TCs, also casa de cambio in Portillo customs building and at Ingeniero Roque Carranza, 13 km from tunnel. **Telephone** Telefónica, O'Higgins 405.

Contents

Valparaíso & Viña del Mar

At a glance

☻ **Getting around** Local buses and *colectivos* pass every few seconds and most other places of interest can be reached by provincial buses. Valparaíso is best explored on foot.

☺ **Time required** 2 or 3 days in either Valparaíso or Viña. 1 day to visit a fishing village and another day or 2 to visit La Campana National Park.

☾ **Weather** Pleasantly warm and dry in summer. Winter is cool but not cold, with sunny days interspersed with cloud and rain.

✘ **When not to go** Viña del Mar and nearby beaches are unpleasantly crowded from New Year until mid-Feb.

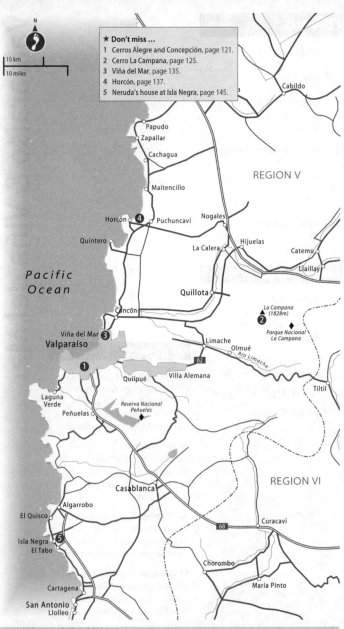

★ Don't miss ...
1 Cerros Alegre and Concepción, page 121.
2 Cerro La Campana, page 125.
3 Viña del Mar, page 135.
4 Horcón, page 137.
5 Neruda's house at Isla Negra, page 145.

N

10 km
10 miles

Cabildo

Papudo
Zapallar
Cachagua

REGION V

Maitencillo

Horcón 4 Puchuncaví

Nogales

Quintero

La Calera

Hijuelas

Catemu

Lliallay

Pacific
Ocean

Quillota

Concón

La Campana
(1828m)
2

Parque Nacional
La Campana

Viña del Mar 3
Valparaíso

Limache
Olmué
Río Limache

1

62

Quilpué

Villa Alemana

Tiltil

Laguna
Verde

Reserva Nacional
Peñuelas

Peñuelas

REGION VI

Casablanca

Algarrobo

El Quisco

Curacaví

68

Isla Negra
El Tabo

5

Chorombo

Cartagena

San Antonio
Llolleo

María Pinto

The coastal strip west of Santiago is one of the most popular destinations for regional tourists. Midway along the coast is Viña del Mar, one of the most famous resorts in South America, awash with Argentines and Chileans strutting their stuff in summer. Near Viña are other popular resorts, such as Reñaca and Concón, plus a host of more secluded spots, including Horcón to the north and Quintay to the south. While the beaches on this stretch of coast are attractive, the water is very cold and swimming is dangerous in many places because of a heavy undertow.

The place that makes this part of Chile really worth visiting is Valparaíso, once the south Pacific's most important port and now the most beguiling city in the country, the capital of Región V and seat of the Chilean House of Parliament, part of which has been declared a UNESCO World Heritage Site. Nearby is the lumpy summit of Cerro La Campana, a high hill between the coast and the Central Valley, which offers some of the best views in Chile and can be climbed in a day. South of Valparaíso, towards the mouth of the Río Maipo, are a number of other centres, including Algarrobo, perhaps the most affluent resort along this coast, and Isla Negra, a village famous as the home of Pablo Neruda, in which the Nobel laureate gathered together a collection of objets d'art from around the world.

Background

This was one of the first areas to be settled by the Spanish, the lands being assigned to prominent *conquistadores* during the 16th century. For most of the colonial period this region was an important exporter of wheat and other foodstuffs to Peru. With Independence and the ending of trade restrictions in the 19th century Valparaíso rose to become the most important port on the Pacific coast of South America, but there were few other large centres of population along this coastline until the 1880s, when the fashion for holidaying near the sea spread from southern Europe. Viña del Mar was established in 1880 and several other resorts followed between 1880 and 1900: Algarrobo, Cartagena, Las Cruces, Zapallar and Papudo, all owing part of their popularity to the building of railway lines linking them to the capital.

Today, this area is one of the major economic centres of the country. Valparaíso and San Antonio are important ports, between them handling much of the country's trade. The region is also a major producer of agricultural products, particularly soft fruit such as avocados, tomatoes, grapes and peaches. The coastline enjoys a Mediterranean-style climate: the cold sea currents and coastal winds produce less extreme temperatures than in Santiago and the Central Valley; rainfall is moderate in winter and the summers are dry. Although the influence of European resorts can still be seen in some of the buildings, especially in Viña del Mar and Zapallar, most of the older buildings have not withstood earthquakes and bulldozers.

Valparaíso

→ *Colour map 3, B2. Population: 300,000.*

Sprawling over a crescent of 42 cerros (hills) that rear up from the sea 116 km west of Santiago, Valparaíso is a one-off. The main residential areas here are not divided into regimented blocks, as in all other Chilean cities; instead Valparaíso is really two cities: the flat, vaguely ordered area between the bus terminal and the port known as 'El Plan', and the chaotic, wasp-nest cerros, in which most porteños (people from Valparaíso) live. It is possible to spend weeks exploring the alleyways of the cerros, where packs of dogs lie sunning themselves, brightly painted houses pile on top of one another and half-forgotten passageways head up and down the hills, offering fantastic views of the Pacific, the city and – on a clear day – right over to the snow-capped cordillera. The Bohemian and slightly anarchic atmosphere of the cerros reflects the urban chaos of the city as a whole. Here you will find such unusual sights as a 'monument to the WC' (Calle Elias) and a graveyard from which all the corpses were shaken out during a severe earthquake. Valparaíso is all about contradictions – the fact that both Salvador Allende and Augusto Pinochet were born and raised here expresses this fact more eloquently than anything else – but the oppositions can also be seen in the juxtaposition of flat El Plan against the labyrinthine cerros; the sea against the views of Aconcagua; and the city's grandiose mansions mingling with some of Chile's worst slums. Given this it is no surprise that Valparaíso has attracted a steady stream of poets and artists throughout the last century. ▸▸ *For listings, see pages 126-134.*

Ins and outs

Getting there There are inter-urban buses to Valparaíso from every major Chilean city (even including connections through to Punta Arenas), and it makes an interesting change to most travellers' itineraries to get a bus to Valparaíso instead of Santiago. Valparaíso also has international connections to Mendoza, Córdoba, Buenos Aires and as far as Rio de Janeiro. Valparaíso can also be reached relatively easy by public transport from Santiago's airport. ▸▸ *See Transport, page 133.*

Getting around You should never have to wait more than 30 seconds to travel anywhere within El Plan (between Plaza Aduana and Avenida Argentina): buses along Pedro Montt are cheap but slow; Errázuriz buses are faster. Valparaíso is the only city in Chile still to have trolleybuses; they are mostly Swiss and from the 1950s. They ply the length of El Plan and cost the same as a local bus fare. Buses to Cerro Alegre and the top of Cerro Concepción leave from calle Chacabuco, behind the bus terminal (No 607) or Avenida Argentina (No 514). Bus 612, popularly known as the 'O', links the hills of Valparaíso from Avenida Argentina all along the Avenida Alemania, down to the port and around the coast to Playa Ancha. Catching it is a sightseeing tour in itself. Taxis and *colectivos* usually wait around at the bottom of each *cerro*; otherwise, you can use the *ascensores* (funicular railways). If you are going to Viña or one of the nearby towns to the north, catch a *micro* from Errázuriz or Brasil; *colectivos* to Viña leave from the same place. Taxis serving a particular *cerro* do not use their meters but are generally reasonable and, if there are three or four of you, sharing a taxi can be cheaper than taking a *colectivo*. Taxis from the bus terminal are metered and can be quite expensive.

Security Robbery is an occasional problem in El Puerto and around the *ascensores* on Avenida Argentina. The upper outskirts of town, as well as Cerro Cordillera, while offering amazing views, are not the safest of places. The poorer and rougher districts tend to be

Neruda on Valparaíso

"The hills of Valparaíso decided to dislodge their inhabitants, to let go of the houses on top, to let them dangle from cliffs that are red with clay, yellow with gold thimble flowers, and a fleeting green with wild vegetation. But houses and people clung to the heights, writhing, digging in, worrying, their hearts set on staying up there, hanging on, tooth and nail, to each cliff. The port is a tug-of-war between the sea and nature, untamed on the cordilleras. But it was man who won the battle little by little. The hills and the sea's abundance gave the city a pattern, making it uniform, not like a barracks, but with the variety of spring, its clashing colours, its resonant bustle. The houses became colours: a blend of amaranth and yellow, crimson and cobalt, green and purple."

Pablo Neruda, *Memoirs*, Penguin, 1978.

those furthest from the centre. Also be aware that Calle Chacabuco (on which some hotels are located) is the pickup point for local rent boys. Keep your personal items secure keep your camera in a bag or rucksack, only taking it out when you want to take a photo. Beware of the mustard trick (see page 52).

Tourist information Offices are located in the **Municipalidad** ⓘ *Av Argentina 864, Mon-Fri 0830-1400, www.ciudaddevalparaiso.cl,* but are not keen on attending to the public. Your best bet are the kiosks by the Plaza Sotomayor and the Plaza Aníbal Pinto, although these are also a bit of a mixed bag. There are also two information offices in the bus terminal, but these are privately run on a commission basis and hence do not give impartial advice. Don't be fooled by the old municipal tourist office sign.

History

Founded in 1542, Valparaíso became, in the colonial period, a small port used for trade with Peru. It was raided at least seven times during the colonial era by pirates and corsairs, including Drake. The city prospered from Independence more than any other Chilean town. It was used in the 19th century by commercial agents from Europe and the US as their trading base in the southern Pacific and became a major international banking centre as well as the key port for shipping between the northern Pacific and Cape Horn. Until the 1840s, the journey from the port to El Almendral (site of the congress and the old road to Santiago) took several hours and passed over wild hills but, as the city's wealth and importance grew, part of the original bay was filled in, creating the modern day El Plan. Fine buildings were erected here, including several banks, South America's first stock exchange and offices of *El Mercurio*, the world's oldest newspaper in the Spanish language, first printed in 1827 and still in publication. (The impressive *Mercurio* building, built in 1900, stands on the site of a famous pirates' cave.) Wealthy European merchants began to populate Cerro Concepción and Cerro Alegre in this period, building churches and fine mansions in every conceivable architectural style.

The city's decline was the result of two factors: the opening of the Panama Canal in 1914 and the breakdown in world trade during the depression in the 1930s. Further decline followed the development of a container port in San Antonio, the shift of banks to Santiago and the move of the middle classes to nearby Viña del Mar. Recently money has been pumped in through UNESCO, the Inter-American Development bank and to some extent tourism, and the city is slowly being restored to its former splendour.

Little of the city's colonial past survived the pirates, tempests, fires and earthquakes, but a remnant of the old colonial city can be found in the hollow known as El Puerto, grouped round the low-built stucco church of La Matriz. Very few wooden buildings predate the devastating earthquake of 1906, which was followed by a series of fires.

Sights

The lower part of the city, El Plan, is the business centre, with fine office buildings on narrow streets that are strung along the edge of the bay and cluttered with buses. Above, covering the hills or *cerros* is a fantastic agglomeration of buildings in every conceivable shape that seem literally to tumble down the slopes. Part of the charm of the *cerros* is the lack of order. It is as if every individual bought a plot of land and built whatever they saw fit, resulting in a hotchpotch of size, style and colour. Spanish colonial mansions lie alongside adobe shacks and neoclassical monoliths.

Superb views over the bay are offered from most of the *cerros*, each of which provides its own unique vista and distinct atmosphere. It is enjoyable to spend an afternoon exploring the hills and, however lost you might feel, a few minutes' walk downhill will always lead you back to El Plan. The lower and upper cities are connected by steep winding roads, flights of steps and 15 *ascensores* (funicular railways) dating from the period 1883-1914.

Plaza Sotomayor and El Puerto

The old heart of El Plan is the **Plaza Sotomayor**, dominated by the former **Intendencia** (Government House), now the seat of the admiralty. Be careful when crossing the plaza, which, although it appears pedestrianized, is in fact criss-crossed by busy roads. Opposite is a fine monument to the 'Heroes of the Battle of Iquique', which also serves as a mausoleum housing the bodies of all who fought in the battle. Visitors are occasionally allowed inside and on 21 May it is the focus of a massive procession of the armed forces through the city celebrating the anniversary of the battle. While excavating under Plaza Sotomayor in order to build a new underground car park, parts of Valparaíso's original **old quay** were uncovered; they can be visited in summer. Alternatively, they can be viewed from above ground through the glass ceiling, although the glass tends to mist up. Look out, too, for the bronze plaques on the ground illustrating the movement of the shoreline over the centuries.

One block away from Plaza Sotomayor is the port entrance (take a boat trip from here around the bay, recommended if sunny; see Activities and tours, page 132) and the **railway station**, from which passenger services run on the newly modernized metropolitan line to Viña del Mar and Limache.

One block northwest of Plaza Sotomayor, on Calle Serrano, is the **Ascensor Cordillera** and the *Escalera de la Muerte* (the Stairs of Death; just try climbing them to find out why). At the top, on Plazuela Eleuterio Ramírez, take Calle Merlet to the left and you will find the **Museo del Mar Almirante Cochrane** ① *Merlet 195, Tue-Sun 1000-1800, free*, which hosts temporary art exhibitions in a small colonial house with excellent views over the bay (the New Year fireworks are filmed from here). Note that thieves and pickpockets are known to work in this area.

Back in El Plan, continue another block along Serrano into the heart of El Puerto to reach **Plaza Echaurren**, Valparaíso's oldest square, tree-lined and with a picturesque fountain. It was once the height of elegance but is now surrounded by cheap restaurants and frequented by a sizeable population of local drunks. Near Plaza Echaurren stands the church of **La Matriz**, built in 1842 on the site of the first church in the city and unusual for its sloping nave and stained-glass windows all depicting Valparaíso themes. Further northwest, along Bustamante, lies Plaza Aduana, named after the customs building, from where the **Ascensor Artillería** takes you up to the Mirador 21 de Mayo and the imposing **Museo Naval y Marítimo** ① *www.museonaval.cl*, Tue-Sun 1000-1730, US$1.30, in the old Naval Academy, which documents naval history 1810-1880, and includes exhibitions on Chile's two naval heroe: Lord Cochrane (see box, page 366) and Arturo Prat.

Playa Ancha and around

To the west of **Cerro Artillería**, the Avenida **Gran Bretaña** winds its way to the municipal stadium on Cerro Playa Ancha, which seats 20,000 people and is home to the local football team Santiago Wanderers. The buildings on Avenida Gran Bretaña are a good example of the suburb's eccentric architecture. Past the stadium the road continues downhill to the foot of Cerro Playa Ancha at **Las Torpederas**, a small bathing beach. Just

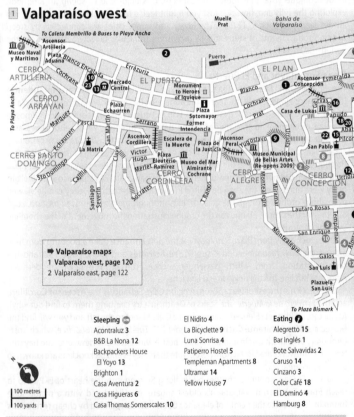

1 Valparaíso west

→ **Valparaíso maps**
1 Valparaíso west, page 120
2 Valparaíso east, page 122

100 metres
100 yards

Sleeping
Acontraluz 3
B&B La Nona 12
Backpackers House
 El Yoyo 13
Brighton 1
Casa Aventura 2
Casa Higueras 6
Casa Thomas Somerscales 10

El Nidito 4
La Bicyclette 9
Luna Sonrisa 4
Patiperro Hostel 5
Templeman Apartments 8
Ultramar 14
Yellow House 7

Eating
Alegretto 15
Bar Inglés 1
Bote Salvavidas 2
Caruso 14
Cinzano 3
Color Café 18
El Dominó 4
Hamburg 8

beyond the beach is a promontory topped by the **Faro de Punta Angeles**, which was the first lighthouse on the west coast of South America. There is a picturesque coastal road back to town, the Avenida Altamirano, passing **Caleta Membrillo**, which has a number of good seafood restaurants.

Around Cerros Alegre and Concepción

Southeast of Plaza Sotomayor, calles Prat, Cochrane and Esmeralda run through the old banking and commercial centre to **Plaza Aníbal Pinto**, around which are some of the city's oldest bars and cafes. Above this part of El Plan are **Cerro Alegre** and **Cerro Concepción**, the heart of the UNESCO-designated area and for many the undisputed symbols of the city. Both are filled with brightly painted mansions and high-ceilinged 19th century houses, some falling down but many now being restored to their former glory and some being extended upwards, despite supposedly restrictive planning regulations, a contentious issue for many in the local community. Cerro Concepción is as posh as Valparaíso gets, while Cerro Alegre has a more artistic, bohemian feel: brightly coloured murals abound, most of the shops seem to double as art galleries and, during university term, students can be seen on practically every street corner sketching buildings or the panoramic views. The two hills are connected to El Plan by three *ascensores*, of which **Ascensor Concepción**, inaugurated on 1 December 1883, is the oldest in Valparaíso. Three miradors offer views of the bay, over to Viña and beyond.

Museo Municipal de Bellas Artes ① *Paseo Yugoslavo, due to reopen soon after eight years of refurbishment, Tue-Sun 1000-1800, free*, is housed in Palacio Baburizza, and has displays of Chilean landscapes and seascapes and some modern paintings. A visit is highly recommended and, if you are lucky, you may get to see the whole of this interesting rococo mansion; the games room, drawing room, shower and servants' quarters provide an insight into the contrasting lifestyles of *porteños* in the early part of the 20th century.

Also worth a visit is the **Casa Mirador de Lukas** ① *Paseo Gervasoni 448, Cerro Concepción, T032-2221344, www.lukas.cl, Tue-Sun 1100-1900, US$1.80*, dedicated to the work of Chile's most famous caricaturist. Lukas (real name Renzo Pecchenino) was originally from Italy but spent most of his life in Valparaíso. The

La Colombina **9**
La Costeñita **10**
La Tertulia **11**
Le Filou de Montpellier **12**
Le Pastis **20**
Los Porteños **13**
Makandrino **7**
Mastodonte **21**
Pasta e Vino **22**

Puerto Viejo **23**
Turri **16**

Bars & clubs ①
Café Vinilo **17**
La Piedra Feliz **19**

museum holds a permanent exhibition of his work, which gives a humorous insight into the political and social history of Valparaíso and Chile. There are also temporary exhibitions and occasional films.

Avenida Alemania and around

Walking uphill along any of the main streets of Cerro Alegre will lead you to the Plazuela San Luis, from where **Avenida Alemania** runs southeast, following the contours of Valparaíso's hills. This is the only road that connects all the hills above Valparaíso and makes a pleasant walk, with ever-changing views, one of the best of which is to be had from **Plaza Bismark**. Calle Cumming heads back down to El Plan from Plaza Bismark passing the former prison (now a cultural centre housing temporary exhibitions and occasional concerts – worth a visit) and three cemeteries, all of which can be visited: **Cementerios I** and **II** are the city's two oldest Catholic cemeteries, while the third, **Cementerio de los Disidentes**, holds the graves of Protestant immigrants. Back on Avenida Alemania, meanwhile, a 20-minute walk

2 Valparaíso east

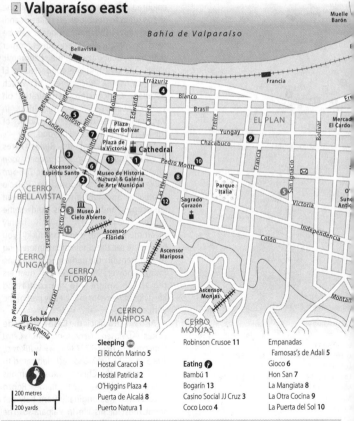

Sleeping
El Rincón Marino 5
Hostal Caracol 3
Hostal Patricia 2
O'Higgins Plaza 4
Puerta de Alcalá 8
Puerto Natura 1

Robinson Crusoe 11

Eating
Bambú 1
Bogarín 13
Casino Social JJ Cruz 3
Coco Loco 4

Empanadas
Famosas's de Adali 5
Gioco 6
Hon San 7
La Mangiata 8
La Otra Cocina 9
La Puerta del Sol 10

N

200 metres
200 yards

will bring you to the former home of Pablo Neruda, **La Sebastiana** ① *Ferrari 692, off Av Alemania, Altura 6900, Cerro Florida, T032-225 6606, www.fundacionneruda.org, Tue-Sun 1030-1430, 1530-1800 (until 1900 in summer), US$4.50, bus 612 from Av Argentina, US$0.65, or colectivo from Plazuela Equador, US$0.65*. It now houses an art gallery as well as a collection of some of his objets d'art, showing his eccentric tastes to the full, and there is a small café in the garden, with fine views.

Plaza de la Victoria and around

From **La Sebastiana**, walk down **Cerro Bellavista** along Calle Ferrari and Calle Héctor Calvo to arrive at the **Museo al Cielo Abierto**. Opened in 1992, this open-air museum consists of large-scale murals painted on the outside walls of buildings in Cerro Bellavista by 17 of Chile's leading artists. Look out for the 6 m by 3 m mural by Chile's most famous contemporary artist, Roberto Matta, situated just before you reach the Ascensor Espíritu Santo; it's a typical example of Matta's later work with sharp-toothed monsters hurtling through space. At the bottom of the museo

is **Plaza de la Victoria** with the cathedral on its east side and the municipal library on Plaza Simón Bolívar just to the north. Plaza Victoria is the official centre of Valparaíso and commemorates Chile's victory in the War of the Pacific; the statues and fountain were looted from Peru during the war.

One block west, on Calle Condell in the 19th-century Palacio Lyon is the **Museo de Historia Natural** ① *Condell 1546, T032-225 7441, www.dibam.cl/sdm_mhn_valpo, Tue-Fri 1000-1300, 1400-1800, Sat-Sun 1000-1400, US$1.10*. Next door is the **Galería de Arte Municipal** ① *Condell 1550, T032-222 0062, Mon-Sat 1000-1900, free*.

Plaza O'Higgins and further east

East of Plaza de la Victoria, Pedro Montt leads to the Parque Italia and **Plaza O'Higgins**. The latter is dominated by the imposing **Congreso Nacional**, a monolithic arch in neo-fascist style, thoroughly out of keeping with the rest of the city. Opposite is the bus terminal, while four blocks north on Errázuriz is the Barón train station and the **Muelle Barón**, the new terminal for cruise ships. A walk to the end of this pier, past kite-flying children, gives a different view of Valparaíso, clearly showing the amphitheatre-like form of the city. Just off the pier is a small colony of sea-lions, and at the pier's base, kayaks can be hired to paddle in the bay. A new coastal

A walk over the *cerros* Alegre and Concepción

From the Plaza Aníbal Pinto walk up Calles Cumming and Elias and take the Ascensor Reina Victoria up to a viewing point. Walk along Paseo Dimalow to the end, then head down Urriola (opposite). After one block, turn right onto Calle Templeman. On the left are two alleyways: Pasaje Templeman has a couple of art workshops, while Pierre Loti has typical English-style houses. Further along Calle Templeman is the Anglican church of San Pablo, built in 1858, which has organ recitals every Sunday at 1230. Follow the church round past the entrance on Pilcomayo and head down to the end of that street, where steps lead down to Paseo Pastor Schmidt, with views of the cemetery opposite. Carry on past the Lutheran church (1897) and along the revamped Paseo Atkinson, once home to merchants and ships' captains and with expansive views. At the end of the walkway, turn right onto Papudo. The next right leads to the Paseo Gervasoni, overlooking the port and the

Turri clock tower, and home to the Lukas museum. Following the paseo round, take the steps down to the labyrinthine Pasaje Galvez, past restaurants, bars and art galleries.

Cross Calle Urriola, and head up Pasaje Bavestrello, ahead and to the right. At the top is an unusual building, four storeys high and 3-m wide. Turn right here onto the Paseo Yugoslavo and the Palacio Baburizza, with views of the Cochrane museum to the left and Playa Ancha beyond. Walk past the Ascensor Peral and follow the road up and round into Pasaje Leighton. The second road on the right is Miramar. Climb 100 m and turn left onto Lautaro Rosas, an avenue lined with fine houses and mansions. After two blocks the road crosses the stair-lined Calle Templeman, boasting one of Valparaíso's classic views.

If you still have any energy left you can climb three blocks to the Plazuela San Luis and begin exploring other hills along the Avenida Alemania.

walkway has recently been built running northeast from here past several small beaches as far as **Caleta Portales**, a small fishing harbour with several seafood restaurants that lies almost at the border between Valparaíso and Viña del Mar.

To the east of the Congress building, Avenida Argentina runs south past four *ascensores* including **Ascensor Polanco** (entrance from Calle Simpson, off Avenida Argentina a few blocks southeast of the bus terminal). This is the most unusual *ascensor* in the city as it is in two sections: walk along a 160-m horizontal tunnel through the rock, then take a vertical lift to the summit on which there is a mirador. Note that the lower entrance is in an area that can be unsafe after dark: do not go alone and do not take valuables. Beyond Polanco the road branches left towards Santiago or continues straight on to Cerro O'Higgins, where there are several mansions built by the British in the 19th century. Nearby is the **Mirador O'Higgins**, from which the Supreme Director, Bernardo O'Higgins, saw the arrival of Cochrane's liberating squadron and proclaimed "On those four craft depends the destiny of America".

South of Valparaíso ⬤➊➋➌ ▸▸ pp126-134.

Laguna Verde, 12 km south of Valparaíso, is a picturesque bay with a huge beach that's peaceful and perfect for picnics, although the wind can get quite fierce in the afternoons and strong undercurrents make swimming dangerous.

Further south, **Quintay** is the least known of the villages on the *central littoral*, and also one of the most picturesque. In its heyday, the village's **whaling station** ① *Tue-Sun 0900-1800, US$0.70*, employed over 1000 workers, mostly from Chiloé, but now only the fishermen remain. Most people ignore the threatening sign warning you not to climb up to the lighthouse. If you take the risk, the view is worth the short climb to watch the sunset.

Quintay has two beaches, the larger of which is being overrun by a housing development. The other, **Playa Chica**, is accessed via an unsignposted route through a eucalyptus wood (entry by the *carabineros*). It is wild and deserted off season and is definitely worth the 20-minute walk.

East of Valparaíso ⬤➊ ▸▸ pp126-134.

Towards Santiago
Reserva Nacional Peñuelas ① *US$2*, encompasses 9260 ha around the artificial Lago Peñuelas and is open to visitors for walking and fishing. The park, which is covered by pine and eucalyptus forest, is situated 30 km southeast of Valparaíso near the main road to Santiago (Route 68). Buses between the two cities pass the entrance where the park administration is located. Beyond the park, Route 68 passes the wine-producing Casablanca valley and through two tunnels (US$3 toll each).

Towards Argentina
The Troncal Sur highway runs through Viña del Mar, climbs out of the bay and passes south of **Quilpué**, Km 16, a dormitory town for Valparaíso and Viña, with an interesting municipal zoo. It crosses a range of hills and reaches the Aconcagua Valley at **Limache**, a sleepy market town, famous for its tomatoes, 40 km from Valparaíso. The Troncal Sur joins Route 60 just before **Quillota**, another fruit-growing centre, continuing to La Calera, Km 88, where it joins the Pan-American Highway; turn southeast and east for Llaillay, San Felipe, Los Andes and the Redentor tunnel to Mendoza.

Parque Nacional La Campana
① *US$2.75 per person.*
Situated north of Olmué (8 km east of Limache), the park covers 8000 ha and includes **Cerro La Campana** (1828 m), which Darwin climbed in 1835, and **Cerro El Roble** (2200 m). It is divided into three main sections, each with its own entrance: in the south are **Sector Granizo** ① *paradero 45, 5 km east of Olmué*, from which the Cerro La Campana is climbed, and **Sector Cajón Grande** ① *paradero 41, reached by unpaved road off the Olmué–Granizo road*, while to the north is **Sector Ocoa** ① *reached by unpaved road (10 km) off the Pan-American Highway between Hijuelas and Llaillay*, which is where the main concentration of Chilean coconut palms (*kankán*) can be found. This native species is now found in natural woodlands in only two locations in Chile. The park can be crossed on foot (six hours) between Ocoa and Granizo or Cajón Grande along well-marked trails through the gamut of Chilean natural vegetation, from cactuses and palm trees to southern beech and lingue. A number of shorter trails lead from all three entrances.

A fair amount of agility is required to climb **Cerro La Campana**. Allow a whole day there and back from Olmué, although fit and experienced hikers could probably do it in around seven hours. There are three places where fresh water is available on the climb, but you should take your own food and drink. From the entrance at Granizo, a path leaves the road to the left just past the CONAF *guardería*, and climbs steeply through forest, fording a clear, rushing stream and providing increasingly fine views of the valley below until reaching an old mining area (two hours from the *guardería*). From here the path is well marked, but becomes more testing; after passing a plaque dedicated by the British community to Charles Darwin on the centenary of his visit, it climbs over loose rock to a pass to the northeast, before doubling back and rising over rocks (where scrambling and a little very basic climbing is required) to the summit. The wonderful views from the top of the Cerro la Campana take in a 300-km stretch of the Andes (including Aconcagua), as well as the rugged outline of the central cordillera losing itself in the haze to the north, the gentler scenes of the southern hills, and, when the haze is not too great, Valparaíso and the Pacific Ocean to the west. It is also possible to ascend La Campana from Quillota, but this route is more difficult and definitely requires a guide.

⊙ Valparaíso listings

For Sleeping and Eating price codes and other relevant information, see Essentials pages 35-42.

⊜ Sleeping

Recent government grants have led to an explosion of new accommodation. While many places look nice on the surface, not all are well run.

Playa Ancha and around *p120, map p120*
B The Yellow House, Capitán Muñoz Gamero 91, Cerro Artillería, T032-233 9435, www.theyellowhouse.cl. One of several hostels and B&Bs in this area, tucked away on a cobbled side street. Quiet, friendly, Australian-run. Some rooms with extensive views. Good showers. Recommended.

Around Cerros Alegre and Concepción *p121, map p120*
There are several *hostales* in the neighbourhood; shop around.
LL-L Acontraluz, San Enrique 473, Cerro Alegre, T032-211 1320, www.hotel acontraluz.cl. Probably the best of the new boutique hotels here. Rooms facing the sea have balconies with tremendous views. Buffet breakfast. Bright, Victorian house fully

restored with attention to detail and no expense spared. English, French, Russian spoken. Recommended.
LL-L Casa Higueras, Higuera 133, Cerro Alegre, T032-249 7900, www.hotelcasa higueras.cl. Another new boutique hotel in a restored building. Rooms are all distinctive, with wooden interiors and some have views over the bay. Good breakfast and fine restaurant. Roof terrace. Spa area with pool. Recommended.
L-AL Casa Thomas Somerscales, San Enrique 446, Cerro Alegre, T032-233 1006, www.hotelsomerscales.cl. Spacious rooms in a restored mansion with period furniture. Basic English spoken. Wi-Fi areas. The rooms on the top floor have lovely views over the bay, although some question whether building an extra storey on a historic building in a protected area can be justified.
AL-A Brighton, Paseo Atkinson 151, Cerro Concepción, T032-222 3513, www.brighton.cl. Bills itself as a typical building in a historic part of Valparaíso, although it's barely a dozen years old. Small rooms, mixed reports on service, 1 room has a balcony with excellent views. There is live tango and bolero music in the bar at weekends, so don't expect much sleep.

A El Nidito, Templeman 833, piso 2, Cerro Alegre, T032-273 4117, www.elnidito.cl. Spacious apartment recently restored with high ceilings, all mod-cons, large fully equipped kitchen and raised bathtub with views over the bay. English spoken, lots of info, advance booking advised. Highly recommended.

A Templeman Apartments, Pierre Loti 65, Cerro Concepción, T032-225 7067, chantal derementeria@gmail.com. Fully equipped, stylish, self-contained apartments sleeping 2-4, one uses an old weaving loom as table and has a wardrobe painted Mondrian style; good if you want a little peace away from the gringo trail. Book in advance for weekends. Highly recommended.

B B&B La Nona, Galos 660, Cerro Alegre, T032-249 5706, www.bblanona.com. Small, friendly family-run bed and breakfast. Some rooms with bath. English spoken, lots of activities and personalized tours. Recommended.

B-C Luna Sonrisa, Templeman 833, Cerro Alegre, T032-273 4117, www.lunasonrisa.cl. **D** singles, **E** per person in shared rooms. Some rooms with bath. Newly restored, bright, comfortable, large kitchen, lots of information, excellent breakfast including wholemeal bread and real coffee, Wi-Fi, tours arranged, English and French spoken, friendly and helpful, and run by the author of this guide. Highly recommended – of course!

C Casa Aventura, Pasaje Gálvez 11, off C Urriola, Cerro Concepción, T032-275 5963, www.casaventura.cl. **F** per person in shared rooms. One of Valparaíso's longest established backpackers' hostels, in a restored traditional house, with good breakfast, German and English spoken, tours, helpful, friendly, informative, kitchen facilities. Highly recommended.

C La Bicyclette, Almte Montt 213, Cerro Alegre. T032-222 2215, www.bicyclette.cl. **E** singles. With breakfast. Basic, bright rooms, lovely patio, French-run, hires out bicycles.

C Patiperro hostel, Templeman 657, Cerro Alegre, T032-317 3153, www.patiperro

hostel.cl. Friendly hostel with doubles and big dorms (**E** per person), all with shared bath. Kitchen facilities and lots of movies. Good choice for the younger crowd. There are several more *hostales*, generally **B** or **C** in Cerro Concepción.

Avenida Alemania and around
p122, maps p120 and p122

AL-A Ultramar, Pérez 173, Cerro Cárcel, T032-221 0000, www.hotelultramar.cl. **A-B** singles. Old brick warehouse tastefully refurbished as an upmarket B&B. The more expensive rooms are spacious and have fantastic views, although they can feel a little stuffy in summer. Rooms are centrally heated, café/bar downstairs. Friendly attentive staff. English spoken. Slightly isolated from the main points of interest.

A Puerto Natura, Héctor Calvo 850, Cerro Bellavista, T032-222 4405, www.puerto natura.cl. In a restored mansion set in large grounds with fruit trees and small swimming pool. Excellent views. There is also a holistic centre with sauna, massages and yoga classes. Recommended.

Plaza de la Victoria and around
p123, maps p120 and p122

LL-AL Robinson Crusoe, Héctor Calvo 389, Cerro Bellavista, T032-249 5449, www.hotels. tk/robinson. Down the hill from the Sebastiana Museum in a large restored old house. Lovely roof terrace with views, peaceful, helpful staff, clean, nice suites with bathrooms, but most rooms have shared bath and these are overpriced.

A Puerta de Alcalá, Pirámide 524, T032-222 7478, www.hotelpuertadealcala.cl. Everything you would expect of a standard 3-star without being spectacular. Rooms at the front can be noisy.

B-C Hostal Caracol, Héctor Calvo 371, Cerro Bellavista, T032-239 5817, www.hostal caracol.cl. **E** per person in dorms. Friendly hostel in a quiet residential hill. Pleasant patio and barbeque area, heating. English spoken. A good choice.

C-D Backpackers House El Yoyo, Ecuador
355, T032-259 1087, ktyoyo@hotmail.com.
F per person in somewhat cramped dorms.
Fun youth hostel for the younger crowd.
Cheap, but cleanliness can be an issue.

Plaza O'Higgins and further east
p123, map p122
The area near the bus terminal can be
unsafe, especially at night.
A O'Higgins Plaza, Retamo 517, T032-223
5616, www.restorantohiggins.cl. A good
business standard, next to the Congress
building but not the most interesting
part of town.
C-D El Rincón Marino, San Ignacio 454,
T032-222 5815, www.rinconmarino.cl.
D-E singles. Uninspiring location, but
clean, friendly, good value and only
4 blocks from the bus terminal.
D Hostal Patricia,12 de Febrero 315, T032-
222 0290, www.hostalpatricia.cl. **E** singles, **F**
per person in dorms. Family accommodation,
hot showers, laundry and kitchen facilities,
Wi-Fi, good local knowledge. Not the nicest
area to say the least, but very convenient
for the bus terminal.

South of Valparaíso *p125*
Camping is possible at Laguna Verde
at **Camping Los Olivos**, which has good
facilities and is well run and friendly.

Parque Nacional La Campana *p125*
There are places to stay in all price categories
in Olmué for easy access to the Granizo
sector of the park.
AL El Copihue, Diego Portales 2203, Olmué,
T033-441544, www.copihue.cl. Small resort
set in pleasant gardens, with gym, games
room, indoor and outdoor pools. Half and
full board available.
C La Alondra, Granizo 8459, Olmué, T033-
441163. **F** singles. A reasonable budget choice.
C Sarmiento, Blanco Encalda 4689, Olmué,
T033-442838. **E** singles. Cheap and cheerful.

Camping
It is possible to camp in all sectors of the park,
US$11 per site with cold showers. In summer
reserve in advance, T033-244 1342.

🍴 Eating

Plaza Sotomayor and El Puerto
p119, map p120
There are countless *fuentes de soda* throughout El Plan and in the market, where the
portions are large (closed in the evenings).
🍴🍴-🍴 **Bote Salvavidas**, Muelle Prat s/n,
piso 2, T032-225 1477. Upmarket seafood
restaurant overlooking the port.
🍴 **La Costeñita**, Blanco 86. Good seafood
restaurant, with incredibly kitsch decor.
Try the *pastel de jaivas*.
🍴 **Los Porteños**, Cochrane 102. Perennial
favourite for fish and shellfish, terse service
but good food.
🍴 **Puerto Viejo**, Cochrane y Valdivia.
Very good-value set-lunch fish dishes.
🍴 **Sandrita**, 2nd floor of the market
(off Plaza Echaurren). Good *carbonada
de mariscos*, friendly, recommended.

Playa Ancha and around *p120*
There are several good fish restaurants at
Caleta Membrillo, 2 km west of Plaza
Sotomayor (take any Playa Ancha bus).
🍴🍴 **Club Social de Pescadores**, Altamirano
1480. A concrete monstrosity by the harbour,
redeemed by views. Busy at weekends.
🍴🍴 **El Membrillo**, Caleta Membrillo.
The oldest restaurant in the Caleta.
Opposite the Club Social.

Around Cerros Alegre and
Concepción *p121, map p120*
🍴🍴🍴 **Le Pastis**, Concepción 280, Cerro
Concepción, T032-249 3319. New bistro
serving exquisite, if expensive duck and
other french classics.
🍴🍴🍴-🍴🍴 **La Colombina**, Paseo Yugoslavo 15,
Cerro Alegre, T032-223 6254. The most
traditional of the area's restaurants.

Good food, wide range of wines, fine views, especially from the top floor. The *ostiones* in particular are recommended.

†††-†† Pasta e Vino, Templeman 352, Cerro Cocepción, T032-249 6187. Closed Mon. Upmarket trendy restaurant serving fresh pasta with a twist. Giant salmon ravioli with curry is a perennial favourite. Slightly haughty service spoils the atmosphere a little. Book 2 days in advance at weekends.

†††-†† Turri, Templeman 147, on Cerro Concepción, T032-225 9198. Wonderful views, reasonable food but a bit of a tourist trap.

†† Alegretto, Pilcomayo 529, Cerro Concepción, T032-296 8839. British-owned pizzeria serving pizzas with excellent bases and unusual toppings. Service can be slow if full.

†† Bar Inglés, Cochrane 851 (entrance also on Blanco Encalada), El Plan, T032-221 4625. Historic bar/restaurant dating from the early 1900s; a chart shows the ships due in port. Good food and drink, traditional, not cheap.

†† Café Vinilo, Almirante Montt 448, Cerro Alegre, T032-223 0665. Inventive lunchtime menus with gourmet interpretations of traditional Chilean dishes. Also a lively bar at night, when it can get a bit smoky.

†† Caruso, Cumming 201, Cerro Cárcel, T032-259 4039. Mostly seafood and fish with a Peruvian touch. Uses inshore fish not found in other restaurants. Good wine list and regular tastings.

†† Cinzano, Plaza Aníbal Pinto 1182, El Plan, T032-221 3043. The oldest bar in Valparaíso, also serving food. Flamboyant live music at weekends, noted for tango performances but no dancing by guests allowed. Service can be awful.

†† Le Filou de Montpellier, Almte Montt 382, T032-222 4663. French-run. Set lunch menu very popular and deservedly so. Also open weekends for dinner. Good value. Recommended.

†† Malandrino, Almirante Montt 532, Cerro Alegre. Traditional pizzas baked in a clay oven using mostly organic ingredients. Cosy atmosphere. Popular with locals as well as tourists.

††-† La Tertulia, Esmeralda 1083, El Plan, T032-221 0905. Good vegetarian options.

† El Dominó, Cumming 67, El Plan. Traditional basic *porteño* restaurant serving *empanadas*, *chorrillanas* and the like.

† Mastodonte, Esmeralda 1139, El Plan, T032-225 1205. No nonsense, very good value, traditional food in kitsch surroundings. Often crowded but still excellent service and cheap locally brewed draught beer.

Cafés

Both the Turri restaurant and the Hotel Brighton have terraces where you can drink coffee while enjoying the views.

Café con Letras, Almte Montt 316, Cerro Concepción. Cosy and friendly no-smoking café with books, magazines and newspapers. Excellent coffee, also soup in winter.

Color Café, Papudo 526, Cerro Concepción. Eclectic, arty café serving tea and real coffee, fresh juice, good cakes and snacks, regular live music, art exhibits, and local art and craft for sale. Slow service.

El Desayunador, Almte Montt 399, Cerro Alegre, T032-275 5735. Opens early for breakfast. Wide range of teas and real coffee, also vegetarian dishes.

Pan de Magia, Almte Montt 738 y Templeman, Cerro Alegre, T032-222 7868. Cakes, cookies and by far the best wholemeal bread in town, all take away.

Riquet, Plaza Aníbal Pinto, El Plan. One of the oldest cafés in Valparaíso, good coffee and breakfast.

Plaza de la Victoria and around
p123, maps p120 and p122

††† Coco Loco, Blanco 1781, pisos 21 y 22, T032-222 7614. Plush revolving restaurant 70 m above the bay. Extensive menu.

†† Hamburg, O'Higgins 1274, T032-259 7037. Owned by an elderly German emigré. Right-wing military memorabilia abounds. The food is apparently good.

†† Hon San, Donoso y Huito. Chinese. Nothing special, but the best of the bunch nevertheless.

♥♥ **Valle de Quintíl**, Rodolfo 254, Cerro Bellavista, T032-246 9631. At the top of the *ascensor* Espíritu Santo. Good fish dishes with extensive views over the city and the bay.

♥ **Bambú**, Independencia 1790, T032-223 4216. Closed Sun. Vegetarian lunches only.

♥ **Casino Social JJ Cruz**, Pasaje Condell 1466, T032-225 0319. A Valparaíso institution: restaurant-cum-museum, famous for its *chorrillanas*, and for being open when everything else is not. Not to be missed unless you are vegetarian.

♥ **Empanadas Famosas's de Adali**, S Donoso 1381, T032-222 7497. Among the best *empanadas* in Valparaíso. Wide range of fillings available.

♥ **Gioco**, Molina 586-B (in a yoga centre). No sign. Excellent-value vegetarian set lunches with fruit juices.

♥ **San Carlos**, Las Heras y Independencia. Traditional family-run restaurant with lots of character that hasn't changed in years. Lunch only. Good food guaranteed. Always full of locals. Recommended.

Cafés

Bogarín, Plaza Victoria 1670. Great juices and good sandwiches and ice cream.

Plaza O'Higgins and further east
p123, map p122

♥♥♥ **Portofino**, Bellamar 301, Cerro Esperanza (above Caleta Portales), T032-262 9939. Fine restaurant with excellent views. One of the best traditional restaurants in Valparaíso. The *tártaro de avestruz* is worth a try. Take *colectivo* 6 from Plaza Victoria.

♥♥♥-♥♥ **Caleta Portales**, Av España s/n, T032-262 5814, www.restaurantcaleta portales.cl. Good seafood restaurant on the road to Viña. There are several other restaurants nearby, mostly ♥♥.

♥♥♥ **La Otra Cocina**, Yungay 2250. Seafood specialities, cosy, good food and service.

♥♥♥-♥ **La Mangiata**, Rodríguez 538, off Pedro Montt. Italian, simple decor, very good food.

♥ **El Rincón de Pancho**, Mercado Cardonal, Yungay y Rawson, 2nd floor. Best of the cheap seafood eateries in this market.

♥ **La Puerta del Sol**, Pedro Montt 2033, T032-223 5158. Traditional Chilean dishes, great chips are served outside.

Cafés

Hesperia, Victoria 2250. A classic old-time coffee emporium with huge comfy bar stools.

South of Valparaíso *p125*

El Galeón restaurant in Laguna Verde serves good simple food. In Quintay try the local speciality *congrio arriero* (fish stew with chips on top!) at any of the reasonably priced restaurants on the harbour (**Miramar** is especially recommended for its huge portions, fresh fish and good service.)

⏿ Bars and clubs

Plaza Sotomayor and El Puerto
p119, map p120

This area can be dangerous at night.

Liberty, Almte Rivero 9, Plaza Echaurren. A real dingy old-timers' bar, where you can see local characters drinking and singing all day. Good cheap food is served.

Pagano, Blanco 236, El Puerto. 80s music and 'anything-goes' atmosphere.

Playa, Serrano 567. An old-fashioned bar, similar to **Bar Inglés** (see Eating), but cheaper, frequented by students and run by slightly snooty staff. There are several bars attracting a similar crowd nearby.

Proa Al Canaveral, Errázuriz 304. Seafood restaurant downstairs, bar upstairs with dancing from 0100, poetry reading on Thu, Latin pop music, mostly students.

Playa Ancha and around *p120*

Bar Roma, Av Playa Ancha. The unofficial drinking hole of the crazy students from the university down the street.

Around Cerros Alegre and
Concepción *p121, map p120*
Axe Bahía, Errázuriz 1084. Cuban *salsoteca*.
El Cielo, Errázuriz 1152. Disco for the
techno-pop generation.
Hotel Brighton (see Sleeping, above) has
a small bar with live music at weekends
2300 to 0300. There are also good bars at
Cinzano and Bar Inglés (see Eating, above).
La Piedra Feliz, Errázuriz 1054. Incorporates
3 areas, each with different decor: a large
pub, a live music area and a dance floor,
serving up everything from jazz to salsa,
bossanova and tango depending on the
evening, entrance US$9.
Poblenou, Urriola 476, Cerro Alegre,
T032-2495245. Open Sun. Intimate wine
bar serving tapas and other snacks.
Vinilo, Almte Montt 448, Cerro Alegre. Café/
bar attracting a friendly 20-30-something
crowd, good place to meet locals and
travellers. Extensive vinyl collection, occasional
live music at weekends. Serves food.

Plaza de la Victoria and around
p123, maps p120 and p122
There are many bars on Subida Ecuador,
but be careful which ones you go into, as in
some of them you risk being eaten alive (only
enter **El Muro**, for example, if you are into
methylated spirits and the sordid elements of
life). **El Coyote Quemado** is by far the best.
El Huevo, Blanco 1386. One of Valparaíso's
most popular nightspots with 3 levels of
dancing and drinking.
El Irlandés, Blanco 1279, T032-259 3675.
Irish-owned pub with a huge variety of
bottled beer as well as bitter and stout from
Britain and Ireland on draught. Live music at
weekends. Good fun.

✪ Entertainment

Valparaíso *p117, maps p120 and p122*
It is worth checking out the 'Invite'
supplement, inside the *Mercurio de
Valparaíso* every Fri.

Cinema
Cinehoyts, Pedro Montt 2111, T032-594709.
Mainstream movies, most from Hollywood.
**Instituto Chileno-Norteamericano de
Cultura** (see below) also shows films, as do
smaller film clubs. The 'Invite' supplement,
inside the *Mercurio de Valparaíso* every Fri
has details of these.

Galleries
In addition to the Galería de Arte Municipal
and the Museo Municipal de Bellas Artes,
occasional free exhibitions are held at the
following galleries:
Cámara Lúcida, Subida Concepción 281,
Cerro Concepción, www.camaralucida.cl.
Photographic exhibitions and workshops.
Consejo de Cultura, Prat and Plaza
Sotomayor. Housed in the former post
office building. Temporary exhibitions
in the basement.
Cult-Art, Almte Montt y Galos, Cerro Alegre.
Contemporary art by local artists.
Fundación Valparaíso, Héctor Calvo, Cerro
Bellavista (between La Sebastiana and ascen-
sor Espíritu Santo). Local contemporary art.
Instituto Chileno-Norteamericano,
Esmeralda 1069. Temporary exhibitions of
photos and paintings from all over Chile.
Sala El Farol, Blanco 1113, El Plan. Art gallery
attached to the Universidad de Valparaíso
with interesting temporary exhibitions.
Wenteche, Templeman 523, Cerro Concep-
ción. Features work by Valparaíso artists.

✪ Festivals and events

Valparaíso *p117, maps p120 and p122*
New Year Celebrated by a 3-day festival
culminating in a superb 40-min firework
display on the bay, which is best seen from
the *cerros*. Over a million visitors and locals
take supper and champagne to celebrate
from vantage points around the bay.
Accommodation can double or even
triple in price at this time and needs
to be booked well in advance.

O Shopping

Valparaíso *p117, maps p120 and p122*
Books
CRISIS, Pedro Montt by the bus terminal. An excellent new and second-hand bookshop.
Cummings no 1, Cumming 1, just off Plaza Aníbal Pinto. Wide selection of new and used books in English and other languages.
Librería Ivens, Plaza Aníbal Pinto. The oldest bookshop in Valparaíso with periodicals in English, French and German, and lots of literature about the city and its history.
Librería Universitaria, Esmeralda 1132. Good selection of regional history.

Crafts

Handicraft shops on the quay are expensive and poor quality. There are several small workshops on *cerros* Alegre and Concepción selling interesting handmade objects:
Design for Valparaíso, Concepción 154, Cerro Concepción. Small textile workshop.
Taller Antiquina, San Enrique y Templeman, Cerro Alegre. Good-quality rustic leather goods ranging from chairs to tea coasters.
Valarte, Pasaje Fischer 68, off Pasaje Gálvez, Cerro Concepción. Glass ornaments as well as paintings in the naïve style.
Victor Hugo, Pasaje Templeman y C Templeman, Cerro Concepción. Silver and lapis lazuli jewellery.

Department stores
Falabella and **Ripley**, both by the Plaza Victoria.

Markets
The fruit and veg market on Av Argentina, Wed and Sat, is colourful and worth a visit; a flea market is held on the same site on Sun. There is also a large antiques market around Plaza O'Higgins on Sun mornings.

▲ Activities and tours

Valparaíso *p117, maps p120 and p122*
A number of tour companies have cropped up recently offering city tours, but it is hard to say if any will last the distance. The best advice is to ask at the place you are staying, but bear in mind that your hosts may recommend the operator that pays the highest commission.

Boat trips
Launches run trips around the harbour from Muelle Prat, 30 mins, US$2.80 per person or US$18 to hire an entire boat, offering a pleasant view of the city, especially when it is sunny. Beware that groups of foreign tourists are liable to be overcharged. Other boats can be hired for fishing. Don't photograph naval ships or installations.

Diving
Austral Divers, Caleta Quintay, T09-9885 5099, www.australdivers.cl. Diving courses and trips for qualified divers.

Horse riding
Ritoque Expediciones, north of Concón, T032-281 6344, www.ritoqueexpediciones.cl. Excellent day trips over a variety of terrain. Galloping encouraged. Also night time rides under the full moon. Recommended. Pickup service from Valparaíso and Viña del Mar.

Kayaking
El Puerto Deportivo, at the Muelle Barón, T032-2592852, www.puertodeportivo.cl, rents sea kayaks by the hour. Also guided tours.

Skiing
Valposki, T09-842 83502, www.valposki.cl. Regular day-trips to El Colorado, Farellones and La Parva ski resorts.

Wine tours
Wine Tours Valparaíso, www.winetours valparaiso.cl. Small-group tours to the Casablanca valley with an English-speaking guide.

⊖ Transport

Valparaíso p117, maps p120 and p122
Air
Santiago airport is 1½ hrs away. A taxi will cost around US$95. To get to Valparaíso from the airport by public transport take the airport bus going to Santiago and get off at the Pajaritos station on the outskirts of the city, from where there are direct buses to Valparaíso and Viña. The total journey time is around 2 hrs, cost about US$10 per person. LanChile, Esmeralda 1048, T600-562 2000, www.lan.com.

Ascensores
Half of Valparaíso's *ascensores* are municipally run and very cheap at US$0.20 per journey; the privately run *ascensores* can charge up to 3 times more. Sometimes you pay on entrance, sometimes on exit.

Bus
Buses and trolley buses, US$0.50 within El Plan, US$0.65 to the *cerros*. There are plenty of buses between the long-distance terminal and Plaza Sotomayor.

Local An excellent and incredibly frequent bus and *colectivo* service from Plaza Aduana, passes along Av Errázuriz to **Viña del Mar**, 20 mins, $0.80. Buses serving **Lago Peñuelas**, **Isla Negra** and **San Antonio** leave every 30 mins from the main terminal, US$5.

Long distance The terminal is at Pedro Montt y Rawson, 1 block from Av Argentina. To **Santiago**, frequent, 1¾ hrs, US$6-8; shop around for the best prices, book return in advance on long weekends and other public holidays. There are also daily services to the following destinations: to **Chillán**, 7 hrs, US$16; to **Concepción**, 8 hrs, US$17; to **Pucón**, 12 hrs, US$22-35; to **Puerto Varas** and **Puerto Montt**, 14 hrs, US$25-44; to **La Serena**, 7 hrs, US$14-28; to **Antofagasta**, 17 hrs, US$40-60; to **San Pedro de Atacama**, 24 hrs, US$50-75; to **Arica**, 30 hrs, US$50-75. La Porteña and Intercomunal run several buses daily north leaving from the Plaza

Victoria to **Pichidangui** and **Los Vilos**, Intercomunal continuing on to **Illapel** and **Salamanca**, although it may be easier to catch any bus to **La Calera** from Errázuriz/ Brasil (every few minutes) and make a connection there.

To Argentina To **Mendoza**, 5 companies, 8 hrs, US$17, leaving early morning. Also overnight service summer only, **Pluma**, continuing on Tue, Fri and Sun to **Buenos Aires**, **Florianopolis**, **São Paulo** and **Rio**. To **Córdoba**, Tas Choapa, daily, US$55.

Car
Car hire from **Automecánica Colón**, Colón 2581, T032-225 6529, www.automecanica colon.cl; **Suzuval**, Colón 2537, T032-225 5505, www.suzuval.cl; many more options in Viña.

Ferry
For boat services from Valparaíso to the Juan Fernández Islands, see page 557.

Taxi
Colectivos, which pickup and set down passengers anywhere en route, operate along the same routes as buses and offer a cheap and quick form of transport. Taxis are more expensive than Santiago.

Train
Regular service on **Merval**, the Valparaíso metropolitan line, to **Viña del Mar**, every 10 mins, 15 mins, US$0.70, and on to **Quilpué** and **Limache**. A special card is needed to travel, which can be purchased at any station.

South of Valparaíso p125
Bus No 120 to **Laguna Verde** can be caught from Pedro Montt via Playa Ancha every 40 mins, 40 mins, US$1.20. A yellow *colectivo* from C 12 de Febrero behind the bus terminal in Valparaíso runs to **Quintay**; it won't go until it's full, but if you're in a hurry you can pay for the extra seats, 45 mins, US$2.20. Buses to Quintay leave from the corner of 12 de Febrero and Yungay.

Parque Nacional La Campana *p125*
The entrances at **Granizo** (paradero 45) and
Cajón Grande (paradero 41) are reached by
local bus/*colectivo* from outside Limache's
train station. There is no public transport to
the entrance at **Palmar de Ocoa** to the north;
bargain with *colectivo*/taxi drivers in La Calera,
expect to pay around US$20-25 for the trip,
arrange return transport if necessary.

⊙ Directory

Valparaíso *p117, maps p120 and p122*
Banks Banks open 0900-1400, closed on
Sat; many Redbanc ATMs on Prat, also one
in the bus terminal; best exchange rates from
Marin Orrego, 3rd floor of the stock exchange
building, Prat y Urriola, only changes US$
and euro cash; for other currencies, there are
several *casas de cambio* along Prat and
Esmeralda. **Consulates** Argentina, Blanco
890, of 204, T032-221 3691; Belgium, Prat
827, piso 12, T032-221 3494; Bolivia, Serrano
579, T032-225 9906; Brazil, Blanco 951, piso 2,
T032-221 7856; Denmark, Errázuriz 940,
T032-226 8379; Ecuador, Blanco Encalada
1623, of 1740, T032-222 2167; Germany,
Blanco 1215, of 1102, T032-225 6749;
Norway, Freire 657, T032-225 2219; Panama,
Blanco 1623, of 1103, T032-22 13592; Peru,
Errázuriz 1178, of 71, T032-225 3403; Spain,
Brasil 1589, piso 2, T032-221 4466; Sweden,
Errázuriz 940, T032-225 0305; UK, Blanco
1199, piso 5, T/F032-221 3063. **Internet**
There are dozens, scattered all over El Plan;
in Cerro Alegre, on Templeman y Urriola.
Language schools Escuela Español
Interactivo, Elias 571, Cerro Carcel,
www.interactive-spanish.cl; Natalislang,
Plaza de la Justicia 45, piso 6, El Plan,
T032-246 9936, www.natalislang.com.
Laundry Las Heras 554, good and
cheap. **Medical services** Hospital Van
Buren, Colón y San Ignacio, El Plan, T032-220
4000, public hospital, for emergencies.
Most private hospitals are in Viña del Mar.
Post office North side of Pedro Montt,
between San Ignacio and Bolívar. Also
on Prat, east of the Plaza Sotomayor.
Telephone There are cheap call
centres all over the plan and a couple
on *cerros* Alegre and Concepción.

Viña del Mar and around

→ Colour map 3, A/B2.

Nine kilometres northeast of Valparaíso via the Avenida España, which runs along a narrow belt between the shore and precipitous cliffs, is Viña del Mar, one of South America's leading seaside resorts. Viña is also famous throughout Chile for its annual international music festival, during which the attention of the entire country is focused on the city; the festival used to bring in some top performers from all over Latin America, but this is no longer the case. In fact, neither the festival nor Viña itself are as wonderful as Chileans like to make out. This is the only place in Chile where road signs are in English as well as Spanish and much of the city feels like suburban North America. That said, with pleasant beaches and shady parks, Viña is a nice enough city to visit, especially if you have some pesos to burn, and makes an interesting contrast to nearby Valparaíso.

North of Viña strung along the coast are several smaller settlements. Reñaca, now a suburb of Viña del Mar, is a well-to-do resort with extensive beaches, while further north, Maitencillo and Zapallar are fashionable seaside destinations, overflowing with tourists in summer. In between are the fishing towns of Concón, famous for its seafood, and Horcón, where horses are still used to tow the fishing boats onto land. ⟩⟩ For listings, see pages 138-143.

Ins and outs

Getting there There are inter-urban buses to Viña del Mar from many cities. The city also has daily connections through to Mendoza in Argentina. Viña del Mar can also be reached relatively easy by public transport from Santiago's airport. ⟩⟩ *See Transport, page 143.*

Getting around Frequent *micros* link Viña and Valparaíso from Libertad or 1 Norte. *Colectivos* also serve these routes, as well as running to many of the city's outlying neighbourhoods and there are numerous buses along the coast. Taxis are plentiful and usually reasonably priced.

Tourist information Sernatur ① *Valparaíso 507, of 303, T032-268 3355, info valparaiso@sernatur.cl.* The municipal tourist office is on the corner of Plaza Vergara and can arrange the rental of private homes in the summer season; there's also a kiosk on calle Valparaíso y Villanelo.

Viña del Mar ⬤🅰🅱🅲🅳❋🅾▲🅱🅲 *pp138-143.*

The older part of Viña del Mar is situated on the banks of a creek, the Marga Marga, which is crossed by bridges. Around Plaza Vergara and the smaller Plaza Sucre are the **Teatro Municipal** (1930) and the exclusive **Club de Viña**, built in 1910. It's a private club, but sometimes hosts public concerts and events. The municipally owned **Quinta Vergara**, formerly the residence of the shipping entrepreneur Francisco Alvarez, lies two blocks further south. The superb grounds include a double avenue of palm trees and encompass a children's playground and a large outdoor amphitheatre where the music festival takes place in February; it also hosts concerts and events throughout the year. Also here is the **Palacio Vergara** ① *T032-268 0618, Tue-Sun 1000-1400, 1500-1800, US$1,* which houses the **Museo de Bellas Artes** and the **Academia de Bellas Artes**. You can take a tour of the city in a horse-drawn carriage from the Plaza Vergara for around US$30 depending on the length of the trip.

Calle Libertad runs north from the plaza, lined with banks, offices and shops. At the junction with 4 Norte is the **Palacio Carrasco**, now a cultural centre housing temporary exhibitions. In the same grounds is the **Museo Fonck** ① *Calle 4 Norte 784, www.museofonck.cl, Mon-Fri 1000-1800, Sat and Sun 1000-1400, US$3*, an interesting archaeological museum, with objects from Easter Island and the Chilean mainland, including Mapuche silver. East of this is the **Palacio Rioja** ① *Quillota 214, T032-689665, Tue-Sun 1000-1400, 1500-1800*, built in 1906 by a prominent local family and now used for official municipal receptions. The ground floor is preserved in its original state and is well worth a visit. Four blocks further east is the **Valparaíso Sporting Club** with a racecourse and playing fields, while to the north, in the hills is the **Estadio Sausalito**, home to Everton football club.

West of the plaza, on a headland overlooking the sea, is **Cerro Castillo**, the president's summer palace; its gardens can be visited. Below, on the coast, Castillo Wulff houses the **Museo de la Cultura del Mar** ① *T032-262542, Tue-Sat 1000-1300, 1430-1800, Sun 1000-1400*, which contains a collection devoted to the life and work of the novelist and maritime historian, Salvador Reyes. Just north, on the other side of the Marga Marga, is

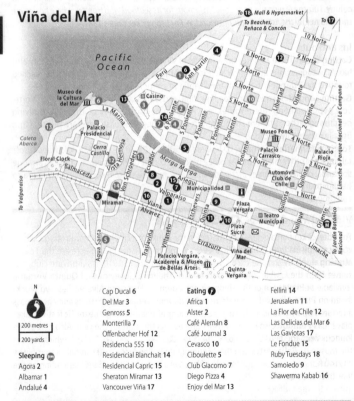

Viña del Mar

	Cap Ducal **6**	**Eating** 🍴
	Del Mar **3**	Africa **1**
	Genross **5**	Alster **2**
N	Monterilla **7**	Café Alemán **8**
	Offenbacher Hof **12**	Café Journal **3**
200 metres	Residencia 555 **10**	Cevasco **10**
200 yards	Residencial Blanchait **14**	Ciboulette **5**
	Residencial Capric **15**	Club Giacomo **7**
Sleeping 🛏	Sheraton Miramar **13**	Diego Pizza **4**
Agora **2**	Vancouver Viña **17**	Enjoy del Mar **13**
Albamar **1**		
Andalué **4**		

Fellini **14**
Jerusalem **11**
La Flor de Chile **12**
Las Delicias del Mar **6**
Las Gaviotas **17**
Le Fondue **15**
Ruby Tuesdays **18**
Samoiedo **9**
Shawerma Kabab **16**

the **casino** ① *open all year, US$2.50*, completely rebuilt after a recent fire and set in beautiful gardens. North of this are the main beaches, Acapulco and Las Salinas (see below), while south of Cerro Castillo is another popular beach at **Caleta Abarca**.

Jardín Botánico Nacional ① *8 km southeast of the city, www.jardin-botanico.cl, US$1.80, bus 203 from Calle Alvarez, get off at the puente El Olivar, cross the bridge and walk 15 minutes*. This was formerly the estate of the nitrate magnate Pascual Baburizza and is now administered by CONAF. Covering 405 ha, it contains over 3000 species from all over the world and is a good picnic spot. Within the gardens is a large collection of Chilean cacti; it's very pretty, but unfortunately the different species are not labelled. There is also a canopy adventure tourism site with ziplines linking trees within the park.

Resorts north of Viña del Mar ⊖🏀🏍❀▲● *pp138-143*.

Reñaca and Cochoa

North of Viña del Mar the coast road runs past **Las Salinas**, a popular beach set between two towering crags. The suburb of **Reñaca** is a popular resort with access to excellent beaches, while to the north at **Cochoa**, there are giant sand dunes and a large sea lion colony 100 m offshore. This route affords lovely views over the sea, but there is also a much faster inland road between Reñaca and Concón.

Concón

Concón lies on the southern shore of a bay 18 km north of Viña del Mar at the mouth of the Río Aconcagua. The town claims to be the oldest settlement in Chile, having been founded by Pedro de Valdivia in 1541, prior to his arrival at what is now Santiago. Concón is famous for its restaurants and is known as the culinary capital of the V region. The area is very popular among Santiaguinos, who often come here for the weekend. A series of six beaches stretches along the bay between Caleta Higuerilla at the western end and La Boca at the eastern end. These beaches include **Playa Amarilla**, which is good for sunbathing; the very peaceful **Playa Higuerillas**, where there are lots of shells; **Playa Los Lilenes**, backed by sand dunes, and **Playa La Boca** itself, which is by far the largest of the six, and excellent for beach sports (horses US$5 for 30 mins; also kayaks for hire). The helpful **tourist office** ① *annexed to the municipal museum, Maroto 1030, www.concon.cl*, can provide maps of the resort.

Quintero

Another 23 km north of Concón, Quintero is a dilapidated fishing town situated around a rocky peninsula with 16 small beaches, all of varying character and quality. The path running along the north side of the peninsula offers a good view of the sunset over the ocean from the Cueva del Pirata at its western end. Good fishing and windsurfing are available at **Playas Loncura** and **Ritoque** to the south of the town, while horses can be hired on **Playa Albatros**. Note that there are many touts and beggars in Quintero in the high season, when the atmosphere can become a little tense. On the opposite side of the bay is **Las Ventanas**, where a power station and copper processing plant rather spoil the outlook from the beach.

Horcón

Set back in a cove surrounded by cliffs, Horcón, also known locally as Horcones, is a pleasant small village, mainly of wooden houses. Although overcrowded in season, during the rest of the year it is a charming place, populated by fishermen and artists, with a tumbledown feel unlike the more well-to-do resorts to the north and south. Across the headland to the south of the village is **Playa Cau Cau**; scramble down a steep flight of log steps to reach the sandy, frequently deserted, tree-lined cove, sadly now dominated by a condominium development.

Maitencillo

Maitencillo, 19 km north of Las Ventanas, is an upmarket resort consisting mainly of chalets and frequented mainly by well-to-do Santiaguinos. There is a wonderful long beach here but the sea is notorious for its strong undercurrents. It is usually deserted off season.

Zapallar

A fashionable resort with a lovely beach, 33 km north of Las Ventanas, Zapallar is an expensive place to stay. The number of fine mansions along Avenida Zapallar are a clue to its luxurious heritage. At **Cachagua**, 3 km south, there are clear views of a colony of penguins on an offshore island from the northern end of the beach; take binoculars.

Papudo

Ten kilometres further north is the site of a naval battle in November 1865, in which the Chilean vessel *Esmeralda* captured the Spanish ship *Covadonga* during the War of Independence. Following the arrival of the railway Papudo rivalled Viña del Mar as a fashionable resort but it has declined a great deal since its heyday in the 1920s. Among the buildings surviving from that period is the **Casa Rawlings**, now the Casa de la Cultura. There are two fine beaches, which are empty except in high summer.

◉ Viña del Mar and around listings

For Sleeping and Eating price codes and other relevant information, see Essentials pages 35-42.

◉ Sleeping

Viña del Mar *p135, map p136*
There are a great many more places to stay in addition to those listed here, particularly in the **AL-A** range, although many are in the business district and not convenient for the beaches. In season, it is generally cheaper to stay in Valparaíso and commute to the beaches around Viña. Note that during the music festival in Feb, accommodation is almost impossible to find. Out of season, furnished apartments can be rented through agencies (with commission).
LL Hotel del Mar, Av Perú y Los Héroes, casino complex, T032-250 0600, www.hoteldelmar.cl. Very expensive luxurious hotel on the upper floors of the casino. Panoramic views. suites, pool, spa, tours, several restaurants.
LL Sheraton Miramar, Av Marina N 15, T032-283 8799, www.starwoodhotels.com. Viña's newest upmarket hotel with exceptional views as well as a swimming pool, gym and restaurant.
L-AL Cap Ducal, Av de la Marina 51, T032-262 6655, www.capducal.cl. Ship-shaped building literally overhanging the sea. Recommended for its unique style and location. Services are also reasonable although the place could do with a revamp. There is a good restaurant at street level.
AL Monterilla, 2 Norte 65, T032-297 6950, www.monterilla.cl. Unpretentious clean carpeted rooms with flat-screen TV and Wi-Fi. Some have king-size beds. Friendly service, some English spoken.
A Agora, 5½ Poniente 253, T032-269 4669, www.hotelagora.cl. On a quiet side street.

Brightly coloured clean rooms, most with full size bath tub. Wi-Fi in all rooms, English spoken, friendly staff. 4 floors but no lifts. A good choice.

A Albamar, San Martín 419, T032-297 5274, www.hotelalbamar.cl. Standard hotel with little charm but well located. Cheaper rooms are on the small side.

A Andalué, 6 Poniente 124, T032-268 4147, www.hotelandalue.cl. Good location, decent carpeted rooms. Restaurant downstairs and heated pool on the roof. Good value.

A-B Genross, Paseo Monterrey 18, off Agua Santa, T032-266 1711, genrosshotel@hotmail.com. Located in a beautiful old mansion, clean airy rooms with bath, garden patio and sitting room, very friendly and informative, homely atmosphere, good breakfast, Canadian-Chilean owned, recommended. Closed in winter.

A-B Offenbacher Hof, Balmaceda 102, Cerro Castillo, T032-262 1483, www.offenbacher-hof.cl. Large wooden house in a quiet residential district overlooking the city centre. The best rooms, with bath and cable TV, are spacious and have views. Good breakfast served on a bright terrace, German and some English spoken. Service a little terse but still recommended.

B Residencia 555, 5 Norte 555, T032-297 2240, residencial555@vtr.net. **C** singles Characterful wooden house with antique furniture. Rooms ranging widely in size have bath and cable TV. Good value. Advance reservations difficult as a deposit is required but credit cards not accepted.

B Vancouver Viña, 5 Norte 650, T032-248 2983, www.hotelvancouvervina.cl. Clean carpeted modest rooms with bath and cable TV. Room 12 is the nicest. Friendly, good value. Also cafetería downstairs. There are 2 similar hotels opposite.

There are lots of cheap *residenciales* around the junction of Von Schroeders and Valparaíso, but this is the red-light district and is particularly insalubrious at night. The best options here are probably the following:

C Residencial Blanchait, Valparaíso 82A, T032-297 4949, www.blanchait.cl. **D-E** singles. Some rooms with bath. Clean, good service. Breakfast extra.

C Residencial Capric, von Schroeders 39, T032-297 8295, hcapricvina@hostelling.cl. **E-F** per person in shared rooms. Run-down rooms with bath and TV, breakfast included, special rates for YHA members.

Reñaca p137

Accommodation here is much cheaper out of season.

L-AL Montecarlo, V MacKenna 136, T032-2830397, www.montecarlo.cl. Comfortable if slightly dated style. Many rooms with sea view.

AL Cabañas Don Francisco, Torreblanca 75, T032-283 4802, cabanasdonfransisco@gmail.com. Helpful service, *cabañas* only available for week-long bookings.

AL Oceanic, Av Borgoño 12925, T032-283 0006, www.hoteloceanic.cl. Comfortable, spacious slightly dated rooms dramatically set on the ocean front. It is worth paying the extra for an ocean-facing room – for the views and also to escape the street noise. Good restaurant (mostly seafood).

AL Piero's, Av Central y Segunda, T032-283 0280, www.pieroshotel.cl. Comfortable, with café, pool, some rooms with sea view.

Concón p137

AL Hostería Edelweiss, Av Borgoño 19200, T032-281 4043, www.edelweiss.cl. Modern *cabañas* sleeping 2-6, clean, sea views, pool, kitchenette (cheaper cabins without), including breakfast, excellent food in attached restaurant, German spoken. Recommended.

B Cabañas Los Romeros, T032-281 3671. Cabins for up to 3 people.

B Cabañas Río Mar, T/F032-281 4644. Many other *cabañas* in this price range.

Camping

Mantagua, 3 km north, T032-811415, www.mantagua.cl. Well equipped but very expensive, also *cabañas*.

Quintero p137

There are lots of cheap *residenciales* here.
A-B Yachting Club, Luis Acevedo 1736, T032-293 0061, www.nhotelq.cl. Hotel with pool and large gardens on the seafront.
C Residencial Brazilian, 21 de Mayo 1336, T032-293 0590, anasatt@yahoo.com. With breakfast, large windows but no view, clean, well maintained, warm sea-water baths for US$6.

Horcón p137

There are many *cabañas* around the village; shop around for the best price, especially off season. Rooms are also available in private houses and, although there's no campsite, camping is possible in people's gardens.
C Cabañas Arancibia, T032-279 6169. Cabins with or without bath, pleasant gardens, good food, friendly. Recommended.
C El Ancla, by the harbour, T032-279 6017. Pleasant *cabañas*, also serves good food.
C Juan Esteban, Pasaje Miramar, Casa 2, T032-279 6056, www.juanesteban.cl. **E** singles. English, Portuguese and Italian spoken, nice terrace with view. Recommended. Also fully equipped *cabañas* (**A**) for 4 people.

Maitencillo p138

LL Marbella Resort, 2 km south, T032-277 2020, www.marbella.cl. 5-star resort, conference centre, restaurants, golf course, tennis courts, pools, and everything else you would expect.
AL-B Cabañas La Mar, Av del Mar 524, T032-277 1036. One of several options in this price range.

Zapallar p138

Accommodation is expensive especially in the centre where it is sparse. There's no campsite.
LL-L Isla Seca, T033-741224, www.hotel islaseca.com. Small, with pool and very expensive suites, good restaurant.
A-B Residencial Villa Alicia, Moisés Chacón 280, T033-741176. Good, and one of the cheapest.

Papudo p138

There are several cheap *residenciales* on Chorillos 100-150.
A Carande, Chorrillos 89, T033-791105, www.hotelcarande.cl. Best in town.
A De Peppino, No 609, T033-791108. *Cabañas* for 4-6 people.

🍴 Eating

Viña del Mar p135, map p136
There are dozens of restaurants in the triangle formed by San Martín, 5 Poniente and 2 Norte, ranging from Mexican to Italian, Austrian, Argentinian and Chinese.
TTT Cap Ducal, in the Cap Ducal hotel (see above). Good seafood, elegant surroundings, excellent views.
TTT Ciboulette, 1 Norte 191, T032-269 0084. Intimate Belgian-owned and run bistro serving traditional French cuisine. Good wine list.
TTT Savinya, Peru 199. Elegant restaurant above the casino.
TTT-TT Diego Pizza, San Martín y 8 Norte, T032-226 81105. Good pizzas but overpriced. Home-delivery service.
TTT-TT Enjoy del Mar, Av Peru s/n, T032-250 0785. Modern restaurant serving everything from gourmet dishes to barbeques and fast food, all on an open terrace on the seafront.
TTT-TT Fellini, 3Norte 88, T032-297 5742. Wide range of fresh pasta in delicious sauces.
TTT-TT Las Delicias del Mar, San Martín 459. Traditional Basque seafood restaurant. Slightly hackneyed menus but good nevertheless.
TTT-TT Ruby Tuesdays, in the mall, 14 Norte. For those of you who can't do without a US-style sports bar.
TT Las Gaviotas, 14 Norte 1248. Chilean meat dishes, inexpensive.
T Africa, Valparaíso 324. Extraordinarily kitsch façade, cheap lunches with a wide range of dishes including soups and salads.
T Café Alemán, Arlegui 228. Good set lunch.
T Café Journal, Agua Santa y Alvarez. Excellent-value set lunch. Recommended.

Cevasco, Valparaíso 700, on the corner of Plaza Vergara. Super-sized fast food. Similar at El Guatón next door.

Club Giacomo, Villanelo 131. A Viña institution. Traditional set lunches with a pool hall annex.

Jerusalem, Quinta 259. Excellent falafel to eat in or take away.

La Flor de Chile, 8 Norte 607 y 1 poniente. Good, typically Chilean food.

Le Fondue, Arlegui 394. Cheap dishes including vegetarian options. Doubles as a bar at night with occasional poetry readings.

Shawerma Kabab, Ecuador 255. Kebabs, stuffed vine leaves and other Arabic specialities.

Cafés

Alster, Valparaíso 225. Elegant, but pricey.

Enjoy Cafe, Av Peru by the casino. Bright café on the seafront. Live jazz outside Sat evenings.

Samoiedo, Valparaíso 637. Old-time café.

Reñaca p137

Hotel Oceanic, see Sleeping. Very good, mostly seafood.

Rincón Marino, Av Borgoño 17120. Good seafood.

El Pancho, Av Borgoño 16180. Excellent seafood and service.

Concón p137

Seafood is the name of the game here. Both Caleta Higuerilla and La Boca are renowned for their restaurants.

Among the most upmarket are located along Av Borgoño, 1 side fronting onto the road, the other onto the beach, including the following in Caleta Higuerilla: **Albatross**, No 21295; **Aquí Jaime**, No 21303; **Bellamar**, No 21505; **Don Chico**, No 21410; **Edelweiss**, No 19200; and **Vista al Mar**, No 21270.

Mid-range options include La Picá de Emeterio, and Las Deliciosas, both on Borgoño in La Boca, while cheaper eateries are to be found in Alto Higuerillas, where *picadas* have been converted by the fishermen into good-value restaurants:

try La Cava de Franz, San Pedro 345; La Picá de Juan Segura, Illapel 15; La Picá El Horizonte, San Pedro 120, and La Picá Los Delfines, San Pedro 130. Look out, too, for tasty seafood *empanadas* served in the resort's bars.

Quintero p137

There are several cheap seafood restaurants down by the harbour.

Horcón p137

Seafood lunches made from the catch of the day are sold at stalls on the seafront, where there also a number of restaurants.

Bahía. Good food, pleasant atmosphere.

El Ancla. Recommended.

Santa Clara. Try the *chupe de mariscos* (cheesy shellfish soup) and *pastel de jaivas* (crabmeat cooked in cheese and breadcrumbs). Recommended.

Reina Victoria. Cheap and good quality.

Roty Schop. Acclaimed for its *empanadas*.

Maitencillo p138

Bar Rest La Canasta, Av del Mar 592. Mediterranean and Moroccan cuisine served in elegant surroundings; expensive but worth it.

Bar Tsunami, Av del Mar 1366. Mid-range seafood.

Café Entre Rocas, Av del Mar s/n. Good drinks and snacks.

Zapallar p138

Isla Seca, see Sleeping, above. Expensive, excellent seafood.

La Culebra. Cheap eaterie.

Los Troncos. Good-value grub.

Natón, Cachagua, south of Zapallar. Cheap restaurant with disco.

Papudo p138

Cava del Mar. Pricey international cuisine.

Gran Azul. Expensive seafood.

La Abeja. Mid-range.

La Maison des Fous, Blanco 151. Unusual bar-restaurant in lovely old house. Friendly

staff, good food and atmospheric candle-lit piano bar with graffiti-covered pillars.
♥ **Don Rota**. Cheap seafood.

🍷 Bars and clubs

Viña del Mar p135, map p136
There are dozens of bars and clubs in the triangle formed by San Martín, 5 Poniente and 2 Norte. They tend to change name and style every other year.
Barlovento, 2 Norte y 5 Poniente. The designer bar in Viña, set over 3 floors with a roof terrace, serves great pizzas and good beer.
Café Journal, Agua Santa y Alvarez. Good beer. Full of students at night.
Oh! Cerveza, 7 Norte y 3 Poniente. Wide variety of draught beer.
Sikaru, 3 Poniente 660. Huge range of bottled beers from all over the world. Also serves pizzas and snacks.
Twister, Av Borgoño. One of many discos. Also try **Kamikaze** and **Neverland** east of town.

Reñaca p137
El Ciervo, Av Central y Segunda. Bar/café with live music in evenings. Recommended.

Papudo p138
Help, Glorias Navales 409. Disco with music from techno to salsa.
La Maison des Fous, see Eating, above.

🎭 Entertainment

Viña del Mar p135, map p136
Cinemas
Cine Arte, Plaza Vergara 42. Also a multiplex in the shopping mall on Libertad (see Shopping, below).

Galleries
Fodigliani, 5 Norte 168.

Mar Pau, Valparaíso 595, local 18.
Palacio Carrasco, Libertad 250.
Sala de Arte Viña del Mar, Arlegui 683.

🎪 Festivals and events

Viña del Mar p135, map p136
Feb Festival Internacional de la Canción, which attracts an audience from all over Chile. Tickets are available from the Municipalidad and should be bought ahead of time; you should also reserve any accommodation well in advance.

Resorts north of Viña del Mar p137
29 Jun Since this area comprises coastal communities, it is no surprise that the Fiesta de San Pedro (the patron saint of fishermen) is an important event.

🛍 Shopping

Viña del Mar p135, map p136
The **market** is held on Wed and Sat at the intersection of Av Sporting and the river. There is a large **mall** on Libertad between 14 and 15 Norte, open till 2300.
La Vinoteca, San Martín 545 y 6 Norte. Stocks a good range of Chilean wine.

🥾 Activities and tours

Viña del Mar p135, map p136
Bowling
Available in the shopping mall on Libertad y 14 Norte (see Shopping, above).

Maitencillo p138
Paragliding
Parapente Aventura, Maitencillo, T09-9561 0048, www.parapente maitencillo.cl. Single tandem flight, US$70; 13 classes, US$500.

Surfing

Café Entre Rojas, see Eating, above.
Surfing classes and biplane tours
(US$60 for 20 mins).

⊖ Transport

Viña del Mar *p135, map p136*
Air
Santiago airport is 1½ hrs away. A taxi will
cost around US$95.

To get to Viña del Mar from the airport by
public transport take the airport bus going
to Santiago and get off at the Pajaritos
station on the outskirts of the city, from
where there are direct buses to Valparaíso
and Viña. The total journey time is around
2 hrs, cost about US$10 per person.

Airline offices Aerolíneas Argentinas,
Ecuador y Marina, T800-610200,
www.aerolineas.com.ar; Air France, Ecuador
125, T032-271 0976; American, 8 Norte 492,
T032-299 0997; LanChile, Valparaíso 280,
T600-526 2000, www.lan.com; Sky, Ecuador
78, T600-600 2828, www.skyairline.cl.

Bus
The bus terminal is 2 blocks east of Plaza
Vergara at Av Valparaíso y Quilpué. To
Santiago, frequent, 1¾ hrs, many companies,
US$6-8, book in advance for travel on Sun
afternoons; to **Pucón**, 12 hrs, US$22-35;
to **Puerto Varas** and **Puerto Montt**, 14 hrs,
US$25-44; to **La Serena**, 7 hrs, US$14-28;
to **Antofagasta**, 17 hrs, US$40-60; to **San
Pedro de Atacama**, 24 hrs, US$50-75;
to **Arica**, 30 hrs, US$50-75.To **Mendoza**
(Argentina), 5 companies, all leave in the
morning and some also at night in summer,
7 hrs, US$17. Buses north from Valparaíso
for destinations including **La Calera**, **La
Ligua**, **Cabildo**, **Pichidangui** and **Los
Vilos** all pass through Viña, and can be
caught on Libertad.

Car
Car hire from Euro Rent-A-Car, in Hotel
O'Higgins, clean cars, efficient; Flota
Verschae, Libertad 10, T032-226 7300,
www.verschae.cl, good value, recommended;
Hertz, Quillota 766, T032-297 1625;
Rosselot, Libertad 892, T032-238 2373,
www.rosselot.cl, well-regarded nationwide
agency. A recommended car mechanic
is Luis Vallejos, 13 Norte 1228.
Automóvil Club de Chile, 1 Norte 901,
T032-268 9509.

Train
Services on the Valparaíso Metropolitan
line (**Merval**) stop at Viña (see page 133).

Resorts north of Viña del Mar *p137*
Buses run from Av Errázuriz in Valparaíso and
from Av Libertad in Viña del Mar: to **Concón**,
bus 601, very frequent, 20-40 mins, US$0.85;
to **Quintero** and **Horcón**, Sol del Pacífico,
every 30 mins, 2 hrs, US$2; to **Zapallar** and
Papudo, Sol del Pacífico, 4 a day (2 before
0800, 2 after 1600), US$4.

⊕ Directory

Viña del Mar *p135, map p136*
Banks Several *casas de cambio* on calles
Arlegui and Valparaíso; shop around for best
rates, and avoid changing money on the street;
many banks (with ATMs) on Arlegui, Valparaíso
and Libertad; ATMs also in the mall; Western
Union money transfer, Libertad 715 (also has
DHL). **Internet and telephone** Several all
along C Valparaíso. **Post office** North of
Plaza Vergara, by the bridge.

Resorts south of Valparaíso

This cluster of resorts stretches along the coast from the mouth of the Río Maipo north towards Valparaíso. The resorts here are not as upmarket as those north of Viña, but every summer tens of thousands of Chileans flock to them from the capital. Beaches range from classic wide white-sand affairs to secluded coves, and a wild, rocky zone around Isla Negra; off season, most are deserted. ▸▸ For listings, see pages 145-146.

Ins and outs

Road links between Valparaíso and the resorts to the south are poor, but there are two good routes from Santiago: one a branch off the main Santiago–Valparaíso highway to Algarrobo and the other, Route 78, direct to San Antonio. Buses link the resorts in this area, but a hire car will allow you to explore more secluded coves.

San Antonio and around

Situated near the mouth of the Río Maipo, 112 km south of Valparaíso, San Antonio was at the epicentre of a large earthquake in 1985. Subsequently, the harbour was rebuilt and has now taken over from Valparaíso as the main container port for this part of the coast. It is the terminal for the export of copper brought by rail from the large mine at El Teniente, near Rancagua (see page 284) as well as being an important fishing port. Many restaurants buy their fish and seafood here and a visit to the docks just after the catch has been unloaded is an interesting experience. **Museo Municipal de Ciencias Naturales y Arqueología** ① *Av Barros Luco, Mon-Fri 0900-1300, 1500-1900*, has displays on nature, pre-colonial culture and geology. There is also a botanical garden.

Nearby to the south are two resorts: **Llolleo**, 4 km, and 7 km further **Rocas de Santo Domingo**, the most attractive and exclusive resort in this area with 20 km of beaches and a golf course; even in high season it is not very crowded.

Cartagena → *For more information on Cartagena, see www.cartagena.cl.*

Eight kilometres north of San Antonio, Cartagena is the biggest resort on this part of the coast, but is a quieter place than San Antonio. It is filled with fish restaurants and ice cream shops and has lovely views sweeping north around the bay towards Isla Negra. In the early years of this century, it was a fashionable summer retreat for the wealthy of Santiago; a number of mansions survive, notably the **Castillo Foster** overlooking the bay. The centre lies around the **Plaza de Armas**, situated on top of the hill. To the south is the picturesque **Playa Chica**, overlooked by many of the older hotels and restaurants; to the north is **Playa Larga**. Between the two a promenade runs below the cliffs; high above hang old houses, some in disrepair but offering spectacular views. Cartagena is a very popular resort in summer but out of season it is a good centre for visiting nearby points of interest; there are many hotels and bus connections are good.

North of Cartagena

The road to Algarrobo runs north along the coast through several small resorts including **Las Cruces**, **El Tabo** and **El Quisco**, a small fishing port with two beautiful white-sand beaches (crowded during Chilean holidays). Just south of Las Cruces is **Laguna El Peral** ① *Sep-Apr daily 0900-1400, 1500-1800; May-Aug daily 0900-1300, 1400-1800*, a nature reserve that protects a wide range of aquatic birds.

Isla Negra

Four kilometres south of El Quisco in the village of Isla Negra is the beautifully restored **Museo-Casa Pablo Neruda** ① *T035-461284, www.funcaciónneruda.org, Tue-Sun 1000-2000 in summer; Tue-Fri 1000-1400, 1500-1800, entry only with guided tours in Spanish, English or French US$6, call in advance for opening hours or to book an English guide.* Bought by Neruda in 1939, this house overlooking the sea was the poet's writing retreat in his later years, and became the final resting place of Neruda and his last wife Mathilde. The house contains artefacts gathered from all over the world and the café specializes in Neruda's own recipes. The museum conveys a powerful sense of the poet and is well worth a visit. However, some Chileans feel that the **Fundación Pablo Neruda** should not be charging such high admission prices. For further information about Pablo Neruda, visit his Santiago house, La Chascona, page 75, and La Sebastiana in Valparaíso, page 122; see also box, page 595.

Algarrobo

Algarrobo is the largest resort north of Cartagena and the most chic, with large houses, a yacht club and a marina. Conveniently located for Santiago, it was the retreat of politicians in the 1960s; both Salvador Allende and Eduardo Frei had summer residences here. Today, it remains one of the most popular spots on the central coast: its shallow waters and sheltered bay ensure that sea temperatures here are much warmer than at most other resorts along the central Chilean coast, while good beaches are supplemented by activities such as fishing, surfing and sailing. From **Playa Canelo** there are good views of pelicans and boobies in a seabird colony on an offshore island. Boat tours circle round it in summer, departing from the jetty.

⊛ Resorts south of Valparaíso listings

For Sleeping and Eating price codes and other relevant information, see Essentials pages 35-42.

⊜ Sleeping

San Antonio and around *p144*
AL Rocas de Santo Domingo, La Ronda 130, Santo Domingo, south of San Antonio, T035-444356, www.hotelrocas.cl. Clean, friendly, with restaurant, cable TV. Good breakfast included in price. Also suites.
B Jockey Club, 21 de Mayo 202, T035-211777, F212922. Best accommodation in town, good views, restaurant.
C Residencial El Castillo, Providencia 253, Llolleo, south of San Antonio, T035-373821.

Cartagena *p144*
D El Estribo, just off Plaza de Armas. Rooms with breakfast, basic, cheap *comedor*.

D Residencial Carmona, Playa Chica, T035-450485. Small rooms, basic, clean, good value.
D Residencial Paty's, Alcalde Cartagena 295, T035-450469. Nice spot, good value.
D Violeta, Condell 110, T035-450372. With swimming pool, good views.

North of Cartagena *p144*
Accommodation is generally more expensive in El Quisco.
A Motel Barlovento, El Quisco, T035-471030. 3-star accommodation.
C Cabañas Pozo Azul, Capricornio 234, El Quisco, T035-471401. Southeast of town, quiet.
C El Quisco, Dubournais 166, El Quisco, T035-481923. With breakfast, clean, open weekends only, with seafood restaurant.

C Gran Italia, Dubournais 413, El Quisco, T/F035-481631. Good beds and pool. Recommended.

C Hotel El Tabo, El Tabo, T035-433719. Good accommodation.

C Motel El Tabo, next door to the hotel El Tabo, T035-212719. Very crowded in Jan-Feb.

C-D Residencial Julia, Aguirre 0210, El Quisco, T035-471546. Very clean, quiet, good value.

Isla Negra *p145*

B Hostería Santa Elena, T035-213439. Beautiful building and location, but some rooms damp and gloomy, also restaurant.

C Casa Azul, Av Santa Luisa, T035-461154. With breakfast, kitchen and living room, English spoken, camping. Recommended.

Algarrobo *p145*

A Uribe, behind Costa Sur, T035-481035. Pleasant, quiet.

⊖ Transport

San Antonio and around *p144*
Bus

Pullman Lago Peñuelas operates direct buses from Valparaíso to **San Antonio**, every 30 mins until 2000, 2 hrs, US$43. The coastal service from Valparaíso to **Algarrobo** and **Isla Negra**, every 30 mins, 2 hrs, US$4, also continues to San Antonio. **Empresa de Buses San Antonio** and **Empresa Robles** run frequent services from Algarrobo to **San Antonio**, until 2000, 30 mins.

Pullman Bus runs services from Santiago to **San Antonio**, every 20 mins in summer, US$6. There are also frequent services from the capital with **Pullman Bus** (from Terminal Alameda) and other companies (from Terminal Sur) to **Isla Negra** and **Algarrobo** (via Cartagena and other resorts).

Contents

Footprint features

From Santiago to La Serena

At a glance

⊖ **Getting around** Good bus services link the main cities and go up the Elqui Valley as far as Pisco. To explore the rugged interior a high-clearance vehicle should be hired.

⊛ **Time required** 3 to 5 days to see the sights around La Serena and the Elqui Valley; more if you want to head off the beaten track.

☼ **Weather** Moderate temperatures on the coast with morning fog not uncommon. Inland blue skies practically every day. The nights are cooler further up the valleys.

⊗ **When not to go** Pleasant all year round, though if you want to star gaze, try to avoid the full moon.

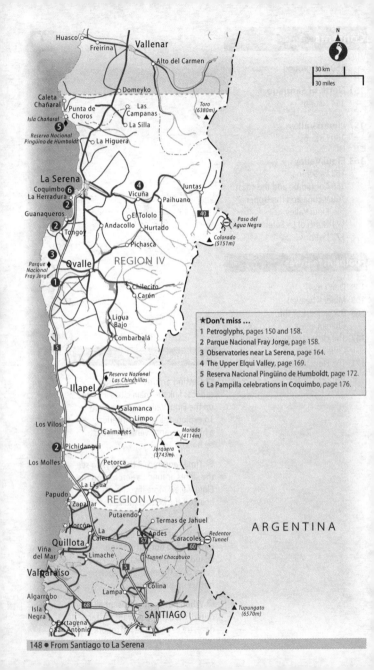

★Don't miss ...

1 Petroglyphs, pages 150 and 158.
2 Parque Nacional Fray Jorge, page 158.
3 Observatories near La Serena, page 164.
4 The Upper Elqui Valley, page 169.
5 Reserva Nacional Pingüino de Humboldt, page 172.
6 La Pampilla celebrations in Coquimbo, page 176.

There is a common saying in Chile, "between Tongoy and Los Vilos". It is a way of saying "in the middle of nowhere". Most Chileans would have you believe that, a handful of coastal resorts aside (Tongoy and Los Vilos among them), the 500 km stretch between Santiago and La Serena is an uninteresting wasteland. Yet this could not be further from the truth. There are rich rewards for those prepared to rough it and take a few risks.

Inland you will find one of the world's highest concentrations of petroglyphs, spectacular mountainsides speckled different colours by rich mineral deposits, and desolate tracks winding through some of Chile's best high-mountain scenery. To the north is the resort of La Serena, the usual centre for visiting the *pisco* distilleries of the fertile Elqui Valley. This valley is one of the world's most important astronomical centres, with five observatories, including two built especially for visitors – it is also the focal point of Chile's New Age movement, and was the birthplace of Nobel laureate Gabriela Mistral. South of La Serena is the lively market city of Ovalle, an ideal centre for forays into the *cordillera* and for visiting the Parque Nacional Fray Jorge, a temperate rainforest that survives in this dry region due to the sea mists that hang almost constantly over its hills.

Background

Stretching north from the Río Aconcagua to the Río Elqui, this area is a transitional zone between the fertile heartland and the northern deserts. Rainfall is rare, and only occurs in winter, while temperatures are relatively stable, with little seasonal variation except at high altitude. North of the Aconcagua, the Andes and the coastal *cordillera* merge in a spectacular lattice of mountains and are crossed by river valleys separated by high ridges. The valleys of the Choapa, Limarí and Elqui rivers are green oases, where the land is intensively farmed and irrigated to produce fruit and vegetables. Elsewhere, the vegetation is characteristic of semi-desert, except in those areas where frequent sea mists provide sufficient moisture to support temperate rainforest. The coastline is generally flat, with many beautiful coves, both rocky and sandy, and good surf, although the water is much colder than you would expect.

Archaeological finds indicate that the river valleys were inhabited at an early stage in prehistory. In fact the recent discovery, south of Los Vilos, of the skeleton of a mastodon that seems to have been slaughtered by humans suggests a presence going back at least 10,000 years. The rise of the Molle culture happened around the same time as the rise of Christianity in Europe; sharing links with northern Argentina, the Molle people produced intricate ceramics and worked with copper. They were superseded by the Diaguitas, who crossed the Andes around AD 900 and settled throughout the area. The pre-Hispanic peoples left their mark in the form of petroglyphs (rock carvings).

Soon after the arrival of the Spanish and the foundation of Santiago, Pedro de Valdivia attempted to secure control over northern Chile by founding La Serena in 1544. Due to the arid climate and the more testing living conditions, the indigenous people here were less numerous than the Mapuche in the south and, despite a few setbacks for the Spanish, they were soon subjugated and wiped out. Throughout the colonial period, La Serena dominated the rest of the region; although small, it was the only city in the north and its leading families had close ties to the main Spanish landowners in the other valleys. After Independence, the area became an important mining zone, producing large amounts of silver, copper and gold.

Mining is an ever more important industry in this area: Although El Indio, inland from La Serena and once the biggest gold producer in Chile, has now closed, El Romeral, north of La Serena, is the most important iron-ore deposit in the country. Many new copper mines are being opened up including a huge mine at Los Pelambres at the top of the Choapa valley. Quartz and the semi-precious stones lapis lazuli and combarbalita are also mined. Despite the dry climate, much of the region's industry is linked to its agricultural produce, notably the distilling of *pisco* from grapes; by law, only grapes grown in the regions of Atacama and Coquimbo can be used to make *pisco*.

North of Santiago

The first stretch of the Pan-American Highway from Santiago heads inland through green valleys with rich blue clover and wild artichokes. North of La Ligua (known for its sweet white cookies as well as its woollen goods), it follows the coast, and the first intimations of the northern deserts appear. From Los Vilos, a paved road turns off the Pan-American Highway towards Illapel, climbing steeply up to a pass, from which there are staggering views of the Andes and the Choapa River.

Illapel is surrounded by barren hills, with good views of the cordillera to the east. While the town is not wildly interesting in itself, it is close to wonderful mountain country, best explored by the adventurous or those with their own transport. The Illapel region is largely ignored by travellers, yet it has some worthwhile attractions. This is the narrowest part of Chile between Arica and Aysén, and the Andes are never far away, with valleys carving right up towards the snowline. There are many examples of pre-Hispanic petroglyphs for those who take the trouble to find them. ▶▶ *For listings, see pages 154-156.*

Ins and outs

Getting there There are direct buses to Los Vilos, Illapel and Salamanca from Santiago, Valparaiso and La Serena.

Getting around There are regular bus services up and down the valley as far as Salamanca from where *colectivos* can be taken to the more remote upper valley. The towns are all small enough to explore on foot.

Los Vilos and the coast

Los Vilos is a small seaside resort 216 km north of Santiago. Set in a wide bay, it is a peaceful, windswept place, disturbed mainly by the noise of the kelp gulls and the waves, except in summer when it fills up with holidaymakers from Santiago. Halfway between the capital and La Serena, it is a good place to break the journey. Los Vilos was founded as a mineral port. Having suffered years of decline as a backwater fishing village, the local economy is being revitalised by the new port at the north tip of the bay serving the recently opened mine at Los Pelambres. There are several attractive *plazuelas* on the *costanera*, with stone benches among aloe and palm trees, from which you can watch the fishing boats bobbing in the sea; the water is cold for bathing. Also on the *costanera* is a small **municipal aquarium** ① *in theory open daily, 0900-1300 and 1430-1700 but often closed off season*. Two blocks inland from here is the **Bodegón Cultural** ① *Elicura 135 (another entrance on Lautaro 207), T053-542581, bodegon culturallosvilos@terra.cl*, in a former port warehouse, now a gallery showing good-quality temporary exhibitions of artwork from the region and around Chile. Entrance is free but donations are welcome. The shop sells stoneware ceramics with diaguita motifs made by local craftswomen.

Offshore are two islands reached by frequent launches: **Isla de Los Huevos**, situated in the bay, and, 5 km south, **Isla de Los Lobos**, where there is a colony of seals. There is a **tourist office** ① *on the main road entering Los Vilos from the Pan-American Highway, www.losvilos.cl, open summer only*.

Pichidangui, 26 km south, is a popular resort on a rocky peninsula, with a beautiful beach to the north. **Los Molles**, 10 km south of Pichidangui, is a fishing village where many wealthy residents of Santiago have their summer homes. Nearby are the **Puguén blow holes** ① *US$2, free off season*, and the **Piscina Los Molles**, a natural swimming pool.

Illapel

Nearly 480 km north of Santiago, Illapel is a poor town that depends on mining in the surrounding mountains for its survival. The lives of the *pirquineros* (see box, page 153) in the nearby hills provide a sobering illustration of the lifestyle that miners in the north of Chile have endured since colonial times. The workers drag rocks from the mine-face in rusting wheelbarrows, living in tumbledown shacks without power, fresh water or public transport, and many of them die tragically young from lung cancer or chagas disease. If you do venture up into these remote areas, bring gifts and humility in abundance.

Illapel is a small town, and can easily be covered on foot. There is a small archaeological museum next to the library in the **Casa de la Cultura** ① *Valdivieso y Constitución, just off the Plaza de Armas, Mon-Fri 0900-1300 and 1400-1800, free*, with a bizarre and disordered collection of arrowheads, jewellery, pottery, miners' boots and newspapers so dusty you almost choke. There is no tourist office (although you could try asking for information at the Municipalidad on the plaza), but there is a very helpful office run by **CONAF** ① *Vicuña Mackenna 93, open Mon-Sat 0830-1730*.

Salamanca and around

This small town lies 32 km southeast of Illapel along the Río Choapa. It is surrounded by the dusty foothills of the Andes and has a large shady plaza where craftspeople display their goods in the evenings. Halfway along the road from Illapel is the **Los Cristales Pass**, from where there are views of distant snowy mountains. Salamanca has lost some of its

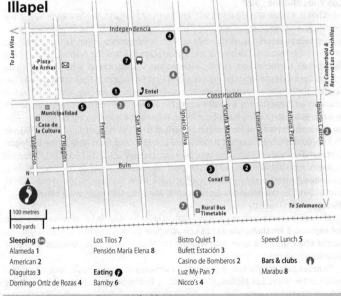

Illapel

Sleeping 🛏	Los Tilos 7	Bistro Quiet 1	Speed Lunch 5
Alameda 1	Pensión María Elena 8	Bufett Estación 3	
American 2		Casino de Bomberos 2	Bars & clubs 🎵
Diaguitas 3	Eating 🍴	Luz My Pan 7	Marabu 8
Domingo Ortíz de Rozas 4	Bamby 6	Nicco's 4	

Mineral heaven

If you are at all interested in geology, you could spend months in this part of Chile and still not be satisfied. The mountains of the cordillera here are brimful of minerals that are easily visible to the naked eye. Near Combarbalá, the colours are white and red, showing that the *combarbalita* – a marble-type rock found nowhere else in the world – is nearby. In the high mountains inland from Ovalle is one of the world's two mines of the brilliant blue stone, lapis lazuli; while at Andacollo, you may have your only chance in Chile to see small-scale gold mining in operation, although the

number of miners working here has declined rapidly in recent years.

Miners in these areas often work independently and they are known as *pilquineros*. They process their findings in two types of small mills. The *trapiche* consists of two heavy vertical wheels in a container half filled with water. As the ore is ground between the wheels, the mineral sticks to mercury, which is spread on the sides of the container. The other type of mill, the *maray*, resembles a large mortar and pestle and is hand driven. Both the *trapiche* and the *maray* are rented by the miner, the rent paid as a share of the ore.

charm since it now doubles as a service town for the new mine at Los Pelambres. Much of the former friendliness to strangers has gone and at nighttime there can be an edge to the atmosphere in town.

Some 2 km north of Salamanca on the Illapel road is a turning for the small town of **Chalinga**, with a church dating from 1750 (ask at the nearby convent if entry is possible). A dusty road continues from Chalinga up into the Chalinga valley, passing plantations of *pisco* grapes, fruit orchards and irrigated vegetable patches before heading up into barren mountain scenery around **Zapallar**. The teacher at the school here has made a study of the petroglyphs in the surrounding area – of which there are many – and may be able to help interested parties seek them out.

North to Combarbalá

From Illapel, a paved road leads 15 km north to the **Reserva Nacional Las Chinchillas** ⓘ *daily 0900-1700 (or until 1800 in summer), US$4*, passing impressive mountains speckled with cacti and minerals. The reserve covers 4229 ha and protects the last remaining colony of chinchillas in this region. The chinchillas and six related species can be viewed from behind two-way mirrors.

After Las Chinchillas, there is a fork in the road. To the left is a decent if sinuous road to Combarbalá via the village of **Los Pozos**. To the right the asphalt disappears and the mountainsides close in – red, purple and white with minerals, and covered with cacti. This poor road (high-clearance vehicle needed) climbs the **Cuesta El Espino** to a height of over 2000 m, from where there are unforgettable views of the multicoloured mountains and the white snows of the Andes. A much worse road – suitable for riders and cyclists only – branches off at the junction for Las Chinchillas and follows the old railway track on an even more remote and dramatic route to Combarbalá, via mining settlements at Farellón Sánchez and Matancillas. Eventually, it rejoins the main road below Cuesta El Espino and reaches the small town of Combarbalá, 73 km north of Illapel.

Combarbalá is set in a dusty bowl surrounded by mountains. The town is famous as the home of the *combarbalita*, a semi-precious stone that was declared the National Stone of

Chile in 1993. However, the town is little known, even to Chileans – the **Senatur** office in Santiago recently told a caller to "phone the appropriate embassy" when asked about Combarbalá. *Combarbalita* is similar in appearance to marble and is found nowhere else in the world. There are lots of workshops on the north side of town, particularly on Calle Flores, where you can see the craftsmen at work and buy their goods. An astronomical observatory, the **Cruz del Sur** has recently been built near the town. At present, visits are by appointment with the municipality, see www.combarbala.net.

◉ North of Santiago listings

For Sleeping and Eating price codes and other relevant information, see Essentials pages 35-42.

● Sleeping

Los Vilos and the coast *p151*
B American Motel, Km 224, T053-541163. Right on the highway and a convenient stopping place between Viña del Mar or Santiago and La Serena, good value.
B-C Cabañas Mar y Sol, Av Los Vilos 20, T053-541705, www.marysol.cl. Snug cabins with kitchenette. Great location although slightly shoddy build quality. The lower cabins are practically on the beach while the upper cabins have a great view. Terrace with small pool and Wi-Fi area. Convenient for **TurBus** and **Pullman**.
B-C Lord Willow, Hostería 1444, Los Vilos, T053-541037. Los Vilos's oldest hotel with a collection of old firearms and fossils, with bath, pleasant, friendly, parking. Small but decent rooms, some with view across the road to the coast, others (quieter) to the good-sized swimming pool. Breakfast extra.
C Cabañas Los Delfines, Lautaro 048, T09-9930 3900. Comfy spacious cabins that sleep 4. With kitchen and cable TV. Views across some wasteland to the Isla de los Huevos.
C-D Bellavista, Rengo 020, Los Vilos, T053-541073. **E** singles. With breakfast, bath and TV in carpeted rooms, hot water, sea views. Pretty tatty but the singles are good value.
D There are 2 cheap, central *residenciales* on Caupolicán in Los Vilos, **Turismo**, No 437, and Residencial Punta de Chungo, No 627, T053-541096.

Camping Campomar, Campusano s/n, Los Vilos, T053-541049. Campsite plus *cabañas* near the town centre.

Pichidangui
Pichidangui has various hotels and *pensiones* at every price.
A Pichidangui, Francis Drake s/n, T053-531114, www.hotel pichidangui.cl. Hotel with swimming pool and restaurant.
C Hostería Puquen, 2 Poniente s/n, T053-531104. **F** singles. Attractive and good value.
Camping Bahía Marina de Pichidangui, T053-531120. Sports facilities and *cabañas*.

Illapel *p152, map p152*
B Domingo Ortíz de Rozas, Ignacio Silva 241, T053-522127, www.hotelortizderozas.cl. Spacious rooms with all mod cons at this attractive 3-star.
B-C American, Carrera 128, T053-523661, american_restaurant@hotmail.com. Nice courtyard, with breakfast, bath and TV.
B-C Diaguitas, Constitución 276, T053-522 587, www.hoteldiaguitas.cl. Noisy, with swimming pool, in-room internet connection.
C Los Tilos, Ignacio Silva 45, T053-523335, hotellostiloss@hotmail.com. With bath, breakfast and TV, friendly, but small rooms. Laundry service and internet.
C-D Alameda, Ignacio Silva 20, T053-522355, hotelalameda@hotmail.com. **E** singles. With bath and TV, without breakfast, friendly, clean, nice patio with lemon and orange trees, cheap laundry service, recommended.
D Pensión María Elena, Esmeralda 54. **F-G** singles. Best of the cheapies, very basic but warm and friendly.

Salamanca and around p152

B My House, Infante 451, T053-552036, www.hotelmyhouse.cl. The nicest of Salamanca's hotels, good rooms, internet access in lobby, can arrange local tours.

C-D Residencial O'Higgins, O'Higgins 430. **E-F** singles. Some rooms with bath. Breakfast extra, friendly, clean, basic, patio.

Camping

There are several basic campsites in the Chalinga Valley, including one at Zapallar.

North to Combarbalá p153

C Reserva Nacional Las Chinchillas. Well-equipped *cabañas*, with kitchen facilities, also a campsite.

C Yagnam, Comercio 252, Combarbalá, T053-741329, hotelyagnam@hotmail.com. Clean, new hotel, friendly, room service, good value, recommended.

D Residencial La Golondrina, Chacabuco y Libertad, Combarbalá. Basic but cheap.

🍴 Eating

Los Vilos and the coast p151

Restaurants in Pichindangui tend to be pricey, although there is a food shop. There are countless places on the seafront in Los Vilos, either in Caleta San Pedro or, further around the coast towards the island, where there are 10 small eateries – watch out, touting for business here is intense!

🍴🍴 Alisio, Elicura 160, Los Vilos. Seafood and fish, good value, probably the best in town.

🍴🍴 Restaurant Turístico Costanera, Caleta San Pedro, Los Vilos. Good views over ocean, good meals and choice of wines, nice warm bread. Also serves a cheap menu.

🍴 El Rey de la Paila Marina Vileña, Caleta San Pedro, Los Vilos. Fish and seafood.

🍴 Pastelería/Heladería Roma, Caupolicán 712, Los Vilos. Excellent cakes and ice cream. The very helpful owners both speak English.

Cafés

Café Entrevientos, Caupolicán 298b, Los Vilos. Intimate café serving decent coffee and cakes. Also serves breakfast but only open from 1000 onwards.

Illapel p152, map p152

🍴🍴 Bistro Quiet, Constitución 200 block. Smart, fills up at weekends.

🍴🍴 Bufett Estación, Buín 452. Smartest in town, good food.

🍴🍴 Nicco's, Ignacio Silva 219. Good pizzas, fancy decor, vegetarian options.

🍴 Bamby Restaurant, Constitución 340. Not great quality but very cheap.

🍴 Casino de Bomberos, Buín 590. Friendly, excellent value, good views of the town, recommended.

🍴 Luz My Pan, San Martín, opposite the bus station. Good bread and cakes.

🍴 Speed Lunch, Constitución 160. Friendly, some vegetarian possibilities (ask for lentils), not as bad as the name suggests.

Salamanca and around p152

Restaurants in Salamanca tend to be basic. There are cheap ice creams at a shop next to ENTEL on the plaza.

🍴 El Americano, O'Higgins y M Montepio. Good lunches, also has information on the surrounding area.

🍴 Restaurant Crillón, on the Plaza on Montepio. Friendly, excellent-value *almuerzos*.

🍸 Bars and clubs

Los Vilos and the coast p151

Several new bars open every year for the summer season.

Pub Cantina, Rengo 86, Los Vilos.

Illapel p152, map p152

Pub Marabú, Ignacio Silva 260. US$3. Bar with free drink, salsa and merengue at the weekends.

☸ Festivals and events

Salamanca and around *p152*
Feb/Mar Holy Week is a big event in
Salamanca, with horse races at La Chilena
and costumed processions through the town.

⛰ Activities and tours

Illapel *p152, map p152*
Turismo Libuca, Independencia 099,
T053-522155. Specializes in tours of the
south for those from Illapel, but can also
arrange visits to Las Chinchillas.

⛴ Transport

Los Vilos and the coast *p151*
Bus There is only 1 bus daily between
Pichidangui and Santiago, but many
north-south buses on the highway also
pass Los Vilos and Pichidangui.

The main long-distance companies
serving Los Vilos each have their own
terminal; they are **Pullman Bus**, Caupolicán
1111, **TurBus**, Caupolicán 898 and **Expreso
Norte**, Caupolicán s/n, each with at least
5 buses daily to **Santiago**, 3½ hrs, US$9, and
La Serena, 4½ hrs, US$9, as well as frequent
buses to **Illapel**, 1 hr, US$2.50, and
Salamanca, US$3. Intercomunal have
5 buses daily to **Valparaíso**, leaving from
Caupolicán 690 and there are 3 buses daily
to **Combarbalá**, from the same location.
Buses from Los Vilos to **Pichidangui** leave
every hour from Rengo at the junction
with Caupolicán.

Illapel *p152, map p152*
Bus The bus station is at San Martín, on
the 200 block. Illapel is served by TurBus,
Pullman Bus and Expreso Norte, all of which
have services to **Santiago**, 4½ hrs, US$9, and
La Serena, 4½ hrs, US$9, via Los Vilos.
Intercomunal has 4 buses daily to **Viña** and
Valparaíso, US$9. Buses to rural destinations

leave from Independencia y Ignacio Silva; the
timetables are posted at the greengrocer's
at the bottom end of Ignacio Silva.

Salamanca and around *p152*
Bus The long-distance bus company offices
are on or around the plaza. There are rural
buses most days from Salamanca to the
mountain communities, as well as *colectivos*
to Illapel (from the plaza) and further up the
valley from Bulnes, 3 blocks east of the plaza.
2 buses an hour, from 0800 to 1800, US$2,
run to **Illapel**, continuing either north to
La Serena or south to **Santiago**.

North to Combarbalá *p153*
Bus Combarbalá can be reached by buses
from **La Serena** and **Ovalle** (page 162), or with
Buses Combarbalá from **Santiago**, **La Calera**,
La Ligua and **Los Vilos**. There are services to
Illapel via **Reserva Nacional Las Chinchillas**
although most of these are at night.

❶ Directory

Los Vilos and the coast *p151*
Bank Banco Estado, Caupolicán y Guacolda,
Los Vilos. MasterCard only. Also changes
money. There is also an ATM that takes visa
in the **Supermercado Los Naranjos**,
Caupolicán. **Post office** Lincoyán, Los Vilos.

Illapel *p152, map p152*
Banks Banco de Chile, Tarcifio Valderrama
s/n. **Laundry** Alondra, Ignacio Silva 370,
only one in town. **Medical services**
Dentist: Vicuña Mackenna 183, T053-521010.
Hospital: Independencia s/n, T053-522312.
Post office Plaza de Armas, Western Union
money transfers.

Salamanca *p152*
Banks Banco Estado, O'Higgins
y Montepio, MasterCard only. There is a
visa ATM in the **Copec** petrol station on
the corner of the plaza. **Post office**
Montepio, on the plaza.

Limarí Valley

→ *Colour map 2, C1.*

The Limarí Valley contains much of the north of Chile in a microcosm: beaches at Tongoy, the mysteriously lush Parque Nacional Fray Jorge, a vibrant market town in Ovalle, countless examples of ancient rock art and wonderful mountain scenery. With remote tracks through the mountains and giant hillsides sprinkled with cacti and multicoloured minerals, it is a fine place to wander for a week or more. ▸▸ *For listings, see pages 160-162.*

Ins and outs

Getting there and around Ovalle is easily reached by regular buses: north from LaSerena and destinations as far north as Arica; south from Illapel, Valparaíso and Santiago. Note that, although Ovalle is a small city, confusingly it has three main bus terminals and several smaller offices. The **Terminal Media Luna** is the only one used by long-distance buses. Numerous local buses and *colectivos* link Ovalle with outlying communities. ▸▸ *See Transport, page 162.*

Ovalle and around → *Colour map 2, C1.*

Situated inland in the valley of the Río Limarí – a fruit-growing and mining district – this lively town is a focal point for the numerous communities in the surrounding mountains and valleys. Edged by dusty hills, which are lined with vines for *pisco* grapes and orchards of avocado trees, it gets busy on market days, when local *campesinos* throng around the market area. That said, Ovalle remains a laid-back town with an almost rural feel to it.

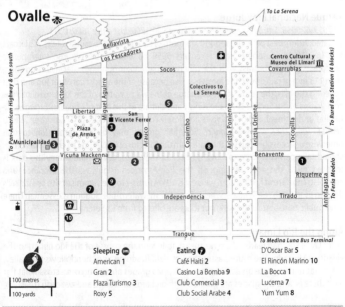

Ovalle

To La Serena

Bellavista
Los Pescadores
Socos
Victoria
Miguel Aguirre
San Vicente Ferrer
Libertad
Plaza de Armas
Arauco
Coquimbo
Ariztia Poniente
Ariztia Oriente
Tocopilla
Socos
Colectivos to La Serena
Centro Cultural y Museo del Limarí Covarrubias
Vicuña Mackenna
Benavente
Riqueme
Independencia
Tirado
Trangue
Antofagasta

To Pan-American Highway & the south
To Rural Bus Station (4 blocks)
To Feria Modelo
To Medina Luna Bus Terminal

100 metres
100 yards

Sleeping
American 1
Gran 2
Plaza Turismo 3
Roxy 5

Eating
Café Haiti 2
Casino La Bomba 9
Club Comercial 3
Club Social Arabe 4

D'Oscar Bar 5
El Rincón Marino 10
La Bocca 1
Lucerna 7
Yum Yum 8

Although not a typical tourist destination it is an excellent window on the traditionally slow pace of life in the Norte Chico. It is famous for its *talabarterías* (saddleries) and for its products made of locally mined lapis lazuli, as well as *queso de cabra* (goat's cheese) and dried fruits (sold in the market). The central part of town can easily be covered on foot. **Museo del Limarí** ① *Covarrubias y Antofagasta, T053-620029, museolimari@adsl.tie.cl, Tue-Fri 0900-1300, 1500-1900, Sat and Sun 1000-1300, US$1, Sun free,* is housed in the old railway station and has displays of petroglyphs and an excellent small collection of Diaguita ceramics and other artefacts. Info in Spanish only. Annexed to the museum is a gallery with temporary art and crafts exhibitions. There is a semi-official **tourist information** centre in one of the kiosks selling *artesanía* on Aritzía. Failing that try the municipalidad just off the Plaza de Armas.

Embalse La Paloma, the largest reservoir in Chile, is 26 km southeast. On the northern shore is the small town of **Monte Patria**, with a *pisco* distillery that can be visited. From Monte Patria, a paved road leads to Chilecito and Carén, where there is the **Parque Ecológico La Gallardina** ① *T053-726009, US$2 (US$3 at weekends),* containing a beautiful collection of roses and other plants and flowers amid the dry mountains.

Monumento Nacional Valle del Encanto ① *about 22 km southwest of Ovalle, open all year 0800-1800, US$3,* is one of the most important archaeological sites in northern Chile. Artefacts from hunting peoples from over 2000 years ago have been found, but the most visible remains date from the Molle culture (AD 700). There are over 30 petroglyphs as well as great boulders, distributed in over sites.

Termas de Socos ① *Pan-American Highway, 35 km southwest of Ovalle, www.terma socos.cl, US$9,* is a popular resort among Chileans. There are swimming pools and individual bath tubs fed by thermal springs, as well as a sauna, jacuzzi and water massage.

Parque Nacional Fray Jorge
① *T053-620058, Sat, Sun and public holidays 0900-1700, last entry 1600, US$5.*
Situated 90 km west of Ovalle and 110 km south of La Serena at the mouth of the Río Limarí, this UN World Biosphere Reserve covers 9959 ha and contains original temperate rainforests, which contrast with the otherwise barren surroundings. Receiving no more than 113 mm of rain a year, the forests survive because of the almost constant fog and mist covering the hills, the result of the discharge of the warm waters of the Río Limarí into the cold waters of the Pacific. The increasingly arid climate of this part of Chile has brought the habitat under threat and hence visits are closely controlled by **CONAF** ① *Cordovez 281, La Serena, T051-211124, www.conaf.cl.* Scientific groups may obtain permission to visit otherwise unaccessible parts of the park from the Director of CONAF in La Serena. All visitors should take particular care to leave no trace of their presence behind them. The park is reached by a dirt road leading off the Pan-American Highway. The entrance and administration are at Km 18, from where it is 10 km further to the summit of the coastal hills (known as the Altos de Talinay), which rise to 667 m. Waterproof clothing is essential. There is no public transport to the park, but tours are offered from La Serena.

Along the Río Limarí
From Ovalle, a road leads 77 km northeast, following the course of the Río Limarí to the village of Hurtado. The route passes the Recoleta Reservoir and then follows the valley, where fat horses graze on alfalfa, vines with *pisco* grapes are strung out across what flat land there is, and the glades are planted with orchards of orange and avocado trees.

The road is paved as far as Samo Alto; shortly after is the turn-off (to San Pedro) for the **Monumento Natural Pichasca** ① *0800-1800, US$4.* Some 47 km northeast of Ovalle at an altitude of 1350 m, this park contains petrified tree trunks and archaeological remains, including a vast cave, comparable to the Cueva Milodón outside Puerto Natales, with remnants of ancient roof paintings. Gigantic rock formations can be seen on the surrounding mountains. Encouraged by the local mayor, a bright green model of a dinosaur has been erected here. Sure to be a magnet for groups of local schoolchildren, the dinosaur is supposed to be the north's answer to the sloth in the Milodon Cave near Puerto Natales, but as yet it is too early to claim that Jurassic Park has come to Pichasca. Note that it is 3 km to the park from the turn-off and about 2 km further to sites of interest.

Beyond the village of **Pichasca** are several plantations, where rickety wooden suspension bridges cross to the far side of the Río Limarí. It is a further 32 km to Hurtado and the road continues winding along the side of the valley, with the Andes now easily visible at the head of the valley. At **Vado Morrillos**, 4 km before Hurtado, is the **Hacienda Los Andes** ① *T053-691 822, www.haciendalosandes.com*, a centre for horse riding in the area, set in a very pretty location, with a 7-km nature trail. The hacienda is run by a German/Austrian couple with previous experience of running horse-riding trips, English and German spoken. Horse-riding tours from one to eight days are offered in the surrounding mountains. If coming by bus to the hacienda, ask the driver to let you off at the bridge at Vado Morrillos – the entrance to the hacienda is just before the bridge on the right.

The road continues on to **Hurtado**, a village set at 1300 m. Excellent accommodation is available at **Tambo de Limarí** (see Sleeping), a *hospedaje* owned by Señora Orieta. Near Hurtado is the only petroglyph in Chile depicting the sun, hinting at possible links to the Incas, and it is also possible to climb the **Cerro Gigante** (2825 m) and visit the site of a Diaguita cemetry.

Valley of the Limarí

Sleeping 🛏
Hacienda Juntas 1
Hacienda Los Andes 2
Tambo de Limarí 3

Eating 🍴
Flor del Valle 1

N

20 km
20 miles

The extremely adventurous may consider continuing from Hurtado into Argentina (permission must be sought from the *carabineros* in Hurtado). It is three days by horse to the pass into Argentina (4229 m); near the pass are the corrals of El Ternero, where a wall built by pre-Hispanic peoples climbs up into the snows. On the far side of the border, the path descends to the Laguna de los Patos, where the Argentines have a police post. However, it is then a further seven to 10 days by horse to the nearest settlement in Argentina and there is no road. It may be possible to find guides for this trip in the village of Las Breas, 22 km beyond Hurtado, where there is a small restaurant.

An easier option is to continue from Hurtado north to Vicuña in the Elqui Valley (see page 169) only 46 km away. This is a stark, desolate but beautiful road road, very poor in places; there is very little traffic and no public transport, but pickups can be hired in Hurtado to make the trip for US$35-40.

To Andacollo

The good road inland between Ovalle and La Serena makes an interesting contrast to Ruta 5, the Pan-American Highway, with a fine pass and occasional views of snow-capped Andes across cacti-covered plains and semi-desert mountain ranges. Some 66 km north of Ovalle, a winding side road runs 27 km southeast, to Andacollo.

Situated in a gorge, Andacollo has been a mining centre since before the arrival of the Spanish (see box, page 153). Ruins of mines and waste tips dot the area. Two mines, one copper and one gold, still operate and there are many independent mines and *trapiches*, small processing plants, which can be visited; the gold has, however, begun to run out and, in recent years, many miners have moved away. Andacollo, however, is more famous as one of the great pilgrimage sites in Chile. In the enormous **Basilica** (1893), 45 m high and with a capacity of 10,000, is a small, carved wooden statue of the Virgen del Rosario de Andacollo, brought from Peru in the 17th century and credited with miraculous powers. Nearby is the **Templo Antiguo**, smaller and dating from 1789. There is also a museum, **Museo de Andacollo** ① *open daily 0900-1300, 1500-1900*. The tourist office on the Plaza de Armas can arrange tours to the Basilica and to mining operations.

---

① Limarí Valley listings

For Sleeping and Eating price codes and other relevant information, see Essentials pages 35-42.

○ Sleeping

Ovalle and around *p157, map p157*
Accommodation is poor in Ovalle itself.
AL Termas de Socos, Panamericana, 35 km southwest of Ovalle, T053-198 2505, www.termasocos.cl. Reasonable hotel offering full board and access to thermal pools.
AL-A Hacienda Juntas, near Monte Patria, Km 38, T053-711290, www.haciendajuntas.cl. Stands in 90 ha of vineyards, with pleasant gardens, spectacular views and a swimming pool. Restaurant open in high season only. Recommended.
AL-A PlazaTurismo, Victoria 295, T053-623258, www.plazaturismo.cl. Spacious rooms, some overlooking the plaza. Wi-Fi in rooms. Not bad, but at this price you would expect a desk and double glazing.
B Hotel American, Mackenna 169, T053-620159, www.hotelamerican.cl. Friendly, small a/c rooms that could do with a revamp. Wi-Fi, parking, overpriced. Get a room with a window onto the patio to avoid street noise.
B-C Gran Hotel, Mackenna 210 (entrance through Galería Yagnam), T053-621084,

www.yagnam.cl/granhotel.htm. Decent rooms with Wi-Fi. Mattresses could be better. Ask to be away from the main road. Friendly and decent service. Probably the best value of all the hotels in town.
C Roxy, Libertad 155, T053-620080. **D** singles. Big basic rooms, clean, friendly, large colonial-style patio covered in vines in summer, a bit run-down. Slightly overpriced but a reasonable choice nevertheless.

Camping
There are camping facilities at Monumento Nacional Valle del Encanto and near the Termas de Socos.

Parque Nacional Fray Jorge *p158*
There is 1 *cabaña* (**A**) sleeping 5 people, which may be hired. Basic accommodation (**C**) is also available in an old hacienda, and at 2 campsites in the national park; 1 at the administration centre, the other 3 km away at El Arrayancito.

Along the Río Limarí *p158, map p159*
AL Hacienda Los Andes, Vado Morrillos, T053-691822, www.haciendalosandes.com. Bed and breakfast. All the rooms have a private bath and there is a sauna and a jacuzzi

that overlooks the river. Camping (including hot showers) is also available, US$8 per person, as well as horse riding, trekking and other outdoor activities.

C Tambo de Limarí, Caupolican 27, Hurtado, T053-1982121. **F** singles. Excellent *hospedaje* with wonderful breakfast. Owner Señora Orieta is very friendly. There is an interesting collection of ancient riding spurs, stirrups and Spanish padlocks. Recommended.

To Andacollo *p160*

There are no hotels, but some *pensiones*. During the festival, private houses rent beds and some let you pay for a shower. Contact the tourist office for details.

🍴 Eating

Ovalle and around *p157, map p157*
🍴 **Club Comercial**, Aguirre 244 (on plaza). Open Sun for general Chilean fare.
🍴 **Club Social Arabe**, Arauco 255, T053-620015. Spacious glass-domed premises, limited selection of Arab dishes, not cheap, often hired out for events at weekends, during the week it is usually empty. Check out the comedy English menu.
🍴 **Casino La Bomba**, Aguirre 364. Very good value *almuerzos*, run by the fire brigade.
🍴 **El Calamar**, in the middle of the Feria Modelo. Good-value lunches – fish and meat. There are many more cheap eateries at the entrance to the market.
🍴 **El Rincón Marino**, Victoria 400 block. One of the better seafood restaurants beside the market.
🍴 **La Bocca Restaurant**, Benavente 110. Specializes in shellfish.
🍴 **Restaurant Lucerna**, Independencia 339 (opposite the market). Opens early for breakfast, popular, interesting place doubling as a doss house for *campesinos*. Next door is Las Tejas, of a similar ilk.
🍴 **Yum Yum**, MacKenna 21. Closes early. Differently themed menu each day, one day serving Arab food, the next Mediterranean, etc.

Cafés
Café Haiti, Victoria 307. Opens early for breakfast.
D'Oscar Bar, Plaza de Armas. Serves good real coffee and is open late.
Frutinor, Mercado Central. Good selection of fresh juices.
Pastelería Tosti, Libertad 427. Good cakes.

Along the Río Limarí *p158, map p159*
🍴 **Restaurant Flor del Valle**, Pichasca. Cheap meals and basic accommodation.

🎵 Bars and Clubs

Ovalle and around *p157, map p157*
El Quijote, Arauco 294. Intimate atmosphere, left-wing old-timers' haunt full of socialist posters and memorabilia.
Eskla, Mackenna 100-block. Disco, often featuring live music.
Pub Katankura, Camino a Sotaqui, km 4, popular disco with restaurant and live music at weekends.

🎭 Entertainment

Ovalle and around *p157, map p157*
Cine Cervantes, Centro Comercial G Corral. Cinema on the plaza.

🎉 Festivals and events

To Andacollo *p160*
23-27 Dec Fiesta Grande attracts 150,000 pilgrims from northern Chile (most important day 26 Dec). The ritual dances date from a pre-Spanish past. Transport is available from La Serena and Ovalle but 'purists' walk (torch and good walking shoes essential). 2 villages are passed on the route, which starts on the paved highway, then goes along a railway track and lastly up a steep, dusty hill.
1st Sun of Oct Fiesta Chica. A smaller festival.

O Shopping

Ovalle and around *p157, map p157*
Market days are Mon, Wed, Fri and Sat, until 1600, Sun morning; the market, **Feria Modelo**, is off Benavente, east of the town centre. Here you can find all kinds of fruit, vegetables, cheese, fish, dried fruit, herbs and spices as well as flowers and cheap clothes. There are many *talabarterías* nearby on Benavente.

For local *artesanía* including worked Combarbalita and Diaguita-style ceramic work try the stalls in the middle of Arítzia or in the Mercado Central.

For articles made of lapis lazuli, try Sr Wellington Vega Alfaro, T09-9475 1004, lapislazuliwellington@hotmail.com. He can usually be found at his stall in the Mercado Municipal and is happy for travellers help him work the stone in his workshop, on the northern outskirts.

▲ Activities and tours

Ovalle and around *p157, map p157*
Tres Valles, Libertad 496, T053-629650, torrejonhnos@adsl.tie.cl. Worth a try for trips to Fray Jorge, Valle del Encanto and other destinations in the area.
Turismec, Coquimbo 140. A travel agent offering aeroplane tickets, etc.

⊙ Transport

Ovalle and around *p157, map p157*
Bus
Local Most of the many rural buses leave from either of 2 terminals outside the feria modelo. Hourly buses to **Carén** serve the **Parque Ecológico La Gallardina**. There is no service to the **Nacional Valle del Encanto**; instead you must take a long-distance southbound bus and ask to be dropped off; it's a 5-km walk to the valley; flag down a bus

to return. The journey from Ovalle to **Andacollo** is US$4 *colectivo* and US$3 bus.

Buses M&R, T053-691866, T09-9822 0320, has an erratic schedule linking Ovalle with **Hurtado**. On Ovalle's market days (Mon, Wed, Fri, Sat), 3 buses leave Hurtado between 0600 and 0630; on Tue and Thu, the buses leave Hurtado at 1000 and 1015, on Sun, at 1230 and 1245. From Ovalle, there are 3 buses to Hurtado on market days (1200, 1230 and 1500), except for Sat, when there is just 1 bus at 1400. On Tue and Thu, buses leave Ovalle at 1615 and 1645, on Sun at 1700 and 1730. The fare is US$3. These buses pass the turn-off to the **Monumento Natural Pichasca** about 42 km from the city.

To **Tulahuén**, 9 daily with Buses Castañeda, Antofagasta y Benavente, 1¾ hrs, US$3. *Colectivos* also serve the outlying towns, leaving from different locations depending on their destination. Many leave from around Av Ariztía.
Long distance Ovalle's main bus terminal is the Terminal Media Luna (by the rodeo ring on Ariztía Oriente) just south of the city centre. There are buses to **Santiago**, mostly mid-morning or late at night, 6½ hrs, US$11; to **La Serena**, 20 a day, 1½ hr, US$3.50 (Horvitur and Via Elqui); also to **Illapel**, 4 hrs, US$8, **Valparaíso**, 6 hrs, US$11, **Antofagasta**, 14 hrs, US$28, and **Arica**, 24 hrs, US$42, mostly at night.

Taxi
Abel Olivares Rivera, T053-620352. Recommended. The round trip to **Parque Nacional Fray Jorge** costs US$75.

ⓘ Directory

Ovalle and around *p157, map p157*
Banks Many Redbanc ATMs on the Plaza de Armas, including Banco de Chile. **Internet** Several in and around the centre. **Post office** MacKenna on the Plaza de Armas. **Telephone** Lots of call centres in and around the centre.

Elqui Valley

A dramatic cleft in the heart of the mountains, the Elqui Valley is home to two of the north's most important cities, Coquimbo and La Serena. Inland, you will find star-filled nights lit up by shooting stars, pisco distilleries and villages in the mountains. The valley of the Río Elqui is one of the most attractive oases in this part of Chile. There are mines, orchards and vineyards set against imposing arid mountains. The contrast between the immense rock formations and the lush valley floor is overwhelming. ▶ *For listings, see pages 172-178.*

Ins and outs

Getting there The cities of Coquimbo and La Serena are easily reached by countless buses from both north and south, from any one of more than 10 companies. Several flights daily from Santiago to Copiapó, Antofagasta and Iquique stop off at La Serena. For transfers to the airport, call T051-295058, US$1.80 per person, or take any Vicuña-bound bus and get off at airport entrance.

Getting around La Serena and Coquimbo are linked by buses that pass down Avenida Francisco de Aguirre in La Serena before travelling along the Pan-American Highway. Taxis are plentiful and cheap.

La Serena ●●❶❶❸❶▲❸❶ ▶ *pp172-178. Colour map 2, C1.*

Situated nearly 500 km north of Santiago, La Serena is the capital of Región IV and is a pleasant if not particularly inspiring city. Built on a hillside 2 km inland from the Bahía de Coquimbo, the city is famous for its numerous churches, while the centre is made up of white buildings of neo-colonial style. Beneath this façade, however, La Serena has a more ancient history and residents often claim to stumble across indigenous burial sites in their backyards. The city has rapidly become a major tourist centre, being popular for its long sandy beach and as a base for visiting nearby attractions. It is full of Chilean and Argentine holidaymakers in January and February, while the city's two universities ensure a vibrant atmosphere all year round.

Ins and outs

Helpful tourist information is available from **Sernatur** ⓘ *Edificio de Servicios Públicos (next to the post office on the Plaza de Armas), T/F051-225199, infocoquimbo@ sernatur.cl, Mon-Fri 0845-1830 (0845-2030 in summer), Sat and Sun 1000-1400 (1000-1400 and 1600-2000 in summer).* Sernatur also has a kiosk at the bus terminal (summer only) which is helpful and has accommodation information.

History

La Serena was founded by Juan de Bohón, aide to Pedro de Valdivia, in 1544, destroyed by the Diaguita in 1546 and rebuilt by Francisco de Aguirre in 1549. The city was sacked by the English pirate Sharpe in 1680. In the colonial period, it was the main staging-post on the route north to Peru; many of the religious orders built churches and convents here providing accommodation for their members. In the 19th century, the city grew prosperous from copper-mining; the neo-classical mansions of successful entrepreneurs from this period can still be seen. The characteristic neo-colonial style of architecture in the centre, however, dates only from the 1950s, when the city was remodelled under the instructions of President González Videla, a lawyer, diplomat and Radical party politician, who was eager to leave his mark on his native city. González Videla ordered the drafting of an urban plan, under which Avenida Francisco de Aguirre was modernized and the Pedro de Valdivia gardens, west of the city, were built. All new buildings in the centre were constructed in Californian colonial style, although his regulation has since been modified, permitting the erection of some modern buildings.

Sights
Around the attractive Plaza de Armas, most of the official buildings can be found, including the post office and the **Casa González Videla**, the great man's residence from 1927 to 1977, which now houses the **Museo Histórico Regional** ⓘ *www.dibam.cl/subdirec_museos/mhr_videla/home.asp, Mon-Fri 1000-1800, Sat 1000-1300, US$1 (ticket also valid for Museo Arqueológico)*, with several rooms dedicated to his life and the history of La Serena. Opposite is the **cathedral**, built in 1844 and featuring a carillon that plays every hour. There are 29 other churches, several of which have unusual towers. **Santo Domingo**, half a block southwest of the Plaza de Armas, built in 1755 with a clock tower dating from 1912, is fronted by a small garden with statues of sea-lions. Southeast of the plaza, on Balmaceda y de La Barra, is **San Francisco**, built between 1586 and 1627, which has a baroque façade and faces a small plaza with arcades. It is home to the **Museo De Arte Religiosa** ⓘ *Mon-Fri 1000-1300, 1600-1800, Sat 1000-1300, US$1*, which includes the funeral mask of Gabriela Mistral.

San Augustín, northeast of the plaza at Cantournet y Rengifo, originally a Jesuit church, dates from 1755 but has been heavily modified. Opposite this church is **La Recova**, the market, which includes a large display of handicrafts and, upstairs, several seafood restaurants. One block south is **Museo Arqueológico** ⓘ *Cordovez y Cienfuegos, T051-224492, www.dibam.cl/sdm_m_laserena/index.asp, Tue-Fri 0930-1750, Sat 1000-1300, 1600-1900, US$1, students free, Sun 1000-1300, free*, which has an outstanding collection of indigenous Diaguita and Molle exhibits, especially of attractively decorated pottery, although they are poorly labelled. There are also some exhibits from Easter Island. Further from the centre, in the University of La Serena, is the **Museo Mineralógico Ignacio Domeyko** ⓘ *A Muñoz 870, Mon-Fri 0930-1230, US$0.80*, for those with a particular interest in geology.

One block west of the Plaza de Armas is the **Parque Pedro de Valdivia** ⓘ *1000-2000*, with the Parque Japonés just south of it. Avenida Francisco de Aguirre, a pleasant boulevard lined with statues and known as the **Alameda**, runs from the centre to the coast, skirting the Parque Japonés and terminating at Faro Monumental, a neo-colonial mock-castle and lighthouse, now a pub. A string of beaches stretch from here all the way to **Coquimbo**, 11 km south, linked by the Avenida del Mar. Many apartment blocks, hotels, *cabañas* and restaurants have been built along this part of the bay. The sectors between 4 Esquinas and Peñuelas are probably the best bet for sunbathing or dipping a toe in the water.

Visiting the observatories
The clear skies and dry atmosphere of the valleys around La Serena have led to the area becoming one of the astronomical centres of the world (see box, page 167). There are five observatories, two built especially to receive visitors. Personal applications for visitor permits to the other three observatories must be made directly to the respective institutions. It is critical to reserve tours to these three in advance – up to three or four months ahead during holiday periods, although off season a few days' notice may be

enough. Be aware that tours are subject to cancellation at short notice if there is inclement weather. Most tour operators in La Serena and Coquimbo arrange tours to Mamalluca. If you can arrange tickets directly with the observatory, taxi drivers will provide transport.

Some visitors to the three large observatories complain that they do not get as much of an insight as they had expected. Bear in mind that trained astronomers have to reserve years in advance to use the equipment and that a day tour will not be the beginning of your astronomical career – it will, though, give you a window onto the workings of some of the most important telescopes on earth.

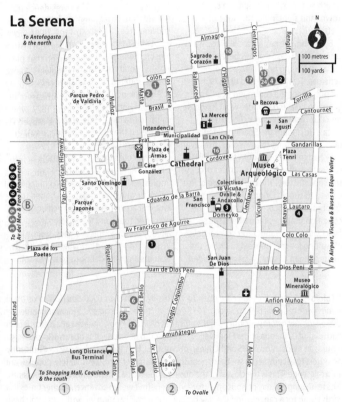

La Serena

Sleeping	Gregoria Fernández 12 C2	Los Balcones de	Donde el Guatón 2 A3
Cabañas Bahía Drake 5 B1	Hostal Colón 1 A2	Aragón 17 A3	El Callejón 3 B2
Camino de Luna 14 B2	Hostal Croata 13 A3	María's Casa 7 C2	Govindas 4 B3
Casa Alejandro Muñoz 4 A3	Hostal del Mar 9 B1	Residencial Suiza 24 A3	La Mía Pizza 8 B1
Costa Real 8 B1	Hostal Familyhome 22 C2		Mai Lan Fan 9 B1
Del Cid 10 A2	Hostal Matta 2 A2	Eating	Porotos 5 B1
El Punto 6 C2	La Serena Plaza 3 B1	Costa Inca 7 B1	Tololo Beach 6 B1
Francisco de Aguirre 11 B2	Londres 16 B2	Daniela 2 1 B2	

Buccaneers of the Chilean coast

Sir Francis Drake was one of the first Europeans to commit piracy along the west coast of South America but his example was soon widely followed. By the second half of the 17th century, free-booting renegades – mostly English, French and Dutch – were roaming the South Seas preying on Spanish coastal towns and shipping in the hope of getting rich quick.

Basil Ringrose has a special place among these desperadoes because he left a fascinating first-hand account of his activities. Towards the end of 1679, he set out, under the command of a Captain Sharp, to take and plunder what Ringrose describes as the "vastly rich town of Arica". On finding the Spanish defence of Arica too strong to overcome, however, they had to continue south to nearby Hilo where they managed to land and occupy the sugar factory. The besieged Spaniards agreed to supply Ringrose and his comrades "four score of beeves" on the condition that they didn't burn the sugar factory to the ground. After several days of waiting for the "beeves" to arrive, the pirates began to smell a rat and decided to burn the factory down regardless and retreated to their ship. It was as well they did because they had no sooner re-embarked than they saw 300 Spanish horsemen advancing on their encampment. But Ringrose was still impressed by Hilo, describing it as "a valley very pleasant being all over set with figs, olives, oranges, lemons, and lime trees, and many other fruits agreeable to the palate". What Ringrose most remembered Hilo for, however, was its "good chocolate" of which they "had plundered some small quantity".

After the double disappointment of Arica and Hilo, the pirates continued south to the Bay of Coquimbo where they discovered the city of La Serena, "most excellent and delicate, and far beyond what we could expect in so remote a place". Ringrose was particularly impressed by the town's seven churches which he and his companions hoped to loot, but again news of their activities preceded them and the Spaniards had already removed the churches' treasures. Instead they "found strawberries as big as walnuts and very delicious to the taste".

El Tololo ① www.ctio.noao.edu, open to visitors by permit Sat 0900 and 1300. For (free) permits write to Casilla 603, La Serena, T051-205200, ctiorecp@noao.edu. Pick your it up before 1200 on the day before your visit from the office at Colina Los Pinos. Situated at 2200 m, 87 km southeast of La Serena in the Elqui Valley, 51 km south of Vicuña, this observatory belongs to Aura, an association of US and Chilean universities. It possesses what was until recently the largest telescope in the southern hemisphere (diameter 4 m), six other telescopes and a radio telescope. This is the closest of the observatories to La Serena and easiest to organise visits to. During holiday periods apply for a visitor permit well in advance; at other times it is worth trying for a cancellation the day before. The administration will insist that you have private transport; you can hire a taxi, US$75, but you will require the registration number when you book, as well as your passport. Motorcycles are, apparently, not permitted to use the access road. Visits last approximately two hours.

La Silla ① www.ls.eso.org, open Sat except in Jul and Aug, 1330-1700. For permits, register in advance at Alonso de Córdoba 3107, Santiago, T02-463 3280, recepstg@ eso.org, or write to Casilla 567, La Serena, T051-224527. Located at 2400 m, 156 km northeast of La Serena, this

The clear skies of northern Chile

With its large expanses of uninhabited desert and its dry, relatively thin atmosphere, northern Chile has become one of the great astronomical centres of the world. In the Elqui Valley alone, there are three large observatories, built by international organizations with important backing from Europe or the USA.

One, La Silla, is owned by European Southern Observatory (ESO), which is financed by the governments of some 10 European governments. The other two are El Tololo, which belongs to a consortium of US and Chilean universities, and Las Campanas, owned by the Carnegie Institute. Visitors are welcome at all these sites, but are not allowed to use the telescopes (see page 164). For this experience, you should go to Mamalluca or El Pangue, two smaller observatories near the town of Vicuña built for the public. They offer night-time visits and provide an opportunity to view the southern skies from the vantage point of the Elqui Valley.

The great powers of astronomy have continued to expand their operations in northern Chile. A new observatory was opened by ESO in March 1999 at Cerro Paranal, 120 km south of Antofagasta (see page 208). Known as the VLT ('very large telescope'), it consists of four 8-m telescopes that together are capable of picking out items on the moon as small as 1 m long. When the lenses arrived at the port of Antofagasta, the city centre was closed down to allow them to be transported to their final destination. Construction is now underway on an even larger project at Chajnantor, over 5000 m up in the Andes; this giant observatory, with 64 12-m radio telescopes, is being financed by ESO along with the governments of the USA and Japan.

These new developments are not without controversy. Construction of Cerro Paranal was held up by local landowners, who refused to renounce their rights to permit mining activity on their land (which would threaten the observatory with increased dust). Eventually, the Chilean government was forced to introduce some new legislation permitting it to buy out the landowners to enable the project to go ahead.

comprises 14 telescopes. To reach La Silla, head north from La Serena for 120 km along the Pan-American Highway to the turn-off, then another 36 km.

Las Campanas ① *www.lco.cl, Sat 1430-1730. For permits, write to Casilla 601, La Serena, T051-207301.* This observatory is at 2510 m, 162 km northeast of La Serena, 30 km north of La Silla. It belongs to the Carnegie Institute, has five telescopes and is altogether a smaller facility than the other two. To get to Las Campanas, follow the Pan-American Highway, take the turning for La Silla and then turn north after 14 km.

Mamalluca ① *bookings through agencies in La Serena as part of a tour or directly from Gabriela Mistral 260, Vicuña, T051-411352, www.mamalluca.org, visits daily at 2100, 2300, 0100 in summer, 1800, 2000, 2200 in winter, US$10 plus optional transport (US$4) per person.* Situated at 1500 m, 6 km north of Vicuña, this municipally owned observatory was built specifically for the public and where visitors can actually look through a telescope at the night sky. The first telescope, diameter 30 cm, was donated by El Tololo. There is also a multimedia centre here. Advance booking is strongly recommended in summer, when groups can be up to 30 people. Tours are given by astronomy students in Spanish and English of variable fluency.

Observatorio del Pangue ① *bookings through agencies in La Serena as part of a tour or directly from Chacabuco 226, Vicuña, T051-543810, www.astronomicasur.org. 2 or 3 visits nightly, US$15 plus US$6 transport.* This new observatory is about 16 km south of Vicuña on the road to Hurtado. Focused exclusively at the visiting public, it limits groups to 12 people. Tours are informative and in good English and French as well as Spanish, and the telescopes are latest-generation and more powerful than those at Mamalluca.

Coquimbo and the coast 🏨🍴🚗❄️🚌🌙 ▸▸ *pp172-178.*

Coquimbo

On the same bay as La Serena and only 84 km from Ovalle, Coquimbo was used during the colonial period as a port for La Serena, attracting attention from English pirates, including Francis Drake, who visited in 1578. Legends of buried treasure at Bahía la Herradura de Guayacán persist to this day. From these small beginnings, Coquimbo grew into a city in the 19th century, when it – and the separate centre of Guayacán – became important in the processing of copper. By 1854, there were two large copper foundries in Coquimbo and in 1858 the largest foundry in the world was built in La Herradura.

Coquimbo

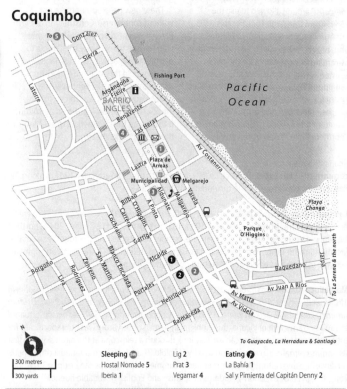

	Sleeping 🛏️	Lig **2**	Eating 🍴
300 metres	Hostal Nomade **5**	Prat **3**	La Bahía **1**
300 yards	Iberia **1**	Vegamar **4**	Sal y Pimienta del Capitán Denny **2**

Today, the city depends on the port for its vitality and economic solvency. It has one of the best harbours on the coast and several major fish-processing plants. The city is strung along the north shore of a peninsula, with most of the commercial life centred on three streets that run between the port and the steep hillside on which are perched many of the poorer houses. The 19th-century mansions of the **Barrio Inglés** along Aldunate to the north of the Plaza de Armas have recently been restored and these are home to much of the city's nightlife. On the south shore of the peninsula lies the suburb of **La Herradura**, where there is an iron-ore loading port, a steel church designed by Eiffel, an English cemetery and a huge cross, the **Cruz del Tercer Milenio**, erected to mark the millennium. It is possible to climb the 83-m cross for a charge of US$2. In 1981, heavy rain uncovered 39 tenth-century burials of humans and llamas, which had been sacrificed; the exhibits are on display in the **Museo del Sitio** ① *Plaza Gabriela Mistral, Jan and Feb only, Mon-Sat 0930-2030, Sun 0930-1400, free*. It doubles as a tourist information office. In summer, it is possible to take **boat trips** ① *regular departures, US$5*, around the harbour and to Punta Lobos on the bay **Municipal tourist office** ① *Las Heras 220, T051-313971*. Travellers should be aware that Coquimbo has a reputation for theft.

The coastal resorts

The coast around Coquimbo has some great beaches; the closest is at **La Herradura**, 2.5 km from Coquimbo, a slightly upmarket suburb that has the best beaches in the bay and numerous *cabañas* and restaurants. Also nearby is a resort complex called **Las Tacas**, with beach, swimming pool, tennis and apartments. Heading south, there are good swimming beaches at **Totoralillo**, 12 km beyond Coquimbo, and a 10-km beach east of **Guanaqueros**, a fishing village on the southern coast of a large bay, 37 km south of Coquimbo. **Tongoy**, 13 km further on is an old fishing port occupying the whole of a small peninsula. It is now a rapidly growing resort and well worth a visit, with two large beaches: the Playa Grande to the south (14 km long) and the Playa Socos to the north.

Vicuña and the Upper Elqui Valley ●❶❸❹❺ ➜ *pp172-178*.

Vicuña, the main town in the Elqui Valley, lies 66 km east of La Serena. The road is paved for another 37 km beyond, as far as Pisco Elqui. Most of the tiny towns here have just a single street. Many tour operators in La Serena offer day trips as far as Pisco Elqui, but you really need to stay overnight to experience the wonder of the upper valley. The valley is the centre of *pisco* production: of the nine distilleries in the valley, the largest is Capel in Vicuña. *Huancara*, a delicious fortified wine introduced by the Jesuits, is also produced in the valley. The Río Elqui has been dammed east of El Molle, 30 km east of La Serena. This has forced the relocation of five small towns in the valley and has also led to increased winds in the valley, according to locals.

Vicuña → *Colour map 2, C2.*

This small, friendly town was founded in 1821. On the west side of the plaza is the Municipalidad, built in 1826 and topped in 1905 by a medieval-style tower – the **Torre Bauer** – prefabricated in Germany and imported by the German-born mayor of the time. Inside the Municipalidad is a gallery of past local dignitaries as well as the **tourist office**. Also on the plaza is the **Iglesia Parroquial**, dating from 1860.

   Museo Gabriela Mistral ① *Gabriela Mistral 759, www.dibam.cl/sdm_mgm_vicuna, Mon-Sat 1000-1900, Sun 1000-1800, shorter hrs off season, US$1, students half price,* contains manuscripts, books, awards and many other details of the poet's life. Next door is the house where she was born. **Museo Entomológico** ① *C Chacabuco 334, daily 1000-2100 in summer; Mon-Fri 1030-1330 and 1530-1930, Sat-Sun 1030-1900 in winter, US$0.50,* has over 3000 insect species displayed. **Solar de los Madariaga** ① *Gabriela Mistral 683, open Jan, Feb and holidays, Mon-Fri 1000-1900, intermittently off season, US$0.70,* is a former residence containing artefacts belonging to a prominent local family. There are good views from Cerro La Virgen, north of town.

The **Capel Pisco distillery** ① *T051-411251, open Dec-May Mon-Sat 1000-1800, no booking required,* lies 1.5 km east of Vicuña, to the right of the main road. There is a small museum dedicated to the history of Pisco (entry US$1) and guided tours of the plant (US$1.50) leave every 30 minutes. Tours in English are sometimes available but phone ahead to make sure. There are two observatories near Vicuña, **Mamalluca**, 6 km north and **El Pangue**, 16 km south.

The upper valley

From Vicuña a *ripio* road (high-clearance vehicle necessary) runs south via **Hurtado** (Km 46), **Pichasca** (Km 85) and the **Monumento Natural Pichasca** to Ovalle (Km 120); see pages 157-158. The main road through the Elqui Valley continues east another 18 km to **Rivadavia**, where the rivers Turbio and Claro meet. Here the road divides, the international road (Route 41) winds through the mountains on a good, partly paved road to the Argentine border at **Paso Agua Negra** (4775 m). **Chilean immigration and customs** ① *open 0800-1700,* are at Juntas, 84 km west of the border (88 km east of Vicuña).

The other branch of the road runs through Paihuano to **Monte Grande**, where the schoolhouse in which Gabriela Mistral lived and was educated by her sister is now a **museum** ① *C Principal s/n, T051-415015, Tue-Sun 1000-1300, 1500-1800 (until 1900 in Jan and Feb), US$0.80.* The poet's tomb is situated at the edge of town, opposite the

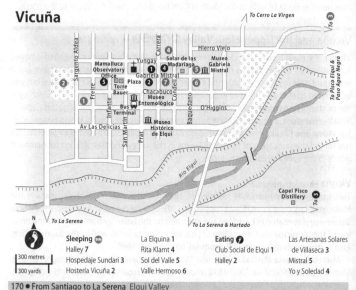

Vicuña

To Cerro La Virgen

To Pisco Elqui & Paso Agua Negra

Hierro Viejo

Mamalluca Observatory Office
Yungay
Solar de los Madariaga
Museo Gabriela Mistral

Plaza
Torre Bauer
Gabriela Mistral

Chacabuco
Museo Entomológico

O'Higgins

Bus Terminal

Av Las Delicias

Museo Histórico de Elqui

Río Elqui

Capel Pisco Distillery

To La Serena

To La Serena & Hurtado

N

300 metres
300 yards

Sleeping		Eating	
Halley 7	La Elquina 1	Club Social de Elqui 1	Las Artesanas Solares de Villaseca 3
Hospedaje Sundari 3	Rita Klamt 4	Halley 2	Mistral 5
Hostería Vicuña 2	Sol del Valle 5		Yo y Soledad 4
	Valle Hermoso 6		

The Elqui Valley in the words of its poet

"It is a heroic slash in the mass of mountains, but so short as to be little more than a green-banked torrent, yet small as it is one comes to love it as perfect. It contains in perfection all that man could ask of a land in which to live: light, water, wine and fruit. And what fruit! The tongue which has tasted the juice of its peaches and the mouth which has eaten of its purple figs will never seek sweetness elsewhere.

The people of the Elqui take remarkable pride in their green soil.

Whenever there is a hump, a ridge or bare patch without greenery, it is because it is naked rock. Wherever the Elquino has a little water and three inches of soil, however poor, he will cultivate something: peaches, vines or figs. That the leafy, polished vines climb only a little way up the mountainsides is because if they were planted higher, they would wither in the pitiless February sun."

Gabriela Mistral, quoted in Jan Reed, *The Wines of Chile* (Mitchell Beazley, 1994).

Artesanos de Cochiguaz *pisco* distillery, which is open to the public. Here the road forks, one branch leading to the **Cochiguaz Valley**. There is no public transport along this road, but there are several New Age settlements – it is said that the valley is an important energy centre – and a number of campsites. At night, there is no better place on earth to stargaze. When the moon is new, or below the horizon, the stars seem to be hanging in the air; spectacular shooting stars can be seen every couple of seconds, as can satellites crossing the night sky. Back on the main road, just south of Montegrande is the **Cavas del Valle** organic winery with free tastings and a salesroom.

Pisco Elqui, with a population of 500, is situated 2 km south of Monte Grande along the main road. It is an attractive village with the newly restored **Iglesia de Nuestra Señora Rosario** fronting onto a shady plaza. Here is the **Tres Erres** *pisco* distillery, which is open to the public and gives guided tours in Spanish for US$4; the vineyards themselves are now covered by nets to protect them from the winds caused by the new dam. Pisco Elqui is famous for its night skies and beautiful scenery and is also a New Age centre, where all sorts of alternative therapies and massages are available. Horses can be hired, for exploring the surrounding area. Ramón Luis, T051-451168, is a recommended guide. At the **Astropub** in the **Hotel Elqui** you can enjoy a few drinks while stargazing through telescopes. Some 4 km further up the valley at **Los Nichos** is a small *pisco* distillery open to the public for visits (closed lunchtime) and a store selling excellent dried fruit and other local products.

North of La Serena ⬤⬤ ↦ *pp172-178.*

It is 218 km north from La Serena to Vallenar, through a sparsely populated district usually bypassed by travellers. Some 35 km north of La Serena is **Caleta Hornos**, an impoverished fishing village with several restaurants where excellent seafood is served. The *Panamericana* then climbs to an arid plateau; 21 km beyond Caleta Hornos is a turning eastwards to **La Higuera**, a small town that once thrived from the iron ore mine at **El Tofo** on the opposite side of the valley. This was once one of the largest iron ore mines in the world; the mine stacks can clearly be seen from the *Panamericana*, as can the eerie eucalyptus trees on top of the hill, kept alive by the coastal fog. Only the guardian of the mine lives here now, but it is worth driving up to El Tofo to see the ghost town and for the spectacular views down to the coast.

To Reserva Nacional Pingüino de Humboldt

Sixteen kilometres north of the turn-off for El Tofo, a road heads westwards from the *Panamericana*, signposted for **Punta de Choros**. This *ripio* road leads through a rugged dry river valley for 20 km before reaching the small village of **Los Choros Bajos**, where the main activity is growing olives; the groves of olive trees provide a beautiful green backdrop to the harshness of the desert. There is a restaurant serving basic meals, but it is better to continue a further 22 km towards the coast to **Punta de Choros**, the departure point for visiting the reserve.

Reserva Nacional Pingüino de Humboldt consists of three islands: **Chañaral**, **Choros** and **Damas**. It was founded to preserve the coast's marine life, which includes many penguins, sea lions and dolphins, as well as wonderful birdlife. The combination of this and the coast's rugged isolation means that visits here will not be quickly forgotten. To visit the reserve, tours are available from La Serena and Vallenar or you can hire a boat with local fishermen (around US$80 for up to 10 people). Isla Damas is the only island at which it is possible to disembark (entrance to the island is US$5) and camping is allowed, but before visiting or camping on the island you must seek permission from **CONAF** in Punta de Choros, T051-272798. There is a toilet on Isla Damas but no drinking water.

From the turning to Punta de Choros, the *Panamericana* continues north, passing several small mining towns. At **Domeyko**, 165 km north of La Serena, a *ripio* road leads west to the coast towards the northern sector of the reserve, based around the small *caleta* at Chañaral.

◉ Elqui Valley listings

For Sleeping and Eating price codes and other relevant information, see Essentials pages 35-42.

◉ Sleeping

La Serena *p163, map p165*
The *Panamericana* from La Serena to Coquimbo is lined with cheaper accommodation and restaurants. There is also good-quality accommodation along Av del Mar, 500 m off the highway.
L-AL Costa Real, Av de Aguirre 170, T051-221010, www.costareal.cl. Supposedly 5-star although without most of the features of a hotel in this category. Excellent restaurant, bar, unheated pool and conference centre. Probably the best hotel in town.
AL-A Francisco de Aguirre, Cordovez 210, T051-222991, www.dahoteles.com. 4-star, refurbished, pool and reasonable restaurant.
AL-A La Serena Plaza, Fransisco de Aguirre 0660, T051-225745, www.hotelserena plaza.cl. Upmarket hotel by the beach with spacious rooms, swimming pool gym and restaurant. Good value.
A Los Balcones de Aragón, Cienfuegos 289, T051-212419, www.losbalconesde aragon.cl. Standard 3-star with rooms arranged around a small neat courtyard. The upstairs rooms at the front of the hotel are bigger but can be affected by noise from the street.
A-B Cabañas Bahía Drake, Av del Mar 1300, T051-223367, www.cabanasbahiadrake.cl. Pleasant fully equipped *cabañas* on the seafront with swimming pool.
A-B Del Cid, O'Higgins 138, T051-212692, www.hoteldelcid.cl. Characterful hotel near the centre with smallish but spotless rooms around a courtyard. Parking available, very friendly, English spoken. Recommended.
A-B Hostal Del Mar, Cuatro Esquinas 0680 (south of town centre, near beach), T051-225559, www.hostaldelmar.cl. Also apartments, clean, friendly.

A-B Londres, Córdovez 550, T051-219066, www.hotellondres.cl. Simple hotel. Bright rooms with good beds, cable TV, Wi-Fi and decent bathrooms. The rooms backing on to the Din shop can be noisy during the day.

B-C El Punto, Andrés Bello 979, T051-228474, www.hostalelpunto.cl. **D-E** singles, **E-F** per person in shared rooms. Recently refurbished rooms with or without bath, with breakfast, tasteful, comfortable, café, laundry, book exchange, parking, English and German spoken, Wi-Fi area, information given and tours arranged. Highly recommended.

B-C Hostal Colón, Colón 371, T051-223979, www.hostaldecolonlaserena.cl. Rooms around a small central courtyard. Nothing exceptional but good value, discounts for payment in dollars and for stays of more than 1 night.

C Casa Alejandro Muñoz, Brasil 720, T051-211619. **F** singles. Accommodation in family home in old part of town, hot showers, good breakfast, garden, some English and French spoken, friendly atmosphere.

C Gregoria Fernández, Andrés Bello 1067, T051-224400, www.hostaldegregoria.cl. **E** singles. Clean, friendly, very helpful, good local information, good beds, some rooms with bath, 3 blocks from bus terminal, garden, good breakfast (charged extra), Wi-Fi, parking.

C-D Camino de Luna, Los Carrera 861, T051-486037, hostalcaminodeluna@gmail.com. **E** singles. Nice clean rooms with cable TV, a bit dark, some with bath. Bright patio. Friendly owner from Valdivia keen to practice English.

C-D Hostal Croata, Cienfuegos 248, T/F051-224997, www.hostalcroata.cl. **D** singles. Some rooms with bath, with breakfast, kitchen and laundry facilities, cable TV, patio, Wi-Fi, hospitable, some English spoken, good value.

C-D Hostal Familyhome, Av Santo 1056, T/F051-224059, www.familyhome.cl. **E-F** singles. Some rooms with bath, kitchen facilities, thin walls and slightly tatty but clean. Far from being the best place in town but it has a 24-hr reception and is close to the bus terminal so useful if you are arriving at night.

C-D Hostal Matta, Matta 234, T051-210014, www.hostalmatta.cl. **D** singles. Pleasant

family-run bed and breakfast. Simple but clean high-ceilinged rooms, some with bath and cable TV. Small garden with barbeque area and use of kitchen. Wi-Fi.

C-D María's Casa, Las Rojas 18, T051-229282, hostalmariascasa.cl. **E-F** singles, **F** per person in dorms. Very welcoming, near bus terminal, kitchen and laundry facilities, Wi-Fi, garden, camping, very helpful. Good value. Some English spoken. Recommended.

C-D Residencial Suiza, Cienfuegos 250, T051-216092, residencial.suiza@terra.cl. With bath and breakfast, good beds. Recommended.

Coquimbo *p168, map p168*

Accommodation is cheaper than La Serena.

B Lig, Aldunate 1577, T051-311171. Comfortable, friendly, with breakfast, overpriced, near bus terminal.

C Hostal Nomade, Regimento Coquimbo 5, T051-315665, www.hostalnomade.cl. **E** singles, **F** per person in dorms. HI-affiliated. Kitchen and laundry facilities, internet, tours arranged, also camping. English spoken.

C Prat, Bilbao y Aldunate, T051-311845. Comfortable, with breakfast, pleasant.

C-D Iberia, Lastra 400, T051-312141. Cheaper without bath. Friendly. Recommended.

D Vegamar, Las Heras 403, T051-311773. Shared bath, basic.

The coastal resorts *p169*

B Cabañas Bahia Club, Guanaqueros, T051-395819, camping1@entelchile.net. *Cabañas* for 3 people with kitchens, on the waterfront. Recommended. Camping also available.

C La Herradura, Av La Marina 200, La Herradura, T/F051-261647. Rooms with bath, restaurant attached.

Camping

Camping La Herradura, La Herradura, T051-263867, mac-food@ctcinternet.cl. Price for up to 5 people.

Camping Oasis, Guanaqueros, T051-395319. On the beach; price per site.

Vicuña *p169, map p170*

Prices are higher in Jan and Feb.

A Hostería Vicuña, Sgto Aldea 101, T051-411144, www.hosteriavicuna.cl. In spacious grounds. Swimming pool, tennis court, poor restaurant, parking. Has seen better days.

B Halley, Mistral 542, T051-412070, turismo halley@yahoo.es. Pleasantly old-fashioned hotel with high-ceilinged rooms, colonial-style courtyard, and a pleasant pool.

C Hospedaje Sundari, C Principal 3, San Isidro (20 mins' walk from Vicuña), T051-412072, www.manos.cl/sundari. Delightful bungalows, with breakfast, spotless, TV, internet, bicycles, pool, in lovely gardens. Aloe and other herbal therapies. Recommended.

C La Elquina, O' Higgins 65, T051-411317. Lovely garden, laundry and kitchen facilities.

C Rita Klamt, Condell 443, T051-419611, rita_klamt@yahoo.es. **D-E** single. Impeccably kept bed and breakfast. Excellent breakfast, ample kitchen facilities, pleasant garden with pool. Friendly and helpful. German and some English spoken. Highly recommended.

C Sol del Valle, Gabriela Mistral 741. T051-411078. With breakfast, bath, TV, vineyard, restaurant, swimming pool, recommended.

C Valle Hermoso, Gabriela Mistral 706, T/F051-411206. Clean, comfortable, parking. Recommended.

Camping

G Unnamed campsite, Gabriela Mistral 152, T09-9428 6158. Hot showers, kitchen.

G Las Tinajas, east end of Chacabuco. Swimming pool, restaurant.

The upper valley *p170*

Accommodation in the valley is much cheaper outside Jan and Feb. If you're heading for the Argentine border, there is basic, clean accommodation at **Huanta** (Guanta on many maps), Km 46 from Vicuña; ask for Guillermo Aliaga. Huanta is also the last chance to buy food.

Pisco Elqui

L-AL Los Misterios de Elqui, A Prat s/n, T051-1982544, www.misteriosde elqui.cl.

Plush *cabañas*, sleep 4, swimming pool, good but expensive restaurant.

AL Elqui Domos, Sector los Nichos s/n, T09-7709 2879, www.elquidomos.cl. Accommodation in geodesic domes. The roofs open allowing a direct view of the night sky from the beds on the mezzanine. English spoken.

A-B Los Dátiles, A Prat s/n, T051-451226, www.losdatileselqui.cl. *Cabañas* with kitchenette, sleep 5, good-sized swimming pool, good restaurant serving Chilean country cooking.

B El Tesoro del Elqui, T051-451069, www.tesoro-elqui.cl. *Cabañas* for up to 4, also shared rooms, **E** per person, pleasant gardens, pool, English and German spoken. Tours arranged, good restaurant. Recommended.

B Refugio La Isla, Sector La Isla, T09-7476 9924, refugiolaisla@gmail.com. Idyllic retreat on a hillside overlooking the village. Simple, rustic accommodation in a colonial house, some rooms with bath. Kitchen facilities, pool, meditation room. Access difficult without transport. Recommended.

C Elqui, O'Higgins s/n, T051-451130. **E-F** singles. Hot shower, good restaurant and bar.

C Hostal Triskel, Baquedano s/n, T09-9419 8680, www.hostaltriskel.cl. **E** singles. With breakfast, shared bathrooms. Decent new hostel located near the town centre.

C La Casa de Don Juan, Prat s/n. **F** singles. Rickety wooden mansion. The upstairs room has spectacular views.

E Hospedaje, Prat 27. **F-G** singles. Cheapest option, friendly, watch out for fleas.

Camping El Olivo, 1 block from the plaza. Small restaurant, pool, excellent facilities. Well-stocked supermarket. Sol de Barbosa. Showers, open all year, price per site.

North of La Serena *p171*

B Cabañas Los Delfines, Pilpilen s/n, sitio 33, Punta de Choros, T09-9639 6678. Cabins for up to 6 people. There are other eating and accommodation options in the area.

🍴 Eating

La Serena *p163, map p165*

Eating tends to be expensive in La Serena – Coquimbo is cheaper. Avoid the restaurants on the upper floor of the Recova market where you will be immediately assailed by numerous waiters and where the food is often poor. Better restaurants are tend to be on the seafront, 2 km west of the centre.

For seafood the best place to go is the Sector de los Pescadores in Peñuelas on the coast halfway between La Serena and Coquimbo. Take any bus to Coquimbo and get off at the junction with Los Pescadores, opposite a mini zoo. Walk 300 m to the coast and there are a dozen or so restaurants. Prices are generally ₸₸.

₸₸-₸₸ **Donde El Guatón**, Brasil 750. Parrillada, paradise for meat eaters, also good seafood, one of the better places in the town centre, but that's not saying much.

₸₸-₸₸ **Porotos**, Av del Mar 900-B, Sector El Faro, T051-210937. Wide variety of well presented dishes (fish, meat and pasta) that manage to combine contrasting flavours. Decent portions and attentive service, although the decor is a bit naff.

₸₸-₸₸ **Tololo Beach**, Av del Mar 5200, Sector Las Gaviotas. On the beach about 4 km south of town. Extensive menu mostly of meat and seafood. You will have to travel a long way to get a better steak!

₸₸ **Costa Inca**, Av del Mar 2500, T051-212802. Without doubt the best Peruvian restaurant in the area. Good value and a range of delicious dishes. Occasional all-you-can-eat deals.

₸₸ **La Mía Pizza**, Av del Mar 2100, T051-212232. Italian, good-value pizzas and also fish dishes, good wine list.

₸₸ **Mai Lan Fan**, Fransisco de Aguirre s/n. The best Chinese in town.

₸₸-₸ **El Callejón**, O'Higgins 635. Bohemian student hangout serving cheap dishes. Popular bar at night.

₸ **Daniela 2**, F de Aguirre 335. Good-quality Chilean home cooking. Recommended.

₸ **Govindas**, Lautaro 841, T051-224289. Open Mon-Fri lunchtime. Incredibly cheap vegetarian food served in a Hari Krishna yoga centre.

Cafés

Café Colonial, Balmaceda 475. Sandwiches fast food and coffee. Also serves breakfast.

Café do Brasil, Balmaceda 461. Good coffee.

Café Morocco, Prat 566. Good coffee and fresh juices.

Diavoletto, Prat 565 and O'Higgins 531. Fast food and ice cream, popular.

Tahití, Cordovez 540, local 113. Real coffee, pastries. Recommended.

Coquimbo *p168, map p168*

According to the tourist office in La Serena, the best cheap seafood is to be had at Coquimbo, especially in the municipal market, Melgarejo, entre Bilbao y Borgoño. The new casino has 3 supposedly top-class restaurants. For more inventive cuisine, try the Barrio Inglés.

₸₸-₸₸ **Sal y Pimienta del Capitán Denny**, Aldunate 769. One of the best in town, pleasant, old fashioned, mainly fish cooked in Chilean style.

₸₸ **Crucero**, Valera. Excellent seafood.

₸₸ **La Picada**, Costanera. Excellent, good *pebre*. Near statue of O'Higgins.

₸₸ **Mai Lai Fan**, Av Ossandón 1. Reasonable Chinese food.

₸₸-₸ **Centro Gastronómico El Suizo**, Fritz Willy Linderman 2427, Guanaqueros. A collection of a dozen small restaurants all serving good-quality fresh seafood in abundant portions.

₸ **La Bahía**, Pinto 1465. Excellent, good value.

₸ **La Barca**, Ríos y Varela. Modest but good.

Vicuña *p169, map p170*

₸₸ **Club Social de Elqui**, Gabriela Mistral 435. Very good, attractive patio, good-value *almuerzo*, real coffee.

₸₸ **Halley**, Gabriela Mistral 404. Specialists in local meat dishes including rabbit and huge portions of goat.

₸₸ **Las Artesanas Solares de Villaseca**, 8 km east of Vicuña in Villaseca, T051-198 2184.

Take a 'Peralillo–Diaguitas' *colectivo* from the bus terminal. Pioneering restaurant in the use of solar ovens. A splinter restaurant has opened up just down the hill after an argument between the shareholders, but the original (painted green) has the better views.

♝ Pizzería Virgos, Prat 234 on the plaza. Mid-range pizzas.
♝ Mistral, Gabriela Mistral 180. Very good, popular with locals, good-value *almuerzo*.
♝ Yo Y Soledad, Gabriela Mistral 364. Inexpensive hearty Chilean food, good.

The upper valley *p170*
♝♝-♝ Miraflores, Camino a Los Nichos. Off season, open weekends only. Excellent meat.
♝ Donde la Elke, O'Higgins y Rodríguez. Well-prepared meat fish and pasta. Recommended.
♝ El Rincón Chileno, O'Higgins s/n. Chilean country fare including roast goat.
♝ Los Jugos, on the plaza. Light snacks and fresh juices.

♬ Bars and clubs

La Serena *p163, map p165*
Most of the clubs are on the Av del Mar and in Peñuelas but in town, you should try:
B-Cool, Av 4 Esquinas s/n. Recommended.
El Callejón, O'Higgins 635. Lounge bar and patio, with a relaxed atmosphere. Young crowd. Fills up with students at weekends.
El Faro, Av del Mar y Av Francisco Aguirre. A pricey but good pub.
El Nuevo Peregrino, Peni y Andrés Bello. Intimate bar with live music at weekends.
Pub-Discosalsa Kamanga, Costanera 4785. University crowd, fun, recommended.

⊕ Entertainment

La Serena *p163, map p165*
There is a multiplex cinema complex in the Mall Plaza (see Shopping, below).
Cultural centres Alliance Française, Matta 665. Centro Latino-Americano de

Arte y Cultura, Balmaceda 824, T051-229344. Music and dance workshops, art gallery, handicraft workshops. **Nueva Acropolis**, Benavente 692, T051-21214. Lectures, discussions, free entry.

Coquimbo *p168, map p168*
There is a new casino at Peñuelas Norte 56, www.casinodecoquimbo.cl.

⊕ Festivals and events

Coquimbo *p168, map p168*
14-21 Sep Coquimbo hosts **La Pampilla**, the biggest Independence Day celebrations in Chile. Between 200,000 and 300,000 people come from all over the country for the fiesta, which lasts for a week. Things get going on 14 Sep, and the partying does not stop until 21 Sep. It costs US$1.50 to gain access to the area where the main dancing tents are to be found, as well as much Chilean food and drink. You have to pay to enter the *peñas*, but there also free communal areas. Big bands such as **Illapu** and **La Ley** have played here in recent years, as well as *cumbia* bands from Argentina and Colombia.

○ Shopping

La Serena *p163, map p165*
For handicrafts try **Cema-Chile**, Los Carrera 562, or **La Recova** handicraft market on Cantournet and Cienfuegos, though many items sold here are imported.

Good supermarkets include **Santa Isabel**, Cienfuegos 500 block, and **Deca**, Balmaceda 1200 block. There is also a **Líder** by the Mall Plaza, on the *Panamericana*, next to the bus station (open from 1030). **Tintos y Blancos**, Prat 630, has a good selection of fine wines and good quality *piscos*. **Librería Inglesa**, Cordovez 309, on the plaza. T051-215699, www.libreriainglesa.cl, is an English-language bookshop, mostly school texts.

▲▲ Activities and tours

La Serena *p163, map p165*
Several agencies offer similar tours of the region. Approximate tour prices: Valle del Elqui US$30, Parque Nacional Fray Jorge US$50, Tongoy US$40, city tour US$20, Mamalluca observatory US$27, Reserva Nacional Los Pingüinos and the Isla Damas US$50. Some operators also offer tours to Valle del Encanto, Andacollo and Isla Chañaral.

Quality varies enormously. The more responsible operators will not lead tours to Mamalluca or Isla Damas in bad weather. Many hostels will arrange tours with the agency that pays them the highest commission, so their recommendations are not always to be taken at face value.

The following are recommended and offer a range of local tours including trekking and climbing options:
Chile Safari, T09-8769 7686, www.chilesafari.com.
Delfines, Matta 591, T051-223624, www.turismoaventuradelfines.cl.
Elqui Total, Parcela 17, El Arrayan at Km 27 along the road from La Serena to Vicuña, T09-92197872, www.elquitotal.cl. Offer short horse-riding trips from their base.
Elqui Valley Tour, Los Carrera 515, T051-214846, www.elquivalleytour.cl.
Jeep Tour La Serena, T09-9291 8105, www.jeeptour-laserena.cl. Private and small group tours (max 6 people) of the area led by Swiss Guide Daniel Russ. Apart from the usual tours he also offers trips to the paso Agua Negra and also a transfer service to San Juan in Argentina (summer only).
Talinay Adventure Expeditions, Prat 470, in the courtyard, T051-218658, www.talinaychile.com.

The upper valley *p170*
Pisco Elqui
Elqui Enduro, Prat s/n, T051-451069, www.elquienduro.com. Enduro motorbike tours.
Mundo Elqui, O' Higgins s/n, T051-451290, www.mundoelqui.cl, offer trekking and mountain-biking trips as well as horse-riding trips in the Cochihuaz Valley.
Turismo Migrantes, O' Higgins s/n, T09-9829 5630, www.turismo migrantes.cl. Tours to the Cochihuaz and Alcohuaz valleys and the observatories.

◉ Transport

La Serena *p163, map p165*
Air
Aeropuerto La Florida, 5 km east of the city, T051-271812. To **Santiago** and **Copiapó**, Lan Chile, 45 mins.

Bicycle
Mike's Bikes, Av de Aguirre 004, T051-224 454, sales, hire, repairs, English spoken, helpful. Also **Cicles Serena**, Colón 452.

Bus
Local The bus terminal is at El Santo y Amunátegui (about 8 blocks south of the centre). City buses cost US$0.75. To **Coquimbo**, bus No 8 from Av Aguirre y Cienfuegos, US$0.90, frequent; to **Vicuña**, with **Via Elqui** and **Servitur**, every 30 mins, 1 hr, US$2.50, most buses continue to **Pisco Elqui**, US$4, until 2000. *Colectivos* to **Coquimbo** from Av Aguirre y Balmaceda; to **Vicuna** from Domeyko y Balmaceda, US$3.50; to **Andacollo** and **Ovalle**, yellow *colectivos* from Domeyko. *Colectivos* also operate on fixed routes throughout town.
Long distance Buses daily to **Santiago**, several companies, 7-8 hrs, US$15-25; to **Arica**, 21 hrs, US$43-55; to **Calama**, 16 hrs, US$30-65; to **Vallenar**, 3 hrs, US$7.50; to **Valparaíso**, 7 hrs, US$15-25; to **Caldera**, 6 hrs, US$14; to **Antofagasta**, several companies, 12 hrs, US$28-43; and to **Iquique**, 17 hrs, US$35-69.
International Covalle, T051-213127, have 2 buses weekly to **Mendoza** and **San Juan** from Infante 538. The buses go via Los Libertadores rather than the more direct route over Aguas Negras.

Car

Hire from **Avis**, Av de Aguirre 063, T051-227171; **Budget**, Balmaceda 3820, T051-290241; **Daire**, Balmaceda 3812, T051-226933, recommended, good service; **Flota Verschae**, Fransisco de Aguirre 0240, T051-27645, good value, recommended; **Hertz**, Av de Aguirre 068, T051-227171, prices range from US$50 to US$80 per day; **La Florida**, at airport, T051-271947; and **Theocar**, Balmaceda 4310, T051-243770, www.theocar.cl, good-value responsible local outfit. Recommended.

Taxi

City taxis charge a flat rate of US$0.55 plus US$0.20 for every 200 m.

Coquimbo and the coast *p168, map p168*
Bus

Terminal at Varela 1300 y Garriga. To **La Serena**, every few mins, US$0.75; to **Guanaqueros**, 45 mins, US$1; to **Tongoy**, 1 hr, US$1.50, with **Ruta Costera**, frequency varies according to day (more on Sun) and season. There are also *colectivos* to **Guanaqueros**, US$2 and to **Tongoy**, US$2.50.

Vicuña and the Upper Elqui Valley *p169, map p170*
Bus

Buses depart from Pisco Elqui to **La Serena**, US$3, on the hour, via Vicuña. From Vicuña to **La Serena**, about 10 a day (more in summer), mostly with **Via Elqui** or **Servitur**, 1st 0800, last 1930, 1 hr, US$3, also *colectivo* from the bus terminal, US$4; to **Santiago** via La Serena, with **Expreso Norte** and **TurBus**, US$20; to **Pisco Elqui**, hourly, with **Vía Elqui** and **Servitur**, 1 hr, US$2.50. There is no public transport beyond towards the border past Rivadavia.

North of La Serena *p171*

There is no public transport to Punta de Choros, but tours are readily available from La Serena; traffic on the road between Punta de Choros, and the Pan-American Highway is relatively frequent, especially at weekends, so hitching is also possible.

⊙ Directory

La Serena *p163, map p165*
Banks Several throughout the city centre. There is an ATM in the bus terminal. *Casas de cambio* at **Inter**, Balmaceda 431; **Cambio Fides**, Caracol Colonial, Balmaceda 460, good rates, changes TCs; also **Cambio Caracol** in the same building. **Consulates** France and Germany, Matta 665. **Internet** Ubiquitous. **Laundry** M & B, Peni 363, T051-211904 US$2.50 per kilo. Will pick up and deliver. Nevada, Los Carrera 635, US$6 for a 5-kg load. **Medical services** Hospitals: San Juan de Dios, Balmaceda 916, T051-200600. Clínica Elqui, Av El Salto 1475, T051-332300, just south of the main bus terminal (for those with insurance). **Police** Carabineros, Cienfuegos 180, T051-225276. **Telephone** Lots of call centres in the town centre.

Coquimbo and the coast *p168, map p168*
Banks Cambios Maya, Portales 305. Also many Redbancs in the centre.
Internet Aldunate 1196, open until 2330.
Telephone CTC, Aldunate 1633. **Medical services** Hospital: San Pablo, Videla s/n, T051-206246. **Police** Carabineros, Varela 1545, T051-311111.

Vicuña and the Upper Elqui Valley *p169, map p170*
Banks There are 2 banks in Vicuña but none further up the valley.

Contents

Into the Atacama

At a glance

⊜ **Getting around** As always there is good public transport between cities. To visit national parks you will have to hire a vehicle or take a tour.

⊚ **Time required** 2 or 3 days to take in the main sights, plus as much time as you want to relax on deserted beaches.

☀ **Weather** Warm on the coast. Inland hot days and cool nights.

⊗ **When not to go** Access to Parque Nacional Tres Cruces is difficult in winter (May-Sep), while the Pan de Azucar tends to fill up with revelling students in Jan and Feb.

★Don't miss ...
1 **Flowering of the desert**, page 184.
2 **Tránsito Valley**, page 184.
3 **The Parque Nacional Tres Cruces**, page 189.
4 **Ojos del Salado**, page 190.
5 **Pan de Azúcar**, page 196.

From La Serena, the shrubs and cacti of the semi-desert stretch north as far as the mining and agro-industrial centre of Copiapó. Beyond this city, the Atacama Desert begins. The main population centres are in the valleys of the rivers Huasco and Copiapó, and in the Salado Valley, where the most important economic activity is mining, especially inland at El Salvador.

Although much of this region appears lifeless and of limited interest to visitors, the area around Vallenar is famous for the flowering of the desert following the rare occasions when there is heavy rainfall; the upper reaches of the Huasco Valley are beautiful and tranquil, and make a good resting point en route to or from the Atacama, as does the beach resort of Bahía Inglesa, while the port of Huasco itself has excellent seafood. All along the coast of this region a variety of excellent inshore fish known as *pescado de roca* are caught. There are also three national parks: the Parque Nacional Pan de Azúcar, which protects a wide range of marine life; the Parque Nacional Llanos de Challe, which safeguards the habitat of one of the very rare flowers that bud with rainfall; and the Parque Nacional Tres Cruces, which covers extensive areas of salt flats northeast of Copiapó. East of the Parque Nacional Tres Cruces is the Paso San Francisco, a desolate yet spectacular border crossing into Argentina; near the pass are some of the highest peaks in the Andes, although most are best tackled from the Argentine side.

Background

Although small groups of Spanish settlers took over the fertile lands in the Huasco and Copiapó valleys in the 16th century, no towns were founded until late in the colonial period. Even the valleys were sparsely populated until the 19th century when the development of mining led to the creation of the ports of Caldera, Chañaral and Huasco and encouraged the building of railways. Mining remains a major economic activity: one of the largest copper mines is at El Salvador and over 50% of all Chilean iron ore is mined around Vallenar. Agriculture is limited to the valleys; the Copiapó Valley is an important producer of grapes, while the lower Huasco Valley is Chile's main olive-growing area. Fishing is centred on Caldera and, on a smaller scale, Chañaral and Huasco.

This part of the country can be divided into two: between the Río Elqui and the Río Copiapó the transitional semi-desert zone continues; north of the Copiapó the Atacama Desert begins and drivers should beware of high winds and blowing sand. The valleys of the rivers Huasco, Copiapó and Salado form oases in this barren landscape. On the coast, temperatures are moderated by the sea and mist is common in the mornings. Inland temperatures are higher by day and cooler by night; Vallenar and the upper valleys of the Copiapó and Huasco can be especially cold on winter evenings. Rainfall is sparse and occurs in winter only, with amounts decreasing as you go north.

East of Copiapó the Andes divide between the eastern range (Cordillera de Claudio Gay) and the western range (Cordillera de Domeyko); a basin collects the waters from the Andes. Here there are salt flats, the most extensive being the Salar de Pedernales. The eastern range has some of the highest peaks in Chile: Ojos del Salado (6893 m-6864 m, see box, page 190), Incahuasi (6615 m), Tres Cruces (6749 m) and San Francisco (6020 m).

Huasco Valley

This valley (known as the Jardín de Atacama) is an oasis of olive groves and vineyards. It is rugged and spectacular, reminiscent of the Cajón del Maipo near Santiago. At Alto del Carmen, 39 km east of Vallenar, the valley divides into the Carmen and Tránsito valleys. There are pisco distilleries at Alto del Carmen and San Félix, both of which have basic residenciales. A sweet wine known as pajarete is also produced. Today the Río Huasco is the last of the unpolluted rivers in the north. However, a huge goldmining project in the upper valley has been approved, to the displeasure of many locals. ➤➤ *For listings, see pages 185-186.*

Ins and outs

The Huasco Valley's main town and transport hub is Vallenar, which is easily reached by regular buses from both north and south. **Tourist information** for the valley is available from the Municipalidad on the Plaza de Armas in Vallenar as well as the Municipalidades in Huasco and Alto del Carmen.

Vallenar → *Colour map 2, B2. Phone code: 051. Population: 47,000.*

Nearly 200 km north of La Serena is Vallenar, the chief town of the Huasco Valley. It was founded in 1789 as San Ambrosio de Ballenary to commemorate the birthplace in Ireland of Ambrosio O'Higgins. The town is centred on a pleasant Plaza de Armas, in which all the benches are made of Chile's purest marble, extracted from the Tránsito Valley. The plaza is dominated by the church, a kitsch monstrosity with its iron girder steeple and electric chimes on the hour. There is a summer-only information kiosk on the plaza. **Museo del Huasco** ① *Sgto Aldea 742, Tue-Fri 1500-1800, US$1,* contains historic photos and artefacts from the valley. Opposite is the northernmost Chilean palm tree in the country.

West of Vallenar

Freirina, founded in 1752, was the most important town in the valley, its prosperity based upon the nearby Capote goldmine and on later discoveries of copper. The pleasant main plaza with the Municipalidad (1870) and the Santa Rosa church (1869) is flanked by streets of multicoloured houses. There are scattered olive groves either side of town, and both olives and olive oil are sold from farmhouses and by the side of the road. It is easily reached by *colectivo*, 36 km west of Vallenar.

Situated at the mouth of the river, **Huasco** lies 56 km west of Vallenar. Those arriving from the desert north and heading down the valley will appreciate the change of scenery – poplars and olive groves with an occasional glimpse of the river below. Destroyed by an earthquake in 1922, Huasco is a modern town with a large beach that is popular in summer, and a further expanse of deserted beach curves round to the north. There is a new coastal promenade with shaded benches looking out to sea and an esplanade for occasional concerts in summer. The port is interesting, as the fishermen unload their catches and hundreds of pelicans hover, waiting to snatch the fish that slip off the crates into the sea. There is a thriving sea-lion colony on the small islands offshore, and fishermen may be willing to take people there for a small charge. However, the best reason to come to Huasco is undoubtedly the seafood. There is good tourist information in the Municipalidad.

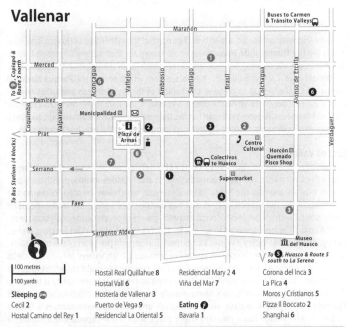

Vallenar

Sleeping 🛏	Hostal Real Quillahue 8	Residencial Mary 2 4	Corona del Inca 3
Cecil 2	Hostal Vall 6	Viña del Mar 7	La Pica 4
Hostal Camino del Rey 1	Hostería de Vallenar 3		Moros y Cristianos 5
	Puerto de Vega 9	Eating 🍴	Pizza Il Boccato 2
	Residencial La Oriental 5	Bavaria 1	Shanghai 6

The flowering of the desert

The average annual rainfall in this region declines as you travel north: in Vallenar it is 65 mm, in Copiapó 20 mm. Most years, the semi-desert appears to support only bushes and cacti and these become sparser as you continue north. However, in years of heavier than usual winter rainfall, this semi-desert breaks into colour as dormant seeds and bulbs germinate to produce blankets of flowers, while insects that normally hide underground emerge to enjoy the foliage.

Although the *desierto florido* (flowering desert) used to occur every seven years or so, changing climatic conditions have led to an increase in the phenomenon.

Although the first traces of the *desierto florido* can be seen as far south as La Ligua and Los Molles, it is particularly worth seeing around Vallenar. From La Serena northwards, the Pan-American Highway is fringed with expanses of different colours: there are great stretches of violet *pata de guanaco*, yellow *corona del fraile* and blue *suspiro del campo*. Not all of these species can be seen at the same time: as the brief spring unfolds, the colours change and new species push through to replace others.

Around Vallenar, however, the colours are more varied as different species compete to celebrate this ever more frequent coming of spring: the Pan-American Highway north of the city as far as Copiapó and the coastal road north of Huasco are both recommended for a prime view. For guided tours, contact **Roberto Alegría**, T051-613865, Vallenar, and for further information, contact Vallenar tourist office see page 182).

Some 9 km east of Huasco, a road branches north at the settlement of Huasco Bajo, near which are the **Humedal de Huasco** wetlands, known for their variety of marine birdlife (there are over 100 species). Some 50 km further north (37 of them *ripio*) is the small *caleta* of **Carrizal Bajo**. Carrizal Bajo is the best place from which to visit the **Parque Nacional Llanos de Challe**, set up to preserve the habitat of the *garra de león* and other flowers during the rare occasions when the desert is in bloom. The park is also home to Copiapoa cacti and guanacos. A decent salt road follows the coastline north of Carrizal Bajo, passing a series of small *caletas* en route to Caldera, including the beautiful beach at Puerto Viejo.

East of Vallenar

East of Vallenar, a paved road leads 39 km to **Alto del Carmen**, the site of the distillery of one of the best *piscos* in Chile. The road clings to arid hillsides sprinkled with cacti and *maitén* bushes, passing the Santa Juana Reservoir, which was created following the damming of the Río Huasco in 1995 and has transformed agriculture in the area. The valley is filled with grapevines for *pisco* and with groves of pepper and eucalyptus trees.

At Alto del Carmen, the road forks: left for the **Tránsito Valley**, right for the **Carmen Valley**. The Tránsito Valley is wilder and extends further into the heart of the mountains, while the Carmen Valley is greener and more populous: both valleys are unlikely clefts in the rocky Andes and reward the traveller who is prepared to make the effort to get to know them. Some 21 km beyond Alto del Carmen along the Tránsito Valley is the *mina de mármol blanco*, where Chile's finest marble is quarried. The peaceful village of **El Tránsito**, where there is basic accommodation and a cheap restaurant, is a further 10 km on. The village has a pleasant shady plaza, with snow-capped mountains as a backdrop in winter. The Carmen Valley stretches 25 km from Alto del Carmen to **San Félix**, the largest town of the valley, and the site of the distillery for Horcón Quemado *pisco*. A 39-km-long path connects the two valleys, from San Félix to the Quebrada de Pinte, 7 km south of El Tránsito, forming part of the Sendero de Chile. Allow two to three days for the trek. The tourist information office in Alto del Carmen's Municipalidad is helpful.

⊙ Huasco Valley listings

For Sleeping and Eating price codes and other relevant information, see Essentials pages 35-42.

⊜ Sleeping

Vallenar *p182, map p183*
A Hostería de Vallenar, Ercilla 848, T051-614379, hostvall@ctcinternet.cl. Decent, with pool, parking, good breakfast and Hertz car hire office. Worth bargaining.
A Puerto de Vega, Ramírez 201, T051-618534, www.puertodevega.cl. Probably the best hotel in town. Only 12 rooms, each with their own individual style. Also pleasant patio and pool.
A-B Cecil, Prat 1059, T051-614071, hotelcecil@hotelcecil.cl. Modern, clean, with bath, hot water, and swimming pool. Recommended.
B Hostal Real Quillahue, Prat 70, T/F051-619992. With breakfast, modern, friendly. Recommended.
C Hostal Camino del Rey, Merced 943, T/F051-613184. Clean, cheaper rooms without bath; friendly, good value. Worth bargaining for longer stays. Recommended.
D Hostal Vall, Aconcagua 455, T051-613380, hostal_vall@yahoo.es. Rooms with breakfast and bath. Friendly, parking, good value.
D-E Residencial Mary 2, Ramírez 631. **F** singles. With private bath, friendly.
E Residencial La Oriental, Serrano 720, T051-613889. **F** singles. Pleasant, friendly, cheap meals, decent value. There are also several *residenciales* in the town.
E Viña del Mar, Serrano 611, T051-611478. Clean, *comedor*, nice rooms. Recommended.

West of Vallenar *p183*
There is no accommodation in Freirina but you'll find options in Huasco.

B Hostería Huasco, Carrera Pinto 110, Huasco, T051-531026. Parking, conference room, with TV and all mod cons.
C Cabañas Skitniza, Craig 833, Huasco, T051-531343, www.skitniza.cl. Parking available.
C Hostal San Fernando, Pedro de Valdivia 176, Huasco, T051-531726. **F** singles. Some rooms with bath. Parking, restaurant. The owner lived for several years in Norway.

Camping
Tres Playitas , 12 km north of Huasco along the coast towards Carrizal Bajo. Also in Huasco near the post office, US$2 per site. Although there is no official campsite, camping is possible at Carrizal Bajo.

East of Vallenar *p184*
F Cabañas Camino al Oro, Serrano y Larraín, San Félix, T051-983173. Cabins, per person.
F Residencial El Azadón del Valle, Alonso García s/n, Alto del Carmen, T051-617695. Price per person.
There is no accommodation in the Tránsito Valley but camping wild is easy.

⊘ Eating

Vallenar *p182, map p183*
†† Bavaria, Serrano 802. Reasonable chain, attentive service.
†† Moros y Cristianos, Panamericana, junction with Huasco road. A good choice.
†† Pizza Il Boccato, Prat 750. T052-614609. Good coffee, clean but lacking in style. At the slightly upmarket end for this town.
† Corona del Inca, Prat 900-block in *local* set aside from road. Cheap meals, good cocktails.

¶ **La Pica**, Brasil y Faez. Seriously cheap but good, serves meals, cocktails and seafood. There are other cheap places along the south end of Av Brasil.
¶ **Shanghai**, Ramírez 1267. Chinese.

West of Vallenar *p183*
Aficionados of Chile's seafood should take a trip to Huasco for lunch; the journey takes only 45 mins from Vallenar. Simply prepared, perfectly fresh seafood is served at many cheap restaurants near Huasco's port. Heading north up the coast, there is also a seafood restaurant at Carrizal Bajo, generally open daily in summer and at weekends out of season.

⊛ Entertainment

Vallenar *p182, map p183*
Bar Bogart, Serrano 925. Popular old-timers' bar with the fattest roundest bar stools you have ever seen. Billboard Pub, Prat 920. Popular with locals. It is also worth checking out the Centro Cultural Vallenar, Vallenar y Colchagua, for cultural events, and occasional exhibitions and concerts.

⊛ Festivals and events

West of Vallenar *p183*
29 Jun Fiesta de San Pedro is celebrated by the fishing community in Huasco.

East of Vallenar *p184*
19 Jul Fiesta del Carmen, Alto del Carmen.
15 Aug Fiesta del Tránsito in Alto del Carmen with a rodeo, market and famous for its ice creams made of snow.

O Shopping

Vallenar *p182, map p183*
Local products are sold in Vallenar's market.
Horcón Quemado, Ercilla 660, Vallenar, T051-610985, sells some of Chile's finest pisco.

▲ Activities and tours

Vallenar *p182, map p183*
Agrotur, Maule 742, Vallenar, T051-617549, T09-2879425. Tours of the Huasco Valley as well as the northern section of the Reserva Nacional Humboldt.

⊙ Transport

Vallenar *p182, map p183*
Bus
Operators include TurBus, Merced 561, and Pullman Bus, opposite. Next door is Vallenar's bus terminal, from which TasChoapa and Flota Barrios depart. To **Arica**, 19 hrs, US\$36-54; to **Iquique**, 15 hrs, US\$33-\$49; to **San Pedro de Atacama**, 14 hrs, US\$27-51; to **Antofagasta**, 9 hrs, US\$21-36; to **Copiapó**, 2 hrs, US\$6; to **Chañaral**, 4 hrs, US\$8; to **La Serena**, 2 hrs, US\$6; to **Valparaíso**, 11 hrs, US\$20; to **Santiago**, 10 hrs, US\$20-49.

Buses to **Junta de Valeriano** (Tránsito Valley) and **San Félix** (Carmen Valley), as well as the intermediate points such as **Alto del Carmen**, leave from Marañon 1289, at 0730, 1100, 1430, 1630, 1730. TurBus runs a daily service between **Huasco** and **Santiago**.

There are also *colectivos* in Vallenar, which may be useful for those with heavy luggage making their way to the bus terminals (catch them on Serrano). *Colectivo* to **Huasco** leave when full, 1 hr 20 mins, US\$3.50.

⊙ Directory

Vallenar *p182, map p183*
Banks Several on Prat, east of the plaza.
Internet and telephone Several in the centre. **Laundry** Lavaseco Rodier, Verdaguer y Ramírez. **Medical services** Clinic: Consulta Médico y Laboratorio Clínico, Pje Nicolás Naranjo 341, T051-616012.

Copiapó Valley

From Vallenar it is 148 km north to Copiapó, the largest city in the valley of the Río Copiapó, generally regarded as the southern limit of the Atacama Desert. This valley is a surprisingly green cleft of farms, vineyards and orchards in the desert, about 150 km long. ➤➤ *For listings, see pages 190-195.*

Ins and outs

Getting there The Copiapó Valley's main centre is Copiapó, which is easily reached by regular buses from both north and south. There are several daily flights serving Copiapó from Santiago and La Serena, continuing on to El Salvador. For a transfer to the airport call **Buses Casther** ① *T052-218889.* ➤➤ *See Transport, page 194.*

Getting around There are many *colectivos* and public buses in Copiapó, which may be useful for those heading for some of the out-of-town sites, such as the Santuario de la Candelaria; the fare for buses is US$0.50.

Tourist information The **Sernatur office** ① *on the north side of Plaza de Armas Los Carrera 691, T052-212838, infoatacama@sernatur.cl, Mon-Fri 0830-1930, Sat 1030-1430, 1630-1930, Sun 1030-1430; out of season Mon-Fri 0830-1730 only,* is extremely helpful. English is spoken. In Copiapó there is also a **CONAF office** ① *Juan Martínez 55, T052-210282.*

Copiapó and around 🖂🎭🏨🍴🍷⛺🛏️🛍️ ➤➤ *pp190-195. Colour map 2, B2.*

The capital of Región III Atacama, Copiapó, with a population of 127,000, is an important mining centre with a big mining school and a backdrop of arid hills to the north. Founded in 1744, Copiapó became a prosperous town after the discovery in 1832 of the third largest silver deposits in South America at Chañarcillo. The wealth from Chañarcillo formed the basis of the fortunes of several famous Chilean families – most notably, the Cousiños – and helped finance the first railway line in the southern hemisphere, linking Copiapó to Caldera (1851). These days, Copiapó's economy still thrives on the large numbers of miners who descend to the city in order to seek distraction and spend their pay cheques. On cool summer nights, people flock to the pleasant, shady Plaza de Armas to chat and watch the world go by.

Sights

The neoclassical **cathedral**, on Plaza Prat, dating from 1851, was designed by William Rogers. Mass is held here every evening. The **Museo Mineralógico** ① *Colipí y Rodríguez, a block east of the plaza, Mon-Fri 1000-1300, 1530-1900, Sat 1000-1300, US$0.80,* is the most impressive museum of its type in Chile. It possesses a collection of weird, beautiful minerals from Chile and also from Asia, Europe and North America, plus a decent set of fossils. There is an unfortunate lack of narrative or explanation but a visit is highly recommended nonetheless; it is extraordinary how, although there are minerals from all over the world, the most colourful or striking are almost always Chilean.

Three blocks further north, at Infante near Yerbas Buenas, is the colonial Jesuit **Iglesia de Belén** ① *Mon-Fri 1630-1830,* remodelled in 1856. Further west, at Atacama y Rancagua, you'll find the **Museo Regional del Atacama** ① *murea@entelchile.net, Mon 1400-1745, Tue-Fri 0900-1745, Sat 1000-1245, 1500-1745, Sun 1000-1245, US$1 (free Sun),* containing collections on local history, especially from the 19th century up to the time of the War of the Pacific; it is also notable for its collection of artefacts from the Huentelauquén people, thought to have flourished 10,000 years ago. On the opposite corner of the same block, at Matta y O'Higgins, is the **Monument to Juan Godoy**, the muleteer, who, in 1832, discovered silver at Chañarcillo. Behind is the **Iglesia de San Francisco**, built in 1872 (the nearby convent is from 1662), which is a good example of a 19th-century construction using Pino Oregón and Guayaquil cane, popular materials of the day. The wealth of the 19th-century mining families is reflected in the **Villa Viña de Cristo**, built in Italian Renaissance style, three blocks northwest on Calle Freire, now part of the University of Atacama. A few blocks further on, the Norris Brothers steam locomotive and carriages used in the inaugural journey between Copiapó and Caldera in 1851 can be seen at the **Universidad de Atacama**; also at the university is an example of an old *trapiche* (see box page 153). Nearby, in the old railway station on Calle Martínez, is the **Museo Ferroviario**, which has photos and artefacts from the railway age, but it opens only sporadically. In fact, the station mostly stands derelict, a sad indictment of how little importance is given to one of the pioneering railway lines in South America. Outside are two small nineteenth century steam locomotives.

On the other side of the city, 3 km southeast of the centre, the **Santuario de la Candelaria** is the site of two churches, the older built in 1800, the other in 1922; inside the latter is the Virgen de la Candelaria, a stone image discovered whole in the Salar de Maricunga by the muleteer Mariano Caro in 1780. The Virgin is said to protect miners, hence her local importance, and is celebrated in the Fiesta de la Candelaria every February (see page 194).

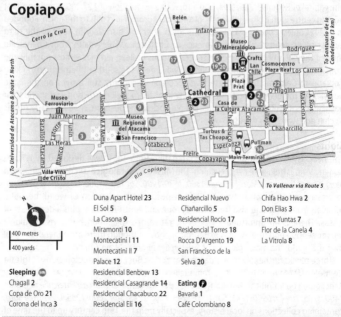

Copiapó

400 metres
400 yards

Sleeping
Chagall 2
Copa de Oro 21
Corona del Inca 3

Duna Apart Hotel 23
El Sol 5
La Casona 9
Miramonti 10
Montecatini I 11
Montecatini II 7
Palace 12
Residencial Benbow 13
Residencial Casagrande 14
Residencial Chacabuco 22
Residencial Elí 16

Residencial Nuevo
 Chañarcillo 5
Residencial Rocío 17
Residencial Torres 18
Rocca D'Argento 19
San Francisco de la
 Selva 20

Eating
Bavaria 1
Café Colombiano 8

Chifa Hao Hwa 2
Don Elias 3
Entre Yuntas 7
Flor de la Canela 4
La Vitrola 8

Around Copiapó

The **Centro Metalúrgico Incaico** is a largely reconstructed Inca bronze foundry, the most complete example in existence, 90 km up the Copiapó Valley by paved road. Further up the valley at Km 98 is the 19th-century **Aquaducto de Amolana**, hidden 300 m off the main road. There is no accommodation in the nearby villages of Valle Hermoso or Las Juntas but there are *cabañas* at Los Loros, which was the site of a clinic for pulmonary diseases at the beginning of the 20th century, attended by the rich and unhealthy from Santiago.

South of Copiapó, about 59 km on the Pan-American Highway, is a signpost for the turning to the ghost town and former silver mine of **Chañarcillo**, along a very poor road. When Chañarcillo was at its peak, the town had a population of 7000; the mine was closed in 1875 but the tips have been reworked and this has destroyed many of the ruins. Now that the silver has gone, only a few goatherds live here among the ruins of dry stone walls. Note there are dozens of dangerously unmarked and unprotected mineshafts, and if you have an accident you are far from help.

East to Paso San Francisco 🌐▲▲ ▶▶ *pp190-195.*

The Argentine border can be crossed at **Paso San Francisco** (4726 m), which is situated just north of **Ojos del Salado** (see box, page 191). The pass can be reached by three poor *ripio* roads (high-clearance vehicle necessary) from Copiapó and by another *ripio* road that runs south and east from El Salvador. All these routes meet up near the northern sector of the **Parque Nacional Tres Cruces** (see below). The road from El Salvador meets the main *camino internacional* from Copiapó near the Salar de Maricunga, 96 km west of Paso San Francisco. The other two routes from Copiapó are branches off the *camino internacional*: the first forks off 10 km east of the Copiapó–Diego de Almagro road and continues southeast through the Quebrada San Miguel to reach the Laguna del Negro Francisco in the southernmost sector of the Parque Nacional Tres Cruces, before turning north. This is a very poor road, where drivers can easily get lost. The second runs through the Quebrada de Paipote and then on through the northernmost sector of the park. Travellers taking either of these alternatives en route to Argentina should note that they will need to deviate north to pass through the Chilean immigration post at the Salar de Maricunga (see page 191). Before setting off it is advisable to speak to the *carabineros* in Copiapó as they will be able to give you information about the state of the various roads.

Parque Nacional Tres Cruces → *Colour map 2, B3.*

Extending over 59,082 ha, this newly designated park is in two sectors: the largest part, the northern sector, includes **Laguna Santa Rosa** and parts of the **Salar de Maricunga**, an expanse of salt flats covering 8300 ha at 3700 m; the southern sector covers the area around **Laguna del Negro Francisco**, a salt lake covering 3000 ha at 4200 m. The lakes are home to some 47 bird species, including all three species of flamingo found in Chile, as well as guanaco and vicuña. The park is stunningly beautiful and, owing to its isolation, rarely visited. The **park administration** ① *summer only 0830-1230, 1400-1800, US$8 (US$5 for Chileans)*, is located at a *refugio* southeast of Laguna del Negro Francisco.

Caldera and Bahía Inglesa 🌐🅕🅝🅞▲🅐🅔 ▶▶ *pp190-195. Colour map 2, B2.*

Caldera, 73 km northwest of Copiapó, is a port and terminal for the loading of iron ore, with a population of 12,000. In the late 19th century, it was a major railway engineering centre

Climbing Ojos del Salado

Ojos del Salado is considered to be the third highest peak in the Americas and the highest active volcano in the world. Its true height is still under debate, with estimates ranging from 6864 m to 6893 m. A permit is required to climb it, available free from the Dirección de Fronteras y Límites, Bandera 52, piso 4, T02-6714110, taking two or three days to issue. Permits can also be arranged at short notice from the Sernatur office in Copiapó.

The ascent is best attempted January-March, though it's possible November and April. In November, December and April it can be hit by the *Invierno Boliviano*, a nasty weather pattern coming from the northeast. Temperatures have been known to drop to -40°C with winds of 150 kph.

Access to the volcano is via a turn-off the main Chile–Argentina road at the former Hostería Murray (burned down). Base camp for the climb is at the old Argentine frontier post (4500 m). There are two *refugios*: Refugio Atacama (four to six beds) at 5100 m and Refugio Tejos (better, 12 beds) at 5750 m. The spur to the former is not easy to find, but can be reached with a high-clearance 4WD vehicle. From Refugio Tejos it is 10 to 12 hours' climb to the summit. The climb is not very difficult (approximately Grade 3), except the last 50 m, which is moderate climbing on rock to the crater rim and summit. Take large quantities of water for the ascent. Guides and equipment can be hired in Copiapó.

and its train station was the southern hemisphere's first. The train station has recently been restored to its former glory and now houses a cultural centre and **tourist information office** ① *summer only, T052-316076*. The **Iglesia de San Vicente de Paul** (1862), on the poorly redesigned Plaza de Armas, was built by English carpenters working for the railway company. Caldera is home to the earliest non-denominational cemetery in Chile, where vestiges of a proud past can be glimpsed in the crumbling graves of European settlers.

Bahía Inglesa, 6 km south of Caldera and 6 km west of the Pan-American Highway, is popular with Chileans for its beautiful white sandy beaches and unpolluted, clear sea. Although the bay is now dominated by a scallop farm, this is not too noticeable from the beach. The water in this sheltered bay is warmer than around the neighbouring coast and it is safe to swim. Bahía Inglesa is rather expensive and can get crowded in January and February and at weekends, but off season makes a perfect, deserted retreat. Given that it lies almost exactly half way between the capital and San Pedro and has two restaurants almost worth making a detour for, it's a good choice to break one's journey. It was originally known as Puerto del Inglés after the visit in 1687 of the English pirate, Edward Davis.

⑩ Copiapó Valley listings

For Sleeping and Eating price codes and other relevant information, see Essentials pages 35-42.

⊜ Sleeping

Copiapó *p187, map p188*
There is often a shortage of accommodation in Copiapó. Advance booking advisable.

AL Duna Apart Hotel, O'Higgins 760, T052-240203, www.dunapart.cl. Comfortable cosy apartments – bathroom, living room, fully equipped kitchen (no oven but there is a microwave). Cheaper if you ask for a *doble factura*.
AL-A Miramonti, Freire 731, T/F052-210440, www.miramonti.cl. All facilities but slightly cold atmosphere. Book in advance as it fills up

Border crossings: Chile–Argentina

Paso San Francisco

Although officially open all year, this pass is liable to closure after snow in winter. Call T052-1981009 for reports of the road condition.

Chilean customs 0900-1900, US$2 per vehicle for crossing Saturdays, Sundays and holidays, are near the Salar de Maricunga, 100 km west of the border. From here a *ripio* road continues along the southern shore of Laguna Verde, where there are thermal springs and a reasonable campsite, en route to the border. On the Argentine side, a paved road continues to Tinogasta.

Argentine border post 0700-1900, is at Fiambalá, 210 km beyond the border, but there is also a police post at La Gruta, 24 km after the border.

with business travellers. That said, there are occasionally cheap walk-in dollar rates. The suites have hydromassage baths.
A Chagall, O'Higgins 760, T052-213775, www.chagall.cl. The best of the executive hotels, central, some rooms with king-size beds and desk, modern fittings, internet, spacious lounge and bar open to public. Recommended.
A-B Montecatini II, Atacama 374, T052-211516, alitor@ctcinternet.cl. Not much character but spacious and comfortable. Cable TV and patio. 10% discount for cash payment. Cheaper when paying in US$.
B Hotel Copa de Oro, Infante 530, T052-216309, hotelcopadeoro@hotmail.com. Big rooms with all mod cons.
B Hotel San Francisco de la Selva, Los Carrera 525, T052-217013, hosanco@entel chile.net. Nice rooms, central, with breakfast, modern cafeteria/bar.
B La Casona, O'Higgins 150, T052-217278, www.lacasonahotel.cl. Clean, friendly, desert colours, restaurant and bar, internet access plug in rooms, good beds, cable TV, pleasant garden, more like home than a hostel. A little overpriced. English spoken. Cheaper for foreigners paying in US dollars. Recommended.
B Rocca D'Argento, Maipú 580, T052-218744, www.atacamachile.com/ hotelrocca. Ugly exterior. Rooms vary in size. Some very spacious doubles are good

value, but there are some overpriced pokey singles. Cable TV, heating, tours and car hire arranged, better prices in dollars, worth bargaining off season.
B-C Corona del Inca, Las Heras 54, T052-363489, sanval@tie.cl. With breakfast, big rooms, friendly, quiet, good value, worth bargaining. No restaurant.
B-C Montecatini I, Infante 766, T052-211363, h.montecatini@terra.cl. Large rooms around beautiful courtyard, swimming pool. Some smaller rooms without TV are cheaper. Helpful, best value in this price bracket. The only downside is that the beds have foam mattresses. Cheaper to pay in dollars. Ask for tax-free rate.
C El Sol, Rodríguez 550, T/F052-215672. Smallish rooms leading off from a central corridor. Rooms with bath and cable TV, quiet, breakfast included, parking.
C Palace, Atacama 741, T052-212852. Comfortable, breakfast extra, parking, central, nice patio. Good value.
D Residencial Benbow, Rodríguez 541, T052-217634. Basic rooms, some with bath, but the best value of the many *residenciales* on this part of Rodríguez. Usually full of mine workers. Excellent value full-board deals.
D Residencial Casagrande, Infante 525, T052-244450. **F-G** singles. Tumbledown colonial building with covered portico around a central courtyard with bougainvillea. Cluttered, with TV in big

rooms. Extremely grumpy unhelpful owner, but browbeaten staff more friendly.

D Residencial Chacabuco, Salas 451, T052-213428. Cheaper rooms with shared bath, with breakfast, simple, quiet, clean.

D Residencial Eli, Maipú 739, T052-219650. **F-G** singles. Friendly, simple rooms, good beds, decent choice.

D Residencial Nuevo Chañarcillo, Rodríguez 540, T052-212368. **E** singles. Dozens of rooms branching off from a seemingly endless corridor, some with bath. Bright central patio. Minimal service, a little stuffy.

D Residencial Rocío, Yerbas Buenas 581, T052-215360. **F** singles. Some rooms with bath and cable TV, common area, clean, patio. Good budget option. Recommended.

D Residencial Torres, Atacama 230, T052-240 727. **F** singles. Without bath, hot water, friendly, quiet. Price per person. Recommended.

There are also several cheap places (**F-G**) per person around the local bus terminal.

East to Paso San Francisco *p189*

F Two **CONAF** *refugios* in the Parque Nacional Tres Cruces: 1 southeast of Laguna Santa Rosa, very basic, another southeast of Laguna del Negro Francisco, with bunk beds, heating, electric light and hot water. Price per person.

Caldera and Bahía Inglesa *p189*

Prices are for off season. In Jan/Feb they can rise by as much as 50%

AL Rocas de Bahía, El Morro 888, Bahía Inglesa, T052-316005, www.rocasdebahia.cl. 4-star hotel with all facilities, reasonable restaurant and swimming pool on the roof.

A Blanco Encalada, Copiapó y Pacífico, Bahía Inglesa, T052-315345, www.bahiainglesa.net. Comfortable, some rooms with balcony, roof terrace with great view, Wi-Fi, tours arranged. Cheap per person deals sometimes offered in low season.

A Hostería Puerta del Sol, Wheelwright 750, Caldera, T052-315205, www.hosteriapuerta delsol.com. *Cabañas* with kitchen, all mod cons, laundry and Wi-Fi service, view over bay.

A Los Jardines de Bahía Inglesa, Av Copiapó, Bahía Inglesa, T052-315359, www.jardinesbahiainglesa.cl. *Cabañas*, open all year, good beds, swimming pool, games rooms, comfortable.

A Portal del Inca, Carvallo 945, Caldera, T052-315252. Fully equipped 4-star *cabañas* with kitchen, English spoken, restaurant not bad, order breakfast on previous night.

B Cabañas, Playa Paraíso, Av Costanera 6000, Bahía Inglesa, T09-8867666, www.cabanasparaiso.cl. On the shore about 6 km south of town. Cosy cabins with kitchenettes and barbecues. Idyllic location, almost like having your own private beach. No public transport, but the owners usually go into town once a day. Reiki and massages available. Recommended.

B Costanera, Wheelwright 543, Caldera, T/F052-316007. Accepts credit cards, simple rooms, friendly.

B El Coral, Av El Morro, Bahía Inglesa, T052-315331. Overlooking sea, good seafood, open all year. Also *cabañas*.

B-C Domo Chango Chile, Av El Morro 610, Bahía Inglesa, T052-316168, www.chango chile.cl. Comfortable accommodation in geodesic domes overlooking the bay. Excellent restaurant and lots of activities offered, including surfing, bike rental and tours. English spoken. Recommended.

D Restaurant Hospedaje Mastique, Panamericana Norte Km 880, outside Caldera. Cabin accommodation, hot showers, breakfast included, comfortable.

D Residencial Millaray, main plaza, Cousiño 331, Caldera, T052-315528. **F** Singles. Friendly, good value, basic. Price per person.

Camping

Camping Bahía Inglesa, Playa Las Machas, T052-315424. Price per site. Also fully equipped *cabañas* for up to 6 persons.

🍴 Eating

Copiapó *p187, map p188*

Ɨ Bavaria, Plaza Prat. Pricey restaurant upstairs, cafeteria downstairs (open 0800 for breakfast), *salón de té* around the corner in Los Carrera.

Ɨ Chifa Hao Hwa, Yerbas Buenas 334, also Colipí 340. One of several reasonably priced *chifas* (Chinese restaurants) in town. Terse service and the typical mix of muzak and western pop, but the food is decent.

Ɨ Entre Yuntas, Vallejos 226. Somewhat rustic but cosy. Peruvian/Chilean food, friendly service, live music Fri and Sat nights.

Ɨ Flor de la Canela, Chacabuco 710. Newly opened Peruvian restaurant.

Ɨ La Carreta, Av Copayapu. Expensive *parrillada*.

ƗƗ-Ɨ La Vitrola, Cosmocentro Plaza Real, 2nd floor. Self-service lunch buffet, good range, reasonably priced, good views overlooking Plaza Prat.

Ɨ Benbow, Rodríguez 543. Very good value *almuerzo*, extensive menu. Recommended.

Ɨ Don Elias, Los Carrera y Yerbas Buenas. Excellent seafood, popular. Recommended.

Cafés

There are several juice bars dotted around the town centre.

Café Colombiano, Cosmocentro Plaza Real 215. Real coffee, snacks, overlooks Plaza Prat, popular meeting place.

Don Gelato, Colipí 506 (northeast corner of plaza). Real coffee, ice cream and fresh juices.

El Bramador, Paseo Julio Aciares (part of Casa de la Cultura). Real coffee, good meeting place. Recommended.

Panadería La Industrial, O'Higgins 984. Good cakes.

Caldera and Bahía Inglesa *p189*

ƗƗƗ-ƗƗ Belvedere, Hotel Rocas de Bahía, Bahía Inglesa. Reasonably elegant Italian/Chilean restaurant, with good service and views.

ƗƗƗ-ƗƗ Domo Chango Chile, El Moro 610, on the Costanera, Bahía Inglesa, T052-316168. Chilean/international fusion served in a geodesic dome with views over the bay. Good wine list and an excellent *pisco sour*. Highly recommended. Café serves breakfasts from 0800 and open all day for snacks, drinks, etc. Free Wi-Fi.

ƗƗƗ-ƗƗ El Plateao, El Morro 756-B on the Costanera, Bahía Inglesa. Local specialities with Peruvian and oriental influences, mostly fish and shellfish, friendly service, Highly recommended, but watch out for the 10% tip automatically added to the bill.

ƗƗ El Teatro, Gana 12, Caldera, T052-316768. Generally considered to be the best restaurant in Caldera.

Ɨ Miramar, Gana 090, Caldera. Good seafood at the pier.

🍸 Bars and clubs

Copiapó *p187, map p188*

Arte Pub, Maipú 641. Intimate bar with wooden interior and tables on 2 levels. Live music every night from 2300, ranging from rock to jazz. US$2 cover charge. Also serves cheap healthy meals at lunchtime.

Costa Cuervos and **Kamikaze**, Circunvalación. 2 discos on the edge of town.

La Tabla, Los Carrera y Salas. Good pub, live music, very popular with locals.

Caldera and Bahía Inglesa *p189*

Bartholomeo, Wheelwright 747, Caldera. Lively bar with dancing at weekends.

🎭 Entertainment

Copiapó *p187, map p188*

Alhambra, Atacama 455, T052-212187. Copiapó's single-screen cinema.

Casa de la Cultura, Plaza Prat, T052-217866. This green colonial-style mansion has a gallery devoted to plastic arts, film screenings and concerts and also organizes workshops. An annexe houses the **Café El Bramador**, and hosts theatre productions and recitals.

Club de Ajedrez, Plaza Prat. Join the locals for a friendly game of chess on the south side of the plaza.

Sala de Cámara, M A Matta 292. New cultural centre hosting exhibitions, concerts, and seminars.

❂ Festivals and events

Copiapó *p187, map p188*
1st Sun in Feb Fiesta de la Candelaria begins, and lasts for 9 days. Up to 50,000 pilgrims and 3000 dancers congregate at the Santuario de la Candelaria in Copiapó (see page 187) from all over the north of Chile for this important religious festival.

◯ Shopping

Copiapó *p187, map p188*
Sporting goods including basic camping equipment from **Albasini**, O'Higgins 420. For handicrafts, visit **Canto de Agua**, Atacama 240. This workshop sells items crafted by local artists out of fish skin, ostrich eggs, lapis lazuli and other materials.

Caldera and Bahía Inglesa *p189*
Fresh seafood can be bought off the pier in Caldera, while live scallops are available from Inglesa's pier. There are no services in Bahía Inglesa. For supermarkets, etc go to Caldera.

▲ Activities and tours

Copiapó *p187, map p188*
A full list of guides, specializing in mountain trekking and climbing, is available from **Sernatur** in Copiapó (see page 187).

Alejandro Aracena, Tierra Amarilla, near Copiapó, T052-320098. Personal tours of small working mines, starting from a town in the valley. You must provide your own transport.
Aventurismo, Atacama 240, Copiapó, T052-232455, T09-9599 2184, www.aventurismo.cl. Mountaineering experts, concession holders for Ojos del Salado, experienced in trips to all of the higher peaks in the region.
Ercio Metafogo, T09-9051 3202. Good-value tours of Parque Nacional Tres Cruces with an English-speaking guide.
Gran Atacama, Mall Plaza Real, Copiapó, T052-219271, www.granatacama.cl. The largest of the regional operators. Offers trips throughout the region, horse riding, mountain climbing, trips to Tres Cruces, etc. Knowledgeable guides who generally speak good English. Also run campsites and cabins in Pan de Azucar.

East to Paso San Francisco *p189*
See above for details of tour operators based in Copiapó operating in this area.
Azimut 360, Arzobispo Casanova 3, Providencia, Santiago, T02-735 8034, www.azimut.cl. Based in the capital, this French-run adventure and ecotourism company offers mountaineering expeditions to Ojos del Salado and Incahuasi.

Caldera and Bahía Inglesa *p189*
During the summer, many activities are available in Bahía Inglesa including kite surfing and boat tours.
Océano Aventura, Gabriela Mistral 57, Caldera, T099-5469848. Diving trips.

❂ Transport

Copiapó *p187, map p188*
Air
Desierto de Atacama Airport is 45 km north west of Copiapó and 15 km east of Caldera. LanChile, Colipí 484, Copiapó, outside the mall, T052-213512, airport T052-214360,

and Sky, fly daily to/from **Santiago**, also to Antofagasta, **El Salvador**, Iquique and Arica.

Bicycle
Bike repairs Bicicletería Biman, Las Carrera 998A, T052-217391. Sales, repairs, parts.

Bus and colectivo
Local Although the major companies run between Copiapó and **Caldera**, the cheapest services are provided by Buses Recabarren and Buses Casther, T052-218889, every 30 mins, US$2, leaving from the street 1 block west of the main bus terminal in Copiapó. Buses Casther also runs a minibus service to Copiapó, US$9 per person, book in advance. *Colectivos* to **Caldera** leave from the same point as the buses. They are much quicker than the bus, cost US$3, and will take you to **Bahía Inglesa** for an extra US$0.75. Otherwise, *colectivos* between **Bahía Inglesa** and **Caldera** cost US$1.50. There are also buses in summer for US$0.75. *Colectivos* run from **Copiapó** to **Chañaral** and **Vallenar** and serve the upper valley as far as the **Nantoco**; you will have to arrange a price if you wish to go higher up the valley. Note that there are no public transport connections to the **Parque Nacional de Tres Cruces**.
Long distance Copiapó's main bus terminal is 2 blocks south of the plaza on Chañarcillo y Chacabuco. The TurBus terminal is opposite and Pullman have their terminal 1 block away on Colipí. To **Arica**, 18 hrs, US$34-63; to **Iquique** 13 hrs, US$30-59; to **San Pedro de Atacama**, 12 hrs, US$25-50; to **Calama** 10 hrs, US$23-$49; to **Antofagasta**, 7 hrs, US$18-$48; to

La Serena 5 hrs, US$11; to **Valparaíso**, 12 hrs, US$23.

Car
Car hire Avis, Peña 102, T/F052-213966. Budget, Freire 4 66, T052-218802. Flota Verschae, Luis Flores y Copayapu, T052-227898. Hertz, Copayapu 173, T052-213522. Rodaggio, Colipí 127, T052-212153.

Caldera and Bahía Inglesa p189
Bus
There are bus services to **Santiago**, several daily, and to **Antofagasta**, 7 hrs, US$17, although to travel north it may be better to take a bus to **Chañaral** (Inca-bus US$2), then change.

ℹ Directory

Copiapó and around p187, map p188
Banks Cambio Fides, Mall Plaza Real, of B123. Mon-Fri 1000-1400, 1600-1900 (closed Sat and Sun). Reasonable rates. There are several banks with Redbanc ATMs around the plaza as well as ATMs in the Plaza Real shopping centre and supermarkets. **Hospital** Los Carrera s/n, T052-212023. **Internet and telephone** Several in and around the centre. **Laundry** Lavandería Añañucas, Chañarcillo 612. **Medical services** Dentist: Eduardo Cáceres, Salas 385, T052-211902. **Post office** Los Carrera y Colipí, on Plaza Prat. Mon-Fri 1000-1400, 1600-2000.

Salado Valley

The 93 km between Caldera and Chañaral are marked by vestiges of vegetation in the desert, but further north there is nothing but unremitting pampa until Antofagasta. The course of the Río Salado is almost permanently dry and the valley is less fertile and prosperous than the Copiapó or Huasco valleys to the south. ** *For listings, see pages 198-200.*

Getting there.

As it is on on the Pan-American Highway, there are regular bus services to Chañaral from as far as Santiago to the south and Arica top the north. Copiapó airport is about 100 km south of Chañaral and there is another airport at El Salvador.

Getting around

There regular bus services between the main towns – Taltal, Chañaral and El Salvador; however, there is no public transport to Pan de Azucar or the Parque Nacional Tres Cruces.

Chañaral → *Colour map 2, B2. Population: 12,000.*

Getting there There are two alternative routes from Copiapó to Chañaral: west to Caldera and then north along the coast, 167 km; or the inland route, known as the Inca de Oro, via Diego de Almagro and then west to meet the *Panamericana* near Chañaral, 212 km.

This is a small, sad town with wooden houses perched on the hillside. In its heyday, Chañaral was the processing centre for ore from the nearby copper mines of El Salado and Las Animas, but those mines have declined, and the town now ekes out a living processing the ores from other mines in the interior. Stone walkways climb up the desert hills behind the main street, Merino Jarpa, reaching platforms where you'll find several stone benches from which to watch the sea; behind the benches are religious murals daubed with the graffiti of impoverished, angry urban youth. There is a beautiful and often deserted white-sand beach just beyond the *Panamericana*, created by waste minerals from the old copper processing plant, stained green by its pollution and causing the bay to be entirely barren of marine life. To assuage their guilt, the copper company built a copper monument in the form of a lighthouse that dominates the bay, but in an ironic twist people started stealing the copper and now the monument can only be viewed through protective railings. Swimming is dangerous here.

Museo de Historia Natural ① *Buín 818, Mon-Fri 0900-1300 and 1530-1900, free*, has exhibits on the mineralogy, hydrobiology and entomology of the region; interesting for naturalists. There is a municipal **tourist information** kiosk on the *Panamericana*, south of town, in summer, while to the north, a new coastal promenade is being built.

Parque Nacional Pan de Azúcar

① *CONAF office, Caleta Pan de Azúcar, daily 0830-1800 (but don't expect anyone to be there at lunchtime), park admission US$6 (US$3 for Chileans).*

This jewel of a national park north of Chañaral manages to combine four incredibly contrasting sets of geographical and ecological features in a stretch of land just 20 km from east to west. Offshore, the **Isla Pan de Azúcar** is home to Humboldt penguins and other sea birds, while fantastic white-sand beaches line the coast; they are popular at weekends and overcrowded in summer. A series of valleys run west to east. In pre-Colombian times they were inhabited by the Chango, a semi-nomadic coastal people. Occasionally archaeological artefacts such as pottery and arrowheads can be found. Dominating the park are coastal hills rising to 800 m, providing spectacular views. To the east the park extends into the desert. The park is inhabited by 103 species of bird as well as guanacos and foxes, and a sea lion colony can be observed by following the signs marked *loberías* from the park entrance. The *camanchaca* (coastal fog) ensures that the park has a unique set of flora that belies its desert location; after rain tall *alstroemerias* of many colours bloom in some of the gullies. The park is also one of the best places in Chile to see the flowering desert (see box, page 184), as well as extremely rare species of cactus.

There are two entrances to the park: either along a side road 20 km from the Pan-American Highway, 45 km north of Chañaral, or by a good secondary road north from Chañaral, 28 km from the village of **Caleta Pan de Azúcar**. The CONAF office here has an exhibition room and cactarium. Basic maps are available, as well as entrance tickets to the park. It's a 2½-hour walk from the office to a mirador with extensive views over the southern section but, to experience the park fully, transport is needed. Although the penguins are sometimes visible from the mainland, for a closer look take a boat trip round Isla Pan de Azúcar from Caleta, US$8.50 per person (minimum total US$85).

Towards El Salvador → *Colour map 2, A2.*
Some 67 km from Chañaral on the El Salvador road is the smaller mining town of **Diego de Almagro**. About 12 km north of here, on a mining track through the desert, is the interesting **Pampa Austral** project, where Codelco, the state mining company, has used water resulting from the process of extracting copper from nearby mines to irrigate the desert, producing a 4-ha extension of plantations in the middle of the desert *pampa*.

El Salvador itself is a modern town, built near one of the biggest copper mines in Chile. Located 120 km east of Chañaral, just north of the valley of the Río Salado, it is reached by a road that branches off the Pan-American Highway, 12 km east of Chañaral. All along the valley people are extracting metal ore from the water with primitive settling tanks. Further east, 60 km by unpaved road is the **Salar de Pedernales**, salt flats 20 km in diameter and covering 30,000 ha at an altitude of 3350 m, where pink flamingos can be seen.

Taltal → *Colour map 2, A2.*
Situated 25 km off the Pan-American Highway and 146 km north of Chañaral, Taltal is the only town between Chañaral and Antofagasta, a distance of 420 km. Along Avenida Prat are several wooden buildings dating from the late 19th century when Taltal prospered as a railhead and mineral port of 20,000 people, exporting nitrates from 21 mines in the area. The town is now a fishing port with a mineral processing plant. There is a tourist information kiosk in the plaza in summer. Off season, ask at the municipalidad.

Although like all towns in the north, Taltal has seen an increase in floating population caused by the mining boom, it still retains its relaxed laid-back air, with small fishing boats bobbing in the bay while pelicans preen themselves on the coastal wall. **Museo Augusto Capdeville** ⓘ *Av Prat 5, free,* is a good local museum in the former *gobernación*, with rooms on prehistory, local history and the saltpetre industry, European immigration, and an exhibition on the Paranal observatory. The curator is very friendly. The surprisingly lush pleasant tree-lined plaza is laid out in the form of the Union Jack in honour of the historical importance of the British community in the town. Just north of town is the cemetery, where the European influence can clearly be seen. The impressive church on the plaza burned down in 2008 but is to be rebuilt. From the plaza walk up to the top of Torreblanca for views over the town and across the bay. South from the plaza along the costanera is an odd shaped bell tower, marking the site of the old pier, which used to sound whenever a ship was about to leave. Further south on Calle O'Higgins is an old steam engine with a pair of carriages behind which are the grounds of the former Taltal Railway Company.

There are excellent trekking opportunities around Taltal and deserted beaches line the coast both north and south, the best known of which is **Cifuncho**, some 40 km south. There's no accommodation here, but camping is easy. North along the coast by 72 km is the **Quebrada El Médano**, a gorge with ancient rock paintings along the upper valley walls.

◉ Salado Valley listings

For Sleeping and Eating price codes and other relevant information, see Essentials pages 35-42.

◉ Sleeping

Chañaral *p196*

B Hostería Chañaral, Müller 268, T052-480050. Dated and rather run-down, but spacious and attentive service, decent restaurant in beautiful dining room, pool room, parking.

B Portal Atacama, Merino Jarpa 1420, T052-489799, portalatacama@hotmail.com. Cold and disinterested staff, but newly refitted to a decent standard. Rooms with bath, TV. Also apartments, **AL**, sleeping 6.

B-C Nuria, Costanera 302, T052-480903. With bath and breakfast, parking, friendly, but a little basic and overpriced. Worth bargaining.

C Carmona, Costanera 402, T052-480522. With bath and TV, friendly, decent value.

C-D Hostal Sutivan, Comercio 365, T052-489123, hostalsutivan@terra.cl. **E-F** singles. Very friendly, clean, nice rooms, good beds, excellent value. Rooms with or without bath. Highly recommended. Also arranges tours to Pan de Azúcar.

C-D Hotel Jiménez, Merino Jarpa 551, T052-480328. Friendly, patio with lots of birds, clean rooms, modern bathrooms (some shared), good-value restaurant, convenient for **Pullman Bus**. Recommended.

D Residencial Molina, Pinto 583, T052-480075. **F** singles. Rooms in a family home. Reasonably basic, but very friendly. Owner Sergio does very good

tours of the park and offers good-value lodging plus tour combos.

E-F La Marina, Merino Jarpa 562. **G** singles. Basic, many parakeets, no hot water.

Parque Nacional Pan de Azúcar *p196*

There are a dozen or so *cabañas* in the park run by **Gran Atacama** in Copiapó (see Activities and tours, page 194), in the **AL-A** range. Reservations and advance payment are essential in high season and if you want to avoid paying VAT as a foreign tourist. The perfectly placed *cabañas* are on a deserted beach behind the *caleta* and sleep 6. Discounts may be possible for fewer people off season.

Some of the fishermen in the *caleta* let out rooms. They are generally quite basic and around the **E-F** per person range.

Camping

There are 3 campsites in the park, 1 in the Caleta, run by the fishermen, and **Camping El Piquero** and El Soldado run by Gran Atacama in Copiapó (see page 194).

Towards El Salvador *p197*

AL Camino del Inca, El Tofo 330, El Salvador, T052-475224, htl_caminodelinca@ hotmail.com. The upmarket choice.

C-G Hostería El Salvador, Potrerillos 003, El Salvador, T052-475749. Cheaper rooms here are without bath.

Taltal *p197*

Advance booking recommended as hotels are often full.

B Cabañas Caleta Hueso, Camino a Paposo 2 km from Taltal, T055-612251, m.finger@entelchile.net. Good cabins.
B Mi Tampi, O'Higgins 138, T055-613605, www.hotelmitampi.cl. Best hotel in town, comfortable spacious rooms, good service, Wi-Fi. Advance booking essential. Recommended.
C Hostería Taltal, Esmeralda 671, T055-611173, btay@entelchile.net. On the seafront with great views and the sounds of waves to send you off to sleep. Passable restaurant, Wi-Fi zone, cheaper rooms without bath. Decent enough on the whole but doesn't do justice to its location.
C-D Hostal del Mar, Carrera 250, T/F055-613539. Clean basic rooms with cable TV and bathroom. Only the front 2 rooms have external windows. Breakfast extra.
D Residencial Paranal, O'Higgins 106. T055-613604, llamilnara@hotmail.com. Next door to Mi Tampi. Basic.
D San Martín, Martínez 279, T055-611088, F055-268159. Without bath, good *almuerzo*.

🍴 Eating

Chañaral *p196*
There are also a couple of restaurants on the *Panamericana*, open 24 hrs.
¶¶ Capely, Merino Jarpa 1140, T052-480477. Simple, but slightly more upmarket than the rest. Serves good fish and usual Chilean fare. Set menu much cheaper than à la carte.
¶ Restaurante de los Pescadores, La Caleta. Good fish, clean, cheap.
¶ Rincón Porteño, Merino Jarpa 567, T052-480070. Good and inexpensive sandwiches, etc.

Parque Nacional Pan de Azúcar *p196*
In Jan and Feb, there is a restaurant in Caleta. Otherwise, buy fish straight from the boats at around 1700 Tue-Sun and prepare it yourself. Take all other food with you.

Taltal *p197*
¶¶ Club Social Taltal, Torreblanca 162, just off the plaza. Good value *menú del día* (à la carte much more expensive). The former club of the British community, with poker room, billiard table and ballroom.
¶ Caverna, Martínez 247. Good seafood.
¶ Las Brisas, Esmeralda y Moreno, by the *caleta*. Large servings, good and cheap. Recommended.

✸ Festivals and events

Chañaral *p196*
15 Jul Fiesta de la Virgen del Carmen, which involves plenty of drumming and dancing around the plaza. The religious groups are dressed in elaborate costumes and vie with one another for the loudest band and the most complex dance; it's a moving manifestation of the faith of this impoverished but proud town.
26 Oct The town celebrates the anniversary of its founding with dancing and a parade.

▲ Activities and tours

Chañaral *p196*
Chango Turismo, Panamericana Norte s/n, T052-480484, www.changoturismo.k25.net. Offers tours to the park as well as kayak trips to the island (entirely at your own risk).
Subsole D'Atacama, kiosk on Merino Jarpa, T09-9972 0077. Sergio Molina and his wife Marcela lead very interesting and informative day tours of the Parque Nacional Pan de Azúcar.

◑ Transport

Chañaral *p196*
There is no main **bus** terminal. The Pullman Bus terminal is at Los Baños y Costanera, TurBus is on Merino Jarpa, 600 block.

To **Arica**, 15 hrs, US$32; to **Iquique**, 11 hrs, US$28; to **San Pedro**, 10 hrs, US$19-26; to **Antofagasta**, frequent, 5 hrs, US$16; to **Santiago**, 13 hrs, US$28-46; to **Copiapó**, 2 hrs, US$5; to **Taltal**, 3 daily, 2 hrs, US$5; *colectivos* to Copiapó depart from Merino Jarpa y Los Baños, US$7, try to leave early in the morning.

Parque Nacional Pan de Azúcar *p196*
Taxi from Chañaral, US$15. Both tour operators also offer a transport-only service. Gates control vehicles in the park, but keys are available from the CONAF office. There are fines for driving in restricted areas.

Towards El Salvador *p197*
Lan Chile and Sky fly to/from **Santiago** via **Copiapó**. There are direct bus services daily to **Santiago**, **Copiapó** and **Chañaral**.

Taltal *p197*
Bus services to **Santiago**, 2 daily, 16 hrs, US$38; to **Antofagasta**, TurBus, 4 hrs, US$10; to **Chañaral** 2 hrs, US$5. There are many more bus services from the Pan-American Highway (taxi US$12).

ⓘ Directory

Chañaral *p196*
Banks Poor rates for cash in BCI on the plaza. Nowhere to change TCs; Redbanc ATMs in the TurBus terminal and ESSO; in summer, money exchange may be offered at the ironmonger's, Consuelo y Merino Jarpa. **Telephone** CTC, Merino Jarpa 506; ENTEL Merino Jarpa 700-block, next to the municipal health centre.

Taltal *p197*
Banks Banco Estado on the plaza (MasterCard only). **Internet** Several along Prat.

Contents

Footprint features

Border crossings

Antofagasta, Calama & San Pedro de Atacama

At a glance

◉ **Getting around** Long distances between towns, but good bus services and regular tours. Some nearby destinations can be visited on mountain bike.

◉ **Time required** 4 days to see the sights around San Pedro; 4 to visit the salt flats in Uyuni, 1 day for travelling.

☼ **Weather** Warm and often overcast (but never wet) on the coast. Inland hot days, cold nights and very dry, except for the occasional storm in winter.

✖ **When not to go** High summer (Jan) can be unpleasantly hot inland. Occasional rain can cause havoc to dirt roads in the altiplano in Feb-Mar and Jul.

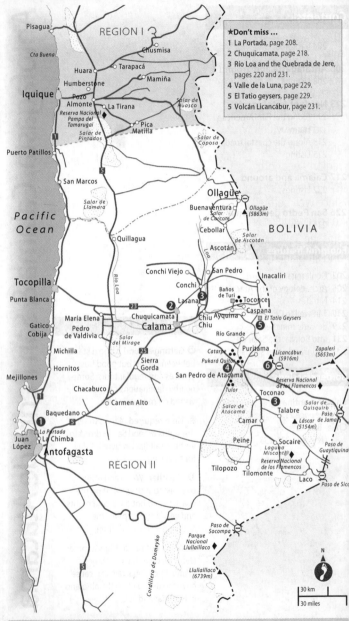

★**Don't miss ...**
1 La Portada, page 208.
2 Chuquicamata, page 218.
3 Río Loa and the Quebrada de Jere, pages 220 and 231.
4 Valle de la Luna, page 229.
5 El Tatio geysers, page 229.
6 Volcán Licancábur, page 231.

This desolate region is one of the most striking in Chile. The Atacama Desert is punctuated by small oases in the all-encompassing yellowness; clefts of green such as the beautiful Quebrada de Jere, near Toconao, or the Alto Loa, from where the lifelessness of the surrounding desert seems somehow impossible.

The main cities are Antofagasta and Calama, both of which are service centres for the mining industry that dominates the region's economy. Most visitors, however, head straight to San Pedro de Atacama, an ancient centre of civilization in the region since well before the Spanish conquest, and the base for trips to spectacular desert landscapes such as the Valle de la Luna and the Salar de Atacama, as well as to the geysers of El Tatio and altiplano lakes. San Pedro is home to one of the north's most important archaeological museums, and trips can also be made over the border into Bolivia to the Salar de Uyuni and to two beautiful lakes, Laguna Colorada and Laguna Verde.

Background

The Atacama Desert stretches 1255 km north from the Río Copiapó to the Chilean border with Peru. The Cordillera de la Costa, at its highest in this region (the highest peak is Cerro Vicuña (3114 m), runs close to the coast, an inhospitable and spectacular cliff face rising sheer from the waters to a height of up to 900 m. Below this cliff, on the edge of the Pacific, is a ledge on which the city of Antofagasta and some smaller towns are situated. In the eastern branch of the Andes, several peaks rise to around 6000 m: Llullaillaco (6739 m), Socompa (6051 m), Licancábur (5916 m), Ollagüe (5863 m). The western branch of the Andes ends near Calama. In between these two ranges the Andean Depression includes several salt flats, including the Salar de Atacama and the smaller Salar de Ascotán.

Before the Spanish conquest, this part of Chile was populated both on the coast and inland. The Chango people fished in the Pacific out of boats made from the pelts of sea lions. They traded fish with the peoples of the interior, from whom they bought coca leaves and quinoa (the staple grain before the arrival of those from Europe); from around the first century AD, there is evidence of an extensive network of paths and trade routes crossing the desert, linking the coastal areas between Taltal and the estuary of the Río Loa with the altiplano of Chile, Argentina and Bolivia.

Until the arrival of the Incas in around 1450, the most important inland civilization was that of the Atacameños, based in the area around San Pedro de Atacama. The Atacameños are believed to have arrived around 9000 BC, and, over the course of the millennia, they managed to adapt to the harsh terrain in which they lived. After the arrival of the Incas, the Atacameños adapted their cultural rituals to suit their new masters.

The first Spanish expedition arrived in 1536, led by Diego de Almagro. Four years later, Pedro de Valdivia took San Pedro de Atacama and the fort at Quitor and, thereafter, the Spanish and the Atacameño peoples enacted the familiar and tragic pattern of subjugation and extinction. San Pedro was the colonial centre but, by the end of the colonial era, the Spanish had established urban settlements only here and in Chiu Chiu. At independence most of the region became part of Bolivia, although the border with Chile was ill-defined. Before the War of the Pacific deprived her of this coastal territory, Bolivia established several towns along the Pacific, notably Cobija (1825), Mejillones (1841), Tocopilla (1843) and Antofagasta (1872). After the war, when the territory passed to Chile, the increased exploitation of nitrates led to the construction of railways and ports and Antofagasta's growth into the north's most important city.

These days, mining is by far the most important economic activity. Fishing is also a major industry, with agriculture limited by the lack of water and poor soils to mainly tropical fruit production on the coast south of Antofagasta. The main towns, Antofagasta and Calama, account for 87% of the population of the area, 97.6% of which is urban. Life in the area is artificial. Water has to be piped for hundreds of kilometres to the cities and the mining towns from the cordillera; all food and even all building materials have to be brought in from elsewhere.

As throughout northern Chile, there are major differences between the climate of the coast and that of the interior. Temperatures on the coast are fairly uniform and the weather is frequently humid and cloudy; *camanchaca*, a heavy sea mist caused by the cold water of the Humboldt current, is common in the morning and, in spite of the fact that this is one of the driest places in the world, it can seem that it is about to rain at any moment, with morning dew a common occurrence in summer. In the interior, the skies are clear day and night, leading to extremes of temperature; winter nights can often be

Archaeology of the Atacama

From early times, people settled along the northern coast of Chile, sustained by the food supply from the Pacific Ocean. Since about 7600 BC, fisherfolk and foragers lived in large groups in permanent settlements, such as the Quebrada de Conchas, just to the north of Antofagasta. They fished with fibre nets, sometimes venturing inland to hunt for mammals.

About 2000 years later, the successors of these people, the 'Chinchorros', developed one of the deepest characteristics of Andean cultures, veneration for their ancestors. The role of the dead in the world of the living was vital to the earliest Andean people. As a link between the spiritual and the material world, the ancestor of each local kin group would protect his clan. The expression of these beliefs came in the form of veneration of the ancestors' bodies; sacrifices were made to them, funeral rites were repeated, and precious grave offerings were renewed. In the arid climate of the Atacama, the people observed how bodies were naturally preserved. The skilled practice of mummification was thus developed, over a period of 3000 years, preserving the dead as sacred objects and spiritual protectors.

Another major cultural practice of northern Chile was the use of hallucinogens. Grave remains found in the region, dating from about AD 1000, include leather bags containing organic powder, wooden tablets and snuffer tubes. The tablets and snuffers were often decorated with supernatural figures, such as bird-headed angels, winged humans, star animals and other characters familiar in altiplano cultures. Although the origins and function of taking hallucinogens is not known for certain, it is thought that the practice may have been brought down to the coast by traders from the highlands. There were also 'medicine men' who travelled throughout the central and south central Andes dispensing the drugs and healing the sick. As with cures practiced in the Andes and Amazonia, it is possible that the drugs were taken as part of religious rituals, and often for a combination of spiritual and physical healing.

cold as -10°C, and colder in the high altiplano. Strong winds, lasting for up to a week, are common, especially, it is said, around the full moon, while between December and March there are sporadic but often violent storms of rain, snow and hail in the altiplano, a phenomenon known as *invierno altiplánico* (highland winter) or *invierno boliviano* (Bolivian winter).

Antofagasta and around

→ *Colour map 1, C1. Population 240,000.*
On the edge of a bay, nearly 700 km south of Arica, Antofagasta is the largest city in northern Chile and the fourth largest in the country. It is not a terribly attractive place, perhaps only worth stopping at to break a long journey. That said, the combination of the tall mountains and the ocean is dramatic, and after a week in the desert interior it is pleasant to breathe the sea air while relaxing on one of the beaches south of town. Apart from the lack of rain, the climate is pleasant; the temperature varies from 16°C in June and July to 24°C in January and February, never falling below 10°C at night. The city's economy depends on the enormous mine at La Escondida in the interior, where 8000 people work, doing week-long shifts at the mine before spending a week in the city; the city's port also acts as the processing point for the copper from La Escondida and Chuquicamata. As well as being the capital of Región II, Antofagasta is also an important commercial centre and the home of two universities.
▶▶ *For listings, see pages 208-212.*

Ins and outs
Getting there Antofagasta is served by many regular buses from both north and south. All major companies serving the north stop here and there are frequent flights with **LanChile**, **Principal** and **Sky** south to Santiago and north to Calama, Iquique and Arica. Taxis to/from the airport cost US$23, but may be cheaper if ordered from a hotel. For airport transfers, call **Aerobus** ① *T055-262727, US$6 to or from the city centre.*
Getting around Antofagasta is one of Chile's largest cities, and you may need to take *colectivos* or buses to get to more out-of-the-way places, particularly the discos and bars in the south and the university campuses. Avenida O'Higgins is also known as Avenida Brasil.
Tourist office ① *Prat 384, in the intendencia on Plaza Colón, T055-451818, infoanto fagasta@sernatur.cl, Mon-Fri 0930-1730, Sat 1000-1400 (although note that these opening hours change regularly).* There is also a kiosk at the airport (open summer only). **CONAF** ① *Argentina 2510, T055-383332, antofaga@conaf.cl.*

Sights
In the main square, **Plaza Colón**, there is a clock tower donated by the British community in 1910. It is a miniature of Big Ben with a carillon that produces similar sounds. The pedestrianised calle Prat, which runs southeast from the plaza, is the main shopping street, full of crowds and busking musicians and performance artists. Two blocks north of Plaza Colón, near the old port, is the former **Aduana**, built as the Bolivian customs house in Mejillones and moved to its current site after the War of the Pacific. Inside is **Museo Regional de Antofagasta** ① *Balmaceda 2786, www.dibam.cl/sdm_m_antofagasta/, Tue-Fri 0900-1700, Sat, Sun and holidays 1100-1400, US$1, children half price, free on Sun,* recently refurbished with displays on marine life, ecology, archaeology, anthropology and mining, as well as the nitrate era and a typically one-sided account of the War of the Pacific. The explanations are in Spanish only. Opposite are the former offices of the **Capitanía del Puerto** (harbourmaster) and the **Resguardo Marítimo** (coastguard).

East of the port are the buildings of the **Antofagasta and Bolivia Railway Company** (FCAB) dating from the 1890s and beautifully restored, but still in use and difficult to visit. These include the former railway station, company offices, workers' housing and the **Museo del Ferrocarril a Bolivia** ① *Bolívar 255, T055-206311, www.fcab.cl (reservations*

Antofagasta

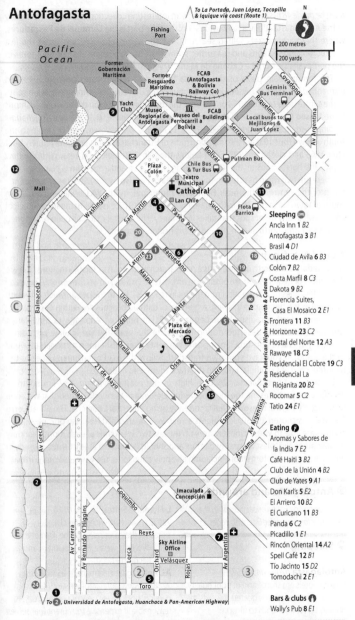

To La Portada, Juan López, Tocopilla & Iquique via coast (Route 1)

N

200 metres
200 yards

Pacific Ocean

Fishing Port

Former Gobernación Marítima

Former Resguardo Marítimo

FCAB (Antofagasta & Bolívia Railway Co)

Géminis Bus Terminal

Yacht Club

Museo Regional de Antofagasta

Museo del Ferrocarril a Bolivia

FCAB Buildings

Local buses to Mejillones & Juan López

Mall

Plaza Colón

Chile Bus & Tur Bus

Teatro Municipal

Cathedral

Lan Chile

Pullman Bus

Flota Barrios

Plaza del Mercado

Imaculada Concepción

Sky Airline Office

To 2, Universidad de Antofagasta, Huanchaca & Pan-American Highway

To Pan-American Highway north & Calama

Sleeping

Ancla Inn 1 *B2*
Antofagasta 3 *B1*
Brasil 4 *D1*
Ciudad de Avila 6 *B3*
Colón 7 *B2*
Costa Marfil 8 *C3*
Dakota 9 *B2*
Florencia Suites,
  Casa El Mosaico 2 *E1*
Frontera 11 *B3*
Horizonte 23 *C2*
Hostal del Norte 12 *A3*
Rawaye 18 *C3*
Residencial El Cobre 19 *C3*
Residencial La
  Riojanita 20 *B2*
Rocomar 5 *C2*
Tatio 24 *E1*

Eating

Aromas y Sabores de
  la India 7 *E2*
Café Haiti 3 *B2*
Club de la Unión 4 *B2*
Club de Yates 9 *A1*
Don Karl's 5 *E2*
El Arriero 10 *B2*
El Curicano 11 *B3*
Panda 6 *C2*
Picadillo 1 *E1*
Rincón Oriental 14 *A2*
Spell Café 12 *B1*
Tío Jacinto 15 *D2*
Tomodachi 2 *E1*

Bars & clubs

Wally's Pub 8 *E1*

must be made 48 hrs in advance), which has an interesting collection relating to the history of the Antofagasta–Bolivia railway. Just north of the port is the **Terminal de Pescadores**, where there are markets selling seafood, fruit and vegetables. Pelicans sit on the fish market roof and sea lions and sea turtles swim in the harbour; there are half-hour tours of the port available from **La Cabaña de Mario** ① *Aníbal Pinto s/n*, US$5.

The former main plaza of the **Oficina Vergara**, a nitrate town built in 1919 and dismantled in 1978, can be seen in the campus of the University of Antofagasta, 4 km south of the centre (take *colectivo* 114 or 333 from the town centre). Also on the university campus is the **Museo Geológico de la Universidad Católica del Norte** ① *Angamos 610, gchong@ socompa.ucn, in theory Mon-Fri 0930-1300, 1530-1800, often closed, free.* On a hill to the south of town (bus 103) are the imposing ruins of **Huanchaca**, a Bolivian silver refinery built after 1868 and closed in 1903. From below, the ruins resemble a fortress. With the new casino and hotel opposite, the ruins are being cleaned up and a museum is planned.

There are two main beaches in town, the **Playa Paraíso** by the Líder supermarket just north of the centre or the nicer **Balneario municipal**, by the McDonald's about 2 km south of town (take bus 103). Alternatively stay on the 103 past the Balneario Municipal and get off at any quiet spot that takes your fancy. The coastal road has been redesigned with cycle paths north and south and is surprisingly pleasant.

Around Antofagasta

La Portada, 16 km north of the city, is a natural arch with fantastic rock formations that are the symbol of Region II and are often seen on postcards up and down the country. Take any bus to Mejillones or Juan López. From the main road it is 2 km to the beach which, although beautiful, is too dangerous to swim. A number of bathing beaches are within easy reach.

A windsurfers' paradise, **Juan López**, is 38 km north of Antofagasta. Popular in summer, it is almost deserted during the rest of the year. The sea is alive with birds, especially at Caleta Constitución opposite Isla Santa María (fishermen there can take you to the island). If you have your own transport, follow the road out of Juan López to the beautiful cove at Conchilla. Keep on the track to the end at Bolsico.

Located on Cerro Paranal, 2600 m high in the coastal *cordillera*, 132 km south of Antofagasta, is, at present, the most powerful telescope in the world, although it will soon be usurped by a rival telescope that is currently being built near La Serena. The site at **Cerro Paranal** was chosen as 350 clear nights a year were guaranteed (see also box, page 167). Tourists are able to visit the observatory on the last two weekends of each month, January to November. Visits last around two hours and should be booked at least three months in advance. For more information, including an application form, see www.eso.org/paranal.

---

① Antofagasta and around listings

For Sleeping and Eating price codes and other relevant information, see Essentials pages 35-42.

● Sleeping

Antofagasta *p206, map p207*
Budget hotels are scarce and of poor quality. Most accommodation is geared towards the mining sector and tends to fill up.

L Florencia Suites, Croacia 0126, T055-789221, www.florenciasuites.cl. Luxury suites on the coast south of the city centre with lovely sea views. Also restaurant and pool. Recommended.
AL Antofagasta, Balmaceda 2575, T055-228811, www.hotelantofagasta.cl. 4-star, parking, pool, lovely view of port and city, reasonable, if expensive restaurant (bar serves

cheaper snacks), convention centre, beach, rooms facing the city are noisy due to all-night copper trains. Understaffed, not great service. English spoken. Rack rates are overpriced.

A Ancla Inn, Baquedano 516, T055-224814, www.anclainn.cl. One of the city's larger hotels with restaurant, car park, pool and sauna. Reasonably good value but avoid the interior rooms.

A Tatio, Av Grecia 1000, T055-419111, consultastatio@123.cl. 1970s concrete construction on the main road south out of town by a small beach. All rooms have a balcony and sea view. Cheaper in dollars than pesos. 10 mins' bus ride from the centre.

B Colón, San Martín 2434, T055-261851, hotel.colon@terra.com. With breakfast, quiet, clean, reasonable value.

B Costa Marfil, Prat 950, T055-225569, hotelcostamarfil@yahoo.es. With breakfast, good service, friendly, English spoken. The rooms are clean though some are a little gloomy. The nicer rooms have full bath tubs.

B Horizonte, Latorre 2450, T055-221886, www.hotelhorizonte.cl. Cable TV, bar, friendly and pleasant, good value though lacking in character, recommended.

B Rocomar, Baquedano 810, T055-261139. Decent sized bright rooms with bath. All have windows out onto the street. With breakfast and room service. A nice option.

B-C Dakota, Latorre 2425, T055-251749, floreriamagnolia@hotmail.com. With breakfast, Wi-Fi and cable TV, friendly, no frills but good value.

C Casa El Mosaico, Casa C18, Sector El Huascar, T09-9938 0743, www.chilegreentours.com. 15 mins south of the centre by bus No 103. Eco-friendly hostel with a wide range of activities including diving and paragliding. Friendly informative English speaking owners. Mosaic classes offered. The perfect place to relax for a few days after spending time in the desert. Highly recommended.

C Ciudad de Avila, Condell 2840, T/F055-221040, hotelciudaddeavila@yahoo.es. **E** singles. Very clean, with bath, TV, basic

restaurant, excellent value. Recommended, considering the alternatives.

C-D Brasil, Ossa 1978, T055-267268. Dark rooms around a central patio. Some rooms have bath and Cable TV. Nothing special, although it is in a quiet part of town with lots of decent restaurants nearby.

C-D Frontera, Bolívar 558, T055-281219. Basic but some rooms with bath and decent beds, TV in rooms. Breakfast at extra cost. Rooms on upper floors are brighter. Convenient for bus terminals and if you are arriving late at night.

C-D Residencial El Cobre, Prat 749, T055-225162. **E-F** Singles. Some rooms with bath Bright but tatty, set around a central courtyard.

D Hostal del Norte, Latorre 3162, T055-251265, hostaldelnorte_aft@hotmail.com. Some rooms with bath, clean, comfortable, quiet, brighter annex at the back.

D-E Residencial La Riojanita, Baquedano 464, T055-381056. **F** singles. Friendly, basic. Older rooms have high ceilings but are run-down. Newer rooms with bath but smaller. Not a bad budget option.

E-F Rawaye, Sucre 762, T055-225399. **F-G** singles, very basic, shared bathrooms, rooms have sinks. Hot water morning only, no towels, a bit grim.

Camping

Las Garumas, Km 6, south of the city on the road to Coloso, T055-247763 ext 42. Also cabins (sleep 4), cold showers and beach. For reservations contact Av Angamos 601, Casilla 606. Price per site (bargain for lower price out of season), wild camping is possible on the beach nearby.

Around Antofagasta p208
C Hostería Sandokan, Juan López, T055-223022. Standard facilities.

❶ Eating

Antofagasta p206, map p207
Note that many bars and restaurants are closed on Sun. The new casino, on Angamos

01455, has a choice of 4 good-quality
(♥♥♥) restaurants.

♥♥♥ **Club de la Unión**, Prat 474, 2 piso,
T055-268371. Excellent *almuerzo*, good
service, traditional atmosphere with
wooden interior and antique mirrors.

♥♥♥ **Club de Yates**, on the costanera.
Exclusive, great sea views and great
seafood. Good service.

♥♥♥-♥♥ **Don Karl's**, A Toro 1093, T055-419401.
Decent German cuisine. Decor a poor
attempt at rustic elegance.

♥♥♥-♥♥ **Picadillo**, Av Grecia 1000. Lively
atmosphere, serves a wide range of
dishes. Good music. Recommended.

♥♥♥-♥♥ **Tomodachi**, Grecia 1730, T055-376552.
The best of the city's sushi restaurants.

♥♥ **Aromas y Sabores de la India**, Copiapó
1294. Recently opened Indian restaurant
and takeaway – the only one of its kind
in the north of Chile.

♥♥ **El Arriero**, Condell 2644, T055-264371.
Grills and traditional hearty criollo food.
Good service, evening menu a little pricy
but cheaper set lunch, popular, live music.

♥♥ **Panda**, Condell 2505, T055-254827. Self-
service, all you can eat for US$9. A mixture
of Chinese and Chilean dishes on offer.

♥♥ **Rincón Oriental**, Washington 2432.
Decent Cantonese, pricey, over-the-top
decor. Recommended.

♥♥ **Spell café**, outdoor food court in the mall.
Varied menu including catch of the day. Good
service. Wide range of drinks, fresh juices.

♥♥ **Tío Jacinto**, Uribe 922. Friendly and serves
good seafood.

♥♥-♥ **El Chico Jaime**, Mercado Central 2nd
floor, local 115, T055-227401. Best of the
restaurants in the central market, good food
and friendly service. The rooms are decorated
with nautically themed antiques.

♥ **El Curicano**, Simón Bolívar 607. Very good
value basic set menu lunches and dinners.

Good fish restaurants are also to be found
in Terminal Pesquero Centro and at Caleta
Coloso, 18 km south (take bus 104).

Cafés
Hotel Antofagasta, Balmaceda 2575, offers
an all-you-can-eat buffet breakfast for US$8.
The only place open early for breakfast.
Café Bahía, Prat 474. Open 0900. Real coffee.
Café del Centro, Galería, Prat 482. Real coffee.
Heladería Latorre, Baquedano y Latorre.
For ice cream.

Around Antofagasta *p208*
♥♥♥ **La Portada**, Camino a la portada, T055-
226423. Open lunchtime and afternoon only.
Expensive seafood restaurant and café.

🍸 Bars and clubs

Antofagasta *p206, map p207*
Thanks to Antofagasta's large student
population, the nightlife is thriving. The most
popular bars and clubs are 16 km south of
the town in Balneario El Huascar. Take Micro
103 from C Matta to get there. Closer to the
centre there is a wide choice on O'Higgins.
Wally's Pub, Toro 982. Closed Sun. British
expat-style with pool, darts and beer.
X3, probably the best of the clubs at
El Huascar, on the road south along
the coast past the universities.

🎭 Entertainment

Antofagasta *p206, map p207*
Teatro Municipal, Sucre y San Martín, T055-
264919. Modern, state-of-the-art theatre.
Teatro Pedro de la Barra, Condell 2495. Run
by University of Antofagasta, this theatre has
a regular programme of high-quality plays,
reviews, concerts and more; details in press.
There is a multi-screen cinema in the mall.

Cultural centres
Instituto Chileno-Alemán de Cultura,
Bolívar 769, T055-225946; Instituto
Chileno-Norte americano de Cultura,
Carrera 1445, T055-263520.

✿ Festivals and events

Antofagasta *p206, map p207*
29 Jun The image of San Pedro, patron saint of the fishermen, is taken out by launch to the breakwater to bless the first catch of the day.
Last weekend of Oct The city's immigrant communities put on a joint festival on the seafront with national foods, dancing and music.

✪ Shopping

Antofagasta *p206, map p207*
The new **Mall Plaza Antofagasta**, Balmaceda y Maipú has a wide variety of shops and a pleasant promenade on the roof, with colourful flowers and views out to the ocean.

Antiques
Galería de Arte Imagen, Uribe 485, sells antiques including artefacts from former nitrate plants.

Bookshops
Antartica, in the mall. Best selection in town.

Camping equipment
Andes gear, in the mall, local A129, T055-533442. Good quality, although on the pricey side.

Handicrafts
Eva Luna, 14 de Febrero 2328, locally made glassware and ceramics.

Markets
Feria Modelo O'Higgins, Av Pinto, next to the fish market. Excellent fruit and vegetables as well as restaurants.
Fish market, Av Pinto, next to the Feria Modelo.
Municipal market, Matta y Uribe.

Supermarkets
Bótica, Latorre 2410.
Infante, Baquedano 800 block.
Korlaert, Ossa y Maipú block.
Líder, A Pinto, north of the port.
Tottus, Balmaceda, south side of the mall. Huge supermarket.

▲ Activities and tours

Antofagasta *p206, map p207*
Tour companies in Antofagasta offer general adventure tourism, including packages to the Atacama, but, on the whole, it is much better value to book directly with an operator in San Pedro (page 237).
Buceo Magallanes, Balmaceda 2615, T055-244873, www.buceomagallanes.cl. Regular diving trips and courses.
Club de Tenis Antofagasta, Av Angamos 906, T055-247756. Phone for details of temporary membership.
Olympic Swimming Pool, Condell y 21 de Mayo. For when the sea is too cold. Mon-Sat 0900-1700, US$5, children half price, swimming cap obligatory.
Soul Surf, Ejercito 155, local 15, near the Balneario Municipal, www.soulsurf.cl gives classes and rents and sells surfing equipment. See www.surfantofagasta.cl for more information on surfing in the area.

⊖ Transport

Antofagasta *p206, map p207*
Air
Cerro Moreno Airport is 22 km north of the city. LanChile, Principal and Sky fly daily to **Santiago**, **Copiapó**, **Iquique** and **Arica**. LanChile also have a daily flight to La Serena.
Airline offices LanChile, Prat 445, T055-265151, T600-526 2000; **Principal**, Sucre 375, T600-425 3510, www.aerolineaprincipal.cl; **American** and **Air France**, Washington 2507, T055-410781; **Lufthansa**, Copiapó 654, T055-263399; **Sky**, Veláquez 890, T055-459090.

Bicycle

Bicycle spares from **Rodrigo Baez Banda**, Condell 3071, also repairs; **Dr Bikes**, Maipú 897.

Bus

No main terminal; each company has its own office in town, some at quite a distance from the centre.

Except for services to Mejillones (see page 216), buses depart from the company offices as follows: **Flota Barrios**, Condell 2682, T055-268559; **Géminis** and **Romani**, Latorre 3055, T055-251796; **Pullman Bus**, Latorre 2805, T055-262591; **TurBus**, Latorre 2751, T055-264487; **Condor Bus**, Bolívar y Latorre.

Numerous companies run services to **Santiago**, 18 hrs, US$39-70, occasional student discounts. Book 2 days in advance during high season. If all seats to the capital are booked, catch a bus to **La Serena**, 12 hrs, US$26-42, then re-book.

To **Valparaíso**, 18 hrs, US$39; to **Arica**, 10 hrs, US$20-37, to **Calama**, several companies, 3 hrs, US$7; to **San Pedro de Atacama**, TurBus, 6 daily, 5 hrs, US$8, or via Calama; to **Copiapó**, 7 hrs, US$18-32; to **Iquique**, 6 hrs, frequent, US$16-21.

To **Salta and Argentina**, Pullman Bus and Géminis, Tue, Fri, Sun at dawn, change at Calama, via San Pedro, Paso Sico and Jujuy, US$44. Immigration check at San Pedro de Atacama. Book in advance for this service, take food and as much warm clothing as possible. There is nowhere to change Chilean pesos en route; take small denomination dollar bills to use in Argentina.

Car

Car rental from **Avis**, Baquedano 366, T055-221073; **Budget**, Balmaceda 2584, of 6, T055-251745; **First**, Bolívar 623, T055-225777; **Hertz**, Balmaceda 2492, T055-269043, offers city cars and jeeps (group D, Toyota Landcruiser) and does a special flat rate, with unlimited mileage. **Andrés Ljubetic Romo**, Atacama 2657, T055-268851, is a recommended mechanic. **Automóvil Club de Chile**, Condell 2330, T055-225332.

Around Antofagasta *p208*

La Portada is reached by minibuses to Mejillones from Latorre, between Sucre and Bolívar (US$4 return), or on from Condell, between Sucre and Bolívar. They will drop you off 2 km from the Portada. Take a hat. Buses go to **Juan López** at weekends in the summer only. These will drop you much closer to La Portada.

Taxis charge US$18. Hitching is easy.

❶ Directory

Antofagasta *p206, map p207*
Banks Several with ATMs around the plaza and the rest of the centre. *Casas de cambio* are mainly on Baquedano, such as **Ancla**, Baguedano 524, Mon-Fri 0900-1400, 1600-1900, Sat 0900-1400, poor rates (if closed try the ice cream shop next door); several exchange agents in the shopping centre at Baquedano 482-498; nearby is also **Nortour**, Baquedano 474; **AFEX**, Latorre 668, open Mon-Fri 0830-2000, Sat 0830-1400, better rates for TCs than Ancla. **Consulates** Argentina, Blanco Encalada 1933, T055-220440; France, Esmeralda 2286; Belgium, Baquedano 299, T055-268669; Bolivia, Washington 2675, piso 13, of 1301, T055-225010; Croatia, Esmeralda 2102; Germany, Pérez Zujovic 4940, T055-251691; Holland, Washington 2675, of 902, T055-266252; Italy, Matta 1945, of 808, T055-227791; Spain, Rendic 4946, T055-269596. **Internet and telephone** Lots in the centre, especially around the bus terminals. **Laundry** Clean clothes, G Lorca 271; La Ideal, Baguedano 660; Laverap, 14 Febrero 1802, efficient, not cheap. **Medical services** Hospital: Clínica Antofagasta, Matta 1945, T055-208103 (emergencies), www.clinicaantofagasta.cl. The best in town for those with insurance. **Police** San Martín y Baquedano. **Post office** Plaza Colón, 0830-1900, Sat 0900-1300.

North of Antofagasta

There are two routes north from Antofagasta: to Iquique along the Pan-American Highway or along the coastal road, Ruta 1, towards Tocopilla and beyond. The coastal route is more picturesque and makes a beautiful alternative to the sterility that accompanies large stretches of the Panamericana. ➤➤ *For listings, see pages 215-216.*

Along the Pan-American Highway ●●● ➤➤ *pp215-216. Colour map 1, C1/2 & B2.*

From Antofagasta, the Pan-American Highway continues north via the former railway post of **Baquedano** (Km 68) where there is a museum and a project underway to restore the station, to **Carmen Alto** (Km 101), where there is a turning to Calama. Four kilometres' walk from the junction is **Chacabuco** (100 km northeast of Antofagasta), a large abandoned nitrate town, opened in 1924 and closed in 1938. It was used as a concentration camp by the Pinochet government between 1973 and 1975. Workers' housing, the church, theatre, stores and the mineral plants can be visited and there is a free guided tour in Spanish. If you visit Chacabuco, be sure to take water and set out early in the morning as you will probably be hitching back.

Another turning 69 km north of Carmen Alto leads to **Pedro de Valdivia**, a nitrate town abandoned in 1996, which has been declared a National Monument and can be visited. From here, a road runs north, parallel to the Pan-American Highway, crossing the Salar del Mirage to **María Elena**, the only nitrate town still functioning. After a half-century or more in the doldrums, the nitrate business is now profitable once again, because the nitrates extracted from the Atacama Desert are thought to be better for the soil than the chemical version. **Museo Arqueológico y Histórico** ① *on the main plaza, free but US$1 donation suggested,* has exhibits on pre-Hispanic cultures.

Some 20 km southeast of María Elena, just off the Pan-American Highway, is the **Balneario Chacance**, where bathing and camping are available on the banks of the Río Loa. North of María Elena, meanwhile, the Highway crosses the Tocopilla–Calama road 107 km north of Carmen Alto. At **Quillagua**, Km 81, there is a customs post where all vehicles heading south are searched. Situated 111 km further north is the southernmost and largest section of the **Reserva Nacional Pampa del Tamarugal**, which contains the **Geoglifos de Pintados**, about 400 figures of humans, animals and geometric shapes on the hillside 3 km west of the highway; the other sections are near La Tirana (see page 248) and 60 km north of Pozo Almonte (see page 247).

Along the coastal road ●②④③⑥ ➤➤ *pp215-216.*

Mejillones and beyond → *Colour map 1, C1.*

Located 60 km north of Antofagasta, Mejillones stands on a good natural harbour protected from westerly gales by high hills. Until 1948, it was a major terminal for the export of tin and other metals from Bolivia. Remnants of that past include a number of fine wooden buildings: the **Intendencia Municipal**, the **Casa Cultural**, built in 1866, and the **church**, 1906, as well as the **Capitanía del Puerto**. The town has been transformed in recent years by the building of the largest port in South America here – the port links Argentina, southern Brazil and Paraguay with the lucrative markets of the Asian Pacific Rim. Although the large port buildings now dominate the northern end of the town, fishing remains

Nitrates

The rise and fall of the nitrate industry played an important role in opening up the northern desert areas between Iquique and Antofagasta to human settlement. In the second half of the 19th century, nitrates became important in Europe and the USA as an artificial fertilizer and for making explosives. The world's only known nitrate deposits were in the Atacama Desert provinces of Antofagasta in Bolivia and Tarapacá in Peru. After the War of the Pacific, Chile gained control of all the nitrate fields, giving a monopoly over world supply. Ownership was dominated by the British who controlled 60% of the industry by 1900. Taxes on the export of nitrates provided Chilean governments with around half their income for the next 40 years.

The processing of nitrates was labour intensive: at its height over 60,000 workers were employed. Using a combination of dynamite and manual labour, the workers dug the nitrate ore from the desert floor. It was then transported to nitrate plants, known as *oficinas*, crushed and mixed with water, allowing pure nitrates to be extracted. The mining and refining processes were dangerous and cost many lives. Wages were relatively high, but workers were paid in special tokens valid only for the particular *oficina* in which they worked. This not only meant that they had no means of leaving the *oficina* with ready cash, but also that they had to buy all their goods from the company stores which were, of course, controlled by the *oficina*.

The development of the Haber-Bosch process, a method of producing artificial nitrates, in Germany during the First World War, dealt a severe blow to the nitrate companies and many mines closed in the 1920s. New techniques were introduced by the Guggenheim company, but the world depression after 1929 led to a collapse in demand and with it the Chilean nitrate industry. Traces of the nitrate era can, however, still be seen: the mining ghost towns of Chacabuco, north of Antofagasta, and Humberstone, near Iquique, can be visited, as can Baquedano, the most important junction of the nitrate railways; most of the other *oficinas* are marked only by piles of rubble at the roadsides north of Antofagasta. Only one mine survives today, at María Elena; paradoxically, its future is secure, as the nitrates from the Atacama are believed to be much better for the soil than those created by the artificial process and demand has increased in recent years.

important, and Mejillones comes alive in the evening when the fishermen prepare to set sail. The sea is very cold around Mejillones because of the Humboldt current.

From Mejillones, the road runs at the foot of 500-m cliffs, with shifting views of the mountains and glistening ocean. Where the cliffs break into jagged rocks on the shoreline, hundreds of cormorants can be seen swarming all over the pinnacles. There are good beach resorts at **Hornitos**, 88 km north of Antofagasta, and **Poza Verde**, 117 km north.

Behind the mountains, the coastal sierra is extensively mined for copper, often by *pirquineros*, small groups of self-employed miners. There are larger mines, with the biggest concentration inland at Michilla. Reminders of the area's mining past can be seen, principally at the ruins of **Cobija**, 127 km north of Antofagasta, founded by order of Simón Bolívar in 1825 as Bolivia's main port. A prosperous little town handling silver exports from Potosí, it was destroyed by an earthquake in 1868 and again by a tidal wave in 1877 before losing out to the rising port of Antofagasta. Adobe walls, the rubbish tip right above the sea and the wreckage of the port are all that remains. The haunting ruins of the port of **Gatico** are at Km 144, just a little way beyond, and about 4 km further north there is an amazing ransacked cemetery. About 152 km north of Antofagasta, a very steep zigzag road winds up the cliffs a further 18 km to the mine at **Mantos de la Luna**. At the top, there are rather dead-looking groves of giant cactus living off the sea mist that collects on the cliffs. Wildlife includes foxes, or *zorros*.

Tocopilla → *Colour map 1, C1.*
Tocopilla lies 187 km north of Antofagasta via the coast road (or 365 km via the Pan-American Highway), and has one of the most dramatic settings of any Chilean town, sheltering at the foot of the coastal mountains that loom inland at heights of up to 2000 m. Tocopilla is dominated by a thermal power station, which supplies electricity to much of the far north, and by the port facilities used to unload coal and to export nitrates and iodine from María Elena. There is a run-down and slightly menacing air to the place, not helped by the 2006 earthquake, which laid waste to a sizeable part of the town. A prolonged stay is not recommended. There are, however, a few interesting early 20th-century buildings with wooden balustrades and façades, while the sloping plaza is an unlikely fiesta of palms and pepper trees amid the otherwise unremitting desert. There are two good beaches: **Punta Blanca**, 12 km south, and **Caleta Covadonga**, 3 km south, which has a swimming pool. A colony of some 20 to 30 sea turtles can often be seen about 3 km north of town. There is also fine deep-sea fishing here, if you can find a boat and a guide. For a spectacular view, head up Calle Baquedano as far as possible until you reach a stone stairway. Walking up this, you reach a minor road, which climbs up behind the town, giving views of the cliffs to the north, the mountains reaching inland and the fishing boats bobbing up and down in the harbour.

Routes north and east of Tocopilla
The coastal road runs north from Tocopilla to **Iquique**, 244 km away, and is a highly recommended journey, offering views of the rugged coastline, sea lions and tiny fishing communities. The customs post at **Chipana-Río Loa** (Km 90) searches all southbound vehicles for duty-free goods; this can take up to half an hour. Basic accommodation is available at **San Marcos**, a fishing village (Km 131). At **Chanaballita** (Km 184), there is a hotel, *cabañas*, camping, restaurant, shops. There are campsites at the former salt mining town of **Guanillos** (Km 126), **Playa Peruana** (Km 129) and **Playa El Aguila** (Km 160).

East of Tocopilla a good paved road climbs a steep, narrow valley 72 km to the Pan-American Highway. From here, the road continues eastwards to **Chuquicamata** (see page 218). Chuquicamata lies 16 km away from Calama, the main city of the interior.

ⓔ North of Antofagasta listings

For Sleeping and Eating price codes and other relevant information, see Essentials pages 35-42.

ⓢ Sleeping

Along the Pan-American Highway *p213*
D Posada Los Arbolitos, 122 km north of Carmen Alto. Rooms, *cabañas* and meals but no running water.

D Residencial Chacance, María Elena, T055-632749. Run-down but the same owners provide nicer rooms round the corner and cheap meals are available at **Casino Social**.

Mejillones *p213*
Wild camping is possible on the beach.
AL Hotel Mejillones, M Montt 086, T055-621590, www.hotelmejillones.cl. New 4-star.

C París, Pje Iquique 095, T055-623061,
iseghe@hotmail.com. **D** singles. Clean,
modern, good.
D Residencial Elisabeth, Alte Latorre 440,
T055-621568. **F** singles. Friendly, basic,
with restaurant. Price per person.
D Residencial Marcela, Borgoño 150,
T055-621464. **F** singles. With bath, pleasant.

Tocopilla *p215*
B-C Atenas, 21 de Mayo 1448, T/F055-
813651. Characterless but comfortable.
With bath and cable TV. Restaurant.
C Croacia, Bolívar 1332, T055-812783.
Modern, helpful. Cheaper without bath.
Opposite on Bolívar is the Sucre, same
ownership, same price.
C-D Hotel Colonial, 21 de Mayo 1717,
T055-811621, F811940. With bath,
breakfast and cable TV, friendly, helpful.
D Hostal Central, A Pinto 1241. Huge
rambling place like something out of a
Hitchcock film, very basic, friendly, vast
rooms, no hot water.

🍴 Eating

Mejillones *p213*
₩-₩ Sion-Ji, Alte Latorre 718. Good-value
Chinese cuisine.
₩ Juanito, Las Heras 241. Excellent
almuerzo and cheap eats.

Tocopilla *p215*
₩₩ Club de la Unión, Prat 1354. Pleasant
atmosphere. Good-value *almuerzo*.
₩₩ Oregón, Rodríguez 1280. Cafeteria,
fine sea views from veranda.
₩ El Chilenito, 21 de Mayo 2042. Few places
open early for breakfast; this is the first up.

🚌 Transport

Along the Pan-American Highway *p213*
Bus Between Antofagasta and Calama,
buses stop at the **Carmen Alto** junction,
1½ hrs, US$4. **María Elena** is served by
TurBus from Iquique, 6 hrs, US$10.

Mejillones *p213*
Bus Buses depart **Antofagasta**, Corsal
terminal, Condell y Sucre, every 30 mins
for Mejillones, 1 hr, US$2. There are also
minibuses to Mejillones departing
from Latorre 2730.

Tocopilla *p215*
Bus
There is no bus terminal in Tocopilla. Bus
offices are located on 21 de Mayo, including
Pullman Bus, **TurBus**, **Flota Barrios** and
Pullman Carmelita, all serving the following
destinations: **Antofagasta**, many daily,
2½ hrs, US$6; **Iquique**, frequent, 3 hrs, US$7.
TurBus also runs services to **Calama**,
3 a day, 3 hrs, US$7. All the above
companies also serve Santiago.
   Note that most buses to southern
destinations are en route from Iquique,
so you're unlikely to be able to leave
Tocopilla before mid-morning.

🛈 Directory

Tocopilla *p215*
Banks BCI, Baquedano y Prat, has a
Redbanc ATM. **Internet** 21 de Mayo 1721,
US$1.20 per hr. **Post office** 21 de Mayo
y A Pinto. **Telephone** CTC call centre near
the post office; also ENTEL, 21 de Mayo 2066.

Calama and around

→ *Colour map 1, B3 & C2.*

Calama is a somewhat seedy city, set at 2265 m in the oasis of the Río Loa, with beautiful views of volcanoes in the Ollagüe area. An expensive and modern town, roughly 200 km northeast of Antofagasta, it acts as a service centre for the large nearby mines of Chuquicamata and Radomiro Tomic. Initially a staging post on the silver route between Potosí and Cobija, Calama superseded San Pedro de Atacama in importance with the development of mining activities at Chuquicamata. Most travellers use Calama as the departure point for San Pedro de Atacama, however, football fans will certainly want to make sure that their visit coincides with a home match of Cobreloa, the most successful Chilean football team outside Santiago in the past 20 years or so. Nearby are oasis villages such as Chiu Chiu and Caspana with their historic churches and altogether slower pace of life.▸▸ *For listings, see pages 222-225.*

Ins and outs

Getting there Calama is easily reached by regular buses from Antofagasta and the south, and by less frequent buses from Iquique and Arica, which often travel overnight. Note that the TurBus terminal is quite a distance from the town centre. For those heading to Uyuni in Bolivia, there are several weekly buses. There are also three weekly buses to Salta in Argentina. The airport is served by daily flights to/from Antofagasta and Santiago. It is about 5 km from the city centre. Taxis to/from the airport cost US$9. Airport transfers are also available. The more expensive hotels may offer courtesy vans.

Getting around The central part of Calama is relatively compact and you should not need to take public transport. There are, however, many *colectivos*, most of which pick up on Abaroa or Vargas.

Tourist office ⓘ *Latorre 1689, T055-531707, www.calamacultural.cl, Mon-Fri 0830-1300, 1400-1800.* They provide maps of the town and can book tours to Chuquicamata. English spoken, helpful staff, but don't expect any info on San Pedro.

Calama

The centre of Calama is Plaza 21 de Mayo, a shady spot in which to relax. The peach-coloured **Catedral San Juan Bautista** on the west side with its copper clad spire makes a pleasant contrast to the colours of the desert. On the northeastern side, the pedestrian walkway of Ramírez continues two blocks east, where visitors will not be able to miss the bright red, phallic statue of **El Minero**, erected as a tribute to the bravery of the region's miners, but also an unlikely piece of kitsch in the Atacama.

This area comes alive at night. In the plaza, teenagers flirt with one another, while Argentine backpackers down on their luck ponder their next move. The pedestrian walkways of Ramírez are awash with young and old, beggars and hippies, not to mention buskers and an old man winding a barrel organ, watched by his pet parakeet.

On Avenida Bernado O'Higgins, 2 km from the centre, is the **Parque El Loa** ⓘ *1000-1800*, which contains a reconstruction of a typical colonial village built around a reduced-scale reproduction of Chiu Chiu church. To get there take bus B or X or *colectivos* 8 or 18 from the centre. In the park is the **Museo Arqueológico y Etnológico** ⓘ *Tue-Fri 1000-1300, 1400-1800, Sat-Sun 1400-1830, US$0.60*, which has an exhibition of local pre-Hispanic cultural history. Nearby is the new **Museo de Historia Natural** ⓘ *1000-1300,*

1500-1830, US$0.90, which has an interesting collection devoted to the *oficinas* and the region's ecology and palaeontology.

Chuquicamata

A visit here is truly memorable. Some 16 km north of Calama, Chuquicamata is the site of the world's largest open-cast copper mine, employing 8000 workers and operated by **Codelco**, the state copper corporation. Although copper has been mined here since pre-Inca times, it was the Guggenheim brothers who introduced modern mining and processing techniques after 1911 and made Chuquicamata into the most important single mine in Chile. In other parts of the plant, 60,000 tonnes of low-grade ore are processed a day to produce refined copper of 99.98% purity. Output is over 600,000

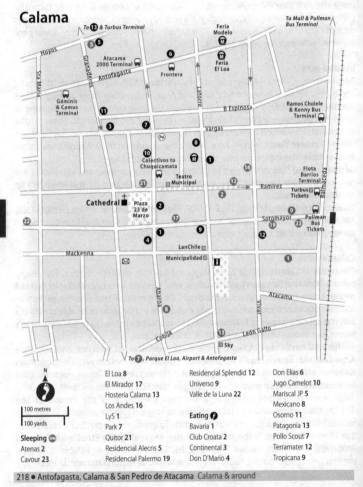

Calama

To 13 & Turbus Terminal

To Mall & Pullman Bus Terminal

Feria Modelo

Hoyos

Sta Maria

Granados

Atacama 2000 Terminal

Antofagasta

Frontera

Feria El Loa

Latorre

Géminis & Camus Terminal

11

B Espinosa

Ramos Cholele & Kenny Bus Terminal

7

Vargas

10 Colectivos to Chuquicamata

8

Pol

21

Teatro Municipal

16

12

Flota Barrios Terminal

Ramirez

Turbus Tickets

Balmaceda

22

Cathedral

Plaza 23 de Marzo

2

17

Sotomayor

19

23

Pullman Bus Tickets

4

1

9

LanChile

12

Mackenna

Municipalidad

i

1

Abaroa

8

Atacama

Cobija

13

León Gallo

Sky

Vivar

To 7, Parque El Loa, Airport & Antofagasta

N

100 metres
100 yards

Sleeping
Atenas **2**
Cavour **23**

El Loa **8**
El Mirador **17**
Hostería Calama **13**
Los Andes **16**
LyS **1**
Park **7**
Quitor **21**
Residencial Alecris **5**
Residencial Palermo **19**

Residencial Splendid **12**
Universo **9**
Valle de la Luna **22**

Eating
Bavaria **1**
Club Croata **2**
Continental **3**
Don D'Mario **4**

Don Elias **6**
Jugo Camelot **10**
Mariscal JP **5**
Mexicano **8**
Osorno **11**
Patagonia **13**
Pollo Scout **7**
Terramater **12**
Tropicana **9**

Farewell to Chuqui

The town of Chuquicamata has always been famous in Chile. Quite apart from the fact that the mine is responsible for a large part of Chile's GDP, miners at 'Chuqui' were treated differently, with free healthcare in a special modern hospital and guaranteed housing close to the mine. The decision to move all those living in Chuqui down to Calama was very sad for those who have grown up and lived in the town, and had a severe impact on both the people of Chuqui and on those living in nearby Calama.

Some 2500 families were moved from Chuqui to new neighbourhoods on the outskirts of Calama, near the road to Chiu Chiu. The town's famous hospital was also transferred to Calama, and is now of great benefit to the city as a whole. The two reasons for the change are the reserves of copper lying beneath the town of Chuqui and the pollution risks for those living there. Certainly, anyone approaching Calama only has to look at the great cloud that hangs to the north to appreciate the dangers of pollution in Chuqui. Nevertheless, the death of the town was a momentous and sad event in the history of northern Chile.

tonnes a year, but the diggers are having to cut ever deeper into the desert, making the extraction process increasingly expensive. In 2005 the town that surrounds the mine was closed and the families moved to Calama, leaving only a small historic centre for visitors. This will enable Codelco to exploit the copper that is buried in the earth beneath the houses and will make Chuquicamata the latest and the largest in the Atacama's long line of ghost towns. The latest plan is to link the three mines in the area, Chuquicamata, mina sur and Radomiro Tomic to create a hole in the earth 14 km long producing 10% of the world's copper supplies.

A visit to the mine at Chuquicamata is highly recommended for the insight it gives into the industry that bankrolls Chile's economy. Although you don't actually go down into the mine you can see right into it, and there are also fantastic views of the desert pampa and the volcanoes to the east. **Guided bus tours** ① *Mon-Fri 1330, less frequently in low season, 1 hr, US$2 donation, passport essential*, depart from the ex-**colegio Chuqui** (the former school). The tours are in Spanish (although guides usually speak reasonable English). Places on tours need to be booked in advance, either by calling the office in Chuquicamata, T055-322122, visitas@codelco.cl, or from the tourist office in Calama. Covered shoes, long trousers and long sleeves must be worn. Arrive 30 minutes early. Note that tours are susceptible to last-minute cancellation due to adverse weather conditions.

North and east of Calama

Chiu Chiu was one of the earliest centres of Spanish settlement in the area. Set in the shadow of the Volcán San Pedro, it is a peaceful oasis village and a nice contrast to the bustle of Calama. In the glades nearby, horses graze on surprisingly lush grasses and the local people cultivate alfalfa. Chiu Chiu's plaza, fringed with pepper trees and opposite the church, is a pleasant place to while away a few hours. The church of **San Francisco**, dating from 1611, has roof beams of cactus and walls over 1 m thick – please leave a donation. Some 10 km away on the road to Caspana is a unique, perfectly circular, very deep lake, also called **Chiu Chiu** or **Icacoia**.

From the village of Chiu Chiu, the road continues north towards Ollagüe. Just beyond the oasis, a small turning branches off the main road and follows the course of the **Río Loa**. Here the canyon is green with crops, and donkeys plough the earth – it seems like a secret valley. This area has been settled for millennia and petroglyphs are clearly visible in the rocks on the right-hand side of the road heading towards **Lasana**. This small hamlet, 8 km north of Chiu Chiu, has striking ruins of a pre-Inca *pukará*, a national monument; drinks are on sale. At **Conchi**, 25 km north of Lasana, the road crosses the Río Loa via a bridge dating from 1890; there is a spectacular view over the river from the bridge, but it is a military zone, so no photographs are allowed. Access to the river is by side tracks, best at Santa Bárbara. There is interesting wildlife and flower meadows and trout fishing in season; you can obtain a permit from Gobernación in Calama.

From Conchi, a road branches east following the valley of the **Río San Pedro**, which has been a route for herders and silver caravans for centuries, to **Inacaliri**, from where a very poor road (4WD essential) runs south to Linzor and the **El Tatio geysers** (see page 229). While there are several direct routes east from Chiu Chiu towards the geysers, only one is in good condition: just north of Chiu Chiu, turn right off the Ollagüe road and continue until you reach a fork some 22 km east of Chiu Chiu. Take the right fork, ignoring the large sign pointing left to El Tatio (this leads to another very bad track via Linzor). At Km 47 a track turns off north to Caspana; again, ignore this turning and continue along the main road as it climbs steeply up the Cuesta de Chita. At about Km 80, branch left to Tatio; this branch meets the main Tatio–San Pedro road some 5 km further north.

Caspana is beautifully set among hills with a tiny church dating from 1641 and a **museum** ① *Tue-Sun 1000-1300, 1500-1730*, with interesting displays on Atacameño culture. Basic accommodation is available. A poor road runs north and east of Caspana through valleys of pampas grass with llama herds to **Toconce**, which has extensive pre-Hispanic terraces set among some interesting rock formations. There are many archaeological sites nearby and the area is ideal for hiking, with the **Cerros Toconce**, **León** and **Paniri** – all over 5500 m – within reach.

Some 20 km west of Toconce is **Ayquina**, in whose ancient church is enshrined the statue of the Virgin of Guadalupe. Her feast day is 8 September, when pilgrims come from far and wide to celebrate and worship. ►► *See Festivals and events, page 223.*

Six kilometres north of Ayquina are the lukewarm thermal waters of the **Baños de Turi** and the ruins of a 12th-century *pukará* that was once the largest fortified town in the Atacama mountains. Close to the village of **Cupo** is a large, ruined pre-Hispanic settlement at **Paniri**, with extensive field systems, irrigation canals (including aqueducts) and a necropolis. Some of the fields are still in use. The area around Cupo is one of the best for seeing the Atacama giant cactus (*Notocereus atacamensis*); flamingos are also visible on the mudflats. Surrounding the *baños* is an oasis of ancient pastoral land, the **Vega de Turi**, now drying up due to the water consumption of the mines. It remains an important site for the llama- and sheep-herders, who believe it has curative properties. At several times in the year, especially September, herders from a wide area congregate here with their flocks.

Border crossings: Chile–Bolivia

Ollagüe–Uyuni → *Bolivian phone code: +591.*
A poor road leads across the Bolivian border from Ollagüe and runs to **Uyuni**, 170 km east. Trucks take a more northerly route across the Salar de Uyuni but motorists are warned against using this latter route into Bolivia. As well as the danger of getting lost on the many tracks leading over the salt lakes, there's no petrol between Calama and Uyuni and little hope of help with a breakdown on the Bolivian side, unless you don't mind waiting for days. After rain the route is impassable and even experienced guides get lost. Maps give widely differing versions of the route. Where the road has been built up, never forsake it for the appealing soft salt beside it. The salt takes a person's weight but a vehicle breaks through the crust into unfathomable depths of plasticine mud below.
Immigration and customs Open 0800-2000.

Ollagüe

Situated 198 km north of Calama on the dry floor of the Salar de Ollagüe at 3696 m, Ollagüe is surrounded by a dozen volcanic peaks of over 5000 m. It is a cold, dusty, windswept place, but remarkable for its sense of remoteness. At this altitude, nights are cold, while the days are warm and sunny, there are only 50 mm of rain a year and water is very scarce.

The road to Ollagüe from Chiu Chiu runs north to Estación San Pedro. This first section is in poor condition, however, from Estación San Pedro to a *carabinero* checkpoint at **Ascotán**, it is worse. This is the highest point of the road at 3900 m. Ask at Ascotán or Ollagüe about weather conditions before setting out, especially in December and January or August. North of Ascotán, the road improves as it crosses the Salares de Ascotán and de Carcote and Ollagüe. There are many llama flocks along this road and flamingos on the *salares*. There is no petrol between Calama and Uyuni in Bolivia, although if you completely run out, you could try buying some from the *carabineros* at Ollagüe or Ascotán, the military at Conchi or the mining camp at Buenaventura.

Some 5 km south of Ollagüe is the sulphur mining camp of **Buenaventura**, which is situated at an altitude of 5800 m, only 150 m short of the summit of Ollagüe Volcano. Camping is possible and there are amazing views over the volcanoes and salt flats. A road leads to the sulphur camp but be wary of walking the route if not coming from Bolivia, as you will not yet be acclimatized for exercise at this altitude. You should also bear in mind that temperatures can drop as low as -37°C.

A road runs west from Ollagüe to the sulphur mines, now closed, of **Aucanquilcha**, where there are the ruins of an aerial tram system. A high-clearance vehicle is needed to drive to the mine but from there you can scramble to the summit of Aucanquilcha, at 6176 m, from which there are superb views. An interesting excursion can also be made north from Ollagüe to the village of **Coska** with its traditional agriculture and herds of llamas and alpacas.

For Sleeping and Eating price codes and other relevant information, see Essentials pages 35-42.

⊜ Sleeping

Calama *p217, map p218*

L Park, Camino Aeropuerto 1392, T055-319900, www.parkplaza.cl/calama. On the edge of town by the airport. 1st class, best hotel in town, pool, bar and restaurant.

A El Mirador, Sotomayor 2064, T/F055-340329, www.hotelmirador.cl. With bath, good atmosphere, clean, helpful. Wi-Fi in common areas. Somewhat convoluted reservation system but one of the few tourist-friendly hotels in Calama. Recommended.

A Hostería Calama, Latorre 1521, T055-341511, www.hosteriacalama.cl. Comfortable if somewhat lacking in charm, good cafetería and service. Buffet breakfast. Rooms have heating, some with king size beds. There is also a gym and a small pool.

A LyS, Vicuña MacKenna 1819, T055-361113, www.lyshotel.cl. Designed for business travellers. Friendly staff, clean rooms, upstairs rooms more spacious. Wi-Fi. Often full Mon-Wed with mining engineers. A good choice.

A Quitor, Ramírez 2116, T055-341716, www.hotelquitor.cl. Central, pleasant, helpful, internet access. Good.

B Residencial Alecris, Félix Hoyos 2143, T055-341616. **C** without bath. No breakfast. Single, double and triple rooms. Well maintained, very clean, family atmosphere, often fully booked with miners. Sunny courtyard. Chatty owner, Alejandro.

B Universo, Sotomayor 1822, T055-361640, hoteluniverso@gmail.com. Decent rooms with bathroom. Unfortunately most face inwards onto a corridor, although there are a couple with windows onto the street, which are much better and good value.

C Atenas, Ramírez 1961, T055-342666, www.hotelatenas.cl. With bath and cable TV, small, somewhat stuffy rooms, pricey laundry service, breakfast extra.

C Residencial Splendid, Ramírez 1961, T055-341841. Central, clean, friendly, hot water, often full, good, cheaper without bath.

C-D Cavour, Sotomayor 1841, T055-314718. With bath and cable TV. No breakfast. Basic, bright and friendly, though rather run-down.

C-D El Loa, Abaroa 1617, T055-341963. Cheaper rooms without bath.

C-D Residencial Palermo, Sotomayor 1889, T055-341283. **F** singles. Some rooms with bath. Friendly, central, very dark.

D Valle de la Luna, Sotomayor 2326, T055-312114. **F** singles. More expensive rooms with bath. Clean, central.

D-E Los Andes, Vivar 1920, T055-341073. **F** singles. As basic as it gets, decent beds.

North and east of Calama *p219*
Chiu Chiu

B Hostal Chiu Chiu, Esmeralda s/n, T055-326386. Friendly and helpful. 3 rooms are also available at the community tourism project in Toconce, providing accommodation for up to 12 people, with full board.

Ollagüe *p221*

There is nowhere official to stay in Ollagüe, but police and border officials will help travellers to find unofficial lodgings.

❷ Eating

Calama *p217, map p218*

Ⅲ Terramater, Vivar 1797, T055-312010. An unlikely elegant restaurant in the city centre. Intimate surroundings and a good wine list. Slightly overattentive staff and a little overpriced, but this is probably Calama's best restaurant.

Ⅲ Bavaria, Sotomayor 2093, T055-3414965. Good restaurant with cafetería downstairs, real coffee, open 0800, very popular, also at Latorre 1935.

Mariscal JP, Félix Hoyos 2127, T055-312559. Closed Mon. Best seafood in town, not cheap but worth it.

Mexicano, Latorre 1986. Mexican cuisine, fairly expensive. Doubles as a pub with live music at weekends.

Patagonia, Granaderos 2549. Lots of meat. Good wine list.

Club Croata, Abaroa 1869, Plaza 23 de Marzo, T055-342126. Excellent-value 4-course *almuerzo*.

Continental, Vargas 2180. Good seafood and fish, cheaper than Mariscal JP but less charm.

Osorno, Espinosa 2198 y Ganaderos, T055-341035. Grill, with live Chilean folk music.

Don D'Mario, Abaroa 1756-A. Basic *picada*, cleaner than most and serving hearty Chilean food.

Don Elias, Antofagasta 2029, opposite the Frontera bus station (no sign). Open 0800 for breakfast. Cheap hearty no-frills Peruvian home-cooking. Packed at lunchtime.

Jugo Camelot, Abaroa 1968. Good fruit juice.

Pollo Scout, Vargas 2102. Clean, friendly, popular, reasonable.

Tropicana, Sotomayor 2043. Good fruit juice.

There are also many very cheap eateries around the **Feria modelo Loa** and in the **Mercado Central** (see below).

North and east of Calama *p219*
Chiu Chiu
Café Tambo. A nice place with old wooden furniture. Mid-range meals.

Bars and clubs

Calama *p217, map p218*
There are decent bars on Ganaderos between the town centre and the **TurBus** terminal.

Calama's discos are all out of town on Av Circunvalación. There are over 10 of them, including **Kamikaze** and **Vox**. Anywhere called a nightclub is actually a strip-joint.

Festivals and events

Calama *p217, map p218*
Jan Festival de Teatro, with a different dramatic production every day at the municipal theatre.
Early Feb Calama's annual festival is a riot of activities and celebrations – recommended for those in the area.
Feb The Parque Loa hosts Calama's annual jazz festival.

North and east of Calama *p219*
8 Sep The feast day of the Virgen de Guadalupe is celebrated in Ayquina, with day-long group dancing to indigenous rhythms on flute and drum. Towards sunset the Virgin is carried up a steep trail to a small thatched shrine, where the image and the people are blessed before the dancing recommences, continuing all the way back to the village. The poor people of the hills gather stones and make toy houses all along the route: miniatures of the homes they hope to have some day.
19 Mar The fiesta of San José is celebrated in Cupo, southwest of Ayquina.

Ollagüe *p221*
19 Jun Fiesta de San Antonio de Padua celebrates the patron saint of Ollagüe, with dancing and Quechua customs, such as the sacrifice of llamas.

Shopping

Calama *p217, map p218*
Económico, Grecia 2314. Supermarket.
El Cobre, Vargas 2148. Supermarket.
Feria El Loa, Antofagasta between Latorre and Vivar. The market sells fruit juices and crafts as well as cheap clothes. There are also craft stalls on Latorre 1600-block.
Shopping mall, Baquedano, north of centre. Reached by bus 1M, *colectivos* 11B and 18B.

▲▲ Activities and tours

Calama *p217, map p218*

Several agencies in Calama run 1-day and longer tours to the Atacama region, including San Pedro; these are usually more expensive than tours from San Pedro and require a minimum number for the tour to go ahead. Reports of tour quality are mixed -- watch out for badly maintained vehicles and poor guides. The tourist office, Latorre 1689, T055-531707, www.calamacultural.cl, has a full list.

Sol del Desierto, grau 723, Local 7A, T055-330428, www.soldeldesierto.cl. A variety of day tours around Chiu Chiu and San Pedro.

☉ Transport

Calama *p217, map p218*
Air

LanChile to **Santiago** via Antofagasta, 5 daily, US$110-430 return depending on season and flexibility. **Sky Airline** is slightly cheaper. Transfer services from the airport are offered by **Transfer City Express**, T055-341022, US$9 per person.

Airline offices LanChile, Latorre 1726, T600-526 2000 and airport, T055-311331; Sky, Latorre 1497, T055-310190.

Bicycle
Repairs from **Ciclos Méndez**, Vívar 2071.

Bus
No main terminal; buses leave from the company offices: TurBus, Granaderos, about 12 blocks north of centre; tickets from Ramírez y Balmaceda; Pullman Bus, Balmaceda 1802; Atacama 2000, Abaroa 2106; Frontera, Antofagasta 2041;Géminis, Antofagasta 2239; Kenny Bus, Vivar 1954; Flota Barrios, Ramírez 2298.

To **Santiago**, 22-24 hrs, US$50-95; to **Antofagasta**, 3 hrs, several companies, US$8; to **Arica**, usually overnight, 9 hrs, US$28, or change in Antofagasta; to

Valparaíso/Viña del Mar, US$50-65; to **Iquique**, TurBus, 3 daily, 6 hrs, via Tocopilla, US$20. To **La Serena**, usually with delay in Antofagasta, 16 hrs, US$35-65. To **San Pedro de Atacama**, 1½ hrs, US$4, TurBus, several daily, Atacama 2000, 3 a day, continuing to Toconao and Peine; Frontera, 6 a day, last bus 2030, often leaves late, but does have a driver who likes to dress up as Spiderman.

To **Salta** (Argentina), 15 hrs, services with both companies leave early morning Tue, Fri and Sun, US$50, Géminis, Pullman Bus.

To **Bolivia**, Buses Frontera and Atacama 2000, between them have daily services to **Ollagüe** for US$12 (see below), either leaving early or late at night with connecting services over the border to **Uyuní**, US$5.

Car
Car hire is not reliable in San Pedro de Atacama, so you're better off picking up a vehicle in Calama. A high-clearance vehicle (necessary for the desert) costs around US$100 per day. Rates are sometimes much lower at weekends. A hired car, shared between several people, is an economic alternative for visiting the Atacama region.

Hire companies include **Alamo**, Hoyos 2177, T055-364543; **Avis**, Gallo 1985A, T055-319757; **Budget**, Granaderos 2925, T341076; **Hertz**, Latorre 1510, T055-341380; IQSA, O'Higgins 877, T055-310281.

Chuquicamata *p218*
Yellow *colectivos* (marked 'Chuqui') depart from Abaroa just north of the Plaza 23 de Marzo in Calama, US$2.75. The service is not particularly reliable and if you are taking the tour of the mine it is probably better to take a taxi, US$12.

North and east of Calama *p219*
Chiu Chiu
Served by minibuses to/from **Calama**, 4 a day, US$3. To catch one, either ring ahead in Calama, T055-343400, or take the Línea 80 *colectivo* on Abaroa to the end of the line in Calama and then catch the next vehicle to

Chiu Chiu. If arranged in advance, the minibuses will continue on to Lasana for an extra charge – you will have to book the return trip, or walk back to Chiu Chiu.

Ollagüe *p221*

There is no fuel in Ollagüe. Buses Frontera from **Calama**, Wed and Sun at 0700, 5 hrs, US$6; returns next day. Ollagüe can also be reached by taking the **Calama–Uyuni train** (see above) but, if you stop off, you will have to hitch back as the daily freight trains are not allowed to carry passengers. Hitching by road is difficult but the police may help you to find a truck.

● Directory

Calama *p217, map p218*
Banks Rates are generally poor especially for TCs. There are several banks with ATMs on Latorre and Sotomayor. *Casas de cambio* include **Moon Valley Money Exchange**, Vivar 1818, and also another exchange at Sotomayor 1837; also on Ramírez, next to Centro Comercial Gala, most open Sat.
Consulates Bolivia, León Gallo 1985A, open (in theory) Mon-Fri 0930-1500, friendly, helpful. **Internet** There are several throughout the centre. Prices US$1 per hr.
Laundry Erika, Espinoza 1930 (charges per kg); Lila, Sotomayor 2077. **Medical services** Hospital del Cobre, Chorrillos 689, T055-342769. **Post office** Granaderos y V Mackenna, open 0830-1300, 1530-1830, Sat 0900-1230, will not send parcels over 1 kg. **Telephone** CTC, Sotomayor 1825; Entel, Sotomayor 2027.

San Pedro de Atacama and around

→ *Colour map 1, C3.*

Situated 103 km by paved road southeast of Calama, San Pedro is an oasis town in the valley of the Río San Pedro at 2436 m. While it is now famous among visitors as the base for excursions in this part of the Atacama, it was important as the centre of the Atacameño culture long before the arrival of the Spanish. There is a definite sense of history in the shady streets and the crumbling ancient walls that drift away from the town into the fields and on into the dust. Owing to the clear atmosphere and isolation, there are wonderful views of the night sky from just outside town. Despite being in the desert, it does rain in San Pedro about three or four times a year, usually around March, as a result of the invierno altiplánico. San Pedro is a good base from which to visit Toconao, the Salar de Atacama and the geysers of El Tatio. → *For listings, see pages 234-238.*

Ins and outs

Getting there San Pedro can be reached by over a dozen buses a day to/from Calama and six daily from Antofagasta. There are three companies: **Atacama 2000**, **Frontera** and **TurBus**. If driving, be aware there is no food, water or fuel along the Calama–San Pedro road. **Turismo Licancabur** ① *T055-334194, transferlicancabur@terra.cl*, run a minibus service from Calama Airport, although the service can be unreliable.

Getting around San Pedro is small so taxis (from by the football field) are only needed for out-of-town trips.

Tourist information **Sernatur** has an office in the plaza (closed on Thursdays). It is worth going there to check out previous travellers' observations on the merits of the various tour companies in the complaints and suggestions book.

Entry charges are levied at most of the natural attractions (around US$4), with the money going to the local communities. ATM machines in town can be unreliable; bring enough cash to cover emergencies

Climate Be prepared for the harsh climate and high altitudes of the interior. Gloves, a hat and a warm coat are essential for excursions from San Pedro, especially for the early morning trip to El Tatio. High-factor suncream and a hat are necessary for the burning daytime sun. Take plenty of water, sunglasses and lip balm on any excursion.

Background

The main centre for the Atacameño culture, which flourished in this region before the arrival of the Incas around 1450, San Pedro was defended by a *pukará* (fortress) at Quitor, 3 km north. The cultivable land around was distributed in 15 *ayllus* (socio-economic communities based on family networks) and irrigation channels were built. San Pedro was visited by both Diego de Almagro and Pedro de Valdivia and the town became a centre of Spanish colonial control; a mission was established in 1557. After Independence, the town became an important trading centre on the route between Cobija on the coast and Salta in Argentina, but the decline of Cobija and the rise of copper-mining led to San Pedro being superceded as an economic centre by Calama.

In the early 20th century, San Pedro's economy was based around mining, with salt mines in the Valle de la Luna (whose ruins are easily visible today) and sulphur mines in the high mountains. Since the 1970s, tourism has been of increasing importance and the town is now dependent on the annual influx of Chilean and foreign visitors. However, travellers should be aware that tourism is a somewhat divisive issue in San Pedro. In many ways the town has lost much of it's Atacameño feel, and with more tourists than locals you may well feel that on entering San Pedro you are leaving Chile behind. Moreover, the tour companies are often run by outsiders and the glut of travel agencies has led to a tenfold increase in rents in the past ten years. Many of the local people still work in agriculture, having lower incomes than those who work with tourism, and, with over 25 tour companies there are dark (and doubtless somewhat exaggerated) rumours that some of these operations are fronts for money laundering and drug running, especially with Bolivia so close.

The road from Calama

At **Paso Barros Arana** (Km 58) there is an unpaved turning to the left, which leads through interesting desert scenery to the small, mud-brick village of **Río Grande**. Look out for guanacos on the pass. The main road continues skirts the Cordillera de la Sal about 15 km from San Pedro. There are spectacular views of the sunset over the western *cordilleras*. The old unpaved road to San Pedro turns off the new road at Km 72 and crosses this range through the Valle de La Luna (see below), but should only be attempted by 4WD vehicles. This road is partly paved with salt blocks.

San Pedro de Atacama

The **Iglesia de San Pedro**, dating from the 17th century, is supposedly the second oldest church in the country. It has been heavily restored and the tower was added in 1964. The roof is made of cactus; inside, the statues of Mary and Joseph have fluorescent light halos. Nearby, on the shady Plaza, is the **Casa Incaica**, the oldest building in San Pedro.

Museo Arqueológico ⓘ *www.ucn.cl/museo, Mon-Fri 0900-1200, 1400-1800, Sat and Sun 1000-1200, 1400-1800, US$3.50*, contains the collection of Padre Gustave Le Paige, a Belgian missionary who lived in San Pedro between 1955 and 1980. It is now under the care of the Universidad Católica del Norte. One of the most important museums in northern Chile, it traces the development of pre-Hispanic Atacameño society. It is well organised, each display having a card with explanations in English. The centrepiece of the collection has always been the Atacameño mummies, fully clothed and perfectly preserved. However these have recently been removed from display at the behest of the local indigenous community and are gathering dust in a storeroom. Nevertheless the museum is well worth a visit.

The **Pukará de Quitor**, 3 km north of San Pedro along the river, US$4, is a pre-Inca fortress that was restored in 1981 and covers 2.5 ha on a hillside on the west bank of the river. It was stormed by the Spanish under Pedro de Valdivia, 1000 defenders being overcome by 30 horsemen who vaulted the walls. The road to Quitor involves fording the river several times, until the *pukará* comes into view on the hill on the left-hand side of the valley. There is a new plaza here, built as a homage to the indigenous people of the region and set amid thorn trees. The road continues along the valley of the Río San Pedro as the canyon climbs further into the Atacama, passing a couple of small farmsteads sheltered by pepper trees where sheep graze in the desert sun. A further 4 km up the river, there are ruins at **Catarpe**, which was the Inca administrative centre for this region. The ruins are on top of a hill on the east side of the valley, and are difficult to find without a guide; horseback tours are offered in San Pedro.

There's another archaeological site 12 km southwest of San Pedro at **Tulor**, US$4, where parts of a village (dated 500-800 BC) have been excavated. The road is *ripio*, and fine for 4WD vehicles. You can sleep in two reconstructed huts or take a tour, US$10. Nearby are the ruins of a 17th-century Spanish-style village, abandoned in the 18th century because of the lack of water.

Baños de Puritama ① *US$9*, just under 30 km north of San Pedro, are pleasant thermal baths. Taxis (US$65) will drop you and wait for two hours. Alternatively take a tour (US$18).

San Pedro de Atacama

	Elim **4** *D2*	La Casa de Don Tomás **9** *D2*	Casa Piedra **1** *C2*
	Hostal Edén Atacameño **3** *C3*	Residencial Chiloé **10** *B1*	Cuna **4** *B2*
	Hostal Katarpe **7** *C1*	Residencial Don Raul **11** *C1*	Empanadium **3** *C2*
	Hostal Lickana **17** *C1*	Residencial La Florida **12** *B2*	La Casona **5** *C2*
	Hostal Mamatierra **18** *C3*	Residencial Vilacoyo **16** *B2*	La Estaka **6** *C2*
100 metres	Hostal Martita **21** *D2*	Takha-Takha **5** *C1*	Les Copains **8** *C2*
100 yards	Hostal Miskanty **14** *C1*		Milagro **12** *C2*
	Hostal Puritama **20** *C1*	**Eating** 🍴	Quitor **11** *B1*
Sleeping	Hostal Sonchek **22** *B2*	Adobe **9** *C2*	
Altiplanico **1** *A1*	Hostelling International **24** *C3*	Bendito Desierto **2** *B1*	
Awasi **2** *D2*	Hostería San Pedro **6** *C3*	Café Etnico **10** *C2*	
Camping Los Perales **13** *D2*	Kimal **8** *C1*	Café Tierra Todo Natural **7** *C2*	
Casa Corvatsch **15** *B1*			

Beware: minefields

An indication of the nature of General Pinochet's geopolitics in the 1970s and 1980s is provided by the numerous minefields that were placed along Chile's border with Bolivia and northern Argentina at that time. The minefields were put down to forestall any possible invasion from Chile's neighbours, which was then perceived to be a very real threat.

Following the Ottowa convention, Chile has begun the slow process of dismantling its extensive minefields. Meanwhile, the danger remains. It is not unknown for people to have been killed

or maimed (often while attempting to smuggle drugs across the border). It is very unwise to make any lone forays into the altiplano without a knowledgeable local guide.

Minefields are known to affect the new **Parque Nacional Llullaillaco** (see page 233) and the Chilean side of **Volcán Licancabur** (see box, page 231) to give just two examples – and there may be other areas that are not known about. Always ask first before heading off into the northern wilderness, keeping in mind that local people are often more knowledgeable than officials.

Valle de la Luna
① *US$4.*

Some 12 km west of San Pedro, this is a valley of fantastic landscapes caused by the erosion of salt mountains. The valley is crossed by the old San Pedro–Calama road. Although buses on the new road will stop to let you off where the old road branches 13 km northwest of San Pedro (signposted to Peine), it is far better to travel from San Pedro on the old road, either on foot (allow three hours each way), by bicycle or high-clearance vehicle. There is a small information centre at the entrance with info in Spanish only, although there is a leaflet in English. The Valle is best seen at sunset. Take water, hat, camera and a torch. Note that camping is prohibited. Agencies in San Pedro offer tours, departing around 1530, returning after sunset, US$15 per person, but make sure the agency departs in time for arrival in the Valle before sunset as they do not always do so. Be aware that most tour groups watch the sunset from the same spot, so do not expect a solitary desert experience. Tours usually include a visit to the **Valle de la Muerte**, a crevice in the Cordillera de la Sal near San Pedro, with red rock walls, contorted into fantastic shapes.

The geysers of El Tatio
① *US$6.*

At an altitude of 4321 m, the geysers of El Tatio are a popular attraction. From San Pedro, they are reached by a road in variable state of repair that runs northeast, past the **Baños de Puritama**, then on for a further 94 km. The geysers are said to be at their best in the morning between 0600 and 0800, although the spectacle varies; locals say the performance is best when weather conditions are stable. A swimming pool has been built nearby. From here, you can hike to surrounding volcanoes if you are adapted to altitude, although it is advisable to take a guide because of the dangers of minefields.

There is no public transport and hitching is impossible. If going in a hired car, make sure the engine is suitable for very high altitudes and is protected with anti-freeze; a 4WD is advisable. If driving in the dark, it is almost impossible to find your way: the sign for El Tatio is north of the turn-off. Following recent accidents a series of stone walls and wooden walkways has been built around the geysers, which some say has taken away from the spectacle. Wrap up warm as it can be extremely cold.

From San Pedro to Toconao

From San Pedro to Toconao, a 37-km journey south, the paved road runs through occasional groves of acacia and pepper trees. There are many tracks leading to the *pozos* (wells), which supply the intricate irrigation system. Most have thermal water but bathing is not appreciated by the local farmers. The groves of trees are havens for wildlife, especially *ñandu* (rhea) and Atacama owls; there are also some llamas.

Toconao and around

This village, at an altitude of 2600 m, is on the eastern shore of the Salar de Atacama. Unlike San Pedro, Toconao's economy is based on agriculture, not tourism. All houses are built of bricks of white volcanic stone, which gives the village an appearance totally different from San Pedro. The 18th-century church and bell tower are also built of volcanic stone. Food is available and there are small shops selling handicrafts. The local church is cared for by nuns who give liturgies. There are no priests.

South of San Pedro de Atacama

Into Bolivia: the Salar de Uyuni and other sights

East of San Pedro, on the border with Bolivia, lies **Volcán Licancábur** (5916 m), a sacred site for the Incas and the focal point of three Inca paths that crossed the altiplano and the Salar de Atacama. The volcano can be climbed only from the Bolivian side, at any time of the year except January and February. At the foot of the volcano on the Bolivian side is **Laguna Verde** (4400 m), which extends over 17 sq km; its wind-lashed waters are an impressive jade, the result, it is said, of magnesium, calcium carbonate, lead or arsenic. There is a *refugio* near the lake (US$2, small, mattresses, running water).

Further north is the equally impressive **Laguna Colorada** (4278 m), which covers 60 sq km; its flaming red waters are the result of the effects of the wind and afternoon sun on the numerous micro-organisms that live in it (up until midday the water is a fairly ordinary colour). The water is less than a metre deep but the mud is very soft, and the shores are encrusted with borax, which provides an arctic white contrast with the waters of the lake. The pink algae in the lake provides food for the rare James flamingos, along with the more common Chilean and Andean flamingos. Some 40 other bird species can also be seen.

Further north still, beyond Ollagüe, is the **Salar de Uyuni**, the largest and highest salt lake in the world and an increasingly popular attraction for visitors. Situated at an altitude of 3650 m and covering 9000-12,000 sq km (depending on who you believe), the Salar is twice as big as the Great Salt Lake in the United States. The depth of the salt varies from 2 to 20 m. Driving across it is one of the most fantastic experiences in South America, especially in June/July when the bright blue skies contrast with the blinding-white salt (be sure to bring good sunglasses). After particularly wet rainy seasons the Salar is covered in water, which adds to the surreal experience.

East of the village is a beautiful gorge called the **Quebrada de Jere** ① US$2, which is almost unimaginably verdant and filled with fruit trees and grazing cattle. At the bottom of the gorge a crystal-clear stream cuts down towards Toconao. There are picnic sites but camping is prohibited. Near the head of the valley on the East side is a petroglyph of a llama. Nearby is the quarry where the stone *sillar* is worked; it can be visited. The stones sound like bells when struck. Also worth visiting are the vineyards, which produce a unique sweet wine.

About 4 km before Toconao, vehicle tracks head east across the sand to a hidden valley 2 km from the road where there is a small settlement called **Zapar**. There are some well-preserved pre-Hispanic ruins on the rocky cliffs above the cultivated valley here. The sand is very soft and a 4WD vehicle is essential.

Around the Salar de Atacama

South of Toconao is one of the main entrances to the Salar de Atacama. Formed by deglaciation some 12,000 years ago it encompasses some 300,000 ha, making it the third largest expanse of salt flats in the world; the air is so dry here that you can usually see right across the Salar, 100 km to the north. Rich in minerals, including borax, potassium and an estimated 40% of world lithium reserves, the Salar is home to three of the world's five species of flamingo – the Andean, Chilean and James – as well as other birds including sandpipers, the Andean gull, and the Andean avocet (although these can only be seen

Border crossings: Chile–Argentina

San Pedro–Paso de Jama
The best crossing and the most northerly, the Paso de Jama at 4200 m, 165 km southeast of San Pedro, is reached by a paved road that runs via the Salar de Tara, which forms a sector of the Reserva Nacional de los Flamencos.

San Pedro–Paso de Sico
The main alternative to this, Paso de Sico at 4079 m, lies further south, 207 km southeast of San Pedro, and is reached by a very poor road which runs via Toconao and Socaire (see page 233). This pass has replaced the higher Paso de Guaytiquina.

San Pedro–Paso de Socompa
The most southerly crossing is Paso de Socompa, 3865 m, which is reached by another very poor road from Pan de Azúcar (see below).
Chilean immigration and customs Open 0800-2300.

Immigration and customs formalities for Paso de Jama and Paso de Sico are dealt with in San Pedro de Atacama, open 0800-2300. Incoming vehicles are searched for meat, fruit and dairy products. If crossing by private vehicle, check road conditions with the *carabineros* and at immigration in San Pedro, as these crossings are liable to be closed by heavy rain in summer and blocked by snow in winter. If hitching, try the immigration post in San Pedro; Spanish is essential.

On the Argentine side of the border, all these roads link up and continue to San Antonio de los Cobres (where Argentine customs and immigration formalities take place) and Salta. Transport using the Paso de Jama crossing usually follows a more northerly alternative via Susques, where there is accommodation, and Jujuy. The most southerly route via Paso de Socompa is perhaps the most spectacular, crossing salt flats and wide expanses of desert, but this route is virtually unused.

when lakes form in winter). The flamingos live by eating algae and tiny shellfish that subsist in the small saline pools in the Salar. Three areas of the Salar are part of the seven-sector **Reserva Nacional de los Flamencos** ① US$4, totalling 73,986 ha, administered by **CONAF** in conjunction with local communities. There is a walkway over part of the salar with information boards in Spanish. You should not leave the path.

From Toconao, a road runs 67 km along the eastern edge of the Salar de Atacama to the attractive village of **Peine**, where you'll find the offices of the lithium extraction company. It is worth asking if the company's access road can be used to visit the Salar de Atacama's spectacular salt formations. Nearby are some prehistoric cave paintings. Local guides in the village offer tours for around US$7 per person. There is also a thermal pool where you can swim. Woollen goods and knitwear are made here. To the east of the village lies a group of beautifully coloured hills, whose colours are more vibrant at sunset, with good views over the Salar de Atacama. A path leads across these hills to **Socaire**; allow two days. Other villages worth visiting include **Tilomonte** and **Tilopozo**, south and west of Peine.

From Peine, a road (64 km) crosses the Salar de Atacama and joins the road that runs from San Pedro down the west side of the Salar, continuing south to **Pan de Azúcar**, an

Border crossings: Chile–Bolivia

San Pedro–Hito Cajones

There are two crossings to Bolivia, the more northerly of which, via Ollagüe, is described on page 221. This, the more southerly crossing, is, 45 km east of San Pedro via a poor road that turns off the paved road towards Paso de Jama at La Cruz, 8 km southwest of the border. Laguna Verde is 7 km north of Hito Cajones. **Chilean immigration and customs** 0800-2300, are in San Pedro. Incoming vehicles are searched for fruit, vegetables and dairy products.

There is no public transport: do not be tempted to hitch to the border as you risk being stranded without water or shelter at sub-zero temperatures. The most practical method of crossing this border is on a tour from San Pedro (see page 237). If you intend to travel independently in this region do not underestimate the dangers of getting stuck without transport or accommodation at this altitude. Do not travel alone and seek full advice in advance.

abandoned railway station. Here it meets the paved road that runs east-west from the Pan-American Highway south of Antofagasta to **Socompa** on the Argentine border, via the vast **La Escondida** copper mine, which has an output of copper higher than any other mine in the world. Ten kilometres east of La Escondida at Imilac, a poor road turns off south to the **Parque Nacional Llullaillaco**. This recently created park covers 263,000 ha and includes **Cerro Llullaillaco** at 6739 m, the second highest peak in Chile, as well as three other peaks over 5000 m: **Cerro de la Pena** at 5260 m, **Guanaqueros**, 5131 m, and **Aguas Calientes**, 5070 m. The park is inhabited by large numbers of guanacos and vicuñas. Visits are by arrangement only with CONAF in Antofagasta, owing to the dangers of minefields in the area. Further along the Pan de Azúcar–Socompa road (poor condition) is **Monturaqui**, the source of the green onyx that is used for carving.

Southeast of Toconao

From Toconao, another road heads south through the villages of **Camar**, where handicrafts made from cactus may be bought, and **Socaire**, which has llama-wool knitwear for sale and a recently restored church built from volcanic rock. From the top of the church tower you can see agricultural land planted on traditional terraces. There are also a couple of places that serve basic lunches. The road is paved as far as Socaire. About 20 km further south, a rough road leaves the main route to the Paso Sico and climbs a hill to the beautiful **Laguna Miscanti** (4240 m), a lake that is part of the **Reserva Nacional Los Flamencos** ① US$4. 'Miscanti' means 'toad' in Atacameño, and refers to when the lake was full of toads. In the 1940s and 1950s, trout were introduced for American fishermen working in Chuquicamata, resulting in the decline of the toad population; today there are none left. There is a path around the lake. Allow four hours for the circuit.

Nearby is the **Laguna Miñiques**. The lakes are on the site of ancient Atacameño hunting grounds and arrowheads can still be found on the shores, which are edged with whorls of calcium salt crystals. The rare Hornet coot can often be seen here. There are clear views of the volcanoes behind the lakes, often snow-capped between April and June, as well as fantastic views down to the Salar.

After the turning to the lakes, the road goes on to the mine at Laco, before proceeding to the **Paso de Sico**, which has replaced the higher, more northerly Guaytiquina pass, at 4295 m (also spelt Huaytiquina) to Argentina.

Some 10 km south of Toconao, the old road branches east towards Guaytiquina. In a deep *quebrada* below Volcán Láscar is the now deserted settlement of **Talabre**, with terracing and an ancient threshing floor. Above the *quebrada* is an isolated, stone-built cemetery. Large flocks of llamas graze where the stream crosses the road below the Láscar Volcano at 5154 m. After a steep climb on a very bad road, you reach the **Laguna Lejía** at 4190 m, once full of flamingos. Mysteriously, the colony declined rapidly immediately after the eruption of Volcán Láscar in 1993. You then pass through the high plains of **Guaytiquina** (4275 m), where only a few herdsmen are found. The Guaytiquina crossing to Argentina is not open to road traffic.

◉ San Pedro de Atacama and around listings

For Sleeping and Eating price codes and other relevant information, see Essentials pages 35-42.

⊖ Sleeping

San Pedro de Atacama *p226, map p228*
San Pedro is an expensive town; accommodation rates rise in Jan and Feb when it may also be scarce. Some hotels offer multi-day packages that are more expensive than paying for accommodation and tours separately.

There are a number of informal, unregistered hostels, usually **F-G** per person, but security is often lax, and thefts have been reported.

LL Awasi, Tocopilla 4, T055-851460, www.awasi.cl. One of several new 5-star resorts in the area. All-inclusive packages. Just 8 cabins, all built with traditional materials, fine food, excellent customer service, professional tours. Recommended.

LL Explora, Av Américo Vespucio Sur 80, 5 piso, Santiago, T055-206 6060, www.explora.com. Luxury full board and excursion programme, 3 nights, 4 nights and 8 nights, advance booking only.

LL Tierra Atacama, Camino Séquitor s/n, Allyu de Yaye, T055-555977, www.tierra atacama.com. The new competition to the Explora. Somewhat removed from the village itself. Very good reports.

LL-L Altiplanico, Atienza 282, T055-851212, www.altiplanico.com. Comfortable boutique hotel on the edge of town (20-min walk). Rooms are independent adobe huts and bathrooms are well designed and spacious. Good reports, but slightly blasé attitude to water usage in the desert.

L Hostería San Pedro, Toconao 460, T055-851011, hsanpedro@chilesat.net. The town's oldest luxury hotel. Pool (residents only), petrol station, cabins. Some rooms with satellite TV. Reasonably comfortable but nothing special.

L Kimal, Atienza 452 y Caracoles, T055-851030, www.kimal.cl. Small intimate hotel near the centre. Nice living room. Some rooms are bigger than others and some have their own terrace. Small swimming pool with jacuzzi and spa. Good restaurant (open to the public) and buffet breakfast. Recommended.

L-AL Alto Atacama, Camino Pucara Suchor, T02-912 3900 (Santiago office reservations), www.altoatacama.com. Spacious rooms, all with private terrace, price includes breakfast.

AL La Casa de Don Tomás, Tocopilla s/n, T055-851176, www.dontomas.cl. Good accommodation, functional and somewhat charmless, bright and spacious lounge, quiet, good sized swimming pool, snacks served. Late check out/and check in. Decent value.

A Hostal Katarpe, Atienza 441, T055-851033, www.katarpe.com. Comfortable and quiet, nice patio, friendly. Some staff speak English. Breakfast extra. Not great value.

A-B Elim, Palpana 6, T055-851567, www.hostalelim.cl. Clean, friendly hostel run by its owners (a definite plus in San Pedro). Good breakfast, laundry service, nice hot showers. Reasonable value for this town. Recommended.

A-C Takha-Takha, Caracoles s/n, T055-851 038, www.takhatakha.com. **B-E** singles. Pretty, lovely garden, pleasant shady patio with tall trees and flowers, clean rooms, those with ensuite bathrooms much nicer than those without. Also camping (US$9 per person). Laundry facilities. Friendly staff. Recommended.

B Casa Corvatsch, Le Paige 178, T/F055-851101, www.corvatschchile.cl. Pleasant views, but several bad reports about the owner. Also has much cheaper rooms.

B Hostal Lickana, Caracoles y Atienza, T055-851940, www.lickanahostal.cl. Impeccable rooms with bath. Slightly impersonal staff. No breakfast. Reasonable choice, although reports that reservations are not always honoured.

B Hostal Sonchek, Le Paige 170, T/F055-851112, sonceksp@hotmail.com. **D-E** singles, **E** per person in dorms. Decent value hostel with kitchen and laundry facilities, a ping-pong table and a café attached. The more expensive rooms have private bathrooms. English and French spoken.

B Residencial Don Raul, Caracoles 130-B, T055-851138, www.donraul.cl. With bath. Pleasant rooms with tiled floors. Better value and slightly airier than most. Kitchen facilities, Wi-Fi. Breakfast extra.

B-C Haramaksi, Coya, near Tulor, 10km southwest of San Pedro, T9-9595 7567, www.haramaksi.cl. Simple accommodation in traditional Atacameño surroundings. An escape from the hubbub of San Pedro.

B-C Hostal Mamatierra, Pachamama 615, T055-851418, hostalmamatierra@sanpedro deatacama.com. **E** per person in shared rooms. 5 mins' walk from the centre, will pick you up from the bus terminals. Some rooms with bath. Kitchen facilities, peaceful.

B-C Hostal Martita, Palpana 4, T055-851394. **D** singles. 5 mins' walk from town centre. Some rooms with bath. Good beds, friendly. Reasonable value.

B-C Hostal Miskanty, Pasaje Mutulera 141, T055-851430, miskanty@hotmail.com. Simple but pleasant rooms with bath. Friendly. Laundry service.

B-C Hostal Puritama, Caracoles 113, T055-851540, hostalpuritama@sanpedrodeata cama.com. Some rooms with bath. Simple but comfortable, with large patio, kitchen facilities, good showers, camping available.

B-C Residencial Chiloé, Atienza 404, T055-851017. Rooms with bath much nicer than those without. Sunny veranda, good clean bathrooms, breakfast extra, laundry facilities, good beds, no single rooms, luggage store.

B-D Hostal Edén Atacameño, Toconao 592, T055-851154. **C-E** singles. Friendly. Rooms without bath are basic. Internet facilities. Unkempt kitchen available for cooking. Also camping.

C Hostelling International, Caracoles 360, T055-851426, www.hostellingatacama.com. **E** per person in dorms. Lively hostel, cramped shared rooms with lockers. Shoddy construction. Bicycle rental.

C-D Residencial Vilacoyo, Tocopilla 387, T055-851006. **E-F** singles. Rooms without bath. Friendly, clean, good kitchen facilities, hammock in courtyard. Laundry service. One of few good budget options in the centre. Recommended.

D Residencial La Florida, Tocopilla 406, T055-851021. **F-G** per person in shared rooms. Without bath, basic, intermittent hot water, kitchen and laundry facilities.

Camping
Alberto Terrazas Oasis Camping at Pozo 3, 5 km east of town, has the best facilities including a swimming pool.
Camping Los Perales, Tocopilla 481.

The geysers of El Tatio p229
There is a workers' camp at El Tatio, which is empty apart from 1 guard, who might let you sleep in a bed in one of the huts; bring food and a sleeping bag.

Toconao and around *p230, map p230*
There are basic *residenciales* in the village.
Cheap accommodation is also offered at the
Restaurant Lascar, which has good, simple
food. Camping is not possible along the
Quebrada de Jere.

🍴 Eating

San Pedro de Atacama *p226, map p228*
Few places are open before 1000. Restaurants
in the centre close at midnight. Drink bottled
water as, owing to its high mineral content,
the local supply is not recommended for
those unaccustomed to it.

¶¶¶-¶¶ Bendito Desierto, Atienza 426.
Inventive food served in a kind of grotto.
Waiters lack some training. Watch out for the
'voluntary' 10% tip automatically added to
the bill. Good *picso sours* with a kick.

¶¶¶-¶¶ La Estaka, Caracoles 259, T055-851201.
Barn-like construction, generally regarded
as one of the best places in town, especially
for meat. The chef tends to get angry if you
send food back!

¶¶ Adobe, Caracoles. A good meeting place
with an open fire, where you can watch the
moon rise. Loud music and somewhat
supercilious service. Greenwich Village/
Islington in the Atacama.

¶¶ Casa Piedra, Caracoles s/n. Open fire,
friendly service, also has a cheap menu,
many of the waiters are musicians who,
if in the mood, will play Inti Illimanni or
Victor Jara songs on panpipes and *queñas*
late at night, good food and cocktails.

¶¶ Cuna, Tocopilla 359, T055-851999.
Understated and warm, interesting menu,
good service. Spacious patio open in summer.

¶¶ La Casona, Caracoles. Good food,
vegetarian options, cheap lunchtime menu,
large portions, interesting Cubist-style
paintings of the desert, popular.

¶¶ Milagro, Caracoles. Good food, vegetarian
options, attentive service. Recommended.

¶¶-¶ Café Étnico, Tocopilla 423, T055-851377.
Good-value set lunch, juice and sandwiches,
internet access. Book exchange.

¶¶-¶ Les Copains, Tocopilla 442, T09-8210
4379. Good sandwiches and juices, plus
excellent pizzas (by Chilean standards).

¶¶-¶ Quitor, Licancabur y Domingo Atienza,
T055-851056. Good, basic home-cooked
Chilean food, relatively inexpensive.

¶ Empanadium, Galería El Peral, Caracoles
317, local 5. Over 100 varieties of *empanada*
with unusual local fillings such as llama,
hare and rabbit. Slow service.

There are several stalls on Licancabur
by the football pitch offering a variety
of inexpensive lunches.

Cafés
Café Tierra Todo Natural, Caracoles.
Much the best choice for breakfast, serving
excellent fruit juices and the best bread in
the Atacama, plus real coffee and yoghurt.
It also opens earliest. It opens for lunch
where it is the best option for vegetarian
dishes. Recommended.

Inti Sol, Tocopilla s/n. Opens 0900. Internet
café serving good coffee and juice.

🍸 Bars and clubs

San Pedro de Atacama *p226, map p228*
Many San Pedro restaurants double as bars at
night, although they close at midnight.

🛍 Shopping

San Pedro de Atacama *p226, map p228*
There are a couple of craft markets, one
a block east of the plaza, and the other in
the Galería el Peral, Caracoles 317. These
days very little *artesanía* is produced in San
Pedro itself and most of what is on offer
comes from Bolivia.

▲ Activities and tours

San Pedro de Atacama *p226, map p228*
San Pedro is awash with tour operators and, with competition so stiff, prices are low. Approximate prices for tours are as follows: Valle de la Luna US$13 (plus US$4 entrance); Salar de Atacama US$20 (plus US$4 entrance); Geysers of Tatio US$35 (plus US$4 entrance) some tours continue to Calama via Chiu Chiu; Altiplano Lakes (including Toconao and Salar de Atacama) US$60 (plus US$10 in entrance fees).

The following advice should help: avoid cut-price operators and try to check out vehicles and guides before booking; if travelling to high altitude make sure that oxygen is being carried; report any complaints to the Municipalidad or to Sernatur; if in doubt, check through the book with travellers' complaints at the Sernatur office. Make sure you get a receipt for any tour.

Spanish speakers may prefer to go with one of the smaller operators to experience better the vastness of the desert, although all the more responsible operators do try to stay away from the well-trodden routes used by the majority. If you want a more solitary experience and are willing to pay a premium, private tours can be arranged, either through agencies or independent guides. There are about 25 agencies, but some are temporary and/or open for only part of the year. Some operators will offer a reduction if you book a series of tours with them.

Atacama Connection, Toconao 460, T055-851548. Usual range of tours. A mixed-bag quality-wise.

Azimut 360, T02-2351519 www.azimut 360.com. A long-established nationwide operator that also offers adventure tours. Book in advance.

Cactus Tour, Atienza 419, T055-851524, www.cactustour.cl. One of the more reputable agencies. Good vehicles. Occasionally offer tours to Bolivia. Most guides speak English. Recommended.

Cordillera Traveller, Caracoles, T055-851291, www.cordilleratraveller.com. Similar tours to those offered by Colque. Perhaps marginally more reliable.

Cosmo Andino Expediciones, Caracoles, T/F055-851069, www.cosmo-andinoexpedi ciones.cl. The yardstick by which other agencies have been measuring themselves for 20 years. English, French, German, Dutch spoken, good vehicles and drivers, experienced guides, highly recommended for non-Spanish speakers. Limited space so book a couple of days in advance. Dutch owner Martin Beeris is very knowledgeable about the region.

Desert Adventure, Caracoles s/n, T/F055-851067, www.desertadventure.cl. Excursions to all the major sites, modern fleet of vehicles, large numbers, mostly good reports.

La Herradura, Tocopilla s/n, T055-851087, laherraduraatacama@yahoo.es. Horseback tours with good local guides, recommended.

Layana, Tocopilla 418, T055-851308, www.turismolayana.cl. Offer the usual range of tours. Fun, but not necessarily the most responsible. Make sure you get a receipt.

Rancho Cactus, Tocopilla 568, T055-851506, www.rancho-cactus.cl. French-Chilean run horseback tours. Recommended, especially for multi-day trips.

Space, Caracoles 166, T055-851935, www.spaceobs.com. Astronomical tours given by a French astronomer who has set up a small observatory in the village of Solor, south of San Pedro. Tours are interesting and informative and compare favourably with those in Mamalluca in the Elqui valley. Tours in English, French and Spanish. US$28. Book in advance from the office (unhelpful receptionist) where you are picked up in the evening. Wear warm clothing. Recommended.

Turismo Colque, Caracoles, T055-851109, www.colquetours.com. Specialists for tours to Bolivia, including 1-day tour to Laguna Verde and 3-day tours to Laguna Colorado and the Salar de Uyuni (US$130 per person, see below); Visa and MasterCard accepted, hires sleeping bags, often recommended but some mixed reports. Has agencies in Uyuni and La Paz.

Vulcano, Caracoles 317, T055-851023, www.vulcanochile.cl. Mountain climbs, guided cycle trips, sandboarding and other adventure tours to infrequently visited areas including bespoke tours, also hire out mountain bikes, English-speaking guides, recommended.

The geysers of El Tatio p229

Tours to El Tatio depart around 0400, arriving at the geysers at 0700, US$35, including breakfast. There are opportunities to swim in the hot thermal pool and to visit the Baños de Puritama on the return journey. Take warm clothing and a swimming costume. Some agencies offer tours to El Tatio and on to Calama, via the villages of the altiplano.

Around the Salar de Atacama p231

Agencies in San Pedro offer excursions to Toconao and the Salar, returning via the Quebrada de Jere, US$20 plus park entry, usual departure 1530, but note that the flamingos are best seen in the morning, so try to get a morning tour, or combine with visiting the altiplano lakes (US$60).

Bolivia tours

The Salar de Uyuni, Laguna Colorada and Laguna Verde are usually visited by tours from the Bolivian town of Uyuni, where accommodation, money exchange and transport to La Paz, Oruro and Potosí are all available. However, **Turismo Colque** (among others) in San Pedro (see above) also offers this tour and will drop passengers off in Uyuni, although some report that, to see the colour changes on Laguna Colorada, the trip is best done from Uyuni. If you are taking a tour to Bolivia, find out if park entrance fees are included. If not, be aware that they are payable in Bolivianos only.

⊙ Transport

San Pedro de Atacama p226, map p228
Bicycle Several agencies offer cycle hire, check prices and condition of bicycles carefully, as quality varies.

Bus There's no terminal. Most buses leave from Licancabur opposite the football field. TurBus terminal on Atienza, north of the centre.

To **Calama**, TurBus, several daily (6 continue on to Antofagasta), also **Frontera** 7 a day, 1½ hrs, first 0900, last 1900, US$4. Frequencies vary with more departures in Jan/Feb and some weekends, fewer out of season. Book in advance if you want to return from San Pedro on Sun evening. **Frontera** also run to **Toconao**, 4 daily at 1240, 1600, 1930, 2030, US$1.50, and to **Peine** and **Socaire** 2 or 3 weekly to each destination, US$3. To **Arica**, daily direct service with TurBus, US$32. To **La Serena**, 16 hrs, US$37-70; to **Valparaíso**, 24 hrs, US$60. To **Santiago**, 24 hrs, US$60-100. **Pullman Bus** and **Géminis** services from Calama to **Salta**, Argentina (see page 224) also stop in San Pedro.

Car Some agencies in San Pedro offer vehicle hire, but you should check vehicle condition and insurance very carefully as there are reports of accidents involving uninsured and badly serviced vehicles; it is better to hire cars in Calama.

⊙ Directory

San Pedro de Atacama p226, map p228
Banks ATMs appear and then disappear and are often out of order anyway. Better to bring pesos from Calama or elsewhere. **Cambio Atacama**, Toconao, daily 1030-1800, rates posted outside, good rates for US$ cash, poor rates for TCs; best not to try changing TCs in San Pedro. The **Géminis** bus terminal will change Bolivianos. **Internet and telephone** Ubiquitous, including Café Étnico, on Tocopilla, book exchange. **Laundry** Alana, Caracoles, near Atienza. **Medical services** Hospital Le Peige s/n, T055-851010. **Post office** Padre Le Peige, opposite Museo Archaeológico.

Contents

Border crossings

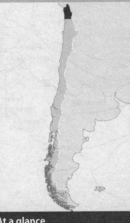

Iquique, Arica & the Altiplano national parks

At a glance

⊖ **Getting around** Good public transport links between towns. A 4WD will allow you to explore the altiplano, though tours from Arica or Putre are an easier option.

◉ **Time required** 4 days to do justice to the altiplano, plus beach and relaxation time on the coast.

☼ **Weather** Moderate temperatures on the coast. Overcast but no rain. The altiplano is cool by day and freezing at night with seasonal rain.

✕ **When not to go** Roads in the altiplano are liable to occasional flooding in Jul and also Jan-Mar.

N

20 km

20 miles

PERU

*Tacora
(5988m)

Visviri

Parque
Nacional
Lauca

Pomerape
(6282m)

Putre

Socoroma

Parinacota

Lago
Chungará

Parinacota (6342m)

Paso Tambo
Quemado

Arica

Río Lluta

Poconchile

Río Azapo

Belén

Tignamar

Guallatiri
(6060m)

Capurata (5990m)

BOLIVIA

Tignamar
Viejo

Guallatiri

Reserva
Nacional
Las Vicuñas

Codpa

Monumento
Natural Salar
de Surire

Río Camarones

Salar de Surire

Surire

Cuya

Geoglifos
de Chiza

Parque Nacional
Volcán Isluga

Isluga
(5530m)

Camiña

REGION I

Isluga

Colchane

Geoglifos
de Tiliviche

British
Cemetery

Cariquima

Pisagua

Reserva Nacional
Pampa del Tamarugai

Alto Toroni
(5982m)

Cta Buena

Gigante del
Atacama

Chusmisa

Pacific
Ocean

Huara

Tarapacá

Iquique

Humberstone

Mamiña

Pozo
Almonte

La Tirana

Pica

Reserva Nacional
Pampa del Tamarugai

Salar de
Huasco

Salar de
Pintados

Matilla

Geoglifos de
Pintados

Salar de
Coposa

The far north of Chile is just as forbidding as the region around Antofagasta and Calama. North of the brash city of Iquique, transport arteries head inland into the desert pampa. There is a strong sense of antiquity here in the few oases and settlements that are sprinkled across the Atacama; the profusion of geoglyphs are testament to the fact that, wherever there is water, people have been living for millennia. These geoglyphs of peoples now vanished and the countless ghost towns of former nitrate *oficinas* stand witness to both the harshness and fragility of life in the region.

Further inland still, towards the altiplano, are some beautiful spots. Mamiña and Pica are two thermal springs resorts near Iquique, each of them remarkable for their tranquillity. There are four remote national parks in the high Andes, the northernmost of which – the Parque Nacional Lauca – offers some of the most stunning scenery in Chile, with a necklace of high lakes, snow-capped volcanoes, lava fields and varied bird life. It is easily reached from Arica, Chile's northernmost city, along the international road to Bolivia. Near Parque Nacional Lauca are small Andean villages, such as Visviri and Parinacota, where most people speak Aymará, and Spanish remains a foreign language.

Background

As elsewhere in northern Chile, there was a widespread and highly developed network of pre-Hispanic cultures in this region. The geoglyphs at sites such as Pintados and Tiliviche are thought to have been markers for caravans of traders making their way from the altiplano to the coast and back again. Circles marked in the hillsides signalled the presence of water. The coastal peoples traded furs and fish with the more highly developed cultures of the interior, maintaining links with Tiahuanaco and the Incas.

Even after the Spanish conquest, the early Spanish settler population was small in number. Settlement was concentrated largely in the oases of the sierra, where the climate was easier and where malaria, the scourge of the coast, was not found. From an early date, Arica became one of the principal ports for the silver trade from Potosí, but the coast remained sparsely inhabited until the 19th century. At the time of Independence, the whole of this area became the Peruvian provinces of Tarapacá and Arica, with the provincial capital at the now ruined city of Tarapacá, near Huara. The region became the focal point for the War of the Pacific (1879-1883), with decisive naval battles fought at Iquique on 21 May 1879, and at Angamos, near Mejillones, on 8 October of the same year. After the war, the area as far north as Tacna came under Chilean control, and became the country's economic powerhouse following the sudden growth of the nitrate industry.

The poor conditions of workers in the nitrate mines led to the development of early left-wing and trade unionist movements in the far northern part of Chile. In 1907, a group of miners from one of the nitrate *oficinas* was executed by the army in the Santa María school in Iquique for campaigning to be paid in hard cash instead of *oficina* tokens. The legacy of the far north's radicalism can be seen in the now infamous 'caravan of death' executed in seven northern cities by one of General Pinochet's henchmen in the days following the 1973 coup (see page 579).

The region's borders were finally delineated in 1929: Tacna voted in a referendum to return to Peru, while Arica opted to remain Chilean. The collapse of the nitrate industry in the 1930s and 1940s was a regional crisis but the quick growth of the fishing industry saved the area from disaster.

The sea still provides the main source of wealth in this region: Iquique is the principal fishing port in Chile, unloading 35% of the total national catch, and has important fish-processing industries. Nowadays, mining is much less important than in other parts of northern Chile; however, silver and gold are mined at Challacollo and copper at Sagasca, near Tarapacá, while the new copper mine at Collahuasi has made a big difference to the region's economy. Over 90% of the population lives in the two coastal cities, Arica and Iquique.

Geography and climate

The Atacama Desert extends over most of the far north. The Cordillera de la Costa slowly loses height north of Iquique, terminating at the Morro in Arica: from Iquique northwards it drops directly to the sea and, as a result, there are few beaches along this coast. Inland, the central depression, the *pampa*, 1000 to 1200 m high, is arid and punctuated by salt flats south of Iquique. Between Iquique and Arica, it is crossed from east to west by numerous gorges, formed by several rivers flowing west from the sierra; the more northerly of these, the Ríos Lluta and San José, provide water for Arica and for the Valle de Azapa. The source of the former is snowmelt from Volcán Tacora. Its sulphurous waters can only support crops such as corn, alfalfa and onions. In contrast the San José brings

Behind the wheel

Do not think of visiting the altiplano in a cheap hire car. A 4WD is essential, with the highest clearance possible. Tyres should not be inflated to more than 30 lbs at sea level. Take extra fuel: cars are much less fuel efficient at high altitude. During the climb from Arica, you should stop several times to release excess pressure in fuel cans and tyres if necessary. There is a private petrol pump at the chemical plant at the Salar de Surire that will nearly always sell petrol or diesel in an emergency.

In the rainy season water levels rise. If a bridge is washed away or the road/path goes through a river or laguna, get out, check the depth and make sure the height of your car's air vents are higher than this. At the Río Lauca crossing this can be as high as 1 m. Drive through the shallowest part. Do not leave the road or well-travelled tracks. Drive slowly and watch out for potholes. On the main road lorry drivers can be erratic. If a vehicle is approaching in the other direction on a *ripio* track, apply pressure to the windscreen with your hand. This will prevent the windscreen from shattering if hit by a stone.

crystal fresh water from the altiplano to the Azapa Valley which is well known for its olive crop and tropical fruit. On the coast, temperatures are moderated by the Pacific Ocean but, in the *pampa*, variations of temperature between day and night are extreme, ranging between 30°C and 0°C. Coastal regions receive *camanchaca* (sea mist) but the *pampa* is permanently rainless.

East of the central depression lies the sierra, the western branch of the Andes, beyond which is a high plateau, the *altiplano* (3500-4500 m), from which rise volcanic peaks, including Parinacota (6350 m), Pomerape (6250 m), Guayatiri (6064 m), Acotango (6050 m), Capurata (5990 m), Tacora (5988 m) and Tarapacá (5825 m). There are also a number of lakes in the altiplano, the largest of which, Lago Chungará, is one of the highest in the world. The main river draining the altiplano, the Río Lauca, flows eastwards into Bolivia. Temperatures in the sierra average 20°C in summer and 9°C in winter. The altiplano is much colder, averaging just 10°C in summer and -5°C in winter. Both the sierra and the altiplano are affected by storms of rain, snow and hail (*invierno boliviano*), usually between January and March.

Iquique and around

→ *Colour map 1, B2.*

Iquique is the the capital of Región I (Tarapacá) and one of the main ports of northern Chile (with a growing population of around 200,000). The city is situated on a rocky peninsula at the foot of the high coastal mountain range, sheltered by the headlands of Punta Gruesa and Cavancha. Iquique is a brash, modern city, with a well-preserved collection of historical buildings in the centre, whose bright wooden façades make a surprising contrast to the lifeless desert and the grey coastal mist.

Inland from Iquique are several small towns that were the early centres of Spanish colonial settlement. They are less crowded than villages near Calama and Arica and are well worth visiting. ►► *For listings, see pages 252-258.*

Iquique ⊖🖉🞂🞊🞖⊙▲🞕🞕 *pp252-258.*

Although the site was used as a port in pre-Hispanic times, it remained sparsely populated throughout the colonial period. Even in 1855, when Iquique had begun to export nitrates, the population was only about 2500. The nitrate trade transformed the city, bringing large numbers of foreign traders and creating a wealthy elite. Although partly destroyed by an earthquake in 1877, the city became the centre of this trade after its transfer from Peru to Chile at the end of the War of the Pacific. Today, the fabulous wealth the nitrate industry brought to the town can be seen in some wonderful buildings. Its coastal position also means that you can enjoy some relaxing days sunning, surfing and swimming, while the hills behind the town have proved to be a perfect jumping-off point for paragliding trips.

Ins and outs → *Iquique is 492 km north of Antofagasta.*

Getting there Iquique is served by all major bus companies from the south and from Arica – most southbound buses take the coastal road to Tocopilla. There are also daily buses up to Oruro and La Paz in Bolivia. National flights to Arica, Antofagasta and Santiago; international to La Paz. The airport transfer service, US$7, is unreliable; it can be just as cheap to get a taxi if there are a few of you, US$16.

Getting around The best way to get around in Iquique is by *colectivo*. Note that the area northeast of the junction of O'Higgins and Ramirez can be rough, especially at night.

Tourist information **Sernatur** ① *Aníbal Pinto 436, T057-312238, infoiquique@sernatur.cl, Mon-Thu 0900-1700, Fri 0900-1630, Sat 1000-1300*, is helpful.

Sights

The old town stretches south and west from **Plaza Prat** with a clock tower and bell dating from 1877. The plaza has recently been remodelled to good effect, with shady benches and newly planted trees. Every Sunday at midday there is a military parade lasting 45 minutes, while on Friday and Saturday nights there are often free theatrical or musical events. On the northeast corner of the plaza is the **Centro Español**, built in Moorish style by the local Spanish community in 1904, and unique in Chile. The ground floor is a restaurant but the upper floors show paintings of scenes from Don Quixote and from Spanish history by the Spanish artist, Vicente Tordecillas. The extravagance of its construction shows the fabulous wealth that nitrates once brought. On the south of the plaza is the **Teatro Municipal**, built as an opera house in 1890 with a façade featuring four women representing the seasons; in its heyday it played host to such famous names as Caruso. Three blocks north of the plaza is the old **Aduana** (customs house) built in 1871 and the scene, in 1891, of an important battle in the Civil War between supporters of President Balmaceda and congressional forces. Part of it now houses the **Museo Naval de Iquique** ⓘ *Esmeralda 250, Tue-Fri 1000-1300, 1600-1900, Sat 1000-1400, US$0.60*, dedicated to the War of the Pacific, and more specifically, to the naval battle of Iquique and its principal hero, Captain Prat. Some info in English. Nearby, is the harbour; there are **cruises** ⓘ *45 mins, US$5, minimum 10 people*, from the passenger pier. Sea lions and pelicans can be seen.

Five blocks east along Calle Sotomayor is the **railway station**, now disused, built in 1883 and displaying several old locomotives. Two blocks south of the railway station, on Bolívar, is the **cathedral**, dating from 1885. It is painted bright yellow and blue and has interesting stained-glass windows. On Amunátegui, behind the **Escuela Santa María** on Zégers, there is a memorial to the workers from the nitrate mines who were killed by the army while sheltering in the school during the strike of 1907.

On Calle Baquedano, which runs south from Plaza Prat, is the highly recommended **Museo Regional** ⓘ *Baquedano 951, T057-411214, Mon-Fri 0830-1300, 1530-1830, Sat 1030-1300, Sun (in summer) 1000-1300 and 1600-2000, free*, which has an excellent collection of pre-Hispanic artefacts (including several mummies). The archaeological section is very well set out, although explanations are in Spanish only, tracing the development of pre-Hispanic civilizations in the region and containing an important ethnographical collection of the Isluga culture of the altiplano (circa AD 400) and of contemporary Aymará cultures. There is also a section devoted to the nitrate era, with exhibits including a collection of *oficina* tokens, a model of a nitrate *oficina* and the collection of the nitrate entrepreneur, Santiago Humberstone.

Elsewhere on the street are the attractive former mansions of the 'nitrate barons'. Adorned with columns, balconies and impressive old doors, these buildings date from between 1880 and 1903 and were constructed from timber imported from California. The finest of these is the **Palacio Astoreca** ⓘ *O'Higgins 350, Tue-Fri 1000-1300, Sat 1000-1330, Sun 1100-1400, US$1*, built in 1903, subsequently the Intendencia and now a museum with fine late 19th-century furniture and exhibitions of shells. Continuing south towards the beach at Playa Cavancha, along Baquedano, Lynch or Obispo Labbé, you'll pass many beautiful old wooden houses painted blue, green, yellow and pink, with white columns and large wooden shutters and doors.

A free tram service runs intermittently up and down Baquedano (1000-1400, 1700-2000). It is incredibly slow (walking would be quicker) but that is not the point. Along this stretch of the road an impromptu market often appears, selling various bits and pieces.

Playa Cavancha is very popular in summer – in spite of the Humboldt Current, the water is almost warm – although surfers and other watersports enthusiasts make for the pounding waves of **Playa Brava** further south (see page 256). Those who enjoy walking or sandboarding may want to climb the large sand dune, **Cerro Dragón**, which rises behind Iquique and gives fantastic views of the city and the sea; take a *colectivo* to Chipana y La Tirana and then walk to the base of the hill. The top of the hill is where most paragliding trips take-off from, before circling the city and landing at Playa Cavancha.

Iquique is a major duty-free centre. North of town is the Free Zone, the **Zofri**, ⓘ *Amunategui, www.zofri.com, Mon-Sat 1100-2100, also Sun in summer, limit on tax-free purchases US$1000, colectivo from the centre US$0.80*. It is a giant shopping centre selling a wide range of duty-free imported products, including electronic and leather goods, perfumes, cars, motorcycles and good-quality camping equipment. Although better than Punta Arenas' equivalent, these days most are a similar price in Santiago. Drivers should note that all vehicles travelling south from Iquique are searched for duty-free goods at Quillagua on the Pan-American Highway and at Chipana on Route 1, the coastal road.

Nitrate towns

Humberstone ① *T057-751213, visits 0830-1830, US$3*, is a large nitrate town, now abandoned, at the junction of the Pan-American Highway and the road to Iquique. At its height in 1940 the town had a population of 3700. Although closed since 1961, you can see the plaza, the church, a well-preserved theatre, the *pulpería* (company stores) and the Olympic-size pool complete with grandstand (built of metal plating from ships' hulls). Recently granted World Heritage status by UNESCO, the town is being slowly restored by former residents who are happy to reminisce with visitors.

Nearby are the ruins of several other mining towns, including **Santa Laura** ① *2 km from Humberstone, T057-751981, 1000-1800, voluntary donation*, which has the skeleton of a nitrate processing plant, the machinery used to crush the minerals and a small, somewhat disorganized mining museum. Both Humberstone and Santa Laura can be visited on tours arranged by local agencies (see Activities and tours, page 256). If you're travelling independently from Iquique, take any bus to Arica or a *colectivo* for Pozo Almonte from Sargento Aldea y Barros Arana, US$3.50 (there is a phone for contacting a taxi company for the return journey or you could probably flag down an Iquique-bound bus or minibus from the highway).

Situated on the Pan-American Highway, 5 km south of the turning to Iquique, **Pozo Almonte** was the main service centre for the nitrate fields of the area. The **Museo Histórico Salitrero** ① *Plaza, Mon-Fri 0830-1300, 1600-1900*, displays artefacts and photographs of the nitrate era.

South along the Pan-American Highway

South of Pozo Almonte, the Pan-American Highway runs to **Quillagua**, 172 km, where there is a customs post. All southbound vehicles are searched. The road continues

N

200 metres
200 yards

Sleeping 🛏
Arturo Prat **2** *B1*
Atenas **17** *E2*
Backpacker's Hostel
  Iquique **1** *E3*
Barros Arana **3** *D3*
Buenos Aires **5** *B2*
Caiti **6** *C2*
Cano **7** *C2*
Casa de Huéspedes
  Profesores **10** *C2*
Cavancha **13** *E2*
Departamento Iquique **19** *E2*
Doña Genoveva **4** *C2*
Gavina **11** *E1*
Hostal Catedral **21** *B2*
Hostal Cuneo **15** *D1*
Hostal Jean IV **16** *A3*
Hostel La Casona 1920 **22** *E2*
Hostal Li Ming **18** *C3*
Hostal Manuel Rodríguez
  Express **14** *E2*
Hostal Nan-King **23** *B2*
Hostal North House **25** *E2*
Inti-Llanka **20** *C2*
Jham **8** *C1*
Riorsa **24** *E2*
Terrado Suites **12** *E2*
YMCA **9** *C1*

El Sombrero **3** *E2*
El Tercer Ojito **12** *E1*
El Viejo Wagon **15** *B1*
Kiru **16** *E3*
La Picada Curicana **5** *C1*
Nan King **13** *B3*
Peña mi Perú **18** *B3*
Pizzería d'Alfredo **7** *E2*

Eating 🍴
Bolivia **9** *B2*
Brasileña **8** *D2*
Casino Español **6** *B1*
Cioccolata **2** *B1*
Claudy **10** *C1*
Club Náutico **1** *E2*
Colonial **17** *C1*
Compañía Italiana de
  Bomberos **11** *B2*
El Barril del Fraile **4** *D2*
El Rincón del
  Cachuperto **14** *E2*

La Tirana

The legend of La Tirana is an intriguing mix of Andean traditions and Catholicism. It is said that, when Diego de Almagro made the first Spanish foray into Chile, one of his companions was an Inca princess. She was a fierce warrior who loathed everything to do with the Spanish and escaped into the pampa to wage war against them. She was so fierce that she became known as 'La Tirana' ('The Tyrant').

La Tirana's techniques were over-thrown when she fell in love with Vasco de Almeyda, a Portuguese soldier enlisted by the Spanish, who persuaded her to convert to Christianity. When her companions discovered her treachery, both the Inca princess and the warrior were killed. The legend goes that a priest, coming some years later to the area to evangelize, discovered a cross on the spot where the couple had died, and built a church there.

Today, the fiesta treads a fine line between commercialism and maintaining these hybrid traditions. The most important day and night occur on 16 July but, for up to a week beforehand, the town is awash with travelling salesmen, who come from all over Chile to sell everything that you could possibly need – clothes, music, bags, hats, cheap meals, ice creams and so on. At the same time, troupes of religious dancers and their accompanying brass bands come from as far away as Peru and Argentina to pay homage to the Virgen del Carmen. Eclecticism is the order of the day: as well as traditional Andean groups, there are also dancers who imitate the Sioux Indians from North America, as well as the 'Ali Baba Christians' dancing with imitation wooden sphinxes. The noise is deafening, day and night, as the brass bands vie with one another to produce the greatest racket. There is even an office set up by the church to perform marriages, and one of the most touching sights at the fiesta is that of happy couples being carried towards the church, amid the dancing, music and the chaos.

towards Antofagasta. At Km 24, the road runs through the largest section of the **Reserva Nacional Pampa del Tamarugal** (the other two sections are around La Tirana and north of Huara), which is administered by CONAF. Covering a total of 100,650 ha, the reserve includes plantations of tamaruga, a tree species adapted to the dry climate and saline soils.

The **Geoglifos de Pintados**, some 400 figures on the hillsides, representing humans, animals and birds, as well as abstract designs, are situated some 3 km west of the Pan-American Highway; take any bus south, US$4, and get off at Km 43. Many other sites around Iquique, including the Gigante del Atacama (see box, page 250), are difficult to visit without a vehicle.

Mamiña

Once a very popular thermal springs resort, Mamiña is reached by a good paved road, which runs 74 km east from Pozo Almonte. Situated on a ridge at 2750 m, this historic village is now dominated by the recently expanded copper mine, some 8 km to the west. Day-trips can be made from Iquique.

Mamiña has pre-Hispanic origins – its name means 'the girl of my eyes' in Aymará – and is inhabited mainly by people of Aymará origin. If you stand on the hill above the village, a circular geoglyph indicating the presence of water is clearly visible on the opposite side of the valley. The Aymará cultural centre, **Kaspi-Kala** ① *1000-1400, 1600-2000*, near the **Hotel Los Cardenales**, includes an *artesanía* workshop and a sales outlet. Legend has it that one of Mamiña's thermal pools once cured an Inca princess; an Inca *pukará* stands on a hilltop 3 km east marked by a white cross that can be seen from the village (it's probably best to hire a guide if you want to visit it). There are also said to be the ruins of a pre-Hispanic settlement further down the valley towards the *pampa*.

The church, built in 1632, is the only colonial Andean church in Chile with twin towers, each topped by a bell tower; ascend the church by steps at the side for a view of the bells linked together by a single rope. Mamiña's abundant thermal springs and unique mud spring *termas* have meant that it has been a popular health resort since the nitrate era; the **Hotel Termas** dates from this period. The thermal springs, classified as being radioactive, are rich in sodium, potassium, sulphur, chlorides and silicates, and are acknowledged to be valuable in treating ailments, such as rheumatoid arthritis and sciatica, as well as respiratory and digestive problems. There is also a mud bath, the **Baño Los Chinos** ① *0930-1300*, which is considered valuable in the treatment of many skin diseases, such as psoriasis. The bath contains radioactive mud with natural deposits of vegetal mineral mud activated by the fermentation of certain algae; the mud is allowed to dry on the skin after the bath and then washed off in one of the thermal springs.

La Tirana

Situated 10 km east of the Pan-American Highway, on a turning 9 km south of Pozo Almonte, La Tirana is famous for a religious festival dedicated to the **Virgen del Carmen**, held annually from 10 to 16 July (see box, page 248), which attracts some 150,000 pilgrims and merrymakers (catapulting the population from around 550). Over 100 groups dance night and day decked out in colourful costumes and spectacular masks, starting on 12 July. All the dances take place in the main plaza in front of the church; no alcohol is served. At other times of year, the church is well worth a visit, and there is a small museum, the **Museo de la Virgen de La Tirana** ① *Mon-Fri 0900-1300, 1600-1930, Sat-Sun 0900-2100, US$0.40*, which contains gifts to the virgin.

Matilla

Some 38 km east of La Tirana, Matilla is an oasis settlement founded in 1760 by settlers from Pica (see below). The village declined after 1912 when the waters of the Quebrada de Quisma were diverted to Iquique. The church (1887) is built of blocks of borax and rears up from over the arid plain like a version of the Sacré Coeur in the desert. It was damaged by an earthquake in 2005 but has now been restored. Nearby is a **museum** ① *Lagar de Matilla, daily 0900-1700*, used in the 18th century for fermenting wine. Get a key from the kiosk in the plaza. Near Matilla, an unpaved, rough road runs southwest to meet the Pan-American Highway.

Pica

Four kilometres northeast of Matilla, Pica, with a current population of 3000, was the most important centre of early Spanish settlement in this region. In colonial times, it produced a famous wine sold as far away as Potosí. Most of the older buildings, including the church, date from the nitrate period when it became a popular resort. It is a leafy oasis, famous for its thermal baths and the fruit grown here – one of the highlights of a stay is drinking fresh fruit juices from any one of numerous stalls near the thermal springs, which

Set in stone

Found as far south as the Río Loa and as far north as the Río Azapa near Arica, as well as along the Peruvian coast as far as Nazca, geoglyphs or *geoglifos* are one of the most visible traces left by ancient civilizations in the Atacama. Dating from an estimated AD 1000-1400, these designs were made on the rocks using two different techniques: by scraping away the topsoil to reveal different coloured rock beneath or by arranging stones to form a kind of mosaic. They exhibit three main themes: geometrical patterns; images of animals, especially camelids, birds and snakes; and humans, often holding or carrying instruments or weapons, such as a bow and arrows. They are easily visible because they were intended to be seen. They are generally located on isolated hills in the desert, on the western slopes of the Cordillera de la Costa or on the slopes of *quebradas* (gorges). Their significance is thought by some experts to be ritual, but the more current theory is that they were often a kind of signpost pointing out routes between the coast and the sierra.

The largest site is at **Pintados**, 96 km south of Iquique, reached by turning off the Pan-American Highway towards Pica and then following a 4-km track from which several panels can be seen, including representations of animals, birds and a large number of humans dressed in ponchos and feather head-dresses, as well as geometrical designs.

Although there are several more sites, the other most important ones are at **Tiliviche**, 127 km north of Iquique, some 600 m south of the Pan-American Highway, where, on the southern side of the quebrada, a 300-m panel can be seen representing a drove of llamas moving from the cordillera to the coast; at **Cerro Rosita**, 20 km north of Huara near the Pan-American Highway, where the 'Sun of Huara' (an Aymara sun emblem) is visible on the eastern side of the hill; and at **Cerro Unitas**, 15 km east of Huara, where geoglyphs are visible on the western and southern sides of an isolated hill. On the western slope of Cerro Unitas is the *Gigante del Atacama* or Giant of the Atacama, probably the most famous of all the images: 86 m high, this is a representation of an indigenous leader with a head-dress of feathers and a feline mask; to his left is a reptile, thought to link him to the earth god Pachamama, to his right is his staff of office.

lie about 1 km from the centre of the town at **Cocha Resbaladero** ① *0700-2000, US$4.* There are changing rooms, a snack bar and a beautiful pool on site and a small tourist information office opposite.

A few kilometres east of Pica on the road to the altiplano, there is a mirador with fine views. There is also a map showing where to find some fossilized dinosaur footprints. Tours are available from Pica.

Iquique to the Bolivian border

Some 30 km north of Pozo Almonte, **Huara** was once a town of 7000 people, serving as a centre for the nearby nitrate towns. Today, the population is reduced to 400 and little evidence remains of the town's former prosperity, apart from the railway station, which is a national monument, and a fascinating small museum preserving a pharmacy from the nitrate era with all the cures and remedies that were then on offer (ask at the

Border crossings: Chile–Bolivia

Colchane

This forlorn and windy border town livens up for the market, which takes place every other Saturday, and provides access to the southern entrance of the Parque Nacional Volcán Isluga, some 6 km northwest.

The border is open 0800-2000 daily. On the Bolivian side, an unpaved road leads to Oruro, 233 km northeast.

municipalidad). The church is also worth a look. The town was badly damaged by the 2005 earthquake and much of it is still in ruins.

At Huara, a road turns off the Pan-American Highway and runs to Colchane, 173 km northeast on the Bolivian frontier. Some 13 km east of Huara, the road passes, on the right, the **Geoglifos de Cerro Unitas**, the most outstanding of which is the **Gigante del Atacama**, a human figure 86 m tall, reported to be the largest geoglyph in the world and best viewed from a distance.

At Km 23, an unpaved road branches off south to **Tarapacá**, settled by the Spanish around 1560 and capital of the Peruvian province of Tarapacá until 1855, now largely abandoned except for the **Fiesta of the Virgen de la Candelaria** on 2 and 3 February. The major historic buildings, the Iglesia de San Lorenzo and the Palacio de Gobierno, are in ruins. At **Chusmisa** (Km 77), there are thermal springs producing water that is bottled and sold throughout northern Chile.

North towards Arica

The Pan-American Highway runs across the Atacama Desert at an altitude of around 1000 m, with several steep hills, best tackled in daylight. At night, *camanchaca* (sea mist) can reduce visibility.

At Zapiga, 47 km north of Huara, a road heads west for 41 km to **Pisagua**, formerly an important nitrate port, now reduced to a small fishing village. Several of the old wooden buildings are national monuments, including the **Municipal Theatre** (1892) and the **Clock Tower** (1887), but the town is now largely abandoned, although a handful of fish restaurants make it a pleasant meal stop. Pisagua was the site of a detention centre after the 1973 military coup; mass graves from that period were discovered near here in 1990.

Heading east from Zapiga, meanwhile, a poor road (deep sand and dust) leads 67 km to **Camiña**, a picturesque village in an oasis. From here, a terrible road runs to the **Tranque de Caritaya**, a dam 45 km further northeast, which supplies water for the coastal towns and which is set in splendid scenery with lots of wildlife and interesting botany (especially *llareta*).

Ten kilometres north of Zapiga is a British cemetery dating from the 19th century: note the fine wrought-iron gates. Nearby, stop for a view of the **Geoglifos de Tiliviche**, representing a group of llamas (signposted to the left and easily accessible). Further north at Km 111, the **Geoglifos de Chiza** can be seen from the bridge that carries the highway over the Quebrada de Chiza. At Km 172, a road runs east to **Codpa**, an agricultural community in a deep gorge surrounded by interesting scenery, with poor roads continuing north and east towards Putre (see page 271), through Tignamar and **Belén**.

This tiny village was founded by the Spanish in 1625 on the silver route between Potosí and the coast. It has two colonial churches: the older one, the **Iglesia de Belén** is one of the oldest (and smallest) churches in Chile; the other, the **Iglesia de Carmen**, dates from the 18th century. There are many pre-Hispanic ruins in the area, with four *pukarás* and a well-preserved stretch of the Camino del Inca. At Tignamar Viejo, an abandoned village 14 km south, there is another colonial church.

⊙ Iquique and around listings

For Sleeping and Eating price codes and other relevant information, see Essentials pages 35-42.

⊜ Sleeping

Iquique *p244, map p246*
Accommodation is scarce in July and also in high summer. At other times, it is always worth bargaining for better rates. There's no campsite in Iquique but wild camping is possible on La Brava beach.
L-AL Terrado Suites, Los Rieles 126, Península de Cavancha, T057-437878, www.terrado.cl. Good sea-view suites with balconies, most expensive, rooftop restaurant, all mod cons. Near beaches but away from the centre.
AL Cavancha, Los Rieles 250, T057-434800, hotelcavancha.cl. 4-star, expensive restaurant, simple but pleasant inside but ugly exterior, south of city on the water's edge; outside is a giant chessboard.
AL Gavina, Prat 1497, T057-413030, www.gavina.cl. Upmarket with bar, pool, sauna and jacuzzi. Spacious rooms, the best are on the upper floors with balconies overlooking the sea. English spoken. Decent if not exceptional. Well located for the beach and the town centre.
AL-A Arturo Prat, Aníbal Pinto 695, T057-427000, www.hotelarturoprat.cl. 4-star, pool, health suite, games room, internet, restaurant, tours arranged. Some rooms have a balcony, rooms in the older part of the hotel are tatty. Reserve in advance for a room with a view over the plaza. Attentive service, good value. Some staff speak English. Can be extremely noisy if the hotel is hosting an event.

A Atenas, Los Rieles 738, Cavancha, T057-431100, atenashotel2002@yahoo.es. Pleasant, personal, good value, good service and food, pool.
A Departamento Iquique, Diego Portales 920, piso 8, Cavancha, T057-428483, www.departamentoiquique.cl. Pleasant fully furnished apartment overlooking the beach. Advance bookings only. Recommended.
A-B Barros Arana, Barros Arana 1302, T057-412840, www.hotelbarrosarana.cl. In 2 parts. The old part is nothing special. The new section has very large rooms and is much more comfortable. Internet, swimming pool, friendly, good value. In a quiet part of town. Recommended.
A-B Jham, Latorre 426, T057-415457, www.hoteljham.cl. Smart, modern, not much character but near the centre. The matrimonial suite has a jacuzzi.
B Manuel Rodríguez Express, Rodríguez 550, T057-427524, www.hotelmanuel rodriguez.cl. **C** singles. Small standard 3 star. Decent rooms with big TVs, bright common areas and Wi-Fi. Near the beach.
B-C Cano, Ramírez 996, T057-315580, www.hotelcano.cl. Friendly, nice atmosphere, decent rooms. Typical 2-star plus.
C Doña Genoveva, Latorre 458, T057-411578, hgenoveva@gtdmail.com. **D** singles. Spacious rooms with breakfast table and cable TV. The rooms with windows onto the street are bright, sunny and the better choice. Bog standard but very good value if you pay in dollars.
C Hostal Catedral, Labbé 253, T057-426372. **D-E** singles. Most rooms with bath and cable TV, quiet, nice balcony and bright patio with plants and seating area, interesting building.

C Hotel Caiti, Gorostiaga 483, T057-423038. Pleasant, with bath, breakfast and all mod cons including Wi-Fi. interior rooms are stuffy. No luggage storage. Recommended if you can get a room with an outside window.

C Hostal La Casona 1920, Barros Arana 1585, T057-413000, www.casonahosteliquique.cl. **E** per person in shared rooms. Recently opened, friendly, fun, clean, in a quiet area of town not far from the beach. English spoken. Good reports.

C Hostal North House, Labbé 1518, T057-427008, miguel.flyiquique@gmail.com. **D** singles. Simple rooms, all with cable TV and bath, although foam mattresses are a drawback. Good location, friendly, English spoken, kitchen facilities. The owner is a paragliding instructor and offers trips.

C Hostal Cuneo, Baquedano 1175, T057-428654, hostalcuneo@hotmail.com. **D-E** singles. Clean with lots of common areas. Some rooms with bath. Lots of 1950s-1970s furnishings. There is an upright piano in the living room. Good value.

C Inti-Llanka, Obispo Labbé 825, T057-311104, www.inti-llanka.cl. **D** singles. Nice rooms with good beds and spacious bathrooms, clean, laundry, good value. Wi-Fi, luggage store. Reduced prices off season. Terse service.

C-D Casa de Huéspedes Profesores, Ramírez 839, T057-314475, iquiquea lojamiento@123mail.cl. **F** singles. With breakfast, doubles with bath. Old building with high ceilings and lots of character. Nice garden, help with tours.

C-D Hostal Li Ming, Barros Arana 705, T057-421912, www.hostal.cl. **E** singles. Clean, simple, some rooms with bath and cable TV, good value, kitchen and laundry facilities, internet, small rooms. Recommended.

C-D Hostal Nan-King, Thompson 752, T057-330691. **E** singles. Clean, small but nice rooms with bath and Cable TV. No breakfast.

D Backpacker's Hostel Iquique, Amunategui 2075, T057-320223, www.hostel iquique.cl. **E** singles, **F** per person in dorms.

With breakfast. Typical lively somewhat formulaic backpackers' affiliated to HI. Clean, cramped bedrooms, good kitchen facilities, internet, games room, activities arranged. Convenient for the beach, south of town centre. Lots of activities. English spoken. Recommended.

D Buenos Aires, Esmeralda 713, T057-472229. **E** singles. With bath, breakfast and cable TV. Meals served. Clean but basic and slightly tatty. Not the nicest area but a good option if arriving late with TurBus as it is by the terminal.

D Hostal Jean IV, Esmeralda 936, T574590, hostaljeaniv@yahoo.es. **F** singles. With bath, breakfast and cable TV, clean, friendly, nice lounge and nice patio, with bath, convenient for buses to Bolivia, excellent value. Highly recommended budget option.

D YMCA, Baquedano 964, T057-573596, www.ymcaiquique.com. **F** per person in shared rooms. The impressive façade hides a modern, though slightly run-down interior. Most rooms are dorm-style with bunkbeds and their own bathroom. Basic, but clean, and right in the town centre.

Nitrate towns p247
C Estancia Inn, Comercial, Pozo Almonte. Basic, geared towards mineworkers.
C Hotel Anakana, Comercio 053, Pozo Almonte, T057-751201. Same as Estancia.

Mamiña p248
It is extremely difficult to find lodging in Mamiña as hotels generally have exclusive contracts with the nearby mine.

La Tirana p249
During the festival, a bed is difficult to find other than in organized campsites (take your own tent), which have basic toilets and showers, and through a few families who rent out rooms for over US$30 a night.

Matilla p249
Complejo Turístico El Parabien, T057-431645. Fully furnished cabañas and a pool.

Pica *p249*

The hotels get full at weekends and at holidays, as well as during La Tirana – it is best to ring ahead.

C Camino del Inca, Esmeralda 14, T/F057-741008, hotelcaminodelinca@hotmail.com. With breakfast, shady patio, table football, good value. Recommended.

C Los Emilios, Cochrane 201, T057-741126. **F** singles. With bath and breakfast, friendly, nice lounge, small pool, interesting old building with photos of the nitrate era, lovely patio. Highly recommended.

C O'Higgins, Balmaceda 6, T057-741524, hohiggins@123mail.cl. **E-F** singles. With bath, modern.

D San Andrés, Balmaceda 197, T057-741319, gringa733@hotmail.com. **F** singles. With bath and breakfast, basic but clean, good restaurant with cheap 4-course *almuerzos*.

Cocha Resbaladero

B-C Hostal Suizo, Ibáñez 210, T057-741551. With bath, popular, modern, very comfy.

C Hostal Casablanca, Ibáñez 75, T057-741410. **E** singles. Smallish rooms with bath and cable TV. Friendly, comfortable, cooking facilities, bright patio with pool, parking.

D Residencial El Tambo, Ibáñez 68, T/F057-741041. **F** singles. Without bath, meals served, somewhat run-down. Also 4-person *cabañas*.

Iquique to the Bolivian border *p250*

Basic accommodation is available in the Restaurant Frontera in Huara and in 4 simple *residenciales* in Colchane.

North towards Arica *p251*

Pisagua Restaurant Acuario, friendly, also has beds (**D**). There is a campsite at the northern end of the beach.

Camiña A simple *hostal* on the plaza.

Belén Food and lodging from **María Martínez**, General Lagos y San Martín.

● Eating

Iquique *p244, map p246*

Beware of the expensive and poor-value tourist restaurants on the wharf on the opposite side of Av Costanera from the bus terminal. Several good, cheap and super-cheap seafood restaurants can be found on the 2nd floor of the somewhat insalubrious central market, Barros Arana y Latorre. There are a number of restaurants near Cavancha beach in Caleta Cavancha. The cafés and restaurants along Calle Baquedano seem to change ownership every couple of years.

♥♥♥ Club Náutico, Los Rieles 110, T057-432951. Seafood, exclusive. Live music on Sat nights.

♥♥♥ El Sombrero, Los Rieles 704, T057-312410. Quality fish and seafood cuisine, elegant setting, not cheap. Buffet lunches.

♥♥♥-♥♥ Casino Español, Plaza Prat 584, T057-423284. Good meals well served in a 1904 Moorish-style palace, which in itself is a reason to eat there.

♥♥♥-♥♥ El Tercer Ojito, Patricio Lynch 1420, T057-471448 Well-presented fish, sushi, pasta and vegetarian options with a Peruvian twist, served in a pleasant courtyard by waiters that are just a little too pleased with themselves. Deservedly popular.

♥♥♥-♥♥ El Viejo Wagon, Thompson 85, T057-341428. Fish and seafood cooked according to traditional northern recipes. Regarded by many as the best restaurant in the town centre.

♥♥♥-♥♥ Kiru, Amunategui 1912. Half elegant restaurant, half sports bar. Smallish portions of Peruvian influenced food. Lots of fish and good pasta. Huge *pisco sours*. Recommended.

♥♥ Brasileña, Vivar 1143, T057-423236. Friendly Brazilian-run restaurant serving seafood during the week and Brazilian food on Sat.

♥♥ Colonial, Plaza Prat. Fish and seafood, popular, a bit of a tourist trap.

¶¶ **El Barril del Fraile**, Ramírez 1181, T057-390334. Good seafood, nice atmosphere, doubles as a lively bar at night.
¶¶ **La Picada Curicana**, Zegers 204, T057-428200. Hearty central Chilean country cooking – *Pernil, costillar, arrollado*, etc. Oven roasted and served in clay pots. Large portions, very good value. A meat-eater's paradise.
¶¶ **Nan King**, Amunategui 533, T057-420434. Deservedly known as the best Chinese in town. Huge portions, good value. Eat as much as you can and take the rest with you.
¶¶ **Pizzeria d'Alfredo**, Los Molles 2290 (Playa Brava). Large variety of pizzas, well-prepared pastas, not cheap, reasonably priced *almuerzo*.
¶¶-¶ **Compañia Italiana de Bomberos**, Serrano 520. Authentic Italian cuisine, excellent value *almuerzo*, otherwise more expensive. Recommended.
¶ **Bolivia**, Serrano 751. *Humitas* and *salteñas*. Recommended. Several other cheap Bolivian restaurants nearby.
¶ **Claudy**, Lynch 749. Simple but hearty lunches at a more than reasonable price.
¶ **El Rincón del Cachuperto**, Valenzuela 125, Peninsula Cavancha. Famed as having the best seafood *empanadas* in Iquique.
¶ **Peña mi Perú**, Bolivar 711. Open 24 hrs. Cheap Chilean and Peruvian staples.

Cafés

Birimbao, Gorostiaga 419. Opens early for breakfast (0800). Fresh juices.
Capuccino, Baquedano y Gorostiaga. Coffee and good ice cream. Pleasant to sit outside and watch the world go by.
Cioccolata, Pinto 487 (another branch in the Zofri). Good coffee and cakes.
Salón de Té Don Luis, Vivar y Latorre. Popular for *onces*, quite expensive, and the peace is often disturbed by the loudspeakers blaring out from the shop opposite.

Mamiña *p248*
¶¶ **Restaurant Cerro Morado**, Av Barros Chino 18. Good variety, traditional dishes,

including rabbit. One of few restaurants open to the general public.

Pica *p249*
Pica is famous for its *alfajores* filled with cream and honey, and you cannot leave without trying some of the fruit juices. Hotels San Andrés and El Tambo (see Sleeping, above) both have good, cheap restaurants.
¶¶ **El Edén de Pica**, Riquelme 12. Best in town, speciality dishes, fine ice cream, lovely surroundings.
¶¶ **Los Naranjos**, Esmeralda y Barbosa. Nice decor, good food.
¶ **La Mía Pappa**, Balmaceda. Good selection of meat and juices, attractive location near the plaza.
¶ **La Palmera**, Balmaceda 115. Excellent *almuerzo*, popular with locals, near plaza.
¶ **La Viña**, Ibáñez 70, by Cocha de Resbaladero. Good cheap *almuerzo*.
¶ **Oasis**, Balamaceda, by the plaza. Ridiculously cheap. Recommended for *alfajores* and fruit juice.

Iquique to the Bolivian Border *p250*
Meals are served in the *residenciales* in Colchane.
¶ **La flor de Huara**, Huara. Good and cheap. Much the best choice in town.

☉ Bars and clubs

Iquique *p244, map p246*
Most discos are out of the town on the road south to the airport.
Hotel Gavina (see Sleeping, above) has a good club on Fri and Sat nights, quite smart.
La Caldera del Sabor, Bajo Molle, south of the city. One of Iquique's most popular clubs, Thu-Sat. Plays salsa and merengue, with dance classes. There are several other choices in the same area.
Pharo's, Av Costanera Sur 3607, Playa Brava. Enormous club with an elaborate design, popular, good.

Rumba, Bolívar y Lynch, T057-318123.
Salsatheque with salsa classes on Fri nights.
Taberna Barracuda, Gorostiaga 601. Nice
decor, good atmosphere, recommended
for late night food and drink.
Taberna Van Gogh, Ramírez y Latorre.
Live music Fri and Sat nights.

Entertainment

Iquique *p244, map p246*
There are occasional recitals in the cathedral.
Casino, Balmaceda 2755. Nightly, *salón* US$3.
Mall las Américas, Av Héroes de la Concep-
ción, T057-432500. Multi-screen cinema.
Teatro Municipal, Plaza Prat, T057-411292.
Plays, ballet, dance and concerts.

Festivals and events

Iquique *p244, map p246*
There are numerous small religious festivals
in the area – ask in Iquique's tourist office
for information.

Shopping

Iquique *p244, map p246*
Most of the city's commerce is in the
Zofri duty-free zone.
Andrés Bello, Héroes de la Concepción 2855,
which stocks an excellent range of books.
Mall de las Américas, south of the centre
on Av Héroes de la Concepción, sells
camping equipment at Tunset, Zofri,
and Lombardi.
Rossi, Tarapacá 579. Supermarket.

Activities and tours

Iquique *p244, map p246*
Landsailing
Civet Adventure, Bolívar 684, T057-428483,
civetcor@vtr.net. Landsailing, altiplano cycling

trips and other special-interest excursions.
English and German spoken. Recommended.

Paragliding
The cliffs directly behind Iquique are a great
place from which to launch off down towards
the coast. Several agencies offer 30- to
40-min tandem flights from around US$60.
Altazor, Via 6, Manzana A, Sitio 3, Bajo Molle,
T057-380110, www.altazor.cl, is generally
considered to be the best and will pick
you up from wherever you are staying.
Also offers week-long courses including
accommodation, as do many other operators.

Surfing
Iquique offers some of the best surfing in
Chile with numerous reef breaks on **Playa
Brava**, south of the city. Surfboard rental and
surf classes are available from a number of
agencies. Lessons cost roughly US$11 per hr.
Try **Vertical**, opposite the Playa Cavancha.
Club de Surf, Av Héroes de la Concepción
1939, T057-447070.

Swimming
The beach at **Cavancha**, just south of
the town centre, is good, and popular
Nov-Mar. There's another bathing beach
at **Huaiquique**, 5 km south, and a fresh-
water pool, **Piscina Godoy**, Av Costanera
at Aníbal Pinto and Riquelme, open
evening, US$1.50.

Tennis
Club de Tenis Tarapacá, Bulnes 140, T057-
412489. Temporary membership available.

Tour operators
The tourist office maintains a list of operators.
Avitours, Baquedano 997, T057-473775,
www.avitours.cl. Tours to Pintados, La Tirana,
Humberstone, Pica, etc, some bilingual
guides, day tours start at US$30, mixed
reports. There are many similar agencies
on the same street.
Extremo Norte, Filomena Valenzuela 712,
T057-760997, www.extremonorte.cl. Good

tours to the Altiplano and desert. Responsible. Also run the Tren Pampino, www.trenpampino.cl, a project to link various ghost towns and saltpeter plants by train. **Iquitour**, Lynch 563, T/F057-412415. Tours of saltpeter *oficinas* and Pica oasis. English spoken.

⊖ Transport

Iquique *p244, map p246*
Air
Diego Aracena International Airport, 35 km south at Chucumata. **Sky**, **Principal** and LanChile fly south to **Santiago**, via Antofagasta, and north to **Arica** – some flights continue on to **La Paz** in Bolivia.
   Airline offices LanChile, Tarapacá 465, T057-427600, www.lan.com, and in the Mall Las Américas; Sky, Tarapacá 530, T600-526200, www.skyairline.cl; TAM, Serrano 430, T057-390600, Principal, Plaza Prat 570, www.aerolineaprincipal.cl.

Bicycle/motorbike
Motorcycle mechanic, **Sergio Cortez**, Civet, Bolívar 684, is recommended. Also repairs bikes. English spoken. **Bianchi**, Bulnes 485, for bike parts, repairs; for sales try the Zofri.

Bus
The bus terminal is at the north end of Patricio Lynch but not all buses leave from here; **TurBus** has its own terminal, Ramírez y Esmeralda, with a **Redbanc** ATM and a good luggage store. Bus company offices are near the market on Sgto Aldea and Barros Arana. All southbound buses are stopped for a luggage check on leaving the duty-free zone of Región I at Quillagua on the Pan-American Highway and at Chipana/Río Loa on the coastal Route 1.
   To **Arica**, buses and *colectivos*, frequent, 4½ hrs, US$11; to **Antofagasta**, 6 hrs, US$14; to **Calama**, 6 hrs, US$16-23; to **Tocopilla** along the coastal road, 3 hrs, US$10; to **La Serena**, 18 hrs, US$35-70;

to **Valparaíso** and **Viña del Mar**, 26 hrs, US$50; to **Santiago**, 25 hrs, US$50-75.
   Most bus companies for international services to **Oruro** and **La Paz** (Bolivia) leave from Esmeralda, near the junction of Juan Martínez (note that some buses go via Arica and Tambo Quemado to La Paz, not via Colchane and Oruro). **Litoral Buses**, T057-423670, daily at 2200 to **Colchane** and **Oruro**, US$10, to **La Paz**, US$15; Salvador Buses at 2300, same price; Géminis from the bus terminal to **La Paz**, via Oruro, more expensive. Delta, Tata Sabaya and Comet all leave from Esmeralda y Juan Martínez 2100-2300 to **Oruro** (via Colchane), bargain for a good price.

Car
Car hire from **Econorent**, Labbé y O'Higgins, T600-200 0000, weekend specials; Hertz, A Pinto 1303, T057-510432; airport office T057-407020; IQSA, Labbé 1089, T057-417068. Jofamar, Libertad 1156, T057-411639; Procar, Serrano 796, T057-413470, at airport T057-410920. Be wary of cheap deals. Many used jeeps are imported from Japan and have their driving wheels moved over to the left hand side for the Chilean market (not a safe thing to do).

Colectivos/taxis
Any car that looks like a taxi serves is a *colectivo* unless it says '*sólo taxi*'. Tell the driver where you are going and, if your destination can combine with that of other passengers, he will take you; if you are the first passenger, tell the driver you want to hire the car as a *colectivo* and he will fit the journeys of subsequent passengers around your destination. The fare is US$0.80 (a little more late at night). Taxi fares are US$2 for journeys within the city centre.

Mamiña *p248*
Two companies run minibuses between **Iquique** and Mamiña; best to book the day before: **Transportes Tamarugal**, Barros Arana 897, departs Iquique daily 0800, 1600, 2½ hrs,

US$7 one-way, returns from Mamiña 0800, 1800; Turismo Mamiña, Latorre 779, departs Iquique Mon-Sat 0800-1600, also Sun 1600, 2½ hrs US$6, returns from Mamiña Tue-Sat 0830, Mon-Sat 1800.

La Tirana *p249*
In ordinary times, buses from Iquique to Pica stop here; during the festival, virtually every taxi and *colectivo* in Iquique seems to be heading for La Tirana, leaving from Sargento Aldea by the market; some bus companies also have services from Antofagasta and Arica.

Pica *p249*
Three bus companies run between **Iquique** and Pica: **Santa Rosa**, Barros Arana 777, departs Iquique daily 0830 and 0930, 2 hrs, US$4, returns from Pica 1700 and 1800; **San Andrés**, Sgto Aldea y Barros Arana, departs Iquique daily 0930, returns from Pica daily 1800, US$4; **Pullman Chacón**, Barros Arana y Latorre, many daily, US$4, 1st return bus from Pica leaves at about 1100.

Iquique to the Bolivian border *p250*
Pullman La Paloma runs daily bus services to **Colchane** at 2300 from Esmeralda y Juan Martínez, US$8. Most services to Ororo can drop you off at Colchane.

North towards Arica *p251*
From **Arica**, Buses La Paloma, German Riesco 2071, T058-222710, runs a service to **Belén**, departing Tue and Fri at 0645, US$6.

⊙ Directory

Iquique *p244, map p246*
Banks Numerous Redbanc ATMs in the centre; lots of ATMs in the Zofri. *Casas de cambio* at **AFEX**, Serrano 396, changes TCs; **Cambio Cambio's**, Lynch 548, Local 1-2; **Wall Street**, in the Zofri, sells and exchanges AmEx TCs. **Consulates** Bolivia, Gorostiaga 215, Departamento E, T057-421777, Mon-Fri 0930-1200; Netherlands, Tarapacá 123, T057-390900, helpful; Peru, Zegers 570, T057-411466; Spain, Manzana 2, Sitio 5 y 9, Zofri, T057-422330. **Internet and telephone** Several in and around the centre. **Language schools** Academia de Idiomas del Norte, Ramírez 1345, T057-411827, www.languages.cl. Swiss-run, Spanish classes, accommodation for students. **Laundry** Barrueto, Zegers 650, T057-762358, charges per kilo. Cruz del Sur, Thompson 553. **Medical services** Dentist: Clinica Dental Lynch, Lynch y Orella, T057-413060. Hospitals: Centro Médico, Orella 433, T/F057-414396; also at Héroes de la Concepción 502, T057-415555. **Police** station at O'Higgins y Labbé. Also on the SW corner of the plaza. **Post office** In the Zofri, there is another branch in the Mall de las Américas.

Arica and around

→ *Colour map 1, A1.*

Arica is the northernmost city in Chile, just 19 km south of the Peruvian border. With Peru so close and Arica being the main port for Bolivian trade, the city has a distinct halfway house sort of feel. It is less ordered than most Chilean cities, with hundreds of street vendors and indoor markets selling cheap, imported goods and has a friendly, laid-back atmosphere. The city centre itself is quite attractive, with long beaches, pleasant gardens and extensive networks of sand dunes all nearby. Rearing up to the south is El Morro, the rock that marks the end of the Chilean coastal range. Inland is the verdant Valle de Azapa with olive groves and a museum housing the world's oldest mummies. Day trips can easily be made across the border to Tacna, the southernmost city in Peru. ⤷ *For listings, see pages 264-270.*

Ins and outs

Getting there Arica is a long way from most of Chile. All major bus companies serving the north make this their final stop; buses take 30 hours to reach Santiago to the south. Arica is a centre for connections to Bolivia and Peru, with a train and frequent *colectivos* north to Tacna in Peru and buses east to La Paz in Bolivia. There is also quite a wide-ranging bus service to villages in the sierra and the altiplano. **Sky** and **LanChile** fly south to Santiago via Iquique and Antofagasta, with some flights continuing on to La Paz in Bolivia or Arequipa in Peru. A taxi to town from the airport costs US$10, *colectivos* cost US$5 per person from Lynch y 21 de Mayo. Be wary if your taxi driver suggests 'a good hotel'. Many are paid commissions to do so.

Getting around Arica is quite a large city, and you may need to take some of the *colectivos* or buses to get to more out-of-the-way places, particularly the clubs, many of which are on the road out to the Azapa Valley.

Tourist information Sernatur ⓘ *Marcos 101 y Parque Baquedano, T058-232101, Mon-Fri 0830-1300, 1500-1830,* is very helpful and can supply a list of tour companies and a good map.

Background

During the colonial period, Arica was important as the Pacific end of the silver route from Potosí. Independence from Spain and the re-routing of Bolivian trade through Cobija led to a decline, but the city recovered with the building of rail links to Tacna (1855) and La Paz (1913) when it became the port of choice for those two cities. The city came under Chilean control at the end of the War of the Pacific. The Morro in Arica was the site of an important Chilean victory over Peru on 7 June 1880.

Arica remains an important route centre and port. Now linked to the Bolivian capital La Paz by road and an oil pipeline, it handles almost half of Bolivia's foreign trade and attracts Bolivians, as well as locals, to its beaches. There are also road and rail connections with the Peruvian city of Tacna, 54 km north. Most of the large fishmeal plants have moved to Iquique, leaving several rusting hulks of trawlers in the bay, now home to a significant local crow population. Regrettably, there are indications that Arica is also becoming a key link in the international drugs trade.

Arica

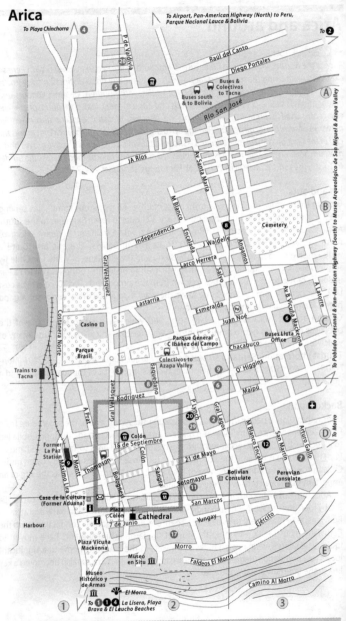

To Playa Chinchorra

To Airport, Pan-American Highway (North) to Peru,
Parque Nacional Lauca & Bolivia

To 2

Raúl del Canto

Diego Portales

Río San José

Buses south
& to Bolivia

Buses &
Colectivos
to Tacna

JA Ríos

Cemetery

Independencia

J Waldelle

Larco Herrera

Lastarria

Esmeralda

Parque General
C Ibáñez del Campo

Juan Noé

Casino

Parque
Brasil

Colectivos to
Azapa Valley

Trains to
Tacna

Buses Lluta
Office

Baquedano

Rodriguez

Former
La Paz Station

Colón
18 de Septiembre

21 de Mayo

Casa de la Cultura
(Former Aduana)

Bolivian
Consulate

Plaza
Colón   Cathedral

Peruvian
Consulate

San Marcos

7 de Junio

Plaza Vicuña
Mackenna

Yungay

Harbour

Morro

Museo
en Situ

Faldeos El Morro

Museo
Histórico y
de Armas

El Morro

Camino Al Morro

To   La Lisera, Playa
Brava & El Laucho Beaches

200 metres
200 yards

Sights

Unlike in most Chilean cities, life is not centred around the main square, but Avenida 21 de Mayo, a mostly pedestrianized street full of banks, shops, restaurants and cafés. Just south of this is the **Plaza Colón**, on which stands the Gothic-style cathedral of **San Marcos**, built in iron by Eiffel. Although small, it is beautifully proportioned and attractively painted. It was brought to Arica from Ilo in Peru as an emergency measure after a tidal wave swept over Arica in 1868 and destroyed all its churches; inside the cathedral is a Christ figure dating from the 12th century. Eiffel also designed the nearby Aduana (customs house), which is now the **Casa de la Cultura** ⓘ *0830-2000, ask for permission to go up into the altillo.* Just north of the Aduana is the La Paz railway station; outside is an old steam locomotive (made in Germany in 1924) once used on this line, while inside is a memorial to John Roberts Jones, builder of the Arica portion of the railway. Hidden away on a small side street behind the cathedral is the private **Museo del Mar** ⓘ *Sangra 315, www.museodel mardearica.cl, Mon-Sat 1100-1900, US$2,* a small, one-room collection of shells and sealife from around the world. If the owner is there he will explain everything to you in English.

To climb **El Morro**, 130 m high, walk to the southernmost end of the Calle Colón, past a small in situ museum displaying a number of recently uncovered Chinchorro mummies, and then follow the pedestrian walkway up to the summit; there are fine views of the city from here. **Museo Histórico y de Armas** ⓘ *www.museomorro arica.cl, daily, 0830-2000, US$1,* on the summit, contains a selection of weapons and military uniforms as well as displays on the War of the Pacific. Basic information in English but most of the exhibits speak for themselves.

Arica centre

A coastal road heads out of Arica to the south. There is no public transport but it makes a pleasant cycle ride. Past the Morro, to the right, is the former Island of Alacrán, now connected to the mainland and a favourite surfing destination. The road passes La Lisera, a beach, crowded in summer, and with a natural pool. Past the empty Playa Brava the air fills with the pungent smell of fishmeal from the processing plant here. At km 7, past further rocky and sandy beaches and a natural blowhole is Playa Corazones, a pleasant beach, quiet except at weekends and in summer. Good cheap seafood is available. Shortly after, the road runs out but a path continues for a further kilometre, past guano-covered rocks, pools full of crabs, starfish and shellfish to the Cuevas de Anzota, a series of caves and fantastic rock formations with crashing waves, a small secluded beach and a sea-lion colony on a small island off-shore.

Valle de Azapa ⊖⊕⦿▲ » pp264-270.

A highly recommended excursion is up the Azapa Valley, a beautiful oasis east of Arica. At Km 12 is the **Museo Arqueológico San Miguel de Azapa** ① *T058-205555, museo@ uta.cl, 0900-2000 (2 Jan-28 Feb), 1000-1800 (1 Mar-31 Dec), US$5,* part of the University of Tarapacá and well worth a visit. Set in a pleasant, shady part of the valley, the museum contains a fine collection of pre-Columbian tools, weaving, pottery, woodcarving and basket work from the coast and the valleys as well as four mummified humans from the Chinchorro culture (8000-10,000 BC), the most ancient mummies yet discovered. In the final room there is an exhibition about the olive oil produced in the valley, including a huge old press. In the forecourt of the museum are several boulders with pre-Columbian petroglyphs and opposite is a garden full of tropical plants and birds. Comprehensive explanations are provided by booklets in English, French, German and Spanish, loaned free at the entrance. Most multi-day tours to the Altiplano make a stop here on the way up.

On the road between Arica and San Miguel several groups of geoglyphs of humans and llamas can be seen to the south of the road. On the opposite side of the valley at San Lorenzo are the ruins of a *pukará* (pre-Inca fortress) dating from the 12th century.

In the nearby village of San Miguel, there are several restaurants with a wide range of prices. The village cemetery is worth a visit, its simple, well-maintained graves protected from the sun by roofs and awnings and decorated with plastic flowers are a stark reminder of the unique conditions here. If you have the energy, a good walk is to climb the desert hill behind the valley, 45 minutes, giving wonderful views of the green oasis and the desolation beyond – running back down the hill takes three minutes and is an exhilarating experience.

Into Peru ⊖ » pp264-270. See box, opposite, for border crossing information.

Tacna is 36 km north of the border. The city was in Chilean hands from 1880 to 1929, when its citizens voted by plebiscite to return to Peru. There is a wide variety of hotels and restaurants here, as well as bus and air services to the rest of Peru. Many Chileans travel to Tacna for optical and dental treatment, which is much cheaper than in Chile, but of dubious quality. There is a **tourist office** ① *Av Bolognesi 2088.*

Border crossing: Chile–Peru

Chacalluta

Chilean immigration At the border post of Chacalluta, is open Sunday to Thursday 0800-2400, 24 hours Friday and Saturday. Immigration is usually fairly uncomplicated, although crossing the border into Peru with a hire car is difficult: make sure you have the correct papers.

Peruvian border post Open 0900-2200. There are no exchange facilities at the border. Good rates are generally available at Tacna's bus station or in the city centre.

Into Bolivia ○⊖ ↠ *pp264-270. See box, page 264, for border crossing information.*

Vía Chungará and Tambo Quemado

There are two routes from Arica to the Bolivian border. **Route 11** (paved to La Paz, although seriously worn in places by overloaded juggernauts) turns off the Pan-American Highway, 12 km north of Arica, and runs through the Lluta Valley, where the **Geoglifos de Lluta** – four groups of geoglyphs representing llamas and humans – can be seen on the hillsides between Km 14 and Km 16. At Km 35 at Pocon Chile there is a Hari Krishna community offering accommodation and good vegetarian food. Further on, at Km 73 is a *centro magnético*, an optical illusion that makes the climbing road seem as if it going downhill. There is a stunning mirador overlooking Copaquilla (Km 89), and Km 99 there is a turnoff for the village of Belén, see page 251. The village of Socoroma lies 9 km up the valley, 4 km north of the main road. At an altitude of 3000m It is a pretty Aymara settlement with a well ordered plaza with bright flowers. The traditional houses look odd with their corrugated zinc roofs. The traditional straw and leather was replaced as it was often home to the bug that causes Chagas disease. Past Socoroma the road continues via Putre and Parinacota through the Parque Nacional Lauca to the border at Chungará. This is the route followed by most transport to Bolivia, including buses and trucks. Estimated driving time to La Paz is six hours.

Vía Visviri and Charaña

The road to Oruro and La Paz (Route 108) is unpaved and should not be attempted in wet weather. It follows the La Paz–Arica railway line to the Chilean immigration post at **Visviri** (altitude 4069 m). Cheap accommodation is available at **Alojamiento Aranda**. There are two routes, both poor, continuing from Charaña towards La Paz, both of which meet at Viacha. Over the border, the route passes through the **Parque Nacional Sajama**, which covers 60,000 ha and contains the world's highest forest, consisting mainly of the rare Kenua tree, which survives at altitudes of up to 5200 m. The scenery is wonderful and includes views of three volcanos: Parinacota (6342 m) and Pomerape (6282 m), both of which are on the border, and Sajama (6530 m), which is Bolivia's highest peak, but can be seen from the Lauca national park in Chile. Park administration is at Sajama village, 14 km off Route 108 (altitude 4200 m), where there is basic accommodation. There is also accommodation at Carahuara de Carangas, 111 km northeast of Tambo Quemado, and at **Patacamaya**, 104 km south of La Paz, where Route 108 joins the main Oruro–La Paz highway.

Border crossings: Chile–Bolivia

Chungará

Chilean immigration 7 km west of the border, open 0800-2000.
Bolivian immigration and customs At Tambo Quemado, just over the border (where there is a local barter market every other Friday). This is a relatively speedy crossing, but very cold; if you're travelling by bus (see page 269), take a blanket or sleeping bag, food, water and a sense of humour.

Visviri

Three kilometres from the Bolivian border and 12 km from Peru (no crossing), T058-261486, open 0800-2000. There is no fuel or accommodation here. Bolivian formalities are conducted behind the railway station at **Charaña**, 10 km east.

ⓘ Arica and around listings

For Sleeping and Eating price codes and other relevant information, see Essentials pages 35-42.

ⓔ Sleeping

Arica *p259, map p260*
Accommodation is cheaper in Arica than in the rest of Chile. For apartment rental on the beach, see local newspapers.
L Arica, San Martín 599, 2 km south on coast (frequent buses, *colectivos*), T058-254540, www.panamericanahoteles.cl. 4-star. Pool, Restaurant, tennis court, beach access. Not great value.
A Americano, General Lagos 571, T058-257752, www.hotelamericano.cl. Airy and spacious rooms, pleasant patio, rooms on upper floor have views to the Morro and these are recommended. Also gym and sauna (extra charge).
B Plaza Colón, San Marcos 261, T058-254424, www.hotelplazacolon.cl. Good location opposite the cathedral. Showing its age a little, otherwise comfortable enough if you avoid the basement rooms. Cheaper to pay in dollars.
B Savona, Yungay 380, T058-231000, www.hotelsavona.cl. Recently refurbished but maintaining much of the original furnishings. Try and get one of the rooms on the upper

floors which are bigger. A/c. Some have giant TV, and full bathtub. Airport transfer service, internet access, Wi-Fi. Airy terrace and pool area. Bike rental. Attentive service. English spoken. Good value. Highly recommended.
B-C Bahía Chinchorro, Luis Berreta Pocel 2031, T058-260676, www.bahiahotel.cl. Located right on the seafront on the southern end of Chinchorro beach. Recently refurbished. Spacious rooms, some with bath and balconies. French and English spoken.
C D'Marie-Jeanne y David, Velásquez 792, T058-258231, www.hoteldmariejeanney david.cl. **D** singles. Fairly comfortable and clean rooms with bath. Some with cable TV. Good location but on a main road so some rooms can be a little noisy. French spoken.
C Hostal Jardín del Sol, Sotomayor 848, T058-232795, www.hostaljardindelsol.cl. **E** singles. With bath and breakfast, comfortable,beds with duvets, friendly, good value, free internet, stores luggage, some info, bike hire. Large kitchen area (US$1 charge). Highly recommended.
C King, Colón 376, T058-232094, hotelking@ chilenet.cl. With bath and breakfast. Incredibly kitsch, in a 1970s timewarp. Lino floor, turquoise wallpaper and a fantastic lamp in the lobby. Some rooms are bigger than others and the brightest face the street.

C Sunny Days, Tomás Aravena 161 y Pedro de Valdivia, población Chinchorro, T058-241038, www.sunny-days-arica.cl. **E** singles, **F** per person in shared rooms. Run by a New Zealander and his Chilean wife. Laundry facilities, some rooms with bath, English spoken, homely atmosphere, lots of info on the area, book exchange, bike rental, will pick you up from the terminal. Convenient for the beach. One of the best hostels in the north of Chile. Warmly recommended.

C-D Maison de France, Aurelio Valdivieso 152, población Chinchorro, T058-223463, atchum turist@hotmail.com. **E** singles. Friendly hostel owned by Christian, a larger-than-life French- man. Breakfast US$2. Good meals. Kitchen facilities, bright patio, info about tours or self- guided trips to the altiplano. Good location for beach and nightlife. Recommended.

C-D Surf House, O'Higgins 661, T058-312213, www.aricasurfhouse.cl. **E** singles. Budget hostel aimed, as the name suggests, at surfers (the owner also runs a surf school). Decent beds and showers, large common areas, kitchen facilities. Tours, jet-ski rental. Good value, recommended.

D Lynch, Lynch 589, T058-231581. **E-F** singles. Basic rooms with bath and cable TV.

D-E Hostal Pacífico, Gen Lagos 672, T058-251616, hostalpacifico672@hotmail.com. **F** singles. A clean, cheap option in the city centre. Some rooms with bath and cable TV.

D-E Hostal Venecia, Baquedano 741, T058-252877, hostalvenecia@gmail.com. **E-F** singles. Small spotless rooms, some with bath, friendly, good value, laundry service.

D-E Residencial América, Sotomayor 430, T058-254148, www.residencialamerica.com. Some rooms with bath, clean, hospitable, good value, recently refurbished. **E-F** singles.

Camping
Playa Corazones, 8 km south, very crowded in summer.

Valle de Azapa *p262*
AL Azapa inn, Sánchez 660, T058-244537, www.azapainn.cl. Set in 4 ha of attractive

grounds out of town in the Azapa Valley, pleasant location, also cheaper *cabañas*, good restaurant. Often used for large conferences.
B Saucache, Sánchez 621, Valle de Azapa, T/F058-241458, desierto300@123click.cl. Fully equipped *cabañas*, sleep 2 or 4.
B Sol de Arica, Avalos 2041, T058-246050, www.hotelsoldearica.cl. Set in large grounds on the edge of the city on the way to Azapa. Sauna, jacuzzi, pool. Recommended.

⑦ Eating

Arica *p259, map p260*
⑪⑪⑪ Maracuyá, San Martín 0321, at the northern end of Playa El Laucho south of the centre, T058-227600. Arica's premier restaurant specializing in fish and seafood. Expensive, but worth it.
⑪⑪-⑪⑪ El Arriero, 21 de Mayo 385, T058-232636. *Parrillada*, also seafood and fish. Large portions.
⑪⑪ Chifa El Mesón, Santa María 1364. One of several good-value Chinese restaurants in the area. Generous portions and clean kitchen in view of the diners.
⑪⑪ Cyclo Public, Diego Portales 1364 T058-262098. Open from 2030. Fashionable seafood and pasta restaurant, reasonably priced. Vegetarian options. Recommended.
⑪⑪ El Rey del Marisco, Colón 565, 2 piso, T058-229232. Seafood specialities. A timeless sort of place. Any restaurant in Chile that lasts 35 years has to be good, and you just know that half of the waiters have been there from the beginning.
⑪⑪ Jalapeño Bar, Baquedano 369, Tex-Mex specialities, relaxed atmosphere. Good value.
⑪⑪ Los Aleros de 21, 21 de Mayo 736, T058-254641. One of the cities oldest established restaurants specializing in Southern Chilean cuisine. Large portions and lots of pork. Also fish options. Tends to fill up with tourists. Good service.
⑪⑪ Mata Rangi, on the pier. Good food in fishy environment, good-value *menú de casa*.

Ψ-Ψ Don Floro, V MacKenna 847,
T058-231481. Popular little seafood
restaurant. Also serves steaks and excellent
Peruvian-style *picantes*, good service.
Recommended, if you don't object to the
television blaring in the background.

Ψ-Ψ El Andén, In the former La Paz railway
station. Good-value inventive menu
Mon-Fri, à la carte weekends. An old train
carriage is used as one of the dining areas.
Service is attentive but a little slow.

Ψ-Ψ Ostión Dorado, Playa Corazones.
A small shack selling fabulous *empanadas*
and other super-fresh seafood.

Ψ Capricho Latino, 18 de Septiembre 250.
Good-value *almuerzo*.

Ψ La Bomba, Colón 357, at fire station,
T058-255626. Good-value, simple Chilean
food. Friendly service, with the chatter of the
on-duty firemen in the background.

Ψ Mercado Colón, Maipú y Colón. Several
stalls offering tasty good value lunches and
fresh juices. Recommended.

Ψ Open Bar, Maipú 500 y Lynch. Fantastically
good-value lunches. Tapas served in the
evening. There is an antique snooker
table in the corner.

Cafés

There are 3 good places on 21 de Mayo, all
offering real coffee and outdoor seating:
Caffelatte, No 248; **Carlos Díaz León Snack
Place**, No 388; and **Di Mango**, No 244, which
also serves juices and lovely ice cream.

Also try **Mi Viejo**, Maipú 436, for cheap
meals and snacks, and **Scala**, 21 de Mayo
201, for excellent fruit juices and real coffee.

Valle de Azapa p262

Ψ La Picada del Muertito, Los Yaganes s/n,
by the cemetery, San Miguel de Azapa,
T058-264189. Closes 2100. known as the
best traditional restaurant in the valley.
Simple no-frills decor, famed for its *pastel de
choclo*, but many other options. Fills up on
Sun with locals. You won't go hungry here
unless you are a vegetarian. Recommended.

ΨΨ Las Tejas de Azapa, Km 1.5, No 4301,
T058-246817. *Parrillada* and other options.

🎵 Bars and clubs

Arica p259, map p260

Carpaccio, Velásquez 510. Restaurant and bar
with live music from 2330 Wed-Sat.
Chill Out, 21 Sep y Lynch. Open till 0400, but
doesn't get going until 2400. Central Arica's
most popular bar. Also **Bar Central**, next door.
Soho, Playa Chinchorro. Disco.
Tunic On the coast past Playa Brava, south of
Arica. Popular with the gay/alternative crowd.

Valle de Azapa p262

Several options, all around 3-4 km out of
town. Open weekends 2300-0430 (taxi US$4).

🎭 Entertainment

Arica p259, map p260
Casino
Casino Municipal de Arica, Velásquez 955.
1200-0300. US$3.50 to enter. Recently
revamped. 3 decent restaurants inside.

Cinemas
Colón, 7 de Junio 190, opposite the
cathedral. T058-231165.

Music
A *peña folklórica* of Andean music is held in
the **Poblado Artesanal**, Fri and Sat 2130.

Theatre
Teatro Municipal de Arica, Baquedano 234.
Theatrical and musical events, exhibitions.

🎪 Festivals and events

Arica p259, map p260
Jan/Feb The Fiesta del Sol, a festival of
Andean dance and music, a slightly more
debauched version of the festival at La Tirana.

Jun The festival of Arica and the national Cueca championships. On 7 Jun, it's the anniversary of the Chilean victory in the Battle of the Morro, with parties and fireworks.

O Shopping

Arica *p259, map p260*
Crafts
Poblado Artesanal, Plaza Las Gredas, Hualles 2825 (take bus 2, 3 or 7). Open at weekends and whenever a cruise ship is in dock. Expensive but especially good for musical instruments. Look out for the replica of the famous church at Parinacota. Otherwise head for Calles Thompson and Bolognesi.

Markets
Feria Turística Dominical, Chacabuco, east of Velásquez Sun flea market, mostly uninspiring bric a brac but good for quinoa and second-hand jeans.
Mercado Central, Sotomayor y Sangra. Recently renovated, fruit and vegetables, mornings only.
Mercado Colón, Maipú y Colón. Fruit and veg. Also excellent cheap restaurants and juice bars.
Terminal del Agro, southeastern edge of town; take bus marked 'Agro' along 18 de Septiembre. Fruit, vegetables and old clothes. An interesting experience.

Supermarkets
There are supermarkets at Baquedano y 18 de Septiembre, San Martín y 18 de Septiembre and at Chacabuco y Lagos.

Into Bolivia *p263*
There are markets in **Visviri** on Wed and Sat mornings; a Sun morning market is held from 0900 north of the town at the border of the 3 countries.

▲ Activities and tours

Arica *p259, map p260*
Boat trips
Several companies offer boat trips around the bay (US$2 per person, only leave when boats are full so better at weekends). For a trip further afield to nearby sea lion and penguin colonies, try Raúl, owner of the **Mata Rangi** restaurant on the pier, turismomarino@ yahoo.es. Access to the pier is via a gate into the port complex marked "*acceso peatonal al terminal pesquero*".

Surfing
There's good surfing at **Playa Las Machas** and **Playa Chinchorro**, north of the city (good for beginners), and at **La Ex Isla Alacrán**. For surfing lessons and equipment rental, try Yoyo Surf School, T058-311120, www.surfschool.cl. English spoken, best to call before 0900.

Swimming
The best beach for swimming is **Playa Chinchorro**, north of town (bus 24). **Playa Las Machas**, further north, has strong currents. Buses 7 and 8 run to beaches south of town; the first 2, **La Lisera** and **El Laucho**, are both small and mainly for sunbathing. **Playa Brava**, also south, is popular for sunbathing but is too dangerous for swimming.
    There's an Olympic pool with a diving pool as well in **Parque Centenario**, Tue-Sat; bus No 5A from 18 de Septiembre.

Tennis
Club de Tenis Centenario, Av España 2640. Open daily.

Tour operators
Most of the following offer local tours and trips to the altiplano at similar prices: city tour US$16; Valle de Azapa US$20; Parque Nacional Lauca, 1 day US$35, 2 days US$100 including food and accommodation; Parque Nacional Lauca and the Salar de Surire, 3 days US$180. Parques Nacional

Lauca and Isluga and the Salar de Surire, 4 days, ending in Iquique or Arica, US$280.

Some agencies pay up to 25% commission to hotels and *residenciales* that refer travellers; to get a lower price form a group of 5 or 6 travellers and negotiate direct with agencies. Make sure that tours advertised as, say, 2 days are 2 full days and do not leave in the afternoon. Shop around as not all operators have the full variety of tours leaving on any specific day. Very few tours leave on Mon. If you want an English-speaking guide you may have to book a couple of days ahead and be prepared to pay a little extra.

Andean Duncan Tours, Yungay 343, Dept 13, T058-314829, www.andeanduncantour. blogspot.com. Interesting day tours geared towards the cruise ship market, including archeological tours, birdwatching, traditional villages and the altiplano. English spoken. Recommended.

Clinamen Safaris y Expediciones, Sotomayor 361, piso 2, T058-232281, www.clinamen.cl. Bespoke small-group expeditions (maximum 3 people) to the Altiplano. Guide Christian Rolf speaks fluent English, German and French.

Geotour, Bolognesi 421, T058-253927, www.geotour.cl. Good altiplano tours.

Latinorizons, Bolognesi 449, T/F058-250007, www.latinorizons.com. Specializes in tours to Lauca and the other altiplano national parks. Not cheap, but one of the better agencies. English and French spoken. Recommended.

Parinacota Expeditions, Thompson y Bolognesi, T/F058-256227, www.parinacota expediciones.cl. One of the oldest operators in Arica. Reasonable reports.

Raices Andinas, Paseo Thompson, local 21, T/F058-233305, www.raicesandinas.com. Well-designed 2- to 4-day trips to the altiplano for 2-6 people, plus bespoke longer trips. Tours generally involve a fair amount of walking as well as contact with local people in the villages. More expensive than most but definitely worth it. English and French usually spoken in the office, though most guides speak Spanish only. Highly recommended.

Ruta de las Aceitunas, Manual Castillo Ibaceta 3689, T/F058-244485, www.rutadela aceituna.com. Day tours of Arica and Azapa valley including an olive oil processing plant.

Suma Inti, Gonzalo Cerda 1366, T058-225 685, www.sumainti.cl. Tours to the altiplano. Recommended guide Freddy Torrejón.

Turismo Lauca, Thompson 200 y Bolognesi, T/F058-252322, www.turismolauca.cl. The biggest of the altiplano agencies. OK for 1-day tours. Not the best option for multi-day trips.

Vientos del Norte, Prat 430, of 1, T058-231331, www.vientosdelnorteadventure.cl. Another small operator offering trips to the Altiplano. English spoken. Good reports.

Valle de Azapa p262
Golf
18-hole course, daily except Mon.

⊕ Transport

Arica p259, map p260
Air
Arica airport, 18 km north of city, Chacalluta, T058-211116. Flights to **La Paz**, with LanChile; to **Arequipa**, Sky; **Santiago**, Sky and LanChile all via Iquique (some via Antofagasta), book well in advance; to **Lima**, LanPerú and others from Tacna (Peru), enquire at travel agencies in Arica.

Airline offices LanChile, Prat 391, T058-251641, www.lan.com; Lloyd Aéreo Boliviano, P Lynch 371, T058-216411; Sky, 21 de Mayo y Sangra, T600-600 2828, www.skyairline.cl.

Bicycle/motorbike
Many hostels hire out bikes. Otherwise try the tour operators in Bolognesi and Thompson. **Bicicletas Wilson**, Diego Portales 1479, repairs, parts, sales, ATB specialists. Recommended.

Pablo Fernández Davils, El Salitre 3254, T058-212863, for motorbike repairs.

Bus

Local City buses run from Maipú, US$0.60. *Colectivos* run on fixed routes within city limits, US$0.80 per person (US$1 per person after 2000). To reach **Valle de Azapa**, take a yellow *colectivo* from outside the international bus terminal or from P Lynch y Chacabuco, US$1.50.

Long distance There are 2 terminals, both northeast of the centre at Av Portales y Santa María, reached by many buses, *colectivos* (including No 8 and 18, US$0.80) and taxis, US$2 (terminal tax US$0.40).

The main terminal is for national services and services to La Paz with Chilean companies. Next door is the terminal for *colectivos* to Tacna and Bolivian services to La Paz. It is advisable to arrive 30 mins before departure for all services.

Apart from the following, bus company offices are located at the bus terminals: **Buses Gutiérrez**, Esteban Ríos 2140, T058-229338; **Buses La Paloma**, Germán Riesco 2071 (bus U from centre); **Bus Lluta**, Chacabuco y V Mackenna; **Litoral**, Chacabuco 454, T058-254702. **Martínez**, 21 de Mayo 575, T058-232265;

To **Antofagasta**, 11 hrs, US$20-32; to **Calama**, 10 hrs, US$21, several companies, most at night; to **San Pedro de Atacama**, daily 2200, 11½ hrs, US$25; to **Iquique**, frequent, 4½ hrs, US$10, also *colectivos*, several companies, all with offices in the terminal; to **Santiago**, 30 hrs, several companies, US$50-85 (most serve meals though these vary in quality; generally better on more expensive services; student discounts often available); to **La Serena**, 23 hrs, US$40-75; to **Viña del Mar** and **Valparaíso**, 29 hrs, US$55. Note that all southbound luggage is carefully searched for fruit prior to boarding and is then searched again at Cuya on the Pan-American Highway. If you are travelling south of Iquique on an evening bus you may well have to get off the bus in the middle of the night.

Car

Car hire from **American**, Gral Lagos 571, T/F058-257752; **Avis**, Chacabuco 314, T058-584820, occasional offers; **Cactus**, Baquedano 635, loc 40, T058-257430, reasonable service; **GP**, Copacabana 628, T058-252594, good reports; **Hertz**, Baquedano 999, T058-231487, reliable; **Klasse**, Velásquez 760, piso 2, Loc 25, T058-254498. good deals.

Hertz provides the most reliable vehicles but check any rental vehicle for jack and lug wrench, and check the condition of the fan belt (often dry and cracked) and spare tyre.

It is periodically forbidden to take fruit products south of Arica: vehicles may be searched at Cuya, 105 km south, and at Huara, 234 km south. There are service stations between the Peruvian border and Santiago at Arica, Iquique, Pozo Almonte, Oficina Victoria, Tocopilla, Oficina María Elena, Oficina Blanco Encalada, Chuquicamata, Calama, Carmen Alto, Antofagasta, La Negra, Agua Verde, Taltal, Chañaral, Caldera, Copiapó, Vallenar, La Serena, Termas de Socos, Los Vilos, then every 30 km to the capital.

Hitchhiking

It's not easy to hitch south: try **Terminal del Agro** off the Pan-American Highway (trucks leave Mon, Thu and Sat before 0700) and the **Copec station** opposite (reached by bus from Arica marked 'Agro' or *colectivo* No 8). To hitch up to the altiplano, try the Bolivian truck centre at the mouth of the Lluta valley.

Taxi

Taxis generally charge US2 between any 2 points in the city, but ask first as there are no meters. Try **Radiotaxis Chacalluta**, T058-254812, for journeys to/from the airport.

Into Peru *p262*
Car

Crossing to Tacna with a hire car can be difficult; the hire firm **Klasse** (see Arica, above) can arrange the paperwork for this.

Colectivo

Regular service from the international terminal in Arica, Diego Portales 1002, to **Tacna**, 1½ hrs, drivers take care of all the paperwork. Bargaining is fierce. Chilean operators generally charge US$4 per person, while Peruvians charge US$3. Supply and demand means that lower prices than these are often on offer. A bus from the terminal, US$2, takes much longer than a *colectivo*.

Train

There is a regular service to the centre of **Tacna**; Arica train station is on Maximo Lira, by the port, and trains leave Mon-Sat 0900 and 2000, 1½ hrs, US$2. Return from Tacna Mon-Sat 0600, 1600. To be safe, buy your ticket at least a day in advance and arrive early. It is interesting to note the different attitudes to border defence adopted by the Chilean and Peruvian governments.

Into Bolivia *p263*
Bus

There are 3 or 4 buses daily between Arica and **La Paz**, via the border towns of **Chungará** (Chile) and **Tambo Quemado** (Bolivia), 8-10 hrs: Humire, Tue-Fri at 0900, US$23; Geminis, Mon, Wed, Fri 1000, US$23 without lunch; ChileBus, daily 1000, US$23; Transalvador, Tue, Thu, Sat, 0900, US$18. If you are going to Putre, these will drop you off 4 km away.

Paloma runs services from Arica to **Putre**, daily, 0700, US$6, via several villages. Book the day before and arrive half an hour early. Services to Putre are also run by Buses Guttierez, Wed, Fri 0630, Sun 2000, leaving from their own office but in theory passing outside the international bus terminal.

Humire buses also runs services from Arica to **Visviri**, Tue and Fri at 1030, US$12, driving often erratic, from where you can take a jeep across the border to **Charaña**. From Charaña, buses to **La Paz** leave before 1000, US$6, 6 hrs.

Hitchhiking

The Chungará border post is a good place for hitching to La Paz; truck transport leaves in the afternoon. Trucks from Arica to La Paz rarely give lifts, and in any case are excruciatingly slow, but another place to try is at the Poconchile control point, 37 km from Arica.

---

❶ Directory

Arica *p259, map p260*
Banks Several all along the pedestrian part of 21 de Mayo, some with ATMs open 24 hrs. *Casas de cambios* are bunched around Colón and 21 de Mayo. **Consulates** Bolivia, Lynch 270, T058-231030; Peru, 18 de Septiembre 1554, T057-231020, T058-231020; Germany, Prat 391, of 101, T058-254663. **Internet and telephone** Several in centre. **Language schools** SW Academy of Arts and Languages, 21 de Mayo 483, T058-258645, www.spanishinchile.blogspot.com. Intensive Spanish classes, Recommended.
Laundry Lavandería A Kilo, Santa Isabel shopping centre, US$6 per 5 kg; Lavandería La Moderna, 18 de Septiembre 457, US$4 per kg, open Sat till 2200. **Medical services** Hospital 18 de Setiembre 1000, T058-232242. **Post office** Prat 375 to send parcels abroad, contents must be shown to Aduana (1st floor of post office), Mon-Fri 0800-1200, packaging sold but take your own tape. CONAF, MacKenna 820, T/F058-250570, Mon-Fri 0830-1730.

Altiplano national parks

→ Colour map 1, A2.

In the Andes and stretching from the border with Bolivia, Parque Nacional Lauca is one of the most spectacular national parks in Chile. Declared a Biosphere Reserve by UNESCO, it is renowned for its bird life, but is equally remarkable for the extraordinary views of snow-capped volcanoes set against the backdrop of Lago Chungará, one of the world's highest lakes, and the profusion of vicuñas and viscachas that live here. The brilliant quality of the light gives colours an intensity that is not easily forgotten and there are many deserted tracks across the altiplano that provide a unique sense of the space and beauty of one of the world's last great wildernesses.

South of Parque Nacional Lauca are three further parks, covering areas of the western range of the Andes. They are best visited from Arica or Putre, as this permits acclimatization in Putre (Colchane and Enquelga, the alternatives, are too high). Furthermore, during the winter months, moving from north to south means you will not have the sun in your eyes as you travel. Tours in this area, lasting two or four days, can also be arranged from here. Guides in Putre charge a fixed price per vehicle per day, so for groups of three or four, arranging a tour from here can be better value than from Arica. ▶▶ For listings, see pages 275-278.

In and outs

Getting there and around Access to Parque Nacional Lauca is easy as Route 11, the main Arica–La Paz road, runs through the park. In January and February, during the rainy season, and in August, when snowfall can occur, some roads in the park may be impassable; check in advance with **CONAF** or the *carabineros* in Arica or Putre. Maps are available from the **Instituto Geográfico Militar** in Santiago. Much of the water in the park is drinkable but you should take bottled water as well.

Parque Nacional Lauca ⊖⊘⊛⊙▲⊖⊙ pp275-278.

Situated 145 km east of Arica, the park covers 137,883 ha and includes a large lake, **Lago Chungará**, a system of smaller lakes, the **lagunas Cotacotani**, and lava fields. Ranging in altitude from 3200 m to four peaks of over 6000 m, Lauca brings significant risks of *soroche*, or altitude sickness (unless you are coming from Bolivia). Because of the extreme height, it is best to rise in stages, spending a night in Putre before going on to Lago Chungará; for this reason one-day tours from Arica are not the best way of seeing the park.

Often, when climbing the road from Arica, it may seem as though the weather is overcast; but vehicles soon gain altitude, climbing through the mist into a sort of lost world above, where the sky is a piercing blue colour and you can gaze down at the grey clouds huddled in the valley as if looking into a different plane of reality. On the way from Arica, at Km 90, there is a pre-Inca *pukará* (fortress) and, a few kilometres further, there is an Inca *tambo* (inn).

Putre

Putre is a scenic Aymará village, 15 km west of the park entrance at 3500 m, and provides an ideal base for exploring and acclimatization. Situated at the base of **Volcán Tarapacá** (Spanish name Nevadas de Putre; 5824 m), it is surrounded by terracing

Lauca National Park

Although the park lies very close to the Atacama Desert, its altitude ensures it receives more rain, which creates a fairyland of volcanoes and highland lakes surrounded by brilliant-green wetlands and vast expanses of puna grassland. The Río Lauca rises near Lago Chungará, then laces slowly through the park leaving marshy cushion bogs and occasional raceways and providing an array of habitats for the varied wildlife of the altiplano.

The camelids are the stars of the park; thousands of domesticated llamas and alpacas, as well as the dainty, graceful, wild vicuña, which now number over 18,000. The charming viscacha, seemingly a long-tailed rabbit, but in fact belonging to the chinchilla family, can be seen perched sleepily on the rocks in the mornings, backside toward the rising sun. Pumas, huemules (deer), foxes, skunks and armadillos are the more elusive mammals, some nocturnal, occupying the more remote reaches.

Lauca birdlife is spectacular, with over 120 species either resident or migrant here. Lago Chungará is home to more than 8000 giant coots, distinguished by their bright orange legs, never-ending nest building and primordial cackling. In addition to coots, ducks and grebes, the wetlands provide a fine habitat for the puna plover, the rare diademed sandpiper plover, the puna ibis, Andean species of avocet, goose and gull, and an assortment of migratory shorebirds. Occasionally, three species of flamingo can be seen at once: the Andean, the James (locally called *parinas*) and the more common Chilean flamingo.

Trips through the drier grasslands can produce glimpses of the puna tinamou, always in groups of three, and the puna rhea, seen in October and November with 20 or 30 miniatures scooting along behind. Passerines occupy all the habitats in the park, some to 5000 m and above. There are also Sierra finches, black siskins, earthcreepers, miners, canasteros, cinclodes, tit-spintails – new names for most birders. And in the skies above, keep your eyes peeled for Andean condors, mountain caracaras, aplomado falcons, black chested buzzard eagles and buteo hawks.

dating from pre-Inca times, which is now used for cultivating alfalfa and oregano. It has a church dating from 1670. The main street, Baquedano, has several shops, restaurants and *residenciales*, and there is a tourist information office on the plaza that will help arrange tours (some English is spoken) but is otherwise not particularly useful. There is also **CONAF** ① *Tte del Campo s/n, in theory open daily 0900-1300, 1400-1730, although the rangers are often out on rounds.* Information on the parks can be obtained here as well as bookings for the CONAF *refugios* on the altiplano. The village, with a population of 1200, is a good centre for hiking: an extensive network of trails lead to numerous villages in the mountains, which provide great opportunities to explore, for those with the necessary time and fitness. In the vicinity, there are four archaeological sites with cave paintings up to 6000 years old. About 11 km east by road are the hot springs of **Jurasi** ① *US$2*, with very hot water, a red mud bath, and views of vicuñas and alpacas. Transport can be organized in Putre. Weather can be poor in January and February, with fog and rain.

Acclimatization for the altiplano

Unless you are entering Chile from Bolivia, the high altitude of the altiplano encountered in the national parks presents specific health problems for the traveller. The risks should not be underestimated; anyone with circulation or respiratory problems should avoid the area. Visitors to the park are advised to spend at least one night, preferably more, in Putre before moving on to higher altitudes. Drinking lots of water and/or *mate de coca* is also advised to compensate for the loss of body fluid. You should, of course, take it easy, limiting exercise before you get that familiar headache associated with *soroche* (altitude sickness), avoid smoking and take steps to get as much fresh air as possible, particularly if spending the night in a *refugio*. In popular *refugios* there can be six to 10 people breathing the same air all night in a small room: to avoid the 0300 headache that often develops in such conditions leave a window open and keep the water bottle nearby. Sleeplessness is a common first-night problem but is not a cause for concern. One-day trips to the national park from Arica cannot really be recommended, either for health or for enjoyment: what should be an unforgettable trip amid incredible scenery can become an unpleasant endurance exercise in a minibus full of passengers all suffering from the dreaded *soroche*.

To minimize symptoms the following tips should be followed during the day before climb to the altiplano:
Eat plain food, avoiding anything that could be hard to digest such as shellfish or rich sauces.
Do not eat any dairy products or drink any fizzy drinks. A glass of wine is fine but travelling to the altiplano with a hangover is a recipe for disaster.
Take lip balm, sunblock, a sun hat, woolly hat and windproof clothing with you.

Exploring the park

From Putre, the road continues to climb and soon enters the park. Some 23 km from Putre is the *sector* **Las Cuevas**, where there is a path and a wooden bridge leading to some rustic thermal springs with water at 40°C. Vizcachas are a common sight. Near here there is a turning south past a *chaku* (corral for llamas) to Cerro El Milagro, a hill ablaze with an incredible range of colours. Back on the main road, past the Cuevas there is a CONAF ranger station. **Parinacota** (4392 m), a small village of whitewashed adobe houses, lies 26 km into the park and 41 km from Putre on two ancient trading routes, one from Potosí to Arica and the other from Belén into Bolivia. The interesting **17th-century church** – rebuilt in 1789 – has frescoes, silver religious objects and the skulls of past priests. Señor Sipriano keeps the key: ask for him at the kiosks and make sure you leave a donation. The **CONAF** office ① *0900-1200, 1230-1700*, which administers the national park is also here. There is a small shop in Parinacota with basic supplies, but most of the handicrafts sold in Parinacota are from Bolivia or Peru: a better place to buy locally made products is **Chucuyo**, 36 km further east, where local residents weave and knit from their own high-quality alpaca wool.

Cerro Guaneguane (5300 m) can be climbed from Parinacota; ask one of the villagers to accompany you as a guide (and pay them). There is also a path to the **Lagunas de Cotacotani**, a walk that would make a good day hike. CONAF maintains a nature trail that covers most plant and bird habitats, beginning at the CONAF pond in Parinacota and ending back in the village. Some 20 km southeast of Parinacota is **Lago Chungará**, one of the highest lakes in the world, at 4512 m, a must for its views of the Parinacota, Pomerape, Sajama and Guallatire volcanoes. Overlooking the lake, there is a CONAF *refugio* and campsite; vicuñas, llamas and alpacas can be seen grazing nearby. From here, it is 3 km to the Chilean passport control point at Chungará and 10 km to the Bolivian border at Tambo Quemado. The border can also be reached via an unpaved road from Parinacota to Visviri, 90 km further north. ▶▶ *See pages 263 and 264 for border crossing information.*

Heading south ◯◯◯◯ *pp275-278.*

A dirt road (A235) turns south off the Arica–La Paz highway, 1 km east of **Las Cuevas**, park-ranger post. It is signed to Chilcaya and Colchane and ends at Huara on the Pan-American Highway, near Iquique (see page 250). There is no public transport on this route and between Las Cuevas and Isluga; the only traffic you will generally see is the occasional tour guide with his group and the odd truck from the Borax plant (see below). The road is open all year round but, between December and February and in August, it may be impassable because of deep mud and water, which can wash out the bridges. If you are planning to travel then, you will find a spade useful. A 4WD is essential; take sleeping bags and stock up on fuel, drinking water and food for emergencies.

Although many maps show roads descending from the altiplano from Surire to the Pan-American Highway and from Colchane to Camiña, do not be tempted to follow them. These roads are terrible in the dry season, dangerous and impassable in the rainy season; if stranded you could wait weeks for help to arrive. The only safe routes between the altiplano and the Pan-American Highway are the international route to Arica through Parque Nacional Lauca (see page 271), from Colchane to Huara (see page 250), and from the Salar de Huasco to Pica or Pozo Almonte.

Reserva Nacional Las Vicuñas

Split off from Parque Nacional Lauca in order to permit mining, this reserve, reached by Route A235 (entrance free), stretches across 209,131 ha, most of it rolling altiplano at an average altitude of 4300 m. The reserve is bisected by the Río Lauca, along which riverine vegetation alternates with *puna tola* (an upland plant) and grasslands, and many camelids can be seen. Keep an eye open, too, for condors, rheas and migrating peregrine falcons. **Mina Choquelimpie** (not operating), one of the world's highest gold and silver mines, can be reached by a 7-km detour (clearly marked) off Route A235. The park administration is in **Guallatire**, a village 96 km south of Las Cuevas at the foot of the smoking Guallatire Volcano (6060 m); the village has a lovely 17th-century altiplano church and a *carabinero* control post. At Km 139, the road reaches the Salar de Surire.

Monumento Natural Salar de Surire

Situated at 4300 m and covering 17,500 ha, the Salar de Surire is a desolate, spectacular drying salt lake split into two sections. The first, with windy and sulphurous thermal springs (together with picnic site) and a year-round population of 12,000 to 15,000 flamingos of three species (nesting season is January) is protected and administered by CONAF. It is open all year, but see advice above. Administration is in **Surire**, 45 km south of Guallatiri and 138 km south of Putre. The other half of the *salar* is mined for borax; sometimes Surire may be reached by getting a ride in a borax truck from Zapahuira, a road junction at Km 100 on the road from Arica to La Paz.

Parque Nacional Volcán Isluga

This park includes some of the best volcanic scenery of northern Chile and covers 174,744 ha at altitudes above 2100 m. Although the lower parts of the park, at its southwestern end, lie in the hills of the *precordillera*, the heart of the park is situated between **Laguna Aravilla** with its flamingos and the village of **Isluga**, where there is a beautiful 18th- century Andean church and bell tower. Route A235 crosses the park, from the northern entrance, 40 km south of Surire, to the southern near Isluga. Northeast of Isluga under the smoking **Volcán Isluga** (5501 m) is the village of **Enquelga**, where Aymaran weavers can be seen working in the sand behind wooden wind breaks. This is also the location of the park administration but there are seldom *guardaparques* there. Just 1 km south of the village is a turn-off to some warm natural thermal springs with changing rooms and a picnic area. Three other peaks over 5000 m in the park are Quimsachata (5400 m), Tatajachura (5252 m) and Latamara (5207 m). Wildlife varies according to altitude; there are large numbers of camelids and birds but fewer than in Parque Nacional Lauca.

South of the park is the border village of Cochrane with basic services and transport to Iquique and Oruro in Bolivia. From here a mostly good road runs southwest 180 km to join the *Panamericana* at Huara. Alternatively a *ripio* road continues south. After 20 km or so there is a turning to the right leading to a hill of giant *Cardón* cactuses. Towering up to 8 m, they flower in September and produce an edible fruit, like a cross between a kiwi and a prickly pear. The road south passes the village of Cariquima and continues on to Lirima through a pass at over 5000 m. This road is new and may not be marked on some maps, but has some of the most spectacular views of the altiplano over the shrubland below. Lodging is available in Lirima, and there are thermal springs 6 km west, with accommodation with a thermal pool in each room. The road from Lirima continues south for 53 km, with microplants turning the flat terrain a radioactive green, before arriving at the **Salar de Huasco**. On the west side there is a radio station in contact with Iquique, and a *refugio* has been built. The view of the sun or full moon rising here is spectacular. In theory it is possible to continue south on the altiplano to Ollagüe and on to San Pedro, but there are also decent roads west to Pica or Pozo Almonte.

◉ Altiplano national parks listings

For Sleeping and Eating price codes and other relevant information, see Essentials pages 35-42.

● Sleeping

Note that many villages marked on maps in the altiplano are uninhabited. Do not expect even the most basic services. CONAF *refugios* should be booked and paid for in advance in the regional office in Arica, T058-201201. CONAF *refugios* do not provide sheets or blankets.

Parque Nacional Lauca *p271*
D Casa Barbarita, Parinacota, T058-300013. Offers 2 bedrooms, cooking facilities, heating, naturalist library.

F CONAF refugio, Lago Chungará. 8 beds, cooking facilities, camping, price per person, reserve in Arica or Putre. Take a sleeping bag, food and candles.

F CONAF refugio, Parinacota. Many beds, cooking facilities. Price per person. Not open to the general public. Bookings only taken for study groups and other delegations.

F-G Residencial Copihue de Oro, Chucuyo. Price per person. 1 room, 4 beds, no showers, meals served.

F-G Residencial Doña Mati, Chucuyo. Price per person. 1 room, 5 beds, no shower, meals served.

F-G Sra Francisca, Parinacota. Price per person. 3 beds, cooking facilities.

F-G Sr Gumercindo Gutiérrez, Lagunillas, 10 km north of Parinacota on road to Visviri, turn left near lake. Price per person. Accommodation and guide.

F-G Uta Maillko, Parinacota. The name means 'home of the condor' in Aymara. Price per person. Dorm, home-cooked Aymara food.

Putre *p271*
AL Las Vicuñas, Baquedano 80, T058-231028, www.chileanaltiplano.cl. Half board, bungalow-style, heating, restaurant, does not accept credit cards. A little overpriced.

A-B Chakana Mountain Lodge, Cochrane s/n, T09-974 59519, www.la-chakana.com. Also shared rooms, **E** per person. Modest clean cabins on the edge of town with pleasant views. English spoken, good breakfast, lots of info. Best choice in town if you don´t mind the walk.

B-C Kukulí, Canto y Baquedano, T09-916 14709. Offering 10 decent rooms, all with their own bathroom. With breakfast. Nothing special but a good choice, given other options in the town centre.

C-D Cali Hostal, Baquedano 399, T09-853 61242, krlos_team@hotmail.com. **E-F** singles. Rooms with or without bath, breakfast extra. The owners are friendly, their sons less so.

C-D Residencial La Paloma, O'Higgins 353, T099-919 79319, lapalomaputre@ hotmail.com. Same owners as the bus company. Some rooms with bath, no heating, also restaurant. Decent standard for the price, but a bit noisy and rather impersonal.

C-D Residencial Rosamel. **E** singles. Clean, pleasant, with hot water and restaurant.

Camping
Sra Clementina Caceres, blue door, Lynch, Camping in the garden and lunch.
Turismo Taki, Copaquilla, 45 km west of Putre (100 km east of Arica). Campsite with a restaurant (serving home-made bread). English and Italian spoken. Also runs trips to nearby *pukarás* (fortress), the Inca *tambo* (inn) and cemetery and the Inca trail, which connected the highlands with the coast.

Reserva Nacional Las Vicuñas *p274*
There is accommodation for up to 7 people at the park administration in Guallatire, T058-250570. Imperative to reserve at least 5 days in advance or it will be closed.
F Don Julián, Guallatire. Price per person. Basic accommodation, with half board, hot water and electricity.

F-G Sra Clara Blanca, 1 km east off A235, 10 km after Chuquelimpie turn-off. Price per person. An Aymaran weaver offers overnight accommodation, food typical of the region and allows travellers to help with llamas and alpacas.

Monumento Natural Salar de Surire *p274*
F CONAF refugio, Surire, 8 km past the borax mine. 15 beds, heating and cooking facilities. Sleeping bags necessary. Advance booking at CONAF in Arica advised (see Directory, page 270). Price per person.

In an emergency, food and lodging will almost always be given at the **Borax mine**.

Camping
Polloquere, 17 km south of Surire. No facilities, no water. Price per site.

Parque Nacional Volcán Isluga *p275*
D Residencial El Volcán, Encuelga. Basic. **F** per person.
F CONAF refugio, Encuelga. 6 beds and cooking facilities, reservation in Arica advised (see Directory, page 270). Price per person.

There are also several basic *residenciales* in Colchane, which lies 6 km south of the southern entrance (see page 251).

🍴 Eating

Parque Nacional Lauca *p271*
🍴-🍴 **Restaurant Kuchumarka**, Baquedano s/n, Putre. Serves local specialities including alpaca and vegetarian options, popular with tour groups.

† **Restaurant Los Payachatas**, Chucuyo. Tasty alpaca dishes.

† **Rosamel**, Latorre y Carrera on the Plaza, Putre. Excellent-value set menus served by its flamboyant owner.

Reserva Nacional Las Vicuñas *p274*

† **Restaurant Sánchez** (no sign), 1 block from *carabineros*, Guallatire. Good lunch stews in an altiplano truckstop.

⊛ Festivals and events

Putre *p271*

Nov Feria de la voz Andina takes place every year, attracting top Andean groups, as well as cultural exhibitions. If going, book accommodation in advance.

O Shopping

Putre *p271*

Buy all food for the park in Putre, which has markets where bottled water, fresh bread, vegetables, meat, cheese and canned foods can be obtained. The **Cooperativo** on the plaza is usually cheapest. Fuel (both petrol and diesel) is available from the **Cali** and **Paloma** supermarkets; expect to pay a premium. **Sra Daria Condori**'s shop on C O'Higgins sells locally made *artesanía* and naturally coloured alpaca wool.

▲ Activities and tours

Parque Nacional Lauca *p271*

Tours are offered by many agencies in Arica (see page 267), daily in season, according to demand at other times, from US$35 with light breakfast and lunch; all 1-day tours make Parinacota their last stop. It is better to spend more than 1 day in the park; longer tours are available. You can leave the tour and continue on another day as long as you ensure that the company will collect you

when you want (tour companies try to charge double for this).

Climbing

The best season for climbing is Aug-Nov; avoid Jan-Feb. Permits are required for climbing Parinacota, Pomerape, Tarapacá and Guallatire volcanoes; these can be obtained from the governor's office in Putre. The procedure is routine (passport required) but expect a delay of 1 or 2 days. To obtain a permit in advance, contact **Departamento de Fronteras y Limites** (DIFROL), Banderas 52, piso 5, Santiago, T02-6794200, listing the mountains you wish to climb. **Arturo Gómez**, who lives next to the Lipigas propane shop in Putre, is a climbing guide and local plant expert.

Putre *p271*

Birding Alto Andino, Baquedano 299, T09-9282 6195, www.birdingaltoandino.com. Specialist birdwatching tours of the area and also walking tours along the Camino del Inca. English spoken, owner is an Alaskan biologist/naturalist, recommended.

Tour Andino, Baquedano s/n, T09-011 0702, www.tourandino.com. Run by recommended tour guide and mountain guide Justino Jirón. There are several other guides, some more knowledgeable than others.

⊖ Transport

Altiplano national parks *p271*

Bus

La Paloma leaves Arica from its own terminal daily at 0700 for **Putre**, US$5, returning from Putre at 1330. The bus often leaves full, so buy your ticket the day before. The journey takes you through several villages on the way. A similar service is run by **Buses Gutiérrez**, Wed, Fri 0630, Sun 2000, returning Mon, Wed, Fri 1700, leaving from their own office but in theory passing outside the international bus terminal.

Alternatively, any bus heading to **La Paz** (page 270) will drop you on the main road, 3 km from Putre. Hitching from here is usually easy with the army or *carabineros*. If you walk, take it easy until you have acclimatized to the altitude.

Jurasi *colectivos*, T058-222813, leave Arica daily at 0700, picking up at hotels, US$12.

Buses Humire run services 1030 Tue and Fri from Arica to **Parinacota**, US$8, slow.

Car
For 5 or more, the most economical proposition is to hire a vehicle in Arica but take at least 1 spare fuel can with a tightly fitting cap. During the climb from Arica, you should stop several times to release excess pressure in fuel cans. For tyre repairs, ask for **Andrés** in Putre. For the Parque Nacional Lauca, 4WD and antifreeze are essential; if you wish to cross from the park into Bolivia you will need a permit from the hire company.

Hitchhiking
Most trucks for Bolivia pass **Parinacota** between 0700-1100. Hitching back to Arica is not difficult and you may be able to bargain with one of the tour buses.

The **Salar de Surire** can sometimes be reached by getting a ride in a borax truck from Zapahuira, Km 100 on the Arica–La Paz road; trucks run sporadically depending on rainfall. The drop-off point is on the mine side of the Salar, 30 km from the hot springs.

⊕ Directory

Putre *p271*
Bank There is a Banco Estado on the plaza, it has an ATM (MasterCard only) but it is inside the bank, access Mon-Fri 0900-1400. **Internet** On the plaza. **Medical services** The Posta, at the east end of Baquedano, will treat you for a small charge if you are feeling the effects of altitude sickness. **Police** There are *carabinero* posts at Chilcaya, Guallatire, and Chungará as well as in Putre and Colchane.

Contents

Footprint features

Central Valley

At a glance

◓ **Getting around** Good bus and train links between cities. Buses also serve national parks in season. Private transport or tours required to visit most vineyards.

◉ **Time required** A couple of days to get a sense of the region and to visit a few wineries. Many more days can be spent trekking in national parks or relaxing on the coast in summer.

◐ **Weather** Hot summers inland. Cooler on the coast. Winter rains are stronger the further south you go.

✖ **When not to go** This area can be visited all year round, although the national parks are often snowed out in winter.

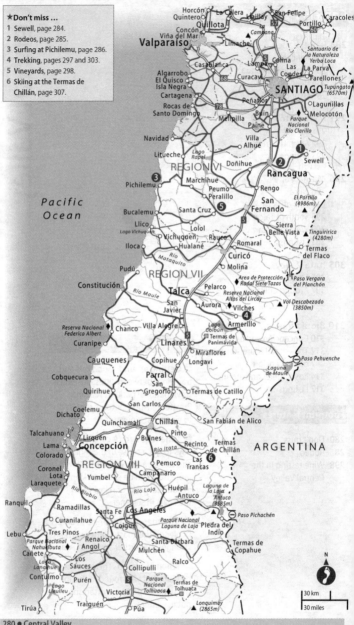

★Don't miss ...
1 Sewell, page 284.
2 Rodeos, page 285.
3 Surfing at Pichilemu, page 286.
4 Trekking, pages 297 and 303.
5 Vineyards, page 298.
6 Skiing at the Termas de Chillán, page 307.

Pacific Ocean

Valparaíso

SANTIAGO

REGION VI

Rancagua

REGION VII

Talca

Curicó

Linares

Concepción

REGION VIII

Los Ángeles

ARGENTINA

30 km
30 miles

N

The Central Valley is the heart of Chile. Stretching from just north of Santiago south to the Río Biobío, this wonderful region climbs from secluded tracks and beaches along the coast to the high Andes in the east, with the fertile valley itself in between.

On clear days, the snowy mountains can easily be seen from the coast, across the woods, fields and vineyards of Chile's agricultural heartland. It is here that the most enduring images of Chilean village life can be found: *huasos* (cowboys) with their long spurs, green valleys speckled with grazing horses and whitewashed houses in colonial style, hinting at that bygone age before cars and motorbikes sounded the death knell for the horse.

Background

The peoples of the Central Valley did not prove as fierce as their Mapuche neighbours; and were conquered by the Incas in about 1470. On his second visit to Chile, Pedro de Valdivia led an expedition southwards, founding Concepción in 1550 and a further seven cities south of the Río Biobío. The Mapuche insurrection of 1598 and the Spanish defeat at Curalabo in 1599 led the Spanish to withdraw north of the Río Biobío and concentrate their efforts in the Central Valley.

Here, the land and its inhabitants were divided up among the colonists to create the forerunner of the hacienda, which was to dominate social and economic life in Chile. The hacienda was a self-contained unit, producing everything it needed. There were no towns in the area but, from the 1740s, the Spanish crown attempted to increase its control over the region by founding settlements, including Rancagua (1743), San Fernando (1742), Curicó (1743), Talca (1742), Cauquenes (1742) and Linares (1755).

After Independence, the Río Biobío continued to be the southern frontier of white settlement until, in 1862, Colonel Cornelio Saavedra led an army south to build a line of 10 forts, each 4 km apart, between Angol and Collipulli. Following the occupation of the coast around Arauco in 1867, another line of forts was built across the Cordillera de Nahuelbuta. By 1881, the railway from Santiago had reached Angol, from where Chilean troops set out on the final campaign against the Mapuche.

Today, the Central Valley is the agricultural heartland of Chile, transformed in the past 30 years by the growth of commercial export agriculture and wine production. Since 1974, over 1,500,000 ha of trees have been planted in Regions VII, VIII and IX, mostly Monterrey Pine. Climatic conditions for forestry are particularly favourable inland from Arauco. The coast between Dichato and Arauco has also seen growth in fishing and fish-processing since the 1980s, while inland, swathes of vineyards are testament to Chile's importance as a producer of fine wines. Despite the decline of coal mining in the 1980s, Concepción and the surrounding area are an important industrial region in Chile.

Geography and climate

Encompassing three of the administrative regions of Chile, Regions VI (O'Higgins), VII (Maule) and VIII (Biobío), the Central Valley is a wide depression located between the Andes to the east and the Cordillera de la Costa to the west. The Andes gradually lose height as they continue southwards, although there are a number of high peaks east of Rancagua: Alto de los Arrieros (5000 m), El Palomo (4986 m), Tingiririca (4280 m). The northern parts of the region enjoy a Mediterranean climate, with a prolonged dry season, but with more rain than Santiago. Rainfall increases gradually from north to south, until around Concepción there is usually some rainfall each month. The Central Valley receives less rain than the coastal mountains, but temperatures vary more inland than in coastal areas. The coastal range is generally under 500 m, but south of the Río Biobío it forms a range of high peaks known as the Cordillera de Nahuelbuta. Five major rivers cross the Central Valley: the Rapel, Mataquito, Maule, Itata and Biobío.

Rapel Valley

→ Colour map 3, B3.

The damming of the Río Rapel has created Lago Rapel, a very popular destination for Santiaguinos taking their summer holidays. There are numerous small and pleasant towns, and several large fundos (farms) south of the town of Rapel, in an area of green hills and stunted thorn trees. Open roads by the coast have wonderful views of the high Andes east of Rancagua, while the beach at Pichilemu is one of the best in Chile for surfing. ▸ *For listings, see pages 287-290.*

Rancagua ●❶❶❶❸❶❶❶ ▸ pp287-290.

The capital of Región VI, Rancagua lies 82 km south of Santiago, on the Río Cachapoal. The city was founded in 1743 and in October 1814 was the scene of an important battle during the Wars of Independence, when Bernardo O'Higgins and his 1700 Chilean patriots were surrounded in the centre of the town by 4500 Royalist (pro-Spanish) troops. O'Higgins managed to break out and escape but was forced into exile in Argentina, only to return within a few years finally to defeat the Spanish forces in Chile (see also page 573).

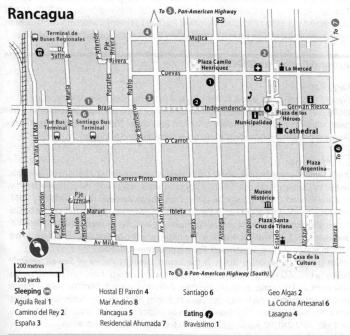

Rancagua

Sleeping 🛏		
Aguila Real 1	Hostal El Parrón 4	Santiago 6
Camino del Rey 2	Mar Andino 8	
España 3	Rancagua 5	**Eating 🍴**
	Residencial Ahumada 7	Bravíssimo 1

Geo Algas 2	
La Cocina Artesanal 6	
Lasagna 4	

Ins and outs

Getting there Rancagua is accessible by bus and train from Santiago (both hourly). There are also connections to the towns further south, especially Talca, Chillán, Concepción, Temuco and Puerto Montt (several daily).

Getting around While the centre of Rancagua is compact, some of the outlying barrios are quite a distance and you may wish to take one of the numerous *colectivos*.

Tourist information ① *Germán Riesco 277, T072-230413, info_ohiggins@sernatur.cl, English spoken. Also municipal office in the Municipalidad on Plaza de los Héroes.*

Sights

At the heart of the city is an attractive tree-lined plaza, the **Plaza de los Héroes** and several streets of single-storey colonial-style houses. In the centre of the plaza is an equestrian statue of O'Higgins. The double-spired cathedral on the south side of the plaza was restored in the 1860s, the original building having been destroyed in the battle of Rancagua, together with most of the other buildings around the plaza. There are several plaques in the city centre marking the sites of the battle and a diagram in the plaza shows the disposition of the troops. One block north is the **Merced** church, from where O'Higgins commanded his beleaguered forces. It dates from 1758 but has been restored several times. The main commercial area lies along Avenida Independencia, which runs west from the plaza towards the bus and rail terminals. **Museo Histórico** ① *Estado 685 y Ibieta, T/F072-221524, www.museorancagua.cl, Tue-Fri 1000-1800, Sat and Sun 0900-1300, US$1.50 (Tue free),* housed in a colonial mansion, contains collections of religious art and late 19th-century furniture. There is also a **Casa de la Cultura** ① *corner of Milán and Cachapoal, T072-230976, daily 0830-1330, 1500-1700,* directly south of Plaza de Los Héroes, which houses temporary exhibitions. In the station there is a small gallery with paintings by local artists for sale.

Around Rancagua ⊕⊘⊕⊕ » pp287-290.

Lago Rapel

West of Rancagua, this lake is 40 km long and feeds the Rapel hydroelectric plant. Most facilities at this popular summer resort are on the east shore around El Manzano, the main town, while the tourist information office is in Las Cabras. There are watersports at Bahía Skorpios, including windsurfing, yachting, waterskiing and fishing.

East of the city

The **El Teniente** copper mine, one of the biggest in the country, is 67 km east of Rancagua. Owned by **Codelco**, it can only be visited by prior arrangement with the company. Nearby, on a private road above El Teniente, is the small **Chapa Verdeski resort** ① *T072-217651, www.chapaverde.cl, lift tickets US$26 per day Mon-Fri, US$35 per day Sat, Sun, ski hire US$26. There is also a small restaurant, and skiing lessons are available. Transport from Ramirez 665, Rancagua, US$12, reservations necessary.* The resort is owned by **Codelco**, but is open to the public in season (June to September). There is no accommodation.

Also part of the Codelco facility is the former mining complex of **Sewell**, recently declared a UNESCO World Heritage Site. The town with its steep stair-cased paths is now a ghost town, and the mine, unusually inverted (shafts lead upwards from the main entrance in the mountainside), which once laid claim to having the biggest underground machine room in the world, is practically deserted. Visits by guided tour only. Contact **VTS** ① *Manuel Montt 192, T072-210290, www.vts.cl.* See www.sewell.cl for more information.

Rodeo

During the summer months, rodeo is one of the most popular sports in central and southern Chile, second only to the inevitable: football. Teams (or *colleras*) of two riders on horseback compete throughout the season, culminating in the national championships in Rancagua at the end of March. Elimination rounds are held in Osorno, Temuco, San Carlos, San Fernando, Vallenar and Los Andes, but most small towns in central southern Chile have their own *media lunas* (stadia, with their own corrals and horseboxes), often used once a year only.

Rodeo owes its origins to the colonial period, when cattle roamed openly and were rounded up once annually to be identified and marked by their owners in a rodeo. Based on the traditional view that heifers need to be broken in, the modern sport of rodeo is a test of the ability of two horses and their riders to work together and control the cattle.

The event takes place inside a stockade of thick upright timbers; although now circular, this is known as a *media luna* (crescent) after the design of the early rings: at two points the walls of the ring are covered by padded sections, with a flag at either end of the section. Each *collera* competes by manoeuvring a heifer around the edge of the ring between the padded sections, stopping it at each padded section by pinning its hindquarters against the fence, before turning it in the opposite direction. This is done three times before the animal is released from the ring.

Three judges give points (on a scale of one to seven) for elegance and horsemanship. It is one of the principles of rodeo that no heifer should be put through this performance more than once; the event should come as a complete surprise to the animal.

Rodeo is a good opportunity to see traditional Chilean rural customs: the *huasos* (cowboys) wearing brightly coloured ponchos, wide-brimmed hats and carved wooden stirrups that were common in the 19th century; the fine horses, and the *cuecas* (traditional dances) that sometimes follow the main event.

South of El Teniente and 28 km east of Rancagua are the thermal springs of **Cauquenes** ① *T072-899010, www.termasdecauquenes.cl*, with a colonial hotel, visited by Charles Darwin in 1835. A bath in the springs costs US$12, massages start at US$18 and a jacuzzi costs US$24. Some 5 km north is the village of **Coya**, where the Chilean President has a summer residence, while to the south is the **Reserva Nacional Río de los Cipreses** ① *T072-297505, US$5.* Situated 50 km southeast of Rancagua, the reserve covers 36,882 ha of the valley of the Río de los Cipreses at altitudes ranging from 900 m to 4900 m. Park administration is at the entrance at the north end of the park.

San Fernando and around

San Fernando lies on the Río Tingiririca, 51 km south of Rancagua. Founded in 1742, it is capital of Colchagua Province and a service town for this fertile valley. There is a small local museum in the **Casa Patronal de Lircunlauta** ① *Jiménez 1595 y Alameda, T072-717326, closed Mon, US$3,* a 17th-century colonial mansion, with local history exhibits.

From San Fernando, a road runs east towards the *cordillera* and divides: the southern branch of the road goes to the resort of **Sierra Bellavista**, a private *fundo* where many Santiago businesspeople have holiday houses, and where there are rodeos in October and November. The northern branch, a treacherous 75 km, runs to the **Termas del Flaco** near the Argentine border, where there are camping facilities, *cabañas* and several hotels and *hospedajes*. The thermal springs (US$3) are only open in the warmer months (October-Easter). Some 500 m from the Termas del Flaco are '*Las huellas de dinosaurios*', dinosaur footprints preserved in the rock, dating from over 120 million years ago. There are good one-day treks starting from the baths, and a four-hour horse ride leads to the site of the Uruguayan plane crash immortalized in the film *Alive*.

Heading west ⊖⊙⊘⊗⊚ ›› *pp287-290*.

West of San Fernando, tracks branch off the main road to Pichilemu southwards through quiet hill country towards Lago Vichuquén (see page 293). Dry thorn trees gradually give way to more fertile land, with the first signs of *copihues* and forests, while ridges high above the valleys provide beautiful routes for cyclists, walkers and horse riders.

Santa Cruz
Fifty kilometres southwest of San Fernando, Santa Cruz is surrounded by some of the country's best vineyards and is the site of the offices of the **Ruta del Vino del Valle de Colchagua** ① *Plaza de Armas 298, of 6, T072-823199, www.rutadelvino.cl* Also in the town is **Museo de Cochagua** ① *Errázuriz 145, T072-821050, www.museocolchagua.cl, Tue-Sun 1000-1800, US$7, concessions US$2-5*, an excellent small museum with exhibits on local history and prehistory as well as winemaking. In summer, a steam train links Santa Cruz with many of the wineries in the Colchagua valley. For reservations, see www.trendelvinochile.cl.

Pichilemu
Pichilemu is a coastal resort with a great many hotels and *residenciales*, 120 km west of San Fernando. It was founded by Agustín Ross Edwards in the 19th century in the style of a European resort. The town is on two levels, one at sea level and the main town above. In summer it is a popular destination for Chileans. During the rest of the year there is a steady flow of foreigners who come to enjoy some of the best surf in South America. This is reflected in the number of shops along the main drag selling surfing accessories.

There is a small go-kart-style motorbike circuit on the south end of the *costanera*, and further along there are three surf schools that also hire equipment. Among several beaches is **Punta Los Lobos**, where international surfing competitions are held. The former train station, made of wood in 1925, is a national monument, and now home to the tourist information office. There is also a small museum, the **Museo del Niño Rural de Ciruelos**, a few kilometres south of town, with three rooms of interesting exhibits from the pre-Hispanic cultures of the region. Fishing is good in nearby lakes. Some 20 km southeast along a *ripio* road is **Pañul**, where interesting pottery is produced using the local clay. Nearby is a watermill, dating from 1904, which locals still use to grind their wheat into flour. It can be visited for US$1. Unless you go by taxi or with a guide, prepare to get lost on the way.

Rapel Valley listings

For Sleeping and Eating price codes and other relevant information, see Essentials pages 35-42.

Sleeping

Rancagua *p283, map p283*

AL Camino del Rey, Estado 275, T072-232314, hotelcaminodelrey@terra.cl. 4-star, suites, full facilities, showing its age a little.

AL Mar Andino, Bulnes 370, T072-645400, www.hotelmarandino.cl. New modern and comfortable hotel. Decent restaurant, business centre, pool. Best in town, though that's not much of an accolade.

AL Santiago, Brasil 1036, T072-230860, www.hotelsantiago.cl. One of the city's oldest hotels, and it is showing its age. There is a restaurant and swimming pool. Overpriced.

A Rancagua, San Martín 85, T072-232663, www.hotelrancagua.galeon.com. Drab but clean rooms with bath and TV, quiet, secure parking.

A-B Aguila Real, Brasil 1045, T072-222047, hotelaguilareal@terra.cl. Modern 3-star. With breakfast, cable TV, laundry, restaurant. Some English spoken.

B España, San Martín 367, T072-230141, noraberriosf@latinmail.com. Bath, cheaper without, central, hot water, pleasant, clean, laundry, food served.

B-C Hostal El Parrón, San Martín 135, T072-758550, www.hostalelparron.cl. New hostel in a 2-story art-deco-style house in the city centre. Rooms with bath and cable TV. Internet, patio.

C Residencial Ahumada, Mujica 125, T072-225892. **F** singles. Kitchen facilities, secure.

Lago Rapel *p284*

C Hostería La Finca, Sector La Carmen caminio Llallauquén, Km 3, T02-289 6676. Pleasant hostel with a pool and restaurant.

Camping

The eastern shore of Lago Rapel around El Manzano is lined with campsites.

Camping Punta Arenas, 3 km north of El Manzano. Basic and cheap.

East of the city *p284*

LL-L Hotel Termas de Cauquenes, Cauquenes, T072-899010, www.termasde cauquenes.cl. Housed in a colonial building. Run-down rooms need a refit. Excellent food is served in the hotel restaurant (full board available). It also has a chapel and gardens.

Camping

There is a site at **Los Maitenes**, 12 km south of the entrance to the Reserva Nacional Río de los Cipreses.

San Fernando and around *p285*

LL Hacienda Los Lingues, Panamericana Sur, Km124, 22 km north of San Fernando, www.loslingues.com. The very expensive accommodation starts at US$250 with an extra charge for breakfast or full board, and is overpriced.

L Viña Casa Silva, Hijuela Norte, T072-710180, www.casasilva.cl. Upmarket accommodation in a colonial building in this well-known vineyard North of San Fernando. Only 7 rooms. Pool, spacious grounds with pleasant views. Relaxing ambiance. Good restaurant.

B Español, Av Rodríguez 959, San Fernando, T072-711098, hotelespanol6@terra.cl. 3-star, with parking and pool.

C Imperio, Av Rodríguez 770, San Fernando, T072-714595. With breakfast and bath (cheaper without), clean, cable TV, parking.

D Pérez, Av Rodríguez 1028, San Fernando, T072-713328. **F** singles, without bath.

Santa Cruz *p286*

Prices are cheaper Apr-Dec.

LL-L Santa Cruz Plaza, Plaza de Armas 286, T072-209600, www.hotelsantacruzplaza.cl. 4-storey building in colonial style on the Plaza. There is a gym, pool and spa as well as a fine restaurant and casino. Spacious rooms and luxurious suites, though some bathrooms on the small side. Disabled-friendly. Tours and visits to wineries arranged. Occasional internet-only specials.

L Viña la Playa, Camino a Quelluque s/n, Peralillo, T02-6759111, www.hotelvina laplaya.cl. Luxurious Lodge some 30 km northwest of Santa Cruz. Pool, tennis court, good meals. Attentive staff.

L-AL Vendimia, Ismael Valdés 92, T072-822464, www.hotelvendimia.com. Filled with antiques, clean, spacious rooms and very attentive staff who can help arrange wine tours. Good breakfast. Recommended.

AL-A Parador de la Viña, Camino Los Boldos s/n, T072-825788, www.paradordelavina.cl. Lovely guesthouse in the heart of wine country, some 2 km west of Santa Cruz. Friendly staff, spacious rooms, good breakfasts. Recommended if you have your own transport.

A Hostal Casa Familia, Los Pidenes 421, T072-825766, www.valledecolchagua.cl/casafamilia. **B** singles. Charming upmarket bed and breakfast. Some rooms a on the small side.

B Hostal Santa Cruz, JJ Carvacho 40, T072-822046, hostalsantacruz@terra.cl. **D-E** singles. Standard rooms with TV and bath. Internet access, Wi-Fi, tours arranged.

Pichilemu *p286*
There are dozens of very cheap places to stay.

A-B Rocas del Pacífico, Gaete 244, T072-841346, www.hotelrocasdelpacifico.cl. With breakfast. Spacious rooms with good bathrooms. Some rooms on the top floor have a decent sea view. Comfortable, if a little plastic.

B Chile-España, Ortúzar 255, T072-841270, www.chileespana.cl. **C** singles. Good option close to the beach. Ample space for storing surf boards. The rooms with bath have cable TV and electric blankets. There is also a café.

B-C Asthur, Ortúzar 540, T072-841072, www.hotelasthur.cl. Traditional hotel dating from the 1930s but redesigned since then. Small comfortable rooms with bath and cable

TV. The best rooms back on to the terrace with extensive views to the north. There is a pleasant bar/breakfast area where meals are served in summer and an unheated pool outside. Recommended.

B-C Surf Hostal, Eugenio Díaz Lira 164, Playa Infernillo, T072-842350, www.pichilemu surfhostal.cl. **E** per person in shared rooms. Comfortable rooms with bath. Some with sea view. Dutch-owned. Good surfing information.

B-C Waitara, Av Costanera 1039, T072-843026, www.waitara.cl. **E** singles. Cabins on the seafront with fully equipped kitchens. Also slightly cheaper rooms with bath. Discounts for longer stays.

D Bahía, Ortúzar 262. **F** singles. With breakfast, clean.

Camping
Pichilemu has several campsites, but at US$12 per site, these are more expensive than the cheaper *residenciales*.

🍴 Eating

Rancagua *p283, map p283*
🍴 **Bravissimo**, Astorga 307. Recommended for ice cream.
🍴 **Geo Algas**, Independencia 677, 2nd floor. Vegetarian food.
🍴 **La Cocina Artesanal**, O'Carrol 60. Traditional meat and seafood dishes.
🍴 **Lasagna**, west end of plaza. Good for bread and *empanadas*.

San Fernando and around *p285*
🍴 **Club Social San Fernando**, Rodríguez 787. Good local food.
🍴 **Restaurante La Carreta**, Rancagua 759. Traditional cuisine.
🍴 **Arenspastycaf**, Chillán y Manuel Rodríguez. The best sandwiches for miles around.

Santa Cruz *p286*
🍴🍴 **Veta Bistro**, Rafael Casanova 570, T072-822401, In a big old house attached to a vineyard and with surprising views over fields

of vines to the rear. Menu that uses traditional ingredients in novel interpretations. Recommended.

Pichilemu p286

¶¶ **La Balaustra**, Ortúzar 289, T072-842458. Has the most innovative menu in town, ranging from lamb ribs with mashed quínoa to fish in garlic sauce. Also serves coffee, sandwiches, pancakes and fresh juice.
¶ There a number of basic restaurants serving fish and traditional Chilean dishes.

◯ Bars and clubs

Rancagua p283, map p283
La Notta, Illanes 303-A. Bar with restaurant.
Pub Restaurant Puerto Girón, Bueras 358. Expensive.
Varadero, O'Carrol 1109. Disco.

San Fernando and around p285
Toscano Pub Disco, Quechereguas 966. Fri and Sat night disco.

Pichilemu p286
Many people come here for the nightlife; there is a good atmosphere after dark, with a dozen or so discos open in summer, and weekends off season.
Delerium Tremens, Ortúzar 215. One of a growing number of micro-brew pubs in Chile.

✸ Festivals and events

Rancagua p283, map p283
Beginning Feb Beans are the most important staple food for *campesinos* in the area and are celebrated in the Festival del Poroto (Bean Festival).
End Mar National Rodeo Championships are held in the Complejo Deportivo, north of the centre, US$18 per day. There are plenty of opportunities for purchasing cowboy items; watch out especially for the fantastic spurs, which are much more important to horsemanship in Chile than elsewhere in Latin America.

Santa Cruz p286
First weekend in Mar Fiesta de la Vendimia (harvest celebration) is held in Santa Cruz around the town's main plaza, where local wine and food can be sampled.

◯ Shopping

Rancagua p283, map p283
There's a shopping mall at Cuevas 483, and a supermarket at **Hipermercado Independencia**, Av Miguel Ramírez 665.

◯ Transport

Rancagua p283, map p283
Air
Airline offices in town include Iberia, Lacsa and United Airlines, Cuevas No 744, T072-220288; LanChile, Astorga 223B, T600-562 2000.

Bicycle
Bike spares at **Gustavo Sepúlveda**, Bueras 481, T072-241413.

Bus
Main terminal in Rancagua is at Doctor Salinas y Calvo just north of the market but most buses for **Santiago** leave from the TurBus terminal at Calvo y O'Carrol. Many services from further south stop on the Pan-American Highway, 2 km outside town.

Local There are too many local buses to list here, but destinations include **Lago Rapel** with Sextur, T072-231342, or Galbus T072-230640, every 20 mins, US$3; **Pichilemu**, US$5 one-way, many companies; and **Termas Del Flaco**, US$20 return with Buses Amistad, T072-229358, booking required 2 days in advance.

Long distance Frequent services to **Santiago**, 1¼ hrs, US$5. To **Valparaíso** and **Viña del Mar**, TurBus, US$9. To **Talca**, 3 hrs, US$6. To **Chillán**, 5 hrs, US$10. To **Concepción**, 5hrs, US$12. To **Temuco**, 9 hrs, US$15-25. To **Valdivia**, 10 hrs, US$16. To **Puerto Varas** and **Puerto Montt**, 12 hrs, US$20-32.

Car

Car hire with **Weber Rentacar**, Membrillar 40, of 2, T072-226005, autorentasweber@tie.cl; **Comercial O'Carrol**, O'Carrol 1120, T072-230041, ocarrolrentacar@yahoo.com. For parts try **Aucamar**, Brasil 1177, T072-223594, and several others around Brasil 1100-1200, although the selection and prices are better in Santiago.
Automóvil Club de Chile, Ibieta 09, T072-239930, F239907.

Train

Rancagua station is at Av La Marina, T072-230361, www.efe.cl. Mainline services between **Santiago** and **Chillán** stop here. Also regular services to/from **Santiago**, 1¼ hrs, and **San Fernando**, 35 mins, on Metrotren, 10-19 a day, US$4.

East of the city *p284*

The thermal springs of **Cauquenes** are served by 5 daily buses from Rancagua with Buses Termas, US$2.50, or a *colectivo* from Rancagua market.

San Fernando and around *p285*
Bus

Many companies have buses to **Santiago**, US$6, including Andimar, T072-711817 and Pullman del Sur, T072-714076. To **Pichilemu**, US$5, with Nilahue, T072-711937 and Galbus, T072-712983; to **Termas del Flaco**, US$14 return, with Amistad, T072-710348, Andibus, T072-711817, and others. Lots of competition to the south, with services running as far as **Chiloé**, US$25, with Cruz del Sur, T072-710348, and most intermediate destinations with TurBus, T072-712923, and Buses Lit, T072-711679.

Train

The station is at Quecheregua s/n, T072-711087. Metrotren runs 10 trains daily to **Santiago**, US$4.50.

Pichilemu *p286*

Andimar and Nilahue buses to **Santiago**, 4 hrs, US$7.

Directory

Rancagua *p283, map p283*
Banks Exchange at Cambios Afex, Av Campos 363, open every day; also several banks on Independencia. **Internet** There are several around the Plaza de Armas.

Mataquito Valley

→ Colour map 3, C2.

The Río Mataquito, formed by the confluence of the Ríos Lontué and Teno, flows through the peaceful heart of Chilean wine country, reaching the Pacific at a wide and serene estuary near Iloca. The Andes can clearly be seen from the cliffs above the largely deserted coast.
» *For listings, see pages 293-295.*

Curicó ⊜⊘⊘⊛⊜❶ » *pp293-295.*

Curicó, which means 'black water' in the Mapuche language, lies between the rivers Lontué and Teno, 54 km south of San Fernando. Founded in 1743, it is the only town of any size in the Mataquito Valley and is the service centre for the region's vineyards. The bustling town centre offers good views towards the mountains and a friendly atmosphere after dark.

Curicó

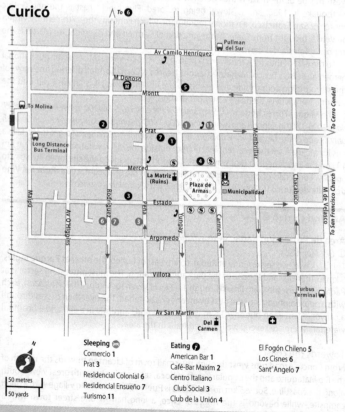

Sleeping ⊜	Eating ❼	El Fogón Chileno 5
Comercio 1	American Bar 1	Los Cisnes 6
Prat 3	Café-Bar Maxim 2	Sant'Angelo 7
Residencial Colonial 6	Centro Italiano	
Residencial Ensueño 7	Club Social 3	
Turismo 11	Club de la Unión 4	

50 metres
50 yards

Ins and outs

Getting there Curicó is easily accessible by bus from Santiago (many times daily). There are also some connections to the towns further south, especially Talca, Chillán, Temuco and Puerto Montt (several daily).

Getting around While the centre of Curicó is quite compact, some of the outlying barrios are quite a distance away, and you may wish to take one of the numerous *colectivos*.

Tourist information Gobernación Provincial ① *Plaza de Armas, Mon-Fri 0900-1330, 1600-1800, helpful, has street map.* **CONAF** ① *Gobernación Provincial building, piso 1, Plaza de Armas, daily 0900-1430.*

Sights

The **Plaza de Armas** is surrounded by about 40 Canary Island palms and has lovely fountains with sculptures of nymphs, black-necked swans and a monument to the Mapuche warrior, **Lautaro**, carved from the trunk of an ancient beech tree. The steel **bandstand** was built in New Orleans in 1904 and is now a national monument. On the western side of the plaza is the church of **La Merced**, which was badly damaged by an earthquake in 1986, and is slowly being restored. Five blocks east is the neo-Gothic church of **San Francisco**, a national monument, which contains the 17th-century Virgen de Velilla, brought from Spain. At the junction of Carmen and Avenida San Martín is the imposing **Iglesia del Carmen**.

To the east of the city is the Avenida Manso de Velasco, with statues of various national heroes, and also a bust of Mahatma Gandhi. Nearby is **Cerro Condell** offering fine views of the surrounding countryside and across to the distant Andes; it is an easy climb to the summit, from where there are a number of short walks.

The **Miguel Torres bodega** ① *5 km south of the city, T075-564100, www.migueltorres.cl, daily 1000-1700 in autumn and winter, daily 1000-1900 in spring and summer, tours in Spanish only,* is one of the biggest wine *bodegas* in Chile and well worth a visit. To get there, take a bus for Molina from the local terminal or from outside the railway station and get off at Km 195 on the Pan-American Highway. There's a good restaurant on the site, open Tuesday to Sunday. For details of other *bodegas* and vineyards in the area, contact the **Ruta del Vino del Valle de Curicó** ① *Prat 301-A, T075-328967, www.rutadelvinocurico.cl.*

Around Curicó ⬤⬤ ⏵⏵ pp293-295.

Area de Protección Radal Siete Tazas
① *Oct-Mar, US$4.*

This park is in two sectors, one at **Radal**, 65 km east of Curicó, the other at **Parque Inglés**, 9 km further east and the site of the park administration. The most interesting sector is at Radal, where the Río Claro flows through a series of seven rock 'cups' (the *siete tazas*), each with a pool emptying into the next by means of a waterfall. The river then passes through a canyon, 15 m deep but only 1.5 m wide, which ends abruptly in a cliff and a beautiful waterfall. There are several well-marked trails in the area.

Towards the coast

From Curicó, a road runs west through the small town of **Licantén** towards the mouth of the Río Mataquito and the popular resort of **Iloca**, set in a wide bay with great views south along the coastline. Some 5 km north of Iloca is **Puerto Duao**, a fishing village with a good campsite, while beyond is the resort of **Llico**, a long narrow one street town with a pleasant dark sand beach and windsurfing facilities. It is reached either by the coastal route or by an unpaved inland road, which branches off at Hualañe, 74 km east of Curicó.

Six kilometres west of Licantén a bridge crosses the Río Mataquito, leading to a road south along the coast to **Putú**, past kilometres of rolling sand dunes, a kind of mini Sahara. Further south, the road reaches the Río Maule, where a ferry crosses to Constitución (see page 300).

Lago Vichuquén and around
Just east of Llico and 114 km west of Curicó, Lago Vichuquén is a large, peaceful lake, set in a bowl surrounded by pinewoods. It is very popular with the wealthy and with watersports enthusiasts and, although parts of the eastern shore of the lake are inaccessible by road, there are full facilities on the western shore, particularly at Aquelarre. The nearby town of **Vichuquén** has some well-preserved colonial architecture and a recommended small **museum** ① US$2, set in a beautiful house with a portico, in the town centre.

Just north of Lago Vichuquén, 120 km west of Curicó, is the **Reserva Nacional Laguna Torca** ① administration and campsite 4 km east of Llico, open Sep-Apr. The reserve covers 604 ha and is a natural sanctuary for over 80 species of bird, especially black-necked swans and other water fowl. To get there take any bus from Curicó to Llico and get out near the administration.

⊙ Mataquito Valley listings

For Sleeping and Eating price codes and other relevant information, see Essentials pages 35-42.

⊖ Sleeping

Curicó *p291, map p291*
AL Turismo, Carmen 727 y Prat, T075-543440, www.hotelturismocurico.cl. Curicó's best hotel, suites, pleasant garden, good restaurant with an extensive wine list.
A Comercio, Yungay 730, T075-310014, www.hotelcomercio.cl. 3-star, newly refurbished with pool, gym, restaurant, Wi-Fi and car hire.
C Prat, Peña 427, T075-311069, hotelpratcurico@yahoo.es. **C-E** singles. Rooms with or without bath. Pleasant patio with grapevines and fig trees, friendly, clean, hot water, laundry facilities, breakfast extra, parking. Recommended.
C-D Residencial Colonial, Rodríguez 461, T075-314103, resicolonial@terra.cl. **F** singles. Clean, patio, friendly, some rooms with bath. Full board available. Good value.

C-D Residencial Ensueño, Rodríguez 442, T075-312648. **D-E** singles. Basic lodging, some rooms with bath. Includes breakfast.

Area de Protección Radal Siete Tazas *p292*
C Hostería La Flor de la Canela, Parque Inglés, 3 km west of Siete Tazas, T075-491613. Breakfast extra, good food. Good value. Highly recommended.

Camping
There's a dirty campsite near the entrance with a shop, US$3 per person. Inside the park is Camping Las Catas, US$19 per site, no shop.

Towards the coast *p292*
B Hotel Iloca, Besoaín 221, Iloca, T075-1983751, www.hoteliloca.cl. **C-D** Singles. Recently restored, with bath. Breakfast, good views. Several *cabañas*, many open in summer only.
B-C Hospedaje El Capricho del Corazón, 35 km west of Curicó on road to Hualañe and Iloca, T075-1976646. Swiss-run, English,

French and German spoken, tours arranged. Recommended.

C Residencial Miramar, Carrera Pinto 48, Llico, T075-400032. At the far end of town. Good seafood restaurant, small rooms with bath, excellent value, full board available.

C-D Hospedaje Marilla, opposite the *carabineros*, Iloca. **F** singles. Simple but clean and friendly. Some rooms with bath.

Camping

El Peñón, 6 km south of Iloca, T072-471026, T02-6336099. US$15 per site. Phone ahead for reservation.

La Puntilla, 2 km north of Iloca, T09-9741 5585. US$12 per site, also *cabañas*.

Lago Vichuquén and around *p293*

A Hostería Vichuquén, Lago Vichuquén, T075-400018, www.lagovichuquen.cl. Spacious rooms with views across the lake. Well equipped, with good food. Rents out bicycles and kayaks.

A Marina Vichuquén, T075-400265, www.marinavichuquen.cl. Fully equipped resort, good. Lots of activities including watersports, tennis, mountain biking, horse riding.

Camping

Vichuquén, east shore of lake, T075-400062. Full facilities.

El Sauce, north shore of lake, T075-400203. Good facilities, US$25 per site.

🍴 Eating

Curicó *p291, map p291*

There are several seriously cheap restaurants with varying standards of cleanliness outside the market on C Donoso. Hotel Turismo and Comercio both have decent restaurants.

🍴🍴-🍴 Club de la Unión, Plaza de Armas. Innovative food in elegant surroundings. Recommended.

🍴 American Bar, Yungay 647. Open daily morning to evening. Real coffee, small pizzas.

🍴 El Fogón Chileno, M Montt 399. For meat and wines.

🍴 Los Cisnes, Rodríguez 1186. *Parilladas* and cheaper *almuerzos*.

🍴 Café-Bar Maxim, Prat 617. Light meals, beer and wine.

🍴 Centro Italiano Club Social, Estado 531. Good, cheap meals.

🍴 Sant' Angelo, Prat 430. Excellent patisserie, also serving good-value set lunches.

🍸 Bars and clubs

Curicó *p291, map p291*

The following are fairly basic drinking holes, and are likely to be shut during the day:

Bar Deportivo, Montt 446.

Crazy Horse, Manso de Velasco.

Scram Pub, Velasco 451.

✹ Festivals and events

Curicó *p291, map p291*

Mid-Mar Fiesta de la Vendimia (wine harvest festival) has displays on traditional winemaking and the chance to try local food and wine. A similar event is also held in nearby Molina at the same time.

🚌 Transport

Curicó *p291, map p291*

Bus

The **main bus terminal** is on Prat y Maipú. Local buses, including those to coastal towns as well as some long-distance services use **Terminal Plaza**, Prat y Maipú. TurBus stop on M De Velasco; their office is also on M De Velasco, 1 block south. Pullman del Sur have their own terminal at Henríquez y Carmen. Many southbound buses bypass Curicó, but can be caught by waiting outside town.

To **Santiago** several companies, frequent, 2½ hrs, US$6. To **Talca**, regular, 1 hr, US$2. To **Temuco**, 7 hrs, US$12-24. To **Puerto Varas** and **Puerto Montt**, 11 hrs, US$18-30. To **Llico**, Buses Díaz, regular in summer, 2 daily off season, 3 hrs, US$3.50. To **Iloca**, every hr in summer, less frequent off-season, 2 hrs, US$3.50.

Car
Automóvil Club de Chile, Chacabuco 759, T075-311156.

Motorbike
Motorcycle spares from **Chaleco López Motos**, San Martín 171, T075-316191.

Train
The railway station is at the west end of Prat, 4 blocks west of Plaza de Armas, T075-310028, www.efe.cl. To/from **Santiago**, 6 a day, 2 hrs, US$10-18; to/from **Chillán**, 6 a day, 2¼ hrs, US$12-22.

Area de Protección Siete Tazas *p292*
Access by car is easy as the road through the park is paved. If you're travelling by public transport, take a minibus from Terminal Plaza to **Molina**, 26 km south of Curicó; from Molina 4 buses run daily to the **Parque Inglés** in summer (last return 1700), 3 hrs, US$4. There's also a daily bus from Curicó in summer at 1330 Mon-Sat (returns 0745) and at 0700 Sun (returns 1900), 4½ hrs.

Directory

Curicó *p291, map p291*
Banks Major banks located around Plaza de Armas. Casa de Cambio, Merced 255, Local 106, no TCs. **Internet and telephone** Several in the city centre. **Laundry** Ecológico, Yungay 411; Lavacentro, Yungay 437; expensive, good. **Post office** Plaza de Armas.

Maule Valley

→ *Colour map 3, C2.*
The Río Maule flows for 240 km from Laguna Maule in the Andes to the sea at Constitución. Its waters have been dammed east of Talca, providing power for the region and creating Lago Colbún. The river itself is particularly beautiful near the coast at Constitución.
↠ *For listings, see pages 301-304.*

Talca ⬤🅿️🄿🄰🄸❄🔺🄰🄲 ↠ *pp301-304.*

Situated on the south bank of the Río Claro, a tributary of the Maule, Talca lies 56 km south of Curicó. The most important city between Santiago and Concepción, it is a major manufacturing centre and the capital of Region VII, Maule. Founded in 1692, it was destroyed by earthquakes in 1742 and 1928. Today, it is a busy, dusty town, with a lively atmosphere day and night.

Ins and outs

Getting there Talca is easily accessible by bus and train from Santiago (both many times daily). There are also frequent connections to the towns further south, especially Chillán, Concepción, Temuco and Puerto Montt (several daily).

Getting around Talca is a sizeable city, and some of the barrios are quite a distance from the centre. Buses and *colectivos* ply the routes to these areas, with their destinations marked in the window.

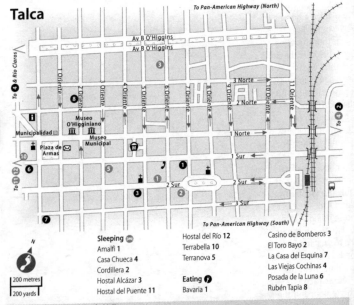

Sleeping	Hostal del Río 12	Casino de Bomberos 3
Amalfi 1	Terrabella 10	El Toro Bayo 2
Casa Chueca 4	Terranova 5	La Casa del Esquina 7
Cordillera 2		Las Viejas Cochinas 4
Hostal Alcázar 3	Eating	Posada de la Luna 6
Hostal del Puente 11	Bavaria 1	Rubén Tapia 8

Tourist information **Sernatur** ① *1 Poniente 1281, T071-233669, infomaule@sern atur.cl, winter Mon-Fri 0830-1730, summer Mon-Fri 0830-1930.*

Sights

In the **Plaza de Armas** are statues that were looted by the Talca Regiment from Peru during the War of the Pacific. Just off the plaza is a **colonial mansion** that belonged to Juan Albano Pereira, tutor to the young Bernardo O'Higgins, who lived here as a child. The house was later the headquarters of O'Higgins' Patriot Government in 1813-1814, before his defeat at Rancagua and is now **Museo O'Higginiano** ① *1 Norte 875, T071-210428, www.dibam.cl/sdm_moba_talca, Tue-Fri 1030-1300, 1430-1845, Sat and Sun 1000-1300, free.* In 1818, O'Higgins signed the declaration of Chilean Independence here: the room Sala Independencia is decorated and furnished in period style. The museum also houses a collection of regional art. The **Casino de Bomberos** ① *2 Sur y 5 Oriente,* has a small museum room with two old fire engines, old firefighting equipment and, for those with an interest in little-known conflagrations, information on important fires in Talca's history.

About 8 km southeast of the centre is **Villa Huilquilemu** ① *T071-242474, Tue-Fri 1500-1830, Sat 1600-1830, Sun 1100-1400, US$1, San Clemente bus,* a 19th-century hacienda, now part of the Universidad Católica del Maule, housing four museums of religious art, handicrafts, agricultural machinery and wine. It is also the office for the **Ruta de Vino del Valle del Maule** ① *T071-246460, www.valledelmaule.cl.*

East of Talca ◉▲◉ ▸▸ *pp301-304.*

Lago Colbún and around

From Talca a good paved road runs 175 km southeast along **Lago Colbún** and up the valley of the Río Maule, passing through some of the finest mountain scenery in Chile to reach the Argentine border at **Paso Pehuenche** ① *open Dec-Mar 0800-2100; Apr-Nov 0800-1900.* On the Argentine side the road continues to Malargüe and San Rafael.

At the western end of Lago Colbún is the town of **Colbún**, from where another road leads south and west to eventually join the Pan-American Highway at Linares. After 5 km it passes through **Panimávida**, where there are thermal springs. While at Panimávida, try the local 'Bebida Panimávida', made from spring water, still or sparkling, flavoured with lemon or raspberry. Artesanal goods are better and cheaper here than in Linares. Further on towards Linares is **Quinamávida**, 12 km south of Colbún, where there are more thermal springs, and an upmarket hotel.

Vilches and around

Some 63 km east of Talca, Vilches is the starting point for the climb to the volcanoes **Quizapu** (3050 m) and **Descabezado** (3850 m). For walks on Descabezado Grande and Cerro Azul, ice axe, crampons and an experienced guide are required. There is also great horse riding in this area. ▸▸ *See Activities and tours, page 303.*

Situated just east of Vilches, the **Reserva Nacional Altos del Lircay** ① *US$3,* covers 12,163 ha and includes peaks up to 2228 m as well as several small lakes. Much of the park is covered with mixed forest including lenga, ñirre, coigüe, roble, raulí and copihue. Near the entrance are the administration and visitor centre; nearby are the **Piedras Tacitas**, a stone construction supposedly built by the indigenous inhabitants of the region, and the **Mirador Del Indio** from where there are fine views over the Río

Wine tasting in the Central Valley

The following is a list of vineyards that can be visited independently. Advance notice is often required, especially for large groups.

Elqui Valley

Falernia, Ruta 41, Km 46, Vicuña, T051-412260, www.falernia.com.
Cavas del Valle, Ruta R-485, Km 14.5, Montegrande, T051-451352, www.cavasdelvalle.cl.

Limarí Valley

Casa Tamaya, Camino Quebrada Seca, Ovalle, T053-686014, www.tamaya.cl.
Tabalí, T02-477 5535, www.tabali.cl.

Aconcagua Valley

Errázuriz, Calle Antofagasta s/n, Panquehue, San Felipe, T034-590139, www.errazuriz.com.
San Esteban, Av La Florida 2200, San Esteban, T034-481050, www.vse.cl.
Von Siebenthal, O'Higgins s/n, Panquehue, San Felipe, T034-591827, www.vinavonsiebenthal.com.

Casablanca Valley

Casas Del Bosque, Hijuelas 2, Ex Fundo Santa Rosa, Casablanca, T02-377 9431, www.casasdelbosque.cl.
Indómita, Ruta 68, Km 72, T032-275 4400, www.indomita.cl.
Veramonte, Ruta 68, Km 64, T032-232 9934, www.veramonte.cl.

Viña Mar, Ruta 68, Km 72, T032-275 4300, www.vinamar.cl.
William Cole, Camino Tapihue, Km 4.5, Casablanca, T032-215 6606, www.williamcolevineyards.cl.

San Antonio Valley

Casa Marín, Camino Lo Abarca Km 4, San Antonio, T02-334 2986, www.casamarin.cl.
Matetic, Fundo Rosario, Lagunillas, T02-232 3134, www.mateticvineyards.com.

Maipo Valley

Almaviva, Av Santa Rosa 821, Paradero 45, Puente Alto, Santiago, T02-270 4200, www.almavivawinery.com.
Aquitania, Av Consistorial 5090, Peñalolén, Santiago, T02-791 4500, www.aquitania.cl.
Chocalán, Parcela 16, Sta Eugenia de Chocalán, Melipilla, T02-437 4763, www.chocolanwines.com.
Concha y Toro, Virginia Subercaseaux 210, Pirque, T02-476 5269, www.conchaytoro.com.
Cousiño Macul, Av Quillín 7100, Peñalolen, Santiago, T02-351 4135, www.cousinomacul.cl.
De Martino, Manuel Rodríguez 229, Isla de Maipo, T02-819 2959, www.demartino.cl.
Odfjell, Camino Viejo a Valparaíso 7000, Padre Hurtado, Santiago, T02-876 2800, www.odfjellvineyards.cl.

Lircay. There are also two good hikes: to **Laguna del Alto**, eight hours via a lagoon in a volcanic crater; and to **El Enladrillado**, 12 hours, a high basalt plateau from where there are great views.

South of Talca ⬤🅿️🅰️🅾️🅱️🅲️ ≫ pp301-304.

Linares

Fifty-three kilometres south of Talca on the *Panamericana*, Linares is a peaceful town with a distinctly *huaso* feel. It boasts the remarkable **Cathedral de San Ambrosio**, built

Pérez Cruz, Liguai de Huelquén. Paine,
T02-824 2405, www.perezcruz.com.
Portal del Alto, Camino el Arpa 119,
Alto Jahuel, Buin, T02-821 9178,
www.portaldelalto.cl.
Santa Carolina, Rodrigo de Araya 1431,
Macul, Santiago, T02-450 3137,
www.santacarolina.cl.
Santa Rita, Camino Padre Hurtado 0695,
Alto Jahuel, Buín, T02-362 2520,
www.santarita.cl.
Undurraga, Camino a Melipilla Km 34,
Talagante, T02-372 2850,
www.undurraga.cl.

Cachapoal Valley
Altair, Totihue, Requinoa, T02-477 5598,
www.altairwines.com.
Anakena, Camino a Pimpinela, Requínoa,
T072-954 207, www.anakenawines.cl.
Gracia, Camino Totihue, Requínoa,
T02-240 7678, www.graciawinery.cl.

Colchagua Valley
Bisquertt, Fundo Lihueimo, Santa Cruz,
T02-756 2508, www.bisquertt.cl.
Casa Lapostolle, Camino Apalta, Km 5,
Santa Cruz, T072-321804,
www.lapostolle.com.
Casa Silva, Hijuela Norte, San Fernando,
T072-710180, www.casasilva.cl.
Estampa, Carretera del vino Km 45,
Palmilla, Santa Cruz, T02-202 7000,
www.estampa.com.

Los Vascos, Camino Pumanque Km 5,
Peralillo, T072-861220,
www.vinalosvascos.com.
Montes, Finca de Apalta, Santa Cruz,
T072-825 417, www.monteswines.com.
Montgras, Camino Isla Yaquíl, T072-822
845, www.montgras.cl.
Siegel, Fundo La Laguna, Santa Cruz,
T072-933 112, www.siegelvinos.com.
Viña Santa Cruz, Camino Lolol Km 25, Santa
Cruz, T02-221 9090, www.vinasantacruz.cl.
Viu Manent, Carretera del vino, Km 37,
T072-858 751, www.viumanent.cl.

Curicó Valley
Alta Cima, Panamericana Km 202,
T075-471 034, www.altacima.cl.
Miguel Torres, Panamericana Km 195,
T075-564 100, www.migueltorres.cl.
Millamán, Peteroa, Curicó, T02-438 0000,
www.millaman.cl.
San Pedro, Panamericana, Km 205,
T075-491 517, www.sanpedro.cl.

Maule Valley
Balduzzi, Balmaceda 1189, San Javier,
T073-322138, www.balduzziwines.com.
Casa Donoso, Camino Palmira Km 3.5, Talca,
T071-341400, www.casadonoso.com.
Gillmore, Camino Constitición Km 20, San
Javier, T073-197 5539, www.gillmore.cl.

Itata Valley
Viña Chillán, Camino Yungay Km 7, Bulnes,
T042-197 1573, www.vinachillan.cl.

between 1934 and 1967 in a Byzantine romantic style. On Letelier 572, in the middle of a row of colonial houses, is the **Museo de Arte y Artesania Nacional** ① *www.dibam.cl/ sdm_maya_linares, Tue-Fri 1000-1730, Sat 1000-1700, Sun 1200-1700, US$1, Sun free*. Here there are exhibits of local, military and prehistoric history, including a 2-ft-long decorative curved spanner, an exploded cannon, horsehair artefacts from the village of Rari, local paintings, petrified wood, old toys and everyday utensils. In the **Mercado Municipal** on Chacabuco, it is possible to buy horsehair art from Rari. Tourist information is available from the Gobernación and Municipalidad, both on the plaza.

Constitución

Lying west of Talca at the mouth of the Río Maule, Constitución is reached by road (89 km) and by a narrow-gauge railway line from Talca, which offers fine views over the wooded Maule Valley. The railway, packed with chatting locals (and as often as not their goats and chickens) is unique in Chile and offers travellers a microcosm of life in the Central Valley. It is not unusual for trains to be flagged down like buses and for the driver to stop in order to share gossip and a coffee with a farmer.

Founded in 1794, the city is situated in a major commercial logging area; there are naval shipyards here and a giant cellulose factory, whose pungent odour hangs over the town on windless days; fishing is also important. Constitución's main appeal, however, is as a seasonal seaside resort. While the town itself is relatively uninteresting, the beach, an easy walk from the centre, is surrounded by picturesque rocks, and the coast both to the north and south is beautiful.

There are good views from **Cerro Mutrún**, at the mouth of the river, accessed via Calle O'Higgins; the **Playa El Cable**, with *cabañas*, is 5 km south. For a pleasant walk or drive, take the quiet track along the south bank of the Maule 8 km east of Constitución to a disused railway bridge over the river; the bridge is open to vehicles, and has great views of the river valley.

Chanco and around

A paved road runs from Constitución along the coast, through thick forest and past a large logging factory, via deserted beaches and fishing villages to the small, peaceful town of Chanco. Chanco is famous for its cheese and its traditional colonial architecture, including the charming adobe-built **Iglesia San Ambrosia**. There is a pleasant 3-km walk to the coast and the unspoilt **Playa Monolito** The land just north of Chanco is the prettiest in this area, with rolling hills, small farmsteads and a small park: the **Reserva Nacional Federico Albert** ① *Apr-Nov 0830-1800, Dec-Mar 0830-2000, US$1*, which covers 145 ha of dunes planted with eucalyptus and cypresses in experiments to control the shifting sands. It has a visitor centre and campsite facilities.

Further south

South of Chanco are two more small resorts at **Pelluhue** and **Curanipe**, 83 km south of Constitución. One kilometre south of Pelluhue a path leads down to a hidden beach, beautiful and deserted off season (although nearby real estate projects will soon put an end to this), while Curanipe has a lovely stretch of black sand. From Curanipe a mostly paved road leads 50 km through wild country past the village of **Buchupureo** to the small seaside town of **Cobquecura**. A tranquil, friendly town with slate-roofed colonial buildings, it has a good beach, a pretty plaza, accommodation, several good seafood restaurants and well-preserved colonial-style houses. About 1 km north of the village is a long curved beach with a large colony of sea lions offshore. At low tide the beach almost extends as far as the rock on which they live and their yelps can clearly be heard. It is worth a detour to see. About 5 km to the north is an impressive *portada* or arch in the cliffs. There are also a few good surfing beaches nearby.

This coast can also be reached by paved road from Parral via Cauquenes. Just north of the road between Cauquenes and Chanco is the **Reserva Nacional Los Ruiles** ① *Dec-Mar 0830-2000, Apr-Nov 0830-1800, US$2, buses from Constitución or Cauquenes*, which covers

45 ha of native flora, including the *ruil* (*Nothofagus alessandri*), an endangered species of southern beech.

⊙ Maule Valley listings

For Sleeping and Eating price codes and other relevant information, see Essentials pages 35-42.

🛏 Sleeping

Talca *p296, map p296*

A Terrabella, 1 Sur 641, T071-226555, www.hotelterrabella.cl. The best hotel in town. Business standard with conference rooms and swimming pool. Basic English spoken.

A-B Casa Chueca, Camino Las Rastras, 4 km east of city centre, T071-1970096, www.trekkingchile.com. **E** per person in shared rooms. European-run colonial-style house with swimming pool, great views, large gardens, mountain bikes, games room. Price includes breakfast, nice rooms with private bathrooms or cheaper rooms with shared bath. Good dinner on request. Trekking and horse-riding tours organized, Spanish classes also available. English, German, French, Portuguese and Swedish spoken. Highly recommended. Closed during winter. Call for instructions on how to get there.

B Terranova, 1 Sur 1026, T071-239608, www.hotelterranova.cl. Another decent business standard with conference room, pool and sauna. Buffet breakfast.

B-C Amalfi, 2 Sur 1265, T071-239292. **D** singles. Old-fashioned, central, good breakfast, cheaper rooms do not have bath.

B-C Cordillera, 2 Sur 1360, T071-221817, www.cordillerahotel.cl. Decent no-frills hotel, serves good breakfast.

B-C Hostal del Puente, 1 Sur 407, T071-220930, www.hostaldelpuente.cl. Lovely gardens, English spoken, parking, with bath, cable TV, breakfast extra.

C Hostal del Río, 1 Sur 411, T071-510218, www. hostaldelrio.cl. Opened by the feuding brother of the owner of the Hostal del

Puente next door, and designed to be just a little better and a little cheaper. Recommended.

C-D Hostal Alcázar, 6 Oriente 1449, T071-711163. **E-F** singles. Without bath, quiet, good value.

Lago Colbún and around *p297*

LL Hotel Termas de Panimávida, Panimávida, T073-211743, www.termas depanimavida.cl. Full board and access to thermal pools. A once grand hotel now partly restored but retaining a feeling of decaying grandeur. In the grounds is a small fountain, where you can drink the sulphourous *agua de la mona*.

L Hotel Quinamávida, Quinamávida, T073-213887, www.termasdequina mavida.cl. In the hotel there are thermal baths, Turkish baths, reflexology, and massage.

Camping

There are several campsites about 12 km east of Colbún on the south shore of Lago Colbún. There are also 3 sites near Panimávida.

Vilches and around *p297*

B-C Complejo Turístico El Roble, Vilches (Sector Seminario), T071-242148/ T09-7411065, www.turismoelroble.cl. Fully furnished comfortable *cabañas* sleeping up to 6, with swimming pool. Horse-riding trips offered.

C Refugio Ecológico Biota Maule, T09-9018 7888, www.biotamaule.blog spot.com. A wooden house in the middle of a forest, with excellent value-for-money accommodation. Meals available.

Linares p298

A Hotel Turismo, Manuel Rodríguez 522, Linares, T073-210636, hturismo@123.cl. Breakfast and bath, restaurant, cable TV.

A-B Hotel Curapalihue, Curapalihue 411, Linares, T073-212516, hotelcurapalihue@tie.cl. Breakfast and bath, cable TV, conference facilities.

B-C Hotel Real, Freire 482, Linares, T073-210834, hotelrealltda@hotmail.com. With bath, without breakfast, cable TV.

E Hostal Linares, Freire 442, Linares, T073-210695. **F** singles. With breakfast.

Constitución p300

B-C Hostería Constitución, Echeverria 460, T071-671450. Overpriced and not as good as it was, but still the best equipped hotel in town. Good lunches.

There are many cheap *residenciales* on Freire 100-300 blocks, including Hostal Maule at No 152, T071-671568, www.hostalmaule.cl; Residencial Familiar at No 160, T071-672940 and Residencial Ramírez at No 209, T071-671233. Book in advance Jan and Feb.

Further south p300

LL La Joya del Mar, Buchupureo, T042-1971733, www.lajoyadelmar.com. Small boutique resort on the coast, accommodation in independent villas, excellent restaurant.

A-B Suhaila Resort, 10kkm south of Curanipe, T09-9304 9329, www.luzdelunasuhaila.cl. Comfortable cabins in an enviable setting on the coast with private access to the beach. Sauna, hot tub and pool (open to day visitors). Massages available in summer. Camping and caravan space. English, German spoken. Recommended.

B Cabañas Campomar, north of Curanipe, T073-541000, www.cabanascampomar.cl. Prices for up to 6 people, kitchen, sea views, swimming pool. English spoken.

B-C Hostería Blanca Reyes, Prat 615, Pelluhue, T073-541061, blancareyes@123mail.cl. With good restaurant, best in town.

C-D Pacífico, Comercio 509, Curanipe, T073-556016. Pleasant, clean.

C-D Piedra Negra, Prat 190, Curanipe. T073-556032. Similar. Good value.

D Residencial La Playa, Prat 510, Pelluhue, T09-9871 4538. **F** singles. Meals served. Also has *cabañas*.

🍴 Eating

Talca p296, map p296

There are many cheap restaurants in the **municipal market**, 3 blocks east of the plaza and several kiosks selling *completos* on 5 Oriente 900 block; some are open 24 hrs.

♯♯ Bavaria, 1 Sur 1370. Plastic Chilean chain serving reasonable steaks and sandwiches.

♯♯ El Toro Bayo, Camino Las Rastras, 2 km east of town, T071-247643. Closed Sun evenings. The best in the area, offering a wide and inventive menu, recommended.

♯♯ La Casa del Esquina, 1 Poniente 708. Spanish food, good.

♯♯ Los Ganaderos, Panamericana, 10 km south of Talca. Great food, a good place to stop for lunch for those with transport.

♯♯ Posada de la Luna, 1 Sur 626. Slightly upmarket restaurant with attractive garden, good seafood.

♯♯ Rubén Tapia, 2 Oriente 1339. Excellent modern cuisine. Good service and very reasonable prices.

♯ Café al Grano, Galería Zaror, local 10. Cosy, good coffee and snacks.

♯ Casino de Bomberos, 2 Sur y 5 Oriente. Good value. There is an interesting museum annexed.

♯ Las Viejas Cochinas, on the banks of the Río Claro, just over the bridge. Famous *picada* serving very good typical Chilean food. Large portions and more than reasonable prices. Lots of others nearby.

Linares p298

♯♯ Fay Chy, Rodríguez 398. Chinese.

♯♯ Las Parrillas de Linares, Lautaro 350. Typical grill.

Estadio Español, León Bustas 01242.
Traditional food.

Constitución *p300*
Some of the town's *posadas* and *hosterías*
provide meals. In addition, you should try:
El Rancho Astillero, open in summer,
on the banks of the river and accessible
only by boat. Wonderful fish cooked over
hot coals between 2 terracotta tiles.

Further south *p300*
Pelluhue is more expensive than **Curanipe**
La Joya del Mar, Buchupureo. T042-197
1733. Seafood. Deservedly known as the
best restaurant in the area.
El Quincho, Prat 560, 1 block from the
Plaza, Pelluhue. Best bet for typical Chilean
food. Generous portions.
Piedra Negra, Prat 190, Curanipe.
T073-556032. Recommended for seafood.

Cafes
Omas Küchen, Condell 823, Pelluhue.
Wonderful cakes.

🟠 Bars and clubs

Talca *p296, map p296*
Varadero, 5 Oriente 985. Good Cuban-
themed pub.
Wurlitzer, 5 Oriente 960. Deservedly
popular pub above a pool hall.

Linares *p298*
El Tablón, Ibáñez y Chacabuco. Basic bar.
Refugio, V Letelier 480. Basic bar.

🟣 Entertainment

Talca *p296, map p296*
Mainstream cinema at 1 Sur 1271 and
Sur 770. Arts cinema at 1 Poniente 685.
Also in Mall Plaza Maule, east of centre.

⚙ Festivals and events

Talca *p296, map p296*
1st week of Jan Regional folklore festival.
4 Oct Fiesta San Francisco, an important
huaso festival, takes place in Huerta del
Maule (southwest of Talca).
First week of Nov Feria del Vino
y la Viticultura (TECVIN) is enjoyable
for those with an interest in Chilean wine.
Last week in Nov Feria Regional
de Folklore y Artesanía is held at Villa
Cultural Huilquilemu.

▲ Activities and tours

Talca *p296, map p296*
Trekking Chile, see Casa Chueca, under
Sleeping, above, www.trekkingchile.com.
Excellent touring information, plus kayaking,
trekking and horse-riding trips Also run a
CO2-offset scheme.
Leonardo Cáceres Rencoret, T09-9892 3625.
Good mountain guide, works for CONAF.

Vilches and around *p297*
La Casa Chueca in Talca (see above).
2 recommended horse guides in Vilches
are **Don Pancho**, T09-9763 5447, and
Don Eladio, T09-9341 8064.

⊖ Transport

Talca *p296, map p296*
Bicycle
Cycle repairs from **Bicimotora Burgos**,
5 Oriente 1185.

Bus
Talca bus terminal is at 12 Oriente y 2 Sur.

Local To **Lago Colbún**, Pullman del Sur,
2 daily, US$1.80; to **Vilches**, Buses Vilches,
5 daily, 2-2½ hrs, US$3; to **Linares**, frequent,
US$1.80; to **Constitución**, Empresa O'Higgins
and Contimar, every 20 mins, 2 hrs, US$1.80.

Hourly buses to **Chanco**, **Curanipe** and **Pelluhue** with Buses Bonanza, US$4, also 3 daily with Contimar, US$4, and 10 daily with Pullman del Sur, US$4. **Long distance** To **Chillán**, frequent service, US$4. To **Temuco**, 5½ hrs, US$10-16. To **Puerto Varas and Puerto Montt**, 9 hrs, US$16-26. Many buses to **Santiago**, 3½ hrs, US$6, and direct services to destinations as far north as Copiapó.

Train
Talca railway station is at 2 Sur y 11 Oriente, T071-226254. Trains run to **Santiago**, 6 a day, US$11-US$22; to **Chillán**, 6 a day, US$9-US$22; to **Constitución**, 2 a day, 2½ hrs, US$3.

Lago Colbún and around *p297*
Buses Villa Prat runs direct services to **Quinamávida** from Santiago's Terminal Sur. For services to/from **Talca** see above.

Linares *p298*
Linares' **bus** terminal is at Espinoza 530. To **Colbún** via Quinimávida and Panimávida, US$1.50. For services to/from **Talca**, see above.

The **railway** station is at Brasil y Independencia, T073-216352. Trains run to **Santiago**, 6 a day, 3¼ hrs, US$12-US$24; to **Chillán**, 6 a day, 1 hr, US$5-US$7.

Constitución *p300*
Empresa Amigo runs buses to **Cauquenes**, 2½ hrs, US$3. For services to/from **Talca**, see above.

Directory

Talca *p296, map p296*
Banks Banco Santander, 1 Sur y 4 Oriente; Edificio Caracol, of 15, 1 Sur 898. For US$ cash. **Internet and telephone** several around the city centre. **Laundry** Lavaseco Donini, 6 Oriente 1120; Lavaseco Flash, 1 Norte 995. **Post office** 1 Oriente s/n.

Linares *p298*
Banks Banco A Edwards, on plaza; Banco Santander, Independencia 555. **Internet and telephone** Chacabuco 491. **Post office** Rodríguez 610.

Itata Valley

→ *Colour map 3, C2.*

The Río Itata and its longer tributary, the Río Nuble, flow west reaching the Pacific 60 km north of Concepción. This is a tranquil valley with some native woods along the banks near the mouth of the river at the tiny hamlet of Vegas de Itata. There is no bridge here, although boats can be hired to make the short crossing in summer; in winter the river swells and no one attempts the crossing. ➤ *For listings, see pages 308-309.*

Chillán ⬤🅿🄵🄷✳🄸🄾🄲 ➤ *pp308-309. Colour map 3, C2.*

Chillán, 150 km south of Talca, is a busy but friendly place. Founded in 1580 and destroyed by the Mapuche, the city has been moved several times, most recently following an earthquake in 1833. Although the older site, now known as Chillán Viejo, is still occupied, further earthquakes in 1939 and 1960 ensured that few old buildings have survived. Nevertheless, this is one of the more interesting cities south of Santiago and has a shady plaza, numerous interesting churches and several museums, as well as a mural of the life of Bernardo O'Higgins. Pleasantly hot in summer, the city is filled with local *campesinos* on market days, creating an atmosphere that is the essence of the Central Valley.

Ins and outs

Getting there Chillán is served by several trains and buses daily from Santiago. There are also frequent connections to the towns further south, especially Concepción, Temuco and Puerto Montt.

Getting around Chillán is a reasonably large city, and some of the outlying barrios and attractions are quite a distance from the centre. Buses and *colectivos* are numerous, with their destinations marked in the window, but taxis are most useful for arranging excursions out of the city.

Tourist information The **municipal office** ① *18 de Sept 455, at side of Gobernación, T042-223272*, can provide a street map of the city and various leaflets on skiing, Termas de Chillán, etc.

Sights

Chillán was the birthplace of Bernardo O'Higgins and today's city is centred around the Plaza O'Higgins and its modern **cathedral**, designed to resist earthquakes. The **San Francisco** church, three blocks northeast, contains a **museum** ① *Tue-Sun 1600-1800, US$1.50*, of religious and historical artefacts. Above the main entrance is a mural by Luis Guzmán Molina, a local artist, which is an interpretation of the life of San Francisco but placed in a Chilean context. The adjoining **convent** (1835) was a big centre for missionary work among the Mapuche.

Five streets west of the plaza is the neo-Gothic **Iglesia Padres Carmelita**, while to the northwest, on Plaza Héroes de Iquique, is the **Escuela México** ① *daily 1000-1300, 1500-1830*, donated to the city after the 1939 earthquake. In its library are outstanding murals by the great Mexican artists David Alvaro Siqueiros and Xavier Guerrero depicting allegories of Chilean and Mexican history. Southwest of the Plaza is the **Museo Interactivo Claudio Arrau** ① *Arrau 568, T042-433390, www.museoarrau.cl, Tue-Fri 0830-1330 and 1500-1900, Sat 1030-1300 and 1600-1900, Sun 1000-1400, US$0.80*, built in honour of the life of the world-famous pianist who was born here. It includes many of the musician's personal affairs as well as a small interactve music room.

Five minutes' walk to the southeast is **Museo Naval El Chinchorro** ① *I Riquelme y Collín, Tue-Fri 0930-1200, 1500-1730*, which contains naval artefacts and models of Chilean vessels.

In Chillán Viejo, southwest of the centre, is a monument and park marking the birthplace of Bernardo O'Higgins; a 60-m-long mural depicts his life (an impressive, but sadly faded mosaic of various native stones), while the **Centro Histórico y Cultural** ① *0830-2000* has a gallery of contemporary paintings by regional artists. Halfway

Chillán

Sleeping		Hostal Marbella 5		Eating		La Sureña 2
Claris 1		Libertador 8		Arcoiris 1		
Cordillera 2		Paso Nevado 9		Café Europa 3		**Bars & clubs**
De la Avenida 6		Quinchamalí 10		Club Comercial 4		Onde El Pala 7
Floresta 3		Residencial		Jai Yang 6		
Gran Isabel		Chi-Can 11		La Copucha 8		
Riquelme 7		Ventura 4		La Motoneta 1 5		

N

200 metres
200 yards

between the centre and Chillán Viejo on Avenida O'Higgins is the **Capilla San Juan de Dios**, a small chapel dating from 1791.

Around Chillán ⊜⊜ ⤞ *pp308-309.*

Quinchamalí

Quinchamalí is a small village of little houses hidden under large fruit trees, located 27 km southwest of Chillán, at the halfway point of the new motorway to Concepción. The village is famous for the originality of its crafts in textiles, basketwork, guitars, primitive paintings and especially black ceramics. These are all on sale in Chillán market and at a handicraft fair in the village during the second week of February.

Termas de Chillán

Situated 82 km east of Chillán by good road (paved for the first 50 km), 1850 m up at the foot of the double-cratered Chillán volcano, are two open-air thermal pools, officially for hotel guests only, and a health spa with jacuzzi, sauna, mud baths and other facilities. There are several trekking oportunities from the *termas*, including a good one- or two-day return hike past some natural hot mud baths (free of charge) to the **Valle de Aguas Calientes**, where there are yet more hot springs, spectacular scenery and solitude.

Above the thermal baths is the largest ski resort in southern Chile, with 11 ski lifts and 32 ski runs (the longest is 13 km in length), rental shops, restaurants, bars, ski school, first aid and a nursery. Experienced skiers can take advantage of nordic skiing, alpine randonnée and heli-skiing, but Chillán is also suitable for families and beginners and is a little cheaper than centres nearer Santiago, although accommodation can be pricey. For further information, contact the **Chillán Ski Centre** ① *Barros Arana 261, www.termaschillan.cl, lift pass US$40 per day, US$30 half day, equipment hire US$30 per day.*

San Fabián de Alico

This pleasant mountain village on the banks of the Río Nuble lies 67 km northeast of Chillán (via San Carlos, daily buses). In summer it is very lively and full of young Chileans. There are several campsites and *hospedajes*, and many opportunities for trekking up the valley. Horses can readily be hired for about US$15 per day. Tourist information is available in the plaza or from the Municipalidad.

Viña Chillán

① *T042-1971573, www.vinachillan.cl.*

Some 35km south of Chillán on the Bulnes-Yungay road is this Swiss-run Vineyard, the southernmost in Chile to produce good quality red (and white) wines. Guided tours are available with advance notice an there is also comfortable accommodation and a good restaurant. If you are driving this is a good place to break the journey on the long trip down to the lakes.

For Sleeping and Eating price codes and other relevant information, see Essentials pages 35-42.

⊙ Sleeping

Chillán *p305, map p306*
There are lots of cheap *hospedajes* on Constitución 1-300.
AL Gran Hotel Isabel Riquelme, Constitución 576, T042-213663, www.hotelisabelriquelme.cl. Slightly overpriced, with cable TV, restaurant, laundry and parking. Spacious suites.
A Paso Nevado, Libertad 219, T042-237666, www.hotelpasonevado.cl. Nice rooms, internet, conference room, bar, tours arranged. A good option in this price range. Check if prices are cheaper in pesos or in dollars.
A Quinchamalí, El Roble 634, T042-423250, www.hotelquinchamali.cl. 5-storey building in the city centre, quiet, clean, hot water, heated lounge.
B Cordillera, Arauco 619, on Plaza de Armas, T042-215211, www.hotelcordillera.cl. Small friendly 3-star.
B De la Avenida, O'Higgins 398 y Bulnes, T042-230256, www.hoteldelaavenida.com. 2-star facilities, including cable TV, Wi-Fi, café, bar and laundry.
B Ventura, O'Higgins 638, T042-227588. 3 star. Clean and with pleasant garden. Good home cooked food (restaurant open to non-residents). A decent choice.
B-C Libertador, Libertad 85, T042-223255, www.hlbo.cl. **C-D** singles. Reasonably spacious rooms, with bath, cable TV, Wi-Fi. Recently refurbished.
C Floresta, 18 de Septiembre 278, T/F042-222253. Quiet, old fashioned, friendly.
C-D Claris, 18 de Septiembre 357, T042-221980. **F** singles. Clean, friendly, run-down.
C-D Hostal Marbella, Libertad 336B, T09-8949 0641. **E** singles. Clean, airy but basic rooms with TV, shared bath and parking. A decent option in this price range, given the alternatives.

D Residencial Chi-Can, Constitución 34. **F** singles. Basic and noisy, but near the central terminal.

Termas de Chillán *p307*
The following are all located at Las Trancas on the road to the *termas*, 70 km southeast of Chillán. Several *cabañas* are also available in the village, usually **A** for up to 6 people, see www.vallelastrancas.cl for more details. Camping is available 2 km from the slopes.
LL Gran Termas de Chillán, T02-2331313, www.termaschillan.cl. 5-star, sports facilities, sauna, thermal pool and spa centre, new casino. Not the most characterful.
L Pirigallo, information T042-434200, www.termaschillan.cl. 3-star. Same ownership as above.
AL Parador Jamón, Pan y Vino, T042-432 100, www.paradorjamonpanyvino.cl. Half board. Recommended horse-riding trips.
AL-A Robledal, T042-214407, www.hotel robledal.cl. Pleasant rooms, including some suites, bar, restaurant, sauna and jacuzzi. Friendly owners. Wide variety of tours offered.
A MI Lodge, T09-9623 0412, www.mi lodge.com. Small lodge with fine views, hot tub and good restaurant.
B-C Hostelling International, T042-244628, j.bocaz@ctcinternet.cl. **E** per person in dorms. Basic European-style youth hostel.

⊙ Eating

Chillán *p305, map p306*
The Chillán area is well known for its *pipeño* wine (very young) and *longanizas* (sausages). There are many cheap restaurants in and around the mercado municipal.
♥♥♥-♥♥ La Sureña, 5 de Abril y Gamero, meat and fish dishes well prepared. Nothing extraordinary, probably the best restaurant here.
♥♥ Arcoiris, El Roble 525. Vegetarian.
♥♥ Café Europa, Libertad 475. Recommended.

¶¶ **Los Adobes**, Parque O'Higgins, Chillán Viejo. Tasty food and good service at reasonable prices.

¶¶-¶ **La Motoneta 1**, Av Padre Hurtado 242, T042-276693. North of the town centre, this *picada* is famous for its hearty home cooked food. If you are feeling adventurous try the *guatitas españolas*. Do not confuse with the restaurant over the road under the same ownership that has a different menu.

¶ **Club Comercial**, Arauco 745. Popular at lunchtime, good value *almuerzo*, popular bar at night. Recommended.

¶ **Jai Yang**, Libertad 250. Good-value Chinese.

¶ **La Copucha**, 18 de Septiembre y Constitución. Inexpensive meals and snacks.

ⓞ Bars and clubs

Chillán *p305, map p306*
Onde El Pala, Flores Millan 31, T042-320705, www.ondelpala.cl. Old-time *chichería* full of character with rustic wooden benches and brick walls. Fills up with locals who come to drink chicha or borgoña. Good live music at weekends. Recommended. Note there is no sign outside.

✸ Festivals and events

Chillán *p305, map p306*
Jan Encuentro International de Teatro, plays are performed in various public spaces.
Third week in Mar Fiesta de la Vendemia is an annual wine festival.

ⓞ Shopping

Chillán *p305, map p306*
Casa Rabie, Maipón 600 block. Supermarket.
Mercado y Feria Municipal, Riquelme y Maipón. Large market selling regional arts and crafts.
Plaza El Roble, El Roble y Riquelme. A modern shopping centre.

⊖ Transport

Chillán *p305, map p306*
Bicycle Repairs at Riquelme 751.

Bus To **Yumbel** and **Quinchamalí**, 30 mins, US$1.80, leave from the terminal near the market, Maipón y Sgto Aldea.

There are 2 long-distance terminals: TurBus, Línea Azul, Tas Choapa and Alsa-LIT all use the central terminal at Brasil y Constitución. Other companies use the modern northern terminal at O'Higgins y Ecuador. To **Santiago**, 5 hrs, US$11; to **Concepción**, TurBus and Línea Azul every 30 mins, 1¼ hrs, US$4; to **Temuco**, 4hrs, US$8-12; To **Puerto Varas** and **Puerto Montt**, 8 hrs, US$13-25.

Motorbike Motorcycle spares from Roland Spaarwater, Ecuador 275, T/F042-232334.

Train Station on Brasil opposite Libertad, 5 blocks west of Plaza de Armas, T042-222424, www.efe.cl. To **Santiago**, 6 daily, 4¼ hrs, US$17-26.

Termas de Chillán *p307*
Dedicated ski buses run Jun-Sep from Libertador 1042 to the slopes at 0800 and from **Chillán Ski Centre**, subject to demand, US$50 (including lift pass). In summer (Jan-mid Mar) there's a bus service from **Anja**, 5 de Abril 594, Thu, Sat, Sun only at 0730, US$12 return, book in advance. Taxis cost US$50 one way, 1½ hrs. At busy periods hitching may be possible from **Chillán Ski Centre**.

ⓘ Directory

Chillán *p305, map p306*
Banks On the Plaza de Armas are Banco BCI, Banco Santander and Banco de Chile, with ATMs, better rates than banks at Casa de cambio, Constitución 550. **Internet and telephone** Ubiquitous. **Post office** Gobernación, Plaza de Armas.

Biobío Valley

→ *Colour map 4, A1/2.*
The Río Biobío flows northwest from the Andes to reach the sea near Concepción. At 407 km, it is the second longest river in Chile. Its more important tributaries include the ríos Laja, Duqueco and Renaico. Apart from Concepción and Talcahuano on the coast, the valley includes several other important cities, notably Los Angeles. This is the southernmost end of the Central Valley, and while you will find grapes and other Mediterranean fruit being cultivated, there are also hints of what the Lake District has to offer to the south, with forests of araucaria and snow-capped volcanos inland. ➤➤ *For listings, see pages 317-322.*

Concepción and around ⊙⊘⊕⊚▲⊕⊙ ➤➤ *pp317-322.*

The capital of Región VIII (Biobío), Concepción is the third biggest city in Chile, with a population of nearly a quarter of a million. Founded in 1550, it was a frontier stronghold in the war against the Mapuche after 1600. The city was destroyed by an earthquake in 1751 and moved to its present site in 1764, but suffered another destructive earthquake and a tidal wave in 1835. Today, although it is one of the country's major industrial centres, Pleasant enough with green, tree-lined streets, Concepción is not in itself a wildly beautiful or fascinating place. Those staying for a long period or getting involved with students at the important university will find doors opening, but otherwise a visit to the port of Talcahuano, Chile's most important naval base (15 km north), is the highlight.

Ins and outs
Getting there Concepción is 15 km from the estuary of the Río Biobío, 516 km south of Santiago. There are flights daily to Concepción from Santiago and Puerto Montt, one or two of which continue on to Punta Arenas. Taxi to airport US$8. Concepción is the transportation hub of the region, and is served by buses to and from Santiago, Temuco, Valdivia and Puerto Montt, as well as to and from other smaller destinations such as Cañete and Lota. There are two long-distance bus terminals and neither is located in the city centre. To get to nearby destinations such as Dichato and Talcahuano, it is easiest to take a *colectivo*.
Getting around *Colectivos* and buses abound; the destinations are signed on the window or roof. Fares are US$0.60 for buses, slightly more for *colectivos*.
Tourist information **Sernatur** ① *Aníbal Pinto 460 on Plaza de la Independencia, T041-274 1337, infobiobio@sernatur.cl*, provides regional information. **CODEF** ① *Caupolicán 346, piso 4, T041-222 6649.*

Sights
In the centre of the city is the attractive **Plaza de la Independencia**, where, in January 1818, Bernardo O'Higgins proclaimed the Independence of Chile. Nearby are many official buildings, including the modern cathedral, the Municipalidad and the Palacio de la Justicia. Also on the plaza is the **Museo de Arte Sagrado** ① *Caupolicán 441, Tue-Fri 1000-1330, 1600-2000, Sat-Sun, 1100-1400, US$1*, containing many fine sacred Christian objects, including priests robes embroidered with gold, and a marble Christ. Southeast of the plaza is the **Parque Ecuador**, where the **Galería de la Historia** ① *Tue-Sun 1000-1330,*

Concepción

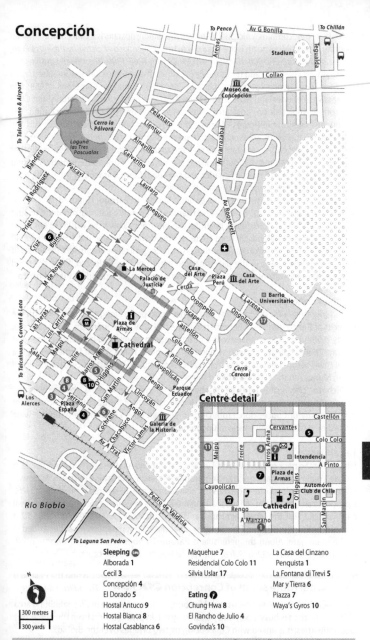

Sleeping
Alborada 1
Cecil 3
Concepción 4
El Dorado 5
Hostal Antuco 9
Hostal Bianca 8
Hostal Casablanca 6

Maquehue 7
Residencial Colo Colo 11
Silvia Uslar 17

Eating
Chung Hwa 8
El Rancho de Julio 4
Govinda's 10

La Casa del Cinzano
Penquista 1
La Fontana di Trevi 5
Mar y Tierra 6
Piazza 7
Waya's Gyros 10

300 metres
300 yards

1500-1830, free, contains a pictorial history of the region; upstairs is a collection of Chilean painting. A few blocks north is the **Casa del Arte** ① *Chacabuco y Paicaví, by the Plaza Perú, T041-2204290, Tue-Fri 1000-1800, Sat 1000-1600, Sun 1000-1300, free*, which contains the University art collection and temporary exhibitions; the entrance hall is dominated by *La Presencia de América Latina* by the Mexican Jorge González Camerena (1965), an impressive allegorical mural depicting Latin American history, famous throughout Chile and often depicted on postcards. Note especially the pyramid representing the continent's wealth, the figures of an armoured warrior and an Indian woman and the wounded cactus with parts missing, representing Mexico's defeat by the USA in 1845-1848. University art students are on hand to provide explanations. There is another fine mural in the entrance hall of the railway station, *La Historia de Concepción* by Gregorio de la Fuente. From the Parque Ecuador you can climb **Cerro Caracol**, to the south, from where there are views over the city and the river.

Sixteen kilometres west of Concepción, **Museo y Parque Hualpén** ① *Tue-Sun 1000-1300, 1400-1900, free*, is a house and garden that is now a national monument. Built around 1885, the house contains beautiful exhibits from all over the world. To get there take a city bus to Hualpencillo from Freire; ask the driver to let you out then walk for 40 minutes (or hitch) along Av Las Golondrinas to the Enap oil refinery, turn left, then right (it is signed). Further west in the park, near the mouth of the Río Biobío, there are good opportunities for walking on the hills and several fine beaches including **Playa Rocoto**.

North of Concepción
A road (nightmare for cyclists) runs north from Concepción along the coast through the suburbs of **Penco** (Km 12), where there is a fine beach, and **Lirquén**, Km 15, a small, old, pretty town of wooden houses with a beach that can be reached by walking along the railway. There is plentiful cheap seafood for sale here. **Tomé**, 13 km further north, is a small town set in a broad bay with long beaches and an interesting cemetery, Miguel Gulán Muñoz, on the cliff overlooking the ocean.

Dichato, 9 km further north along a hilly road offering fine views, is a beautiful fishing village and a busy summer holiday resort. It is also the site of the oceanographic centre of the University of Concepción. From Dichato you can take a local bus around the wide horseshoe bay to the tiny village of **Cocholgüe**.

Talcahuano
Situated at the neck of Península de Tumbes, Talcahuano has the best harbour in Chile. It is Chile's main naval station and an important commercial and fishing port, where crowds of fishermen unload their catches of seafood before a seething mass of buyers, stevedores and hoary, old sailors, snaffling molluscs as they are carried past. In the naval base you can visit the great ship **Huáscar** ① *Tue-Sun 0900-1300, 1400-1700, US$1.50*, a relic of the War of the Pacific. Photography is permitted, but passports must be handed in at the main gate. Along the peninsula is **Parque Tumbes** ① *information from Codeff, Caupolicán 346, T041-2226649, free*, with paths leading along the coast.

The coastal route south of Concepción ●●●●● ›› *pp317-322.*

South of the Río Biobío is the **Costa del Carbón**, until recently the main coalmining area of Chile. The road is busy, noisy and polluted by trucks plying to and from the numerous local industries; it is linked with Concepción by two bridges over the Biobío.

Towards Lota

Just across the Río Biobío from Concepción is the **Laguna Grande**, a watersports centre, and **Laguna San Pedro Chica**, which is good for swimming. **Coronel**, 29 km from Concepción, was the scene of a British naval defeat in 1914, when the *Good Hope* and *Monmouth* were sunk by the German ship *Scharnhorst*. A monument commemorating the defeat was erected in November 1989. The defeat was later avenged at the Battle of the Falklands/Malvinas with the destruction of the German squadron. Close to town on the Bahía de Coronel are the small **Playa Negra**, which has few people and black sand, and **Playa Blanca**, which is bigger with white sand and more crowds, as well as bars, cafés, seafood restaurants and a free campsite.

Forty-two kilometres south of Concepción, **Lota** was, until recently, the site of the most important coal mine in Chile, originally the property of the Cousiño family (see page 71). Even before the mine's closure in April 1997, the town was known to be one of the poorest in Chile and, although the government has invested in retraining for the miners and in trying to open up Lota to tourism, the city still suffers greatly from poverty and neglect. The town is in two parts: **Lota Alto**, on the hill, is the original mining town, while **Lota Bajo**, below, is more recent.

The **Parque de Lota Isidora Cousiño** ① *1000-1800, till 2000 in summer, US$3.50*, covering 14 ha on a promontory to the west of the town, was the life's work of Isadora Cousiño. Laid out by English landscape architects in the 19th century, it contains plants from all over the world, ornaments imported from Europe, romantic paths and shady nooks offering views over the sea; peacocks and pheasants roam freely; no picnicing allowed. The mansion, which was Isadora's home during her stays in Lota, was destroyed in the 1960 earthquake. Near the entrance to the park is the **Museo Historíco de Lota** ① *1000-2000 Nov-Mar, 1000-1800 Apr-Oct, US$1.80*.

The tunnels of the **coal mine** ① *T041-2870682, 1000-1700, US$9*, run almost entirely under the sea (the longest is 11 km) and can be visited on guided tours led by former miners; at the entrance is a small **Museo Minero**. Offshore is an island, **Isla Santa María**, which has basic accommodation and good beaches.

Towards Lebu

South of Lota the road runs past the seaside resort of **Laraquete**, where there are miles of golden sands and lots of Chilean holidaymakers in summer. The road passes a large cellulose factory and then, at Carampangue, Km 64 south of Concepción, it forks: one branch running west to **Arauco**, the site of a great beach but also two pungent cellulose factories; the other branch continuing south, 52 km, to Tres Pinos, where there is a turning towards Lebu.

A fishing port and coal washing centre, **Lebu** lies at the mouth of the Río Lebu, 149 km south of Concepción, and is the capital of Arauco province. There are enormous beaches to both the north and south, popular on summer weekends. About 3 km north, at **Playa Millaneco**, are steep hills and caves offering good walks and majestic views.

Cañete, Contulmo and Lago Lanalhue

Twenty-four kilometres south of Tres Pinos is the small town of Cañete. It is located on the site of the historic **Fort Tucapel** (now being restored), where Pedro de Valdivia and 52 of his men were killed by Mapuche warriors in 1553. About 1 km south on the road to Contulmo, in a modern building supposedly inspired by the traditional Mapuche *ruca*, is the **Museo Mapuche Juan Antonio Ríos** ① *T041-2611093, www.dibam.cl/ sdm_mm_canete, summer*

Mon-Fri 0930-1830, Sat and Sun 1100-1900, closed Mon in winter, US$2. Displays include Mapuche ceramics and textiles. Behind the museum is a reconstruction of a *ruca*.

South of Cañete, **Lago Lanalhue** is surrounded by forested hills from which there has been extensive logging. Much less popular than the Lake District, this area offers good opportunities for walking. A road runs south from Cañete along the north side of the lake to **Contulmo**, a sleepy village at the foot of the cordillera. The **Monumento Natural Contulmo**, 8 km south of the village and administered by CONAF, covers 82 ha of native forest. Access to the lake shore is restricted, as much of it is private property, but **Playa Blanca**, 10 km north of Contulmo, is a popular beach in summer (take any bus between Contulmo and Cañete). The wooden **Casa y Molino Grollmus**, 3 km along the southern side of the lake, are well worth a visit. The splendid garden has a fine collection of *copihue*, the national flower, and the mill, built in 1928, still contains its original wooden machinery. From here, the track runs 9 km north to the **Posada Campesina Alemana**, an old German-style hotel in a fantastic spot at the water's edge.

Twenty kilometres further east, **Purén** is reached by crossing the cordillera through dense forest (do this journey in daylight). Located in a major logging area, Purén was the site of a fortress built by Pedro de Valdivia in 1553 and destroyed soon after. It was again a key stronghold of the Chilean army in the last campaign against the Mapuche (1869-1881) and there is now a full-scale reconstruction of the wooden fort on the original site.

Lago Lleulleu and Tirúa

Lago Lleulleu lies 34 km south of Cañete. It is a peaceful lake covering 4300 ha and offers sandy beaches, many opportunities for camping, fine views of the coastal mountain range and the chance to interact with the local Mapuche community, but there are few facilities. Further south, at the mouth of the Río Tirúa is the town of **Tirúa**, unremarkable in itself, but close to some wonderful country for walking and riding and with a beach that is calm and deserted. The island of **Mocha**, visited by Juan Bautista Pastenes in 1544 and later by Sir Francis Drake, lies 32 km offshore. Most of the island's 800 inhabitants live around the coast, the interior being forest. The main settlement is **La Hacienda** where accommodation is available with families.

Los Angeles and around ⊖❼▲⊖❻ » *pp317-322.*

Situated on the Pan-American Highway, 110 km south of Chillán, Los Angeles is the capital of Biobío province and lies at the heart of a wine, fruit and timber-producing district. Founded in 1739 as a fort, it was destroyed several times by the Mapuche.

Ins and outs

Getting there Los Angeles is easily accessible from north and south by bus; the most common destinations are Santiago, Puerto Montt and Concepción, but all intermediate destinations are also served.

Getting around Los Angeles is not as big as some of the other cities of the central valley, and as a result it is not necessary to take public transport quite as often as in, say, Chillán or Talca.

Tourist information The tourist office is on Caupolicán close to the post office; also try CONAF ① *Ercilla 936, daily 0900-1300.*

Los Angeles

Most visitors find themselves in Los Angeles on their way to Parque Nacional Laguna de Laja and, although there isn't much here in the way of sights, it is a pleasant, expanding city, with a large Plaza de Armas. Colón is the main shopping street and there is a good daily market. The **Museo de la Alta Frontera** ⓘ *Colón 195, Mon-Fri 0815-1830, free,* has some Mapuche silver and colonial artefacts. Swimming is possible in the nearby **Río Duqueco**, 10 minutes south by bus, US$0.80.

Salto del Laja, 25 km north of Los Angeles, is a spectacular waterfall where the Río Laja plunges 15 m over the rocks. Numerous tour groups stop here, and the place is filled with tourist kiosks selling pap. Boat trips are available in the *Buenaventura* ⓘ *T09-9418 1247*.

Parque Nacional Laguna de Laja

A road, paved for the first 64 km, runs east from Los Angeles for 93 km, past the impressive rapids of the Río Laja, to the Parque Nacional Laguna de Laja. Covering 11,600 ha, the park is dominated by the scree slopes of the **Antuco Volcano** (2985 m), which is still active, and the glacier-covered **Sierra Velludac**. There is no clear path to the summit of Antuco. Start out early (0500) from the Refugio Digeder at 1400 m to allow about six hours to ascend and leave plenty of time for the descent, which is exhausting. The volcano slopes are made of black scorias blocks, which are razor sharp, so wear good strong boots and take water; be warned that this sort of terrain is very demanding and can catch out those who are unaware of its severity. From the sulphur fume-cloaked summit of the volcano are fine views over the glaciers and south to the smoking Villarrica Volcano. The valley below is green and wooded, very pleasant and sparsely visited, even in high season. The **visitor centre** is 1 km from the park administration (4 km from the entrance).

Los Angeles

Convento San Francisco

To Long Distance Bus Terminal, Pan-American Highway (North) & Salto del Laja

Tucapel — Av. Ercilla — Mendoza — Valdivia — Rengo — Colón — Almagra — Villagrán — Manso de Velasco

Local — Local

Estero Quilque

Laguna Esmeralda — Colo Colo — Lautaro — Caupolicán

Plaza de Armas — Municipalidad — Museo de la Alta Frontera

Ricardo Vicuña

To 5 & Pan-American Highway

To Pan-American Highway (South)

N

300 metres
300 yards

Sleeping
Caupolicán 651 1
De Villena 2
Gran Müso 3
Residencial Santa María 4

Eating
Di Leone 5

Donde Juanito 1
El Arriero 2
Julio's Pizzas 3

Club de Esquí de los Angeles ① *May-Aug*, has two ski-lifts, giving a combined run of 4 km on the Antuco Volcano. Passing the ski station, the road reaches the turquoise waters of the **Laguna de la Laja**, with views of the Andes stretching towards Argentina; note, however, that it is a walk of several hours from the park entrance to the lake and there is very little passing traffic. The laguna was created by the damming of the Río de Laja by a lava flow and is surrounded by stark scenery. Trees include a few surviving araucarias, and there are 47 species of birds including condors and the rare Andean gull. From the lake, the road continues to the Argentine border at **Paso Pichachén** ① *Oct-Apr, depending on amount of snow*.

Angol
Although of limited interest to travellers, Angol is the main base for visiting the Parque Nacional Nahuelbuta, further west. Reached from the Pan-American Highway by roads from Los Angeles and Collipulli, the town is situated at the confluence of the Ríos Rehue and Picolquén, at the foot of the Cordillera de Nahuelbuta, and is the capital of the province of Malleco. It was founded by Pedro de Valdivia in 1552 and was destroyed seven times by the Mapuche.

Northwest of the attractive Plaza de Armas is the church and convent of **San Buenaventura**. Built in 1863, it became the centre for missionary work among the Mapuche. Also worth visiting is **El Vergel** ① *5 km southeast of Angol, Mon-Fri 0900-1900, Sat and Sun 1000-1900, US$1.80, colectivo No 2*, which was founded in 1880 as an experimental fruit-growing nursery but now incorporates an attractive park with a wide range of trees and the Museo Dillman Bullock with displays on archaeology and natural history. There's an excellent **tourist office** ① *O'Higgins s/n, across bridge from bus terminal, T045-711255*, and an office of **CONAF** ① *Prat 191, piso 2, T045-711870*.

Parque Nacional Nahuelbuta
① *Open all year (snow Jun-Sep).*
Situated in the coastal mountain range at an altitude of 800-1550 m, the park covers 6832 ha of forest and offers views over both the sea and the Andes. There are some good walks: one heads 4 km west of the visitor centre to the **Piedra el Aguila** at 1158 m, where there is a mirador on top of a huge boulder; another goes to **Cormallín**, 5 km north of the visitor centre, from where you may continue to Cerro Anay, 1402 m, and another mirador. Although the forest includes many species of trees, the araucaria is most striking; some are over 2000 years old, 50 m high and with trunks 2 m in diameter. There are also seven species of orchid. Animals include pudú, Chiloé foxes, pumas, kodkod, black woodpeckers and parrots. There is a **visitor centre** ① *spring and summer daily 0800-1300, 1400-2000*, at Pehuenco, 5 km from the entrance. Rough maps are available for US$0.25.

Biobío Valley listings

For Sleeping and Eating price codes and other relevant information, see Essentials pages 35-42.

Sleeping

Concepción *p310, map p311*
Good budget accommodation
is hard to find.
AL Alborada, Barros Arana 457, T041-291 1121, www.hotelalborada.cl. Good 4-star with all mod cons. Large rooms and suites with king size beds. Disabled-friendly. Tours offered.
AL-A El Dorado, Barros Arana 348, T041-222 9400, hoteleldorado.cl. Comfortable business standard, central, spacious rooms, bar and cafeteria, parking.
B Concepción, Serrano 512, T041-222 8851, hotelconcepcion@entelchile.net. Central, comfortable, heating, English spoken.
B-C Hostal Bianca, Salas 643-C, T041-225 2103, www.hostalbianca.cl. Some rooms with bath. With breakfast, food available, parking, student discounts.
C Cecil, Barros Arana 9, near railway station, T041-273 9981. With bath and breakfast, clean, can be noisy at weekends (lots of bars nearby).
C Hostal Antuco, Barros Arana 741, apart 31-33 (entry via the Galería Martínez), T041-223 5485, hostalantuco@hotmail.com. Some rooms with bath. Simple and spartan but clean and reasonable value.
C Hostal Casablanca, Cochrane 133, T041-299 3439. Some rooms with bath, clean. Good value.
C Maquehue, Barros Arana 786, piso 7, T041-221 0261, www.hotelmaquehue.cl. Clean, with bath and cable TV, restaurant, laundry service, parking. Recommended.
C Residencial Colo Colo, Colo Colo 743, T041-222 7118. **E** singles, with bath and breakfast. Meals available.

C Silvia Uslar, Edmundo Larenas 202, T041-222 7449. **F** singles. Good breakfast, quiet, clean, comfortable. Usually lets rooms to university students.

North of Concepción *p312*
B-C Bahía Velero, P Aguirre Cerda 760, Dichato, T041-268 3014. Clean and pleasant rooms with bath and breakfast. Friendly owners. Right by the beach. Parking.
C De la Costa, M Montt 923, Tomé, T041-265 3379. **F** singles. With bath and breakfast.
C Vista Hermosa, Costanera 1135, Tomé, T041-265 0280. On the seafront, with bath, without breakfast.
C-D Residencial Santa Inés, República 540, Dichato. **F** singles. Without bath, basic.

Talcahuano *p312*
B De La Costa, Colón 630, T041-254 5913. Rooms with breakfast.
C France, Av Pinto 44, T041-292 0090, www.hotelfrance.cl. Standard 2-star hotel with café and internet access.
C-D Residencial San Pedro, Rodríguez 22, T041-254 2145. **E-F** singles. With breakfast, some rooms with bath.

Towards Lota *p313*
C-D Angel de Peredo, Aiessandri 169, Lota, T041-287 6824. With bath and breakfast. Good value.
D Residencial Roma, Galvarino 233, Lota, T041-287 6257. **F** singles. Clean, friendly, some rooms with bath. No breakfast.

Towards Lebu *p313*
B Hostería Arauco, Esmeralda 80, Arauco, T041-255 1131, itafesa@hotmail.com. Good restaurant, bar, laundry and parking.
B-C Plaza, Chacabuco 345, Arauco, T041-255 1265. Cheaper rooms without bath.
C-D Central, Pérez 183, Lebu, T/F041-251 1904. **E-F** singles. Most rooms with bath, clean, parking. Recommended.

C-D Hostal La Quinta, Laraquete, T041-257 1993. **F** singles. Helpful, basic, good breakfast.
D Residencial Los Abedules, Los Abedules 144, Laraquete, T041-257 1953. **F-G** singles. Friendly, small rooms, poor bathrooms.

Cañete, Contulmo and Lanalhue *p313*
Lanalhue Turismo, T041-261 3537, www.lanalhueturismo.cl, is an agglomeration of local hotel and *cabaña* owners who also offer tours and information. There are several *cabañas* on the lakeshore. Real coffee is served at **Café Nahuel**, off the plaza in Cañete.
L Hostería Lanalhue, Lago Lanalhue, T041-223 4981. On the south side of the lake, many facilities, good.
A Hotel Licahue, Lago Lanalhue, 4 km north of Contulmo, T09-9870 2822. Full board, attractively set overlooking lake, with pool. Highly recommended. Also owns *cabañas* nearby (connected by boat).
B-C Nahuelbuta, Villagrán 644, Cañete, T041-261 1073, hotelnahuelbuta@lanalhue turismo.cl. Clean, pleasant, parking. Cheaper without bath.
C Central, on the plaza, Purén. Excellent meals, rooms in tourist season only.
C-D Derby, Mariñán y Condell, Cañete, T0412-611 960. **F** singles. Without bath, clean, basic, restaurant.
C-D Gajardo, 7 de la Línea 817 (1 block from plaza), Cañete. **F** singles. Without bath, old fashioned, friendly, pleasant.
D Central, Millaray 131, Contulmo, T041-261 8089, hotelcentral@lanalhue turismo.cl. **F** singles, no sign, hospitable.
D Contulmo, Millaray 116, Contulmo, T041-289 4903. **F** singles. Some rooms without bath, an attractive retreat, friendly and hospitable. Recommended.
D Don Juanito, Riquelme 151, Cañete. **F-G** singles. Very good, friendly. Recommended by the locals, cheap.

Camping
Camping Elicura, Contulmo. Clean, US$6. Recommended.
Camping Huilquehue, 15 km south of Cañete. Lakeside site.
Camping Playa Blanca, Lago Lanalhue.

Lago Lleulleu and Tirúa *p314*
C Residencial Elimar, T041-894902. One of 3 *hospedajes* in Tirúa.

Los Angeles *p314, map p315*
There are several cheap *residenciales* around Colo Colo and Almagra.
A Gran Hotel Müso, Valdivia 222 (Plaza de Armas), T043-313183, www.hotelmuso.cl. 3-star business standard. Good restaurant open to non-residents.
A-B El Rincón, Panamericana Sur Km 494, El Olivo, 2 km east,18 km north of Los Angeles, T09-9441 5019, www. elrinconchile.cl. Beautiful property beside a small river, restful. Good breakfast. South American and European cuisine, including vegetarian, tours arranged, Spanish classes, horse riding, rafting, English, French and German spoken, kitchen facilities.
A-B Hostería Salto del Laja, 30 km north of Los Angeles, T043-321706, www.salto dellaja.cl. With restaurant, 2 swimming pools and chalet-type rooms on an island overlooking the falls, fishing trips arranged, also *cabañas*, for up to 6.
B Complejo Turístico Los Manantiales, 30 km north of Los Angeles, Salto del Laja, T/F043-314275. Also camping.
C Residencial Santa María, Plaza de Armas, T043-328214. Hot shower, TV, friendly but run-down and overpriced.
C-D Caupolicán 651. **F** singles. Private house offering good-value rooms and large breakfast. Opposite is another, also No 651, basic, cheaper.
C-D Hotel de Villena, Lautaro 579, T043-321643. With breakfast.

Parque Nacional Laguna de Laja *p315*
In Antuco, most places are fully occupied by local workers. Take your own food as little is available in Abanico or inside the park. Camping is not permitted on lake shore.
B Cabañas Lagunillas, T043-321086, 2 km from park entrance. Open all year, cabins sleep 6, lovely spot close to the river among pine woods, restaurant, also camping US$5 per person.
D Refugio Digeder, 11 km from the park entrance, T041-2229054. *Refugio* on slopes of Antuco Volcano.
D Refugio Universidad de Concepción, book though the office at O'Higgins 740, Concepción, T041-222 9054. *Refugio* on slopes of Antuco Volcano.

Angol *p316*
B La Posada, El Vergel, T045-712103. With full board, clean, friendly.
C Casa de Huéspedes, Dieciocho 465. **F** singles, with breakfast, friendly.
C Josanh-Paecha, Caupolicán 579, T045-711771. With breakfast, clean, good food.

Camping
There are 2 campsites on the road to Parque Nacional Nahuelbuta at Km 21 and Km 20.

Parque Nacional Nahuelbuta *p316*
There's a campsite near the visitor centre, US$11, and many free campsites along the road from El Cruce to the entrance.

⊕ Eating

Concepción *p310, map p311*
♥♥ **El Rancho de Julio**, O'Higgins 36. Argentine *parrillada*.
♥♥ **La Casa del Cinzano Penquista**, Castellón 881. Characterful restaurant whose walls are covered in old movie memorabilia and antique photos of Concepción. Filling home-style Chilean food, nothing overly special but

recommended for its ambiance and jazz and blues music in the background.
♥♥ **La Fontana di Trevi**, Colo Colo 340. Stylish Italian serving pizzas and fresh pasta.
♥♥ **Novillo Loco**, Portales 539. Traditional food. Good, efficient service.
♥♥ **Piazza**, Barros Arana 631, 2nd floor. Good pizzas.
♥ **Chung Hwa**, Barros Arana 262. Good, cheap oriental food.
♥ **Govinda's**, Angol 451. Good-value vegetarian dishes.
♥ **Mar y Tierra**, Colo Colo 1182. Seafood and fish.
♥ **Waya's Gyros**, Angol 441. Excellent-value kebabs. Recommended. Also on Plaza Perú.

Cafés and snack bars
Café Haití, Caupolicán 515. Open Sun morning. Good coffee.
Cantabria, Caupolicán 415. Pleasant café with outside seating. One of several near the Plaza de Armas.
El Naturista, local 22. Vegetarian food.
Fuente Alemana, Caupolicán 654. *Fuente de soda* near the Plaza de Armas. Recommended.
Gelatería Dimarco, Plaza de Armas. Popular for ice creams.
QuickBiss, O'Higgins between Tucapel and Castellón. Salads, real coffee, good service, good lunches.
Treinta y Tantos, Prat 404. Nice bar, good music, wide selection of *empanadas*, good breakfasts and lunches. Recommended.

North of Concepción *p312*
There are several seafood restaurants on P Aguirre Cerda 600 and 700 blocks in Dichato.
♥♥ **Casino Oriente**, Penco. Good seafood restaurant.
♥♥ **Munot**, Baquedano 1690, Tomé. Swiss food.
♥♥ **Villa Marina**, Riquelme 55, Tomé. Traditional food.

Talcahuano *p312*
The market abounds with fine seafood.

¶¶ **Club Talcahuano**, Colón 446.
For meat dishes.
¶¶-¶ **Benotecas**, on seafront. A row of
4 restaurants facing the harbour. Superb
fish and seafood. Recommended.
¶¶-¶ **Domingo Lara**, Aníbal Pinto 450.
Seafood specialities, excellent.
¶¶-¶ **La Aguada**, Colón 912. Shellfish dishes.

Towards Lota *p313*
¶ **El Greco**, P Aguirre Cerda 422, Lota.
Traditional food, cheap.

Los Angeles *p314, map p315*
¶¶ **Di Leone**, Av Alemania 606. Italian
with good lasagne on the menu.
¶¶ **Donde Juanito**, Colón 720. Good value,
simple fish and seafood. Often packed full.
Recommended.
¶¶ **El Arriero**, Colo Colo 235. Good *parrillas*
and international dishes.
¶ **Julio's Pizzas**, Colón 542. Good pizzeria.

Angol *p316*
¶ **Carloncho**, Lautaro 447. Simple food,
popular with locals.

⊛ Festivals and events

Cañete, Contulmo and Lanalhue *p313*
Jan Semana Musical (music week) is held
in Contulmo.
20 Jan Fiesta de Piedra Santa is a major
Mapuche festival, held in Lumaco.

⊕ Entertainment

Concepción *p310, map p311*
Cultural centres
Alliance Française, Colo Colo y Lamas,
library, concerts, films, cultural events.
Chilean–British Cultural Institute, San
Martín 531, British newspapers, library.
Chilean–North American Institute,
Caupolicán 301 y San Martín, library.

⊙ Shopping

Concepción *p310, map p311*
Feria Artesanal, Freire 777. Craft market.
Galería Internacional, Caupolicán y Barros
Arana. Worth a visit.
Líder, Freire y Prat. Supermarket.
Lippi, Galería Oliveri, O'Higgins 650. For
good-quality camping and outdoor gear.
Mercado Municipal, 1 block west of the
Plaza de Armas. Seafood, fruit and veg.
Plaza del Trebol, near the airport. Large
modern shopping mall and multiplex
cinema. Take any bus for Talcahuano.

▲ Activities and tours

Concepción *p310, map p311*
Alta Luz, S Martín 586, piso 2, T09-9993 3725,
www.altaluz.cl. Tours to national parks.
Viajes Publitur, A Pinto 486, of 202,
T041-224 0800, www.viajespublitur.tk.
City and local tours.

Los Angeles *p314, map p315*
Strong Visión, Caupolicán 506, T43-320448,
www.strongvisionaventura.co.cl. Trekking,
mountain biking, rafting, kayaking, bungee
jumping, fishing.

⊖ Transport

Concepción *p310, map p311*
Air
Concepción airport is north of the city,
off the main road to Talcahuano. In summer,
there are flights daily to and from **Santiago**
(fewer in winter); and connections to
Temuco, **Puerto Montt** and **Punta Arenas**.
   Airline offices LanChile, O'Higgins
648, T041-224 8824; Aerolíneas Argentinas,
O'Higgins 650, of 602.

Bicycle
Spares and repairs from **Ojeda**, Salas 283.

Bus

Local Línea Azul and Costa Azul buses from Concepción pass through the villages north of the city, which can also be reached cheaply by *colectivo* (every 15-20 mins).

To **Talcahuano**, frequent service 30 mins, US$1.50; *colectivos* leave San Martín every 2 mins. Services to **Coronel**, US$1, **Lota**, **Lebu**, **Cañete**, **Tirúa** and **Contulmo** leave from the main terminal.

Long distance The main terminal is known as **Terminal Collao**, 2 km east, Av Gral Bonilla, next to the football and athletics stadium.Many buses to the city centre, US$0.70, taxi US$4.

TurBus, Línea Azul and Buses Bío Bío services leave from **Terminal Camilo Henríquez**, 2 km northeast of main terminal on J M García, reached by buses from Av Maipú in centre, via **Terminal Collao**.

To **Santiago**, 8 companies, 6 hrs, US$15-30; to **Valparaíso**, 8 hrs, US$18 (most go via Santiago). To **Puerto Montt** several companies, about 10 hrs, US$17-30; to **Pucón** direct in summer only, 6 hrs, US$18; to **Valdivia**, 7 hrs, US$13-25, TurBus only; to **Los Angeles**, every 30 mins, US$4.

Best direct bus to **Chillán** is Línea Azul, 2 hrs, US$3. For a longer, more scenic route, take the **Costa Azul** bus, which follows the old railway line, through Tomé, Coelemu and Nipas on to Chillán (part dirt-track, takes 5½ hrs).

Car

Car hire Avis, Chacabuco 726, T041-223 5837; Budget, Castellón 134, T041-222 5377; Dollar, at airport, T041-248 3661; Full famas, O'Higgins 1154, T041-224 8300, airport T09-9440 3300; Hertz, Prat 248, T041-223 0341. **Automóvil Club de Chile**, O'Higgins 630, of 303, T041-224 5884.

Train

The station is at Prat y Barros Arana, T041-222 6925, www.efe.cl. Direct

long-distance services to Santiago are currently suspended although there is a bus that connects with the northbound train service from Chillán. Local services to **Laja** and **Yumbel**, and suburban trains to **Talcahuano** and **Chiguayante**. Booking offices at the station and at **Galería Alessandri**, Aníbal Pinto 478, local 3, T041-222 5286.

Towards Lota *p313*
Bus
To **Concepción**, 1½ hrs, US$2. Many buses bypass the centre of Lota: catch them from the main road.

Cañete, Contulmo and Lanalhue *p313*
Bus
In Cañete, J Ewert, Inter Sur and Thiele use the bus terminal at Riquelme y 7th de la Línea; Jeldres, Erbuc and other companies use the Terminal Municipal, Serrano y Villagrán.

To **Santiago**, 9 hrs, US$18; to **Contulmo**, frequent, US$2; to **Purén**, US$3, sit on right for views of Lago Lanalhue; to **Concepción**, 3 hrs, US$5; to **Lebu** US$2.50; to **Angol** US$5; to **Tirúa**, Jeldres, frequent, and J Ewert, 3 a day, 2 hrs, US$3.50.

Contulmo is also served by buses to/ from **Concepción**, Thiele, 4 hrs, US$7, and **Temuco**, Thiele and Erbuc, US$8.

Tirúa *p314*
Bus
Buses run from Cañete to Tirúa, from where there are **ferries** to **Mocha**, 0600 daily, US$25. Alternatively, you can also ask the police to radio the **plane** to Mocha, US$120.

Los Angeles *p314, map p315*
Bus
Long-distance bus terminal on northeastern outskirts of town, local terminal at Villagrán y Rengo in centre (most services to Ralco and Santa Bárbara).

To **Santiago**, 6½ hrs, US$15-24. To **Viña del Mar** and **Valparaíso**, 8 hrs, US$17; to **Concepción**, US$4, 2 hrs; to Valdivia, 5 hrs,

US$10-22; to **Chillán**, US$4; to **Temuco**, hourly service, 2 hrs, US$6; to **Curacautín**, daily, 3 hrs, US$6. **Salto del Laja** is served by Bus Bío Bío from Los Angeles, frequent, 30 mins, US$2, and from Chillán, US$4.

Car
Automóvil Club de Chile, Villagrán y Caupolicán, T043-322149.

Parque Nacional Laguna del Laja *p315*
Bus
Take ERS Bus, Villagrán 507, from Los Angeles to **Abanico**, then walk 4 km to park entrance. Alternatively take a bus to **Antuco**, 2 hrs, 5 daily Mon-Sat, 2 daily Sun, US$3, then hitch the remaining 24 km to the park.

Angol *p316*
Bus
Local buses use **Terminal Rural**, Ilabaca y Lautaro. Long-distance bus terminal is at Chorrillos y Caupolicán. To **Santiago**, 8 hrs, US$16-38; to **Los Angeles**, US$2; to **Temuco**, Trans Bío-Bío, frequent, US$4.

Car
Car hire Christopher Car, Ilabaca 421, T045-715156.

Parque Nacional Nahuelbuta *p316*
Bus
There is a direct bus to park entrance from Angol, Dec-Feb, Sun 0800, return 1700. Otherwise, take a bus to **Vegas Blancas**

(27 km west of Angol) 0700 and 1600 daily, return 0900 and 1600, 1½ hrs, US$2, and get off at El Cruce, for a steep 7-km walk uphill to the park entrance (US$6). Access is also possible via a dirt road from Cañete, 4WD only Jun-Sep.

Directory

Concepción *p310, map p311*
Banks ATMs at banks on Av O'Higgins; high commission; several *cambios* in Galería Internacional, Barros Arana 565 and Caupolicán 521, check rates first: **Afex**, local 57; **Cambios Fides**, local 58; **Inter-Santiago**, local 31, T041-222 8914. **Consulates** Argentina, San Martín 472, of 52, T041-223 0257. **Internet and telephone** Barros Arana 541, Caupolicán 567, English spoken. Many others. **Laundry** American Cleaning, Freire 817; **Lavandería Radiante**, Salas 283, open 0900-2030, very good. **Police** station at Salas y San Martín. **Post office** O'Higgins y Colo Colo.

Los Angeles *p314, map p315*
Banks Several around the Plaza; best rates at Agencia Interbruna, Caupolicán 350. **Post office** Plaza de Armas. **Telephone** CTC, Colo Colo; **Entel**, Colo Colo 393.

Angol *p316*
Banks Banco Bice, Chorrillas 364; Banco Santander, Lautaro 399.

Contents

Footprint features

Border crossings

Chile–Argentina
see pages 327, 334, 346, 375 and 393

Lake District

At a glance

◉ **Getting around** Extensive bus network and many tour operators. Hiring a car will make things easier.

◉ **Time required** You could do a different activity every day for a week and still have tons left to see.

◑ **Weather** Pleasant daytime during summer and autumn. A bit chilly at night, can rain at any time.

◉ **When not to go** Winter is seriously wet. More popular destinations are crowded in Feb.

★Don't miss ...

Extending from the Río Biobío south to the city of Puerto Montt, the Lake District is one of the most popular destinations for both Chilean and overseas visitors. The main cities are Temuco, Valdivia, Osorno and Puerto Montt, but the most attractive scenery lies further east where a string of lakes stretches down the western side of the Andes. Much of this region has been turned into national parks and the mixture of forests, lakes and snow-capped volcanoes is unforgettable.

Between Temuco and the Pacific coast, meanwhile, is the indigenous heartland of Chile, home to the largest Mapuche communities. Here you will find *rucas* (traditional thatched houses) and communities still fiercely proud of their traditions, hinting at the sort of country that the first *conquistadores* might have found.

The major resorts include Pucón on Lago Villarrica and Puerto Varas on Lago Llanquihue. The cities of Temuco and Puerto Montt are also popular: Temuco for excursions into the Mapuche communities towards the coast and Puerto Montt as the starting point for longer voyages south to Puerto Natales, Puerto Chacabuco and the San Rafael glacier, as well as east across the lakes and mountains to the Argentine resort of Bariloche.

Background

After the Mapuche rebellion of 1598, Spanish settlement south of the Río Biobío was limited to Valdivia, although the Spanish had a right of way north from Valdivia along the coast to Concepción. At independence the only other Spanish settlement in this region was Osorno, refounded in 1796. The Chilean government did not attempt to extend its control into the Lake District until the 1840s. In 1845, all land south of the Río Rahue was declared the property of the state and destined for settlement and, in 1850, Vicente Pérez Rosales was sent to Valdivia to distribute lands to arriving European colonists.

The southern Lake District was settled from the 1850s onwards, mainly by German immigrants (see box, page 380). Further north, Chilean troops began occupying lands south of the Biobío after 1862, but the destruction of Mapuche independence did not occur until the early 1880s when Chilean forces led by Cornelio Saavedra founded a series of forts in the area including Temuco (1881), Nueva Imperial (1882), Freire (1883) and Villarrica (1883). A treaty ending Mapuche independence was signed in Temuco in 1881.

White settlement in the area was further encouraged by the arrival of the railway, which reached Temuco in 1893, reducing the journey time from Santiago to 36 hours; the line was later extended to Osorno (1902) and Puerto Montt (1912). In the 1930s the area became popular as a destination for rich Santiaguinos, and also as an important fishing destination for foreigners.

Today, agriculture is the most important sector of the local economy and the main industries are connected to the region's produce. Proof of Chile's position as a timber producer of international standing is provided by wood-chip piles and cellulose plants dotted along the coast. Fishing is particularly important in the south of the region, where farmed salmon regularly appears on restaurant menus. Tourism is a mainstay in summer (from mid-December to mid-March), when Chileans flock to the Lake District resorts, prices are high, and it is best to book well in advance, particularly for transport. Out of season, however, many facilities are closed.

Geography

The region between the cities of Temuco and Puerto Montt is one of the most picturesque lake regions in the world. There are 12 great lakes, and dozens of smaller ones, as well as imposing waterfalls and snow-capped volcanoes. This landscape has been created by two main geological processes: glaciation and volcanic activity. The main mountain peaks are volcanic: the highest are Lanín (3747 m) and Tronador (3460 m), both on the Argentine border. The most active volcanoes include Llaima and Villarrica, which erupted 22 and 10 times respectively in the 20th century.

Seven main river systems drain the Lake District, from north to south the ríos Imperial, Toltén, Valdivia, Bueno, Maullín, Petrohué and Puelo. The Río Bueno drains Lago Ranco and is joined by the ríos Pilmaiquén and Rahue, thus receiving also the waters of Lagos Puyehue and Rupanco: it carries the third largest water volume of any Chilean river. In most of the rivers there is excellent fishing.

Rain falls all the year round, most heavily further south, but decreases as you go inland: some 2500 mm of rain fall on the coast compared to 1350 mm inland. There is enough rainfall to maintain heavy forests, mostly of southern beech and native species, though there are increasingly large areas of eucalyptus and other introduced varieties to cater for the booming timber industry.

Border crossings: Chile–Argentina

There are several main routes from the Lake District into Argentina:

1 From Curacautín and Lonquimay to Zapala via Paso Pino Pinchado, or Paso de Icalma (see page 334).
2 From Pucón and Curarrehue to Junín de los Andes via Paso Mamuil Malal (also known as the Paso Tromen – see page 346).
3 From Lago Pirehueico to San Martín de los Andes via Paso Huahum (see page 359).
4 From Paso Puyehue to Bariloche (see page 375).
5 The lakes route, from Puerto Montt or Osorno via Ensenada, Petrohué and Lago Todos los Santos to Bariloche (see page 393).

Temuco and around

→ *Colour map 4, A2/3.*

At first sight, Temuco may appear a grey, forbidding place. However, in reality it is a lively industrial and university town. For visitors, it is perhaps more interesting as a contrast to the more European cities in other parts of Chile. Temuco is proud of its Mapuche heritage, and it is this that gives it a distinctive character, especially around the feria (outdoor market). North and east of the city are five national parks and reserves, and several hot springs, while to the west, in the valley of the Río Imperial, are the market towns of Nueva Imperial and Carahue and, on the coast, the resort of Puerto Saavedra. ▶▶ *For listings, see pages 334-339.*

Ins and outs

Getting there Manquehue Airport is 6 km southwest of city. There are several daily flights to/from Santiago, Concepción and Puerto Montt. Taxis from airport to Temuco city centre cost US$8.50; there is no airport bus service. Temuco is the transport hub for the Lake District, and its municipal bus station serves much of the region, as well as the communities towards the coast. The long-distance terminal is on the northern outskirts of town. The city is easily accessible by bus from Santiago (many daily) and has connections to large towns both north and south, especially Talca, Chillán, Concepción, Valdivia and Varas and Puerto Montt (many daily). Train connections to/from Santiago and south as far as Puerto Montt are currently suspended.

Getting around Temuco is a large city. *Colectivos* and buses serve the outlying barrios. However, the centre is relatively compact, and few places are more than a 30-minute walk away. When looking for a specific address, be careful not to confuse the streets Vicuña MacKenna and General MacKenna.

Tourist information Sernatur ① *Bulnes 586, T045-211969, infoaraucania@sernatur.cl, summer daily 0830-2030, winter Mon-Fri 0900-1200, 1500-1700,* has good leaflets in English. There is also a tourist information kiosk in the municipal market and an office of **CONAF** ① *Bilbao 931, T045-234420.*

The Mapuche

The largest indigenous group in southern South America, the Mapuche take their name from the words for 'land' (mapu) and 'people' (che). They were known as Araucanians by the Spanish.

Never subdued by the Incas, the Mapuche successfully resisted Spanish attempts at conquest. At the time of the great Mapuche uprising of 1598 they numbered some 500,000, concentrated in the area between the Río Biobío and the Reloncaví estuary. After 1598, two centuries of intermittent war were punctuated by 18 peace treaties. The 1641 Treaty of Quilín recognized Mapuche autonomy south of the río Biobío.

Although tools and equipment were privately owned, the Mapuche held land in common, abandoning it when it was exhausted by repeated use. This relatively nomadic lifestyle helps explain their ability to resist the Spanish. Learning from their enemies how to handle horses in battle, they became formidable guerrilla fighters. They pioneered the use of horses by two men, one of whom handled the animal, while the other was armed with bow and arrows. Horses also enabled the Mapuche to extend their territory to the eastern side of the Andes and the Argentine pampas.

The conquest of the Mapuche was made possible by the building of railways and the invention of new weapons, especially the breach-loading rifle (which had a similarly disquieting effect in Africa and Asia). The settlement of border disputes between Chile and Argentina enabled Argentine troops to occupy border crossings, while the Chileans subjugated the Mapuche.

Under the 1881 treaty, the Mapuche received 500,000 ha from the government, while 5000,000 ha were kept for Chile. The Mapuche were confined to reservations, most of which were situated near large estates for which they provided a labour force. By the 1930s, the surviving Mapuche, living in more than 3000 separate reservations, had become steadily more impoverished and dependent on the government.

The agrarian reforms of the 1960s provided little real benefit to the Mapuche since they encouraged private landholding – indeed some communal lands were sold off at this time – and the military government made continued encroachments on Mapuche communities, which remain among the poorest in Chile.

It is estimated that the Mapuche now occupy only about 1.5% of the lands they inhabited at the time of the Spanish conquest, mainly in communities south of the Biobío and in reserves in the Argentine cordillera around Lago Nahuel Huapi.

Temuco

The city is centred on the recently redesigned **Plaza Aníbal Pinto**, around which are the main public buildings including the cathedral and the municipalidad; the original cathedral was destroyed by the 1960 earthquake, when most of the old wooden buildings in the city were also burnt down. On the plaza itself is a monument to La Araucanía featuring figures from local history. Nearby are fountains and a small **Sala de Exposiciones**, which stages exhibitions. More compelling, though, is the *feria*, the huge produce market at Lautaro y Aníbal Pinto, always crammed with people (many of them Mapuche), who have come from the countryside to sell their produce (see page 337).

West of the centre, the **Museo de la Araucanía** ⓘ *Alemania 084, Mon-Fri 0900-1700, Sat 1100-1700, Sun 1100-1400, US$1.50 (free Sun), bus 1 from centre*, houses a well-arranged collection devoted to the history and traditions of the Mapuche nation; there's also a section on German settlement.

A couple of kilometres northeast of the centre is the **Museo Nacional Ferroviario Pablo Neruda** ① *Barros Arana 0565, T045-973940, www.museoferroviariotemuco.cl, Tue-Sun 0900-1800, US$2, concessions US$0.50, bus 1 variante or taxi (US$3 from the centre).* Exhibits include over 20 engines and carriages (including the former presidential carriage) dating from 1908 to 1953. The grounds contain rusting hulks and machinery, while the annex houses temporary exhibitions.

On the northern edge of the city is the **Monumento Natural Cerro Nielol** offering views of the city and surrounding countryside. It is a good spot for a picnic. There is an excellent **visitor centre** ① *Open 0830-2030, US$1.50*, run by CONAF, and a fine collection

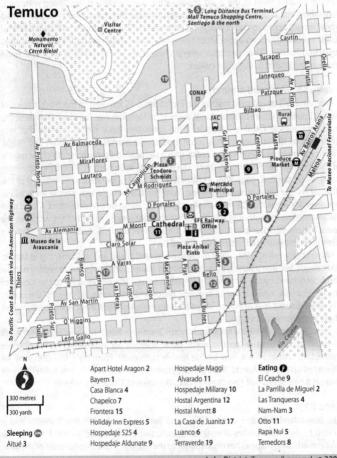

Temuco

To ⑤, Long Distance Bus Terminal, Mall Temuco Shopping Centre, Santiago & the north

Visitor Centre

Monumento Natural Cerro Nielol

To Pacific Coast & the south via Pan-American Highway

To Museo Nacional Ferroviario

N

300 metres
300 yards

Sleeping 🛏
Aitué **3**

Apart Hotel Aragon **2**
Bayern **1**
Casa Blanca **4**
Chapelco **7**
Frontera **15**
Holiday Inn Express **5**
Hospedaje 525 **4**
Hospedaje Aldunate **9**

Hospedaje Maggi
Alvarado **11**
Hospedaje Millaray **10**
Hostal Argentina **12**
Hostal Montt **8**
La Casa de Juanita **17**
Luanco **6**
Terraverde **19**

Eating 🍴
El Ceache **9**
La Parrilla de Miguel **2**
Las Tranqueras **4**
Nam-Nam **3**
Otto **11**
Rapa Nui **5**
Temedors **8**

of native plants in their natural environment, including the copihue rojo, the national flower. A tree marks the spot where peace was finally made with the Mapuche. Note that the hill has a one-way system for drivers (entry by Prat, exit by Lynch) and that bicycles are only allowed in before 1100.

Padre las Casas is a predominantly Mapuche suburb, southeast of the centre, on the other side of the Río Cautín, where you will find the **Casa de la Mujer Mapuche** ① *in the gym, between calles Corvalín and Almte Barroso, T045-233886, Mon-Fri 0930-1300, 1500-1830, bus 8a or 10, colectivo 13a.* Crafts and textiles made by a cooperative of 135 Mapuche weavers are sold here. The items are very good quality, but expensive.

Chol Chol

To get a flavour of the life of the Mapuche, it is well worth making a trip to this dusty, friendly country town in the heart of Mapuche country. Daily buses, laden with corn, vegetables, charcoal and animals as well as locals make the 30-km journey by paved road from Temuco across rolling countryside, with views of five volcanoes on a clear day. You will see people travelling by ox cart on the tracks nearby, and a few traditional round *rucas* (thatched houses). There are also several cheap bars in the town, as well as a small museum dedicated to Mapuche culture.

Puerto Saavedra and around

From Temuco a paved road follows the Río Imperial 35 km west to the market town of **Nueva Imperial**, where cattle auctions are held on Mondays and Tuesdays. From here the road continues to **Carahue**, the site of the Spanish colonial city of Imperial that was destroyed by the Mapuche. It has accommodation, a market, supermarkets and shops. The road continues to **Puerto Saavedra**, which lies behind a sandspit south of the mouth of the Río Imperial. Founded in 1897, the town was destroyed in 1960 by a *maremoto* (tidal wave; see box, page 364). Fortunately the local population were warned of the disaster by the sight of water draining from the bay, and so few people were killed. However, the impact of the *maremoto* on folktales cannot be overestimated. A local man commented to the author of this book, "We thought it was the end of the world, so we spent two months drunk on the hills until the water receded". One of Chile's most famous films in recent years, *La Frontera*, was filmed here.

After the *maremoto*, the centre of the town moved inland and its former site at **Maule**, 2 km south, became a fishing port. Just beyond Maule is a track to the incredibly narrow sandspit created by the *maremoto*. It stretches several kilometres north to the mouth of the Río Imperial, where there's a beautiful beach and uninterrupted views of the ocean. The third distinct area of Puerto Saavedra is the resort of **Boca Budi**, 4 km south, where there's an enormous beach.

From Puerto Saavedra a track leads north 2 km to a free ferry crossing over the Río Imperial to **Nehuentue**, on the north bank (there is an alternative, easier but less interesting crossing via a new bridge further upstream). From here launches may be chartered up the Río Moncul to the pleasant town of **Trovolhue**, four hours. Alternatively there is a half paved half *ripio* road north to the town of **Tirúa**, 70 km away.

Lago Budi

The only inland saltwater lake in Chile, Lago Budi lies south of Puerto Saavedra and is visited by over 130 species of water bird, including black-necked swans. Although the lake is marked on maps as having an outlet to the sea, this is dried up for most of the year, when there is a continuous track along the expanses of sandy beach from Puerto Saavedra south to Porma and Toltén. This was the old right of way for the Spanish between Concepción and Valdivia before their final defeat of the Mapuche; wild and remote, it passes many isolated Mapuche communities.

On the east shore of Lago Budi, 40 km by road south of Carahue, is **Puerto Domínguez**, a picturesque little town famous for its fishing. On the west shore is **Isla Huapi** (also spelt Guapi), a peninsula with a Mapuche settlement of *rucas* and fine views of the lake and the Pacific. This is one of the poorest spots in Chile, but is ideal for camping. It can be reached by *balsa* (ferry) either from 10 km south of Puerto Saavedra or from Puerto Domínguez.

Curacautín and around

Thirty kilometres north of Temuco a paved road branches off the Pan-American Highway and runs east to the Argentine border at Pino Hachado, passing through Curacautín (see page 334 for border crossing information). A small town situated on the Río Cautín, Curacautín lies 84 km northeast of Temuco and 56 km southeast of Victoria by good paved roads. Deprived by new, stricter deforestation laws of its traditional timber industry (until recently there were several sawmills here), Curacautín is trying to recreate itself as a centre for tourism; it is a useful base for visiting the nearby national parks and hot springs, including the indoor and sadly run-down **Termas de Manzanar** ① *17 km east of Curacautín, www.termasdemanzanar.cl, open all year, US$12.* On the way, at Km 6, the road passes a turn-off to **Laguna Blanca** (25 km north, take fishing gear) and the **Salto del Indio** ① *Km 13, US$1.60,* a 30-m-high waterfall, where there are *cabañas.* Some 3 km beyond Manzanar is the **Salto de la Princesa**, a 50-m waterfall, with camping and *hostería.*

Termas and Parque Nacional Tolhuaca

The beautiful pine-surrounded **Termas de Tolhuaca** ① *www.termasdetolhuaca.cl, open all year, US$13,* are 35 km to the north of Curacautín by *ripio* road, or 57 km by unpaved road from just north of Victoria; a high-clearance 4WD is essential out of season. Just 2 km further north is the **Parque Nacional Tolhuaca** ① *open Dec-Apr,* which covers 6374 ha of the valley of the Río Malleco at altitudes of 850 to 1830 m and includes the waterfalls of Malleco and Culebra, and two lakes, Laguna Malleco and Laguna Verde. There's superb scenery and good views of the volcanoes from Cerro Amarillo. Park administration is near Laguna Malleco and there is a campsite nearby. Unfortunately, much of the park, together with the neighbouring **Reserva Nacional Malleco**, was damaged by forest fires in 2002, and will take several decades fully to recover, although some day-trails are open.

Reserva Nacional Nalcas-Malalcahuello

Situated northeast of Curacautín, this 31,305-ha park lies on the slopes of the **Lonquimay Volcano** (2865 m), and is much less crowded than the nearby Parque Nacional Conguillio. The volcano began erupting on Christmas day 1988 and the crater produced was named Navidad. Useful information about the park is available from the **CONAF** office on the main road in Malalcahuello (east of Curacautín) and from **La Suizandina** (see Sleeping below), which is also a good base for treks and for the ascent of the volcano. Several marked trails (varying from one hour to two days) leave from the CONAF office. From Malalcahuello it is a one-day hike to the Sierra Nevada (see below), or a two-day hike to Conguillio national park; less experienced climbers should hire a guide.

Los Arenales ski resort ① *T045-891071, season Jun-Sep, Sat-Tue only, winter access from Lonquimay town, ski pass US$25, equipment hire US$23,* is at Las Raíces Pass on the

The monkey puzzle tree

The Araucaria araucana, known in Chile as the *araucaria* or *pehuén* and elsewhere called variously the Chilean pine, the umbrella tree, the parasol tree and the monkey puzzle tree, is the Chilean national tree and has flourished in this area for 200 million years. Very slow growing, it can grow up to 40 m high; and live for 1200 years. The characteristic cones can weigh up to 1 kg so take care sitting underneath! Though its natural habitat is on both sides of the Andes between 37° and 39° south, it is much more widespread in Chile than in Argentina.

The araucaria was revered by the Mapuche, who ate both its cones and its sharp leathery leaves. Some isolated trees are still seen as sacred by the Mapuche, who leave offerings to the tree's spirit.

road from Malalcahuello to Lonquimay town. It is a pleasant, small resort with a nice restaurant and four lifts that go up to 2500 m with great views. In winter the pass is usually snowed out, and the road from Malalcahuello to Lonquimay town is diverted via the **Túnel Las Raíces** ① *toll US$2*. This former railway tunnel was, until recently, the longest in South America at 4.8 km. There is talk of repairing the tunnel, but for the moment it is in poor condition, unlit and with constant filtration. If travelling by bicycle it is wiser to hitch through the tunnel in a pickup than cycling through yourself.

Access to climb Lonquimay is either from Malalcahuello, 15 km south, or from from the ski resort from where it is a one-hour walk to the municipal *refugio* at the base of the mountain. Walk towards the ski lift and from there head to the spur on the left. Allow four hours for the ascent, one hour for the descent. Crampons and ice-axe are necessary in winter, but in summer it is a relatively simple climb.

Parque Nacional Conguillío

① *Entry US$6, visitor centre (open Dec-Mar) at the park administration by Lago Conguillío. CONAF runs free slide lectures and short guided walks during the summer, covering flora and fauna, Volcán Llaima and other subjects.*

Covering 60,833 ha, the park, situated 80 km east of Temuco, is one of the most popular in Chile though it is deserted outside January and February and at weekends. In the centre is the **Llaima Volcano** (3125 m), which is still active and can be climbed. There are two craters: the western crater was blown out in 1994 and began erupting again in March 1996. The volcano came to life again on New Year's day 2008 and the effects are visible in the massive lava-flow to the north. The last eruption was in April 2009. There are two large lakes, Laguna Verde and Lago Conguillío, and two smaller ones, Laguna Arco Iris and Laguna Captrén. North of Lago Conguillío rise the snow-covered peaks of extinct volcano **Sierra Nevada**, which reaches 2554 m.

Much of the park is covered in forests of southern beech but it is also the best place in Chile to see native **araucaria forest**, which used to cover extensive areas of land in this part of the country (see box, above). Mature araucaria forest can be found around Lago Conguillío and on the slopes of Llaima. Other trees include cypress and *canelo* (winter's bark). Among the park's wildlife are condors, black woodpeckers, the marsupial *monito del monte*, pumas, foxes, pudú and many waterfowl.

There are three **entrances** to the park: the northern entrance is reached by *ripio* road from Curacautín, 28 km north; the southern entrance at Truful-Truful is reached by a *ripio* road from Melipeuco, 13 km southwest, while the western entrance is reached by *ripio* road from Cherquenco (high-clearance vehicle essential). Close by is the **Araucarias ski resort** ① *T045-239999, www.skiaraucarias.cl, US$30*, with four ski lifts, a café, restaurant, bar, *refugio* and equipment rental (US$25).

Trails within the park range from 1 to 22 km in length. Details are available from the park administration or from CONAF in Temuco. One of the best trails is a path round the east side of Lago Conguillío and north towards the Sierra Nevada (allow a full day for the round-trip). The first 10 km are reasonably easy, with two or three miradors offering spectacular views. After this it gets much more difficult for the final 5-km climb. From the western entrance it is a two- to three-day hike around Volcán Llaima to Lago Conguillío – a dusty route, but with beautiful views of Laguna Quepe – then on to the Laguna Captrén *guardería*.

Climb **Llaima** south from **Guardería Captrén**, avoiding the crevassed area to the left of the ridge and keeping to the right of the red scree just below the ridge. From the ridge it is a straight climb to the summit. Beware of sulphur fumes at the top. Allow five hours to ascend, two hours to descend. Crampons and ice-axe are essential except in summer; less experienced climbers should also hire a guide. Further information on the climb is available from **Guardería Captrén**.

Parque Nacional Conguillío

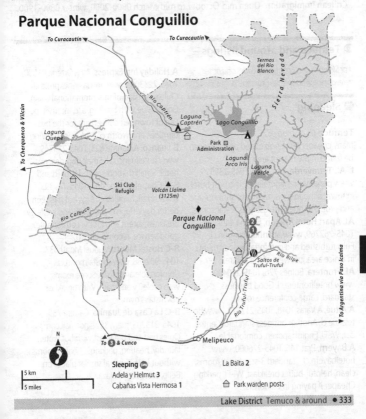

Sleeping
Adela y Helmut **3**
Cabañas Vista Hermosa **1**

La Baita **2**

🏠 Park warden posts

Border crossings: Chile–Argentina

Curacautín/Lonquimay–Zapala via Paso Pino Hachado

Paso Pino Hachado (1884 m) can be reached either by a paved road 73 km southeast from Lonquimay or by a mostly unpaved road 129 km east from Melipeuco. On the Argentine side this road continues to Zapala; some buses from Temuco to Zapala and Neuquén use this crossing.

Immigration and customs At Liucura, 22 km west of the frontier, September to mid-May 0800-2000; winter 0800-1900, can involve very thorough searches, especially when entering Chile.

Curacautín/Lonquimay–Zapala via Paso de Icalma

An alternative route is via Paso de Icalma (1298 m) reached by *ripio* road, 53 km east of Melipeuco, south of Parque Nacional Conguillio, and continuing on the Argentine side to Zapala. This route is often impassable in winter. To see if the pass is open, contact the **Policía Internacional** in Temuco (Prat 19, T045-293890).

Chilean immigration Open mid-October to mid-March 0800-2000; winter 0800-1900.

⊕ Temuco and around listings

For Sleeping and Eating price codes and other relevant information, see Essentials pages 35-42.

⊜ Sleeping

Temuco *p327, map p329*
Many cheaper *residenciales* and *pensiones* can be found in the market area.
L-AL Terraverde, Prat 0220, T045-239999, www.panamericanahoteles.cl. The best hotel in town, although it is starting to show its age and probably does not justify its 5-star status.
AL Apart Hotel Aragon, España 446, T045-262769, www.aparthotelaragon.cl. Fully furbished and comfortable apartments in a nice area just west of the centre.
AL Frontera, Bulnes 726, T045-200400, www.hotelfrontera.cl. Good business standard. Large conference room.
A Aitué, A Varas 1048, T045-212512, www.hotelaitue.cl. Another business standard. Central, bar, Wi-Fi, English spoken, comfortable.
A Bayern, Prat 146, T045-276000, www.hotelbayern.cl. Standard 3-star. Small rooms, clean, helpful, buffet breakfast, Wi-Fi, parking. Cheaper if paying in US dollars.

A Holiday Inn Express, Av R Ortega 01800, T045-223300, www.holidayinnexpress.cl. Chilean version of this international chain. Good value with heating, a/c, internet, pool. Out of town but convenient for the bus terminal, and worth considering if driving.
B Luanco, Aldunate 821, T045-213749, www.hotelluanco.cl. Small non-descript hotel. Smallish rooms with TV, bath and Wi-Fi.
B-C Chapelco, Cruz 401, T045-749393 www.hotelchapelco.cl. Airy, but has seen better days. Rooms with bath and cable TV. Breakfast, internet in lobby, comfortable, good service, recommended.
B-C Hostal Montt, Manuel Montt 637, T045-982488, www.hostalmontt.cl. Comfortable and clean. Some rooms with cable TV and bath. With breakfast, downstairs gym.
B-C La Casa de Juanita, Carrera 735, T045-213203, juany362@hotmail.com. Quiet bed and breakfast with hot water, laundry, heating, parking. Cheaper rooms without bath. Several similar places on Bello, west of the plaza.

C Hospedaje Maggi Alvarado, Recreo 209, off Av Alemania, T045-409804, cppacl@gmail.com. **E** singles. Small rooms, but very clean, friendly, helpful, in a pleasant part of town. Also has a good-value *cabaña* sleeping 4.

C Hostal Argentina, Aldunate 864, T045-624238. Run-down. With breakfast, hot water, parking and TV.

C-D Casa Blanca, Montt 1306 y Zenteno, T045-277799, hostalcasablancatemuco@gmail.com. **F** singles. With breakfast, friendly, slightly run-down, but good value for rooms with bath.

C-D Hospedaje 525, Zenteno 525, T045-233982. **F** singles. Without breakfast, some rooms with bath, large rooms, clean, poor beds but good value. TV lounge.

C-D Hospedaje Aldunate, Aldunate 187, T045-270057, cristorresvalenzuela@hotmail.com. **E** singles. Friendly, cooking facilities, some rooms with TV and bath.

C-D Hospedaje Millaray, Claro Solar 471, T045-645720, hostalmillaray_tco@yahoo.es. **F** singles. Simple, basic, unfriendly. Other houses on this street in the same price range.

Puerto Saavedra *p330*

B Hotel Boca Budi, Boca Budi, T045-352990. With bath and breakfast. Sea views, heating, room service, heated swimming pool. Tours offered. Mid-price restaurant.

C Cabañas Miramar, Miramar 3, Puerto Saavedra, T045-634290, www.miramarchile.com. Fully equipped *cabañas* for 2-8 people, with picnic and barbeque areas. Also camping, US$10 per site.

D Hospedaje Santa Rita, Las Dunas 01511, T045-634171, ritasandovalm@hotmail.com. **E-F** singles. Lovely, knowledgeable host, home-cooked food served.

D Lago Los Cisnes, Boca Budi, T045-251891. Cheap option with restaurant.

Lago Budi *p330*

C Hostería Rucaleufú, Alessandri 22, Puerto Domínguez, T045-687794. With good meals, often serves fresh lake-caught fish, clean, lake views. Highly recommended.

The only other accommodation is the Puaucho campsite on Isla Huapi.

Curacautín and around *p331*

L-AL Termas de Manzanar, Termas de Manzanar, 17 km from Curacautín, T045-881200, www.termasdemanzanar.cl. Simple rooms with bath, includes access to thermal pools, full board available. Overpriced.

B Anden Rose, 5 km west of Manzanar (Km 68) on the banks of the river Cautín, T09-9869 1700, www.andenrose.com. Rooms with bath and central heating. With breakfast, restaurant, bike, horse, kayak rental, tours arranged, camping, good restaurant. German owners. Good reports.

B-C Hostal Las Espigas, Miraflores 315, Curacautín, T045-881138, rivaseugenia@hotmail.com. **E** singles. Good rooms with bath, kitchen, breakfast, dinner available on request.

B-C Plaza, Yungay 157, main plaza, Curacautín, T045-881256. Overpriced. Restaurant is okay but pricey.

C Hostería Abarzúa, Termas de Manzanar, 18 km from Curacautín, T045-870011. Simple, friendly. *Cabañas*, also cheaper rooms without bath. Full board available (good food).

C Hostería La Rotunda del Cautín, Termas de Manzanar, 17 km from Curacautín, T045-881569, www.rotondadelcautin.cl. Rooms and good mid-range restaurant, friendly.

D Residencial Rojas, Tarapacá 249, Curacautín. **F** singles. Without bath, good meals. Recommended.

D Turismo, Tarapacá 140, Curacautín, T045-881116 hotelturismocuracautin@gmail.com. **E-F** singles. Clean, good food, comfortable, best value.

Termas and Parque Nacional Tolhuaca *p331*

L Termas de Tolhuaca, Termas de Tolhuaca, T045-881164, www.termasdetolhuaca.cl. With full board, includes use of baths and horse riding, jacuzzi and massage also available. Very good.

D Residencial Roja, Termas de Tolhuaca.
F singles. Hot water, food, camping near
the river, good.

Reserva Nacional Nalcas-Malalcahuello *p331*

A-B La Suizandina, Km 28, Curacautín-
Lonquimay rd (3 km from Malalcahuello),
T045-1973725, www.suizandina.com. Double
rooms, hostel accommodation (price per
person) and camping. Laundry, large swiss
breakfast with home-baked bread, English and
German spoken, TCs accepted, good meals.
Hiking, horse riding, travel and trekking tours
or just information. Car hire. It's been described
as "like being in Switzerland". Recommended.
C Residencial Los Sauces, Estación 510, in
Malalcahuello village, on the edge of the park,
T09-7497 8706. **F** singles with shared bath
and use of kitchen, hot water. Also good-
value *cabañas*. Full board available.
Señora Naomi Saavedra arranges lifts
to destinations within the reserve.
C-D Hostal Lonquimay, Pinto 555,
Lonquimay, T045-891324. **E-F** singles.
Basic rooms with shared baths and breakfast.
D Hospedaje Navidad, Caupolicán 915,
Lonquimay, T045-891111. **F** singles.
More of the same. With restaurant.

Parque Nacional Conguillio *p332, map p333*

A La Baita, 3 km south of Laguna Verde,
T045-581253/T09-9733 2442,
www.labaitaconguillio.cl. *Cabañas* with
electricity, hot water, kitchen and wood
stove. Charming, lots of information as
well as nature trails and a good restaurant.
Italian/Chilean owned, recommended.
A-B Cabañas Vista Hermosa, 10 km from
the southern entrance, T09-9444 1630. Clean
but spartan wooden cabins, each with a
wood stove and fantastic views to the
volcano. Electricity pm only. Run by a friendly
horse-riding guide (he's a former champion
equestrian). Good food. Recommended.
B Centro Turístico Los Pioneros, 1 km
east of Melipeuco, T045-581005, turismo

pioneros@araucaniaandina.cl. **D** Singles.
Rooms and *cabañas*. Full board available,
tours to the park offered.
C Adela y Helmut, Faja 16000, 5 km north
of Temuco–Cunco rd, west of Melipeuco,
T09-8258 2230,www.adelayhelmut.com.
Cosy guesthouse (upgraded in 2007) and
restaurant on a Mapuche/German-owned
farm, English spoken, room for families and
for backpackers in 6-bed dorm (**E**pp), meals
extra, kitchens, hot showers, solar heating,
mountain bike rental. Pick-up from Temuco
US$34. Tours to Conguillio National Park,
hot springs, Mapuche and other sites,
US$125-177 pp all-inclusive from Temuco.
Also arrange horse-riding and fly-fishing
packages. Website has directions, phone
for pick-up from bus stop. Good reports.
D Hospedaje Icalma, Aguirre Cerda 729,
Melipeuco, T045-581108. **E-F** singles.
Spacious, basic rooms with bath and
breakfast. Recommended.

Camping

There are several campsites in the park,
one on the west side of Laguna Captrén
and 5 dotted around Lago Conguillio. All
are administered by CONAF, T045-298210,
parque.conguillio@conaf.cl for information
and reservations. There is a free municipal
campsite in Melipeuco and Camping
Los Pioneros, 1 km from Melipeuco, T045-
581005. On road to the park, hot water.

🍴 Eating

For places to eat in Puerto Saavedra, Curacautín
and the national parks, see Sleeping, above.

Temuco *p327, map p329*

Those on a very strict budget should make for
the **Mercado Municipal**, Aldunate y Portales,
where there are several restaurants and fierce
touting for business, or the rural bus terminal,
where countless restaurants serve very cheap
set meals at lunch. *Humitas* are on sale in the
street in summer/autumn.

La Caleta, Mercado Municipal, Aldunate y Portales. One of the better choices in the covered market serving fish and seafood.

La Cumbre del Cerro Nielol, Cerro Nielol. Food and dancing on top of the hill, not always open.

La Parrilla de Miguel, Montt 1095, T045-275182. Good for large servings of meat and wine. One of the better restaurants in the town centre.

Las Tranqueras, Alemania 0888, T045-385 044. One of several good mid-priced restaurants on Av Alemania (take bus 1). Meat specialists, great grills, vegetarian options available.

Otto, V Mackenna 530. German dishes, cakes, etc.

El Ceache, Cruz 231. Typical Chilean food. Good-value set lunch.

Nam-Nam, Portales 802. Good sandwiches and snacks.

Rapa Nui, Aldunate 415. For take-away lunches and snacks, recommended.

Restaurante Temedors, San Martín 827. Good-value lunch.

Cafés

Café Marriet, Prat 451, Local 21. Excellent coffee.

Il Gelato, Bulnes 420. Delicious ice cream.

✪ Bars and clubs

Temuco *p327, map p329*
Banana bliss, Montt 1031. Bar and disco.
El Túnel, Caupolicán y M Blanco. Restaurant with dancing.
Mr Jones, Bello 844. Pub-café-disco.
Sol y Luna, 10 km south on road to Pucón. Late-night disco.

✪ Entertainment

Temuco *p327, map p329*
There is a cinema on the south side of the plaza, and another on the 3rd floor of the Almacenes Paris building, Montt y Prat.

It is also worth checking out the Instituto Chileno-Francés, Varas 736, and the Instituto Chileno-Norte Americano, Gen MacKenna 555, for films and events.

✪ Shopping

Buy supplies in Temuco, Curacautín or Melipeuco, where they are much cheaper than in the shop in the Parque Nacional Conguillio.

Temuco *p327, map p329*
Crafts
Mapuche crafts and textiles are sold inside and around the **Mercado Municipal**, Aldunate y Portales, and also in the **Casa de la Mujer Mapuche**.

Food
Frutería Las Vegas, Matta 274. Dried fruit (useful for climbing/trekking).
Las Brisas, Rodríguez 1100 block. Supermarket.
Santa Isabel, Bulnes 279. Supermarket.
Super, Rodríguez 1400 block. Supermarket.
Temuco feria, Lautaro y Aníbal Pinto. One of the most fascinating markets in Chile, where people from the surrounding countryside come to sell their wares. You will find excellent cheap fruit and vegetables, local spices such as *merquén* (made from smoked chillies), fish, grains, cheese and honey; there are many inexpensive bars and restaurants nearby.

✪ Activities and tours

Temuco *p327, map p329*
Most companies in Temuco offer tours to Parque Nacional Conguillio, 1 day, US$60; to Puerto Saavedra and Villarrica volcano (US$90), but unless you are in a hurry it is better and cheaper to book a tour closer to the destination. Some also offer skiing and snowboarding trips.
Amity Tour, Bucalemu 01220, T045-285290, www.amitytours.cl. A wide range of tours throughout the region.

Tribu Piren, Prat 069, T045-985711, www.tribupiren.cl.

Curacautín and around p331
Turismo Christopher, Yungay 260, T045-882471.
Turismo Tolhuaca, Calama 240.

● Transport

Temuco p327, map p329
Air
LanChile, Bulnes 687, on plaza, T600-526 2000, www.lan.com; and Sky, T600-600 2828, fly to Manquehue Airport to/from **Santiago**, 1¼ hrs, from US$85 return; **Concepción**, 40 mins, **Osorno**, 40 mins, and **Puerto Montt**, 45 mins.

Bus
Local Services to neighbouring towns leave from **Terminal Rural**, Pinto y Balmaceda or from bus company offices nearby: Erbuc, Miraflores y Bulnes; JAC, NarBus and Igi Llaima, Balmaceda y Aldunate; TurBus, Lagos 549.

To **Panguipulli**, Power and Pangui Sur, 2½ hrs, US$5. Pangui Sur also has services to **Loncoche**, US$3, **Los Lagos**, US$4, and **Mehuín**, summer only. To **Curacautín** via Lautaro, Erbuc, 4 daily, 2½ hrs, US$5, continuing to **Lonquimay**, 3½hrs, US$6. Narbus has hourly services daily to **Nueva Imperial**, **Carahue** and **Puerto Saavedra**. JAC runs buses to **Villarrica** and **Pucón**, many daily 0705-2045, 1½ hrs, US$6, and to **Coñaripe**, 3 hrs, and **Lican-Ray**, 2 hrs. Erbuc and Thiele run buses to **Contulmo**, 2 hrs, US$5, **Cañete**, US$5 and **Lebú**. To **Chol Chol**, Huincabus, 4 daily 1100-1800, 1 hr, US$2.

Long distance The long-distance terminal is north of city at Pérez Rosales y Caupolicán; to get there, take buses 2, 7 or 10 from the centre. To **Santiago** several companies, 8-9hrs, many overnight, US$18-48; to **Castro**, Cruz del Sur, 3 a day; to **Puerto Montt**, 10 a day, 5½ hrs, US$10-18; to **Valdivia**, JAC, several daily,

2½ hrs, US$6; to **Osorno** 4 hrs, US$8; to **Concepción**, Bío Bío, 4½ hrs, US$9; to **Chillán**, 4 hrs, US$9.

International To **Junín de los Andes** via Pucón, Igi Llaima and Narbus, daily between them, leaves early morning, advance booking required, US$27. To **Neuquén** via Curacautín, Lonquimay and the Paso Pino Hachado, Igi Llaima, Buses Caraza and Buses El Valle, daily between them, US$33; Buses Caraza have connecting services to **Buenos Aires**, **Bahía Blanca** and **Mar del Plata**, US$58. To **Bariloche** via Osorno, Tas Choapa, daily, US$30.

Car
Car hire from **Budget**, Lynch 471, T045-214911; **Christopher Car**, Varas 522, T/F045-215988; **Dollar**, at airport, T045-336512; **Euro**, MacKenna 426, T045-210311, helpful, good value; **Full Famas**, at airport and in centre T045-215420, recommended; **Hertz**, Las Heras 999, T045-235385. Several others.

Motorbike/bike
Motorbike mechanic: **Terremoto**, Claro Solar 358, T045-312828. Bicycles parts can be bought at Oxford, Andrés Bello 1040, T045-211869; repairs at Bulnes 228, Lautaro 1370, Portales 688. Also many on Balmaceda, Nos 1266, 1294 and 1448.

Train
The station is at Barros Arana y Lautaro Navarro, T045-233416, www.efe.cl. At the time of writing, services north to Santiago and south to Puerto Montt are suspended.

Puerto Saavedra p330
To **Temuco** (Terminal Rural), **Narbus**, hourly, 3 hrs, US$3.

Lago Budi p330
There are buses to **Puerto Domínguez** from Temuco, 3 hrs.

The Carlos Schalchli ferry leaves Puerto Domínguez for **Isla Huapi**, Mon and Wed 0900 and 1700, returning 0930 and 1730, free, 30 mins.

Curacautín and around *p331*
The bus terminal is on the main street, by the plaza. TurBus and Inter Sur have daily direct services to **Santiago**. Erbuc services from Temuco and Los Angeles continue on to **Malalcahuello** and **Lonquimay**.

Parque Nacional Tolhuaca *p331*
There are bus services from Victoria to **San Gregorio** (19 km from park entrance) Mon, Wed, Fri 1715; return same day 0645.

Reserva Nacional Nalcas-Malalcahuello *p331*
Erbuc runs bus services from Temuco via Lautaro and Curacautín, 4 daily, to **Malalcahuello**, 3 hrs, US$5.50, and **Lonquimay** town, 3 ½ hrs (or 4 hrs via Victoria), US$6.

Parque Nacional Conguillio *p332, map p333*
There are daily buses from Temuco to **Cherquenco**, but no onward public transport into the park.

Taxi from Curacautín to the **northern entrance**, US$35 one-way. Transport to the **southern entrance** can be arranged from Melipeuco (ask in grocery stores and *hospedajes*), US$35 one-way. For touring, hire a 4WD in Temuco or join an agency tour, see Activities and tours, above.

Directory

Temuco *p327, map p329*
Banks ATMs at several banks on or around Plaza A Pinto. Also try the following *casas de cambio*: Christopher, Prat 696, of 419; Comex, Prat 471; Inter-Santiago, Bulnes 443, Local 2; Turcamb, Claro Solar 733; also at Bulnes 667, Local 202, and at Prat 427. There are many *cambios* around the Plaza; all deal in dollars and Argentine pesos. **Consulates** Netherlands, España 494, honorary consul, Germán Nicklas, is friendly and helpful. **Internet** Several throughout the city, generally US$0.75 per hr. **Laundry** Alba, Zeneto 480, opposite the church, and at Aldunate 324 and Aldunate 842; Marva, M Montt 415 and 1099, Mon-Sat 0900-2030. **Post office** Portales 839. **Telephone** CTC, A Prat just off Claro Solar and plaza, open Mon-Sat 0800-2400, Sun and holidays 1030-2400; Entel, Bulnes 303, daily 0830-2200; also call centres at Lautaro 1311 and Montt 631.

Lago Villarrica and around

→ *Colour map 4, B2/3.*
Wooded Lago Villarrica, 21 km long and about 7 km wide, is one of the most beautiful lakes in the region, with the active and snow-capped Villarrica Volcano (2840 m) to the southeast. Villarrica and Pucón, resorts at the lake's southwest and southeast corners, are among the more expensive in the region, but are definitely worth a visit. ➤➤ *For listings, see pages 346-355.*

Villarrica ⊖⊘⊕⊛▲⊙⊙ ➤➤ *pp346-355. Colour map 4, B2.*

Pleasantly set at the extreme southwest corner of the lake, Villarrica can be reached by a paved road southeast from Freire, 24 km south of Temuco on the Pan-American Highway, or from Loncoche, 54 km south of Freire, also paved. Less significant as a tourist resort than nearby Pucón, it is a little cheaper. Founded in 1552, the town was besieged by the Mapuche in the uprising of 1599: after three years the surviving Spanish settlers, 11 men and 13 women, surrendered. The town was refounded in 1882.

There is a small museum, **Museo Histórico** ① *Pedro de Valdivia 1050 y Zegers, Mon-Sat 0900-1730, 1800-2200, Sun 1800-2200, reduced hrs in winter, US$0.50,* containing a collection of Mapuche artefacts. Next to it is the **Muestra Cultural Mapuche**, featuring a Mapuche *ruca* and stalls selling good quality handicrafts in summer. The **tourist office** ① *Valdivia 1070, T045-411162, open daily in summer, Mon-Fri off season,* has information and maps. There are good views of the volcano from the *costanera;* for a different perspective over the lake, go south along Aviador Acevedo and then Poniente Ríos towards the **Hostería La Colina**. Just south of town (500 m along Avenida Matta), there is a large working farm, **Fundo Huifquenco** ① *T045-412200, www.fundohuifquenco.cl,* with trails, horse riding, carriage rides and meals (book in advance).

Pucón ⊖⊘⊘⊕⊛⊙▲⊙⊙ ➤➤ *pp346-355. Colour map 4, B2.*

On the southeastern corner of the lake, 26 km east of Villarrica, Pucón is one of the most popular destinations in the Lake District, famous above all as a centre for visiting the 2840 m Villarrica Volcano, which dominates the view to the south. Built across the neck of a peninsula, the town has two black-sand beaches, which are popular for swimming and water sports. Whitewater rafting is also offered on the nearby rivers and excursions can be made into the Parque Nacional Huerquehue or the Cañi Nature Reserve as well as a number of thermal springs, all of which lie east of the town.

Ins and outs

Getting there Pucón is served by four daily buses from Puerto Montt and Valdivia and several daily (many overnight) from Santiago. There are regular services from Temuco and Villarrica. The airport, 2 km east of Pucón on the Caburga road, has several flights a week to/from Santiago in summer.
Getting around Pucón is small enough to walk around. Taxis for out-of-town trips.
Tourist information Do not confuse the **Municipal Tourist Office** ① *Municipalidad, O'Higgins 483, T045-293002, ofturismo@municipalidadpucon.cl,* which provides information and sells fishing licences, with the Chamber of Tourism at the entrance to Pucón from Villarrica and other private operators displaying 'Tourist Information' signs.

The town also has a **CONAF** office ① *Lincoyan 336*, with leaflets and information on the national parks.

Sights and activities

The Pucón of today is very different from the town of 30 years ago, when it was a small, pleasant, quiet village with some seasonal Chilean tourism, but no foreign backpackers. It is now a thriving tourist centre, full of Chileans in summer and gringos in the autumn. Within easy reach of town are an active climbable volcano where you can also ski in

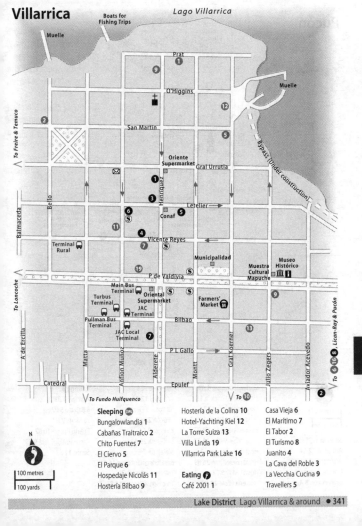

Villarrica

Lago Villarrica

Boats for Fishing Trips

Muelle

Prat ①

O'Higgins

Muelle

To Freire & Temuco

San Martín

⑨

✝

⑫

Oriente Supermarket

Gral Urrutla

⑤

Bypass (Under construction)

✉

❶

Henríquez

Letelier

❸

Conaf

⑥ ⑪ ⑤

Bello

❹

Vicente Reyes

⑦ ⑤

Balmaceda

Terminal Rural

⑲

Municipalidad

P de Valdivia

Muestra Cultural Mapuche

Museo Histórico 🏛 ❶

To Loncoche

Main Bus Terminal ⑤ ⑤

Turbus Terminal

Oriental Supermarket

JAC Terminal

Farmers' Market 🛒

⑨

A de Ercilla

Pullman Bus Terminal

JAC Local Terminal ⑦

Bilbao

⑬

To 6 16 8, Lican-Ray & Pucón

Catedral

Matta

Antón Muñoz

Alderete

P I Gallo

Montt

Gral Koerner

Julio Zegers

Aviador Acevedo

Epulef

To Fundo Huifquenco

To 10

❷

N

100 metres
100 yards

Sleeping 🛏

Bungalowlandia 1
Cabañas Traitraico 2
Chito Fuentes 7
El Ciervo 5
El Parque 6
Hospedaje Nicolás 11
Hostería Bilbao 9

Hostería de la Colina 10
Hotel-Yachting Kiel 12
La Torre Suiza 13
Villa Linda 19
Villarrica Park Lake 16

Eating 🍴

Café 2001 1

Casa Vieja 6
El Marítimo 7
El Tabor 2
El Turismo 8
Juanito 4
La Cava del Roble 3
La Vecchia Cucina 9
Travellers 5

winter, rivers for whitewater rafting and fly-fishing, canopy tours in native forests, quadbike excursions, lakes and waterfalls, two national parks and a private nature sanctuary as well as a dozen thermal springs. This makes Pucón an excellent base for visiting the northern lake district.

Every other house in the town centre seems to offer accommodation, while the main drag is awash with tour operators. Neon signs are forbidden and road signs and telephone kiosks are made of wood, but the streets are full of bars, restaurants, boutiques and *artesanía*. The commercial centre lies between **Avenida O'Higgins**, the main thoroughfare, and the **Gran Hotel Pucón**. Private land (ask for permission at the entrance)

Pucón

100 metres
100 yards

Sleeping
Antumalal 2 *C1*
Araucarias 1 *B1*
Donde Germán 6 *C3*
Gran Pucón 8 *A2*
Gudenschwager 4 *A1*
Hospedaje Graciela 13 *C2*
Hospedaje Lucía 17 *C2*
Hospedaje M@yra 10 *B3*
Hospedaje Sonia 18 *B2*
Hospedaje Victor 11 *C2*
Hostal Backpackers 3 *C2*
Hostal Gerónimo 26 *B3*
Hostal Willy 5 *C3*
Hostería école 21 *B3*
Interlaken 24 *C1*
Kernayel 12 *C3*
La Posada Plaza-
  Pucón 28 *B1*
La Poza 9 *C1*
La Tetera 29 *B2*
Malalhue 7 *C3*
Residencial Lincoyán 16 *B2*
Tr@vel Pucón 15 *C3*
Tree House Hostel 14 *B3*

Eating
Arabian 1 *B2*
Il Baretto 5 *B2*
La Maga 7 *B2*
Puerto Pucón 10 *B2*
Rap Hamburguesa 9 *B3*
Senzo 11 *B2*

leads west from the centre of town to **La Península**, where there are fine views of the lake and volcano, as well as a golf course. There is also a pleasant walk, along the **Costanera Otto Gudenschwager**, starting at the northern end of Calle Ansorena and following the lakeside north.

Boat trips ① *daily 1500 and 1900, summer only, 2 hrs, US$8,* on the lake leave from the landing stage at La Poza at the western end of O'Higgins. Walk a couple of kilometres north along the beach from here to the mouth of the Río Trancura for views of volcanoes. Or take a **boat** ① *summer only, US$15,* to the mouth of the river from near the **Gran Hotel**.

To cross the Río Pucón, head east out of Pucón along the main road, then turn north on an unmade road leading to a new bridge. There are pleasant walks from here along the north shore of the lake to the Mapuche settlement of **Quelhue** and the beach at **Río Plata**, or northeast towards **Caburga** (the round trip makes a perfect day's outing by mountain bike). You can also strike up into the hills through farms and agricultural land, with views of three volcanoes and the lake (if possible, ask permission to cross first).

From the road to the Villarrica Volcano, a *ripio* road branches off for 5 km to some privately managed **Cuevas Volcánicas** (volcanic caves') ① *T045-442002, www.cuevas volcanicas.cl, US$18,* surrounded by a small attractive park with tunnels and a museum, as well as paths through the forest. Entry to the site is expensive, but it's recommended as a bad-weather option. Snowmobile tours are also offered.

East of Lago Villarrica

Within easy reach of Villarrica and Pucón are two more lakes, two national parks and several hot springs. Busy with Chilean tourists in summer, these are among the most dramatic spots in the Lake District, and well worth a visit for those in the area.

Parque Nacional Villarrica

This park, which covers 61,000 ha, stretches from Pucón to the Argentine border near Puesco. There are three sectors: Villarrica Volcano sector, Quetrupillán Volcano sector (see page 345) and the Puesco sector, which includes the slopes of the Lanín Volcano on the Argentine border. Each sector has its own entrance and ranger station.

The **Villarrica Volcano** ① *access US$5,* 2840 m high and still active, lies 8 km south of Pucón. Access to this sector is in theory restricted only to groups with a guide and there is no public transport, although several agencies offer trips and to individuals who can show proof of membership of a mountaineering club in their own country. Entry is refused if the weather is poor. Good boots, crampons and ice picks are essential; these can be rented for US$12 per day from tour operators, but will be generally be included in the price of a tour. You should also take sunglasses, sun block, plenty of water and chocolate or some other snack; equipment is checked at the park entrance. ▶▶ *See Activities and tours, page 352.*

It is a three- to four-hour trek to the summit, but you can skip the first part of the ascent by taking the **ski lift** ① *US$10.* In summer this is recommended as it saves 400 m climbing scree. If the conditions are right, at the summit you can look down into the crater at the bubbling molten lava below, but beware of the sulphur fumes; take a cloth mask moistened with lemon juice. On exceptionally clear days you will be able to see six or more other volcanoes. Conditions permitting, groups may carry ski and snowboard equipment for the descent; otherwise just slide down down the many toboggan shutes.

Between July and September (and occasionally October) it is possible to ski at the **Pucón resort**, which is situated on the eastern slopes of the volcano and reached by a badly maintained track (see page 352). The slopes are run by Enjoy who own the casino and Gran Hotel. Randonée skiing is usually possible until December.

Lagos Caburga and Colico

Lago Caburga (spelt locally Caburgua) is a very pretty lake in a wild setting 25 km northeast of Pucón. It is unusual for its beautiful white-sand beach (other beaches in the area have black volcanic sand), and is supposedly the warmest lake in the Lake District. The western and much of the eastern shores are inaccessible to vehicles, but the village of **Caburga**, at the southern end of the lake, is reached by a turning off the main road to Argentina, 8 km east of Pucón. If walking or cycling, there is a very pleasant alternative route: turn left 3 km east of Pucón, cross the Puente Quelhue, then turn right and follow the track for 18 km through beautiful scenery. Just off the road from Pucón, at Km 15, are the **Ojos de Caburga** ① *US$1*, beautiful pools fed from underground, particularly attractive after rain. The northern tip of the lake can be reached by a road from Cunco, which runs east along the northern shore of **Lago Colico**. This is one of the less accessible lakes, and lies north of Lago Villarrica in a remote setting.

Parque Nacional Huerquehue

① *Open all year but often closed after heavy snowfall, US$6, parking 500 m along the track.*

Located a short distance east of Lago Caburga, Parque Nacional Huerquehue covers 12,500 ha at altitudes rising to 1952 m at Cerro San Sebastián in the **Nevados del Caburga**. It also encompasses about 20 lakes, some of them very small, and many araucaria trees. The entrance and administration is on the western edge, near **Lago Tinquilco**, the largest lake in the park. From the entrance there is a well-signed track north up a steep hill to **Lago Chico**, where the track divides left to **Lago Verde** and right to

Lagos Villarrica, Caburga & Colico

Lago Toro. Both paths eventually meet up, making a circuit. The lakes are surrounded by trees and are very beautiful. At **Lago Huerquehue**, a further 20 km of trails begin. None of the routes is particularly taxing, making the park a good warm-up for the Volcán Villarrica hike. An adequate map may or may not be provided at entrance. The warden is generally very helpful. People in the park rent horses and boats. Take your own food.

Getting there Take the Caburgua road from Pucón; 3 km before Caburgua turn right along a *ripio* road to Paillaco, from which another road leads 7 km to the park administration. **Buses Caburgua** has services from Pucón.

Termas de Quimey-co, de Huife and los Pozones

South of Parque Nacional Huerquehue and reached via turning off the Pucón-Caburga road are three sets of thermal baths. The most expensive and ostentatious are the **Termas de Huife** ① *Km 33, T045-441222, www.termashuife.cl, US$18*, where entry includes the use of one modern, pleasant pool. Closer to Pucón are the recently refitted **Termas de Quimey-co** ① *Km 29, T045-441607, www.termasquimey co.com, US$12*, while further on are the **Termas los Pozones** ① *Km 35, US$7 per day, US$9 at night*, which have six natural rock pools but little infrastructure and are very popular with travellers, especially at night.

Reserva Forestal Cañi

① *Park entrance is US$5 per person.*

Situated south of Parque Nacional Huerquehue and accessed from the road to the Termas de Huife, this is a private nature reserve covering 500 ha, owned by the non-profit **Fundación Lahuén**. It is a three- to four-hour trek to its highest peak, **El Mirador**. The first part of the trek to a basic *refugio* at the park entrance is straightforward, along a wide path winding upwards through ancient native forests of coigue and lenga, with occasional views back to Lagos Villarrica and Caburga. Inside the reserve there are 17 small lakes, snow-covered for much of the year. Between these lakes are dotted millennial araucaria trees. From here it is a steep climb to **El Mirador** (1550 m) from where there are panoramic views over neighbouring parts of Argentina and Chile, including four volcanoes: **Lanín, Villarrica, Quetrupillán** and **Llaima**. As the reserve is above the snowline for much of the year, independent visits are normally restricted to summer, although guided visits are possible off season. ▸▸ *See also Activities and tours, page 352.*

Towards Argentina

From Pucón a road runs southeast along the southern bank of the valley of the Río Trancura to **Curarrehue** and the Argentine border, providing access en route to thermal springs and a number of hikeable *saltos* (waterfalls).

At Km 18, a *ripio* road heads south 10 km to the **Termas de Palguín** ① *T045-441968, www.termasdepalguin.cl, US$8*, and a series of spectacular waterfalls. A hidden 200-m path leads to **Salto Palguín** (which can be seen from the road), and beyond that is the impressive **Salto China** ① *Km 26, US$1.50*, where there's a restaurant and camping. **Saltos del Puma** and **del León** ① *US$2 for both*, are 800 m from the Termas. From the springs, a rough dirt road runs south to Coñaripe, with access to the Volcán Quetrupillán section of the **Parque** Nacional Villarrica. If you're driving, a high-clearance 4WD vehicle is necessary to reach the national park, and the road is often impassable in winter; but travelling on horseback is best. The treks in this sector are not physically demanding. Palguín is also the starting point for a three-day hike to Puesco, with vistas over the Villarrica and Lanín volcanoes.

Border crossing: Chile–Argentina

Pucón/Curarrehue–Junín de los Andes via Paso Mamuil Malal
Chilean immigration and customs are 1 km from the border, open 0800-1900.
Argentine customs are 3 km from the border. The road continues south through
Argentina to Junín de los Andes, San Martín de los Andes and Bariloche.

Further along the road, on the other side of the park are the new **Termas Geométricas**
① *T02-2141214, www.termasgeometricas.cl, US$22*, 17 architecturally designed pools of
different sizes and geometrical shapes. There is a small café. Because of the poor state of
the road, access is easier from Coñaripe.

Back on the Curarrehue road, at Km 23, a turning leads north to the indoor and outdoor
pools at **Termas de San Luis** ① *www.termasdesanluis.cl, US$9*, and **Termas Trancura**
① *www.termastrancura.com, US$9 or US$13 including transport from Pucón*, from where it
is 30 minutes' walk to **Lago del León**. At Km 35 another turning leads north for 15 km to
the **Termas de Panqui** ① *US$10*, where there are three pools beautifully situated in the
mountains as well as accommodation.

Beyond the small town of Curarrehue, 36 km east of Pucón, where there is a small but
interesting Mapuche museum, the road continues unpaved, climbing south past Puesco
to Lago Quellelhue, a beautiful area for trekking, tranquil and with well marked trails. This
is probably the easiest area to see Araucaria forest close-up from the comfort of a car. Six
kilometres southeast is the border at **Paso Mamuil Malal** (also known as the Paso
Tromen), see box above for border-crossing information. To the south of the pass rises the
graceful cone of **Volcán Lanín** (3747 m), one of the world's most beautiful mountains.
Currently dormant, Lanín is geologically one of the youngest volcanoes in the Andes and
is climbed from the Argentine side. A four-hour hike from Argentine customs leads to a
refugio at 2400 m. The climb from here to the summit is not difficult but crampons and ice
axe are needed.

⊕ Lago Villarrica and around listings

*For Sleeping and Eating price codes and other
relevant information, see Essentials pages 35-42.*

⊖ Sleeping

Villarrica *p340, map p341*
Price codes are based on high-season rates
(Jan-Feb); off-season prices are 30-40% lower.
More upmarket accommodation tends to be
on the lakefront.
LL Villarrica Park Lake, Km 13 on road
to Pucón, T045-450000, www.vplh.cl.
5-star. Rooms are spacious and all have
balconies overlooking the lake. Conference
rooms, banquet halls, spa with pools,

sauna, solarium, tours. Helpful staff.
Recommended, but only if you have
your own transport.
AL El Ciervo, Koerner 241, T045-411215,
www.hotelelciervo.cl. 4-star. Comfortable
rooms with heating. In pleasant grounds.
German-style breakfasts. German and some
English spoken, pool, terrace, Wi-Fi. Probably
the best hotel in the town centre.
Recommended.
AL Parque Natural Dos Ríos, 13 km west
of Villarrica, T09-94198064, www.dosrios.de.
With full board. Tranquil 40-ha nature park
with *cabañas* on the banks of the Río
Toltén (white-sand beach), horse riding,

birdwatching, children-friendly, German and English spoken.

AL-A Hostería de la Colina, Las Colinas 115, overlooking town, T045-411503, www.hosteriadelacolina.com. With breakfast, large gardens, good service, Wi-Fi, good restaurant (the owner makes fresh ice cream every day), fine views, especially from the spacious suites. English spoken, very attentive friendly service. Highly recommended.

AL-A Hotel y Cabañas El Parque, 3 km east on Pucón road, T045-411120, www.hotelelparque.cl. Lakeside with beach, tennis courts, breakfast, good restaurant with set meals. Recommended.

B Bungalowlandia, Prat 749, T045-411635, www. bungalowlandia.cl. *Cabañas* for 2, with *comedor*, good facilities and service. Better value off season.

B Cabañas Traitraico, San Martín 380, T045- 411064, traitraico@hotmail.com. 100 m from lake, sleeps 2-6, TV, heating, kitchenette, parking.

B Hostería Bilbao, Henríquez 43, T045-411 186, www.interpatagonia.com/bilbao. Clean, small rooms, pretty patio, good restaurant.

B Hotel-Yachting Kiel, Koerner 153, T045-411631, www. yachtingkiel.cl. Small 6-room hotel, 3 with views across the lake to the volcano. The others are smaller and much cheaper. Spacious bathrooms, cable TV and heating. Clean, friendly, German and some English spoken. Good Restaurant.

C La Torre Suiza, Bilbao 969, T045-411213, www.torresuiza.com. **E** per person in dorms. Some rooms with bath. Excellent breakfast, kitchen and laundry facilities, camping, bike rental, book exchange. Lots of info. German and English spoken. Recommended.

C Villa Linda, Pedro de Valdivia 678, T045-411392, www.villalinda.tk. **E** singles. Slightly tacky charmless interior. Hot water, clean, basic, cheap, good restaurant.

C-D Hospedaje Nicolás, Anfion Muñoz 477, T045-410232. F singles. Basic rooms with cable TV and bath. With breakfast. Good value, although the walls are thin. One of several on Muñoz 400 and 500 blocks.

D Chito Fuentes, Vicente Reyes 665, T045-411595. **F** singles. Basic rooms above a restaurant.

There are also rooms in private homes usually **C**, or **F** singles; several on Koerner 300 block and O'Higgins 700 and 800 blocks.

Camping

Many sites east of town on Pucón road, but these are expensive and open in season only. It may be cheaper to stay in a *hospedaje*; those nearest to town are **El Edén**, 1 km southeast of centre, T045-412772, US$6 per person, recommended.

Pucón p340, map p342

Rooms may be hard to find in high season (Dec-Feb) but there are plenty of alternatives in Villarrica. There are also rooms in private houses – look for the signs or ask in bars/restaurants. Price codes are based on high season rates; off season prices can be 20-40% lower and it's often possible to negotiate.

LL Antumalal, 2 km west, T045-441011, www.antumalal.com. Very small, picturesque Bauhaus chalet-style, set in 5 ha of parkland, magnificent views of the lake, tennis court, lovely gardens, excellent, with meals, open year-round, with pool and hot tub.

LL-L Gran Hotel Pucón, Holzapfel 190, T045-913300, www.granhotelpucon.cl. Once Pucón's best, this hotel has seen better days. It has recently been taken over by the casino, however, and improvements are promised. Rooms at the back have beautiful lake views.

L Interlaken, Caupolicán 720, T045-441276, www.hotelinterlaken.cl. Chalets, pool, water-skiing, tours arranged, no restaurant.

AL Malalhue, Camino Internacional 1615, T045-443130, www.malalhue.cl. One of the better hotels in town, about 15 mins' walk from the centre. Staff are generally helpful and most speak English. Rooms at the back are quieter and have views of the volcano.

AL-A Gudenschwager, Pedro de Valdivia 12, T045-442025, www.hogu.cl. Refurbished 1920s hotel. 20 simple centrally heated rooms (thin walls), some with lake and volcano view. Cheaper rooms with exterior bathroom. Reasonable rates off season. Living room with big screen TV and Wi-Fi area. English spoken.

A Araucarias, Caupolicán 243, T045-441286, www.araucarias.cl. Clean, comfortable, indoor pool and spa, Wi-Fi area.

A La Posada Plaza-Pucón, Valdivia 191, T045-441088, www.hotelplazapucon.cl. Simple, somewhat dated rooms with bath, restaurant, also spacious cabins, gardens and a pool. Cheaper when paying in dollars. Great location but could do with a refit.

A-B Hostal Gerónimo, Alderete 665, T045-443762, www.geronimo.cl. Recently refurbished. Rooms with bath and cable TV. Comfortable, friendly, quiet, with restaurant, bar and terrace. Avoid the pokey rooms on the ground floor. Recommended.

B Kernayel, 1 km east at Camino International 1510, T045-442164, www.kernayel.cl. 8 rooms with bath heating and cable TV and more expensive *cabañas*, pool, comfortable, but nothing special.

B-C Hostal Willy, Arauco 565, T045-444578, www.hostalyturismowilly.com. **D** singles. Pleasant carpeted and heated rooms with cable TV and spacious bathrooms. Breakfast available, internet, use of kitchen. Friendly, information given, good value, recommended.

B-C Hostería école, Urrutia 592, T045-441 675, www.ecole.cl. **E** per person in dorms without breakfast, rooms on the small side, some with bath, good vegetarian restaurant, ecological shop, forest treks, rafting, biking,

information, language classes, massage. Staff a mixed bag – some friendly, others less so.

B-C La Tetera, Urrutia 580, T045-441462, www.tetera.cl. Rooms with and without bath. Good breakfast with real coffee, friendly, English spoken, Spanish classes, book swap, lots of info. Recommended, book in advance.

C Donde Germán, Brasil 640, T045-442444, www.dondegerman.cl. **F** per person in dorms. Comfortable hostel relocated in a new building. Good beds, nice common areas, clean, kitchen facilities. Friendly, tours arranged. Recommended.

C Hospedaje M@yra, Colo Colo 485, T045-442745, www.myhostelpucon.com. **E** singles. Some rooms with bath and cable TV. Kitchen facilities, internet, information, laundry, parking, tours. Good backpackers' hostel.

C Hospedaje Victor, Palguín 705, T045-443 525, www.pucon.com/victor. **E-F** per person in 4-bed dorms. Some with bath. Kitchen facilities, TV, laundry. Friendly. A decent choice.

C Hostal Backpackers, Palguín 695, T045-441373 www.backpackerspucon.com. Kitchen facilities, internet, bike hire, information, also run their own trips.

C Residencial Lincoyán, Av Lincoyán 323, T045-441144, www.lincoyan.cl. **E** singles. With bath, cheaper without, clean and comfortable, breakfast extra.

C Tr@vel Pucón, Blanco Encalada 190, T045-444093, www.interpatagonia.com/ travelpucon. **F** singles. English, German, French spoken, near the **TurBus** terminal, garden, kitchen facilities, Spanish classes.

C The Tree House Hostel, Urrutia 660,
T045-444679, www.treehousechile.cl. **E** per
person in dorms. Fun and lively hostel Good
mattresses but mostly bunk beds. Breakfast
extra. English run. Lots of info. Kitchen
facilities and large patio. Good reports
C-D Hospedaje Graciela, Pasaje Rolando
Matus 521 (off Av Brasil). **F** singles.
Comfortable rooms, good food.
C-D Hospedaje Lucía, Lincoyán 565,
T045-441721. **E** singles. Some rooms with
bath. Friendly, quiet, garden, cooking facilities.
C-D Hospedaje Sonia, Lincoyán 485, T045-
441269, www. pucon.com/sonia. **F** singles.
Basic but clean rooms, some with bath. Use
of kitchen, noisy and somewhat crowded,
friendly. Basic English spoken.

Camping
Ainoha, 12 blocks north of town centre.
Lakeside site.
La Poza, Costanera Geis 769, T045-441435.
Hot showers, clean, quiet, good kitchen
facilities, open all year. Recommended.
L'etoile, Km 2 towards Volcán Villarrica,
T045-442188. Attractive forest site.
Los Boldos, Pasaje Las Rosas. East of town.
Millaray, Km 7 west of Pucón, T045-212336.
Lakeside campsite.
Saint John, Km 7 west of Pucón, T045-
441165, casilla 154. Beside Lago Villarrica.

Lagos Caburga and Colico *p344*
L-AL Trailanqui, 20 km west of Lago Colico
(35 km north of Villarrica), T045-578218, www.
trailanqui.com. Luxurious hotel on the riverbank, with suites and restaurant, also equipped
cabañas, campsite, horse riding golf course.
AL-A Landhaus San Sebastián, east of Lago
Caburga, F045-1972360, www.landhaus-
chile.com. With bath and breakfast, tasty
meals, laundry facilities, good walking base,
English and German spoken, Spanish classes.

Camping
The southern end of Lago Caburga is lined
with campsites; there are a couple of basic
shops, open summer only. There are 2 sites

about halfway along north shore of Lago Colico: **Quichelmalleu**, Km 22 from Cunco, T045-573187; and **Ensenada**, Km 26, T045-221441.

Parque Nacional Huerquehue *p344*

B-C Parque Tinquilco, southwest shore of Lago Tinquilco, 2 km from park entrance, T045-441480, www.parquehuerquehue.cl. Breakfast included. Large rooms, private bathrooms with hot water, restaurant, rowboats for hire. Also *cabañas*.
B-C Refugio Tinquilco, 3.5 km from park entrance, T09-9539 2728, www.tinquilco.cl. Doubles with bath available, **E** per person in dorms, meals served, cooking facilities, heating.
C Braatz and Soldans, southern end of Lago Tinquilco near the park entrance. 2 German-speaking families offer accommodation, no electricity, food and camping (US$6); they also rent rowing boats on the lake.

Camping

There are several campsites near the park entrance, US$10. Inside the park, camping is allowed at 'el refugio'.

Termas de Quimey-Co, de Huife and los Pozones *p 345*

LL-L Hostería Termas de Huife, Termas de Huife, T045-1975666, www.termashuife.cl. The most upmarket of the spa hotels.
A Hotel Termas de Quimey-Co, Termas de Quimey-Co, T045-441903, www.termas quimeyco.com. Also a campsite and 2 cabins.

Towards Argentina *p345*

AL Termas de San Luis, T045-443965, www.termasdesanluis.cl. *Cabañas* with TV, heating, sauna, restaurant. Pickup service for hotel guests from Pucón. Cheaper in pesos than in dollars. Extra for full board.
A-F Cabañas La Tranquera, Puesco. Cabins for 6, also dorm accommodation, restaurant, campsite.
B-C Hotel Termas de Panqui, T049-94436741, panquihotsprings@hotmail.com. **D** singles. in rooms or tepees that sleep 3.

Also camping facilities. Breakfast extra. Good vegetarian meals, trekking, aromatherapy, English spoken.
C Kila Leufu, Km 20, Pucón–Currarrehue road, T09-91337657, www.kilaleufu.cl. **F** per person in shared rooms. Rooms on the Martínez family farm. The owners are Mapuche and staying here will offer insights into their way of life. Full board available including lamb in the *ruca* and other home-grown food. Recommended.
C Rancho de Caballos, 36 km southeast of Pucón on the dirt road to Coñaripe, T09-8346 1764 (limited signal), www.rancho-de-caballos.com. Restaurant with vegetarian dishes, laundry and kitchen facilities; also *cabañas* and camping, self-guided trails, horse-riding trips US$70 per day, English and German spoken, recommended.
C Ruca Rayen, T09-9711 8064. Idyllic spot on the banks of the Río Palguín, 15 mins' walk from the main road (regular buses to Pucón). Some rooms with bath. Good breakfast included. Friendly English-speaking Austrian-Mapuche hosts (Margot's parents own Kila Leufu, above). The perfect choice if you want to avoid the hustle and bustle of Pucón. Meals served, Horse-riding trips. Offers trekking information and mountain-bike hire, camping possible. Highly recommended.

Camping

There is a **CONAF** campsite at Puesco, free, no facilities.

❶ Eating

For eating options in the national parks and lakes east of Pucón, see Sleeping, above.

Villarrica *p340, map p341*
¶¶¶ **El Tabor**, Epulef 1187, T045-411901. Fish and seafood specialities. Long-standing reputation. Elegant, but quality perhaps not as good as the past. Somewhat overpriced.
¶¶¶ **La Cava del Roble**, Valentín Letelier 658, piso 2, T045-416446. Excellent grill. Specializes in exotic meat and game with

unusual local ingredients such as *piñones*.
Extensive wine list. Recommended.
♦♦ **La Vecchia Cucina**, Pedro de Valdivia 1011,
T045-411798. Surprisingly good Italian
serving the usual range of pizza and pasta.
♦♦ **The Travellers**, Letelier 753, T045-413617.
Varied menu including vegetarian and Asian
food, bar, English spoken.
♦♦-♦ **Juanito**, Vicente Reyes 678. Closed Sun.
Good, and cheap end of the range.
♦ **Casa Vieja**, Letelier y Muñoz. Good-value
set lunch. Family-run, friendly.
♦ **El Marítimo**, Alderete 769, T045-412034.
Unpretentious restaurant serving traditional
fish and seafood. Generally 1st-rate.
♦ **El Turismo**, Epulef 1201 y Rodriguez. Normal
range of Chilean dishes. No frills, just good
food. Best of the cheapies. Recommended.

Cafes

Café 2001, Henríquez 379. Best coffee in
town. Also good cakes and friendly service
at a reasonable price. For ice cream,
try the stall next door.

Pucón *p340, map p342*
For other options, see Sleeping. Vegetarians should check out the delicatessen
at O'Higgins y Fresia, which serves fresh
vegetarian food. New boutique restaurants
open every year along Fresia, while there
are several cheap restaurants around the
junction of Urrutia and Ansorena.
♦♦♦ **Puerto Pucón**, Fresia 251. One of Pucón's
older restaurants. Spanish, stylish.
♦♦♦-♦♦ **La Maga**, Alderete 276 y Fresia,
T045-444277. Uruguayan Parillada serving
possibly the best steak in Chile. So good
that several imitations have opened up
nearby to take the overspill.
♦♦♦-♦♦ **Senzo**, Fresia 284, T045-449005. Fresh
pasta and risotto prepared by a Swiss chef.
♦♦ **Arabian**, Fresia 354-B, T045-443469. Arab
specialities – stuffed vine leaves, falafel, etc.
♦♦ **Ecole**, Urrutia 592, T045-441675, the best
option in town for vegetarians.

♦♦ **il Baretto**, Fresia 124, T045-443515.
Stone-baked pizzas. Much better value
than Buonatesta across the road.
♦ **Rap Hamburguesa**, O'Higgins 625.
Open late. Freshly made hamburgers,
chips and Chilean fast food.

Cafés

Also try **Hostería école**, see Sleeping.
Café de la P, O'Higgins y Lincoyán. Real coffee.
Cassis, Fresia 223. Chocolates, ice creams,
pancakes and snacks as well as coffee.

🍸 Bars and clubs

Pucón *p340, map p342*
At weekends in summer, there are discos
2-3 km east of town, near the airport,
at **Kamikaze** and **La Playa**, plus several
more in the same area.
Mamas and Tapas, O'Higgins y Arauco.
Drink and snacks. There are several others
on O'Higgins.

⊛ Festivals and events

Villarrica *p340, map p341*
Jan-Feb Many events are organized,
including music, regattas, rodeo and the
Festival Cultural Mapuche, with a market,
based around the **Muestra Cultural
Mapuche**, usually in 2nd week of Feb.

Pucón *p340, map p342*
Feb Pucón is home to an international
triathlon competition every year as well as
mountain-bike races and other events.

⦾ Shopping

Pucón *p340, map p342*
There is a large handicraft market just south of
O'Higgins on Ansorena. The local specialities
are painted wooden flowers. Camping
equipment is available at **Eltit Supermarket**,

O'Higgins y Fresia, and from **Outdoors and Travel**, Lincoyán 36. **Pucon Express**, O'Higgins y Colo Colo, is a 24-hr supermarket. There is a large **Eltit Supermarket** on the Camino Internacional on the eastern outskirts of town.

▲ Activities and tours

Villarrica p340, map p341
Prices are fairly standard: to Parque Nacional Villarrica, US$25; to climb Volcán Villarrica, US$65-80; to Valdivia US$60; to Termas de Coñaripe, US$40.
Karina Tour, Letelier 825, T045-412049.
Novena Región, Parque Ecológico 3 Esteros, 20 km from Villarrica towards Panguipulli, T09-8901 2574, www.novena-region.com. Mushing and husky trekking on the winter snow with Siberian Huskies. Also igloo building. Unique in Chile.
Politur, Anfión Muñoz 647, T045-414547, www.politur.cl. Small branch of the reputable Pucon agency. Recommended.
Ríos Family, T045-412408. Birdwatching and fishing trips.
Rodrigo Puelma, T09-9625 1345. Private guide, speaks basic English, recommended.
Trancura, Camilo Henríquez y Reyes, www.trancura.com. Wide range of excursions and competitive prices but tend to cut corners on safety and are not to be trusted with adventure tourism.
Turismo Coñaripe, P Montt 525, T045-411111.

Pucón p340, map p342
Canopy tours
Several agencies offer canopy tours – ziplining through treetops in native forests.
Bosque Aventura, Arauco y O'Higgins, T045-444030, www.canopypucon.cl. Has one of the longest runs as well as being the most responsible safety-wise.

Climbing
Sierra Nevada, O'Higgins 524-A, T045-444210, www.sierranevadapucon.cl.

The only company currently offering *Via Ferrata*, a kind of climbing up sheer rock faces for beginners using metal hand-and-foot-holds imbedded in the rock.

Fishing
Pucón and Villarrica are celebrated as bases for fishing on Lago Villarrica and on the beautiful Lincura, Trancura and Toltén rivers. The local tourist office will supply details on licences and open seasons, etc. Some tourist agencies also offer trips as well as fly-fishing classes. Prices although not cheap are much more reasonable than further south.
Mario's Fishing Zone, O'Higgins 580, T045-444259, www.flyfishingpucon.com. Expensive, but good fishing guide.
Off Limits, O'Higgins 560, T045-442681, www.offlimits.cl. Fishing specialists, English and Italian spoken, offer fly-fishing excursions and courses between half and 3 days. Birdwatching trips and cycle hire also offered.

Horse riding
Horse hire is about US$30 half day, US$50 full day with guide.
Campo Antilco near Quelhue, T09-97139758, www.antilco.com. Small groups, excursions ranging from half- to 12-day trips to Argentina.
Centro de Turismo Ecuestre Huepil-Malal, T09-96432673, www.huepil-malal.cl. Similar.
Ruca Rayen, see under Sleeping, offer good day rides east of Pucón.

Skiing
Pucón resort, 35 mins from Pucón on the slopes of the Villarrica Volcano, T045-441901, www.skipucon.cl. The resort is owned by Gran Hotel Pucón, which can provide information on snow, ski lifts and, perhaps, transport; otherwise consult the tourist office in Pucón. There are 8 lifts (day ticket US$28-40, depending on the season, US$12 to the restaurant only), though rarely do more than 2 or 3 work and piste preparation is mediocre. The snow is generally soft and good for beginners, though more advanced skiers can try the steeper areas. The season

runs from the beginning of Jul to the end of Sep (longer during exceptionally good years). The ski centre offers equipment rental (US$23 per day, US$120 per week), ski instruction, first aid, and has a restaurant and bar with wonderful views from the terrace. Some tour operators in town offer ski hire and transport to slopes for around US$30 per person.

Sky diving
Skydive Pucón, at the airport, T09-9820 0194, www.skydivepucon.cl. Flights over Volcán Villarrica and tandem skydives as well as skydiving courses.

Thermal springs
There are dozens of thermal springs around Pucón ranging from the rustic Termas de Pozones to the hip Termas Geométricas and upmarket Termas de Huife. Most operators arrange tours to a variety of termas.

Travel agency
Travel Aid, Ansorena 425 local 4, T045-444040, www.travelaid.cl. Helpful general travel agency selling trekking maps, guidebooks, gps routes with waypoints, lots of other information, also can organize transport to trailheads and are agents for Navimag and other boat trips. English and German spoken.

Whitewater rafting and Volcán Villarrica trek
Most operators can arrange a variety of trips, including climbing Villarrica, 12 hrs, US$65-85 including park entry, equipment provided. Whitewater rafting, Trancura bajo (basic, Grade II-III) US$30, Trancura alto (advanced, Grade III-IV) US$45. Shop around, prices vary, as well as the quality of guides and equipment. Unfortunately, while several agencies offer acceptable levels of service, none is exceptional. To reach the falls, lakes and termas it is cheaper for groups to flag down a taxi and negotiate a price.

Trancura is the biggest agency in Pucón with several branches. They offer very competitive prices, but safety-wise they range from lax to dangerously irresponsible, with more than their fair share of accidents. Do not consider any sort of adventure tourism with this company if you value your personal safety.

Aguaventura, Palguín 336, T045-444246, www.aguaventura.com. Long-standing reputable French-run agency specializing in kayaking and rafting, but offer other activities as well. Ski equipment available for rent.

Enjoy Tour, In the Gran Hotel, T045-442303, www.enjoytour.cl. Owned by the casino. Prices are slightly above average, but equipment is generally first rate.

Kayak Chile, O'Higgins, T09-8837 3253, www.kayakchile.net. Day trips and classes for all levels. All guides are UK or US trained. Maximum of 2 students per instructor. Responsible. Recommended. Also sell used equipment.

Mountain Life Adventure, Palguín 360, T045-444564, www.mountainlife-adventure.com. Villarrica hike plus treks and climbs up other volcanoes in the region.

Paredón, T045-444663, www.paredon expeditions.com. Specialize in small-group excursions to VolcánVillarrica. English spoken. Good equipment. Recommended.

Politur, O'Higgins 635, T045-441373, www.politur.com. Good for volcano treks and rafting. A little more expensive than most, but generally responsible.

Ronco Track, O'Higgins 615, esq Arauco, T045-449597, www.roncotrack.cl. Small group quad-bike excursions from 1½ hrs to 1½ days. Good fun. Also hires out good quality bicycles and offers a wide range of other tours.

Sol y Nieve O'Higgins, esq Lincoyán, T/F045-441070, www.solynieve.cl. Generally decent long-standing operator. Most guides speak English. Equipment mostly good.

Sur Expediciones, O'Higgins 615, www.surexpediciones.com. One of the better agencies for the volcano trip.

Watersports
Equipment for water-skiing (US$16 for 15 mins), dinghy sailing (lasers US$16 per hr),

jet-skis and windsurfing (sailboards US$16 per hr) can be hired in summer at Playa Grande, the beach by the Gran Hotel. Rowing boats can also be hired for US$8 per hr. The outlets on La Poza beach are more expensive and not recommended.

Parque Nacional Villarrica *p343*
Tours from Pucón cost US$65-85, including park entry, guide, transport to park entrance and hire of equipment (no reduction for those with their own equipment). Bargain for group rates. Travel agencies will not start out if the weather is bad and some travellers have experienced difficulties in obtaining a refund: establish in advance what terms apply in the event of cancellation and be prepared to wait a few days. For information on independent guides, all with equipment, ask for recommendations at the tourist office.

Reserva Forestal Cañi *p345*
Hostería école, see Sleeping above, offers good tours.

⊖ Transport

Villarrica *p340, map p341*
Bus
The main terminal is at Pedro de Valdiva y Muñoz; JAC has 2 terminals, at Muñoz y Bilbao (long-distance) and opposite for Pucón and Lican-Ray (local). Other services leave from the Terminal Rural, Matta y Vicente Reyes.

To **Santiago**, 10 hrs, US$18-55, several companies; to **Pucón**, Vipu-Ray (main terminal) and JAC, every 15 mins in summer, 40-min journey, US$1; to **Puerto Montt**, US$11; to **Valdivia**, JAC, 5 a day, 2½ hrs, US$6; to **Lican-Ray**, services in summer, JAC and Vipu-Ray, US$2; to **Coñaripe**, US$2.50, and **Liquiñe** at 1600 Mon-Sat, 1000 Sun; to **Temuco**, JAC, every 30 mins in summer, US$5; to **Loncoche** (Route 5 junction for hitching), US$3. There are also occasional direct buses to **Panguipulli**, via Lican-Ray.

To Argentina Buses from Temuco to **Junín** stop in Villarrica en route to the **Paso Mamuil Malal**; fares are the same as from Temuco, see page 338.

Car/bicycle
Car hire from **Castillo Propiedades**, Anfion Muñoz 417, good value. Bike hire from **Mora Bicicletas**, Körner 760, helpful.

Pucón *p340, map p342*
Air
Lan Express and Sky fly to **Santiago**, twice weekly each in summer.

Bicycle
Repairs at El Pelao, Colo Colo 430. Hire for US$1.50 per hr or US$10 per day from several travel agencies, many on O'Higgins; shop around as quality varies.

Bus
There is no municipal terminal; each company has its own: JAC, Uruguay y Palguín; TurBus, O'Higgins 910, east of town; Igi Llaima and Condor, Colo Colo south of O'Higgins.

JAC has services to **Villarrica**, every 15 mins, US$1; to **Valdivia**, 5 daily, US$7; to **Temuco** hourly, 2 hrs, US$5, or *rápido*, 1½ hrs, US$6; to **Puerto Montt**, 6 hrs, US$12, daily, or change at Valdivia. To **Santiago**, several companies, morning and evening, 11 hrs, US$20-60.

To Argentina Buses from Temuco to **San Martín** arrive in Pucón at 1000; fares are the same as from Temuco, see page 338.

Car
Hire prices start at US$32 per day; **Avis**, Arauco 302, T045-465328, www.avischile.cl; **Hertz**, in the Gran Hotel, T045-441664; **Kilometro Libre**, Alderete 480, T045-444399, www.rentacarkilo metrolibre.com; **Pucón Rent A Car**, Colo Colo 340, T045-443052, www.puconrentacar.cl.

Taxi
Araucaria, T045-442323.

Lagos Caburga and Colico *p344*
Buses Caburgua run minibuses every 30 mins from Pucón to **Caburga**, US$1.50; there are also minibuses every 30 mins from **Ansorena y Uruguay** in **Pucón**; a taxi day trip costs US$35 return.

Parque Nacional Huerquehue *p344*
Buses Caburgua from **Pucón**, 3 daily, 1½ hrs, US$3. Tour agencies arrange transport for groups, US$12. Taxis cost US$40 return.

Termas de Quimey-Co, de Huife and los Pozones *p345*
A taxi from Pucón costs US$35 return, US$25 one-way; **Termas de Huife** and **Termas de Quimey co** have their own transport and will pick people up from **Pucón**, US$18. Buses Caburgua have 3 daily services to Los Pozones, passing by the entrances of the other 2 termas on the way.

Reserva Forestal Cañi *p345*
Buses Caburgua service to Los Pozones passes near the entrance.

Towards Argentina *p345*
Several minibuses daily to **Curarrehue** from Pucón. 3 buses weekly from Pucón to **Puesco**.

❶ Directory

Villarrica *p340, map p341*
Banks There are ATMs at Banco BCI, Pedro de Valdivia y Alderete; Banco de Chile, Pedro de Valdiva y Pedro Montt; Banco Santander, Pedro de Valdiva 778. In general, rates through *casas de cambio* are poor. Carlos Huerta, Muñoz 417; Central de Repuestos, Muñoz 415, good rates; Cristopher, Valdivia 1061, good rates for TCs; Turcamb, Henríquez 570, poor rates for TCs. **Internet** Cybercafé Salmon, Letelier y Henríquez. **Language lessons** Language Pucón, Uruguay 306, T045-444967, www.languagepucon.com.
Laundry Lavacenter, Alderete 770; Lavandería y Lavaseco Villarrica, Andrés Bello 348; Todo Lavado, Urrutia 669. **Post office** Muñoz y Urrutia, open Mon-Fri 0900-1300, 1430-1800, Sat 0900-1300.
Telephone CTC, Henríquez 544; Chilesat, Henríquez 473; Entel, Henríquez 440 and 575.

Pucón *p340, map p342*
Banks There are 3 or 4 banks with ATMs and several *casas de cambio* on O'Higgins, although *cambio* rates are universally poor. Much better to change money in Temuco.
Internet Several on O'Higgins.
Laundry At Urrutia 520; Palguín 460; Fresia 224; Colo-Colo 475 and 478, several others. All close for 2 hrs for lunch.
Post office Fresia 183.

The Seven Lakes

→ *Colour map 4, B2.*

This group of lakes, situated south of Lago Villarrica, provides a beautiful necklace of water, surrounded by thick woods and with views of distant snows giving a picture-postcard backdrop. Six of the lakes lie in Chile, with the seventh, Lago Lácar, in Argentina. After the final peace settlement of 1882 the area around these lakes was reserved for Mapuche settlements. Lago Riñihue is most easily reached from Valdivia and Los Lagos and is dealt with in a later section (see page 367). Most of the lakes have black-sand beaches, although in spring, as the water level rises, these can all but disappear. ▸▸ *For listings, see pages 359-361.*

Lago Calafquén ⊖⊙▲⊖ ▸▸ *pp359-361.*

The most northerly of the seven lakes, Lago Calafquén is a popular tourist destination for Chileans, readily accessible by a paved road from Villarrica, along which there are fine views of the Volcán Villarrica. Wooded and dotted with small islands, the lake is reputedly one of the warmest in the region and is good for swimming. A mostly paved road runs around the lake.

The Seven Lakes

The legend of Lican-Ray

At the height of the wars between the Spanish and the Mapuche a young Spanish soldier lost the rest of his unit and strayed into the forests near Lago Calafquén. Suddenly he saw a beautiful young Mapuche woman drying her hair in the sun and singing. As he did not want to frighten her he made himself visible at a distance and began to sing along. Singing, smiling and exchanging glances, they fell in love. She called him Allumanche, which means white man in Mapuche, and, pointing to herself, indicated that her name was Lican-Rayan, meaning the flower of magic stone. They began to live together near the lake.

Lican Rayan's father, Curtilef, a powerful and fearsome chief, feared she might be dead. One day a boy came to him and said: "Lican Rayan is alive. I have seen her near the lake with a white man but she is not a prisoner: it is clear they are in love".

Lican Rayan saw the warriors coming to look for her. Knowing her father she feared what might happen, so she persuaded the soldier that they should flee. They escaped by riding on logs to one of the islands. There they felt safe, but they could not light a fire against the cold because the smoke would give them away. The weather grew cooler, the north wind blew and it rained heavily. After several days, unable to bear the cold and thinking that the warriors would have given up the search, they lit a fire. The smoke was spotted by Curtilef's men, so Lican Rayan and the solider fled to another island but again they were discovered and had to escape. This happened so many times that, although they were never caught, they were never seen again.

In the town of Lican-Ray, it is said that on spring afternoons it is sometimes possible to see a distant column of smoke from one of the islands, where Lican Rayan and the soldier are still enjoying their love after over 400 years.

Abridged and translated from *Lengua Y Costumbres Mapuches* by Orietta Appelt Martin, Imprenta Austral, Temuco, 1995.

Lican-Ray

Situated 30 km south of Villarrica on a peninsula on the north shore, Lican-Ray is the major resort on the lake and is named after a legendary Mapuche woman (see above). There are two beaches, one on each side of the peninsula. Boats can be hired for US$5 per hr, and there are **catamaran trips** ① *US$7 per hr or US$23 to the islands*. Although crowded in season, Lican-Ray can feel like a ghost town by the end of March, when most facilities have closed. Some 6 km to the east is the river of lava formed when Volcán Villarrica erupted in 1971. There is a **tourist office** ① *daily in summer, Mon-Fri in winter*, on the plaza.

Coñaripe

Lying 21 km southeast of Lican-Ray at the eastern end of Lago Calafquén, Coñaripe is another popular Chilean tourist spot. At first sight the village is dusty and nondescript, but its setting, with a black-sand beach surrounded by mountains, is beautiful. Most services are on the Calle Principal. The **tourist office** on the plaza ① *mid Nov-mid Apr daily; late Apr-early Nov Sat and Sun only*, can arrange trips to local thermal springs.

From Coñaripe a road (mostly *ripio*) around the lake's southern shore leads to **Lago Panguipulli**, see below, 38 km west, and offers superb views over Volcán Villarrica, which can be climbed from here. Another dirt road heads northeast through the Parque Nacional Villarrica to Pucón, see page 340; the first few kilometres are good *ripio*. There are several thermal springs here. After the Termas Geométricas the road worsens and is suitable for high-clearance 4WD only.

Southeast of Coñaripe

From Coñaripe a road runs southeast over the steep Cuesta Los Añiques offering views of **Lago Pellaifa**, a tiny lake with rocky surroundings covered with vegetation and a small beach. **Termas de Coñaripe** ① *Km 15, 2 km from the lakeshore, T063-431407, www.termas conaripe.cl*, has six pools, accommodation, restaurant, cycles and horses for hire. They can organize transport from the town of Coñaripe.

Further south are the **Termas de Liquiñe** ① *Km 32, T063-317377, US$6-10 per person*, with eight thermal springs and accommodation (but little other infrastructure), surrounded by a small native forest. About 8 km north of Liquiñe is a road going southwest for 20 km along the southeast shore of **Lago Neltume** to meet the Choshuenco–Puerto Fuy road.

The **Paso Carirriñe** across the **Argentine border** ① *open 15 Oct-31 Aug*, is reached by unpaved road from the Termas de Liquiñe. On the Argentine side the road continues to San Martín de los Andes.

Lago Panguipulli ◉⑦❸▲◉❶ » *pp359-361.*

Covering 116 sq km, Lago Panguipulli, the largest of the seven lakes, is reached either by paved road from Lanco or Los Lagos on the Pan-American Highway or by *ripio* roads from Lago Calafquén. A road leads along the beautiful northern shore, which is wooded with sandy beaches and cliffs, but most of the lake's southern shore is inaccessible by road.

Panguipulli

The site of a Mapuche settlement, Panguipulli, meaning 'hill of pumas', is situated on a hillside at the northwest corner of the lake. It grew as a railway terminal and a port for vessels carrying timber from the lakesides, and is now the largest town in the area.

On Plaza Prat is the **Iglesia San Sebastián**, built in Swiss style with twin towers by the Swiss Padre Bernabé; its belltower contains three bells from Germany. By the plaza there is a **tourist office** ① *Dec-Feb daily, otherwise week days only, T063-310435, www.sietelagos.cl*.

From Plaza Prat the main commercial street, Martínez de Rozas, runs down to the lakeshore. In summer, catamaran trips are offered on the lake and excursions can be made to Lagos Calafquén, Neltume, Pirehueico and to the northern tip of Lago Riñihue, see page 367. The road east to Coñaripe, on Lago Calafquén, offers superb views of the lake and of Volcán Villarrica.

Choshuenco and around

Choshuenco lies 45 km east of Panguipulli on the Río Llanquihue, at the eastern tip of the lake and can only be reached by road from Panguipulli or Puerto Fuy. To the south is the **Reserva Nacional Mocho Choshuenco** (7536 ha), which includes two volcanoes: Choshuenco (2415 m) and Mocha (2422 m). On the slopes of Choshuenco the **Club Andino de Valdivia** runs a small ski resort and three *refugios*. (The resort is reached by a turning from the road that goes south from Choshuenco to Enco at the east end of Lago Riñihue, see page 367.) From Choshuenco a road leads east to **Neltume** and **Lago Pirehueico**, via the impressive waterfalls of **Huilo Huilo**. The falls are a three-hour walk from Choshuenco, or take the Puerto Fuy bus and get off at **Alojamiento Huilo Huilo**, from where it is a five-minute walk to the falls.

Lago Pirehueico ●● *pp359-361.*

Lago Pirehueico is a 36-km long, narrow and deep glacial lake surrounded by virgin *lingue* forest. It is beautiful and largely unspoilt, although there are plans to build a huge tourist complex in Puerto Pirehueico.

There are two ports on the lake: **Puerto Fuy** at the northern end and **Puerto Pirehueico** at the southern end. The ports are linked by a ferry service (the crossing is beautiful; see page 361) and can also be reached by the road that runs east from Neltume to the Argentine border crossing at Paso Huahum. The road south from Puerto Fuy, however, is privately owned and closed to traffic. This is a shame because it is a beautiful route passing around Volcán Choshuenco and through rainforest to Río Pillanleufú, Puerto Llolles on Lago Maihue and Puerto Llifén on Lago Ranco.

Paso Huahum ① *all year, Chilean immigration summer 0800-2100, winter 0800-2000*, is 11 km southeast of Puerto Pirehueico. On the Argentine side the road leads alongside Lago Lacar to San Martín de los Andes and Junín de los Andes.

◉ The Seven Lakes listings

For Sleeping and Eating price codes and other relevant information, see Essentials pages 35-42.

● Sleeping

Lican-Ray *p357*
There are plenty of options along the north shore of Lago Calafquén towards Coñaripe.
B Cabañas Los Nietos, Manquel 125, T045-431078. Self-catering cabins.
B Hostería Inaltulafquen, Casilla 681, Playa Grande, T045-431115, www.hotel-refugio.com. With breakfast and bath, English spoken, trips to thermal springs.
C Cabañas Cacique Vitacura, Urrutia 825, Playa Grande, T02-2355302, tradesic@intermedia.cl. For 2, also larger cabins with kitchen.
C-D Residencial Temuco, G Mistral 515, Playa Grande, T045-431130. **F** singles, with breakfast. Clean, without bath, good.

Camping
There are also 6 sites just west of town.
Foresta, 500 m east of town, T045-211954. Sites for up to 6 people.
Prado Verde, 1 km east of town, T045-431161.

Coñaripe *p357*
A Entre Montañas, on the Plaza, T063-408300. Overpriced, poor food.
C Hospedaje Chumay, Las Tepas 201, T063-317287, turismochumay@hotmail.com. **F** singles. Restaurant, internet, tours.

Camping
There are campsites on the north and south sides of the lake, US$15 per site. Free camping is possible on the beach outside town.
Isla Llancahue, 5 km east, T063-317360. Campsite with *cabañas* on an island in Río Llancahue.

Southeast of Coñaripe *p358*
AL Termas de Liquiñe, Km 32, T/F063-317377. Price per person, full board, cabins, restaurant, tours offered. There is also accommodation in private houses.

Panguipulli *p358*
B Hostal España, O'Higgins 790, T063-311166, www.hostalespana.cl.kz. Rooms with breakfast.
B-C Hostería Rayen Trai, María Alvarado y O'Higgins. **D-E** singles. Former yacht club serving good food, open all year.
C Etchegaray 464. **F** singles. Clean, good breakfast. Reduced rates for longer stays.

C Hospedaje Familiar, Los Ulmos 62, T063-311483. **F** singles. English and German spoken, kitchen facilities, helpful, good breakfast.
C Hotel Central, Valdivia 115, T063-311331/ 09-98823955. **F** singles. Clean, breakfast.
C Residencial La Bomba, J M Carrera y R Freire. Quiet.
F-G Albergue Juvenil, Gabriela Mistral 1112, T063-311282. Youth hostel opposite bus terminal. Price per person.

Camping

There are also 3 sites at Chauquén, 6 km southeast on the lakeside.
Camping Lago Riñihue, T063-461344, F063-461111.
El Bosque, P Sigifredo 241, T063-311489. Clean, hot water.

Choshuenco and around *p358*

B-C Hostería Ruca Pillán, San Martín 85, T063-318220, www.rucapillan.cl. Also cabins, **A**. Family-run hotel overlooking the lake. English spoken, tours.
C-D Hostal Choshuenco, Bernabé s/n, T063-318214, jcarrilloh@telsur.com. **F** singles. A little run-down but clean, good meals, breakfast included. Also *cabañas*.
C-D Restaurant Robles, in Neltume, east of Choshuenco. **F** singles without bath.
D Alojamiento Huilo Huilo, Huilo Huilo, near Neltume. **F-G** singles. Basic but comfortable and well situated for walks.

Lago Pirehueico *p359*

Beds are available in private houses, and free camping is possible on the beach.
D Hospedaje Pirehueico Puerto Pirehueico. **F-G** singles.
D Restaurant Puerto Fuy, Puerto Fuy. **F** singles. Cold water, good restaurant.

🍴 Eating

For eating options in Coñaripe, Choshuenco and around, see Sleeping.

Lican-Ray *p357*

¶¶-¶ Café Naños, Urrutia 105. Very good, reasonable prices, helpful owner.
¶¶-¶ Restaurant-Bar Guido's, Urrutia 405. Good value.
¶ Coyote, on the plaza. Cheap, open off season.

Panguipulli *p358*

Cheap restaurants on O'Higgins 700 block.
¶¶ Didáctico El Gourmet, Ramón Freire s/n. Restaurant linked to a professional hotel school. Excellent food and wine, mid-price but high quality, open in school terms only.
¶¶-¶ Café Central, M de Rozas 750. Good cheap lunches, expensive evening meals.
¶¶-¶ El Chapulín, M de Rozas 639. Good food, good value, friendly.

🎉 Festivals and events

Panguipulli *p358*

Last week of Jan La Semana de Rosas, with dancing and sports competitions.

▲ Activities and tours

Coñaripe *p357*

Hospedaje Chumay, see Sleeping, organizes hikes to Villarica volcano and trips to various thermal springs.
Rucapillán Expediciones, San Martín 85, T063-318220, www.rucapillan.cl. Rafting in the rivers Fuy, Enco ands San Pedro as well as volcano treks.

Panguipulli *p358*
Fishing

The following fishing trips on Lago Panguipulli are recommended: Puntilla Los Cipreses at the mouth of the Río Huanehue, 11 km east of Panguipulli, 30 mins by boat; the mouth of the Río Niltre, on east side of lake. Boat hire US$10, licences from the **Municipalidad**, **Librería Colón**, O'Higgins 528; or from the **Club de Pesca**.

Rafting

Good rafting opportunities on the Río Fuy, Grade IV-V; Río San Pedro, varying grades, and on the Río Llanquihue near Choshuenco.

○ Transport

Lican-Ray *p357*

There is no central bus terminal; buses leave from offices around plaza. To **Villarrica**, JAC, frequent, 1 hr, US$2; to **Santiago**, TurBus (summer only) and JAC, 11 hrs, US$20-50; to **Temuco**, JAC, 2½ hrs, US$7; to **Coñaripe**, 7 daily (4 off season).

Coñaripe *p357*

Buses run to **Panguipulli**, 7 daily (4 off season), US$2; to **Villarrica**, 16 daily, US$2.50; to **Lican-Ray**, 45 mins, US$1. Also a nightly bus direct to **Santiago** run by TurBus (summer only) and JAC, 11½ hrs, US$20-50.

Panguipulli *p358*

The bus terminal is at Gabriela Mistral y Portales. To **Santiago** daily, US$21-50; to **Valdivia**, Mon-Sat, 4 only on Sun, several companies, 2 hrs, US$7; to **Temuco**, frequent, Power and Pangui Sur, US$6; to **Puerto Montt**, US$10; to **Calafquén**, 3 daily at 1200, 1545 and 1600; to **Choshuenco**, **Neltume** and **Puerto Fuy** (3 hrs), 3 daily, US$5; to **Coñaripe**, for connections to Lican-Ray and Villarrica, 7 daily, 4 off season.

Lago Pirehueico *p359*

Bus Puerto Fuy to **Panguipulli**, 3 daily, 3 hrs, US$5; Puerto Pirehueico via Paso Huahum to **San Martín de los Andes**, daily in summer, weekly in winter (out Sat 0930, back Sun 1330).

Ferry The Hua Hum sails from **Puerto Fuy** across lake to **Puerto Pirehueico**, 2 daily in summer, twice a week, other times, 2-3 hrs, foot passengers US$2, cars US$28. For reservations and information see www.sietelagos.cl. This is a recommended journey and compares with the famous lakes crossing from Puerto Montt to Bariloche but at a fraction of the price.

○ Directory

Panguipulli *p358*

Banks ATM at the BCI, M de Rozas y Matta.

Valdivia and around

→ *Colour map 4, B2.*

Surrounded by wooded hills, Valdivia is one of the most pleasant cities in southern Chile and a good place to rest after arduous treks in the mountains. In the summer tourist season the city comes to life with activities and events, while off season this is a pleasant verdant city with a thriving café culture. With a high student population (its total population is 127,000), it is also one of the best cities for meeting young Chileans, who will be at the pulse of anything in the way of nightlife in the city. Valdivia lies nearly 839 km south of Santiago at the confluence of two rivers, the Calle Calle and Cruces, which form the Río Valdivia. To the northwest of the city is a large island, Isla Teja, where the Universidad Austral de Chile is situated. West, along the coast, are a series of important Spanish colonial forts, while to the north are two nature reserves with native forests and a wide range of birdlife. Inland there are two lakes off the beaten tourist path. ►► *For listings, see pages 367-371.*

Ins and outs

Getting there There are daily flights north to Santiago and Concepción. The bus network is very wide, with numerous daily services to Santiago and south to Puerto Montt, as well as to cities such as Temuco, Pucón, Concepción and Chillán. By road access to the Panamericana is north via Mafil or south via Paillaco.

Getting around Valdivia is quite sizeable: *colectivos* and buses serve the outlying barrios. However, like many Chilean cities, the centre is relatively compact, and few places are beyond walking distance, even those across the river on the Isla Teja.

Tourist information The **tourist office** ⓘ *Prat 555, by dock, T063-239060, info valdivia@sernatur.cl, daily in summer, weekdays off season*, has good maps of the region and local rivers, a list of hotel prices and examples of local crafts with artisans' addresses. There's also a **CONAF office** ⓘ *Ismael Valdez 431, T063-218822*.

History

Valdivia was one of the most important centres of Spanish colonial control over Chile. Founded in 1552 by Pedro de Valdivia, it was abandoned as a result of the Mapuche insurrection of 1599 and was briefly occupied by Dutch pirates. In 1645 it was refounded as a walled city and the only Spanish mainland settlement south of the Río Biobío. The Spanish continued to fortify the area around Valdivia throughout the 1600s, developing the most comprehensive system of defence in the South Pacific against the British and

Valdivia centre

Casino
Carampangue
Alemania
Buses to Niebla
Independencia
Chacabuco
O'Higgins
Henríquez
Municipal
Municipalidad
Picarte
Libertad
Feria Fluvial
Cathedral
Plaza de la República
Sernatur
Yungay
Lan Chile
Maipú
Río Valdivia
Muelle Fluvial
Arauco
Rosales
San Carlos

➡ **Valdivia maps**
1 Valdivia centre, page 362
2 Valdivia, page 363

N

100 metres
100 yards

Eating 🍴
Café Haussmann **2**
Café Moro **1**
Camino de Luna **6**
Chester's **3**
Delicias **5**
Entrelagos **4**

Dutch navies. Seventeen forts were built in total. They were reinforced after 1760, but proved of little avail during the Wars of Independence, when the Chilean naval squadron under Lord Cochrane seized control of the forts in two days. From independence until the 1880s Valdivia was an outpost of Chilean rule, reached only by sea or by a coastal route.

Valdivia

The city is centred around the tree-lined **Plaza de la República**. In the cathedral, the **Museo de la Catedral de Valdivia** ⓘ *Independencia 514, Tue-Sun 1000-1300, 1600-1900 in summer; Mon-Fri 1000-1300, 1600-1900, Sat 1000-1300 in winter*, covers four centuries of Christian history. Three blocks east is the **Muelle Fluvial**, the dock for boat trips down the river. From the Muelle Fluvial there is a pleasant walk north along the *costanera* (Avenida Prat) and under the bridge to Isla Teja and on round the bend in the river (where boats can be hired for US$6 per hour) as far as the bus terminal.

On the western bank of the river, **Isla Teja** has a botanical garden and arboretum with trees from all over the world. West of the botanical gardens is the **Parque Saval** ⓘ *open daylight hours, US$0.80*. Covering 30 ha it has areas of native forest as well as a small lake, the Lago de los Lotos. There are beautiful flowers in spring. It often hosts events like Rodeos, and a Mapuche market and craft market in summer. Also on the island are two museums. The **Museo Histórico y Antropológico** ⓘ *T063-212872, museohistorico@uach.cl, Tue-Sun*

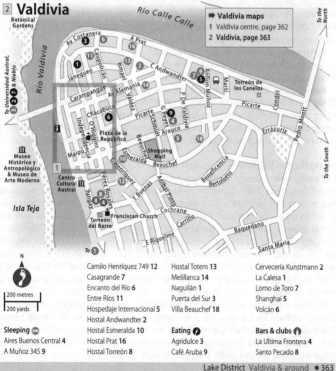

2 Valdivia

➡ **Valdivia maps**
1 Valdivia centre, page 362
2 Valdivia, page 363

Sleeping 🛌
Aires Buenos Central **4**
A Muñoz 345 **9**
Camilo Henríquez 749 **12**
Casagrande **7**
Encanto del Río **6**
Entre Ríos **11**
Hospedaje Internacional **5**
Hostal Andwandter **2**
Hostal Esmeralda **10**
Hostal Prat **16**
Hostal Torreón **8**
Hostal Totem **13**
Melillanca **14**
Naguilán **1**
Puerta del Sur **3**
Villa Beauchef **18**

Eating 🍴
Agridulce **3**
Café Aruba **9**
Cervecería Kunstmann **2**
La Calesa **1**
Lomo de Toro **7**
Shanghai **5**
Volcán **6**

Bars & clubs 🍸
La Ultima Frontera **4**
Santo Pecado **8**

The 1960 earthquake

Southern Chile is highly susceptible to earthquakes: severe quakes struck the area in 1575, 1737, 1786 and 1837, but the tremor that struck around midday on 22 May 1960 caused the most extensive damage throughout southern Chile and was accompanied by the eruption of four volcanoes and a *maremoto* (tidal wave) that was felt in New Zealand and Japan.

Around Valdivia the land dropped by 3 m, creating new lagunas along the Río Cruces to the north of the city. The *maremoto* destroyed all the fishing villages and ports between Puerto Saavedra in the north and Chiloé in the south. The earthquake also provoked several landslides. The greatest of these blocked the Río San Pedro, near the point where it drains Lago Riñihue, and the lake rose 35 m in 24 hours. Over the next two months all available labour and machinery was used to dig channels to divert the water from the other lakes and to drain off the waters of Lago Riñihue, thus averting the devastation of the San Pedro Valley.

1000-1300, 1400-1800, daily 1000-2000 in summer, US$2.50, is beautifully situated in the former mansion of Carlos Andwandter, a leading German immigrant. Run by the university, it contains sections on archaeology, ethnography and German colonization. Next door, in the former Andwandter brewery, is the **Museo de Arte Moderno** ① *Jan-Feb Tue-Sun, 1000-1300, 1400-1800, off season only open for temporary exhibitions, US$2*. Boat trips can be made around Isla Teja, offering views of birds and seals.

Kunstmann Brewery ① *just out of town on the Niebla road, T063-292969, www.cerveza-kunstmann.cl*, offers tours of the working brewery and its beer museum; it also has a good restaurant.

Every Sunday during January and February there is a special **steam train service** ① *departs on Equador 2000, T063-214978, Sun, 1½ hrs, return from Antilhue 2 hrs later, US$8 return, advance booking essential*, to **Antilhue**, 20 km to the east. The train is met by locals selling all sorts of local culinary specialities. The engine dates from 1913. Special additional trips are often made on public holidays; check departure times before travelling.

Along the Río Valdivia → Colour map 4, B1/2.

The various rivers around Valdivia are navigable: pleasant journeys can be made by rented motor boat south of town on the Ríos Futa and Tornagaleanes around the **Isla del Rey**, while at the mouth of the Río Valdivia are interesting and isolated villages that can be visited by road or by river boat. The two main centres are **Niebla** on the north bank and **Corral** opposite on the south bank, site of two of the most important 17th-century Spanish forts on the Río Valdivia (see page 362). There is a frequent boat service between the two towns. Midstream, between Niebla and Corral is **Isla Mancera**, a small island dominated by the Castillo de San Pedro de Alcántara, the earliest of the Spanish forts. Inside the fort there is a small church and convent. The island is a pleasant place to stop over on the boat trips, but it can get crowded when an excursion boat arrives.

Eighteen kilometres west of Valdivia, **Niebla** is a resort with seafood restaurants and accommodation. To the west on a promontory is the **Fuerte de la Pura y Limpia Concepción de Monfort de Lemus** ① *daily in summer 1000-1900, closed Mon in winter, US$1, free on Sun*, with a museum on Chilean naval history, a tourist information office and a telephone office. Around Niebla the north bank is dotted with campsites and *cabañas*.

About 6 km further round the coast is **Los Molinos**, a seaside resort set among steep wooded hills. There is a campsite and lots of seaside restaurants. The road continues, rising and falling along the coast, with fine views of beaches deserted outside summer. The paved road runs out about 6 km north of Los Molinos but a *ripio* road continues past Curiñanco as far as the Parque Oncol.

Corral lies 62 km west of Valdivia by road and is the main port serving the city. It is much quieter and more pleasant than Niebla, and its fort, **Castillo de San Sebastián** ① *US$5 Jan-Feb, US$1.50 off season*, has a dilapidated, interesting atmosphere. It was built in 1645 as one of the main fortifications on the estuary, and during the 17th century its 3-m-thick walls were defended by a battery of 21 guns. Inside is a museum, and in summer re-enactments of the 1820 storming of the Spanish fort by the Chilean Republican forces in period costume are held daily 1200 and 1800.

Further north near the mouth of the river are pleasant beaches and the remains of two other Spanish colonial forts, the **Castillo San Luis de Alba de Amargos** and the **Castillo de San Carlos**. The coastal walks west and south of Corral, along very isolated and forested roads above the ocean, are splendid and very rarely visited. The friendly tourist office on the pier can provide some trekking information.

North of Valdivia

Some 27 km to the northwest is the **Parque Oncol** ① *T09-96441439, www.parqueoncol.cl, US$1.80, daily buses in summer, US$7 including park entry, T063-278100 for bookings*. It consists of 754 ha of native Valdivian forest with several easy trails and lookouts with fine views, canopy ziplines, a picnic area, a good café and campsite.

Stretching from the outskirts of the city, 30 km north, is the **Santuario de la Naturaleza Carlos Anwandter**, along the Río Cruces, which was flooded as a result of the 1960 *maremoto* and now attracts many bird species. Boat trips to the reserve are available from Valdivia aboard the **Isla del Río** ① *daily 1415, 6 hrs, US$22 per person*.

Lagos Ranco & Maihue

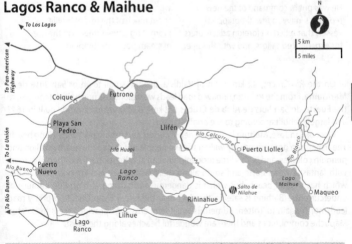

Lord Cochrane

Lord Thomas Alexander Cochrane (1775-1860) was born into a Scottish aristocratic family and began his career in the British navy during the Napoleonic Wars, rising rapidly through the officer ranks. He was elected to Parliament in 1806 as MP for Honiton and in 1807 as MP for Westminster. Cochrane had never been on good terms with his naval superiors, and when he used his position in the House of Commons to accuse the naval commander, Lord Gambier, of incompetence, he precipitated his own downfall. Gambier was court-martialled and acquitted; Cochrane was retired on half-pay and spent the next three years exposing corruption and abuses in the navy. His links with a financial scandal in 1814 provided his enemies with an opportunity for revenge: he was dismissed from the navy, expelled from Parliament and sentenced to 12 months' imprisonment.

Cochrane was recruited for the Chilean armed forces by an agent in London and quickly became friendly with Chile's independence leader Bernardo O'Higgins. He was put in command of the new republic's 'navy', a few ill-equipped vessels that relied on foreign adventurers for experienced sailors, and with this fleet harassed the Spanish-held ports along the Chilean coast. His audacious storming of the fortresses of Corral, San Carlos and Amargos led to the capture of the key Spanish base of Valdivia (see page 362).

Later that year Cochrane transported Peruvian liberation troops, led by José de San Martín, along the Pacific coast to invade Peru, but his relations with San Martin were poor and he became very critical of the Peruvian's cautious strategy. Afterwards Cochrane continued to attack Spanish shipping in the Pacific, sailing as far north as Mexico in 1822.

In 1823 the new government of Brazil appointed Cochrane to head its navy in the struggle for independence from Portugal. Once again leading a motley collection of boats manned largely by foreigners, Cochrane drove the colonial fleet from Bahia and pursued it back to Portugal. In 1825 he fell out with the Brazilian government and returned to Britain. Two years later he volunteered to help the Greeks in their struggle for independence from Turkey. He was reinstated in the British navy in 1832, was promoted to Rear-Admiral and spent much of the rest of his life promoting developments in the use of steam power in shipping.

On the Río Cruces, 42 km north of Valdivia, lies the small town of **San José de la Mariquina**. From the town an unpaved road leads west along the north side of the river to the **Fuerte de San Luis de Alba de Cruces** (22 km), a colonial fortification built in 1647 and largely rebuilt according to the original plans.

West of San José, **Mehuín** is a small, friendly resort and fishing port with a long beach. The fishermen here are usually willing to take people out to see the nearby sealion and penguin colonies, and with a little luck dolphins can also be spotted. A clifftop *ripio* road, with fantastic views north and south along the coastline, leads 6 km north to **Queule**, which has a good beach, but which is dangerous for bathing at high tide because of undercurrents. (Bathing is safer in the river near the ferry.) From Queule, a pretty road leads north again to **Toltén**; numerous small ferry crossings provide access to isolated Mapuche communities and there are wonderful beaches along the coast.

East of Valdivia

The route east from Valdivia to the lakes passes through what is, perhaps, the least interesting part of the Lake District, consisting largely of wheatfields and dairy farms. Some 93 km east of Valdivia, beyond Antilhue (where there are picnic sites) and Los Lagos, is **Lago Riñihue**, the southernmost of the Seven Lakes. **Riñihue**, a beautiful but small and isolated village at its western end, is worth visiting but the road around the southern edge of the lake from Riñihue to Enco is poor and there is no road around the northern edge of the lake.

South of Lago Riñihue is **Lago Ranco**, one of the largest lakes, covering 41,000 ha, and also one of the most accessible as it has a road, poor in many places, around its edge. The road is characterized by lots of mud and animals. However it is worth taking the opportunity to escape the gringo trail and witness an older lifestyle while admiring the beautiful lake, starred with islands, and the sun setting on the distant volcanoes. There is excellent fishing on the southern shore; several hotels organize fishing expeditions.

From the Pan-American Highway the north side of the lake can be reached from Los Lagos or from a better road 18 km further south. These two roads join and meet the road around the lake some 5 km west of **Futrono**. This is the main town on the northern shore and has a daily boat service to **Huapi**, the island in the middle of the lake. From Futrono the road (paved at this point) curves round the north of the lake to **Llifén**, Km 22, a picturesque place on the eastern shore. From Llifén, it is possible visit **Lago Maihue**, 33 km further east, the south end of which is surrounded by native forests. From Llifén the road around Lago Ranco continues via the Salto de Nilahue (Km 14) to **Riñinahue**, Km 23, at the southeast corner, with access to beaches. Further west is **Lago Ranco**, Km 47, an ugly little town on the south shore, which has a museum with exhibits on Mapuche culture. On the western shore is **Puerto Nuevo**, where there are watersports and fishing on the Río Bueno. Further north, 10 km west of Futrono, is **Coique**, where there are more good beaches. Paved roads lead to Río Bueno and the Pan-American Highway.

⓪ Valdivia and around listings

For Sleeping and Eating price codes and other relevant information, see Essentials pages 35-42.

⓪ Sleeping

Valdivia *p362, maps p362 and p363*
Accommodation is scarce during Semana Valdiviana. In the summer, accommodation is widely available in private homes, usually **C**, or **F** singles.

L-AL Puerta del Sur, Los Lingues 950, Isla Teja, T063-224500, www.hotelpuertadelsur. com. 5-star, set in large grounds, all facilities including pool, sauna, restaurant, tennis courts, activities and tours offered, very good.
AL Melillanca, Alemania 675, T063-212509, www.melillanca.cl. 4-star. Decent business standard. Spacious rooms could do with a refit. With restaurant, sauna, Wi-Fi zones.

AL Naguilán, Gral Lagos 1927, T063-212851, www.hotelnaguilan.com. Pleasant 4-star, south of the city centre along the river. Clean, quiet, nice views, outdoor pool, good restaurant.
A Encanto del Río, Prat 415, T063-225740, www.hotelencantodelrio.cl. Small new hotel, comfortable if lacking in character. Rooms on the middle floor have balconies and river views. Disabled access, Wi-Fi, central heating.
B Casagrande, Andtwandter 880, T063-202035, www.hotelcasagrande.cl. Cramped rooms with bath, heating and cable TV. Attractive old house, recently refurbished. Great views from the breakfast area. Internet, Wi-Fi and laundry facilities. Convenient for bus terminal.
B Entre Ríos, Anwandter 337, T063-259310, www.hostalentrerios.cl. Refurbished old wooden house inexplicably painted a

faux-wooden colour. Decent business standard hotel. Pleasant garden at the back.
B-C Hostal Prat, Prat 595, T063-222020. With good breakfast and bath, cable TV. Views to an industrial zone across the river.
B-C Hostal Torreón, P Rosales 783, T063-212622, mrprelle@gmail.com. **D-E** singles. With breakfast. Creaky old German-style wooden villa with 17 rooms. Spacious living and dining room with period furniture. Nice atmosphere, cable TV, parking. Rooms on the top floor are more airy and a couple have pleasant views.
C Aires Buenos Central, García Reyes 550, T063-222202, www.airesbuenos.cl. Small doubles, **E** per person in dorms. Good HI-affiliated hostel. Friendly English-speaking staff, Wi-Fi, book exchange, kitchen facilities, pleasant garden with pet duck! Lots of info. Recommended.
C Hospedaje Internacional, García Reyes 660, T063-212015, www.hostalinternacional.cl. Some rooms with bath, **E** singles. With breakfast, without bath, clean, helpful, use of kitchen, barbeque area, book exchange, tours offered. Also *cabañas*.
C Hostal Anwandter, Anwandter 601, T063-218587, hostalanwandter@hotmail.com. Good-value rooms with bath and breakfast, cheaper without. Internet and laundry facilities.
C Hostal Esmeralda, Esmeralda 651, T063-215659. **F** singles. A little run-down, spacious rooms, some with bath, also *cabañas*, parking.
C Hostal Totem, Anwandter 425, T063-292849, www.turismototem.cl. Simple rooms with bath, French and basic English spoken, friendly, clean, tours arranged. Recommended.
C Villa Beauchef, Beauchef 844, T063-216044, www.villabeauchef.cl. **E** singles. Some rooms with or without bath and breakfast, cable TV. Thin walls.
C-D Camilo Henríquez 749, casa 6, T063-222574. **F** singles. Charming tumbledown mansion that survived the 1960 earthquake at the expense of wildly sloping floors. Large basic rooms, kitchen,

laundry, internet. Basic English spoken. Recommended, if only for its unique qualities.
D A Muñoz 345, opposite bus terminal. **F** singles. Very basic accommodation. Several similar places on the same street, or on Picarte.

Camping
Camping Centenario, rowing club on España. Overlooking the river.
Isla Teja, T063-213584. Views over the river.

Along the Río Valdivia *p364*
B Cabañas Fischer, Niebla, T063-282007. *Cabañas* and camping. Worth bargaining out of season.
C Hostería Los Alamos, Corral. **F** singles. Perfect for a quiet life.
C Residencial Mariel, Tarapacá 36, Corral, T063-471290. **F** singles. Modern, clean, friendly, good value.
C Villa Santa Clara, Niebla, T063-282018. With breakfast, also *cabañas*, cooking and laundry facilities.

North of Valdivia *p365*
The following are all in Mehuín. There are also 2 simple *residenciales* in Queule.
B El Nogal, T/F063-451352. With bath and breakfast, good.
D Hospedaje Marbella. **F-G** singles. Clean and the cheapest option.

East of Valdivia *p367*
Some of the houses around Lago Ranco are available for let in summer.
AL Hostería Huinca Quinay, 3 km east of Riñihue, Lago Riñihue, T063-1971811, gcristi@hotmail.com. 4-star *cabañas* with restaurant and lots of facilities.
AL Hostería Riñinahue, Casilla 126, Riñinahue, near Lago Ranco, T063-491379. Organizes fishing expeditions.
AL Hotel Puerto Nuevo, Puerto Nuevo, Lago Ranco, T064-375540, www.hotelpuerto nuevo.cl. Leisure complex in large grounds by the lake, with restaurant.
AL-A Hostería Chollinco, 3 km out of Llifén, on the road towards Lago Maihue in the Lago

Ranco area, T063-1971979, www.hosteria chollinco.cl. Remote country lodge with swimming pool, trekking, horse riding, fishing, hunting and other activities.

AL-A Riñimapu, northwest edge of Lago Riñihue, T063-311388, www.rinimapu.cl. Comfortable rooms and suites with views over the lake, excellent food.

A Huequecura, Llifén, T09-96535450. Includes meals and fishing services, good restaurant.

C-D Hospedaje Futronhue, Balmaceda 90, Futrono, T063-481265. Good breakfast.

Camping

There are campsites all around Lago Ranco as well as several on Lago Maihue, though many are open in summer only and prices are high.

Bahía Coique, 9 km west of Futrono, T063-481264. Autocamping, US$50 per site in summer, US$35 per site off season.

Bahía Las Rosas, 1 km east of Futrono. US$20 per site.

Camping Lago Ranco. US$18 per site.

Maqueo, eastern shore of Lago Maihue, US$20 per site.

Nalcahue, 1 km west of Futrono, T063-481663. US$20 per site.

Playa Ranquil, Riñinahue, US$12 per site.

🍽 Eating

For places to eat in the coastal resorts and around the lakes, see Sleeping, above.

Valdivia p362, maps p362 and p363
There are plenty of very cheap restaurants serving good food down by the waterfront, facing the boat dock, and in the market.

††† Restaurante Camino de Luna, Prat s/n. A floating restaurant next to the *costanera*, unique in Chile.

†††-†† Agridulce, Prat 327, T063-433435, www.agridulcevaldivia.cl. Perfect mix of sophisticated dishes using local produce, tapas and generous sandwiches. Good service and good value. Recommended.

†††-†† Lomodetoro, Los Robles 170, Isla Teja, T063-346423. Probably the best steak in town. Good wine list.

†† Café Haussmann, O'Higgins 394. A Valdivian institution famous for its raw meat dishes.

†† Cervecería Kunstmann, on the road to Niebla, T063-292969, www.cerveza-kunst mann.cl. German food, brewery with 5 varieties of beer, recommended.

†† Delicias, Henríquez 372. Recommended for meals, cakes and real coffee.

†† La Calesa, O'Higgins 160, T063-225467. Elagant and intimate Peruvian and international resataurant. Good *pisco sours*. Recommended.

†† Shanghai, Andwandter y Muñoz. Pleasant Chinese.

† Café Aruba, Picarte 766. Good-value, filling sandwiches.

† Chester's, Henríquez 314. Good-value pizzas and fast food. Open late.

† Restaurant Volcán, Caupolicán y Chacabuco. *Pichangas, cazuelas*. Great food at a good price.

Cafés

Café Moro, Independencia y Libertad. Airy café with a mezzanine art gallery. Good-value lunches (Wed *pastel de jaiva* particularly recommended). Popular bar at night.

Entrelagos, Pérez Rosales 622. Ice cream and chocolates, expensive.

La Baguette, Yungay y Libertad. Bakery selling French-style cakes and brown bread. Repeatedly recommended.

Mi Pueblito, San Carlos 190, Wholemeal bread and vegetarian snacks to take away.

Along the Río Valdivia p364

†† Las Delicias, Niebla, T063-213566. A restaurant with 'a view that would be worth the money even if the food wasn't good'. Also *cabañas* and camping.

††-† Las Terrazas de Centinilla, 8 km north of Niebla, T063-247426. Open Fri-Sun. Picada specializing in *empanadas* (it serves over a dozen kinds) and other seafood. Great views.

⚬ Bars and clubs

Valdivia *p362, maps p362 and p363*
Bunker, Av Los Robles 1345, Isla Teja.
Lively student bar.
La Bomba, Caupolicán. Pleasant old Valdivian
bar, serves *empanadas* and other dishes.
La Ultima Frontera, Pérez Rosales 787 (in
Centro Cultural 787). Fills up with alternative
20- and 30-something crowd. Cheap beer
as well as a large variety of sandwiches
(including falafel) and filling soups. Friendly
but slow service and very smoky.
Ocio Restobar, Arauco 102, loud music.
Popular with young professionals.
Santo Pecado, Yungay 745. Refined but
laid-back bar also serving a variety of
sandwiches and exotic dishes.

◉ Entertainment

Valdivia *p362, maps p362 and p363*
There's a cinema in the Mall on Calle Arauco.
Cine Club UACH, on the university campus
on Isla Teja, T063-215622, www.uach.cl/
extension/cineclub/cartelera.php. Shows
films at the weekend (not in summer).

◉ Festivals and events

Valdivia *p362, maps p362 and p363*
Mid-Feb Semana Valdiviana, with a series
of sporting and cultural activities such a as
a triathlon, theatre and music, culminates
in **Noche Valdiviana** on the Sat with a
procession of elaborately decorated
boats that sail past the Muelle Fluvial.
Sep A well-regarded film festival.

Along the Río Valdivia *p364*
Mid-Feb Niebla hosts a Feria Costumbrista,
with lots of good food including *pullmay*,
asado and *paila marina*.

⚬ Shopping

Valdivia *p362, maps p362 and p363*
Bookshops
There is a Sun books and antiques fair
at the Torreón del Barro.
Librería de Valdivia, Lautaro 177. Excellent
bookshop with a small selection of maps as
well as literature in English and French.
Librería Chiloé, Caupolicán 410.

Chocolate
Valdivia is famous for its chocolate and there
are several shops in the centre that sell it.
Entre Lagos is the best known, but also the
most expensive.

Supermarkets
Hiper-Unico, Arauco 697.
Las Brisas, Henríquez 522 (on plaza).

▲ Activities and tours

Valdivia *p362, maps p362 and p363*
The tourist boats to Isla Mancera and Corral,
depart from the Muelle Fluvial, Av Prat 555,
Valdivia. Several companies offer trips.
They will only leave with a minimum of 10
passengers, so off season organize in advance.
There is a full list of operators in the tourist
information office. Prices per person: city US$6,
Isla Teja US$10, Corral-Mancera US$25-40.
There are several other destinations.
Fundo Teja Norte, next to the Parque Saval,
T063-293439, offer guided horse rides
through the Valdivian forests.
Nauticentro Koch, On the costanera
opposite the heliport, T09-8505 0558. Hire
pedalos, kayaks and motor boats.
Pueblito Expediciones, San Carlos 188,
T063-245055, www.pueblitoexpediciones.cl.
Offers classes and trips in sea kayaks in the
waters around Valdivia, US$25-35 for 4-5 hrs.
Tourist House, Camilo Henríquez 266, T063-
433115, www.casadelturista.com. Offer a
range of excursions and give good advice.

✈ Transport

Valdivia *p362, maps p362 and p363*
Air
LanChile, Maipú 271, T60-5262000,
www.lan.com runs several flights daily to/from
Santiago except during winter via Temuco or
Concepción. **Sky Airline** have an office at
Walter Schmidt 303, local 5, T600-600 2828

Bus
Terminal at Muñoz y Prat, by the river.
For local services along the Río Valdivia
or to Lago Ranco, see below.
   To **Santiago**, several companies, 11 hrs,
most services overnight, US$25-65; to
Osorno, every 30 mins, 2 hrs, several
companies, US$5; to **Panguipulli**, Empresa
Pirehueico, about every 30 mins, US$5; to
Puerto Montt, many daily, 3 hrs, US$6; to
Castro, 7 hrs, US$14; to **Temuco**, US$5; to
Puerto Varas, 2¾ hrs, US$6; to **Frutillar**,
2¼ hrs, US$6; to **Villarrica**, JAC, 6 a day direct,
2½ hrs, US$6, continuing to **Pucón**, US$7,
3 hrs; to **Mehuin**, 2 hrs, US$3.
   To Argentina   To **Bariloche** via
Osorno, 7 hrs, Bus Norte, US$24; to **Zapala**,
Igi-Llaima, Mon, Thu, Sat, 2300, change in
Temuco at 0200, arrive Zapala 1200-1500,
depending on border crossing, US$45.

Car
Hire from **Autovald**, Henríquez 610, T063-
212786; **Hertz**, Picarte 640 and at the airport,
T063-272273/T063-218316; **Salfa Sur**, Picarte
2225, T063-230324, www.salfasur.cl. Good

value, recommended. Turismo Méndez,
Gral Lagos 1335, T063-213205.

Along the Río Valdivia *p364*
Boat
There is an hourly ferry service between
Niebla and **Corral**, 30 mins, US$1.

Bus
Bus to **Niebla** from Chacabuco y Yungay,
Valdivia, every 20 mins between 0730 and
2100, 30 mins, US$1.20; the service continues
to **Los Molinos**, with 3 buses a day carrying
on further as far as Curiñanco. Also *colectivos*.

East of Valdivia *p367*
Buses from Valdivia to **Llifén** via Futrono,
Cordillera Sur, 4 daily, US$3; to **Riñihue** via
Paillaco and Los Lagos, frequent; from Osorno
to **Lago Ranco**, Empresa Ruta 5, 6 daily.

❸ Directory

Valdivia *p362, maps p362 and p363*
Banks   Several banks with ATMs in the
centre. Turismo Cochrane, Arauco 435; Casa
de Cambio, Carampangue 325, T063-213305;
Turismo Austral, Arauco y Henríquez, Galería
Arauco, accepts TCs. **Internet**   Several
throughout the centre, around US$0.60 per
hr. **Laundry**   Au Chic, Arauco 436; Lavazul,
Chacabuco 300, slow; coin laundry at
Lavamatic, Schmidt y Picarte, Mon-Sat
0930-2030; Manantial, Henríquez 809.

Osorno and around

→ *Colour map 4, B2.*

Situated at the confluence of the Ríos Rahue and Damas, 921 km south of Santiago, Osorno was founded in 1553 before being abandoned in 1604 and refounded by Ambrosio O'Higgins and Juan MacKenna O'Reilly in 1796. It later became one of the centres of German immigration; their descendants are still of great importance in the area. Although Osorno is an important transport hub and a reasonable base for visiting the southern lakes, it is a drab uninspiring city, and is likely to be a place that you will pass through. ▶▶ *For listings, see pages 375-378.*

Ins and outs

Getting there Osorno is a key crossroads for bus routes in southern Chile. Passengers heading overland to Bariloche, Neuquén, Coyhaique or Punta Arenas will pass through here before making for the Puyehue Pass into Argentina; buses tend to leave from Puerto Montt, and travellers from Santiago may well change buses here. There are also hourly local services to Puerto Montt, as well as frequent services north to Temuco and Valdivia.

Getting around Most of the places visitors are likely to visit are within easy walking distance. Taxis or *colectivos* may be useful for longer trips.

Tourist information Information is available from the provincial government office of **Sernatur** ① *Plaza de Armas, O'Higgins s/n, piso 1, T064-234104.* The municipal tourist office is based in the bus terminal and in a kiosk on the Plaza de Armas, both open December to February. There is also a **CONAF** office ① *Rosas 430, T064-234393.*

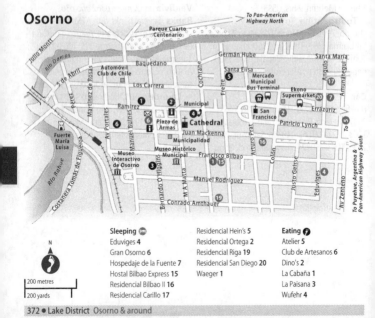

Osorno

Sleeping 💤
Eduviges 4
Gran Osorno 6
Hospedaje de la Fuente 7
Hostal Bilbao Express 15
Residencial Bilbao II 16
Residencial Carillo 17

Residencial Hein's 5
Residencial Ortega 2
Residencial Riga 19
Residencial San Diego 20
Waeger 1

Eating 🍴
Atelier 5
Club de Artesanos 6
Dino's 2
La Cabaña 1
La Paisana 3
Wufehr 4

Osorno

On the large **Plaza de Armas** stands the modern, concrete and glass cathedral, with many arches and a tower that is itself an open, latticed arch with a cross superimposed. West of the centre on a bend overlooking the river is the **Fuerte María Luisa**, built in 1793 and restored in 1977; only the river front walls and end turrets are still standing. East of the main plaza along Calle MacKenna are a number of late 19th-century wooden mansions built by German immigrants, now preserved as national monuments. Two blocks south of the Plaza is the **Museo Histórico Municipal** ① *Matta 809, Mon-Sun 1100-1900 in summer; Mon-Fri 0930-1730, Sat 1500-1800 in winter, US$1.50*, which has displays on natural history, Mapuche culture, the refounding of the city and German colonization. Three blocks southwest of the plaza, in the former train station is the **Museo Interactivo de Osorno (MIO)** ① *T064-212996, www.municipalidadosorno.cl, Mon-Thu 0815-1300, 1445-1815, Fri 0815-1300, 1445-1715, Sat 1415-1745*, an interactive science museum designed for both children and adults.

North and west of Osorno

Río Bueno, 30 km north, is celebrated for its scenery and fishing. The Spanish colonial fort, dating from 1777, is situated high above the river and offers fine views. Just over 20 km further west on the Río Bueno is **Trumao**, a river port with a river launch service to La Barra on the coast. There are beaches at **Maicolpue**, 60 km west of Osorno, and **Pucatrihue**, which are worth a visit in the summer. Further north is the **Monumento Natural Alerce Costero**, a park covering 2307 ha in the coastal mountain range and protecting an area of alerce forest (though a fire in 1975 destroyed some of the forest). Access is by a poor ripio road which runs northwest for 52 km from La Unión. There is a CONAF *guardería* and *refugio* at the entrance, from which a 3-km trail leads to a 3500-year-old alerce tree.

East of Osorno

From Osorno Route 215 runs east to the Argentine border at the Puyehue Pass via the south shore of Lago Puyehue, Anticura and the Parque Nacional Puyehue (see below). **Auto Museo Moncopulli** ① *Route 215, T064-210744, www.moncopulli.cl, 1000-1900, US$2.75, bus towards Entre Lagos*, 25 km east of Osorno is the best motor museum in Chile. Exhibits include a Studebaker collection from 1852 to 1966. There is also a 1950s-style cafetería.

Lago Puyehue and the Parque Nacional

Surrounded by relatively flat countryside, 47 km east of Osorno, **Lago Puyehue** extends over 15,700 ha. The southern shore is much more developed than the northern shore, which is accessible only by unpaved road from **Entre Lagos** at the western end. On the opposite side of the lake are the **Termas de Puyehue** ① *www.puyehue.cl, 0900-2000 daily, US$50-60 including meals, drinks and access to all facilities.*

Stretching east from Lago Puyehue to the Argentine border, **Parque Nacional Puyehue** covers 107,000 ha, much of it in the valley of the Río Golgol. On the eastern side are several lakes, including Lago Constancia and Lago Gris. There are two volcanic peaks: **Volcán Puyehue** (2240 m) in the north (access via a private track US$10) and **Volcán Casablanca** (also called Antillanca, 1900 m). Leaflets on walks and attractions are available from the park administration at Aguas Calientes and from the ranger station at Anticura.

At **Aguas Calientes**, 4 km south of the Termas de Puyehue in a thickly forested valley, is an open-air pool (dirty) with very hot thermal water beside the **Río Chanleufú** ① *Mon-Fri*

0830-1230, 1400-1800 in summer only; Sat, Sun and holidays 0830-2030 all year; outdoor pool US$5, children US$2.50; indoor pool US$12, children US$6.

From Aguas Calientes the road continues 18 km southeast past three small lakes and through forests to **Antillanca** on the slopes of Volcán Casablanca. In winter a one-way traffic system operates on the last 8 km: ascending traffic from 0800 to 1200 and 1400 to 1730; descending traffic from 1200 to 1400 and after 1730. This is a particularly beautiful section, especially at sunrise, with views over Lago Puyehue to the north and Lagos Rupanco and Llanquihue to the south, as well as the snow-clad peaks of Calbuco, Osorno, Puntiagudo, Puyehue and Tronador forming a semicircle. The tree-line on Casablanca is one of the few in the world made up of deciduous trees (*nothofagus* or southern beech). From Antillanca it is possible to climb Casablanca for even better views of the surrounding volcanoes and lakes; there's no path and the hike takes about seven hours there and back; information from **Club Andino** in Osorno. On the south side of the volcano there are caves (accessible by road, allow five hours from **Hotel Antillanca**).

The paved Route 215 continues from the Termas de Puyehue to **Anticura**, northeast of Aguas Calientes. In this section of the park are three waterfalls, including the spectacular 40-m wide **Salto del Indio**. Legend has it that an Indian, enslaved by the Spanish, was able to escape by hiding behind the falls. Situated just off the road, the falls are on a marked path through dense forest which includes a 800-year-old Coigüe tree known as 'El Abuelo'.

Lago Rupanco

Lying south of Lago Puyehue and considerably larger, this lake covers 23,000 ha and is far less accessible and less developed for tourism than most of the other larger lakes. Access from the northern shore is via two unpaved roads that branch off Route 215. **El Paraíso**

Lagos Puyehue & Rupanco

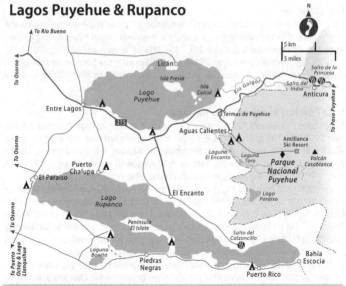

Border crossing: Chile–Argentina

Paso Puyehue

The Chilean border post is 4 km east of Anticura at Pajaritos. Immigration is open from the second Saturday in October to the second Saturday in March 0800-2100, otherwise 0800-1900. From here it's a further 22 km east to the border at Paso Puyehue, although this route is liable to closure after snow. For private vehicles entering Chile, formalities are quick (about 15 minutes), but include a search for fruit, vegetables and dairy produce. On the Argentine side the road continues to Bariloche.

(aka Marina Rupanco), at the western tip of the lake, can be reached by an unpaved road south from Entre Lagos. A 40-km dirt road runs along the southern shore, via **Laguna Bonita**, a small lake surrounded by forest, and **Piedras Negras** to **Bahía Escocia** at the eastern end. From the south, access is from two turnings off the road between Osorno and Las Cascadas.

⦿ Osorno and around listings

For Sleeping and Eating price codes and other relevant information, see Essentials pages 35-42.

⬤ Sleeping

Osorno *p372, map p372*
AL-A Waeger, Cochrane 816, T064-233721, www.hotelwaeger.cl. Probably the best in town. Room sizes vary from spacious to tiny, and rooms facing the street can be noisy.
A-B Gran Hotel Osorno, O'Higgins 615, T064-232171, granhotelosorno@entel chile.net. Cable TV, well furnished but ageing. Comfortable 3-star.
B Eduviges, Eduviges 856, T064-235023, www.hoteleduviges.cl. Cheaper rooms with out bath. Spacious, clean, quiet, attractive, gardens, also *cabañas* and restaurant. Laundry and internet facilities. Recommended.
C Hostal Bilbao Express, Bilbao 1019, T064-262200, pazla@telsur.cl. With bath and breakfast, parking, restaurant. Also Residencial Bilbao II, MacKenna 1205, T064-264444.
C Residencial Riga, Amthauer 1058, T064-232945, resriga@telsur.cl. Clean, pleasant. Internet access. Recommended but heavily booked in season.

C Residencial Hein's, Errázuriz 1757, T064-234116. **E** singles. Some rooms with bath. Old-fashioned, spacious, family atmosphere.

There are lots of cheap options near the bus terminal, including the following:
D Hospedaje de la Fuente, Los Carrera 1587. **F** singles. Basic, friendly.
D Residencial Ortega, Colón 602. **F** singles. Parking, basic, clean, friendly.
D Residencial San Diego, Los Carrera 1551. **F** singles with breakfast.
D Residencial Carillo, Angulo 454. **F-G** singles. Basic, clean.

Camping
Municipal site off Pan-American Highway near southern entrance to city, open Jan-Feb only, poor facilities, US$9 per site.

North and west of Osorno *p373*
C Hostería Miller, Maicolpue, 60 km west of Osorno, T064-197 5360. On the beach, clean, with good service, also a recommended campsite.

Lago Puyehue and the Parque Nacional *p373, map p374*

A private house close to the *termas* provides cheap accommodation, either room only or full board.

LL Hotel Termas de Puyehue, Termas de Puyehue, T064-232157, www.puyehue.cl. Large resort containing 2 thermal swimming pools (one indoors, very clean), theatre, conference centre, well maintained, meals expensive, beautiful scenery, heavily booked Jan-Feb (cheaper May to mid-Dec).

A-B Hotel Antillanca, at foot of Volcán Casablanca, T064-235114, www.skiantillanca.com. Attached to the antillanca ski resort, decent restaurant/café, pool, sauna, friendly club-like atmosphere, also *refugio*.

A Cabañas Nilque, on the southern lakeshore, T064-371218, www.turismonilque.cl. Cabins (half-price May-Oct), fishing trips, watersports, car hire.

B Hospedaje Millaray, Ramírez 333, Entre Lagos, T064-371251. **E** singles. With breakfast, excellent, clean, friendly.

B-C Hostal y Cabañas Miraflores, Ramírez 480, Entre Lagos, T064-371275, olivia.hostal miraflores@gmail.com. Pleasant rooms and cabins.

B-C Hostería Entre Lagos, Ramírez 65, Entre Lagos, T064-371225. Rooms with lake view.

D Ruta 215 Gasthaus, Osvaldo Muñoz 148, Entre Lagos, T064-371357. **F** singles with bath and good breakfast. Clean, friendly, German spoken. Good value.

Camping

Camping No Me Olvides, Km 56, on southern lakeshore. US$15, also *cabañas*.

Chanleufu, Aguas Calientes, T064-236988. US$20 per site with hot water, also *cabañas*, an expensive café and a small shop.

Los Derrumbes, 1 km from Aguas Calientes. No electricity, US$25 per site.

Playa Los Copihues, Km 56.5, on southern lakeshore. Hot showers, good.

There is also a **CONAF** *refugio* on Volcán Puyehue (check with CONAF in Anticura whether it is open) and a campsite beside the Río Chanleufú (US$5 per person).

Lago Rupanco *p374, map p374*

There is no accommodation on the northern shore of the lake.

AL Puntiagudo Lodge, Bahía Escocia, T064-1974731, www.puntiagudolodge.cl. With breakfast, very comfortable, good restaurant, fly-fishing, horse riding, boat excursions. Advance bookings only.

B Refugio Club de Pesca y Caza, Sector Islote, 7 km east of Piedras Negras, T064-232056, cpc.osorno@entelchile.net. Basic *refugio* with breakfast and bath.

Camping

There are several campsites on the southern shore, including at Puerto Rico.

Desague del Rupanco, just south of El Paraíso. No facilities.

Puerto Chalupa, on northern shore, T064-232680. US$32 per site.

● Eating

For other eating options in the area, see Sleeping above. Good cheap restaurants can be found in the market

Osorno *p372, map p372*

The bakery at Ramírez 977 sells good wholemeal bread.

♥♥ Atelier, Freire 468, T064-213735. Fresh pasta and other Italian delights.

♥♥ Dino's, Ramírez 898, on the plaza. Good restaurant upstairs, bar/cafeteria downstairs.

♥♥ La Paisana, O'Higgins 827, piso 2. Arab specialities including vegetarian options.

♥♥ Wufehr, Ramirez 959, local 2. Local raw meat specialities as well as filling sandwiches. Popular with locals.

♥♥-♥ Club de Artesanos, MacKenna 634. A good choice for hearty traditional Chilean fare.

♥ La Cabaña, Ramirez 774, T064-272479. Wide variety of super cheap lunches ranging from Chinese to home-cooked Chilean. Excellent value.

Cafés
Café Lierario Hojas del Sur, MacKenna 1011 y Cochrane, more like a living room than a café. cosy, friendly. Wi-Fi.

Lago Puyehue and the Parque Nacional *p373, map p374*
¶¶ **Jardín del Turista**, Km 46, Entre Lagos, T064-371214. Very good restaurant set in spacious grounds.
¶¶ **Pub del Campo**, Entre Lagos, T064-371220. Highly recommended restaurant.

O Shopping

Osorno *p372, map p372*
There is a mall on C Freire 542 with 3 internet cafés and a bookshop, **CM Books**, which sells some English titles.
Alta Artesanía, MacKenna 1069. Excellent handicrafts, not cheap.
Climet, Angulo 603. Fishing tackle.
Ekono, Colón y Errázuriz. Supermarket.
The Lodge, Los Carrera 1291, local 5. Fishing tackle.

▲ Activities and tours

Osorno *p372, map p372*
Skiing
Club Andino, O'Higgins 1073, T064-235114. Information and advice on skiing in the area.
Hotel Antillanca, see Sleeping, above, is attached to one of Chile's smaller ski resorts; 17 pistes are served by 3 lifts, ski instruction and first-aid available. Piste preparation is unreliable. Skiing is not difficult but quality depends on the weather: though rain is common it often does not turn to snow. See www.skiantillanca.cl for information on the state of the pistes.

Lago Rupanco *p374, map p374*
Fishing
Lago Rupanco is very popular for fishing.
Bahía Escocia Fly Fishing offers excursions from the **Puntiagudo Lodge** (see Sleeping). Advance booking required.

⊜ Transport

Osorno *p372, map p372*
Air
LanChile, E Ramírez 802, T600-526 2000, flies daily to **Santiago** via Temuco.

Bus
Main terminal 4 blocks from Plaza de Armas at Errázuriz 1400, bus from centre, US$0.50. Left luggage open 0730-2030.

To **Santiago**, frequent, 11 hrs, US$20-55; to **Valparaíso** and **Viña del Mar**, Tas Choapa, US$25; to **Concepción**, 9 hrs, US$16-30; to **Temuco**, US$10; to **Panguipulli**, Buses Pirehueico, 4 a day; to **Pucón** and **Villarrica**, US$13; to **Valdivia**, frequent, 2 hrs, several companies, US$5; to **Frutillar**, US$3, **Llanquihue**, **Puerto Varas** and **Puerto Montt**, every 30 mins, US$4; to **Puerto Octay**, Vía Octay, every 30 mins, US$3; to **Lago Ranco** (town), 6 a day, Empresa Ruta 5, 2 hrs, US$4; to **Punta Arenas**, several each week, US$65; to **Anticura**, 2 or 3 buses daily, 3 hrs, US$8.

Some local services leave from the Mercado Municipal terminal, 1 block west of the main terminal. To **Entre Lagos**, frequent in summer, reduced service off season, **Expreso Lago Puyehue**, T064-234919, and **Buses Barria**, 45 mins, US$2; buses by both companies also continue to **Aguas Calientes**, off season according to demand, 2 hrs, US$4. To **Puyehue**, 4-5 daily, 1½ hrs, US$4. Also frequent buses to **Río Bueno** and daily services to **Maicolpué** and **Pucatrihue** on the coast.

Car

Car hire from **Salfa Sur**, Av Fuschlocher, T064-240124, www.salfasur.cl. Also at airport. Good value, recommended.

Car mechanics at **Automotriz Amthauer**, Amthauer 1250; **Automotriz Salfa Sur SA**, Fco Bilbao 857. **Automóvil Club de Chile**, Bulnes 463, T064-232269, information and car hire.

Train

The station is 3 blocks west of the Plaza de Armas at Variante Mackenna 555, T600-585 5000, www.efe.cl. All services are suspended at the time of writing.

North and west of Osorno *p373*

River launches run between **Trumao** on the Río Bueno, 22 km west of Osorno to **La Barra** on the coast, 0900 Wed and Sat only, 5 hrs, return 0900 Thu and Sun, US$12, no service in winter. For bus services from Osorno, see above.

Lago Puyehue and the Parque Nacional *p373, map p374*

Note that buses from Osorno (see above) to **Entre Lagos** and **Aguas Calientes** do not stop at the lakeside (unless you want to get off at **Hotel Termas de Puyehue** and clamber down). There is no public transport from Aguas Calientes to **Antillanca**; hitching is always difficult, but it is not a hard walk.

Border with Argentina *p375*

Several bus companies run daily services from Puerto Montt via Osorno to **Bariloche** along this route (see page 403). Although less scenic than the ferry journey across Lake Todos Los Santos and Laguna Verde this crossing is far cheaper, reliable and still a beautiful trip. Best views are from the right-hand side of the bus.

Lago Rupanco *p374, map p374*

Bus from Osorno to **Piedras Negras** from the main terminal, leaves 1230 Mon-Fri, 1630 on Sat, returns from Piedras Negras early morning.

❶ Directory

Osorno *p372, map p372*

Banks Several banks with ATMs around the plaza. Casas de cambio at **Cambio Tur**, MacKenna 1004; **Turismo Frontera**, Ramírez 949, local 11 (Galería Catedral); if stuck try Travels bar in bus terminal. **Internet** Several throughout the city centre. **Laundry** Prat 678, allow at least a day. **Post office** O'Higgins 645. **Telephone** Ramírez at central plaza, Juan MacKenna y Cochrane.

Lago Llanquihue

→ *Colour map 4, C2.*

The second largest lake in Chile and the third largest natural lake in South America, Lago Llanquihue is one of the highlights of the Lake District. Three snow-capped volcanoes can be seen across the vast expanse of water: the perfect cone of Osorno (2680 m), the shattered cone of Calbuco (2015 m), and the spike of Puntiagudo (2480 m), as well as, when the air is clear, the distant Tronador (3460 m). On a cloudless night with a full moon, the snows reflect eerily in the lake and the peace and stillness are hard to match. ▶▶ *For listings, see pages 384-390.*

Ins and outs

Getting there Access from the south is from nearby Puerto Montt, while there are direct transport links with Santiago along the Pan-American Highway. The northern tip of the lake is also easily reached from Osorno.

Getting around The largest towns, Puerto Varas, Llanquihue and Frutillar are all on the western shore, linked by the Pan-American Highway. Although there are roads around the rest of the lake, the eastern shore is difficult to visit without transport, and beyond Las Cascadas, the road is narrow with lots of blind corners, necessitating speeds of 20-30 kph at best in places (see below). Beware of lorries that ply the route servicing the salmon farms. There no public transport between Las Cascadas and Ensenada and hitching is very difficult.

Lago Llanquihue

German colonization in the Lake District

The most important area of German agricultural colonization in Chile was around Lago Llanquihue. The Chilean government declared the area as destined for colonisation in 1845, and to encourage settlement, gave each adult male 75 cuadras of land, an extra 12 cuadras for each son, a milking cow, 500 planks of timber, nails, a yoke of oxen, a year's free medical assistance and Chilean citizenship on request.

The first groups of German colonists arrived in the area in 1852: one group settled around Maitén and Puerto Octay, another helped found Puerto Montt. The lives of these early settlers were hard and the risks great, yet within 10 years the settlers had cleared much of the forest round the lake and soon they were setting up small industries. In 1880, when the offer to colonists ended, unsettled land was auctioned in lots of 400-800 ha. By then the lake was ringed by a belt of smallholdings and farms. The legacy of this settlement can be seen in the German-looking farmhouses around Puerto Octay and in many of the older buildings in Frutillar and Puerto Varas.

Valdivia was another centre for German colonization. A small number of German and Swiss colonists settled in the city, exerting a strong influence on the architecture agricultural methods, education, social life and customs of the area. They established most of the industries that made Valdivia an important manufacturing centre until the 1950s. According to an 1884 survey of Valdivia, all breweries, leatherworks, brickworks, mills, bakeries, and machine shops belonged to families with German surnames.

Little of the architectural heritage of this period survived the 1960 earthquake, but the city's German heritage can still be seen in some of its best cafés and restaurants and in the names of its streets.

Tourist information There is no general information centre for the lake, but each town has its own municipal tourist office.

Puerto Octay ●●●● ▶ pp384-390.

Puerto Octay is a peaceful and picturesque small town at the north tip of the lake 56 km southeast of Osorno, set amid rolling hills, hedgerows and German-style farmhouses with views over Volcán Osorno. Founded by German settlers in 1852, the town enjoyed a boom period in the late 19th century when it was the northern port for steamships on the lake: a few buildings survive from that period, notably the church and the enormous German-style former convent. Since the arrival of railways and the building of roads, the town has declined. Much less busy than Frutillar or Puerto Varas, Puerto Octay offers an escape for those seeking peace and quiet. Rowing boats and pedalos can be hired for trips on the lake.

Museo el Colono ① *Independencia 591, www.museopuertooctay.cl, Dec-Feb only Tue-Sun 1000-1300, 1500-1900* , has displays on German colonization. Another part of the museum, housing agricultural implements and machinery for making *chicha*, is just outside town on the road towards **Centinela**. This peninsula, about 3 km south (taxi US$2 one way) along an unpaved road, has accommodation, camping, a launch dock, bathing beaches and watersports. It is a very popular spot in good weather, especially for picnics, with fine views of the Osorno, Calbuco and Puntiagudo volcanoes.

Puerto Octay to Volcán Osorno

The eastern lakeside, with Volcán Osorno on your left is very beautiful. From Puerto Octay two roads run towards Ensenada, one *ripio* along the shore, and one paved. (They join up after 20 km.) At Km 10 along the lakeside route is **Playa Maitén**, a lovely beach, often deserted, with a marvellous view of Volcán Osorno. Continue for another 24 km past **Puerto Fonck**, which has fine 19th-century German-style mansions, and you'll reach **Las Cascadas**, surrounded by picturesque agricultural land, old houses and German cemeteries. To reach the waterfalls that give the village its name turn east at the school along a *ripio* road to a car park, continue along a footpath over two or three log bridges over a stream before arriving at an impressive jungle-like 40-m-high natural cauldron, with the falls in the middle. The round trip takes about 1½ hours.

Volcán Osorno

The most lasting image of Lago Llanquihue is the near-perfect cone of Volcán Osorno, situated north of Ensenada on the eastern edge of the lake. Although the peak is on the edge of the Parque Nacional Pérez Rosales (see page 391), it is climbed from the western side, which lies outside the park. Access is via two roads that branch off the Ensenada–Puerto Octay road along the eastern edge of Lago Llanquihue. The northern one is at Puerto Klocker, 20 km southeast of Puerto Octay and only suitable for 4WDs, while the main entrance is 2 km north of Ensenada along a good paved road.

Guided ascents of the volcano (organized by agencies in Puerto Varas) set out from the *refugio* at **La Burbuja** where there is a small ski centre in winter and pleasant short walks in summer to a couple of craters and with great views of the lake and across to Puerto Montt. From here it is six hours to the summit. The volcano can also be climbed from the north (La Picada); this route is easier and may be attempted without a guide, although only experienced climbers should attempt to climb right to the top as ice climbing equipment is essential, and there are many craters hidden below thin crusts of ice.

Ensenada

Despite its lack of a recognizable centre, Ensenada is beautifully situated at the southeast corner of Lago Llanquihue, almost beneath the snows of Volcán Osorno. A good half-day trip from Ensenada itself is to **Laguna Verde**, about 30 minutes from **Hotel Ensenada**, along a beautiful circular trail behind the lake (take first fork to the right behind the information board), and then down the road to a secluded campsite at Puerto Oscuro on Lago Llanquihue.

Frutillar

Lying about half-way along the western side of the lake, Frutillar is in fact two towns: **Frutillar Alto**, just off the main highway, and **Frutillar Bajo**, beautifully situated on the lakeside, 4 km away. The latter is possibly the most attractive and expensive town on the lake, with superb views from the *costanera* over the water with volcanoes Osorno and Tronador in the background. The town's atmosphere is very German and somewhat snobbish, but the **tourist office**① *on the lakeside, T065-420198, summer only*, is helpful. In the square opposite is an open-air chess board and the **Club Alemán** restaurant. After eight years of construction work, the new concert hall on the lakeside is now complete. It plays host to the town's prestigious music festival in late January.

Away from the waterfront, the appealing **Museo Colonial Alemán** ① *Vicente Pérez Rosales s/n, T065-421142, museofrutillar@uach.cl, summer 1000-1930 daily, winter 1000-1730 daily, US$3.50*, is set in spacious gardens, with a watermill, replicas of two German colonial houses with furnishings and utensils of the period, and a blacksmith's shop selling personally engraved horseshoes for US$9. It also has a *campanario*, a circular barn with agricultural machinery and carriages inside, as well as a handicraft shop. At the northern end of the town is the **Reserva Forestal Edmundo Winckler**, run by the Universidad de Chile and extending over 33 ha, with a guided trail through native woods. Named after one of the early German settlers, it includes a very good collection of native flora as well as plants introduced from Europe.

Llanquihue

Twenty kilometres south of Frutillar, Llanquihue lies at the source of the Río Maullín, which drains the lake. The site of a large dairy processing factory, this is the least touristy town on the lake, and makes a cheaper alternative to Puerto Varas and Frutillar. It has uncrowded beaches. Just north of town is the Colonos brewery, which has a restaurant and can be visited.

Puerto Varas and around
⬤🅿🅷🔺🅾🅾🅾 ‣‣ *pp384-390.*

Situated on the southwestern corner of the lake, Puerto Varas, with a population of 25,000, is the commercial and tourist centre of Lago Llanquihue. It also serves as a residential centre for Puerto Montt, 20 km to the south. The self-styled "city of the roses" was recently voted the best place to live in Chile. In the 19th century, Puerto Chico (on the eastern outskirts) was the southern port for shipping on the lake. With the arrival of the railway the settlement moved to its current location

Frutillar Bajo

To Reserva Forestal Edmundo Winckler
To ⑤⑧⑪, Playa Maqui & Puerto Octay (Ripio)

Caupolicán ①

To Frutillar Alto & Pan-American Highway

S Junginger

18 de Septiembre

Av Philippi

Carlos Richter

🏛 Museo Colonial Alemán
Prat

⑬

⑫
Balmaceda

Av Alemania

Lago Llanquihue

⑨

San Martín ①
Municipalidad ⬛ ③
Pier

O'Higgins

⑥
J Montt

Las Piedras

③
A Varas

①②
Concert Hall
Pérez Rosales

M Rodríguez

P Aguirre ②
⑦

21 de Mayo

Lautaro

N
200 metres
200 yards
To Llanquihue

Sleeping 😴
Apart Hotel Frutillar **2**
Ayacara **7**
Bayernhaus **9**
Casona del 32 **1**
Hospedaje Angélica **12**
Hospedaje Tía Clarita **4**
Hospedaje Vivaldi **6**
Hostal Cinco Robles **5**
Hostería El Arroyo **3**
Lagune Club **8**
Residenz am See **13**
Salzburg **11**

Eating 🍴
Andes **1**
Casino de Bomberos **2**
Club Alemán **3**

and is now a resort, popular with Chilean as well as foreign tourists; in February especially, the town clogs up with oversized jeeps from Santiago. Despite the numbers of visitors, though, it has a friendly, compact feel, and is one of the best bases for exploring the southern Lake District, near centres for trekking, rafting, canyoning and fly-fishing.

Ins and outs

Getting there Puerto Varas is served by many buses from Puerto Montt; there are also connections north to Osorno, Valdivia, Temuco and all the way to Santiago. A taxi from Puerto Montt airport costs US$28. Minibuses from the airport charge US$10 per person but will often stop in Puerto Montt first. The bus terminal is on the southwestern outskirts. Only local minibus services enter the town centre.

Tourist information The tourist office is in the **Municipalidad** ① *San Fransisco 413, T065-321330, securismo.puertovaras@munitel.cl.* Not very helpful. Information is

Puerto Varas

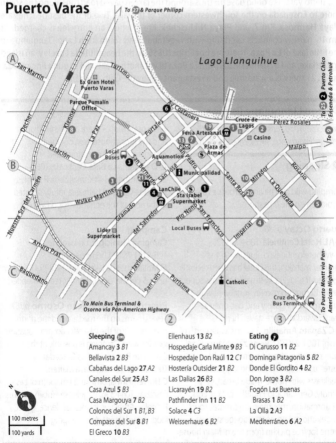

Sleeping		Ellenhaus **13** *B2*	Eating
Amancay **3** *B1*		Hospedaje Carla Minte **9** *B3*	Di Carusso **11** *B2*
Bellavista **2** *B3*		Hospedaje Don Raúl **12** *C1*	Dominga Patagonia **5** *B2*
Cabañas del Lago **27** *A2*		Hostería Outsider **21** *B2*	Donde El Gordito **4** *B2*
Canales del Sur **25** *A3*		Las Dalias **26** *B3*	Don Jorge **3** *B2*
Casa Azul **5** *B3*		Licarayén **19** *B2*	Fogón Las Buenas
Casa Margouya **7** *B2*		Pathfinder Inn **11** *B2*	Brasas **1** *B2*
Colonos del Sur **1** *B1, B3*		Solace **4** *C3*	La Olla **2** *A3*
Compass del Sur **8** *B1*		Weisserhaus **6** *B2*	Mediterráneo **6** *A2*
El Greco **10** *B3*			

100 metres
100 yards

available on the **Parque Pumalín** ① *Klenner 299, T065-250079, www.pumalinpark.org*, see page 436.

Sights

Puerto Varas is small and easily navigable on foot. **Parque Philippi**, on top of a hill, is a pleasant place to visit, although the views are a bit restricted by trees and the metal cross at the top is unattractive. Also in the park is an electric clock that chimes the quarter-hours during daylight hours. To reach the summit walk up to **Hotel Cabañas del Lago** on Klenner, cross the railway and the gate is on the right. The centre lies at the foot of the hill, but the town stretches east along the lake to **Puerto Chico**, where there are hotels and restaurants. The imposing **Catholic church** was built by German Jesuits in 1918 in baroque style as a copy of the church in the Black Forest. North and east of the former **Gran Hotel Puerto Varas** (1934) are a number of German-style mansions.

Puerto Varas is a good base for trips around the lake. A paved road runs along the south shore to Ensenada on the southwestern corner of the lake. Two of the best beaches are **Playa Hermosa**, Km 7, and **Playa Niklitschek**, Km 8, where an entry fee is charged. At Km 16, narrow channels overhung with vegetation lead south from Lago Llanquihue to the little lake of **La Poza**. There are boat trips (US$5) to the beautiful **Isla Loreley**, an island on the lake, and a channel leads from La Poza to yet another lake, the **Laguna Encantada**. At Km 21 there is a watermill and a restaurant run by the **Club Alemán**.

⊚ Lago Llanquihue listings

For Sleeping and Eating price codes and other relevant information, see Essentials pages 35–42.

⊜ Sleeping

Camping wild and having barbecues are forbidden on the lake shore.

Puerto Octay *p380*
L-AL Hotel Centinela, T064-391326, www.hotelcentinela.cl. Built in 1914 as a summer mansion, this hotel has been recently restored. It is idyllically situated and has superb views, 12 rooms, *cabañas*, restaurant with grand minstrels' gallery and bar, open all year. Edward VIII once stayed here.
B-C Zapato Amarillo, 35 mins' walk north of town, T064-210787, www.zapatoamarillo.cl. **F** per person in shared rooms. Excellent hostel, use of spotless kitchen, great breakfasts with home-made bread, very friendly, German and English spoken. Lots of information, mountain-bike rental, tours, canoes and sailing boat, luggage storage, phone for free pickup from town. Main house

has a grass roof or there are mini *cabañas* and the roundhouse next door with restaurant. Highly recommended.
C-D Hostería La Baja, Centinela, T064-391269, irisbravo1@hotmail.com. **F** singles, with breakfast and bath. Beautifully situated at the neck of the peninsula. Good value.

Camping
Camping Municipal, on lakeside, T09-9171 7819. US$18 per site.
El Molino, beside lake, T064-391375. US$20 for up to 5 people, clean, friendly, recommended.

Puerto Octay to Volcán Osorno *p381*
Several farms on the road around the north and east side of the lake offer accommodation; look for signs. Camping is possible at the **Centro de Recreación Las Cascadas**, T064-235377, and at **Playa Maitén**.
C Hostería Irma, on lake, 2 km south of Las Cascadas, T064-396227, julietatrivino@yahoo.es. **F** singles. Attractive former residence, good food, very pleasant. Also camping.

Volcán Osorno p381

There are 2 *refugios* (**E**), both of them south of
the summit and reached from the southern
access road: **La Burbuja**, the former ski-club
centre, 14 km north of Ensenada at 1250 m)
and **Refugio Teski Ski Club**, www.teskiclub.cl,
just below the snowline. Price per person,
meals served. **Refugio La Picada**, marked
on the northern slopes on many trekking
maps, burned down several years ago.

Ensenada p381

LL Yan Kee Way Lodge, T065-212030,
www.southernchilexp.com. Understated
resort specializing in fly-fishing expeditions.
Excellent restaurant.

L-AL Ensenada, Casilla 659, Puerto Montt,
T065-212028, www.hotelensenada.cl. Closed
in winter. With bath, old-world style, lots of
antiques, good food, good view of lake and
Volcán Osorno, runs tours, hires mountain
bikes (guests only). Also much cheaper *hostal*
in the grounds with cooking facilities.

AL-B Cabañas Brisas del Lago, Km 42,
T065-212012, www.brisasdellago.cl.
On the beach, rooms and cabins sleeping
2-6, good restaurant nearby. Recommended.

B Hospedaje Ensenada, Km 43, T065-
212050, www.hospedajensenada.blog
spot.com. **D** singles. Most rooms with bath.
Very clean, excellent breakfast.

B-C Casa Ko, Km 37, 3 km north of the
main road.T09-77036477, www.casako.com.
Best of the hostels around Ensenada. Good
meals served. Good-value camping, lots of
info, English and French spoken. Call for
pickup from main road.

Camping

Montaña, centre of town. Price per site,
good beach space.

Playa Larga, 1 km east of Hotel Ensenada,
US$15 per site.

Puerto Oscuro, 2 km north of Ensenada,
US$12 per site.

Trauco, 4 km west of Ensenada, T065-
212033. Large site with shops, fully
equipped, US$5-10 per person.

Frutillar p381, map p382

During the annual music festival
accommodation should be booked well in
advance; alternatively stay in Frutillar Alto or
Puerto Varas. In most cases on Av Philippi you
are paying a premium for the view. If you are
staying here, try and ensure your room has
one. There are several cheap options along
Carlos Richter (main street) in Frutillar
Alto and at the school in Frutillar Alto in
Jan-Feb (sleeping bag required).

AL Casona del 32, Caupolicán 28,
Frutillar Bajo, T065-421369. With breakfast,
comfortable old house, central heating,
English and German spoken. Groups only
off season. Recommended.

AL Salzburg, on the road to Playa Maqui,
1 km north of Frutillar Bajo, T065-421589,
www.salzburg.cl. Excellent restaurant (open
to public), plus sauna, swimming pool,
mountain bikes, tours and fishing.

AL-A Ayacara, Philippi y Pedro Aguirre
Cerda, T065-421550, www.hotelayacara.cl.
Typical German-style wooden construction
on the lakefront. 8 airy rooms, 6 with views.
A good choice.

AL-A Bayernhaus, Philippi, Frutillar Bajo.
Old house with period furniture. Only 2 of
8 rooms have views. One has a balcony and
this is by far the best option.

AL-A Hostal Cinco Robles, 1 km north of
Frutillar Bajo, T065-421351, www.cinco-robles.
com. Small hotel in pleasant large grounds
with views and access to a private beach.
Rooms with wooden interiors. With
breakfast, restaurant, parking, Wi-Fi.

A Residenz am See, Philippi 539,
Frutillar Bajo, T065-421539, hotelamsee.cl.
Good breakfast and views. Café downstairs
serving German specialities.

A-B Lagune Club, 3 km north of Frutillar
Bajo, T065-330033, www.interpatagonia.com/
laguneclub. In an old country house in 16 ha
of land by the lake (private beach), fishing trips,
free pickup from terminal. Disabled-visitor
friendly. Also *cabañas*. Good value in dollars.

B Apart Hotel Frutillar, Philippi 1175,
Frutillar Bajo, T065-421388, www.aparthotel

frutillar.cl. Also cabins, good breakfasts, meals available.

B Hospedaje Vivaldi, Philippi 851, Frutillar Bajo, T065-421382. **D** singles. Quiet, comfortable, excellent breakfast and lodging, also family accommodation. Recommended.

B Hostería El Arroyo, Philippi 989, Frutillar Bajo, T065-421560, alarroyo@surnet.cl. With breakfast. Recommended.

C Hospedaje Angélica, Pérez Rosales 590, Frutillar Bajo. *Cabañas* and excellent breakfast.

C Hospedaje Tía Clarita, Pérez Rosales 648, Frutillar Bajo, T065-421806, hospedaje tiaclarit@hotmail.com. **E** singles, kitchen facilities, very friendly, good value.

C-D Hospedaje Juana Paredes, Aníbal Pinto y Winkler, Frutillar Alto, T065-421407. **F** singles. Recommended. Also *cabañas* for up to 5 and parking.

Camping

Los Ciruelillos, 2 km south of Frutillar Bajo, T065-339123. Most services.

Playa Maqui, 7 km north of Frutillar, T065-339139. Fancy, expensive site.

Llanquihue *p382*
Camping

Baumbach, 1 km north of Llanquihue, T065-242643. On lakeside, meals available.

El Totoral, 8 km north of Llanquihue, T065-339123. Campsite and *cabañas*.

Playa Werner, 2 km north Llanquihue, T065-242114. On lakeside.

Puerto Varas *p382, map p383*

There are many hotels along the lake front, but in high season they tend to be tourist traps.

L Bellavista, Pérez Rosales 060, T065-232011, www.hotelbellavista.cl. 4-star, with good views over the lake, reasonably spacious rooms with king size beds, restaurant and bar, sauna, parking. Unfortunately the rooms with a view also face the main street, which can be noisy.

L Cabañas del Lago, Klenner 195, T065-232291, www.cabanasdellago.cl. 4-star hotel on Philippi hill overlooking lake, superb

views. Heating, sauna, swimming pool, games room, bar and restaurant. Often full with package groups.

L Colonos del Sur, Del Salvador 24, T065-235555, www.colonosdelsur.cl. Refurbished good-quality 4-star on the lakeside. Owns another hotel at Estación 505, overlooking the town, which has seen better days.

L-AL Licarayén, San José 114, T065-232305, www.hotelicarayen.cl. Most rooms good sized. Superior rooms have lake view. cosy, comfortable, clean, gym and sauna.

L-AL Solace, Imperial 0211, T065-364100, www.solacehotel.cl. One of several new upmarket hotels in town, this is probably the best. Spacious rooms, clean, attentive staff. Recommended.

AL-A El Greco, Mirador 134, T065-233880, www.hotelelgreco.cl. Recently refurbished German-style mansion with wooden interior and full of artworks. Simple rooms with bath and cable TV. A good choice.

A Weisserhaus, San Pedro 252, T065-346479, www.weisserhaus.cl. Cosy family-run 10-room hotel right in the town centre. Heated rooms, good breakfast, Wi-Fi. A good choice.

A-B Hostería Outsider, San Bernardo 318, T065-232910, www.turout.com. With bath, breakfast with real coffee, meals, friendly, comfortable. German and English spoken, book in advance.

B Amancay, Walker Martínez 564, T065-232201, cabamancay@chile.com. With bath and breakfast. Friendly, German spoken, also *cabañas*, sleep 4. Recommended.

B Canales del Sur, Pérez Rosales 1631A, 1km east of town, T065-717618, www.canalesdelsur.cl. Pleasantly set on the lakeside. Very friendly and helpful family-run guesthouse, tours arranged. Good breakfast, garden, laundry, internet and car hire service. Recommended.

B-C Casa Azul, Manzanal 66 y Rosario, T065-232904, www.casaazul.net. **E** per person in shared rooms. Some rooms with bath. German/Chilean owners, good buffet breakfast with home-made muesli (US$5 extra), large kitchen, good beds with duvets, central heating, internet, book exchange, comfortable common area, English and German spoken, tours organized. Highly recommended, although some reports that service can be terse.

B-C Compass del Sur, Klenner 467, T065-232044, www.compassdelsur.cl. **E** per person in shared rooms. Chilean/Swedish-run, kitchen facilities, internet, cable TV in comfortable lounge, breakfast with muesli and real coffee, friendly, helpful, lots of information, tours, German, English, Swedish spoken, highly recommended. Also camping and car hire.

C Casa Margouya, Santa Rosa 318, T065-237640, www.margouya.com. **E** per person in shared rooms. Bright and colourful fun hostel in the town centre with breakfast and kitchen facilities. Friendly, lots of info, though slightly cramped. French-run, English spoken. Spanish classes offered.

C Ellenhaus, Walker Martínez 239, T065-233577, www.ellenhaus.cl. Some rooms with bath. **F** per person in dorms. Kitchen and laundry facilities, luggage stored, lounge, tours offered. German and English spoken.

C Hospedaje Carla Minte, Maipo 1010, T065-232880, www.interpatagonia.com/carlaminte. **E** singles. Rooms with bath and breakfast in a family home. Cable TV, Wi-Fi, very comfortable.

C Las Dalias, Santa Rosa 707, T065-233277, las_dalias@hotmail.com. **E** singles. Some rooms with bath. In a family home, peaceful, clean, good breakfast with real coffee, parking, German spoken.

C Pathfinder Inn, Walker Martínez 561, T065-312515, www.pathfinderinn.com. **E** per person in dorms. New small HI-affiliated hostel, with bunkbeds only. Good location, internet.

D Hospedaje Don Raúl, Salvador 928, T065-310897, hospedajedonraul@hotmail.com. **E-F** singles. Laundry and cooking facilities, very friendly, garden with hammock, clean. Recommended. Camping by main road.

Camping
Los Troncos, 10 km east of Puerto Varas, T09-920 6869. US$15 per site, no beach access.
Playa Hermosa, 7 km east of Puerto Varas. Fancy ground, US$22 per site, bargain off season, take own supplies. Recommended.
Playa Niklitschek, 8 km east of Puerto Varas, T065-338352. Full facilities.
Casa Tronador, Tronador y Manzanal, T09-9078 9631. Expensive but central.

Eating

Puerto Octay *p380*
♦♦ **El Rancho del Espanta-Pajaros**, 6 km south on the road to Frutillar, T065-330049. In a converted barn with wonderful views over the lake, serves all kind of spit-roasted meat. All you can eat, with salad bar and drinks included, for US$14. Also arranges horse-riding trips. Recommended.
♦♦ **Fogón de Anita**, 1 km out of town, T064-391455. Mid-priced grill. Also German cakes and pastries.
♦ **Restaurante Baviera**, Germán Wulf 582. Cheap and good. Salmon and *cazuelas*.

Ensenada *p381*
♦♦♦ **Latitude 42**, Yan Kee Way resort, T065-212030. Expensive, excellent and varied cuisine, very good-quality wine list. Views over the lake.
♦ **Canta Rana**. Recommended for bread and *küchen*.
♦ **Donde Juanito**, west of Ensenada. Excellent-value cheap set lunch.

Frutillar *p381, map p382*
♦♦ **Andes**, Philippi 1057, Frutillar Bajo. Good set menus and à la carte.
♦♦ **Club Alemán**, Av Philippi 747. Good but not cheap, and hostile to backpackers.
♦ **Casino de Bomberos**, Philippi 1060, Frutillar Bajo. Open all year. Upstairs bar/restaurant, memorable painting caricaturing firemen in action. Great value but service can be poor.

Cafés

There are several German-style cafés on C Philippi, including **Salón de Te Frutillar**, at No 775 and **Guten Apetit**, at No 1285.

Puerto Varas *p382, map p383*
The expensive motel restaurants at the end of the *costanera* aren't worth visiting, although the service is friendly.

¶¶-¶¶ Mediterráneo, Santa Rosa 068, T065-237268. On the lakefront, varied and interesting menu with a Mediterranean influence, often full. Quality has not kept up with price increases.

¶¶ Di Carusso, San Bernardo 318, T065-233478. Italian trattoria. Good fresh pasta dishes on Fri. Recommended.

¶¶ Dominga Patagonia, Walker Martínez 551, T065-238981. Interesting fusion cuisine with Peruvian elements. Tapas and also main dishes. Cosy atmosphere, generous *pisco sours*. Reasonably priced. Recommended.

¶¶ Fogón Las Buenas Brasas, San Pedro 543, T065-214553. Popular Argentinian-style *parrillada*. Decent when uncrowded but service a bit of a disaster when full.

¶¶ La Olla, Pérez Rosales 1071, T065-233540. 1 km east of centre along the lakefront. Seafood and traditional Chilean cuisine. Recommended.

¶¶-¶ Donde El Gordito, downstairs in market. Large portions, good range of meat dishes, no set menu.

¶ Don Jorge, San Bernardo 240. Sandwiches and good-value lunches.

Cafés

Café Danés, Del Salvador 441. Good coffee and cakes.
El Molino, on road to Ensenada, 22 km east. Café next to an old water mill.
Punto Café, Del Salvador 348. Café with internet and art gallery.

🍸 Bars and clubs

Puerto Varas *p382, map p383*
Barómetro, Walker Martínez 500 block. Probably the most popular bar in the centre.
Pim's, San Francisco near C Imperial. Spacious US-style pub with food.

🎉 Festivals and events

Frutillar *p381, map p382*
Jan/early Feb A highly regarded classical music festival is held in the town; tickets must be booked well in advance from the Municipalidad, T065-421290.

Llanquihue *p382*
End Jan A German-style beer festival with oom-pah music is held here.

🛍 Shopping

Ensenada *p381*
There are several shop selling basic supplies. Most places are closed off season, other than a few pricey shops, so take your own provisions.

Frutillar *p381, map p382*
Services and shops are generally much better in Frutillar Alto, although in Frutillar Bajo, seek out **Der Volkladen**, O'Higgins y Philippi, for natural products, including chocolates, cakes and cosmetics.

Puerto Varas *p382, map p383*
Líder, Gramado 565. Supermarket with a good selection, reasonably priced.
Mamusia, San José 316. Chocolates.
Santa Isabel, Salvador 451. Supermarket.

▲▲ Activities and tours

Most tours operate in season only (Sep-May).

Volcán Osorno p381
Weather permitting, agencies in Puerto
Varas organize climbing expeditions with
a local guide, transport from Puerto Montt
or Puerto Varas, food and equipment, US$200
per person, payment in advance (minimum
group 2, maximum 6 with 3 guides). Weather
conditions are checked the day before. A full
refund is given if the trip is cancelled, and
a 50% refund is available if the trip is
abandoned due to weather before the real
climbing begins. Those climbing from La
Burbuja must register with **CONAF** at La
Burbuja, and show they have suitable
equipment. Those climbing from the north
(La Picada) are not subject to any checks.

Also based at La Burbuja is a small skiing
centre, with 11 pistes and 5 ski lifts, usually
open Jun-Sep. Ski ticket US$30, equipment
rental US$30, ski school. See www.volcan
osorno.com for conditions.

Ensenada p381
Southern Chile Expeditions, T065-213030,
www.southernchilexp.com. Expensive
fly-fishing tours.

Frutillar p381, map p382
Viajes Frutillar, Richter y Alissandre,
Frutillar Alto. Travel and tour agent.

Puerto Varas p382, map p383
Fishing
The area around Puerto Varas is popular
for fishing. A licence (obligatory) is obtainable
from the Municipalidad. Fishing expeditions
are organized by many operators (see below).
The Río Pescado (25 km east of Puerto
Varas) is a good easy alternative for those
who do not want to hire a guide.

Horse riding
Campo Aventura, San Bernardo 318,
T065-232910, www.campo-aventura.com.

English and German spoken, offers 1-, 3-
and 10-day trips on horseback (see Cochamó,
page 394).
Quinta del Lago, Km 25, T065-330193,
www.quinta del Lago. Generally
recommended day rides. Good views.

Scuba-diving
Diving Sur, Blanco Encalada 1160, Puerto
Chico, T065-284399, www.divingsur.cl.
Guided diving trips including night diving
in Lago Llanquihue.

Tour operators
Al Sur, Aconcagua y Imperial, T065-232300,
www.alsurexpeditions.com. Rafting on Rió
Petrohue. Official tour operator to the
Parque Pumalín. Sells trekking maps.
Aqua Motion, San Fransisco 328,
T065-232747, www.aquamotion.cl.
Rafting, trekking, mountain biking,
fishing, birdwatching.
Cruce de Lagos, Del Salvador 72,
T065-232811, www.crucedelagos.com.
Operates 'lakes' trip to Bariloche, Argentina
via Lago Todos los Santos, Peulla, Cerro
Tronador, plus other excursions.
Kokayak, Km 40T09-93105272,
www.kokayak.com, French/Chilean-run,
offers bike hire, whitewater rafting and
sea kayaking. Good 1-day trips
Yak Expediciones, T065-234409, www.seakay
akpatagonia.com. Repeatedly recommended
for multi-day sea-kayak trips around the
Seno de Reloncaví and the Gulf of Ancud.

⊝ Transport

Puerto Octay p380
Buses to **Osorno**, every 30 mins, US$3; to
Las Cascadas Mon-Fri 1730, return next
day 0700. **Thaebus** runs 5 daily services to
Frutillar, 1 hr, US$1.50, **Puerto Varas**, 2 hrs,
and **Puerto Montt**, 2¼ hrs, US$3.

Ensenada *p381*
Frequent minibuses run from **Puerto Varas** in summer. Buses from Puerto Montt via Puerto Varas to **Cochamó** also stop here. Hitching from Puerto Varas is difficult.

Frutillar *p381, map p382*
Bus *Colectivos* run between the 2 towns, 5 mins, US$0.60. Most buses to other destinations leave from Alessandri y Richter in Frutillar Alto. **Thaebus** and others have frequent services to **Puerto Varas**, US$1.50, and **Puerto Montt**, US$1.80. To **Osorno**, Turismosur, 1¼ hrs, US$3; to **Puerto Octay**, Thaebus, 5 a day.

Car Mechanic, **Toirkens**, Los Carrera 1260, is recommended if expensive.

Train Train station at Alessandri s/n, although services to Temuco and Puerto Montt are currently suspended.

Puerto Varas *p382, map p383*
Airline office Sky Airline, San Bernardo 430, www.skyairline.cl.

Bicycle Bike hire is available from many tour operators, see above, for around US$18 per day; check equipment carefully.

Bus Minibuses to **Ensenada** and **Petrohué** leave from San Bernardo y Martínez; regional buses stop on San Fransisco 500 block; long-distance buses leave from the new terminal on the northern edge of town.

To **Santiago**, TurBus, Pullman, Cruz del Sur and several others, US$30-75. Thaebus, Full Express and others have services to **Puerto Montt**, every 15 mins, 30 mins, US$1.20; same companies, same frequency to **Frutillar**, 30 mins, US$1.50, and **Osorno**, 1 hr, US$4. Same companies hourly to **Petrohue**, US$3. To **Valdivia**, 3 hrs, US$7; to **Temuco**, US$10; to **Cochamó** via Ensenada,

5 a day, US$5. Services from Puerto Montt to **Bariloche** (Argentina) also stop here. For the **Andina del Sud** lakes route via Lago Todos los Santos, see page 396.

Car Car-hire companies include **Adriazola Expediciones**, Santa Rosa 340, T065-233477, www.adriazolaflyfishing.com; **Hunter**, San José 130, T065-237950; **Turismo Nieve**, Gramado 560, T065-346115. A recommended car mechanic is **Raúl Gómez**, Prat 100 block.

Train Train station at Klenner 350. Services to Temuco and Puerto Montt are currently suspended.

❶ Directory

Frutillar *p381, map p382*
Banks Banco Santander, Philippi, at the lakeside, with Redbanc ATM taking Visa and other cards. **Post office** San Martín y Pérez Rosales, Mon-Fri 0930-1230, 1430-1800, Sat 0900-1230. **Telephone** Call centre at Philippi 883.

Puerto Varas *p382, map p383*
Banks Several banks with ATMs in the town centre. *Casas de cambio* include Exchange Ltda, Del Salvador 257, local 11, Travel Sur, San José 261, local 4, Turismo Los Lagos, Del Salvador 257 (Galería Real, local 11), open daily 0830-1330, 1500-2100, Sun 0930-1330, accepts TCs, good rates. **Internet** Several in the centre, although if you want coffee while you browse try Punt Café, Del Salvador 348. **Laundry** Gramado 1090; Lavandería Delfín, Martínez 323, expensive. **Medical services** Clínica Alemana, Otto Bader 810, T065-232336, emergencies T065-232274, usually has English-speaking doctors. **Post office** San José y San Pedro; Del Salvador y Santa Rosa. **Telephone** Several call centres around town.

Parque Nacional Vicente Pérez Rosales

→ Colour map 4, C2/3.

Established in 1926, this is the oldest national park in Chile, stretching east from Lago Llanquihue to the Argentine border. The park is covered in woodland and contains a large lake, Lago Todos los Santos, plus three major volcanic peaks: Osorno, Puntiagudo and Tronador. Several other peaks are visible, notably Casablanca to the north and Calbuco to the south. Near the lake are the Saltos de Petrohué, impressive waterfalls on the Río Petrohué. A memorable journey by road and water takes you through the park from Puerto Montt to Bariloche in Argentina. South of the park is the beautiful Seno de Reloncaví.
⤷ *For listings, see pages 394-396.*

Ins and outs

Getting there In season, take one of the hourly minibuses from Puerto Montt and Puerto Varas via Ensenada to Petrohué. They generally allow you to break your journey at the waterfalls at no extra cost. It is impossible to reach the national park by public transport

Parque Nacional Pérez Rosales & the lakes route to Argentina

out of season: there are buses only as far as Ensenada, little traffic for hitching and none of the ferries takes vehicles. Entrance to the park is free.

Getting around A combination of walking and hitching rides in locals' boats is the best way to explore the park. In wet weather many treks in the park are impossible and the road to Puerto Montt can be blocked.

Tourist information CONAF has an office in Petrohué with a visitor centre, small museum and model of the park. There is also a *guardaparque* office in Puella. No maps of treks are available in the park; buy them from a tour operator in Puerto Varas (see page 389).

Lago Todos los Santos 🌐🕐🌐 ➤ *pp394-396.*

The most beautiful of all the lakes in southern Chile, Lago Todos los Santos is a long, irregularly shaped sheet of emerald-green water, surrounded by a deeply wooded shoreline and punctuated by several small islands that rise from its surface. Beyond the hilly shores to the east are several graceful snow-capped mountains, with the mighty Tronador in the distance. To the north is the sharp point of **Cerro Puntiagudo**, and at the northeastern end **Cerro Techado** rises cliff-like out of the water. The lake is fed by several rivers, including the Río Peulla to the east, the ríos Techado and Negro to the north, and the Río Blanco to the south. At its western end the lake is drained by the Río Petrohue. The lake is warm and sheltered from the winds, and is a popular location for watersports, swimming and for trout and salmon fishing. There are no roads round the lake. The only scheduled vessel on the lake is the **Cruce de Lagos** service between Petrohue and Peulla, with connections to Bariloche (Argentina, see opposite), but private launches can be hired from locals for trips.

Petrohué and around

At the western end of the lake, 16 km northwest of Ensenada, Petrohué is a good base for walking tours with several trails around the foot of Volcán Osorno, or to the miradors that look over it, such as Cerro Picada. Near the Ensenada–Petrohué road, 6 km west of Petrohué, is the impressive **Salto de Petrohué** ① *US$2*, which was formed by a relatively recent lava flow of hard volcanic rock. Near the falls are a snack bar and two short trails, the **Sendero de los Enamorados** and the **Sendero Carileufú**. In Petrohué, boats can be hired (US$100) to visit the **Termas de Callao** – actually two large Alerce tubs in a cabin – north of the lake. The boat will drop you at the uninhabited El Rincón (arrange for it to wait or collect you later), from where it's a 3½-hour walk to the baths through forest beside the Río Sin Nombre. The path twice crosses the river by rickety hanging bridges. Just before the baths is a house, doubling as a comfortable *refugio*, where you collect the keys and pay. From the termas there is a two-day trail northwards to Lago Rupanco.

Peulla and around

Peulla, at the eastern end of the lake, is a good starting point for hikes in the mountains. The **Cascadas Los Novios**, signposted above the **Hotel Peulla**, are a steep walk away, but are stunning once you reach them. There is also a good walk to **Laguna Margarita**, which takes four hours.

Cayutué and around

On the south shore of Lago Todos Los Santos is the little village of Cayutué, reached by hiring a boat from Petrohué, for US$50. From Cayutué (no camping on the beach but

Border crossing: Chile–Argentina

Puerto Montt–Bariloche
Chilean customs In Peulla, open summer 0800-2100 daily; winter 0800-2000 daily.
Argentine customs In Puerto Frías.

there are private sites) it is a three-hour walk to **Laguna Cayutué**, a jewel set between mountains and surrounded by forest, where you can camp and swim. From the laguna it is a five-hour hike south to Ralún on the Reloncaví Estuary (see page 394): the last half of this route is along a *ripio* road built for extracting timber and is part of the old route used by missionaries in the colonial period to travel between Nahuel Huapi in Argentina and the island of Chiloé.

The lakes route to Bariloche ☺ ⤮ *pp394-396*.

This popular and ever-more expensive route from Puerto Montt to Bariloche, involving ferries across Lago Todos los Santos, Lago Frías and Lago Nahuel Huapi, is outstandingly beautiful. The journey starts by bus via Puerto Varas, Ensenada and the Petrohué falls (20-minute stop) to Petrohué, where you board the catamaran service (1¾ hours) across Lago Todos Los Santos to **Peulla**. During the summer there is a two-hour stop in Peulla for lunch and for **Chilean customs**, see box, above, followed by an hour-long bus ride through the **Paso Pérez Rosales** to Argentine customs in **Puerto Frías**. Then it's a 20-minute boat trip across Lago Frías to **Puerto Alegre**, and a short bus journey (15 minutes) to **Puerto Blest**. A catamaran departs from Puerto Blest for the beautiful one-hour trip along Lago Nahuel Huapi to **Puerto Panuelo**, from where there is a final one-hour bus journey to Bariloche. (The bus drops passengers at hotels, camping sites or in the town centre.)

Bariloche is a popular destination and centre for exploring the Argentine Lake District. Beautifully situated on the south shore of Lago Nahuel Huapi, the streets rise steeply along the edge of a glacial morraine. West of the city on the shores of the lake is the resort of **Llao Llao**, where the famous **Hotel Llao Llao** looks out over chocolate-box scenery. Nearby are two ski resorts. Boat excursions can be made from Bariloche to other parts of the Argentine Lake District. There is a wide range of accommodation as well as air and bus connections to Buenos Aires and other destinations in Argentina. ⤮ *For more details, consult Footprint's Argentina Handbook, Patagonia Handbook, or the South American Handbook.*

Seno de Reloncaví ☺☺▲☺ ⤮ *pp394-396*.

The Seno de Reloncaví, situated east of Puerto Montt and south of the Parque Nacional Pérez Rosales, is the northernmost of Chile's glacial inlets. It is a quiet and beautiful estuary, often shrouded in mist and softly falling rain, but stunning nonetheless, and recommended for its wildlife, including sea lions and dolphins, and for its peaceful atmosphere. It is relatively easily reached from Puerto Montt by a road that runs along the wooded lower Petrohué Valley south from Ensenada and then follows the eastern shore of the estuary for almost 100 km to join the Carretera Austral.

Ralún and around

A small village situated at the northern end of the estuary, Ralún is 31 km southeast from Ensenada by a poorly paved road. There is a village shop and post office, and on the outskirts are **thermal baths** ① *US$2, reached by boat, US$3.50 across the Río Petrohué*. Ralún is the departure point for a five-hour walk north to **Laguna Cayutué** in the Parque Nacional Vicente Pérez Rosales (see page 392). From Ralún you can either travel along the eastern shore of the estuary to Cochamó (see below) or take the road that branches off and follows the western side of the estuary south, 36 km to Lago Chapo and the Parque Nacional Alerce Andino (see page 435).

Cochamó and further south

Some 17 km south of Ralún along a poor *ripio* road is the pretty village of Cochamó. It's situated in a striking setting, on the east shore of the estuary with the volcano behind, and has a small, frequently deserted waterfront, where benches allow you to sit and admire the view. Cochamó's fine wooden church dates from 1900 and is similar to those on Chiloé. It has a clock with wooden hands and an unusual black statue of Christ.

Further south, on the south bank of the Río Puelo (crossed by a new bridge), is **Puelo**, a most peaceful place. From here the road continues 36 km further southwest to Puelche on the Carretera Austral (see page 436).

Gaucho Trail

The Gaucho Trail east from Cochamó to **Paso León** on the Argentine border was used in the colonial period by the indigenous population, Jesuit priests and later by *gauchos*. It runs along Río Cochamó to La Junta, then along the north side of Lago Vidal, passing waterfalls and the oldest surviving Alerce trees in Chile at El Arco. The route takes three to four days by horse or five to six days on foot, depending on conditions and is best travelled between December and March. A road is due to be built which will allow access by jeep. From the border crossing at Paso León it is a three-hour walk to the main road towards San Carlos de Bariloche.

⦿ Parque Nacional Vicente Pérez Rosales and around listings

For Sleeping and Eating price codes and other relevant information, see Essentials pages 35-42.

● Sleeping

Lago Todos los Santos *p392*
The CONAF office in Petrohué can help find cheaper family accommodation.
LL Hotel Petrohué, T065-212025, www.petrohue.com. Burned down in 2002, but is now rebuilt. Half board available. Magnificent views, log fires, cosy. Sauna and heated swimming pool. Hiking, fishing and other activities arranged.

L Hotel Natura, Peulla, T065-367094, www.hotelnatura.cl. Recenty opened luxury hotel, contrasts with traditional Hotel Peulla (see below) under the same ownership.
AL Hotel Peulla, Peulla, T065-367094, www.hotelpeulla.cl. Price includes dinner and breakfast, cheaper out of season. Beautiful setting by the lake and mountains, restaurant and bar, poor meals, cold in winter, often full of tour groups, showing its age.
D Residencial Palomita, 50 m west of **Hotel Peulla**. Price per person for half board, lunches available. Family-run, simple, comfortable but not spacious, separate shower, book ahead in season.

Camping

In Petrohué, there's a campsite beside the lake, US$10 per site, no services (local fishermen will ferry you across for US$3). Camping wild and picnicing is forbidden at Petrohué; car parking US$4 per day.

The campsite in Peulla is opposite the CONAF office, US$7 per site. There's also a good campsite 1¾ hrs' walk east of of the village, or ask at the *carabineros* station if you can camp on the beach; no facilities.

Seno de Reloncaví *p393*

Accommodation in Puelo is also available with families.

LL Río Puelo Lodge, Puelo, T02-2298533, www.rio-puelo-lodge.cl. Plush lodge recently refurbished, offering all-in fly-fishing packages.

A Campo Aventura, 4 km south of Cochamó, T065-232910, www.campo-aventura. com. For details of riding and trekking expeditions, see below. Accommodation is offered at the base camp (signpost on road) with great breakfast, kitchen, sauna. Camping is also possible. Very fresh milk from Campo Aventura's cow, herb garden, expensive but good food using local produce, vegetarian also available, book exchange. There's another base in a renovated mountain house in the valley of La Junta. Office at San Bernardo 318, Puerto Varas.

C-D Cochamó, T065-216212. **F** singles. Basic but clean, friendly, often full with salmon farm workers, good meals, recommended.

C-D Mercado Particular Sabin, Catedral 20, Cochamó. One of several *pensiones*, next to Hotel Cochamó.

C-D Navarrito, Ralún. **F** singles in basic accommodation. Also restaurant.

D Hospedaje Edicar, Cochamó. **F** singles. Breakfast available. Without bath, spacious, recommended.

D Hospedaje Maura, JJ Molina 12, Cochamó. **F** singles. Some rooms with bath. Beautifully situated, good food.

D Posada Campesino, Ralún. **F** singles. Without breakfast, very friendly, simple, clean.

Camping

Camping Los Castaños, Cochamó, T065-216212.

🍴 Eating

Lago Todos los Santos *p392*
See Sleeping, above, for hotel restaurants. There is a small shop in the **Cruce de Lagos** building in Petrohué, with basic supplies and some of the houses sell fresh bread, but if you're camping it's best to take your own food.

Seno de Reloncaví *p393*
Eateries in Cochamó include **Donde Payi,** opposite the church and **Reloncaví**, on the road down to the waterfront. On the seafront there is a cheap fish/seafood restaurant, which also hires out canoes, US$2.50 for 30 mins.

▲▲ Activities and tours

Seno de Reloncaví *p393*
Horse riding/trekking

Campo Aventura, 4 Km south of Cochamó, T065-232910, www.campo-aventura.com. Specializes in all-inclusive riding and trekking expeditions with packhorses along the Gaucho trail between the Reloncaví Estuary and the Argentine border, 2-10 days, roughly US$100 per person per day; good guides, spectacular scenery, English, French and German spoken, highly recommended. It also organizes other activities including combined sea kayaking-horse riding trips with Kokayak in Puerto Varas.

Miralejos, San Pedro 311, Puerto Varas, T065-234892, www.miralejos.cl, runs a variety of small group and bespoke tours around the Cochamó area from 1 to 10 days, including horse-riding, sea-kayaking, and treks across the border to El Bolsón in Argentina.

Sebastián Contreras, C Morales, Cochamó, T065-216220. An independent guide who

offers tours on horseback and hires out
horses, recommended.

⊖ Transport

Lago Todos los Santos p392
Boat
The Cruce de Lagos catamaran sails between
Petrohué and Peulla, departing Petrohué
1030 Mon-Sat, departing Peulla Mon-Sat
1500, 2 hrs, US$50 per person one way,
bicycles free (book in advance); most seating
indoors, no cars carried, commentaries in
Spanish and English, expensive refreshments.
This is the only public service across the lake
and it connects with the Cruce de Lagos tour
bus between Puerto Montt and Bariloche
(see page 403). Local fishermen also make
the trip across the lake and for a group this
can be cheaper than the public service,
allow 3½ hrs.

Bus
Minibuses from **Puerto Varas** to Ensenada
continue to **Petrohué** in summer; last return
bus from Petrohue to Puerto Varas, 1800.
There is a reduced service to **Ensenada**
only in winter.

The lakes route to Bariloche p393
The trip may be cancelled if the weather
is poor; there are reports of difficulty in
obtaining a refund. This journey is operated
only by **Cruce de Lagos** (see page 402)
whose buses depart from company offices
in **Puerto Montt** daily at 0800; the fare is
US$230 one way (not including lunch in
Peulla). From 1 May to 30 Aug this trip is done
over 2 days with an overnight stay in Peulla.
Add another US$108 to the fare for a double
room in the **Hotel Peulla**. Baggage is
automatically taken here but for cheaper
alternatives see Sleeping, above.

Seno de Reloncaví p393
Bus
Buses Fierro and Bohle from Puerto Montt
via Puerto Varas and Ensenada, to **Ralún**,
Cochamó and **Puelo**, 5 daily all year.

Boat
In summer boats sail up the estuary from
Angelmó. Get a group of people together
and convince one of the fishermen to take
you. For information on (irregular) scheduled
trips, contact the Regional Sernatur office
in Puerto Montt.

Puerto Montt and around

→ *Colour map 4, C2.*

The capital of Región X (Los Lagos), Puerto Montt lies on the northern shore of the Seno de Reloncaví, 1016 km south of Santiago. The jumping-off point for journeys south to Chiloé and Patagonia, it is a busy, modern and often windy city, flourishing with the salmon-farming boom. As the fastest growing city in Chile, it sometimes seems as if it is buckling under the pressure, with infrastructure struggling to keep up with population growth. It was founded in 1853, as part of the German colonization of the area, on the site of a Mapuche community known as Melipulli, meaning four hills. Good views over the city and bay are offered from outside the Intendencia Regional on Avenida X Región. There is a wide range of accommodation, but most people will prefer to stay in Puerto Varas, more picturesque and only 20 minutes away by bus. ►► *For listings, see pages 400-404.*

Ins and outs

Getting there El Tepual Airport is 13 km northwest of town, served by **ETM buses** ① *T065-294292, 1½ hrs before departure, US$3*, from the bus terminal; there's also a minibus service to/from hotels, US$7 per person. There are several daily flights north to Santiago, Concepción and Temuco, and south to Chaitén, Coyhaique and Punta Arenas. Ferries and catamarans serve Chaitén (four to six times weekly) and Puerto Chacabuco (one or two weekly); there's also a weekly service south to Puerto Natales. Puerto Montt is the departure point for bus services south to Coyhaique and Punta Arenas, and for buses north to Santiago and all the intermediate cities.

Getting around Puerto Montt is quite a large city, with many *colectivos* and buses serving the *barrios* on the hill above the town. The cental area is down by the port, though, and everything here is within walking distance.

Tourist information **Sernatur** ① *Regional office in the Intendencia Regional, Av Décima Región 480, Casilla 297, T065-254580, infoloslagos@sernatur.cl, Mon-Fri only.* There's also an **information kiosk** ① *Plaza de Armas, open until 1800 on Sat*, run by the municipality, which has town maps and poor information. **CONAF** is on Ochogavia 458, but cannot supply details of conditions in the national parks.

Puerto Montt

The **Plaza de Armas** lies at the foot of steep hills, one block north of Avenida Diego Portales, which runs east-west parallel to the shore. The **Teatro Municipal Diego Rivera** ① *Quillota 116, off the Plaza de Armas, T065-261817*, hosts temporary exhibitions, concerts and plays. Two blocks west of the square is the **Iglesia de los Jesuitas**, on Calle Gallardo, dating from 1872, which has a fine blue-domed ceiling; behind it on a hill is the **campanario** (clock tower). Further west, near the bus terminal, is the **Museo Regional Juan Pablo II** ① *Diego Portales 997, 1030-1800, US$1*, documenting local history. It has a fine collection of historic photos of the city and memorabilia of Pope John Paul II's visit in 1988. Next to the museum is a small park with an old crane and a couple of rusting steam engines.

The little fishing port of **Angelmó**, 2 km west along Avenida Diego Portales, has become a tourist centre thanks to its dozens of seafood restaurants and handicraft shops. Launches depart from Angelmó (US$2), for the wooded **Isla Tenglo**, offshore from Puerto Montt. It's a favourite place for picnics, with views from the summit. The island is famous for its *curanto*, served by restaurants in summer. Boat trips round the island from Angelmó last for 30 minutes and cost US$9. A longer boat trip (two hours) will take you to **Isla Huar**, an island in the Seno de Reloncaví, departing at 1600 and returning from the other end of the island at 0730. If you are lucky you can stay at the island's church, but it may be best to camp.

West of Puerto Montt

Monumento Nacional Lahuen Nadi (US$3) lies between Puerto Montt and the airport, along a *ripio* road going north signed 'Lagunillas' branching off the main road 5 km before the airport. There is a pleasant, short and easy (30-minute) trail through mixed native forest. This is perhaps the most easily accessible place in Chile to see Alerce forests, although they are nowhere near as old or impressive as in other parts. Note that it is easy to get lost on the way back to the main road from the park.

The old coast road west from Puerto Montt is very beautiful. **Chinquihue** (the name means 'place of skunks'), beyond Angelmó, has many seafood restaurants, oysters being a speciality. Further south is **Calbuco**, scenic centre of the fishing industry. It is situated on an island linked to the mainland by a causeway and can be visited direct by boat or by road. West of here is the Río Maullín, which drains Lago Llanquihue, and has some attractive waterfalls and good salmon fishing. At its mouth is the little fishing village of **Maullín**, founded in 1602. On the coast to the southeast is **Carelmapu**, with an excellent beach and *cabañas* at windswept Playa Brava, about 3 km away.

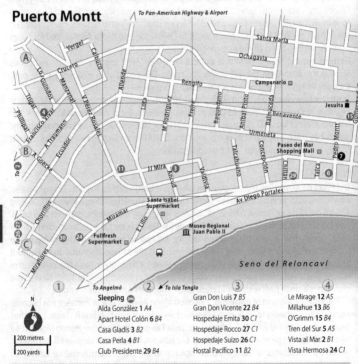

Puerto Montt

To Pan-American Highway & Airport

Seno del Reloncaví

N
200 metres
200 yards

Sleeping		
Alda González 1 *A4*	Gran Don Luis 7 *B5*	Le Mirage 12 *A5*
Apart Hotel Colón 6 *B4*	Gran Don Vicente 22 *B4*	Millahue 13 *B6*
Casa Gladis 3 *B2*	Hospedaje Emita 30 *C1*	O'Grimm 15 *B4*
Casa Perla 4 *B1*	Hospedaje Rocco 27 *C1*	Tren del Sur 5 *A5*
Club Presidente 29 *B4*	Hospedaje Suizo 26 *C1*	Vista al Mar 2 *B1*
	Hostal Pacífico 11 *B2*	Vista Hermosa 24 *C1*

Sea routes south of Puerto Montt

Puerto Montt is the departure point for several popular voyages along the coast of southern Chile. All sailings are from Angelmó; timetables should be checked carefully in advance as schedules change frequently. ▸▸ *See Transport, page 404. For ferry routes, refer to the colour maps at the back of the book.*

To Puerto Natales One of the highlights of many journeys to Chile is the 1460-km voyage between Puerto Montt and the southern port of Puerto Natales, made by the Navimag *M/N Evangelistas*; it is quicker and cheaper to fly or go by bus via Argentina but the voyage by boat is spectacular given a little luck with the weather. The route south from Puerto Montt crosses the Seno de Reloncaví and the Golfo de Ancud between the mainland and the large island of Chiloé, then continues south through the Canal Moraleda and the Canal Errázuriz, which separate the mainland from the outlying islands. It then heads west through the Canal Chacabuco to Bahía Anna Pink and across the open sea and the infamous Golfo de Peñas (Gulf of Sorrows), where seasickness pills come in more than handy, to reach a series of channels – Canal Messier, Angostura Inglesa, Fiordo del Indio and Canal Kirke – which provide one of the narrowest routes for large shipping in the world, making a short detour to the massive Pio XI (southbound) or Amalia (northbound) glacier. There are spectacular views of the wooded fjords, weather permitting, particularly at sunrise and sunset, and a sense of peace pervades everything except the ship, which is filled with people having a good time.

The only regular stop on this route is at the fishing village of **Puerto Edén** on Isla Wellington, one hour south of the Angostura Inglesa. It has three shops (scant provisions), one off-licence, one café, and a *hospedaje* for up to 20 people (open intermittantly). The population of 250, includes five *carabineros* and a few remaining native Alacaluf people. Puerto Edén is the drop-off point for exploring **Isla Wellington**, which is largely untouched, with stunning mountains. If you do stop here, take all food; maps (not very accurate) are available in Santiago. The onward fare to Puerto Natales is US$150.

This is a ferry that also carries cargo rather than a cruise liner; standards of service and comfort vary, depending on the number of passengers and weather conditions. Economy-class accommodation is basic but comfortable, in 22-berth dormitories, and although economy class and cabin passengers eat the same food, they are confined to separate areas (economy class is cramped) except when on deck. The food is variable and served in large portions, and,

Eating 🍴
Café Central **2** *B4*
Café Haussman **1** *B5*
Café Real **2** *B4*
Centro Español **3** *B5*
Club Alemán **4** *B5*
Club de Yates **8** *C6*
Cotele **5** *C6*
Dino **7** *B4*
Pazos **6** *C6*

apart from videos and a few talks, organized entertainment on board is limited. There is a bar on board, but you are welcome to bring your own drinks.

To Puerto Chacabuco and Laguna San Rafael Navimag also runs a twice-weekly ferry service between Puerto Montt and **Puerto Chacabuco**, 80 km west of Coyhaique. This beautiful voyage passes forested cliffs, seemingly within touching distance, and offers glimpses of distant snows. However, taking this route south means that travellers miss out on the attractions of much of the Carretera Austral. From Puerto Chacabuco there are further services to visit **Laguna San Rafael**. However, it may well be cheaper, and is certainly more comfortable, to take a catamaran service to the Laguna from Puerto Chacabuco (see page 466) or to charter a small plane from Coyhaique. A luxury alternative is to board *Skorpios II* for a cruise to Chiloe and Laguna San Raphael. Generally, service is excellent, the food superb and, at the laguna, you chip ice off the face of the glacier for your whisky. After San Rafael the ship visits **Quitralco fjord**, where there are thermal pools and boat trips. The fare varies according to season, type of cabin and number of occupants. There are also four- to six-day tours from Puerto Montt with **Patagonia Connection**, which visit Puerto Chacabuco, Laguna San Rafael and the Termas de Puyuhuapi (see page 465). ▶▶ *See Transport, page 404.*

◉ Puerto Montt and around listings

For Sleeping and Eating price codes and other relevant information, see Essentials pages 35-42.

⬤ Sleeping

Puerto Montt *p397, map p398*
Accommodation is expensive in season; much cheaper off season. There are lots of *cabañas* on the outskirts of the city and in Pelluco.
L Gran Hotel Don Vicente, Varas 447, T065-432900, www.granhoteldonvicente.cl. Business-class hotel. Some rooms noisy, restaurant serves seafood, fine views.
AL Club Presidente, Portales 664, T065-251666, www.presidente.cl. Comfortable 4-star with breakfast. Large rooms or suites, many with views. English spoken. Recommended.
AL Gran Hotel Don Luis, Quillota 146, T065-259001, www.hoteldonluis.cl. A comfortable 4-star hotel with decent restaurant, gym and sauna.
AL O'Grimm, Gallardo 211, T065-252845, www.ogrimm.com. Pleasant, spacious, slightly dated rooms with lounge area, cosy restaurant with occasional live music, central.

A Apart Hotel Colón, Pedro Montt 65, T065-264290, www.aparthotelcolon.cl. Fully furbished studio apartments, good value, especially when paying in dollars.
A-B Le Mirage, Rancagua 350, T065-255125, www.hotellemirage.cl. A basic business-class hotel with breakfast, small rooms, clean.
A-B Tren del Sur, Santa Teresa 643, T065-343939, www.trendelsur.cl. Self-styled boutique *hostal*. Pleasant spacious lobby and cosy common areas, decorated with objects recycled from the old railway, but rooms a tad overpriced, especially those with no windows. Very helpful English-speaking owner.
B Hostal Pacífico, J J Mira 1088, T065-256229, www.hostalpacifico.cl. With bath, some rooms a little cramped, breakfast included, cable TV, parking, comfortable. Discounts for foreign tourists.
B Millahue, Copiapó 64, T065-253829, www.hotelmillahue.cl. With breakfast and bath, slightly run-down, restaurant, also apartments at Benavente 959, T/F065-254592.
B-C Hospedaje Suizo, Independencia 231, T/F065-252640, rossyoelckers@yahoo.es. **F** singles, with breakfast. Some rooms with bath. Attractive house near the bus terminal,

clean, German and Italian spoken, painting and Spanish classes. Convenient for Navimag. Recommended.

C Alda González, Gallardo 552, T065-253334. **F** singles. Some rooms with bath, breakfast included, cooking facilities, English and German spoken, good value.

C Hospedaje Emita, Miraflores 1281, T065-250725, hospedaje_emita@hotmail.com. With breakfast, including home-made bread. Some rooms with bath. Clean, friendly, safe, near the bus terminal.

C Hospedaje Rocco, Pudeto 233, T/065-272897, www.hospedajerocco.cl. **D-E** per person in shared rooms. All rooms with shared bath. Impeccably clean but no frills. Excellent breakfast included, real coffee, English and Italian spoken, friendly atmosphere, laundry. Quiet residential area, convenient for Navimag. A little overpriced but still recommended.

C Vista al Mar, Vivar 1337, T065-255625, www.hospedajevistaalmar.unlugar.com. **E** singles. Friendly, helpful, welcoming, good breakfast. Phone for lift from bus terminal.

C-D Casa Perla, Trigal 312, T065-262104, www.casaperla.com. **F** per person in shared rooms. With breakfast. Slightly ramshackle house uphill from the bus terminal, helpful, friendly, meals, laundry, internet, pleasant garden, English spoken, Spanish classes offered, good meeting place. Recommended.

D Casa Gladis, Ancud y Mira. Some double rooms. **F** per person for dorm beds, kitchen and laundry facilities, near bus terminal.

D Vista Hermosa, Miramar 1486, T/F065-268001, vistahermosa@mixmail.com. **F** singles without bath, 10 mins' walk from bus terminal. Peaceful neighbourhood. The room at the front has the best views although these have been somewhat compromised by the new high-rise block.

Camping

Wild camping is possible along the seafront. Several official sites west of Puerto Montt. **Anderson**, 11 km west. American-run, hot showers, private beach, home-grown fruit, vegetables and milk products.

El Ciervo, 3 km west. Good site.
Municipal, Chinquihue, 10 km west. Open Oct-Apr, fully equipped with tables, seats, barbecue, toilets and showers, small shop, no kerosene, bus service from town.

West of Puerto Montt p398

B Cabañas El Pangal, 5 km from Maullin, T065-451244, m_essedin@hotmail.com. Campsite and cabins on the beach.
B Hotel Colonial, Calbuco, T065-461546, www.hotelcolonial@hotmail.com. One of several decent hotels.
C Huelmo, un destino no turistico, T09-8314 2656, www.rocio.cl. **E** Singles. Simple cabins near Huelmo, a small seafront village completely off the beaten track. English spoken. Recommended.

❼ Eating

Puerto Montt p397, map p398
For seafood enthusiasts, the only place to go is Angelmó, where there are many seafood restaurants in the old fishing port past the fish market, serving excellent lunches only. Look out for local specialities such as *curanto* and *picoroco al vapor*, a giant barnacle whose flesh looks and tastes like a crab, and ask for *té blanco* (white wine; the stalls are not legally allowed to serve wine).

The centre of Puerto Montt is full of unpretentious, cheap restaurants. Most upmarket restaurants tend to be around Pelluco along the coast on Puerto Montt's southeastern outskirts (10 mins from the centre by *colectivo*).

♥♥♥ Club de Yates, Juan Soler s/n. Fancy restaurant on a pier serving expensive seafood with pretty much the best view in town.
♥♥♥-♥♥ Cotele, Juan Soler s/n, Pelluco, T065-278000. Only serves one thing – beef, but serves it as well as anywhere in southern Chile. Recommended. Reservations advised.
♥♥♥-♥♥ Club Alemán, Varas 264, T065252551. Old fashioned, good food and wine.

ⅢⅢ-Ⅲ Pazos, Pelluco, T065-252552. Serves the best *curanto* in the Puerto Montt area.
Ⅲ Café Haussman, San Martín y Urmeneta. German-style cake, beer and *crudos* (raw meat).
Ⅲ Centro Español, O'Higgins 233, T065-343753. Decent traditional Chilean and Spanish food. Vegetarian options.
Ⅲ Dino, Varas 550, T065-252785. Restaurant upstairs, snacks downstairs (try the lemon juice). Often has an all-you-can-eat buffet.
Ⅰ Café Central, Rancagua 117, T065-482888. Spartan decor, generous portions (sandwiches and *pichangas*). Giant TV showing football.
Ⅰ Café Real, Rancagua 137, T065-253750. For *empanadas, pichangas, congrío frito* and cheap lunches.
Ⅰ Restaurant de las Antigüedades, Av Angelmó. Attractive and unusual decor, real coffee, interesting menu.

Cheap food is also available at Puerto Montt bus terminal.

Cafés

Asturias, Angelmó 2448. Limited menu but often recommended.
Café Alemana, Rancagua 117. Real coffee.

West of Puerto Montt *p398*
Ⅲ Kiel, Chinquihué, T065-255010. Good meat and seafood dishes.

🟠 Bars and clubs

Puerto Montt *p397, map p398*
Note Several of the 'bars' near the port and along Pérez Rosales have more to them than meets the eye.
Star, Ruta 5 north of the city. Disco. Several more in Pelluco, east of Puerto Montt.

O Shopping

Puerto Montt *p397, map p398*
Woollen goods and Mapuche-designed rugs can be bought at roadside stalls in Angelmó and on Diego Portales opposite

the bus terminal. Prices are much the same as on Chiloé, but quality is often lower.
Fullfresh, opposite bus terminal. Supermarket, open 0900-2200 daily.
Paseo del Mar, Talca y Antonio Varas. Large modern shopping mall. There is also a new mall, the **Paseo Costanera** on the seafront which also has a multi-screen cinema.
Sotavento, Diego Portales 570. Bookshop with a small selection of English novels, also maps and local-interest books.

▲ Activities and tours

Puerto Montt *p397, map p398*
There are many agencies. Most offer 1-day excursions to Chiloé (US$45) and to Puerto Varas, Isla Loreley, Laguna Verde, and the Petrohué Falls: these tours are cheaper from bus company kiosks inside the bus terminal. Some companies offer 2-day excursions along the Carretera Austral to Hornopirén, US$120, with food and accommodation.
Andina del Sud, Varas 437, close to central tourist kiosk, T065-257797. Sells a variety of tours, and through its subsidiary **Cruce de Lagos** (www.crucedelagos.com) also offers the lakes trip to Bariloche (see page 393).
Ecosub, Panamericana 510, T065-263939, www.ecosub.cl. Scuba-diving excursions.
Eureka Turismo, Gallardo 65, T065-250412, www.chile-travel.com/eureka.htm. Helpful, German and English spoken.
Kayaking Austral, T09-96980951, or book through **Casa Perla**. Guided sea kayaking.
Travellers, General Bulnes 1009, 22 de Mayo, T065-262099, www.travellers.cl. Booking office for **Navimag** ferry to Puerto Natales, bespoke excursions, also sells imported camping equipment and runs computerized tourist information service, book swap ("the best south of Santiago"), map display, TV, real coffee, English-run.

West of Puerto Montt *p398*
Marina del Sur (MDS), Chinquihué, T/F065-251958, www.marinadelsur.cl.

Sailing courses, noticeboard for *tripulante* (crew) requests, modern building with bar and restaurant. The MDS charters office specializes in chartering boats for cruising the Patagonian channels: US$3200-10,000 per week depending on size of boat.

⊙ Transport

Puerto Montt *p397, map p398*
Air
LanChile and Sky have several flights daily to **Santiago**, from US$95 return (best one-way prices with Sky); to **Balmaceda** for Coyhaique, from US$75 return; to **Punta Arenas**, from US$100 return. In Jan, Feb and Mar you may be told that flights are booked up, however, cancellations are sometimes available from the airport. To **Stanley** (Falkland Islands/Islas Malvinas), from Santiago via Punta Arenas, **LanChile**, Sat, US$700 return.

Airline offices Aerotaxis del Sur, A Varas 70, T065-731315, www.aerotaxis delsur.cl; Cielomar Austral, Quillota 245, loc 1, T065-264010; LanChile, O'Higgins 167, T600-526 2000; Sky, T600-600 2828 for information.

Bus
The very crowded terminal on the seafront at Diego Portales y Lota has telephones, restaurants, a *casa de cambio* and left luggage (US$2.50 per item for 24 hrs). Theft is a common problem here, so keep a tight hold of your baggage.

Expreso Puerto Varas, Thaebus and Full Express run minibuses every few mins to **Puerto Varas**, US$1.20, **Llanquihue** and **Frutillar**, US$2, and to **Osorno**, US$3. Buses and *colectivos* Nos 2, 3 and 20 ply the route to **Anglemó**, US$0.60 each way.

To **Ensenada** and **Petrohué**, several companies, hourly; to **Ralún**, **Cochamó** and **Puelo**, Buses Fierro and Buses Bohle, 5 daily via Puerto Varas and Ensenada, US$6; to **Pucón**, JAC, several daily, 6 hrs;

to **Santiago**, several companies, 13 hrs, US$30-75; to **Temuco**, US$10; to **Valdivia**, US$8; to **Concepción**, US$13. For services to Chiloé, see page 411.

To **Punta Arenas**, Pacheco and Queilen Bus, 1-3 weekly, 32-38 hrs, approximately US$80 (bus goes through Argentina via Bariloche; take US$ cash to pay for meals, etc in Argentina); book well in advance in Jan-Feb and check if you need a multiple-entry Chilean visa; also book any return journey before setting out. To **Coyhaique** via Bariloche, 2 weekly, **Turibus**, US$55.

International To **Bariloche** via Osorno and the Puyehue pass, daily, 7hrs, **Andes Mar**, Río de la Plata and Tas Choapa, US$23. Andes Mar also has through services to **Buenos Aires**, **Nequén** and **Bahía Blanca**; services are reduced out of season. Buy tickets for international buses from the bus terminal, not through an agency. The best views are from the right hand side of the bus. For the route to Argentina via **Lago Todos los Santos**, see page 393.

Bicycle
For repairs, try Kiefer (*la casa del ciclista*), Pedro Montt 129.

Car/motorbike
Hire from Autovald, Sector Cardenal, Pasaje San Andrés 60, T065-256043, www.autovald.cl, cheap rates; Avis, Benavente 670, T065-367840, and at airport; Budget, Antonio Varas 162, T065-286277, www.budget.cl, and at airport; Egartur, Benavente 575, loc. 3, T065-257336, www.egartur.cl, good service, recommended, will deliver your car to your hotel for free; First, Antonio Varas 447, T065-252036; Full Famas, Diego Portales 506, T065-258060, F065-259840, and airport, T065-263750, friendly, helpful, good value, has vehicles that can be taken to Argentina; Hertz, At the airport, T065-268944, www.auto rentas.cl; Salfa Sur, Pilpilco 800, also at Airport, T065-290224, www.salfasur.cl. Good value.

For motorcycle repairs, visit **Miguel Schmuch**, Urmeneta 985, T/F065-258877.

Ferry

Shipping offices **Catamaranes del Sur**, Diego Portales 510, T065-267533, www.catamaranesdelsur.cl; **Navimag**, Naviera Magallanes SA, Angelmó 2187, T065-253318, www.navimag.com; **Skorpios**, Angelmó 1660 y Miraflores (Castilla 588), T065-252619, www.skorpios.cl.

Train

The station is 2 km north of the city centre at Cuarta Terraza s/n, La Paloma, T600-585 5000, www.efe.cl. At the time of writing all services have been suspended.

Sea routes south of Puerto Montt *p399*

To Puerto Natales Navimag *Ferry Evangelistas* sails once a week, Nov-Apr, departing Puerto Montt Mon 1600, returning Fri 0400 (although departures are frequently delayed, or even advanced, by weather conditions), 3½ days, economy from US$555 per person, private cabin with view US$1720 (double US$1750), all prices include meals, 10% discount for ISIC holders in cabin class only, fares 10-20% lower Apr-Oct. Book well in advance for cabin class departures Dec-Mar (more than 2 weeks in advance in Feb), especially for the voyage south; Puerto Natales to Puerto Montt is less heavily booked; it is worth putting your name on the waiting list for cancellations at busy periods. Tickets can be bought in advance through **Travellers** in Puerto Montt (see Activities and tours, above), from **Navimag** offices in Puerto Montt, Puerto Natales and Punta Arenas, from travel agencies throughout the country, or online at www.navimag.cl (occasional offers).

To Puerto Chacabuco and Laguna San Rafael Navimag sails to Puerto Chacabuco throughout the year, usually once a week, 24 hrs, accommodation from US$60 to US$210, cars US$230, motorcycles US$100, cycles US$50. In the summer (Sep-Apr) the *Magallanes* continues 1 a week (usually at the weekend) from Puerto Chacabuco to **Laguna San Rafael**, 21-24 hrs, return fare Puerto Montt–Laguna San Rafael US$400-800; better offers are available from Puerto Chacabuco to Laguna San Rafael (see page 466).

Skorpios Cruises luxury ship *Skorpios 2* leaves Puerto Montt Sat 1100 for a 6-day cruise to **Laguna San Rafael**, returning to Puerto Montt Fri, double cabin from US$1300 per person. For further details (and information about routes sailed by *Skorpios II*), consult www.skorpios.cl.

Other sea routes To **Chaitén**, Naviera Austral, 2-4 ferries weekly, 10 hrs, passenger reclining seat US$35, bunk US$50, cars US$150, bicycles US$15.

O Directory

Puerto Montt *p397, map p398*
Banks ATMs at several banks and supermarkets in the centre and in both malls; commission charges for TCs vary widely. Good *casas de cambio* rates at **Galería Cristal**, Varas 595; **Afex**, Portales 516; **La Moneda de Oro**, at the bus terminal, exchanges Latin American currencies Mon-Sat 0930-1230, 1530-1800; Turismo Los Lagos, Varas 595, local 13. **Consulates** Argentina, Cauquenes 94, piso 2, T065-253996, quick visa service; Germany, Antonio Varas y Gallardo, piso 3, of 306, Tue-Wed 0930-1200; Netherlands, Chorillos 1582, T065-253003; Spain, Rancagua 113, T065- 252557.
Internet Several in the centre and on Av Angelmó. **Laundry** Center, Antonio Varas 700; **Lavatodo**, O'Higgins 231; **Narly**, San Martín 187, local 6, high prices, US$7 for 3 kg; **Nautilus**, Av Angelmó 1564, cheaper, good; Unic, Chillán 149; Yessil't, Edif Caracol, Urmeneta 300, service washes. **Medical services** Seminario s/n, T065-261134.
Post office Rancagua 126, open 0830-1830 Mon-Fri, 0830-1200 Sat. **Telephone** Several in the centre and along Av Angelmó.

Contents

Footprint features

Chiloé

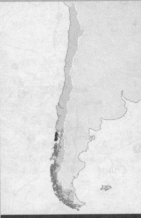

At a glance

⊖ **Getting around** Good public transport between towns. Private transport needed for some out-of-the-way places, be it a sturdy car or mountain bike.

◉ **Time required** A day for a brief glimpse, 3 or 4 to see most of the sights and at least a week to begin to appreciate something of Chilote culture.

☼ **Weather** Lots of rain. Showers in summer and prolonged downpours the rest of the year.

✕ **When not to go** Winter (May-Aug) is generally dark and very wet. *Tábanos* (horseflies) can be a problem in Dec and Jan.

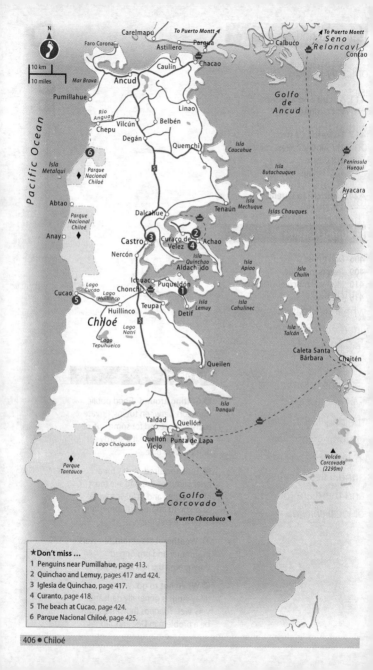

★Don't miss ...
1 Penguins near Pumillahue, page 413.
2 Quinchao and Lemuy, pages 417 and 424.
3 Iglesia de Quinchao, page 417.
4 Curanto, page 418.
5 The beach at Cucao, page 424.
6 Parque Nacional Chiloé, page 425.

The mysterious archipelago of Chiloé is one of the most fascinating areas of Chile. Consisting of one main island, officially known as La Isla Grande de Chiloé, and numerous islets, its rolling hills, covered in patchwork fields and thick forest, provide a lasting sense of rural calm. Here you are almost always within sight of the sea, with dolphins playing in the bay and, on a clear day, there are views across to the twisting spire of Volcán Corcovado on the mainland.

Just under half the population of 155,000 live in the two main towns, Ancud and Castro, and there are also many fishing villages. The Cordillera de la Costa runs at low altitudes along the Pacific side of the island. South of Castro a gap in the range is filled by two connected lakes: Lago Huillinco and Lago Cucao. Thick forests cover most of the sparsely populated western and southern parts of the island; elsewhere hillsides are covered with wheat fields and dark green plots of potatoes and the roads are lined with wild flowers in summer. East of the main island are several groups of smaller islands, where the way of life is even more peaceful.

Chiloé is famous for its legends and rich mythology; here witches are said to fly around at night, identifiable as lights in the dark sky. Chiloé is equally well known for its painted wooden churches, some of them dating back to the late colonial period. In January and February, most towns and villages celebrate their annual fiestas; traditional dishes, such as *curanto*, are served and there are rodeos and dancing, as well as much drinking of local *chicha*.

Background

History

The original Chilotes (inhabitants of Chiloé) were the Chonos tribe, who were pushed south by the Huilliches, invading from the north. The first Spanish sighting of the islands was by Francisco de Ulloa in 1553 and, in 1567, Martín Ruiz de Gamboa took possession of the islands on behalf of Spain. The small settler population divided the indigenous population and their lands between them, but the Huilliche uprising after 1598 drove the Spanish out of the mainland south of the Río Biobío, isolating the 200 Spanish settlers on Chiloé. Following a violent earthquake in 1646, the Spanish population asked the viceroy in Lima for permission to leave, but this was refused. Much of Chiloé's distinctive character derives from 200 years of separation from mainstream Spanish colonial development.

The islanders were the last supporters of the Spanish Crown in South America. When the Chilean patriot leaders rebelled, the Spanish governor fled to the island and, in despair, offered it to Britain. George Canning, the British foreign secretary, turned the offer down; Chiloé finally surrendered to the patriots in 1826. Visiting less than a decade later, Charles Darwin still clearly distinguished Chiloé from the rest of Chile, saying that here the Andes were not nearly "so elevated as in Chile".

Throughout the 19th and the first part of the 20th century, Ancud was the capital of Chiloé. All that changed with the earthquake and *maremoto* (tidal wave) of 1960. This drastically altered the landscape in Ancud, bringing petrified trees to the surface and causing forests to submerge. The whole of the lower town was destroyed, except for the cathedral, which was badly damaged and then blown up rather than renovated; until then, this had been the second largest cathedral in South America. The capital was moved back to its former site at Castro, which is the only place in Chiloé that really feels urban today. The *maremoto*, and the rivalry between Ancud and Castro that it spawned, have never entirely been forgotten.

The relatively high birth rate and the shortage of employment in Chiloé have led to regular emigration, with Chilotes settling across Chile; they were prominent as shepherds in late 19th-century Patagonia and as sailors and fishermen along the coast. However, with the recent growth in the salmon farming industry, more Chilotes are choosing to stay.

Climate

The appalling climate of Chiloé is almost as legendary as the witches that are said to live there. The west coast has particularly vile conditions – it can rain here for three weeks at a time – while the sheltered east coast and offshore islands are only a little drier. Some of the best weather is in early December and late March. The main benefits of the climate are culinary: the Humboldt Current and the sheltered east coast ensure a wide variety of fresh shellfish is available all year. Chiloé also has indigenous elephant garlic, which is used to make a very tasty garlic sauce, as well as several dozen endemic varieties of potato.

Art and architecture

The availability of wood and the lack of metals on the islands have left their mark on Chilote architecture. Some of the earliest churches were built entirely of wood, using pegs instead of nails. These churches often displayed German influence as a result of the missionary work of Bavarian Jesuits. Four notable features were the *esplanada* or porch that ran the length of the front of the church, the not-quite semi-circular arches, the central position of the tower directly above the door and the fact that they have three

Jesuits in Chiloé

The Jesuits arrived in Chiloé in 1608 and the first Jesuit residence was established four years later. Although in Chiloé they introduced few of the missions for which they became famous in Paraguay, at their expulsion in 1767 there were 79 churches on the island.

The key to the Jesuits' influence lay in their use of *fiscales*: indigenous people who were trained to teach Christian doctrine and to ensure that everyone observed religious duties. One fiscal was appointed for every 50 inhabitants. On 17 September each year, two missionaries set sail from Castro in small boats, taking with them statues of saints and essential supplies. They spent the next eight months sailing around the islands of Chiloé, visiting all the parishes in a set order. In each parish they would spend three days officiating at weddings and baptisms, hearing confessions and reviewing the work of the *fiscales*.

Most of the old churches for which Chiloé is famous date from after the expulsion of the Jesuits, but some writers claim that their influence can still be seen, for example in the enthusiasm for education on the island, which has long boasted one of the highest literacy rates in the world. Many villages in Chiloé still have *fiscales* who are, according to tradition, responsible for keeping the church keys.

levels representing the Holy Trinity. Few of the oldest churches have survived, but there are still over 150 on the islands and even small villages almost invariably have churches with pretty cemeteries – in 2001, UNESCO declared them World Heritage sites.

The *rucas* (houses) of the indigenous population were thatched; thatch continued in widespread use throughout the 19th century. The use of thin *tejuelas* (shingles) made from alerce wood was influenced by the German settlers around Puerto Montt in the late 19th century; these tiles, which are nailed to the frame and roof in several distinctive patterns, overlap to form effective protection against the rain. *Palafitos*, or wooden houses built on stilts over the water, were once popular in all the main ports, but are now mainly found at the northern end of Castro, to the west of the *Panamericana*.

The islands are also famous for their traditional handicrafts, notably woollens and basketware, which can be bought in all the main towns and on some of the smaller islands, as well as in Puerto Montt and Angelmó.

Folklore

Chiloé's distinctive history and its maritime traditions are reflected in the strength of its unique folklore. There is widespread belief in a mermaid (*pincoya*); witches, who are said to meet at caves near Quicaví (between Dalcahue and Quemchi); and a ghost ship, the *Caleuche*, which whisks shipwrecked sailors aboard (see box, page 410). The *Caleuche* is said to transform itself into a log, brought ashore by its crew (who become birds) when it needs repairs. Legend has it that Chiloé's dead are rowed along the reaches of Lago Huillinco and Lago Cucao in a white ship, out into the Pacific. For further information about the myths associated with the islands, read *Casos de Brujos de Chiloé* by Umiliana Cárdenas Saldivia (1989, Editorial Universitaria) and *Chiloé, Manual del Pensamiento Mágico y Creencia Popular* by Renato Cárdenas and Catherine Hall (1989, El Kultrún).

Mythical mischief-makers

Visitors to Chiloé should beware of these four unlikely mythological hazards.

El Trauco A small, ugly and smelly man who wears a little round hat made of bamboo and clothing of the same material; he usually carries a small stone hatchet, with which he is reputed to be able to fell any tree in three strokes. He spends much of his time haunting the forests, sitting on fallen tree trunks and weaving his clothes.

El Trauco specializes in seducing virgins and is – conveniently – held to be responsible for unwanted pregnancies. He uses his magic powers to give them erotic dreams while they are asleep; they wake and go to look for him in the forest and are seduced by his eyes. Despite his ugliness, he is irresistible and the girl throws herself on the ground. You should be careful not to disturb the Trauco while he is thus occupied: those who do so are immediately deformed beyond recognition and sentenced to die within 12 months.

La Fiura A small ugly woman who lives in the forests near Hualdes, where she is reputed to bathe in the streams and waterfalls, combing her hair with a crystal comb. Known as the indefatigable lover of bachelors, she attracts her victims by wearing colourful clothes. As the man approaches he is put to sleep by her foul breath. After La Fiura has satisfied her desire, the unfortunate man goes insane. Refusing her advances is no escape either: those who do so, whether animals or men, become so deformed that they are unrecognizable.

La Sirena and **El Caleuche** A dangerous double act for those travelling by sea. La Sirena is a mermaid who lies alluringly on rocks and entices sailors to their deaths. Once shipwrecked, sailors are whisked into the bowels of *El Caleuche*, the ghost ship that is said to patrol the channels of the archipelago. Both the Chilean navy and merchant ships have reported sightings of the *Caleuche*. The author of this book has also met several people on Chiloé who claim to have seen the ghost ship; but a word of warning was sounded by an old cynic in Castro: "I knew a fisherman who used to walk along the beach shouting 'I've seen La Sirena'. All the other fishermen fled, and then he stole their fish."

Modern Chiloé

Although fishing and agriculture remain mainstays of the economy, salmon farming has become just as important, and seaweed is also harvested for export to Japan. Tourism provides a seasonal income for a growing number of people, especially in Ancud and Castro, with agrotourism also available in rural areas. This consists of staying with local families and sharing their way of life, whether it be farming or fishing. The host families are invariably friendly and welcoming, and the stays are highly recommended as a fascinating way to immerse yourself in Chilote life. Prices per person are all **E** with breakfast, **D** for half board and **C** for full board. Reservations should be made a day or two in advance. An updated list of agroturism operators is available from the **Fundación Con Todos** ① *Ramírez 207, T065-630247, agroturismochiloe@gmail.com*, and also at the **Sernatur** office in Ancud, page 411.

Ins and outs

Getting there

Ferry and catamaran services connect the island with Chaitén and the Carretera Austral (see page 428), but the main sea link is the frequent **vehicle ferry service** ① *30 mins, cars US$16 one way (more expensive at night), foot passengers US$1,* between Pargua on the mainland (55 km southwest of Puerto Montt) across the Chacao straits to Chacao. Dolphins often follow the boat. There have been plans to build a bridge to the mainland for a number of years although these have not gone beyond the planning stages.

Getting around

Frequent bus services, which connect with ferry sailings, operate between Ancud and Castro (the main towns on Chiloé) and Puerto Montt. It is possible to travel direct to many cities, including Santiago, Osorno, Valdivia, Temuco and Los Angeles. Inter-urban bus transport is dominated by **Cruz del Sur**, who also owns **Trans Chiloé**, operating from their own terminals in Ancud and Castro. **Cruz del Sur** also operates its own ferries to the mainland, which give priority to **Cruz del Sur** buses. The only independent long-distance bus operator to the island is **Queilen Bus** (cheaper but less regular). Provincial bus services are crowded, slow and often wet, but provide a good picture of life in rural Chiloé. Mountain bikes and horses are ideal for travelling slowly through remote parts of the archipelago.

Ancud and around

→ *Colour map 4, C1.*

Situated on the northern coast of Chiloé, 34 km west of the Straits of Chacao, Ancud lies on a great bay, the Golfo de Quetalmahue. It is a little less characterful than some of the other towns on the island but is nevertheless the best centre for visiting the villages of northern Chiloé. There is a friendly small-town feel; everyone knows each other and everything happens in its own time. Tourism is slowly reviving Ancud's fortunes following the disaster of the maremoto in 1960. Within striking distance are white-sand beaches, Spanish colonial forts and an important colony of Magellanic and Humboldt penguins. ▸▸ *For listings, see pages 414-416.*

Ins and outs

Getting there There are buses every 30 minutes from Castro and Quellón, and hourly from Puerto Montt. **Cruz del Sur** have buses to and from Valdivia, Temuco and Santiago (several daily). There are two bus terminals, the Terminal Municipal, on the outskirts of town, 1.5 km east of the centre, and the much more convenient Cruz del Sur terminal.

Getting around Ancud is big enough for you to want to take the occasional *colectivo*; there are many of these, with their destinations signed on the roof (US$0.60, US$90 after 2100). Rural buses serve nearby beaches and villages.

Tourist information **Sernatur** ① *Libertad 665, T065-622800, infochiloe@serna tur.cl, Mon-Fri 0830-2000, Sat and Sun (summer only) 0900-1800.*

Ancud

The port is dominated by the **Fuerte San Antonio**, the fort where the Spanish surrendered Chiloé to Chilean troops in 1826. Close to it are the unspectacular ruins of the Polvorín del Fuerte (a couple of cannon and a few walls). A kilometre north of the fort is a secluded beach, **Arena Gruesa**, where public concerts are held in summer. The small fishing harbour at Cochrane y Prat is worth a visit, especially towards the end of the morning when the catch is landed. On the road west, along the coast, you can see concrete pillars, remnants of the old railway, destroyed by the 1960 earthquake.

Near the Plaza de Armas is the **Museo Regional** ① *Libertad 370, T065-622002, www.dibam.cl/sdm_mr_ancud, Jan-Feb daily 1000-1930, otherwise Tue-Fri 1000-1730, Sat, Sun and holidays 1000-1400, US$1, children US$0.50,* with an interesting collection on the early history of Chiloé. It also displays a replica of a traditional Chilote thatched wooden house and of the small sailing ship *Ancud*, which claimed the Straits of Chacao for Chile, pipping the French to the post by a day. In the patio is a skeleton of a blue whale. There's a good craft shop and café on site and activities for children are provided. Excellent wooden toys and clocks are made by **Lucho Troncoso** ① *Prat 342, T09-9263 9383.*

Ancud

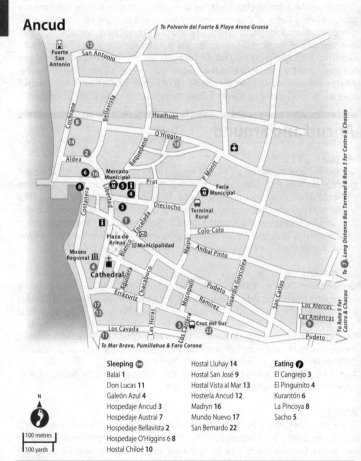

Sleeping 💤
Balai **1**
Don Lucas **11**
Galeón Azul **4**
Hospedaje Ancud **3**
Hospedaje Austral **7**
Hospedaje Bellavista **2**
Hospedaje O'Higgins 6 **8**
Hostal Chiloé **10**

Hostal Lluhay **14**
Hostal San José **9**
Hostal Vista al Mar **13**
Hostería Ancud **12**
Madryn **16**
Mundo Nuevo **17**
San Bernardo **22**

Eating 🍴
El Cangrejo **3**
El Pinguinito **4**
Kurantón **6**
La Pincoya **8**
Sacho **5**

The **Faro Corona** lighthouse lies 34 km west of Ancud along a beach, which, although unsuitable for swimming (absolutely freezing water and dangerous currents), offers good views with interesting birdlife. There isn't much there so take something to eat and drink. To the south is **Fuerte Ahuí**, an old fort with good views of Ancud.

East of Ancud

Most people travelling to Chiloé will arrive in **Chacao** on the north coast. The town has a small, attractive plaza; and there's a pretty church and old wooden houses in Chacao Viejo, east of the port. Black-necked swans arrive here in summer from their winter habitat in Paraguay and Brazil. The *Panamericana* heads west from here to Ancud, while a coastal road branches south, towards Quemchi. Turn north off the *Panamericana* along the coast to reach **Caulín**; the road is only passable at low tide. There are good beaches here; in Caulín you can see many black-necked swans in summer and flamingos in autumn.

Pumillahue

Pumillahue is 27 km southwest of Ancud, on the Pacific coast. About 10 km before is **Mar Brava**, a vast, deserted curved beach, wonderful for horse riding. About 3 km away from Pumillahue at Puñihuíl, there is colony of both Humboldt and Magellanic penguins as well as sea otters, sea lions and a wide range of marine birdlife, situated on an island facing the beach. Guided tour with local fishermen (in Spanish and often with exaggerated hand gestures making up for the lack of informed commentary), US$7. The penguins are there from October to late March. The best time to see them is in the early morning or evening. For an account of penguin-watching at Puñihuíl, read Ben Richards' *The Mermaid and the Drunks* (Weidengeld, 2003). Catch one of the two or three buses that leave daily from Ancud, take a tour, taxi, or hitch.

South of Pumillahue a poor road continues south some 5 Km to Duhatao. From here it is a a wild coastal walk of seven hours to Chepu (see below). The route is difficult to follow so take extra food and a tent and wear light-coloured clothes in summer to protect against *tábanos* (horseflies).

Chepu and around

Twenty six kilometres south of Ancud, a dirt road heads west from the Pan-American Highway to the coast at Chepu, famed for its river and sea fishing. It is a base for exploring the drowned forest and the waterways of the Río Chepu and its tributaries (a result of the 1960 *maremoto*). There is a wide range of bird life here and excellent opportunities for kayak and boat trips and horse riding. Chepu is also the entrance to the northern sector of the **Parque Nacional Chiloé** (see page 425). From here, it is a 1½-hour walk to Playa Aulén, which has superb forested dunes and an extinct volcano. At **Río Anguay** (also known as Puerto Anguay), there is a campsite and *refugio*.

Boat trips can be organized in Río Anguay to **Laguna Coluco**, one hour up the Río Butalcura (a tributary of the Río Chepu). Two-day trips, navigating the ríos Grande, Carihueco and Butalcura, usually start further inland and finish at Río Anguay. These can be arranged in Ancud (see page 415).

For Sleeping and Eating price codes and other relevant information, see Essentials pages 35-42.

⊜ Sleeping

Ancud *p411, map p412*

In summer the school on C Chacabuco is used as a cheap *albergue*. Many people wait at the bus station offering accommodation in private homes. These are generally decent and in the **F-G** range per person.

AL-A Hostería Ancud, San Antonio 30, T065-622340, www.panamericanahoteles.cl. Overlooking bay, wonderful views, attractive, reasonably comfortable, though rooms are dark and past their prime, friendly and helpful, restaurant, traditional Chilote carvings, English spoken, tours offered.

A Galeón Azul, Libertad 751, T065-622567, www.hotelgaleonazul.cl. Cramped heated rooms with cable TV. Rather basic for the price but excellent views. Bright restaurant.

A-B Don Lucas, Costanera 906, T065-620950, www.hoteldonlucas.cl. Newly renovated. Nice rooms, some with sea view, though these can be stuffy in summer. Disabled access, Wi-Fi. A good choice.

B Hostal Vista al Mar, Costanera 918, T065-622617, www.vistaalmar.cl. **C-D** singles. With bath, **E-F** per person in dorms with shared bath, also self-catering apartments. Views over the bay, heating, internet, laundry, dinner served in barn in summer.

B-C Balai, Pudeto 169, T065-622541, www.hotelbalai.cl. With heating, laundry, parking, restaurant, cable TV, interesting local paintings, models and artefacts on display. Tours arranged.

B-C Mundo Nuevo, Costanera 748, T065-628383, www.newworld.cl. **C-D** singles, **F** per person in dorms. Some rooms with bath. With breakfast, comfortable, great views over the bay, lots of info, heating, good showers, Wi-Fi, kitchen facilities, bike rental, car hire, 1 room has a boat-bed. Tours offered. English, German spoken. Highly recommended.

C Hostal Chiloé, O'Higgins 274, T065-622869, hchiloe@yahoo.es. **E** singles. With bath, food served, laundry service, Wi-Fi.

C Hostal Lluhay, Cochrane 458, T/F065-622656, www.hostal-lluhay.cl. **D-E** singles. Meals served, friendly, attentive, heating, Wi-Fi, nice lounge, views. Recommended.

C Madryn, Bellavista 491, T065-622128, www.hotelmadryn.cl. With bath, cable TV and breakfast, also meals, clean. Laundry, internet, tours arranged.

C-D Hospedaje Bellavista, Bellavista 449, T065-622384. With bath. **F-G** per person in dorms with shared bath. Good breakfast, very friendly, meals served.

C-D Hostal San José, Las Américas 661, T065-629944, hostalsanjose6@hotmail.com. **E-F** singles. With breakfast, good family atmosphere, nice views from lounge, clean, hot water, some rooms with bath, use of kitchen, internet, tours offered, bicycle hire, friendly. Recommended.

D Hospedaje Ancud, Los Carrera 821, T065-622296, macriser@latinmail.com. **F** singles. Nice house, clean, friendly, kitchen facilities.

D Hospedaje Austral, Aníbal Pinto 1318, T065-624847, hospedajeaustral@hotmail.com. **F** singles. Cosy wooden house, friendly owners, with breakfast. laundry and kitchen facilities (US$1 charge). Convenient for municipal bus terminal but not Cruz del sur.

D Hospedaje O'Higgins 6, O'Higgins 6, T065-622266. **F** singles. With breakfast, bath, spacious, interesting objets d'art, near the sea, nice views, recommended.

F-G San Bernardo, Errázuriz 395, T065-622657. Price per person in dorms, clean.

Camping

Arena Gruesa, Costanera Norte 290, Arena Gruesa beach, at north end of Baquedano, T065-623428, arenagruesa@yahoo.com.

Chiloé, Arena Gruesa beach, at north end of Baquedano, T065-622961.

Playa Gaviotas, 5 km north, T09-9653 8096. Also has *cabañas*.

Playa Larga Huicha, 9 km north. Hot water and electricity.

East of Ancud p413
A Caulín Lodge, Caulín, T09-9643 7986, www.caulinlodge.cl. Native Chilote trees grow in the garden, *cabañas* and a sauna available. Decent restaurant. Horse riding and other trips offered.

Pumillahue p413
AL-C Pinguinland Cabañas, at Puñihuil, between Mar Brava and the penguin colony, T09-90194273, pinguinland@hotmail.com. Clean *cabañas* for 5-7 people, also double rooms and expensive meals. Spectacular view if the weather is good.

Chepu and around p413
Armando Pérez and **Sonia Díaz**, T09-9653 9241, offer agrotourism stays. Make cheese, tend cattle and sheep, and go for good walks in the Chepu area. To get there from Ancud, travel 26 km south on Route 5, turn right (east) for 5 km to Coipomó, there turn left, and after 3.5 km turn right. The farm is on the left after 2 km.

Eating

Ancud p411, map p412
Restaurants in Ancud tend to be inconsistent in the quality of their food.
*** Kurantón**, Prat 94, T065-623090. Serves good *curantos* and seafood.
*** Restaurant Quetalmahue**, 12 km west of Ancud on the road to Faro Corona and Fuerte Ahui, T09-9033 3930. The best place for traditional *curantos al hoyo* (cooked in the ground, daily in summer). Excellent but service tends to slacken when the owner is absent.
***-* Sacho**, Mercado Municipal, local 7, T065-622918. Renowned for its *curantos*. Huge portions, not fancy but very reasonable; several similar places in the same arcade.
* **El Cangrejo**, Dieciocho 155. Highly recommended for seafood.

* **El Pinguinito**, off Prat, near the market. Seriously cheap, lunches only. Also look in the market area, where there are *colaciones*.
* **El Timón**, Yungay y Allende. Small, cheap and good value.
* **Hamburguería**, Av Prat. Much better than name suggests, good seafood.
* **La Pincoya**, Prat 61, T065-622613. Seafood next to harbour.

Bars and clubs

Ancud p411, map p412
Lumière, Ramírez 278, The place to be seen for the younger crowd. Also serve good food.
Retro's Pub, Maipú 615, off Pudeto, T065-626410. Open Mon-Fri 1100-0300, Sat 2000-0400, Sun 2000-0400 in summer. Appealing ambience, food (including vegetarian fare) and good cocktails.

East of Ancud p413
***-* Ostras Caulín**, Caulín, T09-9643 7005, www.ostrascaulin.cl. Excellent, very fresh oysters served in any number of ways.
** Restaurant Pilón de Oro**, Sommermier 20, Chacao, T09-9839 3651. Good Chilote fare.
There's also restaurant and *hospedaje* at Freire 35.

Pumillahue p413
There are 3 restaurants at Puñihuil with similar menus and prices. The best of these is probably **Bahía Puñuhuil**, T09-9655 6780, punihuil@gmail.com, who also offer trips to see the penguins.

Activities and tours

Ancud p411, map p412
There is a travel agent at Bellavista 493, selling airline tickets. For bicycle hire try the shop at Ramírez 311, US$1.50 per hr or US$8 per day.

Tour operators
Aki Turismo, patio of Mercado Municipal, T065-545253, www.akiturismo chiloe.cl. Good-value trips to the penguin colony.
Austral Adventures, Costanera 904, T065-625977, www.austral-adventures.com. Small-group bespoke tours of the archipelago and northern Patagonia (including Parque Pumalín), hiking or by sea, bilingual guides, US-run. Recommended.
Patagón Chiloe, Bellavista 491, T065-622128, www.patagonchiloe.cl. Tours to the Penguin colony, Chepu and other parts of Chiloé.

Chepu and around *p413*
This area offers great opportunities for horse riding, with long beaches that are perfect for a windswept gallop.
Alfonso Bergara, Chepu, T099-9517 0358. Fishing trips around Chepu.
Carlos Oyarzún, T09-9657 4021. An independent guide based in Ancud offering sit-on-top kayak tours.
Mirador de Chepu, T09-9227 4517, www.chepu.cl, privately run information centre with its own pier with views of the wetlands, information on flora and fauna, café, kayak rentals, boat trips, trekking info. Also transport to and from Ancud.
Sr Zuñipe or **Sr Uroa**, ask at the *refugio* in Río Anguay. US$6 per hr for horse riding.

O Shopping

Ancud *p411, map p412*
There are 2 covered markets both selling a mixture of fresh produce and handicrafts: Mercado Municipal, Prat y Libertad, and the Feria Municipal, Prat y Pedro Montt.
El Gran Pez, Ramírez y Blanco, has a good selection of books.

⊖ Transport

Ancud *p411, map p412*
For ferry services between the mainland and Chacao, see page 411.

Bus
Local Buses leave Ancud from Terminal Rural, Pedro Montt 538. To **Pumillahue** and **Mar Brava**, 2 buses daily Mon-Fri with **Buses Mar Brava**, 1 bus Sat; to **Faro Corona** and **Fuerte Ahui**, 2 buses each daily Mon-Sat; to **Quemchi** (via Linao and coast), 2 hrs, US$2.
Long distance Municipal terminal on eastern outskirts of Ancud at Av Prat y Marcos Vera, reached by bus No 1 or **Pudeto colectivos** Cruz del Sur terminal on Los Carrera in the town centre. To **Castro**, frequent, 1½ hrs, **Cruz del Sur**, US$3, or **Queilen Bus**, US$2.50; to **Chonchi**, US$5; to **Quellón**, Cruz del Sur, 11 daily, US$7. To **Santiago**, Cruz del Sur, 24 hrs, US$40, salón cama US$60; to **Puerto Montt**, 3 hrs, frequent, with Cruz del Sur, US$7 and Queilén Bus, US$6.

Car
Mechanic Errázuriz 414, (spare parts have to be ordered in from Puerto Montt).

Taxi
Taxis charge US$22 to the penguin colony at Puñihuil.

⊕ Directory

Ancud *p411, map p412*
Banks ATM at Banco BCI, Ramírez, 1 block from the plaza; *casa de cambio* on same block. **Laundry** Lava Fresh, Prat 171, T065-628844. Same-day service, home delivery;. **Police** Baquedano y O'Higgins. **Post office** Pudeto y Blanco Encalada, corner of Plaza de Armas. **Telephone** Plaza de Armas, open Mon-Sat 0700-2200; ENTEL, Pudeto 219, with internet; Los Carrera 823.

Towards Castro

There are two alternative routes from Ancud to Castro: direct along the Pan-American Highway, crossing rolling hills, forest and agricultural land, or the more leisurely route via the east coast. This is a dramatic journey on unpaved roads that plunge up and down forested hills. The route passes through small farming and fishing communities and offers a real insight into rural life in Chiloé. The two main towns along the coastal route, Quemchi and Dalcahue, can also be reached by roads branching off the Pan-American Highway.
▸▸ *For listings, see pages 420-423.*

Along the east coast ●❼⊛❺▲● ▸▸ pp 420-423.

Quemchi and around

South of Chacao is the small village of **Hueihue**, where fresh oysters can be bought, US$25 for 100. Further south, before Quemchi, is a small lake with model sailing boats. Quemchi itself is a quiet town with long beaches, overlooking a bay speckled with wooded islands. There is a small tourist information booth in the plaza. A short walk up the road north towards **Linao** leads to high ground from where there are views to the temperate rainforest on the mainland. Miniature ornamental boats are made in the village. Some 4 km from Quemchi is **Isla Aucar**, once linked by bridge (now ruined), where black-necked swans can be seen.

The road from Quemchi to Dalcahue (50 km) passes many places that are the essence of Chiloé. The road rises up and down steep forested hills, rich with flowers, past salmon farms and views of distant bays. Some 20 km from Quemchi is a turn-off to **Quicaví**, legendary as the home to the witches of Chiloé; a further few kilometres brings you to **Tenaún**, a beautiful village with a church dating from 1837, which is now a UNESCO World Heritage Site – trips to neighbouring islands such as Mechuque are easy to arrange here. You will pass numerous small communities with churches and views to the coast before you reach Dalcahue.

Dalcahue and around

Some 74 km south of Ancud via the Pan-American Highway, Dalcahue is more easily reached from Castro, 30 km further south. The wooden church on the main square dates from the 19th century and is a UNESCO World Heritage Site. There is a tourist kiosk in season. Dalcahue is one of the main ports for boats to the offshore islands, including Quinchao (see below) and the **Chauques Islands**. These are a group of 16 islands east of Dalcahue, interconnected by sandbars, which are accessible at low tide. The largest is **Mechuque** (reached by bus from Tenaún), which has one village and offers splendid walking country. There are beautiful views of the mainland in good weather.

Quinchao → population 3500.

The island of Quinchao is a short ferry journey from Dalcahue. Passing the pretty village of Curaço de Velez, you reach the main settlement, **Achao**, 25 km southeast of Dalcahue. This is a large fishing village serving the smaller islands offshore, with a boarding school attended by pupils from outlying districts. Its wooden church, built in 1730, is the oldest surviving church in Chiloé. Saved by a change of wind from a fire that destroyed much of the town in 1784, it is a fine example of Chilote Jesuit architecture and contains a small

Curanto

Particularly associated with Puerto Montt and Chiloé, *curanto* is a very filling fish, meat and seafood stew, which is delicious despite the rather odd combination of ingredients. Though of pre-Hispanic origins, it has developed by adding new ingredients according to new influences. In its original pre-Conquest form, a selection of fish was wrapped in leaves and baked over hot stones in a hole – some specialists wonder if this way of cooking may have come from the Pacific islands, where pit baking is still practised. With the arrival of the Spanish, the dish was modified to include pork, chicken and white wine. Today, it is often cooked in a large pan and advertised as *pullmay* or *curanto en olla*, to distinguish it from the pit-baked form.

museum ① *US$1*. Achao has a seasonal **tourist office** ① *Serrano y Progreso, Dec-Mar only*. A beautiful road leads 9 km south of Achao to the small village of **Quinchao** in a secluded bay at the foot of a hill; an important religious festival is held in the fine church here on 8 December (see page 422). For more information, see www.islaquinchao.com.

With patience and persistence, boats can be found to take you from Achao to outlying islands, where facilities are basic and shops non-existent but lodging can be found with families; ask around. It is recommended to go with a local friend, if possible.

Castro ◗◗◗◗▲◗◗ » pp420-423.

The capital of Chiloé, with a population of just under 30,000, lies 88 km south of Ancud on a fjord on the east coast. It is a small, friendly town, full of bars and seafood restaurants where Chilotes from remote regions sit drinking *chicha*, eating *cazuela* and swapping tall stories. The centre is on a promontory, from which there is a steep drop to the port. Castro is the major tourist centre on the island.

Ins and outs

Getting there Castro is Chiloé's transport hub. There are many buses south to Quellón (hourly) and north to Ancud and Puerto Montt. **Cruz del Sur** have buses continuing north to Valdivia, Temuco and Santiago (several daily). Many buses serve the more isolated Chilote communities from the Municipal Bus Terminal. Although most services leave from Quellón, Castro is occasionally used as a port for passenger services to Chaitén and Puerto Montt.

Getting around There are some *colectivos* and public buses serving the barrios high above the town near the *media luna*, but it is unlikely that you will need to use these. It is only a half-hour walk up there in any case.

Tourist information A kiosk is run by hotels and agencies on the Plaza de Armas, opposite the cathedral. **CONAF** is in Gamboa behind the Gobernación building.

Sights

On the Plaza de Armas is the large wooden **cathedral**, unmissable in bright lilac and orange, designed by the Italian architect, Eduardo Provosoli, and dating from 1906. One block south is the **Museo Regional** ① *C Esmeralda, summer Mon-Sat 0930-2000, Sun 1030-1300, winter Mon-Sat 0930-1300, 1500-1830, Sun 1030-1300*, with displays on the history, handicrafts and mythology of Chiloé, as well as photos of the effects of the 1960 earthquake. Further south, on the waterfront, is the **Feria de Artesanía**, where local woollen articles, such as hats, sweaters, gloves, can be bought, although many of the articles sold are imported from elsewhere in South America. Nearby are several new *palafito* restaurants, built on stilts above the water. More traditional *palafitos* can be seen on the northern side of town and by the bridge over the Río Gamboa.

There are good views of the city from **Mirador La Virgen** on Millantuy hill above the cemetery. **Museo de Arte Moderno** ① *T065-635454, www.mamchiloe.cl, Jan-Feb daily 1000-1800, Nov, Dec, Abr 1100-1400, closed May-Oct*, is in the Parque Municipal, about 3 km northwest of the centre, and is reached by following Calle Galvarino Riveros up the hill west of town, from where there are fine views. Passing the Parque Municipal, Calle Galvarino Riveros becomes a small track heading out into the thick forests of the interior, with several small farmsteads. There is also a pleasant two-hour circular walk through woods and fields

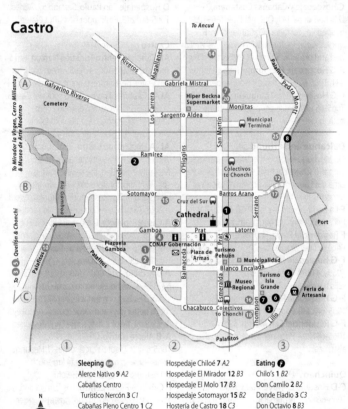

Castro

Sleeping
Alerce Nativo **9** *A2*
Cabañas Centro
  Turístico Nercón **3** *C1*
Cabañas Pleno Centro **1** *C2*
Cabañas Trayen **5** *C1*
Casa Blanca **2** *C2*
Casita Española **4** *B2*
Hospedaje América **16** *C3*

Hospedaje Chiloé **7** *A2*
Hospedaje El Mirador **12** *B3*
Hospedaje El Molo **17** *B3*
Hospedaje Sotomayor **15** *B2*
Hostería de Castro **18** *C3*
Lidia Low **14** *A2*
Palafito Hostel **10** *C1*
Residencial Capullito **20** *A2*
Unicornio Azul **25** *B3*

Eating
Chilo's **1** *B2*
Don Camilo **2** *B2*
Donde Eladio **3** *C3*
Don Octavio **8** *B3*
El Curanto **4** *C3*
La Playa **6** *C3*
Sacho **7** *C3*

N

200 metres
200 yards

to **Puntilla Ten Ten** and the peninsula opposite Castro; turn off the Pan-American Highway 2 km north of town. **Nercón**, 4 km south, has a wooden church, which was restored in 1996.

⊙ Towards Castro listings

For Sleeping and Eating price codes and other relevant information, see Essentials pages 35-42.

⊕ Sleeping

Quemchi and around *p417*

C Hospedaje y Cabañas Costanera, D Bahamonde 141, Quemchi, T065-691230, hospedaje_costanera@latinmail.com. **F** singles. *Cabañas* for up to 5 people, as well as bed and breakfast in rooms with shared bath.
F-G Hospedaje El Embrujo, Pedro Montt 431, T065-651262. Basic, price per person.
F-G Hospedaje La Tranquera, Yungay 40, T065-651250. Price per person without bath, basic.

Dalcahue and around *p417*
On Mechuque, accommodation is available with the schoolteacher's son or with Señora Dina del Carmen Paillacar, who also serves good meals.
F La Feria, Rodríguez 17, T065-641293. Price per person without bath, basic.
F Residencial Playa, Rodríguez 9. Price per person. Basic.
F-G Hospedaje Mary, Tte Merino 10, T065-641260. Price per person. Also sells handicrafts.
F-G Hospedaje Puteman, Freire 305, T065-641330. Price per person. Clean, basic.
F-G Residencial San Martín, San Martín 1, T065-641207. Price per person. Basic, clean, also meals.

Quinchao *p417*
C-D Hostería La Nave, Prat y Aldea, Achao, T065-661219, hosterialanave@latinmail.com. Breakfast provided, cheaper rooms without bath, restaurant with fine views over bay.

C-D Plaza, Plaza de Armas, Achao, T065-661283. With bath and breakfast, clean, good.
D Hospedaje Achao, Serrano 061, Achao, T065-661373. Without bath, good, clean.
D Hospedaje Chilhue, Zañartu 021, Achao. Without bath, with breakfast, clean.
D Hospedaje São Paulo, Serrano 52, Achao, T065-661245. Basic, poor beds, hot water.

Castro *p418, map p419*
AL Cabañas Centro Turístico Nercón, Km 5 south of Castro, T065-632985. With bath, hot water, heating, restaurant, tennis court.
AL-A Cabañas Trayen, Km 5 south of Castro, T065-633633, www.trayenchiloe.com. Cheaper off season, *cabañas* with lovely views over the Fiordo de Castro.
AL-A Hostería de Castro, Chacabuco 202, T065-632301, www.hosteriadecastro.cl. Recently expanded, the new section is spacious and comfortable, with wonderful views and nice suites. Good restaurant. Avoid the tired and noisy rooms in the old section.
A Casita Española, Los Carrera 359, T/F065-635186, www.hosteriadecastro.cl/ce. Same ownership as the Hostería de Castro. Heating, cable TV, parking.
A Unicornio Azul, Pedro Montt 228, T065-632359, www.hotelunicornioazul.cl. Good views over bay, comfortable, but has seen much better days and some rooms are pokey. Restaurant, helpful staff, some English spoken.
A-B Alerce Nativo, O'Higgins 808, T065-632267, hotelalerc@surnet.cl. Heating, breakfast, also has *cabañas* (4 km south of Castro), and restaurant. Helpful.
B Cabañas Pleno Centro, Los Carrera 346, T065-635092. 2-person *cabañas*, also larger version with kitchen.
B Palafito Hostel, Riquelme 1210, T065-531 008, www.palafitohostel.com. With bath. Located over the water in a restored

traditional *palafito* building. Friendly, helpful staff, good breakfast, Wi-Fi. Tours arranged. Recommended.

B-C Casa Blanca, Los Carrera 308, T/F065-632726, nelysald@surnet.cl. With breakfast, cheaper rooms without bath (**E** per person), clean, modern, warm, also *cabañas*, sleep 6.

C Hospedaje El Mirador, Barros Arana 127, T065-633795, maboly@yahoo.com. **E** singles. Good breakfast, kitchen facilities, good views, internet, laundry, very clean and friendly, highly recommended.

C Hospedaje Sotomayor, Sotomayor 452, T065-632464. **F** singles. With breakfast, quiet, small beds.

C Serrano 407. **F** singles. With breakfast, friendly, warm water.

C-D Hospedaje América, Chacabuco 215, T065-634364. **F** singles. With breakfast. Friendly, very good food – "our tourists arrive thin and leave fat" – cable TV, shared bath.

C-D Hospedaje Chiloé, San Martín 739. **F** singles. With breakfast, clean. Recommended.

C-D Hospedaje El Molo, Barros Arana 140, T065-635026, elmolochiloe@gmail.com. **F** singles. With breakfast, clean, comfortable, cooking facilities, friendly, secure. Recommended.

C-D Residencial Capullito, San Martín 709. **F** singles. Clean, friendly, quiet.

D Lidia Low, San Martín 890. **F-G** singles. With good breakfast, warm showers, use of kitchen.

D San Martín 879. **F-G** singles. With big breakfast, central, clean. Recommended.

Camping

Llicaldad, Esmeralda 269, Km 6 south of Castro, T065-635080. One of several sites along road south towards Chonchi. *Cabañas* also available.

Pudú, 10 km north on the Pan-American Highway, T/F065-632476. Hot showers, sites with light, water, children's games, also *cabañas*.

❶ Eating

Along the east coast *p417*
There are numerous small restaurants along the harbour and around the market in Dalcahue, serving excellent and cheap seafood. Note that if you ask for *té*, you will be served a mug of white wine.

❦ **Hostería La Nave**, Quinchao, see Sleeping, above.

❦ **Restaurant Centenario**, Bahamonde 360, Quemchi. Good, cheap fare.

❦ **Restaurant Central**, Achao. Simple, good.

❦ **Restaurant La Dalca**, Freire 502, Dalcahue. Good cheap food. Recommended.

Castro *p418, map p419*
You may have difficulty tracking down some breakfast before 0900. Palafito restaurants near the **Feria Artesanía** on the waterfront offer good food and good value, including Brisas del Mar, La Amistad and Rapu Nui. There are also very cheap restaurants by the municipal bus terminal. In the market, try *milcaos*, fried potato cakes with meat stuffing.

❦❦ **Años Luz**, Plaza de Armas. Classic pub and restaurant.

❦❦ **Donde Eladio**, Lillo 97. Meat and seafood specialities.

❦❦ **La Playa**, Lillo 93. Recommended for fish and meat.

❦ **Chilo's**, San Martín 459. Good lunches.

❦ **Don Camilo**, Ramírez 566. Good food, not expensive.

❦ **Don Octavio**, Pedro Montt 261. Good food, good value.

❦ **El Curanto**, Lillo 67. Seafood including *curanto*. Recommended.

❦ **Sacho**, Thompson 213. Good sea views. Recommended.

Cafés

La Brújula del Cuerpo, Plaza de Armas. Good coffee and snacks.

Stop Inn Café, Martín Ruiz shopping centre, Gamboa s/n. Good coffee.

🍸 Bars and clubs

Castro *p418, map p419*
Kaweshkar Lounge, Blanco Encalada 31, Minimalist bar with wide range of cocktails and occasional live music. Also serves food.

✳ Festivals and events

Quinchao *p417*
8 Dec People come from all over Chiloé for Día de la Virgen and watch as a huge model of the Virgin is carried with great reverence to the church.

🛍 Shopping

Dalcahue *p417*
Dalcahue weekly market is held Sun 0700-1300. It has quality goods, but bargaining is practically impossible, and in recent years it has become somewhat overrun with tourists. It's good for *curantos*, though.

Castro *p418, map p419*
CDs of typical Chilote music are widely available around town.
Annay Libros, Serrano 357 and **El Tren Libros**, Thompson 229. Both of these bookshops sell books on Chilote history and culture, mostly in Spanish and cheaper than in Santiago bookshops.
Hiper Beckna, Sargento Aldea y O'Higgins. Supermarket with good bakery.
Mercado Artesanal, on the wharf. Good-quality woollens at reasonable prices.
Mercado Municipal, Yumbel, off Pilato Samuel Ulloa. Good fish and vegetables.

🚶 Activities and tours

Dalcahue and around *p417*
Altue Active Travel, 3 km south of Dalcahue, reservations from Encomenderos 83, piso 2,

Las Condes, Santiago, T02-232 1103, www.altue.com. Sea kayaking.

Castro *p418, map p419*
Tour operators usually charge around US$25 to Parque Nacional Chiloé.
Costa Sur, O'Higgins 670, piso 3, of 11, T065-632788, www.turismocostasur.cl. Offers a variety of tours throughout the island. Also trekking.
Sergio Márquez, Felipe Moniel 565, T065-632617. Very knowledgeable local guide with transport.
Turismo Isla Grande, Thompson 241, Transmarchilay and Navimag agency.
Turismo Pehuén, Blanco Encalada 208, T065-635254, www.turismopehuen.cl. LanChile agents, also offer horse-riding excursions and trips to the national park, the penguin colony and the smaller islands.

🚌 Transport

Dalcahue and around *p417*
Buses to **Castro**, hourly, 40 mins, US$1.50; daily bus to **Puerto Montt**, via Ancud, US$9. *Colectivos* to **Castro** and **Achao**, US$2.
To reach **Mechuque**, catch the bus from Tenaún, departs Wed 1730, returns Thu, 2½ hrs, US$3.50 one-way.

Quinchao *p417*
Arriagada buses to **Ancud**, 5 daily; to **Castro**, 4 daily, US$2.50. There's a frequent ferry service to **Dalcahue**, free for pedestrians and cyclists.

Castro *p418, map p419*
Bus
There are 2 bus terminals. Cruz del Sur services depart from Cruz del Sur terminal, San Martín behind the cathedral, T065-632389. Other services, including most buses to rural communities, leave from the Municipal Terminal, San Martín, 600 block (2 blocks further north).

To **Quemchi**, 1 daily, with Quilen Bus; to **Dalcahue**, frequent, with Gallardo and Arriagada, also *colectivos* from San Martín 815; to **Tenaún**, daily 1200; to **Achao** via Dalcahue and Curaço de Vélez, 4 daily Mon-Sat, 3 daily Sun, with Arriagada, US\$3, last return from Achao 1730. To **Chonchi**, frequent, with Cruz del Sur, Queilén Bus, minibuses and *colectivos* (from Ramírez y San Martín and Esmeralda y Chacabuco); to **Puqueldón**, 4 daily Mon-Sat, with Gallardo, US\$2; to **Queilen**, 6 daily, with Queilén Bus, US\$3.50; to **Quellón**, frequent, with Cruz del Sur/Trans Chiloé, US\$3.50. To **Cucao** for the Parque Nacional Chiloé, 6 daily in summer, 1 daily in winter, with Arroyo and Ocean Bus, US\$3, avoid Fri, when the service is crowded with school children.

There are also frequent services to **Ancud**, 1 hr, US\$3 and **Puerto Montt**, 3 hrs, US\$9, with Cruz del Sur, Trans Chiloé and Queilén Bus, US\$6. Cruz del Sur also runs to **Osorno**, **Valdivia**, **Temuco**, **Concepción** and **Santiago**. Bus Norte serves **Ancud**, **Puerto Montt**, **Osorno** and **Santiago** daily. Cruz del Sur and Queilén Bus run weekly services to **Punta Arenas**, 36 hrs, US\$70.

Ferry

If for whatever reason the Quellón ferry port is out of action, the Naviera Austral services to **Chaitén** on the mainland depart from Castro, 4 per week Dec-early Mar, reduced service off season, 5 hrs, passengers US\$33, cars US\$135, cycles US\$13. Some ships continue from Chaitén to **Puerto Montt**. Schedules are subject to last-minute changes due to inclement weather.

⊙ Directory

Castro *p418, map p419*
Banks Banco de Chile, Plaza de Armas, ATM, accepts TCs (at a poor rate); BCI, Plaza de Armas, MasterCard and Visa ATM; Julio Barrientos, Chacabuco 286, cash and TCs, better rates than the banks. **Internet** Throughout the town centre. **Laundry** Clean Centre, Serrano 440 ; Lavandería Adolfo, Blanco Encalada 96, quick, reasonably priced; Lavaseco Unic, Gamboa 594. **Medical services** Muñoz de Las Carreras, near police station, surgery Mon-Fri 1700-2000, recommended. **Post office** West side of Plaza de Armas. **Telephone** Latorre 289; Entel, O'Higgins between Sotomayor and Gamboa; also private centre at Latorre 275.

Chonchi to Quellón

→ *Colour maps 4, C1/5, A2.*

The Pan-American Highway continues south to Quellón, the southernmost port in Chiloé, with paved side roads leading east to Chonchi and west to Cucao. From Chonchi, a partially paved road continues southeast to Queilen. Winding across forested hills, this is probably the most attractive route on the island, especially in autumn; numerous tracks branch off to deserted beaches where you can walk for hours and hear nothing but the splashing of dolphins in the bay. The ferry to Lemuy sails from a port just south of Chonchi on this road.
➠ *For listings, see pages 426-428.*

Chonchi and around

A picturesque fishing village 23 km south of Castro, Chonchi is a good base for exploring the island. Known as the *Ciudad de los Tres Pisos* (city built on three levels), it was, until the opening of the Panama Canal in 1907, a stopping point for sailing ships. In the years that followed, it was the cypress capital of Chile: big fortunes were made in the timber industry and grand wooden mansions were built in the town. In the 1950s, Chonchi boomed as a free port but, in the 1970s, it lost that status to Punta Arenas. Its harbour is now a supply point for salmon farms almost as far south as Coyhaique.

On the main plaza is the **church**, built in neoclassical style in 1880. Its impressive tower was blown off in a storm in March 2002 and has been rebuilt. There is a **tourist information kiosk** one block uphill from here in summer. From the plaza, **Calle Centenario** drops steeply to the harbour, lined with several attractive but sadly neglected wooden mansions. The small **Museo de Tradiciones Chonchinas** is located in an old house at No 116, with videos on the churches of Chiloé, including the 18th-century church 5 km north of Chonchi at Vilopulli. Fishing boats bring in the early morning catch, which is carried straight into the new **market** on the seafront.

In the bay opposite Chonchi lies the island of **Lemuy**. It covers 97 sq km and offers many good walks along quiet unpaved tracks through undulating pastures and woodland. From the ferry dock (free crossing for pedestrians), a road runs east across the island, passing a fine 19th-century wooden church at **Ichuac** before reaching **Puqueldón**. This is the main settlement on the island and is built on a very steep hill stretching down to the port. There's a post office and a telephone centre here. From Puqueldón, the road continues a further 16 km on a ridge high above the sea, passing small hamlets, with views of the water and the patchwork of fields. There are old churches at **Aldachildo**, 9 km east of Puqueldón, and at **Detif**, in the extreme south of the island.

Some 46 km southeast of Chonchi, **Queilen** is a pretty fishing village on a long finger-shaped peninsula. On the north side is a sandy beach, which curves round the head of the peninsula, while on the south side is the old wooden pier, which doubles as the port. There are fine views across the straits to Tanqui Island and the mainland.

The west coast

West of Chonchi at Km 12 is **Huillinco**, a charming village on Lago Huillinco. Beyond here the narrow and sinuous paved road continues west to **Cucao**, one of the few settlements on the west coast of Chiloé. The immense 20-km-long beach is battered by thundering Pacific surf and dangerous undercurrents, making it one of the most dramatic places along the whole coast of Chile.

Cucao lies at the edge of the southern sector (35,207 ha) of the **Parque Nacional Chiloé** ① *T065-532501/T09-9932 9193, US$3*. The park, in three sections, covers extensive areas of the wild and uninhabited western side of the island, much of it filled by temperate rainforest. Wildlife includes the Chilote fox and pudú deer. There are over 110 species of bird resident here, including cormorants, gulls, penguins and flightless steamer ducks.

You can take a car as far as the **administration centre** ① *1 km north of Cucao, T099-9932 9193, daily*, at the entrance, which has limited information and a guest bungalow for use by visiting scientists; applications to **CONAF** via your embassy. There are also decent camping facilities. The centre provides maps of the park, but they are not very accurate and should not be used to locate *refugios* within the park.

A path, affording great views, runs 3 km north from the administration centre to **Laguna Huelde** and then north for a further 12 km to **Cole Cole**. Once you reach **Río Anay**, 9 km beyond Cole Cole, you can wade or swim across the river to reach a beautiful, secluded beach from where you can enjoy the sight of dolphins playing in the huge breakers. The journey can also be made on horseback; allow nine hours for the round trip. Take lots of water and your own food. There are several other walks in the national park, but signposts are limited and *tábanos* are bad in summer, so wear light-coloured clothing.

Quellón

The southernmost port in Chiloé, located 92 km south of Castro, Quellón has suffered its fair share of misfortunes in recent years. In 2002, the arrival of the lethal *marea roja* microorganism (see page 39) caused the collapse of the shellfish industry, provoking demonstrations from fishermen and dockers who destroyed part of the pier. As a result,

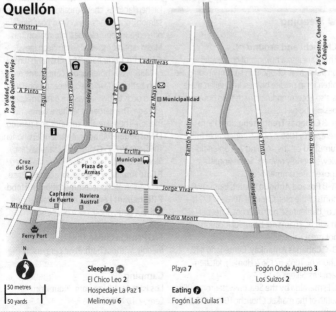

Quellón

Sleeping 🛏	Playa **7**	Fogón Onde Aguero **3**
El Chico Leo **2**		Los Suizos **2**
Hospedaje La Paz **1**	Eating 🍴	
Melimoyu **6**	Fogón Las Quilas **1**	

the passenger ferry services from Quellón to Chaitén and Puerto Montt were suspended and have only recently returned to normal. **Tourist information** ⓘ *Vargas y García* is often closed, even in summer. Note that the street numbering system in Quellón is unfathomable.

There is not much to interest the traveller here, although the **Museo Amador Cardenas Paredes** ⓘ *Pedro Montt 309*, has an odd collection of antique typewriters and sewing machines, and there are pleasant beaches nearby: **Viejo**, 4 km west, where there is an old wooden church; **Punta de Lapa**, 7 km west, and **Yaldad**, 9 km west along a pretty road over the hills. The launch *Puerto Bonito* sails around the bay in summer from the pier, three times daily in summer, US$16, passing Punta de Lapa, Isla Laitec and Quellón Viejo. A trip can be made to **Chaiguao**, 11 km east, where there is a Sunday morning market.

The far south of the island has been bought by a private foundation and has been turned into a nature sanctuary known as the **Parque Tantauco**. Covering some 120,000 ha of native woodland, wetlands, lagoons and rivers, it is home to a range of endangered wildlife. There are two campsites (no electricity) and 12 shortish trails. At present access is by sea only, from Quellón to **Inio** on the south coast. Transport can be arranged through the **park office** ⓘ *in Quellón, Av La Paz 068, T065-681064, www.parquetantauco.cl*, and further information is available from the **Fundación Futuro** ⓘ *Av Apoquindo 3000, piso 19, Las Condes, Santiago*.

◉ Chonchi to Quellón listings

For Sleeping and Eating price codes and other relevant information, see Essentials pages 35-42.

◉ Sleeping

Chonchi and around *p424*
There are also a number of *hospedajes* on Irarrázaval, Chonchi. In summer rooms are often let in private homes. In Queilen there is also accommodation in the big house beside the pier.
A-B Cabañas Treng Treng, José Pinto Pérez 420, T065-672532. Impeccable fully furnished cabins sleeping 2-7. Splendid views, friendly owners. Some English spoken. Recommended.
A-B Posada Antiguo Chalet, Irarrázaval s/n, north of the pier, Chonchi, T065-671221, fco_barrientos@hotmail.com. Cheaper in winter, charming, beautiful location, not great value.
B-C Cabañas Amankay, Centenario 410, Chonchi, T065-671367. Homely, kitchen facilities. Sleeps 4-10.
C Esmeralda by the Sea, on waterfront 100 m south of the market, Chonchi, T065-671328,

www.esmeraldabythesea.cl. **F** per person in dorms. Breakfast available, English spoken, kitchen facilities, cheap meals served (excellent salmon), good beds, canoe and boat trips offered, also rents bicycles, information. Mixed reports, especially as to cleanliness.
C Huildin, Centenario 102, Chonchi, T065-671388, www.hotelhuildin.com. Some rooms with bath, old fashioned, decent rooms with good beds but windows are onto an interior passage. The garden does have views though. There are also *cabañas* and parking.
D Hospedaje Mirador, Alvarez 198, Chonchi, T065-671351. **F-G** singles. With breakfast, friendly, clean, good value. Recommended.
F Café Amancay, Puqueldón, Lemuy. Price per person. Basic accommodation and food.
F Restaurant Lemuy, Lemuy. Clean, without bath, good, price per person. Food served only in high season.
F-G Pensión Chiloé, Queilen, is basic, friendly, without bath. Price per person.

Camping
Los Isleños, 1.5 km from Puqueldón, Lemuy, T099-9654 8498.

Los Manzanos, Aguirre Cerda y Juan Guillermo, T065-671263.

The west coast p424

There's a cheap *residencial* in Huillinco with good food, or you can stay at the post office. In the Parque Nacional, there is a *refugio* and camping at Cole Cole and another *refugio* at Anay, 9 km further north. The following accommodation is all in Cucao.

C Parador de Darwin, at park entrance, Cucao sector, T09-9799 9923. With breakfast, good food with vegetarian options, real coffee. Recommended camping also available.

C Posada Cucao, T065-633040/T09-8969855. With breakfast, hot water, great seafood meals, friendly. Recommended.

F Provisiones Pacífico. Small grocery store offering full board or demi-pension, friendly, good, clean, meals and homemade bread, but no hot water. Price per person. Recommended.

Camping

Lago Mar, 2 km east of Cucao, T065-635552, US$15 per site. One of several campsites in the area; check prices carefully first.

Quellón p425, map p425

The school on la Paz becomes a cheap *albergue* in summer, with dormitory accommodation.

B Melimoyu, Pedro Montt 369, T065-681250. Clean, good beds, parking.

C El Chico Leo, Pedro Montt 325, T065-681567, elchicoleo@telsur.cl. Cheaper without bath.

C-D Playa, Pedro Montt 427. **F** singles. With breakfast, without bath. Clean.

D Hospedaje La Paz, La Paz 370, T065-681207. **F** singles. With breakfast, hot water.

Camping

There are 5 sites at Punta de Lapa and sites without services at Chaiguao and Yaldad.

🍴 Eating

Chonchi and around p424

🍴-🍴 There are 6 *cocinarías* on the top floor of the new market serving traditional seafood.

🍴 **El Alerce**, Candelaria 308. Excellent value.

🍴 **El Trébol**, Irarrázabal 187, T065-671203. Good views over the harbour.

🍴 **La Quila**, Pedro Andrade 183, T065-671389. Cheap, good, popular with locals.

The west coast p424

🍴-🍴 **Las Luminarias** in Cucao sells excellent *empanadas de machas* (*machas* are local shellfish). There are several other cheap seafood restaurants in Cucao, among them El Caleuche, América and Brisas del Pacífico.

Quellón p425, map p425

🍴 **Fogón Las Quilas**, La Paz 053, T065-681206. Famous for shellfish. Recommended.

🍴 **Los Suizos**, Ladrilleros 399. Swiss cuisine.

🍴 **Fogón Onde Aguero**, La Paz s/n. Good cheep traditional food. Popular at lunchtime.

🍴 **Rucantú**, Pedro Montt. Good food and value. Lots more cheap seafood restaurants on the same street.

🍸 Bars and clubs

Chonchi and around p424

There are a couple of summer-only discos.

✺ Festivals and events

Chonchi and around p424

2nd week of Feb La Semana Chonchina is one of the series of Chilote festivals.

○ Shopping

Chonchi and around p424

Handicrafts are sold from the **Feria artesanal**, on the waterfront, and from the *parroquia*, next to the church (open Oct-Mar only).

In the summer many *artesanal* stalls open, a speciality being traditional woollen clothes.

Quellón *p425, map p425*
Traditional wooden carvings are sold at **Tallados Noly**, Gómez Garcia 361. Handicrafts from the **Feria Artesanal** on Ladrilleros y Gómez García.

▲ Activities and tours

The west coast *p424*
Many houses in Cucao rent horses at US$3.50 per hr, US$28 per day. It usually costs US$45 a day for the round trip on horseback to **Río Anay**. Bear in mind that the horses will be of varying tameness, and that if you hire a guide, you pay for his horse too.

Quellón *p425, map p425*
Horses can be hired for US$3.50 per hr; kayaks with a guide, US$4 per hr from the beach.

☻ Transport

Chonchi and around *p424*
Bus
Services depart from the main plaza to **Castro**, frequent, US$1; to **Puerto Montt**, US$7. Services to **Quellón** and **Queilen** (from Castro and Puerto Montt) and to **Cucao** (from Castro) also stop in Chonchi.

There are 4 buses daily Mon-Sat from Castro to **Lemuy**, and 6 daily Mon-Fri, 4 daily Sat, 3 daily Sun, from Castro to **Queilen**, Queilen Bus, 2 hrs, US$3.

Ferry
Services to **Lemuy** depart from Puerto Huicha, 4 km south of Chonchi, approximately every 30 mins, foot passengers travel free.

The west coast *p424*
6 buses a day to **Cucao** from Castro via Chonchi in season, US$3, last departure 1600, reduced service off season; hitching is very difficult.

Quellón *p425, map p425*
Bus
To **Castro**, frequent, 2 hrs, Cruz del Sur, US$3.50; also services to **Ancud**, US$7 and **Puerto Montt**, US$12.

Ferry
Naviera Austral services, Pedro Montt 457, T065-681331/T065-682207, www.navier austral.cl, to **Chaitén** on the mainland depart from Quellón, 4 per week Dec-early Mar, reduced service off season, 5 hrs, passengers US$33, cars US$135, cycles US$13. To **Puerto Chacabuco**, via Melinka, Raúl Marín Balmaceda and Puerto Cisnes, weekly, 24 hrs, reclining seat US$43, bunk US$72, cars US$230, bicycles US$16. All services leave from Castro when Quellón's port is out of commission and schedules are subject to last-minute changes due to inclement weather. **Navimag** is at Pedro Montt 383.

❶ Directory

Chonchi *p424*
Banks Banco del Estado, Centenario 28, ATM accepts MasterCard but not Visa. *Casas de cambio* Nicolás Alvarez, Centenario 429, cash only. **Telephone** San Martín y Mistral.

Quellón *p425, map p425*
Banks Banco del Estado, Ladrilleros. MasterCard only, no commission on US$ cash. Banco de Chile, Ladrilleros 315, ATM accepts Visa. **Laundry** Lavandería Ruck-Zuck, Ladrilleras 392.

Contents

Footprint features

Border crossings

At a glance

● **Getting around** Boat, minibus, air taxi, or ideally mountain bike. You will need a lot of patience.

● **Time required** At least a week and twice as much as you think.

☀ **Weather** Cold in winter, wet on the coast but surprisingly pleasant in summer.

✖ **When not to go** Winter is unforgiving, while the road is liable to flooding in spring and autumn.

★Don't miss ...
1 Mountain biking the Carretera Austral, page 434.
2 Parque Pumalín, page 436.
3 Trekking near Futaleufú and Chile Chico, pages 440 and 459.
4 Lago General Carrera, page 456.
5 Laguna San Rafael, page 465.

Travelling along the Carretera Austral is one of the greatest journeys South America has to offer. It is a largely unpaved *ripio* road stretching almost 1200 km through spectacular ever-changing scenery and with a similar length of branch roads heading either to the fjords or the mountains and Argentinian Patagonia beyond. Before the opening of the road, this part of Chile was largely inaccessible; it remains breathtaking. The journey will take you past trees growing up out of vertical cliffs; impenetrably thick millennial forests; burned pastures dotted with glacial debris; innumerable waterfalls rushing right down to the road's edge, while spiralling volcanoes and sparkling glaciers feed turquoise lakes and fast-flowing rivers, all rich with southern Chile's unique flora.

The only town of any size, Coyhaique, lies in the valley of the Río Simpson. South of Coyhaique are Lago General Carrera, the largest lake in Chile, and the Río Baker, one of the longest rivers in the country, which reaches the sea at Caleta Tortel. Further south still is Villa O' Higgins and the icefields of the Campo de Hielo Sur, which feed several magnificent glaciers and prevent further road building, although a route (by boat and on foot or mountain bike) exists that goes on to El Chaltén in Argentina. Coyhaique enjoys good air connections with Puerto Montt and Santiago, while nearby Puerto Chacabuco can be reached by ferry or catamaran from Puerto Montt, Chaitén and Chiloé. The most appealing parts of this region, however, can only be visited by travelling along the Carretera Austral.

The recent eruptions of Volcán Chaitén have caused considerable damage to the town of Chaitén, which has been evacuated save for the ferry terminal, and to the southern section of the Parque Pumalín, which remains closed at the time of writing. With further eruptions a possibility, it is hard to say when normal services will resume. See the relevant text for more detail.

Background

The original inhabitants of northern Patagonia were Alacalufes (Kaweshkar or *canoeros*), who were coast dwellers living off the sea (see page 570), and Tehuelches (Tzónecas, or Patagones), who lived on the pampa hunting guanacos, *ñandúes* (rheas) and *huemules* (an indigenous deer, now almost extinct; see box, page 458). There are some fine cave paintings in the vicinity of Lago General Carrera, for example at the Manos de Cerro Castillo, and Cueva de las Manos, on the Argentine side of the border near Chile Chico.

The Spanish called the region Trapalanda, but initially explored little more than the coast. This was the last territory to be occupied by the Chilean state after Independence from Spain. In the late 19th century, expeditions up the rivers led by George Charles Musters (1869) and Enrique Simpson Baeza (1870-1872) were followed by a failed attempt to found a settlement at the mouth of the Río Palena in 1884. Fearing that Argentina might seize the territory, the Chilean government appointed Hans Steffen to explore the area. His seven expeditions (1892-1902) were followed by an agreement with Argentina to submit the question of the frontier to arbitration by the British crown.

The Chilean government granted concessions to three large cattle companies in an attempt to occupy the area. One of these ranches, on the Río Baker, was managed by E Lucas Bridges, of the Bridges family from Tierra del Fuego and author of *Uttermost Part of the Earth* (for more details, see *South* by AF Tschiffely). Until the 1920s, there were few settlers; early pioneers settled along the coast and brought supplies from Chiloé. The estimated population of northern Patagonia in 1907 was just 197 people. By 1920, this had risen to 1660 and, by 1930, 8886 inhabitants were in the region. Although the first town, Baquedano (modern-day Coyhaique), was founded in 1917, followed by Puerto Aisén in 1924, the first road, between Puerto Aisén and Coyhaique, was not built until 1936. It was not until the 1960s, when new roads were built and airstrips were opened, that this region began to be integrated with the rest of the country.

Although the road has helped transform the lives of many people in this part of Chile, the motivation behind its construction was mainly geopolitical. Ever since Independence, Chilean military and political leaders have stressed the importance of occupying the southern regions of the Pacific coast and preventing any incursion by Argentina. Building the Carretera Austral was seen by General Pinochet as a means of achieving this aim: a way of occupying and securing territory, just as colonization had been in the early 20th century.

Begun in 1976, the central section of the Carretera Austral, from Chaitén to Coyhaique, was opened in 1983. Five years later, the northern section, linking Chaitén with Puerto Montt, and the southern section, between Coyhaique and Cochrane, were officially inaugurated. Since then, the Carretera has been extended south of Cochrane to Puerto Yungay and Villa O'Higgins. Work is continuing, building branch roads (which currently amount to around 1300 km) and widening and paving the most important sections. The road is the work of the army corps of engineers and dotted along the route are memorials to the dozens of young recruits who died during its construction.

Despite recent growth, this remains one of the most sparsely populated areas of Chile, with barely 100,000 inhabitants, most of whom live in Coyhaique or in nearby Puerto Aisén. Agriculture is limited by the climate and poverty of the soil, but fishing remains important as a source of employment in the inland channels, with salmon farming providing most income. Forestry plays a growing role in the economy: wood is used for construction and winter fuel. Zinc, lead and copper are mined, but only zinc is extracted in large quantities. A project for a huge aluminium plant, which would have had both

Tips for travelling along the Carretera Austral

Travelling the length of the Carretera Austral can be quite a challenge. The first and most important piece of advice is to take enough cash. While there are Cirrus and MasterCard ATMs in Chaitén and Cochrane, Coyhaique is the only place between Puerto Montt and Villa O'Higgins with Visa ATMs.

Off season, much of the northern section of the Carretera is rendered inaccessible when the Arena–Puelche and Hornopirén–Caleta Gonzalo ferry services are suspended. You will have to go to Chaitén directly from Puerto Montt or Chiloé instead. If you are driving, take a 4WD vehicle and fill up your tank whenever possible. Take spare parts – the road is unforgiving. After heavy rain, parts of the Carretera are liable to flood, so check the weather carefully and be prepared to be stuck in one place for a few days while conditions improve.

Most of the buses that ply the Carretera Austral are minibuses (and in more than one case, converted transit vans) operated by small companies, and often they are driven by their owners. Services are less reliable than elsewhere in Chile and timetables change frequently as operators go out of business and new ones start up. Booking your ticket in advance means that if your bus does not leave, for whatever reason, the company is liable to pay for your accommodation until the bus is ready to depart. Complaints should be directed to SERNAC, the government consumer rights department, in Coyhaique.

economic and ecological repercussions, was recently abandoned after continued protests. Disturbingly, the Chilean government seems to view hydroelectric power as a solution to the petrol and natural gas crises and studies are underway as to the feasibility of damming some of Chile's most spectacular rivers, including the Baker and Futaleufú.

Geography and climate

South of Puerto Montt the sea has broken through the coastal cordillera and drowned the central valley. The higher parts of the coastal cordillera form a maze of islands, stretching for over 1000 km and separated from the coast by tortuous fjords and *senos* (inlets). There is no real dry season near the coast, with annual rainfall of over 2000 mm on the offshore islands. Westerly winds are strong, especially in summer, and temperatures vary little day to night.

The Andes are much lower in this region than they are further north, and eroded by glacial action: towards the coast they rise in peaks such as San Valentín (4058 m), the highest mountain south of Talca; inland they form a high steppe around 1000 m, where the climate is drier, warm in summer and cold during the winter months. The shores of Lago General Carrera enjoy a warm microclimate that allows the production of fruit.

To the south of Coyhaique are two areas of highland covered by ice, known as *campos de hielo* (icefields). The Campo de Hielo Norte, over 100 km from north to south and some 50 km from east to west, includes the *ventisqueros* (glaciers) San Rafael, Montt and Steffens. The Campo de Hielo Sur covers a larger area, stretching south from the mouth of the Río Baker towards Puerto Natales.

Five main rivers flow westwards: from north to south these are the Futaleufú or Yelcho, the Palena, the Cisnes, the Simpson or Aisén and the Baker. This last, at 370 km, is the third longest river in Chile and carries more water than any other. The three largest lakes in this region, lagos General Carrera, Cochrane and O'Higgins, are shared with Argentina.

Travelling along the Carretera Austral

The road can be divided into three sections: **Puerto Montt to Chaitén** (143 km), plus two ferry crossings; **Chaitén to Coyhaique** (445 km); and **Coyhaique to Villa O'Higgins** (559 km), plus one ferry crossing. There is also a main branch that runs along the southern shore of **Lago General Carrera** from Puerto Guadal to Chile Chico, as well as important branches to Futaleufú, Palena, Raúl Marín Balmaceda, Lago Verde, Puerto Cisnes, Puerto Aisén, Bahía Exploradores and Tortel. The Puerto Montt–Chaitén section can only be travelled in summer, when the ferries are operating, but three alternative routes exist year round, either direct by ferry from Puerto Montt to Chaitén, through Chiloé and then by boat to Chaitén, or overland through Argentina via Osorno, Bariloche, Esquel and Futaleufú. The road is paved just south of Chaitén and around Coyhaique, from just north of Villa Amengual to Villa Cerro Castillo and Puerto Ibáñez.

The condition of the road can vary dramatically depending on the time of year and amount of traffic. Some sections can be difficult or even impossible after heavy rain or snowfall, and widening/paving/repair work is constantly being undertaken. Although tourist infrastructure is growing rapidly and unleaded fuel is available all the way to Villa O'Higgins, drivers should carry adequate fuel and spares, especially if intending to detour from the main route, and should protect their windscreens and headlamps.

Hitching is popular in summer, but extremely difficult out of season, particularly south of Cochrane. Watching the cloak of dust thrown up by the wheels from the back of a pickup, while taking in the lakes, forests, mountains and waterfalls, is an unforgettable experience, but be prepared for long delays, carry a tent and plenty of food and allow at least three days from Chaitén to Coyhaique.

The Carretera Austral is highly recommended for **cycling** as long as you have enough time and are reasonably fit. A good mountain bike is essential and a tent is an advantage. Most buses will take bicycles for a small charge.

Puerto Montt to Chaitén

→ *Colour map 4, C2.*
This 242-km section of the Carretera Austral is perhaps the most inaccessible and secluded stretch along the entire route, passing through two national parks and the private Parque Pumalín. Beautiful old trees close in on all sides, the rivers and streams sparkle and, on (admittedly rare) clear days, there are beautiful views across the Golfo de Ancud to Chiloé.
▶▶ *For listings, see pages 438-439.*

Ins and outs

This section of the route includes two ferry crossings at La Arena and Hornopirén. Before setting out, it is imperative to check when the ferries are running (generally only in January and February) and, if driving, to make a reservation for your vehicle: do this at the **Transmarchilay** and **Naviera Austral** offices in Puerto Montt, rather than in Santiago. Hitching to Chaitén takes several days, and there is a lot of competition for lifts: you must be prepared for a day's wait if you find yourself out of luck. The experience of riding in the back of a pickup, however, will make the hanging around worthwhile. An alternative route to Chaitén is by ferry from Puerto Montt or Castro/Quellón (see page 423).

South of Puerto Montt

The Carretera Austral heads east out of Puerto Montt through **Pelluco**, where there is a polluted bathing beach with black sand and some good seafood restaurants, and then follows the shore of the beautiful Seno de Reloncaví (Reloncaví Estuary, see page 393). Between the sound to the south and west and Lago Chapo to the northeast is **Parque Nacional Alerce Andino** ① *entrances 2.5 km from Correntoso (35 km west of Puerto Montt) and 7 km west of Lenca (40 km south of Puerto Montt), US$8*. The park covers 39,255 ha of steep forested valleys rising to 1500 m and containing ancient alerce trees, some over 1000 years old (the oldest are estimated to be 4200 years old). There are also some 50 small lakes and many waterfalls in the park. Wildlife includes pudú, pumas, *vizcachas*, condors and black woodpeckers. **Lago Chapo** (5500 ha) feeds a hydroelectric power station at Canutillar, east of the park. There are ranger posts at Río Chaicas, Lago Chapo,

Parque Nacional Alerce Andino

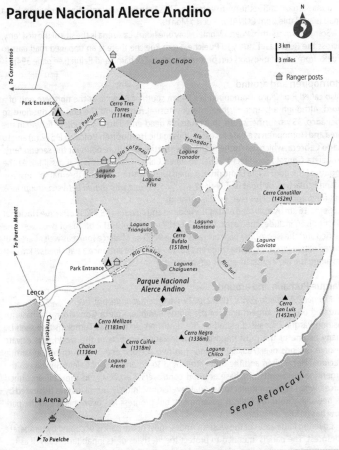

The price of settlement

In 1937, desperate to encourage settlement in this isolated region, the Chilean government passed a law offering settlers ownership of land provided it was cleared of forest. The people came, and smoke from the forest fires that followed could be seen from the Atlantic coast. The legacies of this law are still apparent to the visitor.

Firstly, in the large expanses of burnt tree stumps to be seen, especially around the Río Palena and Mañihuales, and also in the shifting of the port facilities from Puerto Aisén to Puerto Chacabuco, as so much soil was washed into the rivers that the Río Aisén silted up, preventing vessels from reaching Puerto Aisén.

Laguna Sargazo and at the north entrance. These can provide very little information, but a map is available from **CONAF** in Puerto Montt.

Some 45 km south of Puerto Montt (allow one hour), **La Arena** is the site of the first ferry, across the Reloncaví Estuary to **Puelche**. From Puelche there is an unpaved road east to Puelo, from where transport can be found north to Cochamó and Ralún (see page 394).

Hornopirén and around

Also called Río Negro, Hornopirén lies 54 km south of Puelche at the northern end of a fjord. Although a branch of the Carretera Austral runs round the edge of the fjord to Pichanco, 35 km further south, that route is a dead-end. There is excellent fishing in the area and Hornopirén is a base for excursions to the **Hornopirén Volcano** (1572 m) and to **Lago Cabrera**, which lies further north. It is also the departure point for the second ferry, to Caleta Gonzalo (or direct to Chaitén when Caleta Gonzalo is not accessible). At the mouth of the fjord is **Isla Llancahué**, a small island with a hotel and thermal springs. The island is reached by **boat** ① *T09-9642 4857, US$60 one way shared between group*; look out for dolphins and fur seals on the crossing.

Some 16 km by *ripio* road east of Hornopirén and covering 48,232 ha, **Parque Nacional Hornopirén** includes the **Yates Volcano** (2187 m) as well as the basins of two rivers, the Blanco and the Negro. The park protects some 9000 ha of alerce forest as well as areas of mixed native forest including lenga and coigue. From the entrance a path leads 8 km east up along the Río Blanco to a basic *refugio*.

Parque Pumalín and around

① *Klenner 299, Puerto Varas, T065-250079, www.pumalinpark.org, free.*
Situated on the southern edge of the Fiordo Reñihue, **Caleta Gonzalo** is the base for visiting Parque Pumalín. Created by the US billionaire Douglas Tompkins and seen by many as one of the most important conservation projects in the world, this private reserve extends over 700,000 ha and is in two sectors: one just south of the Parque Nacional Hornopirén and the other stretching south and east of Caleta Gonzalo to the Argentine border. Its purchase aroused controversy, especially in the Chilean armed forces, who saw it as a threat to national sovereignty. Initially Tompkins was frustrated by stonewalling from the Chilean government, but progress has been made and the park now has nature sanctuary status.

Covering large areas of the western Andes, most of the park is occupied by temperate rainforest. The park is intended to protect the lifestyles of its inhabitants as well as the physical environment. Tompkins has established a native tree nursery, producing 100,000 saplings of native endangered species, and developed apiculture; in 2002 the Pumalín bee stations produced 30,000 kg of honey. There are treks ranging from short trails into the temperate rainforest to hikes lasting for several days (these are very arduous). The trail heads are all on the main road. Three marked trails lead to a waterfall, **Cascadas Escondidas**; to an area of very old alerce trees; and to **Laguna Tronador**. The road through these forests was only built in the 1980s, meaning that, unlike areas to the north and south, endangered trees have been protected from logging (laws protecting alerces, araucaria and other native species were passed in the 1970s). As a result, Parque Pumalín is home to perhaps the most diverse temperate rainforest in the world, and is the only place where alerce forests remain intact just a few metres from the main road. It is a truly humbling experience looking up from the base of a 3000-year-old, 3-m-wide alerce, and this, in itself, is a reason to visit the park. There are only three buses a week, but hitching is not difficult in season.

Much of the this section of the park was covered in ash after the recent eruptions of Volcán Chaitén and at the time of writing, the southern half of the park between Caleta Gonzalo and Chaitén is closed. Repair work is underway and the hope is that the park will open again at some point in the not too distant future. However, this is dependent on the volcano calming down.

The Carretera Austral runs through the park, climbing steeply before reaching two lakes, **Lago Río Negro** and **Lago Río Blanco**. The coast is reached at **Santa Bárbara**, 48 km south, where there is a black sand beach. Towards sunset dolphins often swim right up to the beach. You can join them, although the water is very cold.

Chaitén
Chaitén lies in a beautiful spot, with a forest-covered hill rising behind it, and a quiet inlet leading out into the Patagonian channels. In many ways Chaitén is a cultural crossroads. Until relatively recently, the town had more contact with Argentina than the central Chilean mainland, while a Chilote influence is clear in the town's architecture. Indeed until the construction of the Carretera this area was known as Chiloé Continental and was governed as part of the island opposite.

In May 2008, Volcán Chaitén, previously thought to be extinct, erupted, spewing a 20-cm layer of ash over the surrounding countryside and causing the Río Blanco to shift its banks and flood most of the town of Chaitén, destroying many buildings and covering much of the town with a thick layer of volcanic mud. A further eruption followed in February 2009. The government decided to abandon the town, making plans to rebuild Chaitén 10 km to the north, at Santa Barbara. The population was evacuated to Puerto Montt and Chiloé, and most have stayed away either because they fear a future eruption may entirely destroy the town, or because they have no work to return to. The seat of provincial government has been moved to Futaleufú taking with it the bank, and an important source of local employment.

Out of an original population of over 4000, about 80 diehard locals remain in the remnants of the town, mostly in the northwestern sector that survived relatively unscathed. At the time of writing the ferry terminal is still in use, with connecting bus services to Futaleufú and the south. Despite having to use generators for electricity, there are basic amenities such as food and lodging. Whether Chaitén has a future on its present site is ultimately dependent on the future activity of its eponymous volcano. In the meantime construction work on the new town is well underway at Santa Barbara.

Chaitén remains important as a port for ferries to Puerto Montt and to Chiloé (see page 423), and when the new town is rebuilt will once again be a growing centre for adventure tourism, and trips to the Parque Pumalín as well as nearby thermal springs and glaciers. There is excellent fishing nearby, especially to the south in the ríos Yelcho and Futaleufú and in lagos Espolón and Yelcho.

⊙ Puerto Montt to Chaitén listings

For Sleeping and Eating price codes and other relevant information, see Essentials pages 35-42.

⊜ Sleeping

South of Puerto Montt *p435*
There are basic *refugios* at Río Pangal, Laguna Sargazo and Laguna Fría in the Parque Nacional Alerce Andino, and campsites at Río Chaicas and the northern entrance; no camping is permitted inside the boundaries of the park.

Hornopirén and around *p436*
There are lots of *cabañas* and *residenciales* here, including the following:
AL-A Termas de Llancahue, Llancahue Island, T09-9642 4857, www.termasde llancahue.cl. **B** singles. Full board, good food, access to thermal springs.
B-C Hostería Catalina, Ingenieros Militares s/n, T065-217359, www.hosteriacatalina.cl. Simple, spacious rooms with breakfast and bath. Recommended.
C Hornopirén, Carrera Pinto 388, T065-217256. Rooms with shared bathrooms. Recommended, also *cabañas*.

Camping
There's a good site on Ingenieros Militares, US\$14 per site, and 4 more sites south of Hornopirén on the road to Pichanco.

Parque Pumalín and around *p436*
There is a restaurant, *cabañas* and a campsite in Caleta Gonzalo, as well as a visitor centre (not always open) and demonstrations of agricultural techniques in the region. Camping is available in the park at several well-run sites from US\$8 per tent.

(Accommodation in the park suspended at the time of writing).

Chaitén *p437*
At the time of writing, accommodation is being offered in Chaitén in 3 or 4 basic *hostales*, which also offer food.

▲ Activities and tours

Chaitén *p437*
Chaitur, O'Higgins 67, T09-7468 5608, www.chaitur.com. General travel agent selling bus and boat tickets. Also bespoke excursions, trekking, horse riding, fishing and trips to Parque Pumalín as well as trips to the Termas de Amarillo and Yelcho Glacier. English spoken, friendly and helpful. Lots of information. Highly recommended. Most buses leave from here.

⊝ Transport

South of Puerto Montt *p435*
Bus
To reach the northern entrance of the **Parque Nacional Alerce Andino**, take Fierro or Río Pato bus from Puerto Montt to **Correntoso** (or **Lago Chapo** bus, which passes through Correntoso), several daily except Sun, then walk. To reach the southern entrance, take any Fierro bus to **Chaicas**, **La Arena**, **Contau** and **Hornopirén**, US\$2.50, getting off at **Lenca** sawmill, then walk (signposted).

Ferry
30-min crossing from La Arena to **Puelche**, 10 daily Dec-Mar, reduced service off season.

Arrive 30 mins early for a place; buses have priority, cars US$17, bicycles US$5. See www.transmarchilay.cl for more details.

Hornopirén and around p436
Bus
Fierro runs 2 buses daily from Puerto Montt in season. There are no buses south from Hornopirén.

Ferry
In Jan and Feb only, **Naviera Austral** operates a ferry from Hornopirén to **Caleta Gonzalo**, 1600 daily, 6 hrs, return departures 0900 daily, cars US$110 one way, foot passengers US$18, bicycles US$11. Advance booking required: there can be a 2-day wait. See www.navieraustral.cl for more details. Chaitur organizes connecting transport between the ferry port in Caleta Gonzalo and Chaitén (see Activities and tours, above). With the current situation, the Hornopirén ferry is bypassing Caleta Gonzalo and sailing direct to Chaitén via Ayacara. Fares are 20% more than to Caleta Gonzalo.

Chaitén p437
Bus
Terminal at Chaitur Office, O'Higgins 67. Recent disruptions mean that there is no permanent schedule for buses from south from Chaitén. However, minibuses are running along the Carretera Austral to **Coyhaique**, 3 weekly, 12 hrs, direct in summer or with an overnight stop in La Junta or Puyuhuapi in winter, departures usually 0800-0900, US$30. Minibuses usually travel full, so can't pick up passengers en route. **Chaitur** acts as an agent for all these services (see Activities and tours, above). There are also buses to **Futaleufú**, 3 weekly, 4 hrs, US$12; change here for buses to the Argentine border.

Ferry
The ferry port is about 1 km north of town. Schedules change frequently and ferries are infrequent off season. **Naviera Austral**, Corcovado 266, T065-731272, www.navieraustral.cl.

To **Chiloé**, Naviera Austral operates ferry services to **Castro** or **Quellón**, 4 per week in summer (Dec-Mar), reduced service off season, 5 hrs, passengers US$32 one way, cars US$132, bicycles US$12.

To **Puerto Montt**, Naviera Austral, 4 weekly, 10 hrs, passengers US$35, US$50 with bunk, car US$141, bike US$16.

Chaitén to Coyhaique

→ *Colour map 5, A3.*

This section of the Carretera Austral, 422 km long, runs through long stretches of virgin rainforest, passing small villages, the perfectly still waters of Lago Yelcho, and the Parque Nacional Queulat, with its glaciers and waterfalls. Roads branch off east to the Argentine border and west to Puerto Cisnes. Near Coyhaique, the road passes huge tracts of land destroyed by logging, where only tree stumps remain as testament to the depredations of the early colonists. ▶▶ *For listings, see pages 443-446.*

Towards Puerto Cárdenas

At Amarillo, 25 km south of Chaitén, there is a turning to the **Termas de Amarillo** ⓘ *5 km east, US$5,* which consists of two wooden sheds with a very hot pool inside, and an outdoor swimming pool, worth a visit. There is superb salmon fishing in the nearby rivers. From here, it is possible to hike along the old trail to Futaleufú (see below). The hike takes four to seven days and is not for the inexperienced; be prepared for wet feet all the way. The trail follows the Río Michinmawida, passing the volcano of the same name, to **Lago Espolón** (see below). A ferry with a sporadic schedule crosses the lake, taking cargo, foot passengers and bicycles to Futaleufú.

Situated 46 km south of Chaitén and surrounded by forest, **Puerto Cárdenas** lies on the northern tip of **Lago Yelcho**, a beautiful glacial lake on the Río Futaleufú, surrounded by hills and with views of the stunning Yelcho glacier. The lake is frequented by anglers. Further south at Km 60, a path leads to the **Yelcho glacier**, a two-hour walk each way (there is a viewing station halfway up). There is a campsite here, and the administrator charges US$3.50 to people walking to the glacier. Whether he is legally allowed to do this is a contentious issue.

Into Argentina via Futaleufú or Palena

Southeast of Chaitén the Argentine border is reached in two places, Futaleufú and Palena, along a road that branches off the Carretera Austral at **Villa Santa Lucía** (Km 81), named after General Pinochet's wife, where there are 30 houses, a military camp and one small shop; bread is available from a private house. The road to the border is *ripio* of variable standard, passable in a regular car, but best with a good, strong high-clearance vehicle. The scenery is beautiful. See box, opposite, for border crossing information.

At **Puerto Ramírez**, at the southern end of **Lago Yelcho**, the road divides: the north

Futaleufú

Sleeping
Adolfo B&B 1
Cabañas la Escondida 10
Cabañas Río Espolón 2
Cabañas Veranada 3
Continental 4
El Barranco 5
Hostería Río Grande 6
Los Troncos 7
Posada la Gringa 8
Sur Andes 9

Eating
Futaleufú 1
Martín Pescador 2
Sur Andes 3

Border crossings: Chile–Argentina

Futaleufú–Trevelin
Chilean immigration, open 0800-2000, is on the border, 8 km east of Futaleufú, at the bridge. If entering Chile, change money in Futaleufú (poor rates but there is nowhere at the border), and then continue from Futaleufú towards Puerto Ramírez; outside Ramírez, take the right turn to Chaitén, otherwise you'll end up back at the border in Palena.

Palena–Trevelin
Chilean immigration, open 0800-2000, is 8 km west of the border. It is much quieter than the crossing at Futaleufú.

Trevelin is 45 km east of Futaleufú, 95 km east of Palena. It is an offshoot of the Welsh Chubút colony on the Atlantic side of Argentine Patagonia, as featured in Bruce Chatwin's *In Patagonia* (see page 611). It has accommodation, restaurants, tea rooms and a tourist office, but there is a much wider range of services at **Esquel**, 23 km northeast. Esquel is a base for visiting the Argentine Parque Nacional Los Alerces. There are also transport connections to Bariloche and other destinations in Argentine Patagonia.

branch runs along the valley of the Río Futaleufú to Futaleufú, while the southern one continues to Palena. Futaleufú, the new capital of Palena province, has established itself as the centre for the finest whitewater rafting in the southern hemisphere. Every year, hundreds of fanatics travel to spend the southern summer here and there is no shortage of operators offering trips. The river is an incredible deep blue colour and offers everything from easy Grade II-III sections downstream to the extremely challenging Grade V Cañón del Infierno (Hell Canyon). Although the town is only at 350 m, the spectacular mountain scenery makes you feel as if you were up in the High Andes. The Río Espolón provides a peaceful backdrop to this pleasant town, with wide streets lined with shrubs and roses and Chilote-style houses. There is **tourist information** ① *T065-721241, www.futaleufu.cl, daily in summer, 0900-2100, sells fishing licences*, on the plaza. **Lago Espolón**, west of Futaleufú, is reached by a turning 41 km northeast of Puerto Ramírez. It is a beautiful lake and enjoys a warm microclimate, regularly reaching 30°C in the day in summer. The lake is even warm enough for a quick dip, but beware of the currents.

La Junta and around
From Villa Santa Lucía, the Carretera Austral follows the Río Frío and then the Río Palena to La Junta, a tranquil, nondescript village at the confluence of Río Rosselot and Río Palena, 151 km south of Chaitén. Fuel is available here. There is a **tourist office** ① *Mon-Fri 1000-2100 summer only*, on the plaza. Some 9 km east is **Lago Rosselot**, surrounded by forest and situated at the heart of a *reserva nacional* (12,725 ha) with a well-equipped campsite and cabins. From here, the road continues east for 74 km, to the border crossing at picturesque **Lago Verde** ① *summer 0800-2200, winter 0800-2000*, and on to Las Pampas in Argentina. There is also a new road leading northwest from La Junta, past some rustic thermal springs (not always open), across the broad expanse of the Río Palena

(four ferry crossings daily) and on to **Puerto Raúl Marín Balmaceda** on the coast, a tranquil fishing village with more than its share of rainfall. Different species of dolphin can be seen and when it is clear there are wonderful views of Volcán Melimoyu from the beach. Accommodation is available and camping is possible. Raúl Marín forms one apex of the blue whale triangle, and the giant cetacean can sometimes be sighted on the ferry to Quellón.

Puyuhuapi and around

From La Junta, the Carretera Austral runs south along the western side of Lago Risopatrón, past several waterfalls, to Puyuhuapi (also spelt Puyuguapi), 45 km further south. Located in a beautiful spot at the northern end of the Puyuhuapi fjord, the village is a tranquil stopping place, about halfway between Chaitén and Coyhaique. It was founded by four Sudeten German families in 1935, and its economy is based around fishing, ever-increasing tourism and the factory where Puyuhuapi's famous handmade carpets are produced and which can be visited. **Alfombras de Puyuhuapi** ① *T067-325131, www.puyuhuapi.com, daily in summer 0830-1930, closed lunch, English spoken*. By the municipalidad on the main street there is a decent **tourist information office** ① *Mon-Sat in season, 1000-1400, 1600-1900*. A bus timetable is pinned up here. If you are travelling in your own vehicle ask at the police station about road conditions and temporary road closures.

From Puyuhuapi, the road follows the eastern edge of the fjord along one of the most beautiful sections of the Carretera Austral, with views of the **Termas de Puyuhuapi** ① *18 km southwest of Puyuhuapi, US$20 per person, under 12s US$15*. This resort is on the western edge of the fjord and is accessible only by boat. It has several 40°C springs filling three pools near the beach. Take food and drink. The resort can also be visited on a four- or six-day tour with **Patagonia Connection SA** (see pages 445 and 469) and day trips are possible from Puyuhuapi. More easily accessible are the new **Termas del Ventisqero** ① *6 km south of Puyuhuapi by the side of the Carretera overlooking the fjord, www.termasventisqueropuyuhuapi.cl*. In season the baths are open until 2300 and during the day there is a café.

Covering 154,093 ha of attractive forest around Puyuhuapi, the **Parque Nacional Queulat** ① *administration at the CONAF office in La Junta, T067-314128, US$5*, is, supposedly, the former location of the legendary Ciudad de los Césares, a fabulously wealthy mythological city built between two hills made of gold and diamonds and inhabited by immortal beings. According to legend, the city was protected by a shroud of fog and hence was impossible for strangers to discover. The Carretera Austral passes through the park, close to **Lago Risopatrón** north of Puyuhuapi, where boat trips are available. Some 22 km south of Puyuhapi, a road turns off to the main entrance of the park, continuing for 3.5 km past the guardaparques' hut to a campsite and car park. Three walks begin from here: a short stroll through the woodland to a viewpoint of the **Ventisquero Colgante** hanging glacier; or cross the river where the path begins to **Laguna Tempanos**, where boats cross the lake in summer. The third trail, 3.25 km, takes 2½ hours to climb to a panoramic viewpoint of the **Ventisquero**, where you can watch the ice fall into huge waterfalls. From here the Carretera Austral climbs out of the Queulat valley through a series of narrow hairpin bends surrounded by an impressive dense jungle-like mass of giant Nalcas. There are fine views of the forest and several glaciers. Near the pass (250 m off the main road) is the **Salto Pedro García** waterfall, with the **Salto del Cóndor** waterfall some 5 km further on. Steep gradients mean that crossing the park is the hardest part of the Carretera for those travelling by bicycle.

Border crossing: Chile–Argentina

La Tapera
Chilean immigration is 12 km west of the border and is open summer 0800-2200, winter 0800-2000.

On the Argentine side, the road continues to meet up with Route 40, the north-south road at the foot of the Andes.

On the southern side of the pass there is a sign labelled **Bosque Encantado** with a small parking area. A path leads west through a forest of Arayanes, like something out of a fairytale. After crossing a series of small bridges the path runs out at the river. Follow the river bank around to the right to get to a beautiful laguna with floating icebergs and a hanging glacier. The trek to the laguna and back should not take more than three hours and is well worth the effort.

South of the Río Cisnes

Stretching 160 km from the Argentine border to the coast at Puerto Cisnes, the Río Cisnes is recommended for rafting or canoeing, with grand scenery and modest rapids – except for the horrendous drop at Piedra del Gato, about 60 km east of Puerto Cisnes. Good camping is available in the forest. Possibly the wettest town in Chile, **Puerto Cisnes** is reached by a 33-km winding road that branches west off the Carretera Austral about 59 km south of Puyuhuapi. Once a peaceful fishing port where traditional knitted clothes were made, it is now an important salmon-farming centre. Fuel is available. Heading south again on the main spine of the Carretera the paved section of the road begins at Km 77.

Fifteen kilometres further on, at Km 92, south of **Villa Amengual**, a road branches west for 104 km to the **Argentine border** via La Tapera, see box, above.

Reserva Nacional Lago Las Torres is 98 km south of Puyuhuapi and covers 16,516 ha. There are no trails, but it includes the wonderful **Lago Las Torres**, which offers good fishing and a small *hospedaje* and campsite. Further south, at Km 125, a road branches east to **El Toqui**, where zinc is mined.

Villa Mañihuales, at Km 148, is a small, nondescript town with a Copec petrol station and several basic *residenciales* and restaurants. Most buses stop here for 15 to 30 minutes. Nearby is the **Reserva Forestal Mañihuales** ① *US$5*. The reserve covers 1206 ha and encompasses a huemul sanctuary. Fires largely destroyed the forests in the 1940s but the views are good.

① Chaitén to Coyhaique listings

For Sleeping and Eating price codes and other relevant information, see Essentials pages 35-42.

⊜ Sleeping

Towards Puerto Cárdenas *p440*
AL-A Cabañas Yelcho en La Patagonia, Lago Yelcho, 7 km south of Puerto Cárdenas,

T065-576005, www.yelcho.cl. Cabins and rooms on the lake shore. Also expensive campsite and cafeteria.
A Termas de Amarillo, Termas de Amarillo, T065-731326. Also camping and *cabañas*.
C Residencial Yelcho, Puerto Cárdenas, T065-264429. Clean, full board available.

D Residencial Marcela, Amarillo, T065-264442. Also *cabañas* and camping.

Futaleufú *p440, map p440*

L-AL El Barranco, O'Higgins 172, T065-721314, www.elbarrancochile.cl. Probably the best rooms in town, but still a little overpriced. There is a bar, restaurant, outdoor swimming pool, Wi-Fi and free bicycles for the guests. Disabled access. Fishing trips organized. Rather nonchalant staff.

AL Hostería Río Grande, O'Higgins 397, T065-721320, www.pachile.com. Overpriced though comfortable, en suite bathrooms, friendly, bar, good restaurant, arranges tours and activities.

A Posada la Gringa, Sargento Aldea 498, T065-721260, http://lagringa.homestead.com/h.html. Elegant and charming guesthouse set in large gardens and with the best view in town. Price includes a large brunch. The owner is of Basque descent and speaks perfect English. Recommended, but she may be moving back to Santiago soon.

B Cabañas Río Espolón, PA Cerda s/n, 5 mins' walk west of centre, T065-721216, rioespolon@yahoo.es. Secluded cabins with bar and restaurant overlooking the river, the sound of which is a constant in the background. Book ahead as it often fills up with rafting groups.

B Cabañas Veranada, Sargento Aldea 480, T065-721266, www.turismofutaleufu.cl. Well-equipped cabins with excellent beds and good kitchens. All have slow-burning wood stoves except one with an open fireplace. Friendly owners. Recommended.

B Sur Andes, Cerda 308, T065-721405. Rustic but tasteful apartment, fully equipped and with Wi-Fi, but with no kitchen.

B-C Cabañas la Escondida, Rodriguez 57, T065-721219. Decent no-frills cabins with good beds. Sleep 4.

C-D Adolfo B&B, O'Higgins 302, T065-721256, lodeva@surnet.cl. **F** singles. Well-kept and friendly family home. With breakfast and kitchen facilities.

C-D Los Troncos, Carmona 541, T065-721269. **F** singles. Basic clean *hospedaje* on the northern edge of town. With breakfast and kitchen facilities.

E-F Continental, Balmaceda 595, T065-721222. **G** singles. Pokey rooms, creaky floors, squeaky beds and no toilet paper provided, but clean and you can't ask for more at this price.

Camping Aldea Puerto Espolón, Sector La Puntilla, 400m from town, T09-94477448, www.aldeapuertoespolon.blogspot.com. Accommodation in pre-erected teepees and dome-tents.

Los Copihues, T065-721413, is on the river, 500 m from Futaleufú. Horse-riding trips.

There is a decent, if basic campsite on the west edge of town next to Laguna Espejo, US$5 per person with hot water.

Villa Santa Lucía

E Sra Rosalía Cuevas de Ruiz, No 7. Basic, meals available. One of several options on the main street; none has hot water.

Palena *p440*

D Residencial La Chilenita, Pudeto 681, T065-741212. Simple rooms.

La Junta and around *p441*

AL Espacio y Tiempo, La Junta, T067-314141, www.espacioytiempo.cl. Attractive garden, friendly, English spoken, good restaurant, internet, fishing expeditions and other tours.

C Residencial Copihue, Varas 611, T09-9501 8874. **E** singles. Some rooms with bath, with breakfast, good meals, changes money at very poor rates.

C-D Hostería Valdera, Varas s/n, T067-314 105, luslagos@hotmail.com. **E-F** singles. Breakfast and bath, meals served. Excellent value.

D-E Residencial Patagonia, Lynch 331, T09-7702 8181. **C-D** singles. Good meals, small rooms, limited bathrooms.

Puyuhuapi and around p442

There's a CONAF campsite at Lago Risopatrón.

LL-L Fiordo Queulat Ecolodge, Seno Queulat, Parque Nacional Queulat, T067-233302, www.aisen.cl. ½ board. Good reputation, offers hikes and fishing trips. Campsite nearby.

LL-L Puyuhuapi Lodge and Spa, T067-325 103, www.patagonia-connection.com. Reserve directly, or contact **Patagonia Connection**, Fidel Oteiza 1921, of 1006, Santiago. Price includes use of baths and boat transfer to/from the hotel. Good restaurant. Recommended. Boat schedule on jetty, 2 hrs' walk from town, frequent in season, US$5 one way, 10-mins. Independent transport to the hotel can be arranged via hydroplane from Puerto Montt.

L Cabañas El Pangue, north end of Lago Risopatrón, Carretera Austral Norte, Km 240, Parque Nacional Queulat, T067-325128, www.elpangue.com. Cabins sleep 4, private bathrooms, hot water, heating, telephone, parking, swimming pool, fishing trips, horse riding, mountain bikes.

B Aonikenk, Hamburgo 16, T067-325208, aonikenkturismo@yahoo.com. Pleasant newly built heated *cabañas*. Good beds, friendly service, good information, bike hire. Noise insulation non existent within each cabin.

B Casa Ludwig, Av Otto Uebel s/n, on the southern edge of town, T067-325220, www.casaludwig.cl Excellent, English and German spoken. Recommended.

B-C Hostería Alemana, Av Otto Uebel 450, T067-325118, www.hosteríaalemana.cl. With bath. A large, comfortable, wooden house on the main road, owned by Señora Ursula Flack Kroschewski. Recommended, closed in winter.

D Sra Leontina Fuentes, Llantureo y Circunvalación. **F** singles. Clean, hot water, good breakfast for US$3.

Camping

CONAF, reservations T067-212125, runs a basic campsite (cold water) 12 km north of Puyuhuapi on the shores of Lago Risopatrón, and another near the Ventisquero Colgante. There is also a dirty campsite by the fjord behind the general store in Puyuhuapi.

South of the Río Cisnes p443

B Cabañas Río Cisnes, Costanera 101, Puerto Cisnes, T067-346404. Cabins sleep 4-8. Owner, Juan Suazo, has a boat and offers good sea trout/salmon fishing.

C Hostería El Gaucho, Holmberg 140, Puerto Cisnes, T067-346514. With breakfast, dinner available, hot water.

E Hospedaje, Café y Restaurante El Encanto, Villa Amengual. One of several cheap options in the town.

E Residencia Bienvenido, Ibar 248, Villa Mañihuales. Clean, friendly, with a restaurant.

E Villa Mañihuales, E Ibar 200, Villa Mañihuales, T067-234803. Friendly, with breakfast.

🍴 Eating

Futaleufú p440, map p440

† Futaleufú, Cerda 407, T065-721295. All the normal Chilean fare plus, of course, trout.

† Martín Pescador, Balmaceda y Rodríguez, T065-721279. Decent meat and fish.

†-† Sur Andes, Cerda 308, T065-721405. Pleasant little café serving real coffee as well as a variety of cakes, sweets, snacks and light meals. Local handicrafts also sold.

Puyuhuapi and around p442

† Café Rossbach, Costanera, Puyuhuapi. Limited menu, including excellent salmon; also good for tea and *küchen*; building is in the style of a German Black Forest inn.

† Restaurante Marili, Otto Ubel s/n, Puyuhuapi. Cheaper option.

South of the Río Cisnes p443

† K-Cos Café Restaurante, Prat 270, Puerto Cisnes. Good snacks.

⛰ Activities and tours

There are good fishing opportunities on Río Futaleufú and Lago Espolón (ask for the Valebote family's motorboat on the lake) and around Puerto Cisnes. For the latter, contact **German Hipp**, Costanera 51, Puerto Cisnes, T067-346587, or **Cabañas Río Cisnes** (see Sleeping, above). For further information, contact **Turismo Lago Las Torres**, 130 km Carretera Austral Norte, T067-234242.

Towards Puerto Cárdenas p440
Isla Monita Lodge, near Puerto Cárdenas, www.islamonita.cl, offers packages on a private island on Lago Yelcho (see page 440), as well as fishing in many nearby locations.

Futaleufú p440, map p440
Tour operators can arrange whitewater rafting (see page 441). Prices start from US$75 per person. There are several local fishing guides who can be contacted in the village.
Earth River, www.earthriver.com. Excellent choice for river rafting and kayaking trips, book in advance.
Expediciones Chile, Mistral 296, T065-721 386, www.exchile.com. Offers the best multi-day trips. Book in advance. Day trips can be booked on site. Also offer trekking and horse riding.
Futaleufú Expediciones, O'Higgins 397, T/F065-258634. Organizes rafting, canyoning, trekking and horse-riding expeditions.
Futaleufú Explore, O'Higgins 772, T065-721411, www.futaleufuexplore.com. Another respected rafting company.

Puyuhuapi and around p442
Patagonian Waters, main road in Puyuhuapi, T09-9777 1820, www.patagonianwaters.com, offers canoeing and sea kayak trips in the fjord, as well as trekking and horse riding. There is also an office in La Junta.

⊖ Transport

Futaleufú p440, map p440
Buses to the border depart O'Higgins 234, Mon Wed and Fri 0845 and 1815, 30 mins, US$4; from the Argentine side there are connecting services to **Trevelin** and **Esquel**, US$3. Direct to **Puerto Montt** via Argentina,

2 weekly, 12 hrs, US$37. To **Chaitén** 3 weekly, 5 hrs, US$9; to **La Junta** 3 weekly, 6 hrs, US$13; to **Coyhaique** 3 weekly, 12 hrs, US$34; to **Palena** 3 weekly, 3 hrs, US$7. The café on Balmaceda y Prat acts as agent for flights and catamarans to **Puerto Montt**.

Palena p440
Transporte Patagonia Norte, T065-741257, runs a weekly service to **Puerto Montt** via Argentina, Mon 0630, 13 hrs, US$28.

La Junta and around p441
No bus terminal. Daily buses to **Coyhaique**, 8 hrs, US$16; 2 weekly to **Puerto Cisnes**, US$10, 3 weekly to **Chaitén**, 4 hrs, US$10.

Puyuhuapi and around p442
3 buses weekly from Puyuhuapi north to **Chaitén**. Daily service south to **Coyhaique**, plus 2 weekly to **Lago Verde**.

South of the Río Cisnes p443
Transportes Terra Austral, T067-346757, runs services from Puerto Cisnes to **Coyhaique**, Mon-Sat 0600, US$11. **Buses Norte**, T067-346440, offers the same route once a week, US$11. There are also daily buses to Coyhaique from **Villa Mañihuales**, 1½ hrs.

❀ Festivals and events

Futaleufú p440, map p440
Late Feb Futa Festival. Rafting and kayaking races on the river. See www.futafest.org.

❶ Directory

Futaleufú p440, map p440
Banks Banco del Estado, ATM accepts MasterCard but not Visa. Changing foreign currency is difficult, but US dollars and Argentine pesos are accepted in many places.
Medical services Hospital, Balmaceda y Aldea, T065-721231

Coyhaique and around

→ *Colour map 5, B3.*

Located 420 km south of Chaitén, Coyhaique (also spelt Coihaique) lies in the broad green valley of the Río Simpson. The city is encircled by a crown of mountains and, for a few hours after it has rained, the mountainsides are covered in a fine layer of frost – a spectacular sight. Founded in 1929, it is the administrative and commercial centre of Región XI and is the only settlement of any real size on the Carretera Austral (with a population of just over 40,000). The constant call of chickens in people's gardens gives away the fact that much of the population comprises recent arrivals from a very distinct and slowly disappearing lifestyle in the surrounding countryside, while the number of bow-legged elderly men making their way slowly about town is indicative of a generation who feel more comfortable on horseback than on foot. A rapidly growing and increasingly lively city, it also provides a good base for day excursions in the area. Rafting down the Río Simpson is a memorable experience, while in the Reserva Nacional Río Simpson there are picturesque waterfalls and the occasional sighting of the elusive huemul. Note that there are no Visa ATMs south of Coyhaique, so stock up on cash here if you are heading south. ►► *For listings, see pages 450-455.*

Ins and outs

Getting there There are two airports in the Coyhaique area: **Teniente Vidal** ① *5 km southwest of town, taxi US$7*, handles only smaller aircraft; **Balmaceda** ① *56 km southeast of Coyhaique via paved road, 5 km from the Argentine border at Paso Huemules, 1 hr*, is the most direct way into Coyhaique from Santiago or Puerto Montt, with several flights daily. There are also flights to Punta Arenas (more often in summer). There is no bus service between Coyhaique and Balmaceda; instead minibuses, known as *transfers*, ply this route, stopping at hotels; contact **Transfer & Turismo** ① *Cochrane 387, T067-256000*, or **Transfer Valencia** ① *Lautaro 828, T067-233030, both US$7 per person*. **Ferries** (one or two a week) make the journey from Puerto Montt or Chiloe to Puerto Chacabuco, 77 km west of Coyhaique. **Buses** (several weekly) from Puerto Montt have to take the route via Argentina, which is long and expensive. There are also one or two weekly buses to Comodoro Rivadavia and south to Punta Arenas. Within Región XI, Coyhaique is the transport hub. There are regular minibuses north to Chaitén or Futaleufú, and daily services south to Cochrane, as well as minibuses connecting with the ferry at Puerto Ibáñez for Chile Chico (five weekly).

Getting around Coyhaique is small enough to be easily covered on foot; taxis are only useful for out-of-town excursions.

Tourist information English is spoken at the very helpful **Sernatur office** ① *Bulnes 35, T067-231752, infoaisen@sernatur.cl, Mon-Fri 0830-1700, weekends in summer*, which has up to date bus timetables. See www.patagoniachile.net for more information. There's also a privately run information kiosk on the plaza in summer, as well as **CONAF** ① *Ogana 1060, T067-212125, Mon-Fri 0830-1730*.

Coyhaique

Although a visit to the tourist office will throw up far more attractions outside Coyhaique than in the town itself, this is a pleasant, friendly place, perfect for relaxing for a couple of days or as a base for day trips. The town is centred around an unusual pentagonal plaza, on which stand the cathedral, the Intendencia and a handicraft market. The plaza was built in

1945, supposedly inspired by the Place de l'Étoile in Paris. Two blocks northeast of the plaza at Baquedano y Ignacio Serrano, there is a monument to El Ovejero (the shepherd). Further north on Baquedano is a display of old military machinery outside the local regimental headquarters. In the Casa de Cultura the **Museo Regional de la Patagonia Central** ① *Lillo 23, T067-213174, Tue-Sun summer 0900-2000, winter 0830-1730, US$1,* has sections on history, mineralogy, zoology and archaeology, as well as photos of the construction of the

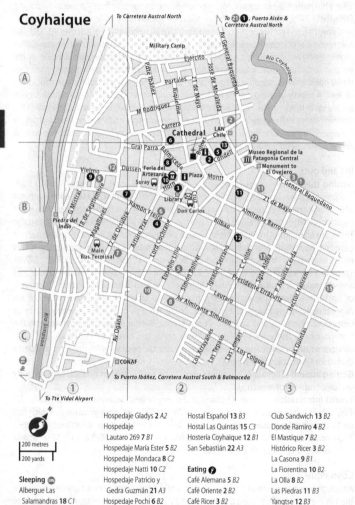

Coyhaique

To Carretera Austral North

To 21 ① , Puerto Aisén & Carretera Austral North

Military Camp

Ejército

Pte Ibáñez

Portales

21 de Mayo

José de Moraleda

Av General Baquedano

Río Coyhaique

M Rodríguez

Riquelme

Carrera

Cathedral

LAN Chile

Gral Parra

Balmaceda

Bilbao

Condell

Museo Regional de la Patagonia Central

Monument to El Ovejero

Vielmo

Dussen

Feria del Artesanía

Plaza

Montt

Av General Baquedano

JM Carrera

18 de Septiembre

Magallanes

12 de Octubre

Suray

Horn

Library

Don Carlos

21 de Mayo

Almirante Barroso

Piedra del Indio

Ramón Freire

Arturo Prat

Lord Cochrane

Eusebio Lillo

Gilbao

Simón Bolívar

Ignacio Serrano

C Colón

Almirante Barroso

Presidente Errázuriz

Sgta Aldea

P Aguirre Cerda

Héctor Hanen

Main Bus Terminal

Lautaro

Av Almirante Simpson

Los Ñadanes

Los Tepas

Las Lengas

Los Colgues

Las Quintas

CONAF

To Puerto Ibáñez, Carretera Austral South & Balmaceda

To Tte Vidal Airport

200 metres
200 yards

Sleeping 🛏
Albergue Las Salamandras **18** C1
Cabañas Mirador **1** B3
El Reloj **3** B3

Hospedaje Gladys **2** A2
Hospedaje Lautaro 269 **7** B1
Hospedaje María Ester **5** B2
Hospedaje Mondaca **8** C2
Hospedaje Natti **10** C2
Hospedaje Patricio y Gedra Guzmán **21** A3
Hospedaje Pochi **6** B2
Hostal Araucarias **9** B1
Hostal Bon **11** B3

Hostal Español **13** B3
Hostal Las Quintas **15** C3
Hostería Coyhaique **12** B1
San Sebastián **22** A3

Eating 🍴
Café Alemana **5** B2
Café Oriente **2** B2
Café Ricer **3** B2
Casino de Bomberos **6** A2
Cipres **1** A3

Club Sandwich **13** B2
Donde Ramiro **4** B2
El Mastique **7** B2
Histórico Ricer **3** B2
La Casona **9** B1
La Fiorentina **10** B2
La Olla **8** B2
Las Piedras **11** B3
Yangtse **12** B3

Border crossings: Chile–Argentina

Coyhaique Alto

This crossing is 43 km east of Coyhaique, 6 km west of the border, open summer 0800-2200, winter 0800-2000. It is reached by a *ripio* road that runs east of Coyhaique past the **Monumento Natural Dos Lagunas**, US$2, camping US$15 per site, a small park that encompasses Lagos El Toro and Escondido with black-necked swans among the wildlife that can be seen from the short interpretive trails.

On the Argentine side, the road leads through Río Mayo and Sarmiento to Comodoro Rivadavia on the Atlantic seaboard. Chilean **immigration** is at Coyhaique Alto.

Paso Huemules

This crossing is 61 km southeast of Coyhaique, open summer 0800-2200, winter 0800-2000. It is reached by a paved road, Route 245, which runs southeast from Coyhaique, via Balmaceda airport. There is no accommodation at the frontier or at the airport and no public transport from the border to the airport. On the Argentine side, a *ripio* road runs via Lago Blanco (has fuel) to join Route 40, 105 km east of Paso Huemules.

See page 453 for transport details between Coyhaique and these crossings.

Carretera Austral (no information in English). Near the city, on the east bank of the Río Simpson, is the **Piedra del Indio**, a rock outcrop which, allegedly, looks like a face in profile. This is best viewed from the Puente Simpson, west bank of the Río Simpson.

There are two national reserves close to Coyhaique: 5 km northwest off the Carretera Austral is **Reserva Nacional Coyhaique**, which covers 2150 ha of forest (mainly introduced species) and has a number of well marked trails of between 20 minutes and five hours, while around the valley of the Río Simpson west of Coyhaique (take any bus to Puerto Aisén) is the **Reserva Nacional Río Simpson**, covering 40,827 ha of steep forested valleys and curiously rounded hills rising to 1878 m. One of these, near the western edge of the park, is known as '*El Cake Inglés*'. There are beautiful waterfalls, lovely views of the river and very good fly-fishing here, as well as trekking options. Wildlife includes pudú, pumas and huemul, as well as a variety of birds, ranging from condors to several species of duck. The administration office is 32 km west of Coyhaique, just off the road. On the southern side of the Reserva, 12 km west of Coyhaique reached by a separate *ripio* road, is the **Cerro Huemules**, where lots of wildlife can be seen including 23 bird species, foxes, wildcats and of course, the huemul.

Puerto Aisén and around

Puerto Aisén lies at the confluence of the rivers Aisén and Palos. First developed in the 1920s, the town grew as the major port of the region although it has now been replaced by Puerto Chacabuco, 15 km downriver. Few vestiges of the port remain today: boats lie high and dry on the riverbank when the tide is out and the foundations of buildings by the river are now overgrown with fuchsias and buttercups. To see any maritime activity you have to walk a little way out of town to **Puerto Aguas Muertas**, where the fishing boats come in.

The town is linked to the south bank of the Río Aisén by the Puente Presidente Ibáñez, once the longest suspension bridge in Chile. From the far bank a paved road leads to **Puerto**

Chacabuco; a regular bus service runs between the two. There is a helpful **tourist office** ① *Prat y Sgto Aldea, Dec-Feb only*, in the Municipalidad. For information on shipping, see www.portchacabuco.cl.

A good 10-km walk north along a minor road from Puerto Aisén leads to **Laguna Los Palos**, calm, deserted and surrounded by forested hills. En route is a bridge over a deep, narrow river; it's freezing cold but offers the chance for a bracing swim. **Lago Riesco**, 30 km south of Puerto Aisén, can be reached by an unpaved road that follows the Río Blanco. In season, the *Apulcheu* sails regularly from Puerto Chacabuco to **Termas de Chiconal** ① *US$50, 1 hr, on the northern shore of the Seno Aisén*, offering a good way to see the fjord; take your own food.

⊕ Coyhaique and around listings

For Sleeping and Eating price codes and other relevant information, see Essentials pages 35-42.

⊜ Sleeping

Coyhaique *p447, map p448*
The tourist office has a list of accommodation, but look for notices in windows since any place with fewer than 6 beds does not have to register with the authorities.
L-AL El Reloj, Baquedano 828, T067-231108, www.elrelojhotel.cl. Small boutique hotel in a former saw mill. Good restaurant, nice lounge, conference room, some rooms have wonderful views. English spoken. Best hotel in town. Highly recommended.
AL Hostería Coyhaique, Magallanes 131, T067-231137, www.hotelcoyhaique.cl. Bills itself as Coyhaique's premier hotel although it is showing its age. Set in spacious gardens, with decent rooms, doubles have full-size bathtub.
A Cabañas Mirador, Baquedano 848, T067-233191, www.miradorcoyhaique.blog spot.com. Fully equipped cabins sleeping 2-4. The end cabin has tremendous views. Advance booking essential in season (deposit required). Long-term lets off season.
A Hostal Español, Sargento Aldea 343, T067-242580, www.hostalcoyhaique.cl. New, small family-run hotel. 7 rooms all with views, carpets, bathrooms and cable TV. Spacious living room downstairs. Recommended, though there have been reports that reservations are not always honoured.

A San Sebastián, Baquedano 496, T067-233427, www.sansebastianhotel.cl. Small hotel with spacious rooms, all with view, good breakfast. Recommended, though could do with a refit.
B Cabañas Río Simpson, 3 km north of town, T067-232183, www.cabanasriosimpson.cl. Fully equipped cabins for 2-6 people plus 1 luxury cabin, **L** sleeping 7. Horse riding, fishing and tours. Several tame alpacas in the grounds.
B Hospedaje Gladys, Parra 65, T067-251076. **D** singles. Clean and well-kept rooms with cable TV. Some with bathrooms. Breakfast extra. Doubles as a beauty salon. A little dark and somewhat overpriced.
B Hostal Araucarias, Vielmo 71, T067-232707. Spacious, slightly creaky rooms with bath and TV, pleasant lounge with good view, quiet.
B Hostal Bon, Serrano 91, T067-231189, hostal_bon@hotmail.com. With breakfast, friendly, clean, cramped rooms, good meals.
C Albergue Las Salamandras, 2 km south of town, T067-211865, www.salamandras.cl. Double rooms, dorm beds are **E-F**, *cabañas* **B** and camping in attractive forest location. With breakfast, kitchen facilities, winter sports, trekking and tours. Maps, including good trekking maps, and cycling information provided. Wood-fired hot tub. English spoken. Informative website. Highly recommended.
C Hostal Las Quintas, Bilbao 1208, T067-231173. **D** singles. Spartan, but clean and extremely spacious rooms with bath and breakfast. Some rooms are architecturally

C Hospedaje Patricio y Gedra Guzmán,
Baquedano 20, T067-232520,
www.balasch.cl/cabanas. Small but
comfortable self-contained cabins on the
edge of town with extensive views. English
spoken. Good value. Range in quality from
tatty to excellent. Recommended. Preference
given to those taking Spanish classes.
C-D Hospedaje Natti, Av Simpson 417, T067-
231047. **F** singles. Clean, kitchen facilities,
breakfast US$2 extra. Also good-value
camping including access to hot showers.
C-D Hospedaje Pochi, Freire 342, T067-
256968. **F** singles. Rooms in a family home
with bath and cable TV, breakfast included.
Cluttered garden, very pleasant owners,
English spoken by the daughter. Good
value. Recommended.
D Hospedaje Lautaro 269, T067-237184.
F singles. Large old creaky wooden house, with
parking, internet access and kitchen facilities.
Camping available in the front garden.
D Hospedaje María Ester, Lautaro 544,
T067-233023. **F** singles. Some rooms with
bath and TV. Friendly, local information given,
laundry facilities, good value but breakfast
is extra and kitchen use charged for.
D Hospedaje Mondaca, Av Simpson 571,
T067-254676. **F** singles. Small (only 3 rooms)
but spotless family home. Friendly, breakfast
extra, will heat up pre-prepared food.

Campsites

Sernatur in Coyhaique (see page 447) has
a full list of all sites in Región XI. Also see
Albergue las Salamandras, Hospedaje Natti
and Hospedaje Lautaro 269, above. There are
several other campsites in Coyhaique and on
the road to Puerto Aisén, including:
Camping Alborada, Km 1 towards Puerto
Aisén, T067-238868. US$14, with hot shower.
Camping Río Correntoso, Km 42 towards
Puerto Aisén, T067-232005. US$20, showers
and fishing.
  In the Reserva Nacional Coyhaique, there
are basic campsites, US$7, at Laguna Verde
and at Casa Bruja, 4 km and 2 km
respectively from the entrance, and a

refugio, US$2, 3 km from the entrance.
There's also a campsite near the turning
to Santuario San Sebastián, US$7, in the
Reserva Nacional Río Simpson.

Puerto Aisén and around p449

Accommodation can be hard to find, most is
geared towards workers in the fishing industry
in both Puerto Aisén and Puerto Chacabuco.
There's no campsite but free camping is easy.
LL-L Parque Turístico Loberías de Aisén,
Carrera 50, Puerto Chacabuco, T067-351112,
www.loberiasdelsur.cl. Recently rebuilt 5-star
complex, the best hotel serving the best food
in this area. Climb up the steps direct from
the port for a drink or a meal overlooking
boats and mountains before boarding
your ferry. Car hire available.
A Patagonia Green, 400m from bridge
(on Pto Chacabuco side), T067-336796,
www.patagonia green.cl. Nice cabins for up
to 5, kitchen, heating, TV, gardens, arranges
tours to Laguna San Rafael, fishing, mountain
biking, riding, trekking, etc, English spoken.
A-B Hotel Caicahues, Michimalonco 660,
Puerto Aisén, T067-336633. With bath,
heating, telephone and internet; book
in advance. Recommended.
B-C Hotel Plaza, O'Higgins 613, Puerto
Aisén, T067-332784. **E** singles. Basic, without
breakfast, some rooms with no windows.
C Mar Clara, Carrera 970, Puerto Aisén,
T067-330030. **F** singles. More expensive
with bath. Basic, clean, thin walls, looks
nicer from the outside than from within.
D Moraleda, O'Higgins 82, Puerto
Chacabuco, T067-351155. **F** singles.
Basic. Full board available.

Eating

Coyhaique p447, map p448

₩₩₩ Restaurant Histórico Ricer, Horn 48 y 40,
piso 2, T067-232920. Regional specialities,
historical exhibits, recommended, though
somewhat overpriced and a bit of a
tourist trap.

₸₸-₸₸ Cipres, Baquedano 022, T067-25183. Bizarre entrance through someone's house leading to a restaurant with as breathtaking a view as any in Coyhaique. Aims for rustic elegance, occasionally at odds with the music. Patagonian-Mediterranean cuisine. Abundant portions, decent food, wine sold by the glass.

₸₸ El Reloj, Baquedano 444, T067-231108. Unusual dishes using all local ingredients. Good service, recommended.

₸₸ La Casona, Obispo Vielmo 77, T067-238894. Good lamb and fish dishes, long-standing reputation, popular with locals, considered by many to be the best in town, recommended.

₸₸ La Olla, Gral Prat 176, T067-242588. Spanish, excellent cuisine, not cheap but there are good-value lunches. Recommended.

₸₸ Las Piedras, 21 de Mayo 655, T067-233243. Slightly upmarket but with good-value set lunches. Dishes include venison and emu. Fills up at weekends. Recommended.

₸₸ Yangtse, Bilbao 715, T067-242173. Better than average (in Chilean terms) Chinese. You can hear your food being stir-fried fresh to order. Reasonable prices but the quantity of MSG leaves you almost happy to fork out for the exorbitantly expensive drinks.

₸₸-₸ Casino de Bomberos, Gral Parra 365, T067-231437. Wide range, large portions, very good value. Slow service, especially if the overdressed tip-hungry waiters are doting on a table of cruise ship tourists.

₸₸-₸ Donde Ramiro, Freire 319, T067-256885. Decent basic set lunches. Big screen TV. A good place to watch football matches.

₸₸-₸ La Fiorentina, Prat 230, T067-238899. Good value pizza and pasta.

₸ El Mastique, Bilbao 141. Cheap but good pasta and Chilean food.

₸ Club Sandwich, Moraleda 433. 24-hr fast food.

Cafés

Café Alemana, Condell 119. Excellent cakes, coffee, vegetarian dishes. Recommended.
Café Oriente, Condell 201 y 21 de Mayo. Good bakery, serves tea.
Café Ricer, Horn 48. Also serves light food.

Puerto Aisén and around *p449*
There are many cheap places on Aldea, between Municipal and Dougnac.

₸₸ Café Restaurante Ensenada, O'Higgins 302, Puerto Chacabuco. Basic grub.

₸₸ Restaurante La Cascada, Km 32 between Coyhaique and Puerto Aisén. Waterfalls nearby. Recommended for meat and fish.

⦿ Bars and clubs

Coyhaique *p447, map p448*
Bar West, Bilbao y 12 de Octubre. Western-style bar.
El Boliche, Moraleda 380. A bar for the beer-drinking crowd. Many bars on the same street.
Pepe le Pub, Parra 72. Good cocktails and snacks, relaxed, live music at weekends.
Piel Roja, Moraleda y Condell. Friendly, laid-back atmosphere, meals served, not cheap.

Puerto Aisén and around *p449*
The following are all in Puerto Aisén. There are a couple of smaller bars on Sargento Aldea; one has a wildly sloping pool table.
Crazzy Pub, Aldea 1170. Make up your own mind how 'crazzy' it is.
Dina's, Carrera 1270. Disco.

⦿ Festivals and events

Puerto Aisén and around *p449*
2nd week of Nov Local festival of folklore is held in Puerto Aisén.

O Shopping

Coyhaique *p447, map p448*
Food, especially fruit and vegetables, is more expensive here than in Santiago. For *artesanía* try the **Feria de Artesanía** on the plaza or **Manos Azules**, Riquelme 435. **Kaienk**, Plaza 219-A, T067-2245216, www.telaresdela patagonia.cl, sells good-quality locally produced knitware. Decent camping

equipment can be obtained from **Condor Explorer**, Dussen 357, T067-670349. There are large supermarkets at Prat y Lautaro and Lautaro y Cochrane. Good sheep's cheese is occasionally available from a kiosk by the plaza. **El Rincón del Poeta**, Moraleda y Parra has a good selection of local-interest books as well as a small selection of second-hand books in English. **Fly Fishing Suray**, Prat 231, for fly-fishing equipment.

▲ Activities and tours

Coyhaique *p447, map p448*
A full list of specialist tours and fishing guides is available from **Sernatur**, see page 447. There is also an association of independent local guides who offer (as a rule) good-value and well-informed excursions within the region. See www.escueladeguias.cl for more information.
Albergue Las Salamandras, see Sleeping, page 450. Excursions and good trekking information available.
Casa del Turismo Rural, Dussen 357-B, T067-214031, www.casaturismorural.cl, Mon-Fri 1000-1330, 1530-2000 (also weekends in high season). An association of 40 or so families, mostly in the countryside, who offer activities such as horse riding and fishing. Many of these people do not have telephones or internet so make reservations here.

Fishing
There are excellent opportunities for fishing in the Coyhaique area, especially southwest at Lagos Atrevesado (20 km) and Elizalde (also yachting and camping), and southeast at lagos Frío, Castor and Pollux. In addition to those listed below, most of the general tour operators offer specialist fishing trips.

Tour operators
Andes Patagónicos, Horn 48 y 40, local 11, T067-216711, www.ap.cl. Trips to local lakes as well as Tortel, historically based tours and bespoke trips all year round. Good, but not cheap. General tourist information.

Aysen Tour, Gral Parra 97, T067-237070, www.aysentour.cl. Typical range of tours along the Carretera Austral.
Cabot, Lautaro 339, T067-230101, www.cabot.cl. Horse-riding excursions to Cerro Castillo and other tours.
Camello Patagón, Moraleda 463, T067-244327, www.camellopatagon.cl. Trips to Capilla de Marmol in Río Tranquilo.
Condor Explorer, Dussen 357, T067-573634, www.condorexplorer.com. Good small-scale agency who specialize in trekking but also do general Carretera tours. English spoken. Recommended.
Expediciones Coyhaique, Portales 195, T067-231783, www.coyhaiqueflyfishing.com. Fly-fishing experts.
Geo Turismo, Balmaceda 334, T067-573460, www.geoturismopatagonia.cl. Offers wide range of tours throughout the region, English spoken, professional, recommended.
Turismo Prado de la Patagonia, 21 de Mayo 417, T067-231271, www.turismoprado.cl. Tours of local lakes and other sights, Laguna San Rafael trips and historical tours. Also offers general tourist information and accepts TCs.

Skiing
El Fraile, office in Coyhaique at Dussen y Plaza de Armas 376, T067-231690. Near Lago Frío, 29 km southeast of Coyhaique, this ski resort has 5 pistes, 2 lifts, a basic café and equipment hire (season Jun-Sep).

Puerto Aisén *p449*
Turismo Rucaray, on the plaza, rucaray@ entelchile.net. Recommended for local tours. Internet access.

⊖ Transport

Coyhaique *p447, map p448*
Air
From Tte Vidal airport, **Don Carlos** flies to **Chile Chico**, Mon-Sat, US$50; to **Cochrane**, Mon and Thu, 45 mins, US$75, and to **Villa O'Higgins**, Mon and Thu, US$100, recommended only for

those who like flying, have strong stomachs, or are in a hurry. Note that a number of Don Carlos' planes have gone down in the last couple of years. There are also flights to **Tortel**, Wed, US$35, but these are subsidized for residents of the village; foreigners may fly if there's a free seat, but expect to pay more.

Balmaceda airport is used by LanChile and Sky for flights to **Santiago**, several daily, US$90-270 return plus tax (depending on season and flexibility), and **Puerto Montt**, several daily, US$55-215 return plus tax. Sky also flies to **Punta Arenas**, 3 flights weekly, US$85-170 return plus tax. The best one-way fares are generally with Sky. For details of transport to/from the airport, see page 447.

Airline offices Sky, Prat 203, T067-240827, local calls T600-600 2828; LanChile, Moraleda 402, T067-231188, local calls T600-526 2000; Don Carlos, Subteniente Cruz 63, T067-231981.

Bus

Local A full listing of bus timetables is posted outside the Sernatur office (see page 447). The main terminal is at Lautaro y Magallanes but many companies use their own offices. In the terminal there is a left-luggage store as well as the following companies: Bus São Paulo, T067-255726; Bus Sur, T067-211460, www.bus-sur.cl; Don Oscar, T067-254335, Giobbi, T067-232607; Interlagos, T067-240840, www.patagonia interlagos.cl; Queilen Bus, T067-240760; Trans Austral, T067-232067; Transportes Terra Austral, T067-254335; Via Bariloche, T067-253841. Other companies are Bus Bronco, Lautaro 728; Buses Becker, Parra 335, T067-2321670; Buses Daniela, Baquedano 1122, T067-231701; Buses Queulat, Parra 329, T067-242626; Don Carlos, Subteniente Cruz 63, T067-232981; Suray, Prat 265, T067-238387.

Long distance To **Puerto Montt**, via Bariloche and Osorno, all year, Trans Austral, Tue and Fri 1645, US$50; Queilen Bus, Mon, Wed, Fri, Sat, US$50, with connections to Valdivia, Temuco, Santiago and Castro, often heavily booked. To **Punta Arenas** via Coyhaique Alto and Comodoro Rivadavia,

Bus Sur, Tue, US$55. To **Bariloche** (Argentina), Via Bariloche, Daily, 0730, US$21. To **Comodoro Rivadavia** (Argentina), Trans Austral, Mon, Fri, 0800, 12 hrs, US$35.

Carretera Austral Suray and São Paulominibuses run to **Puerto Aisén** every 15 mins between them, 1 hr, US$2, with connections for Puerto Chacabuco. There are also a few buses daily to **Mañihuales**.

Colectivos to **Puerto Ibáñez** on Lago General Carrera will pick you up at 0700 from your hotel to connect with *El Pilchero* ferry to Chile Chico, 2 hrs, book the day before, US$7; operators include Bus Carolina, T067-219009; Bus Freddy, T09-6503593; Dario Figueroa, T067-233286; Miguel Acuña, T067-251579.

Bus services further afield vary according to demand: north to **Chaitén** via Puyuhuapi and La Junta, Buses Queulat and Buses Becker, 3 weekly between them, US$34. To **Futaleufú** via La Junta, Buses Becker, Buses Queulat and Buses Daniela, US$34. To **Lago Verde** via La Junta, Gerardo Valenzuela, (T09-8197 8793), US$18; also Bus Bronco, Wed, Fri, Sat. To **Puerto Cisnes**, Transportes Terra Austral and Don Oscar, each Mon-Sat, US$9.

South to **Cochrane**, Sao Paulo, and Don Carlos, and Acuario 13, US$19. Buses to Cochrane stop at **Cerro Castillo**, US$6, **Bahía Murta**, US$10, **Puerto Río Tranquilo**, US$13, and outside **Puerto Bertrand**, US$15. To **Tortel**, direct services on Wed and Sat.

Bicycle hire

Manuel Iduarte, Parra y Bulnes, check condition first; Bilbao 500 block, poor supply of spares but good repair service; Motortech, Baquedano 131; Tomás Enrique, Madrid Urrea, Pje Foitzick y Libertad, T067-252132. Bicycle spares repair services are also available from several shops on Simpson.

Car hire

AGS, Av Ogana 1298, T067-253225; Automotriz Varona, Carrera 330, T067-216673, www.varona.cl; Automundo AVR, Bilbao 510,

T067-231621; **Sur Nativo Renta Car**; Baquedano 457, T067-231648; **Turismo Prado**, 21 de Mayo 417, T067-231271, www.turismoprado.cl.

Mechanic at **Automotores Santiago**, C Los Nires 811, T067-238330, T099-640 6896, speaks English, can obtain spare parts quickly.

Ferry

Shipping offices are at are at **Navimag**, Horn 47-D, T067-233306, www. navimag.com; **Catamaranes del Sur**, Carrera 50, Puerto Chacabuco, T067-351112, www.catamaranes delsur.cl; **Naviera Austral**, Terminal de Transbordadores, Puerto Chacabuco, T067-351493, www.navieraustral.cl; **Navimag**, Terminal de Transbordadores, Puerto Chacabuco, T067-351111, www. navimag.cl.

Taxi

Hailing a taxi on the street is expensive and fares are 50% extra after 2100. It is cheaper to call a radio taxi T067-242424, any journey within the city limits US$2. *Colectivos* congregate at Prat y Bilbao, fare US$0.70.

Puerto Aisén *p449*
Bus

To **Puerto Chacabuco**, Suray, every 20 mins, US$0.75. For services to **Coyhaique**, see above.

Ferry

Shipping offices are at **Catamaranes del Sur**, Carrera 50, Puerto Chacabuco, T067-351112, www.catamaranes delsur.cl; **Naviera Austral**, Terminal de Transbordadores, Puerto Chacabuco, T067-351493, www.navieraustral.cl; **Navimag**, Terminal de Transbordadores, Puerto Chacabuco, T067-351111, www.navimag.cl.

Navimag have year-round ferry services from Puerto Chacabuco to **Puerto Montt** via the Canal Moraleda 1 or 2 a week in summer, irregular off season, 24 hrs, from US$55, cars US$235. See also page 423. **Naviera Austral** have a service from Puerto Chacabuco to **Quellón** via Puerto Cisnes, Raúl Marín Balmaceda and Melinka, irregular off season, from US$55, cars US$220.

Several companies offer trips of varying length to **Laguna San Rafael**. **Patagonia Connection SA**, Fidel Oteíza 1921, of 1006, Providencia, Santiago, T02-225 6489, www.patagonia-connection.com, operates all-inclusive 3-day tours from Puerto Chacabuco to Laguna San Rafael, from US$990 per person, including the Patagonia Express catamaran service from Puerto Chacabuco via **Termas de Puyuhuapi** (see page 442), overnight accommodation at Termas de Puyuhuapi and a day excursion to Laguna San Rafael. Boat information is posted at **Turismo Rucaray**. Also, contact **Navimag**, Terminal de Transbordadores, Puerto Chacabuco, T067-351111, www.navimag.cl.

O Directory

Coyhaique *p447, map p448*
Banks Several with **Redbanc** ATMs in centre, for dollars, TCs and Argentine pesos. Both the following *casas de cambio* are recommended: **Casa de Cambio Emperador**, Bilbao 222, and Lucía Saldivia, Baquedano 285. **Internet** Ciber Patagonia, 21 de Mayo 525, best value; several others. **Language schools** Baquedano Language School, Baquedano 20, T067-232520, www.balasch.cl. US$400 per week, including 4 hrs 1-to-1 tuition daily, lodging and all meals, other activities organized at discount rates, friendly, informative, highly recommended. **Laundry** Lavandería, Simpson 417-A; QL, Bilbao 160. **Medical services** Hospital, C Hospital 068, T067-233172. **Post office** Cochrane 202, Mon-Fri 0900-1230, 1430-1800, Sat 0830-1200. **Telephone** Several call centres; shop around as prices are relatively expensive.

Puerto Aisén *p449*
Banks BCI, Prat, for Visa; Banco de Chile, Plaza de Armas, only changes cash, not TCs. There's a Redbanc ATM in Puerto Chacabuco. **Post office** South side of bridge. **Telephone** Plaza de Armas, next to Turismo Rucaray; ENTEL, Libertad 408, internet access.

Lago General Carrera

→ *Colour map 5, B3.*

The section of the Carretera Austral around the north and western sides of Lago General Carrera is reckoned by many people to be the most spectacular stretch of all. Straddling the border with Argentina, this is the largest lake in South America after Lake Titicaca and is now believed to be the deepest lake on the continent; soundings in 1997 established its maximum depth as 590 m.

The lake is a beautiful azure blue, surrounded at its Chilean end by predominantly alpine terrain and at the Argentine end by dry pampa. The region prides itself on having the best climate in southern Chile, with some 300 days of sunshine a year; much fruit is grown as a result, especially around Chile Chico, where rainfall is very low for this area. In general, the climate here is more similar to Argentine Patagonia than to the rest of the Carretera Austral region.
▶▶ *For listings, see pages 460-463.*

Ins and outs

Getting there The main towns, Puerto Ibáñez on the north shore and Chile Chico on the south, are connected by a ferry, *El Pilchero*. Overland routes between Coyhaique and Chile Chico are much longer, passing either through Argentina, or along the Carretera Austral, which runs west around the lake.

Getting around Minibuses run along the Carretera Austral in summer and air taxis link the small towns of the region.

Reserva Nacional Cerro Castillo and around

Beyond Coyhaique, the Carretera Austral runs through slightly wilder, more rugged land, with the occasional cow or wild horse feeding by the side of the road. Some 40 km south of Coyhaique, the carretera enters the Reserva Nacional Cerro Castillo, which extends over 179,550 ha. The park is named after the fabulous **Cerro Castillo** (2675 m), which resembles a fairy-tale castle with rock pinnacles jutting out from a covering of snow. It also includes Cerro Bandera (2040 m) just west of Balmaceda and several other peaks in the northern wall of the valley of the Río Ibáñez. The park offers a number of excellent day treks and some of the best self-contained multi-day trekking in Patagonia. There is a *guardería* at the northeastern end of the park near Laguna Chinguay and a **CONAF** campsite ① *T067-237070, US$8 per site*, nearby. At Km 83 the road crosses the **Portezuelo Ibáñez** (1120 m) and drops through the **Cuesta del Diablo**, a series of bends with fine views over the Río Ibáñez.

The principal port on the Chilean section of the lake, **Puerto Ibáñez** (officially Puerto Ingeniero Ibáñez) is reached by taking a paved branch road, 31 km long, from La Bajada 97 km south of Coyhaique. You will probably just pass through to reach the ferry. It is, however, a centre for distinctive pottery, leather production and vegetable growing (you can visit potters and buy salad from greenhouses). Local archaeology includes rock art and the largest Tehuelche cemetery in Patagonia. There are some fine waterfalls, including the **Salto Río Ibáñez**, 6 km north.

From the turning to Puerto Ibáñez the Carretera Austral goes through **Villa Cerro Castillo** (Km 8), a quiet village in a spectacular setting beneath the striking, jagged peaks of Cerro Castillo, overlooking the broad valley below. There's a petrol station, public phone, several food shops and a tiny tourist information kiosk by the road side (January-February only), with details of guides offering trekking to the Cerro, and horse rides.

The village is a good place to stop for a few days with two appealing attractions. There's a truly spectacular four-day trek around the fairytale castle peaks of Cerro Castillo, in the Reserva Nacional Cerro Castillo. The walk starts at Las Horquetas Grandes, a bend in the river Río Ibáñez, 8 km south of the park entrance, where any bus driver will let you off. It follows Río La Lima to the gorgeous Laguna Cerro Castillo, then follows animal trails around the peak itself, returning to the village (accommodation or bus back to Coyhaique). This is a challenging walk: attempt it only if fit, and ideally, take a guide, as trails are poorly marked (IGM map essential, purchase in advance in Coyhaique). The *guardería* is on the Senda Ibáñez, 50 m to the left of the main road (as you head south), opposite Laguna Chinguay to the right, with access to walks and **campsite** ① *camping US$5, November-March, beware of the biting dog*, take equipment – there are no *refugios*. The picnic ground is open summer 0830-2100, winter to 1830. A new, equally if not more spectacular five-day trekking route around Monreal has recently been opened up. Ask in Villa Cerro Castillo for details.

A few kilometres south of the village is the **Monumento Nacional Manos de Cerro Castillo** ① *US$1 charged Dec-Apr*. In a shallow cave, a few handprints have been made on

Lago General Carrera

Native deer

The Andean huemul (*Hippocamelus bisulcus*) is a mountain deer native to the Andes of southern Chile and Argentina. Sharing the Chilean national crest with the Andean condor, the huemul (pronounced 'way-mool') is a medium-sized stocky cervid adapted to survival in rugged mountain terrain. Males grow antlers and have distinctive black face masks.

Human pressures have pushed the huemul to the brink of extinction and current numbers are estimated at 1000-1500. The huemul has become the focal point of both national and international conservation efforts, carried out primarily by **CONAF** and the **Comité pro la Defensa de la Fauna y Flora de Chile** (CODEFF).

Your best chance of seeing the huemul is in one of two reserves managed by CONAF: the **Reserva Nacional Río Claro**, which lies on the southeastern corner of the larger Reserva Nacional Río Simpson just outside

Coyhaique, and the **Reserva Nacional Tamango**, near Cochrane. To visit either of these you will need to be accompanied by a warden: ask in Coyhaique or Cochrane to make sure someone is available.

The Carretera Austral area is also one of the best places for trying to spot the equally rare pudú. This miniature creature, around 40 cm tall and weighing only 10 kg, is the smallest member of the deer family in the world. Native to southern Argentina and Chile, the pudú is listed in Chile as vulnerable to extinction, largely due to habitat loss, but also because its unique appearance (the males grow two short spiked antlers) has made it a target for poaching for zoos. Reddish-brown in colour, the pudú is ideally adapted to the dense temperate rainforests of Chile and Argentina, scooting along on trails through the undergrowth, leaving behind minuscule cloven tracks.

the side of vertical rocks high above the Río Ibáñez. There's no clue to their significance, but they're in a beautiful place with panoramic views. This makes a delightful two-hour walk. The site is accessible all year, signposted clearly from the road. There is also a small **local museum** ① *2 km south of Villa Cerro Castillo, open Dec-Mar 0900-1200.*

The road climbs out of the valley, passing the emerald-green **Laguna Verde** and the Portezuelo Cofré. It descends to the boggy Manso Valley, with a good campsite at the bridge over the river; watch out for mosquitoes.

The western shore

Some 5 km from the Carretera Austral, at Km 203, is **Bahía Murta**, situated on the northern tip of the central arm of Lago General Carrera. This sleepy, almost forgotten village dates from the 1930s, when it exported timber to Argentina via Chile Chico. There is a tiny tourist information hut, which in theory opens summer 1000-1430, 1500-1930. Back on the carretera, the road follows the lake's western shore. At Km 207 from Coyhaique is a small privately owned forest of ancient and gnarled Arrayanes, worth a visit, US$3.50. Some 20 km further south is **Río Tranquilo**, where the buses stop for lunch and fuel is available. The lake reflects the mountains that surround it and the clouds above. Close to Río Tranquilo is the unusual **Catedral de Mármol**, a peninsula made of marble, with fascinating caves that can be visited by boat ① *2 hrs for the whole tour, US$45 to hire a boat with guide and be prepared to get wet. The best time to go is early in the morning when the lake is calmer.* The village also has an unusual cemetery made up of mausolea in the form of miniature Chilote-style houses. A new branch of the Carretera Austral heads northwest from Río Tranquilo to **Puerto Grosse** on the coast at Bahía Exploradores. At Km 52 on this road is a *refugio* from which a well-maintained path (US$5 entry) leads to a lookout opposite the Exploradores glacier. **Guided hikes** ① *US$45 per person, 6 hrs including 2-3 hrs on the glacier, crampons provided*, are available. The hike can be treacherous in bad weather. Book though **El Puesto** in Río Tranquilo.

South to Puerto Bertrand

The road continues along the edge of the azure lake, with snow-covered mountains with pointed peaks visible in the distance. At the southwestern tip of Lago General Carrera, at Km 279, is **El Maitén**, from where a road branches off east along the south shore of the lake towards Chile Chico. South of El Maitén, meanwhile, the Carretera Austral becomes steeper and more winding; in winter this stretch is icy and dangerous. The picturesque tranquil village of **Puerto Bertrand**, 5 km away, is a good place for fishing and the best base in the region for whitewater rafting and kayaking. Day hikes are possible along decent trails. Nearby is a sign showing the *Nacimiento del Río Baker*: the place where the turquoise Río Baker begins. This area is home to the most impressive hydrological system in Chile, with its most voluminous river, its biggest lake to the north and a huge icefield to the west. Beyond Puerto Bertrand, the road climbs up to high moorland, passing the confluence of the ríos Neff and Baker, before winding south along the east bank of the Río Baker. On a sunny day it is hard to imagine more pleasant surroundings. The road is rough but not treacherous and the scenery is splendid all the way to Cochrane. Watch out for cattle and hares on the road (and the occasional huemul) and take blind corners slowly.

The southern shore of Lago General Carrera

Some 10 km east of El Maitén, **Puerto Guadal** is a friendly, picturesque town that is a centre for fishing. It also has shops, accommodation, restaurants, a post office, petrol and a lovely stretch of lakeside beach. Further east along the shore, just past the nondescript village of **Mallín Grande**, Km 40, the road runs through the **Paso de las Llaves**, a 30-km stretch carved out of the rock face on the edge of the lake. The south side of the lake is much drier than the rest of the Carretera but there are still gorges and waterfalls dotted along the route. The landscape is more open as there is less of an influence from the icefields. The road climbs and drops, narrow and poor in places, offering wonderful views across the lake and the icefields to the west. At Km 74, a turning runs to **Fachinal**. A further 5 km east is the **Garganta del Diablo**, an impressive narrow gorge of 120 m with a fast-flowing stream below. Further on there is an open-cast mine, which produces gold and other metals.

Chile Chico and around → *www.chilechico.cl.*

Chile Chico is a quiet, friendly but dusty town situated on the lake shore 122 km east of El Maitén, close to the Argentine border. The town dates from 1909 when settlers crossed from Argentina and occupied the land, leading to conflict with cattle ranchers who had been given settlement rights by the Chilean government. In the showdown that followed (known as the war of Chile Chico) the ranchers were driven out by the settlers, but it was not until 1931 that the Chilean government finally recognized the town's existence.

Now the centre of a fruit-growing region, it has an annual festival at the end of January and a small **museum** (summer only); outside is a boat that carried cargo on the lake before the opening of the road along the southern shore. There are fine views from the **Cerro de las Banderas** at the western end of town. The **tourist office**, on O'Higgins, is helpful.

Border crossings: Chile–Argentina

Chile Chico

Chilean immigration Open September-April 0730-2200, May-August 0800-2000.
A road runs 2 km east from Chile Chico to the border and on for 5 km to **Los Antiguos**, a town with a cherry festival in January. **Perito Moreno**, 67 km east of the border, has accommodation, a restaurant and money exchange services. About 120 km south is **Cueva de las Manos**, where the walls of a series of galleries are covered with painted human hands and animals, 10,000 years old. All but 31 of the 800 hands are left hands.

To the south and west of Chile Chico is good walking terrain, through weird rock formations and dry brush scrub. The northern and higher peak of **Cerro Pico del Sur** (2168 m) can be climbed by the agile from Los Cipres (beware dogs in the farmyard). You will need a long summer's day and the 1:50,000 map. Follow the horse trail until it peters out, then navigate by compass or sense of direction until the volcano-like summit appears. After breaching the cliff ramparts, there is some scrambling and a 3-m pitch to the summit, from where you'll enjoy indescribable views of the lake and the Andes.

About 20 km south of Chile Chico towards Lago Jeinimeni is the **Cueva de las Manos**, a cave full of Tehuelche paintings, the most famous of which are the *manos azules* (blue hands). From the road, climb 500 m and cross the Pedregoso stream. The path is difficult, and partly hidden, so you're recommended to take a guide.

Reserva Nacional Lago Jeinimeni

ⓘ *53 km south of Chile Chico, open all year but access may be impossible Apr-Oct due to high river levels, US$4, camping US$8. Lifts from Chile Chico; see CONAF office.*
This park covers 160,000 ha and includes two lakes, **Lago Jeinimeni** and **Lago Verde**, which lie surrounded by forests in the narrow valley of the Río Jeinimeni. Impressive cliffs, waterfalls and small glaciers provide habitat for huemul deer, pumas and condors. Activities include fishing for salmon and rainbow trout, trekking and rowing. Access is via an unpaved road, which branches south off the road to Los Antiguos and crosses five rivers, four of which have to be forded. At Km 42, there is a small lake, **Laguna de los Flamencos**, where large numbers of flamingos can be seen. The park entrance is at Km 53; just beyond is a ranger station, a campsite and fishing area at the eastern end of Lago Jeinimeni. Take all supplies, including a good map.

⊕ Lago General Carrera listings

For Sleeping and Eating price codes and other relevant information, see Essentials pages 35-42.

⊜ Sleeping

Reserva Nacional Cerro Castillo and around *p456*
B Cabañas Shehen Aike, Risopatrón 55, Puerto Ibáñez, T067-423284, www.aike.cl.

Children-friendly cabin complex run by a Swiss-Chilean family. Lots of information on the local area as well as horse riding and fishing trips. English, German, French spoken. Recommended.
C Residencial Villarrica, O'Higgins 59, Villa Cerro Castillo, T067-419500. **F** singles. Basic good-value accommodation, good mid-price meals and a grocery store. Also cabins, **A-B**.

D Cabañas Don Niba, Los Pioneros 872, Villa Cerro Castillo, T067-419920. **F** singles. Another friendly but basic *hospedaje*. Good value. Recommended.

D Residencial Ibáñez, Bertrán Dixon 31, Puerto Ibáñez, T067-423227. **F** singles. Clean, warm, hot water. Similar next door at No 29.

D Vientos del Sur, Bertrán Dixon 283, Puerto Ibáñez, T067-423208. **F** singles. Cheap meals available, good.

Camping

Municipal campsite, Puerto Ibáñez, T067-423234. Open Dec-Mar, US$10 per site.

The western shore p458

In February there is often a lack of accommodation in Río Tranquilo.

AL Hostal el Puesto, Pedro Lagos 258, Río Tranquilo, T02-1964555, www.elpuesto.cl. No doubt the most comfortable place in the area. The owners can organize a variety of tours.

A Hostal Los Pinos, Godoy 51, T067-411576, Río Tranquilo. Family run, well maintained, basic rooms with bath. Overpriced, but better standard than most. Mid-price meals served (check price first).

B Campo Alacaluf, Km 44 on the Río Tranquilo–Bahía Exploradores side road. Wonderful guesthouse hidden miles away from civilization and run by a very friendly eccentric German family. Good-value camping. Meals served, boxed lunches available. Recommended.

C Cabañas Jacricalor, Carretera Austral 245, Río Tranquilo, T067-419500 (public phone). **F** singles. Tent-sized *cabañas*.

C Hostería Carretera Austral, 1 Sur 223, Río Tranquilo, T067-419500 (public phone), lopezpinuer@yahoo.es. Serves cheap meals.

C-D Hospedaje y Cabañas Silvana, Godoy 197, Río Tranquilo. Basic accommodation. Clean and good value.

E Hostería Lago General Carrera, Av 5 de Abril 647 y Colombia, Bahía Murta, T067-419 600 (public phone). **F-G** singles. Cheap meals.

E Residencial Patagonia, Pasaje España 64, Bahía Murta, T067-419600 (public telephone). **F-G** singles. Very basic, without bath.

Camping

Free camping is possible by the lake in Bahía Murta, with good views of Cerro Castillo.

Camping Pudú, 1km south of Río Tranquilo, www.puduexpediciones.cl.

South to Puerto Bertrand p459

LL Mallín Colorado, 2 km west of El Maitén, T02-2741807, www.mallincolorado.cl. *Cabañas*, adventure activities, horse riding, rafting, fishing, English and German spoken.

L Hacienda Tres Lagos, 2 km west of Cruce El Maitén, Chile Chico, T067-411323, T02-333 4122 (Santiago) www.haciendatres lagos.com. Set in spacious grounds on the lakeshore. With a capacity of only 34 guests, this boutique resort is an unexpected piece of luxury in the middle of Patagonia. The

bungalows and suites are much nicer than the standard cabins. Good restaurant, games room, wide range of excursions offered, sauna, jacuzzi. Good service. English spoken. Recommended.

AL Patagonia Baker Lodge, Orillas del Río Baker, 3 km north of Puerto Bertrand, T067-411903, www.pbl.cl. Fishing lodge. Advance booking only.

A Río Baker Lodge, Costanera s/n, Puerto Bertrand, T067-411499, riobaker@ hotmail.com. Fly-fishing lodge.

C Hostería Puerto Bertrand, Sector Costanera, Puerto Bertrand, T067-419900 (public phone). **E** singles. Also meals, cabañas, and activities.

D Doña Ester, Casa 8, Puerto Bertrand. Rooms in a pink house. **F** singles. Full board available. Good.

Camping is available in the village, basic, but with access to hot water.

Chile Chico *p459*
C Hostería de la Patagonia, Camino Internacional s/n, T067-411337. **D** singles; full board available. Clean, excellent food, English, French and Italian spoken, trekking, horse riding and whitewater rafting organized, also camping.

C Ventura, Carrera 290, T067-411311. **E** singles. Unprepossessing rooms with bath.

C-D Casa Quinta No Me Olvides, Camino Internacional s/n, Sector Chacra. **E-F** singles. Without bath, clean, cooking facilities. Also camping. Tours arranged.

C-D Plaza, Balmaceda 102 y O'Higgins, T067-411215. Basic, clean.

E Hospedaje Don Luis, Balmaceda 175, T067-411384. **F-G** singles. Clean, meals available.

Camping

Free campsite at Bahía Jarra, 5 km from Chile Chico, then 12 km north. **Camping del Sol** at the eastern end of the town.

🍴 Eating

Most *hosterías* and *residenciales* will serve meals (see Sleeping, above).

Chile Chico *p459*
🍴 **Café Holiday**, C González. Good coffee, friendly service.
🍴 **Cafetería Loly y Elizabeth**, González 25, on plaza. Serves coffee, ice cream and cakes.

🍷 Bars and clubs

Chile Chico *p459*
Pub El Minero, Carrera 205. Recommended for a drink.

🎉 Festivals and events

South to Puerto Bertrand *p459*
3rd weekend of Feb Semana de Bertrand. 3 days of drunken revelry.

Chile Chico *p459*
Last week of Jan The town hosts the Festival Internacional de la Voz.

🎫 Activities and tours

The western shore *p458*
El Puesto Expediciones, Lagos 258, Río Tranquilo, T02-1964555, www.elpuesto.cl. Fishing, icehiking, kayaking and other trips.

South to Puerto Bertrand *p459*
Horse riding, fishing guides and whitewater rafting in the Río Baker (generally easy with a few Grade-III rapids) can all be arranged at the tourist information office, T067-419900 (public phone). Advance booking helpful.
Hacienda Tres Lagos, see Sleeping, run a series of Canopy zip lines, US$30.
Patagonia Adventure Expeditions, T067-411330, www.adventurepatagonia.com. Professional outfit running exclusive fully

supported treks to the Campo de Hielo Norte and the eastern side of Parque Nacional Laguna San Rafael. Expensive but a unique experience and recommended. Also organize rafting on the Río Baker and provide general help organising tours, treks and expeditions.

The southern shore *p459*
Pascual Díaz, Puerto Guadal, cabalgasur@hotmail.com, leads trips to nearby fossil fields.

Chile Chico *p459*
Jaime Berrocal, O'Higgins 501. Fishing and climbing guide.

⊖ Transport

Reserva Nacional Cerro Castillo and around *p456*
Bus
Minibuses and jeeps meet the ferry in Puerto Ibáñez for connections to **Coyhaique**, 2 hrs, US$7. There is also a road from Puerto Ibáñez to **Perito Moreno** in Argentina. It is poor-quality *ripio*, suitable for 4WD only and there is no public transport. Tomás Urreta, T09-9950 0276, provides transport from Villa Cerro Castillo to **Coyhaique**, US$6.

Ferry
The car ferry, *El Pilchero*, sails from **Puerto Ibáñez** to **Chile Chico**, Tue 1000, Wed 1000, Fri 1000, Sat 1100, Sun 1500, return departures Mon 0800, Tue 1500, Thu 1300, Fri 1500, Sun 1200, 2½ hrs, cars US$47, passengers US$8, motorbikes US$9 and bicycles US$4. The number of passengers is limited to 75 plus 5 cars; arrive 30 mins before departure. Reserve at least 2 days in advance through **Mar del Sur**, Baquedano 146, Coyhaique, T067-231255 (southbound) or at the **Terminal de Transbordadores**, Chile Chico, T067-411864 (northbound). This is a very cold crossing even in summer: take warm clothing. Buses and jeeps meet the ferry in Puerto Ibáñez for connections to Coyhaique.

South to Puerto Bertrand *p459*
Buses do not enter Purto Bertrand, stopping instead 1 km away on the main *carretera*.

Chile Chico *p459*
Air
Don Carlos flies to **Coyhaique**, 5 weekly, US$50, from an airstrip just outside Chile Chico.

Bus
There are 5 minibuses a week along the south side of the lake to **Puerto Guadal**, US$12, and **Cochrane**, US$20.

Minibuses to **Los Antiguos** (Argentina), 45 mins including formalities, US$4 (payable in Chilean pesos only), are run by Arcotrans, T067-411841, and Transportes Padilla, T067-411904. The buses depart when they are full – usually about 5 times daily each.

Car
Hire from **Jaime Acuña Vogt**, Grosse 150, T/F067-411553.

Ferry
For services to **Puerto Ibáñez**, see above.

Into Argentina *p460*
From Los Antiguos buses run weekdays to **Comodoro Rivadavia** via Perito Moreno, 7 hrs, US$25. There are also direct buses to **Río Gallegos** and **El Calafate** from Los Antiguos, and 1 flight a week to **Río Gallegos** from Perito Moreno.

⊕ Directory

Chile Chico *p459*
Banks It's best to change money in Coyhaique or Argentina, but dollars and Argentine pesos can be changed in small amounts (at poor rates) at shops and cafés in Chile Chico, including Cafetería Loly y Elizabeth. **Medical services** Hospital: Lautaro s/n, T067-411334.

Cochrane and further south

→ *Colour map 5, C2/3.*
Travelling by bus along the final 224-km stretch of the Carretera Austral from Cochrane to Villa O'Higgins can be frustrating, as you will undoubtedly want to stop every 15 minutes to marvel at the views. This is a beautiful trip through thick forest, with vistas of snow-capped mountains and waterfalls. ►► *For listings, see pages 467-469.*

Ins and outs

Getting there Cochrane can be reached by air taxi or bus from Coyhaique, or on a poor unpaved road from Perito Moreno in Argentina. The southern tip of the Carretera at Villa O'Higgins is linked in summer by a ferry service to Calendario Mansilla, from where it is a day long journey to/from El Chaltén in Argentina.

Getting around Public transport is scarce. Only two weekly buses ply the route from Cochrane to Villa O'Higgins. Hitching is a possibility in summer (be prepared for long waits), but a pick-up or 4WD vehicle will make getting around much easier. Better still, travel by mountain bike. ►► *See Transport, page 469.*

Tourist information ① *San Valentín 555, www.cochranepatagonia.cl, Cochrane, summer Mon-Fri 0830-2000, Sat-Sun 1100-2000, off season Mon-Fri 0830-1730.* **CONAF** at the end of Calle Steffens.

Cochrane and around

Sitting in a hollow on the northern banks of the Río Cochrane, 343 km south of Coyhaique, Cochrane is a simple, somewhat godforsaken place. However with its pleasant summer climate it is a good base for walking and fishing in the nearby countryside. There is a small **museum** ① *San Valentín 555, Mon-Fri 0900-1300, 1500-1900,* with displays on local history. On the same street is an odd, *mate*-shaped house. Fuel is available.

Just 4 km northeast of Cochrane is the entrance to the **Reserva Nacional Tamango** ① *Dec-Mar 0830-2100, Apr-Nov 0830-1830, US$5, guided visits to see the huemul, Tue, Thu, Sat, US$80 for a group of 6 people.* The reserve covers 6925 ha of lenga forest and is home to one of the largest colonies of the rare huemul as well as guanaco, foxes and lots of species of bird, including woodpecker and hummingbird. There are marked paths for walks between 45 minutes and five hours, up to **Cerro Tamango** (1722 m) and **Cerro Temanguito** (1485 m). Take water and food, and windproof clothing if climbing the Cerros. The views from the reserve are superb, over the town, the nearby lakes and to the Campo de Hielo Norte to the west. Tourist facilities, however, are rudimentary. Excursions can be made to **Lago Cochrane**, which straddles the frontier with Argentina (the Argentine section is called **Lago Puerredón**). The lake, which covers over 17,500 ha, offers excellent fishing all year round; boats can be hired for US$18 per person.

Some 17 km north of Cochrane, a road runs east through Villa Chacabuco to enter Argentina at **Paso Roballos** ① *78 km, Chilean immigration summer 0730-2200, winter 0800-2000,* before continuing on to Bajo Caracoles. There isn't any public transport along this route and, although the road is passable in summer, it is generally in a poor state, and often flooded in spring.

Tortel and Puerto Yungay

Built on a hill at the mouth of the river 135 km from Cochrane, Tortel has no streets, the village being connected by 7 km of stairs and walkways made of cypress wood. There are a couple of beaches and two plazas built on stilts, roofed for protection from the almost constant drizzle. Its main industries are wood, for trade with Punta Arenas, shellfish, and now tourism. At the entrance to the village is a small tourist information office with information on the dozen or so *residenciales* and a useful map. A branch of the Carretera Austral, beginning 2 km south of Vagabundo and reaching south 23 km to Tortel, was completed in early 2003, making the village accessible by road. From Tortel, you can hire a boat to visit two spectacular glaciers: **Ventisquero Jorge Montt**, five hours southwest by boat, or **Ventisquero Steffens**, north on the edge of the Parque Nacional San Rafael, 2½ hours by boat and then a three-hour trek on a very wet, but well-signed trail including a river crossing by rowing boat to a viewing point from which the glacier can be seen across the lake. Trips can also be made to the nearby **Isla de los Muertos**, where some 100 Chilote workers died in mysterious circumstances early in the 20th century.

The main spine of the Carretera continues southwards to **Puerto Yungay** (allow 1¼ hours by car from Tortel under normal conditions), a tiny village with a military post and a pretty church. This section of the road is hilly and in places very bad; it is not advisable to drive along here at night. From Puerto Yungay, there is a **ferry crossing** ⓘ *45 mins, free, southbound 1000, 1200 and 1800, northbound 1100, 1300, 1900, check timetables locally off season*, to Río Bravo, run by the army If you miss the last boat the *carabineros* will help you find accommodation. After the ferry crossing, the road continues south. After 9 km there is a turn-off marked 'Ventisquero Montt'. This road is still under construction and at the time of writing is a dead end. Carry on through more spectacular scenery – lakes, moors, dense forest, swamps, rivers and waterfalls, often shrouded in mist – before arriving at the Carretera's final destination, Villa O'Higgins.

Villa O'Higgins

Villa O'Higgins lies 2 km from the northeastern end of an arm of **Lago O'Higgins**, which straddles the Argentine border (it's known as **Lago San Martín** in Argentina), see box, page 466 for border crossing information. With a population of around 500, the people are friendly, and there is something of a frontier feel about the town. **Tourist information** ⓘ *T067-211849*, is available in the plaza in summer or from the Municipalidad ⓘ *www.voh.cl*, which can provide trekking guides. There is also a good guide to the town at www.villaohiggins.com.

On rare sunny days, Villa O'Higgins' pleasant setting can be fully appreciated. Half way up a wooded hill behind the town, a mirador affords spectacular views of nearby mountains, lakes and glaciers. There are large numbers of icebergs in Lago O'Higgins, which have split off the glaciers of the Campo de Hielo Sur to the west. There is a tiny museum, the **Museo de la Patagonia Padre Antonio Ronchi**, on the plaza. Fuel is available from the ECA store (Monday to Saturday). A six-hour trek from the town goes through native forest to the **Mosco Glacier**. Allow two days for a return trip. Fresh water is plentiful and there is a *refugio* on the way, but the route is difficult after heavy rain. From Villa O'Higgins, the road continues 7 km south to **Bahía Bahamóndez** on the shores of Lago O'Higgins.

Laguna San Rafael

Getting there from Puerto Montt   Official cruises from Puerto Montt are run by Skorpios (see pages 400 and 404). Various private yachts for 6-12 passengers can also be chartered.

Border crossing: Chile–Argentina

Villa O'Higgins–El Chaltén

Chilean immigration From Bahía Bahamóndez there is a US$3 transfer (often but not always a minibus), connecting with a boat that departs to Chilean immigration at **Candelario Mancilla**. The boat service runs from November to April, with frequency varying between once a fortnight and three a week depending on the season (contact the Municipalidad in Villa O'Higgins for details). After docking at Calendario Mancilla, the boat makes a return trip to the face of the spectacular glacier O'Higgins before heading back to Villa O'Higgins in the evening. There is also a catamaran to Calendario Mancilla, 2½ hours, US$45; with glacier visit 8½ hours, US$70; return to Villa O'Higgins via the glacier 11½ hours, US$90.

Argentine control post From Calendario Mansilla, it is 23 km to the Argentine control post at the northern end of Lago del Desierto.

From Candelario Mancilla to the northern edge of the lake, horses can be hired for US$26 to carry your packs – usually one horse can carry two or three people's equipment. Approximate journey times: five hours on foot (without packs), 3½ hours by bike (unladen) and seven hours by bike (fully laden). Note that the last 2 km are treacherous and you may well have to carry your bike for part of the way.

There is a boat service across Lago del Desierto scheduled to coincide with the arrivals from Chile, which takes 45 minutes and costs US$30. The lake can also be skirted on foot (five hours) but not by bike.

El Chaltén On the south side of the lake there is a bus service along a *ripio* road for the remaining 37 km to El Chaltén, taking one hour and costing US$28. In theory it if you take both boats and the bus, you should arrive in El Chaltén at 2100 on the same day you set off from Villa O'Higgins. Add an extra day if you want to visit the glacier. With the opening of this route, it is now possible to travel along the whole of the Carretera Austral and on to Torres del Paine without having to double back on yourself. The journey is much easier to coordinate from north to south as there are regular last-minute disruptions to the Catamaran schedule due to inclement weather.

Getting there from Puerto Chacabuco Although it's now nearly as cheap to fly, official cruises to the Laguna are run by **Navimag**, all year, reduced service off season, 24 hours, from US$324, and Catamaranes del Sur, one to three weekly from September to April, one-day trips US$299, three-day trips from US$550, see page 455 for company contact details. Local fishing boats from Puerto Chacabuco and Puerto Aisén take about 18-20 hours each way and charge a little less than the tourist boats, ask at the port. Note that these unauthorized boats may have neither adequate facilities nor a licence for the trip. Trips to Laguna San Rafael out of season are very difficult to arrange. ▶ *See Transport, page 469.*

Situated west of Lago General Carrera and some 200 km south of Puerto Aisén, Laguna San Rafael is one of the highlights for many travellers to Chile. The **Ventisquero San Rafael**, one of many glaciers from the giant **Campo de Hielo Norte**, flows into the laguna, which, in turn, empties into the sea northwards via the Río Tempano. About 45 km in length and towering 30 m above water level, the deep blue glacier groans and cracks as it carves off icebergs, which are carried across the laguna and out to sea. Around the shores of the lake is thick vegetation and above are snowy mountain peaks.

Laguna San Rafael and the Campo de Hielo Norte are part of the **Parque Nacional Laguna San Rafael** ① *US$6*, which extends over 1,740,000 ha, and is a UN World Biosphere Reserve. In the national park are puma, pudú, foxes, dolphins, occasional sea lions and sea otters, and many species of bird. Walking trails are limited (about 10 km in all) but a lookout platform has been constructed, with fine views of the glacier. There is also a small ranger station that provides information, and a pier. The rangers are willing to row you out to the glacier in calm weather, an awesome three-hour adventure, past icebergs and swells created when huge chunks of ice break off the glacier and crash into the laguna.

Sadly, the San Rafael Glacier is rapidly disintegrating and is likely to have disappeared entirely by 2013. While this shrinkage is symptomatic of what has happened to many glaciers in Patagonia, some blame the motorized tourist boats that go too close to the glacier, creating a greater force of erosion against the ice. It is vital for visitors to act responsibly if considering a boat trip to this spectacular site.

◉ Cochrane and further south listings

For Sleeping and Eating price codes and other relevant information, see Essentials pages 35-42.

◒ Sleeping

Cochrane *p464*
In summer it is best to book rooms in advance. The accommodation is generally mediocre.
AL Ultimo Paraíso, Lago Brown 455, T067-522361. Regarded as the best place to stay. Also arranges fishing trips. Not always open.
A Cabañas Rogeri, Tte Merino 502, T067-522264. Small but decent cabins sleep 4, with kitchen facilities. Bigger cabins opposite, same owners, also good.
A Hotel Wellmann, Las Golondrinas 36, T067-522171. Good-sized rooms, comfortable, warm, meals served. Recommended.
C Hostal Latitud 47 sur, Lago Brown 564, T067-522280. **E** singles. Friendly, family-run *residencial*. Simple rooms but pleasant atmosphere. With internet, tours offered.
C Residencial Cero a Cero, Lago Brown 464, T067-522158, ceroacero@ze.cl. **E** singles, with decent breakfast, cheaper without bath, avoid downstairs rooms, those on upper floor are much better (though floorboards are creaky).

C Residencial Sur Austral, Prat 334, T067-522150. **E** singles, with breakfast and hot water. Some rooms with bath. Often full as it doubles as the Don Carlos bus terminal.
C-D Hospedaje Ana Luz, Los Nadis 569, T09-7787 4011. **F** singles. Neat but basic cabins sleeping 2-3. Also basic rooms in the main house. Friendly. Recommended.
D Hospedaje Cochrane, Dr Steffens 451, T067-522377. **F** singles. Good meals, also camping (popular).
D Hospedaje Paola, Lago Brown 150, T067-522215. **F** singles. Run down. Also camping.

Camping
In the **Reserva Nacional Tamango**, there are campsites and *cabañas* at **Los Correntadas**, US$14 per site, and **Los Coigües**, US$18 per site. Details and booking through **CONAF**, Av Ogana 1060, T067-212125.
Camping Río Nadis, 9 km west of the carretera, (turn of at Puente Barrancoso, 45 km south of Cochrane), lillischindele@ yahoo.de, or contact through **Casa Turismo Rural** in Coyhaique.

Tortel and Puerto Yungay *p465*

All accommodation in Tortel also serves meals. There is camping at sector Junquillo at the far end of town.

AL Entre Hielos lodge, sector centro, Tortel. T02-1960271, www.entrehielostortel.cl. Newly built, the only upmarket accommodation in town.

C Estilo, Sector Centro, Tortel, tortelhospe dajeestilo@yahoo.es. Warm and comfortable. Good food. Very friendly, funny and talkative host (if your Spanish is up to it). Recommended.

C Hospedaje Costanera, Sector Centro, Tortel, T067-211876 (public phone). Price includes breakfast (also open to non-residents). Clean, warm, with attractive garden. The end room has good views.

D La Sureña, Sector Playa Ancha, Tortel. **F** singles. One guest comments: "Expect fresh mutton meals and if you are squeamish ... don't look out of the window when they butcher 2 lambs a day on the front porch."

Villa O'Higgins *p465*

There are about 6-8 beds available in local houses in Calendario Mancilla.

B El Mosco, at the northern entrance to the town, T067-431819, patagoniaelmosco@ yahoo.es, **E-F** per person in dorms. Spanish run, kitchen facilities, games, laundry facilities, trekking maps and information. Can help with bike repairs. Overpriced singles, camping available, English spoken. More expensive than the rest, but nothing else competes in terms of infrastructure. Recommended.

C Cabañas San Gabriel, Lago O'Higgins 310. Nice cabins. A good Choice for small groups.

D Residencial Campanario, Lago O'Higgins 72, Opposite El Mosco, friendly, kitchen facilities, camping.

E Los Nirres, Lago O'Higgins 72, **F** singles. Basic accommodation. Goods meals served. Several other similar places in town.

Camping

There are very basic camping areas at either end of Lago del Desierto.

Eating

For other eating options, see Sleeping, above.

Cochrane *p464*

Café Tamango, Esmeralda 464, on the Plaza. Good fresh juices, quiches and cakes. Avoid the coffee.

El Fogón, San Valentín 653, T067-522240. One of few eating places in town. Basic southern Chilean fare.

Tortel and Puerto Yungay *p465*

Café Celes Salom, Tortel. Basic cheap meals and disco on Sat with occasional bands.

Villa O'Higgins *p465*

Entre Patagones, at the northern entrance to the town, T067-431810. The only restaurant in town with any sort of style.

Activities and tours

Cochrane *p464*

Excursions can be arranged through Guillermo Paso at **Transportes Los Nadis** (see Transport); fishing tours are available from **Hotel Ultimo Paraíso** (see Sleeping).

Casa del Turismo Rural, Dussen 357-B, Coyhaique, T067-524929, www.casaturismo rural.cl. Has many members in this area.

Don Pedro Muñoz, T067-522244. Hires horses for trips in the surrounding countryside.

Expediciones San Lorenzo, Fundo San Lorenzo, 60 km southeast of Cochrane. T067-522326, or contact through the Casa del Turismo Rural, above. Offer the best horse-riding trips in the area.

Tortel and Puerto Yungay *p465*

Charter boats can easily be arranged. Prices to **Ventisquero Jorge Montt**, US$275 for up to 8 people. To **Ventisquero Steffens**, US$225 for up to 8 people. To **Isla de los Muertos** US$85 for up to 8 people. The condition of the boats varies. Check first. In theory the harbourmaster will only allow boats out in good conditions, however the weather can change very quickly and occasionally boats will have to turn back mid-trip. Make sure you agree beforehand with your guide whether you get any sort of refund if this happens.

Villa O'Higgins *p465*
Alberto Guinao, horse-riding guide. Horse rides from ½ a day to a week can be arranged, but note that the horses in Villa O'Higgins are not the best. **Nelson Henríquez**, Lago Cisnes 5, T067-431820. Fishing trips on Lagos Ciervo, Cisnes and El Tigre.

Laguna San Rafael *p465*
Patagonia Connection SA, Fidel Oteíza 1921, of 1006, Providencia, Santiago, T02-225 6489. Operates a 3-night catamaran tour to Laguna San Rafael via **Puyuhuapi Lodge and Spa** (see pages 442 and 445) on board the *Patagonia Express*. Also offers special fly-fishing programmes and other excursions.

⊖ Transport

Cochrane and around *p464*
Air Don Carlos flies to **Coyhaique**, Mon, Thu, US$75, from an airstrip just north of town.

Bus To **Coyhaique**, **Sao Paulo**, **Don Carlos** and **Acuario**, 13, 6 days a week between them, US$19. To **Chile Chico**, Buses Ali, Thu, Sun, US$15. To **Tortel**, Gabriel Becerra and Buses Aldeas, daily between them, US$10. To **Villa O'Higgins**, Don Carlos, 2 weekly, Tue, Fri, 0800, US$19.

Tortel and Puerto Yungay *p465*
Air Don Carlos to **Coyhaique**, Mon and Wed, US$35. This is a subsidized price for residents of the village. Other travellers must buy a standby ticket and should expect to pay much more.

Bus To **Cochrane**, daily, US$10.

Villa O'Higgins *p465*
Air Don Carlos air taxi flies to Villa O'Higgins from **Coyhaique**, via Cochrane, Mon, Thu, US$100.

Boat Hielo Sur, www.hielosur.com, contact Hans Silva. Catamaran to **Calendario Mancilla** 2½ hrs, US$45; with glacier visit 8½ hrs, US$70; return to Villa O'Higgins via glacier 11½ hrs, US$90. Tickets for the connecting boat and bus in Argentina can be paid here or directly in Argentina.
Bus There are 1 or 2 buses weekly to **Cochrane**, US$19 as well as a local fortnightly bus to **Lago Cristi**, US$16 return. Bus terminal at Res Cordillera, Lago Salto 302, T06-743 1829. If you have a return bus ticket northwards, reconfirm on arrival at Villa O'Higgins.

Laguna San Rafael *p465*
Air Don Carlos provides air taxis from **Coyhaique** (addresses under Coyhaique), US$200 each for party of 5. Other air-tour options are sometimes available from Coyhaique. Note that the planes are tiny and not particularly safe in bad weather.

❶ Directory

Cochrane and around *p464*
Banks Banco del Estado, on the plaza, changes dollars. ATM accepts MasterCard and Cirrus but not Visa. **Internet** On the western side of the plaza. **Supermarket** Melero, Las Golondrinas 148.

Tortel and Puerto Yungay *p465*
Banks There is no bank in Tortel but a mobile bank comes twice a month. **Medical services** Medical centre staffed by doctors, nurses and dentists visits Tortel monthly. **Post office** Mon-Fri 0830-1330, post leaves Tortel weekly by air.

Contents

Footprint features

Far South

At a glance

⊕ **Getting around** Good bus links between the 2 main cities and to Torres del Paine. Hiring a 4WD will give you a little more freedom, but mostly you will be travelling on foot.

◉ **Time required** A couple of days for a whistlestop tour, 5 or 6 to make the most of your trip, and more if you want to hike the circuit.

☀ **Weather** Unpredictable. Can range from gorgeous sun to bitingly cold frozen rain in a few hours. Winter is calmer but cold.

✖ **When not to go** Winter is beautiful, but trekking is complicated due to the short days and snowfall that closes many (but not all) trekking routes in Torres del Paine.

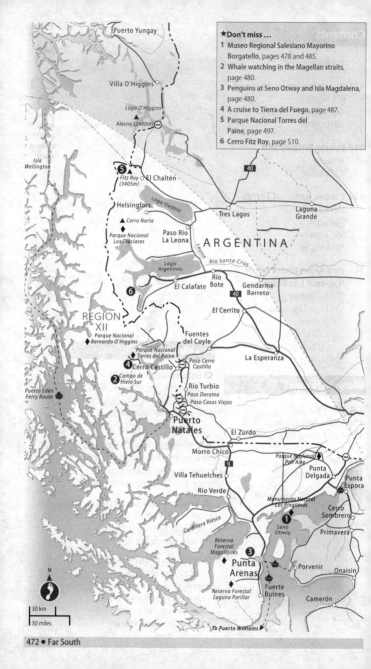

★**Don't miss ...**
1 Museo Regional Salesiano Mayorino Borgatello, pages 478 and 485.
2 Whale watching in the Magellan straits, page 480.
3 Penguins at Seno Otway and Isla Magdalena, page 480.
4 A cruise to Tierra del Fuego, page 487.
5 Parque Nacional Torres del Paine, page 497.
6 Cerro Fitz Roy, page 510.

Puerto Yungay

Villa O'Higgins

Lago O'Higgins

Alesna (2480m)

Isla Wellington

40

⑤ El Chaltén
Fitz Roy (3405m)

Helsingfors

Lago Viedma

Cerro Norte

Tres Lagos

Laguna Grande

Parque Nacional Los Glaciares

Paso Río La Leona

ARGENTINA

Lago Argentino

Río Santa Cruz

⑥ El Calafate

Río Bote

Gendarme Barreto

40

REGION XII

El Cerrito

Parque Nacional Bernardo O'Higgins

Fuentes del Coyle

Parque Nacional Torres del Paine

④ Cerro Castillo

Paso Cerro Castillo

La Esperanza

② Campo de Hielo Sur

Río Turbio
Paso Dorotea
Paso Casas Viejas

Puerto Edén Ferry Route

Puerto Natales

El Zurdo

Morro Chico

Parque Nacional Pali Aike

9

Villa Tehuelches

Punta Delgada

Punta Espora

Río Verde

Monumento Natural Los Pingüinos

Cerro Sombrero

Cordillera Riesco

① Seno Otway

Primavera

Reserva Forestal Magallanes

③ **Punta Arenas**

Porvenir

Onaisin

Reserva Forestal Laguna Parillar

Fuerte Bulnes

Camerón

N

30 km
30 miles

To Puerto Williams ▶

A spectacular land of fragmenting glaciers and teetering icy peaks, southern Patagonia feels like nowhere else on earth. Although Chileans posted here will often say that they are a 'long way from Chile', this is the country's most popular destination for visitors.

The jewel in the crown is the Parque Nacional Torres del Paine, a natural magnet for travellers from all over the world. The 'towers', three massif-like fingers after which the park is named, point vertically upwards from the Paine, surrounded by glaciers, turquoise-coloured lakes and thick forests of native trees.

Puerto Natales is the base for exploration of Torres del Paine and for boat trips to the glaciers in the Parque Nacional Bernardo O'Higgins. It also provides access to El Calafate and the Parque Nacional Los Glaciares in Argentina. Further south, Punta Arenas is a European-style city with a lively Chilote community and remnants of earlier English and Croatian influences.

Background

Southern Patagonia was inhabited from the end of the Ice Age, mainly by the Tehuelche people, who roamed from the Atlantic coast to the mountains (see box, page 476). The first Europeans did not visit until the 16th century. When Magellan sailed through the Straits in 1520, the strategic importance was quickly recognized: soon Spanish ships were using the route, as were mariners from other countries, including Francis Drake on his world voyage (1578). The route became less important after 1616 when Dutch sailors Jacob le Maire and Cornelius van Schouten discovered a quicker route into the Pacific round Cape Horn.

At Independence, Chile claimed the far southern territories along the Pacific coast but little was done to carry out this claim until 1843 when, concerned at British activities in the area and at rumours of French plans to start a colony, President Bulnes ordered the preparation of a secret mission. The expedition, on board the vessel *Ancud*, established Fuerte Bulnes; the fort was abandoned in 1848 in favour of a new settlement 56 km north, called Punta Arenas. The development of sheep farming in Patagonia and on Tierra del Fuego (with the help of arrivals from the nearby Falkland Islands), and the renewed importance of the Magellan Straits with the advent of steam shipping, led to the rapid expansion of Punta Arenas at the end of the 19th century, when it took the first steps towards being the city that it is today.

Sheep farming remains vital to the local economy, although wool exports have dropped in recent years. Forestry has become more important, but is controversial, as native forests are used for woodchips to export to Japan, Taiwan and Brazil. This is especially serious on Tierra del Fuego. Although oil production has declined, large quantities of natural gas are now produced and about 33% of Chilean coal comes from large open-cast coal mines on the Brunswick Peninsula. Tourism is growing rapidly, making an increasingly important contribution to the local economy.

Geography and climate

Chilean southern Patagonia stretches south from the icefields of the Campo de Hielos Sur to the Estrecho de Magallanes (Straits of Magellan), which separate continental South America from Tierra del Fuego. The coastline is heavily indented by fjords; offshore are numerous islands, few of which are inhabited. The remnants of the Andes stretch along the coast, seldom rising above 1500 m, although the Cordillera del Paine has several peaks over 2600 m and Cerro Balmaceda is 2035 m. Most of the western coast is covered by thick rainforest but further east is grassland, stretching into the arid Patagonian plateau across the Argentine border. Together with the Chilean part of Tierra del Fuego, Isla Navarino and Chilean Antarctica, this part of Chile is administered as Región XII (Magallanes); the capital is Punta Arenas. The region covers 17.5% of Chilean territory, but the population is only around 150,000, under 1% of the Chilean total.

People from Punta Arenas say they often have four seasons in one day. Frequently, however, the only season appears to be winter. Cold winds, often exceeding 100 km per hour, blow during the summer bringing heavy rain to coastal areas. Further east, the winds are drier; annual rainfall at Punta Dungeness at the east end of the Straits is only 250 mm compared to over 4000 mm on the offshore islands. Coastal temperatures seldom rise above 15°C in summer. In winter, snow covers the whole region, except those parts near the sea, making many roads impassable. Recent times, however, have seen a general warning trend and Punta Arenas has not seen heavy snow for years. Moreover there is little wind in the winter months, and this means that tourism remains possible for most of the year.

Punta Arenas and around

→ *Colour map 7, B1. Population: 116,000.*

Capital of Región XII, Punta Arenas lies 2140 km due south of Santiago. The city was originally named 'Sandy Point' by the English, but adopted the Hispanic equivalent under Chilean colonization. A centre for natural gas production, sheep farming and the fishing industry as well as an important military base, it is also the home of Polar Austral, one of the most southerly breweries in the world. Although Punta Arenas has expanded rapidly, it remains a tranquil and pleasant city. The climate and architecture give it a distinctively northern European atmosphere, quite unlike anywhere else in Chile. ➤➤ *For listings, see pages 480-487.*

Ins and outs

Getting there Punta Arenas is cut off from the rest of Chile. Puerto Natales aside, the only road connections are via the Argentine towns of Comodoro Rivadavia and Río Gallegos either to Coyhaique and the Carretera Austral (20 hours; one or two buses weekly in summer) or to Bariloche and on to Puerto Montt (36 hours, daily buses in summer); it is quicker, and often cheaper, to take one of the many daily flights to/from Puerto Montt or Santiago instead. Carlos Ibáñez del Campo Airport is 20 km north of town. Buses from Puerto Natales to Punta Arenas will only stop at the airport if they are scheduled to drop passengers there. There are minibuses operated by **Transfer Austral** ① *Lautaro Navarro 975, T061-615100, www.transferaustral.com*, costing US$5 which will drop you anywhere near the city centre. A taxi ordered at the airport costs US$13, while a radio taxi ordered in advance from the city is a little cheaper. There is a ferry service between Punta Arenas and Porvenir on Tierra del Fuego on the **Melinka** ferry (six weekly). Buses to Tierra del Fuego use the more northerly ferry crossing, at Punta Delgada (many daily) to Puerto Espora. There are also direct flights to Porvenir, Puerto Williams and Ushuaia. Puerto Natales, 247 km north, is easily reached on a paved road (many buses daily). ➤➤ *See Transport, page 485.*

Getting around Punta Arenas is not a huge city and walking about is a pleasant way of getting to know it. Buses and *colectivos* are plentiful and cheap (US0.60): a taxi is only really necessary for out-of-town excursions. Be careful not to confuse the streets Pedro Montt with Jorge Montt and Carrera with Carrera Pinto.

Tourist information The **municipal tourist office** ① *On the plaza, T061-200610, is good.* **Sernatur** ① *In temporary offices at Lautaro Navarro 999 (permanent location not yet decided), T061-225385, www.patagonia-chile.com, open 0830-1845, closed Sat and Sun off season*, is reasonably helpful, English spoken. **CONAF** ① *Bulnes 0309, opposite the shepherd monument, between the racetrack and the cemetery, T061-238544, Mon-Fri*, doesn't have much useful information. **Falkland Islands Tourist Board** ① *Old Philomel Store, PO Box 618, Stanley, FIQQ 1ZZ, T+500 22215/27019, www.visitorfalklands.com.*

History

After its foundation in 1848, Punta Arenas became a penal colony modelled on Australia. In 1867, it was opened to foreign settlers and given free-port status. From the 1880s, it prospered as a refuelling and provisioning centre for steam ships and whaling vessels. It also became a centre for the new sheep *estancias* as it afforded the best harbour facilities. The city's importance was reduced overnight by the opening of the Panama Canal in

The original big foots

The dry Patagonian plateau was originally inhabited by one principal indigenous group, the Tehuelches, who lived along the eastern side of the Andes, as far north as modern-day Bariloche, and were hunters of guanaco and rheas. In the 18th century, they began to domesticate the wild horses of the region and sailed down the Patagonian rivers to reach the Atlantic coast.

The Tehuelches were very large: it is said that when the Spanish first arrived in this area, they discovered Tehuelche footprints in the sand, exclaiming 'qué patagón' ('what a large foot'), hence the name Patagonia.

In the 18th and early 19th centuries, the Tehuelche interacted with European whalers and were patronizingly described as 'semi-civilized'. The granting by the Chilean government of large land concessions in the late 19th century, combined with Argentine President Julio Roca's wars of extermination against Patagonian native peoples in the 1870s, spelled the end for the Tehuelches. They were hunted and persecuted by settlers and only a few survived diseases and the radical change of lifestyle.

Towards the end of the 20th century, a belated sense of moral guilt arose among the colonizers, but it was too late to preserve the Tehuelche way of life. Today, only a few isolated groups remain in Argentine Patagonia.

For details of the indigenous groups further south and in the Patagonian fjords, see the Tierra del Fuego chapter.

1914. Although immigrants from Britain and Croatia were central in the growth of Punta Arenas (their influence can be seen to this day), most of those who came to work in the *estancias* were from Chiloé; many people in the city have relatives in Chiloé and feel an affinity with the island (the barrios on either side of the upper reaches of Independencia are known as Chilote areas); the Chilotes who returned north took Patagonian customs with them, hence the number of *maté* drinkers on Chiloé.

Sights

Around the attractive **Plaza Muñoz Gamero** are a number of mansions that once belonged to the great sheep-ranching families of the late 19th century. A good example is the **Palacio Sara Braun** ① *Tue-Sun, US$2*, built between 1894 and 1905 with materials from Europe; the Palacio has several elegantly decorated rooms open to the public and also houses the **Hotel José Nogueira**. In the centre of the plaza is a statue of Magellan with a mermaid and two Fuegian Indians at his feet. According to local wisdom, those who rub or kiss the big toe of one of the Indians will return to Punta Arenas.

Just north of the plaza is the **Museo de Historia Regional Braun Menéndez** ① *Magallanes 949, T061-244216, www.dibam.cl/sdm_mr_magallanes, summer Mon-Sat 1030-1700, Sun 1030-1400; winter Mon-Sun 1030-1300, US$2, children half price*, the opulent former mansion of Mauricio Braun, built in 1905. A visit is recommended. Part of the museum is set out as a room-by-room regional history; the rest of the house has been left with its original furniture. Guided tours are in Spanish only, but a somewhat confusing information sheet in English is also available. In the basement there is a permanent exhibition dedicated to the indigenous people of southern Patagonia, somewhat ironic considering the leading part the Braun Menéndez family played in their demise.

Punta Arenas

To **6** & Instituto de la Patagonia, Free Port, Airport,
Puerto Natales & Ferry to Porvenir

A Carrera

Senoret

Angamos

Cemetery

Carrera

Jorge Montt

Quillota

13

11

9

Av Bulnes

19 **4**

Maipú

8

23

Museo Regional Salesiano
Mayorino Borgatello

1 **5**

Sarmiento de Gamboa

B Mejicana

Armando Sanhueza

Chiloé

Borjes

Magallanes

14

Croacia

16

Mejicana

4 **5**

2 **2**

Carrera Pinto

7

Almirante Senoret

4
6 **20**

17 **21**

Teatro
Cervantes

18

10

27

2

O'Higgins

Av Colón

Lautaro Navarro

J Menéndez

C Arauco

11
Lan Chile

10

Museo Braun-
Menéndez

18

J Montt

St James

3

Waldo Seguel

British
School

15

Pedro Montt

10 **i**

i

Museo Naval
y Marítimo

9

7

25

24

Av Costanera

Mirador
Cerro de
la Cruz

Cathedral

Plaza
Muñoz
Gamero

1

Roca

Fagnano

12

22

3

15

12

To Museo Militar

28

Noguera

Errázuriz

D Balmaceda

13

21 de Mayo

Casino

*Estrecho de
Magallanes*

26

Av España

Av Independencia

2

3

Muelle A Prat

To **16**

To Parque María Behety &
To Fuerte Bulnes & Puerto del Hambre

14

Port

To Reserva Forestal
Magallanes

N

300 metres

300 yards

Sleeping
Backpackers Paradise **2** C3
Cabo de Hornos **1** C2
Carpa Manzano **5** B2
Chalet Chapital **3** C1
Cóndor del Plata **20** C2
Finis Terrae **21** C2
Hospedaje Miramar **28** D1
Hostal Ainil **4** B2

Hostal al Fin del
    Mundo **25** C3
Hostal de la Avenida **6** C2
Hostal del Estrecho **18** C3
Hostal del Sur **7** B1
Hostal Dinka's House **11** A3
Hostal El Conventillo **24** D3
Hostal Independencia **26** D1
Hostal Keoken **19** B2
Hostal La Estancia **27** C3
Hostal Luna **14** B3
Hostal Paradiso **8** B3
Hostal Quo Vadis **16** D1
Hostal Sonia Kuscevic **9** A2
Hostal Taty's House **23** B3

José Nogueira (Palacio
    Sara Braun) **10** C2
Mercurio **12** D2
Oro Fueguino **15** C1
Pink House **13** A3
Plaza **22** D2
Tierra del Fuego **17** C2

Eating
Carioca **11** B2
Damiana Elena **1** B2
Dino's Pizza **16** B2
El Asador Patagónico **2** C3
El Estribo **4** C2
El Quijote **7** C2

La Luna **9** C3
La Marmite **5** C2
La Tasca **3** D2
Lomit's **10** C2
Parrilla Los Ganaderos **6** A2
Puerto Viejo **12** D2
Remezón **14** D2
Sabores de Chiloé **13** D2
Santino **18** C2
Sotitos **15** D3

Buses
Fernández **4** C2
Pacheco **2** C2
Sur **1** C2

Three blocks east of the plaza, the **Museo Naval y Marítimo** ① *Pedro Montt 981, T061-205479, terzona@armarda.cl, Jan-Feb Tue-Sun 0930-1700; Mar-Dec Tue-Sun 0930-1230, 1400-1700, US$1.50,* houses an exhibition of local and national maritime history with sections on naval instruments, cartography, meteorology, and shipwrecks. There is a video in Spanish and an information sheet in English.

West of the plaza Muñoz Gamero on Waldo Seguel are two reminders of British influence in the city: the **British School** and **St James's Anglican Church** next door. Nearby on Calle Fagnano is the **Mirador Cerro de La Cruz** offering a view over the city and the Magellan Straits complete with its various shipwrecks.

Three blocks further west is the **Museo Militar** ① *Zenteno y Balmaceda, T061-247133, Tue-Sun, 0900-1300, 1500-1700, free,* at the Regimiento Pudeto. Lots of knives guns, flags and other military memorabilia are displayed here plus many items brought from Fuerte Bulnes. Explanatory notes in excruciating English.

North of the centre along Bulnes is the **Museo Regional Salesiano Mayorino Borgatello** ① *Colegio Salesiano, Av Bulnes 336, entrance next to church, T061-221001, www.museomaggiorinoborgatello.cl, Tue-Sun 1000-1230, 1500-1800, hours change frequently, US$3.50,* an excellent introduction to Patagonia with a large collection of stuffed birds and animals from the region, exhibits on local history, geology, anthropology, aviation and industry. Easily the most complete and fascinating regional museum in Chile. Three blocks further on, the **cemetery** ① *Av Bulnes, 0800-1800 daily,* is one of the most interesting places in the city, with cypress avenues, gravestones in many languages that bear testimony to the cosmopolitan provenance of Patagonian pioneers, and many mausolea and memorials to pioneer families and victims of shipping disasters. Look out for the statue of Indicito, the little Indian, on the northwest side, which is now an object of reverence, bedecked with flowers. Further north still, the **Instituto de la Patagonia** houses the **Museo del Recuerdo** ① *Av Bulnes 1890, Km 4 north, T061-207056, Mon-Fri 0830-1130, 1430-1815, Sat 0830-1300, US$2, children free,* an open-air museum with artefacts used by the early settlers, pioneer homes and botanical gardens. Opposite is the Zona Franca with a mall and ice rink.

On 21 de Mayo, south of Independencia, is a small ornate Hindu temple, one of only two in Chile, while further along the same street, on the southern outskirts of the city, the wooded **Parque María Behety** features a scale model of Fuerte Bulnes, a campsite and children's playground, popular for Sunday picnics. In winter, there is an ice rink here.

Reserva Forestal Magallanes ① *7 km west of town, US$5,* known locally as the Parque Japonés, extends over 13,500 ha and rises to 600 m. Although getting there by taxi is the easiest option, it can also be reached on foot or by bike: follow Independencia up the hill and take a right for Río de las Minas, about 3 km from the edge of town; the entrance to the reserve is 2 km beyond. Here you will find a self-guided nature trail through lenga and coigue trees. The road continues through the woods for 14 km passing several picnic sites. From the top end of the road a short path leads to a lookout over the **Garganta del Diablo** (Devil's Throat), a gorge with views over Punta Arenas and Tierra del Fuego. From here a slippery path leads down to the Río de las Minas Valley and then back to Punta Arenas.

Around Punta Arenas

Reserva Forestal Laguna Parrillar

About 25 km south of Punta Arenas, there is a fork in the road to the right; 21 km further on is the very peaceful Parrillar reserve, covering 18,814 ha and surrounded by

Port Famine (Puerto Hambre)

In 1582, Felipe II of Spain, alarmed by Drake's passage through the Straits of Magellan, decided to establish a Spanish presence on the Straits. A fleet of 15 ships and 4000 men, commanded by Pedro Sarmiento de Gamboa, was despatched in 1584. Before the ships had left the Bay of Biscay, a storm arose and scattered the fleet, sinking seven ships and killing 800 people. Further depleted by disease, the fleet of three remaining ships at length arrived at the Straits, with just 300 men on board. Led by Sarmiento this small force founded two cities: Nombre de Jesús on Punta Dungeness at the eastern entrance to the Straits and Rey Don Felipe near Puerto Hambre.

Disaster struck when their only remaining vessel broke its anchorage in a storm near Nombre de Jesús; the ship, with Sarmiento on board, was blown into the Atlantic, leaving many of Sarmiento's men stranded on land. After vain attempts to re-enter the Straits, Sarmiento set sail for Río de Janeiro where he organized two rescue missions: the first ended in shipwreck, the second in mutiny. Captured by English corsairs, Sarmiento was taken to England where he was imprisoned. On his release by Elizabeth I, he tried to return to Spain via France, but was jailed again. Until his death in 1608, Sarmiento besieged Felipe II with letters urging him to rescue the men stranded in the Straits.

When the English corsair Thomas Cavendish sailed through the Straits in 1587 he found only 18 survivors at Rey Don Felipe. With the English and Spanish at war, only one – Tomé Hernández – would trust Cavendish when he first arrived. A sudden spell of fine weather arose, and Cavendish set sail, leaving the rest of the men to die. He named the place Port Famine as a reminder of their grisly fate.

snow-capped hills. It has older forest than the Magallanes Reserve and sphagnum bogs, and offers excellent salmon and trout fishing. There is a three-hour walk to the treeline, as well as along poorly marked, boggy paths, and fine views from the mirador. There are CONAF-administered campsites and picnic sites. Note that there is no public transport to the reserve and hitching is virtually impossible; a radio taxi will cost about US$50.

Fuerte Bulnes and further south

Some 56 km south of Punta Arenas, Fuerte Bulnes is a replica of the wooden fort erected in 1843 by the crew of the Chilean vessel *Ancud*. Built in the 1940s and originally designed to house a museum, nearly all the interesting exhibits and artefacts were moved to museums in Punta Arenas and Santiago in 1986 and now only the empty shells of the various buildings remain. Several agencies run half-day tours to here, but hitching is not difficult at weekends or in summer, as there are many holiday camps in the area.

Nearby is **Puerto Hambre**, where there are ruins of the church built by Sarmiento de Gamboa's colonists in 1584. This is a very beautiful area with views towards the towering ice mountains near Pico Sarmiento; it was of Puerto Hambre that Darwin wrote: "looking due southward … the distant channels between the mountains appeared from their gloominess to lead beyond the confines of this world". Southern dolphins can often be seen in the straits around this point.

At the intersection of the roads to Puerto Hambre and Fuerte Bulnes, 51 km south of Punta Arenas, is a small monolith marking the **Centro Geográfico de Chile**, the midway point between Arica and the South Pole. Bypassing Fuerte Bulnes, the road continues past a memorial to Captain Pringle Stokes, Captain of the Beagle, who committed suicide here in 1829, being replaced as captain by Fitz Roy. The road carries on, past San Juan to the light house at San Isidro. The last part of this journey can only be done in a high-clearance vehicle and at low tide and in summer, as it involves crossing an estuary at the mouth of the Río San Pedro. Alternatively leave your vehicle on the north side of the estuary, ford the river (at low tide) and walk 2½ hrs to San Isidro. From here, it is a day hike to **Cape Froward**, the southernmost point of the continent of South America, marked by a 24-m-high cross. There is no path, and a guide is essential (this can be arranged by the hostería at San Isidro with advance notice). Some 70 km west of Cape froward along the Magellan Straits is Isla Carlos III, a popular base for humpback whale watching.

North of Punta Arenas

Some 70 km north of Punta Arenas, **Seno Otway**ⓘ *Oct-mid Mar, US$5*, is the site of a colony of around 11,000 Magellanic penguins. There are beautiful views across the sound to the mountains to the north and rheas skunks and foxes can also be seen. Several agencies offer trips to the colony lasting five hours (US$15 plus entry fees at peak season); if you wish to visit independently, a taxi from Punta Arenas will cost US$40 return. It is best to go early in the day. Try to avoid going at the same time as the large cruise ship tours – it is not much fun having to wait behind 200 people for your turn at the viewing stations. Access to the colony is via a private road where a toll of US$1.75 per person is charged.

A small island, 30 km northeast, **Isla Magdalena** is the location of the **Monumento Natural Los Pingüinos**, a colony of 150,000 penguins, administered by **CONAF**. Deserted apart from during the breeding season from November to early February, Magdalena is one of a group of three islands visited by Drake (the others are Marta and Isabel), whose men killed 3000 penguins for food. Boat trips to the island are run by **Comapa**ⓘ *Tue, Thu, Sat, 1600 (Dec-Feb), 2 hrs each way with 2 hrs on the island, US$34, subject to cancellation if windy (full refund given)*. Take a hat, coat and gloves.

Beyond, Route 255 heads northeast past Kimiriaike (from where a road branches south towards Tierra del Fuego) to Punta Delgada. From here there is a turn-off north along a *ripio* road for 26 km to Parque Nacional Pali Aike, a fantastic volcanic landscape dotted with small cones and craters. There are five easy marked trails, all of which can be done in a day. From Punta Delgada Route 255 continues to the Argentine border and then along Argentine Route 3 to Río Gallegos, an unappealing city. For routes to Calafate in Argentina, see page 506.

◉ Punta Arenas and around listings

For Sleeping and Eating price codes and other relevant information, see Essentials pages 35-42.

● Sleeping

Punta Arenas *p475, map p477*
Hotel prices are substantially lower during winter months (Apr/May-Sep). Most hotels include breakfast in the room price. Accommodation is also available in many

private houses; ask at tourist office.
There are no campsites in or near the city.
LL Cabo de Hornos, Muñoz Gamero 1039 on the plaza, T061-715000, www.hoteles-australis.com. 4-star, newly refurbished and comfortable. Bright and spacious rooms. Good views from the 4th floor up, either of the Magellan Straits or the plaza.
LL-L Finis Terrae, Colón 766, T061-228200, www.hotelfinisterrae.com. Typical large hotel;

some rooms are small, as are the bathrooms. Expensive suites. Views from the top 2 floors. Best thing about the hotel is the rooftop café/bar. English spoken, parking.

LL-L José Nogueira, Bories 959, in former Palacio Sara Braun, T061-711000, www.hotelnogueira.com. Beautiful *loggia*. Small rooms, but high ceilings. The rooms on the 2nd floor are best. Good suites, lovely dining room, parking. Probably the nicest hotel in town. Recommended.

L Tierra del Fuego, Colón 716, T061-226200, www.puntaarenas.com. Good breakfast, parking. Decent-sized rooms, some rooms with kitchenette. Café 1900 is downstairs.

AL Plaza, Nogueira 1116, piso 2, T061-241300, www.hotelplaza.cl. Historic building on the corner of the main plaza with high ceilings and old-fashioned charm, redone recently. English spoken. Limited parking and no elevators. Recommended.

A Carpa Manzano, Lautaro Navarro 336, T061-710744, www.hotelcarpamanzano.com. Small hotel with comfortable but slightly cramped carpeted rooms. Good beds (king-size in superior rooms). There is a wild garden at the back. Generally helpful staff, Wi-Fi, basic English spoken.

A Chalet Chapital, Sanhueza 974, T061-730100, www.hotelchaletchapital.cl. Small well-run hotel. Rooms are on the small side (although there is a common lounge area) and the stairs are a bit creaky, but the staff are friendly and helpful. A good choice in this price range. Recommended.

A Cóndor del Plata, Colón 556, T061-247987, www.condordeplata.cl. Small hotel often used by polar expeditions. Rooms with cable TV and full bathtubs. Slightly disinterested staff. Cash discounts sometimes offered.

A Mercurio, Fagnano 595, T061-242300, www.chileaustral.com/mercurio. Kitch 1970s rooms with full bathtub, TV and phone. Reasonable value.

A Oro Fueguino, Fagnano 356, T061-249401, www.orofueguino.cl. Recently refurbished, TV and phone. Some rooms with no windows. Good breakfast. Often

fills up with groups so book ahead. Cheaper in US dollars than pesos.

A-B La Casa Escondida, Parcela 26A, Sector Ojo Bueno, T061-223003, www.lacasa escondida.cl. Cosy rustic guesthouse hidden in the woods 15 km north of Punta Arenas towards the airport. Free pickup from town/airport. Very friendly and helpful owners, sauna, meals served. English spoken. Recommended.

B Hostal de la Avenida, Colón 534, T061-247532. Heated rooms with bath and cable TV. Good breakfast. Homely feel but some staff not so friendly.

B Hostal del Estrecho, Menéndez 1048, T061-241011, www.chileanpatagonia.com/estrecho. With large breakfast and bath (cheaper without), central heating, cable TV, Wi-Fi. Slightly overpriced and has seen better days.

B Hostal del Sur, Mejicana 151, T061-227249, hostaldelsur@hotmail.com. Homely and impeccably kept late-19th-century house. The living room is top of the range 1960s, but the rooms are modern. Excellent breakfast with cereal and cakes. Not central, but in a peaceful neighbourhood. Advance booking advised in summer. Good value. Recommended.

B Hostal Sonia Kuscevic, Pasaje Darwin 175, T061-248543, www.hostalsk.cl. One of the oldest guesthouses in Punta Arenas. Impeccably kept rooms with TV and bath. Very quiet, information given. Good breakfast including omelette. Slightly overpriced but good value off season or long stay.

B-C Hostal Ainil, Lautaro Navarro 230, T061-220962, www. www.hostalainil.com. Comfy bed and breakfast with smallish rooms. The ones at the front of the house are brightest. At the back are 2 lovely cabins, **A-B**, sleeping 3-4 people and good value.

B-C Hostal La Estancia, O'Higgins 765, T061-249130, www. estancia.cl. Simple but comfortable rooms, some with bath. Heating in passageways but not in rooms. Very good kitchen facilities, internet, lots of information, friendly. English spoken. Excellent breakfast with real coffee. Recommended.

B-C The Pink House, Caupolicán 99, T061-222436, www.chileanpatagonia.com/pink house. **D-E** singles. Impeccable rooms with or without bath, breakfast included. Pickup from bus station. English spoken, internet.

C Hostal al Fin del Mundo, O'Higgins 1026, T061-710185, www.alfindelmundo.cl. **E** singles, **F** per person in dorms. With breakfast. Bright cosy and friendly. Shared baths, central, helpful, laundry service, book exchange, internet, cooking facilities, English spoken, helpful, recommended.

C Hostal Dinka's House, Caupolicán 169, T061-244292, www.dinkashouse.cl. Heated rooms with bath, breakfast, use of kitchen, laundry.

C Hostal Keoken, Magallanes 209, T061-244086, www.hostalkeoken.cl. **D-E** singles. Bizarre construction on 3 floors each with its own entrance up rickety outside staircases. With breakfast. Some rooms with bath, kitchen facilities, Wi-Fi. Good value, friendly. Some info. Top floor rooms with shared bathroom have paper-thin walls.

C Hostal Luna, O'Higgins 424, T061-221764, hostalluna@hotmail.com. Rooms with or without bath. Breakfast included, use of kitchen, laundry facilities; dorm beds available, **F**.

C Hostal Parediso, Angamos 1073, T061-224212, hostalparediso@hotmail.com. **C-E** singles. Decent rooms with cable TV and heating, with or without bath (some cheaper rooms have no window). Good breakfast, parking, use of kitchen. Friendly, basic information given, some English spoken. Recommended.

C Hostal Quo Vadis, Paraguaya 150, T061-247687, www.hostalquovadis.cl. **E** singles. Motorcycle parking, meals, safe, quiet. Recommended.

C Hostal Taty's House, Maipu 1070, T061-241525, www.hostaltatyshouse.cl. Decent rooms with bath and cable TV. Good beds, decent value, a good choice in this price bracket. Basic English spoken.

C-D Hostal El Conventillo, Pasaje Korner 1034, T061-242311, www.hostalel conventillo.com. New 'hip' hostel. Rooms for 2-6 with shared bath, none with outside windows. Cheerful, good value, free internet. Good location.

D Backpackers Paradise, Carrera Pinto 1022, T061-240104, backpackersparadise@ hotmail.com. **G** per person in basic dorms. Fun cheap backpackers' with cooking facilities, limited bathroom facilities, lots of info, good meeting place, luggage store, internet, laundry service, little privacy, book exchange. Expensive bike rental. Recommended.

D Hospedaje Miramar, Almte Senoret 1190, T061-215446. **G** per person in dorms. Slightly exotic location on the edge of the red-light district. Friendly staff, good views over the bay. Breakfast extra.

E Hostal Independencia, Independencia 374, T061-227572, www.chileaustral.com/ independencia. **F-G** per person in shared rooms. Friendly, small basic rooms. Breakfast extra, kitchen facilities, laundry service, internet, bike rental and cheap camping. Also *cabañas* away from the centre. Good value. Recommended.

Fuerte Bulnes and further south *p478*

L Hostería Faro San Isidro, 75 km south of Punta Arenas, booking office Lautaro Navarro 1163, Punta Arenas, T061-710511, www.hosteriafarosanisidro.cl. The southernmost lodging on the American continent and within striking distance of Cape Froward. Excursions offered.

⊕ Eating

Punta Arenas *p475, map p477*
Visitors to Punta Arenas and the surrounding region should be especially wary of eating shellfish. In recent years, the nearby waters have been sporadically affected by a *marea roja* (red tide) of poisonous algae. While the *marea roja* only affects bivalve shellfish, infected molluscs can kill humans almost instantly. Mussels should not be picked along the shore of Punta Arenas; foreigners who

have done this have died. However, all shellfish sold in restaurants have been inspected and so are theoretically safe.

There are seasonal bans on *centolla* (king crab) fishing to protect dwindling stocks; out of season *centolla* served in restaurants will probably be frozen.

Many eateries here are closed on Sun.

TTT Remezón, 21 de Mayo 1469, T061-241029, www.patagoniasalvaje.net. Regional specialities such as krill. Very good, and so it should be given the exorbitant prices.

TTT-TT Damiana Elena, Magallanes 341, T061-222818. Stylish restaurant serving Mediterranean food with a Patagonian touch. Menu changes on a daily basis. Popular with locals. Advance booking essential at weekends, recommended.

TTT-TT El Asador Patagónico, O'Higgins 694, T061-222463. A new branch of the well-regarded **Natales** restaurant specializing in spit-roasted lamb.

TTT-TT El Estribo, Carrera Pinto 762, T061-244714. Specializes in local and exotic dishes such as *guanaco*. Something of a tourist trap.

TTT-TT José Nogueira hotel, see Sleeping, has a restaurant widely regarded as among the best in town.

TTT-TT La Tasca, Centro Español, Plaza Muñoz Gamero 771. Large helpings, limited selection, quite expensive. Decent lunch menu.

TTT-TT Puerto Viejo, O'Higgins 1167, T061-225296. By the port. Once the most traditional of the seafood restaurants, now relocated and more upscale. Service could be a lot better.

TTT-TT Sotitos, O'Higgins 1138. Good service and old fashioned elegance. Recommended.

TT La Luna, O'Higgins 1017, T061-228555. Fish and shellfish including local specialities, huge *pisco sours*, lively atmosphere.

TT La Marmite, Plaza Sampaio. Intimate restaurant decorated in desert pastel colours. Self-styled 'mestizo' restaurant – regional food with an international touch. Friendly service, relaxed atmosphere. Good value for Punta Arenas. Recommended.

TT Parrilla Los Ganaderos, Bulnes 0977, T061-222818. Best place for spit-roast lamb. It's a long walk past the hippodrome from the town centre. Take a taxi or a *colectivo* going towards the Zona Franca.

TT Santino, Colón 657, T061-220511. Good pizzas, large bar, good service.

T Carioca, Menéndez 600 y Chiloé. Cheap lunches, snacks and beer, good service.

T Cocinerías, Lautaro Navarro, south of the port entrance. Stalls serving cheap fish meals.

T Dino's Pizza, Bories 557. Good pizzas, huge sandwiches. For something different, try the rhubarb juice. Recommended.

T El Quijote, Lautaro Navarro 1087, T061-241225. Good burgers, sandwiches and fish dishes. Good-value set lunch. Recommended.

T Lomit's, Menéndez 722. A Punta Arenas fast-food institution serving cheap snacks and drinks, open when the others are closed, always busy, recommended.

T Sabores de Chiloé, Chiloé esq Balmaceda. Chilote food, as the name implies.

Cafés

Café 1900, Tierra del Fuego hotel, Colón 716.

Café Montt, Pedro Montt 976. With Wi-Fi.

Chocolatta, Bories 852. Probably the best coffee in town.

Coffeenet, Waldo Seguel 670. Proper internet café serving espresso.

Entre Fierros, Roca 875, T061-223436. Open until 1900. Small diner, colloquially known as the *Kiosko Roca*, that by all accounts has remained unchanged since the 1950s. It is famous for its banana milkshakes and tiny *choripan* (spicy sausage-meat sandwiches).

🎶 Bars and clubs

Punta Arenas *p475, map p477*
Be aware that anywhere that calls itself a 'nightclub' is in fact a brothel.

Kamikaze, Bories 655. Disco.

La Taberna del Club de la Unión, Plaza Muñoz Gamero y Seguel. Atmospheric pub in the basement of the **Nogueira** hotel, smoky.

Olijoe, Errázuriz 970. Reasonably plush British-style pub, leather interior. Recommended.
Pub 1900, Av Colón esq Bories. Friendly, relaxed atmosphere.
Santino, Colón 657, T061-220511, www.santino.cl Pizzeria that doubles as a popular bar at night.

⊛ Entertainment

Punta Arenas *p475, map p477*
There is a single-screen **cinema** at Mejicana 777. The new **casino** is on O'Higgins just north of the port.

⊛ Festivals and events

Punta Arenas *p475, map p477*
Late Jan/Early Feb Muestra custumbrista de Chiloe, when the Chilote community celebrates its culture.
21 Jun Carnaval de invierno is the winter solstice marked by a carnival on the weekend closest to 21 Jun.

O Shopping

Punta Arenas *p475, map p477*
Zona Franca, 3½ km north of the centre, on the right-hand side of the road to the airport, take bus E or A from Plaza Muñoz Gamero or a *colectivo*. Open Mon-Sat 1000-1230, 1500-2000.

Punta Arenas has certain free-port facilities. Cheap perfume and electrical goods are especially worth seeking out, as is camping equipment and cameras. The quality of most other goods is low and the prices little better than elsewhere. There is a new mall, the **Espacio Urbano**, 2 km to the west of the town centre. Take *colectivo* 300, 777 or 800.

Camping equipment
Alfgal, Errázuriz y Lautaro Navarro, camping gear.
Andes gear, Espacio Urbano mall, the best store for outdoor equipment.
Sports Nativa, Colón 614. Camping and skiing equipment.
The North Face, Bories 887. Outdoor gear.

Handicrafts and local products
Punta Arenas is famous for the quality of its chocolate. Delicious handmade chocolate is for sale at several shops on Calle Bories.
Chile Típico, Carrera Pinto 1015, T061-225827. Chilean souvenirs
Chocolates Norweisser, Carrera 663. Good chocolate factory.
Pingüi, Bories 404. Crafts and books on Tierra del Fuego, Patagonia and Antarctica.
The Wool House Patagonia, Fagnano 675, by the plaza. Good-quality, reasonably priced woollen clothes.

Supermarkets
Abu Gosch, between Magallanes and Bories north of Carrera Pinto.
Cofrima, Lautaro Navarro 1293 y Balmaceda.
Cofrima 2, España 01375.
Listo, 21 de Mayo 1133.
There are also Líder and Cofrima hyper-markets 2 km northwest of the city centre.

▲ Activities and tours

Punta Arenas *p475, map p477*
Golf
There's a 9-hole golf course 5 km south of town on the road to Fuerte Bulnes.

Skiing
Cerro Mirador, 9 km west of Punta Arenas in the Reserva Nacional Magallanes, is one of the few places in the world where you can ski with a sea view. Season Jun to Sep, weather permitting. Daily lift-ticket, US$11; equipment rental US$9 per adult. There's a mid-way lodge with food, drink and equipment. For

cross-country skiing facilities, contact the **Club Andino**, T061-241479, www.club andino.tierra.cl. However, the ski centre is often closed due to lack of snow. There's also a good 2-hr hike here in summer; the trail is clearly marked and flora is labelled.

Skiing is also available at **Tres Morros**.

Tour operators

Most organize tours to Fuerte Bulnes, the *pingüineras* on Otway sound and Torres del Paine. Note that a 1-day tour to the latter involves leaving at 0500 and returning around 2300. Several also offer bespoke tours; shop around as prices vary. Specify in advance if you want a tour in English. There are many more tour operators than these listed; for more information, ask at the **Sernatur** office.

Arka Patagonia, Señoret 1597, T061-248167, www.arkapatagonia.com. General agent offering all types of tours, rafting, fishing, etc.

International Tours & Travel, 1 Dean St, Stanley, T+500-22041, www.falklandislands. travel. LanChile agents on the Falkland Islands, book FIGAS flights and organize tailor-made and special-interest tours.

Pali Alke, Lautaro Navarro 1125, T061-223301, www.turismopaliaike.com. Wide range of tours including horse-riding trips.

Solo Expediciones, Nogueira 1255, T061-710219, www.soloexpediciones.com. Bespoke and off-the-beaten-track excursions on and around the Magellan Straits.

Turismo Aonikenk, Magallanes 619, T061-221 982, www.aonikenk.com. Expensive but very good bespoke excursions. Recommended.

Turismo Aventour, Patagonia 779, T061-241197, www.aventourpatagonia.com. General excursions and multi-day tours.

Turismo Comapa, Magallanes 990, T061-200200, www.comapa.com. Tours to Torres del Paine, Tierra del Fuego and Isla Magdalena, also agents for trips to the Falklands/Malvinas, Ushuaia and Cape Horn.

Turismo Ruta Club Internacional, Carrera Pinto 1142, T061-229000, www.turismo rutaclub.cl. General travel agent also offering local tours. Cycle hire, US$2 per hr.

Turismo Viento Sur, Fagnano 585, T061-226930, www.vientosur.com. For camping equipment, fishing excursions, sea kayaking, cycle hire, English spoken, good tours.

Whale Sound, Lautaro Navarro 1163, T061-710511, www.whalesound.com. Whale-watching trips in the Magellan Straits.

● Transport

Punta Arenas *p475, map p477*
All transport is heavily booked from late Dec through to Mar; advance booking is advised.

Air
Flights arrive at **Carlos Ibáñez del Campo Airport**, 20 km north of town.

Airline offices Aerovías DAP, O'Higgins 891, T061-616100, www. dap.cl, 0900-1230, 1430-1930; LanChile, Bories 884, T600-526 2000, www.lan.cl; Sky Airline, Roca 933, T600-600 2828, www.skyairline.cl.

Domestic To **Balmaceda** (for Coyhaique), with LanChile (LanExpress), daily in summer, and Sky Airline, 3 weekly all year, US$80. To **Puerto Montt**, with LanChile (LanExpress) and Sky Airline, 10 daily, from US$120 return. Cheapest one-way tickets with **Sky**. To **Santiago**, LanChile (LanExpress) and Sky Airline several daily, from US$200 return, via Puerto Montt (sit on the right for views). To **Porvenir**, Aerovías DAP, 2-3 daily Mon-Sat, US$34 one-way, plus other flights, with Twin-Otter and Cessna aircraft, 10 kg baggage allowance. To **Puerto Williams**, Aerovías DAP, daily in summer (book well in advance), US$95 one-way, 10 kg baggage allowance.

International To **Ushuaia** (Argentina), Lan Chile, 3 weekly in summer, 1 hr, from US$200 one-way; reserve well in advance from mid-Dec to Feb. To **Falkland Islands/ Islas Malvinas**, LanChile, Sat, US$600 return. International Tours & Travel, T+500-22041, www.falklandtravel.com (see Tour operators, above), serves as LanChile agents on the Falkland Islands.

Bicycle and motorbike
Bike parts from José Aguila Quezada, Arauco 2675, T061-265399. Motorbike parts from Violic, Sanhueza 285, T061-241606, also in the Zona Franca.

Bus
Buses depart from the company offices as follows: Bus Sur, Menéndez 552 T061-227145, www.bus-sur.cl; Cruz del Sur, Pingüino and Fernández, Sanhueza 745, T061-242313, www.busesfernandez.com; Gesell, Menéndez 556, T061-222896; Ghisoni, Queilen Bus and Tecniaustral, Lautaro Navarro 971, T061-222078, www.ghisoni. terra.cl; Pacheco, Colón 900, T061-242174, www.busespacheco.com.

Services and frequencies change every year, so check on arrival at the helpful Sernatur office. Timetables are also printed daily in *El Austral*. The services detailed below are for high season only. There is a project to build a new bus terminal north of town by the Zona Franca to be shared by all bus companies.

Fernández, Buses Pacheco (best buses) and Bus Sur (cheapest), all run several services each day to **Puerto Natales**, 3 hrs, last departure 2000, US$9 one-way, US$16 return (although this means you have to return with the same company). Buses may pick up at the airport with advance booking and payment. To **Coyhaique**, 24 hrs, Bus Sur, 1 per week via Argentina, US$55, meals not included. Pacheco (*semi cama* and *salon cama*), Queilen Bus and Cruz del Sur have services through Argentina to **Osorno**, **Puerto Montt** and **Castro**, several weekly, 36 hrs to Castro, US$50-75.

To Argentina To **Río Gallegos**, Pingüino, Ghisoni and Pacheco, 2 or 3 daily between them. All cost US$12 and take about 5 hrs. For services to **Buenos Aires** it is cheaper to go to Río Gallegos and buy an onward ticket from there. Pacheco and Tecni Austral have buses most days to **Río Grande** via Punta Delgada, 8 hrs, US$33, heavily booked. To **Ushuaia** via Punta Delgada, US$50, 12-14 hrs, book any return at same time, Tecni Austral and Pacheco, Mon-Sat between them.

Car
Car hire Try looking in the local newspaper for special deals and bargain if you want to hire a car for several days. Budget, O'Higgins 964, T061-202720, www.budget patagonia.com; Econorent, Waldo Seguel 443, T600-200 0000, www.econorent.cl; EMSA, Roca 1044, and at the airport, T061-222 9049, www.emsarentacar.cl. Avis agents; Hertz, O'Higgins 931, T061-613087, www.autorentas.cl; Lubag, Colón 975, T061-242023, www.lubag.cl; Magallanes Rent a Car, O'Higgins 949, T061-220780,

www.magallanesrentacar.cl; **Payne Rent a Car**, Menéndez 631, T061-240852, www.payne.cl, try bargaining, friendly.

Boat

For ferry services to **Tierra del Fuego**, see page 536. **Transbordadores Austral Broom**, Bulnes 05075, T061-218100, www.tabsa.cl, has a weekly ferry service to **Puerto Williams**, leaves Wed, 34 hrs, US$175 in a reclining seat, US$210 in a bunk.

Cruceros Australis operate a pair of luxury cruise ships, sailing twice weekly from Punta Arenas to **Ushuaia** via Cape Horn and Puerto Williams. The trip lasts 4 days with daily excursions and, weather permitting, fantastic views of glaciers and wildlife; details from **Comapa** in Punta Artenas or direct from **Cruceros Australis SA**, Miraflores 178, piso 12, Santiago, T02-6963211, www.aust ralis.com. Advance booking advised.

Government supply ships are only recommended for the young and hardy; take a sleeping bag, extra food and travel pills. For transport on navy supply ships to **Cape Horn**, ask at **Tercera Zona Naval**, Lautaro Navarro 1150, be prepared to be frustrated by irregular sailings (about 1 every 3 months) and inaccurate information. You will almost certainly need a letter of recommendation. During the voyage across the Drake Passage, albatrosses, petrels, cormorants, penguins, elephant seals, fur seals, whales and dolphins can all be sighted.

Most cruise ships to **Antarctica** leave from Ushuaia (Argentina). However, there are a few operators based in Punta Arenas, for example **Antárctica XXI**, Lautaro Navarro 987, piso 2, T061-228783, www.antarctica xxi.com who offer a flight/cruise package.

Taxi

Ordinary taxis have yellow roofs. Reliable service is available from **Radio Alce vip**, T061-710999, and **Taxi Austral**, T061-247710/T244409. *Colectivos* (all black) run on fixed routes within the city, US$0.70 for anywhere on the route.

ⓘ Directory

Punta Arenas p475, map p477
Banks Several on or around Plaza Muñoz Gamero many 24 hrs, all have ATMs. Banks open Mon-Fri 0830-1400, *casas de cambio* open Mon-Fri 0900-1230, 1500-1900, Sat 0900-1230; good rates at **Cambio Gasic**, Roca 915, of 8, T061-242396. German spoken; **La Hermandad**, Lautaro Navarro 1099, T061-243991, excellent rates; **Scott Cambios**, Colón y Magallanes, T061-227145; **Sur Cambios**, Lautaro Navarro 1001, T061-225656.
Consulates Argentina, 21 de Mayo 1878, T061-261912, open weekdays 1000-1530, visas take 24 hrs; Belgium, Roca 817, of 61, T061-241472; Brazil, Arauco 769, T061-241093; Germany, Pasaje Korner 1046, T061-241082, Casilla 229; Italy, 21 de Mayo 1569, T061-221596; Netherlands, Magallanes 435, T061-248100; Norway, Magallanes 990, T061-241437; Paraguay, Bulnes 0928 Dp14 piso 1, T061-211825; Spain, Menéndez 910, T061-243566; Sweden, Errázuriz 891, T061-224107; UK, Catarates de Niaguara 01325, T061-211 535, helpful, with information on Falkland Islands; Uruguay, José Nogueira 1238, T061-241594. **Internet** Lots of places offer access, including at Magallanes y Menendez, and below **Hostal Calafate** on Magallanes, ½ block north of Plaza. Prices are generally US$1 per hr.
Laundry Lavaseco Josseau, Carrera Pinto 766; Lavasol, O'Higgins 969, the only self-service laundry, Mon-Sat 0900-2030, Sun (summer only) 1000-1800, US$6 per machine, wash and dry, good but busy. **Medical services** Dentist: Rosemary Robertson Stipicic, Roca 932, T061-22931, speaks English. Hospitals: Hospital Regional Lautaro Navarro, Angamos 180, T061-244040, public hospital, for emergency room ask for *urgencias*; Clínica Magallanes, Bulnes 01448, T061-211527, private clinic, medical staff the same as in the hospital but fancier surroundings and more expensive; minimum charge US$45 per visit. A list of English-speaking doctors is available from Sernatur. **Post office** Bories 911 y Menéndez, Mon-Fri 0830-1930, Sat 0900-1400.

Puerto Natales and around

→ *Colour map 6, B3. Population 19,000.*

From Punta Arenas, a good paved road runs 247 km north to Puerto Natales through forests of southern beech and prime pastureland; this is the best area for cattle- and sheep-raising in Chile. Nandúes and guanacos can often be seen en route. Puerto Natales lies between Cerro Dorotea (which rises behind the town) and the eastern shore of the Seno Ultima Esperanza (Last Hope Sound), over which there are fine views, weather permitting, to the Peninsula Antonio Varas and the jagged peaks and receding glaciers of the Parque Nacional Bernardo O'Higgins beyond. Founded in 1911, the town grew as an industrial centre and, until recent years, the town's prosperity was based upon employment in the coal mines of Río Turbio, Argentina. Today, Puerto Natales is the starting point for trips to the magnificent O'Higgins (see page 490) and Torres del Paine national parks (see page 497), and tourism is one of its most important industries; the town centre has a prosperous if somewhat touristy atmosphere. ▶▶ For listings, see pages 490-496.

Ins and outs

Getting there Puerto Natales is easily reached by many daily buses from Punta Arenas, as well as by buses from Río Turbio (Argentina) and El Calafate (two to four daily). There are also two buses weekly from Río Gallegos. The town is the terminus of the *Navimag* ship to Puerto Montt. In summer, there are flights from Santiago via Puerto Montt. If driving between Punta Arenas and Puerto Natales, make sure you have enough fuel. Note that buses from Argentina invariably arrive late. In theory buses from Punta Arenas to Puerto Natales will pick passengers up at Punta Arenas airport as long as reservations have been made with advance payment through an agency in Puerto Natales. In practice though they are often unreliable. ▶▶ *See Transport, page 496.*

Getting around Puerto Natales is small; taxis needed only for journeys out of town.

Tourist office There is a **Sernatur kiosk** ① *on the waterfront, Av Pedro Montt y Philippi, T061-412125*; information is also available from the **Municipalidad** ① *Bulnes 285, T061-411263*, and from **CONAF** ① *O'Higgins 584*.

Sights

The **Museo histórico municipal** ① *Bulnes 285, T061-411263, museonat@123mail.cl, Mon-Fri 0800-1900, Sat 1000-1300, 1500-1900, closed Sat off season, US$1*, houses a small collection of archaeological and native artefacts as well as exhibits on late-19th-century European colonization. Reasonable descriptions in English.

South of the town centre past the end of calle Baquedano is the **Museo de Fauna Patagónica** ① *Colegio Salesiano, Padre Rossa 1456, T061-411258, museo@fagnano.cl, Mon-Sat 0900-1315, 1430-1930 in summer, US$1.50*. It houses a collection of around 350 stuffed animals from the region.

The colourful old steam train in the main square was once used to take the workers to the the meat-packing factory at **Puerto Bories**, 5 km north of town. It is a pleasant hour-long walk along the shore to Bories (US$4 by taxi), with glimpses of the Balmaceda Glacier across the sound. In its heyday the plant was the biggest of its kind in Chile with a capacity for 250,000 sheep. Bankrupted in the early 1990s, much of the plant was dismantled in 1993. Belatedly the plant was given National Monument status and is slowly being restored. The remaining buildings and machine rooms can be visited. **Museo Frigorífico**

Puerto Bories ① T061-414328, www.museopuertobories.cl, Mon-Sun 1000-1900 in summer, US$6 with an audioguide in several languages.

The slab-like **Cerro Dorotea** dominates the town, with superb views of the whole Seno Ultima Esperanza. It can be reached on foot or by any Río Turbio bus or taxi (recommended, as the hill is further away than it seems). The trail entrance is marked by a

Puerto Natales

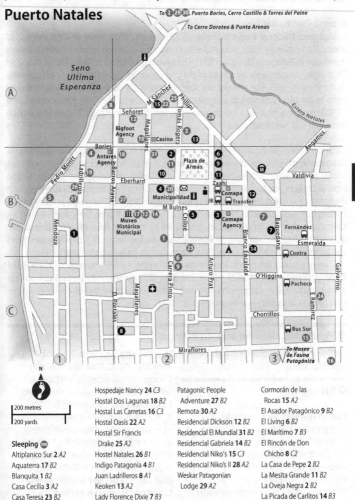

N
200 metres
200 yards

Sleeping
Altiplanico Sur **2** A2
Aquaterra **17** B2
Blanquita **1** B2
Casa Cecilia **3** A2
Casa Teresa **23** B2
Charles Darwin **21** B1
Costaustralis **5** B1
Glaciares **19** B1
Hospedaje Chila **6** C2

Hospedaje Nancy **24** C3
Hostal Dos Lagunas **18** B2
Hostal Las Carretas **16** C3
Hostal Oasis **22** A2
Hostal Sir Francis
  Drake **25** A2
Hostel Natales **26** B1
Indigo Patagonia **4** B1
Juan Ladrilleros **8** A1
Keoken **13** A2
Lady Florence Dixie **7** B3
Los Inmigrantes **9** C2
Martín Gusinde **10** A2
Natalino **20** B2
Patagonia Adventure **11** B2

Patagonic People
  Adventure **27** B2
Remota **30** A2
Residencial Dickson **12** B2
Residencial El Mundial **31** B2
Residencial Gabriela **14** B2
Residencial Niko's **15** C3
Residencial Niko's II **28** A2
Weskar Patagonian
  Lodge **29** A2

Eating
Afrigonia **4** B2
Andrés **1** B1
Angelicas **3** B2

Cormorán de las
  Rocas **15** A2
El Asador Patagónico **9** B2
El Living **6** B2
El Marítimo **7** B3
El Rincón de Don
  Chicho **8** C2
La Casa de Pepe **2** B2
La Mesita Grande **11** B2
La Oveja Negra **2** B2
La Picada de Carlitos **14** B3
La Repizza **12** B3
La Ultima Esperanza **10** B2
Masay **5** B2
Parrilla Don Jorge **13** A2

sign that reads 'Mirador Cerro Dorotea'. Expect to be charged US$5-8 in one of the local houses, where you will be given a broomstick handle which makes a surprisingly good walking stick. It is a 1½-hour trek up to the 600-m lookout along a well-marked trail. In theory you can continue along the top of the hill to get better views to the north, but the incredibly strong winds often make this dangerous.

Around Puerto Natales

Monumento Nacional Cueva Milodón ⓘ *25 km north, US$6, buses JB US$8, taxi US$30 return. Most Torres del Paine tours stop at the cave.* This is the end point of Bruce Chatwin's travelogue *In Patagonia* (see page 611). The cave, a massive 70 m wide, 220 m deep and 30 m high, contains a plastic model of the prehistoric ground-sloth whose remains were found there in 1895. The remains are now in London, although there is talk of returning them to the site. Evidence has also been found here of occupation by Patagonians some 11,000 years ago. Nearby, a visitor centre has summaries in English. There's also a good restaurant and handicraft store.

Parque Nacional Bernardo O'Higgins Often referred to as the **Parque Nacional Monte Balmaceda**, this park covers much of the Campo de Hielo Sur, plus the fjords and offshore islands further west. A three-hour boat trip from Puerto Natales up the Seno de Ultima Esperanza takes you to the southernmost section, passing the Balmaceda Glacier, which drops from the eastern slopes of **Monte Balmaceda** (2035 m). The glacier is retreating; in 1986 its foot was at sea level. The boat docks further north at **Puerto Toro**, from where it is a kilometre walk to the base of the Serrano Glacier on the north slope of Monte Balmaceda. On the trip, dolphins, sea lions (in season), black-necked swans, flightless steamer ducks and cormorants can often be seen. Take warm clothes, including a hat and gloves.

There is a route from Puerto Toro on the eastern side of the Río Serrano for 35 km to the Torres del Paine administration centre (see page 497); guided tours are available on foot or on horseback. It is also possible to travel to the Paine administration centre along the river by boat or zodiac (four hours, US$85).

ⓞ Puerto Natales and around listings

For Sleeping and Eating price codes and other relevant information, see Essentials pages 35-42.

ⓢ Sleeping

Puerto Natales *p488, map p489*
Most prices include breakfast. Hotels in the countryside are open only in the summer months; specific dates vary. In season, cheaper accommodation fills up quickly after the arrival of the *Navimag* ferry from Puerto Montt. Most of the more expensive hotels in the town centre are much of a muchness, give or take the view. Occasionally one of these will have a special offer. Call around for quotes.

LL Altiplánico Sur, Huerto 282, T061-412525, www.altiplanico.cl. Minimalist hotel with a unique design built into the hillside 1 km north of town, with views across the sound.
LL Costaustralis, Pedro Montt 262, T061-412000, www.hoteles-australis.com. The most expensive hotel in the town centre, but no better than the other big hotels. In effect you are paying for the view, which, to be fair, is the best there is. The rooms facing inland are an expensive waste of money.
LL Indigo Patagonia Hotel and Spa, Ladrilleros 105, T061-413620, www.indigo patagonia.com. Old 3-storey house on the waterfront with fantastic views, expanded and converted into a boutique hotel,

together with restaurant (open to the public, serving seafood and vegetarian options) and roof-top spa.

LL Remota, Huerto 279, 1 km north of town along the coast, T061-412727, www.remotahotel.com. Expensive all-inclusive packages of 3 days or more with a wide range of activities inside and outside Torres del Paine. Rooms are spacious with extensive views.

L Weskar Patagonian Lodge, Km 1, road to Bories, T061-414168, www.weskar.cl. Quiet lodge overlooking the bay, understated wooden interior. Rooms are simple but most have extensive views. With a good but expensive restaurant for guests, and bike rental. Helpful staff. A pleasant out-of-town place to relax.

L-AL Charles Darwin, Bulnes 90, T061-412478, www.hotelcharlesdarwin.com. Newly refurbished comfortable 3-star standard. Some rooms with partial views. Permanently empty restaurant downstairs. Good rates off-season.

L-AL Martín Gusinde, Bories 278, T061-412770, www. hotelmartingusinde.com. Comfy 3-star, although the carpets could do with a change and rooms do not have a view. Good-value off-season rates.

AL Aquaterra, Bulnes 299, T061-412239, www.aquaterrapatagonia.com. Understated design. No frills but thought and effort have gone into it. Not cheap, but unlike many other places in the same price bracket you get the feeling that the staff are there to help and are able to answer your questions. Living room upstairs and a bar downstairs. Alternative therapies also offered. Thin walls a drawback.

AL Glaciares, Eberhard 104, T061-411452, www.hotelglaciares.com. A standard 3-star. Comfortable enough, some rooms have a partial view. Good day tours to Torres del Paine.

AL Juan Ladrilleros, Pedro Montt 161, T061-411652, www.hoteljuanladrilleros.com. Small basic often tatty rooms with bath, no TV, but great views. Rack rates overpriced but often willing to give discounts.

AL-A Lady Florence Dixie, Bulnes 655, T061-411158, www. hotelflorencedixie.cl. 3-star. Helpful staff. The standard rooms are a bit cramped and cold, but the superior rooms are bigger, carpeted and good value.

A Hostal Sir Francis Drake, Philippi 383, T061-411553, www.hostalfrancisdrake.com. Simple, smallish but comfortable rooms with bath and cable TV. There is a pleasant living room on the upper floor with views. Wi-Fi, French spoken. Recommended.

A Keoken, Señoret 267, T061-413670, www.keokenpatagonia.com. New homely upmarket bed and breakfast. Spacious living room. Some rooms with views. All rooms have their own bathroom but note that not all are en suite. Some English spoken.

A Patagonic People Adventure, Bulnes 280, T061-412014, www.patagonicpeople adventure.com. Set up as a boutique hostel. Nice mininalist rooms and common areas with Wi-Fi. Pretty, but somewhat lacking in character. Singles overpriced.

A-B Hostel Natales, Ladrilleros 209, T061-411081, www.hostelnatales.cl. **D-E** per person in dorms. All rooms with bath. Formerly a decent hotel, converted into a luxury hostel. The place has been fully refurbished and is very comfortable, even if the dorm beds are a little overpriced.

B Hostal Oasis, Señoret 332, T061-411675, www.hostaloasis.cl. Comfortable rooms, with or without bath, cable TV. Breakfast included. Some rooms have no window and can get a little stuffy.

B-C Casa Cecilia, Tomás Rogers 60, T061-613560, www.casaceciliahostal.com. **D** singles. With good breakfast, some rooms with bath, clean, cooking facilities, Wi-Fi, English, French and German spoken, heating, luggage store, camping equipment rental, information on Torres del Paine, tours organized, bus tickets sold, credit cards accepted. Better value in US dollars. Warmly recommended.

B-C Hostal Las Carretas, Galvarino 745, T061-414584, www.lascarretashostal.com. Tastefully decorated and impeccably clean bed and breakfast. Comfortable rooms, some with bath, good beds, kitchen facilities, Wi-Fi, friendly staff. Some English spoken. Recommended. However, it is a 15-min walk to the centre – not nice in bad weather.

C Blanquita, Carrera Pinto 409, T061-411674. **E** singles. Basic quiet hotel that looks like a giant portacabin. With bath, heating and breakfast, friendly.

C Hospedaje Nancy, E Ramírez 540, T061-4510022, www.natateslodge.cl. **F** singles. Some rooms with bath. Cooking facilities, internet access, laundry service, helpful, tours, lots of information. Good budget option. Recommended.

C Hostal Dos Lagunas, Barros Arana 104, T061-415733, doslagunas@hotmail.com. **D** singles. Simple clean unpretentious *residencial*. All rooms with shared bathrooms. Very friendly English speaking owner eager to help with travellers' needs. Good breakfast including real coffee. Recommended.

C Patagonia Adventure, Tomás Rogers 179, T061-411028, www.apatagonia.com. **E-F** per person in dorms. Shared bathrooms. Friendly, clean, English spoken, camping equipment for hire, luggage store, book exchange. Good bike and kayak tours offered. Also a general agent selling trips to Torres del Paine. Breakfast is served in the café annex.

C-D Residencial Dickson, Bulnes 307, T061-411871, patagoniadickson@hotmail.com. **F** singles. Some rooms with bath. Good breakfast, clean, helpful, cooking and laundry facilities, internet.

C-D Residencial Niko's, Ramírez 669, T061-412810, nikoresidencial@hotmail.com. **E-F** singles. With breakfast, basic rooms, some rooms with bath, good meals, also dorm accommodation. Recommended.

C-D Residencial Niko's II, Philippi 528, T061-411500, www.nikostwoadventure.com. With good breakfast. Some rooms with bath and cable TV, English spoken, tours, tent hire, book exchange, free internet if you can get the owners' children off the PC. Recommended.

D Los Inmigrantes, Carrera Pinto 480, T061-413482, losinmigrantes@hotmail.com. **F** singles. Good breakfast, clean, kitchen facilities, equipment rental, luggage store.

D Natalino, Eberhard 371, T061-411968. Clean and very friendly. Rooms with bath and breakfast, parking.

D Residencial El Mundial, Bories 315, T061-412476, omar@fortalezapatagonia.cl. **F-G** singles. Some rooms with bath. Some use of kitchen, good-value meals, luggage stored.

D Residencial Gabriela, Bulnes 317, T061-411061. **F** singles. Clean, good breakfast, helpful, luggage store, heating. Recommended.

E Casa Teresa, Esmeralda 463, T061-410472, freepatagonia@hotmail.com. **G** singles. Good value, warm, cheap meals, quiet, friendly. Tours to Torres del Paine arranged. Recommended.

E Hospedaje Chila, Carrera Pinto 442, T061-412328. **G** singles. Use of kitchen, welcoming, laundry facilities, luggage store, home-baked bread. Recommended.

Around Puerto Natales p490

L-AL Cisne de Cuello Negro, 6 km north of town, Km 275 near Puerto Bories, for bookings contact Av Colón 782, Punta Arenas, T061-244506, pehoe1@ctcinternet.cl. Clean, decent food. Recommended.

AL Estancia Tres Pasos, 40 km north of town, T061-221930, www.trespasos.cl. Simple and beautiful lodge between Puerto Natales and Torres del Paine. Horse-riding trips offered.

AL Hostal Río Penitente, on the road from Punta Arenas, Km 138, T061-331694. In an old *estancia*.

AL Hostería Río Verde, on the road from Punta Arenas, Km 90, east off the highway on Seno Skyring, T061-311122. Private bath, heating.

A Cabañas Kotenk Aike, 2 km north of town, T061-412581. Sleeps 4, modern, very comfortable, great location.

A Hostería Llanuras de Diana, on the road from Punta Arenas, Km 215 (30 km south of Puerto Natales), T061-410661. Hidden from road, beautifully situated. Recommended.

B Hotel Rubens, Km 183, T061-226916. Popular for fishing.

Camping There is a campsite in town on Esmeralda y Prat with hot water and tent hire.

Parque Nacional Bernado O'Higgins

L Hostería Monte Balmaceda, T061-220174. Although the park is uninhabited, guest accommodation is available here.

❶ Eating

Puerto Natales p488, map p489

₮₮₮ **Afrigonia**, Eberhard 343, T061-412232, afrigonia@hotmail.com. A totally unexpected mixture, Patagonia meets East Africa in this new Kenyan/Chilean-owned fusion restaurant, considered by many to be the best, and certainly the most innovative, in town.

₮₮₮-₮₮ **Angélicas**, Bulnes 501, T061-410365, angelicas@rest.cl. A sign that Puerto Natales is now a boutique town. Elegant Mediterranean-style restaurant originally from Santiago. Quality ingredients well prepared. Pricey

but more than reasonable for Natales, and customers invariably leave satisfied. Staff can be a little flustered when the restaurant is full. Recommended.

₮₮₮-₮₮ **Cormoran de las Rocas**, Miguel Sánchez 72, T061-413723, www.cormoran delasrocas.com. Patagonian specialties with an innovative twist. Wide variety of well-prepared dishes. 1st-rate *pisco sours*. Good service and attention to detail, and incomparable views. Recommended.

₮₮₮-₮₮ **El Asador Patagonico**, Prat 158 on plaza. Specializes in spit-roast lamb. Book in advance as space us limited. Recommended.

₮₮₮-₮₮ **Parrilla Don Jorge**, Bories 430 on plaza, T061-410999. Another restaurant specializing in *Cordero al Palo*, but also serving fish, etc. The open plan leaves you feeling a little exposed when the restaurant is not full. Decent service.

₮₮ **El Marítimo**, Baquedano 379. One of the best places in town to eat fish and seafood.

₮₮ **El Rincón de Don Chicho**, Luis Cruz Martínez 206, T061-414339. All-you-can-eat *parrillada*. Vegetarian options on request. 15 mins' walk from town centre. Recommended.

₮₮ **La Casa de Pepe**, Tomás Rogers 131 on the plaza. For those who want to sample the traditional food of central Chile – *pernil, pastel de choclo*, etc. Uncomfortable seats.

₮₮ **La Mesita Grande**, Prat 196 on the plaza, T061-411571, www.mesitagrande.cl. 1st-rate pizzas made in a wood-burning clay oven. Also pasta, salads and good desserts. Not much atmosphere, but there's a fantastic antique till.

₮₮ **La Oveja Negra**, Tomás Rogers 169, on the plaza. Typical Chilean dishes, book swap. Ownership of this restaurant seems to change every year.

₮₮-₮ **La Picada de Carlitos**, Blanco Encalada y Esmeralda. Good, cheap traditional Chilean food. Often full of locals at lunchtime. Service can be slow when full.

₮₮ **La Ultima Esperanza**, Eberhard 354. Recommended for salmon, seafood, huge portions, not cheap but worth it.

₮ **Andrés**, Ladrilleros 381. Excellent, good fish dishes, good service.

¶ **La Repizza**, Blanco Encalada 294, T061-410361. Good-value sarnies and light meals.
¶ **Masay**, Bulnes 429. Cheap sandwiches.

Cafés
Aquaterra, Bulnes 299. Cosy, good, also a shiatsu and reiki centre.
Café + Books, Blanco Encalada 224. Cosy café with an extensive 2-for-1 book exchange.
Cerritos, Miguel Sánchez 11. Tiny hidden café with friendly owners and a fantastic view.
El Living, on the plaza. Cosy, British-run, with English newspapers and magazines. Wide variety of cakes, good tea and coffee, wine and vegetarian food. Book exchange.
Emporio de la Pampa, Eberhard 302, T061-413279. Small café/delicatessen selling wine and local gourmet products.
Patagonia Adventure, Tomás Rogers 179 on the plaza. Opens at 0630 for early risers.
Patagonia Dulce, Barros Arana 233, T061-415285, www.patagoniadulce.cl. For the best hot chocolate in town.

❶ Bars and clubs

Puerto Natales *p488, map p489*
There are a couple of clubs on Blanco Encalada.
Casino, Bories 314, T061-411834. Daily 1300-0400. Modest, tables open from 2100.
El Bar de Ruperto, Bulnes 371. Good, English-run pub with a lively mix of locals and tourists. For a kick, try the chile vodka.
Iguana, Magallanes y Eberhard. There is invariably a bar here, but it seems to change name and ownership each year.
Kaweshkar, Eberhard 161. European-style lounge bar.
Murciélagos, Bulnes 731. Popular bar with late-night music and dancing.
Toore, Eberhard 169. Another popular bar.

◯ Shopping

Puerto Natales *p488, map p489*
Camping equipment
Camping gas is available in hardware stores, eg at Baquedano y O'Higgins. Wares tend to be more expensive than the Zona Franca in Punta Arenas. **Alfgal**, Barros Arana 299, T061-413622; **Balfer**, Bulnes 660; **La Maddera**, Prat 297, T061-41331, outdoor clothing; **Torres del Paine**, Baquedano 622, trekking gear. **Casa Cecilia** and **Patagonia Adventure** (see Sleeping) have a reputation for hiring out good-quality gear, but there are an increasing number of alternatives mostly with tour agencies and hostels. Shop around and check all equipment and prices carefully. Average charges, per day: tent US$8, sleeping bag US$4-6, mat US$2, raincoat US$1, also cooking gear US$2. Deposits sometimes required: tent US$200, sleeping bag US$100. Note that it is often difficult to hire walking boots.

Food
Food prices are variable, so shop around, although everything tends to be more expensive than in Punta Arenas. The biggest supermarket is **Abu Gosch** at Bulnes y Ramirez. Also **Don Bosco**, Baquedano 358. The town markets are also good.

Handicrafts
El Toque Campero, Eberhard 148. Good-quality and reasonably priced leather and woolen handicrafts as well as locally produced cakes jams, etc sold from a characterful old shepherd's wagon. Friendly owners.
Nandu, Eberhard 586 y Magallanes. Popular craft store. Another branch at the Milodon Cave.
Pueblo Artisanal Etherh Aike, Philippi y Valdivia. Covered market with many handicraft stalls.

▲ Activities and tours

Puerto Natales *p488, map p489*
Reports of the reliability of agencies, especially for their trips to Parque Nacional Torres del Paine, are very mixed. It is better to book tours in Puerto Natales than through agents in Punta Arenas or Santiago, where huge commissions may be charged. While most tours can be booked direct with the operators, there are several agencies in Puerto Natales who can make bookings with all of the operators below as well as transport and accommodation within the park.

Some agencies offer 1-day tours to the Perito Moreno glacier in Argentina (see page 512), 14-hr trip, 2 hrs at the glacier, US$65 excluding food and park entry fee; take US$ cash or Argentine pesos as Chilean pesos are not accepted. However, if you have more time it is better to break the trip by staying in Calafate, and organizing a tour from there.

As most organised activities within Torres del Paine such as horse riding and ice trekking are operated by exclusive licence holders, many other agencies are concentrating on the area to the south of the park around the Río Serrano and the route between Puerto Natales and the Park.

Tour operators

Antares, Barros Arana 111, T061-414611, www.antarespatagonia.com. Kayaking and trekking.

Baguales Group, Galvarino 661, T061-412654, www.bagualesgroup.com. Specialists in the route from the park back to Puerto Natales. Tailor made multi-activity tours that can incorporate zodiacs, horse riding, kayaking and trekking, mostly off the beaten track. A real experience. Recommended.

Bella Patagonia, Barros Arana 160, T061-412 489, www.bellapatagonia.com. Belgian-run operator specializing in kayak trips and trekking.

Chile Nativo, Eberhard 230, T061-411835, www.chilenativo.com. Specializes in multi-day and bespoke tours of Torres del Paine and surroundings.

Comapa, Eberhard 555, T061-414300, www.comapa.com. Large regional operator offering decent day tours to the park.

Criollo Expediciones, Huerto 157-B, T09-85284225, www.criolloexpediciones.com. Guided horse rides around Natales and Last Hope Sound as well as the edge of Parque Nacional Torres del Paine and multi-day trips to the wild Sierra Baguales. US/Chilean-run. Friendly attentive guides. Well-kept horses. Recommended.

Erratic Rock, Baquedano 719, T061-410355, www.erraticrock.com. Trekking experts offering interesting and alternative expeditions from half a day to 2 weeks. Also hire out good-quality equipment.

Estancia Travel, Casa 13B, Puerto Bories, 5 km north of Puerto Natales, T061-412221, www.estanciatravel.com. English/Chilean operator offering horse rides around Puerto Natales. Bilingual guides and well-kept horses. Good half-day trips to the cueva del Milodón. Prices start from US$35 for 2 hrs. Multi-day trips only for the well off. Book direct or through agencies in Natales.

Indomita, Bories 206, T061-414525, www.indomitapatagonia.com. Kayak trips ranging from 3 hrs to 12 days.

Punta Alta, Punta Alta, Blanco Encalada 244, T061-411015, www.puntaalta.cl. Runs trips along the same route as 21 de Mayo but in a faster boat and then a zodiac to the Pueblito Serrano at the park's southern edge. There is an option to return to Natales on the same day by minibus along the southern access road, thus avoiding park entry fees.

Rutas Patagonia, Blanco Encalada 353, T061-613874, www.rutaspatagonia.com. The concession holders for ice hiking on the Grey Glacier and kayaking on Lago Grey. Book direct or through an agency.

Sendero Aventura, Hostal Patagonia Adventure, Tomás Rogers 179, T061-415636, sendero_aventura@terra.cl. Trekking in Torres del Paine, cycle and kayak trips to the park, boats to Parque Nacional Bernado O'Higgins, camping equipment and bike hire.

Serrano Aventura, Prat 379, T061-410100, www.serranoaventura.cl. Ice hiking and kayaking on and around Glaciar Serrano.
Skorpios, www.skorpios.cl. 2-3 day cruises up the southern fjords to Puerto Eden and the Pio XI Glacier. No office in Puerto Natales. Book online or through an agency.
Tour Express, Bulnes 769, T061-410734, www.tourexpress.cl. Daytrips to Torres del Paine.
Turismo 21 de Mayo, Eberhard 554, T061-411476, www.turismo21demayo.cl. Offer boat trips to Parque Nacional Bernado O'Higgins and Glaciar Serrano and on to the southern entrance of Torres del Paine national park in motor zodiac. This can be combined in a very long day with a trip to the park returning by public bus. US$125 one-way including food but excluding park entry.
Tu Travesia, Bulnes 37, T061-415747, www.tutravesia.com. Kayaking and jetski trips around Last Hope Sound and Península Varas.

⊖ Transport

Puerto Natales *p488, map p489*
Air
Flights arrive at the tiny **Teniente Julio Gallardo Airport**, 7 km north of town.
   To **Santiago** via **Puerto Montt**, Sky Airline, Bulnes 684, T600-600 2828, www.skyairline.cl, 3 weekly in summer.

Bike
Hire from Patagonia Adventure, see Sleeping. Repairs at El Rey de la Bicicleta, Ramírez 540. Good, helpful.

Bus
Punta Arenas is served by Bus Fernández, Eberhard 555, T061-411111; Bus Sur, Baquedano 668 (poor buses); and Bus Pacheco, Baquedano 500 (best buses); several daily, 3 hrs, US$9, book in advance. Bus Sur runs to **Coyhaique**, Mon, 24 hrs, US$50. For details of buses to **Torres del Paine**, see page 505.

To Argentina Buses Sur has 2 weekly direct services to **Río Gallegos**, US$18. Cootra runs services to **Río Turbio**, 2 hrs (depending on customs), US$5. To **Calafate**, Bus Zaahj, 4½ hrs, US$19 1 or 2 daily.

Car
Hire agents can arrange permission to drive into Argentina, but this is expensive and takes 24 hrs to arrange. Avis, Bulnes 632, T061-410775; Motor Cars, Blanco 330, T061-413 593, www.motorcars.cl; Punta Alta, Blanco 244, T061-410115, www.puntaalta.cl, good reports; Ultima Esperanza, Blanco Encalada 206, T061-410461. Carlos González, Ladrilleros entre Bories y Eberhard, is a recommended car mechanic.

Ferry
Navimag, Pedro Montt 262, Loc B, Terminal Marítimo, T061-411421, operates the *M/V Evangelistas* every Fri in summer to **Puerto Montt**, less frequently off season (see page 399); confirmation of reservations is advised.

⊕ Directory

Puerto Natales *p488, map p489*
Banks Shop around as some *casas* offer very poor rates (much better to change money in Punta Arenas). Banks offer poor rates for TCs, which cannot be changed into US$ cash.
Banco Santander Santiago, Bulnes y Blanco Encalada, MasterCard and Visa, ATM; Banco de Chile, Bulnes 544, MasterCard and Visa, ATM; Cambio Stop, Baquedano 380; Enio America, Blanco Encalada 266, Argentine pesos can be changed here; there are 2 more at Bulnes 683 and 1087 (good rates, also change Argentine pesos), and others on Prat. **Internet** Several around town. **Laundry** Servilaundry, Prat 337, express service; Milodón, Baquedano 642; Laundry Express, Eberhard 320. **Medical services** Hospital: Ignacio Carrera Pinto 537, T061-411583. **Post office** Eberhard 417, Mon-Fri 0830-1230, 1430-1745, Sat 0900-1230.

Parque Nacional Torres del Paine

→ *Colour map 6, B2.*

Covering 242,242 ha, 145 km northwest of Puerto Natales, this national park is a UNESCO Biosphere Reserve and a huge, huge draw for its diverse wildlife and spectacular surroundings. Taking its name from the Tehuelche word Paine, meaning 'blue', the park encompasses stunning scenery, with constantly changing views of peaks, glaciers and icebergs, vividly coloured lakes of turquoise, ultramarine and grey, and quiet green valleys filled with wild flowers. In the centre of the park is one of the most impressive mountain areas on earth, a granite massif from which rise oddly shaped peaks of over 2600 m, known as the Torres (towers) and Cuernos (horns) of Paine. ▸▸ *For listings, see pages 503-505.*

Ins and outs

Getting there

The most practical way to get to Torres del Paine is with one of the many bus or tour companies that leave Puerto Natales daily. If you want to drive, hiring a pickup from Punta Arenas or Puerto Natales is an economical proposition for a group, US$400 for four days. There are two *ripio* roads to the park from Puerto Natales; it takes about 3½ hours along the old road to the administration via Cerro Castillo and Lago Sarmiento. This is the route taken by public buses. The new road links Natales to the south side of the park via the pueblito Serrano. While it is a more direct route (total journey time to the administration is around 1½ hours), the road is narrow with lots of blind corners and sudden gusts of wind and can be rough in patches. There are entrances at Laguna Amarga, Lago Sarmiento Laguna Azul and the Puente Serrano, foreigners' entrance fee US$25 payable in Chilean pesos only (proceeds are shared between all Chilean national parks). If you are based outside the park and plan on entering and leaving several times explain this when you are paying your entrance. Your ticket will be given a stamp allowing multiple entry. Otherwise you will have to pay each time you enter the park. ▸▸ *See Transport, page 505.*

Getting around

Allow a week to 10 days to see the park properly. Most visitors will find that they get around on foot, however, there are minibuses between the CONAF administration and Guardería Laguna Amarga, as well as boats across Lago Pehoé. Bus travel between two points within the park (eg Pudeto–Laguna Amarga) is US$6. Services are provided by **Bus Gómez** ① *Prat 234, T061-411971;* **JB** ① *Prat 258, T061-410242;* and **Trans Via Paine** ① *Bulnes 518, T061-413672.* At other times, services by travel agencies are subject to demand; arrange your return date with the driver and try to coincide with other groups to keep costs down. In season there are minibus connections from Laguna Amarga to the Hostería Los Torres, US$66, and from the administration centre to Hostería Lago Grey, US$15.

Roads inside the park are narrow and bendy with blind corners. In theory, rangers keep a check on the whereabouts of all visitors: you are required to register and show your passport when entering the park or setting off on any hike. There is an **administration centre** ① *at the northern end of Lago del Toro near the head of the Río Serrano, T061-691931, summer daily 0830-2000, off-season 0830-1230, 1400-1830,* with interesting videos and information on request. There are nine *guarderías* (ranger stations) in the park staffed by *guardaparques*, who give advice. The outlying *guarderías* are open October to

Parque Nacional Torres del Paine

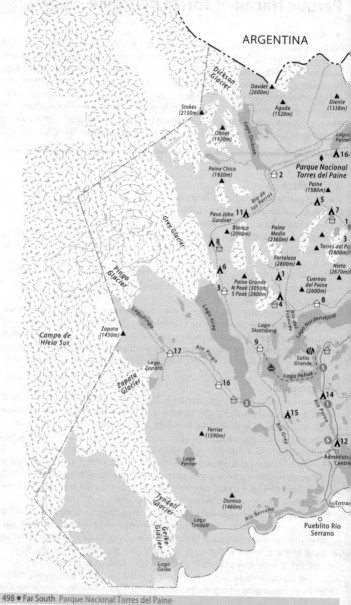

ARGENTINA

Dickson Glacier

Davdet (2600m)

Aguda (1520m)

Diente (1338m)

Stokes (2150m)

Ohnet (1920m)

Lago Dickson

Lago Paine

16

Paine Chico (1920m)

2

Parque Nacional Torres del Paine

Río de los Perros

Paine (1580m)

11 Paso John Gardner

Blanco (2090m)

5

7

Grey Glacier

8

6

Paine Medio (2360m)

Fortaleza (2800m)

3 Torres del Pe (2800m)

Pingo Glacier

3 Paine Grande N Peak (3050m) S Peak (2600m)

1

4

Cuernos del Paine (2600m)

Nieto (2670m)

8

Lago Nordenskjold

Campo de Hielo Sur

Zapata (1450m)

Lago Pingo

Lago Grey

Lago Skottsberg

9

Río del Francés

17

Río Pingo

Lago Zapata

16

3

Salto Grande

Lago Pehoé

5

14

Zapata Glacier

15

Río Paine

Río Grey

6

12

Administra Centre

Ferrier (1590m)

Lago Ferrier

Tyndall Glacier

Donaso (1460m)

Lago Tyndall

Río Serrano

Entra

Gelke Glacier

Lago Gelke

Pueblito Río Serrano

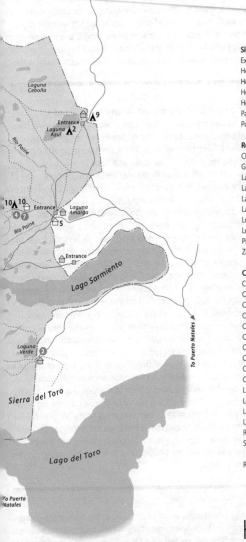

Sleeping 🛏️

Explora **1**
Hostería Lago Grey **3**
Hostería Las Torres **4**
Hostería Mirador del Payne **2**
Hostería Pehoé **5**
Patagonia Ecocamp **7**
Posada Río Serrano **6**

Refugios ⌂

Chileno (Fantástico Sur) **1**
Grey (Vertice) **3**
Lago Dickson (Vertice) **2**
Lago Paine **4**
Laguna Amarga **5**
Las Torres (Fantástico Sur) **10**
Lodge Paine Grande (Vertice) **9**
Los Cuernos (Fantástico Sur) **8**
Pingo **16**
Zapata **17**

Camping 🅰

Campamento Británico **1**
Campamento Cairon **16**
Campamento Chileno **3**
Campamento Italiano **4**
Campamento Japonés **5**
Campamento Lago Paine **2**
Campamento Las Carretas **15**
Campamento Las Guardas **6**
Campamento Las Torres **7**
Campamento Paso **8**
Lago Pehoé **14**
Laguna Azul **9**
Las Torres **10**
Los Perros **11**
Río Serrano **12**
Serón **13**

Ranger stations (*guarderías*) ⌂

April only. There are a limited number of lockers available for storing luggage at the **Hostería Las Torres**.

Best time to visit

The weather in the park can change in a few minutes. The warmest time is from December to March, although it can be wet and windy. The spring months of October and November are recommended for wild flowers. Rain and snowfall are heavier the further west you go and bad weather sweeps off the Campo de Hielo Sur without warning. Snow may prevent access in winter, but well-equipped hikers can do some good walking when conditions are stable. For information in Spanish on weather conditions, phone the administration centre.

Sights

There are 15 peaks above 2000 m, of which the highest is **Cerro Paine Grande** (3050 m). Few places can compare to its steep forested talus slopes topped by 1000-m vertical shafts of basalt with conical caps. These are the remains of frozen magma in ancient volcanic throats, everything else having been eroded. On the western edge of the park is the enormous **Campo de Hielo Sur** icefield. Four main *ventisqueros* (glaciers) – Grey, Dickson, Zapata and Tyndall – branch off it, their meltwater forming a complex series of lakes and streams, which lead into fjords extending to the sea. Two other glaciers, Francés and Los Perros, descend on the western side of the central massif.

A micro-climate exists especially favourable to plants and wildlife. Over 200 species of plant have been identified and, although few trees reach great size, several valleys are thickly forested and little light penetrates. The grassland here is distinct from the monotony of the pampa and dispersed sclerophyl forest. Some 105 species of bird call the park home, including 18 species of waterfowl and 11 birds of prey. Particularly noteworthy are condors, black-necked swans, rheas, kelp geese, ibis, flamingos and austral parakeets. The park is also one of the best places on the continent for viewing rheas and guanacos. Apart from the 3500 guanacos, 24 other species of mammal can be seen here, including hare, fox, skunk, huemul and puma (the last two only very rarely).

Torres del Paine has become increasingly popular with foreigners and Chileans alike, receiving well over 100,000 visitors a year, most during the summer months of January and February, which, if possible, should be avoided due to overcrowding, especially at *refugios* and campsites, and the unpredictability of the weather. Many parts of the park are now open all year round; visiting in winter is becoming increasingly popular as, although the temperature is low, there is little wind. Efforts to manage the ever-growing number of visitors have been poor and the impact of such a large influx is showing. Litter is a serious problem, especially around *refugios* and camping areas on the 'W': please take all of your rubbish out of the park and remember that this also includes toilet paper. Most importantly, if you are using your own cooking stove, only cook in designated areas. The negligence of one backpacker caused around 14,000 ha of forest to burn down in the northeastern sector of the park in 2005.

Trekking

There are about 250 km of well-marked trails. Visitors must keep to the trails: cross-country trekking is not permitted. It is vital not to underestimate the unpredictability of the weather, nor the arduous nature of some stretches on the long hikes. Some paths are confusingly marked and it is all too easy to end up on precipices with glaciers or churning rivers awaiting below; be particularly careful to follow the path at the Paso John Gardner on El Circuito (see below). The only means of rescue are on horseback or by boat; the nearest helicopter is in Punta Arenas and high winds usually prevent its operation in the park.

Equipment
It is essential to be properly equipped against the cold, wind and rain. A strong, streamlined, waterproof tent is essential if doing El Circuito (although you can hire camping equipment for a single night at the *refugios* on the 'W'). Also essential are protective clothing, strong waterproof footwear, sunscreen, compass, good sleeping bag and sleeping mat. In summer also take shorts. You are strongly advised to bring all necessary equipment and your own food from Puerto Natales, although all running water within the park is fine to drink. Do not to rely on availability of food at the *refugios* within the park; the small shops at the *refugios* (see below) and at the **Posada Río Serrano** are expensive and have a limited selection. Rats and mice are occasionally a problem around camping sites and the free *refugios*, so do not leave food in your pack (which may be chewed through). The safest solution is to hang food in a bag on a wire. You are not allowed to make open fires in the park, so take a camping stove. A decent map is provided with your park entrance ticket; other maps (US$7) are obtainable in many places Puerto Natales but most have one or two mistakes. The map produced by **Patagonia Interactiva** has been recommended as more accurate.

El Circuito
The park's most emblematic trek is a circuit round the Torres and Cuernos del Paine. Although most people start at the *guardería* at **Laguna Amarga**, it is probably best done anticlockwise starting from Lodge Paine Grande at the western edge of Lago Pehoe. Some walkers advise doing the route clockwise so that you climb to Paso John Gardner with the wind behind you. The route normally takes between five days and a week. The circuit is often closed in winter because of snow; major rivers are crossed by footbridges, but these are occasionally washed away. From Laguna Amarga the route is north along the western side of the Río Paine to **Lago Paine**, before turning west to follow the pastures of the valley of the Río Paine to the southern end of **Lago Dickson** (it is possible to add a journey to the *campamento* by the Torres on day one of this route); the *refugio* at Lago Dickson lies in a breathtaking position in front of the icy white lake with mountains beyond. From Lago Dickson the path runs along the wooded valley of the **Río de los Perros**, past the Glaciar de los Perros, before climbing through bogs and up scree to **Paso John Gardner** (1241 m, the highest point on the route), then dropping steeply through forest to follow the Grey Glacier southeast to **Lago Grey**, continuing to **Lago Pehoé** and the administration centre. There are superb views en route, particularly from the top of Paso John Gardner.

The longest stretch is between Refugio Laguna Amarga and Refugio Dickson (30 km, 10 hours in good weather; two campsites on the way at Serón and Cairon), but the most difficult section is the very steep, slippery slope from Paso John Gardner down to the Campamento Paso; the path is not well signed at the top of the pass, and some people (including the author) have got dangerously lost. Camping gear must be carried, as many of the campsites do not have *refugios*.

The W
A more popular alternative to El Circuito, this four- to five-day route can be completed without camping equipment as there is accommodation in *refugios* en route. In summer

this route is very crowded and far from being the solitary Patagonian experience many people expect. It combines several of the hikes described separately below. From Refugio Laguna Amarga the first stage runs west via **Hostería Las Torres** and up the valley of the **Río Ascensio** via Refugio Chileno to the base of the **Torres del Paine** (see below). From here return to the **Hostería Las Torres** and then walk along the northern shore of **Lago Nordenskjold** via **Refugio Los Cuernos** to **Campamento Italiano**. From here climb the **Valley of the Río del Francés** (see below) before continuing to **Lodge Paine Grande**. From here you can complete the third part of the 'W' by walking west along the northern shore of **Lago Grey** to **Refugio Grey** and the Grey Glacier before returning to **Lodge Paine Grande** and the boat back across the lake to the **Refugio Pudeto**.

To the base of the Torres del Paine

From **Refugio Laguna Amarga**, this six-hour route follows the road west to **Hostería Las Torres** (1½ hours), before climbing along the western side of the **Río Ascensio** via **Refugio Chileno** (two hours) and **Campamento Chileno** to **Campamento Las Torres** (two hours), close to the base of the **Torres del Paine** (be careful when crossing the suspension bridge over the Río Ascensio near **Hostería Las Torres**, as the path is poorly marked and you can end up on the wrong side of the ravine). The path alongside the Río Ascensio is well marked, and the **Campamento Las Torres** is in an attractive wood (no *refugio*). A further 30 minutes up the morraine takes you to a lake at the base of the towers themselves; they seem so close that you almost feel you could touch them. To see the Torres lit by sunrise (spectacular but you must have good weather), it's well worth carrying your camping gear up to **Campamento Torres** and spending the night. One hour beyond **Campamento Torres** is **Campamento Japonés**, another good campsite.

Valley of the Río del Francés

From **Lodge Paine Grande** this route leads north across undulating country along the western edge of **Lago Skottberg** to **Campamento Italiano** and then follows the valley of the Río del Francés, which climbs between Cerro Paine Grande and the Ventisquero del Francés (to the west) and the Cuernos del Paine (to the east) to **Campamento Británico**; the views from the mirador, a half-hour's walk above **Campamento Británico**, are superb. Allow 2½ hours from **Lodge Paine Grande** to **Campamento Italiano**, 2½ hours further to **Campamento Británico**.

Treks from Guardería Grey

Guardería Grey, 18 km west by road from the administration centre, is the starting point for a five-hour trek to **Lago Pingo**, recommended if you want to get away from the crowds, and one of the best routes in the park for birdwatching. From the *guardería* follow the **Río Pingo**, via **Refugio Pingo** and **Refugio Zapata** (four hours), with views south over Ventisquero Zapata (look out for plenty of wildlife and for icebergs in the lake) to reach the lake. **Ventisquero Pingo** can be seen 3 km away over the lake. Note there is a bridge over a river here, marked on many maps, which has been washed away. The river can be forded when it is low, however, allowing access to the glacier.

Two short signposted walks from Guardería Grey have also been suggested: one is a steep climb up the hill behind the ranger post to **Mirador Ferrier**, from where there are fine views; the other is via a suspension bridge across the Río Pingo to the peninsula at the southern end of **Lago Grey**, from where there are good views of the icebergs on the lakes.

To Laguna Verde

From the administration centre follow the road north 2 km, before taking the path east over the **Sierra del Toro** and then along the southern side of Laguna Verde to the Guardería Laguna Verde. Allow four hours. This is one of the easiest walks in the park and may be a good first hike.

To Laguna Azul and Lago Paine

This route runs north from Laguna Amarga to the western tip of **Laguna Azul**, from where it continues across the sheltered **Río Paine** valley past Laguna Cebolla to the Refugio Lago Paine at the western end of the lake. Allow 8½ hours. Good birdwatching opportunities.

◉ Parque Nacional Torres del Paine listings

For Sleeping and Eating price codes and other relevant information, see Essentials pages 35-42.

● Sleeping

Parque Nacional Torres del Paine

p497, map p498

Accommodation is available on several levels inside the park itself: there are hotels (all are expensive, some feel overpriced); 6 privately run *refugios*, well-equipped, staffed, offering meals and free hot water for tea, soup, etc; 3 free very basic *refugios*, 10 campsites with amenities, some of which have pre-pitched tents available, and10 basic *campamentos*. All options fill up quickly in peak summer months, Jan-Feb, so plan your trip and book hotels and *refugios* in advance. Paying in US dollars (you must show your passport) means you will save 19% tax, but check prices in pesos as well as they may be cheaper.

As accommodation space is limited within the park and prices exorbitant, there is an increasing amount of better value accommodation springing up around the park limits, especially to the south at the Pueblito Río Serrano.

LL Explora, Salto Chico on edge of Lago Pehoé, T061-411247, reservations from Av Américo Vespucci 80, piso 7, Santiago, T02-206 6060, www.explora.com. Ugly building but the most luxurious and comfortable hotel in the park, offering all inclusive packages, spectacular views, pool, gym, tours and transfer from Punta Arenas.

LL Hostería Lago Grey, reservations T061-712100, www.turismolagogrey.com. Small rooms on edge of Lago Grey with views of the Grey Glacier, decent restaurant.

LL Hostería Las Torres, T061-360364, reservations T061-363636, www.lastorres.com. Probably the best of the *hosterías* in the park. Recently expanded. Nice rooms, although none has a particularly good view, good restaurant, disabled access, English spoken, horse riding, transport from Laguna Amarga ranger station. There is a limited number of standard rooms, which are much cheaper.

LL Patagonia Ecocamp, reservations T02-232 9878, www.ecocamp.travel. Luxury all-inclusive tented camp with geodesic design and powered by renewable energy. Offers 4- to 10-day walking and wildlife-watching packages.

LL-AL Hostería Pehoé, 5 km south of Pehoé ranger station, 11 km north of park administration, T061-411390, www.pehoe.com. On an island with spectacular view across the lake to Cerro Paine Grande and Cuernos del Paine, this place does not make the most of its stunning location, run-down, overpriced.

AL Posada Río Serrano, reservations advisable; book through Baqueano Zamora, Baquedano 534B, Puerto Natales, T061-412911, www.baqueanozamora.com. An old *estancia*, much improved recently, some rooms with bath, some with shared facilities, breakfast extra, near park administration, with expensive but good restaurant and a shop.

Private refugios

There are 2 companies running the 6 private *refugios* in the park, providing dormitory space only (bring your own sleeping bag or hire one for US$8). Prices are around US$40 per person with full board about US$35 extra. *Refugios* have kitchen facilities, hot showers and space for camping. Most will hire out tents for around US$12 per night. In high season, accommodation and meals in the non-CONAF *refugios* should be booked in advance in Puerto Natales, or by asking staff in one *refugio* to radio another. In winter most of the *refugios* close, although 1 or 2 may stay open depending on the weather.

Fantástico Sur refugios Book in agencies in Puerto Natales or direct on T061-710050, www.wcircuit.com.
Refugio Las Torres, next to the Hostería Las Torres (see above).There are 2 *refugios* here, the **Torre Norte** and the newer, more comfortable and slightly more expensive **Torre Central**.
Refugio Los Cuernos, on the northern shore of Lago Nordenskjold, which also has a few small 2-person cabins.
Refugio Chileno, valley of the Río Ascensio at the foot of the Torres.

Vertice refugios Book through agencies in Puerto Natales or via www.verticepatagonia.cl.
Lodge Paine Grande, new and large on the northwestern edge of Lago Pehoe. In theory the most comfortable of all, but in practice has had teething troubles and several complaints regarding customer service.
Refugio Grey, on the eastern shore of Lago Grey.
Refugio Lago Dickson, on the northern part of the circuit.

Campsites The wind tends to increase in the evening so it is a good idea to pitch tents early (by 1600). Fires are not allowed. These restrictions should be observed as forest fires are a serious hazard. Use camping stoves. *Guardaparques* also require campers to have a trowel to bury their waste. Equipment can be hired in Puerto Natales (see Shopping).These sites are in addition to sites at the private *refugios*:
Lago Pehoé, www.campingpehoe.com, US$7 per person, hot showers, shop, restaurant.
Laguna Azul, hot showers.
Las Torres, run by Fantástico Sur, US$7, hot showers.
Los Perros, run by Vertice, with shop and hot showers.
Serón, run by Fantástico Sur, US$7, hot showers.

Free camping is permitted in 10 other locations in the park; these are known as *campamentos* and have very basic facilities.

Outside the park

LL Cabañas del Paine, T061-243354, www.cabanasdelpaine.cl. Lodge-style cabins on the edge of the Río Serrano. Decent restaurant.
LL Río Serrano, T061-240528, www.hotelrioserrano.cl. Monstrous construction. The new wing has blocked the view for many neighbours. Decent rooms, many with great views. Poor, canteen-style restaurant. Mixed reports on service.
LL-L Hostería Lago Toro, www.lagodeltoro.com. Decent rooms and rustic cabins with kitchen facilities. Some of the view has been blocked by the expansion of the hotel in front. Friendly staff and reasonable food. Good value given the alternatives.
L Hostería Mirador del Payne (Estancia Lazo), reservations at Fagnano 585, Punta Arenas, T061-226930, www.miradordelpayne.com. Beautifully situated on Laguna Verde with spectacular views and good fishing, restaurant. Recommended but an inconvenient base for visiting the park; own transport essential, or you can trek to it from within the park.

Campsites Camping Río Serrano, www.camping chile.com. Peaceful campsite with fine views. With advance notice owners can prepare spit-roasted lamb dinners. Good-value cabin accommodation also available as well as horse riding and transport within the park. Recommended.

▲ Activities and tours

Parque Nacional Torres del Paine
p497, map p498

Before booking a tour check all the details carefully and get a copy in writing, as there have been increasingly mixed reports of the quality of some tours. Many companies who claim to visit the Grey Glacier, for example, only visit Lago Grey (you see the glacier in the distance). After mid-Mar there is less public transport and trucks are irregular.

Several agencies in Puerto Natales offer 1-day tours by minibus, US$35 plus park entry; these give a good impression of the lower parts of the park, although you spend most of the day in the vehicle and many travellers would argue that you need to stay several days, or at least overnight, in the park to appreciate it fully. Recommended agencies include **Comapa**, **Los Glaciares** and **Tur Express**. Cheaper tours are also available, but both guide and vehicle may not be as good as the established operators. There are many more operators based in Puerto Natales offering trekking, kayaking, ice-hiking, boat trips and other tours in the park (see page 495). The following do not have offices in Puerto Natales.

Cascada Expediciones, T02-861 1777, www.cascada-expediciones.com, based in Santiago, offers small-group tours to Torres del Paine.

Experience Chile, T02-570 9436, www.experiencechile.org. Itineraries and accommodation in the region can be arranged by this UK-based operator.

Hostería Lago Grey, see Sleeping, above, provides excursions by boat to the face of the Grey Glacier at 0900 and 1500 daily, 3½ hrs, US$70 per person. Book direct or through agencies in Puerto Natales.

⊖ Transport

Parque Nacional Torres del Paine
p497, map p498

Bus

From early Nov to mid-Apr daily bus services run from **Puerto Natales** to the park, leaving between 0630 and 0800, and again at around 1430, 2½ hrs to **Laguna Amarga**, 3½ hrs to **Refugio Pudeto** and 4½ hrs to the administration centre, US$15 one-way, US$24 open return (return tickets are not interchangeable between different companies); return departures are usually around 1300 and 1800. Generally, buses will stop at Laguna Amarga and continue to the administration centre before returning via the same route. The buses also stop at Refugio Pudeto to connect with the boats to/from Refugio Lago Pehoé.

To go from Torres del Paine to **Calafate** (Argentina), either return to Puerto Natales and catch a bus, or take a bus or hitch from the park to Villa Cerro Castillo and try to link with the Natales–Calafate bus schedule. In season, there is a direct bus service from the park to Calafate with **Chaltén Travel**, US$60.

Boat

A catamaran service runs across **Lago Pehoé** from near the **Lodge Paine Grande** to **Refugio Pudeto**, 30 mins, US$19 one-way with 1 piece of baggage free, US$6 per bag thereafter, tickets available on board. Daily departures from Paine Grande 1000, 1230, 1830; from Pudeto 0930, 1200, 1800. Reduced service off season, no service May-Oct. For information call T061-411380, maclean@entelchile.net.

Into Argentina: Parque Nacional Los Glaciares

→ *Colour map 6, A2.*

Of all Argentina's impressive landscapes, the sight of the immense glaciers stretching out infinitely and silently before you, may stay with you longest. This is the second largest national park in Argentina, extending along the Chilean border for over 170 km. Almost half of it is covered by the Southern Ice Cap; at 370 km long, it's the third largest in the world. From it, 13 major glaciers descend into two great lakes: Lago Argentino in the southeast and Lago Viedma to the northeast.

There are two main areas to explore: the glaciers can be visited by bus and boat trips from El Calafate, while from El Chaltén, 230 km northwest, there is superb trekking around the dramatic Fitz Roy massif and ice climbing near its summit. The central section, between Lago Argentino and Lago Viedma, is the Ice Cap National Reserve, inaccessible to visitors apart from a couple of estancias.

East of the ice fields, there's southern beech forest before the land flattens to the wind-blasted Patagonian steppe. Birdlife is prolific; often spotted are black-necked swans, Magallenic woodpeckers, and, perhaps, even a torrent duck diving in the rivers. Guanacos, grey foxes, skunks and rheas (a large flightless bird) can be seen on the steppe, and the rare huemul (a deer-like animal) inhabits the forest. ►► *For listings, see pages 514-523.*

Ins and outs

Getting there Access to the park is via El Calafate, 50 km from the park's eastern boundary, for the glaciers, or via El Chaltén, 230 km northwest, for trekking, near Fitz Roy on the northeastern edge of the park. There are buses from Río Gallegos and Puerto Natales. El Chaltén is three hours' drive north then west, with several buses daily from El Calafate and Río Gallegos. El Chaltén can also be reached from Villa O'Higgins on the Carretera Austral in Chile. ►► *See Transport, page 522.*

Best time to visit Although this part of Patagonia is generally cold, there is a milder microclimate around Lago Viedma and Lago Argentino, which means that summers can be reasonably pleasant, with average summer temperatures between 5°C and 22°C, though strong winds blow constantly at the foot of the cordillera. In the forested area, around 1500 mm of rain falls annually, mainly between March and late May. In winter, the whole area is inhospitably cold and most tourist facilities are closed. The best time to visit, therefore, is between November and April, avoiding January and early February, when Argentines take their holidays, campsites are crowded and accommodation is hard to find. Park entry US$9. For further information contact T02962 491477, peritomoreno@apn.gov.ar, or see www.losglaciares.com.

Río Turbio → *Colour map 6, B3.*

A charmless place you're most likely to visit en route to or from Torres del Paine in Chile. The site of Argentina's largest coalfield hasn't recovered from the recent depression hitting the industry. It has a cargo railway connecting it with Punta Loyola, and visitors can see Mina 1, where the first mine was opened. There's a small ski centre nearby, **Valdelén**, which has six pistes and is ideal for beginners; there's also scope for cross- country skiing between early June and late September. The **tourist office** is in the municipal building on San Martín. For more information, see www.welcome argentina.com/rioturbio.

Parque Nacional Los Glaciares

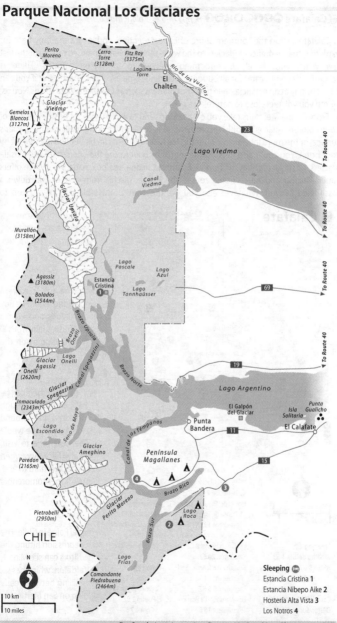

To Route 40

Sleeping
Estancia Cristina **1**
Estancia Nibepo Aike **2**
Hostería Alta Vista **3**
Los Notros **4**

El Calafate sits on the southern shore of Lago Argentino, and, as it's the only base for exploring the magnificent glaciers to the west, the town has expanded rapidly in the last few years, with hotels mushrooming everywhere to exploit tourism. There is accommodation to cater for all budgets, including some excellent hostels, but if you can afford it, stay at an estancia-style hotel out of town such as **Eolo**, **Alta Vista** or **Los Notros**, where you will feel close to nature.

From El Calafate, tours take you on boat trips and to walkways right beside the wall of Perito Moreno glacier. Highly recommended is the **Minitrekking** walk on the glacier's surface, or the more intrepid six-hour **Big Ice** hike. All these can be booked in town, or by your hotel. You could also head further north by boat to see the Spegazzini and Upsala glaciers, or stay a night at the remote **Estancia Cristina**, see box, page 515, which offers superb hiking and horse riding to see the Upsala glacier from above, and down a fossil-filled canyon. Whatever else you do, this is an unmissable part of any trip to

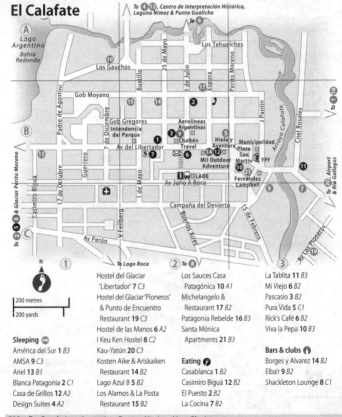

El Calafate

Sleeping 🛏
América del Sur 1 *B3*
AMSA 9 *C3*
Ariel 13 *B1*
Blanca Patagonia 2 *C1*
Casa de Grillos 12 *A2*
Design Suites 4 *A2*

Hostel del Glaciar 'Libertador' 7 *C3*
Hostel del Glaciar 'Pioneros' & Punto de Encuentro Restaurant 19 *C3*
Hostel de las Manos 6 *A2*
I Keu Ken Hostel 8 *C2*
Kau-Yatún 20 *C3*
Kosten Aike & Ariskaiken Restaurant 14 *B2*
Lago Azul B 5 *B2*
Los Alamos & La Posta Restaurant 15 *B2*

Los Sauces Casa Patagónica 10 *A1*
Michelangelo & Restaurant 17 *B2*
Patagonia Rebelde 16 *B3*
Santa Mónica Apartments 21 *B3*

Eating 🍴
Casablanca 1 *B2*
Casimiro Biguá 12 *B2*
El Puesto 2 *B2*
La Cocina 7 *B2*

La Tablita 11 *B3*
Mi Viejo 6 *B2*
Pascasio 3 *B2*
Pura Vida 5 *C1*
Rick's Café 6 *B2*
Viva la Pepa 10 *B3*

Bars & clubs 🍸
Borges y Alvarez 14 *B2*
Elba'r 9 *B2*
Shackleton Lounge 8 *C1*

Francisco Moreno, El Perito

You can't miss the name of Argentina's favourite son as you travel around Patagonia. Francisco Pascasio Moreno (1852-1919) is commemorated by a national park, a town, countless streets and a world-famous glacier. Moreno, a naturalist and geographer, explored areas previously unknown to the authorities. At the age of 20, he travelled up the Río Negro to Lago Nahuel Huapi, along the Río Chubut, and then up the Río Santa Cruz to reach the giant lake which he named Lago Argentino. Expeditions such as these were dangerous: apart from physical hardships, relations with the indigenous population were poor. On one expedition, Moreno was seized as a hostage, but escaped on a raft which carried him for eight days down the Río Limay to safety.

His fame established, Moreno was elected to congress and became an expert (*perito*) adviser to the Argentine side in the negotiations to draw the border with Chile. His reward was a grant of land near Bariloche, which he handed over to the state to manage, the initial act in creating the national parks system in Argentina, and an inspiring gesture at a time when anyone who could was buying up land as fast as possible. Moreno's remains are buried in a mausoleum on Isla Centinela in Lago Nahuel Huapi. For a good read while you are travelling Argentina seek out *Perito Moreno's Travel Journal: A Personal Reminiscence* (published by Elefante Blanco). It is a fascinating read about his travels, and his escape from capture.

Patagonia. You can visit the Perito Moreno glacier all year round, but weather close to the glacier can make it unpleasant.

Ins and outs

Getting there Bus travel is convenient, with buses from Río Gallegos and Ushuaia and from Puerto Natales, via Cerro Castillo, if you want to get directly to/from Torres del Paine. The bus terminal is centrally located up a steep flight of steps off the main street, and has a small, not very helpful, tourist office. ▶▶ *See Transport, page 522.*

Getting around El Calafate is so small it's easy to get around on foot.

Tourist information El Calafate **tourist office** ⓘ *in the bus terminal, T02902-491090, www.elcalafate.gov.ar in English, daily Oct-Apr 0700-2200, May-Sep 0800-2100,* may look disorganized, but the staff speak several languages and have a good map with accommodation shown, as well as information on estancias and tours. There's another branch at the airport, T02902-491230. There's also an **Intendencia del Parque** (park office) ⓘ *Libertador 1302, T02901-491005, losglaciares@apn.gov.ar, Mon-Fri 0800-1600.*

Around El Calafate

Just west of the town centre is **Bahía Redonda**, a shallow part of Lago Argentino that freezes in winter, when ice-skating and skiing are possible. From the **Intendencia del Parque**, an hour's stroll will take you to **Laguna Nimez** at the eastern edge of the bay, where there's a bird reserve with flamingos, black-necked swans and ducks. To get there, follow Calle Bustillo up the new road among cultivated fields and orchards to cross the bridge. Keep heading north: the laguna is signposted. Hike to the top of the **Cerro Calafate**, behind the town (2½ to three hours), for views of the silhouette of the southern end of the Andes, Bahía Redonda and Isla Solitaria on Lago Argentino. There is also scope for good hill-walking to the south of the town, while **Cerro Elefante**, to the west, on the road to the Perito Moreno glacier, is good for rock climbing.

In addition to the glaciers, El Calafate provides access to some other good places for trekking, horse riding and exploring by 4WD, if you're here for a few days. There are several estancias within reach of the town, which offer a day on a working farm, a lunch of superb Patagonian lamb, cooked *asado al palo*, and outdoor activities. **El Galpón del Glaciar** offers displays of sheep shearing, walking and horse-riding trips to the Perito Moreno glacier and Cerro Frias. Overnight accommodation is available in the lovely house with views of Lago Argentino.

Lago Roca, 40 km southwest of El Calafate, is set in beautiful open landscape, with hills above offering panoramic views. The lake is perfect for lots of activities, including trout and salmon fishing, climbing and walking.

Lago Argentino and the glaciers ⊖ ⇥ pp514-523.

Perito Moreno glacier

Perito Moreno is one of the few glaciers in the world that is still advancing. Some 30 km long, it reaches the water at a narrow point on one of the fjords, **Brazo Rico**, opposite **Peninsula Magallanes**. Every few years, the glacier blocks the fjord and, as water pressure builds up behind the ice wall, the ice suddenly breaks, reopening the channel and sending huge *témpanos* (icebergs) rushing down the Canal de los Témpanos. Naturally, there are concerns about the effects of climate change on the glacier, but these are not straight-forward, and it is believed that the glacier's calving has no relationship with increased temperature.

Upsala glacier

The fjords at the northwestern end of Lago Argentino are fed by four other glaciers. The largest is the Upsala glacier, named after the Swedish university that commissioned the first survey of this area in 1908. It's a stunning expanse of untouched beauty, covering three times the area of the Perito Moreno glacier, and is the longest glacier flowing off the Southern Patagonian ice fields. Unusually it ends in two separate frontages, each about 4 km wide and 60 m high, although only the western frontage can be seen from the lake excursion. The best way to see the glacier is to stay at **Estancia Cristina** (see box, page 515) and take the trip up to the viewpoint, where vermillion rocks have been polished smooth by the glacier's approach. The estancia can be reached only by boat from Punta Bandera, 50 km west of El Calafate. Further south, the **Spegazzini** glacier has a frontage 1.5 km wide and 130 m high. In between are **Agassiz** and **Onelli**, both of which feed into **Lago Onelli**, a quiet and very beautiful lake, full of icebergs of every shape and size, surrounded by beech forests on one side and ice-covered mountains on the other.

Cerro Fitz Roy ⊜ ⇥ pp514-523.

The soaring granite of **Cerro Fitz Roy** (3405 m) rises up from the smooth baize of the steppe, more like a ziggurat than a mountain, surrounded by a consort of jagged snow-clad spires, with a stack of spun-cotton cloud hanging constantly above them. It is one of the most magnificent mountains in the world and it towers above the nearby peaks: **Torre** (3128 m), **Poincenot** (3076 m) and **Saint-Exupery** (2600 m). Its Tehuelche name was El Chaltén ('smoking mountain' or 'volcano'), perhaps because at sunrise the pink towers are occasionally lit up bright red for a few seconds in a phenomenon known as the *amanecer de fuego* ('sunrise of fire'). Perito Moreno named the peak after the captain of the *Beagle*, who saw it from afar in 1833, and it was first climbed by a French expedition in 1952. It stands in the northern end of Parque Nacional Los Glaciares at the western end of Lago Viedma, 230 km north of El Calafate, in an area of lakes and glaciers

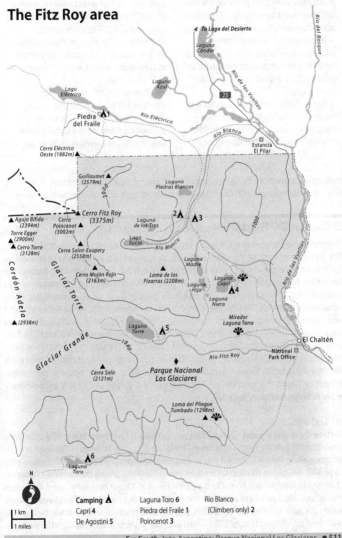

The Fitz Roy area

Camping ▲

Capri **4**
De Agostini **5**

Laguna Toro **6**
Piedra del Fraile **1**
Poincenot **3**

Río Blanco
(Climbers only) **2**

Hiking

→ **Equipment** A map is essential, even on short walks. Take plenty of warm clothes and a four-season sleeping bag, if you're camping. A gas or alcohol stove is essential, as fires are prohibited. It is possible to rent equipment in El Chaltén; ask at the park office or Rancho Grande.

→ **Information** The park's *Intendencia* provides a good map, showing walks and campsites. *Guardaparques* can advise on walks and the state of the paths. Some speak English.

→ **Paths** Paths are well marked. Stick to the centre of the path so as not to make it any bigger and walk in single file (this may mean that you're walking in a rut).

→ **Rubbish** Take all rubbish back down the mountain with you.

→ **Water** All river water in the national park is drinkable. Don't bathe in rivers and lakes; do not wash or bury waste within 70 m of a water source. Never go to the toilet near water sources.

→ **Weather** The weather changes hourly, so be prepared for a sudden deterioration in conditions. Always wear sunscreen (SPF 30 at least).

→ **Wildlife** As you leave El Chaltén, don't let the dogs follow you, as they frighten the huemules (a rare and endangered species of deer). For more information, see www.elchalten.com.

that makes marvellous trekking country. The base for walking and climbing around Fitz Roy is the modern town of El Chaltén, which has been built right next to the mountains.

El Chaltén ◉❶❷❸◉▲◉◉ » *pp514-523. Colour map 6, A2.*

The small modern town of El Chaltén is set in a wonderful position at the foot of Cerro Fitz Roy and at the mouth of the valley of the Río de las Vueltas but, having been founded in 1985 in order to pre-empt Chilean territorial claims, it has grown with little thought for aesthetics. Now hugely popular as a centre for trekking and climbing in summer, and for cross-country skiing in winter, it's an expensive place and can be unattractive, especially when the harsh wind blows. But the steady stream of visitors creates a cheerful atmosphere and, from the town, you can walk directly into breathtaking landscapes. Tourist infrastructure is still developing in El Chaltén and, so far, there are no ATMs, so take sufficient cash. Accommodation ranges from camping and hostels to not-quite-luxurious *hosterías*. Food can be expensive, though there is increasingly plenty of choice. Credit cards are only accepted in larger establishments. El Chaltén is also the base for two unique expeditions onto the Southern Ice Field; Consult the guides at **Fitz Roy Expediciones**. » *See Activities and tours, page 522.*

Ins and outs

Getting there and around The quickest way to reach El Chaltén is on one of the frequent buses from El Calafate (about four hours).There are also daily buses to El Chaltén from Los Antiguos along Ruta 40, useful if you've crossed into Argentina from Chile Chico (see box, page 460). El Chaltén can also be reached from Villa O'Higgins on the Carretera Austral in Chile (see box, page 466). Access to the park is free and it is not necessary to register before you set out. Most paths are very clear and well worn but a map is essential, even on short walks: the park information centre has photocopied maps of treks but the best is one published by *Zagier and Urruty*, US$5, and is available in shops in El Calafate and El Chaltén.

Best time to visit Walking here is only really viable mid-October to April, with the best months usually March to April when the weather is generally stable and not very cold, and the autumn colours of the beech forest are stunning. Mid-summer (December and January) and spring (September to October) are generally very windy. And in December and January the campsites can be full to bursting, with many walkers on the paths.

El Chaltén

To ⑬ & Lago del Desierto

Sleeping 🛏
Albergue Patagonia 1
Aylen-Aike 2
Cóndor de los Andes 3
Estancia La Quinta 12
Hospedaje La Base 6
Hostería El Pilar 13
Hostería El Puma
  & Restaurant Terray 5
Hostería Posada
  Lunajuim 7
Inlandsis 4
Los Cerros 10
Mi Rincón 8
Northofagus 9
Pioneros de Valle 14

Eating 🍴
Ahonikenk Chaltén 3
El Muro 7
Estepa 9
Fuegia 6
Josh Aike 1
Pangea 4
Patagonicus 5

Bars & clubs 🍸
Elal Resto-Bar 8
La Cervecería 10

Tourist information The **Intendencia del Parque** ⓘ *T02962-493004*, is in El Chaltén, across the bridge at the entrance to the town. It hands out helpful trekking maps of the area, with paths and campsites marked, giving distances and walking times. El Chaltén's **tourist office** ⓘ *Güemes 21, T02962-493011, www.elchalten.com, Mon-Fri 0900-2000, Sat and Sun 1300-2000*, has an excellent website, with accommodation lists. Most services in El Chaltén and some hotels close out of season.

Hiking around Cerro Fitz Roy

→ *These are the most popular walks from El Chaltén.*

▲▲ **Laguna Torre** (short: two hours each way) Walk west to Mirador Laguna Torre (1½ hours) for views of Cerro Torre then continue to busy **Camping De Agostini** (30 minutes) on the lake shore, where there are fantastic views of the dramatic peaks of Cordón Torre.

▲▲ **Laguna de Los Tres** (four hours each way) Walk up to Laguna Capri (two hours), with great views of Fitz Roy, then continue to **Camping Poincenot** (one hour) and **Camping Río Blanco** (only for climbers, by prior arrangement). From Río Blanco you can head southwest to Laguna de los Tres, where you'll get a spectacular view on a fine day (one hour) but in bad weather, you're better off walking to Piedras Blancas.

▲▲ **Laguna Torre** (long: seven hours each way) A marvellous walk with views of both mountain groups. Climb past Laguna Capri and take the signed path to your left, passing two lakes (Madre and then Hija), to reach the path that leads to Laguna Torre.

▲▲ **Loma del Pliegue Tumbado** (four hours each way) A marked path from the *guardería* (park ranger's office) leads southwest to this viewpoint where you can see both condors and Lago Viedma. This is a good day walk, best in clear weather. More experienced trekkers can continue to the glacial Laguna Toro (six hours from El Chaltén).

▲▲ **Río Blanco to Piedra del Fraile** (seven hours each way) This beautiful walk starts at **Camping Río Blanco** and runs north along the Río Blanco and then west along the Río Eléctrico to **Camping Piedra del Fraile** (four hours), just outside the national park. From here a path leads south, up Cerro Eléctrico Oeste (1882 m) towards the north face of Fitz Roy (two hours); it's tough going but with spectacular views. You should take a guide for the last bit. Ask at **Hostería El Pilar** and outdoor centre, www.hosteriaelpilar.com.ar.

Climbing Cerro Fitz Roy → *Colour map 2, C2.*

Base camp for ascents of Fitz Roy (3375 m) is **Camping Río Blanco**. Other peaks include Cerro Torre (3128 m), Torre Egger (2900 m), Cerro Solo (2121 m), Poincenot (3002 m), Guillaumet (2579 m), Saint-Exupery (2558 m), Aguja Bífida (2394 m) and Cordón Adela (2938 m): all of these are for very experienced climbers only. However, most climbers can try ice climbing at the foot of Cerro Torre; contact **Fitz Roy Expediciones**, page 522. The best time to climb is mid-February to the end of March; November and December are very windy and the winter (May to July) months are extremely cold. Permits for climbing are available at the national park information office and guides are available in El Chaltén.

Around El Chaltén

The main attraction here is the trekking around Fitz Roy, but there is also stunning virgin landscape to explore outside the park, around **Lago del Desierto**, 37 km north. The long skinny lake is fjord-like and surrounded by forests. It's reached by unpaved Route 23, which leads along the Río de las Vueltas via **Laguna Cóndor**, where flamingos can be seen. A mirador at the end of the road gives fine views over the lake and a path runs along the east side of the lake to its northern tip, from where a trail leads west along the valley of the Río Diablo to **Laguna Diablo**, and north to Lago O'Higgins in Chile, see page 465.

En route to the lake is **Hostería El Pilar**, www.hosteriaelpilar.com.ar, in a stunning position with views of Fitz Roy. Accommodation is available here but you can also visit for tea or use it as an excellent base for trekking up **Río Blanco** or **Río Eléctrico**.

Lago Viedma to the south of El Chaltén can also be explored by boat. The trips usually pass Glaciar Viedma, with the possibility of ice trekking on some excursions. ▶▶ *See Activities and tours, page 521.*

⊕ Into Argentina: Parque Nacional Los Glaciares listings

For Sleeping and Eating price codes and other relevant information, see pages 35-42.

⊜ Sleeping

El Calafate *p508, map p508*
From Dec to Feb most hotels are generally booked out. Reserve ahead of time. Low

season (May to Sep) is a great time to find a great deal at one of the top hotels. For more hotels see www.todocalafate.com.
LL Design Suites, C 94 No 190, T02902-494525, T011-5199 7465 in Buenos Aires, www.designsuites.com. Large stylish hotel with one of the best views of Lago Argentino. Heated pool, spa treatments and

Estancia Cristina

For many visitors, a visit to historical Estancia Cristina is the highlight of their trip. A boat leaves Puerto Bandera early in the morning and travels for two hours to the northernmost reaches of Lago Argentina, strewn with mighty icebergs, to see the Upsala glacier from the water. Then, having taken in the sheer size of and unspoilt beauty, the boat continues to the remote estancia situated in isolation on the shores of the lake under a crown of mountains. Visit for the day to enjoy a real Patagonian *asado*, or better still, stay overnight in comfortable rooms with superb views. An overnight stay allows for a wonderful horse-riding trip, or an excursion by 4WD to a viewpoint high above the Upsala glacier, with the still milky Prussian blue lake below, and fire coloured rocks all around. From here hike down the staggering Canyon de los Fosiles, with your own private guide: mind-blowingly beautiful. Day trips cost from US$110, all included. For more information on Estancia Cristina, T02902-491133, www.estanciacristina.com.

gym. A little out of town but worth the short drive. Low season prices move this hotel down a category (**L**). Recommended.
LL Los Sauces Casa Patagónica, Los Gauchos 1352/1370, T02902-495854, T011-43485189 in Buenos Aires, www.casalossauces.com. Incredibly stylish and welcoming boutique hotel close to town. Attention to detail and great accommodation packages make this a hotel a must. Member of Small Luxury Hotels. Highly recommended.
L Kosten Aike, Gob Moyano 1243, T02902-492424, www.kostenaike.com.ar. A special place, relaxed and yet stylish with large elegant rooms, king-size beds throughout, jacuzzi and gym. The restaurant Ariskaiken is open to non-residents and has an excellent chef; there's a cosy bar with a wood fire, and a garden. The staff are extremely attentive and speak English.
L Los Alamos, Gobernador Moyano and Bustillo, T02902-491144, www.posada losalamos.com. Located in 2 separate chalet-style buildings, this is an extremely comfortable large hotel, with charming rooms, beautifully decorated and equipped, good service, lovely gardens, golf course and without doubt the best restaurant in town, La Posta. Recommended.

AL Blanca Patagonia, Parque Nacional Los Glaciares No.149, T02902-493370, www.blancapatagonia.com. With only 13 rooms, this small hosteria offers cabins for 2 and 4 people, as well as doubles. Fantastic views from the main building, as it is situated within the city heights. Recommended.
AL Patagonia Rebelde, José Haro 442, T02902-494495, www.patagonia rebelde.com. Charming building in traditional Patagonian style, resembling an old inn with its corrugated zinc walls and rustic decor, all looking pretty basic though offering good comfort with well-heated bedrooms and comfy sitting rooms.
A Michelangelo, Espora and Gobernador Moyano 1020, T02902-491045, www.michelangelohotel.com.ar. A lovely, quiet and welcoming place, modern and stylish in design, with a really excellent restaurant. The menu is innovative, and includes hare, steak, and ink squid ravioli. All rooms have TV, bath and minibar, breakfast included. Excellent value. Recommended.
A Santa Mónica Apartments, Josefa Freile 42, T02902 491835, www.santamonica aparts.com.ar. Located right in the middle of town, just off the main street, this little collection of wooden cabins is perfect

for couples or groups of up to 4. Very convenient. Open all year.

B Ariel, Av del Libertador 1693, T02902-493131, www.hotelariel.com.ar. A modern functional place west of centre, very clean and well-maintained rooms with bath and TV. Breakfast included.

B Casa de Grillos, Los Cóndores 1215 corner of Las Bandurrias, T02902-491160, www.casadegrillos.com.ar. Marta and Alejandro are the welcoming hosts at this B&B situated in the calm green area, next to Nímez nature reserve. It has all the comfort and charm of a family house.

E pp Lago Azul 'B', Perito Moreno 83, T2902-491419. Cheapest in the area, this pioneer house with a couple of simple and spotless rooms to share is the most welcoming budget choice, with charming Mrs Echeverría and her husband offering traditional Patagonian hospitality. Recommended.

Camping

AMSA, Olavarría 65 (50 m off the main road, turning south at the fire station), T02902-492247, US$5 per person, hot water, security, open only in summer.

There are 2 campsites in the park en route to Lago Roca: **El Huala**, 42 km from El Calafate, free with basic facilities and open all year round; and **Lago Roca**, 50 km from El Calafate, T02902-499500. Beautifully set, with hot water, public phone, restaurant, bike hire, US$6 per person.

Hostels

E-F Hostel del Glaciar 'Libertador', Av del Libertador 587 (next to the bridge on the access to town), T02902-491792, www.glaciar.com. Open Jul-May. Clean and modern with good, functional, well-heated rooms, private doubles or rooms to share among 4, all with own bath. Breakfast is only included in the high-season rate for the private rooms; free transfer from bus station. Discounts to HI members. Price per person. Recommended.

F América del Sur, Puerto Deseado153, T02902-493525, www.americahostel.com.ar. A short walk from the centre of town on a hilltop, each room in this hostel has uninterrupted lake views. Price per person. Friendly staff, and a no-shoes policy makes this a great choice.

F Hostel del Glaciar 'Pioneros', Los Pioneros 251, T/F02902-491243, www.glaciar.com. Larger, older, a bit further from the centre and than its sister hostel **Libertador**, this long-established hostel is open only in high season (Oct-Mar), and offers a great range of accommodation for all budgets: shared dorms for up to 4 people, **C** standard private doubles (also for 3 and 4) with bath, and **B** larger superior doubles with bath. They also run Patagonia Backpackers agency with the **Alternative Glacier Tour** (see below), and organize a booking service for **Navimag**, hotels and transport throughout Patagonia, and run free shuttle service from the bus terminal. Book well in advance. Price per person.

F I Keu Ken Hostel, FM Pontoriero 171, T02902-495175, www.patagoniaikeuken.com.ar. Basic dorms, but well-equipped kitchen, and fantastic views. 2 cabins (**B**) attractively decorated and great for a couple or group. Price per person.

G Hostel de las Manos, Egidio Feruglio 59, T02902-492996, www.hosteldelas manos.com.ar. Clean, comfortable private rooms and basic dorms (**F**) available at this welcoming hostel 6 blocks from the main street. Take a taxi from the bus station and they will reimburse you. Call first to arrange. Price per person.

Around El Calafate p509
Estancias

LL Hostería Alta Vista, 35 km west of El Calafate (on the way to Lago Roca–Ruta 15), T02902-499902, www.hosteriaalta vista.com.ar. Set within the land of Estancia Anita, the largest estancia in the area (a staggering 74,000 ha) Alta Vista is a famous estancia with all facilities you could possibly need, and only 15 guests. Favoured by celebrities and politicians, the lovely house was built in the 1930s and mostly retains its original style. Full-board is possible with excellent cuisine and wines included. There are attractive walks and a great range of excursions in all within the vast expanse of the ranch. Recommended.

LL Kau-Yatún, Estancia 25 de Mayo (10 blocks from town centre, east of arroyo Calafate), T02902-491059, T011-4783 2930 in Buenos Aires, www.kauyatun.com. The easiest way to stay at an estancia from town, this is a very comfortable renovated main house of an old estancia, now on the outskirts of town, and surrounded by 4 ha of very well-kept gardens, where vegetables are grown for the meals served in its 2 excellent restaurants. The welcoming hosts successfully combine a homely feel with rustic decor, typical of a traditional Patagonian estancia. Either half board or all-inclusive programmes with excursions in the Park included.

LL Los Notros, www.losnotros.com (in Buenos Aires: T011-4814 3934). An exclusive retreat by the lake with luxurious accommodation in spacious, well-designed rooms. The only option if you want to wake up to views directly of the Perito Moreno glacier. You can walk, hike, trek, and ride horses. Expensive, but there are all inclusive packages with free transfers to the glacier *pasarelas* included.

AL Estancia Nibepo Aike, in the far south of the park on the shores of Brazo Sur of Lago Argentino, T02966-436010 in Río Gallegos, www.nibepoaike.com.ar, www.lagosan martin.com. Open Oct-Apr. A spectacular setting inside the national park, near the shores of the lake, the house has just 15 simple rooms, decorated with lovely old furniture, and there's a cosy sitting room. Lots of activities are possible in the park, or the surrounding 12800 ha. Premises are open for day visits too.

Camping

Bahía Escondida, 7 km east of the glacier. Facilities include fireplaces, hot showers and a shop. Crowded in summer, US$3 per person.

Correntoso, 10 km east of the glacier. An unmarked site with no facilities but a great location. No fires. US$3 per person.

Lago Roca, 50 km from El Calafate, T02902-499500. Beautifully set, with hot water, public phone, restaurant, bike hire, US$4 per person.

Cerro Fitz Roy *p510, map p511*

There are campsites in the park at **Poincenot**, **Capri** and **Laguna Toro**. **Río Blanco** is for climbers with prior permission. Campsites have no services but all have latrines, apart from Toro. A gas/alcohol stove is essential as fires are prohibited. See box, page 512.

Camping Piedra del Fraile, on Río Eléctrico, just north of the park boundary. Privately owned with *cabañas* and hot showers (**E** per person) as well as camping (US$6 per person).

El Chaltén *p512, map p513*

See www.elchalten.com for a full list. Most hotels close from April/May to Sept and from December to March finding accommodation can be challenging. Book ahead.

LL Los Cerros, T02962-493182, www.loscerros delchalten.com. On a hill above the town, this large hotel is by far the most sophisticated choice. Stylish, yet informal, all rooms are very comfortable with impressive attention to detail. Half-board and all-inclusive packages with excursions run by **Fitz Roy Expediciones**.

AL Hostería El Puma, Lionel Terray 212, T02962-493095, www.hosteriaelpuma.com.ar. The most desirable place in town, set a little apart, and with splendid views up the valley, a welcoming lounge with log fire and tasteful furnishings, spacious rooms and plush bathrooms. Transfers and breakfast included. Tours arranged through their agency **Fitz Roy Expediciones**, see Activities and tours, page 522. Recommended.

AL Hostería Posada Lunajuim, Trevisán s/n, T/F02962-493047, www.posadalunajuim. com.ar. Stylish, relaxed and welcoming, with comfortable rooms (thick duvets on the beds) with bathrooms and a lovely big lounge with wood fire. Full breakfast included. Charming hosts. Recommended.

B-C Northofagus, Hensen s/n T02962-493087, www.elchalten.com/northofagus. A small cosy B&B, with simple double rooms with shared bath, including breakfast. Welcoming and good value.

C Hospedaje La Base, Lago de Desierto 97, T02962-493031. A friendly little place with basic en suite doubles or dorms for 3-4 (**E**). Tiny kitchen for guests to use, self-service breakfast included, and a great video lounge.

C Inlandsis, Lago del Desierto 480, T02962-493276, www.elchalten/inlandsis. This small B&B has 8 cosy rooms, some with magnificent views. Quiet, clean and good value. Recommended.

C Mi Rincón, Cabo Gracia 115, T02962-493099, www.mirincon-elchalten.com.ar. Simple, clean and inviting doubles and triples with a view of Fitz Roy. Good value.

Hostels

E Albergue Patagonia, San Martín 493, T/F02962-493019, www.elchalten.com/patagonia. HI-affiliated. The most appealing hostel. Cosy and friendly with rooms for 4-6, kitchen, video room, bike hire and laundry. Information and excursions available. Next door is restaurant **Fuegia**. Price per person.

E Aylen-Aike, Trevisan 125, T02962-493142, www.elchalten.com. Closed late-Apr to Oct. Large, modern yellow building on one of the quieter streets, has friendly staff. 4- or 10-bed dorms. Price per person.

E Cóndor de los Andes, Av Río de las Vueltas y Halvorsen, T02962-493101, www.condordelosandes.com. Closed mid-Apr to Sept. Friendly, small and modern, with nice little rooms for 4-6 or en suite doubles, sheets included, breakfast extra. Washing service, library, kitchen facilities. Quiet atmosphere. HI-discount.Price per person. Recommended.

E Pioneros de Valle, San Martín 451, T02962-493079. Central, large new hostel with basic, clean but slightly cramped dorms, and a modern kitchen. Price per person.

Around El Chaltén *p514 map p511*
There is a campsite at the southern end of Lago del Desierto and *refugios* at its northern end and at Laguna Diablo.

L Estancia La Quinta, on RP 23, 2 km south of El Chaltén, T02962-493012, www.estancialaquinta.com.ar. Oct-Apr. A spacious pioneer house with renovated rooms and beautiful gardens. A superb breakfast is included and the restaurant is open for lunch and dinner. Free transfer to/from El Chaltén bus terminal.

AL-A Hosterías El Pilar, on RP 23, Km 17, T/F02962-493002, www.hosteriaelpilar.com.ar. A special place to stay a little way out of town on the road to Lago del Desierto. This simple country house, in a spectacular setting with views of Fitz Roy, offers the chance to access less visited parts of the park. Spacious rooms and great food. Tailor-made trekking tours. Recommended.

AL Estancia Lago del Desierto, Punto Sur, southern tip of Lago del Desierto, T02962-493010. Basic place with *cabañas* for 5, camping US$5 per person, hot showers, kitchen. Recommended.

❶ Eating

El Calafate *p508, map p508*
For cheap meals, there are 2 lively, packed places on the main street, Av del Libertador, with good atmosphere and cheapish food: Rick's Café, No 1091, T02902-492148, serving *parrilla tenedor libre* for US$15, and Casablanca, Av del Libertador and 25 de Mayo, T02902-491402. A welcoming place, serving omelettes, hamburgers and vegetarian food, US$11 for steak and chips.

♥♥♥ Casimiro Biguá, Av del Libertador 963, T02902-492590. A popular upmarket place with quality food, including the excellent stew *cazuela de cordero*.

♥♥♥ El Puesto, Gobernador Moyano y 9 de Julio, T02902-491620. Tasty thin-crust pizzas in a cosy old house. Also pricier regional meals and takeaway service. Recommended.

₸₸₸ Pascasio, 25 de Mayo 52, T02902-492055. Cosy, exclusive and a very good spot for romantic dinners.

₸₸ La Cocina, Av del Libertador 1245, T02902-491758. Pizzería, a large variety of pancakes, pasta, salads, in cosy warm atmosphere. Good wine list.

₸₸ Mi Viejo, Av del Libertador 1111, T02902-491691. Popular *parrilla*, try the grilled lamb for US$9.

₸₸ Punto de Encuentro, Los Pioneros 251 (at Hostel del Glaciar 'Pioneros'). Ideal for meeting fellow travellers, over creative meals that include veggie options.

₸₸ Pura Vida, Av del Libertador 1876. Recommended for a relaxed place to eat well, with comfortable sofas, homemade Argentine food, lots of veggie options, and a lovely warm atmosphere with lake view.

₸₸ Viva la Pepa, Emilio Amado 833, T02902-491880. Closed Wed. Mainly vegetarian café with great sandwiches and crêpes with special fillings.

El Chaltén *p512, map p513*

₸₸₸ Los Cerros, Hotel Los Cerros T02962-493182. Top cuisine in a sophisticated atmosphere, where regional meals such as *puchero patagónico* and *carbonada de liebre* sit well among other more international standards. The wine list includes produce from the best *bodegas*.

₸₸ Ahonikenk Chaltén, Güemes 23, T02962-493070. Centrally located small café with large portions of pizza and pasta.

₸₸ El Muro, San Martín 948, T02962-493248. Inviting restaurant/bar serving pasta, pizza, and home-made beers. Strangely there is a climbing wall to practice on– before you try the beer.

₸₸ Estepa, Cerro Solo and Antonio Rojo. Open from 1500, closed Mon. Small, intimate place with a varied menu that includes excellent lamb, selected wines and imaginative vegetarian options.

₸₸ Fuegia, San Martín. T02962-493243. The usual international menu in a warm atmosphere, plus some Patagonian dishes

and more imaginative options, such as curries and veggie food. Great breakfast menu, served until 1430 in high season.

₸₸ Josh Aike, Lago del Desierto 105. Excellent *confitería*, delicious homemade food, in a beautiful building. Recommended.

₸₸ Pangea, Lago del Desierto and San Martín, T02962-493084. Open for lunch and dinner, drinks and coffee, in calm comfortable surroundings with good music, a varied menu, from pastas to steak, trout and pizzas. Recommended.

₸₸ Patagonicus, Güemes and Madsen, T02962-493025. Open 1200-2400. A lovely warm cosy stylish place with salads, home made pastas and the best pizzas. Great family photos of mountain climbers on the walls. Recommended.

₸₸ Terray, Lionel Terray 212, **Hostería El Puma**, T02962-493095. Climbers, trekkers and other visitors chat about their expeditions, over excellent food in a homely atmosphere.

⚑ Bars and nightclubs

El Calafate *p508, map p508*

Borges y Alvarez, Av del Libertador 1015, 1st floor, Galería de los Gnomos. T02902-491464. Cosy wooden bar with huge windows over the shopping street below. Affordable, and delicious lunch and dinner, as well as live music, and books for sale. A must.

Elba'r, 9 de Julio 57, T02902-493594. Just off the main street, this café/bar serves hard to find waffles, and juices as well as home-made beer and sandwiches.

Shackleton Lounge, Av del Libertador 3287, T02902-493516. On the outskirts of town (US$2.50 in taxi). A great place to relax, lovely views of the lake, old photos of Shackleton, great atmosphere, good music. Highly recommended for a late drink or some good regional dishes. Afternoon tea served.

El Chaltén *p512, map p513*

Elal Resto-bar, Lago del Desierto 410, T02962-493106. Open 0730-2400. Live shows

attract large crowds in summer, and they follow a good night with a great breakfast.
El Bodegón Cervecería, San Martín 724. Packed-out café/bar serving home-brewed beers from their own microbrewery, as well as great vegetarian pizzas, sandwiches, and soups. The wooden interior feels homely.

❀ Festivals and events

El Calafate *p508, map p508*
15 Feb People flock to the rural show Lago Argentino Day, and camp out with live music, dancing and *asados*.
10 Nov Displays of horsemanship and *asados* on Día de la Tradición.

○ Shopping

El Calafate *p508, map p508*
All along Libertador there are souvenir shops selling hats and gloves for those chilly boat rides to the glacier. There are lots of fine quality handicrafts; look out for Mapuche weavings and woollen items. Handicraft stalls are on Libertador at around 1200.
Abranpampa, Libertador 1341, T02902-491697. Clothing, and camping gear rentals from backpacks, to tents to cookers.
Ferretería Chuar, a block away from bus terminal. The only place selling white gas for camping and camping supplies.
La Anónima, Av del Libertador and Perito Moreno. Supermarket.

El Chaltén *p512, map p513*
Camping Center, San Martín, T02962-493264. Buy or rent equipment for climbing, trekking and camping.
El Gringuito, Av San Martín. The best of many supermarkets. All are expensive and have little fresh food. Fuel is available.
Eolia rental and Outdoor shop, San Martín and Fonruge, T02962-493066. Equipment hire, advice on personalised APN-certified guides. These guys know their stuff when it

comes to ice and rock climbing and glacier trekking.
El Súper, Lago del Desierto and Av Güemes, T02902-493039. A supermarket that also rents and sells camping and climbing equipment, maps, postcards, books and handicrafts.
Viento Oeste, Av San Martín s/n (northern end of town), T02962-493021. Equipment hire such as tents and sleeping bags. Also arranges mountain guides and sells handicrafts.

▲ Activities and tours

El Calafate *p508, map p508*
Ballooning
Kau Yatún (see Sleeping, page 517). Organizes balloon trips over El Calafate and Lago Argentino, weather permitting, US$150 per hr for a group of up to 7 people.

Birdwatching
Cecilia Scarafoni, T02902-493196, ecowalks@cotecal.com.ar. Expert-led birdwatching walks to Laguna Nimez, lasting 2 hrs, US$6, Mon-Sat.

Boat trips
Boat trips are also run by Hielo y Aventura, see below.
Fernández Campbell, Av del Libertador 867, T02902-491298, www.solopatagonia.com.ar. The main operator for trips on Lago Argentino to the Perito Moreno and Upsala glaciers.
Mar Patag, www.crucerosmarpatag.com or call T02902-492118 or T011-5031 0756 in Buenos Aires. Run the *Spirit of the Glaciers* luxurious boat trip, a recommendable 2-day exclusive experience for viewing Moreno, Upsala and Spegazzini glaciers (US$365 per person, full board).

Fishing
Calafate Fishing, C Espora 33, T02902-496545, 9 de Julio 29, www.calafate fishing.com. From half-day excursions to 3-day expeditions.

Horse riding

Cabalgata en Patagonia, Av del Libertador 3600, T02902-493203, www.cabalgataen patagonia.com. For 2-hr rides (US$25 per person) or 6-hr excursions (US$45per person, lunch included) to see the Gualicho cave paintings by the lake.

Ice trekking

Always Glaciers, Gobernador Moyano 1226, T02902-492450, www.alwaysglaciers.com. Prolific agency that offers tours in the area. Their speciality is the packages they offer combining several tours in one. HI cardholders receive a discount.

Hielo y Aventura, Av del Libertador 935, T02902-492205, www.hieloyaventura.com. *Safari Náutico* 1-hr boat trip for viewing Moreno glacier from the south side, leaves from Bajo de las Sombras pier, US$9 (tickets also sold at the pier); *Brazo Sur* boat trip, the same as Safari plus a landing to give you the chance to see more glaciers, US$32; the famous *minitrekking*, with 90 mins on the glacier with crampons, US$88, and *Big Ice*, a much longer walk on ice in the same area of the *minitrekking*, US$119. Recommended. Note that people under 18 and over 45 are not permitted to attempt the ice trekking.

Mountain bikes

On Rent a Car, Av del Libertador 1831, T02902-493788, www.onrentacar.com.ar. US$21/day.

Offroading

Mil Outdoor Adventure, Av del Libertador 1029, T02902-491437, www.miloutdoor.com. Exciting excursions in 4WD to see wild places with wonderful views, 3-6 hrs, US$42-70.

Rafting

Nonthue Aventura, Libertador 1177, T02902-491179. Rafting on the Río Santa Cruz, 4-5 hrs, US$41 with transport.

Tour operators

Most agencies charge the same rates for excursions: to the Perito Moreno Glacier

US$21; to Lago Roca, a full-day including lunch at Estancia Anita, US$30; horse riding to Gualichó caves, 2 hrs, US$21.

Chaltén Travel, Av del Libertador 1174, T2902-492212, www.chaltentravel.com. The most helpful, with a huge range of tours: glaciers, estancias, trekking, and trips to El Chaltén with a visit to Torres del Paine, US$69; also sells tickets along Ruta 40 to Los Antiguos. English spoken. Highly recommended.

Lago San Martín, Av del Libertador 1215, 1st floor, T02902-492858, www.lagosanmartin.com. Specializes in reservations to estancias in Santa Cruz province, very helpful.

Leutz Turismo, Av del Libertador 1341, T02902-492316, www.leutzturismo.com.ar. Daily excursion to Lago Roca 1000-1800, US$ 36 per person, plus US$18 for optional lunch at Estancia Nibepo Aike, and an interesting tour of the sheep and fruit. **Estancia Quien Sabe** with a traditional *cordero asado* for dinner.

Patagonia Backpackers, at Hostels del Glaciar: Los Pioneros 251 or Av del Libertador 587, T/F2902-491243, www.glaciar.com. Offers the 'Alternative Tour to Moreno Glacier'. Highly recommended, it includes lots of information on the landscape and wildlife, followed by the boat trip, to see it up close. US$40. Other trips include 'Supertrekking El Chaltén', a 2-day hiking trip, featuring the best treks in the Fitz Roy massif, including camping and ice trekking; and a 2-day visit to Torres del Paine including camping and trekking (US$190). They also sell tickets for the **Navimag** ferries in the Chilean fjords. Highly recommended.

El Chaltén *p512, map p513*
Boat trips

Patagonia Aventura, San Martín 56, T02962-493110 www.patagonia-aventura.com.ar. Boat trips along Lago Viedma to see Glaciar Viedma, informative; transfers US$12 extra. Also a good full-daytrip along Lago Viedma, with ice trekking on Glaciar Viedma. They also operate Lago del Desierto crossings, US$18 per person.

Tour operators and trekking guides
Fitz Roy Expediciones, Lionel Terray 212 (next to **Hostería El Puma**), T02962-493017, www.fitzroyexpediciones.com.ar. The best and most experienced company with excellent guides. Trekking, rock climbing and ice-climbing courses, adventure expeditions, including 2-day ascents of Cerro Solo (2121 m), 3-day trekking crossing from Lago Viedma to Lago San Martín, and 8-day trekking expeditions on the Campo de Hielo. Also organizes superb kayaking down the Río de las Vueltas from its wonderful adventure camp, the FRAC, on the way to Lago del Desierto. Great *asados*, hiking, biking, and guides on hand too. Highly recommended.

⊖ Transport

Río Turbio *p506*
Bus
To **Puerto Natales**, 1 hr, US$3.50, several daily with **Cootra**, Tte del Castillo 01, T02902-421448. **Bus Sur**, Baquedano 534, Pto Natales, T+56(0)61-411859, www.turismozaahj.co.cl. **Lagoper**, Av de Los Mineros 262, T02902-411831, El Pingüino. To **El Calafate**, Cootra, Taqsa, www.taqsa.com.ar, daily, US$14, 4½ hrs. To **Río Gallegos**, Taqsa, daily, 4 hrs, US$11. Taqsa also run a year-round service from El Calafate, via El Chalten (weather permitting) to Bariloche stopping at Perito Moreno, Los Antiguos, Esquel and El Bolson. It is long, and the bus is basic, but it is a great way to see the famous Ruta 40. Bring your own food. US$90, 28 hrs. Or an alternative route to Bariloche via the coast, which is cheaper and takes less time, is offered by **Las Lengas**, Viedma 95, T02962-493023, laslengaselchalten@yahoo.com.ar. Unlike most companies, instead of transiting through El Calafate and then Río Gallegos on the way to Bariloche, the bus travels directly through Piedra Buena to the north (5hrs, US$30) with connections to Bariloche and Puerto Madryn. Only in high season.

El Calafate *p508, map p508*
Bus
The terminal is on Roca, 1 block up steep stairs from Libertador.

Long-distance To **Ushuaia** take a bus to Río Gallegos; (the **Taqsa** 0300 is the best connection). To **Río Gallegos**, daily with **Interlagos**, T02902-491179, **Sportman**, T02902-492680, and **Taqsa**, T02902-491843, 4 hrs, US$8-11. To **El Chaltén**, daily with **Cal-Tur**, **Chaltén Travel**, T02902-491833, and **Taqsa**, 4-4½ hrs, US$16-18. To **Perito Moreno glacier**, daily with **Cal-Tur**, T02902-491842, 1½ hrs, US$12. **Taqsa**, goes only in summer. To **Perito Moreno** and **Los Antiguos**, contact **Chaltén Travel**. To **Bariloche** along Ruta 40 with **Overland Patagonia**, www.overlandpatagonia.com, 4 days via the Perito Moreno national park, Cueva de las Manos, Estancia Melike, Río Mayo and Fitz Roy, US$96 plus accommodation at US$6 per day; bookings in El Calafate from **Patagonia Backpackers** (Hostels del Glaciar), T02902-491243, www.glaciar.com.

To Chile To **Puerto Natales**, daily with either **Cootra** T02902-491444, or **Bus Sur** T02902-491631, US$18, advance booking recommended. **Bus Sur** (Tue, Sat 0800) and **Zaahj** (Wed, Fri, Sun 0800) also run to Puerto Natales via **Cerro Castillo**, where you can pick up a bus to **Torres del Paine** in summer. Take your passport when booking tickets.

Car hire
Adventure Rent a Car, Av del Libertador 290, T02902-492595, www.adventurerentcar.com. **On Rent a Car**, Av del Libertador 1831, T02902-493788, www.onrentacar.com.ar. Average US$55 per day for a small car including insurance.

Taxi
To **Río Gallegos**, 4 hrs, US$110 for up to 5 people.

Perito Moreno glacier *p510*
Bus
The cheapest way to get to the glacier is on the regular daily bus services run by **Taqsa** T02902-491843, and **Cal-Tur** T02902-491842, to the car park above the walkways.

Minibus Many agencies in El Calafate (see Activities and tours) also run minibus tours (park entry not included) leaving 0800 and returning 1800, giving you 3 hrs at the glacier; the return ticket is also valid if you come back next day (student discount available). **Patagonia Backpackers** run an extended alternative itinerary.

Boat
Boat trips for up to 60 passengers are run by **Fernández Campbell** (see Activities and tours). **Safari Náutico** offers the best views, US$12 pp, 1 hr. Boats leave from the tourist pier signposted from the car park in Parque Nacional Los Glaciares, bus travel is included.

Car
Out of season, trips to the glacier are difficult to arrange, but you can gather a party and hire a taxi (*remise* T02902-491745/492005). These will charge US$50 for 4 passengers, round trip.

Upsala glacier *p510*
Tour boats usually run daily. The main operator is **Fernández Campbell** (see Activities and tours) who charges US$25, including transfer bus and park entry fees. The bus departs at 0730 from El Calafate for Punta Bandera, with time allowed for lunch at the restaurant (not included, so take your own food) near the Lago Onelli track. The return bus to El Calafate is at 1930. A more expensive but also more spectacular trip is offered by **Estancia Cristina**, see box, page 515.

El Chaltén *p512, map p513*
Bus
In summer, buses fill quickly, so book ahead. The following are high-season services; they are less frequent in winter. Daily buses to **El Calafate**, 4-4½ hrs, US$16-18 one-way: run by **Chaltén Travel**, San Martín 635 (at Albergue Rancho Grande), T02902-493005, www.chaltentravel.com, **Cal-Tur**, San Martín 520 (at Fitz Roy Inn), T02902-493062, and **Taqsa**, Av Güemes 68, T02902-493068. To **Los Antiguos** along the Ruta 40, **Itinerarios y Travesías**, T02902-493088 overnight, even dates (ie 2nd, 4th, 6th), includes trip to Cueva de las Manos in the early morning. **Chaltén Travel** runs a service Nov-Mar, leaving on odd days to go along Ruta 40 up to Bariloche, with a stopover at the small town of Perito Moreno, US$114 transport only.

Overland Patagonia does trips to **Bariloche** in 4 days, staying at estancias and visiting Cueva de las Manos.

O Directory

El Calafate *p508, map p508*
Banks Best to take cash as high commission is charged on exchange. Plenty of ATMs. Change money at **Thaler**, 9 de Julio 57, www.cambio-thaler.com. **Post office** Av del Libertador 1133. **Telephone** Open Calafate, Libertador 996, huge *locutorio* for phones and internet. **Centro Integral de Comunicaciones**, Av del Libertador 1486, is cheaper.

El Chaltén *p512, map p513*
Banks There are no banks or ATMs in El Chalten, and you will have a hard time trying to change a TC or pay with credit card, so bring ready cash. **Internet/telephone** Rancho Grande, San Martín 724. Open late. There are also 3 *locutorios* with phones, and internet on Av Güemes at the entrance to the town. There is no cellular phone coverage here, and you will find the internet excruciatingly slow.

Contents

Footprint features

Border crossing

Tierra del Fuego

At a glance

◉ **Getting around** Local buses will take you to the local attractions but not much further afield.

◉ **Time required** 3-4 days will allow you to visit Ushuaia and surrounds. Add another 5 days to trek the Dientes de Navarino.

☼ **Weather** Windy during the warmer months. Snow Jun and Jul.

✕ **When not to go** The height of winter (May-Aug) can be unpleasantly cold, unless you want to ski.

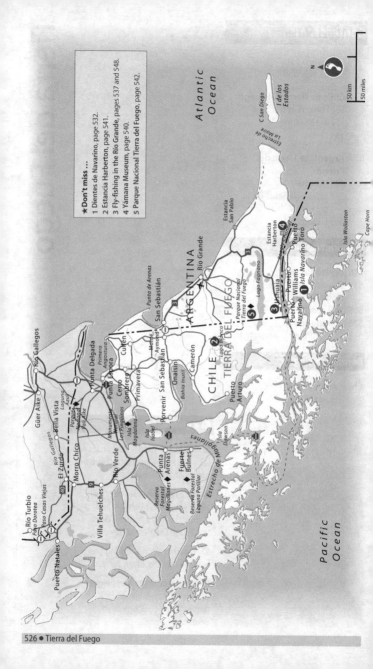

★ **Don't miss ...**

1 Dientes de Navarino, page 532.
2 Estancia Harberton, page 541.
3 Fly-fishing in the Río Grande, pages 537 and 548.
4 Yámana Museum, page 540.
5 Parque Nacional Tierra del Fuego, page 542.

The island of Tierra del Fuego is the most mysterious and captivating part of all Patagonia. At the very foot of the South American continent and separated from the mainland by the intricate waterways of the Magellan Straits, this is America's last remaining wilderness and an indispensable part of any trip to the south. The island is divided between Argentina and Chile by a north-south line, which grants Argentina the Atlantic and southern coasts, and gives Chile an expanse of wilderness to the west, where the tail of the Andes sweeps east in the form of the mighty Darwin range.

The Chilean side is largely inaccessible, apart from the small town of Porvenir, though expeditions can be organized from Punta Arenas to take you hiking and trout fishing. Glaciers and jagged peaks give a dramatic backdrop to the Argentine city of Ushuaia, the island's main centre, set in a serene natural harbour on the Beagle Channel, with views of the Dientes de Navarino mountains on the Chilean island of Navarino opposite, with some of Patagonia's most demanding trekking routes. Sail from Ushuaia along the channel to the pioneer home of Harberton; to Cape Horn; or even to Antarctica. Head into the small but picturesque Parque Nacional Tierra del Fuego, for hikes around Bahía Lapataia and steep climbs with magnificent views out along the channel. The mountain slopes are covered in lenga forest, and if you visit in autumn you might think the name 'Land of Fire' is derived from the blaze of scarlet and orange. Elsewhere on the island, lakes and valleys can be explored on foot or on horseback, and in winter the valleys are perfect for cross-country skiing, while the slopes at Cerro Castor (www.cerrocastor.com) offer good powder snow, and skiing with spectacular views of the end of the world.

Ins and outs

Getting there

Air Argentine Tierra del Fuego is easy to reach with several flights daily from Buenos Aires to Río Grande and Ushuaia, and less frequent flights from El Calafate, and some other towns in Patagonia. Flights are heavily booked in advance throughout the summer months. Chilean Tierra del Fuego is less easily accessed by air, daily flights from Punta Arenas to Porvenir, and five to six a week to Puerto Williams on Isla Navarino.

Ferry and bus There are two places where ferries cross to Tierra del Fuego: from **Tres Puentes**, just north of Punta Arenas to **Porvenir**, and further east across **Primera Angostura** at Punta Delgada, both crossings on Chilean territory. All buses from mainland Argentina use the quicker and more frequent Punta Delgada crossing, and from Punta Arenas, buses take the road northeast to Punta Delgada, and cross by ferry there. There's a cosy tea room **Bahía Azul** on the northern side, with hot snacks and toilets. There is a daily ferry crossing (summer) from Tres Puentes, just north of Punta Arenas to Porvenir, and from here a 225 km road runs east to Río Grande (six hours) via the border at San Sebastián. (By road, Punta Arenas and Punta Delgada are connected by a good road, RN255). ▶▶ *See box, opposite.*

Getting around

Buses between Punta Arenas and Río Grande do not pick up passengers en route. From Porvenir there is limited public transport to Cerro Sombrero and Camaron. Otherwise you will need your own high-clearance vehicle. Argentine Tierra del Fuego is much easier to get around, via Route 3 between Río Grande and Ushuaia with several buses a day. A fan of roads spreads out south and west from Río Grande to the estancias in the Argentine side, but these are unpaved, and best attempted in a 4WD vehicle. A good *ripio* road leads from 40 km east of Ushuaia to Harberton and Estancia Moat on the south coast, and part of the way along the north coast to Estancia San Pablo; no public transport here either.

Background

Tierra del Fuego's narrated history began with the early 16th-century explorers, but the island had been inhabited for some 10,000 years by four indigenous groups who survived until the early 20th century, when white settlers wiped them out. The most numerous of these four groups, the Onas (also known as the Selk'nam), were hunter-gatherers in the north, living mainly on guanaco, which they shot with bow and arrow. The southeastern corner of the island was inhabited by the Haus or Hausch, also hunter-gatherers, of whom very little is known. The Yaganes or Yámana lived along the Beagle Channel and on the islands further south, and were seafaring people who survived mainly on seafood, fish and seabirds, physically smaller than the Onas but with a strongly developed upper body for rowing long distances. The fourth group, the Alacalufe, lived in the west of Tierra del Fuego as well as on the Chonos Archipelago, surviving by fishing and hunting seals.

The first Europeans to visit the island came with the Portuguese navigator Fernão Magalhães (Magellan), who, in 1520, sailed through the channel that now bears his name. It was Magellan who named the island Land of Fire when he saw the smoke from many fires lit along the shoreline. As a result of numerous maritime disasters, including the failure of Sarmiento de Gamboa's attempt at colonizing the Straits in 1584, the indigenous population were left undisturbed for three centuries.

Border crossing: Chile–Argentina

San Sebastián (Argentina)

The Chilean/Argentine border is at the Argentine town of San Sebastián, 128 km south of where the ferry arrives at Punta Espora, and – confusingly – 14 km east of a Chilean town also called San Sebastián. The border at Argentine San Sebastián is open 24 hours, with a basic ACA motel, T02964-425542, and a service station open 0700 to 2300. From here Route 3 is paved to Río Grande.

Fitzroy and Darwin's visits for scientific surveying in 1832 and 1833 recorded some fascinating interaction with the indigenous peoples. Their visits were a precursor to determined attempts to convert the indigenous groups to Christianity so that the island could be used by white settlers without fear of attack by uncontrolled natives. Several disastrous missions followed, and encountered naturally stiff resistance from the inhabitants; the first successful mission was finally established in 1869 and, in 1884, the Reverend Thomas Bridges founded a mission at Ushuaia. But Bridges soon realized that his original task was a destructive one. He was the first European to learn the Yámana language, and soon had many Yámana settled around Ushuaia and compiled his Yámana–English dictionary for the ease of conversion. The purpose of the missionary work had of course been to facilitate lucrative sheep farming on the island. The Ona were attracted to the 'white guanacos' on their land and hunting sheep proved far easier than the faster-footed guanaco. The colonists responded by offering two sheep for each Ona that was killed (proof was provided by a pair of Ona ears). The indigenous groups were further ravaged by epidemics of European diseases. In a desperate attempt to save the Ona, Salesian missionaries founded three missions in the Magellan Straits in the early 20th century but, stripped of their land, the Ona lost the will to live; the last Ona died in 1999. The Hausch also died out. One old Yámana lady presently survives near Puerto Williams and there are a few Alacalufe at Puerto Edén in the Chonos Archipelago.

Imprecision in the original colonial land division and the greed of the rush southwards led to border disputes between Argentina and Chile. These still rumble on today. The initial settlement of the dispute in 1883 was followed by a desire by both governments to populate the area by allocating large expanses of land for sheep farming. The main beneficiaries of this policy on Tierra del Fuego were the Menéndez and Braun families, already established in Punta Arenas.

Argentine government tax incentives to companies in the 1970s led to the establishment of new industries in Río Grande and Ushuaia and a rapid growth in the population of both cities; the subsequent withdrawal of incentives has produced rising unemployment and migration. Tourism is increasingly important in Ushuaia.

For a detailed narrative account of Tierra del Fuego, the best book is the classic by Lucas Bridges, *Uttermost Part of the Earth*. Colin McEwan's *Patagonia, Natural History, Prehistory and Ethnography at the Uttermost Part of the Earth* (British Museum press, 1997) is brilliantly informative and utterly fascinating. Also recommended is *Savage – The Life and Times of Jemmy Button* by Nick Hazelwood (Hodder & Stoughton, 2000).

Chilean Tierra del Fuego

The Chilean half of Tierra del Fuego is in two sections: the western half of Isla Grande, the main island, and the whole of Isla Navarino, to the south of the main island. Much less developed than the Argentine side of Tierra del Fuego, there are just two small towns where Chile's Fuegians are mostly concentrated: Porvenir, on Isla Grande, easily reached by ferry from Punta Arenas, and Puerto Williams on Isla Navarino, which can either be reached from Punta Arenas, or across the Beagle Channel from Ushuaia. The northern part of Isla Grande is flat steppe, but the south is dominated by the Darwin range of mountains, which provide a dramatic visual backdrop, even if you can't easily get to them. Tourism on Chilean territory is very limited, but it's possible to organize trekking tours from Punta Arenas, and there are plenty of fishing lodges offering magnificent trout fishing, particularly on Río Grande.
➽ *For listings, see pages 534-536.*

Porvenir and around ⊜❼▲◉❶ ➽ *pp534-536. Colour map 7, B1.*

Chilean Tierra del Fuego has a population of 7500, most of whom live in the pretty small town of Porvenir (population 5500), the only town on the Chilean half of the main island. The airstrip and port are both about 5 km from town, transfer is US$5 per person. Founded in 1894 in the gold boom, when many people came seeking fortunes from Croatia and Chiloe, Porvenir is a quiet place with a wide-open pioneer feel, streets of neat brightly painted houses of corrugated zinc, and quaint tall domed trees lining the main avenue. The small but interesting museum **Museo Fernando Cordero Rusque** ① *Zavattaro 402, on the plaza, T061-580098, US$1,* has archaeological and photographic displays on the Selk'nam (Onas) and a good collection of Selk'nam ceremonial masks as well as good displays on natural history and the early gold diggers and sheep farmers. A fair bit of information is in English. There's little else to do here, but you could visit the pretty cemetery on the north edge of town before strolling around the plaza, with its **Iglesia San Francisco de Sales**, and down to the shore-side promenade, where there's a strange collection of 19th-century farm machinery and a striking wooden monument to the Selk'nam. There is tourist information in the museum, but more helpful information can be found at a kiosk on the waterfront, which when open sells fine handicrafts. There's a bank on the plaza.

Beyond Porvenir

Beyond Porvenir there is wonderfully wild virgin territory to explore. However, if you want an adventure, by far your best bet is to arrange a trip through tour operators in Punta Arenas, since there's still very little infrastructure on the Chilean side of the island. The tour operator **Aonikenk** is recommended (see page 445), offering several days' trekking into the remote mountainous south of the island, which is otherwise unreachable, horse riding expeditions and also fly-fishing. There is one tour operator in Porvenir itself, offering fairly traditional tours through the Cordón Baquedano to see the areas where gold was mined – recommended for great views of the Magellan Straits, and to traditional *estancias*.

Until recently the secret haunt of Hollywood stars, it's now possible to stay in several comfortable fishing lodges in Río Grande, Lago Escondido and Lago Blanco. This area is famous for its brown trout, sea-run brook trout and steelheads, weighing 2 to 14 kg. See specialist fly-fishing tour operators, or **Aonikenk** (page 445). The season runs from 15 October to 14 April, with the best fishing from January to April.

Shipwrecked in the Magellan Straits

The Estrecho de Magallanes, 534 km long, is a treacherous sea passage with a long history of claiming victims. The hostile conditions are eloquently conveyed in the words of Sir John Narborough: "horrible like the ruins of a world destroyed by terrific earthquakes".

From the Atlantic, the first navigational problem facing sailors is simply the difficulty of entering the straits against the fierce westerly gales that prevail. Once in the straits the dangers are far from over: many ships have fallen victim to the notorious *Williwaws*, winds with the ferocity of tornados that spring up from nowhere; no less vicious are the *Pamperos*, which blow off the land with enough force to capsize a vessel.

Although in 1520 Magellan succeeded in passing through the straits that bear his name, few others managed to do so in the years that followed; of the 17 ships that attempted the passage in the early 16th century, only one, the Victoria, succeeded in reaching the Pacific and returning to Europe. Twelve were lost near the eastern entrance and four returned in failure. The reason these early navigators chose to attempt the dangerous voyage was the lure of a short route between Europe and the spices of the East. Even when it became clear that there was no such short route, the straits still provided a useful means for Europeans to reach the rich Pacific ports of Peru and Chile without disembarking to cross Mexico or Panama overland.

Even with the development of advanced navigation techniques in the 19th century, losses continued: in 1869, the Santiago, an iron paddle-steamer built in Glasgow and owned by the Pacific Mail line, went down off Isla Desolación at the western end of the straits with a cargo of gold and silver. While the Panama Canal now provides a shorter route between the Atlantic and Pacific Oceans, the size of modern ships means that the straits are still a busy shipping route. The most common cargo is now oil; casualties still occur but now, of course, with the added risk of environmental disaster from oil spillage.

Camerón → *Colour map 7, B1.*

About 90 km east of Porvenir, roads head north to San Sebastián and south to Camerón. This large farm settlement, which is the only other community of any size on the Chilean part of the island, lies 149 km southeast of Porvenir on the opposite shore of Bahía Inútil. The wonderful windswept bay, with views of distant hills and the snow-capped Darwin range all along the horizon, was named 'useless' by British engineers making a hydrographic survey here in 1827 because it has no useful port. Nevertheless, as you near Camerón, the southern mountains loom ahead and the road passes secluded canyons and bays, interspersed with a few farms, and the whole feel is dramatic, isolated and somehow rather magical. The road has little traffic, but there are a few vehicles daily in summer, so hitching is possible – if you don't mind waiting on an exposed windswept plain for hours. There's not much at Camerón itself, although 650 people live scattered among the farm buildings all around, but at the eastern end of the bay, at **Caleta Josefina**, you can visit a handsome ex-estancia built in 1833 by the powerful sheep farming Menéndez family, where some old buildings remain.

From Camerón a road runs southeast past an airfield and on for a further 40 km to a junction, where roads head north to San Sebastián and south to Sección Río Grande (7 km from the junction) and Estancia Vicuña (35 km further on) – there is very little traffic here.

The road south climbs into the hills, through woods where guanacos hoot and run off into glades and the banks are covered with red and purple moss. The north shores of **Lago Blanco** can be reached by cutting through the woods from Sección Río Grande, with superb views of the mountains surrounding the lake and the snows in the south, or from Estancia Vicuña. In the centre of the lake is Isla Victoria, which has accommodation. The lake area can be very cold, even in mid-summer; biting winds sweep in from the south, so wrap up warmly. It's essential to organize any trip to this area through a reliable tour operator with the infrastructure.

From **Estancia Vicuña** a trail leads southwest to the **Río Azopardo**, which also offers trout fishing (sleeping at **Estancia Almirantazgo**). South of here trails run across the Darwin Range to the **Estancia Yendegaia** near the Beagle Channel, a wonderful area for horse riding. For trips into this wild and undiscovered country, contact **Aonikenk** in Punta Arenas, www.aonikenk.com.

Isla Navarino ⊜🖐🔺⊜⊙ ⏩ pp534-536.

Situated on the southern shore of the Beagle Channel, Isla Navarino is totally unspoilt and beautiful, offering great geographical diversity, thanks to the Dientes de Navarino range of mountains, with peaks over 1000 m, covered with southern beech forest up to 500 m and, south of that, great plains covered with peat bogs, and many lagoons abundant in flora. The island was centre of the indigenous Yaganes culture, and there are 500 archaeological sites, the oldest dated as 3000 years old. Guanacos and condors can be seen inland, as well as large numbers of beavers, which were introduced to the island and have done considerable damage. The flight from Punta Arenas is beautiful, with superb views of Tierra del Fuego, the Cordillera Darwin, the Beagle Channel and the islands stretching south to Cape Horn.

Puerto Williams → Colour map 7, C2. Phone code: 061. Population: 2500.

The only settlement of any size on the island is Puerto Williams, a Chilean naval base situated about 50 km east of Ushuaia in Argentina, across the Beagle Channel. Puerto Williams is the southernmost permanently inhabited town in the world; 50 km east-southeast is Puerto Toro, the southernmost permanently inhabited settlement on earth. Some maps mistakenly mark a road from Puerto Williams to Puerto Toro, but it doesn't exist; access is only by sea. Due to the long-running border dispute with Argentina here, Puerto Williams is controlled by the Chilean Navy. Outside the Naval headquarters, you can see the bow section of the *Yelcho*, the tug chartered by Shackleton to rescue men stranded on Elephant Island (see box, page 533).

Your main purpose for visiting the island is likely to be the trekking on the Dientes de Navarino, but you should take time to explore the indigenous heritage here too. It's beautifully documented in the **Museo Martín Gusinde** ① Mon-Thu 1000-1300, 1500-1800, Sat and Sun 1500-1800, US$1, known as the **Museo del Fin del Mundo** (End of the World Museum), which is full of information about vanished indigenous tribes, local wildlife and the famous voyages by Charles Darwin and Fitzroy of the *Beagle*. A visit is highly recommended. A kilometre west of the town is the yacht club (one of Puerto Williams' two nightspots), whose wharf is made from a sunken 1930s Chilean warship. There is **tourist information** ① Municipalidad de Cabos de Hornos, Presidente Ibañez 130, T061-621011, isotop@mitierra.cl, where you can ask for maps and details on hiking. The town also has a bank, supermarkets and hospital.

Endurance in the Antarctic

Ernest Shackleton's 1914-1916 Antarctic expedition is one of the epics of polar exploration. Shackleton's vessel, *Endurance*, which left England in August 1914 with 28 men aboard, became trapped in pack-ice in January 1915. After drifting northwards with the ice for eight months, the ship was crushed by the floes and sank. With three boats, supplies and the dogs, the group camped on an ice floe which continued to drift north for a further eight months. In April 1916, after surviving on a diet largely of seals and penguins, the party took to the boats as the ice broke up. After seven days at sea they reached Elephant Island. From there, Shackleton and five other men sailed 1300 km to South Georgia, where there were whaling stations. At first Shackleton, from whom nothing had been heard for 18 months, was not recognized.

The British government sent a rescue vessel to Elephant Island. After ice had prevented three rescue attempts Shackleton persuaded the Chilean authorities to permit a fourth attempt using the tug *Yelcho*. Leaving Punta Arenas on 25 August 1916, the small vessel encountered thick fog but, unusually for the time of year, little ice and it quickly reached Elephant Island where the men, who had endured an Antarctic winter under upturned boats, were down to four days of supplies.

Although the expedition failed to cross Antarctica, Shackleton's achievement was outstanding: the party had survived two Antarctic winters without loss of life. Shackleton himself returned to the region in 1921 to lead another expedition but, in January 1922, aged only 47, he suffered a fatal heart attack in South Georgia.

Exploring the island

For superb views, climb **Cerro Bandera**, which is reached by a path from the dam 4 km west of the town (a three- to four-hour round trip, it's steep, and you'll need warm clothes). There is excellent trekking around the **Dientes de Navarino** range, the southernmost trail in the world, through impressive mountain landscape, frozen lagoons and snowy peaks, giving superb views over the Beagle Channel. It's a challenging hike, over a distance of 53 km in five days, possible only from December to March, and a good level of fitness is needed. There is no equipment rental on island; ask for information in the tourist office at Puerto Williams, but it's best to go with an organized expedition from Punta Arenas. There are views of Cape Horn in clear weather but conditions change quickly and it can snow on the hills, even in summer. Charter flights are available over Cape Horn and to King George Island on the northern tip of the Antarctic peninsula, where you can see the curvature of the earth on the horizon, with excursions to penguin and sea lion colonies.

Beyond Cerro Bandera, a road leads 56 km west of Puerto Williams to Puerto Navarino. There is little or no traffic on this route and it is very beautiful, with forests of lengas stretching right down to the water's edge. You can also visit **Villa Ukika**, 2 km east of town, the place where the last descendants of the Yaganes people live, relocated from their original homes at Caleta Mejillones, which was the last indigenous reservation in the province, inhabited by hundreds of Yagana descendents. At **Mejillones**, 32 km from Puerto Williams, is a graveyard and memorial to the Yámana people. Just before Estancia Santa Rosa (10 km further on), a path is said to cross the forest, lakes and beaver dams to Wulaia (four to six hours), where the *Beagle* anchored in 1833; however, even the farmer at Wulaia gets lost following this track.

At **Puerto Navarino** there are a handful of marines and an abandoned police post, where you may be allowed to sleep. There are beautiful views across to Ushuaia and west to icebound Hoste Island and the Darwin Massif. A path continues to a cliff above the Murray Narrows; blue, tranquil and utterly calm. If trekking alone in wild parts of the island, beware of sinking mud caused by beaver dams; note also that there is quite a high incidence of rabies among domestic and wild animals (including beavers).

Cape Horn

You can catch a boat from Isla Navarino to Cape Horn (the most southerly piece of land on earth apart from Antarctica). There's a pebbly beach on the north side of the island; boats anchor in the bay and passengers are taken ashore by motorized dinghy. A rotting stairway climbs the cliff above the beach to the building where three marines run the naval post. A path leads to the impressive monument of an albatross over looking the churning waters of the Drake Passage below. **▸▸** *See Transport, page 536.*

ⓔ Chilean Tierra del Fuego listings

For Sleeping and Eating price codes and other relevant information, see Essentials pages 35-42.

● Sleeping

Porvenir *p530*

B-C España, Croacia 698, T061-580160. **C** singles. The largest hotel in town, decent standard, recently refitted and with spacious rooms. Slightly aloof service.
B-C Rosas, Philippi 296, T061-580088, hotelrosas@chile.com. With bath, hot water, heating, restaurant and bar, internet, laundry facilities.
C Hostel Kawi, Pedro Silva 144, T061-581638, hostalkawi@yahoo.com. **D** singles. A comfortable *hostal*, with rooms for 3, all with bath, and offering fly-fishing trips on the island.
E Residencial Dalmacia, Croacia 469, T061-580008, angelacardenas1945@ hotmail.com. **F-G** singles. Basic *residencial*.

Beyond Porvenir *p530*

If you get stuck in the wilds, note that it is almost always possible to camp or bed down in a barn at an estancia.
B-E Hostería de la Frontera, San Sebastián, T061-696004, escabini@tie.cl. Rooms with bath and a decent restaurant. Avoid the more basic accommodation in an annexe.

B-E Hostería Tunkelen, Prat 101, Cerro Sombrero, 46 km south of Primera Angostura, T061-212757, hosteria_tunkelen@ hotmail.com. Rooms and dorm accommodation. Recommended.
E Posada Las Flores, Km 127 on the Porvenir–San Sebastián road.
F Pensión del Señor Alarcón, Cerro Sombrero, 46 km south of Primera Angostura. Good, friendly.
F Refugio Lago Blanco, Lago Blanco, T061-241197. The only accommodation on the lake.

Puerto Williams *p532*

You can also stay at private houses.
LL Lodge Lakutaia, on the edge of Lauta bay, 2 km out of town, T061-621733, www.lakutaia.cl. The only upmarket place on the island. Simple but attractive rooms, lovely views from spacious common areas. Splendid walks in the area. A range of activities is offered.
A Bella Vista Hostal, Teniente Muñoz 118, T061-621010, www.victory-cruises.com/ bella_vista_hostal.html. **B-C** Singles. Some rooms with views, English spoken, sailing trips offered. Also camping, US$10.
B Hostal Yagan, Piloto Pardo 260, T061-621334, hostalyagan@hotmail.com. **D** singles. Good meals available, clean and comfortable, friendly, tours offered.

B-C Hostal Akainij, Austral 22, T061-621173, www.turismoakainij.cl. Smallish but comfortable rooms with bath. Very friendly hosts, excellent, filling meals served. Kitchen facilities, basic English spoken, tours offered. Recommended.

B-C Hostal Coirón, Maragaño 168, T061-621227, hostalcoiron@hotmail.com. Some rooms with bath, kitchen and laundry facilities, also organizes sailing trips, treks and other activities.

C Hostal Camblor, Capedeville 41, T061-621033, hostalcamblor@hotmail.com. Full board available, gets very booked up. Good value.

C Hostal Pusaki, Piloto Pardo 222, T061-621116, pattypusaky@yahoo.es. **D-E** singles. Friendly, good meals served.

C Residencial Onashaga, Uspashun 15, T061-621564, run by Señor Ortiz – everyone knows him. Accommodation is basic, but the welcome is warm. Good meals, helpful, full board available.

🍴 Eating

Porvenir *p530*

¶¶ Club Croata, Senoret y Philippi. On the waterfront, good food, lively.

¶¶-¶ El Chispa, Señoret 202, T061-580054. Seafood and other hearty home-cooked fare. Friendly service, good value.

Puerto Williams *p532*

There are several grocery stores; prices are high because of the remote location. Most hostels will serve food.

▲ Activities and tours

Porvenir *p530*

For adventure tourism and trekking, it's best to go through tour operators in Punta Arenas. **Turismo Cordillera de Darwin**, Señoret 511, T061-580450, jebr_darwin@hotmail.com. Day tours of the area around Porvenir.

Puerto Williams *p532*

Sailing

Captain Ben Garrett, www.victory-cruises.com. Offers recommended adventure sailing in his schooner *Victory* in Dec and Jan, including special trips to Ushuaia, cruises in the canals and voyages to Cape Horn, the glaciers, Puerto Montt and Antarctica.

Crucero Australis, www.australis.com, run cruises that call at Wulaia Bay on the west side of Isla Navarino after visiting Cape Horn; you can disembark to visit the museum and take a short trek.

Tour operators

Turismo Akainij, see Sleeping. Adventure expeditions and transfers.

Sea, Ice and Mountains, Ricardo Maragaño 168, T061-621150, www.simltd.com. Sailing trips, trekking tours and many other adventure activities, including kayaking and wildlife spotting.

Shila, O'Higgins 322 (a hut at entrance to Centro Comercial), T061-621366, www.turismo shila.com. Luis Tiznado Gonzales is an adventure guide, trekking and fishing. Equipment hire: bike US$10 per day, tent US$4-8, sleeping bag US$10, stove US$10, and more. Lots of trekking information, US$1.60 for photocopied maps.

🚌 Transport

Porvenir *p530*

Air

Aerovías DAP, Señoret s/n, Porvenir, T061-580089, www.aeroviasdap.cl, fly from **Punta Arenas** (weather and bookings permitting), 2 to 3 times daily Mon-Sat, 15 mins, US$35 one-way. Heavily booked so make sure you confirm your return reservation.

Bus

Buses from Punta Arenas to Ushuaia don't take on passengers in Chilean Tierra del Fuego. Local buses run to **Camerón** from Manuel Señoret, in theory Tue and Fri 1600,

2 hrs, return at 2030, US$3. There is also a service to **Cerro Sombrero**, leaving from opposite the Municipalidad, Mon, Wed, Fri 0800, 1¾ hrs, return service at 1700 or 1800, US$4.50.

Ferry

The *Melinka* sails from **Tres Puentes** (5 km north of Punta Arenas; catch bus A or E from Av Magallanes, or *colectivo* 15, US$1; taxi US$3) to Bahía Chilota, 5 km west of Porvenir, Tue-Sun 0900 with an extra afternoon sailing Tue-Thu in season, 2½ hrs, pedestrians US$9, bicycles US$12, cars US$55. The boat returns from Porvenir in the afternoon Tue-Sun. Timetable dependent on tides and subject to change; check in advance. The crossing can be rough and cold. Watch for dolphins. Reservations are essential especially in summer (at least 24 hrs in advance for cars); obtainable from **Transbordadora Austral Broom**, Bulnes 05075, Punta Arenas, T061-218100 (T061-580089 in Porvenir), www.tabsa.cl.

The ferry service from **Punta Delgada** on the mainland to Punta Espora, 80 km north of Porvenir, departs usually every 40 mins 0830-2300 (schedules vary with the tides) and takes just 15 mins, pedestrians US$3, cars US$21. This is the principal route for buses and trucks between Ushuaia and mainland Argentina. Before 1000, most space is taken by trucks.

Puerto Williams *p532*
Air

Aerovías DAP, Centro Comercial s/n, T061-621051, www.aeroviasdap.cl, flies 20-seater Cessna aircraft from **Punta Arenas** Mon-Sat, departure time varies, 1¼ hrs, US$96 one-way. Book well in advance; there are long waiting lists. Luggage allowance 10 kg (US$2 per kg extra). DAP or Aeropetrel will charter a plane from **Puerto Williams** to Cape Horn (US$2600 for 8-10 people).

Ferry

The following all depart from **Punta Arenas**: Austral Broom ferry Cruz Australis, www.tabsa.cl, 1 a week, 36 hrs, US$175 for a reclining seat, US$210 for a bunk, meals included; **Navarino** (contact Carlos Aguilera, 21 de Mayo 1460, Punta Arenas, T061-228066), 3rd week of every month, 12 passengers, US$210 one-way. Some cruises to **Ushuaia** also stop at Puerto Williams. There are also irregular services by small operators in yachts, zodiacs and small catamarans from Ushuaia to Puerto Williams, US$80-150 per person.

Cape Horn *p534*

Crucero Australis cruises from **Ushuaia** stop at Cape Horn. In addition, the naval vessel *PSG Micalvi*, which sails once every 3 months from **Punta Arenas** via **Puerto Williams**, may take passengers to Cape Horn for US$250 (letters of recommendation required). Navy and port authorities in Puerto Williams may deny any knowledge, but everyone else knows when a boat is due; ask at the Armada in Punta Arenas. Otherwise ask at the yacht club about hitching a ride to Cape Horn.

🅞 Directory

Porvenir *p530*

Banks There's a bank on the plaza, ATM accepts MasterCard but not Visa. Currency exchange is available at **Estrella del Sur**, Santos Mardones and at Señoret 346. Poor rates.

Puerto Williams *p532*

Post Closes 1900. **Telephone** CTC, Mon-Sat 0930-2230, Sun 1000-1300, 1600-2200.

Argentine Tierra del Fuego

Argentine Tierra del Fuego belongs to the province of Tierra del Fuego, Antártida y Las Islas del Atlántico Sur, the capital of which is the welcoming tourist centre Ushuaia. The population of the Argentine sector is around 85,000, most of whom live in the two towns of Río Grande and Ushuaia. Both bigger and more developed than the Chilean side of the island, it provides good territory for guided explorations of the wilderness. ▸▸ *For listings, see pages 543-552.*

Ins and outs

Getting there The main point of entry is **Aeropuerto Internacional Malvinas Argentinas** ① *4 km from Ushuaia, on a peninsula in the Beagle Channel, T02901-423970, www.tierradel fuego.org.ar/aeropuerto*, which receives daily **flights** from Buenos Aires (four hours), frequent flights from El Calafate and Punta Arenas, as well as weekly flights with army airline **LADE** from many towns in Patagonia. This is by far the easiest way to get to the Argentine side of the island and the view from the plane as you land over jagged mountains onto the quiet channel below is magical. From the airport, a taxi to the centre of town costs US$3. There is another airport at Río Grande with flights to/from Buenos Aires and Ushuaia. **Buses** from mainland Argentina and from Punta Arenas in Chile travel to Río Grande and Ushuaia via Punta Delgada and San Sebastián. There are also buses from Porvenir to Río Grande.

Getting around Buses from Río Grande and Ushuaia are frequent, but are heavily booked in summer. There are abundant tours from Ushuaia to suit most needs, and some great hiking adventures on offer, too. If you fly in and out of Ushuaia, you can get around fine by bus and boat for the national park and visits along the Beagle Channel, including Harberton. However, if you want to visit Lago Fagnano or more remote estancias or hike in places not visited by the many adventure tourism companies, you could consider hiring a car. ▸▸ *See Transport, page 551.*

Río Grande → *Colour map 7, B2.*

Río Grande grew rapidly in the oil boom of the 1970s and suffered when tax benefits were withdrawn, leading to increasing unemployment and emigration and leaving a rather sad, windy town today. It is a sprawling modern coastal town, and the centre for a rural sheep-farming community. The people are friendly but there's little culture, and you're most likely to visit in order to change buses. There are a couple of good places to stay, however, and two small museums: the **Museo de Ciencias Naturales e Historia** ① *El Cano 225, Tue-Fri 0900-1700, Sat and Sun 1500-2000*, and the **Museo de la Ciudad** ① *Alberdi 555, T02964-430414, Tue-Fri 1000-1700*, which recounts the city's history through sheep, missions, pioneers and oil. In the blue-roofed hut on the plaza is the small but helpful **tourist office** ① *Rosales 350, T02964-431324, www.tierradel fuego.org.ar, Mon-Fri 0900-2100, Sat 1000-1700*.

The Salesian mission **La Candelaria** ① *11 km north on Route 3, T02964-421642, Mon-Sat 1000-1230, 1500-1900, Sun 1500-1900, US$2, afternoon tea US$3*, was founded in 1893 by José Fagnano to try to protect the Ona people from gold prospectors and sheep farmers. It now houses displays of natural history and indigenous artefacts, with strawberry plantations, piglets and an aviary.

Building bridges

The story of the first successful missionary to Tierra del Fuego, Thomas Bridges, is one of the most stirring in the whole history of pioneers in Argentina. An orphan from Bristol, Thomas Bridges was so called because he was found as a child under a bridge with a letter 'T' on his clothing. He was adopted by a reverand and, as a young man, was taken to start a Christian mission in wild, uncharted Tierra del Fuego where no white man had survived.

Until his death in 1898, Bridges lived near the Beagle Channel, first creating the settlement of Ushuaia and then Harberton. He devoted his life to working with the Yámanas (Yaghanes) and gave up converting them in favour of compiling a dictionary of their language,

and protecting them from persecution. Thomas's son Lucas (1874-1949), one of six children, spent his early life among the Yámanas and Onas, living and hunting as one of them, learning their language, and even, almost fatally, becoming involved in their blood feuds and magic rituals. Lucas became both defender and protector of the indigenous people whose culture he loved, creating a haven for them at Harberton (see page 541 and Estancia Viamonte (see below), at a time when most sheep farmers were more interested in shooting them. His compelling memoirs, *Uttermost Part of the Earth* (1947) trace the tragic fate of the native population with whom he grew up.

South of Río Grande

A fan of roads spreads out south and west from Río Grande to numerous estancias; these are unpaved and best attempted in a 4WD vehicle. **Estancia Viamonte**, on the coast 40 km south, is a working sheep farm with a fascinating history. Here, Lucas Bridges, son of Tierra del Fuego's first settler, built a home to protect the large tribe of indigenous Onas, who were fast dying out. The estancia is still inhabited by his descendants, who can take you riding and to see the life of the farm. Accommodation is also available. It's highly recommended for an insight into Fuegian life and a cosy place to read *Uttermost Part of the Earth*, see box, above.

The paved road south, Ruta 3, continues across wonderfully open land, more forested than the expanses of Patagonian steppe further north, and increasingly hilly as you near Ushuaia. After around 160 km, you could turn left along a track to the coast, to find **Estancia Cabo San Pablo**, 120 km from Río Grande. This simple working estancia is in a beautiful position, surrounded by native woodland for walking and riding, birdwatching and fishing. It's open all year, but reserve well in advance.

Ruta 3 then climbs high above **Lago Fagnano**, a large expanse of water at the heart of Tierra del Fuego, which straddles the border with Chile. In the small settlement of **Tolhuin** there's a YPF service station just off the main road and a tiny, friendly **tourist office**. Drive into the village to visit the famous bakery **La Unión**, where you can buy all kinds of bread, great *empanadas* and delicious fresh *facturas* (pastries), before heading down to the tranquil lake shore, There's a quiet stretch of beach and a couple of good places to stay.

Further along Ruta 3, about 50 km from Ushuaia, a road to the right swoops down to **Lago Escondido**, a long, fjord-like lake with steep green mountains descending into the water on all sides. There are *cabañas* and a couple of *hosterías*, one with a good restaurant for lunch.

Ushuaia ⬤🅿🅾⛺🅾🅲 ➤ pp543-552. Colour map 7, C2.

Ushuaia's setting is spectacular. Its brightly coloured houses look like toys against the dramatic backdrop of snow-covered Cerro Martial to the north. Opposite are the forbidding peaks of Isla Navarino, and between flows the green Beagle Channel. Sailing these waters, it is easy to imagine what it was like when Darwin arrived here in 1832 and when the Bridges family first settled here in 1871. Although the town has expanded in recent years, sprawling untidily along the coast, Ushuaia still retains the feel of a pioneer town, isolated and expectant. There are lots of places to stay (which fill up entirely in January) a fine museum and some great fish restaurants. There is dramatic landscape to be explored in all directions, with good treks in the Parque Nacional Tierra del Fuego just to the west of the city and more adventurous expeditions into the wild heart of the island, trekking, climbing or riding. There's splendid cross-country skiing nearby in winter, as well as downhill skiing at **Cerro Castor**. And to the east, along a beautiful stretch of coastline is the historic Estancia de Harberton (see page 538), which you can reach by a boat trip along the Beagle Channel.

Tourist information ⓘ *San Martín 674, corner with Fadul, T/F02901-432000, www.tierradelfuego.org.ar, Mon-Fri 0800-2200, Sat, Sun and holidays 0900-2000.* Quite the best tourist office in Argentina. The friendly and helpful staff speak several languages and will find you somewhere to stay, even in the busiest period. They also have a great series of leaflets in English, French, German and Dutch about all the things to see and do, including bus and boat times. There's also an office at the **airport** ⓘ *T02901-423970.* **Tierra del Fuego National Park Office** ⓘ *San Martín 1395, T02901-421315,* has a useful little map of the park.

Background

Missionary Thomas Bridges first established a mission here in 1884 and the fledgling settlement soon attracted pioneers in search of gold. A penal colony, on nearby Staten Island, moved to the town in 1902, and Croatian and Spanish immigrants, together with shipwreck survivors, began to settle here. However, the town remained isolated until planes arrived in 1935. When the prison closed it was replaced by a naval base and, in the 1970s, a wave of new inhabitants arrived, many of them from Buenos Aires, attracted by reduced income taxes and cheap car prices. Now the city is capital of Argentina's most southerly province and, although fishing still plays a key role in the local economy, Ushuaia has become an important tourist centre as the departure point for voyages to Antarctica.

Sights

It's easy to walk around the town in a morning, since all its sights are close together. You'll find banks, restaurants, hotels and shops along calle San Martín, which runs parallel to the shore, a block north of the coast road, Maipú. Boat trips leave from the **Muelle Turístico** (tourist pier) by a small plaza, 25 de Mayo, on the seafront. There are several museums worth looking at if bad weather forces you indoors. The most fascinating is **Museo del Fin del Mundo** ⓘ *on the seafront at Maipú and Rivadavia, T02901-421863, www.tierradel fuego.org.ar/museo, Nov-Apr daily 0900-1900, May-Oct Mon-Sat 1200-1900, US$4,* in the 1912 bank building, which tells the history of the town through a small collection of carefully chosen exhibits on the indigenous groups, missionaries, pioneers and shipwrecks. There's also a stuffed collection of Tierra del Fuego's birdlife and an extensive reference library. Further east, the old prison, Presidio, at the Naval Base, houses the **Museo Marítimo**

ⓘ *Yaganes and Gob Paz, www.museomaritimo.com, daily 1000-2000, US$8,* which has models and artefacts from seafaring days, and, in the cells, the **Museo Penitenciario**, which details the history of the prison. **Museo Yámana** ⓘ *Rivadavia 56, T02901-422874, www.tierra delfuego.org.ar/mundoyamana, daily 1000-2000 (winter 1200-1900), US$2,* has interesting scale models of everyday indigenous life.

For exhilarating views along the Beagle Channel and to Isla Navarino beyond, don't miss a trip on the chair lift up to **Cerro Martial** ⓘ *daily 1000-1800 (winter 1030-1630), US$8.50,* about 7 km behind the town. From the top of the lift, you can walk for 90 minutes through *lenga* forest to Glaciar Martial, where there's limited skiing in winter. There's also a splendid tea shop, *refugio* and *cabañas* at the Cerro. Several companies run minibuses from the corner of Maipú and Roca to the bottom of the chairlift, hourly in summer, US$4 return, last buses return at 1900 and 2100. Otherwise it's a 1½-hour walk from town via Magallanes.

The **Tren del Fin del Mundo** ⓘ *station 8 km west of Ushuaia (bus US$2 from Maipú and Roca, taxi US$3), T02901-431600, www.trendelfindelmundo.com.ar, 50 mins, 2 departures daily in summer, 1 in winter, US$23 return, plus US$8 park entrance,* is the world's southernmost steam train, running new locomotives and carriages on track first laid by prisoners to carry wood to Ushuaia. It travels into the Tierra del Fuego National Park (see page 542) and is an unashamedly touristy experience with relentless commentary in English and Spanish. However, it might be fun for children and is one way of getting into

Ushuaia

Sleeping
Albergue Cruz del Sur 1
Antárctica 2
B&B Nahuel 5
Canal Beagle 7
Cap Polonio 8
Familia Velásquez 11
Freestyle 4
Galeazzi-Basily 12

Hostal Malvinas 13
Hostería Posada Fin
del Mundo 14
La Casa de Tere 6
Lennox 16
Los Troncos 17
Mil810 9
Posada del Duende 10
Tzion 15

Yakush 3

Eating
137 Pizzas & Pastas 12
Bodegón Fueguino 9
Café Bar Banana 6
Café de la Esquina 1
Café Tante Sara 2
El Turco 4

200 metres
200 yards

the national park to start a walk. Sit on the left on the outbound journey for the best views. Tickets are available at the station or from travel agencies in town.

Estancia Harberton

ⓘ *85 km east of Ushuaia (2 hrs' drive), T02901-422742, www.acatushun.org, 15 Oct-15 Apr daily except holidays. Tour of the estancia US$5, museum entrance US$2.*

In a land of extremes and superlatives, Harberton still stands out as special. The oldest estancia in Tierra del Fuego was built in 1886 on a narrow peninsula overlooking the Beagle Channel by the missionary Thomas Bridges (see box, page 538). He was granted the land by President Roca for his work with the indigenous people and for rescuing victims of shipwrecks in the channels. Harberton is named after the Devonshire village where Thomas's wife Mary was born; the farmhouse was pre-fabricated by her father in England and assembled on a spot chosen by the Yámana. The English connection is evident in the neat garden of lawns, shrubs and trees between the jetty and the farmhouse; behind the buildings is a large vegetable garden, a real rarity on the island.

Still operating as a working farm, Harberton is run by Thomas Goodall, great-grandson of the founder. Visitors receive an excellent guided walk (bilingual guides) through protected forest around the estancia, where there are reconstructions of the Yámana dwellings, plus a tour of the impressive **Museo Acatushun**, founded by Thomas' wife, Natalie Goodall. The museum is the result of 23 years' scientific investigation into the area's rich marine life and contains the complete skeletons of dolphins, whales and seals. Tea or lunch (if you reserve ahead) are served in the room overlooking the bay. You can camp free, with permission from the owners, or rent one of the two simple cottages on the shore. There are wonderful walks along the coast, and noticeably more wildlife here than in the Tierra del Fuego National Park, probably owing to the estancia's remoteness. ▸▸ *See Transport, page 552.*

Beagle Channel

A sea trip along the Beagle Channel can be rough but is highly recommended. Excursions leave from the Muelle Turístico in Ushuaia. Destinations include the sea lion colony at **Isla de los Lobos**, **Isla de los Pájaros**, **Les Eclaireurs lighthouse** and the penguin colony at **Isla Martillo**. You can visit Estancia Harberton by boat but always check that your tour actually includes the estancia and not just Harberton Bay. ▸▸ *See Activities and tours, page 548.*

Kaupé **5**
La Cabaña **3**
La Estancia **7**
Martinica **14**
Moustacchio **10**
Parrilla La Rueda **11**
Ramos Generales **18**
Sandwichería Kami **19**
Tía Elvira **13**

Volver **15**

Bars & clubs 🎵
Küar **21**
Lennon Pub **22**
Ushuaia Che **20**

Parque Nacional Tierra del Fuego 💿 » pp543-552.

ⓘ *Park administration: San Martín 1395, Ushuaia, T02901-421315, www.parques nacionales.gov.ar, US$7. Park entrance 11 km west of Ushuaia. Note there are no legal crossing points into Chile from the national park.*

Covering 63,000 ha of mountains, lakes, rivers and deep valleys, this small but beautiful park stretches west to the Chilean border and north from Bahía Lapataia on the Beagle Channel to beyond Lago Fagnano. Large areas are closed to tourists to protect the environment, but there are marvellous walks for every level of fitness. Lower parts of the park are forested with lenga, ñirre and coihue and are rich in birdlife, including geese, the beautiful torrent duck, Magellanic woodpeckers and austral parakeets. Even if you have just a couple of hours to spare, take a bus or taxi to Lago Roca or Bahía Lapataia.

Walking in the park

Senda Costera (6.5 km, three hours each way) This lovely easy walk along the shore of the Beagle Channel gives you the essence of the park: its rocky coastline, edged with a rich forest of beech trees and glorious views of the low islands and steep mountains. Start at **Bahía Ensenada** (where the bus can drop you off and where boats leave for trips to Bahía Lapataia, daily 1000-1700, two hours, US$20, reservation essential). Walk along a well-marked path along the shoreline and then rejoin the road briefly to cross Río Lapataia (ignoring signs to Lago Roca to your right). After crossing the broad green river and a second stretch of water (where there's a small camping spot and the *gendarmería*), it's a pleasant stroll inland to the beautifully tranquil **Bahía Lapataia**, an idyllic spot, with views across the sound.

Lago Roca or Sendo Hito XXIV (4 km, 1½ hours one way). Another easy walk, this time alongside peaceful Lago Roca, where there's a very helpful *guardaparque*, plus camping

Parque Nacional Tierra del Fuego

1 km
1 miles

🚌 Bus stop

and a *confitería*. It takes in lovely pebble beaches and dense forest, with lots of bird life and is especially recommended in the evening, when most visitors have left. Get off the bus at the junction for Lago Roca, turn right along the road to the car park (passing the *guardaparque's* house) and follow the lake side.

Cerro Guanaco (4 km, four hours one way). Starting at the car park for Lago Roca, this is a challenging, steep hike up through forest to a *mirador* with splendid views over Lago Roca, the Beagle Channel and far-off mountains. The ground is slippery after rain: take care and don't rush. Allow plenty of time to return in daylight, especially in winter.

⊙ Argentine Tierra del Fuego listings

For Sleeping and Eating price codes and other relevant information, see pages 35-42.

⊙ Sleeping

Río Grande *p537*
Book ahead, as there are few decent choices. Several estancias offer full board and some, mainly on the northern rivers, have expensive fishing lodges, others offer horse riding: see www.tierradelfuego.org.ar and www.estanciasfueguinas.com.
A Posada de los Sauces, Elcano 839, T02964-432868, www.posadadelossauces.com.ar. By far the best choice. Breakfast included, beautifully decorated and comfortable rooms, good restaurant and cosy bar. Recommended.
B Hotel Isla del Mar, Güemes 963, T02964-422883, www.hotelguia.com/hoteles/isladelmar. Right on the sea shore, looks very bleak in bad weather and is frankly run-down, but cheap, with bathrooms and breakfast included, and the staff are welcoming.
B Villa, Av San Martín 281, T02964-424998, hotelvillarg@hotmail.com. Central, modern, restaurant/confitería, internet, TV, parking, discount given for cash.
C Hotel Argentina, San Martín 64, T02964-422546, hotelargentino@yahoo.com. Quite the best cheap place to stay. Set in a beautifully renovated 1920s building close to the sea with kitchen facilities, a bright sunny dining room and welcoming owner, Graciela, who knows all about the local area. Highly recommended. Parking, Wi-Fi and book exchange. Price per person.

Estancias around Río Grande
LL Estancia María Behety, 15 km from Río Grande. Established in 1897 on a 40-km stretch of river that has become legendary for brown trout fishing. 18 comfortable rooms and good food. At US$5350 per week, this is one of the country's priciest fishing lodges, apparently deservedly so. Reservations through **Fly shop**, www.maribety.com.ar.
L Estancia Rivadvia, 100 km from Río Grande, on route H, www.estanciariva davia.com, T02901-492186. A 10,000-ha sheep farm, owned by descendants of the original Croatian pioneer who built the place. Luxurious accommodation in a splendid house near the mountains and lakes at the heart of Tierra del Fuego, where you can enjoy a trip around the *estancia* to see wild horses and guanacos, good food, and trekking to the trout lake of Chepelmul and Yehuin.
L Estancia Viamonte, some 40 km southeast on the coast, T02964-430861, www.estancia viamonte.com. For an authentic experience of Tierra del Fuego. Built in 1902 by pioneer Lucas Bridges, this working estancia is run by his descendants. You'll be warmly welcomed as their guest, in traditional, beautifully furnished rooms, with comfortable bathrooms, and delicious meals (extra cost). Also a spacious cottage for 7, US$310. Join in the farm activities, read the famous book by blazing fires, ride horses over the estate and completely relax. Warmly recommended. Reserve a week ahead.

Camping
Club Náutico Ioshlelk-Oten, Montilla 1047, 2 km from town on river. Clean, cooking

facilities, camping in heated building in cold weather. YPF petrol station has hot showers.

South of Río Grande *p538*
AL-A Cabañas Khami, T02964-15611243, www.cabaniaskhami.com.ar. Isolated in a lovely spot at the head of the lake. Very comfortable and well-equipped *cabañas*, nicely decorated and with great views of the lake. Good value at US$40 per day for 6. Recommended.

A Hostería Petrel, RN 3, Km 3186, Lago Escondido, T02901-433569, hosteria.petrel@hotmail.com. The only place to stay in this secluded forest position on a tranquil beach of the lake. Decent rooms with bath, and a good restaurant overlooking the lake which serves delicious lamb, open to non-residents. Also has tiny *cabañas* right on the water.

D Parador Kawi Shiken, off the main road on the way to Ushuaia, 4 km south of Tolhuin on RN 3, Km 2940, T02964-424380 . Rustic, with 3 rooms, shared bathrooms, *casa de té* and restaurant. Phone ahead to arrange a *cordero al asador* (barbecued lamb). Horse riding.

D Terrazas del Lago, RN 3, Km 2938, T02964-432300, terrazas@uol.com.ar. A little way from the shore, smart wooden *cabañas*, well decorated, and also a *confitería* and *parrilla*.

F pp Refugio Solar del Bosque, 18 km from Ushuaia, RN 3, Km 3020, Lago Escondido, T02901-421228, solardelbosque@tierradel fuego.org.ar. Further along the road is this basic hostel for walkers, with shared bathrooms in dorms for 4, breakfast included.

Camping
Camping Hain del Lago, T02964-425951, T02964-15603606, robertoberbel@hotmail.com. Lovely views, fireplaces, hot showers, and a *quincho* for when it rains.

Camping La Correntina, T156-05020, 17 km from Tolhuin. In woodland, with bathrooms, and horses for hire.

Ushuaia *p539, map p540*
The tourist office has lists of all accommodation, and can help find you somewhere to stay, but in Jan you must reserve ahead.

L Canal Beagle, Maipú y 25 de Mayo, T02901-432303, www.hotelcanalbeagle.com.ar. ACA hotel (discounts for members), comfortable and well attended, with a small pool, gym, sauna and clear views over the channel from some rooms (others see the container dock), good restaurant.

L Lennox, San Martín 776, T02901-436430, www.lennoxhotel.com.ar. Boutique hotel on the main street, with breakfast, services include internet, hydromassage, TV, frigobar, restaurant and *confitería* on 4th floor.

L Mil810, 25 de Mayo 245, T02901-437710, www.hotel1810.com. City hotel with 30 standard rooms, 1 with disabled access, no restaurant but breakfast and *confitería*, all rooms with flat-screen TV, minibar, safe, quite small but cosy, calm colours, good views, business centre and multiple-use room where you can hang out while waiting for your flight.

AL Cap Polonio, San Martín 746, T02901-422140, www.hotelcappolonio.com.ar. A smart central modern city hotel with very comfortable minimalist rooms, all with bath, phone, TV, Wi-Fi; some have views of the canal. There's a chic restaurant downstairs.

B Hostal Malvinas, Gob Deloqui 615, T/F02901-422626, www.hostal malvinas.net. Neat, comfortable if rather small rooms with excellent bathrooms, and good views, in this central and well-run town house hotel. A basic breakfast is included, and all-day tea and coffee. Recommended.

B Hostería Posada Fin del Mundo, Gob Valdez 281, T02901-437345, www.posada findelmundo.com.ar. A relaxed family atmosphere in a quiet residential area close to centre, homely rooms and friendly staff. Good value.

C La Casa de Tere, Rivadavia 620, T02901-422312, www.lacasadetere.com.ar. Shared bath, with breakfast, home-made bread and cake, use of kitchen, some rooms get lots of sun, singles, doubles and triples, hot water, helpful owner. Price per person.

C Tzion, Gob Valdez 468, T02901-432290, tzion_byb@hotmail.com. B&B with 3 rooms, 1 with bath (**B**), high above town, 10 mins' walk from centre, nice family atmosphere (contact Daniel Pirruccio at **Tolkar Turismo**), cheaper in low season, laundry service, English and French spoken.

D B&B Nahuel, 25 de Mayo 440, T02901-423068. byb_nahuel@yahoo.com.ar. A family house, views over channel, with brightly painted and tastefully decorated rooms, and a lovely welcome from the charming and talkative owner. Great value. Recommended.

Outside the city

LL Cabañas del Beagle, Las Aljabas 375, T02901-432785/T1-551 1323, www.cabaniasdelbeagle.com. 3 rustic-style cabins 1.3 km above the city, fully equipped with kitchen, hydromassage, fireplace, heating, phone, self-service breakfast, very comfortable, personal attention.

LL Finisterris Lodge Relax, Monte Susana, Ladera Este, 7 km from city, T02901-1561 2121 (mob), Buenos Aires T011-5917 8288, www.finisterris.com. In 17 ha of forest, 5-star luxury in individual cabins, with top-of-the-range fittings, hydromassage and private spa, rustic style but spacious, 'home-from-home' atmosphere, 24-hr attention from owner, given mobile phone on arrival. Meals can be ordered in, or private chef and sommelier can be booked for you.

LL Las Hayas, Martial 1650 (road to Glaciar Martial), T02901-430710, www.lashayas.com.ar. A 5-star hotel, in a spectacular setting, high up on the mountainside with outstanding views over the Beagle Channel. Light, tasteful, impeccable rooms. Breakfast included and use of pool, sauna, gym, squash court, 9-hole golf course, shuttle from town in high season, and transfer from airport. A lovely calm atmosphere, friendly staff, recommended.

LL Los Cauquenes, at Bahía Cauquen, C Reinamora 3462, T02901-441300, www.los cauquenes.com. High-quality 5-star hotel overlooking Beagle Channel, room price depends on room size and view, with spa, very tastefully decorated, prize-winning restaurant with US$13 lunch menu, regional food on dinner menu.

LL Los Yámanas, Costa de los Yámanas 2850, western suburbs, T02901-445960,

www.hotelyamanas.com.ar. In the same group as Canoero tour operator, all rooms with Channel view, spacious, well-decorated with DirectTV, Wi-Fi, hydromassage, fitness centre, spa and conference centre in wooded grounds, shuttle to town. Very pleasant.

LL-L Cumbres del Martial, Luis F Martial 3560 (7 km from town), T02901-424779, www.cumbresdelmartial.com.ar. A charming cottage by a mountain stream in the forested slopes of Martial range with comfortable rooms and balconies looking out to the Beagle Channel. Homely, relaxed and in a secluded location, there are also 4 *cabañas* with fireplace and big windows opening on to the woods. Superb fondues are served.

L Tierra de Leyendas, Tierra de Vientos 2448, T02901-443565, www.tierradeleyendas.com.ar. Western suburbs. 5 comfortable rooms with views of the Beagle Channel, or the mountains at the back, 1 room with jacuzzi, others with shower, excellent restaurant serving regional specialities, open only for guests for breakfast and dinner. Free internet, no cable TV, but DVDs, living room with games, library, deck overlooking Río Pipo's outflow. Only for non-smokers. Recommended. In **Rusticae** chain.

Hostels

D-E Antárctica, Antártida Argentina 270, T02901-435774, www.antarcticahostel.com. Price per person. Welcoming and central hostel with a spacious chill-out room and an excellent bar open till late. Dorms are rather basic and cramped, with larger private doubles (**C**). Cooking facilities, breakfast and the use of internet are included. Bikes for hire (US$8.50 per day).

E Freestyle, Gob Paz 866, T02901-432874, www.ushuaiafreestyle.com. Price per person. Very busy, good, central hostel, with laundry (US$3), TV room, DVDs and pool table. Also has doubles with bath (**B**), TV and kitchenette, which will move to new **Alto Andino** hotel, which is being built in front.

E-F Yakush, Piedrabuena and San Martín, T02901-435807, www.hostelyakush.com.ar. Price per person. A very well-run hostel with spacious rooms to share and a few private ones, a light kitchen and dining room, and a steep garden with views.

F Albergue Cruz del Sur, Deloqui 636, T02901-434099, www.xdelsur.com.ar. Relaxed Italian-owned *hostal* with a very friendly atmosphere, cosy dorms, use of kitchen and a lovely quiet library. Price per person. Recommended.

F Posada del Duende, Deloqui 1482, T432562, posadadelduende@hotmail.com. Price per person. Also has doubles with bath (**C**), kitchen, email, hot water and heating, laundry service.

Private homes

C Galeazzi-Basily, Gob Valdez 323, T02901-423213, www.avesdelsur.com.ar. The best option by far. A cosy, stylish family home, with welcoming owners who speak excellent English, in a pleasant residential area 5 blocks from the centre. Delicious breakfast included. There are also excellent-value *cabañas* (**A**) in the garden. Highly recommended.

C-D Familia Velásquez, Juana Fadul 361, T02901-421719, almayo@arnet.com.ar. Basic rooms with breakfast in cosy cheerful pioneer family home, where the kind owners look after you.

D Los Troncos, Gob Paz 1344, T02901-421895, lostroncos@speedy.com.ar. A welcoming house run by charming Mrs Clarisa Ulloa, with simple rooms, breakfast, TV and free internet.

Estancias

L Estancia Rolito, Route 21 (ex 'A'), Km 14, T02901-437351, www.tierradelfuego.org.ar/rolito. A magical place on the wooded heart of the island, with cosy accommodation in traditionally built houses, and friendly hosts Annie and Pepe, booked through **Turismo de Campo**, www.turismodecampo.com. Also day visits with recommended walks or horse rides in mature southern beech forest.

A-B Harberton, T02901-422742, estancia harberton@tierradelfuego.org.ar. 2 impeccably restored historical buildings on the tranquil lakeside, giving space and privacy from the

main house. Simple accommodation, but wonderful views, and beautiful walks on the estancia's coastline. 90 km east of Ushuaia, along RN 3 and 33, a spectacular drive. Open mid-Oct to mid-Apr.

Camping

Camping del Solar del Bosque, RN 3, Km 19, heading to Río Grande, T02901-435276 . US$3 per person. At a small ski resort that in summer offers plenty of activities. Hot showers, and also a large dorm with good facilities.

Camping Haruwen, Haruwen Winter Sports complex (Km 36), en route to Río Grande, T02901-431099. US$4 per tent, electricity, shop, bar, restaurant in a winter sports centre, open also in summer for outdoor activities.

Parque Nacional Tierra del Fuego
p542, map p542
Camping

Camping Lago Roca, T02901-433313 (entry fee to park US$ 13), 21 km from Ushuaia. By the forested shore of tranquil Lago Roc, this is a beautiful site with good facilities, reached by bus Jan-Feb, expensive small shop, *cafetería*, US$4 per person. Tents and sleeping bags for hire.

There are also various sites with no facilities: Bahía Ensenada Camping, 14 km from Ushuaia; Río Pipo, 16 km from Ushuaia, and **Camping Las Bandurrias**, Cauquenes and **Camping Laguna Verde**, 20 km from Ushuaia.

🍴 Eating

Río Grande *p537*
🍴 El Rincón de Julio, next to Posada de los Sauces, Elcano 800 block. For excellent *parrilla*.
🍴 La Nueva Colonial, Av Belgrano and Lasserre. Half a block from the plaza, next to **Casino Club**, where the locals go for delicious pasta in a warm family atmosphere.
🍴 La Nueva Piamontesa, Belgrano y Mackinlay, T02964-426332, to the side of the charming 24-hr grocery store. Cheap set menus and also delivers food.

⍦ La Rueda, Islas Malvinas 998, 1st floor. Excellent *parrilla* in a welcoming place. Has another branch on O'Higgins 200 block.

Cafés

El Roca, Espora entre Av San Martín y Rosales, ½ a block from Plaza. *Confitería* and bar in the historic original cinema, good and popular.
Tío Willy, Alberdi entre Espora y 9 de Julio. Serves *cerveza artesanal* (microbrewery).

South of Río Grande *p538*

La Unión, Tolhuin. Famous bakery. Open 24 hrs, daily except Mon 2400-Tue 0600. On the same block there are pizzas at Pizzería Amistad, and more of a range at La Posada de los Ramírez, a cosy restaurant and *rotisería*, open weekends, lunch and dinner.

Ushuaia *p539, map p540*

⍦⍦⍦ Bodegón Fueguino, San Martín 859, T02901-431972. In a stylishly renovated 1896 house in the main street, this stands out from the crowd by serving *picadas* with delicious and imaginative dips, good roast lamb, and unusual *cazuelas*, *picadas* and dips. A buzzy atmosphere and welcoming staff.
⍦⍦⍦ Kaupé, Roca 470 y Magallanes, T02901-437396. The best restaurant in town, with exquisite food. King crab and meat dishes all beautifully served in a lovely environment – a great treat.
⍦⍦⍦ La Cabaña, Luis F Martial 3560, T02901-434699. Open every day. The cosy restaurant and tea room of **Cumbres del Martial** hotel serves several excellent types of fondue for dinner, that may be preceded at teatime by a rich list of cakes, scones and brownies.
⍦⍦⍦ Tía Elvira, Maipú 349, T02901-424725. Open Sun. Retains its reputation for excellent seafood, with a good choice of fresh fish and views over the channel.
⍦⍦⍦ Volver, Maipú 37, T02901-423977. In an atmospheric old 1898 house, with ancient newspaper all over the walls (read intriguing fragments while you eat). Cosy stoves and an intimate atmosphere. Delicious salmon and *arroz con mariscos*.

⍦⍦⍦-⍦⍦ La Estancia, San Martín 253, T02901-432700. Cheery and good-value *parrilla tenedor libre*. Packed in high season.
⍦⍦⍦-⍦⍦ Parrilla La Rueda, San Martín and Rivadavia, T02901-436540. A good *tenedor libre* for beef, lamb and a great range of salads. US$13 with dessert per person.
⍦⍦ 137 Pizzas and Pastas, San Martín 137. A brightly lit functional place with tasty filling food. Also takeaway *empanadas* and pizzas.
⍦⍦ Moustacchio, San Martín 272 and Gob Godoy, T02901-423308. Long-established, good for seafood, cosy atmosphere. Next door is a cheaper all-you-can-eat sister restaurant.
⍦⍦-⍦ Martinica, San Martín entre Antártida Argentina and Yaganes. Open 1130-1500, 2030-0000. Cheap, small, busy, sit at the bar facing the *parrilla* and point to your favourite beef cut. Takeaway (T02901-432134) and good meals of the day, pizzas and *empanadas*.
⍦ El Turco, San Martín 1410. One of few good and cheap places, popular with locals, serves generous *milanesas*, pastas, steaks and pizzas.

Cafés

Café Bar Banana, San Martín 273, T02901-424021. Quite small, always busy, with a pool table at the back, offers good fast food, such as burgers, small pizzas, puddings, breakfasts and an all-day *menú* for US$7.50.
Café de la Esquina, San Martín y 25 de Mayo. Lunch choices, specials, sandwiches, tortas, *picadas*, *lomitos*, café and bar. Open for 15 years.
Café Tante Sara, Fadul and San Martín. The most appealing of the cafés on San Martín. Smart and modern with an airy feel, serving good coffee and tasty sandwiches.
Ramos Generales, Maipú 749, T02901-424317, www.ramosgeneralesushuaia.com. An old warehouse, with wooden floor and shelves and a collection of historic objects and dusty ledgers. Sells breads, pastries, wines and drinks, cold cuts, sandwiches, salads, ice cream and coffee. Breakfasts till 1300, teas 1300-2000. Not cheap but atmospheric. Recommended.
Sandwichería Kami, San Martín 54. Open 0800-2130. Friendly, simple sandwich shop, selling rolls, baguettes and *pan de miga*.

Going further ... Antarctica

Ushuaia is the starting point for a number of excellent expeditions to Antarctica. These usually run from mid-November to mid-March and last between eight and 11 days, taking in the Antarctic peninsula and the Wedell sea. Some offer extra activities, such as camping and kayaking. Its not exactly a luxury cruise: trips are usually made in non-tourist boats used for scientific exploration, so the accommodation is informal and simple and the food is reasonable but not excessive. The expedition leader organizes lectures during the three-day journey to reach the Antarctic, with at least two disembarkations a day in a zodiac to see icebergs and penguins. When selecting your trip, bear in mind that there's most ice in November and December, more baby penguins in January and February, and whales in March. The landscape, however, is always impressive.

A longer trip of 18 to 19 days, combines the Antarctic with the Malvinas/Falklands and South Georgia islands. There are weekly departures in season. It's worth turning up in Ushuaia and asking the major tour operators for availability; there's a 30% discount if you book last minute in Ushuaia.

For further information and bookings contact Rumbo Sur, Turismo de Campo and All Patagonia, see Tour operators, below. Seats can also sometimes be purchased on Chilean Naval supply vessels heading for Antarctica, though this requires patience and a long period of waiting in Punta Arenas.

🍸 Bars and clubs

Ushuaia *p539, map p540*
Küar, Av Perito Moreno 2232, east of town. Great setting by the sea, restaurant, bar and brewery open from 1800.
Lennon Pub, Maipú 263. A lively friendly atmosphere and live music.
Ushuaia Che, San Martín 452. A lively place with Mexican and Brazilian food.
For a bit of Irish loving try **Galway Irish Pub**, Lasserre 108, or **Dublin Bar Irlandés**, 9 de Julio. Both are favourites of locals and tourists alike.

✸ Festivals and events

Río Grande *p537*
Jan The sheep-shearing festival is definitely worth seeing, if you're in the area.
2nd week of Feb Rural exhibition with handicrafts.
1st week of Mar Shepherd's day, with impressive sheepdog display.

20-21 Jun Winter solstice, the longest night, has fireworks and ice-skating contests, though this is a very inhospitable time of year.

⛰ Activities and tours

Río Grande *p537*
Mariani Travel Rosales 259, T02964-426010, mariani@netcombbs.com.ar.
Tecni Austral, Moyano 516, T02964-432885. Bus tickets to Ushuaia.

Ushuaia *p539, map p540*
Boat trips and cruises
All short boat trips leave from the Muelle Turístico. Take your time to choose the size and style of boat you want. Representatives from the offices are polite and helpful. All have a morning and afternoon sailing and include Isla de los Lobos, Isla de los Pájaros and Les Eclaireurs lighthouse, with guides and some form of refreshment. Note that weather conditions may affect sailings, prices can change and that port tax is not included.

Barracuda, T02901-437233, barracuda@
speedy.com.ar. On a lovely old motor yacht, the
first tourist boat in Ushuaia, US$32; their other
boat, Lanín, includes Isla Bridges, US$36; all trips
include a discount at the **Acuario**.

Canoero, T02901-433893, losyamanas@
arnet.com.ar. Catamarans for 60-100 passengers, 2½-hr trips to the 3 main sites and Isla
Bridges, US$36. Thay also have a 5-hr trip
almost daily to the Pingüinera on Isla Martillo
near Estancia Harberton (Oct-Mar only). Boats
stay for 1 hr, but you cannot land on Martillo.
Passengers can return to Ushuaia by bus: US$65
without stops on bus ride, US$76 with stops.

Paludine, T02901-434865, navegandoelfin
delmundo@gmail.com. Fast boats with 12
passengers, US$40. Also has all-day trips on a
sailing boat, 1000-1700 with lunch, prepared
during a trek on Bridges, US$56 all inclusive.

Patagonia Adventure Explorer, T02901-
1546 5842, www.patagoniaadvent.com.ar.
Has a sailing boat and motor boats for the
standard trip, plus Isla Bridges: US$50 sailing,
US$40 motoring. Good guides.

Pira-Tour, T02901-1560 4646, piratour@
gmail.com. Runs 2-3 buses a day to Harberton,
from where a boat goes to the Pingüinera on
Isla Martillo: 15 people allowed to land (maximum 45 per day – the only company licensed
to do this). US$85 for a morning tour, including
lunch at Harberton and entry to Acatushún
museum; US$70 for afternoon tour.

Tres Marías, T02901-421987, www.tresmarias
web.com. The only company licensed to visit
Isla H, which has archaeological sites,
cormorants, other birds and plants. Also has
sailing boat, no more than 10 passengers;
specialist guide, café on board, US$40 on
Tres Marías, US$50 on sailing boat.

Also **Rumbo Sur** and **Tolkeyen**; see
Tour operators, below.

Sea trips and Antarctica Ushuaia is the
starting point, or the last stop, en route to
Antarctica for several cruises from Oct-Mar
that usually sail for 9-21 days along the
western shores of the Antarctic peninsula
and the South Shetland Islands. Other trips

include stops at **Falkland/Malvinas**
archipelago and at South Georgia. Agencies
sell 'last-minute tickets', but the price is
entirely dependent on demand (available
1 week before sailing). Coordinator for
trips is **Turismo Ushuaia**, Gob Paz 865,
T02901-436003, www.ushuaiaturismo
evt.com.ar, which operates with IAATO
members only. Approximate prices:
1-day flight, US$3000, 8 passengers
from Punta Arenas, 2-day plane and
ship from Punta Arenas, US$9000,
all-ship tours from about US$4000.
To **Chile Cruceros Australis**, www.australis.
com, operates 2 luxury cruise ships between
Ushuaia and Punta Arenas, with a visit to
Cabo de Hornos, frequently recommended.

Ushuaia Boating, Deloqui 302 y Godoy,
T436153 (or at the Muelle Turístico), T02901-
436193, ushuaiaboating@argentina.com.ar.
Operates all year round a channel crossing
to **Puerto Navarino** (Isla Navarino), 20-90
mins depending on weather, and then bus
to **Puerto Williams**, 1 hr, US$100 1-way,
plus US$6.60 taxes. At Muelle AFASYN, near
the old airport, T02901-435805, ask about
possible crossings with a club member to
Puerto Williams, about 4 hrs, or if any
foreign sailing boat is going to Cabo de
Hornos or Antarctica. From Puerto Williams
a ferry goes once a week to Punta Arenas.

Fishing
The lakes and rivers of Tierra del Fuego offer
great fishing for brown and rainbow trout
and stream trout in Lago Fagnano. Both fly-
casting and spinning are allowed, and permits
must be bought. The trout season is 1 Nov-
Apr (though this varies slightly every year),
licences US$10 per day (an extra fee is charged
for some rivers and lakes). Contact **Asociación
de Caza y Pesca**, Maipú 822, cazapescush@
infovia.com.ar. Mon, Wed, Fri 1700-2100 and
they sell licences and are very helpful.

Hiking and climbing
Club Andino, Fadul 50, T02901-422335,
www.clubandinoushuaia.com.ar. For advice,

Mon-Fri 1000-1200, 1400-2030. Sells maps and trekking guidebooks; free guided walks once in a month in summer; also offers classes, eg yoga, dancing, karate-do and has exercise bikes. The winter sports resorts along Ruta 3 (see below) are an excellent base for summer trekking and many arrange excursions.
Nunatak, 25 de Mayo 296, T02901-430329, www.nunatakadventure.com. Organizes treks, canoeing, mountain biking and 4WD trips to lagos Escondido and Fagnano.

Horse riding
Centro Hípico, Ruta 3, Km 3021, T02901-443996/T1556 9099 (mob), www.centrohipico ushuaia.com.ar. Rides through woods, on Monte Susana, along coast and through river, 2 hrs, US$35; 4-hr ride with light lunch, US$70; 7-hr ride with *asado*, US$105. Gentle well-cared-for horses; all guides have first-aid training. Very friendly and helpful. All rides include transfer from town and insurance. Hats provided for children; disabled children welcome. They can arrange long-distance rides of several days, eg on Península Mitre.

Tour operators
All agencies charge the same fees for excursions; ask the tourist office for a complete list: Tierra del Fuego National Park, 4 hrs, US$30 (entry fee US$6.65 extra); Lagos Escondido and Fagnano, 7 hrs, US$45 without lunch. With 3 or 4 people it might be worth hiring a *remise* taxi.
All Patagonia, Juana Fadul 40, T02901-433622, www.allpatagonia.com. Trekking, ice climbing, and tours; trips to Cabo de Hornos and Antarctica.
Canal, 9 de Julio 118, local 1, T02901-437395, www.canalfun.com. Huge range of activities, trekking, canoeing, riding, 4WD excursions. Recommended.
Comapa, San Martín 245, T02901-430727, www.comapa.com. Conventional tours and adventure tourism, bus tickets to Punta Arenas and Puerto Natales, trips to Antarctica, agents for **Curceros Australis** and **Navimag** ferries for Puerto Natales–

Puerto Montt (10% ISIC discount for **Navimag**). **Hertz** also here.
Compañía de Guías de Patagonia, San Martín 628, T02901-437753, T1549 3288 (mob), www.companiadeguias.com.ar. The best agency for walking guides, expeditions for all levels, rock and ice climbing (training provided), also diving, sailing, riding, 7-day crossing of Tierra del Fuego on foot and conventional tours. Recommended.
Límite Vertical, T02901-1560 0868, www.limiteverticaltdf.com.ar. 4WD adventures off-road to the shores of lagos Escondido and Fagnano, taking logging trails and *ripio* roads, seeing beaver damage in the forests, etc. Lunch is an *asado* at an old saw mill; similar tours by other companies stop for lunch on shore of Fagnano. Good fun.
Rumbo Sur, San Martín 350, T02901-422275, www.rumbosur.com.ar. Flights, buses, conventional tours on land and sea, plus Antarctic expeditions, mid-Nov to mid-Mar, English spoken.
Tolkar, Roca 157, T02901-431412, www.tolkarturismo.com.ar. Flights, bus tickets to Argentina and Chile, conventional and adventure tourism, canoeing and mountain biking to Lago Fagnano.
Tolkeyen, San Martín 1267, T02901-437073, www.tolkeyenpatagonia.com. Bus and flight tickets, catamaran trips (50-300 passengers), including to Harberton (Mon, Wed, Fri, US$65) and Parque Nacional, large company.
Travel Lab, San Martín 1444, T02901-436555, travellabush@speedy.com.ar. Conventional and unconventional tours, mountain biking, trekking, etc, English and French spoken, helpful.
Turismo de Campo, Fuegia Basket 414, T/F02901-437351, www.turismode carnpo.com. Adventure tourism, English- and French-speaking guides, boat and trekking trips in the national park, birdwatching, sailing and trips to Antarctica.

Winter sports
Ushuaia is becoming popular as a winter resort with 11 centres for skiing, snowboarding and husky sledging.

Cerro Castor complex, Ruta 3, Km 27, T02901-499301, www.cerro castor.com, is the only centre for alpine skiing, with 24 km of pistes, powder snow and an 800-m vertical drop. Attractive centre with complete equipment rental, also for snowboarding and snowshoeing.

The other centres along Ruta 3 at Km 18-36 east of Ushuaia offer excellent cross-country skiing (and alternative activities in summer). **Kawi Shiken at Las Cotorras**, Ruta 3, Km 26, T02901-444152, T02901-1551 9497 (mob), www.tierradelfuego.org.ar/hugo flores, specializes in sled dogs, with 100 Alaskan and Siberian huskies: 2-km ride on snow US$20, 2-hr trips with meal US$56. In summer offers 2-km rides in a dog cart, US$13.50.
Tierra Mayor, 20 km from town, T02901-423240, or T02901-155 13463, is the largest and recommended. In a beautiful wide valley between steep-sided mountains, offering half- and full-day excursions on sledges with huskies, as well as cross-country skiing and snow-shoeing. Equipment hire and restaurant.

⊖ Transport

Book ahead in summer, as flights fill up fast. In winter, poor weather often causes delays. Passport needed to buy tickets.

Río Grande *p537*
Air
The airport is 4 km west of town, T02964-420600. A taxi to the centre costs US$2. To **Buenos Aires**, Aerolíneas Argentinas, San Martín 607, T02901-424467, daily, 3½ hrs direct. LADE flies to **Ushuaia**, once a week and to other Patagonian towns.

Bus
Buses leave from the terminal Elcano and Güemes, T02964-420997, or from the office of Tecni Austral, Moyano 516, T02964-430610. To **Porvenir** (Chile), 5 hrs, Gesell, Wed and Sun 0800, US$10, passport and luggage control at San Sebastián. To **Punta Arenas**

(Chile), via Punta Delgada, 10 hrs, Pacheco, Tue, Thu, Sat 0730, US$16. To **Río Gallegos** for connections to **El Calafate**, Tecni Austral, 3 times a week, US$15. To **Ushuaia**, Tecni Austral, 3-4 hrs, 2 daily (heavily booked in summer), US$14; also Tolkeyen, US$8.

Ushuaia *p539, map p540*
Air
Schedules change from season to season, so call airline offices for times and prices: Aerolíneas Argentinas, Roca 116, T02901-422267, www.aerolineas.com.ar; Aerovías DAP, 25 de Mayo 64, T02901-431110; LADE, Lasserre 445, T02901-422968 www.lade.com.ar.

Aerolíneas and LADE fly to **Buenos Aires**, 3½-5 hrs depending on whether service is direct, and **El Calafate**, 1¼ hrs. Also flights to **Río Gallegos**, 1 hr, and **Río Grande**, 1 hr, but check with agents. To **Punta Arenas** (Chile), Aerovías DAP, 1 hr.

Bus
Long distance Buses arrive at offices around town: Tecni Austral/Tolkar, Roca 157, T02901-431412; Líder, Gob Paz 921, T02901-436421; Tolkeyen, Maipú 237, T02901-437073. To **Buenos Aires**, 36 hrs, US$72, TAC, Don Otto, El Pingüino and Transportadora Patagónica. To **Río Grande**, 4 hrs, Tecni Austral and Líder, both US$10, 2 daily; Tolkeyen, US$11. No through services from Ushuaia to **Río Gallegos**; instead, go to Río Grande, and change (total 8-10 hrs); book a ticket for the journey with Tolkar in Ushuaia, US$18.

To **Punta Arenas** (Chile), via Punta Delgada (15-min ferry crossing), 12 hrs, Tecni Austral, Mon, Wed, Fri 0600, US$30; Tolkeyen/Pacheco, Tue, Thu, Sat, 0630, US$36; also less frequent via **Porvenir**, 12 hrs (2½-hr ferry crossing), US$52.

Local Ebenezer and Bella Vista, daily to **Lago Escondido**, US$10 return, and **Lago Fagnano**, US$13. In summer, various companies, hourly to **Lago Roca**, US$3 return, and **Bahía Lapataia**, US$9, from the tourist pier; last return 2000/2100. **Ebenezer and Gonzalo** to the **Fin del Mundo station** (see page 540) 0800, 0900, 1400; return 1700, US$4.

Urban buses from west to east across town, most stops along Maipú, US$0.45. Tourist office provides a list of minibus companies that run daily from town (stops along Maipú) to nearby attractions. To the national park: in summer buses and minibuses leave from the bus stop on Maipú at the bottom of Fadul. Pasarella, 9 a day from 0800, last back 1900, US$11.50 return, US$13.30 to Lapataia; Ebenezer 8 a day from 0830, last back 2000. From same bus stop, many other *colectivos* go to the Tren del Fin del Mundo, Lago Escondido, Lago Fagnano and Glaciar Martial, leave when full. For Harberton, check the notice boards at the station at Maipú y Fadul.

Car hire
Most companies charge US$50 per day including insurance and 150 km per day. **Europcar**, Av Belgrano 423, T02901-430365, www.europcar.com. Localiza, San Martín 642, T02901-430191.

Taxi
Remise Carlitos, T02901-422222; Tienda Leon, San Martín 995, T02901-422222.

Estancia Harberton *p541*
Access by car is along a good unpaved road which branches off Route 3, 40 km east of Ushuaia. Marvellous views en route but no petrol beyond Ushuaia. **Boat** trips twice weekly in summer from the Muelle Turístico, US$25 for a day trip. Daily **minibuses**, Bella Vista and Lautaro, from Maipú and Juana Fadul, US$16 return. **Tours**, US$42 plus entrance.

❶ Directory

Río Grande *p537*
Banks 4 banks with ATMs on San Martín between 100 and 300. **Post office** Piedrabuena y Ameghino. **Telephone** *Centro de llamada* at San Martín 170 and 458.

Ushuaia *p539, map p540*
Banks ATMs are plentiful along San Martín. Changing TCs is difficult but possible at Banco de Tierra del Fuego, San Martín 396. **Consulate** Chile, Malvinas Argentinas and Jainen, Casilla 21, T02901-421279. **Internet and telephone** Cyber cafés and *centros de llamada* along San Martín. **Post office** San Martín, Mon-Fri 0900-1300, 1700-1900, Sat 0830-1200.

Contents

Footprint features

Chilean Pacific Islands

At a glance

◉ **Getting around** Walking and by boat on Juan Fernández; walking or hiring a car on Easter Island.

◉ **Time required** 3 days to a week for each island.

◑ **Weather** Warm and humid with occasional rain all year round.

✕ **When not to go** Juan Fernández can be pretty wet in winter (Jun-Aug).

Far out in the Pacific are two Chilean island possessions; the Juan Fernández Islands, famed for Alexander Selkirk's enforced stay in the 17th century (the inspiration for Defoe's *Robinson Crusoe*), and the Polynesian island of Rapa Nui, better known as Easter Island, the most isolated inhabited spot on earth. Both possess dramatic views of the Pacific. Juan Fernández is famous for the huge cliffs that rise sheer from the ocean, while Easter Island is home to hundreds of mysterious and imposing *mo'ai*. Although the cost of getting to these islands is prohibitive for many visitors, both can be reached relatively easily by air from Santiago.

Islas Juan Fernández

→ Phone code: 032. Colour map 3, B2. Population: 500.

Situated 667 km west of Valparaíso, this group of small volcanic islands is a national park administered by CONAF and was declared a UN World Biosphere Reserve in 1977. There are three islands: Isla Alejandro Selkirk (4952 ha), the largest; Isla Robinson Crusoe (4794 ha); and Isla Santa Clara (221 ha), the smallest. The islands enjoy a mild climate and the vegetation is rich and varied: the Juan Fernández palm, previously used widely for handicrafts, is now a protected species, but the sandalo (sandalwood tree), once the most common tree on the islands, is now extinct owing to its overuse for perfumes. Fauna includes wild goats, hummingbirds and seals. The islands are famous for langosta de Juan Fernández *(a pincerless lobster) that is prized on the mainland. In summer, a boat goes once a month between Robinson Crusoe and Alejandro Selkirk if the langosta catch warrants it, so you can visit either for a few hours or a whole month.* ➤➤ *For listings, see pages 556-557.*

Background

The islands are named after João Fernández, a Portuguese explorer in the service of Spain, who was the first European to visit them (in 1574). For the next 150 years, they were frequented by pirates and *corsairs* resting up before attacking Spanish America. In 1704, Alexander Selkirk, a Scottish sailor, quarrelled with his captain and was put ashore from HMS *Cinque Ports* on what is now Isla Robinson Crusoe, where he stayed alone until 1709, when he was picked up by the *Duke*; his experience inspired *Robinson Crusoe*.

From 1750 the Spanish took steps to defend the archipelago, founding San Juan Bautista and building seven fortresses. During the Wars of Independence the islands were used as a penal colony for Chilean independence leaders captured after the Battle of Rancagua. In 1915, two British destroyers, HMS *Kent* and *Glasgow* cornered the German cruiser, *Dresden*, in Bahía Cumberland. The German vessel was scuttled and still lies on the bottom; a monument on shore commemorates the event and, nearby, unexploded shells are embedded in the cliffs. Some of the German crew are buried in the cemetery.

Isla Robinson Crusoe

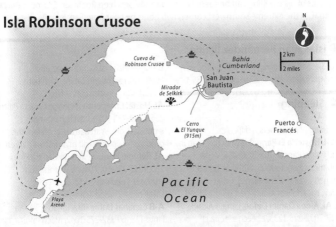

Legends of buried pirate treasure have abounded over the years and several attempts have been made to find it. In recent years a team using a Chilean-built robot with a penetrative sensor claimed to have discovered signs of the treasure, leading to massive media interest, but so far have failed to unearth anything of interest.

Ins and outs

Getting there The best time for a visit is between October and March. Air taxis from Santiago land on an airstrip in the west of the island, from where passengers are taken by boat to San Juan Bautista. (The boat transfer should be included in the price of the air ticket.) There are also boats to the islands from Valparaíso.

Getting around Isla Robinson Crusoe is small enough to explore on foot. You will need a boat on the other islands. Take insect repellent.

Tourist information San Juan Bautista has a **CONAF office** ① *Mon-Fri 0800-1800*, with information and advice on the island.

Sights

The only settlement in the archipelago is **San Juan Bautista**, a fishing village of simple houses. Located on Bahía Cumberland on the north coast of Isla Robinson Crusoe, it has a church, schools, post office, police station and radio station. San Juan Bautista is overlooked by the remains of the **Fuerte Santa Bárbara**, the largest of the Spanish fortresses, while in the village itself is a **Casa de la Cultura** ① *Mon-Fri 1000-1300, 1700-2100*, with exhibition rooms. Nearby are the **Cuevas de los Patriotas**, home to the deported Chilean independence leaders. The island's other famous cave, where Alexander Selkirk spent his years of isolation, is 4 km north west of the village and can be visited by boat.

South of the village is the **Mirador de Selkirk**, the hill where Selkirk lit his signal fires. A plaque was set in the rock at the lookout point by British naval officers from HMS *Topaze* in 1868; nearby is a more recent plaque placed by Selkirk's descendants. The mirador is the only easy pass between the north and south sides of the island. A footpath leads further south to the anvil-shaped **El Yunque**, 915 m, the highest peak on the island, where Hugo Weber, a survivor from the *Dresden*, lived as a hermit for 12 years: some remains of his dwelling can be seen. The only sandy beach on Robinson Crusoe is **Playa Arenal**, in the extreme southwest corner, two hours by boat from San Juan Bautista.

① Islas Juan Fernández listings

For Sleeping and Eating price codes and other relevant information, see Essentials pages 35-42.

◉ Sleeping

Lodging with villagers is difficult.

LL-L Hostería El Pangal, east of San Juan in the Caleta Pangal, T02-273 1458, www. robinsoncrusoetours.cl. With half board; owned by one of the airlines. Great views, pool, bar and restaurant, best on the island.

L-AL Aldea Daniel Defoe, Larraín Alcalde 449, T032-275 1233, ebeeche@terra.cl.

B singles. Half board (full board also available), rooms and cabins, with bath, bar, laundry service, tours offered.

AL Hostal Charpentier, Ignacio Carrera Pinto 256, T032-275 1020, hostalcharpentier @hotmail.com. With bath, kitchen facilities, *cabañas* for up to 4, half board, tours offered.

AL Refugio Náutico, Ignacio Carrera Pinto 280, T032-275 1077, www.islarobinson crusoe.cl. Food served, tours offered, kayak hire included in the price.

A-B Cabañas Dafne Rita, Ignacio Carrera Pinto 118, T/F032-275 1042, ritachamorro_g

@hotmail.com. Wooded *cabañas* for 2, with views, laundry facilities.

A-B Hostería Martínez Green, El Castillo 116, T032-275 1039, www.hosteriamartinez green.cl. Rooms with bath and TV, restaurant (half- and full-board options also available), views, tours offered.

B Hostería Villa Green, Larraín Alcalde 246, T/F032-275 1044. Basic lodging with breakfast, bath and TV.

⊛ Festivals and events

Feb A yachting regatta visits the islands. It sets out from Algarrobo (see page 145) to Isla Robinson Crusoe and thence to Talcahuano and Valparaíso. At this time, Bahía Cumberland is full of colourful and impressive craft, and prices in restaurants and shops double.

⚠ Activities and tours

The following tour operators offer all-inclusive packages, some including flights:
Ecoturismo Los Colonos, El Castillo s/n, T032-275 1216, www.colonosdejuan fernandez.cl.
Endémica Expeditions, Sector del Muelle s/n, T032-275 1003, www.endemica.com.
Marooned, La Falda s/n, T032-275 1030, lactorisfernandeziana@hotmail.com, offers guided day hikes. English spoken.
Refugio Náutico, see Sleeping.
Rutas de Robinson Crusoe, Larraín Alcalde 390, T032-275 1137, www.rutasdeirc.cl.

⊖ Transport

Air

Air taxis from **Santiago**, 2½ hrs, are operated by 2 companies; services can be erratic, especially off season. All leave from **Tobalaba Aerodrome** in La Reina (eastern outskirts of the city). Prices are about US$250-300 1-way, US$500-600 return, luggage allowance 10 kg.
Aerolíneas ATA, Av Larraín 7941, Hangar 3, Aeródromo de Tobalaba, Santiago, T02-275 0363, aerolineasata.cl.
LASSA, Av Larraín 7941, La Reina, Santiago, T02-273 5209, www.lassahelicopteros.com.

Ferry

Boats from **Valparaíso** are operated by **Naviera del Sur of Valparaíso** (Blanco Encalada 1041, of 18, Valparaíso, T032-259 4304, www.navieradelsur.cl), US$300 return including meals, leaving in the 1st week of each month; preference is given to islanders, and passages are sometimes difficult to obtain.

The Chilean Navy also has a monthly boat to the islands and may take passengers with appropriate credentials (a letter of recommendation or introduction); contact the **Armada**, Prat 620, Valparaíso, T032-225 2094.

To explore the archipelago, it is possible to charter the municipal launch, *Blanca Luz*, which goes to different places including Selkirk Island; contact Larraín Alcalde 320, T032-275 1001. The fishermen's union has several launches between them, some of which can be hired.

⊕ Directory

There are no exchange facilities on the island. No credit cards, no TCs; only pesos and US$ cash are accepted. The **post office** is at Alcalde Larraín s/n.

Rapa Nui (Easter Island)

→ Phone code: 032. Population 3800.

Isla de Pascua, or Rapa Nui, lies in the Pacific Ocean just south of the Tropic of Capricorn and 3790 km west of Chile; its nearest neighbour is Pitcairn Island. The island is triangular in shape, with an extinct volcano at each corner. The original inhabitants called the island Te Pito o te Henua, 'the navel of the world'. The unique features of the island are the many ahu *(ceremonial altars) on top of some of which stand 600 (or so)* mo'ai, *huge stone figures up to 10 m in height, representing the deified ancestors of the Rapa Nui people. The islanders have preserved their indigenous songs and dances and are extremely hospitable.*
➤➤ *For listings, see pages 563-566.*

Background

It is now generally accepted that the island was colonized from Polynesia about AD 800. Thor Heyerdahl's theories that the first inhabitants came from South America are less widely accepted than they used to be and South American influence is now largely discounted.

Indigenous Polynesian society was competitive, and it seems that the five clans that originally had their own lands on Rapu Nui demonstrated their strength by erecting complex monuments representing deceased leading figures of the tribes, facing inwards as to protect the tribesfolk. These *mo'ai* were sculpted at the Rano Raraku quarry and transported on wooden rollers over more or less flat paths to their final locations; their red topknots were sculpted at Puna Pau and then brought to the coast. Rounded pebbles were all collected from the same beach at Vinapu and laid out checkerboard fashion at the *ahu*. The sculptors and engineers were paid out of the surplus food produced by the sponsoring family. The population grew steadily, until around the 16th or 17th century it

Rapa Nui - Easter Island

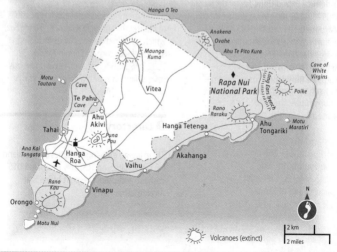

Easter Island geology and the making of the *mo'ai*

In geological terms Easter Island is a youthful 2.5 million years old. It is located above a tectonic 'hot spot', an active upwelling of magma emerging from beneath the crust of the earth and solidifying. Enough molten rock has poured out to form a mountain nearly 3000 m high, the altitude of Easter Island if measured from the sea bed. There are, however, no records of volcanic activity since humans arrived. The three high peaks are all volcanic in origin and are mostly basalt. In the cliffs of Rano Kau, different layers of basalt can be identified, indicating the existence of distinct lava flows. Caves have been formed where the lava has solidified on the outside but continued to flow downhill on the inside. On Terevaka, where the roofs of some of these caves have collapsed, long caverns up to 10 m high can be seen.

The volcanic nature of the island contributed to the carving of the *mo'ai*. Extremely hard basalt from Terevaka was used to make the tools for carving and sharp-edged implements were fashioned using obsidian, volcanic glass formed by lava cooling very rapidly. The *mo'ai* were carved from tuff, a porous rock much softer than basalt but also volcanic. Tuff can be found at Rano Raruka, a secondary cone on the side of Terevaka.

passed the limits of the islands natural resources, causing a century of warfare and famine between the tribes during which most of the *mo'ai*, seen to have failed their descendents, were destroyed or at the very least knocked off their plinths. At one point the population was reduced to as few as 111 inhabitants. War was finally ended with the introduction of the cult of the Bird Man at Orongo, and the population slowly recovered.

European contact with the island began with the visit of the Dutch admiral, Jacob Roggeven, on Easter Sunday 1722, who was followed by the British navigator James Cook in 1774 and the French sailor Le Perouse in 1786. The population of the island remained stable at around 4000 until the 1850s, when Peruvian slavers, smallpox and emigration to Tahiti (encouraged by plantation owners) reduced the numbers. Between 1859 and 1862, over 1000 islanders were transported as slaves to work in the Peruvian guano trade. The island was annexed by Chile in 1888 and from 1895 to 1952 most of it was leased to a private company that bred sheep on its grasslands: a wall was built around the Hanga Roa area, which islanders were forbidden to cross.

Now, about half the island is used for grazing and agriculture, while the other half constitutes a national park. Of the current population, about 1000 are from the mainland. Tourism has grown rapidly since the air service began in 1967 and is now also regularly visited by cruise ships. Many of the *mo'ai* have now been restored to their original positions.

Ins and outs

Getting there The high tourist season is September to April, although there are tourists year-round. The only ways to reach the island is by **Lanchile** plane from Santiago or on a cruise ship. Easter Island's airport is just south of Hanga Roa. Most flights continue from Easter Island to Tahiti.

Getting around There are numerous taxis available on the island and an unreliable summer bus service. Horses, bicycles, motorbikes and cars can all be hired.

Tourist information Sernatur ① *Tu'u Maheke, T032-210 0255, ipascua@sernatur.cl. Mon-Fri 0830-1300, 1400-1730, Sat 1000-1300, 14300-1730. English spoken.*

Bird Man cult of Orongo

Easter Island shows the extent of unique development possible for a people left wholly in isolation. Its older altars (*ahu*) are similar to those of French Polynesia, and its older statues (*mo'ai*) similar to those of the Marquesas Islands, but the very precise stone fitting of some of the *ahu*, and the tall gaunt *mo'ai* with elongated faces and ears for which Easter Island is best known were later developments.

The Bird Man cult of Orongo developed in the early 18th century after the islanders had lost their clan territoriality and were concentrated at Hanga Roa, but still needed a way to simulate inter-clan rivalry.

Central to the Bird Man cult was an annual ceremony in which the heads of the clans, or their representatives, raced to the islets of Motu Nui, Motu Iti and Motu Kao off the southwest coast of Rapa Nui to obtain the first egg of the sooty tern (known as the Manutara), a migratory seabird that nests there. The winner was then named Bird Man, Tangata Manu, for the following year.

It appears that, in the cult, the egg of the tern represented fertility, although the actual status of the Tangata Manu on the island is less clear. The petroglyphs at Orongo depict the half-man, half-bird Tangata Manu, the creator god Make Make and the symbol of fertility, Komari.

Climate Unlike most Polynesian islands, Easter Island has no coral reef as winter temperatures are too cold for coral to survive. As a result, the coastline has been eroded in parts to form steep cliffs, around Poike, Rano Kao and on the northern side of Terevaka. There is no high central plateau and consequently little gully erosion, which would normally lead to the development of streams and rivers. Moreover, much of the island's rainfall drains away underground into the huge caverns formed by the collapse of basalt caves. As a result, although annual rainfall is usually above 1000 mm, there is always a severe shortage of water and in many years several months of drought. Humidity is usually high, and the rainy season is March to October, with the wettest weather in May. Average monthly temperatures range from 15-17°C in August, up to 24°C in February, the hottest month.

Hanga Roa and around

There is one village on the island, Hanga Roa, where most of the population live. The **Museo Antropológico Sebastián Englert** ① *T032-255 1020, www.museorapanui.cl, Tue-Fri 0930-1230, 1400-1730, Sat and Sun 0930-1230, US$2, US$1 concessions, valid for unlimited visits within a 30-day period*, has good descriptions of island life, although most of the objects are reproductions because the originals were removed from the island. Free guided visits are available with advance notice. There is also an interesting modern church with locally stylized religious art and carvings, mixing catholic themes with elements of the cult of the Bird Man. Services are held on Sundays with hymns sung in Rapa Nui. A taxi journey within any two points in town should not cost more than US$3.

A six-hour walk from Hanga Roa north along the west coast passes **Ahu Tahai**, just outside town, where there is a cave house and a *mo'ai* with eyes and topknot in place. Two caves can be reached north from here: the one inland appears to be a ceremonial centre, while the other (nearer the sea) has two 'windows' (take a strong flashlight and be careful). Further north is **Ahu Te Peu**, with a broken *mo'ai* and ruined houses. Beyond here you can join the path to Hanga o Teo (see below), or turn right, inland to **Te Pahu** cave and the seven *mo'ai* at **Akivi**. Either return to Hanga Roa or continue to the **Puna Pau** crater (two hours), where the *mo'ai*'s distinctive red topknots were carved.

South of Hanga Roa is **Rano Kau**, the extinct volcano where the curious Orongo ruins can be seen. The road south from Hanga Roa passes the two caves of **Ana Kai Tangata**, one of which has paintings, and continues southeast. If, however, you're on foot, take the path just past the CONAF sign for a much shorter route to the impressive Rano Kau crater. A lake with many reed islands lies 200 m below the rim of the crater. Locals occasionally

Hanga Roa

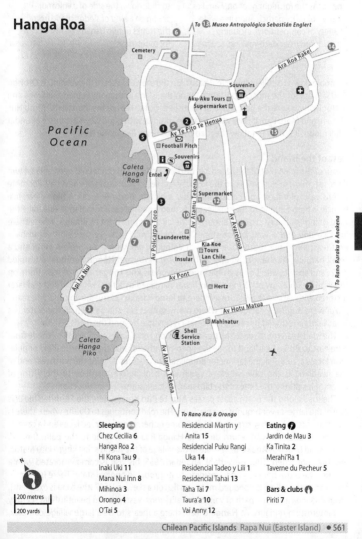

Sleeping	Residencial Martín y	Eating
Chez Cecilia 6	Anita 15	Jardín de Mau 3
Hanga Roa 2	Residencial Puku Rangi	Ka Tinita 2
Hl Kona Tau 9	Uka 14	Merahi'Ra 1
Inaki Uki 11	Residencial Tadeo y Lili 1	Taverne du Pecheur 5
Mana Nui Inn 8	Residencial Tahai 13	
Mihinoa 3	Taha Tai 7	Bars & clubs
Orongo 4	Taura'a 10	Piriti 7
O'Tai 5	Vai Anny 12	

200 metres
200 yards

Tapati, or Semana Rapa Nui

Held each year in late January/early February, Tapati is organized as a huge competition between groups, many of them families, each of which elects a beauty queen. It begins slowly but gets better as the fortnight goes on. Families score points by participating in a wide variety of competitions, including gastronomy, necklace-making, sculpting

mo'ai, body painting, dancing, singing, horse racing, swimming and a modified decathlon. In the most spectacular event, men, dressed only in the traditional thong and with their bodies painted, compete to slide down the side of a volcano, sitting on a kind of sledge made from the trunks of two banana plants. Only for tough guys!

scramble down to collect medicinal herbs. On the seaward side of the volcano is **Orongo** ⓘ US$9, one of the most important sites on the island with many ruined buildings and petroglyphs, where the bird man cult flourished. Out to sea are the 'bird islets', Motu Nui, Motu Iti and Motu Kao. It is very windy at the summit, with good views at sunset or under a full moon. It is easy to follow the road back to Hanga Roa in the dark.

Rest of the island

A tour of the main part of the island can be done on foot, but this would need at least two days, returning to Hanga Roa on the first day and setting out again the next day. For more extensive exploration you could hire either a bicycle, horse or a car. A high-clearance vehicle is better suited to the smaller roads than a normal car. From Hanga Roa, take the road going southeast past the airport; at the oil tanks turn right to **Vinapu**, where there are two *ahu* and a wall whose stones are joined with Inca-like precision. Head back northeast along the south coast to reach **Vaihu**, an *ahu* with eight broken *mo'ai* and a small harbour, **Akahanga**, an *ahu* with toppled *mo'ai*, and **Hanga Tetenga**, a toppled *mo'ai* and an *ahu*, with bones visible inside. Beyond is **Ahu Tongariki**, largest platform on the island with a row of 15 *mo'ai*, which was damaged by a tidal wave in 1960 and later restored with Japanese aid. Turn left here to **Rano Raraku** (2 km), the volcano where the *mo'ai* were originally carved and where many statues can still be seen. In the crater is a small lake surrounded by reeds; swimming is possible beyond the reeds.

The road heads north past 'the trench of the long ears'; an excursion can be made from here east to **Poike** headland to see the open-mouthed statue that is particularly popular with local carvers. Ask the farmer for permission to cross his land. At the northeast end of the headland is the cave where a virgin was kept before marriage to the victor of ceremonies during the time of the bird man cult; ask someone for directions.

The road along the north coast passes **Ahu Te Pito Kura**, where the 10-m-tall *mo'ai* is one of the largest ever brought to a platform. The road continues to **Ovahe** where there is a very attractive beach with pink sand and some rather recently carved faces and a cave.

From Ovahe, you can return direct to Hanga Roa or continue to the palm-fringed, white-sand beach at **Anakena**, the site of the village of the island's first king, Hotu Matua, and the spot where Thor Heyerdahl landed in 1955; his visit is commemorated with a plaque. The *mo'ai* here has been restored to its probable original state. There is a picnic area and a stall selling barbequed meat and fish on a skewer, US$7 (the tuna is excellent). From Anakena a coastal path of variable quality runs west, passing beautiful cliff scenery and interesting remains. At **Hanga o Teo**, there appears to be a large village complex,

Money matters

When travelling to Easter Island make sure you take both dollars and Chilean pesos in cash. Most purchases can be made in either currency, but in some cases it is much better to pay in one and in other cases the other. Always ask for the price in dollars and pesos and see which is better value. Credit card transactions have up to 10% surcharge added.

with several round houses, while further on is a burial place, built like a long ramp with several ditches containing bones. From Hanga o Teo the path goes west then south, inland from the coast, to meet the road north of Hanga Roa.

⊚ Rapa Nui listings

For Sleeping and Eating price codes and other relevant information, see Essentials pages 35-42.

⊜ Sleeping

Hanga Roa and around *p560, map p561*
Unless it is a particularly busy season there is no need to book in advance; some mainland agencies make exorbitant booking charges. That said, the advantage of an advance booking is that you will be met at the airport, given a traditional welcome necklace and a free transfer to your hotel or hostel. Flights are met by large numbers of hotel and *residencial* representatives but it is often cheaper to look for yourself. There are even reports of touts approaching passengers at Santiago airport prior to their flight to the island. Accommodation is much more expensive than anywhere else in Chile, ranging from about US$25-150 per person for bed and breakfast. There is no accommodation outside Hanga Roa. The tourist office has a full list of accommodation and prices.

LL Hanga Roa, Av Pont s/n, T032-210 0299, www.hotelhangaroa.cl. In its time the best hotel with one of the best locations on the island. Currently being refurbished and due to reopen in 2010.

LL Taha Tai, Api Na Nui s/n, T032-255 1192, www.hoteltahatai.cl. Well-kept bright hotel with ceramic floors and cabins with a sea view. There is a small swimming pool, and expensive tours are offered. English spoken.

L O'Tai, Te Pito Te Henua s/n, T032-210 0250, otairapanui@entelchile.net. Great location 2 mins from sea, lovely gardens, pool, restaurant. English spoken. Rooms vary in quality. The better rooms have a terrace and a/c; 133-137 are the most spacious.

L-AL Cabañas Christophe, Mataveri, T032-210 0826, www.cabanaschristophe.com. Comfortable stone cabins south of the town centre. Very friendly and helpful French owner. Tours offered (some included in the price). Recommended.

L-AL Taura'a, C Principal s/n, T032-210 0463, www.tauraahotel.cl. Upmarket B&B. Comfortable rooms with good beds and spacious bathrooms. Good breakfast, pleasant garden. English and French spoken, good service, tours offered. Recommended.

AL Cabañas Pikera Uri, Tahai s/n, T032-210 0577, www.pantupikerauri.cl. Simple spacious cabins in a quiet sector north of town. Sea views, very friendly service. Horse-riding tours offered.

AL Mana Nui Inn, Tahai s/n, opposite the cemetery, T032-210 0811, www.rapanuiweb.com/mananui. **B** singles. Pleasant cabins on the north edge of town with fine views. Friendly, good breakfast with local specialities, tours offered.

AL Residencial Martín y Anita, Simon Paoa s/n, opposite hospital in Hanga Roa, T032-

210 0593, www.hostal.co.cl. With breakfast, clean, good food, tours offered.

AL Residencial Tadeo y Lili, Apina Ichi s/n, T032-2100422, tadeolili@entelchile.net. Simple but clean, French/Rapa Nui-run. All rooms have sea view and a small terrace. Excellent location, good breakfast, tours offered including trips on horseback. Recommended.

AL-A Chez Cecilia, near Tahai Moai, T032-210 0499, www.rapanuichezcecilia.com. With breakfast, English and French spoken, excellent food, also *cabañas* and good-value camping. Nice view from the grounds. Not as friendly as some.

A HI Kona Tau, Avareipua s/n, T032-210 0321, www.konataurapanui.com. **D** per person in dorms. Hostelling International affiliated. All rooms with bath and breakfast. Kitchen facilities, meals served, terrace with interesting views inland.

A Inaki Uki, C Principal s/n, opposite Taura'a, www.inakiuki.cl. **C** singles. Simple, clean rooms with shared bathrooms and kitchen facilities. No breakfast. Central, a good budget option.

A Orongo, Atamu Tekena s/n, T/F032-210 0572, www.hotelorongo.com. Half-board available (excellent restaurant), good service, pleasant garden. Good value.

A Residencial Puku Rangi Uka, Puku Rangi Uka s/n, T032-210 0405, www.rapanuiweb. com/pukurangiuka. Simple but spacious rooms, some with bath.

A Residencial Tahai, Sector Tahai s/n, T032-210 0395. With breakfast, full board available, nice garden. Good value.

B Vai Anny, Tuki Haka He Viri s/n, T032-210 0650, www.vaianny.com. Good-value, family-run *cabañas*.

B-C Mihinoa, Av Pont s/n, T032-511593, www.mihinoa.com. This campsite also has a few rooms, breakfast extra, excellent fresh fish barbeques, clean, kitchen facilities, hot showers, laundry, internet, friendly, exceptional value. Fishing trips offered. Recommended.

Camping

Camping is only officially allowed in **Hanga Roa**, where there are several sites. Many people have campsites in their gardens,

US$8-12 per person, check availability of water first; some families also provide food.
Mihinoa, Av Pont s/n, T032-511593, www.mihinoa.com. Campsite with good facilities and friendly owners. Also hire out camping equipment. Recommended.

❶ Eating

Hanga Roa and around *p560, map p561*
Food, wine and beer are expensive, often twice the price of the mainland, due to freight charges, but local fish, vegetables, fruit and bread are cheap and vegetarians will have no problems on the island. Average prices: coffee/tea US$1.50, meals about US$10 or more, bread and fruit US$2 per kg, beer/cola US$3.50 in most bars and restaurants. Bring all you can from the mainland, but not fruit. Fish can be bought from the *caleta* for around US$6.50 per kg. Restaurants tend to serve their fish well done. If you don't want to be chewing leather, ask for it *no tan cocido*.

Some *residenciales* offer full board. Coffee is generally instant. It is worth booking a table in advance for evening meals.

♦♦♦ Jardín de Mau, Atanu Tekena s/n. Pasta/fusion using mostly local ingredients. Some of the pasta is made fresh. Excellent tuna carpaccio. Clean, friendly staff, sea view, better wine list than most.

♦♦♦ Taverne du Pecheur, Caleta Hanga Roa. By far the most expensive restaurant on the island – prices in line with the owner's ego – this is the self-proclaimed "best restaurant in Chile"! To be fair the food is excellent – lobster, fish and meat all cooked excellently with inventive sauces using ingredients brought specially from all over the world. Full selection of wines and spirits.

♦♦ Ka Tinita, Te Pito Te Henua s/n. Closed Sun. Fish, prepared simply but well, large salads and side dishes. Good value by island standards.

♦♦ Merahi'Ra, Te Pito Te Henua s/n. Closed Thu. Well known for its fish. Service can be a bit lax.

♦ Kiosk, by football pitch. *Empanadas* and cheap sandwiches.

🌙 Bars and clubs

Hanga Roa and around p560, map p561
There are 2 discos in Hanga Roa. The action begins after 0100. Drinks are expensive: a *pisco sour* costs US$6, canned beer US$3.50.
Piriti, near airport. Open Thu-Sat. **Toroko**, by the coast in Caleta Hanga Roa. Open daily.

🎭 Entertainment

Hanga Roa and around p560, map p561
There are shows of traditional dancing from the island at **Hotel Hanga Roa** (see Sleeping), and at **Kopakabana Restaurant**. Music at the **church**, Av Te Pito Ote Henua, for the 0900 Sun mass has been described as 'enchanting'.

🎉 Festivals and events

Rapa Nui p558, map p558
Jan-Feb Tapati, or Semana Rapa Nui from the end of Jan for 2 weeks, see box, page 562.

🛍 Shopping

Hanga Roa and around p560, map p561
On **Av Policarpo Toro**, the main street, there are lots of small shops and market stalls, which close when it rains, and a couple of supermarkets; the cheapest are **Kai Nene** or **Tumukai**. Some local produce can be found free, but ask first. This includes wild guava fruit, fish, '*hierba luisa*' tea and wild chicken. Film is readily available but cannot be developed on the island.

Handicrafts and souvenirs

Wood carvings and stone *mo'ai* are sold throughout Hanga Roa. Good pieces cost US$50-200. Bargaining is only possible if you pay cash. The municipal market, left of the church, will give you a good view of what is available. The cheapest handicrafts are available from the jail, behind the airport,

where prisoners earn money by carving and selling semi-finished items to market stall owners. With a couple of days' notice you can ask for practically any design at modest prices.

There are several souvenir shops on Av Policarpo Toro including **Hotu Matuu's Favorite Shoppe**, where prices are 'top dollar and she will not bargain', but she does have the best T-shirts. Handicrafts are sold at Tahai, Vaihu, Rano Raraku and Anakena. The airport shop is expensive.

⛰ Activities and tours

Rapa Nui p558, map p558
Hiking

Allow at least a day to walk the length of the island, 1 way, taking in all the sites. It is 5 hrs' easy walk from Hanga Roa to Rano Raraku; 5 hrs to Anakena. You can hitch back to Hanga Roa, especially at weekends, although there are few cars at other times. Anyone wishing to spend time exploring the island would be well advised to speak to **CONAF**, T032-210 0236, first; they give good advice on special interests (biology, archaeology, handicrafts, etc). Maps are sold on Av Policarpo Toro for US$15-18.

Riding

This is the best way to see the island, provided you are fit. Horses can be hired for US$65 a day (including a guide; cheaper without).
Pantu Cabalgatas, T032-100577, www.pantupikerauri.cl, is the only officially licenced operator, although several other local guides can be hired privately and charge a little less. Ask at the tourist office.

Tours

Over 20 agencies as well as several *residenciales* and local individuals arrange excursions around the island. Some provide transport (tour prices around US$40 per person per day). others will accompany tourists in hired vehicles (usually around US$110 for a full day). The English of tour guides is often poor. Recommended operators include:

Aku-Aku Tours, Tu'U Koihu s/n, T032-210 070, akuakuturismo.cl. Wide range of half- and full-day tours.
Archaeological Travel Service, Tu' U Koihi s/n, T032-210 0364, archeots@rapanui.cl. Archaeological and scientific tours. English, French, German spoken.
Hanga Roa Travel, T032-210 0158, hfritsch@ entelchile.net. English, German and Spanish spoken, good-value all-inclusive tours. Recommended.

Tour operators

Mike Rapu, Caleta Hanga Roa, T032-255 1055, www.mikerapu.cl. Offers diving expeditions and courses as well as fishing trips.
Orca, Caleta Hanga Roa, T032-100375, www.seemorca.cl. Offers guided diving trips as well as excursions by boat, kayaking and windsurfing. English and French spoken.

⊖ Transport

Rapa Nui *p558, map p558*
Air
LanChile, Poilcarpo Toro Y Av Pont, T032-210 0279 flies from **Santiago** 4-6 times a week, depending on the season, 5-5½ hrs. Some flights continue to Papeete on Tahiti. LanChile will not allow you to fly to Easter Island unless you have a confirmed flight off the island (note that planes to Tahiti are more crowded than those back to Santiago). You should reconfirm your booking on arrival on the Island.

If booked well in advance, the cheapest off-season fare in 2009 was approximately US$530 return from Santiago, with occasional special deals available through travel agents. Special deals may be available on flights originating outside Chile, or for those booking in advance. Under 24s and over 65s are often eligible for a 28% discount on some fares.

Flying from Santiago to Easter Island incurs domestic tax of US$20. Airport tax for international flights from Easter Island to Tahiti is US$9. Don't take pesos to Tahiti, as they are worthless in French Polynesia.

Bicycle/motorcycle
Bicycles (some in poor condition) are available for rent for US$12 per day on main street or from *residenciales*. Motorbikes can be hired for about US$30 a day plus fuel (Suzuki or Honda 250 are recommended).

Boat
Many pacific cruises stop at Easter Island, but there is no scheduled passenger service. Freight is brought by sea 3 times a year.

Car
Cars and jeeps are available from *residenciales*, hotels and hire companies. There are many companies (**Policarpo Toro** is a good place to start) and vehicles vary in size and condition; shop around. Jeep hire US$60 per day, US$110 with driver. There is no insurance; drive at your own risk (be careful at night, many vehicles drive without lights). US$5-10 will buy enough fuel for a 1-day trip around the island.

Taxi
Taxis can be hired to take you around but it is much better value either to take a tour or hire some means of transport.

⊙ Directory

Hanga Roa and around *p560, map p561*
Banks 1 bank on Atamu Tekena s/n with an ATM. Accepts MasterCard and Cirrus but not visa. Cash can be exchanged in shops, hotels, etc, at about 5% less than in Santiago. Poor rates on TCs at **Afex** on the main street but no commission. Credit cards are widely accepted, but all transactions incur a 10% service charge. **Internet** There are several internet cafés which, although expensive, have good broadband connections. **Medical services** A hospital, 3 doctors, a trained nurse and 1 dentist. **Post office** Mon-Fri 0900-1300, 1430-1800, Sat 0900-1200. **Telephone** ENTEL, Atamu Tekena s/n. Phone calls to the Chilean mainland are subsidized, at US$0.50 per min. Calls to Europe cost US$1 per min.

Contents

Footprint features

Background

History

Origins

Some 50,000 years ago, the very first people crossed the temporary land bridge spanning Asia and America at the Bering Straits and began a long migration southwards. They were hunters and foragers, following in the path of huge herds of now-extinct animals, such as mammoth, giant ground sloth and ancestors of the camel and horse. The first signs that these people had reached South America date from around 14,000 BC, if not earlier.

As sources of game in forested valleys dried up, some groups settled along the coasts, particularly drawn by the abundance of marine life provided by the cold Humboldt current in the Pacific. Some of the earliest evidence of humans in Chile has been found in the north, both on the coast and in the parched Atacama Desert. The coastal people lived on shellfish gathered by the shore and on fish and sea-lions speared from inflated seal-skin rafts.

One such group, the Las Conchas people, migrated from the inland valleys to the coast near Antofagasta around 7500 BC. They were one of the first peoples in South America to take hallucinogenic drugs. Many graves excavated in this region contain mortars, which may have been used to grind up seeds also found nearby. These seeds contained an alkaloid similar to that found in the ayahuasca plant, which is still used for its hallucinogenic effects by the Shuar in Peru – indeed, the Shuar are believed by some to be descendants of these Atacameño peoples, having migrated to the Amazon in order to hide from the Spanish. Some specialists believe that the many geoglyphs of the Atacama Desert (see box, page 250) – the most famous ones being the Nazca Lines in Peru – were maps for shamans undergoing the hallucinatory experience of flight after taking drugs such as ayahuasca.

The beginnings of agriculture

Gradually, the settled life of agricultural subsistence took over from the more nomadic hunting lifestyle. Remains of slingshot stones and what seem to be *bolas* (weights attached to cords used to bring down prey by entangling their legs) have been found alongside bones of mastodons in Monte Verde, near Puerto Montt. Other remains found nearby included agricultural tools and medicinal plants, hearths and house foundations, all indications that the site was inhabited for some time by one community. Crop seeds have also been found, including those of potatoes, evidence of very early contact with cultures from as far afield as the Central Andes. Some of these remains were found in a remarkable condition, owing to being buried in a peat bog; mastodon bones even had traces of meat on them. It is widely agreed that the site was settled 10,000 years ago, although lower levels have been controversially dated from as early as 34,000 years ago.

By about 2500 BC, agriculture was practised throughout much of Chile, as it was across the rest of the continent. Maize, beans and squash have been found in northern Chile from as early as 5000 BC. However, people in the south only turned definitively to agriculture at a much later date. In Araucanía, horticulture was not practised until around AD 500. These people also had unusual burial practices, placing the body in an urn inside a funerary canoe, perhaps reflecting the local dependence on fishing for their livelihood. Elaborate artefacts found in some graves, such as stone and copper jewellery and ceramic offerings, suggest a stratified society of both rich and poor.

Northern influences

In the north, the extremely dry climate is a great preservative, allowing archaeologists to build up a detailed picture of early life. The people in the Atacama lived in solidly built adobe houses, arranged in complexes around inner courtyards and corridors, such as can be seen in the village of Tulor near San Pedro de Atacama.

These northern peoples had contact with neighbouring highland communities, shown by the presence there of plants and other goods found only in the adjacent regions. The important *altiplano* culture of **Tiahuanaco** in present-day Bolivia is thought to have had particularly close links with northern Chile, helping to stimulate the growth of settlements such as that at San Pedro de Atacama. Trade with Tiahuanaco, through llama caravans bringing highland goods and produce, boosted the wealth and cultural development of the desert people. Some very fine textiles were found in this area, showing distinct design similarities with those of Tiahuanaco. The textiles were hand-spun and coloured with vegetable and cochineal dyes. Clothing and jewellery adornments containing feathers suggested contact even with tropical regions, although these may have been obtained through their *altiplano* intermediaries. Local ceramics were mostly plain and highly polished, but some items decorated with elaborate dragon-like figures had probably been traded with Tiahuanaco.

Mummification was practised from as early as 2500 BC by the Chinchorro people. They buried their dead stretched out straight, in contrast to the foetal position used by other Chilean and Peruvian cultures. Internal organs and the brain were removed and the body was stuffed with a variety of materials to preserve it. Sticks were attached to the limbs to keep them straight. A mask was placed over the face and a wig of real human hair was attached to the head. The body was then coated in a layer of clay and wrapped in animal skins or mats. According to the person's status, they were often buried with their personal possessions: clothing, jewellery, musical instruments and copper items.

In the period AD 500-900 the association between San Pedro de Atacama and Tiahuanaco had become even stronger. In return for trading their agricultural produce and other goods, it is thought that the Tiahuanaco people sought copper, semi-precious stones and the use of grazing lands in northern Chile. As with the Araucanía in the south, some graves from this period contained bodies with more elaborate clothing, jewellery, imported ceramics and other valuables, suggesting the existence of a wealthy elite, which was also common in central Andean cultures.

Following the demise of Tiahuanaco in about AD 1100, a number of cultures arose in the adjacent area bordering southern Bolivia, northern Chile and Argentina, practising derivative agriculture, with terraces and irrigation, and producing ceramics in similar styles. In the Quebrada de Humahuaca in present-day Argentina, several small defensive towns were built with fortified walls and stone houses. Grave remains have revealed that metallurgy was well developed here; some bodies were adorned with pectorals, bracelets, masks and bells, made of copper, silver and gold. Shells from the Pacific and ceramics from present-day Bolivian cultures, such as the Huruquilla, show the existence of widespread trade links.

Inca expansion

The next major empire to touch northern Chile was that of the Incas, which, at the peak of its growth in the 16th century, stretched as far south as the Aconcagua Valley near modern-day Santiago. The advancing armies of Inca Topa Yupanqui suppressed resistance in the valleys of the central region and replaced local structures with their own military administration. They were finally stopped by hostile forest tribes at the Río Maule near present-day Talca. This was the southernmost limit of the Inca Empire, some 3840 km south of the equator and the deepest that any imperial movement had penetrated into the southern hemisphere.

One major group that survived the Inca incursion and resisted conquest by the Europeans right up until the 19th century was the **Mapuche** (see box, page 328). They were concentrated in the central valley south and east of the Cordillera de Nahuelbuta. The Mapuche were primarily farmers but also hunted and fished, both inland and along the coasts and lake shores. Their large cemeteries contained a variety of burial sites, some in canoes or stone chambers and some in simple earthen graves. Grave goods were plentiful, with elaborate ceramics, wooden and stone artefacts and jewellery made of copper and semi-precious stones.

The Far South
Despite the apparently inhospitable conditions, these regions were home to a sizeable population of hunting, fishing and gathering peoples from very early times continuously up to the 19th century AD. Bones of horses and extinct giant sloths, dating from approximately 8000 BC, have been found near to stone arrowheads in sites such as Fells's Cave and Pali Aike Cave on the Magellan Straits – evidence of the earliest hunters.

Four distinct cultures developed here: the Haush, Ona, Yámana and Alacalufe. The oldest of these was the **Haush**, nomadic hunters of the guanaco mainly confined to the farthest southeastern tip of Tierra del Fuego, in present-day Argentina. The Haush hunted with bows and arrows, using guanaco skins for clothing and sometimes for covering their stick-framed houses. They also gathered shellfish and caught fish by the shore, using spears and harpoons.

The **Ona** people also hunted guanaco, ranging on foot across most of the Isla Grande of Tierra del Fuego in family groups. They were strong runners and tall people, some of them 6 ft tall; in fact, all these hunters and gatherers are thought to have been the tallest of the first South American peoples. They wore guanaco skin robes, fur side out, and also guanaco fur moccasins, known as *jamni*. They made open-topped shelters out of guanaco skins, which were weatherproofed with a coating of mud and saliva, and sometimes painted red. The Ona did not use harpoons or spears and only collected shellfish from beaches at low tide.

The **Yámana** were nomadic coastal hunters, travelling in canoes up and down the coasts of the Beagle Channel and around the islands southwards to Cape Horn. They caught otters, fish and seals, using spears and harpoons, and used slings and snares to catch birds. The Yámana houses were simple, made of sticks and grass, and they wore little clothing, perhaps a small seal skin and skin moccasins in winter.

Like the Yámana, the **Alacalufes** were also nomadic coastal peoples, roaming from Puerto Edén in the Chilean channels, to Yendegaia in the Beagle Channel. There was some contact with the Yámana, with whom they would sometimes exchange goods and inter-marry. The Alacalufes had similar lifestyles to the Yámana but developed various additions, such as raising a sail on their canoes and using a bow and arrow in addition to the sling when hunting birds or guanaco.

Spanish conquest and early settlement
The first Spanish expeditions to Chile were led by **Diego de Almagro** and **Pedro de Valdivia**, both of whom followed the Inca road from Peru to Salta and then west across

the Andes. Almagro's expedition of 1535-1537, which included 100 Spaniards, African slaves, crypto-Jews and some thousands of indigenous Americans – many of whom perished – reached the heartland but, bitterly disappointed at not finding gold, returned to Peru almost immediately. Valdivia's expedition then carried out what initially appeared to be a swift and successful conquest, founding Santiago in February 1541 and a series of other settlements in the following years. But, in the 1550s, these Spanish settlements were shaken by a Mapuche rebellion, which led to the death of Valdivia.

The two major indigenous figures in this early resistance to the Spaniards were the *caciques* Lautaro and Caupolicán. Lautaro was an interesting case: initially an adjutant of Pedro de Valdivia (known by the conquistador as Felipe), he turned against Validivia and led the expedition that captured him in 1553. Lautaro went on to lead several successful campaigns, before being killed by the Spaniards in the Mataquito Valley in 1557. Caupolicán fought alongside Lautaro, but was eventually captured in the *cordillera* in 1558 and impaled on a stake by the Spaniards. Nevertheless, the two Mapuche heros had successfully undermined the Spanish colony and their struggles set the tone for the colonial period in Chile. Lacking precious minerals, threatened by the warlike Mapuche and never less than four months' journey from Europe, the colony was of relatively little importance to Spain, except as a frontier zone.

The motivation of these early expeditions – as in Mexico and Peru – was greed. The Spanish crown did nothing to finance the ventures, so all the risk was shouldered by those who participated, who therefore had a pressing need to find silver and gold to recompense themselves. Nevertheless, a fifth of all gold and silver that was found in the New World went into the royal coffers; an influx of precious metal that was urgently needed to prop up the falling value of coinage in Europe at this time.

The greedy motivations of the early arrivals made control in distant Chile difficult for the Castillian crown to exercise. Chile was effectively run by men such as **Francisco de Aguirre**, a conquistador who had accompanied Pedro de Valdivia's initial expedition. As one of the first Spaniards on the scene, Aguirre was made Governor of Tucumán – just across the Andes in modern-day Argentina – and later founded La Serena. He was, however, deeply anti-clerical and proclaimed himself "Pope and King" in Chile, saying that he would rather have a farrier than a priest. The Inquisition eventually caught up with Aguirre in the Río de la Plata in the 1570s and he died poor, bitter and disgraced in La Serena.

In addition to trying to exert effective control over the Spaniards in their territory, one of the main concerns of Chile's Spanish governors after Valdivia was the war against the Mapuche successors to Lautaro and Caupolicán. Known by the Spanish as Araucanos, the Mapuche were fearsome opponents. In 1598, they began a general offensive that destroyed all of the Spanish settlements south of the Río Biobío, revealing the weakness of a colony whose Spanish population was under 8000. Pushed back into the northern part of the Central Valley, the Spanish were forced to build a string of forts along the Río Biobío, guarded by a frontier army of 2000 men, the only force of its type in Spanish America, financed by a special subsidy from the viceregal capital of Lima. However, Chile was not important enough to warrant a full-scale Spanish assault on the Mapuche and, for the rest of the colonial period, the Spanish presence south of the river would be limited to the island of Chiloé and to the coastal city of Valdivia.

Town planning in the 16th century

Perhaps the most obvious influence of Spanish colonial settlement for a visitor is the characteristic street plan of towns and cities. Colonial cities were founded by means of an official ceremony, which involved tracing the central square and holding a mass. A series of Royal Ordinances issued in Madrid in 1573 laid down the rules of town planning: the four corners of the main plaza had to face the four points of the compass; the plaza and the main streets had arcades and, away from the plaza, the streets were traced out with a cord and ruler in the now-familiar grid-pattern. Once this was done, building lots near the plaza were distributed, allocated by lottery to those settlers who had rights to be there.

The Ordinances specified the principles underlying the distribution of the major public buildings. Churches were to be distant from the plaza and built on high ground, so that they were easy to see and people had to climb up to them on steps, thereby forcing a greater reverence. The *cabildo* and the customs house were to be built nearby, while the hospital of the poor and those sick with non-contagious diseases was to be north-facing, planned so that the inmates could enjoy southern exposure.

The Ordinances also advised settlers on how to deal with local suspicion and hostility: "While the new town is being built the settlers … shall try to avoid communication and intercourse with the Indians. Nor are the Indians to enter the circuit of the settlement until the latter is complete and in condition for defence and the houses built, so that when the Indians see them they will be filled with wonder and will realize that the Spaniards are settling there permanently and not temporarily."

'Royal Ordinances Governing the Laying Out of New Towns' by Zelia Nuttall, Hispanic American Historical Review, May 1922.

The Chilean colony

As in the other colonies in the Americas, Chilean society under Spanish rule was not the two-sided world of Spanish settlers and Amerindian peoples that official histories would have us believe. From very early on, two other groups became increasingly important: *marranos* – or forced converts from Judaism to Christianity, who had fled Inquisitional persecution in Spain and Portugal – and slaves from West Africa. The *marranos* controlled large parts of the trade in South America and suffered bouts of persecution from the Inquisitional office in Lima, while the Africans did much of the manual labour in the colony. Although both groups eventually became absorbed into Chile, the legacy of their presence can perhaps be felt today in the widespread stereotyping of Africans and Jews in mainstream Chilean society.

African slaves started arriving from very early on in the colonial period, principally because the Spanish found that the indigenous people were not hardy enough to do the work required of them. By the end of the 16th century, Africans in Chile were working as cattle ranchers and as *stevedores*, and as blacksmiths, tailors, carpenters and servants in every city. They were mostly sold as contraband, brought over from Buenos Aires instead of through the 'official' port of entry at Cartagena, Colombia, and originated from all parts of the West African coast, from Senegambia to Angola.

By the turn of the 17th century, much of the trade of the fledgling colony was in the hands of the *marranos*, who were prohibited from holding positions of authority. Their main port of entry was Buenos Aires, from where they travelled overland to Potosí and Lima by way of Tucumán.

In the following years, colonial Chile achieved a degree of stability and developed as a compact society; most of its population inhabited the Central Valley and most trade was through Valparaíso. By the end of the 17th century, there were few people of pure indigenous blood, most having died, inter-married or escaped south of the Río Biobío. The majority of the population was *mestizo* (mixed race), though the society was dominated by a small white elite. Chile was, however, highly isolated, being cut off from the rest of the continent in winter. People dared not use the lower passes to the south for fear of the Mapuche, and the high passes near Mendoza and Santiago were blocked by snow for months at a time.

During the colonial period, the *hacienda*, or landed estate, was the most important feature of rural society in the Central Valley. In the 17th century, Chilean agriculture expanded to meet demands for wheat, tallow, salted beef and cattle hides from Peru; hides were also sent to Potosí and mules to the great fair in Salta. These exports and the need to feed the frontier army led to the development of large-scale agriculture. As the *haciendas* grew, small farmers and tenants were gradually forced to become *inquilinos*, a class of peasants tied to the land. The *inquilino* is regarded as the ancestor of the *huaso*, the Chilean cowboy, a figure seen as resourceful, astute, cunning and archetypally Chilean.

Although *haciendas* grew in response to food shortages, they were very self contained, with their own supplies of food and clothing, their own vineyards, forges and workshops. Ownership of a *hacienda* was one of the clearest marks of upper-class status, although many were the property of religious orders. The *hacienda* remained at the centre of rural life in the Central Valley and social relations between landowners and *inquilinos* changed little until the Agrarian Reforms of the 1960s. Although no colonial *haciendas* remain, a few dating from the 19th century can be visited, notably Villa Huilquilemu, near Talca (see page 297).

Chile was governed as part of the Viceroyalty of Peru, with its capital in Lima; until the 18th century, all trade with Spain had to pass via Lima and trade with other countries was forbidden. This led to uncontrolled smuggling and, by 1715, there were 40 French vessels trading illegally along the Chilean coast. In 1740, direct trade with Spain was permitted for the first time and, in 1750, Chile was allowed to mint her own currency.

The War of Independence

Independence came to Spanish America as a direct result of Napoleon's invasion of Spain. As Spanish guerrilla forces fought to drive the French out, these events led the colonial elites to debate where their loyalties lay: to Napoleon's brother Joseph, now officially King? Or to the overthrown king, Ferdinand VII, now in a French prison? Or to the Spanish resistance parliament in Cádiz?

In 1810, a group of leading Santiago citizens appointed a Junta to govern until Ferdinand returned to the throne. Although they protested loyalty to Ferdinand, their move was seen as a challenge to the crown by the viceregal government in Lima, which sent an army to Concepción. War broke out between the Chilean Patriots and the Royalist troops supporting Lima. The defeat of the Patriot army led by **Bernardo O'Higgins** at Rancagua in October 1814 led to a restoration of colonial rule, but O'Higgins was able to

War of the Pacific, 1879-1883

One of the few major international wars in Latin America after Independence, the War of the Pacific had its roots in a dispute between Chile and Bolivia over national boundaries in the Atacama Desert. There had already been one military conflict in 1836-1839, when Chile defeated Peru and Bolivia, but relations were further complicated by the discovery of nitrates in the Atacama in the 1860s, particularly in the then-Bolivian province of Antofagasta.

The war also has to be put into the wider international context of the late 1870s. The years 1873-1875 saw a serious recession, with plunging commodity prices around the world. This was followed in 1876 by one of the most severe El Niño weather patterns the world has ever seen, leading to the deaths of tens of millions of people from famine. Santiago had its lowest ever barometric reading in 1877, Peru suffered widespread floods and there were devastating droughts in the Bolivian altiplano.

The Bolivian government was forced to impose port taxes to support its weak economy and, in 1878, attempted to tax the Chilean-owned Antofagasta Railroad and Nitrate Company. When the company refused to pay, its assets were seized, sparking claims of foul play by the Chilean government. Peru announced that it would honour a secret alliance with Bolivia, so the Chilean president, Aníbal Pinto, declared war on both states.

None of these three countries was prepared for military conflict; they lacked skilled officers and adequate weapons. Control of the sea was vital: when the Chileans blockaded the Peruvian nitrate port of Iquique with two wooden ships, the Esmeralda and the Covadonga, Peru retaliatied with her two best iron-clad ships, the Huáscar and the Independencia. In the Battle of Iquique, 21 May 1879, the Esmeralda was sunk, but the Independencia ran aground and was captured, thus altering the balance of power between the two navies. Later in October 1879, the two Chilean iron-clads, Blanco Encalada and Cochrane, captured the Huáscar off Angamos, near Antofagasta. (The ship can now be visited in the harbour at Talcahuano.)

Rather than attack the Peruvian heartland, the Chileans invaded the southern Peruvian province of Tarapacá and then took the town of Tacna, in May 1880, before capturing Arica, further south. In January 1881, fresh Chilean armies seized control of Lima. Bolivia signed a ceasefire, giving up her coastal province, and eventually, under the 1883 peace settlement, Peru gave up Tarapacá to Chile. The provinces of Tacna and Arica were occupied by Chile for 10 years, and it was not until 1929 that an agreement was reached under which Tacna was returned to Peru.

The war gave Chile a monopoly over the world's supply of nitrates and enabled her to dominate the southern Pacific coast. Some idea of its importance in official Chilean history can be gained by the number of streets and squares named after the war heroes, especially Arturo Prat and Aníbal Pinto, and after the two Chilean vessels Esmeralda and Blanco Encalada. Chile's relations with her northern neighbours, however, remain sour. There is widespread racism in Chile towards the indigenous peoples in Peru and Bolivia, while signs in Bolivia proclaim that the Pacific coastline is still Bolivian.

escape across the Andes to join forces with Buenos Aires' liberation hero, José de San Martín. The turning point came in 1817, with the invasion of Chile from Mendoza by San Martín's Army of the Andes, a force of 4000 men, which defeated the Royalists at Chacabuco on 12 February 1817. A Royalist counter-attack was defeated at Maipó, just south of Santiago, on 5 May 1818, putting an end to Royalist power in the Central Valley. The victory of the small Patriot navy led by **Lord Cochrane** at Valdivia in January 1820 helped clear the Pacific coast of Royalist vessels and paved the way for San Martín to launch his seaborne invasion of Peru.

Nineteenth-century expansion

In most of former Spanish America, Independence was followed by a period of political turmoil, marked by civil wars and dictatorship, which in some cases lasted until the 1860s. Many Independence heroes had tragic ends: disgusted at the chaos, San Martín retired to France; Simon Bolívar died penniless and in hiding in a boarding house in Santa Marta, Colombia; and O'Higgins was quickly overthrown. O'Higgins' demise was followed by a brief period of instability in Chile but, in 1830, conservative forces led by Diego Portales restored order and introduced the Constitution of 1833, which created a strong government under a powerful president. Portales, a Valparaíso merchant, who never became president, explained his actions thus: "If one day I took up a stick and gave tranquillity to the country it was only so that the bastards and whores of Santiago would let me get on with my work in peace."

Chile became famous throughout Latin America as the great example of political stability: the army was reduced to 3000 men and kept out of politics; after 1831, four successive presidents served the two five-year terms permitted under the constitution. However, this stability had another side: civil liberties were frequently suspended, elections rigged, opponents exiled and power lay in the hands of a small landowning elite. Neither was the stability perfect: there were short civil wars in 1851, 1859 and 1891.

The latter half of the 19th century saw Chile's great period of expansion. In 1881, when victory over Peru in the War of the Pacific was assured (see box, page 574), the much-enlarged army was sent to put an end to Mapuche independence and thus secure continuous Chilean control over the entire Pacific coastline south of Arica. In the few short years between 1879 and 1883, Chilean territory had expanded both northwards and southwards. However, some Chileans still argue that the victory over Peru and Bolivia came at the price of losing both the region around Mendoza and most of Patagonia to Argentina; according to some, this should, by dint of colonial land divisions under the Viceroyalty, be Chilean territory. It is certainly true that maps from the early 19th century show Chilean territory crossing the Andes and advancing halfway to the Atlantic Ocean, while early colonial documents speak of "the city of Mendoza in Chile".

From the 1860s onwards, conflict between President and Congress became a constant feature of political life. The War of the Pacific brought the Chilean government a new source of income through the tax levied on nitrate exports coming from the new territories of the Atacama (see box, page 574) but it also increased rivalry for control of this income. When, in 1890, Congress rejected the budget, President Balmaceda announced he would use the 1890 budget for 1891. Congressional leaders denounced this as illegal and fled to Iquique, where they recruited an army, which defeated Balmaceda's forces and seized the capital. Balmaceda took refuge in the Argentine embassy, where he committed suicide. His defeat was important: between 1891 and 1924 Chilean presidents were weak figures and real power lay with Congress, ruled by the elite.

Twentieth-century politics

In the years before the First World War, the income from nitrates helped build a large railway network, roads and ports and the best education system on the continent. However, the collapse of the industry during the First World War led to worker and student unrest, which brought down the constitutional system in 1924 when the military intervened. A new constitution restored the strong presidency, which had apparently served Chile so well in the 19th century, but the Great Depression brought further economic stress, which resulted in a series of short-lived governments, including a military-led 100-day Socialist Republic in 1932.

As economic conditions recovered in the 1930s, Chile once again became a model of political stability. Between 1932 and 1970, Chile developed a complex multiparty system: two left-wing parties, the Socialists and Communists, representing the urban workers and miners; the Conservative and Liberal parties, dating from the 19th century, representing the landowners; and the Radicals, a centre party representing the middle classes. The Radicals became the key to power, winning the presidency in 1938, 1942 and 1946. However, one major group remained excluded from political life: the peasants, whose votes, controlled by their landlords, gave the Liberals and Conservatives their representation in Congress and enabled the landlords to block rural reform.

In the 1958 election, the Socialist **Salvador Allende** (see box, opposite) only narrowly failed to defeat the Conservative Jorge Alessandri. This shook both the right-wing parties and (in the aftermath of the Cuban Revolution), the US government. In 1964, the US and the Chilean right-wing threw their weight behind **Eduardo Frei Montalva**, a Christian Democrat who promised a 'revolution in freedom'. Frei Montalva's achievements in office were impressive: state ownership of 51% of the copper industry; minimum wage and unionization rights for agricultural workers; and the 1967 agrarian reform, which began replacing the *haciendas* with family farms. However, these measures raised hopes that could not be satisfied, especially in the countryside where workers now enjoyed rights and pushed for faster land reform. Hostility from the landowners was reflected in Congress where the National Party, formed in 1966 by the merger of the Conservatives and Liberals, denounced the government. The President's Christian Democrat Party was divided between supporters and opponents of reform. Nevertheless, Frei Montalva has been an enduringly popular President – his memory was widely seen as a key factor in the landslide victory of his son, Eduardo Frei Ruiz-Tagle, in the 1993 presidential elections.

The 1970 election was narrowly won by Salvador Allende, polling just over 36.3% of the vote, with the electorate split in three. Allende headed a left-wing alliance called Unidad Popular, which launched an ambitious programme of reforms: banking, insurance, communications, textiles and other industries were taken over in the first year and the nationalisation of copper was completed (this last even with the support of the right-wing parties). After that, the government ran into major problems: the nationalisations had depleted Chile's currency reserves, while hostility by domestic business groups and the US caused capital flight and a US-led boycott on international credit. In Congress, an alliance between the Christian Democrats and National Party impeached several ministers. At grassroots level, a series of anti-government strikes by truck drivers and professional groups brought the country to a halt in October 1972 and again in August 1973, while the supplies in shops were unable to keep pace with the wider purchasing power of many social classes, leading to long queues for foodstuffs and a rise in annual inflation to over 300% in 1973.

Salvador Allende Gossens

Born in 1908 into an upper-middle-class Valparaíso family, Salvador Allende's childhood ambition was to be a doctor, like his grandfather Ramón Allende Padín, a respected Radical politician who became Serene Grand Master of the Chilean freemasons. While studying medicine, Salvador discovered first-hand the appalling living conditions of the poor and the links between poverty and disease. Even before he qualified as a doctor, he became active in politics and was briefly imprisoned during the Ibáñez dictatorship. He was a founder member of the Chilean Socialist party in 1933; at about the same time he also became active in the Freemasons.

Elected to Congress for Valparaíso at the age of 29, he served as Minister of Health in Aguirre Cerda's Popular Front government of 1939-1942 and was elected to the Senate in 1945, becoming Senate president in 1965. Allende was a candidate in four presidential elections. In 1952, he gained only 5.45% of the votes but, in 1958, as candidate of the Front for Popular Action, an alliance between the Socialists and Communists, he lost narrowly to the right-wing candidate, Jorge Alessandri. Easily defeated in 1964 by the Christian Democrat, Eduardo Frei, he finally won the presidency in 1970. However, without a majority in Congress, heading a broad but divided coalition of eight parties, and facing the hostility of much of the Chilean population and of Washington, Allende found himself with increasingly little room for political manoeuvre.

When news of the military revolt came through in the early hours of 11 September 1973, Allende went to the Moneda Palace and spoke twice on the radio before communications were cut. Although he was offered a flight out of the country in return for his resignation, Allende refused, and the palace was bombed by three Hawker Hunter jets. Most accounts now accept that Allende committed suicide. He was buried in an unmarked grave in Viña del Mar. In September 1990, following the return to civilian rule, his body was exhumed and transported to Santiago for a state funeral, thousands of people lining the route from the coast.

Despite these negative effects, Allende's Socialist experiment did have a measure of success: agricultural production increased and, by 1972, there were 27% more foodstuffs available in Chile than there had been in 1970. However, even this increase in supply was outstripped by the demand caused by a real rise in wages among the poor. This was a sign that Allende's goal of eradicating poverty was bearing some fruit, with per capita consumption rising for all foodstuffs except red meat. The upper and middle classes who bemoaned the queues in the shops were, in fact, venting frustration that their customary position at the head of affairs was finally being usurped.

The Pinochet era

Allende's popularity in some quarters was demonstrated by the March 1973 Parliamentary elections, at which the Unidad Popular polled 43.4% of the vote, 7% more than in 1970. Nevertheless, the coup of 11 September 1973, led by **General Augusto Pinochet** (born 1915), was widely expected, the armed forces having received open encouragement from Allende's opponents in Congress, including the Christian

Democrats, and from opposition groups on the streets; it later became clear that the CIA had had a major role in fomenting the unrest that led to the pre-coup stand-off.

The brutality of the coup shocked people who were accustomed to Chile's peaceful traditions. Left-wing activists and people mistakenly identified as leftists were arrested, thousands were executed, torture was widespread, with at least 7000 people held in the national football stadium, and, by 1978, there were 30,000 Chilean exiles in Western Europe alone. With political parties and labour unions banned, the government adopted neo-liberal economic policies under the influence of the 'Chicago Boys' – local economists who had been trained at the University of Chicago under the tutelage of Milton Friedman.

Pinochet installed himself as the undisputed head of a military junta. Those who did not approve of his methods often met grisly ends, including the former head of the Army, Carlos Prats, who was assassinated by a car bomb in Buenos Aires in 1974. Pinochet increased his hold on power by his control over the regime's notorious secret police, the DINA, which was headed by a close colleague, General Manuel Contreras, while silencing exiles and international critics through Operation Condor, an international anti-leftist terrorist movement. Under a new constitution, adopted in 1980, Chile became a 'protected democracy' based on the exclusion of political parties and the 'guardianship' of the armed forces, who put forward a single candidate for an eight-year presidential term in 1981. To no one's surprise that candidate was Pinochet, who, during his second term (1981-1989) became the longest-serving Chilean president. With his stern features enhanced by dark glasses, Pinochet became the stereotype of the South American dictator. Often seen as a bluff, no-nonsense character, he was also noted for his astuteness, his suspicious mind, his ruthlessness, his hatred of communism and distrust of democracy.

It would be wrong to see his dominance as merely the result of repression and fear. For many Chileans, who had hated Allende and feared his liberal policies, the human rights abuses and destruction of democracy were seen as a price worth paying. In spite of his widespread vilification in much of the Western press, Pinochet retained popularity among many Chileans, polling 44% of the vote in a plebiscite in 1988. This bid for a further eight-year term was unsuccessful but, when the first results came in, the military government initially tried to maintain that the 'si' vote (yes to Pinochet) had triumphed. Even when this position became untenable, the constitution of 1980 ensured that Pinochet still had 18 months before he had to relinquish power.

Eventually, presidential and congressional elections were held in 1989. A veteran Christian Democrat politician, **Patricio Aylwin Azócar**, the candidate of the Coalition of Parties for Democracy (CPD, or Concertación), was elected President and took office in March 1990 in a peaceful transfer of power. General Pinochet remained as Army Commander, although other armed forces chiefs were replaced. The new Congress set about revising many of the military's laws on civil liberties and the economy, but in December 1990, questions in Congress and in the press about financial scandals involving army officers and Pinochet's own son-in-law led the Army Commander to order all troops to report to barracks. In May 1993, Pinochet surrounded the Ministry of Defence with soldiers and ordered generals to wear battle dress to work for a day.

In 1991, the National Commission for Truth and Reconciliation (the RETTIG Commission) published a report detailing those who had been killed under the military regime. The RETTIG commission established that 3197 people had died as the result of the violation of human rights, but opposition by the armed forces and an amnesty law protecting members of the military prevented mass human rights trials. At this time, prosecution of those guilty of human rights abuses in Chile was widely seen as impossible.

Presidential elections in December 1993 resulted in victory for the Christian Democrat, Eduardo Frei Ruiz-Tagle, candidate of the Concertación coalition but, in congressional elections held at the same time, the Concertación failed to achieve the two-thirds majority required to reform the constitution, replace the heads of the armed forces and end the system of designated senators whose votes enabled the right-wing parties and the military to block reform. As a result Frei's presidency became an exercise in balancing the demands of the parties of the Concertación against the entrenched power of the military and the right-wing. Although the Concertación won a comfortable victory in congressional elections in December 1997, it still failed to achieve the majority necessary to break the deadlock; the position of the military was strengthened in March 1998 when General Pinochet retired as Army Commander-in-Chief and, as a former president who had held office for six years, took up his lifetime seat in the Senate.

In October 1998, General Pinochet was arrested in London at a private clinic, while recovering from a back operation. The arrest warrant had been issued by a Spanish judge, Baltasar Garzón, for murder and torture of Spanish citizens under the military regime. Pinochet's arrest put the Frei government under great pressure: Pinochet's supporters demanded action, while some of the government's supporters, especially those in the Socialist party, were privately delighted. Meanwhile, the families of those who had disappeared during Pinochet's regime continued to demand news of the whereabouts of the victims' corpses, and the prosecution of those responsible. Combined with the worsening economic situation and the choice of the first Socialist to head the Concertación into presidential elections, these dramatic events made the December 1999 poll unexpectedly close. The Concertación candidate, Ricardo Lagos, eventually won with a tiny majority in a second-round ballot against the populist Mayor of Las Condes, Joaquín Lavín (one of the bright young 'Chicago boys' of the 1970s), although Lavín had won more votes in the first round of polling.

The ructions caused by the Pinochet affair were significant. Having allowed the extradition process to continue, Jack Straw, the British Home Secretary, permitted Pinochet to return to Chile on grounds of ill health in March 2000. However, a legal case started by Judge Juan Guzmán Tapia in the Chilean courts in January 1998 meant that Pinochet still faced a legal challenge. In July 1999, the Supreme Court ruled that, in cases where the fact of death could not be certified, amnesty did not apply, thereby laying Pinochet and the military open to charges regarding the 'disappeared'. This was followed in June 2000 by an Appeal Court ruling that stripped Pinochet of his immunity from trial. The decision was confirmed by the Supreme Court in August, and Pinochet was finally indicted by Judge Guzmán on 29 January 2001. The charges of kidnapping and murder related to the infamous 'caravan of death' in 1973, when many political detainees 'disappeared' in the north of the country. However, in July 2001, the court ruled narrowly that Pinochet's worsening health meant that he was not capable of mounting a proper defence and that the case could not be continued. Judge Guzmán was soon forced to take sick leave as a result of stress induced by the case. Although appeals were mounted by the families of victims of the military government, Pinochet eventually won the right not to stand trial under a Supreme Court Ruling in July 2002, although he resigned his position as senator for life.

Recent history

It appeared that the July 2002 ruling would finally allow some distance to be put between Chile and its troublesome former President. However over the next two years a series of human rights abuse charges were made against Pinochet, Each followed the same course as the last; first Pinochet had to be stripped of immunity for a particular charge, then he was indicted and placed under house arrest before being ruled too infirm to stand trial. For some time Chileans had been cynical about the prospects of 'Pinocchio' ever being brought to justice and the ruling simply seemed to confirm most people's suspicions. Indeed, 'the old man' still retained sizeable support amongst large sectors of the population who maintained that his acts were justified in as much as they were borne of patriotic ideals and served to save Chile from communism and transform it into the modern country of today. However all this changed in 2004 when it was discovered that Pinochet had stashed away US$27 million in secret foreign bank accounts. He was charged along with his wife and four of his children (one of whom laughably tried to claim political asylum in the US) for tax evasion and holding false passports. Now, suddenly, the same people who had defended Pinochet's murders were aghast at the idea that he may have been stealing money from them. To add further fuel to the fire, in July 2006, Manuel Contreras, the former head of the DINA, claimed that Pinochet made this money by the large-scale production and sale of cocaine to Europe and North America. This new case was never resolved, Pinochet dying under house arrest on 10 December 2006 to a bizarre mixture of raucous celebration and quasi-religeous grief, never having been brought to justice but equally failing to end his life with the respect and authority he had tried to develop. Denied the state burial he craved, he was nevertheless buried with full military honours.

Back to 2002 and President Lagos urgently needed to concentrate on important national economic issues: in particular, the impact of the economic meltdown in neighbouring Argentina – Chile's main trading partner and the source of the majority of its overseas visitors. As political uncertainty increased across the continent – with coups and counter-coups in Venezuela, the collapse of Argentina and the victory of the left in presidential elections in Brazil – 2002 was a difficult year to be steering the Chilean ship. The government's decision in August 2002 to freeze the minimum wage in an effort to reduce unemployment caused widespread protests, largely because most people's experience of economic realities did not match the government's subsequent statements as to the "improving situation".

The early months of 2003, however, saw Lagos able to reassert his statesmanship through his renewed importance on the global stage: Chile now occupied one of the 15 seats on the UN Security Council. As the international crisis over Iraq reached a head, Lagos did not desert his old support base, with Chile proving to be one of the most intractable of the "six undecided council members", and putting forward a strong case against pre-emptive military invasion. This resistance to pressure from the 'yanquis' and the Brits reflected the mood in the country and enhanced Lagos's popularity. But opposition to war in Iraq did not come without a price; the Americans subsequently postponed signing a free trade agreement with Chile.

In his last two years of office, president Lagos concentrated on important social and democratic themes. The Plan Auge aimed to create a more European-style healthcare system heavily subsidising treatment for an increasing number of illnesses to low-income families and in some cases allowing them access to private clinics, while the justice system was shaken up in an effort to speed up processes that had often seen prisoners on remand for longer than they were finally sentenced for. Agreement was finally reached to phase out the system of appointed senators, paving the way for a return to true democracy, while in 2005 the president was at last given the authority to dismiss leaders of the armed forces, once again making the military subordinate to democratic institutions. When President Lagos finally stepped down, he enjoyed the highest popularity rating of any Chilean leader.

The most recent elections, at the end of 2005 threw up a three-way contest. The Concertación put forward the Socialist Michelle Bachelet, while the right put up two candidates, Joaquín Lavín for the UDI and Sebastián Piñera for the RN. After Lavín was knocked out in the first round, the final result seemed too close to call. Over a series of television debates, Piñera, owner of Chile's national airline and a major television channel, came across as a slightly false patronising and domineering figure, and in the end Bachelet won by a comfortable 7%.

In many ways Bachelet has broken the mould in Chilean politics. A woman president in a still very much male-dominated country, Bachelet was not a career politician. Tortured alongside her father (a military man who had remained loyal to Allende), she worked for many years as a paediatrician before being made Health and then Defence Minister under Lagos. Although she had a quiet start to her presidency she has continued the progressive reforms of her predecessor. On the domestic front she has the advantages of record copper prices filling the treasury coffers enabling the country to weather the 2009 global economic crisis much better than most of her South American neighbours, while internationally she has tried to balance Chile's reputation as a stable neo-liberal trading partner with her relations with ever more left-leaning populist governments in the region.

Modern Chile

An overview
The Pinochet affair forced Chileans to confront their recent past. Although old wounds reopened, the increasing political apathy of the young, which was apparent in the early 1990s, was nipped in the bud. While the presidencies of the Concertación continued the Pinochetista neo-liberal policies that made Chile such a banker's favourite in the 1980s, these have been accompanied by a genuine attempt at more inclusive government, including significant increases in the national minimum wage, at rates well above that of inflation. With a pension system on which countries such as Britain have modelled their own 'stakeholder' schemes, urban Chile is now, for the most part, modern and dynamic.

There are, however, several problems that the government needs to address. While there has been a limited rise in living standards among the inhabitants of Santiago's *callampas* (shanty towns), urban poverty remains widespread. Problems in Santiago are due in large part to the over-centralisation of the country: over a third of the population live in the capital or the surrounding Región Metropolitana, and Chile's unusual geography means that Santiago is a natural focal point, on which the rest of the country is all too dependent.

Chile managed to weather the short '*crisis económica*' at the beginning of the decade caused largely by weaknesses among Chile's main trading partners: the crisis in the Far East had major ramifications in Chile, while the devaluation in Brazil, followed by the subsequent economic crisis in Argentina, led to the temporary rise of the US dollar against the Chilean peso from 2001 to 2004. The government did extremely well to stave off the inflationary pressures of these developments, and buoyed by the rise in copper prices the steady constant growth and prosperity that characterised the 1990s has in some senses returned. However, although this might be the case on a macro level and although Chile's economy remains the most stable in South America, the economic situation of the lower and middle classes remains tough. There is an all too apparent wealth gap, while the working week is a hefty 45 hours (reduced from 48 by Lagos). In order to avoid having to make redundancy payments, jobs are often offered on short-term contracts, and it is not surprising that people talk about the difficulty of finding – and keeping – work.

Chile's income tax system is symptomatic of the country's traditional conservatism. Direct income tax is exceptionally low and business tax is almost non-existent. While Chile's lower and middle classes can clearly not afford to pay more income tax, this is far from true of the country's upper classes. The inability of recent governments to tackle this subject is evidence both of the oligarchic stranglehold that the Chilean aristocracy retains on the state and of the taboo status of even the slightest economic redistribution – thanks to the 'anti-Communist wars' waged by the military government in the 1970s and 1980s and to the psychological scars caused by the Allende government's economic policies and their consequences.

Perhaps the most fundamental long-term problem, however, is that Chile's wealth depends in part on the ongoing rape of its extensive natural resources, often by multinational companies; industries such as logging and intensive fishing, while successful at present, have the potential to ruin Chile's future. One example is the ongoing plan to built a series of huge hydroelectric plants in the Aysen region in the far south, which would destroy the pristine ecosystems of Chilean Patagonia. There has been widespread local opposition (see www.patagoniasinrepresas.cl for more details). According to one estimate, Chile lost 80% of its marine life in the 1980s and its native forests continue to disappear at alarming rates. Environmentalists have joined forces with farmers to highlight the environmental damage caused by introduced species such as the eucalyptus, which extracts most of the goodness from the soil, and by plantations of pine, which acidify the soil. Chile's Free Trade Agreements with Europe, North America and China are not seen as beneficial in all quarters.

However, these moves are symbolic of Chile's increasingly outward-looking mentality. After four centuries characterized by isolation and insularity, the ramifications of Chile's recent history have put the country onto the international map in an unprecedented manner. Whereas, until recently, Chileans compared themselves to Europeans, they now take increasing national pride in their own achievements. Even though Pinochet was not put on trial in Chile, the case and its consequences mean that the country is at the vanguard of one of the most significant human rights movement in history; one that, in a short space of time, has already had repercussions for repressive former heads of state in the Central African Republic and Yugoslavia.

Constitution and government

Chile is governed under the 1980 Constitution, introduced by the military government of General Pinochet and approved in a plebiscite on 11 September 1980, although important amendments were made during the transition to civilian rule in 1989-1990. The constitution provided for an eight-year non-renewable term for the President of the Republic, a bicameral legislature with a Congress and a Senate and an independent judiciary and central bank, although it was only after the rejection of Pinochet in the 1988 vote that most of the provisions of the constitution come into operation. A two-thirds majority in both houses of legislature is required to reform the constitution. In February 1994, the legislature cut the presidential term of office from eight years to six, and in 2006 it was further reduced to four years. Presidents are prohibited from holding two consecutive terms of office. The legislature is composed of a 120-seat Chamber of Deputies and a 47-seat Senate.

The dominant political party in Chile is the Christian Democrats, a centre party that grew rapidly after its foundation in 1957. The Christian Democrats welcomed the overthrow of Allende but later became the focus of opposition to the dictatorship. Not strong enough to rule on its own, since 1990 the party has contested elections in an alliance known as the **Concertación**. The other members are the Socialists, a centre-left party traditionally split between the Radicals and the Partido por la Democracía, a centre-left grouping led by ex-Socialists. The main opposition to the Concertación comes from the right wing, which is divided into two main parties, Renovación Nacional and the ever stronger Unión Democrática Independiente. In recent elections, they have formed an alliance called the **Alianza para Chile**.

Chile is divided into 15 regions, usually referred to by Roman numerals (although they also have names). The government of each region is headed by an *intendente*, who is appointed by the president.

Economy

Chile's economy is dependent on the mining sector. Mineral ores account for half of total export revenue. Copper is the most important mineral, with Chile being the world's largest producer. Although the Pinochet government of 1973-1990 sold off most state-run industries to the private sector, CODELCO (the state copper mining company) was not touched. The biggest new mine is La Escondida, where production began in 1990, which produces an output of 800,000 tonnes a year, making it the world's leading mine (see page 233), while Chuquicamata is the biggest open-cast mine in the world. Other mineral resources in Chile include a quarter of the world's known molybdenum ore reserves and around 40% of the world's lithium reserves. Fluctuations in world prices for minerals can have a great impact on the country's balance of payments.

The country's diverse environment means that agriculture is also of great importance. Traditional crops, such as cereals, pulses and potatoes, and industrial crops, such as sugar beet, sunflower seed and rape seed, account for about a third of the value of agriculture, while vegetables account for a quarter. Fruit growing has expanded rapidly, with fresh fruit now accounting for over US$1 billion in exports a year, while timber and wood products make up the third place in exports. Chile is the most important fishing nation in Latin America and the largest producer of fishmeal in the world; it is also one of the world's leading salmon farmers.

Chile is fortunate in possessing reserves of oil, natural gas and coal, and abundant hydroelectricity potential. Almost all the country's hydrocarbon reserves are in the extreme south, on Tierra del Fuego, in the Strait of Magellan. Two pipelines are planned and six new gas-fired power plants have recently been built. Manufacturing activity is mostly food processing, metalworking, textiles, footwear and fish processing.

The government follows anti-inflationary policies, accompanied by structural adjustment and reform. Privatization has been widespread, although certain key companies, such as Codelco, remain in state hands. Rising investor confidence has brought reasonably stable economic growth since the late 1980s and the Chilean model has been held up as an example for other debtor countries.

Culture

Chilean culture is rooted in the nation's hybrid soul. European guitars blend with panpipes and *queñas*; religious art flourishes alongside traditional crafts; literature scales the heights of modernism, while never losing track of the natural beauty from which it is born.

Society

Chile is a deeply conservative country: it was the first newly independent state in Latin America fully to embrace the Catholic church and has the most stable 'democratic' (or, until the 1950s, oligarchic) tradition in the region.

There is less racial diversity in Chile than in most Latin American countries. Over 90% of the population of 16 million is *mestizo* (mixed race). There are hardly any people of African origin – in sharp contrast to, say, Brazil or Colombia – and there has been much less immigration from Europe than in Argentina and Brazil. The German, French, Italian and Swiss immigrants came mostly after 1846 as small farmers in the forest zone south of the Biobío. Between 1880 and 1900, gold-seeking Serbs and Croats settled in the far south and the British took up sheep farming and commerce in the same region.

There is disagreement over the number of indigenous people in Chile. Survival International estimate the **Mapuche** population to be one million, but other statistics – including the official ones – put it at much less. There are also 45,000-50,000 **Aymara** in the northern Chilean Andes and 4500 **Rapa Nui** on Easter Island. A political party, the Party for Land and Identity, unites many indigenous groupings, and legislation is proposed to restore indigenous people's rights.

The population is far from evenly distributed: Middle Chile, from La Serena to Concepción, consisting of 20% of the country's area, is home to over 77% of the population, with the Metropolitan Region of Santiago containing, on its own, about 40% of the total. Population density in 2002 ranged from 393 per sq km in the Metropolitan Region to 0.84 per sq km in Región XI (Aisén). Since the 1960s, heavy migration from the countryside has led to rapid urbanisation. By 2002, 86.6% of the population lived in urban areas.

According to the most recent (2002) census the population is 70% Catholic and 15% Protestant. Membership of Evangelical Protestant churches has grown rapidly in recent years. There are also small Jewish communities in Santiago and Temuco especially.

Chilean literacy rates are higher than those of most other South American states; according to the 2002 census over 95% of the population above the age of 10 is literate. Census returns also indicated that, among the over-25s, 16% had completed higher education, 52% had completed secondary education and 41% had only completed primary education. Higher education provision doubled in the 1980s through the creation of private universities.

In November 2004, and to the consternation of the Catholic church and most conservative politicians Chile became one of the last countries in the world to legalise divorce. Until then, couples that wanted to separate had to go through the farcical process of getting a notary to swear that they were married in an inappropriate municipality and that their marriage certificate is therefore invalid. Even now the process is not cheap and the upshot for impoverished rural populations is that divorce – and remarriage – is still, in effect, impossible.

Traditional arts and crafts

Chile's traditional crafts are often specific to particular places and all have a long history. Present-day handicrafts represent either the transformation of utilitarian objects into works of art, or the continued manufacture of pieces that retain symbolic value. A number of factors threaten these traditions: the loss of types of wood and plant fibres through the destruction of forests; the mechanisation of farm labour, reducing the use of the horse; other agricultural changes, which have, among other things, led to reductions in sheep farming and wheat growing; and migration from the countryside to the city. On the other hand, city dwellers and tourists have created a demand for 'traditional' crafts so their future is to some degree assured.

Basketry Mapuche basketry is made for domestic, agricultural and fishing uses in Lago Lanalhue and the Cautín region. Apart from the Mapuche areas, one of the great centres of basket-making is Chimbarongo, just south of San Fernando in the Central Valley. Here, weaving is done in almost every household, usually by the men. One of the main materials used is willow, which is collected in June when it is still green and then soaked in water for four months, at the end of which the bark peels off. The lengths of willow are split into four and finished with a knife. Baskets, chairs and lamps are the most common objects made. Willow is not the only fibre used. Many items are made from different types of straw, including little boxes made of wheat; although the latter are produced throughout the country, the most famous are from La Manga, Melipilla. Note also the yawl made for fishing, typical of Chiloé. Other important centres of basket-making are Ninhue-Hualte in Nuble (Región VIII), Hualqui, 24 km south of Concepción, and San Juan de la Costa, near the coast of Osorno, Región X.

Carving and woodwork The people of the Atacama region edge trays with cactus wood and make little churches – traditionally the doors of the old churches were made of cactus – and they also use cactus for drums, while bamboo is used for flutes of various sizes. Different types of wood are used in the construction of guitars, *guitarrones*, harps and *rabeles* (fiddles), mainly in the Metropolitan Region. Villarrica (see page 340) is a major producer of wooden items: plates, kitchen utensils, but especially decorative objects like animals and birds, jointed snakes and *picarones* (small figures, which, when picked up, reveal their genitals). Wooden ships in bottles are made in Coronel, while in Loncoche, south of Temuco, a workshop specialises in fine carvings, in native wood, of country and Mapuche scenes. Another craft from the Mapuche region is the carving of horn or antler (*asta*) in Temuco, to make animals, birds, cups, spoons, etc.

Ceramics The two most famous places for ceramics are Quinchamalí near Chillán, where the traditional blackware is incised with patterns in white, and Pomaire, west of Santiago (see page 104), which is renowned for heavy terracotta household items that are used in many Chilean homes. Less well known is the pottery of the Atacama zone, the clay figures of Pañul and Lihueimo (Región VI), the household items, clay figurines and model buildings of Pilén de Cauquenes-Maule (Región VII) and the scented pottery of the nuns of the Comunidad de Santa Clara (Convento de Monjas Claras in Santiago and Los Angeles). These highly decorated pieces have been made since colonial times, when they achieved great fame.

Cowboy equipment and clothing Items can be found in any part of the country where there are *huasos*: Rancagua, San Fernando, Chillán, Curicó, Colchagua, Doñihue and also in Santiago. Saddles of leather, wood and iron, carved wooden stirrups in the old style, leather reins, spurs (some of them huge and very elaborate – *huasos* are always proud of their spurs) and hats of straw or other materials are the types of equipment you will see. The clothing comprises ponchos (long, simple in colour and design, often with one or two coloured stripes), *mantas* (shorter, divided into four with a great variety of colour), *chamantos* (luxurious *mantas*, double-sided, decorated with fine patterns of vines, leaves, flowers, small birds etc) and sashes/*fajas* (either single or tri-coloured, made to combine with *mantas* or *chamantos*).

Knitwear and textiles Chiloé is famous for its woollen goods, hand-knitted and coloured with natural dyes. With the atrocious weather, clothing (such as sweaters, knitted caps, *mantas*, socks) is very popular; this and rugs, blankets and patch dolls are all sold locally and in Puerto Montt. The main knitting centres are Quinchao, Chonchi and Quellón. Other crafts of Chiloé are model-boat building and basketware from Quinchao and Quellón, where mats and figurines such as birds and fish are also made.

The Mapuche are also weavers of sheep's wool, making ponchos, *mantas*, sashes (*fajas*), reversible rugs (*lamas*) with geometric designs and bedspreads (*pontros*). The colours come from natural dyes. The main producing areas are around Lago Lanalhue, Chol Chol, Nueva Imperial and other small settlements in the Mapuche heartland between Temuco and the coast.

Silverware Although silverware is one of the traditional crafts of the Mapuche, its production is in decline owing to the cost of the metal. Traditional women's jewellery includes earrings, headbands, necklaces, brooches and *tupus* (pins for fastening the *manta* or shawl). Nowadays, the most common items to be found for sale are *chawai* (earrings), but these are smaller and in simpler shapes than those traditionally worn by Mapuche women. It is a matter of debate whether Mapuche silversmiths had perfected their skills before the arrival of the Spaniards; certainly the circulation of silver coins in the 18th century gave great impetus to this form of metalwork. The Universidad Católica in Temuco is in charge of a project to ensure the continuance of the art.

Specialist crafts The Mapuche make musical instruments: the *trutruca*, a horn 1½ to 4 m long; *pifilka* (or *pifüllka*), a wooden whistle; the *kultrún* drum; *cascahuilla*, a string of bells; and *trompe*, similar to a Jew's harp. The village of Rari, near the Termas de Panimávida, some 25 km northeast of Linares (Región VII), specializes in beautiful, delicate items made from dyed horsehair: bangles and brooches in the shape of butterflies, little hats, flowers, etc.

Mined in the Cordillera de Ovalle, lapis lazuli is a blue stone, only found otherwise in Afghanistan. It is set in silver to make earrings, necklaces and bracelets. Many shops in

Santiago sell the semi-precious stone and objects that incorporate it. Of growing popularity in recent years, combarbalita is a smooth, marble-like stone found only around the remote town of Combarbalá in Región IV. A very beautiful stone that comes in a variety of hues, it is used to make everything from jewellery and cutlery holders to bedside tables and can be very good value.

Fine art and sculpture

The colonial period

There was little home-grown art during the colonial period in Chile but trade with other regions was extensive and Santiago in particular has good collections of non-Chilean art. The Catholic church inevitably dominated fine art and sculpture; the new religious foundations needed images of Christ and the saints to reassure Christian settlers and also to instruct new converts. The importation of works from Spain was very costly, so most patrons relied instead on the major colonial artistic centres of Cuzco, Potosí and Quito.

The churches and monasteries of Santiago give a vivid sense of the thriving art market in colonial Spanish America: sculptures were shipped down the coast from Lima and from Quito via Guayaquil; canvasses were carried across the Andes on mule trains from Cuzco and Potosí; and occasionally an itinerant Spanish-trained artist would pass through in search of lucrative commissions. Extensive cycles of the lives of Christ, the Virgin and selected saints were popular: a cycle of 40 or 50 large canvasses representing the exploits of, say, St Francis, provided instant cover for large expanses of bare plaster, a good clear narrative and an exemplary life to follow.

San Francisco in Santiago (see page 70) has a cycle of 53 paintings of the life of St Francis painted in Cuzco in the late 17th century. These are based on a similar cycle in the Franciscan monastery in Cuzco by the indigenous artist Basilio de Santa Cruz Pumacallao, which is in turn derived from a series of European engravings. One of the Santiago paintings, the Funeral of St Francis of 1684, is signed by **Juan Zapaca Inca**, an indigenous artist and follower of Santa Cruz, who probably oversaw production of the whole series. Wherever possible the artist has introduced bright-coloured tapestries and rich fabrics embellished with lace and gold embroidery, a mark of the continuing importance of textiles in Andean culture. This is a typical pattern for colonial art: a set of European engravings forms the basis for a large painted cycle which in turn becomes the source for further copies and derivatives. The narrative content and general composition remain constant, while the setting, attendant figures, costume and decorative detail are often translated into an Andean idiom.

There are, of course, many different categories of colonial art. The big painted cycles were produced more for the educated inhabitants of the monastic establishments than for a lay audience, and were intended for edification rather than devotion. Popular devotion tends to create increasingly decorated and hieratic images. A good example is that of the so-called Cristo de Mayo. Early in the 17th century Pedro de Figueroa, a friar of the Augustinian monastery in Santiago, carved a figure of the crucified Christ, which still hangs in the church of **San Agustín** (Estado 170, not far from Cerro Santa Lucía). This passionate, unusually defiant image was credited with miraculous powers after it survived a serious earthquake in Santiago in May 1647 (hence the popular name de Mayo). The only damage was that the crown of thorns slipped from Christ's head and lodged around his neck. A cult quickly grew up around the image, creating a demand for painted copies, which are identifiable by the upward gaze, the distinctive necklace of thorns and the evenly distributed lash marks across the body. The Carmelite convent of San José has a locally produced 18th-century example of the Cristo de Mayo that includes attendant saints and garlands of bright flowers, the latter like pious offerings. The Jesuits established a school of sculpture on Chiloé, where, up until the late 19th century, native craftsmen continued to produce boldly expressive Christian images.

After Independence

In the 19th century, Chile's distance from the old colonial centre of viceregal power worked to its advantage in the field of art. The Lima-born artist **José Gil de Castro** (died 1841), known as El Mulato Gil, accompanied Bernardo O'Higgins on the campaign for Chilean Independence from 1814, working both as engineer and map-maker and as a portrait painter. His portrait of O'Higgins of 1820 in the **Museo Histórico Nacional** in Santiago represents the hero as a towering giant of a man, immovable as the rocky mountains behind him. Another 1818 painting in the **Municipalidad of La Serena** shows San Martín standing beside a writing desk, his hand inside his jacket in a distinctively Napoleonic pose.

The 19th century also brought European traveller-artists to Chile, who helped to confirm the Chilean landscape, peoples and customs as legitimate subjects for paintings, including the German Johann Moritz Rugendas, who lived in Chile from 1833 to 1845, and the Englishman Charles Wood (in Chile from 1819 to 1852). Examples of both artists' work can be seen in the **Museo Nacional de Bellas Artes** (see page 69). The Frenchman Raymond Monvoisin also spent many years in Chile, from 1843 to 1857. His perceptive portraits of members of the government and the literary elite are interesting for the way in which they link the Chilean tradition of Gil de Castro with European sources. After his return to France he produced the first major painting dedicated to an event from colonial history, the Mapuche hero Caupolicán taken prisoner by the Spaniards (1859). Caupolicán was celebrated in Chile 10 years later in a bronze statue by Nicanor Plaza (1844-1914) erected on the Cerro Santa Lucía in Santiago, and although it originated as an entry for a competition organised by the US government for a statue to commemorate the Last of the Mohicans, it represents the incorporation of indigenous people into the national mythology.

The **Chilean Academy of Painting** was founded in 1849 and, although its first presidents were mediocre European artists, they too helped to make Chilean subject matter respectable. The Academy also acted as a focus for aspiring young artists. **Antonio Smith** (1832-1877) rebelled against the rigidity of the academic system, working as a political cartoonist as well as a painter, but his dramatic landscapes grew out of the gradual awakening of interest in Chilean scenery. He transformed the picturesque view into a heroic vision of mountains and valleys, full of air and space and potential. Cosme San Martín (1850-1906), Pedro León Carmona (1853-1899), Pedro Lira (1845-1912), Alfredo Valenzuela Puelma (1856-1909) and English-born Thomas Somerscales (1842-1927) extended the range of possible national subjects in the fields of landscape, portraiture, history and genre. The late 19th century saw a number of important commissions for nationalistic public statuary including the peasant soldier *El Roto Chileno* in Santiago's Plaza Yungay by Nicanor Plaza's pupil Virginio Arias (1855-1941), and several monumental works by Rebecca Matte (1875-1929).

The 20th century

From the later 19th century until well into the 20th century, Chilean painting was dominated by refracted versions of Impressionism. Artists such as **Juan Francisco González** (1853-1933) and **Alfredo Helsby** (1862-1933) introduced a looser technique and more luminous palette to create landscapes full of strong contrasts of sunlight and shadows, a tradition continued by, for example, **Pablo Burchard** (1873-1964), **Agustín Abarca** (1882-1953), **Arturo Gordon** (1883-1944) and **Camilo Mori** (1896-1973).

The Chilean avant garde has been dominated by artists who have lived and worked for long periods abroad, many as political exiles. After studying with Le Corbusier in Switzerland and encountering the Surrealists in Paris, **Roberto Matta** (1911-2002) moved to New York in 1939 and began painting uniquely unsettling space-age monsters and machines that circulate in a multi-dimensional chaos; he is perhaps the most famous artist to have come from Chile. **Nemesio Antúnez** (1918-1993) developed more earth-bound abstractions of reality: volcanic landscapes viewed through flames and falling rocks, or milling crowds, faceless and powerless.

The younger generation includes **Eugenio Dittborn** (born 1943), who sends 'Airmail Paintings' around the world in an exploration of ideas of transition and dislocation and, because many contain photographs of victims of political violence, of anonymity and loss. **Alfredo Jaar** (born 1956) creates installations using maps and photographs to document the destructive exploitation of the world's resources, both human and natural – most recently focusing on the aftermath of the Rwandan genocide.

In recent years many exiles have returned home and Santiago is now a cultural centre of growing importance, with women particularly well represented (for example **Carmen Valbuena**, born 1955, and **Bernarda Zegers**, born 1951). Chile is the home of an interesting ongoing project called '**Cuerpos Pintados**' (Painted Bodies), whereby artists from Chile and other Latin American countries are invited to Santiago to paint nude models in the colours and designs of their choice. It is worth watching out for exhibitions of the stunning photographs that are the project's permanent outcome; and also for one-off exhibitions up and down the country of the many very talented local artists (especially in cultural centres such as Valparaíso and Concepción).

Literature

From colonial times to Independence

The long struggle of the Spaniards to conquer the lands south of their Peruvian stronghold inspired one of the great epics of early Spanish American literature, *La Araucana* by **Alonso de Ercilla y Zúñiga** (1533-1594). Published in three parts (1569, 1578 and 1589), the poem tells of the victories and defeats of the Spaniards. Nothing like an apologia, the work endures because it recognises the brutal actions of the Spaniards. Like a subsequent work, *Arauco domado* (1596), by the *criollo* **Pedro de Oña** (1570-1643), the point of view is that of the conquering invader, not a celebration of Chilean, or American identity, although Ercilla does show that the people who resisted the Spaniards were noble and courageous. After Ercilla, literature written in what was to become Chile concentrated on chronicling either the physical or the spiritual conquest of the local inhabitants.

Writers in the 18th and early 19th centuries tended to mirror the colonial desire to consolidate the territory that was in Spanish, rather than Mapuche hands. Post-Independence, the move was towards the establishment of the new republic. To this end, the Venezuelan **Andrés Bello** (1781-1865) was invited to Santiago from London in 1829 to oversee the education of the new elite. Already famous for his literary journals and strong views on Romantic poetry, Bello made major contributions to Chilean scholarship and law. His main work was *Gramática de la lengua castellana destinada al uso de los americanos* (1847). As Jean Franco says, "He was one of the first of many writers to see that a general literary Spanish could act as an important cohesive factor, a spiritual tie of the Hispanic peoples".

A cultural haven

Chile's relative political stability in the 19th century helped Santiago to become a cultural centre that attracted many foreign intellectuals, such as the Argentine Diego Sarmiento and the Nicaraguan Rubén Darío. At this time, Chilean writers were establishing a national literary framework to replace the texts of the colonial era. This involved the spreading of *buenas costumbres*, a movement to shift literary subject matter onto Chilean territory, a republican education for the middle classes and the founding of a national identity. Realist fiction captured the public interest. **José Victorino Lastarria** (1817-1888) wrote *costumbrista* stories, portraying national scenes and characters, while **Alberto Blest Gana** (1829-1904) enjoyed two periods of success as a novelist, heavily influenced by Balzac. His most popular novel was *Martín Rivas* (1862), the love story of a young man who wins a wife of a higher class. For some, Blest Gana's presentation of Santiago and its class structure is a worthy imitator of the French *comédie humaine*; for others, his realism fails either to unite his themes to his sketches of Chilean life or to rise above a pedestrian style.

Twentieth-century prose writing

Realism remained the dominant mode of fiction until well into the 20th century, but it appeared in several guises. **Baldomero Lillo** (1867-1923) wrote socialist realist stories about the coal miners of Lebu: *Sub terra* (1904) and *Sub sole* (1907). Lillo and other regionalist writers shifted the emphasis away from the city to the countryside and the miserable conditions endured by many Chileans. Other novelists, including **Luis Orrego Luco** (1866-1948) and **Joaquín Edwards Bello** (1887-1968), concentrated on the crisis of aristocratic values and the gulf between the wealthy and the deprived.

Another strand was *criollismo*, a movement seeking to portray Chile and the tribulations of Chileans without romanticism, championed especially by short story writers like **Mariano Latorre** (1886-1955). His main interest was the Chilean landscape, which he described almost to the point of overwhelming his characters. A different emphasis was given to regionalism and *criollismo* by **Augusto d'Halmar** (Augusto Goeminne Thomson, 1882-1950), whose stories in *La lámpara en el molino* (1914) were given exotic settings and were labelled *imaginismo*. D'Halmar's followers, the Grupo Letras (1920s and 1930s), became openly antagonistic towards the disciples of Latorre: **Luis Durand** wrote books in the 1920s and 1940s that described *campesino* life in detail. Another branch of realism was the exploration of character through psychology in the books of **Eduardo Barrios** (1884-1963), such as *El niño que enloqueció de amor* (1915), *El hermano asno* (1922) and *Los hombres del hombre* (1950).

The anti-fascist views of a group of writers known as the Generation of 1938 (**Nicomedes Guzmán**, 1914-1965, **Juan Godoy**, **Carlos Droguett**, born 1915, and others) added a politically committed dimension, which coincided with the rise to power of the Frente Popular, a Socialist movement. At the same time, *Mandrágora*, a journal principally dedicated to poetry, introduced many European literary ideas, notably those of the surrealists. Its influence, combined with a global decline in Marxist writing after the Second World War and the defeat of the Frente Popular, contributed to the rise of a new generation of writers in the 1950s, whose main motivation was the rejection of all the 'ismos' that had preceded it. These novelists, short story writers and dramatists were characterised by existential individualism and political and social scepticism. Many writers started publishing in the 1950s; among them was **Volodia Teitelboim** (born 1916), a communist exiled to the USSR after 1973, whose novels *Hijo del salitre* (1952) and *La semilla en la arena* (1957) were portrayals of the struggles of the Chilean masses. In 1979 he published *La guerra interna*, which combined real and imaginary characters in a vision of post-coup Chile.

From the 1920s on, a significant development away from *criollismo* was the rise of the female voice. The first such novelist to achieve major recognition was **Marta Brunet** (1901-1967), who brought a unique perspective to the rural themes she handled (including the need to value women), but who has also been described as a writer of the senses (by Nicomedes Guzmán). Her books include *Montaña adentro* (1923), *Aguas abajo* (1943), *Humo hacia el sur* (1946) and *María Nadie* (1957). Also born in 1901, **María Flora Yáñez** wrote about the alienation of women with great emphasis on the imagination as an escape for her female protagonists from their routine, unfulfilled lives (*El abrazo de la tierra*, 1934; *Espejo sin imágen*, 1936; *Las cenizas*, 1942). **María Luisa Bombal** (1910-1980) took the theme of alienated women even further (*La última niebla*, 1935; *La amortajada*, 1938, and various short stories): her narrative and her characters' worlds spring from the subconscious realm of female experience and are expressed through dreams, fantasies and journeys loaded with symbolic meaning.

Manuel Rojas (1896-1972) was brought up in Argentina, but his family moved to Chile in 1923. His first short stories, such as *Hombres del sur* (1926), *Travesía* (1934) and the novel *Lanchas en la bahía* (1932) were undoubtedly *criollista* in outlook, but he devoted a greater importance to human concerns than his *criollista* contemporaries. By 1951, Rojas' style had changed dramatically, without deserting realism. *Hijo de ladrón* (1951) was perhaps the most influential 20th-century Chilean novel up to that time. It describes the adventures of Aniceto Hevía, the son of a Buenos Aires jewel thief, who crosses the Andes to Valparaíso, ending up as a beachcomber. Nothing in his life is planned or motivated by anything other than the basic necessities. Happiness and intimacy are only brief moments in an unharmonious, disordered life. Aniceto's adventures are continued in *Mejor que el vino* (1958), *Sombras contra el muro* (1963) and *La obscura vida radiante* (1971). To describe the essential isolation of man from the inside, Rojas relaxes the temporal structure of the novel, bringing in memory, interior monologue and techniques to multiply the levels of reality (to use Fernando Alegría's phrase).

The demise of *criollismo* coincided with the influence of the US Beat Generation and the culture epitomized by James Dean, followed in the 1960s by the protest movements in favour of peace, and black and women's rights. The Cuban Revolution inspired Latin American intellectuals of the left and the novel-writing 'boom' gained momentum. At the same time, the national political process that led ultimately to Salvador Allende's victory in 1970 was bolstered by writers, folk singers and painters who questioned everything to do with the Chilean bourgeoisie.

José Donoso (1924-1996) began publishing stories in 1955 (*Veraneo y otros cuentos*), followed two years later by his first novel, *Coronación*. This book describes the chaos caused by the arrival of a new maid into an aristocratic Santiago household and introduces many of Donoso's recurring themes: the closed worlds of old age and childhood, madness, multiple levels of reality, the inauthenticity of the upper classes and the subversion of patriarchal society. The stories in *Charleston* (1960), *El lugar sin límites* (1966), about a transvestite and his daughter who live in a brothel near Talca, and *Este domingo* (1966) mark the progression from *Coronación* to *El obsceno pájaro de la noche* (1970), a labyrinthine novel (Donoso's own term) narrated by a schizophrenic, throwing together reality, dreams and fantasy, darkness and light. Donoso achieved the same status as Gabriel García Márquez, Julio Cortázar and Mario Vargas Llosa with this, his most experimental novel. Between 1967 and 1981 he lived in Spain; in the 1970s he published several novels, including *Casa de campo* (1978), which relates the disintegration of a family estate when the children try to take it over. Back in Chile, he published, among others, *El jardín de al lado* (1981), which chronicles the decline of a middle-aged couple in exile in Spain, *Cuatro para Delfina* (1982), *La desesperanza* (1986) about the return of a left-wing singer from Paris to the daily horrors of Pinochet's regime.

Another writer who describes the bad faith of the aristocracy is **Jorge Edwards** (born 1931). His books include *El patio* (1952), *Los convidados de piedra* (1978), *El museo de cera* (1980), *La mujer imaginaria* (1985) and *Fantasmas de carne y hueso* (1993). His book *Persona non grata* (1973) describes his experiences as a diplomat, including his expulsion from Cuba. **Fernando Alegría** (born 1918) spans all the movements since 1938, with a variety of work including essays, highly respected literary criticism, poetry and novels. He was closely associated with Salvador Allende and was his cultural attaché in Washington 1970-1973. *Recabarren* was published in 1938, after which followed many books, among them *Lautaro, joven libertador del Arauco* (1943), *Caballo de copas* (1957), *Mañana los guerreros* (1964), *El paso de los gansos* (1975), about a young photographer's experiences in the 1973 coup, *Coral de guerra* (1979), also about brutality under military dictatorship, *Una especie de memoria* (1983), Alegría's own memoir of 1938 to 1973, and *Allende: A Novel* (1992). Having been so close to Allende, Alegría could not write a biography, he had to fictionalise it, he said. But the rise and fall of Allende becomes a realisation that history and fiction are intimately related, particularly in that Chilean epoch.

The death of Salvador Allende in 1973, and with it the collapse of the left's struggle to gain power by democratic means, was a traumatic event for Chilean writers. Those who had built their careers in the 1960s and early 1970s were for the most part exiled, forcibly or voluntarily, and thus were condemned to face the left's own responsibility in Allende's failure. René Jara says that before 1970 writers had not managed to achieve mass communication for their ideas and 1970-1973 was too short a time to correct that. Once Pinochet was in power, the task became how to find a language capable of expressing the usurping of democracy without simplifying reality. Those in exile still felt part of Chile, a country temporarily wiped from the map, where their thought was prohibited.

There are many other contemporary male novelists who deserve mention: **Antonio Skármeta** (born 1940) was exiled in Germany until 1980, writing short stories and novels and directing theatre and film. His short-story collections include *El entusiasmo* (1967), *Desnudo en el tejado* (1969), *Tiro libre* (1973) and his novels *Soñé que la nieve ardía* (975), *No pasó nada* (1980), *Ardiente paciencia* (1985) and *Match-ball* (1989). *Ardiente paciencia*, retitled *El cartero de Neruda* after its successful filming as *Il postino*, is a good example of Skármeta's concern for the enthusiasms and emotions of ordinary people, skilfully weaving the love life of a postman and a bar owner's daughter into the much bigger picture of the death of Pablo Neruda and the fall of Allende. A different take entirely on the legacy of Neruda and Chilean letters in general is provided by **Roberto Bolaño** – also

Ariel Dorfman

As expressed in the subtitle of his fascinating recent memoir, *Heading South, Looking North* (1998), the literary and political career of Ariel Dorfman has taken the form of a 'bilingual journey', between the United States and South America, between English and Spanish. Born in Buenos Aires in 1942, as the son of Russian Jewish immigrants, Dorfman and his family were expelled from Argentina in the mid-1940s due to his father's political activism. They took up residence in New York, until McCarthyism sent the Dorfmans once more south in 1954, this time to Chile. Here, the monolingual, English-speaking adolescent gradually focused his attention on the Spanish language and on Chilean politics and culture, until the military coup of 1973 drove Dorfman once again into exile, where he became one of the most articulate, bilingual voices against the military regime.

Since the return to civilian government in 1990, Dorfman has divided his time between Santiago and a professional post at Duke University, writing and broadcasting in both Spanish and English. Dorfman's work, as a poet, novelist, short story writer, essayist, playwright and more recently scriptwriter, is concerned, in his words, with, "on the one hand, the glorious potential and need of human beings to tell stories and, on the other, the brutal fact that in today's world, most of the lives that should be telling those stories are generally ignored, ravaged and silenced". He is perhaps best known for his early critique of US cultural imperialism, *How to Read Donald Duck* (1971) and for *Death and the Maiden* (1990), later filmed by Roman Polanski, which deals with torture and resistance.

He often adapts his own work to different genres: *Widows* started as a poem, became a novel and later a play. Much of the work focuses on torture, disappearance, censorship and the exile condition, but also demonstrates staunch rebellion and resistance and optimism for our future. For further details, see page 612.

an exile – whose satirical novel *Nocturno de Chile* (2003 – English translation, *By Night in Chile*) provides both an understanding of the fate of the Chilean literary world under Pinochet and of the nature of that world itself.

Another famous Chilean exile is **Ariel Dorfman** (see box, above), whose work exemplifies the struggle of the exile to find a bridge between their social reality overseas and their Chilean identity. His prolific output includes the novels *Moros en la costa*, 1973 (Hard Rain), *La última canción de Manuel Sendero*, 1982 (The Last Song of Manuel Sendero), *Mascara*, 1988, *Viudas*, 1981 (Widows), *Konfidenz*, 1995 and *The Nanny and the Iceberg*, 1999; the plays *Death and the Maiden*, *Reader* (1995), *Widows* (1997) and two further dramas co-written with his son Rodrigo; several volumes of essays and many poems (some collected in English as *Last Waltz in Santiago and other poems of Exile and Disappearance* (1988). Most of Dorfman's work is currently in print in English.

The most successful Chilean novelist today is **Isabel Allende** (born 1942). Her book *La casa de los espíritus* (1982) was a phenomenally successful novel worldwide. Allende, a niece of Salvador Allende, was born in Peru and went into exile in Venezuela after the 1973 coup. *The House of the Spirits*, with its tale of the dynasty of Esteban Trueba interwoven with Chilean history throughout much of the 20th century, ends with a thinly disguised description of 1973. It was followed in 1984 by *De amor y de sombra*, a disturbing tale set during the Pinochet regime. The main motivation behind these novels is the necessity to preserve historical reality (see the brief prologue to *Of Love and Shadows*, "Here, write it, or it will be erased by the wind"). The same thing applies in *Paula* (1994), Allende's letter to her daughter in a coma, where possible salvation from the devastation of not being able to contact Paula comes through the "meticulous exercise of writing". She has also written *Eva Luna* (1987) and *Los cuentos de Eva Luna* (1990), about a fictional Venezuelan storyteller and her stories, *El plan infinito* (1991), *Daughter of Fortune* (1998), *Portrait in Sepia* (2002), and *Mi país inventado* (2002), a look at Chile and her people.

Like her predecessors, Allende employs the marvellous and the imaginary to propose alternatives to the masculine view of social and sexual relations. The same is true of **Lucía Guerra** (born 1942), who published *Más allá de las máscaras* in exile in 1984. Another example might be **Daniela Eltit** (born 1949), who did not leave Chile after 1973 and was actively involved in resistance movements. Her provocative, intense fiction confronts issues of exploitation, violence, the oppression of women and volatile mental states. In *Vaca sagrada* (1991) at least, the protagonist's vulnerability is expressed through her body, by her blood, her two lovers' effects upon it, the brutality inflicted upon it and her obsession with her heartbeat. The main characters live out their obsessions and fears in a city in which there are no jobs and no warmth. Three earlier novels, *Lumpérica* (1983), *Por la patria* (1986) and *El cuarto mundo* (1988) maintain the same experimental, challenging approach to contemporary Chilean society.

Twentieth-century poetry

In many ways, poetry is the lifeblood of Chilean culture; the country's poetic output is prodigious, with poetry circles thriving even in remote rural areas. In the first half of the 20th century, four figures dominated Chilean poetry, Gabriela Mistral, Vicente Huidobro, Pablo Neruda and Pablo de Rokha. The three men were all socialists, but their politics and means of expression followed different trajectories. Neruda overshadows all other Chilean poets on an international level, and for this reason he is discussed separately, see box, opposite.

Gabriela Mistral wrote poetry that rejected elaboration in favour of a simple style using traditional metre and verse forms. Her poetry derives from a limited number of personal roots: she fell in love with Romelio Ureta who blew his own brains out in 1909. This inspired the *Sonetos de la muerte* (1914), which were not published at the time. She never lost the grief of this tragic love, which was coupled with her love of God and her "immense martyrdom at not being a mother". Frustrated motherhood did not deprive her of tenderness, nor of a deep love for children. The other main theme was her appreciation of nature and landscape, not just in Chile, but also in North and South America and Europe, which she visited as a diplomat. Her three principal collections are *Desolación* (1923, but re-edited and amplified frequently), *Tala* (1938) and *Lagar* (1954). She also wrote many poems for children.

If Gabriela Mistral relied on tradition and verse to present her unique view of a lone woman trying to find a place in a male-oriented world, **Vicente Huidobro** (1893-1948) wanted to break with all certainties. He made grand claims for the poet's role as nothing short of a quest for the infinite and for the language to liberate it. From Santiago he moved to Buenos Aires, then Paris, where he joined the Cubists, collaborated with Apollinaire and others, began to write in French and got involved in radical politics. Between the 1920s and 1940s he moved from Europe to the USA to Chile, back to Spain

Pablo Neruda

Pablo Neruda was born in Parral on 12 June 1904 as Ricardo Neftalí Reyes. Two months later, his mother died and his father and stepmother subsequently moved the family to Temuco. Neruda's childhood memories were dominated by nature and, above all, rain, "my only unforgettable companion", as he described it in *Confieso que he vivido*. Among his teachers in Temuco was Gabriela Mistral. In 1921, he went to study in Santiago, but he had already decided on a literary career. His first book of poems *Crepusculario* (1923), was published under the pseudonym Neruda, borrowed from a Czech writer; it was postmodernist in style but did not yet reveal the poet's own voice. His next volume, *Veinte poemas de amor y una canción desesperada* (1924) catapulted him into the forefront of Latin American poetry. The freedom of the style and the natural, elemental imagery invoking the poet's two love affairs, made the collection an immediate success. Three books followed in 1926 before Neruda was sent to Rangoon as Chilean consul in 1927. His experiences in the Orient, including his first marriage, inspired one of his finest collections, *Residencia en la tierra*, in which the inherent sadness of the Veinte poemas becomes despair at the passing of time and human frailty. Reinforcing this theme is a kaleidoscope of images, seemingly jumbled together, yet deliberately placed to show the chaos and fragmentary nature of life.

In the 1930s, Neruda moved to Spain, where he met many poets. The Civil War, especially the death of Federico García Lorca, affected him deeply and his poetic vision became more direct, with a strong political orientation. 'Explico algunas cosas' in *Tercera residencia* (1947) explains the move towards militancy.

Between 1938 and the election of Videla to the Chilean presidency, Neruda worked with the Frente Popular and was consul general in Mexico. He also composed his epic poem of Latin American and Chilean history, from a Marxist stance, *Canto general* (1950). Its 15 cantos chronicle the natural and human life of the Americas, from the conquered pre-Columbian inhabitants to the 20th-century labourers. One of its most famous sections is 'Alturas de Machu Picchu', which mirrors the poet's own development: from the universal to 'minuscule life' from introspection to a new-found role as the voice of the oppressed. *Canto general* defined Neruda's subsequent enormous output.

The political commitment remained but did not submerge his respect for and evocation of nature in *Odas elementales* (1954), *Nuevas odas elementales* (1957) and *Tercer libro de odas* (1959), which begins with 'El hombre invisible'. He also never tired of writing lyric verse, such as *Los versos del capitán* (1950), *Cien sonetos de amor* (1959), and wrote memoirs such as *Memorial de Isla Negra* (1964) and *Confieso que he vivido* (1974). *Extravagaria* (1958), whose title suggests extravagance, wandering and variety, is full of memory, acceptance and a world-weary joy.

Neruda was awarded the Nobel Prize in 1971 but died of cancer two years' later. His death was hastened by the coup and the military's heartless removal of him from Isla Negra to Santiago. The poet's three houses were either ransacked or shut up by the dictatorship, but many of the Chileans for whom the poet spoke visited Isla Negra to leave messages of respect, love and hope until democracy returned. See Ariel Dorfman's 'Afterword' in *The House in the Sand*, translated by Dennis Maloney and Clark Zlotchew, 1990, Milkweed).

during the Civil War, before retiring to Llolleo to confront time and death in his last poems, *Ultimos poemas*, 1948. Huidobro considered himself at the forefront of the avant garde, formulating *creacionismo*, a theory that the poet is not bound by the real world, but is free to create and invent new worlds through the complete freedom of the word. Nevertheless, all the experimentation and imagery which "unglued the moon", was insufficient to achieve the language of revelation. So in 1931 he composed *Altazor*, a seven-canto poem that describes simultaneously the poet's route to creation and the ultimate frustration imposed by time and the human condition.

Pablo de Rokha (Carlos Díaz Loyola, 1894-1968) was deeply concerned for the destiny of the Chilean people and the advance of international socialism. His output was an uncompromising epic search for Chilean identity and through his work, for all its political commitment, there runs a deep sense of tragedy and inner solitude (especially true in *Fuego negro*, 1951, written after the death of his wife). *Los gemidos* was his first major book (1922); others included *Escritura de Raimundo Contreras* (1929), a song of the Chilean peasant, *Jesucristo* (1933) and *La morfología del espanto* (1942).

Although these poets, and Neruda especially, furthered the Chilean poetic tradition, those who came after were not necessarily keen to emulate his style or his politics. From the 1950s, poets were still critical of society but, taking their cue from **Nicanor Parra**, they did not elevate the writer's role in denouncing inhumanity, alienation and the depersonalisation of modern life. Instead writer and reader are placed on the same level; rhetoric and exuberant language are replaced by a conversational, ironic tone. **Parra** (born 1914; see also box, opposite), a scientist and teacher, called this attempt to overcome the influence of Neruda *antipoesía* (anti-poetry). In the poem '*Advertencia al lector*' in *Poemas y antipoemas* (1954), he writes:

> *According to the doctors of the law this book should not be published:*
> *The word rainbow does not appear in it,*
> *Let alone the word grief,*
> *Chairs and tables, yes, there are aplenty,*
> *Coffins! Writing utensils!*
> *Which fills me with pride*
> *Because, as I see it, the sky is falling to bits.*

Obra gruesa anthologises his work to 1969, followed by *Emergency Poems* (1972, bilingual edition, New York), which contain a darker humour and satire, but remain compassionate and socially committed, *Artefactos* (1972) and *Artefactos II* (1982), *Sermones y prédicas del Cristo de Elqui* (1979) and *Poesía política* (1983).

The adherents of *antipoesía* continually sought new means of expression, so that the genre never became institutionalised. There are too many poets to list here, but **Gonzalo Rojas** (born 1917), **Enríque Lihn** (1929-1988), **Armando Uribe** (born 1933) and **Miguel Arteche** (born 1926) are perhaps the best known.

Another poetic development of the 1950s onwards was *poesía lárica*, or *de lares*, poetry of one's place of origin (literally, of the gods of the hearth). Its founder and promoter was **Jorge Teillier** (1935-1996), whose poems describe a precarious rural existence, wooden houses, fencing, orchards, distant fires, beneath changing skies and rain. The city dweller is an exile in space and time who returns every so often to the place of origin. See especially '*Notas sobre el último viaje del autor a su pueblo natal*', which evokes the lost frontier of his youth, the changed countryside and his city life. As for the future, "if only it

Violeta Parra

Violeta Parra was brought up in Chillán as one of 11 children. Her father, Nicanor, was a music teacher, while her mother, Clarisa, was a seamstress who played the guitar and sang. Violeta sang with her sister Hilda in Santiago bars for several years. She also worked in the circus. Another child, Nicanor, became a professor of maths and physics, and a poet (see page 596).

Violeta travelled the length of Chile and abroad with the Chilean poet Pablo de Rokha (see page 596), collecting material and promoting their idea of Chilean-ness. While de Rokha expressed himself in the lyrical epic, Violeta sang, wrote songs, made tapestries, ceramics, paintings and sculpture. All her work was based on a philosophy of helping those in need. In France she was recognized as a great artist and her works were exhibited in the Louvre in 1964, but at home recognition was only grudgingly given.

In the 1960s Violeta set up La Carpa de la Reina as a centre for popular art in the capital. It was here, in February 1967, that she committed suicide, her head resting on her guitar. The national grief at her funeral far outweighed the acclaim given her during her life. Neruda called her 'Santa Violeta'; the Peruvian novelist Jose María Arguedas described her as 'the most Chilean of all Chileans I could possibly know, but at the same time the most universal of all Chile'.

For Violeta, folklore was a form of class struggle. Her influence on a whole generation of Latin American folk singers was enormous and long-lasting. Without her, Salvador Allende would not have had the folkloric backing of Victor Jara, Inti-Illimani, Los Quilapayún and the Parras themselves. After Violeta's death, her brother Nicanor published *Décimas*, a sort of autobiography in verse, full of simple humanity.

---

could be as beautiful as my mother spreading the sheets on my bed", but it is only an unpaid bill; "I wish the UFOs would arrive." In his later poems, the violence of the city and the dictatorship invade the *lares*. Among Teillier's books are *Para angeles y gorriones* (1956), *Para un pueblo fantasma* (1978), *Cartas para reinas de otras primaveras* (1985) and *Los dominios perdidos* (1992). A variation on this type of poetry comes from **Clemente Riedemann** (born 1953), whose *Karra Maw'n* deals with the Mapuche lands and German immigration in the area.

Many poets left Chile after 1973 but others stayed to attack the dictatorship from within through provocative, experimental works. In a country with such a strong poetic tradition and such a serious political situation, poets understood that their verses had to mutate in order to reflect and comment on their contemporary realities. A more experimental and opaque poetry developed as a result, dealing with themes such as the reaffirmation of colloquialism, the city (developed through the slang of *antipoesía*), and poetry itself, unravelling contexts and bridging the past and the present. Several writers were members of the Grupo Experimental de Artaud, including Daniela Eltit (see above), Eugenia Brito, Rodrigo Cánovas and **Raúl Zurita**, perhaps the most celebrated poet in Chile today: his verse is a complex and at times difficult union of mathematics and poetry, logical, structured and psychological. *Purgatorio* (1979) had an immediate impact and was followed by *Anteparaíso* (1982), *El paraíso está vacío* (1984), *Canto a su amor desaparecido* (1986) and *El amor de Chile* (1987). 'Pastoral de Chile' in *Anteparaíso* reveals most of Zurita's obsessions: Chilean landscapes, love, Chile's distress, sin and religious terminology.

Other significant poetic works of the 1980s include *La Tirana* (1985) by **Diego Maquieira**, a complex, multireferential work, dealing with a Mapuche virgin, surrounded by a culture that oppresses her and with which she disguises herself. It is irreverent; a 'black mass', threatening to the régime. Carmen Berenguer's *Bobby Sands desfallece en el muro* (1983) is a homage to the IRA prisoner and thus to all political prisoners. She also wrote *Huellas del siglo* (1986) and *A media asta* (1988). Carla Grandi published *Contraproyecto* in 1985, an example of feminine resistance to the coup.

Poetry continues to be significant in Chile. There are numerous workshops and organisations for young poets; the *Taller de Poesía de la Fundacion Pablo Neruda* is particularly influential. There are also important underground literary movements. Interesting contemporary poets include **Carolina Cerlis** and **Javier del Cerro**, both maintaining the experimental and free verse tradition of Zurita and others.

Cinema → See also page 24.

Not many months after the first screening organized by the Lumière brothers in Paris in December 1895, moving pictures were exhibited in Chile on 25 August 1896. Initially all the films were imported, but from 1902 local artists and entrepreneurs began to produce short documentaries. The first narrative movie, *Manuel Rodríguez*, was screened in September 1910. From about 1915, with European production semi-paralysed by war, the pre-eminence of Hollywood cinema was established. The modern dreams of Hollywood were often more complex, technologically superior and more entertaining than the products of rudimentary national cinemas. The historian of Chilean silent films, Eliana Jara Donoso, quotes a publicity handout for a local movie that read, "it's so good that it doesn't seem Chilean".

But despite the overwhelming presence of Hollywood, local film-makers in the silent era could still establish a small presence in the market. In the main they made documentaries, for this was a niche free of international competition: regional topics, football competitions, civic ceremonies, military parades. Almost 100 feature films were also made, but these are the domain of the film historian, since only one such movie has survived (carefully restored by the University of Chile in the early 1960s): *El húsar de la muerte* (The Hussar of Death), directed by Pedro Sienna in 1925. It was, like many movies in Latin America at the time, a historical melodrama, exploring the fight for Chilean independence from Spanish rule in the 1810s through the heroic exploits of the legendary Manuel Rodríguez. It achieved great box office success in a year when 16 Chilean films were screened. Never again would so many national movies be produced annually.

The coming of synchronized sound created a new situation in Latin America. In those countries with a large domestic market – in particular Mexico, Argentina and Brazil – investment was made in expensive machinery, installations and rudimentary studios. Elsewhere, and Chile is a telling example, sound devastated local production due to its cost and complexity. Local entrepreneurs were usually unwilling to make the risky capital investment, and the history of Chilean cinema thereafter is littered with tales of self-sacrifice on the part of cast and crew. The first non-silent film made in Chile was *Norte y Sur*, directed by **Jorge Délano** in 1934, telling the story of a love triangle where a woman is the object of the attentions of a Chilean and an American engineer. It was a rare example of sophisticated cinema at a time when Chilean film output was reverting to often formulaic stories of young men seducing innocent ladies, or the naïve idealisation of rural landscapes. Délano stood out in this age – another film of his, *Escándalo* (1940) dealt with the lives of the middle class, rather than those of the aristocracy or the peasantry. Nevertheless, Tobías Barros, an important director of the time, summed up the mood when he sarcastically described his *Río Abajo* as a film "where there are neither illegitimate nor lost children".

An attempt was made in the 1940s to stimulate cinema through state investment. The state agency CORFO saw cinema as an important growth industry and in 1942 gave 50% finance to set up **Chile Films**. Costly studios were erected, but the plan proved over-ambitious and Argentine film-makers ended up using most of the facilities; by 1947 Chile Films had collapsed. In 1959, however, the Universidad de Chile set up a Centre for Experimental Cinema under the direction of a documentary film-maker Sergio Bravo, which trained aspirant directors from Chile and elsewhere in Latin America (notably the Bolivian Jorge Sanjinés).

Cinema became intricately involved in the wider political discussions of the 1960s. The years 1968-1969 saw the maturity of Chilean cinema. Five features came out: **Raúl Ruiz**'s *Tres tristes tigres* (Three Sad Tigers); Helvio Soto's *Caliche sangriento* (Bloody Nitrate); Aldo Francia's *Valparaíso mi amor* (Valparaíso My Love); Miguel Littín's *El chacal de Nahueltoro* (The Jackal of Nahueltoro) and Carlos Elsesser's *Los testigos* (The Witnesses). These film-makers came from different ideological and aesthetic tendencies, from the inventive maverick Raúl Ruiz to the sombre neo-realism of Francia, but they can be seen as a group, working with very scarce resources: the films by Ruiz, Elsesser, Francia and Littín were made, consecutively, with the same camera; furthermore, many of the directors sought to break down the traditionally melodramatic themes of Chilean cinema, employing more realistic language and situations more reflective of everyday social problems. Aldo Francia, a doctor by profession, also organized a famous 'Meeting of Latin American Film-makers' at the Viña del Mar film festival in 1967. This would be one of the key events to cause growing awareness of cineastes across the continent that they were working with similar ideas and methods, producing 'new cinemas'.

The narrow victory of the Popular Unity parties in the election of 1970 was greeted by film-makers with an enthusiastic manifesto penned by **Miguel Littín**; Littín himself was put in charge of the revived state institution Chile Films. He lasted for only 10 months, tiring of bureaucratic opposition and inter-party feuding, as the different members of Popular Unity all demanded a share of very limited resources. Few films were made between 1970 and 1973; Raúl Ruiz was the most productive film-maker of the period, with a number of films in different styles. Littín was working on an historical feature *La tierra prometida* (The Promised Land) when the 1973 coup occurred and post-production took place in Paris.

The most ambitious film to trace the radicalization of Chile in 1972 and 1973 was Patricio Guzmán's three-part documentary *La batalla de Chile* (The Battle of Chile), which was edited in exile in Cuba. In the first years of exile, this film became Chile's most evocative testimony abroad and received worldwide distribution. Paradoxically, Chilean cinema, which had little time to grow under Popular Unity, strengthened in exile.

Policies following the coup practically destroyed internal film production for several years. Film personnel were arrested, tortured and imprisoned and many escaped into exile. Severe censorship was established: even *Fiddler on the Roof* was banned for displaying Marxist tendencies. It is from the exiled directors that the continuity of film culture can be seen. Littín took up residence in Mexico, supported by Mexican President, Echeverría, and became an explicit spokesman for political Latin American cinema, making the epic *Actas de Marusia* (Letters from Marusia) in 1975 and several other features in Mexico and later in Nicaragua. In the mid-1980s he returned clandestinely to Chile with several foreign film crews to make the documentary *Acta General de Chile* in 1986, a perilous mission documented by Gabriel García Márquez in his reportage *Clandestine in Chile* (1986). Raúl Ruiz took a less visible political role, but since his exile to France, he has produced a body of work that has earned him a reputation as one of the most innovative directors in Europe, the subject of a special issue in 1983 of France's distinguished journal *Cahiers du Cinéma*. He makes movies with great technical virtuosity and often great speed: on a visit to Santiago to celebrate the return to civilian rule in 1990, he shot a film, entitled *La telenovela errante* (The Wandering Soap Opera), in less than a week for US$30,000. Other exile directors to make their mark include Ruiz's wife Valeria Sarmiento, Gastón Ancelovici and Carmen Castillo, all based in France, Patricio Guzmán in Spain, Marilú Mallet in Canada, Angelina Vásquez in Scandinavia, Sebastián Alarcón in the Soviet Union and Antonio Skármeta in Germany.

Inside Chile, the output under censorship varied from maritime adventures such as *El Ultimo grumete* to Silvio Caiozzi's *Julio comienza en julio* (Julio begins in July, 1979), one of the first films made in the period, set carefully in a turn-of-the-century historical location and self-financed through Caiozzi's work in commercials. It would take him a further 10 years to produce a second feature, *La luna en el espejo* (The Moon in the Mirror), evocatively set in Valparaíso, which was screened in 1990. An example of increased critical debate within Chile in the last years of the Pinochet régime can be found in Pablo Perelman's *Imagen latente* (Latent Image, 1987) which tells of a photographer's search for a missing brother who disappeared after the coup; although the film was not released in Chile until 1990, it was possible to make the film in the country in the mid-1980s. Another case is that of *Hijos de la Guerra Fría* by Gonzalo Justiniano (1985), which is replete with metaphors of a society asphyxiated by a repressive system.

The return to civilian rule had some benefits for film-makers, most notably the easing of censorship. The Viña del Mar Film Festival was symbolically reinstated after 20 years and saw the emotional return of many exiled directors, but that, in itself, could not solve the problems of an intellectual community dispersed around the world and the chronic underfunding and under-representation of Chilean films in the home market. New names have emerged and some internationally successful films have been made, most notably Ricardo Larraín's *La Frontera* (The Frontier, 1991), one of the best Chilean films ever made, which tells of a school teacher's internal exile in the spectacular scenery of southern Chile in the late 1980s, which as Gustavo Graef-Marino's *Johnny Cien Pesos* (1993), which deals with violence in Chilean society. The latter was produced by Chile Films, a short-lived production company made up of film directors and producers financed by a State Bank credit loan. The loan was withdrawn, however, when other productions failed at the box office.

The last few years have seen the screening of one or two Chilean features a year, the best received being the political thriller *Amnesia* (1994), directed by Gonzalo Justiniano, Andrés Wood's vogue-ish *Historias de Futbol* (1997) and Sergio Castillo's 1997 *Gringuito*, which focuses on the problems of children brought up in exile, returning as foreigners to Chile. This gentle comedy of reintegration has been made to seem somewhat tame by the demonstrations in Chile surrounding the Pinochet extradition process. Larraín's latest feature *El entusiasmo* (Enthusiasms, 1999) did not live up to its title among local audiences but it garnered international recognition, as did Andrés Wood's new films, *Loco Fever,* an engaging comedy about two conmen's frenzied search for as many 'locos' – the shellfish, not the crazies – as possible, and most recently *Machuca,* a socio-political drama centred around the friendship of two boys, one rich and one poor, during the final doomed days of Allende's regime. While there are many talented young filmmakers, and although government art grants are becoming more available, the increasing globalisation of the culture industry, however, means that the pattern of scarce local production is likely to continue.

Music and dance

Traditional forms

As far as **traditional dance** goes, at the very heart of Chilean music is the *cueca,* a courting dance for couples, both of whom make great play with a handkerchief waved aloft in the right hand. The man's knees are slightly bent and his body arches back; in rural areas, he stamps his spurs together for effect. Guitar and harp are the accompanying instruments, while handclapping and shouts of encouragement add to the atmosphere. The dance has a common origin with the Argentine *zamba* and Peruvian *marinera* via the early 19th-century *zamacueca,* in turn descended from the Spanish *fandango.* The most traditional form of song is the *tonada,* with its variants the *glosa, parabienes, romance, villancico* (Christmas carol) and *esquinazo* (serenade), in common with the *custon* in Argentina, this may be heard in the form of a *contrapunto* or *controversia,* a musical duel. Among the most celebrated groups are **Los Huasos Quincheros**, Silvia Infante with **Los Condores** and the **Conjunto Millaray**, all of which are popular at rural dances, with their poignant combination of formal singing and rousing accordian music. Famous folk singers in this genre are the **Parra family** from Chillán (see box, page 597), **Hector Pávez** and **Margot Loyola**.

In the north of the country the music is Amerindian and closely related to that of Bolivia. Groups called 'Bailes' dance the *huayño, taquirari, cachimbo* or *rueda* at carnival and other festivities as well as pre-Columbian rites like the *cauzulor* and *talatur.* Instruments are largely wind and percussion, including *zampoñas* (pan pipes), *lichiguayos, pututos* (conch shells), *queñas* (flutes) and *clarines.* There are some notable religious festivals that attract large crowds of pilgrims and include numerous groups of costumed dancers. The most outstanding of these festivals are those of the **Virgen de La Tirana** near Iquique (see box, page 248), the **Virgen de la Candelaria** of Copiapó (see page 187) and the **Virgen de Andacollo** (see page 161).

In the south the Mapuche nation have their own songs, dance-songs and magic and collective dances, accompanied by wind instruments like the great long *trutruca* horn, the shorter *pifilka* and the *kultrún* drum. Further south still, Chiloé has its own unique musical expression: wakes and other religious social occasions include collective singing, while the recreational dances, all of Spanish origin – such as the *vals, pavo, pericona* and *nave* – have a heavier and less syncopated beat than in central Chile. Accompanying instruments here are the *rabel* (fiddle), guitar and accordion.

Nueva canción

The most famous Chilean movement on the international stage was that of the *nueva canción,* or new song, which arose in the late 1960s and early 1970s under such luminaries as **Violeta Parra** (see box, page 597) and **Victor Jara**. This movement, which scorned commercialism and sought to give a political meaning to its songs – whether overt or suggested – gave a whole new dimension to the Chilean musical scene, and was part of a wider movement across the continent, involving people such as Mercedes Sosa in Argentina and Sílvio Rodríguez in Cuba.

Facing the music

There are many famous Chilean groups whose music is still widely distributed and available internationally. These include Illapu, Inti Illimani, Quilapayún and the late Victor Jara. All these groups were involved in some way in the movement of La Nueva Canción, and went into exile after the military coup.

One of the best albums is Illapu's *Despedida del Pueblo*, of which the most popular and resonant song is *'Vuelvo'*, dealing with the emotions of the returning exile. Compilations of Victor Jara are usually good, and the collection of *Cantos de Pueblos Andinos* by Inti Illimani is a haunting, melodic introduction to their music.

Among the standard bearers of La Nueva Canción and one of Inti Illimani's most popular songs was *'El pueblo unido jamás será vencido'* ('The people, united, will never be divided') – a good old-fashioned protest song. Later Inti Illimani music demonstrates the influence of dance rhythms from the Caribbean, yet retains its Chilean roots – a good example is *'Andadas'*.

Chilean pop music scene has been dominated by the rock band La Ley. Los Prisioneros, an older band, were more political, producing music that expressed the feelings of the Chilean youth that grew up in the 1980s under the Pinochet dictatorship.

Beginning as an underground movement, faraway from the usual round of publicity and radio stations, the *Nueva Canción* protagonists rose to prominence during the 1970 election campaign, which resulted in the victory of Salvador Allende. Although related to folk rhythms, the movement sought to be dynamic and not confined to any particular style. Violeta Parra's suicide and the subsequent coup of 1973 forced its protagonists into exile – Inti Illimani to Italy, Illapu to France. But Victor Jara was imprisoned in the National Stadium after the coup and was hauled to his death, singing Violeta Parra's famous song, 'Gracias a la vida' (I give thanks to life). Now back in Chile, the ageing Intis and other nueva canción folk groups of the early 1970s still play regular concerts throughout the country.

Land and environment

Chile is smaller than all other South American republics except Ecuador, Paraguay, Uruguay and the Guianas. It is 4329 km long and, on average, no more than 180 km wide. In the north Chile has a short (150 km) east-west border with Peru. In the far north its eastern frontier is with Bolivia – 750 km long – but from San Pedro de Atacama south to Tierra del Fuego it shares over 3500 km of border with Argentina. In the main this frontier follows the water margin of the Andes but, in the far south, where the Andes are lower, or where icefields cover the border area, there have been frequent frontier disputes with Argentina; these still rumble on. Chilean sovereignty over the islands south of Tierra del Fuego gives it control over Isla Navarino, on which Puerto Williams is the most southerly permanent settlement in the world (apart from scientific bases in Antarctica). Various island archipelagos in the Pacific, including Easter Island/Rapa Nui and the Juan Fernández group, are under Chilean jurisdiction.

Geology

The Quaternary Period, 1.6 million years ago, was marked by the advance and retreat of the Antarctic Ice Sheet which, at its maximum extent, covered all of the Chilean Andes and the entire coastline south of Puerto Montt. However, although there are surface remnants of older rock formations, most have disappeared with the dramatic creation of the Andes, which started around 80 million years ago and continues to this day. The South American Plate, moving westwards, meets the Nazca and Antarctic plates, which are moving eastwards and sinking below the continent. These two plates run more or less parallel between 26°S and 33°S and the friction between them creates a geologically unstable zone, marked by frequent earthquakes and volcanic activity. The area of Concepción has been particularly susceptible to both land and undersea quakes and the city was twice destroyed by tidal waves in the 18th century before being moved to its present site.

All of the Chilean Pacific islands were formed by underwater volcanoes associated with fracture zones between the Nazca and Antarctic Plates. Easter Island gained its characteristic triangular shape from the joining together of three lava flows.

Northern desert

Northern Chile has a similar form to Peru immediately to the north: the coastal range rises to 1000-1500 m; inland are basins known as *bolsones*, east of which lie the Andes. The Atacama Desert is, by most measures, the driest area on earth, and some meteorological stations near the coast have never reported precipitation. Water is therefore at a premium as far south as Copiapó; it is piped in from the east and, in the Andean foothills, streams flow into alluvial fans in the inland basins, which can act as reservoirs and may be tapped by drilling wells. One river, the Río Loa, flows circuitously from the Andes to Calama and then through the coastal range to the coast; however, for most of its length it is deeply entrenched and unsuitable for agriculture. East of Calama and high in the Andes are the geysers of El Tatio, more evidence of volcanic activity, which are fed by the summer rains that fall in this part of the Andes.

In the past, notably as the ice sheets retreated, there were many lakes in the depressions between the Coastal Range and the Andes. These dried out, leaving one of

Glacial landscapes

Southern Chile provides some of the best examples of glacial landscapes on earth. One common sign of the region's glacial past is the U-shaped valleys. Good examples can be seen throughout the south, but perhaps one of the best is the Río Simpson between Coyhaique and Puerto Aisén. High above these valleys, sharp mountain ridges can often be seen, which have been caused by the eroding action of the ice on two or more sides. In some places, the resulting debris or 'moraine' formed a dam, blocking the valley and creating a lake, as in he Lake District at Lagos Calafquén, Panguipulli and Riñihue.

The drowned coastline south of Puerto Montt also owes its origin to glaciation. The ice that once covered the southern Andes was so heavy that it depressed the relatively narrow tip of South America. When the ice melted and the sea level rose, water broke through, leaving the western Andes as islands and creating the Chilean fjords, glaciated valleys carved out by the ice and now drowned.

the greatest concentrations of salts in the world, rich in nitrates: there has been extensive mining activity here since the late 19th century.

Central Chile

South of Copiapó the transition begins between the Atacama and the zone of heavy rainfall in the south. At first, the desert turns to scrub and some seasonal surface water appears. The Huasco and Elqui rivers follow deep trenches to reach the sea, allowing valley bottoms inland to be irrigated for agriculture. Further south, near Santiago, the Central Valley between the Coastal Range and the Andes reappears, the rivers flowing westwards across it to reach the Pacific. Further south is the Lake District, with its many lakes formed by glaciation and volcanic activity, its attractive mountain scenery, its rich volcanic soils and fertile agricultural land.

Southern Chile

South of Valdivia, the Coastal Range becomes more broken until near Puerto Montt it becomes a line of islands as part of a 'drowned coastline' that extends all the way south to Cape Horn. The effects of glaciation can be seen in the U-shaped valleys and the long deep fjords stretching inland. This is a land of dense forests with luxuriant undergrowth that is virtually impenetrable and difficult to clear owing to the high water content. Further south in Chilean Patagonia, coniferous forests are limited in expanse because glaciers have stripped the upper slopes of soil. Some of the remaining glaciers reach sea level, notably the San Rafael, which breaks off the giant icefields of the *Campo de Hielo Norte*.

The Andes

The whole of Chile is dominated by this massive mountain range, which reaches its highest elevations in the border region between Chile and Argentina. In the north, near the Peruvian border, the ranges that make up the Andes are 500 km wide, but the western ranges, which mark the Chilean border, are the highest. Sajama, the highest peak in Bolivia, lies only 20 km east of the border, along which are strung volcanoes including Parinacota (6330 m). Further south, to the southeast of San Pedro de Atacama, lies the highest section of the Andes, which includes the peaks of Llullaillaco (6739 m) and Ojos del Salado (altitude 6864 m or 6893 m depending on your source). Still further south, to the northeast of Santiago and just inside Argentina, lies Aconcagua (6960 m).

South of Santiago, the Andes begin to lose altitude. In the Lake District, the mountain passes are low enough in places for crossing into Argentina. South of Puerto Montt, the Andes become more inhospitable, however, as lower temperatures bring the permanent snowline down from 1500 m at Volcán Osorno near Puerto Montt to 700 m on Tierra del Fuego. Towards the southern end of the Andes stand Mount Fitz Roy (3406 m) – in Argentina – and the remarkable peaks of the Paine massif in Chilean territory.

Climate

It is only to be expected that a country that stretches over 4000 km from north to south will provide a wide variety of climatic conditions. Annual rainfall varies from zero in northern Chile to over 4000 mm on the offshore islands south of Puerto Montt. Rainfall is heavier in the winter months (May to August) throughout the country, except for in the northern *altiplano* where January and February are the wettest months.

Variations in the Chilean climate are concentrated by two significant factors: altitude and the cold waters of the Humboldt Current. The Andes, with their peaks of over 6000 m, are rarely more than 160 km from the coastline. On average, temperatures drop by 1°C for every 150 m you climb. The Humboldt Current has perhaps even more impact. The current flows in a northeasterly direction from Antarctic waters until it meets the southern coast of Chile, from where it follows the coastline northwards. Cold polar air accompanies the current on its journey, eventually colliding with warmer air moving in from the southwest. The lighter warm air is forced to rise over the dense cold air, bringing rainfall all year round to the area south of the Río Biobío and rain in winter further north in the Central Valley.

Paradoxically, the ocean also has a moderating effect on temperatures, which are not generally extreme and decrease less than might be expected from north to south. As a result of the Humboldt Current, temperatures in northern Chile are much lower than they are for places at corresponding latitudes, such as Mexico. In the far south, the oceans have the opposite effect and temperatures rarely fall below -6°C despite the high latitude. Detailed temperature and rainfall patterns are given in the text.

Flora

The diversity of Chilean flora reflects the geographic length and climatic variety of the country. Although the Andes constitute a great natural barrier, there are connections between the flora of Chile and that of the eastern side of the mountain range, most notably in the far north with the Bolivian *altiplano* and in the south with the temperate forests of Argentina.

Far North

The arid central plain of northern Chile forms one of the driest areas on earth. Vegetation is limited to cacti, among them the *cardon* (*Echinopsis atacamensis*) and, in the Pampa de Tamarugal around Iquique, the *tamarugo* (*Proposis tamarugo*), a tree specially adapted to arid climates. On the western slopes of the Andes, ravines carry water, which has permitted the establishment of small settlements and the planting of crops. The only native tree of this area, *queñoa* (*Polylepis tomentella*) – heavily over-exploited in the past – grows in sheltered areas, mainly near streams, at altitudes between 2000 and 3500 m. Among cacti are the *candelabros* (genus *Browningia*) and, at higher altitudes (between 3000 and 4000 m) the *ayrampus* (genus *Opuntia*).

The northern *altiplano* supports only sparse vegetation. Many plants found in this area, such as the *llareta* (genus *Laretia*) and the *tola* (genus *Baccharis*) have deep root systems and small leaves. Near streams, there are areas of spongy, wet salty grass, known as *bofedales*.

To the west of the central plain, the Pacific coastal area is almost complete desert, although in places the influence of the Humboldt Current is offset by the *camanchaca*, an early morning coastal fog that comes off the sea and persists at low altitudes, permitting the growth of vegetation, notably in the Parque Nacional Pan de Azúcar, north of Chañaral, and around Poposo, south of Antofagasta, where about 170 flowering plants, including shrubs, bromeliaceae and cacti can be found.

Norte Chico

Lying between the northern deserts and the matorral of central Chile, the Norte Chico is a transition zone: here annual rainfall averages from 30 to 100 mm, increasing southwards. In the main dry areas native flora, such as *pingo-pingo* (*Ephedra andina*), *jarilla* (*Larrea nitida*) and *brea* (*Tessaria absinthoides*) can be found. On the rare occasions when there is spring rainfall, the desert comes to life in a phenomenon known as the 'flowering of the desert' (see box, page 184). The central plain is crossed by rivers; in the valleys irrigation permits the cultivation of fruit, such as chirimoya, papaya and grapes.

On the coast near Ovalle, sea mists support a forest of evergreen species, including the *olivillo* (*Aextoxicon punctatum*), *canelo* or winter's bark (*Drimys winteri*) and *arrayán* (*Luma chequen* or *Myrtus chequen*) in the Parque Nacional Fray Jorge.

Central Chile

The Central Valley, with its dry and warm summers and mild winters, is home to the *matorral*, a deciduous scrubland ecologically comparable to the chaparral in California and consisting of slow-growing drought-resistant species with deep roots and small spiny sclerophyllous leaves. The original plant cover has been modified by human impact, particularly in the form of livestock agriculture, charcoal-burning and irrigation. In many areas, from the Río Limari in the north to the Río Laja in the south, the result is *espinal* (*Acacia cavan*), usually considered to be a degraded form of the original matoral and characterised by open savanna scattered with *algarrobo* trees (*Prosopis chilensis*). Along ravines and on western facing slopes, there are areas of evergreen sclerophyllous trees, including the *peumo* (*Cryptocarpa alba*), *litre* (*Lithrea caustica*) and *boldo* (*Peumos boldos*) and, along the banks of the great rivers, the *maiten* (*Maytenus boaria* or *Maytenus chilensis*) and a local species of willow can be found.

Towards the coast more hygrophilous species grow on hills receiving coastal fogs: among these are *avellano*, *lingue* (*Persea lingue*), *belloto* or northern acorn (*Beilschmiedia miersii*) and *canelo* as well as bromeliads and epiphytic lichens and mosses. Species of southern beech (*Nothofagus*) and the formerly endemic Chilean or ocoa palm (*Jubea chilensis*), grow under protection in the Parque Nacional La Campana between Santiago and Valparaíso.

Subantarctic temperate forests

As a result of the fragmentation of the great landmass of Gondwana some 120 million years ago, some of the species in these forests (*Araucaria araucana*, *Nothofagus* and *Podocarpus salingus*) share affinities with flora found in Australia and New Zealand as well as with fossils uncovered in Antarctica. Similar affinities of some insect groups have also been established. However the isolation of these subantarctic forests, with the nearest neighbouring forests 1300 km away in northwestern Argentina, has led to the evolution of many unique endemic species, with volcanic activity also having had an important influence.

Nowadays these forests are mainly of broad-leafed evergreen species; in contrast to temperate forests in the northern hemisphere there are few species of conifers. The dominant genus is the Nothofagus or southern beech, of which eight species are found in Chile. In the Maule area *roble* (*Nothofagus obliqua*) and *hualo* (*Nothofagus glauca*) can be found, while further south there is a gradual transitional change via the Valdivian rainforest (see below), to the southern deciduous Nothofagus forests. The latter, which can also be found at higher altitudes along the Andes, include the Patagonian and Magellanic forests. From the Valdivian forest south to the Magellanic forests all species of Nothofagus attract fungis from the genus Cyttaria and, especially in the south, the *misodendron* or South American mistletoe.

Around the Río Biobío, the Valdivian rainforest predominates. This is a complex and diverse environment, which includes ferns, bromeliads, lichens including old man's beard, and mosses, as well as a variety of climbing plants including the *copihue* or Chilean bell flower (*Lapageria rosea*), the national flower of Chile. Colourful flowering plants that can easily be identified include the firebush or *ciruelillo* (*Embothrium coccineum*), several species of alstroemeria and berberis and the fuschia. Near the Andes, for example in the Parque Nacional Puyehue, the forests are dominated by two species of Nothofagus, the evergreen *coihue* or *coigüe* (*Nothofagus dombeyi*) and the deciduous *lenga* (*Nothfagus pumilio*) as well as by the Podocarpus (*Podocarpus salingus*) and, near water, myrtle trees like the *arrayán*. The under-storey is dominated by tall *chusquea* bamboos. However many of these endemic species of flora are currently under threat from the proposed damming of the Río Biobío by Endesa, the Chilean electricity company, in violation of a law of 1993 which safeguards people from signing away their lands if they do not want to.

In the northern parts of the Valdivian forest, at altitudes mainly between 900 m and 1400 m, there are forests of monkey puzzle trees (*Araucaria araucana*), Chile's national tree. The most important of these forests are in the Parque Nacional Nahuelbuta in the coastal *cordillera* and in the Parque Nacional Huerquehue in the Andean foothills (see also box, page 332).

Other species include the giant larch (*Fitzroya cupressoides*), known as the *alerce* or *lahuén*, which has some of the oldest individual specimens on earth (3600 years). Athough this conifer grew extensively as far south as the 43° 30' south, excessive logging has destroyed most of the original larch forest. Some of the best examples of *alerce*, which is now a protected species, can be seen in the Parque Nacional Andino Alerce and in the Parque Pumalín.

The Patagonian and Magellanic forests are less diverse than their Valdivian counterpart, mainly due to lower temperatures. The Magellanic forest, considered the southernmost forest type in the world, includes the evergreen Nothofagus betuloides, the deciduous *lenga* (*Nothofagus pumilio*) and Nothofagus antarctica, and the *canelo*.

Firebush and berberis can also be found, as well as several species of orchids and beautiful species of Calceolaria or slipper plants. Shrubland in the south is mainly characterised by mounded shrubs, usually found in rocky areas. Common species include *mata barrosa* (*Mullinum spinosum*), a yellow-flowered shrub, and *mata guanaco* (*Anartrophyllum desideratum*), a red-flowered shrub of the legume family.

Pacific Islands

In the Juan Fernández Islands and Easter Island there are endemic species. In the forests of the Juan Fernández Archipelago, at altitudes above 1400 m, important species of fern can be found, as well as tree species such as *luma*, *mayu-monte*, giant *naranjillo* and the *yonta* or Juan Fernández palm, which, along with the ocoa palm, is one of only two palms native to Chile. The native forests of Easter Island were destroyed, first by volcanic activity and later by human impact, leaving land covered partially with pasture. Although native species, such as the *toromiro*, can be found, introduced species such as the eucalyptus are more common.

Fauna

Chile is an ecological island. Fauna that is commonplace in neighbouring countries has not been able to migrate here because of the Andes, the desert, the ice and the sea. This explains why there are no land tortoises, squirrels, jaguars or poisonous snakes in the country. Surrounded by natural barriers on all sides, its isolation has contributed to a range of endemic wildlife – something that Darwin glimpsed in microcosm on Chiloé in 1835, when he observed a fox unique to that island.

The one geographical constant from top to bottom of the country is the **Pacific Ocean**, the world's richest ocean for marine species. Coldwater species live near Chile's mainland, feeding off the rich nutrients in the Humboldt Current, while subtropical species inhabit the warmer waters around the Juan Fernández archipelago, and tropical species can be found in the waters around Easter Island. This explains the diversity of Chilean marine life, from hake, swordfish, bream and bass to countless shellfish, such as abalones, mussels, sea urchins, lobsters and a variety of crabs. Nine of the world's 18 species of **penguins** also live in Chile. The Humboldt penguins can be found between Arica and Chiloé, while the King, Adelia and Emperor penguins live solely in Antarctica. There are numerous colonies of sea-lions up and down the coast; dolphins are often seen off the shore of Chiloé and even killer whales abound.

Inland, there are some 680 species of mammal, amphibian, reptile and bird. In the north, the **camelids** predominate among mammals: the alpacas, guanacos, llamas and vicuñas, with the guanaco also being found as far south as Tierra del Fuego. These South American camels are adapted for the mountainous terrain by having narrower feet than the desert forms of the species. All four species can be seen in Chile, although three are found only in the north. Like horses and donkeys, all the camelids can breed with one another, arising to some confusion as to their origins. There is a long-held view that both the llama and the alpaca are descended from wild guanaco.

Guanaco, coffee coloured with a dark head and tail and weighing up to 55 kg, were once found throughout Chile except in rainforest areas. Both grazers and browsers, they live in deserts, shrub land, savannah and occasionally on forest fringes. In many areas hunted to extinction, an estimated 20,000 now survive in the far north, especially in the Parque Nacional Lauca, in coastal and mountain areas between Antofagasta and Lago Rapel and in parts of the far south, such as the Parque Nacional Torres del Paine.

Vicuña, weighing up to 20 kg, are like half-sized guanaco, although with a much finer yellower coat and coffee-coloured head and tail. Hunted almost to extinction, there were only around 400 in Chile in 1970. Protection has increased their numbers to around 12,000, mainly in the far north at altitudes of 3700-4800 m.

Alpaca are domesticated animals, weighing 20-30 kg, but seeming to be much larger because of their wool. Colours vary between black, coffee coloured, mahogany, grey and white. An estimated 20,000 can be found in drier parts of the northern altiplano.

Llama are also domesticated and are usually found with alpacas. Larger than alpacas and weighing up to 55 kg, their wool varies in colour but is shorter than that of alpacas. They are found only in the area of their domestication, which first occurred around Lake Titicaca some 4000-5000 years ago. Used as pack animals, males can carry loads of up to 40 kg. There are some 40,000 in the Tarapacá and Antofagasta regions of Chile.

Perhaps surprisingly, the north is also one of the avian capitals of Chile, with three of the world's six species of **flamingo** – the James, Chilean and Andean – all to be found around the saltpans of the Atacama. The **Parque Nacional Lauca** is also exceptional for birdlife, with over 120 species of either resident or migrant birds (see box, page 272).

As the land becomes more humid, south of the desert, there are naturally many changes in wildlife. One of the few constants is the famous **puma**, which is found in the *cordillera* all the way from Arica to the Straits of Magellan, albeit in increasingly small numbers; the puma is understandably shy of humans, and is rarely spotted. There are several species of fox, particularly in the mountains, and the Central Valley is also a haven for spiders, including dangerous **arañas de rincón** and tarantulas.

Further south, in the lush forests of the Lake District and down towards the Carreterra Austral, two of the most interesting creatures are the **huemul** and the **pudú**. Both are species of deer. The huemul's northernmost group is found around Chillán; it is a medium-sized creature, well adapted for life in the mountains. The pudú is an extraordinary creature, a deer just 40 cm high, very shy and extremely difficult to spot, although it can sometimes be seen in the more remote parts of Chiloé and the Carreterra Austral.

The **Parque Nacional Torres del Paine** is a haven for wildlife, sheltering guanacos, condors, pumas and foxes. On Isla Magdalena and Seno Otway, both near Punta Arenas, there are famous Magellanic penguin colonies, while Isla Navarino has a colony of beavers (unintentionally introduced from Canada), as well as some fantastic birdlife including petrels and even – on a good day – albatrosses.

Wine → *See also pages 16-17.*

Chile is a major producer and exporter of fine wines. The fine wine-producing area stretches from the valley of the Río Aconcagua in the north to the Maule Valley in the south. Grapes are also produced outside this area, notably around Ovalle and in the Elqui Valley near La Serena, which is the main production centre for *pisco*, a clear distilled spirit commonly drunk with lemon as *pisco sour*, although the distillery that many hold to be the best is Alto del Carmén, in the upper reaches of the Huasco Valley.

The great majority of Chilean wines come from the Central Valley. The hot, dry summers guarantee exceptionally healthy fruit. Chilean wine is famous for being free from diseases such as downy mildew and phylloxera. As a result, growers are spared the costs of spraying and of grafting young vines onto phylloxera-resistant rootstocks.

There are eight denominated wine-growing regions, based around the valleys of the Ríos Limarí, Aconcagua, Casablanca, Maipo, Cachapoal, Colchagua, Curicó, Maule and

Biobío. The heartland of Chilean red wine production is the Maipo Valley, just south of Santiago, which is home to many of the most prestigious names in Chilean wine. Although the Maipo produces far less wine than the regions to the south, it is considered by many experts to produce the best wines in Chile as a result of the lime content of its soils. For visits to vineyards in this area, see page 105. In recent years the Casablanca Valley has emerged as a fine producer of Chardonnay and crisp Sauvignon blancs, while the recent rediscovery of the lost Carmenere grape is helping to give Chilean wine its own identity.

The main harvest period begins at the end of February, for early maturing varieties such as Chardonnay, and runs through to the end of April for Cabernet Sauvignon, although there are regional variations. Harvest celebrations are often accompanied by two drinks: *chicha*, a partly fermented grape juice, and *vino pipeño*, an unfiltered young wine which contains residue from the grapes and dried yeast.

Although the vine was introduced to Chile in the mid-16th century by the Spanish, the greatest influence on Chilean vineyards and wine making has been exerted by the French. In the 1830s, one prominent Frenchman, Claudio Gay, persuaded the Chilean government to establish the Quinta Normal in Santiago as a nursery for exotic botanical specimens including vines. In the 1970s domestic consumption of wine dropped and wine prices fell, leading to the destruction of many vineyards. In the last two decades, however, large-scale investment, much of it from the United States and Europe has led to increases in wine production, increasingly of quality wines destined for export. Chilean wines are now widely available around the world; they are also very popular within Latin America.

Chileans are justly proud and are increasingly becoming connoisseurs of their wines. More and more top-end wines are sold on the domestic market each year. However, there remains a marked distinction between these fine wines and wines sold in tetrapacks and grown exclusively for mass domestic consumption. The most commonly planted grape variety is still the dark-skinned *Pais*, found only in Chile, and thought to be a direct descendant of cuttings imported by Spanish colonists. Although Chilean wines, especially those produced for export, are typically very clean and fruity, they have only recently developed a full-bodied structure. Most export wines are red Cabernet Sauvignon, Merlot and Carmenere and white Chardonnay and Sauvignon Blanc.

Books → See also page 24.

Travelogues

Chatwin, Bruce, *In Patagonia* (1977), Pan. A modern classic for those visiting the far south, although it concentrates mainly on Argentina.

Cooper, Marc, *Pinochet and Me* (2001), Verso. Fascinating account of the 1973 coup by Salvador Allende's English translator, intermingled with his account of modern Chile and the coup's legacy.

Darwin, Charles, *The Voyage of the Beagle* (1989), Penguin. Still fascinating reading of the great naturalist's voyage and adventures from Cape Horn to Copiapó in the 1830s.

Giménez Hutton, Adrian, *La Patagonia de Chatwin* (1999), Editorial Sudamericana. Interesting Argentine perspective on Chatwin and Patagonia (both Argentine and Chilean).

Green, Toby, *Saddled with Darwin* (2000), Phoenix House. A former author of this book retraces Darwin's route in South America on horseback.

Keenan, Brian and McCarthy, John, *Between Extremes* (2000), Black Swan. The 2 friends from Lebanon travel together again, this time through Chile.

Lucas Bridges, E, *Uttermost Part of the Earth* (1948), Hodder & Stoughton. Brilliant and beautiful account of his adventurous life in Tierra del Fuego with the Yámana and Ona peoples; the classic text on Tierra del Fuego.

Pilkington, John, *An Englishman In Patagonia* (1991), Century. Heavily critical of Chatwin.

Reding, Nick, *The last cowboys at the end of the world* (2001), Random House. Quirky yet evocative and highly readable account of the lives of the dying breed of gauchos in central Patagonia.

Souhami, Diana, *Selkirk's Island* (2001), Weidenfeld & Nicolson. The extraordinary story of Alexander Selkirk and his island, inspirations for Robinson Crusoe and for the community of San Juan Bautista on modern-day Isla Robinson Crusoe. A prize-winning account.

Swale, Rosie, *Back to Cape Horn* (1988), Fontana. Swale tells of her epic journey from Antofagasta to Cape Horn on horseback.

Wheeler, Sara, *Travels in a Thin Country* (1994), Little, Brown & Co. Popular account of the author's 6-month stay in Chile.

Fiction and poetry

Allende, Isabel, the doyenne of modern Chilean letters. Her books include: *The House of the Spirits* (1994), Black Swan. Brilliant, evocative, allegorical magical-realist account taking the reader through 20th-century Chilean history. *Of Love and Shadows* (1988), Black Swan. Painful story about a journalist uncovering evidence of military atrocities under the military regime. *Paula* (1996), Flamingo. A beautiful 'letter' written from Allende to her daughter, who is stuck in a coma after a car accident, taking in the modern history of Chile and Allende's emotional roots. More recent books include *Daughter of Fortune* (2000), Flamingo, and *Portrait in Sepia* (2002), Flamingo, both of which are lyrical prequels to the story that made Allende's name: *The House of the Spirits*.

Bolaño, Roberto, *By Night in Chile* (2003), Harvill. A caustic, brilliant novel, as an ageing Chilean priest lives through the last night of his life, and recalls teaching Marxism to General Pinochet and various surreal encounters with the Chilean literary establishment – thereby exposing the complicity of so many in the 'normality' that accompanied the military government.

Donoso, José, *The Garden Next Door* (1994), Grove Press. Evocative novel that deals with the ageing process of a couple in Spain. *The Obscene Bird of the Night* (1995), Grove Press.

Donoso's most famous, experimental novel, which gained him international acclaim across Latin America.

Dorfman, Ariel, *Death and the Maiden* (1996), Nick Hern Books (also in the collected volume *The Resistance Trilogy*; 1998). Subtle, moving tale of torture and resistance, an allegory for the state of Chile. *The Nanny and the Iceberg* (1999), Sceptre. Cross-cultural story of Chile and North America told with Dorfman's usual eloquence.

Neruda, Pablo, *Selected Poems* (trans/ed Ben Bellit (1961), New York Grove Press. Bilingual anthology of the master's work.

Richards, Ben, *The Mermaid and the Drunks* (2003), Weidenfeld & Nicolson. An English novel set in Chile, which gives an entertaining picture of modern Chile from the perspective of a longtime friend of the country.

Skármeta, Antonio, *Il Postino* ('The Postman', 1996), Bloomsbury. Beautiful novel about the relationship between Neruda and his postman while the poet is in exile in Italy, made into a famous film. *Watch Where the Wolf is Going* (1991), Readers' International. Another novel in Skármeta's trademark style of eloquence and emotional honesty.

Adventure sports

Biggar, John, *The High Andes* (1996), Castle Douglas, Kirkudbrightshire. Andes contains 3 chapters with information on Chilean peaks.

CONAF, *Guía de Parques Nacionales y Otras Areas Silvestres Protegidas de Chile*, US$12, a very useful guide to the main parks, with information on access, campsites, flora and fauna. It also publishes *Chile Forestal*, a monthly magazine with articles on the parks and ecological issues.

Fagerstrom, René Peri, *Cuentos de la Carretera Austral*, on the Camino Austral. *Regata*, a monthly sailing magazine. Climbers will also find *Cumbres de Chile* of interest: 2 books with accompanying tapes, each covering 20 peaks.

Mantellero, Alberto, *Una Aventura Navegando Los Canales del Sur de Chile*, a guide to sailing the southern coast, with maps.

Reference and background

Almarza V, Claudio, *Patagonia* (Punta Arenas: GeoPatagonia). A book of photographs, with text, on the region.

Araya, B and Millie, G, *Guía de Campo de Las Aves de Chile*. Bird-lovers will appreciate this guide to Chile's feathered population.

Bahn, Paul and Flenley, John, *Easter Island, Earth Island* (1992), Thames and Hudson. A comprehensive appraisal of Easter Island's archaeology.

Cárdenas Saldivia, Umiliana, *Casos de Brujos de Chiloé* (1989), Editorial Universitaria. Fascinating tales of witchcraft on Chiloé.

Castillo, Juan Carlos (ed) *Islas Oceánicas Chilenas* (1987), Ediciones Universidad Católica de Chile. Much information on the natural history and geography of Juan Fernández and Easter Islands.

Clissold, Stephen, *Chilean Scrapbook* (1952), The Cresset Press. Gives an evocative historical picture of Chile, region by region.

Collier, S and Sater, WF, *A History of Chile 1808-2002* (2004), Cambridge University Press. The definitive single-volume history of Chile in English.

Coña, Pascal, *Memorias de un Cacique Mapuche* (1930), publisher unmarked. An account of Mapuche traditions and history by a Mapuche chief in his 70s.

Constable, Pamela and Valenzuela, Arturo, *Chile: A Nation of Enemies* (1991), Norton. Excellent and readable take on the Pinochet years.

Dinges, John, *The Condor Years* (2004), The New Press. Thorough examination of the Condor anti-leftist terrorist operation set up by South American dictators, including Pinochet.

Dorfman, Ariel, *Unending Terror: The Incredible Unending Trial of General Augusto Pinochet* (2003), Pluto Press. A gripping account of the Pinochet affair from one of the most perceptive living writers on Chile. His memoir *Heading North, Looking South* (1998) is also essential reading.

Goni, Uki, *The Real Odessa: How Perón Brought the Nazi War Criminals to Argentina* (2002), Granta. Although based on the Argentine hiding of Nazi war criminals, this book has a continent-wide significance, as it reveals how this movement shaped the fascist attitudes of military governments of the 1970s.

Haslam, Jonathan, *The Nixon Administration and the Death of Allende's Chile* (2005), Verso. This book examines the involvement of Nixon and the CIA in the 1973 coup.

Hazlewood, Nick, *Savage: The Life and Times of Jemmy Button* (2001), Sceptre. Interesting if hyperbolic history of Jemmy's tale.

Heyerdahl, Thor, *Aku-Aku, The Art of Easter Island* (1975), New York: Doubleday.

Kornbluh, Peter, *The Pinochet File* (2003), The New Press. Declassified CIA documents together with editorial explanations relating to US government involvement and collusion in the 1973 coup.

Montecino, Sonia, *Historias de Vida de Mujeres Mapuches* (1985), Centro de Estudios de la Mujer. Interviews with Mapuche women giving a real insight into their lives.

O'Shaughnessy, Hugh, *Pinochet: The Politics of Torture* (2000), Latin American Bureau. Informed and up-to-date analysis of the whole Pinochet affair.

Porteous, J Douglas, *The Modernization of Easter Island* (1981), Department of Geography, University of Victoria, BC, Canada. A very thorough illustrated book.

Read, Jan, *The Wines of Chile* (1994), Mitchell Beazley. A gazetteer of the vineyards and wineries of Chile, ideal for the specialist.

Rector, John, *The History of Chile* (2005), Palgrave MacMillan. A readable general history of Chile.

South American Explorers Club, *The South American Explorer* (126 Indian Creek Road, Ithaca, New York 14850, USA). This journal regularly publishes articles on Chile including Easter Island.

Spooner, MH, *Soldiers In A Narrow Land* (1994), University of California Press. A readable account of the Pinochet dictatorship by a North American journalist resident in the country at the time.

Wearne, Philip, *Return of the Indian: Conquest and Revival in the Americas* (1996), Cassell/Latin America Bureau. Information on the Mapuche within the entire Amerindian context.

Maps and guidebooks

Chiletur, published by Copec, www.copec.cl, is very useful for roads and town plans, but not all distances are exact. It is published annually in 3 parts; Norte, Centro, and Sur (in Spanish only), alongside a separate volume dedicated to national parks. It contains a wealth of maps covering the whole country and neighbouring tourist centres in Argentina, and is well worth getting, particularly for those with their own transport. Each volume costs around US$10, but buying the whole set is better value. Available from larger Copec service stations.

Sernatur publishes a free *Guía Turística/ Tourist Guide* in Spanish and English, with good maps, useful text, while **CONAF** publishes a series of illustrated booklets in Spanish/English on Chilean trees, shrubs and flowers, as well as *Juventud, Turismo y Naturaleza*, which lists national parks, their facilities and the flora and fauna of each. A recommended series of general maps are published by **International Travel Maps** (ITM), *345 West Broadway, Vancouver, V5Y 1P8, Canada, T604-8793 621*, compiled with historical notes, by Kevin Healey.

Contents

Footnotes

Basic Spanish for travellers

Learning Spanish is a useful part of the preparation for a trip to Latin America and no volumes of dictionaries, phrase books or word lists will provide the same enjoyment as being able to communicate directly with the people of the country you are visiting. It is a good idea to make an effort to grasp the basics before you go. As you travel you will pick up more of the language and the more you know, the more you will benefit from your stay.

General pronunciation

Whether you have been taught the 'Castilian' pronunciation (*z* and *c* followed by *i* or *e* are pronounced as the *th* in think) or the 'American' pronunciation (they are pronounced as *s*), you will encounter little difficulty in understanding either. Regional accents and usages vary, but the basic language is essentially the same everywhere

Vowels

a	as in English *cat*
e	as in English *best*
i	as the *ee* in English *feet*
o	as in English *shop*
u	as the *oo* in English *food*
ai	as the *i* in English *ride*
ei	as *ey* in English *they*
oi	as *oy* in English *toy*

Consonants

Most consonants can be pronounced more or less as they are in English. The exceptions are:

g	before *e* or *i* is the same as *j*
h	is always silent (except in *ch* as in *chair*)
j	as the *ch* in Scottish *loch*
ll	as the *y* in *yellow*
ñ	as the *ni* in English *onion*
rr	trilled much more than in English
x	depending on its location, pronounced *x*, *s*, *sh* or *j*

Spanish words and phrases

Greetings, courtesies

hello	*hola*
good morning	*buenos días*
good afternoon/ evening/night	*buenas tardes/noches*
goodbye	*adiós/chao*
pleased to meet you	*mucho gusto*
see you later	*hasta luego*
how are you?	*¿cómo está?* *¿cómo estás?*
I'm fine, thanks	*estoy muy bien, gracias*
I'm called...	*me llamo...*
what is your name?	*¿cómo se llama?* *¿cómo te llamas?*
yes/no	*sí/no*
please	*por favor*

thank you (very much)	*(muchas) gracias*
I speak Spanish	*hablo español*
I don't speak Spanish	*no hablo español*
do you speak English?	*¿habla inglés?*
I don't understand	*no entiendo/ no comprendo*
please speak slowly	*hable despacio por favor*
I am very sorry	*lo siento mucho/ disculpe*
what do you want?	*¿qué quiere?* *¿qué quieres?*
I want	*quiero*
I don't want it	*no lo quiero*
leave me alone	*déjeme en paz/ no me moleste*
good/bad	*bueno/malo*

Questions and requests

Have you got a room for two people?
¿Tiene una habitación para dos personas?
How do I get to_?
¿Cómo llego a_?
How much does it cost?
¿Cuánto cuesta? ¿cuánto es?
I'd like to make a long-distance phone call
Quisiera hacer una llamada de larga distancia
Is service included?
¿Está incluido el servicio?

Is tax included?
¿Están incluidos los impuestos?
When does the bus leave (arrive)?
¿A qué hora sale (llega) el autobús?
When? *¿cuándo?*
Where is_? *¿dónde está_?*
Where can I buy tickets?
¿Dónde puedo comprar boletos?
Where is the nearest petrol station?
¿Dónde está la gasolinera más cercana?
Why? *¿por qué?*

Basics

bank	*el banco*	market	*el mercado*
bathroom/toilet	*el baño*	note/coin	*le billete/la moneda*
bill	*la factura/la cuenta*	police (policeman)	*la policía (el policía)*
cash	*el efectivo*	post office	*el correo*
cheap	*barato/a*	public telephone	*el teléfono público*
credit card	*la tarjeta de crédito*	supermarket	*el supermercado*
exchange house	*la casa de cambio*	ticket office	*la taquilla*
exchange rate	*el tipo de cambio*	traveller's cheques	*los cheques de viajero/*
expensive	*caro/a*		*los travelers*

Getting around

aeroplane	*el avión*	insured person	*el/la asegurado/a*
airport	*el aeropuerto*	to insure yourself against	*asegurarse contra*
arrival/departure	*la llegada/salida*	luggage	*el equipaje*
avenue	*la avenida*	motorway, freeway	*el autopista/la*
block	*la cuadra*		*carretera*
border	*la frontera*	north, south, west, east	*norte, sur, oeste*
bus station	*la terminal de*		*(occidente), este*
	autobuses/camiones		*(oriente)*
bus	*el bus/el autobús/*	oil	*el aceite*
	el camión	to park	*estacionarse*
collective/		passport	*el pasaporte*
fixed-route taxi	*el colectivo*	petrol/gasoline	*la gasolina*
corner	*la esquina*	puncture	*el pinchazo/*
customs	*la aduana*		*la ponchadura*
first/second class	*primera/segunda clase*	street	*la calle*
left/right	*izquierda/derecha*	that way	*por allí/por allá*
ticket	*el boleto*	this way	*por aquí/por acá*
empty/full	*vacío/lleno*	tourist card/visa	*la tarjeta de turista*
highway, main road	*la carretera*	tyre	*la llanta*
immigration	*la inmigración*	unleaded	*sin plomo*
insurance	*el seguro*	to walk	*caminar/andar*

Accommodation

air conditioning	el aire acondicionado	power cut	el apagón/corte
all-inclusive	todo incluido	restaurant	el restaurante
bathroom, private	el baño privado	room/bedroom	el cuarto/la habitación
bed, double/single	la cama matrimonial/sencilla	sheets	las sábanas
		shower	la ducha/regadera
blankets	las cobijas/mantas	soap	el jabón
to clean	limpiar	toilet	el sanitario/excusado
dining room	el comedor	toilet paper	el papel higiénico
guesthouse	la casa de huéspedes	towels, clean/dirty	las toallas limpias/sucias
hotel	el hotel		
noisy	ruidoso	water, hot/cold	el agua caliente/fría
pillows	las almohadas		

Health

aspirin	la aspirina	diarrhoea	la diarrea
blood	la sangre	doctor	el médico
chemist	la farmacia	fever/sweat	la fiebre/el sudor
condoms	los preservativos, los condones	pain	el dolor
		head	la cabeza
contact lenses	los lentes de contacto	period	la regla
contraceptives	los anticonceptivos	sanitary towels	las toallas femeninas
contraceptive pill	la píldora anti-conceptiva	stomach	el estómago
		altitude sickness	el soroche

Family

family	la familia	boyfriend/girlfriend	el novio/la novia
brother/sister	el hermano/la hermana	friend	el amigo/la amiga
daughter/son	la hija/el hijo	married	casado/a
father/mother	el padre/la madre	single/unmarried	soltero/a
husband/wife	el esposo (marido)/la esposa		

Months, days and time

January	enero	Monday	lunes
February	febrero	Tuesday	martes
March	marzo	Wednesday	miércoles
April	abril	Thursday	jueves
May	mayo	Friday	viernes
June	junio	Saturday	sábado
July	julio	Sunday	domingo
August	agosto		
September	septiembre	at one o'clock	a la una
October	octubre	at half past two	a las dos y media
November	noviembre	at a quarter to three	a cuarto para las tres/a las tres menos quince
December	diciembre		
		it's one o'clock	es la una

it's seven o'clock	*son las siete*	in ten minutes	*en diez minutos*
it's six twenty	*son las seis y veinte*	five hours	*cinco horas*
it's five to nine	*son las nueve menos cinco*	does it take long?	*¿tarda mucho?*

Numbers

one	*uno/una*	sixteen	*dieciséis*
two	*dos*	seventeen	*diecisiete*
three	*tres*	eighteen	*dieciocho*
Four	*cuatro*	nineteen	*diecinueve*
five	*cinco*	twenty	*veinte*
six	*seis*	twenty-one	*veintiuno*
seven	*siete*	thirty	*treinta*
eight	*ocho*	forty	*cuarenta*
nine	*nueve*	fifty	*cincuenta*
ten	*diez*	sixty	*sesenta*
eleven	*once*	seventy	*setenta*
twelve	*doce*	eighty	*ochenta*
thirteen	*trece*	ninety	*noventa*
fourteen	*catorce*	hundred	*cien/ciento*
fifteen	*quince*	thousand	*mil*

Food

avocado	*el aguacate*	goat	*el chivo*
baked	*al horno*	grapefruit	*la toronja/el pomelo*
bakery	*la panadería*	grill	*la parrilla*
banana	*el plátano*	grilled/griddled	*a la plancha*
beans	*los frijoles/ las habichuelas*	guava	*la guayaba*
beef	*la carne de res*	ham	*el jamón*
beef steak or pork fillet	*el bistec*	hamburger	*la hamburguesa*
boiled rice	*el arroz blanco*	hot, spicy	*picante*
bread	*el pan*	ice cream	*el helado*
breakfast	*el desayuno*	jam	*la mermelada*
butter	*la mantequilla*	knife	*el cuchillo*
cake	*el pastel*	lime	*el limón*
chewing gum	*el chicle*	lobster	*la langosta*
chicken	*el pollo*	lunch	*el almuerzo/la comida*
chilli or green pepper	*el ají/pimiento*	meal	*la comida*
clear soup, stock	*el caldo*	meat	*la carne*
cooked	*cocido*	minced meat	*el picadillo*
dining room	*el comedor*	onion	*la cebolla*
egg	*el huevo*	orange	*la naranja*
fish	*el pescado*	pepper	*el pimiento*
fork	*el tenedor*	pasty, turnover	*la empanada/ el pastelito*
fried	*frito*	pork	*el cerdo*
garlic	*el ajo*	potato	*la papa*

prawns	los camarones	spoon	la cuchara
raw	crudo	squash	la calabaza
restaurant	el restaurante	squid	los calamares
salad	la ensalada	supper	la cena
salt	la sal	sweet	dulce
sandwich	el bocadillo	to eat	comer
sauce	la salsa	toasted	tostado
sausage	la longaniza/el chorizo	turkey	el pavo
scrambled eggs	los huevos revueltos	vegetables	los legumbres/vegetales
seafood	los mariscos	without meat	sin carne
soup	la sopa	yam	el camote

Drink

beer	la cerveza	ice/without ice	el hielo/sin hielo
boiled	hervido/a	juice	el jugo
bottled	en botella	lemonade	la limonada
camomile tea	la manzanilla	milk	la leche
canned	en lata	mint	la menta
coffee	el café	rum	el ron
coffee, white	el café con leche	soft drink	el refresco
cold	frío	sugar	el azúcar
cup	la taza	tea	el té
drink	la bebida	to drink	beber/tomar
drunk	borracho/a	water	el agua
firewater	el aguardiente	water, carbonated	el agua mineral con gas
fruit milkshake	el batido/licuado	water, still mineral	el agua mineral sin gas
glass	el vaso	wine, red	el vino tinto
hot	caliente	wine, white	el vino blanco

Key verbs

to go	**ir**		there is/are	hay	
I go	voy		there isn't/aren't	no hay	
you go (familiar)	vas				
he, she, it goes,			**to be**	**ser**	**estar**
you (formal) go	va		I am	soy	estoy
we go	vamos		you are	eres	estás
they, you (plural) go	van		he, she, it is,		
			you (formal) are	es	está
to have (possess)	**tener**		we are	somos	estamos
I have	tengo		they, you (plural) are	son	están
you (familiar) have	tienes				
he, she, it,					
you (formal) have	tiene				
we have	tenemos				
they, you (plural) have	tienen				

This section has been assembled on the basis of glossaries compiled by André de Mendonça and David Gilmour of South American Experience, London, and the Latin American Travel Advisor, No 9, March 1996

Index → *Entries in bold refer to maps*

Advertisers' index

Acknowledgements

As always, numerous people have helped in making this book as precise and relevant as possible. Wholehearted thanks go to the regional SERNATUR offices throughout Chile as well as to CONAF and municipal tourist offices who gave their time, expertise and local knowledge to ensure that the information on their area was thorough and complete.

Special thanks go to the following for providing help and information: Ross in Arica for his hospitality and helpful information; Emily and Rodrigo for taking me around some of Arica's hidden gems; Marcelo for showing me that Antofagasta is not as much of a dump as I thought; Víctor in San Pedro; Sol in Copiapó for her hospitality; Pato in Santiago for his time and help as ever; Armin for good food tips in the capital; Berlin in Litueche; Hans in Pucón, a mine of local information as always; Peter and Margot for good company in one of my favourite places in the Lake District; Mauro and Malin for five days of home life during a hectic journey and a couple of unexpected day-trips; Chave and Lore in Valdivia; Armin for rescuing me and my clapped-out car and Nadia for nursing me through the flu; Nico for keeping me up to speed on the disaster-zone around Chaitén; Jorge and Conzuelo for being talked into a road trip down the Carretera Austral; Juan Pablo for a fine day on horseback and teaching me how to splay and spit-roast a lamb. Thanks also to Ben Box, editor of the South American Handbook, for help and advice, Ria, Sarah, Kassia and all at Footprint for working tirelessly and to a very tight schedule on the production of this book and to the countless readers whose letters and emails have helped to make this guide as up-to-date as possible.

Finally, thanks to Juan Carlos, Sol, Vero, Rubén and the rest of the team for holding the fort at Luna Sonrisa these past months, and to my wife, Lorena for her help, support and company.

This book is dedicated to the memory of Claudia Castañeda Navarrete 1977-2009.

About the author

Janak Jani was born in London. Travelling is in his genes and he has lived and worked in several countries in four continents. He arrived in Chile eight years ago and, enchanted by the magic of Valparaíso, he decided to settle down, following in the family tradition of westward migration. He now owns and runs a guesthouse with his wife, Lorena, and spends his spare time breaking down in his car on gravel roads in the middle of nowhere and getting lost with his dog in the Andes.

Credits

Footprint credits

Editor: Ria Gane
Map editor: Sarah Sorensen
Colour section: Kassia Gawronski

Managing Director: Andy Riddle
Commercial Director: Patrick Dawson
Publisher: Alan Murphy
Editorial: Sara Chare, Nicola Gibbs, Jen Haddington, Alice Jell, Felicity Laughton, Jo Williams

Cartography: Emma Bryers, Kevin Feeney, Robert Lunn
Cover design: Robert Lunn
Design: Mytton Williams
Marketing: Liz Harper, Hannah Bonnell
Sales: Jeremy Parr
Advertising: Renu Sibal
Finance and administration: Elizabeth Taylor

Photography credits

Front cover: David Norton/Alamy
Back cover: Yadid Levy/Alamy

Printed in India by Aegean Offset Printers, New Delhi

Footprint feedback

We try as hard as we can to make each Footprint guide as up to date as possible but, of course, things always change. If you want to let us know about your experiences – good, bad or ugly – then don't delay, go to www.footprintbooks.com and send in your comments.

Publishing information

Footprint Chile
6th edition
© Footprint Handbooks Ltd
December 2009

ISBN: 978 1 906098 780
CIP DATA: A catalogue record for this book is available from the British Library

® Footprint Handbooks and the Footprint mark are a registered trademark of Footprint Handbooks Ltd

Published by Footprint
6 Riverside Court
Lower Bristol Road
Bath BA2 3DZ, UK
T +44 (0)1225 469141
F +44 (0)1225 469461
www.footprintbooks.com

Distributed in the USA by Globe Pequot Press, Guilford, Connecticut

Every effort has been made to ensure that the facts in this guidebook are accurate. However, travellers should still obtain advice from consulates, airlines, etc about travel and visa requirements before travelling. The authors and publishers cannot accept responsibility for any loss, injury or inconvenience however caused.

Map 1

PERU

Visviri

Tacora (5988m) ▲

Pomerape (6282m) ▲
Putre ○ Parinacota
Parque
Nacional Parinacota (6342m) ▲
Lauca Paso Tambo Quemada
Acotango
Geoglifos (6050m) ▲ Capurata (5990m)
de Lluta Gualláiri ▲
Arica Guallatiri ▲
Poconchile Belén ○ Guallatiri
Geoglifos
de Azapa Reserva
Río Azapa Nacional
Tignamar Las Vicuñas ◆
Tignamar
Viejo
Codpac Salar de Surire ◆ Monumento
Natural Salar
Surire ○ de Surire

A

Río Camarones

Cuya ○
Geoglifos
de Chiza Parque
Nacional Isluga
Volcán (5530m) ▲
Camiña Isluga Colchane

British
Cemetery Isluga
Geoglifos REGION I Cariquima
de Tiliviche
Pisagua Reserva Nacional
Pampa del Tamarugal
Gigante del Chusmisa Alto Toroni
Atacama (5982m) ▲
Caleta Buena Huara Tarapacá
Humberstone Mamiña
Iquique Pozo
Almonte La Tirana Salar de
Reserva Nacional Huasco
Pampa del
Tamarugal Salar de
Geoglifos de Pica Pintados Matilla
Pintados

B

Puerto Patillos Salar de
Caposa

San Marcos

BOLIVIA

*Pacific
Ocean* Ollagüe ○
Buenaventura Ollagüe
Salar de (5863m) ▲
Carcote
Quillagua ○ Cebollar
Salar
de Ascotán
Ascotán

Conchi Viejo
San
Pedro
Tocopilla Conchi Inacaliri
Punta Blanca Baños Linzor
Mantos de la Luna Layana de Turi
Gatico Ayquina Toconce
Cobija María Elena Chiu Chiu Caspana ○ El Tatio Geysers
Pedro Chuquicamata Calama
Michilla de Valdivia Río Grande
Salar
Hornitos Miraje Putama
Sierra Gorda Catarpe Lincancabur Zapaleri
Pukará Quitor (5916m) ▲ (5653m) ▲
Mejillones Chacabuco San Pedro de Atacama
Carmen Alto Reserva Nacional
de los Flamencos ◆
Baquedano Tulor
Salar de
Bolsico Toconao Salar de
Juan López La Portada Quisquiro
Antofagasta La Chimba Camar Paso
de Jama
Salar de Talabre Lascar
REGION II Atacama (5154m) ▲

Peine Socaire Paso de
Guatiquina
Tilopozo Laguna
Miscanti
Tilomonte Reserva Nacional Laco
de los Flamencos ◆ Paso de Sico

N

30 km
30 miles

1 **2** **3**

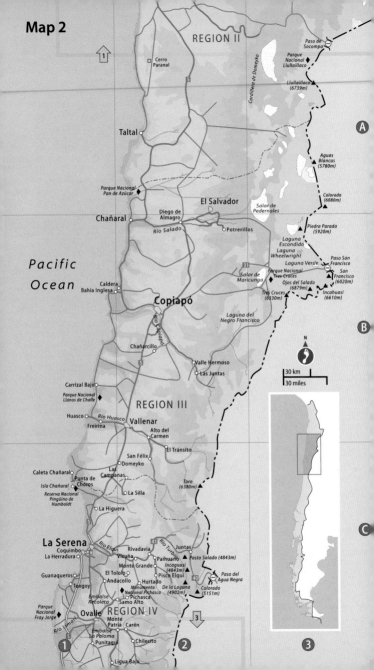

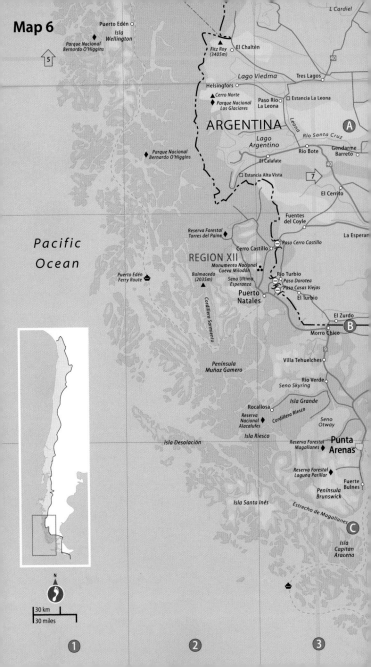

Distance chart

Antofagasta																		
701	**Arica**																	
2552	3253	**Castro**																
1880	258	801	**Concepción**															
566	1261	1992	1320	**Copiapó**														
3011	3712	414†	1260	2451	**Coyhaique***													
492	316	3044	2372	1058	3503	**Iquique**												
887	1588	1665	993	333	2124	1377	**La Serena**											
2274	2975	284	523	1708	743	2766	1387	**Osorno**										
2150	2851	515	399	1584	974	2641	1263	227	**Pucón**									
2377	3078	175	626	1811	634	2869	1490	109	340	**Puerto Montt**								
4464	5165	2472‡	2707	3904	1593	4956	3577	2190	2639	2299	**Puerto Natales***							
4451	5152	2461†	2700	3890	1580	4943	3564	2177	2404	2286	254	**Punta Arenas***						
320	719	2870	2198	876	3329	515	1209	2592	2470	2605	4784	4769	**San Pedro de Atacama**					
1361	2062	1191	519	801	1649	1853	474	913	789	1016	3103	3090	1679	**Santiago**				
1618	2319	934	262	1052	1393	2110	731	656	532	759	2844	2833	1936	257	**Talca**			
2038	2738	514	287	1472	973	2530	1151	236	112	339	2424	2413	2356	677	420	**Temuco**		
2202	2903	391	452	1640	850	2694	1313	107	145	210	2295	2177	2520	839	584	162	**Valdivia**	
1319	2020	1312	639	759	1769	1811	432	1033	909	1136	3223	3210	1637	120	377	797	961	**Valparaíso**

* via Carretera Austral
† via Ferry Quellón-Chaitén
‡ via Puerto Montt

Distances in kilometres 1 kilometre = 0.62 miles

Map symbols

- □ Capital city
- ○ Other city, town
- International border
- Regional border
- ⊖ Customs
- Contours (approx)
- ▲ Mountain, volcano
- Mountain pass
- Escarpment
- Glacier
- Salt flat
- Rocks
- Seasonal marshland
- Beach, sandbank
- Waterfall
- Reef
- Motorway
- Main road
- Unpaved or *ripio* (gravel) road
- Track
- Footpath
- Railway
- Railway with station
- ✈ Airport
- Bus station

- Ⓜ Metro station
- Cable car
- Funicular
- Ferry
- Pedestrianized street
- Tunnel
- → One way-street
- Steps
- Bridge
- Fortified wall
- Park, garden, stadium
- Sleeping
- Eating
- Bars & clubs
- Building
- Sight
- Cathedral, church
- Chinese temple
- Hindu temple
- Meru
- Mosque
- Stupa
- Synagogue
- Tourist office
- Museum
- Post office

- Police
- Ⓢ Bank
- @ Internet
- Telephone
- Market
- Medical services
- Ⓟ Parking
- Petrol
- Golf
- Archaeological site
- National park, wildlife reserve
- Viewing point
- Campsite
- Refuge, lodge
- Castle, fort
- Diving
- Deciduous, coniferous, palm trees
- Mangrove
- Hide
- Vineyard, winery
- Distillery
- Shipwreck
- Historic battlefield
- Related map

Index